S0-ARK-645

THE AMERICAN

COUNTRY INN
and
BED & BREAKFAST

COOKBOOK

VOLUME TWO

THE AMERICAN

COUNTRY INN

and

BED & BREAKFAST

COOKBOOK

VOLUME TWO

Kitty and Lucian Maynard

ð&. ð&. ð&.

More than 1,800 crowd-pleasing
recipes from 600 inns

Julia M. Pitkin, Editor

RUTLEDGE HILL PRESS
Nashville, Tennessee

Copyright © 1990 by Kitty E. Maynard and Lucian Maynard

All rights reserved. Written permission must be secured from the publisher to use or reproduce any part of the book, except for brief quotations in critical reviews or articles.

Published in Nashville, Tennessee, by Rutledge Hill Press, Inc., 513 Third Avenue South, Nashville, Tennessee 37210.

Typography: Bailey Typography, Inc., Nashville, Tennessee
Jacket: Harriette Bateman
Art: Tonya Pitkin Presley, Studio III Productions

Library of Congress Cataloging-in-Publication Data

Maynard, Kitty, 1955-
  The American country inn and bed & breakfast cookbook.

  Includes indexes.
  1. Breakfasts. 2. Bed and breakfast accommodations—
United States—Directories. I. Maynard, Lucian,
1952-   . II. Pitkin, Julia M. III. Title.
TX733.M43 1987   641.5′0973   87-10105
ISBN 0-934395-50-0 (v. 1)
ISBN 1-55835-059-2 (v. 2)

Manufactured in the United States of America
1 2 3 4 5 6 7 8 — 96 95 94 93 92 91 90

Table of Contents

Dedicated to:

The inn guests:
Without them, the inn industry would not continue to flourish.

The innkeepers:
Without them, friendships would be lost.

The country inns and bed and breakfasts:
Without them, comfort, creativity, and the personal touch would be hard to find.

The chefs:
Without them, the world would be tasteless.

🐚 🐚 🐚

A special thanks to our children: Kelly, Barry, and Nick. They keep our feet firmly on the ground.

Preface

*T*he *American Country Inn and Bed & Breakfast Cookbook, Volume Two,* is a unique resource. It provides you with an accurate picture of the food and accommodations each inn offers its guests and presents you with a collection of recipes for the finest in United States and Canadian eating.

For that reason we have organized the volume alphabetically by state and province, and by city within each. Every inn and its facilities are described; where appropriate, historical information and a brief sketch of nearby attractions are included. Addresses are provided, and except in those rare instances where an inn prefers to be contacted by mail, telephone information is included as well.

The recipes are printed with the inns that submitted them, providing you with information about the kind of food you might expect should you visit there. For each inn, the recipes follow a sequence common in cookbooks: breakfast dishes; jams, jellies and butters; appetizers; beverages; soups; sauces; salads and dressings; breads; entrees; vegetables; and desserts.

The exhaustive index begining on page 600 indexes each recipe in alphabetical order, under its main ingredient or ingredients (such as strawberries, potatoes, bananas, or chicken), and with its food category (such as appetizers, cakes, soups, or desserts).

What was true with the first volume of *The American Country Inn and Bed & Brakfast Cookbook* became even more obvious as we created this volume: Time and space limitations have prevented us from including every inn and recipe we wanted to list. To have done so would have required a volume two or three times larger than this book. What we can say, however, is that we have taken great care to provide you with a superior cookbook and with a travel guide that is as reliable as we can make it. No one should assume that because an inn does not appear in *The American Country Inn and Bed & Breakfast Cookbook, Volume Two,* that we are implying that it is inferior to those which do. Space limitations prevented us from including many excellent inns and recipes; we can only hope that we will be able to include them in subsequent editions.

Introduction

The glow of the fireplace warms you. The laughter dancing in the air from the kitchen brings a smile to your face. The aromas of spices and warm, fragrant bread remind you of happy times with your family. The sights, smells, and sounds make you feel warm, comfortable, and welcome, just as you were at home or at grandma and grandpa's place when you were a child. Every day, guests at inns across the United States and Canada experience these wonderful feelings, and more.

It has been our pleasure to watch the growth of interest in country inns and bed and breakfasts in recent years. When volume one of *The American Country Inn and Bed & Breakfast Cookbook* was published in 1987, there were approximately five thousand such establishments; soon there will be twenty thousand. Those of us who have been a part of this explosion know that its key is the innkeepers who graciously open their doors to us travelers.

Innkeepers are not in the "business" for the love of money; their financial rewards are far less than one might imagine. To those of us who know this hardy bunch, it is obvious that their love of innkeeping is what keeps them going. They are open, friendly people whose warm, gentle ways provide their guests with pleasant memories.

This warmth became vividly clear to us when we attended the First Annual Professional Association of Innkeepers International Convention in April 1990. There we met unique, happy people who generously shared anecdotes and information about their inns. Anyone who arrived as a stranger left with many friends! This happens every day as countless innkeepers and guests across the United States and Canada greet one another or go their separate ways. If you have never stayed at a inn while traveling, we encourage you to try the experience. We think you'll like it.

One of the small additions we want to contribute here is a substitution guide which we have developed since compiling the first volume. At our bakery and restaurant, we cater to lowfat, low-sugar, low-cholesterol, low-sodium lifestyles. Many times our chefs have had to prepare recipes to fit special diets; and although at first it sounds complicated, it doesn't have to be that difficult. Modifying recipes for healthier eating or for special diets is simple if you follow a few rules. Ours are as follows:

1. Use a minimum of fat. Decrease the use of butter or shortening and substitute vegetable oil, rice bran oil, or lowfat/no cholesterol margarine.
2. Substitute nonfat yogurt for sour cream.
3. Use cocoa powder in place of chocolate.
4. Minimize the use of hydrogenated fat and lard.
5. Use lowfat, skim milk cheeses instead of aged cheese; this will include ricotta and mozzarrella cheese.
6. Minimize the use of whole eggs.
7. Avoid nondairy substitute creamers and whipped toppings; these are made with coconut and palm oils. With the fat substitutes that will be available in the near future, there soon will be an opportunity to make your favorite recipes fat-free.
8. Use lowfat or nonfat (skim) milk rather than whole milk, cream, or half-and-half.
9. Avoid organ meats such as liver, kidney, and sweetbreads.
10. Minimize the use of avocados, olives, and nuts. Even though they are not saturated fats, you should use restraint with them.
11. Avoid mayonnaise, gravies, and heavy cream sauces. We have successfully substituted nonfat yogurts in recipes calling for mayonnaise and cannot tell the difference in the end product. Also be careful of "lite" mayonnaise; be sure to read the ingredients for saturated fats.
12. Prepare meat by braising, broiling, roasting, and grilling without additional fat; skim fat when you stew meat. Always avoid frying foods.
13. When looking for recipes, read the wording carefully; for there you will get the hints regarding what you should modify or avoid. Some of these words are creamy, buttery or buttered, breaded, fried or deep-fried, in its own gravy or pan gravy, au gratin, and rich. Words that may signal a lower fat content are grilled, broiled, poached, steamed, roasted, baked, and stir-fried.

We are delighted with *The American Country Inn and Bed & Breakfast Cookbook, Volume Two.* We are proud of the first volume and its continued success, and we believe volume two is every bit as good. Some of you will like it better. The recipes are marvelous, and the inns sound just like the kind of places you always dreamed of visiting. So delight in reading about them, and enjoy some truly great recipes. Travel as often as you can, and enjoy life to its fullest.

—Kitty E. Maynard
Lucian E. Maynard

THE AMERICAN

COUNTRY INN
and
BED & BREAKFAST

COOKBOOK

VOLUME TWO

Alabama

The Victoria

1604 Quintard
Anniston, Alabama
(205) 236-0503

The Victoria, situated midway between Atlanta and Birmingham, is one of the most picturesque Victorian estates in the South. Built in 1888, it was home to three prominent Anniston families before its preservation as a country inn. The main house includes elegant dining facilities and three upstairs guest suites featuring period antiques, carved fireplace mantels, parquet floors, brass hinges, and etched glass. A newly completed inn that blends esthetically with the original mansion offers forty-four sleeping accommodations. Connecting the new inn and the main house is a system of covered walkways, verandahs, and gazebos carefully designed to flow naturally among the massive trees, gardens, courtyard, and pool. Room service, a complimentary daily newspaper, turndown service with imported chocolates, and complimentary valet parking are a few of the personal services offered to guests of the Victoria. Breakfast, lunch, and dinner are served in the restaurant.

The guest house has been converted into a one-bedroom suite ideal for honeymooners. Also on the grounds in the carriage house is the Wren's Nest Gallery, which features the work of internationally known wildlife artist Larry K. Martin.

Potato and Leek Soup

2 to 3 tablespoons butter
½ pound leeks, thinly sliced (white part only)
1½ pounds potatoes, peeled and diced
1½ teaspoons dried thyme
2 quarts chicken stock
1 quart heavy cream
Salt and white pepper to taste

In a large soup kettle melt the butter. Add the leeks and sauté until translucent. Add the potatoes and thyme, and sauté for 5 minutes. Add the chicken stock and bring to a boil. Reduce the heat and cook until the potatoes are tender. Remove the potatoes and leeks from the stock, reserving the stock. In a food processor or blender, purée the potatoes and leeks. Slowly add the stock to the purée mixture, blending until smooth. Add the cream and season to taste. The soup may be returned to the soup kettle and heated over low heat, or served chilled. Serve with a fresh garnish of snipped chives or parsley.

Serves 10.

🐦 🐦 🐦 🐦 🐦

New England Crab Cakes

6 cups French bread crumbs
Salt and pepper to taste
¼ teaspoon nutmeg
4 tablespoons chopped shallots
½ cup lemon juice
1½ cups butter, softened
2 pounds lump blue crab meat
1 cup freshly chopped parsley
1 egg
1 tablespoon water

In a large bowl combine 4 cups of bread crumbs, the salt, pepper, nutmeg, shallots, lemon juice, butter, crab meat, and parsley. Mix well. Taste and adjust the seasonings. Divide into eight 5-ounce portions and form into patties. Don't press them together too tightly. In a shallow bowl beat the egg with the water. Dip the patties into the egg mixture and then into the remaining bread crumbs. In a skillet sauté the patties over low heat until golden brown and heated through.

Serves 8.

Bittersweet Chocolate Terrine

1 cup shelled pistachio nuts
½ cup golden raisins, softened
½ cup glacéed cherries, cut in half
1 8½-ounce package butter cookies, broken into ½-inch pieces
6 ounces semisweet chocolate
1 cup granulated sugar
¼ cup water

The Victoria

1 cup cocoa powder
¾ cup unsalted butter, very soft
1½ teaspoons Grand Marnier
1 egg plus 3 egg yolks, lightly
   beaten

Butter a 5x8-inch rectangular terrine or loaf pan. Peel the pistachio nuts by placing them in boiling water. Turn off the heat and let them sit for 5 minutes. Remove the nuts to a kitchen towel and rub them briskly to remove the skins. In a medium bowl mix together the nuts, raisins, cherries, and butter cookie bits, and set aside. In the top of a double boiler melt the chocolate. Set aside. In a saucepan combine the sugar and water, and stir over very low heat until the sugar is completely dissolved and the syrup is very clear. Set aside. In a large bowl combine the cocoa and softened butter and stir together until smooth. Stir in the sugar syrup, melted chocolate, and Grand Marnier. Add the eggs and mix well. Gently fold in the nuts, fruit, and cookie bits, and fold the mixture into the prepared mold. Tap the mold on a cloth covered counter to ensure that the contents are settled. Cover and refrigerate overnight. To unmold, run a knife around the sides of the terrine. Dip the mold into a bowl of hot water, then invert onto a serving

platter. Let the terrine reharden in the refrigerator until firm. To serve, cut several slices of the terrine and let them overlap, showing the handsome mosaic of nuts, fruit, and cookie bits.
   Serves 10.

Sundried Tomato Marinara

This is a wonderful topping for oysters, chicken, or fresh fish.

2 red sweet peppers, diced
2 green sweet peppers, diced
2 yellow sweet peppers, diced
¼ cup clarified butter
1 12-ounce jar sundried tomatoes
10 whole tomatoes, peeled and
   diced
1 46-ounce can tomato juice
¼ cup lemon juice
2 tablespoons ground oregano
2 tablespoons Worcestershire sauce
2 tablespoons Tabasco sauce
1 tablespoon horseradish
Salt and white pepper to taste

In a large skillet cook the peppers in clarified butter until translucent. Add the sundried tomatoes and their juice, and cook for 5 minutes. Set

aside. In a saucepan over low heat combine the remaining ingredients. Bring the mixture to a boil, reduce the heat, and simmer for 30 minutes. Add the peppers and simmer to the desired temperature.
   Makes about 3 quarts.

Victoria's Signature Snapper

2 tablespoons clarified butter
1 6 to 7-ounce fillet American Gulf
   Red Snapper
Salt and white pepper to taste
All-purpose flour
2 ounces lump blue crab meat
1 teaspoon toasted almonds
1 teaspoon chopped parsley
½ cup white Zinfandel wine
4 wilted spinach leaves

In a medium sauté pan heat the clarified butter until translucent. Salt and pepper the snapper fillet to taste. Dredge the fillet in flour. Place the fillet skin-side up in the pan and sear for about 30 seconds. Turn over and sprinkle the crab, almonds, and parsley over the fillet and deglaze with white zinfandel. Place in a 400° oven for 3 to 4 minutes or until the fish flakes easily. Remove and serve on a bed of wilted spinach leaves.
   Serves 1.

Blue Shadows

Box 432, Route 2
Greensboro, Alabama
(205) 624-3637

Blue Shadows, nestled in a country setting, is in a designated Alabama Treasure Forest. Set on 320 acres, its elegant accommodations are complemented by a formal garden, a private fish pond, a bird sanctuary, and a nature trail. Nearby attractions include ante-bellum homes, historical sites, Marion Military Institute, the University of Alabama, Indian mounds, and much more. Afternoon tea is served daily. There is no smoking inside.

Janet's Farm-raised Catfish Jambalaya

6 slices bacon, diced
6 sausages
2 large onions, chopped
2 cloves garlic, minced
2 ribs celery, chopped
1 green pepper, chopped
1½ pounds farm-raised catfish fillets
1 32-ounce can stewed tomatoes
1 tablespoon Worcestershire sauce
1 teaspoon salt
1 tablespoon chili powder

In a large skillet sauté the bacon, sausages, onions, garlic, celery, and pepper until the onions are golden. Add the catfish fillets and sauté for 10 minutes. Add the remaining ingredients and adjust the seasonings. Simmer for 10 more minutes. Serve over cooked rice.
Serves 6.

"Country Sunshine"

Route 2, Box 275
Leeds, Alabama 35094
(205) 699-9841

Situated on a secluded four-and-one-half-acre retreat with a quiet country atmosphere, "Country Sunshine" offers its guests four bedrooms with private baths, each decorated

differently. There is room here to board and pasture horses, and a screened patio provides for relaxing or dining.

Alabama Country Grits

1 quart water
2 tablespoons butter
1 teaspoon salt
1 cup quick cooking Jim Dandy Grits

In a saucepan bring the water to a boil. Add the butter and salt, and stir until the butter melts. Add the grits and reduce the heat to medium-low. Stir constantly with a wooden spoon until the consistency of pudding. Serve hot.
Serves 4.

Fresh Fruit Bowl

1 quart strawberries
3 tablespoons sugar

🐦 🐦 🐦

½ cantaloupe, cut into bite-sized pieces
½ pound seedless grapes

1 orange, peeled and cut up
1 apple, pared and cubed
1 pear, pared and cubed
1 kiwi fruit, peeled and cut up

Peel, wash, and cut up the strawberries. In a bowl combine the strawberries and sugar, tossing to coat. Cover and refrigerate overnight.
Add the remaining ingredients, mixing well.
Serves 2 to 4.

The Malaga Inn

359 Church Street
Mobile, Alabama 36602
(205) 438-4701

Situated in the historic district of downtown Mobile, the Malaga Inn was originally two townhouses. Built in 1862 by two brothers-in-law when the Civil War was going well for the South, since then the two homes have been connected and restored around a quiet patio and garden. All the forty

Malaga Inn

rooms and suites, with private baths and air conditioning, have been furnished with the finest in southern amenities. Many of the rooms retain their original hardwood floors.

The courtyard is a sublime feature of the Malaga. Beautifully landscaped, quiet, and private, this gas-lit area is perfect for weddings, receptions, intimate dinners, cocktail parties, or warm spring evenings of jazz. Octavia's Restaurant and Lounge adds to the ambience of the Malaga.

Featuring regional seafood specialties and courteous service in an elegant atmosphere, Octavia's is one of Mobile's culinary landmarks.

Lump Crab Meat Pestalozée

2 tablespoons butter
1 pound lump crab meat
1 tablespoon chives

Salt to taste
1 to 2 tablespoons white wine
Sliced almonds

In a skillet or sauté pan melt the butter. Sauté the crab meat with the chives and salt. Add the wine, cooking until heated through.

In a separate skillet toast the almonds in a small amount of butter. Place the crab meat in an au gratin dish and top with the toasted almonds.

Serves 4 to 6.

Alaska

North Face Lodge and Camp Denali

Late May to early September:
Post Office Box 67
Denali National Park, Alaska 99755
(907) 683-2290

Early September to late May:
Post Office Box 216
Cornish, New Hampshire 03746
(603) 675-2248

With spectacular views of Mount McKinley, North Face Lodge and Camp Denali are set in the heart of Denali National Park in the Alaska wilderness. The inn provides modern lodging with a small country inn flavor and features two- and three-night stays. Camp Denali is a rustic, elegant wilderness lodge designed for those who desire an extended vacation. Costs include transportation from the Denali Park Rail Station, a five-hour bus trip. Meals are provided, and a variety of outdoor activities are encouraged.

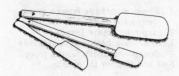

Chocolate Cinnamon Buns

¾ cup lukewarm water (110° to 115°)
¼ cup sugar
1 ¼-ounce package active dry yeast

&ha; &ha; &ha;

2¼ to 2½ cups unbleached all-purpose flour
⅓ cup cocoa
¼ cup oil
1 teaspoon salt
1 egg

&ha; &ha; &ha;

1 tablespoon butter, softened
1½ teaspoons cinnamon
1 tablespoon sugar
½ cup chopped pistachios, almonds or pecans

&ha; &ha; &ha;

¾ cup sifted confectioners' sugar
Milk or cream

In a large bowl combine the water and sugar. Add the yeast. Let the mixture stand until foamy, about 10 minutes. Add 1 cup of flour, the cocoa, oil, salt, and egg. Stir vigorously, about 200 strokes. Gradually stir in 1¼ to 1½ cups of flour, until a soft dough forms. Knead the dough on a floured surface until smooth. Place the dough in an oiled bowl and cover. Let the dough rise in a warm place until very light and almost doubled.

Grease a 9x13-inch pan. Punch the dough down and turn out onto a floured surface. Roll into a 9x12-inch rectangle. Spread with softened butter. Sprinkle cinnamon, 1 tablespoon of sugar, and the pistachio nuts over the butter. Roll the dough jelly-roll fashion, beginning with a long edge. Pinch the edges together. Cut into 12 pieces and place the rolls in the greased pan. Cover and let the rolls rise in a warm dry area until very light and almost doubled.

Bake the rolls in a 375° oven for 20 minutes.

Combine the confectioners' sugar with enough milk or cream to make a spreadable glaze and frost the rolls while still hot.

Makes 12 buns.

Orange Rye Rolls

1¼ cups lukewarm water (110° to 115°)
⅓ cup molasses
2 tablespoons honey
2 tablespoons active dry yeast

&ha; &ha; &ha;

¾ cup orange juice concentrate
1 tablespoon finely grated orange rind
1½ cups rye flour
1½ cups whole wheat flour
½ cup vegetable oil
2 eggs
¾ teaspoon baking soda
1 teaspoon salt
3 cups unbleached all-purpose flour

&ha; &ha; &ha;

1 egg
1 teaspoon water

In a large bowl combine 1¼ cups of water, the molasses, and honey. Add the yeast. Let the mixture stand until foamy, about 10 minutes. Add the orange juice concentrate, orange rind, rye flour, whole wheat flour, oil, 2 eggs, baking soda, and salt. Stir vigorously, about 200 strokes. Gradually stir in the all-purpose flour, enough to form a soft dough. Knead the dough on a floured surface until smooth. Place the dough in an oiled bowl and cover. Let the dough rise in a warm dry place until doubled in bulk.

Grease a large baking sheet. Punch the dough down and shape into rolls. Arrange the rolls on the baking sheet about ½ inch apart. Cover and let the rolls rise in a warm dry place until very light and almost doubled. (Rye rolls take extra rising time.)

Beat together one egg and 1 teaspoon of water. Brush the rolls with the egg mixture. Bake in a 350° oven for 20 to 25 minutes. The bottoms overbrown easily, so watch carefully during baking.

Makes about 3 dozen rolls.

Russian Black Bread

2 cups lukewarm water (110° to 115°)
1 tablespoon sugar
¼ cup molasses
2 ¼-ounce packages active dry yeast

&ta; &ta; &ta;

1 tablespoon instant coffee granules
3 cups rye flour
3 cups unbleached all-purpose flour
1 cup bran
¼ cup cocoa
1 tablespoon dried onion flakes
2 teaspoons crushed caraway seeds
1 teaspoon crushed fennel seeds
¼ cup vinegar
¼ cup oil
2 teaspoons salt

&ta; &ta; &ta;

1 teaspoon cornstarch
½ cup cold water

Grease two 9-inch cake or pie pans. In a large bowl combine the water, sugar, and molasses. Add the yeast. Let the mixture stand until foamy, about 10 minutes. Add the instant coffee, 2 cups of rye flour, 1 cup of all-purpose flour, bran, cocoa, dried onion flakes, caraway seeds, fennel seeds, vinegar, oil, and salt. Stir vigorously, about

200 strokes. Gradually stir in the remaining rye flour and all-purpose flour, until a kneadable dough forms. Knead the dough on a floured surface, adding all-purpose flour until the dough is smooth but still slightly sticky. Place the dough in an oiled bowl and cover. Let the dough rise in a warm dry place until doubled in bulk. Punch down and divide the dough in half. Shape each half into a round, tucking the seams underneath. Place each round in a prepared cake or pie pan. Cover and let rise in a warm place until almost doubled.

Bake the rounds in a 350° oven for 40 to 45 minutes, or until they sound hollow when the bottoms are tapped.

To glaze the tops, in a small saucepan mix together the cornstarch and cold water. Cook over medium heat, stirring constantly until the mixture boils, thickens, and clarifies. As soon as the bread is baked, brush the mixture over the tops of the loaves and return them to the oven for 2 to 3 minutes.

Makes 2 large round loaves.

Lentil Stew

5 cups water or stock
1 heaping cup lentils, rinsed
½ teaspoon thyme
½ teaspoon marjoram
1 bay leaf

&ta; &ta; &ta;

2 to 4 tablespoons olive oil
2 onions, chopped
4 carrots, diced

&ta; &ta; &ta;

1 15-ounce can whole tomatoes, cut up
¼ cup dry sherry
Salt and pepper to taste

&ta; &ta; &ta;

¼ cup chopped fresh parsley
Grated Swiss, Monterey Jack, or Cheddar cheese

In a large pot bring the water, lentils, thyme, marjoram, and bay leaf to a boil. Cover and simmer for 20 to 30 minutes, or until the lentils are tender.

Meanwhile, heat the olive oil and

sauté the onions and carrots. Cover and simmer until the carrots are crispy-tender. Stir the carrots and onions into the lentil mixture, along with the tomatoes, sherry, salt, and pepper. Simmer for 1 hour.

Just before serving, stir in the parsley. Place the cheese in the bottom of each bowl and fill with stew.

Serves 4 to 6.

Sour Cream Halibut

⅓ cup butter or margarine
2 tablespoons lemon juice
4 to 5 pounds halibut or other white fish, filleted and cut in pieces
Lemon pepper

&ta; &ta; &ta;

2 cups sour cream
½ cup yogurt
¾ cup mayonnaise

&ta; &ta; &ta;

1 cup crushed soda crackers
Paprika

Melt the butter or margarine in a 9x13-inch enamel baking dish. Add the lemon juice. Arrange the halibut pieces in the dish and sprinkle with lemon pepper.

In a bowl combine the sour cream, yogurt, and mayonnaise. Spread the sour cream mixture over the halibut pieces. Bake in a 375° oven for 20 minutes.

Remove the halibut from the oven. Top with the crushed crackers and paprika. Return the dish to the oven and bake for 15 to 20 minutes, or until the fish is done and the cracker crumbs are golden brown.

Serves 8 to 10.

Green Beans with Lemon Thyme

1 10-ounce package frozen green beans (or canned or fresh)
2 teaspoons thyme leaves
1 tablespoon butter or margarine
3 tablespoons fresh lemon juice
Salt and pepper to taste

Prepare the green beans according to the package directions. Add the remaining ingredients to the beans and toss together. Serve immediately.

Serves 4.

Muldrow Mud Cake

1½ cups strong coffee
¼ cup coffee-flavored liqueur
5 ounces unsweetened baking chocolate
1 cup butter
2 cups sugar

🍃 🍃 🍃

2 cups unbleached all-purpose flour
1 teaspoon baking soda
¼ teaspoon salt

🍃 🍃 🍃

2 eggs
1 teaspoon vanilla extract
Chocolate Glaze

Grease a bundt pan or 10-inch springform pan and dust with sifted cocoa.

Heat the coffee and liqueur in the top of a double boiler over simmering water. Add the chocolate and butter. Heat until melted, stirring frequently. When the mixture is smooth, add the sugar and stir until dissolved. Cool until lukewarm.

Sift together the flour, baking soda, and salt. Gradually add the coffee-chocolate mixture, beating well after each addition to avoid lumps in the batter. Add the eggs and vanilla. Beat with an electric mixer at medium speed for 2 minutes. Pour the batter into the prepared pan. Bake in a 275° oven for about 1 hour and 30 minutes, or until a toothpick inserted in the center comes out clean. Glaze with Chocolate Glaze.

Serves 14.

Chocolate Glaze

4 ounces semisweet chocolate
1 tablespoon butter or margarine
2 tablespoons milk, cream, or strong coffee

Melt the chocolate and butter in the top of a double boiler over simmering water. Add the milk, adding more if necessary to achieve a spreadable consistency. Glaze the Muldrow Mud Cake.

Makes about ⅓ cup.

🐚 🐚 🐚 🐚 🐚

Banana Sour Cream Pie

1⅓ cups crushed vanilla wafers
⅓ cup melted butter

🍃 🍃 🍃

1 ¼-ounce envelope unflavored gelatin
½ cup sugar
1 cup boiling water

🍃 🍃 🍃

12 ounces cream cheese, softened
1 ripe banana, mashed

🍃 🍃 🍃

½ cup sour cream
2 tablespoons fresh lemon juice
1 teaspoon vanilla extract

🍃 🍃 🍃

Sliced banana

Combine the vanilla wafer crumbs and the melted butter. Press the crumbs into the bottom of a 9-inch pie plate. Bake in a 350° oven for 10 minutes. Cool.

In a small bowl combine the gelatin and sugar. Add the boiling water and set aside.

In a large bowl beat the cream cheese until fluffy. Add the mashed banana, beating until blended. Add the gelatin mixture and beat again. Add the sour cream, lemon juice, and vanilla extract. Beat until very

smooth. Turn the mixture into the baked pie shell and chill for several hours or overnight. Before serving, garnish each serving with banana slices.

Variations: For the crust, use ginger snaps, chocolate wafers, or graham crackers. Add ¼ cup of sugar when using graham crackers.

Serves 6 to 8.

Walnut Honey Butter

½ cup butter or margarine
½ cup honey
¼ cup chopped walnuts

Cream the butter and honey until very light. Stir in the walnuts. Cover and store in the refrigerator.

Makes approximately 1 cup.

The Glacier Bay Country Inn

Post Office Box 5
Gustavus, Alaska 99826
(907) 697-2288

The Glacier Bay Country Inn blends the comforts of old-fashioned country living with the rustic wilderness that is Alaska.

Less than a half hour by air from Juneau, Alaska's capital, Gustavus and the Glacier Bay Country Inn seem generations away—a place apart, where life passes at a different pace, slower, somehow richer. Set in a clearing surrounded by trees with a majestic mountain backdrop, the inn is an idyllic setting that is further enhanced by the warm, personal attention given guests.

The Glacier Bay Country Inn

Country Inn Braided Bread

5 to 5½ cups all-purpose flour
¼ cup sugar
2 teaspoons salt
1 ¼-ounce package active dry yeast

&ε &ε &ε

1½ cups milk
¼ cup butter, cut in small pieces
2 eggs

&ε &ε &ε

1 egg white
1 tablespoon water
Sesame seeds

Grease a baking sheet. In a large mixing bowl combine 1 cup of flour, the sugar, salt, and dry yeast. Heat the milk and butter in a saucepan (or microwave) just until the milk is warm; the butter does not need to melt. Add the eggs and the warm milk mixture to the flour mixture. Mix very well until thoroughly moistened; beat on medium speed of mixer for about 3 minutes. Stir in enough of the remaining flour to make a stiff dough. Turn out onto floured board; knead the dough until it is smooth and elastic (about 5 minutes). Work into a ball; place in a greased bowl, turning to coat all sides. Cover and let rise in a warm, draft-free place until light and doubled in bulk, about 1 to 1½ hours.

Punch the dough down and let rest for about 10 minutes. Divide dough into six equal portions. Roll each into a thin cylinder about 8 to 10 inches long. Take three strips and braid them together. Place on a greased baking sheet. Braid the remaining three strips and place about 6 inches away from the other loaf. Cover the loaves and let rise until doubled in bulk, about 1½ hours.

Lightly beat the egg white with the water. Brush the loaves with the mixture, and sprinkle with sesame seeds. Bake in a 375° oven for 35 to 40 minutes, or until the loaves sound hollow when tapped on the bottom and have a nice golden color.

Makes 2 loaves.

Halibut Bisque

1 cup butter
2 cups chopped onions
3 cups chopped celery
2 teaspoons white pepper
6 cups cold chicken stock
3 tablespoons cornstarch
2 teaspoons salt
4 cups cream
2 cups milk
4 pounds halibut, cut in bite-sized chunks
Parsley or paprika for garnish

In a large saucepan melt the butter and sauté the onions, celery, and white pepper until tender. Dissolve the cornstarch in the chicken stock and add with the salt to the vegetables. Heat to boiling, stirring constantly. Boil and stir until thickened. Reduce the heat and stir in the cream and milk. Bring to a simmer. Add the halibut and turn off the heat. This prevents the halibut from overcooking and giving the bisque a "fishy" taste. Ladle into bowls and garnish with sprigs of parsley or paprika.

Note: To make paprika designs on the soup, make a stencil from paper or mylar. Hold the stencil about ½-inch above the bowl and lightly sprinkle paprika over the top.

Serves 12.

Shrimp Salad

12 ounces seashell macaroni, cooked, drained and cooled
½ pound small shrimp, cooked
½ cup chopped onions
1 cup diced celery
2 tomatoes, seeded and diced
½ green pepper, seeded and diced
2 dozen snow peas, cut in 1-inch pieces

&ε &ε &ε

2 cups mayonnaise
2 tablespoons chopped fennel
2 tablespoons chopped dill
½ teaspoon white pepper
½ teaspoon salt

In a large bowl combine the macaroni, shrimp, and vegetables. In a separate bowl combine the mayonnaise and remaining ingredients. Blend the mixture with the shrimp mixture, tossing well. Chill well before serving.

Serves 12.

Halibut Mousse
with Shrimp, Crab, and Mushroom Sauce

1½ pounds fresh halibut, boned and
   skinned
1 tablespoon salt
3 to 4 egg whites
2 cups heavy cream
½ teaspoon Tabasco sauce
2 tablespoons fresh dill

⁍ ⁍ ⁍

3 tablespoons unsalted butter
½ cup all-purpose flour
2 cups milk

⁍ ⁍ ⁍

8 ounces shrimp
8 ounces crab meat
3 tablespoons oil
2 tablespoons minced shallots
1 clove garlic, minced
6 ounces crushed tomato
4 ounces brandy
8 ounces white wine

⁍ ⁍ ⁍

8 ounces mushroom caps
8 ounces morel mushrooms
Salt
White pepper

⁍ ⁍ ⁍

Chopped dill for garnish

Dice the halibut into small pieces and place in a food processor. Add the salt and purée until smooth; add the egg whites and purée until incorporated. Do not overwork. Remove to a bowl and work in the cream a little at a time. Fold in the Tabasco and the chopped dill. Cover and refrigerate.

To prepare the sauce, melt the butter in a small saucepan. Add the flour and cook for 2 to 3 minutes. Add the milk and stir until smooth. Bring the mixture to a simmer and cook for 15 to 20 minutes. Set aside.

Clean the shrimp and crab meat, reserving any shells. Set the shrimp and crab meat aside. Heat the oil in a small saucepan over high heat. Add the reserved shells from the shrimp and crab meat. Reduce the heat and cook for about 2 minutes. Add the shallots and garlic and cook for 1 minute. Add the crushed tomato and cook until almost dry. Add the brandy

and flame. Add the white wine and reduce to almost dry. Fold in the white sauce and simmer for 15 to 20 minutes. Strain and set aside.

Butter a ring mold. Place the chilled mousse mixture in the prepared mold. Place the mold in a hot water bath and bake in a 300° oven until firm, about 25 to 30 minutes.

During the last 10 minutes of cooking time, sauté the shrimp in a saucepan with a little butter. Add the mushrooms and cook 2 to 3 minutes. Add the reserved sauce and the crab meat. Season to taste with salt and white pepper. Simmer for 2 to 3 minutes. When the mousse is cooked, turn it upside down on a platter and remove the mold. Fill the center with the sauce, spooning any extra sauce around the outside. Garnish with chopped dill.

Serves 8.

Salmon with Garden Vegetable Stuffing

1 8- to 10-pound whole salmon,
   cleaned
Salt and pepper

⁍ ⁍ ⁍

1½ cups chopped celery
1 cup chopped green onions
2 cloves garlic, minced
1 teaspoon white pepper
¼ cup butter or oil
2 cups grated carrots
½ cup chopped fresh chives
¼ cup chopped dill
¼ cup minced fresh parsley
3 eggs
¼ cup chicken broth
1½ cups dry bread crumbs

⁍ ⁍ ⁍

Oil
½ cup butter, melted
¼ cup lemon juice

Wash the fish quickly in cold water and pat dry. Rub the cavity with salt and pepper.

Sauté the celery, green onions, garlic, and white pepper in butter or

oil. Add the carrots and sauté until the vegetables are tender. Stir in the chives, dill, and parsley, and remove from the heat. Stir in the eggs, chicken broth, and bread crumbs. Stuff the salmon with the mixture and close the opening with skewers.

If you have extra stuffing, place the mixture in a baking dish and refrigerate. Cover and place in a 350° oven for 20 minutes before serving.

Brush the fish with oil and place in a shallow roasting pan. Bake in a 350° oven for 1 hour and 30 minutes or until the salmon flakes easily with a fork. Baste occasionally with a mixture of butter and lemon juice during baking.

Serves 10 to 12.

Stir-fried Peas

2 cups snow peas
1 tablespoon oil
1 large onion, sliced
2 to 3 stalks celery, sliced
   diagonally
4 ounces mushrooms, sliced
2 chicken bouillon cubes
Water
1 tablespoon cornstarch
½ teaspoon sugar
2 tablespoons soy sauce

Wash the peas and remove the ends. Heat the oil in a large skillet. Add the onion, celery, mushrooms, and peas. Cook until the onion is translucent, stirring constantly. Add the chicken

bouillon plus enough water to make ½-inch depth in the skillet. Boil for 3 minutes. Dissolve the cornstarch and sugar in the soy sauce and add to the pea mixture. Stir until thick and remove from the heat.

Note: This is good served with rice.

Serves 8.

Country Inn Sautéed Potatoes

4 cups diced potatoes (preferably new potatoes)
½ cup butter
¼ cup chopped chives
¼ cup chopped parsley
1 teaspoon salt
½ teaspoon white pepper
½ teaspoon fresh dill weed (optional)

In a large saucepan heat 1 inch of water to boiling. Add the potatoes. Cover and heat to boiling. Cook just until tender, about 20 minutes. Drain and plunge the potatoes in cold water to stop the cooking process. In a large skillet melt the butter. Add the potatoes and seasonings. Stir gently to coat the potatoes. Heat through and serve immediately.

Serves 8.

Pumpkin Cookies

3 cups brown sugar
1½ cups oil
3 cups pumpkin (1 large can)
1 tablespoon vanilla extract
6 cups all-purpose flour
1 tablespoon baking soda
1 tablespoon baking powder
1½ teaspoons salt
1½ teaspoons cinnamon
1½ teaspoons nutmeg
¾ teaspoon ginger
3 cups raisins
1½ cups chopped nuts

Beat together the brown sugar, oil, pumpkin, and vanilla. Sift together the dry ingredients and add to the pumpkin mixture. Stir in the raisins and nuts. Drop by rounded teaspoonfuls onto a greased baking sheet. Bake in a 350° oven for 8 to 10 minutes or until lightly browned.

Makes about 5 dozen.

Sugar Crinkles

½ cup sugar
½ cup brown sugar
1 cup shortening
1 teaspoon vanilla extract
1 egg
2 cups all-purpose flour
1 teaspoon cream of tartar
½ teaspoon baking soda
1 teaspoon salt
Sugar

Cream together the sugar, brown sugar, shortening, vanilla, and egg. Add the flour, cream of tartar, baking soda, and salt. Mix well. Roll into 1-inch balls and roll in sugar. Place the balls about 2 inches apart on an ungreased baking sheet. Bake in a 350° oven for 10 minutes or until lightly browned.

Makes about 4 dozen.

🐦 🐦 🐦 🐦 🐦

Rhubarb Strawberry Mousse

1 ¼-ounce package unflavored gelatin
¼ cup cold water
1 cup hot rhubarb syrup (recipe follows)
½ cup confectioners' sugar
🐦 🐦 🐦
1 cup whipping cream
1 cup egg whites (approximately 8)
1 pound whole strawberries, chilled

In a large bowl soften the gelatin in the water. Add the rhubarb syrup and confectioners' sugar, and beat until smooth.

In a separate bowl beat the whipping cream until stiff, and refrigerate until chilled. In another bowl beat the egg whites until stiff peaks form. Gently fold the whipping cream into the egg whites. Reserve 10 of the strawberries for garnish. Gently add the remaining strawberries and the rhubarb syrup mixture to the whipped mixture. Spoon into 10 dessert dishes and garnish with the reserved berries.

Variation: Substitute fresh raspberries for the strawberries.

Serves 10.

Rhubarb Syrup

Fill an 8-quart stockpot with chopped rhubarb, to within 2 inches of the top. Cover with water. Simmer until very tender, about 30 minutes. Mash the rhubarb and drain, saving the liquid.

Add an equal amount of sugar to that of liquid and bring to a boil. Simmer for 30 minutes or until the consistency of a thick syrup.

Spruce Tip Syrup

Young, tender Sitka spruce tips
Cold water
Sugar

In the early spring, gather a large quantity of Sitka spruce tips, being sure to pick only the young, tender tips. They should still have the light brown sheath visible on the tips. (If they are too old, your syrup will have a kerosene flavor.)

Fill your largest pot with the spruce tips; rinse once in cold water. Cover the tips with water, bring to a boil and simmer until the water turns amber, about 1 hour.

Drain, saving the liquid and discarding the tips. Measure the liquid and add an equal amount of sugar to it. (For each cup of liquid, add one cup of sugar.) Bring to a boil and simmer until syrup is of desired thickness.

Serve with pancakes or waffles.

Gustavus Inn

Post Office Box 60
Gustavus, Alaska 99826
(907) 697-2254
(907) 697-2291 (FAX)

The Gustavus Inn combines a traditional homestead atmosphere and a magnificent Alaskan setting with modern accommodations and convenient transportation. It is the perfect retreat from which to base a Glacier Bay adventure. The Gustavus Inn began in 1928 as a farm homestead for a nine-child family carving a home out of the Alaskan wilderness. Today, its attractive and comfortable accommodations retain the spirit of the early pioneers.

Salmon Chowder

¼ cup olive oil
1 bunch green onions, chopped
1 or 2 cloves garlic, crushed
½ cup sliced or chopped celery
1 quart fish stock (canned clam juice works well)
1 28-ounce can tomatoes with basil
Handful chopped celery leaves
1 tablespoon basil
1 tablespoon oregano
1 bay leaf
1 tablespoon lemon juice
Salt and pepper
2 cups left-over cooked salmon

In a large soup pot heat the olive oil over medium heat. Add the onions, garlic, and celery. Stir and cook until the onions are limp. Add the fish stock, tomatoes, celery leaves, basil, oregano, bay leaf, lemon juice, salt, and pepper. Bring all to a boil and simmer for 15 minutes.

Add the cooked salmon, stir, and simmer for a few minutes. Serve in large heated soup bowls.

Serves 6 to 8.
Recipe courtesy Chef David Lesh.

Stir-fried Halibut

1 pound halibut
2 teaspoons cornstarch
1 egg white, beaten
1 tablespoon rice wine or sherry
1 teaspoon salt
4 tablespoons oil
1 teaspoon finely chopped gingerroot
1 scallion, finely chopped

Cut the fish into small squares, about 1" by ½". Place the cornstarch in a bowl, add the halibut and toss until each piece is lightly coated. Add the egg white, wine, and salt. Toss again.

Heat a wok and add the oil. Add the gingerroot and scallion. Stir-fry for 1 minute. Add the halibut and stir-fry gently until firm and white. Serve at once.

Serves 4.
Recipe courtesy Chef David Lesh.

Minted Mayonnaise

1 egg
¼ cup vegetable oil
2 tablespoons mint vinegar (see note)

1 bunch fresh mint leaves
½ teaspoon salt

❧ ❧ ❧

¾ cup vegetable oil

In a blender combine all of the ingredients except ¾ cup of oil. At low speed, add the oil slowly. Turn the blender off as soon as all of the oil has been added.

Serve chilled.

Note: To make mint vinegar, place a couple of sprigs of mint into a bottle of vinegar and let the mixture stand for one week or more.

Serve with Cold Minted Trout or any whole pieces of poached fish.

Makes about 1 cup.
Recipe courtesy Chef David Lesh.

Cold Minted Trout

Fill a poaching kettle with mint tea. When it boils, add whole cleaned and scaled trout. Cook very gently, do not boil again. (You may turn off the heat after adding the trout and cook to 120° on an instant-reading thermometer.) Poach until tender. Let the trout cool

Gustavus Inn

in the poaching liquid until cold. Gently remove the fish, bone and filet it, and place it carefully on a bed of lettuce leaves.

Decorate the platter with nasturtium flowers and serve with minted mayonnaise on the side. Serve chilled on chilled plates.

Recipe courtesy Chef David Lesh.

The Summer Inn Bed and Breakfast

247 Second Avenue
Post Office Box 1198
Haines, Alaska 99827
(907) 766-2970

The Summer Inn Bed and Breakfast is a five-bedroom historical house situated near the heart of downtown Haines. Providing an excellent view of the Lynn Canal, home to whales, seals, and sea lions, the house was built by Tim Vogel, a member of Skagway's notorious Soapy Smith gang. Nearby mountainsides and glacial river valleys provide habitats for bald eagles, moose, mountain goats, bears, foxes, and wolves. The Summer Inn is a nonsmoking establishment.

Coffee Squares

½ cup butter
1 cup brown sugar
1 egg
1 teaspoon vanilla extract
1½ cups all-purpose flour
¼ teaspoon salt
½ teaspoon baking powder
½ cup hot coffee

🐛 🐛 🐛

1½ cups confectioners' sugar
1 tablespoon cocoa
¼ teaspoon salt
¼ cup melted butter
Cold coffee

In a large bowl cream the butter and sugar. Add the egg and vanilla, and mix well. Into a separate bowl sift the flour, salt, and baking powder. Alternately add the flour mixture and the hot coffee to the creamed mixture. Mix well and pour the batter into a 9-inch square pan. Bake in a 350° oven for 30 minutes.

Into a small bowl sift together the confectioners' sugar, cocoa, and salt. Pour in the melted butter, and add the cold coffee one tablespoon at a time, mixing well, to make a spreadable icing. Frost the cake when completely cooled.

Serves 9.

Magic Canyon Ranch

40015 Waterman Road
Homer, Alaska 99603
(907) 235-6077

Overlooking magnificent Kachemak Bay, Magic Canyon Ranch provides opportunity for a variety of experiences, including nature walks on the seventy-five acres of property, relaxing on the sundeck, soaking in the outdoor hot tub, fishing, reading, and visiting with the horses and other animals. Three deluxe dormered rooms upstairs are filled with country crafts and antiques; a guest cottage provides welcomed privacy. The hosts will help their guests arrange for recreational activities available in the area. There is no smoking indoors.

Herb Waffles with Seafood Sauce

2 cups unbleached all-purpose flour
1 tablespoon baking powder
½ teaspoon salt

🐛 🐛 🐛

2 cups milk
2 egg yolks
1 tablespoon fresh parsley
1 tablespoon finely chopped onion
1 teapoon fresh sage
1 teaspoon fresh thyme
6 tablespoons melted butter
2 egg whites

🐛 🐛 🐛

¼ cup butter
¼ cup chopped onion
¼ cup chopped celery
Salt and cracked pepper
3 tablespoons all-purpose flour
1 cup chicken broth
1 cup milk
1 pound fresh seafood (shrimp, crab, or salmon), cooked
1 tablespoon lemon juice
Fresh parsley for garnish

In a large bowl combine the dry ingredients. In a separate bowl beat the milk, eggs, and spices. Add the milk mixture to the dry ingredients alternately with the melted butter. Beat the egg whites until fluffy and gently fold into the batter. Bake in a hot waffle iron until golden.

In a saucepan melt ¼ cup of butter. Sauté the onion, celery, salt, and pepper in the butter. Add the flour, stirring to blend. Add the broth and the milk. Bring to a boil, stirring constantly. Stir in the seafood and lemon juice, and heat through. Serve over the waffles, garnishing with parsley.

Serves 4.

Magic Canyon Quiche

3 cups whole wheat pastry flour
1 cup wheat germ
1 tablespoon salt
1 cup shortening
1 egg
1 tablespoon vinegar
1 tablespoon honey
Warm water

🍂 🍂 🍂

6 cups shredded Swiss cheese
1 pound cooked salmon
1 pound fresh broccoli flowerettes
Fresh chives, chopped
Salt
6 cups milk
9 eggs
Cracked pepper

In a large bowl combine the flour, wheat germ, and salt. Cut in the shortening. Combine one egg, the vinegar, honey, and enough water to make 1 cup of liquid. Add the liquid ingredients to the dry ingredients. Form the dough into 3 balls and wrap each in plastic wrap. Refrigerate the dough overnight.

Roll the dough out between sheets of waxed paper. Line 3 large quiche pans with pastry and sprinkle shredded cheese over the bottoms. Divide the salmon, broccoli, chives, salt, and remaining cheese among the 3 pans. Blend 2 cups of milk and 3 eggs for each quiche, and pour over the mixture in each pan. Top with cracked pepper. Bake in a 375° oven for 15 minutes. Reduce the heat to 350° and bake for 45 minutes. Cool before serving.

Note: Quiches refrigerate and reheat well, but do not freeze. We use local shrimp, crab, or halibut sometimes.

Serves 18, 6 servings per quiche.

Arizona

The Mine Manager's House Inn

Number 1 Greenway Drive
Ajo, Arizona 85321
(602) 387-6505

The Manager's House Inn

Bed 'n Breakfast in Arizona

5995 East Orange Blossom Lane
Phoenix, Arizona 85018
(602) 994-3759

Perched atop a hill overlooking the southwestern Arizona desert, the Manager's House Inn affords its guests vistas that give a sense of forever. Near the historic town of Ajo, the birthplace of Arizona's mining industry, the inn was built as a home for the manager of the New Cornelia Mining Company. The atmosphere of the Manager's House is relaxed and informal, the decor a mixture of antiques and contemporary furnishings. The coffee pot is always on, and refreshments are served afternoons on the patio or in front of the fireplace. Each bedroom suite has a different motif and its own bath. A hot tub/spa awaits those who wish to soak aching muscles.

Breakfast Casserole

4 cups cubed day old bread
2 cups (8 ounces) shredded mixed

white and yellow cheese
10 eggs
4 cups milk
1 teaspoon dry mustard
Salt
½ teaspoon garlic powder
½ cup diced peeled tomatoes
10 slices bacon, cooked and crumbled
½ cup mushroom slices

Butter a 9x13-inch baking dish. Arrange the bread cubes in the prepared dish and sprinkle with the cheese. In a large bowl combine the eggs, milk, dry mustard, salt, and garlic salt. Pour the mixture over the cheese and bread. Sprinkle with tomatoes, bacon, and mushrooms. Cover and refrigerate overnight.

Bake uncovered in a 325° oven for 30 minutes. Remove from the oven, form a tent over the baking dish with foil to prevent burning, and return to the oven for 30 minutes. Let the casserole cool for 10 minutes before serving. Cut into squares.

Serves 10.

This charming home, situated in the exclusive Arizona Country Club area of Phoenix, is furnished with an eclectic mixture of contemporary and collectors' items. Breakfast often features such delicious specialties as Swedish pancakes with crêpe suzette sauce, German apple pancakes with fruit topping, almond French toast, tropical and apple spice Belgian waffles, and fruit and fiber bran bread. Arizona State University, Desert Botanical Gardens, and the fashionable Fifth Avenue Scottsdale shops are nearby.

Cinnamon Raisin Toast

1 cup skim milk
2 eggs
1 teaspoon vanilla extract
4 slices cinnamon raisin bread

14

Combine the milk, eggs, and vanilla in a flat bowl. Mix well. Dip the bread in the mixture to coat both sides. Heat a skillet or griddle coated with nonstick spray. Brown the toast over medium heat for approximately 2 minutes, then turn to brown on the other side. There are 131 calories per slice.

Serve with Three Berry Sauce. Serves 4.

Three Berry Sauce

    1 cup fresh strawberry halves
    ⅔ cup raspberries
    2 teaspoons sugar
    2 teaspoons cornstarch
    2 teaspoons cold water
    ⅓ cup bing cherries (or
        blueberries)

Combine the strawberries, raspberries, and sugar in a medium saucepan. Let the mixture stand until the sugar dissolves. Cook over medium heat for 5 minutes. Combine the cornstarch with the water and add to the berry mixture. Increase the heat to high, and stir constantly until thickened and clear. Remove the sauce from the heat and stir in the cherries or blueberries. Serve immediately with the Cinnamon Raisin Toast.

Makes 1⅓ cups.

60 Minute English Muffin Loaf

    Cornmeal
    5 cups all-purpose flour
    1 tablespoon sugar
    2 teaspoons salt
    ¼ teaspoon baking soda
    2 ¼-ounce packages active dry yeast
    2 cups milk
    ½ cup water

Grease two 9x5-inch microwave-safe loaf pans, and sprinkle with cornmeal. Set aside 1 cup of flour. In a large bowl combine the remaining flour, sugar, salt, baking soda, and yeast. Heat the liquids until very warm (125° to 130°). Add the heated liquids to the dry mixture, and beat well. Stir in the reserved flour to make a stiff batter. Spoon the batter into the prepared pans. Sprinkle the tops with cornmeal. Cover and microwave on medium power (50%) for 1 minute. Let the dough rest for 10 minutes. Repeat cooking and resting, allowing the loaf to double in size. To bake, microwave each loaf separately on high (100%) for 6 minutes and 30 seconds. The surface of the loaves will be flat and pale in color. Allow the loaves to rest in the pan for 5 minutes, remove, and cool.

Makes 2 loaves.

The Prescott Country Inn

503 S. Montezuma
U.S. Highway 89 South
Prescott, Arizona 86303
(602) 445-7991

The Prescott Country Inn is not the typical bed and breakfast. Situated just three blocks south of the old downtown courthouse square, its eleven separate, private cottages with private baths are fully equipped and offer a variety of comfortable sleeping accommodations. Breakfast is brought to each cottage so that it may be enjoyed in privacy, indoors or on a patio. To facilitate "getting away" from everything, all eleven cottages are phone free. There are many recreational and entertainment opportunities in the area.

Baked Mustard Ham

    2 center slices of ham, ½-inch thick
    ¼ cup prepared mustard
    ½ cup brown sugar
    1 cup milk (evaporated or whole)

Place the ham slices in a 12x9-inch glass baking dish. Spread the prepared mustard evenly over the ham slices. Sprinkle brown sugar over the mustard. Pour the milk into the baking dish. The milk should barely overlap the top of the ham slices. Bake in a 350° oven for 45 minutes or until the liquid becomes a sauce.

Serves 4.

Morrissio
(Hot Rum Mocha)

    Water to fill 1 mug
    1 teaspoon dark, rich instant coffee
    ½ envelope (½ ounce) Carnation
        Hot Cocoa Mix
    1 ounce rum (light or dark)
    Cool Whip or whipped cream

Boil the water and heat the rum. Place the instant coffee and cocoa mix in a mug. Pour the rum into the mug, stirring to dissolve the dry ingredients. Add the boiling water to fill the mug. Top with Cool Whip or whipped cream.

Pull up a comfortable chair in front of the fireplace, sit back, sip slowly, and enjoy the warm feeling on cold nights.

Serves 1.

Salmon Mousse

    1 ¼-ounce envelope unflavored
        gelatin
    2 tablespoons lemon juice
    1 slice onion
    ½ cup boiling water
    ❧ ❧ ❧
    ½ cup mayonnaise
    1 16-ounce can red salmon, drained

¼ teaspoon paprika
1 teaspoon dill

ча   ча   ча

1 cup heavy cream

In a blender combine the gelatin packet, lemon juice, slice of onion, and boiling water. Cover the blender and blend on high speed for 40 seconds. Turn off. Add the mayonnaise, salmon, paprika, and dill. Cover and blend on high speed until well blended. Turn the blender to low speed, remove the cover, and gradually add the heavy cream. Blend for 30 seconds. Pour into a 4-cup ring mold and chill until firm. Unmold on a platter and garnish the center of the ring with fresh watercress. Serve with slices of rye and pumpernickel bread.

This mousse has a very pretty delicate color.

Serves 6 to 8.

Orange Marmalade Muffins

1½ cups all-purpose flour
½ cup sugar
1 teaspoon baking powder
1 teaspoon baking soda
1 teaspoon salt

ча   ча   ча

½ cup orange juice
⅓ cup orange marmalade
6 tablespoons butter, melted
1 egg

ча   ча   ча

½ cup golden raisins

Grease and flour muffin tins or line with paper liners. In a small bowl sift together the flour, sugar, baking powder, baking soda, and salt. Set aside. In a medium mixing bowl combine the orange juice, marmalade, melted butter, and egg. Sift the flour mixture into the orange mixture, and stir until just combined. Fold in the raisins. Divide the batter into the prepared muffin tins. Bake in a 400° oven for 15 to 20 minutes.

Makes 12 muffins.

Country Fruit Squares

1 8-ounce can refrigerated crescent rolls
1 3-ounce package cream cheese, softened
¾ cup sugar
1 tablespoon lemon juice
2 eggs
½ cup coconut
1 8¼-ounce can crushed pineapple, well drained

Separate the dough into 2 long rectangles. Place in an ungreased 9x13-inch pan, pressing over the bottom to form the crust. Seal the perforations. Bake in a 375° oven for 5 minutes.

In a small bowl combine the cream cheese, sugar, lemon juice, and eggs. Blend until smooth. Stir in the coconut and pineapple; mix well. Pour the mixture over the partially baked crust, spreading evenly. Bake an additional 20 to 28 minutes or until the crust is golden brown and the filling is set. Cool completely and cut into squares.

Variations: If desired, sprinkle with confectioners' sugar and garnish with slices of kiwi or strawberries. Cherry or blueberry pie filling may be substituted for the pineapple. If so, leave out the ¾ cup of sugar.

Makes 12 squares or 36 bars.

Beef Bourguignon

This is a favorite of our guests. To take the best advantage of the sauce serve over steamed rice or noodles. We usually add a green salad tossed with olive oil and wine vinegar dressing, and serve cheesecake or sour cream lemon pie for dessert.

2 cups sliced onions
4 to 6 tablespoons olive or peanut oil
1 cup all-purpose flour
1 teaspoon garlic powder
2 tablespoons sweet paprika
4 pounds beef sirloin, cut into 2-inch cubes
1¾ cups Burgundy wine
1¾ cups beef consommé
¼ teaspoon ground fresh pepper
1 bay leaf
½ teaspoon thyme

ча   ча   ча

1 pound fresh mushrooms, thickly sliced
4 tablespoons butter
½ teaspoon garlic powder
¼ cup chopped parsley

In a skillet sauté the onions in olive oil. Transfer to a casserole dish. In a bowl combine the flour, garlic powder, and paprika. Toss the beef in the flour mixture. In the same skillet used for the onions, brown the beef. Add more oil if needed. Transfer the beef to the casserole dish. In the skillet heat the wine and consommé, then pour over the beef. Add the pepper, bay leaf, and thyme. Cover and bake in a 350° oven for 2 hours.

Sauté the mushrooms in butter and garlic powder. Remove the casserole from the oven and add the mushrooms. Return the casserole to the oven and bake for an additional hour. Garnish with parsley.

Serves 12.

Carrot-Prune-Raisin Cake

2 cups all-purpose flour
2 teaspoons baking soda
2 teaspoons baking powder

1 teaspoon salt
¼ teaspoon nutmeg
¼ teaspoon allspice
1 tablespoon cinnamon
7 large pitted prunes, chopped
¾ cup chopped pecans

&amp#x25AB; &amp#x25AB; &amp#x25AB;

4 large eggs
2 cups sugar
1½ cups oil
5 medium carrots, grated
¾ cup golden raisins

&amp#x25AB; &amp#x25AB; &amp#x25AB;

2 tablespoons confectioners' sugar

Grease and flour a 12-cup bundt pan. In a mixing bowl sift together the flour, baking soda, baking powder, salt, and spices. Add the chopped prunes and toss to coat. Add the nuts. In a separate mixing bowl beat the eggs and sugar until frothy. Add the oil while continuing to beat. Add the carrots and raisins, and mix well. Add the dry ingredients a little at a time, mixing until well combined. Pour the batter into the prepared pan. Bake in a 350° oven for 55 minutes. Cool in the pan for 10 minutes, then invert onto a wire rack. Cool completely. Sift the confectioners' sugar over the cake.

Note: This can be baked in three 8-inch round pans and frosted with cream cheese frosting.

Serves 12 to 18.

Arkansas

The Great Southern Hotel

127 West Cedar
Brinkley, Arkansas 72021
(501) 734-4955

Built in 1915 as the Rusher Hotel, the Great Southern Hotel was resurrected as a hotel in 1981 and restored to its former use. The large, spacious lobby has fifteen-foot pressed-tin ceilings and marble wainscotting. Breakfast is served in the rooms; lunch and dinner are available in the hotel's Victorian Tea Room.

Spinach-Cheese Grits

    4 cups water
    ½ teaspoon salt
    ½ teaspoon garlic powder
    1 cup quick grits
    1 10-ounce package frozen chopped
        spinach, thawed
    2 cups grated Cheddar cheese
    4 eggs
    Grated cheese for garnish

Grease a 3-quart baking dish. Bring the water, salt, and garlic powder to a boil. Stir in the grits. Cook for 2 minutes. Remove from the heat and stir in the spinach and cheese. Beat the eggs and stir into the grits mixture. Pour the grits into the prepared baking dish. Bake in a 350° oven for 30 to 45 minutes or until the grits are puffy. Top with grated cheese and return to the oven to melt the cheese.

This dish can be served at any meal from brunch to dinner.
Serves 4 to 6.

Delta Pork

    2 pounds pork tenderloin, thinly
        sliced
    4 tablespoons butter
    1 apple, sliced
    1 8-ounce carton heavy cream
    Rosemary or tarragon
    Pepper

Pound the slices of pork very thin. Melt the butter in a skillet. Add the pork and cook until the edges are slightly brown and the pork is done but not overcooked. Add the apple slices and simmer on low heat for 1 to 2 minutes. Increase the heat to medium and add the cream. Add rosemary or tarragon and pepper to taste. Remove from the heat when the butter and cream are well blended and thickened slightly.

Note from the innkeeper: Delta Pork is very quick and easy to fix. We use this for a dinner menu, but it could be prepared with rosemary and served over biscuits.
Serves 4.

Tender Comfort Steak

    2 ounces Southern Comfort
    1 tablespoon brown sugar
    2 8-ounce fillets beef tenderloin
    4 tablespoons butter
    6 peppercorns
    Dash rosemary
    Dash basil

Combine the Southern Comfort and brown sugar. Marinate the beef in the mixture for 30 minutes. Melt the butter in a skillet and add the steaks. Reserve the marinade. Cook covered over low heat. Watch closely. The sugar content is high and they will burn if the heat is too high. Cook until almost done, and add the peppercorns and other seasonings. Pour in the marinade and heat through. Be careful; the marinade is flammable. Serve the liquid poured over the steak.
Serves 2.

Arkansas Derby Pie

    3 eggs
    ¾ cup sugar
    1 cup dark corn syrup
    1 tablespoon melted butter
    ½ teaspoon salt
    2 tablespoons Southern Comfort
    1 teaspoon vanilla extract

        🍂 🍂 🍂

    ¼ cup coconut
    ½ cup chocolate chips
    ½ cup pecans

        🍂 🍂 🍂

    1 unbaked 9-inch pie crust

Beat the eggs slightly with an electric mixer. Add the sugar, corn syrup, butter, salt, Southern Comfort, and vanilla extract. Combine the coconut, chocolate chips, and pecans. Sprinkle the pecan mixture over the unbaked pie shell. Pour the syrup mixture over the pecan mixture. Bake in a 375° oven for 45 minutes.

Serves 6 to 8.

Bridgeford Cottage

263 Spring Street
Eureka Springs, Arkansas 72632
(501) 253-7853

Bridgeford Cottage, nestled in the heart of Eureka Springs's historic residential district, is a Victorian delight. The gracious hospitality of that era has been carefully rekindled in this 1884 gingerbread house. Outside, shady porches invite guests to pull up a wicker chair, relax, and enjoy the panorama of Spring Street. Bridgeford Cottage is within walking distance of downtown Eureka Springs, but far enough away from its hustle and bustle to afford guests a peaceful, calm visit.

Frozen Fruit Salad

1 cup sugar
1 8-ounce package cream cheese, softened
1 16-ounce can apricots, drained
1 11-ounce can Mandarin oranges, drained
½ cup chopped pecans
1 8-ounce carton whipped topping
Lettuce leaves

Blend the sugar and cream cheese. Add the fruit and pecans, mixing well.

Fold in the whipped topping. Spread the salad into a 9x13-inch pan. Cover with plastic wrap and freeze.

Cut into squares and serve on lettuce leaves.

Serves 10 to 12.

Ozark Corn Scallop

1 16-ounce can whole kernel corn
1 16-ounce can cream-style corn
2 eggs, slightly beaten
⅔ cup evaporated milk
¼ cup corn liquid
¼ cup butter, melted
2 tablespoons minced onion
½ teaspoon salt
¼ teaspoon pepper
2 cups coarsely crushed saltines
12 ounces diced Cheddar cheese
1 8-ounce can oysters, drained (optional)

Butter a 10-inch casserole dish. Drain the whole kernel corn, reserving ¼ cup of liquid. Combine the corn with the reserved liquid and remaining ingredients, and turn the mixture into the prepared dish. Bake in a 325° oven for 1 hour.

Serves 6.

Dairy Hollow House

515 Spring Street
Eureka Springs, Arkansas 72632
(501) 253-7444

An award-winning country inn and restaurant, Dairy Hollow House is in two homes, the Farmhouse (a small restored 1880s Ozark farmhouse) and

Bridgeford Cottage

Suites on Spring/The Restaurant at Dairy Hollow (a large 1940s bungalow-style home with additions). Named after the "hollow," or valley, on the outskirts of town where several small dairies were once located, the inn reflects the love for historic preservation of its owners, Ned Shank and Crescent Dragonwagon, noted author of cookbooks, fiction, and children's books.

Apple-glazed Rock Cornish Game Hens

We do a slightly different version of this recipe with various fruits in season. This and Game Hens Glazed with Blueberry Chutney are our favorites.

    4 game hens, thawed if frozen
    1 tart apple (Granny Smith),
        unpeeled, cored and quartered
    4 green onions
    4 stalks celery, with leaves
    4 tablespoons raisins
    4 small sticks cinnamon
    Paprika

        ❧ ❧ ❧

    1 gallon fresh-pressed cider, boiled
        down to 1 quart
    1 cup Bleumarie Tarragon Mustard
    ½ cup honey
    ½ cup Tamari soy sauce
    ¼ cup cider vinegar

        ❧ ❧ ❧

    1 to 2 cups chicken broth
    Salt and pepper

        ❧ ❧ ❧

    4 herb sprigs with stiff stem, such
        as fresh thyme or tarragon
    1 apple, unpeeled, cored and
        quartered

Grease a baking dish. Stuff each game hen with ¼ of an apple, a green onion folded in half, a stalk of celery folded in half, 1 tablespoon of raisins, and a stick of cinnamon. Tie the legs. Place the game hens breast-side-down in the prepared baking dish. Sprinkle with paprika. Place the hens in a 325° oven.

Meanwhile, in a large nonstick skillet combine the reduced cider, mustard, honey, soy sauce, and cider vinegar, and stir over medium heat until a consistency similar to honey. This takes about 30 minutes.

After the hens have baked 30 to 45 minutes, turn them over. Take care not to puncture the breast skin if possible. If the pan juices seem in danger of burning, add chicken broth. Continue baking for 15 minutes. Baste with the cider glaze. Baste every 10 to 15 minutes with glaze and/or pan juices until the hens are done, about 1 hour and 15 minutes to 1 hour and 30 minutes. Salt and pepper the hens with the last basting.

When the hens are done, untruss the legs. Heat the remaining glaze. Pour a little glaze on the serving plates, then place a hen on each plate. Ladle a little glaze over the hens. Garnish with an herb sprig poked in where the drumstick joins the body. Place an apple quarter on the plate.

Serves 4.

Dairy Hollow House Iced Herbal Cooler

This cooler is refreshing, caffeine-free, and delicious. In hot weather, each room is provided with a pitcher of cooler at check-in.

    4 cups boiling water
    8 Red Zinger (or similar) tea bags

    1 12-ounce can apple juice
        concentrate, reconstituted
    Juice of 1 orange
    1 lemon, sliced
    1 orange, sliced
    Sprigs of fresh mint and/or
        honeysuckle

Pour the boiling water over the tea bags. Let the tea steep until the water is lukewarm, making a very strong tea. Wring out the tea bags to get even more flavor. In a large pitcher combine the tea, apple juice, and orange juice. Garnish the pitcher with lemon and orange slices. Garnish each serving with a mint or honeysuckle sprig.

Serves 6 amply.

Vegetable Stuffing
for Vegetarian Harvest Platter

Often vegetarians feel overlooked at a restaurant. We try to make them feel otherwise with our Harvest Platter of Three Stuffed Vegetables. This consists of any three of the following: a tomato stuffed with a spinach-parmesan mixture, an eggplant quarter stuffed with a garlicky ratatouille, a couple of mushrooms stuffed with sautéed mushrooms, onions, and nuts, and a stuffed zucchini half or blanched cabbage leaf stuffed with the mixture below.

    1 purple onion, sliced
    1 carrot, grated
    4 tablespoons olive oil
    3 to 4 cups cooked Uncle Ben's
        Converted Rice
    ½ cup raisins
    3 tablespoons dried dill weed
    3 tablespoons fresh parsley
    Salt and freshly-ground black
        pepper
    ½ cup cooked, well-drained chick
        peas (optional)
    ¾ cup toasted walnuts

        ❧ ❧ ❧

    Sour cream
    1 cup diced canned tomatoes (or
        peeled, diced fresh tomatoes)

        ❧ ❧ ❧

    6 ounces grated Cheddar cheese

In a skillet sauté the onions and carrots in olive oil. In a large bowl combine the onion and carrot mixture with the next 7 ingredients.

For stuffed cabbage leaves: Blanch 6 to 8 large outer cabbage leaves for 3 minutes in boiling water. Roll ¼ cup of stuffing mixture in each leaf. Place seam side down in a greased baking dish. Dot with sour cream and scatter with the diced tomatoes. Bake in a 325° oven for 30 minutes.

For stuffed zucchini: Halve 3 to 4 zucchini or summer squash. Remove the seeds and make a hollow with a melon baller. Steam the zucchini over boiling water for 2 minutes. Stuff the zucchini with the stuffing mixture, top with grated Cheddar cheese, and press the cheese into the stuffing. Place the zucchini in a greased baking dish. Bake in a 325° oven for 30 minutes.

Leftover stuffing is delicious as a side dish, or reheated for lunch the next day.

Serves 3 to 4.

The Heartstone Inn and Cottages

35 Kingshighway
Eureka Springs, Arkansas 72632
(501) 253-8916

Called the "best breakfast in the Ozarks" by the *New York Times,* this restored two-story Victorian home with wrap-around verandahs was voted one of the ten best new inns for 1985 by the *National Inn Review.* Each carefully restored room has a private bath, antique furnishings, air conditioning, and cable television. A full gourmet breakfast is served in the new breakfast room. Coffee or cold drinks are available throughout the day or evening in the cozy guest lounge or under umbrellas on the deck overlooking a wooded ravine. The inn has ample off-street parking, and the trolley stops at the front door.

Zippy Artichoke Oven Omelet

¾ cup hot picante sauce or salsa
1 cup chopped artichoke hearts
¼ cup grated Parmesan cheese
1 cup shredded Monterey Jack cheese
1 cup shredded sharp Cheddar cheese
6 eggs
1 8-ounce carton sour cream
Tomato wedges (optional)
Parsley sprigs (optional)

Grease a 10-inch quiche dish. Spread the picante in the bottom. Distribute the chopped artichokes evenly over the picante sauce. Sprinkle Parmesan cheese over the artichokes. Sprinkle the Monterey Jack and Cheddar cheese over all. Place the eggs in a blender container and blend until smooth. Add the sour cream and blend. Pour the egg mixture over the cheeses. Bake uncovered in a 350° oven for 30 to 40 minutes, or until set. Cut into wedges and serve garnished with tomato wedges and parsley.

Serves 6.

Cornucopia Muffins

4 eggs
2 cups sugar
2 tablespoons vanilla extract
1 cup vegetable oil
2 cups unpeeled shredded zucchini
2 cups shredded carrot

🍂 🍂 🍂

4 cups all-purpose flour
2 teaspoons baking soda

The Heartstone Inn and Cottages

½ teaspoon baking powder
1 teaspoon salt
3 teaspoons cinnamon

🍂 🍂 🍂

2 cups dried mixed fruit bits
1 cup chopped pecans

Grease muffin cups. Combine the first 4 ingredients, mixing well. Stir in the shredded zucchini and carrot. Set the mixture aside. Combine the next 5 ingredients in a large bowl. Measure ⅓ cup of flour mixture and toss with the dried fruit and pecans. Make a well in the center of the flour mixture and add the zucchini-carrot mixture, stirring until just moistened. Stir in the dried fruit and pecans. Spoon the mixture into the muffin cups, filling ⅔ full. Bake in a 350° oven for about 20 minutes.

Makes about 3 dozen muffins.

Singleton House Bed & Breakfast Inn

11 Singleton
Eureka Springs, Arkansas 72632
(501) 253-9111

Singleton House is an old-fashioned inn in a restored country Victorian home. Its light, airy guest rooms are furnished with ceiling fans and handmade quilts on antique brass and iron bedsteads. Although the atmosphere "feels" secluded, the quaint shops and cafes of Eureka Springs's historic district are but a short walk away. Breakfast is served on the balcony, where one also can watch the animals playing in the gardens.

Lemon Sherbet

This is great with sliced green grapes or chopped strawberries.

1½ cups apple juice
2½ cups water or more
½ teaspoon lemon juice
¼ cup kuzu or arrowroot

In a saucepan dilute the apple juice with water until very little apple taste remains and the taste is only slightly sweet. Add the lemon juice. In a separate container place 1 cup of this liquid with the kuzu, and set aside. Bring the mixture in the saucepan to a boil, reduce the heat, and simmer for 15 to 20 minutes. Add the diluted kuzu and stir until transparent. Freeze until firm.

Serves 4.

Singleton House

Light Lemon Pie

⅔ cup arrowroot
2 teaspoons agar-agar
1 teaspoon sea salt
3½ cups water
2 cups rice syrup
4 teaspoons pure maple syrup
½ cup fresh lemon juice
1½ teaspoons grated lemon rind
1 teaspoon pure vanilla extract
1 10-inch baked pie shell

In a medium saucepan combine the arrowroot, agar-agar, and salt. Slowly add the water, stirring to dissolve all of the ingredients. Bring the mixture to a boil over medium heat, stirring often. Reduce the heat to low and simmer for 10 minutes, stirring often. Add the rice syrup, maple syrup, lemon juice, and lemon rind, and simmer for a few minutes more. Add the vanilla and set aside to cool. Stir the cooled lemon filling and pour into the baked pie shell. Cool completely and refrigerate for 4 hours or until set.

Serves 6 to 8.

Tofu Whipped Cream

1 cup tofu
Boiling water
6 tablespoons rice syrup
1 tablespoon oil
Pinch sea salt
3 tablespoons agar-agar
½ cup apple juice
1 teaspoon vanilla extract

In a saucepan bring water to a boil and drop the tofu into the water. Remove from the heat and cool for 2 to 3 minutes. Squeeze the liquid out of the tofu. In a bowl blend the tofu, rice syrup, oil, and sea salt together until creamy. Set aside. In a saucepan combine the agar-agar and apple juice, and bring to a boil. Lower the heat and simmer until the agar-agar dissolves. Remove from the heat. Add the vanilla and the tofu mixture. Set aside to gel. When the mixture has almost set, beat again. Set aside for a few hours to mellow. Chill. To freshen, beat again before using.

Makes about 1½ cups.

Corn Cob Inn

Route 1, Box 183
Everton, Arkansas 72633
(501) 429-6545

This historical stone house sits beside Clear Creek in the Ozarks. The Corn Cob Inn originally was built as a general store for a mining community, then was used as a corn cob pipe factory, and now is a comfortable home situated on eighteen acres. The Corn Cob Inn is a perfect place to relax; its three bedrooms share a bath. A country-style breakfast is served in the dining room or on the patio. Lunch and dinner are also available on request. The creek offers fishing, swimming, and floating. The Corn Cob Inn is near many Ozark attractions.

Whole Wheat Pancakes

½ cup wheat germ
2 cups whole wheat flour
2 teaspoons baking powder
1 tablespoon brown sugar
1 teaspoon salt
2 large eggs
2½ to 3 cups milk
2 tablespoons oil
Sesame seeds
Blueberry Sauce (recipe follows)
 and sour cream

Stir together all of the dry ingredients with a fork. Beat the eggs lightly and add the milk. Add the egg mixture to the dry ingredients and stir briefly. Stir in the oil with a few strokes. Heat a griddle (do not grease it) and sprinkle with some sesame seeds. Pour ½ cup of batter onto the griddle. Cook at medium heat, turning the pancakes over when the edges are dry and bubbles come to the surface.

Serve with hot Blueberry Sauce and sour cream.
Serves 6 to 8.

Blueberry Sauce

¾ cup water
¼ cup sugar
1 tablespoon lemon juice
1 teaspoon cornstarch
1 cup fresh blueberries

In a small saucepan bring the water and sugar to a boil. Stir until the sugar has dissolved. Add the lemon juice. Mix the cornstarch with 1 tablespoon of water and then add to the syrup. Cook, stirring constantly, for 1 minute. Add the blueberries and cook for 30 seconds.
Serve warm over Whole Wheat Pancakes with a dollop of sour cream.
Serves 6 to 8.

Australian Pancakes

1 cup all-purpose flour
Pinch salt
2 eggs
1 cup milk

🐦 🐦 🐦

Lemon juice
Sugar

Sift together the flour and salt. Make a well in the center and add the eggs. Work the flour from the sides. Add the milk a little at a time. Beat well until the bubbles rise to the surface. Let the batter stand for 1 hour.
Heat a lightly greased griddle. Pour 2 to 3 tablespoons of batter onto the griddle in a very thin layer. Cook slowly, loosening the edges with a knife until set and lightly brown underneath. Toss or carefully turn and brown on the other side. Sprinkle with lemon juice and sugar. Roll up and keep warm while preparing the remaining batter.
Serves 4.

Pepper and Cheese Custard

This is a crustless quiche.

2 bell peppers, diced
3 to 4 hot peppers, diced
1 tablespoon oil
2 cups cottage cheese
4 cups grated Cheddar cheese
10 eggs
1 cup milk

In a skillet sauté the peppers in oil until soft. Combine the peppers, cottage cheese, and grated Cheddar. Place the mixture in a casserole dish or quiche pan. Beat the eggs with the milk and pour the mixture over the cheese mixture. Bake in a 350° oven for 35 to 40 minutes, until golden on top and a knife inserted in the center comes out clean.
Serves 8, or makes 64 appetizers.

🐦 🐦 🐦 🐦 🐦

Baked Garlic Soup

2 cups diced fresh tomatoes
1 15-ounce can garbanzo beans,
 undrained
4 to 5 summer squash, sliced
2 large onions, sliced
½ green pepper, diced
1½ cups dry white wine
4 to 5 cloves garlic, minced
1 bay leaf
2 teaspoons salt
1 teaspoon basil
½ teaspoon paprika

🐦 🐦 🐦

1¼ cups grated Monterey Jack
 cheese
1¼ cups heavy cream

Combine all of the ingredients except the cheese and cream in a 3-quart baking dish. Cover and bake in a 375° oven for 1 hour. Stir in the cheese and cream and lower the heat to 325°. Bake 10 to 15 minutes longer, making sure it doesn't boil.
Serves 4 to 6.

Thomas Quinn Guest House

814 North B Street
Fort Smith, Arkansas 72901
(501) 782-0499

The Thomas Quinn Guest House is on the edge of Fort Smith's historic district. The first story was built in 1863, with the second floor and Corinthian columns added in 1916. There are seven two-bedroom suites and two one-bedroom suites. All suites have a furnished compact kitchen with bar, living room, full private bath, cable TV, and private phones. The Thomas Quinn House offers a large patio area complete with Jacuzzi and large fish pond. Complimentary coffee is provided in each suite with a continental breakfast across the street Monday through Friday. Horse-drawn carriage rides to local points of interest are available.

Applesauce-Orange Salad

1 46-ounce can applesauce
1 6-ounce package orange gelatin
Grated rind and juice of 1 orange

In a saucepan heat the applesauce until bubbly. Add the gelatin, grated rind, and orange juice. Stir to combine and dissolve the gelatin. Pour into a 6-cup mold. Refrigerate the salad until firm.
Serves 8.

Mandarin Orange Salad

1 6-ounce package orange gelatin
2 cups hot water
1 pint orange sherbet
1 11-ounce can Mandarin oranges, drained
1 8½-ounce can crushed pineapple

Dissolve the gelatin in the hot water. Add the remaining ingredients and pour the mixture into an 8-cup mold. Refrigerate until firm.
Serves 8.

Raspberry Salad

1 3-ounce package raspberry gelatin
1 cup hot water
1 10-ounce package frozen raspberries
1 cup miniature marshmallows
1 1¼-ounce package Dream Whip, prepared
1 3-ounce package cream cheese, softened

Dissolve the gelatin in the hot water. Add the frozen raspberries and cool the mixture to room temperature. Add the marshmallows and chill until firm. Combine the Dream Whip and cream cheese, and spread the mixture over the salad. Chill.
Serves 4 to 6.

ᔗ ᔗ ᔗ ᔗ ᔗ

Fools Cove Ranch

Post Office Box 10
Kingston, Arkansas 72742
(501) 665-2986

Situated on 160 acres of Ozark mountain land, Fools Cove Ranch provides its guests with a spectacular view. Presently there are three bedrooms with a shared bathroom; soon a suite will be added, with its own sitting area, bath, and private entrance.
Fools Cove Ranch is situated near Eureka Springs and Fayetteville, Arkansas, a short drive south of Branson, Missouri. Corrals on the property accommodate guests who wish to bring their own horses to ride. The ranch is close to the headwaters of the Buffalo River National River Wilderness Area, a popular canoeing venue.

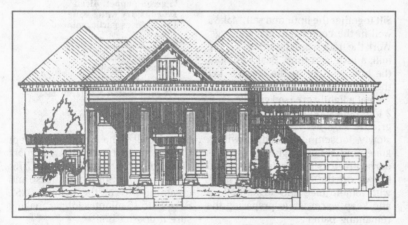

Thomas Quinn Guest House

Sullivan Special Baked Beans

Excellent for large picnics.

¼ pound bacon, chopped
1 large onion, chopped
1⅓ cups packed dark brown sugar
2 tablespoons prepared mustard
2 6-pound 10-ounce cans pork and
  beans

In a large skillet brown the bacon until crisp. Reserve some of the bacon grease and sauté the onion until translucent. Combine the brown sugar and mustard. Add some of the liquid from the beans to soften the brown sugar. Combine all of the ingredients in large casserole dishes. Bake in a 325° oven for 2 hours or until thickened.
Serves about 45 to 50.

Double Chocolate Zucchini Cake

½ cup butter, softened
½ cup oil
1¾ cups sugar

2 eggs
1 teaspoon vanilla extract
½ cup sour milk
2½ cups all-purpose flour
4 tablespoons cocoa
1 teaspoon baking soda
½ teaspoon cinnamon
½ teaspoon cloves
½ teaspoon salt
2 cups grated zucchini

❧   ❧   ❧

1 cup chopped nuts
1 cup miniature chocolate chips

Grease a 9x13-inch pan. In a large bowl combine all of the ingredients except the nuts and chocolate chips in the order given. Pour the batter into the prepared pan. Top with the nuts and chocolate chips. Bake in a 325° oven for 45 minutes.
Serves 10.

Peachy Peach Cobbler

2 cups peeled sliced peaches
Dash allspice
Sugar to taste

❧   ❧   ❧

¾ cup sugar
3 tablespoons butter or margarine
1 teaspoon baking powder
¼ teaspoon salt
½ cup milk
1 cup all-purpose flour

❧   ❧   ❧

1 cup sugar
1 tablespoon cornstarch

❧   ❧   ❧

⅔ cup boiling water

Toss the peaches with the allspice and sugar to taste. Arrange the peaches in the bottom of an 11x7-inch pan.
Combine ¾ cup of sugar, the butter, baking powder, salt, milk, and flour. Spread the mixture over the peaches. Combine the remaining ingredients and sprinkle the mixture over the cobbler. Pour the boiling water over all. Bake in a 375° oven for 45 minutes.
Serves 6.

California

Forest Manor

415 Cold Springs Road
Angwin, CA 94508
(707) 965-3538

Forest Manor is a beautiful, secluded twenty-acre estate in the hills above St. Helena in the renowned Napa Valley wine country. Adjoining a 100-acre vineyard, it offers a tranquil environment, picnic areas, and extensive paths through a forest that abounds with deer and wildlife. The manor has three stories of guest rooms and features spacious air-conditioned rooms, high vaulted ceilings, and massive hand-carved beams. Furnished with English antiques, Persian carpets, and Oriental art, it provides guests with feelings of warmth and openness. It also features fireplaces, decks, coffee pots in every room, a game room, a swimming pool, and outdoor Jacuzzi.

In the area are historic wineries, superb restaurants, antique shops, hot air ballooning, glider flights, and Robert Louis Stevenson Museum and State Park.

Rice Delight

1 cup butter
2 cups George Washington broth
2 14½-ounce cans Mexican-style stewed tomatoes
½ can (5 ounces) tomato soup, undiluted
1 tablespoon Pickapeppa or Worcestershire sauce
2 cups shredded Cheddar cheese
2 cups chopped or sliced olives
2 cups uncooked rice

In a saucepan melt the butter and add the broth. Combine the remaining ingredients in a casserole dish. Pour the broth over all. Cover and bake in a 350° oven for 1 hour.
Serves 8.

❧ ❧ ❧ ❧ ❧

Corlene's Baked Beans

2 cups dried small Navy beans
½ cup oil
1 cup boiling water
½ cup catsup
1 onion, diced
2 tablespoons molasses
1 tablespoon salt
1 teaspoon paprika
½ cup brown sugar

In a bean pot soak the beans overnight in water to cover. Cook the beans until tender, about 30 to 45 minutes.

Combine the remaining ingredients, blending well. Add the mixture to the beans. Cook over low heat for 7 hours, or bake in a 375° oven for 1 hour.
Serves 8.

The Guest House Bed and Breakfast Inn

120 Hart Lane
Arroyo Grande, California 93420
(805) 481-9304

The Guest House, situated in the charming old village of Arroyo Grande, was built in the 1850s by a sea captain from New England. Hosts Mark Miller and Jim Cunningham have kept the flavor of old New England alive with many family heirlooms to create a mellow and inviting home. A crackling fire in the fireplace and easy chairs make the living room a haven for relaxation and easy conversation, adding to the enjoyment of afternoon wine and cheeses.

Several of these recipes are taken directly from *Miss Parloo's New Cook Book* published in Boston, Massachusettes, in 1883. I have found them a pleasant change from some of our modern dishes, and a definite part of our colonial heritage, as well as those "good old days."

❧ ❧ ❧ ❧ ❧

Eggs Broville

2 mushrooms, diced
1 tablespoon butter

🍂 🍂 🍂

6 eggs
1 teaspoon salt
Pepper to taste
Dash nutmeg
½ cup heavy cream
3 tablespoons butter

In a small skillet sauté the mushrooms in 1 tablespoon of butter. Beat the remaining ingredients together and transfer to a saucepan. Add the mushrooms. Cook over moderate heat, stirring constantly, until the mixture begins to thicken. Remove from the heat and beat rapidly until quite thick and creamy. Serve at once on heated dishes.
   Serves 4.

Flannel Cakes

These were a great favorite for the 6 a.m. breakfast on my grandfather's farm and are favored by our guests here at The Guest House. . . . Eggs

Broville or Scotch Eggs are a perfect companion for them.

3 cups milk
1 cup cornmeal
2 tablespoons butter

🍂 🍂 🍂

¼ cake compressed yeast
4 tablespoons cold water

🍂 🍂 🍂

2 cups all-purpose flour
1 teaspoon salt
1 tablespoon sugar

Bring the milk to a boil. In a bowl, combine the cornmeal and butter. Pour the hot milk over the cornmeal, stirring constantly. In a separate bowl dissolve the yeast in the water. When the cornmeal mixture has cooled, add the yeast and and remaining ingredients. Let the mixture rise overnight.
   Cook the mixture on a hot griddle as you would griddle cakes.
   Serves 6 to 8.

Potato Fritters

2 cups mashed potatoes
½ cup hot milk

3 tablespoons sugar
1 teaspoon salt
Pinch nutmeg
2 eggs, well-beaten

🍂 🍂 🍂

2 eggs, well-beaten
1 cup bread crumbs

Butter an 8-inch square pan. In a large bowl combine the potatoes with the next 5 ingredients. Stir until very smooth and light. Spread the mixture into the prepared pan. Set aside to cool. When the mixture is firm, cut into 9 squares. Dip the squares into the egg, then into the bread crumbs. Fry in hot oil until golden. Serve immediately.
   Makes 9 squares.

The Village Inn

407 El Camino Real
Arroyo Grande, California 93420
(805) 489-5926

The Village Inn offers a delightful blend of yesterday's charm and hospitality with today's comforts and conveniences. Featuring Victorian farm-style architecture, the inn is decorated with Laura Ashley prints and wallcoverings and antiques. Each of the seven bedrooms has a private bath, and sitting area, as well as its own color scheme and style. Wine and cheese (or tea and cookies) are served in the late afternoon in the parlor, where guests gather. Television, games, and puzzles are provided for enjoyment. Smoking is not permitted indoors.
   The Village Inn is situated near the Central Coast of California, affording guests ample opportunity for touring wineries, shopping quaint shops, riding horseback on the beach, visiting the nearby Hearst Castle, and much more.

Forest Manor

Mexican Quiche

10 eggs, beaten
½ cup all-purpose flour
1 tablespoon baking powder
Dash salt
2 4-ounce cans diced green chilies
1 pint cottage cheese
4 cups shredded Monterey Jack and/
or Cheddar cheese
½ cup melted butter

Grease a 13x9-inch Pyrex dish. In a large bowl mix the ingredients in the order given. Pour into the greased dish. Bake in a 400° oven for 15 minutes. Reduce the heat to 350° and continue to bake for 20 minutes or until a knife inserted in the center comes out clean.

Serves 14.

Scrambled Eggs and Zucchini

½ onion, sliced
3 tablespoons parsley
2 tablespoons oil
6 to 8 small zucchini, sliced
Salt to taste
4 eggs, beaten

2 tablespoons Parmesan cheese

In a medium skillet fry the onion and parsley in oil until the onion is golden. Add the sliced zucchini, cover, and cook until tender. Salt to taste. Add the eggs and Parmesan cheese. Reduce the heat and cook, turning often until the eggs are set.

Serves 4 to 6.

Union Hotel

401 First Street
Benicia, California 94510
(707) 746-0100

Built in 1882 and active as a twenty-room bordello from then until the early 1950s, the Union Hotel was completely renovated in 1981 into a twelve-room inn that mixes the best of a hotel and a bed and breakfast. Each uniquely decorated room has a

queen- or king-size bed, temperature control, private bath with Jacuzzi bathtub, and television. The stained glass windows in the bar and dining room are particularly beautiful.

The Restaurant at the Union has received national acclaim for Chef Lev Dagan's modern cuisine. Situated between San Francisco and the wine country, Union Hotel is forty-five minutes from San Francisco airport.

Grilled Chicken Kebabs
with Strawberry Chutney

⅓ cup brown sugar
1 tablespoon water
½ cup raspberry vinegar
1 medium green apple, peeled,
cored, and finely chopped
1 teaspoon grated fresh ginger
1 clove garlic, pressed or minced
½ small jalapeño pepper, seeded
and minced
¼ teaspoon fresh cilantro, minced
Pinch ground cloves
Pinch ground cinnamon
Pinch salt and pepper
1 pint strawberries, rinsed,
stemmed and chopped

⁂

6 chicken kebabs

In a heavy saucepan combine the sugar and water. Bring to a boil over medium-high heat. Boil for 2 or 3 minutes, until the mixture caramelizes. Stir in the vinegar and apples, and return to a boil. Reduce the heat to medium-low. Add the seasonings. Simmer for 5 minutes. Remove from the heat and pour the mixture into a food processor or blender. Add half the strawberries. Process lightly for about 10 seconds. The mixture should be chunky. Pour into a bowl, mix in the remaining strawberries, and set aside.

Grill the chicken kebabs and place on individual plates. Top with several spoonfuls of chutney.

Serves 6.

The Village Inn

The Union Hotel

Butter a 9x5-inch baking dish. Dip the bread slices in the melted butter. Place half of the bread in the prepared baking dish. Add half of the crab and half of the cheese. Cover with buttered bread slices, and top with the remaining crab and cheese. Beat the eggs and milk, and pour over the cheese. Cover and refrigerate overnight. Uncover and bake in a 350° oven for 45 minutes.

Serves 6.

Fairview Manor

245 Fairview Avenue
Ben Lomond, California 95005
(408) 336-3355

Nestled in the heart of the San Lorenzo Valley, Fairview Manor offers two and one-half acres of privacy on landscaped grounds with winding pathways that lead to quiet rest areas. Once the site of the old Ben Lomond Hotel that was destroyed by fire in 1906, the present home was built in 1924 by a prominent San Francisco family that used it as their summer residence. In 1981 it was acquired and opened as an inn. Fairview Manor is near Henry Cowell Park with its giant redwoods, Fall Creek Park, Roaring Camp Railroad, and Boulder Creek with its famous Big Basin Park.

Crab and Cheese Soufflé

6 slices white bread
2 tablespoons butter, melted
1 pound crab meat (or 2 cans)
4 cups grated sharp Cheddar cheese
6 eggs, beaten
3 cups milk

Brannan Cottage Inn

109 Wapoo Avenue
Calistoga, California 94515
(707) 942-4200

Built in 1860 and listed on the National Register of Historic Places, Brannan Cottage Inn is the only guest house built by Sam Brannan for his Calistoga Hot Springs Resort still remaining on its original site. Carefully reconstructed, the inn is decorated in country cottage style, with light oak floors, primitive pine antiques, and fresh white wicker. The parlor is elegantly furnished, and relaxing lawns and gardens surround the inn. Its six rooms (two suites) all have private baths, private entrances, queen-size

beds, down comforters, ceiling fans, and air conditioning. Smoking is permitted outside only.

Orange Marney French Toast

8 eggs
4 egg whites
1 cup sugar
½ teaspoon salt
6 cups milk
2 tablespoons Grand Marnier
Grated zest of 2 oranges
2 loaves sweet French bread
Nutmeg

In a large mixing bowl whisk together the first 4 ingredients. Add the milk, Grand Marnier, and orange zest. Whisk again. Slice the bread into 1-inch slices and dip in the mixture until the bread is saturated, approximately 1 minute. Arrange on a baking sheet and set aside for 1 hour. If time permits, prepare this the night before and refrigerate overnight.

In a large, lightly-oiled frying pan or griddle, slowly brown both sides of the bread for about 2 to 3 minutes on each side. Remove to a clean cookie sheet and sprinkle lightly with nutmeg. When all of the slices are browned, place in a 425° oven and bake for 20 minutes. Arrange on a warm platter and sprinkle generously with powdered sugar and nutmeg. Serve immediately.

Serves 12.

Foothill House

3037 Foothill Boulevard
Calistoga, California 94515
(707) 942-6933

The Foothill House setting is distinguished by the wide variety of lovely old trees that surround it, keeping it comfortably shaded and cool. The inn offers views across the valley of wooded hills and Mount St. Helena. The Foothills' vicinity abounds with such wildlife as quail, hummingbirds, and hawks. Three cozy, yet spacious, suites are individually decorated with country antiques. The color scheme for each room complements the handmade quilt that adorns the queen-size four-poster bed.

Foothill House Fiesta Rollups

2 8-ounce packages cream cheese
1 1.25-ounce package taco seasoning mix
1 4-ounce can diced green chilies, drained
1 4-ounce can chopped ripe olives
10 flour tortillas, approximately 8 inches in diameter

In a food processor mix the cream cheese, taco seasoning, green chilies, and ripe olives until blended, about 1 minute. Spread the mixture on the tortillas and roll up. Place the rolls on a plate and refrigerate overnight. Just before serving, slice each roll into 1-inch sections. Use party toothpicks to serve. A real crowd pleaser.
Serves 80.

Baked Brie in Puff Pastry
Stuffed with Pesto

1 cup packed basil leaves
5 cloves garlic
2 tablespoons olive oil
½ cup toasted pine nuts
1 8-ounce wedge Brie
1 package puff pastry
1 egg, beaten

In a food processor chop the basil and garlic until fine. Add the olive oil

and mix for 15 seconds. Transfer to a small bowl and add the pine nuts. Cut the Brie wedge in half horizontally. Spread the pesto mixture on half, and top with the other half. Roll the puff pastry to ⅛-inch thickness. Wrap the Brie carefully in the pastry, removing any air pockets. Seal with beaten egg. Place the Brie on a plate with overlapped edges on the bottom. Brush with egg. Decorate with pastry shapes such as a grape cluster or leaves. Freeze uncovered for 1 hour. Place on a cookie sheet and bake in a 375° oven for 25 minutes or until golden brown. Cool for 5 minutes before serving.

If you want to make this ahead, after freezing the Brie for 1 hour uncovered, wrap it in foil. It will keep for up to 2 weeks.

Serve with crackers. Bon Appetit! Serves 20.

Foothill House Hot Mulled Wine

4 cups apple cider
1 cup sugar
1 orange, sliced
1 lime, sliced
1 lemon, sliced
8 whole cloves
1 stick cinnamon
2 750-ml bottles inexpensive red wine

Boil the apple juice and sugar, and stir until the sugar is completely dissolved. Reduce the heat to a simmer, and add the sliced fruit, cloves, and cinnamon stick. Simmer for 10 minutes. Remove from the heat and pour into a crock pot. Add the wine and warm for 1 hour to 1 hour and 30 minutes.

Serves 18 (6 ounce servings).

Scarlett's Country Inn

3918 Silverado Trail North
Calistoga, California 94515
(707) 942-6669

Scarlett's Country Inn is an intimate retreat tucked away in a small canyon in the heart of the famed Napa Valley wine country. Tranquility, green lawns, and a refreshing swimming pool await guests in this woodland setting. The continental breakfast is served by request on the deck, under the apple trees, at poolside, or in the cozy sitting room. The inn has two suites and one room, with separate entrances, queen-size beds, private baths, and special touches. Complimentary refreshments are served in the afternoon.

Scarlett's Buttermilk French Toast

8 eggs
1¼ cups buttermilk
1¼ teaspoons vanilla extract
Dash salt, optional
14 thick pieces white bread
Cinnamon
Confectioners' sugar
Strawberries for garnish

In a mixing bowl beat together the eggs, buttermilk, and vanilla with a fork. Add salt if desired. Grease a hot griddle or frying pan with butter. Dip pieces of bread in the egg mixture and place on the hot griddle. Spoon more mixture on top of the bread and sprinkle cinnamon on each. Fry over medium-high heat until brown on the bottom and turn over to brown the other side. Place immediately on plates or a platter and sprinkle generously with confectioners' sugar. Garnish with strawberries.

Serves 6.

Sausage-Prune Turkey Stuffing

**1 pound pitted prunes
1 cup water
1 cup vinegar**

🦐 🦐 🦐

**4 tablespoons butter
2 onions, minced
1 pound sausage
3 cups fresh bread crumbs
⅓ cup chopped parsley
1 teaspoon thyme
1 teaspoon salt
Pepper to taste**

In a small saucepan bring the prunes, water, and vinegar to a boil. Remove from the heat and allow the prunes to plump for 1 hour. Drain and cut the prunes into quarters.

In a large sauté pan cook the butter and onions over low heat until the onions are soft but not browned. Add

the sausage meat, breaking it apart and spreading it as it cooks. Simmer until the meat is crumbly and beginning to color. Remove from the heat. Drain the prunes, and stir into the sausage mixture with the remaining ingredients.

Stuffs a 12 to 15 pound turkey.

Scarlett's Holiday Chestnut Purée

**1 pound fresh chestnuts
1 13¾-ounce can chicken stock
¼ cup butter**

Place the chestnuts in a large pot with cold water. Slowly bring to a boil over medium heat. Remove from the heat, keeping the chestnuts in the warm water. Peel and skin the chestnuts. In a saucepan combine the chestnuts and chicken stock, and simmer until the chestnuts are soft. Drain, reserving the broth. Push the chestnuts through a sieve or purée in a food mill. Heat in a saucepan with butter and about ½ cup of broth until bub-

bly, stirring constantly until smooth and creamy. If the mixture is too thick, add milk or more broth.

Serve as a side dish for turkey. This can be made ahead and reheated.

Serves 4 to 5.

Scarlett's Creamy Cheesecake

**1 individual packet graham
    crackers, crumbled
¼ cup butter, melted**

🦐 🦐 🦐

**2 eggs
12 ounces cream cheese, softened
¾ cup sugar
2 teaspoons vanilla extract**

🦐 🦐 🦐

**1 cup sour cream
3 tablespoons sugar
1 teaspoon vanilla extract**

Stir together the graham cracker crumbs and melted butter. Press into a 9-inch pie pan. In a large bowl beat the eggs and cream cheese with an electric mixer on low speed. Add the sugar and 2 teaspoons vanilla. Pour into the pie shell. Bake in a 350° oven for 15 to 20 minutes, until slightly set around the edges. Cool for 5 minutes.

In a small bowl beat together the sour cream, 3 tablespoons of sugar, and 1 teaspoon vanilla. Pour over the cheesecake. Bake an additional 5 minutes. Refrigerate for at least 5 hours or overnight.

Serves 6 to 8.

Scarlett's Country Inn

Wine Way Inn

1019 Foothill Boulevard
Calistoga, California 94515
(707) 942-0680

Situated in the Napa Valley, Wine Way Inn was built in 1915 as a family home. Since 1980 it has served as an inn offering comfort and hospitality to its guests. From the warm, beamed-ceiling living room with its fireplace to the six guest rooms, all with private baths and individualized climate control, guests are treated to a homey experience reinforced by the innkeepers' hospitality. A charming gazebo on the backyard hillside affords a spectacular mountain view and an ideal place for breakfast, a picnic, or an intimate dinner. The innkeepers are gourmet cooks who have a repertoire of baked delights to accompany full breakfasts. Many recreational activities abound in the area, as do fine restaurants and shops.

Italian Sausage Casserole

½ cup butter
½ pound fresh mushrooms, sliced
1¼ cups thinly sliced yellow onions
1½ pounds mild Italian sausage
12 slices buttered bread, crusts removed
4 cups grated sharp Cheddar cheese

    ❦ ❦ ❦

5 eggs
2 cups milk
3 teaspoons Dijon mustard
1 teaspoon dry mustard
½ teaspoon nutmeg
½ teaspoon salt
½ teaspoon pepper
2 tablespoons chopped parsley

Grease a 9x13-inch casserole. In a skillet melt the butter and brown the mushrooms and onions until tender, 6 to 8 minutes. Set aside. Cook the sausage and cut into pieces. In the greased casserole place 6 slices of bread, half of the mushroom mixture, half of the sausage, and half of the cheese. Repeat the layers, ending with cheese. Mix together the eggs, milk, mustards, nutmeg, salt, and pepper. Pour over the casserole. Cover and refrigerate overnight. When ready to bake, sprinkle parsley on top and bake uncovered in a 350° oven for 1 hour. Serve immediately.
Serves 6.

Tomato Quiche

2 cups shredded Swiss cheese
1 unbaked 9-inch pie shell
3 tomatoes, peeled, chopped and drained
¼ cup chopped onion
Salt and pepper
1 teaspoon dried basil
¼ teaspoon garlic powder
2 eggs
¾ cup milk
3 tablespoons grated Parmesan cheese

Sprinkle the Swiss cheese over the bottom of the pie shell. Layer the tomatoes and onion over this. Sprinkle with salt, pepper, basil, and garlic powder. Beat the eggs and milk together, and pour the mixture over the tomatoes. Sprinkle the Parmesan cheese over the top. Bake in a 350° oven for 45 to 50 minutes.
Serves 6.

Orange Cranberry Nut Bread

2 cups all-purpose flour
1 cup sugar
1½ teaspoons baking powder
½ teaspoon baking soda
1 teaspoon salt
¼ cup margarine
2 teaspoons grated orange peel
¾ cup fresh orange juice
1 egg, well beaten
1¼ cups cranberries, finely chopped (or whole cranberry relish)
¾ cup chopped nuts

Wine Way Inn

Grease a 9x5-inch loaf pan. In a large bowl sift together the dry ingredients. Cut in the margarine. Combine the orange peel, juice, and egg. Add to the dry ingredients. Mix just enough to moisten. Fold in the cranberries and nuts. Pour into the prepared loaf pan or 3 mini loaf pans. Bake in a 350° oven for 1 hour and 10 minutes, or 50 minutes for mini pans.

Makes 1 large or 3 mini loaves.

The J. Patrick House

2990 Burton Drive
Cambria, California 93428
(805) 927-3812

This log home takes one back to a time when life moved more slowly. Each guest room has a wood burning fireplace and full private bath, with no televisions, radios, or telephones to disturb privacy or comfort; and the path to the guest rooms passes through a colorful garden with an arbor and surrounding pine trees. In the evenings guests enjoy relaxed refreshments by the fireplace in the living room.

Situated just off scenic Highway 1 on the central California coast, The J. Patrick House is six miles south of Hearst Castle and near vineyards, Morro Bay, San Luis Obispo, and Big Sur.

Sour Cream Soda Bread

1 cup butter, softened
6 tablespoons sugar
1½ teaspoons baking soda
1 teaspoon salt
4 cups all-purpose flour
1 cup raisins

2 tablespoons caraway seeds
2 cups sour cream
Milk

In a large bowl combine the butter, sugar, baking soda, salt, and flour. Mix with an electric mixer on low speed until crumbly. Fold in the raisins, seeds, and sour cream. Mix until a dough forms. Divide the dough in half and place each half on a foil-lined baking sheet. Pat each into a smooth round, using milk to create a shiny crust. Bake in a 375° oven for 50 to 60 minutes.

Makes 2 loaves, 12 servings.

The Cobblestone Inn

Post Office Box 3185
Carmel-by-the-Sea, California 93921
(408) 625-5222

The Cobblestone Inn invites guests to experience a unique country inn nestled romantically in the heart of Carmel-by-the-Sea. One of the oldest inns in the area, it presents an ideal vacation retreat setting and a quality weekend get-away for rest and relaxation. The English country garden atmosphere is enhanced by the personal attention given to each guest.

Salmon Mousse

1 ¼-ounce envelope unflavored gelatin
¼ cup cold water
½ cup boiling water
½ cup mayonnaise
1 tablespoon lemon juice
1 tablespoon finely grated onion
Dash Tabasco

The Cobblestone Inn

¼ teaspoon paprika
1 teaspoon salt
2 tablespoons dill
2 cups finely flaked fresh salmon
1 cup whipped cream

Soften the gelatin in cold water. Stir in the boiling water and stir slowly until the gelatin is dissolved. Cool. Whisk in the mayonnaise, lemon juice, grated onion, Tabasco, paprika, salt, and dill. Stir to blend well. Refrigerate for about 20 minutes, or until the mixture slightly thickens. Fold in the salmon. Whip the cream until thick and fluffy and fold gently into the salmon mixture. Chill for at least 4 hours.

Serves 4 to 6.

Italian Vegetable Chowder

3 large onions, chopped
4 tablespoons butter
6 stalks celery, chopped

❧ ❧ ❧

4 cups quartered artichoke hearts
2 28-ounce cans whole tomatoes
3 16-ounce cans garbanzo beans
2 teaspoons oregano
Salt and pepper
1 cup chicken stock
4 cups white wine

❧ ❧ ❧

6 medium zucchini, chopped
2 cups cream
1 cup Parmesan cheese

In a large stock pot sauté the onions in butter until tender. Add the celery and sauté for a few minutes. Add the artichoke hearts, tomatoes, garbanzo beans, seasonings, chicken stock, and wine. Cook for about 10 minutes. Add the zucchini and cook for a few minutes. Add the cream and heat through, but do not boil. Just before serving add the Parmesan cheese.

Serves 24.

White Sulphur Springs

Post Office Box 136
Highway 89
Clio, California 96106
(916) 836-2387

Guests of White Sulphur Springs ranch and bed and breakfast enjoy an expansive view of Mohawk Valley and the surrounding peaks as they relax by the pool or on the balcony of this luxuriously restored stagecoach stop. Built in the 1850s, it was later established as a ranch and hotel for the Truckee-Quincy stage. Many of the furnishings in its six rooms were made by one of the original owners. Guests are served a lavish breakfast in the dining room. Golf, hiking, tennis, racquetball, horseback riding, fishing, downhill and cross-country skiing are available nearby.

Praline Pumpkin Pie

⅔ cup nuts
⅔ cup brown sugar
4 tablespoons butter
1 9-inch unbaked pie shell

🍂 🍂 🍂

2 eggs, well beaten
1 16-ounce can pumpkin
⅔ cup brown sugar
1 tablespoon all-purpose flour
⅛ teaspoon mace
¼ teaspoon cloves
½ teaspoon salt
½ teaspoon ginger
½ teaspoon cinnamon
1 cup light cream or evaporated milk

In a small bowl combine the first 3 ingredients. Press the mixture into the bottom of the pie shell. Bake in a 450° oven for 10 minutes. Cool.

Combine the remaining ingredients and pour into the cooled pie shell. Bake in a 325° oven for 40 to 45 minutes.

Serves 8.

Ye Olde' Shelford House

29955 River Road
Cloverdale, California 95425
(707) 894-5956

Ye Olde' Shelford House provides its guests with a turn-of-the-century experience that will make a stay in the wine country especially memorable. Once a stagecoach stop, this restored Victorian home features high ceilings, gleaming hardwood floors, and period furniture. The six rooms (four with a private bath) are furnished with carefully selected Victorian pieces. In the mornings, breakfast is served on a prized collection of Depression glass dishes. The mood in the evenings is one of rest and relaxation.

White Sulphur Springs

Eggs Florentine Quiche

10 eggs, well beaten
12 ounces creamed cottage cheese
8 ounces Feta cheese
1 cup grated Swiss cheese
4 tablespoons butter
1 teaspoon nutmeg
2 10-ounce boxes frozen chopped spinach, thawed

Spray 2 large quiche pans with cooking spray. In a large bowl combine all of the ingredients except the spinach. Drain the spinach and add to the egg mixture. Pour the quiche mixture into the prepared pans. Bake in a 350° oven for 30 minutes.
Serves 12.

Oatmeal Pancakes

1 cup rolled oats
1 cup whole wheat flour
¼ cup wheat germ
¼ cup nonfat dry milk
1 teaspoon baking soda
¼ teaspoon salt
1 tablespoon brown sugar

  ⨎ ⨎ ⨎

2 eggs
2 cups buttermilk
¼ cup melted butter

  ⨎ ⨎ ⨎

Cider Sauce (recipe follows)

In a large bowl combine the dry ingredients. In a separate bowl combine the eggs, buttermilk, and butter. Stir the wet ingredients into the dry ingredients until well blended. Heat a skillet or griddle. Pour ½ cup of batter onto the hot skillet. Turn the pancakes when the edges are dry and bubbles come to the surface. Serve with Cider Sauce.
Serves 6.

Cider Sauce

½ cup sugar
2 tablespoons cornstarch
¼ teaspoon cinnamon

¼ teaspoon nutmeg
2 cups apple cider or apple juice
2 tablespons lemon juice

  ⨎ ⨎ ⨎

¼ cup butter

In a saucepan combine all of the ingredients except the butter. Cook the sauce over medium heat until boiling. Boil for 1 minute, stirring constantly. Add the butter and stir until melted. Remove from the heat and serve immediately.
Serves 6.

The City Hotel

Main Street
Post Office Box 1870
Columbia, California 95310
(209) 532-1479

The City Hotel in Columbia continues to provide hospitality to wayfarers as was traditionally extended 100 years ago. Small and intimate, with nine lovely and luxuriously appointed guest rooms, the hotel appears to have been left behind intact as the gold miners left and the twentieth century dawned. The service is attentive, the atmosphere warm and personal, the food and drink most satisfying, and the lodging intimate.

Buckwheat Cakes
with Maple Syrup, Apples, and Cream Cheese

These pancakes are very flavorful and make a wonderful brunch or rainy day breakfast entree.

3 cups all-purpose flour
1 teaspoon baking powder
1 teaspoon salt
2 teaspoons baking soda
1 cup buckwheat flour

  ⨎ ⨎ ⨎

4 eggs, beaten
5 cups buttermilk
3 tablespoons melted butter

  ⨎ ⨎ ⨎

2 cored, peeled large Pippin apples, cut into thin wedges
3 tablespoons butter

The City Hotel

1 cup maple syrup
1 8-ounce package cream cheese
Melted butter

In a large bowl combine the first five ingredients and mix well. In a separate bowl combine the eggs, buttermilk, and 3 tablespoons of melted butter. Pour the liquid mixture into the dry ingredients. Whisk until smooth and set aside for 30 minutes.

Meanwhile, sauté the apples with the remaining 3 tablespoons of butter and a little of the maple syrup until the apples are soft.

Pour the batter onto a hot griddle, turning when the edges are dry and bubbles come to the surface.

To serve, spread cream cheese on a pancake, cover with apples, and top with another pancake. Drizzle with melted butter and maple syrup.

Serves 8.

Recipe courtesy Chef Daniel Malzhan.

Raspberry, Pear, and Ginger Cobbler

1 cup fresh raspberries, washed
2½ cups peeled, diced Bosc pears
¼ cup sugar
2 tablespoons sweet butter
Juice and zest of 1 lemon
1 tablespoon minced fresh
    gingerroot

&a   &a   &a

1 cup unbleached all-purpose flour
2 tablespoons sugar
Pinch salt
1 teaspoon baking powder
4 tablespoons cold butter, diced
6 tablespoons buttermilk

&a   &a   &a

1 egg yolk
2 tablespoons water

&a   &a   &a

Whipping cream

Butter a 9x13-inch baking dish. Combine the fruits with the sugar, butter, lemon, and gingerroot. Place the fruit mixture in the baking dish. In a bowl combine the flour, sugar, salt, and

baking powder. Cut the butter into the dry ingredients and work together until the consistency of coarse meal. Add the buttermilk and work just until the dough holds together. Wrap the dough in plastic and refrigerate for 1 hour. Roll the dough to ⅛-inch thickness. Cut into 1-inch strips the length of the baking dish and place in a cross-hatch pattern over the fruit. Beat the egg yolk with the water and brush the dough with the mixture. Bake in a 350° oven for 20 to 25 minutes.

Serve warm with lightly whipped cream.

Serves 6 to 8.

Recipe courtesy Chef Daniel Malzhan.

The Carter House

1033 Third Street
Eureka, California 95501
(707) 445-1390

The Carter House is a recreated Victorian mansion modeled after a nineteenth-century banker's home in San Francisco destroyed in the 1906 earthquake and fire. The magnificent structure has been rebuilt in Old Town Eureka by its innkeepers, who offer unrivaled hospitality, comfort, and cuisine acclaimed nationally in such magazines as *Bon Appetit, Travel & Leisure,* and *Gourmet.* Four

of the seven guest rooms have private baths, while the remaining three share a bath.

Grilled Skewered Rabbit
with Phyllo-wrapped Chevre in a Honey-Mustard Sauce

Fresh rabbit has never been so stylish and savory! The herbal panache of this dish will wow even the most jaded gastronome.

½ cup red wine
2 cloves garlic, crushed
¼ cup extra virgin olive oil
1 tablespoon fresh rosemary
1 fresh organic rabbit, boned and
    cut into chunks

&a   &a   &a

1 cup white wine
3 shallots, chopped
3 cloves garlic, crushed
3 cups heavy cream
3 tablespoons Dijon-style mustard
1 tablespoon pure clover honey
Salt and white pepper to taste

&a   &a   &a

6 strong rosemary twigs

&a   &a   &a

4 ounces fresh chevre
2 tablespoons chopped fresh chives
1 tablespoon minced garlic
1 tablespoon fresh parsley
Phyllo dough
Clarified unsalted butter

&a   &a   &a

Rosemary leaves for garnish
Chive flowers

In a small bowl combine the red wine, 2 crushed cloves of garlic, olive oil, and rosemary. In a shallow dish marinate the rabbit chunks in the mixture for at least a couple of hours, or overnight if possible.

In a saucepan combine the white wine, shallots, and 3 crushed cloves of garlic. Reduce the mixture over medium heat until just 2 tablespoons of liquid remain. Add the heavy cream and reduce slowly over medium heat until the mixture thickens and reduces to half of its former volume, or to about 2 cups of liquid. Pour the mixture into a food processor and blend until smooth. Add the mustard and honey. Blend well, and add salt and pepper to taste. Strain through a fine mesh.

Remove the leaves from the rosemary twigs. Skewer the marinated rabbit on the rosemary twigs. Grill over a hot barbecue grill for a few minutes on each side.

In a small bowl mix together the chevre, chives, 1 tablespoon garlic, and parsley until smooth. Cut the phyllo dough into 5-inch squares. Stack four squares together, brushing with butter between layers. Place 1 tablespoon of the chevre mixture in the middle of each 4-tiered square. Gather the outer edges of the dough into a pouch around the chevre filling, and pinch together at the top. Place the bundles on an ungreased baking sheet. Bake in a 375° oven for 3 to 4 minutes or until the dough is golden brown.

Coat the bottom of a warmed plate lightly with the honey-mustard sauce. Place two skewers of grilled rabbit onto the sauced plate. Place 3 chevre purses to the side of the skewered rabbit. Sprinkle with fresh rosemary leaves and chive flowers.

Serves 4 to 6.

Black Bean and Butternut Squash Soup

Finally, a soup with flair! Actually a duet of two stylish bisques, this dish injects true culinary interest back into the too-often blasé soup course.

1 pound black turtle beans
1 onion, peeled and chopped
1 carrot, peeled and chopped
1 stalk celery, chopped
6 cloves garlic, chopped
2 tablespoons fresh cilantro
2 tablespoons fresh thyme
2 tablespoons fresh parsley
2 tablespoons whole peppercorns
1 large ham bone, or 1 cup ham scraps
2 to 3 quarts chicken stock
1 tablespoon ground cumin
2 teaspoons chili powder
4 tablespoons unsweetened cocoa

🍃 🍃 🍃

2 large fresh butternut squash
1 large onion, chopped
4 cloves garlic, chopped
1 carrot, chopped
1 stalk celery, chopped
¾ cup white wine
¾ cup champagne vinegar
4 cups heavy cream
Salt and white pepper to taste

🍃 🍃 🍃

Crème fraîche for garnish
Cilantro sprigs for garnish
Homemade salsa for garnish

Soak the beans overnight in cold water. Drain. In a heavy soup pot, combine the beans, 1 chopped onion, 1 chopped carrot, 1 chopped stalk celery, 6 chopped cloves garlic, the cilantro, thyme, parsley, peppercorns, ham bone, and chicken stock. Cover and bring to a boil. Skim off the excess fat. Simmer slowly, loosely covered, until the beans are tender, about 2 hours. Add more stock if necessary to keep the liquid level as high as the beans. Stir often to ensure that the beans cook evenly and do not burn.

Place the cooked mixture into a meat grinder, food mill, or processor to purée. Blend in the ground cumin, chili powder, and unsweetened cocoa.

In a baking pan place the squash in ½ inch of water. Cover the pan with foil and bake in a 350° oven until the squash becomes very, very soft, approximately 1 hour. Remove from the oven and cool. Peel the squash and place in a food processor. Purée very well.

In a separate pan mix the remaining onion, garlic, carrot, and celery with the white wine and champagne vinegar. Reduce over high heat until there are just a few drops of liquid in the pan. Add 4 cups of cream. Reduce the sauce over high heat to approximately 3 cups in volume, creamy but not thick. Mix in the squash purée, and salt and pepper to taste.

To serve, pour 1 ladle of the black bean soup and 1 ladle of the squash soup simultaneously into opposite sides of a bowl. The dark and light soup should remain separate, filling the soup bowl evenly and forming a distinct line down the approximate center of the bowl. Garnish the soup with crème fraîche, a sprig of cilantro, and a touch of homemade salsa.

Serves 10 to 12.

Individual Hazelnut-Mocha Torte
with Mocha Butter Cream and Mocha Sauce

The meal you serve has to be pretty impressive not to be overshadowed by this spectacular dessert!

1 cup hazelnuts, roasted and skinned
2 tablespoons cornstarch
¾ cup sugar
6 large egg whites
½ teaspoon cream of tartar

🍃 🍃 🍃

2 cups butter, room temperature
1 cup sugar
1 cup very strong instant coffee
3 to 4 tablespoons Grand Marnier
6 egg yolks

≈ ≈ ≈

2 cups heavy cream
¼ cup strong coffee or espresso
3 tablespoons Grand Marnier

≈ ≈ ≈

Chopped hazelnuts for garnish
Chocolate shavings for garnish
Edible flowers for garnish

Grease an 11x17-inch cake pan and line the bottom with parchment paper. In a food processor mix together the hazelnuts, cornstarch, and ¾ cup of sugar until the consistency of fine powder. In a separate bowl whip the egg whites with the cream of tartar until they hold a nice peak. Fold the powder mixture into the egg whites. Pour the mixture into the prepared cake pan. Bake in a 350° oven for 20 to 25 minutes or until a toothpick inserted in the center comes out clean. Cool the cake and remove from the pan onto another piece of parchment paper. Remove the paper from the bottom of the cake. Cut into 3-inch circles.

Prepare the Mocha Butter Cream. With an electric mixer beat the butter until soft and creamy. Set aside. In a saucepan bring to a boil 1 cup of sugar, 1 cup of coffee, and 3 to 4 tablespoons of Grand Marnier. Boil for 5 minutes. With an electric mixer beat the egg yolks at medium speed, adding the coffee mixture very slowly. Beat for 10 minutes, until the mixture assumes a light mayonnaise-like texture. Add the butter slowly and beat at medium speed.

For the Mocha Sauce, in a medium bowl whip together the cream, ¼ cup of coffee, and 3 tablespoons Grand Marnier with a hand whisk.

To serve, place Mocha Butter Cream between 3 cake circle layers, cover with chopped hazelnuts, and serve with Mocha Sauce. Garnish with chocolate shavings and edible flowers.

Serves 4.

Chalet de France

Kneeland Post Office
Eureka, California 95549
(707) 443-6512
(707) 444-3144

The Chalet de France is a traditional Swiss-Tyrolean all-wood chalet on a three thousand-foot mountaintop overlooking the Pacific Ocean and providing thirty-mile views covering a thousand square miles of ranch and timber wilderness. An exclusive private residence for years, the Chalet now provides two rooms in a remote hide-away behind locked gates. Hiking, fishing, swimming, rides in antique automobiles, Swedish massage, croquet, darts, and French gourmet cuisine are part of the experience. No smoking is permitted.

Pâté de Foies de Volaille
(Chicken Liver Pâté)

¼ cup butter
½ pound chicken livers, halved
3 ounces chopped mushrooms
2 tablespoons chopped green
    onions or shallots
2 tablespoons chopped parsley
¼ teaspoon crushed thyme
Dash salt

≈ ≈ ≈

1 tablespoon brandy
¼ cup Madeira wine
½ cup butter, cut in pieces
3 ounces black olives, chopped
French bread or crackers

In a frying pan over medium heat melt ¼ cup of butter. Add the next 6 ingredients and cook, stirring constantly until the livers are browned on all sides and well done. Warm the brandy, pour over the livers, and ignite. Shake the pan until the flame dies. Add the wine, and simmer briefly. In a blender, purée the liver mixture, adding ½ cup of butter a few pieces at a time. If the mixture seems a little too dry, add a little more wine. Blend until smooth. Remove from the blender and add the olives. Pour the mixture into a large terrine or small individual terrines and chill until firm, several hours or overnight.

The pâté keeps for 2 to 3 days if covered and refrigerated. Serve with crusty French bread or crackers.

Serves 6 to 8.

Potage aux Poireaux
(Cream of Leek Soup)

6 cups sliced leeks, white part only
3 cups diced potatoes
3 cups chicken broth or water
2 cups half and half
3 to 4 tablespoons butter
Salt and pepper to taste
Chives or parsley for garnish

In a stock pot combine the leeks, potatoes, and chicken broth. Bring to a boil. Reduce the heat and simmer for 20 to 30 minutes, until the leeks are tender. Purée the mixture in a blender or food processor. Return the mixture to the pot and slowly add the half and half. Heat, but do not boil. Add the butter, salt, and pepper to taste. If the soup appears too thick, add milk. Serve hot and garnish with chives or parsley if desired.

Serves 6.

Articho aux Crevettes

(Artichokes with Bay Shrimp)

4 large artichokes
1½ cups basic white sauce
½ to ¾ cup dry white wine
1 cup grated Swiss cheese
1 cup bay shrimp, cooked
Dash lemon juice

Cut the stem and ⅓ of the top off the artichokes and discard. Cut the tips off the remaining leaves. Steam the artichokes in a large pot for about 45 minutes or until tender but not over-cooked. While the artichokes are steaming, prepare the white sauce. Add the wine and Swiss cheese, and stir until the cheese is melted. Add the shrimp and lemon juice. Keep warm.

Drain the artichokes and place on individual plates. Open the leaves gently until all are fanned outward. Remove the yellow leaves and scrape the chokes. Spoon the shrimp sauce into the center of the artichokes.

This can be served instead of a salad or as a main course.

Serves 4.

Belgian Pain Cramique

(Egg and Raisin Bread)

I learned this recipe from my grand-mother while growing up in Ypres, Flandres (Belgium). This was a fes-tive bread baked for Sundays and hol-idays. This bread is excellent for French toast.

2 ¼-ounce packages active dry yeast
½ cup warm water (110° to 115°)
⅓ cup sugar
2 cups seedless golden raisins
1 cup milk
¼ cup butter
2 tablespoons dough enhancer
(optional)

1 teaspoon salt
3 eggs
5 to 6 cups flour (bread flour preferred)

🍃 🍃 🍃

1 egg yolk
1 tablespoon water

Dissolve the yeast in ½ cup of warm water. Add 1 tablespoon of the sugar and let the mixture stand for 5 to 10 minutes, until the yeast begins to foam. Soak the raisins in water until plumped. In a saucepan combine the milk, butter, and remaining sugar. Heat to lukewarm, about 110°. Pour into a large bowl and add the dough enhancer, salt, eggs, dissolved yeast, and drained raisins. Stir until well mixed. Gradually beat in 5 cups of flour using an electric mixer with dough hooks. Add more flour until the dough leaves the sides of the bowl and is smooth and satiny. Remove from the mixing bowl and form into a ball. Place in a greased bowl and turn the dough to grease the top. Cover and let rise until doubled, about 30 to 40 minutes.

Grease two 9x5-inch loaf pans. Punch the dough down, knead briefly on a floured board, and divide into 2 equal parts. Shape each half into a loaf and place in the prepared loaf pans. Cover the loaves and let rise in a warm place until almost doubled in bulk, about 30 minutes. Beat the egg yolk with 1 tablespoon of water and brush the loaves with the mixture. Bake in a 375° oven for 40 minutes or until browned. When done, the loaves will sound hollow when tapped on the bottom.

Makes 2 loaves.

Crème Renversée au Caramel

(Upside-down Caramel Custard)

½ cup sugar
4 eggs
¼ cup sugar
½ teaspoon vanilla extract
2 tablespoons rum (optional)
2 cups milk, scalded

In a small frying pan over low heat melt ½ cup of sugar. Shake the pan as the sugar liquifies. Divide the melted sugar into four 6-ounce or six 4-ounce custard cups. Set the cups in a baking pan.

Beat the eggs, remaining sugar, va-nilla, and rum together. Add the scalded milk. Divide the egg mixture among the custard cups. Pour boiling water in the baking pan around the custard cups to a depth of 1 inch. Bake in a 350° oven for 25 minutes or until the center of the custard jiggles when the dish is shaken. Remove from the water and cool at room tem-perature until serving time. The custards can be refrigerated for up to 2 days. To serve, run a knife around the custard in the dish and invert onto a serving plate.

Serves 4 or 6.

Hotel Carter Country Inn

301 L Street
Eureka, California 95501
(707) 444-8062

Hotel Carter, a warm and inviting European-style inn, provides the charm and personalized hospitality of a country inn with the services one would expect from a modern hotel. Opened in 1986, the Hotel Carter is a reconstruction of a circa 1880 Victorian building that was known as the Old Town Cairo Hotel in its heyday. Inside, the Hotel Carter sports a lobby with marble fireplace, imported antique pine furniture, and striking art. The rooms all feature queen-size beds and modern bathrooms. While the continental breakfast has attracted the attention of *Gourmet* magazine, the Hotel Carter Restaurant has been featured in many publications.

Smoked Duck, Mozzarella, and Fresh Wild Blackberry Sandwich

Warm smoked duck breast smothered in smoked Mozzarella cheese, balsamic blackberries, and topped with fresh sage. Rediscover the sandwich!

1 pint fresh wild blackberries
¼ cup balsamic vinegar
Granulated sugar to taste
1 teaspoon fresh squeezed lemon juice
8 slices good homemade bread
1½ pounds smoked duck breast (6 ounces per sandwich)
4 generous slices smoked Mozzarella cheese
Fresh sage to taste

In a bowl toss the blackberries, vinegar, sugar, and lemon juice. Leave the mixture to marinate for 30 minutes at room temperature. Lightly toast the bread. Thinly slice the duck breast and layer on 4 slices of the toasted bread with the cheese. Bake the sandwiches open-faced in a 350° oven until the cheese is slightly

melted. Top the sandwiches with a generous portion of the balsamic blackberry mixture, sprinkle lightly with sage, and place the remaining slices of toast on top.

Serves 4.

Poached Pears in Zinfandel Sauce

A simple yet tasty and uncommon dish. A very fine way to elevate any meal to a "beyond the pale" status.

1 quart Zinfandel wine
1 cup sugar
1 dozen cloves
1 tablespoon cinnamon
Juice of 1½ lemons
1 teaspoon nutmeg
4 pears (or 1 pear per person)
Mint and apple, cherry, or pear blossoms for garnish

In a large saucepan combine the wine, sugar, cloves, cinnamon, lemon juice, and nutmeg. Mix well and bring to a boil. Peel and halve the pears. Add the pears to the boiling wine mixture and cook until tender. Remove the pears. Continue boiling the wine mixture until it reduces to a fine syrup consistency. Remove from the heat and strain through a fine screen. Place the pears on serving plates, cover with wine sauce, and garnish with a sprig of mint and an apple, cherry, or pear blossom.

Serves 4.

Fresh Salmon with Tri-colored Salsa

A colorful and unique way to prepare fresh salmon. Impressive visually and singularly delicious.

1 sweet golden pepper
1 jalapeño pepper
1 yellow onion
3 cloves garlic
6 yellow tomatoes
1 teaspoon fresh lemon juice
1 tablespoon fresh cilantro
1 tablespoon fresh parsley
1 teaspoon cumin
1 tablespoon coarse-grain yellow mustard
Salt and white pepper to taste

≈ ≈ ≈

1 Anaheim pepper
1 green bell pepper
1 jalapeño pepper
2 green onions
1 white onion
2 cloves garlic
6 tomatoes
1 teaspoon lime juice
2 tablespoons cilantro
1 tablespoon green mustard
Salt and white pepper to taste

≈ ≈ ≈

1 red onion
1 red sweet pepper
1 cayenne pepper
3 cloves garlic
3 large red tomatoes
1 teaspoon raspberry vinegar
1 teaspoon cumin
1 tablespoon tomato paste
Salt and white pepper to taste

≈ ≈ ≈

6 8-ounce fillets (not steaks) salmon
Extra virgin olive oil
18 corn husks
Fresh cayenne pepper for garnish

Prepare the yellow salsa. Chop the golden pepper, 1 jalapeño pepper, yellow onion, and 3 cloves of garlic into large chunks. Mix well. Dry roast the mixture in a 350° oven for around 45 minutes, or until the ingredients are softened well.

Score the yellow tomato skins. In a large pot boil the tomatoes in water to cover until the skins begin to peel away from the tomatoes. Remove the tomatoes and place in cold water.

Once cool, peel and seed the tomatoes and cut into chunks. Mix the tomato chunks with the roasted ingredients and add the lemon juice, 1 tablespoon of cilantro, parsley, 1 teaspoon of cumin, and mustard. Process the mixture briefly in a food processor, leaving the mixture somewhat chunky. Salt and pepper to taste.

Prepare the green salsa. Cut the Anaheim pepper, green bell pepper, 1 jalapeño pepper, green and white onions, and 2 cloves of garlic into chunks. Roast in a 350° oven for about 45 minutes, or until the ingredients are softened well.

Score the tomato skins. In a large pot boil the tomatoes in water to cover until the skins begin to peel away from the tomatoes. Remove the tomatoes and place in cold water. Once cool, peel and seed the tomatoes and cut into chunks. Mix the tomato chunks with the roasted green pepper mixture and add the lime juice, 2 tablespoons of cilantro, and green mustard. Process the mixture briefly in a food processor, leaving the mixture somewhat chunky. Salt and pepper to taste.

Prepare the red salsa. Cut the red onion, red sweet pepper, cayenne pepper, and 3 cloves of garlic into chunks. Roast in a 350° oven for about 45 minutes, or until the ingredients are softened well.

Score the tomato skins. In a large pot boil the tomatoes in water to cover until the skins begin to peel away from the tomatoes. Remove the tomatoes and place in cold water. Once cool, peel and seed the tomatoes and cut into chunks. Mix the tomato chunks with the roasted red pepper mixture and add the raspberry vinegar, 1 teaspoon cumin, and tomato paste. Process the mixture briefly in a food processor, leaving the mixture somewhat chunky. Salt and pepper to taste.

Heat a grill and brush the salmon fillets with olive oil. Cook the salmon skin-side up first, for approximately 4 minutes per side. Place 3 corn husks on each plate and arrange the salmon fillets on husks. Pour the salsas in 3 parallel diagonal lines across the top of the salmon. The sauces should be side by side but not mixing together. Garnish with cayenne pepper.

Serves 6.

Old Town Bed & Breakfast Inn

1521 Third Street
Eureka, California 95501
(707) 445-3951

This inn, which was built in 1871, is one of the few remaining Greek Revival buildings in the area. The original home of William Carson, the local lumber baron, it was moved when he built the Carson Mansion, centerpiece of the Old Town district. The decor combines period pieces with a touch of whimsy and the fun-loving nature of its innkeepers. Every bed has its own teddy bear, and the antique claw-foot tubs come complete with bubble bath and rubber ducks. Beds are covered with afghans made by the innkeeper and her grandmother.

Old Town Eggs Derelict

2 cups milk
2 tablespoons cornstarch
3 tablespoons sherry
1 cup grated cheese

🍃 🍃 🍃

4 sliced English muffins
Butter
Grated Parmesan cheese
8 slices smoked turkey breast
8 basted eggs (poached are fine, too)
Chopped fresh dill

In a saucepan warm the milk. Dissolve the cornstarch in a small amount of warm milk and add back to the saucepan. Add the sherry, and blend well. Stir over medium heat until the sauce begins to thicken. Add the cheese and stir until melted. Keep the sauce warm.

Butter the English muffins and sprinkle with Parmesan cheese. Heat

Old Town Bed & Breakfast Inn

a large skillet and toast the English muffins buttered-side down until browned. On 4 serving plates, place the English muffins toasted-side up. Top each with 2 turkey slices, 1 egg, and cheese sauce. Garnish with chopped dill. Serve immediately.

Heart-healthy modification: Substitute corn oil margarine for butter, reduce the amount of cheese in the sauce, and use basted egg whites rather than whole eggs.

Serves 4.

Cast Iron Breakfast Pie

    1½ pounds potatoes
    3 tablespoons bacon drippings
    1 small onion, chopped
    ¼ green bell pepper, chopped
    Salt and pepper to taste
    8 slices bacon, cooked and
        crumbled
    8 eggs
    ½ cup milk

Boil the potatoes until done, and dice. In a 10-inch cast iron skillet heat the bacon drippings over moderate heat. Add the onion and bell pepper. Cook for 5 minutes, until lightly browned. Add the diced potatoes and cook for 10 minutes, until the potatoes are spotted brown. Season to taste. Sprinkle the crumbled bacon over the potato mixture and reduce the heat to low. Beat the eggs and milk together. Pour the egg mixture over the potatoes, cover the skillet (with foil if necessary) and cook over low heat for 5 minutes. Uncover the pan and bake in a 425° oven for 15 minutes or until just set.

Variation: Crumbled sausage, diced turkey ham, or sautéed sliced fresh mushrooms may be used instead of bacon.

Heart-healthy modification: Substitute olive oil for the bacon drippings, turkey ham or mushrooms for the bacon, and egg substitute for the eggs.

Serves 6 to 8.

The Gingerbread Mansion

400 Berding Street
Ferndale, California 95536
(707) 786-4000

Exquisitely turreted, carved, and gabled and colorfully landscaped with lush English gardens, the Gingerbread Mansion is a visual masterpiece. One of Northern California's most photographed buildings, this grand lady of the Victorian village also possesses a beautifully restored interior, where guests are welcomed to enjoy such amenities as twin claw-footed tubs for "his & her" bubble baths. A very special experience.

Applesauce Muffins

    ½ cup butter, softened
    1 cup sugar
    1 egg
    1 cup unsweetened applesauce
    1½ teaspoons cinnamon
    1 teaspoon allspice
    ½ teaspoon cloves
        ⋙ ⋙ ⋙
    2 cups all-purpose flour
    1 teaspoon baking soda
    ½ teaspoon salt
    ½ cup chopped nuts
        ⋙ ⋙ ⋙
    Grape Nuts cereal

In a large bowl cream together the butter and sugar. Add the egg. Stir in the applesauce and spices. In a separate bowl sift together the flour, bak-

The Gingerbread Mansion

ing soda, and salt. Add the dry ingredients to the applesauce mixture and beat just until mixed. Stir in the nuts. Pour the batter into greased muffin tins, filling tins ⅔ full. Sprinkle Grape Nuts cereal over the top. Bake in a 350° oven for 8 to 10 minutes. (If the batter has been refrigerated, bake for 25 to 30 minutes.)

Notes: This recipe can be doubled easily, and will keep several days in the refrigerator. As with all muffin recipes, do not overmix the batter or the muffins will be "tough."

Makes about 15 muffins.

Gingerbread's Bran Muffins

This is a good recipe to prepare in several batches and store for up to 2 weeks, an advantage for busy inn-keepers.

    1 cup raisins
    1 tablespoon baking soda
    1 cup boiling water
        ❧ ❧ ❧
    1 cup sugar
    ½ cup butter
    2 eggs
    2 cups all-purpose flour
    ½ teaspoon salt
    1 cup All Bran cereal
    2 cups Raisin Bran cereal
    ¾ cup coarsely chopped walnuts
    2 tablespoons sugar
    1 teaspoon cinnamon
        ❧ ❧ ❧
    2 cups buttermilk
    Grape Nuts cereal

Generously butter large muffin tins. In a small bowl combine the raisins, baking soda, and boiling water. Let cool. In a large mixing bowl cream together 1 cup of sugar, butter, and eggs. Add the flour and salt. Stir until blended. Stir in the cooled raisin mixture just until combined. Pour the cereals, walnuts, 2 tablespoons of sugar, and cinnamon over the mixture. Do not stir. Cover and refrigerate for up to 2 weeks, if desired.

When ready to serve, add the buttermilk and stir just until blended. Fill each muffin cup ⅔ full. Sprinkle with about ½ teaspoon of Grape Nuts cereal. Bake in a 375° oven for 20 minutes or until a toothpick inserted in the center comes out clean.

Makes about 3 dozen muffins.

Brandy Fruitcake

    2 20-ounce cans diced fruit
        (peaches, pineapple, fruit
        cocktail)
    2½ cups sugar
        ❧ ❧ ❧
    1 20-ounce can diced fruit (use a
        different kind)
    2½ cups sugar
        ❧ ❧ ❧
    1 16-ounce jar Royal Ann cherries
        (or a can of fruit)
    2½ cups sugar
        ❧ ❧ ❧
    3 18-ounce boxes yellow or lemon-
        pudding cake mix
    2 cups oil
    12 eggs
    3 6-ounce packages vanilla instant
        pudding mix
    1 cup chopped nuts

In a 1-gallon glass jar combine 2 cans of fruit and 2½ cups of sugar. Do not use a metal container. Do not seal the lid on the jar. Keep it loosely on the top because air is needed for the fermentation process. Allow the mixture to rest at room temperature for 10 days, stirring daily.

On the tenth day, add 1 can of fruit and 2½ cups of sugar. Allow the mixture to rest for 10 days, stirring daily.

On the twentieth day, add the cherries and 2½ cups of sugar. Allow the mixture to rest for 10 days, stirring daily.

On the thirtieth day, in each of 3 large mixing bowls combine 1 box of cake mix, ⅔ cup of oil, 4 eggs, 1 package of pudding mix, ⅓ of the drained fruit, ½ cup of the juice from the fruit, and ⅓ of the nuts, if desired. The batter will be very thick. Grease and flour five 5x9-inch loaf pans or 3 bundt pans. Pour the batter into the prepared pans. Bake in a 325° oven for 60 to 70 minutes.

Save 1½ cups of the juice from the fruit mixture for the next starter, and give the rest away to friends.

Makes 5 loaves, 3 round cakes, or about 36 servings.

Lord Bradley's Inn

43344 Mission Boulevard
Mission San Jose
Fremont, California 94539
(415) 490-0520

Guests at Lord Bradley's are warmly greeted by the lord or lady of the inn in the common room, where a traditional social hour is observed in late afternoon. Adjacent to Mission San Jose and its ancient olive trees, the inn is but a short walk from various shops and a noted winery. From nearby Mission Peak hikers can view the San Francisco Bay area. The inn's eight rooms, all with private baths, are decorated in Victorian flavor; two of the rooms have handicapped access.

Anne McMuffins

To serve in the evenings.

    2 bunches green onions, chopped
        (stems and all)
    2 cups grated Cheddar cheese
    1 cup mayonnaise
    1 5¾-ounce can olives, chopped
    2 tablespoons curry powder
        ❧ ❧ ❧
    6 English muffins

In a large bowl combine the chopped green onion, Cheddar cheese, mayonnaise, olives, and curry powder. Spread the mixture on the English muffins. Bake in a 350° oven for 10 minutes or until bubbly.

Serves 4 to 6.

Lord Bradley's Inn

Emma's Crackers

A hit at wine time.

　　1 12-ounce box oyster crackers
　　⅓ cup oil
　　1 package dried Italian dressing
　　2 tablespoons dillweed

In a large bowl combine all of the ingredients. Stir 5 or 6 times during the day. This mixture keeps well, is not greasy, and needs no baking.
　　Serves 10 to 12.

The Campbell Ranch Inn

1475 Canyon Road
Geyserville, California 95441
(707) 857-3476

The spectacular view from Mary Jane and Jerry's hilltop home is the highlight of their ranch. The beautiful rolling vineyards and the abundance of flowers in Mary Jane's garden provide a photographer's dream. During warm weather, breakfast is served on the terrace so guests can enjoy the view while dining on a scrumptious meal. What distinguishes the Campbell Ranch from the traditional bed and breakfast inn are the professional

tennis court, the twenty-by-forty-foot swimming pool, and the hot tub spa. Evening dessert of homemade pie or cake is offered daily.

Wild Blackberry Pie

　　3 cups all-purpose flour
　　1½ cups shortening
　　1 teaspoon salt
　　5 tablespoons water
　　1 extra-large egg
　　1 teaspoon vinegar

　　　　🍃　🍃　🍃

　　6 cups blackberries (or
　　　　blueberries), rinsed and drained
　　1 cup sugar
　　¼ cup tapioca
　　¼ teaspoon salt
　　½ teaspoon nutmeg
　　½ teaspoon cinnamon
　　1½ teaspoons lemon juice
　　1½ tablespoons margarine

In a large bowl cut together the flour, shortening, and salt until the mixture resembles peas. In a cup, whip the water, egg, and vinegar with a fork until well mixed. Pour over the flour mixture. Mix with a fork and then by hand until the mixture forms a ball. Divide the dough into thirds and place each third of the dough between 2 pieces of floured waxed paper. Roll out, and place one in a 9-inch pie pan. Use one third for the top, and the other for an extra bottom or top to be frozen. Chill. (Remember, the secret of tender, flaky pie crusts is to handle the dough as little as possible and to chill before baking. It is convenient to double or even quadruple this pie crust recipe and make stacks of bottoms and tops. Store in the refrigerator or freezer during apple or peach harvest. With the crusts made ahead, it's much easier to just prepare the fruit filling and bake!)
　　In a large bowl combine the blackberries and remaining ingredients except the margarine. Mix well. Pour the blackberry mixture into the pie shell, dot liberally with margarine, and cover with a top pie crust. Crimp the edges decoratively. Sprinkle with

sugar. (It helps to cut a "B" in the top of the crust to identify the type of pie, when freezing these pies after they're baked.) Bake in a 425° oven for approximately 45 minutes, until nicely browned.
　　This pie freezes well. Freeze on a cookie rack overnight, and then wrap tightly in foil the next day. Return to the freezer until needed. Warm the pie in a 140° oven until heated through.
　　Serves 6 to 8.

Lemon Whipples

　　1 18-ounce box lemon cake mix
　　2 cups Cool Whip, thawed
　　1 extra-large egg
　　½ cup confectioners' sugar

Grease a cookie sheet. Combine the first three ingredients in a large mixing bowl. Drop by tablespoonfuls into the confectioners' sugar and roll into balls. Place the balls on the cookie sheet. Bake in a 350° oven for 15 minutes.
　　To make wonderfully soft chewy cookies, remove them from the oven while the cookies look wet on the top and just slightly brown on the edges.
　　Makes 2 dozen cookies. If you like lemon, you'd better double the recipe.

The Hope-Merrill House/Hope-Bosworth House

Post Office Box 42
Geyersville, California 95441
(707) 857-3356

These vintage Victorian turn-of-the-century inns welcome travelers in grand style to the California wine country. The twelve rooms each have private baths, two with Jacuzzi tubs. Beautiful gardens, a gazebo, vineyards, and a swimming pool enhance a stay at these two inns. They were featured in *Country Homes, Sunset,* and *House Beautiful.*

The Best Gingerbread Ever

1 cup sugar
1 cup molasses
1 cup butter, melted
3 eggs
3 cups sifted unbleached all-purpose flour
1 tablespoon baking soda
1 tablespoon ginger
2 teaspoons cinnamon
1 teaspoon cloves
1 teaspoon grated fresh nutmeg
½ teaspoon salt
1¼ cups boiling water
Confectioners' sugar
Whipped cream

Grease and flour a 9-inch fluted tube pan. In a large bowl beat together the sugar, molasses, butter, and eggs. In a separate bowl combine the dry ingredients. Add the dry ingredients alternately with the boiling water to the egg mixture. Pour the batter into the prepared pan. Bake in a 350° oven for 40 minutes, or until a toothpick inserted in the center comes out clean. Cool in the pan on a wire rack for 15 minutes. Loosen the cake from the edges of the pan with a knife. Invert the cake onto the wire rack and sprinkle with confectioners' sugar. This is excellent served with whipped cream.
Serves 14 to 16.

Rosalie's Summer Fruit Tart

1 cup butter
2 tablespoons sugar
½ teaspoon salt
2 egg yolks, beaten
2 cups all-purpose flour

🍃 🍃 🍃

6 cups fruit (sour cherries, blueberries, peaches, plums, gooseberries, or rhubarb)
2½ cups sugar
½ cup plus 2 tablespoons flour

🍃 🍃 🍃

2 eggs
½ cup cream

In a food processor blend the first 5 ingredients. Press the crust into the bottom and sides of a 10-inch tart pan or a 9x13-inch cake pan.

In a large bowl combine the fruit, sugar, and flour, tossing until well combined. Pour the fruit mixture into the unbaked tart. Beat together the eggs and cream, and pour over the fruit filling. Bake in a 350° oven for 45 minutes.
Serves 18.

Pear Tart

½ cup butter
1½ cups all-purpose flour
¼ cup ice water
1 tablespoon sugar

🍃 🍃 🍃

3 eggs, beaten
⅔ cup sugar
⅓ cup all-purpose flour
⅓ cup melted butter
1 teaspoon almond extract

🍃 🍃 🍃

3 large pears

In a food processor blend together the first 4 ingredients. Roll out on a lightly floured board to fit a 10-inch tart pan. Place the dough in the tart pan and trim the excess.

In a large bowl combine the eggs, sugar, flour, melted butter, and almond extract. Peel, core, and thinly slice the pears. Arrange the pear slices in tart pan in 2 concentric circles, starting with the outside circle. Pour the filling over the pears. Bake in a 350° oven for about 45 minutes. Cool on a rack for 5 to 50 minutes. Serve warm.

Serves 12 to 14.

Old Thyme Inn

779 Main Street
Half Moon Bay, California 94019
(415) 726-1616

Old Thyme Inn is an authentic 1899 Queen Anne Victorian house restored and decorated by the British-born hosts, Anne and Simon Lowings. All of the seven rooms have private baths (three with whirlpools). In the late afternoon sherry or tea is served; a continental plus breakfast is provided.

Nearby attractions include whale and sea watching excursions, Año Nuevo State Reserve, Fitzgerald Marine Reserve, Fioli Estate Gardens, and a wide variety of outdoor activities.

Simon's Scones

3 cups flour (unbleached all-purpose, whole wheat pastry, or a mixture)
⅓ cup sugar
½ teaspoon baking soda
2½ teaspoons baking powder
¾ cup cold butter, cut in pieces
1 cup buttermilk
Cinnamon sugar (see below)
Butter, jam, or lemon curd

Grease a cookie sheet. In a mixing bowl stir together the flour, sugar, baking soda, and baking powder. Drop the pieces of cold butter into the bowl and cut into the dry ingredients with 2 forks until the mixture resembles cornmeal. (It will look a little lumpy, which is just how it should be.) Make a well in the center of the mixture and add the buttermilk. Stir with a fork until the mixture leaves the sides of the bowl. Add more buttermilk (about 1 tablespoon) if necessary to bind the mixture. Divide the dough into 2 equal portions. Shape each into a ¾-inch high round on the cookie sheet. The rounds will fit on 1 sheet. Score each round with a knife into 6 or 8 equal sections, cutting almost to the bottom of the dough. Brush the tops with a little milk or cream, then sprinkle with cinnamon sugar until lightly covered. Bake in a 350° oven for about 30 minutes, until golden brown. Serve warm with butter, jam, or lemon curd.

Cinnamon Sugar: For every cup of sugar, add 4 tablespoons of cinnamon. Keep the mixture in a shaker that has fine holes.

Serves 12.

Scotch Eggs

Guests always ask "How did you get the egg into the middle of the sausage?"

3 tablespoons all-purpose flour
1¼ tablespoons finely chopped sage
1 teaspoon fresh thyme (or ½ teaspoon dried)
1 pound sausage
1½ cups bread crumbs
Salt and pepper
2 eggs, lightly beaten
8 small hard-boiled eggs, shelled
Vegetable oil for deep frying

Spread the flour on a piece of waxed paper. Mix the herbs into the sausage meat and divide into 8 pieces. In a small bowl combine the bread crumbs, salt, and pepper. Place the beaten eggs in a separate bowl. Roll each hard-boiled egg in flour to coat all over. Flatten each piece of sausage meat. Place a boiled egg in the center of each sausage circle and press the sausage around the egg, covering the egg entirely. Dip the sausage-covered eggs into the beaten eggs and then into the bread crumbs. Roll the eggs to coat all sides. Heat the oil in a deep pan to 360°. Fry the eggs in enough oil to cover until golden brown. This will only take a few minutes. Drain on paper towels. Serve warm or refrigerated.

To serve, cut the eggs in half, exposing the concentric circles of egg yolk, white, and sausage meat.

Serves 8.

Healdsburg Inn on the Plaza

116 Matheson Street
Healdsburg, California 95448
(707) 433-6991

This historic Wells Fargo building of 1900 now serves as a delightful bed and breakfast. Situated in the center of town, it has two gift shops, a bakery, and an art gallery on the main floor. A grand staircase in the art gallery leads to the guest suites, all with private baths and some with fireplaces. The solarium and roof garden provide a charming common area for guests to meet for coffee, tea, and cakes every afternoon and a full breakfast in the morning. Books, puzzles, games, and television are available in the lounge.

Country Egg Casserole

2 cups diced frozen potatoes
8 hard-boiled eggs, sliced
8 cooked link sausages, cut in
**   thirds**
1 4-ounce can mushrooms
1 10¾-ounce can cream of
**   mushroom soup**
5 ounces (½ soup can) milk
Monterey Jack cheese
3 green onions, chopped
Salt and pepper to taste

In a greased 9x11-inch casserole dish layer the potatoes, eggs, sausages, and mushrooms. Combine the soup and milk, and pour over the casserole. Sprinkle the cheese, onions, salt, and pepper over the top. Bake in a 350° oven for 20 to 30 minutes, until heated through.

Serves 8.

Easy Oven Pot Roast

1 3- to 4-pound pot roast
1 medium onion, thinly sliced
2 tablespoons chopped parsley
1 10¾-ounce can mushroom soup
10¾ ounces (1 soup can) Burgundy
Potatoes, peeled and quartered
Carrots, peeled and sliced
**   lengthwise**

In a Dutch oven place the pot roast and sprinkle with onions and parsley. Mix the soup and wine, and pour over the meat. Cover and bake in a 325° oven for 5 hours. During the last hour add the potatoes and carrots.

Serves 6 to 8.

Chocolate Chip Cheesecake

1½ cups finely crushed Oreos
**   (about 18)**
¼ cup melted butter
3 8-ounce packages cream cheese,
**   softened**
1 14-ounce can sweetened
**   condensed milk**
3 eggs
2 teaspoons vanilla extract
1 cup miniature chocolate chips
1 teaspoon all-purpose flour

In a small bowl combine the Oreo cookie crumbs and butter. Pat firmly onto the bottom of a 9-inch springform pan. In a large mixing bowl beat the cream cheese until fluffy. Add the sweetened condensed milk, and beat until smooth. Add the eggs and vanilla. In a small bowl toss together ½ cup of chocolate chips and the flour. Stir the coated chips into the cream cheese mixture. Pour over the crust and sprinkle the remaining chocolate chips over the top. Bake in a 300° oven for 1 hour or until the cake springs back when lightly touched. Cool to room temperature. Chill the cheesecake overnight before removing from the pan.

Serves 12.

Madrona Manor

1001 Westside Road
Healdsburg, California 95448
(707) 433-4231

Constructed as a summer home in the late 1800s by wealthy San Francisco businessman John Paxton, in the early 1980s it was completely renovated and opened as a country inn. In 1987 it was placed on the National Historic Registry as a Historical District. The manor is nestled on eight acres of terraced, landscaped grounds; its twenty rooms are elegantly decorated, with original and antique reproduction furniture in the manor house. The full breakfast is a European-style buffet; a gourmet restaurant on the premises serves California nouvelle cuisine. Nearby attractions include magnificent redwood trees, the Russian River, wineries, and many shops.

Thai Soup with Salmon

1 pound fresh salmon
1 yellow onion, sliced
Peanut oil
2 cups chopped bok choy
4 cloves garlic, minced
1 tablespoon julienned ginger
1 quart fish stock or clam juice
1 12-ounce can coconut milk
6 stalks lemon grass, cut lengthwise
**   and into 2-inch lengths**
1 tablespoon sugar
¼ cup rice wine vinegar
2 tablespoons Szechwan oil
**   (Mongolian hot oil)**

Bone, skin, and cube the salmon. In a saucepan sweat the onions (cook covered over low heat) in the peanut oil. Add the bok choy, garlic, and ginger, and cook until soft. Remove the mixture from the pan. Cook the salmon in the saucepan briefly. Remove the salmon. Add the fish stock, coconut milk, and lemon grass. Simmer for 20 minutes. Add the salmon, bok choy mixture, and remaining ingredients. Simmer for 40 minutes more.

Serves 6.

Recipe courtesy of Chef Todd Muir.

Roasted Cornish Game Hens
and Sundried Tomato Pasta with Fall Vegetables

Sundried tomato pasta (see below)

🍂 🍂 🍂

Dash thyme
Dash marjoram
Dash sage
¼ cup honey
2 tablespoons vinegar
Salt and pepper to taste
2 tablespoons minced garlic
3 Cornish game hens

🍂 🍂 🍂

Fall vegetables (baby carrots, green
    and yellow squash, red and
    yellow bell pepper, cherry
    tomatoes, Japanese eggplant,
    red onions, basil leaves, garlic)
2 tablespoons olive oil
Salt and pepper to taste
2 tablespoons grated Parmesan
    cheese

Prepare the sundried tomato pasta using any pasta recipe and adding 2 tablespoons of sundried tomato paste per cup of flour. Cut the pasta into strips and dry according to the recipe.

Combine the thyme, marjoram, sage, honey, vinegar, salt and pepper, and garlic. Marinate the game hens for 4 hours.

Cook the game hens over a spit or oven roast for 1 hour.

Blanch the vegetables, using any combination or all of the vegetables mentioned. Cook the pasta. Toss the cooked pasta with the blanched vegetables, olive oil, and salt and pepper to taste. Divide the pasta among 6 plates. Sprinkle the Parmesan over the pasta. Cut the game hens into halves and place each half on a nest of pasta, arranging the vegetables around the hens.

Serves 6.

Recipe courtesy Chef Todd Muir.

Strawberry Creek Inn

Post Office Box 1818
Idyllwild, California 92349
(714) 659-3202

Strawberry Creek Inn is a rambling home in the mountains, its shingled exterior blending in quietly with the surrounding pines and oaks. The inn grounds extend to Strawberry Creek, offering peaceful shaded areas for relaxation. Idyllwild affords ample opportunities for hiking, walking, and exploring the mountains. Because every effort has been to give the inn a feeling of quiet retreat, no telephones or televisions are in the rooms. The spacious living room with its large fireplace provides comfort and warmth.

🐦 🐦 🐦 🐦 🐦

Strawberry Creek Inn

German French Toast

3 eggs
2 cups milk
1 teaspoon grated lemon rind
12 slices thick day-old French bread
2 cups bread crumbs

🍂 🍂 🍂

3 to 4 links smoked bratwurst,
    thinly sliced
1 to 2 slices onion
2 to 3 tart apples, cored and sliced
3 to 4 cups water
1 tablespoon lemon juice

🍂 🍂 🍂

⅓ cup cinnamon-sugar mixture
Maple syrup

Separate the eggs. In a medium bowl combine the yolks, milk, and lemon rind. Mix well. Soak the bread slices in the egg yolk mixture. Dip the soaked bread in the egg whites, then in the bread crumbs, and place on a greased cookie sheet. Bake in a 425° oven for 15 minutes. Remove from the oven and turn the toast. Bake an additional 15 minutes.

Sauté the bratwurst and onions until lightly browned. In a saucepan combine the apple slices, water, and lemon juice. Bring to a boil and remove from the heat. To serve, place the toast on serving plates, sprinkle with cinnamon-sugar, cover with cooked apples, and serve with the bratwurst. Garnish as desired and serve with maple syrup.

Serves 6.

Wilkum Inn

26770 Highway 243
Post Office Box 1115
Idyllwild, California 92349
(714) 659-4087

This snug inn invites its guests to enjoy warm hospitality and personal service. One of its four guest rooms has a private bath, and all four have been individually furnished with the innkeepers' personal antiques and collectibles. The river rock fireplace in the common room and the pine interior enhance the inn's warm, homey atmosphere. Evening refreshments consist of hot cider, teas, chocolate, with popcorn and snacks. Nearby are a variety of outdoor activities such as hiking, fishing, swimming, and riding.

Fruit Bake

2 16-ounce cans pear halves in juice
1 16-ounce can peach halves in juice
1 tablespoon cinnamon
1 teaspoon nutmeg
½ teaspoon cloves
¼ cup brown sugar
6 ounces frozen cranberries
2 to 3 apples, peeled if desired
Cornstarch (optional)
Rum extract (optional)
½ cup Quaker Natural cereal

Drain the juices from the canned pears and peaches into a large saucepan. Add the spices and brown sugar. Bring to a boil and add the cranberries. Cook until the cranberries begin to pop.

Thinly slice the apples and add to the cranberry mixture. Cook over medium heat until the apples are slightly tender. Slice the pears and peaches and arrange in an 8-inch square glass pan. Remove the apples and cranberries from the juice with a slotted spoon. Top the pears and peaches with the cranberries and apples. Continue cooking the juices until thickened, or add the cornstarch if desired. Add rum extract, if desired. Sprinkle the cereal over the fruit. Pour the thickened juice over all. Bake in a 350° oven for 35 minutes.

This may be prepared the night before it is needed. Cover the dish with plastic wrap and refrigerate. Place in a cold oven and increase the baking time to 45 minutes.

Serves 4.

Quicky Baked Apples

4 baking apples (Granny Smith, Rome or Jonathan)
3 tablespoons orange juice concentrate
¼ cup apple juice
1 tablespoon cinnamon
1 teaspoon nutmeg
¼ teaspoon cloves
¼ cup grated orange zest
½ cup raisins
¼ teaspoon rum extract (optional)

&a &a &a

Flavored yogurt, nutmeg, parsley, or orange slices

Wash and core the apples. Peel the apples halfway from the top. Arrange in a circle in a round glass microwavable dish. Combine the next eight ingredients and pour over the apples. Cover with plastic wrap. Microwave on high for 8 minutes. Baste every 2 minutes with the sauce and rotate the dish ¼ turn. Remove the apples from the microwave when tender. Let the apples rest, covered, for 5 minutes before serving. Place in individual dishes and top with yogurt. Garnish

with nutmeg and parsley or orange slices.

Serves 4.

Sesame Cheese Bread

2 cups buttermilk biscuit mix
1½ tablespoons grated Parmesan cheese
1½ tablespoons grated Romano cheese
¼ cup sugar (optional)
1 egg
⅔ cup milk
⅔ cup sour cream
¼ cup butter or margarine, melted
¼ cup sesame seeds

Grease a 9x13-inch baking pan, preferably glass. Mix the biscuit mix, sugar, and cheeses. In a small bowl beat the egg and add the milk and sour cream. Add the egg mixture to the dry ingredients. Add the melted butter and mix well. Pour into the greased pan, spreading into the corners. Sprinkle the sesame seeds over the batter. Bake in a 350° oven for 35 minutes, until browned and firm in the center.

Makes 35 to 40 pieces.

Cheesecake Brownies

1½ cups all-purpose flour
1 cup sugar
¼ cup cocoa
¼ teaspoon salt (optional)
1 teaspoon baking soda

&a &a &a

1 egg
1 cup water
5 tablespoons oil
1 tablespoon vinegar

&a &a &a

1 egg
8 to 12 ounces cream cheese
¼ cup sugar
1 6-ounce package chocolate chips
½ cup chopped walnuts (optional)
Chocolate chips and walnuts for topping (optional)

In a large bowl mix the flour, 1 cup of sugar, the cocoa, salt, and baking soda. In a separate bowl beat together 1 egg, the water, oil, and vinegar and add to the dry ingredients. Pour the mixture into a 9x13-inch pan. Combine the egg, cream cheese, and ¼ cup of sugar for the cheesecake mixture. Add the chocolate chips and walnuts if desired. Drop the cheesecake mixture into the brownie mixture by heaping tablespoons. Top with chocolate chips and walnuts, if desired. Bake in a 350° oven for 25 minutes, until the brownie mixture is set.

Makes 24 brownies.

Ten Inverness Way

Post Office Box 63
Inverness, California 94937
(415) 669-1648

Ten Inverness Way is the perfect inn for people who like books, long walks, and a full garden. The rooms have queen beds, private baths, handmade quilts, and flowers. There's a private hot tub in the garden. The living room has overflowing bookcases, comfortable couches, and brass reading lamps; the floors and walls are the original Douglas fir.

Crème Caramel French Toast

2 tablespoons corn syrup
1 cup brown sugar
¼ cup butter
1½ pounds cinnamon raisin bread
6 eggs
2 cups milk
2 cups light cream
⅓ cup sugar
1 tablespoon vanilla extract
½ teaspoon salt
Sour cream

In a saucepan combine the corn syrup, brown sugar, and butter. Melt until smooth and bubbly. Spread in the bottom of an 11x17-inch glass baking pan. Overlap the bread like dominoes on the syrup. In a large bowl combine the eggs, milk, light cream, sugar, vanilla, and salt. Pour the mixture over the bread. Refrigerate the mixture overnight. Bake in a 350° oven for 50 to 55 minutes, uncovering for the last 10 minutes. The toast should be puffed and golden. Cut into 8 pieces and invert to serve. Top each piece with 2 tablespoons of sour cream and accompany with fresh berries or a raspberry or cranberry sauce.

Serves 8.

The Heirloom

Post Office Box 322
214 Shakeley Lane
Ione, California 95640
(209) 274-4468

Built about 1863 and hidden away in the historic Gold Country is a treasure called the Heirloom. Comfortable twin, double, queen, or king-size beds, private or shared baths, cozy fireplaces, and balconies overlooking the spacious English romantic garden are offered to guests.

Spiced Apple Crepes

This crepe batter recipe has been passed down from my French grandmother. Many members of the family use it regularly. It was our first entree served at the Heirloom, and continues to be one of the favorites.

4 eggs
½ cup sugar
1 teaspoon salt
2 teaspoons vanilla extract
4 cups milk
2½ cups all-purpose flour
3 tablespoons oil

🍂 🍂 🍂

2 cups lowfat cottage cheese
2 cups cream cheese
¼ cup confectioners' sugar

🍂 🍂 🍂

¾ cup margarine or butter
1 cup firmly packed light brown sugar
2 teaspoons cinnamon
½ teaspoon nutmeg
12 to 14 apples, peeled and thinly sliced
1 cup chopped walnuts

In a large bowl combine the first 4 ingredients with a beater. Add the milk alternately with the flour. Add the oil. Heat a black iron skillet. Pour in several tablespoons of batter and tilt the pan so that the batter spreads evenly. Cook until the bottom is lightly browned and the edges lift easily. Turn and cook the other side. Repeat until all of the batter is used.

Beat the cottage cheese, cream cheese, and confectioners' sugar together. Set aside.

In a heavy pan melt the margarine and add the brown sugar and spices. Add the apples and walnuts. Sauté lightly, but do not overcook the apples.

To assemble, place 3 to 4 teaspoons of the cheese filling on each crepe and fold or roll the crepes.

The Heirloom

Place the filled crepes in a baking pan. Bake in a 300° oven for 10 minutes, until heated through. Top with spiced apples.

Serves 12 to 16.

Grampa Adrien's Baked Eggs
in Tomato Shells

4 medium-ripe tomatoes
Salt and pepper to taste
½ teaspoon dried basil, crumbled
2 tablespoons butter, melted
4 eggs
Salt
¼ cup grated Swiss or Monterey Jack cheese
Fresh parsley

Cut a thin slice from the top of each tomato. Scoop out the pulp and seeds. Turn the tomatoes upside down to drain for 10 minutes. Sprinkle the tomato shells with a little salt, pepper, and basil. Butter a baking dish with the melted butter. Place the tomatoes in the prepared dish cut-side up. Break an egg into each tomato shell. Sprinkle again with a little salt. Bake in a 350° oven for 35 minutes, or until the egg whites have set. Sprinkle the grated cheese over the eggs, and bake until the cheese melts, about 2 minutes. Serve immediately. Garnish with fresh parsley or another fresh herb.

Serves 4.

Raquel's Scrumptious Chicken Sandwich

2 cups cooked diced chicken
1 cup diced apple
½ cup coarsely chopped cashews
Mayonnaise to moisten
Salt, pepper, and curry to taste
Bread or toast

In a large bowl combine all of the ingredients, adding mayonnaise to achieve a spreadable consistency. Serve on bread or toast.

Serves 4.

Gate House Inn

1330 Jackson Gate Road
Jackson, California 95642
(209) 223-3500

Gate House is a charming turn-of-the-century Victorian inn offering its guests three rooms, a two-room suite, or a private summer house, all with private baths. Each evokes the past, with lace curtains, handmade afghans, brass or Early American queen-size beds, and Victorian furnishings to complete the comfortable decor. Guests may relax on the wide porches, picnic on the lovely grounds, or enjoy the swimming pool on warm summer days. The Gate House Inn has a three-star Mobil rating.

Oven-baked Omelet

6 eggs
½ cup lowfat cottage cheese
½ cup sour cream
🍃 🍃 🍃
½ cup mild salsa
1 cup shredded Monterey Jack cheese
1 cup shredded Cheddar cheese

Spray a 9-inch pie pan with nonstick cooking spray. Whip together the eggs, cottage cheese, and sour cream in a medium bowl. Spread the salsa over the bottom of the pie pan, and sprinkle the cheeses over the salsa. Pour the egg mixture over the cheese. Bake in a 350° oven for 45 minutes.

Serves 5 to 6.

The Wedgewood Inn

11941 Narcissus Road
Jackson, California 95642
(209) 296-4300
1-800-WEDGEWD for reservations

The Wedgewood Inn is nestled on five acres of pines and oaks ten minutes east of Jackson off Highway 88 in the Sierra foothills. This lovely Victorian replica stirs memories of early times, yet provides the comfort of contemporary living. A parlor grand piano dominates the living room, and tapestries from Belgium and Germany grace the dining room walls. The six guest rooms, with private baths adjoining, are decorated with a Victorian touch. On cool days the New England parlor stove accentuates the warmth the hosts provide their guests.

Eggs à la Wedgewood

12 eggs
3 teaspoons chopped fresh parsley
1 teaspoon nutmeg
Salt and pepper to taste
½ cup sour cream
Green onions, finely chopped
½ to 1 pound bacon, cooked and crumbled
12 or more whole button mushrooms
1 to 2 cups grated Cheddar cheese

In a large skillet scramble the eggs with the parsley and nutmeg. In a 9-inch square baking dish layer the scrambled eggs, salt and pepper to taste, sour cream, green onions, bacon pieces, mushrooms, and Cheddar cheese. Refrigerate the casserole overnight.

Bake in a 300° oven for 20 to 30 minutes, until the cheese is melted. Do not overbake.
Serves 6.

The Wedgewood Inn

Hot Mulled Cranberry Drink

½ gallon cranberry juice
1 cup pineapple juice
1 teaspoon whole cloves
1 teaspoon whole allspice
1 stick cinnamon
Ginger ale or club soda

In a large saucepan combine the cranberry and pineapple juices with the spices. Mull over low heat for 40 to 50 minutes. Remove the spices. Pour into serving cups and add ginger ale or club soda to taste.

Variation: For iced Crantea, prepare the mixture as above, and store in the refrigerator. To serve, pour equal amounts of cranberry mixture and prepared presweetened lemon iced tea into a serving glass. Serve over ice with a shot of ginger ale or club soda. Add a slice of lemon.
Serves 16 to 20.

The Carriage House

1322 Catalina Street
Laguna Beach, California 92651
(714) 494-8945

The Carriage House is a charming old New Orleans-style bed and breakfast inn just several houses away from the beautiful beaches of the Pacific Ocean. One of Laguna Beach's designated historical landmarks, the colonial-style Carriage House is situated in the heart of the village within pleasant walking distance to shops and galleries.

Cream Cheese Danish

So easy to make!

2 8-count packages refrigerated crescent rolls
1 8-ounce package cream cheese
1 cup sugar
1 teaspoon almond extract
1 egg, separated
Cinnamon-sugar mixture
Slivered almonds

Grease a 9x13-inch baking pan. Unroll 1 package of crescent rolls and spread in the prepared pan. Beat together the cream cheese, sugar, almond extract, and egg yolk. Spread over the crescent rolls. Cover with the remaining package of crescent rolls. Beat the egg white and brush over the top of the dough. Sprinkle with cinnamon-sugar and slivered almonds. Bake in a 350° oven for 20 minutes or until browned. Cool for 30 minutes before cutting into squares.
Serves 16.

Hot Spicy Applesauce

5 cups homemade applesauce
1 teaspoon cinnamon
½ teaspoon cloves
2 16-ounce cans whole-berry
  cranberry sauce
Nuts or raisins, optional

In a saucepan combine all of the ingredients, stirring until blended and heated through. Serve warm.
Serves 12 to 16.

Kolachy

1 cup butter or margarine, softened
1 8-ounce package cream cheese,
  softened
1 tablespoon milk
1 tablespoon sugar
1 egg yolk, well beaten
1½ cups all-purpose flour
½ teaspoon baking powder

⁓ ⁓ ⁓

1 8-ounce can Solo cake and pastry
  filling (almond is good)
Confectioners' sugar

Cream together the butter, cream cheese, milk, and sugar. Add the egg yolk. In a separate bowl sift together the flour and baking powder and add to the creamed mixture. Refrigerate for several hours or overnight.

Turn the dough out onto a floured board and roll to ¼-inch thickness. Cut with a round cookie cutter and make a depression in the center of each. Place 1 teaspoon of cake filling in each indentation. Place on a cookie sheet. Bake in a 400° oven for 15 to 20 minutes. Sprinkle with confectioners' sugar before serving.
Makes 2 dozen.

Simple Stollen

1 8-ounce package cream cheese,
  softened
¼ cup sugar
1½ to 2 teaspoons rum flavoring
¼ cup chopped blanched almonds

½ cup raisins
¼ cup chopped Maraschino cherries
2 8-ounce cans crescent rolls

⁓ ⁓ ⁓

1 cup confectioners' sugar
2 tablespoons milk
Candied red and green cherries

Grease a large cookie sheet. In a small bowl beat the cream cheese with the sugar. Stir in the rum flavoring. Fold in the almonds, raisins, and Maraschino cherries. Set aside. Unroll the crescent rolls into 4 long rectangles on the prepared sheet. Overlap the long sides and press the edges to seal. Pat to form a 13x13-inch square. Spread the cream cheese filling down the center. Fold the ends of the dough 1 inch over the filling. Bring two sides of the dough over the filling, overlapping the edges to form a 6x13-inch loaf. Bake in a 375° oven for 25 to 30 minutes, or until golden brown. Cool.

Combine the confectioners' sugar and milk and drizzle over the cooled stollen. Garnish with cherries.
Serves 12 to 14.

⁓ ⁓ ⁓ ⁓ ⁓

Eiler's Inn

741 South Coast Highway
Laguna Beach, California 92651
(714) 494-3004

In the heart of Laguna Beach but just a few steps from the Pacific Ocean, Eiler's Inn offers elegant yet casual sophistication with an unhurried, peaceful setting. The inn's European hosts provide guests with hospitality in the Old World tradition.

Each of the inn's eleven rooms and one suite has a private bath, and no two are alike. Fresh flowers, fruit, and candles are in each room (a complimentary bottle of champagne is presented at check-in), and from the sun deck guests can enjoy an ocean view. On Saturdays and special occasions, guests are entertained by a classical guitarist.

⁓ ⁓ ⁓ ⁓ ⁓

The Carriage House

Rhubarb-Banana-Fig Jam

    1 pound rhubarb
    ¼ pound dry figs
    ½ pound peeled bananas
    1 teaspoon cinnamon
    2 pounds sugar
    2 3-ounce packages liquid Certo
    Dry sherry

In a large saucepan bring the fruits, cinnamon, and sugar to a boil. Boil for 3 minutes. Add the Certo and bring to a boil again. Boil for 1 minute. Remove the jam from the heat and add dry sherry to taste. Pour into sterilized jars and seal at once. Cool upside down.

Apple Strudel

    6 to 8 cooking apples, cored, peeled
        and sliced
    2 tablespoons sugar
    2 tablespoons cinnamon
    1 cup raisins
    7 sheets filo dough
    ½ cup butter, melted
    6 slices whole wheat bread, toasted
    ½ cup brown sugar
    1 cup chopped walnuts

    🍃 🍃 🍃

    Whipped cream
    Cognac
    Vanilla extract
    Confectioners' sugar

In a bowl toss together the apples, sugar, cinnamon, and raisins. Place 3 sheets of filo dough on a fresh towel and brush with melted butter. Crumble the bread and mix with the brown sugar and walnuts. Scatter ⅓ of the crumb mixture over the buttered filo dough. Place 2 more sheets of filo dough over the first layer, brush with melted butter, and sprinkle ⅓ of the crumb mixture over the buttered filo dough. Repeat with the last 2 sheets of filo dough, butter, and remaining crumb mixture. Place the apple slices in a row along the right edge of the filo dough. Using the towel, roll the dough and apples toward the left.

Place the strudel on a baking sheet and brush with butter. Bake in a 350° oven for about 35 minutes, or until golden.

Combine the whipped cream, cognac, vanilla, and confectioners' sugar. Serve with the strudel.

Serves 12.

Bluebelle House Bed and Breakfast

263 South State Highway 173
Post Office Box 2177
Lake Arrowhead, California 92352
(712) 336-3292

The cozy elegance of European decor in an Alpine setting welcomes guests to Bluebelle House, where they enjoy immaculate housekeeping, exquisite breakfasts, warm hospitality, and relaxing by the fire or out on the deck. The lakeside village, boating, swimming, and restaurants are within walking distance. The private beach club and ice skating are nearby; winter sports are thirty minutes distant.

Double Chocolate Chip Cookies

    2 cups butter
    2 cups brown sugar
    2 cups sugar
    2 tablespoons vanilla extract
    1 tablespoon maple extract
    4 eggs

    🍃 🍃 🍃

    4 cups all-purpose flour
    5 cups oatmeal (finely ground in
        blender)
    1 tablespoon baking soda
    1 tablespoon baking powder
    ½ to 1 tablespoon salt
    2 12-ounce packages semi-sweet
        chocolate chips
    1 8-ounce Hershey bar, finely grated
    3 cups finely chopped walnuts

In a very large bowl cream together the butter, sugars, vanilla, maple, and eggs. In a separate bowl combine the flour, ground oatmeal, baking soda, baking powder, and salt. Add the dry ingredients to the butter mixture. Fold in the remaining ingredients. Place golf ball-sized amounts on a cookie sheet. Bake in a 375° oven for 6 to 10 minutes. These cookies may be frozen.

Makes 8 dozen.

Hot Fudge Sauce

For Christmas gifts, pour the fudge sauce into gift jars and wrap in sparkling cellophane. Serve hot over chocolate chip cookies and ice cream, or as fondue for fresh fruit.

    1 12-ounce package semi-sweet
        chocolate chips
    1 14-ounce can evaporated milk
    1 cup light corn syrup
    1 cup butter

In the top of a double boiler over simmering water, melt the chocolate chips until smooth. Add the remaining ingredients and stir until the butter is melted. Cook for 30 minutes. Remove from the heat and beat with an electric mixer.

Makes 5 cups.

Eagle's Landing

27406 Cedarwood
Lake Arrowhead, California

Post Office Box 1510
Blue Jay, California 92317
(714) 336-2642

Situated on the exclusive west shore of Lake Arrowhead, Eagle's Landing offers its guests four unique, charming rooms in which to enjoy the ambience of a small European-style mountain inn. Each room has its private bath. Guests may enjoy each other's company in the evening on the spacious decks overlooking the lake or in the Hunt Room by a roaring fire. Eagle's Landing is just a short distance from the village of Blue Jay with its open-air-style ice skating rink and from the new Arrowhead Village that offers fine restaurants and boutique shopping. Smoking is not permitted.

Mountain Cinnamon Popovers

3 eggs
1 cup milk
1 cup all-purpose flour
3 tablespoons butter, melted
1 teaspoon cinnamon
¼ teaspoon salt

Eagle's Landing

Grease 6 to 8 muffin or custard cups. Combine all of the ingredients and blend in a blender for 30 seconds. Fill the muffin or custard cups ½ full. Bake in a 400° oven for 40 minutes.

Serves 6 to 8.

Wine and Roses Country Inn

2505 West Turner Road
Lodi, California 95242
(209) 334-6988

Nestled in a secluded, two and one-half-acre setting of towering trees and old-fashioned flower gardens, the Wine and Roses Country Inn is a beautiful, charming historical estate that has been converted into a nine-room inn and restaurant. The inn and guest rooms are filled with handmade comforters, antiques, art, collectibles, and fresh flowers. Overnight guests enjoy late afternoon wine in the sitting room while warming by the crackling fire or browsing through the library. Breakfasts, all specialties of the inn, are served in the dining room.

Kris's Cookie Brittle

1 cup Imperial margarine
1 cup sugar
1 teaspoon vanilla extract
1 teaspoon butter flavoring or extract
1 teaspoon salt
2 cups all-purpose flour
1 cup nuts
1 cup Hershey's chocolate bits

In a saucepan melt the margarine and cool to room temperature. Add the remaining ingredients and stir by hand until blended together. Press the mixture onto a cookie sheet. Bake in a 350° oven for 23 to 25 minutes. Cool and break into pieces.

Serves 24.

Brie en Croute
with Apples and Raisins

1½ pound wedge Brie
1 sheet puff pastry
1 egg yolk
2 tablespoons cream

Encase the Brie in the puff pastry and place on a cookie sheet. Combine the egg yolk and cream, and brush the pastry, using the mixture to seal the edges. Use pieces of the pastry to make decorations, affixing them with the egg wash. Bake in a 400° oven for about 30 minutes or until the pastry is puffed and golden brown. Serve warm with the Apple Raisin Compote and crackers.

Serves 20.

Apple Raisin Compote

½ cup butter
⅓ cup sugar
Pinch salt
2 apples, chopped
½ cup walnuts
½ cup raisins
1 squeeze lemon juice

In a saucepan melt the butter and add the remaining ingredients. Cook, stirring constantly, until the sugar is dissolved and the apples are starting to soften. Remove from the heat and pour onto a serving platter. Top with the Brie en Croute. Serve immediately.

Makes about 3 cups.

Wine and Roses Country Inn

Persimmon Pudding

½ cup butter, melted
1 cup sugar
1 teaspoon vanilla extract
1 cup raisins
½ cup ground walnuts
1 teaspoon lemon juice
1 cup all-purpose flour
1 teaspoon cinnamon
2 teaspoons baking soda
2 teaspoons baking powder
¼ teaspoon salt
3 very ripe persimmons, seeded
2 eggs

Butter a pudding mold or coffee can. In a large bowl combine the butter, sugar, vanilla, raisins, walnuts, and lemon juice. In a separate bowl sift the dry ingredients, and fold into the butter mixture. Beat the persimmon pulp with the eggs until well combined, and add to the batter. Pour the batter into the prepared mold, filling the mold ⅔ full. Cover with aluminum foil, and steam for 2 hours and 30 minutes in simmering water.
Serves 12.

Terrace Manor

1353 Alvarado Terrace
Los Angeles, California 90006
(213) 381-1478

Built in 1902, Terrace Manor reflects its rich past with original stained and leaded glass windows, tiger oak paneling, and an Ionic-columned fireplace with a built-in clock that melodiously chimes the hours. It is furnished with unusual collectibles, period objets d'art, beautiful floral arrangements, and artwork. Each of its five beautiful rooms has a private bath. Near the Convention Center, Coliseum, and Dodger Stadium, it is centrally located to many Southern California attractions.

Juices

This is the basic recipe for juices served at Terrace Manor. We vary it by adding leftover fresh fruit such as pears, peaches, raspberries, or strawberries, or by combining orange and pineapple juice.

1 quart juice (orange, pineapple, or cranberry)
1 cup piña colada yogurt
1 banana
Nutmeg, cinnamon, or vanilla extract (optional)

Combine the juice, yogurt, and banana, blending well. Serve in juice glasses. Add a dash of nutmeg, cinnamon, or vanilla if desired.
Serves 4 to 6.

Pineapple Lemon Muffins

¼ cup sugar
¼ cup lemon juice
1 tablespoon water

❧ ❧ ❧

½ cup butter or margarine, softened
½ cup sugar
¾ teaspoon grated lemon peel
½ teaspoon vanilla extract
2 eggs, room temperature
1¼ cups all-purpose flour
½ teaspoon baking powder
½ teaspoon baking soda
½ teaspoon salt
¾ cup finely ground almonds
½ cup piña colada yogurt
½ cup well-drained crushed pineapple
¼ cup brown sugar, packed

To make Lemon Syrup, in a small saucepan stir together ¼ cup of sugar, lemon juice, and water over medium heat until the sugar dissolves and the mixture boils. Simmer until the mixture reduces to almost half. Set aside.

Grease and lightly flour 12 muffin cups. In a large bowl cream together the butter and ½ cup of sugar until fluffy. Beat in the lemon peel and vanilla. Add the eggs, one at a time, beating well after each addition. In a separate bowl combine the flour, baking powder, soda, salt, and ½ cup of almonds. Add the dry ingredients to the butter mixture alternately with the yogurt, beating well after each addition. Fill each muffin cup ⅔ full. Poke 1 teaspoon pineapple into the center of the muffin batter, and sprinkle the remainder on top of each muffin. Mix the remaining ¼ cup of almonds and the brown sugar, and sprinkle over the muffins. Bake in a 350° oven for 25 minutes.

Using a fork, pierce the top surface of the muffins and slowly spoon the Lemon Syrup over the hot muffins. Cool on a rack.

Makes 12 muffins.

Southwestern Corn Cakes

½ cup chopped onions
1 tablespoon oil
1 tablespoon margarine
1 clove garlic, chopped
½ cup mixed chopped red, green, and yellow peppers

1 17-ounce can cream-style corn
3 eggs
1 cup all-purpose flour
2 teaspoons baking powder
¼ teaspoon salt
1 cup shredded Cheddar cheese
Guacamole
Salsa
Sour cream
Olives (optional)

In a skillet sauté the onions in oil and margarine until soft. Add the garlic and peppers and cook for about 5 minutes.

In a large bowl beat together the corn, eggs, flour, baking powder, and salt. Blend in the onion mixture and Cheddar cheese. Pour enough batter to make dollar-sized pancakes on a greased hot griddle. Cook until bubbles rise to the surface and the edges are browned. Turn and brown the other side. To serve, overlap 3 pancakes in a circle. Top with about 2 tablespoons of salsa, 1 tablespoon of guacamole, 1 tablespoon of sour cream, and an olive.

Serves 4 to 6.

Blintz Soufflé

½ cup butter or margarine, softened
½ cup sugar
6 eggs
1½ cups sour cream
½ cup orange juice
1 cup all-purpose flour
2 teaspoons baking powder

1 8-ounce package cream cheese, cut up
2 cups small curd cottage cheese
2 eggs
2 tablespoons sugar
1 teaspoon vanilla extract
Fruit Sauce (see recipe)
Sour cream

Butter a 9x13-inch baking pan. In a blender or food processor combine the butter, ½ cup sugar, 6 eggs, sour cream, orange juice, flour, and baking powder. Pour half of the mixture into the prepared pan.

In a blender or food processor combine the cream cheese, cottage cheese, 2 eggs, remaining sugar, and vanilla. Mix well. Drop by heaping spoonfuls over the batter. Smooth evenly with a spatula. Pour the remaining batter over the filling. At this point the unbaked soufflé may be covered and refrigerated for several hours or overnight. Before baking, allow the soufflé to stand for 1 hour or until it reaches room temperature.

Bake in a 350° oven for 50 to 60 minutes or until puffed and golden. Top with Fruit Sauce and sour cream.

Makes 8 to 10 servings.

Fruit Sauce

½ cup sugar
2 tablespoons fresh lemon juice
½ teaspoon vanilla extract
2 cups fruit (orange, blueberries, strawberries, or peaches)
1 tablespoon orange liqueur, optional

In a saucepan combine the sugar and lemon juice, and heat until the sugar melts. Add the vanilla and ¼ cup of fruit. Simmer until the sauce thickens

slightly, about 5 to 10 minutes. Add the liqueur. Cool slightly, then add the remaining fruit.

For orange sauce, add ¼ cup of orange juice with the sugar and lemon juice.

The sauce keeps well for up to a week in the refrigerator.

Makes about 2 cups.

Fudgerama

8 cups miniature marshmallows
1 12-ounce can evaporated milk
½ cup butter or margarine
3 cups sugar
½ teaspoon salt

2 12-ounce packages semi-sweet chocolate pieces
2 teaspoons orange liqueur
2 tablespoons grated orange peel
1 cup chopped nuts

Grease a 9x13-inch pan. In a saucepan combine the marshmallows, milk, butter, sugar, and salt. Cook, stirring constantly, until the mixture comes to a full boil. Boil for 5 minutes over medium heat, stirring constantly. Remove from the heat and add the chocolate chips, beating until melted. Fold in the liqueur, orange peel, and nuts. Pour into the prepared pan. Chill until firm. Cut into pieces.

This fudge stores well refrigerated in an airtight container. Leave in large pieces and cut as needed. Add whole marshmallows for a rocky road effect.

Makes 5 pounds.

Pear Torte

½ cup butter or margarine
⅓ cup sugar
¼ teaspoon vanilla extract
¾ cup all-purpose flour
⅔ cup chopped nuts

1 8-ounce package cream cheese
¼ cup plus 1 teaspoon sugar
1 egg
½ teaspoon vanilla extract
2 to 3 ripe pears
1 teaspoon ground cinnamon

In a large bowl cream together the butter and ⅓ cup of sugar. Add ¼ teaspoon of vanilla, the flour, and nuts. Press into a 9-inch tart pan with a removable bottom. Pierce the crust with a fork. Bake in a 350° oven for 10 minutes. Do not overbake.

In a small bowl beat the cream cheese, ¼ cup of sugar, egg, and vanilla until smooth. Spread the mixture over the cooled crust. Pare and thinly slice the pears. Arrange over the cream cheese mixture. Combine the cinnamon and remaining sugar. Sprinkle over the pears. Bake in a 375° oven for 25 minutes. Remove from the oven and cool. Refrigerate before serving.

Serves 6 to 8.

The Headlands Inn

Howard and Albion Streets
Post Office Box 132
Mendocino, California 95460
(707) 937-4431

The Headlands Inn, originally built in 1868 as a barbershop, is centrally located within Mendocino Village's Historical Preservation District. The inn has five guest accommodations, including a private cottage immediately to the rear. All accommodations have wood burning fireplaces, king- or queen-size beds, and private baths. Some have spectacular ocean views overlooking the English-style garden, while one has a large private balcony. Full, gourmet breakfasts, served directly to each room, feature a different hot entree daily.

🐦 🐦 🐦 🐦 🐦

Crustless Salmon-Dill Quiche

12 large eggs

🐦 🐦 🐦

½ cup all-purpose flour
2 teaspoons seasoned salt
2 teaspoons paprika
3 cups milk
¼ teaspoon Tabasco sauce
2 teaspoons dill weed
2 8½-ounce cans boneless, skinless pink salmon
2 cups shredded Gruyère cheese
2 cups shredded mild Cheddar cheese
1 cup chopped green onions

🐦 🐦 🐦

Sour cream
2 large green or red bell peppers, sliced into 10 circles
Fresh parsley
Paprika

In a large bowl beat the eggs slightly with an electric mixer. In a separate bowl combine the flour, salt, and paprika. Add the flour mixture to the eggs, beating with the electric mixer until well mixed. Beat in the milk and Tabasco until blended. Stir in the dill weed, salmon, cheeses, and onions. Cover the bowl and refrigerate overnight.

In the morning, spray 10 individual 5-inch quiche dishes lightly with cooking spray. Stir the quiche mixture and ladle evenly into the prepared dishes, filling within ¼ inch of the rim. Bake in a 350° oven for 25 minutes, or until the centers are set and the quiches have risen above the rims. Garnish with a dollop of sour cream placed in the center of a bell pepper ring with a parsley sprig and lightly sprinkled with paprika. Serve immediately.

Serves 10.

Mincemeat Oat Muffins

1 large egg
¾ cup milk

2 cups prepared mincemeat
½ cup oil
1¼ cups all-purpose flour
1¼ cups quick oats
⅓ cup sugar
1 tablespoon baking powder

Line muffin cups with paper liners. In a large bowl beat the egg and milk. Stir in the remaining ingredients. Mix just until moistened. Pour the batter into the prepared tins. Bake in a 400° oven for 20 to 25 minutes, or until a toothpick inserted in the center comes out clean.

Makes 14 to 16 muffins.

Spicy Egg Boats

10 oval-shaped sourdough French bread rolls or hard rolls
6 tablespoons butter, melted

🐦 🐦 🐦

4 cups white sauce
2 tablespoons ground cumin
2 tablespoons chopped fresh chives
1 teaspoon salt, or to taste
¼ teaspoon white pepper

🐦 🐦 🐦

12 hard-boiled eggs, shelled and sliced

The Headlands Inn

4 slices bacon, cooked and
crumbled
Paprika

🐚 🐚 🐚

Edible flowers or parsley sprigs for
garnish

Cut a thin horizontal slice from the
top of each roll and set aside for the
"sails." Carefully hollow out the rolls,
saving the bread and crumbs for future use. Brush the insides and the
"sails" with melted butter.

Season the white sauce with the
cumin, chives, salt, and white pepper.
Gently fold the sliced eggs into
the white sauce. Fill the rolls with the
mixture and sprinkle with the
crumbled bacon and paprika. Place a
small amount of sauce in the center of
10 individual au gratin dishes, and
place the rolls on the sauce. Put the
"sails" buttered-side-up on a foil-
lined cooking sheet. Bake the egg
boats in a 350° oven for 25 to 30 minutes. During the last 10 minutes,
place the "sails" in the oven to lightly
brown. When cooked, stand a "sail"
upright in each boat, garnish with an
edible flower or parsley sprig, and
serve.
Serves 10.

sheets, crystal, china, and silver are
part of the special touches of this inn.
The house abounds with antiques,
from the 1827 parlor piano, once part
of Alexander Graham Bell's piano collection, to original light fixtures
throughout.

Shrimp Puff

10 eggs
½ cup all-purpose flour
1 teaspoon baking powder
¼ teaspoon salt
2 cups cottage cheese
½ cup butter, melted
4 cups grated hot pepper Monterey
Jack cheese
4 green onions, chopped
1 tablespoon mixed herbs (basil,
tarragon, thyme)
1 4-ounce can mushrooms, stems
and pieces, drained
1 4½-ounce can shrimp, well
drained

In a large bowl whip the eggs until
fluffy. Add the flour, baking powder,
salt, cottage cheese, melted butter,
and half of the grated Monterey Jack
cheese. Blend well. Add the onions,
spices, and mushrooms, and blend.
Gently fold in the shrimp.

Grease a 9x13-inch pan or twelve 4-
ounce ramekins. Pour the shrimp
mixture into the prepared pan or
ramekins and top with the remaining
cheese. Bake the large pan in a 400°
oven for 15 minutes. Reduce the heat
to 375° and bake an additional 30 minutes. For the ramekins, place in a
large baking dish and add water to ⅓
the depth of the ramekins. Bake in a
375° oven for 30 minutes.
Serves 12.

Artichoke Frittata

Margarine
1 cup Ricotta cheese
1 cup grated Mozzarella cheese
1 cup grated Monterey Jack cheese
12 eggs
1 4-ounce can of mushrooms, stems
snd pieces, pressed dry
1 8-ounce can artichoke hearts,
quartered and pressed dry
Salt and pepper to taste
1 tablespoon mixed herbs (basil,
tarragon, thyme)
Parmesan cheese
Paprika

Grease twelve 4-ounce ramekins with
margarine. Mix together the cheeses

Whitegate Inn

Post Office Box 150
499 Howard Street
Mendocino, California 95460
(707) 937-4892

The Whitegate Inn sits behind a
white picket fence amidst an English
garden, just steps from the magic of
historic Mendocino Village. Great
cypress trees bend close to shelter
the old mansion, built in 1880. The
feeling of comfort and welcome, even
wellness, is strong at the Whitegate
Inn. Down comforters, lace-edged

Whitegate Inn

and eggs until well blended. Add the mushrooms, artichokes, salt, pepper, and herbs. Mix until just blended. Place the mixture in the prepared ramekins. Bake in a 300° oven for 30 minutes. Sprinkle with grated Parmesan cheese and a dash of paprika. Serve immediately.

Serves 12.

The Goose and Turrets Bed and Breakfast

835 George Street
Post Office Box 370937
Montara, California 94037

The Goose and Turrets was built around 1908 in the Northern Italian villa style. Since then it has housed the Spanish-American War Veterans' Country Club, a music and dance studio, and a speakeasy during Prohibition. The large common area offers a wood stove, piano, stereo, games, books, and plenty of space to read and write. The five guest rooms are provided with German down comforters, English towel warmers, and bath robes. Breakfast is abundant and delicious; its two courses may feature French, Italian, English, southern, or California dishes.

Sausage Biscuit Pinwheels

4 cups all-purpose flour, divided
1¼ teaspoons baking powder
½ teaspoon baking soda
¼ teaspoon salt
1 cup shortening

1½ cups buttermilk
2 pounds bulk sausage

Sift 3½ cups of flour into a large mixing bowl. Make a well in the center and add the baking powder, baking soda, and salt. Cut in the shortening. Add the buttermilk and mix well. Add the last ½ cup of flour. Blend completely until smooth and not sticky. If the dough is wrapped in waxed paper and chilled for 1 hour, it is easier to use.

Divide the dough in half. On a floured surface roll each half to an 18x8-inch rectangle, ¼-inch thick. Spread half of the sausage on each dough half. Leave ½ inch of the dough uncovered on one long side. Starting at one long side, roll up jelly roll fashion, ending with the uncovered edge of dough. Seal the dough. (The rolls can be refrigerated overnight at this point, if needed.) Chill for at least 30 minutes so the logs will cut cleanly. A bread knife works best. Cut into ½-inch slices. Place the dough on cookie sheets, or if the sausage is fatty, use a broiler pan, so the grease drains away. Bake in a 450° oven for 15 minutes or until the sausage is cooked and the dough is golden.

Makes 40 to 60, or 10 to 15 servings.

Zucchini-Onion-Dill Bread

3 cups all-purpose flour
1 teaspoon salt
1 teaspoon baking powder

¾ teaspoon baking soda
2 cups shredded unpeeled zucchini
½ cup chopped onion
½ teaspoon dill weed, or to taste
¼ cup chopped fresh basil

🍂   🍂   🍂

3 eggs
1 cup oil

Grease a 9x5-inch loaf pan. In a large bowl stir together the flour, salt, baking powder, baking soda, zucchini, onion, dill, and basil. In a separate bowl, beat the eggs and oil. Pour the egg mixture over the flour mixture and stir until moistened. Pour the batter into the prepared pan. Bake in a 350° oven for 1 hour and 30 minutes, or until a toothpick inserted in the center comes out clean. Cool in the pan for 10 minutes. Invert onto a rack, turn topside up, and cool completely.

Variations: In place of basil, use up to ⅛ cup chopped cilantro, or 1 teaspoon dried cumin powder.

Makes 1 loaf, or 12 servings.

Dunbar House, 1880

Post Office Box 1375
271 Jones Street
Murphys, California 95247
(209) 728-2897

Dunbar House will seem familiar to fans of the TV series "Seven Brides for Seven Brothers" because it was filmed here. Now it is an inviting bed and breakfast inn that makes a perfect base of operations for exploring the old town of Murphys, one of the best preserved and least changed of the early mining towns of Calaveras County and the Mother Lode.

Dunbar House was built in 1880 and is a lovely example of Italianate style, with wide porches and beautiful gardens.

Shirred Egg with Salsa

1 teaspoon bread crumbs or crackers
2 slices Swiss cheese
1 tablespoon high quality salsa
1 tablespoon shredded ham
1 egg
5 to 6 slices sautéed mushrooms
1 tablespoon half and half
Parmesan cheese

Spray a 1-cup ramekin with cooking spray. Sprinkle the bread crumbs over the bottom. Arrange the cheese slices so that the bottom and sides of the ramekin are covered. In order, add the salsa, shredded ham, and egg. Place the mushrooms over the egg, and top with cream. Sprinkle the Parmesan cheese over all. Bake in a 350° oven for 15 to 20 minutes, or until the egg is firm.
Serves 1.

Orange Juice Spritzer

1 6-ounce can frozen country-style orange juice concentrate
1 cup cold water
1 tablespoon lemon juice
1 12-ounce can lemon-lime soda
Orange and lime slices

In a large pitcher combine the orange juice, water, and lemon juice. Just prior to serving, slowly add the soda and stir gently to blend. Serve over ice, and garnish with orange and lime slices.
Serves 8.

The Napa Inn

1137 Warren Street
Napa, California 94559
(707) 257-1444

The Napa Inn is a three-story Queen Anne Victorian home built in 1899 and opened in 1981 following extensive restoration. The inn is furnished primarily in Victorian antiques, and each room has a queen-size bed, sitting area, and private bath. Situated on a quiet residential street, the inn is only minutes away from vineyards, wineries, and the renowned restaurants of the Napa Valley.

Eggs Florentine

9 eggs
2 cups cottage cheese
2 cups grated Swiss cheese
8 ounces Feta cheese
4 tablespoons melted butter
2 10-ounce packages frozen chopped spinach, thawed and drained
1 teaspoon nutmeg

Grease a 9x13-inch pan. In a large bowl beat the eggs slightly, and add the cheeses and butter. Mix well. Stir in the spinach and nutmeg. Pour into the prepared pan. Bake in a 350° oven for 1 hour or until a knife inserted in the center comes out clean.
Serves 8 to 10.

Chili Pepper Casserole

3 eggs
1 cup milk
½ cup baking mix
½ teaspoon salt

2 4-ounce cans chopped green chilies
2 cups chopped tomatoes
2 cups shredded cheese

Grease an 8x8-inch baking dish. In a bowl beat together the eggs, milk, baking mix, and salt until foamy. Place the chilies in the prepared dish. Top with the tomatoes, and sprinkle with cheese. Pour the egg mixture over all. Bake in a 350° oven for 40 to 45 minutes or until golden brown.
Serves 4 to 6.

Dunbar House, 1880

Delicate Lemon Squares

1 cup all-purpose flour
½ cup butter, melted
½ cup confectioners' sugar
Dash salt

ఆ ఆ ఆ

2 eggs, beaten
1 cup sugar
2 tablespoons all-purpose flour
2 tablespoons lemon juice
½ teaspoon grated lemon rind
Confectioners' sugar

In a small bowl combine 1 cup of flour, the butter, confectioners' sugar, and salt. Spread the mixture in an 8x8-inch baking pan. Bake in a 350° oven for 15 to 20 minutes.

In a small bowl combine the eggs, sugar, 2 tablespoons of flour, lemon juice, and lemon rind. Pour over the baked layer and bake in a 350° oven for 20 to 25 minutes. Sprinkle with confectioners' sugar. Cool in the pan before cutting.

Serves 9.

Chocolate-filled Peanut Butter Bars

1 18-ounce box yellow or white cake
   mix
½ cup butter or margarine
2 eggs
1 cup peanut butter

ఆ ఆ ఆ

2 tablespoons butter or margarine
1 12-ounce package chocolate chips
1 14-ounce can sweetened
   condensed milk

ఆ ఆ ఆ

1 cup coconut
½ cup chopped nuts
1 teaspoon vanilla extract

In a large bowl combine the cake mix, ½ cup of butter, eggs, and peanut butter. Reserve ⅓ cup of the dough, and press the remaining mixture into the bottom of a 9x13-inch cake pan.

In a microwave safe dish, combine 2 tablespoons of margarine, the choc-olate chips, and sweetened condensed milk. Microwave on high until the chocolate chips are melted. Fold in the remaining ingredients, and pour the chocolate mixture over the dough. Crumble the reserved dough over the top. Bake in a 350° oven for 20 to 25 minutes.

Serves 24.

The Old World Inn Bed and Breakfast

1301 Jefferson Street
Napa, California 94559
(707) 257-0112

The historic Old World Inn was built in 1906 by local contractor E. W. Doughty for his private town residence. The home is an eclectic combination of architectural styles detailed with wood shingles, wide shady porches, clinker brick, and leaded and beveled glass. The inn is furnished throughout with painted Victorian and antique furniture. Most bedrooms have clawfoot tubs and showers and some have canopy beds. There is a custom built Jacuzzi available for guests' use in an enclosed patio area. Homemade hors d'oeuvres are served throughout the day.

Apricot Nut Bread

¾ cup dried apricots
Lukewarm water
1 orange

ఆ ఆ ఆ

½ cup raisins
Boiling water
⅔ cup sugar

2 tablespoons butter, melted
1 egg
2 cups all-purpose flour
2 teaspoons baking powder
1 teaspoon salt
1 teaspoon baking soda
½ cup chopped walnuts
1 teaspoon vanilla extract

Lightly grease a 9x5-inch loaf pan. In a bowl cover the apricots with lukewarm water and set aside for 30 minutes. Drain. Using a vegetable peeler, remove the outer peel from half the orange. Cut the orange in half and squeeze all of the juice from both halves. Reserve the juice. Put the apricots, orange peel, and raisins through a food grinder or chop finely with a knife. To the orange juice add enough boiling water to make 1 cup and pour into a bowl. Add the ground fruit. Stir in the sugar and butter. Beat in the egg.

In a separate bowl stir together the flour, baking powder, salt, baking soda, and walnuts. Add the dry ingredients to the fruit mixture along with the vanilla and stir until well blended. Pour into the prepared pan. Bake in a 350° oven for 55 to 60 minutes.

Makes 1 loaf, or 12 servings.

Shortbread Cookies

2 cups butter
1 cup sugar
1 teaspoon vanilla extract
1 teaspoon almond extract
4 cups all-purpose flour

In a large bowl cream together the butter, sugar, vanilla, and almond extract. Add the flour and mix until the dough is easy to work with, soft yet firm. Roll out on a floured board to about ¼-inch thickness. Cut into any shape desired. Place the cookies on a cookie sheet and prick with a fork. Bake in a 350° oven for 8 minutes or until the edges are golden brown.

Makes approximately 2 dozen.

ఆ ఆ ఆ ఆ ఆ

Downey House

517 West Broad Street
Nevada City, California 95959
(916) 265-2815

Downey House is a romantic 1869 Eastlake-style Victorian dwelling atop Nabob Hill overlooking Nevada City. Each of the six comfortable, sound-proof rooms has its own private bath with tub and shower and a queen or double bed. The downstairs parlor provides a common meeting place. Depending on the weather and a guest's preference, breakfast may be served in the kitchen, parlor, sun room, garden, terrace, or veranda. The outside garden area provides ample room for sunning and casual conversation. Downey House is just a few steps from the shops, fine restaurants, galleries, and museums of downtown Nevada City, where the streets are lit by gas lights.

Top Knot Rolls

1 ¼-ounce package active dry yeast
¼ cup warm water (110° to 115°)
¼ cup sugar
2¾ cups all-purpose flour
1 teaspoon salt
6 tablespoons melted butter
1 egg
½ cup warm milk (110° to 115°)

Grease 24 mini muffin cups, 18 small muffin cups, or 12 regular muffin cups. In a large mixing bowl combine the first 3 ingredients. Let the mixture stand in a warm place until bubbly, about 15 minutes. Add the remaining ingredients and mix with the dough hook of an electric mixer until the dough forms a ball. Let the dough rise in a warm dry place until doubled in bulk. For each roll, knead a small amount of dough in the palm of your hand to form a roll. Place in each cup to fill half full. Roll small pieces of dough into marble-sized balls. Make a small indentation in the top of each roll and insert the small ball to make the top knot. Cover and let rise until doubled in bulk. Bake in a 400° oven for 8 minutes for mini rolls, 10 minutes for small rolls, or 15 minutes for regular rolls.
Serves 12 to 14.

Cinnamon Rolls

1 recipe Top Knot Roll dough
6 tablespoons butter
4 tablespoon water
⅔ cup packed brown sugar
4 teaspoons cinnamon
½ cup raisins (optional)
½ cup nuts (optional)

Grease a 9x13-inch baking pan. Divide the dough in half and roll half on a floured board into a 9x15-inch rectangle. Reserve the remainder in the refrigerator for another batch of Cinnamon or Top Knot Rolls. In a small saucepan melt the butter, and add the water, brown sugar, and cinnamon. Stir until the mixture boils, and remove from the heat. Spread half of the mixture over the rectangle, and pour the remaining mixture in the bottom of the prepared pan. Sprinkle raisins and nuts over all. Roll the dough starting with the 15-inch side. Cut into 1¼-inch slices and place cut-side down on the brown sugar syrup in the prepared pan. Cover and let rise in a warm place until doubled in bulk, about 45 minutes.
    Bake in a 400° oven for 15 to 18 minutes. To serve, invert the rolls onto a serving platter.
Serves 12 to 14.

Grandmere's Bed & Breakfast Inn

449 Broad Street
Nevada City, California 95959
(916) 265-4660

Grandmere's Inn is situated in one of California's most charming gold mining communities. The inn's lovely three-story Colonial Revival architecture complements the grounds containing a large garden area, shrubs, trees, and many flowers. On the National Register of Historic Places, the inn is decorated in country style. All guest rooms have queen-size beds and private bathrooms; guests frequently label the breakfasts "legendary" and call the inn the perfect place for grown-ups who need to be spoiled.

Monterey Soufflé

12 slices white bread, crusts removed and cubed
1 16-ounce can whole kernel corn, drained
2 4-ounce cans green chilies, diced
4 cups grated Monterey Jack cheese
ꝋ   ꝋ   ꝋ
4 eggs, beaten
3 cups milk
½ teaspoon white pepper

Butter a 4-quart dish. Layer half of the bread, half of the corn, one can of chilies, and half of the cheese. Repeat the layers. Combine the eggs, milk, and pepper. Pour over the top of the layers. Refrigerate for at least 4 hours, or overnight.
    Bake in a 350° oven for 1 hour to 1 hour and 30 minutes, until golden.
Serves 12.

Red Castle Inn

109 Prospect Street
Nevada City, California 95959
(916) 265-5135

Strains of Mozart echo through lofty hallways, breezes linger on wide verandahs, chandeliers sparkle, and the aura of another time prevails in this California Gold Country inn. The "Castle" was named by the people of Nevada City as it was rising on Prospect Hill in 1857. Later this legendary pre-Civil War landmark became one of the first bed and breakfast lodgings

Red Castle Inn

in California, and today guests can savor the experience of life as it once was, tranquil, romantic, and genteel.

Alpha Chi Omega Chicken

2 6-ounce packages seasoned croutons
4 cups cooked chicken
6 ounces frozen chopped onions
1 cup mayonnaise
3 tablespoons fresh parsley, chopped
½ teaspoon dried basil
8 eggs, beaten
2 cups milk

ɜ ɜ ɜ

24 ounces cream of mushroom soup, undiluted
1 cup sliced almonds
2 cups grated Cheddar cheese

Grease two 7x11-inch baking pans. Arrange the croutons in the bottoms of the prepared pans. Mix together the chicken, onions, mayonnaise, parsley, and basil. Spread evenly over the croutons. Combine the eggs and milk, and pour carefully over the mixture in both pans. Refrigerate overnight. Bake in a 350° oven for 15 minutes, then top with the soup, almonds, and finally cheese. Return to the oven and bake for 1 hour.
Serves 16.

Julie Olson's Southwestern Soufflé

At the Red Castle we often name our recipes for the friends who give them to us.

3 tablespoons melted margarine
12 slices sourdough bread
½ pound fresh mushrooms, sliced
1 4-ounce can diced green chili peppers
4 cups grated Cheddar cheese
⅓ cup minced green pepper

4 eggs
3 cups milk
½ teaspoon salt
Dash pepper
½ teaspoon paprika

Spray a 9x13-inch baking pan with cooking spray. Spread the melted butter on the bread. Cut the bread slices in half and arrange 12 halves in the bottom of the prepared pan. Add half of the mushrooms, half of the chilies, half of the cheese, and half of the green peppers. Cover with the remaining bread and repeat the layers. Combine the eggs, milk, and seasonings and blend well. Pour over the layers, cover, and refrigerate overnight. Bring the dish to room temperature before baking. Bake uncovered in a 350° oven for 50 to 60 minutes.
Serves 8.

Heart's Desire Inn

3657 Church Street
Post Office Box 857
Occidental, California 95465
(707) 874-1311

Nestled against a hillside of berry bushes and fruit trees, Heart's Desire Inn is a two-story Victorian structure built in the 1860s that has been carefully renovated by its owners. Situated in Occidental, originally a lumbering and narrow gauge railroad center near the Sonoma coast and wine country, it blends the old and the new with elegant appointments of a wine country inn. Each room features antique pine furnishings and a private bath. The romantic Honeymoon Suite, with its own fireplace, four-poster bed, and private deck, provides the perfect setting for a special time. Outside is a walled garden with fountain. The covered porches with wicker furniture and balustered railings remind one of times long past.

Robin's Heart's Desire Inn Zucchini Muffins

3 eggs, beaten
1 cup oil
2½ cups sugar
1 tablespoon vanilla extract
2½ cups diced zucchini

   🍃 🍃 🍃

3 cups all-purpose flour
2 tablespoons cinnamon
1 teaspoon baking soda
1 teaspoon salt
¼ teaspoon baking powder

Spray muffin tins with cooking spray. In a large bowl beat the eggs, oil, sugar, and vanilla. Add the zucchini. Mix well. In a separate bowl combine the flour, cinnamon, baking soda, salt, and baking powder. Fold the liquid mixture into the dry mixture, stirring until just combined. Bake in a 350° oven for 20 to 25 minutes.
Makes 18 muffins.

Peach Cobbler
with Strawberry-Rhubarb Sauce

1 pound rhubarb
½ cup apple juice
1 pint strawberries
¾ cup brown sugar

   🍃 🍃 🍃

6 cups sliced peaches
1⅓ cups sugar
2 eggs, beaten

   🍃 🍃 🍃

3½ cups all-purpose flour, sifted
1 teaspoon salt
2 tablespoons baking powder
2 tablespoons sugar

Heart's Desire Inn

¾ cup butter
1 to 1¼ cups milk or cream

   🍃 🍃 🍃

2 to 4 tablespoons butter, melted
2 tablespoons sugar
1 tablespoon cinnamon

Trim and cut the rhubarb into 1-inch pieces. In a saucepan combine the rhubarb and apple juice, and bring to a boil. Simmer until tender. If the strawberries are large, cut them in half. Add the strawberries to the saucepan and simmer until tender. Add brown sugar to taste and mix well. Extra sauce may be prepared and frozen.

In a saucepan combine the peaches, 1⅓ cups of sugar, and the eggs. Heat but do not boil. Set aside. In a bowl combine the flour, salt, baking powder, and 2 tablespoons of sugar. Cut in the butter with a pastry blender, and gradually add the milk or cream. The dough should be the consistency of thick batter. Place the hot peach mixture in an ungreased 9x13-inch glass baking dish. Spoon the dough over the peaches and drizzle with the melted butter, 2 tablespoons of sugar, and cinnamon. Bake in a

425° oven for about 30 minutes or until the cobbler turns golden brown. Place in small bowls and spoon the Strawberry-Rhubarb Sauce over the individual servings. Serve warm.
Serves 12.

The Gosby House Inn

643 Lighthouse Avenue
Pacific Grove, California 93950
(408) 375-1287

The Gosby House, built in 1887, is an example of Queen Anne style, with the rounded corner tower, varied surface textures, and bay windows. The Victorian atmosphere has been retained. An open-hearth fireplace entices visitors to gather to enjoy afternoon tea, sherry, fresh fruits, and hors d'oeuvres.

The Gosby House Inn

Apricot or Date Scones

    4 cups all-purpose flour
    ½ cup sugar
    4 teaspoons baking powder
    1 teaspoon salt
    ½ teaspoon cream of tartar
    ¾ cup butter
    2 tablespoons grated orange peel
    1 cup chopped dried apricots or
        dates

        🐦 🐦 🐦

    1 egg
    1 cup cream
    ½ cup orange juice
    Cream
    Sugar

Grease a large baking sheet. In a large bowl combine the flour, sugar, baking powder, salt, and cream of tartar. Cut in the butter until the mixture resembles coarse crumbs. Add the orange peel and apricots or dates.

In a small bowl beat together the egg, cream, and orange juice. Add the liquid ingredients to the dry ingredients, and mix lightly with a fork until a soft dough forms. Turn the dough out onto a lightly floured surface and knead gently 5 to 6 times. Divide the dough into quarters, and roll each to ½-inch thickness. Cut into wedges. Place the scones on the prepared baking sheet. Brush with cream and sprinkle with sugar. Bake in a 425° oven for 15 to 18 minutes.

Serves 6.

Country Salmon Pie

    1 sheet puff pastry
    Parmesan cheese
    1 large onion, diced
    1 clove garlic, finely chopped
    2 tablespoons butter

    2 cups sour cream
    4 eggs
    1 16-ounce can salmon, cleaned and
        broken into pieces
    1 cup finely chopped, sautéed
        mushrooms
    1½ cups shredded Swiss cheese
    1 teaspoon dill
    ¼ teaspoon salt

Roll the pastry out to fit a 9-inch springform pan and make 2-inch sides. Place the pastry in the pan, shaping the dough around the bottom and sides of the pan. Sprinkle with Parmesan cheese. Set aside.

Sauté the onion and garlic in butter until soft. In a large bowl, beat together the sour cream and eggs until well blended. Stir in the salmon, mushrooms, sautéed onion and garlic, 1 cup of Swiss cheese, dill, and salt. Pour the mixture into the pastry lined pan. Top with the remaining ½ cup of cheese. Turn the sides of the dough in to form an edge. Bake in a 375° oven for 40 to 50 minutes, until set.

Serves 14.

🐦 🐦 🐦 🐦 🐦

Shrimp Pâté

    2 pounds cooked tiny shrimp
    1 8-ounce package cream cheese
    1 bunch green onions
    ½ red pepper
    1 tablespoon tomato paste
    1 tablespoon mustard
    1 tablespoon horseradish
    Salt and pepper to taste
    Parsley

Squeeze out the liquid from the shrimp and pat dry. Place all of the ingredients in a food processor and blend until everything is finely chopped. Line a mold with plastic wrap. Fill with shrimp pâté. Refrigerate for 2 to 4 hours. Unmold and serve with crackers, melba toast, or a baguette.

Serves 10 to 12.

Green Gables

104 Fifth Street
Pacific Grove, California 93950
(408) 375-2095

The Green Gables, built in 1888, is situated at the corner of 5th Street and Ocean View Boulevard in Pacific Grove, California. It is an excellent example of Queen Anne Victorian architecture in a fairy tale setting by the sea. The special touches at Green Gables provide for each guest's comfort. Each room is elegantly appointed with antiques of burnished wood, soft quilts, fresh fruit, and garden flowers. Most rooms have excellent ocean views, and six have working fireplaces.

7-Layer Nacho Dip

    1 16-ounce can refried beans
    1 2½-ounce package taco seasoning
        mix
    2 ripe avocados, peeled and
        chopped
    1 cup sour cream
    Chopped ripe black olives
    2 large tomatoes, diced
    1 small onion, finely chopped
    1 4-ounce can green chilies
    1½ cups shredded Monterey Jack
        cheese

Combine the beans and taco seasoning, and spread in the bottom of an 8x12-inch dish. Layer the remaining ingredients in order over the beans. Serve with real nachos.
Serves 8.

Hummus Dip

    6 cloves garlic
    3 16-ounce cans garbanzo beans,
        drained, reserving liquid from 1
        can
    4 ounces fresh chopped parsley
    Juice of 4 lemons

    3 tablespoons tahini butter (sesame
        seed butter)
    Salt to taste
    2 tablespoons olive oil

    ❧ ❧ ❧

    Parsley for garnish
    Dill pickle slices
    Pine nuts
    Cherry tomatoes
    Whole garbanzo beans
    Cumin
    Paprika

    ❧ ❧ ❧

    Sliced pita or French bread, or
        vegetable sticks

In a food processor combine the garlic and garbanzo beans, and process to a rough paste consistency. Add the parsley. Add the liquid from the garbanzo beans in small amounts, alternately with the lemon juice. Add the tahini butter, salt, and olive oil. The paste should be thick enough to spread. Place the mixture on a 9x13-inch platter. Garnish with parsley, dill pickle slices, pine nuts tossed in olive oil, cherry tomatoes, and whole garbanzo beans. Sprinkle with cumin and paprika. Serve with sliced pita or French bread, or vegetable sticks.
Serves 12 to 16.

Seven Gables Inn

555 Ocean View Boulevard
Pacific Grove, California 93950
(408) 372-4341

Seven Gables Inn is a landmark Victorian mansion furnished throughout with fine European antiques matched by gracious hospitality. The inn's spectacular setting offers dramatic views of the ocean and coastal mountains from every room. All guest rooms are bright and sunny, and each has its own private bath. Colorful gardens surround Seven Gables Inn. En-

glish-style high tea is served at four o'clock each afternoon; in the morning the generous sit-down breakfast is served in the grand dining room. Pebble Beach, Carmel-by-the-Sea, Big Sur, Point Lobos, and the many attractions of Monterey are a short drive away.

Honey Apple Muffins

    6 cups all-purpose flour
    1⅓ cups sugar
    3 teaspoons baking soda
    1½ teaspoons baking powder
    ¾ teaspoon salt
    2 cups oil
    1¼ cups honey
    5 eggs
    1½ teaspoons vanilla extract
    1 cup milk
    3 large apples, peeled and diced
    2 cups raisins
    1½ cups chopped nuts

Grease muffin tins. In a large bowl combine the flour, sugar, baking soda, baking powder, and salt. Add the oil, honey, eggs, vanilla, and milk. Stir until just blended. Fold in the apples, raisins, and nuts. Pour the dough into the prepared muffin tins. Bake in a 350° oven for 20 to 25 minutes.
Makes 3½ dozen muffins.

Country Scones

    Hot water
    ½ cup raisins or currants

    ❧ ❧ ❧

    2 cups all-purpose flour
    6 tablespoons sugar
    2 teaspoons baking powder
    ¾ teaspoon salt
    ½ teaspoon baking soda

    ❧ ❧ ❧

    5 tablespoons butter, cut in pieces

    ❧ ❧ ❧

    1 cup sour cream
    1 egg

    ❧ ❧ ❧

    1 teaspoon sugar
    ⅛ teaspoon cinnamon

Grease a cookie sheet. In a small mixing bowl pour enough hot water over the raisins or currants to cover. Let the raisins stand for 5 minutes. Drain well and set aside. In a food processor combine the dry ingredients and pulse 3 or 4 times to mix. Add the butter and process for 1 minute, until the mixture resembles cornmeal and the butter is completely blended. Transfer to a large mixing bowl.

Add the sour cream, raisins, and egg. Stir just until the dough clings together. On a floured surface, knead the dough gently 10 to 12 times. Roll or pat the dough to 1-inch thickness. Cut with a round or patterned cutter. Place on a cookie sheet. Combine the remaining teaspoon of sugar with the cinnamon and sprinkle over the scones. Bake in a 350° oven for 20 to 25 minutes or until lightly browned.

Serves 16.

Fleming Jones Homestead Bed & Breakfast Inn

3170 Newton Road
Placerville, California 95667
(916) 626-5840

Nestled on eleven acres in the Sierra foothills of the Mother Lode, Fleming Jones Homestead provides guests with the opportunity to relax on an old porch swing, farmhouse balcony, or bunkhouse deck. The farm's warm hospitality extends to the parlor where guests may play the old church pump organ or sink into a comfortable rocker to read or think. The Fleming Jones Homestead is well situated as a base for day trips to Gold Rush mining towns, museums, mines, and foothill wineries.

Baked Herb Cheese Egg

    1 tablespoon melted butter
    1 egg
    1 to 2 tablespoons half and half
    1 tablespoon grated sharp Cheddar,
        Monterey Jack, or Swiss cheese
    Pinch Italian herbs (oregano, basil,
        marjoram, etc.)
    Pinch parsley
    Dash Parmesan cheese
    Dash ground black pepper
    Dash paprika

Pour the melted butter into a ramekin or custard dish. Break the egg into the dish. Pour the cream around the edges of the yolk. Arrange the grated cheese around the edge. Sprinkle herbs, parsley, Parmesan cheese, black pepper, and paprika on top. Place the ramekin in 1 inch of hot water in a baking pan. Bake uncovered in a 350° oven for 15 to 20 minutes, until the cream and cheese "froth up," or bubble. Remove from the oven and serve immediately. The egg will remain quite hot in the dish for several minutes.

Serves 1.

Herb Sausage Cheese Balls

A convenience food for breakfast, brunch, or a party.

    2½ pounds freshly ground pork
        sausage
    8 cups grated sharp Cheddar cheese
    3 cups biscuit mix
    10 tablespoons dried Italian herbs
        (oregano, basil, marjoram, etc.)
    3 to 5 tablespoons curry powder

Allow the sausage and Cheddar cheese to reach room temperature, for easier mixing. In a large bowl combine all of the ingredients and shape into 1-inch balls. To store until needed, freeze in bags.

Remove from the freezer and place on a cookie sheet or cake pan. Bake in a 350° oven for 15 to 20 minutes until brown. Serve hot.

Makes 40 to 50.

Homestead Bran Muffins

This recipe won a blue ribbon at the 1983 El Dorado County Fair.

    3 cups All Bran
    ⅔ cup hot water
    3 tablespoons frozen orange juice
        concentrate
    ½ cup oil
    2 eggs, slightly beaten
    🍂 🍂 🍂
    2½ cups all-purpose flour
    ¾ cups sugar
    2½ teaspoons baking soda
    2 cups buttermilk
    1 cup currants
    🍂 🍂 🍂
    Ground walnuts

Grease muffin tins. In a bowl combine 1 cup of All Bran, hot water, orange juice concentrate, and oil. Add the eggs. In a large bowl combine the flour, sugar, and baking soda. Add the buttermilk and the All Bran mixture. Stir in the remaining All Bran and the currants. Pour into the prepared muffin tins, filling ⅔ full. Sprinkle ground walnuts over the batter. Bake in a 350° oven for 15 to 20 minutes. Serve hot.

Makes 15 to 20.

Orange Butter

    ½ cup butter, softened
    1 3-ounce package cream cheese,
        softened
    2 tablespoons grated orange rind
    1 tablespoon frozen orange juice
        concentrate

In a mixing bowl combine all the ingredients and beat with an electric mixer until smooth.

Serve at room temperature. Store in the refrigerator. If crumbly, bring to

Fleming Jones Homestead

room temperature and beat again.

Variation: Lemon rind may be substituted for orange rind. Finely ground walnuts may be added.

Makes about ¾ cup.

East Brother Light Station

117 Park Place
Point Richmond, California 94801
(415) 233-2385

Situated on one of four rocky islands that mark the straits separating San Francisco Bay from San Pablo Bay, East Brother Light Station was constructed in 1873-1874 as one of seventeen lighthouses eventually built in the San Francisco Bay area. It has been restored as a living museum.

Guests savor the "California French" cuisine and enjoy the finest in California wines and champagnes; candlelight adds to the magic of the dining experience. Victorian furnishings, brass beds, and fresh flowers highlight the four guest rooms that once served as the lighthouse keepers' quarters. Included in the fees are transportation from the Point San Pablo Yacht Harbor, as well as dinner and breakfast. The keepers will provide a tour of the island if requested.

Salmon in Chive Sauce

1 4½-pound fresh salmon fillet
4 cups chicken stock
1 cup dry white wine
1 cup dry sherry

❧ ❧ ❧

Pinch thyme
1 bay leaf
1 cup heavy cream
1 bunch chives, chopped

Cut the salmon into 8 individual fillets, approximately 1½x5-inches each. Divide the salmon fillets between 2 glass baking dishes. Pour 2 cups of chicken stock, ½ cup of dry white wine, and ½ cup of sherry over each dish. Bake in a 375° oven for 20 minutes. Do not overcook, the white fat should bubble to the surface of the fish. Remove the fish from the stock and set aside. Transfer the stock to a large skillet. Add the thyme and bay leaf, and reduce the stock to ¼ the original amount. Remove the bay leaf. Add the cream and reduce over medium heat until the sauce begins to thicken. Return the salmon to the cream sauce and heat through.

One minute prior to serving, add the chopped chives. Spoon the sauce over the salmon fillets.

Serves 8.

Recipe courtesy of Chef Leigh Hurley.

Chicken and Sausage in Puff Pastry

4 chicken breast fillets, cut into
    ¾-inch pieces
12 inches Hillshire Farms
    precooked hot sausage, skinned
    and finely chopped
1 large apple pear, pared, cored and
    chopped
1 cup finely chopped bell peppers
    (red, green, yellow, or orange)
1 package Near East Rice Pilaf
3 medium onions, coarsely chopped
1 cup shiitake mushrooms
1 clove garlic, pressed
6 tablespoons butter
½ teaspoon salt
1 teaspoon black pepper
1 8-ounce package cream cheese
2 sheets Pepperidge Farms puff
    pastry
2 egg whites, lightly beaten

Grease a cookie sheet. In a large bowl combine the chicken, sausage, apple pear, and bell peppers. Prepare the rice according to the package directions and add to the mixture. Sauté the onion, mushrooms, and garlic in the butter. Add the salt and pepper, and cook until the onions are translucent. Add the onion mixture to the chicken mixture. Cut the cream cheese into chunks, and distribute throughout the chicken mixture.

Roll out the puff pastry to 12x18-inch rectangles. Place one sheet of pastry on the cookie sheet. Spread the chicken mixture over the pastry, leaving a 1½-inch border. Top with the remaining sheet of pastry, moistening the edges and folding them in toward the center, sealing the ingredients within the pastry. Bake in a 350° oven for 30 minutes. Remove from the oven and brush with the egg whites. Bake an additional 15 minutes.

Cut into 8 equal portions and garnish with tomato roses.

Serves 8.

Recipe courtesy Chef Leigh Hurley.

Black Bean Soup

1 16-ounce package black beans
2 quarts chicken stock, approximately
1 teaspoon cumin
½ teaspoon garlic powder
1 teaspoon oregano
1 teaspoon chili powder
1 teaspoon black pepper
1 teaspoon salt, or to taste

🌿 🌿 🌿

Red tomatoes, chopped
Yellow tomatoes, chopped
Red onion, chopped
Fresh cilantro, chopped
Salt and black pepper
Sour cream thinned with heavy cream

Soak the beans overnight in water. Drain the water and cover with chicken stock. Add the seasonings and simmer for 5 to 6 hours or until the beans are tender. Continue to add chicken stock during cooking, until the soup is the desired consistency. Toss together the chopped vegetables, salt, and pepper. Garnish individual servings of soup with the salsa mixture and the thinned sour cream.

Serves 6 to 8.

Recipe courtesy Chef Leigh Hurley.

Crème Brûlée

2½ cups whipping cream
½ cup sugar
6 egg yolks
1 teaspoon vanilla extract

🌿 🌿 🌿

Sugar
Fresh strawberries for garnish

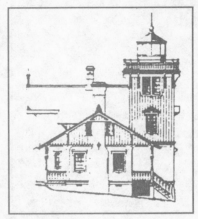

East Brother Light Station

Heat the cream almost to the boiling point. In a bowl combine the sugar with the egg yolks until the mixture is smooth. Pour the heated cream very slowly into the egg mixture, stirring constantly. Add the vanilla and place in 8 individual serving dishes. Place the dishes in a pan of hot water. Bake in a 350° oven for 45 minutes. Chill.

Sprinkle sugar lightly over each dish and place under the broiler until the sugar browns lightly and bubbles. Chill again. Garnish with fresh strawberries, sliced and fanned.

Serves 8.

Recipe courtesy Chef Leigh Hurley.

Christmas House

9240 Archibald Avenue
Rancho Cucamonga, California 91730
(714) 980-6450

Christmas House is an elegant, spacious three-story Victorian home built in 1904 for H. D. Cousins, who raised Thoroughbred horses on the surrounding acreage. The next owners, the Whitson family who bought the house in 1910, gave many lavish Yuletide parties. For this reason, and because of the numerous red and green stained glass windows, the mansion became known as the "Christmas House," the name retained when the present owners began a two-year restoration in 1983. Christmas House accommodations include two suites with private baths and three bedrooms with one shared bath, all uniquely furnished.

Sweet Cheese Crepes
with Cranberry Sauce

4 large eggs
1 cup all-purpose flour
1 tablespoon oil
1½ cups milk
Butter

🌿 🌿 🌿

1 8-ounce package cream cheese
⅓ cup sugar
4 cups small curd cream-style cottage cheese
2 teaspoons vanilla extract

🌿 🌿 🌿

3 cups fresh cranberries
½ cup sugar
2 tablespoons cornstarch
1 cup water

🌿 🌿 🌿

Banana spears
Hazelnuts
Whipped cream
Holly sprigs for garnish

In a blender whirl the eggs, flour, and oil until smooth. Add the milk and whirl until blended. In a 7-inch nonstick skillet prepare the crepes. Coat the skillet with butter between each crepe.

In a large bowl blend the cream cheese, ⅓ cup of sugar, cottage cheese, and vanilla with an electric mixer. Set aside.

In a saucepan combine the cranberries, ½ cup of sugar, cornstarch, and water. Cook over medium heat until boiling and thickened.

Spread a large tablespoon of cheese filling in each crepe. Fold the crepes in half, and then in half again to form a triangle. Serve 3 crepes on each plate, arranged with the points of the triangles toward the center of the plate. Spoon warm cranberry sauce over all. Garnish with banana spears between each crepe, sprinkle with hazelnuts, and top with whipped cream. Garnish with a sprig of holly. Serves 4.

Eggnog Coffee Cake

½ cup softened butter
⅓ cup sugar
2 eggs
3 cups all-purpose flour
1 tablespoon baking powder
1½ teaspoons nutmeg
2 cups eggnog
1 cup chopped nuts

❧ ❧ ❧

1½ cups confectioners' sugar
¼ teaspoon nutmeg
¼ teaspoon cinnamon
Eggnog to moisten

Grease a fluted cake pan. In a large bowl cream together the butter and sugar. Beat in the eggs. In a separate bowl combine the flour, baking powder, and 1½ teaspoons nutmeg. Add the flour mixture and the eggnog alternately to the butter mixutre. Fold in the nuts. Pour into the prepared pan. Bake in a 325° oven for 30 minutes.

In a small bowl combine confectioners' sugar, ¼ teaspoon nutmeg, and cinnamon. Gradually add enough eggnog to make the frosting the consistency to drizzle. Drizzle over the cooled cake.

Variation: To make muffins, pour the batter into 24 greased muffin cups. We use "Christmas-shaped" muffin cups, such as wreaths, trees, etc.
Serves 12.

❧ ❧ ❧ ❧ ❧

Palisades Paradise B & B

1200 Palisades Avenue
Redding, California 96003
(916) 223-5305

This fine contemporary home overlooks the Sacramento River and provides a spectacular view of the city, Shasta Bally, and the surrounding mountains. Although the inn is in a quiet residential neighborhood, it is near many fine restaurants. Guests can watch the wide-screen television in the living room, relax in the old-fashioned porch swing under the oak tree, or soak in the garden spa. Many outdoor activities, such as rafting, swimming, fishing, and boating, are available nearby.

Palisades Fruit Puff
with Bananas Amaretto

4 eggs
⅔ cup all-purpose flour
⅔ cup milk
¼ teaspoon salt
¼ teaspoon vanilla extract
4 tablespoons butter, melted
Confectioners' sugar

❧ ❧ ❧

2 tablespoons butter
1 tablespoon light brown sugar
4 firm bananas
¼ cup Amaretto
Nutmeg
Whipped cream or sour cream

In a medium bowl, beat the eggs with an electric mixer on high speed until frothy. Slowly add the flour, beating on medium speed until blended. Stir in the milk, salt, and vanilla. Divide the melted butter in four 8-inch skillets. Pour the egg mixture into the hot skillets. Bake in a 450° oven for 12 to 15 minutes or until brown and puffed.

Remove from the oven and sprinkle with confectioners' sugar.

In a skillet melt 2 tablespoons of butter. Add the brown sugar and sauté the bananas until slightly soft, but not mushy. Gently stir in the Amaretto. Gently sprinkle with nutmeg. Serve the puffs with the bananas, garnished with whipped cream.

Variations: Top the puffs with strawberries and sliced kiwi, sliced peaches and blueberries, or canned apples with brown sugar and cinnamon. Top with whipped cream, Cool Whip, or yogurt.
Serves 4.

Cajun Corn Salad

1 teaspoon sugar
2 tablespoons mayonnaise
1 teaspoon Creole mustard
½ teaspoon Tabasco sauce
¼ cup herbed white wine vinegar
1 tablespoon dried leaf basil
½ teaspoon fresh ground pepper
½ teaspoon salt
½ cup olive oil

❧ ❧ ❧

3 cups canned whole kernel corn
6 green onions, sliced
1 large green bell pepper, chopped
1 cup cherry tomato halves
1 cup thinly sliced hot pickled okra
½ cup minced parsley

In a 2-quart bowl whisk together the first 8 ingredients. Add the olive oil in a slow steady stream, whisking until slightly thickened.

In a salad bowl, toss together the remaining ingredients. Pour the dressing over the salad, tossing gently. Cover and refrigerate overnight or up to 3 days before serving.
Serves 6 to 8.

Bread Pudding
with Whiskey Sauce

4 cups torn French bread pieces
2 cups milk
½ cup chopped dates or raisins

❧ ❧ ❧

3 eggs, slightly beaten
1 cup sugar
¼ cup melted butter
1 tablespoon vanilla extract
2 teaspoons cinnamon

    ❧   ❧   ❧

¼ cup butter
½ cup sugar
1 egg yolk
2 tablespoons water
2 tablespoons bourbon

In a large bowl combine the bread pieces, milk, and raisins. Let the mixture stand for 5 minutes or until the bread is softened, stirring often.

Grease an 8-inch square baking pan. Beat together the 3 eggs, 1 cup of sugar, ¼ cup of butter, vanilla, and cinnamon. Stir into the bread mixture until blended. Pour into the prepared pan. Bake in a 350° oven for 40 to 45 minutes, or until a knife inserted in the center comes out clean.

In a small saucepan, melt ¼ cup of butter. Stir in ½ cup of sugar, the egg yolk, and water. Cook over medium heat, stirring often, for 5 to 6 minutes or until the sugar dissolves and the mixture thickens. Remove from the heat and stir in the bourbon. Makes ⅔ cup.

Serves 9.

Amber House

1315 22nd Street
Sacramento, California 95816
(916) 444-8085

Amber House is a stately old mansion in the heart of Sacramento. Sheltered by towering elm trees, it is an elegant sanctuary where a guest's needs receive personal attention. The area nearby has many turn-of-the-century houses that make an evening stroll a pleasurable experience. A variety of restaurants are within a few blocks. Each of the five guest rooms

has a private bath. In the common areas plush Oriental rugs accent the hardwood floors, and fragrant flowers harmonize with classical music. Antique pocket doors, a boxed beam ceiling, and clinker brick fireplace complete the setting.

Mushroom Crustless Quiche

½ pound mushrooms, sliced
1 bunch green onions, chopped
3 tablespoons margarine

    ❧   ❧   ❧

3 eggs
½ cup plus 1 tablespoon Bisquick
½ teaspoon salt
¼ teaspoon pepper
½ teaspoon nutmeg
1½ cups milk

    ❧   ❧   ❧

1½ cups shredded Monterey Jack cheese

Butter a 9-inch round cake pan. In a skillet sauté the mushrooms and onions in margarine. Set aside.

Beat the eggs, and add the Bisquick. Mix until smooth. Add the spices and blend for 1 minute. Slowly add the milk to the egg mixture. Mix thoroughly. Layer the bottom of the pan with half of the mushrooms and onions. Add the Monterey Jack cheese and top with the remaining mushrooms and onions. Pour the egg mixture over all. Bake in a 350° oven for 30 to 35 minutes.

Serves 6 to 8.

Swiss Mustard Eggs

3 eggs
2 tablespoons milk
1 tablespoon stone-ground mustard
⅛ teaspoon pepper
2 strips bacon
½ tablespoon butter
¼ cup grated Swiss cheese
1 English muffin, split and toasted
1 tablespoon grated Parmesan cheese
Tomato slices and sprouts for garnish

In a small bowl mix the eggs, milk, mustard, and pepper, using a wire whisk. In a skillet cook the bacon until crisp. Crumble and set aside. Melt the butter in the skillet. Add the egg mixture and scramble. Just before the eggs are done, add the Swiss cheese and crumbled bacon. Cook until the cheese melts. Place the toasted muffin halves on a serving plate, spoon the eggs onto each half, and sprinkle with Parmesan cheese. Garnish the plate with quartered tomato slices and sprouts.

Serves 1.

Aunt Abigail's

2120 "G" Street
Sacramento, California 95816
(916) 441-5007

Aunt Abigail's, a Colonial Revival mansion built in downtown Sacramento in 1912, has been a home away from home throughout its history. Situated within walking distance of Sutter's Fort, Almond Plaza, the Convention Center, and the state capitol, it is just minutes away from many fine restaurants, Old Town, and the Railroad Museum. Popular with business travelers who prefer the comforts of home while traveling, its large living and sitting rooms provide a relaxing atmosphere. The patio provides a relaxing place for visiting on warm evenings. The five guest rooms are large and luxurious.

Berry Bundt Cake

1½ cups sifted cake flour
1½ teaspoons baking soda
3 tablespoons instant dry nonfat milk
½ teaspoon salt
1 teaspoon cinnamon
½ teaspoon nutmeg

Aunt Abigail's

Jami's Famous Hazelnut Coffee

**2 heaping tablespoons Viennese
    coffee beans
1 heaping tablespoon hazelnut
    coffee beans
12 cups cold water**

In a coffee bean grinder, grind the beans together, counting slowly to 20. In an electric drip coffee maker, add the water and brew. Remove the coffee immediately and serve or store in a thermal carafe.
    Serves 12.

Chicken Rice Salad à la Bartels

Great for an easy luncheon or light supper.

**1 6¾-ounce package wild rice mix,
    cooked and cooled
½ cup chopped green onions,
    including tops
1 cup fresh mushrooms, sliced
½ cup diced red sweet peppers (or
    pimientos)
1 7¼-ounce can whole ripe olives
2 cups large chunks cooked chicken
1½ cups fresh snow peas (or 1
    package frozen snow peas,
    thawed)
⅔ cup mayonnaise
½ cup sour cream
Salt and pepper to taste
Lettuce leaves
Fruit for garnish**

In a large bowl combine all of the ingredients except the lettuce leaves, tossing until well combined. Serve on a bed of lettuce leaves with fruit for garnish.
    Serves 6.

**½ teaspoon cloves
½ cup oat bran
½ cup chopped almonds**

🙣 🙣 🙣

**1½ cups sugar
¾ cup plain lowfat yogurt
3 eggs, beaten
¾ cup corn oil
½ teaspoon orange extract
1 cup berries of your choice**

Grease and flour a 12-cup Bundt pan. In a medium bowl mix together the flour, baking soda, dry milk, salt, cinnamon, nutmeg, cloves, and oat bran. Mix in the chopped nuts. In a separate bowl combine the sugar and yogurt. Beat in the eggs, corn oil, and orange extract. Fold in the berries. Add the dry ingredients, stirring until just blended. Pour into the prepared Bundt pan. Bake in a 350° oven for 45 to 50 minutes. Cool for 15 minutes.
    Serves 12.

Bartels Ranch and Country Inn

1200 Conn Valley Road
St. Helena, California 94574
(707) 963-4001

Situated in the heart of the Napa Valley wine country, Bartels Ranch is nestled away in a private, peaceful setting. Solitude and romance are the magnets that draw guests from all over the United States and many foreign countries. The award winning accommodations set on "100 acres with a 10,000-acre view" provide a large entertainment room, bicycles, fireplace, terraces overlooking the pool-spa, and vineyard. The three guest rooms have private baths. Golf, tennis, wineries, and a lake are nearby. Tailored itineraries included.

The Wine Country Inn

1152 Lodi Lane
St. Helena, California 94574
(707) 963-7077

Perched on a knoll overlooking manicured vineyards and nearby hills, the Wine Country Inn offers twenty-five individually decorated guest rooms. All rooms are decorated with antique furnishings and lovely, fresh colors reflecting the seasonal moods of the Napa Valley. Each room has its own private bathroom, but no television. The agricultural beauty of the valley contrasts with the rugged, tree-covered hills surrounding it. Century-old stone bridges, pump houses, barns, and rock buildings afford artists and photographers a wide variety of subjects. Within a short distance of the Wine Country Inn are over 100 wineries, tennis courts, hot air balloon rides, mineral baths, several Robert Louis Stevenson sites, antique shops, and over fifteen excellent restaurants serving luncheon and dinner.

Poppy Seed Cake

2 cups sugar
1½ cups oil
4 eggs
1 teaspoon vanilla extract
3 cups all-purpose flour
¼ teaspoon salt
1½ teaspoons baking soda
1 12-ounce can evaporated milk
1 2½-ounce can or package poppy
  seeds
1 3-ounce package walnuts (or
  pecans)

Grease a bundt pan. In a large bowl combine the sugar, oil, eggs, and vanilla. Add the remaining ingredients and mix well. Pour into the prepared pan. Bake in a 350° oven for 1 hour and 10 minutes.

Serves 10.

The Wine Country Inn Granola

2 cups oats
1 cup sliced almonds
¼ cup honey
¼ cup melted butter
½ cup brown sugar
Cinnamon
Salt
¾ cup coconut
1 cup raisins

Combine the oats and almonds in a large baking pan. Combine the honey and melted butter, and pour over the oats and almonds. Stir to coat the oat mixture. Sprinkle the brown sugar, cinnamon, and salt over all. Bake in a 300° oven, stirring frequently until lightly toasted. Add the coconut. Continue baking and stirring until the granola is a nice golden color. Remove from the oven and add the raisins.

Makes about 5 cups.

The Wine Country Inn

Casa de Flores

184 Avenue La Cuesta
San Clemente, California 92672
(714) 498-1344

Casa de Flores is in the heart of Southern California's coastal communities. In less than five minutes guests can be strolling sandy beaches or swimming in the Pacific Ocean. Situated halfway between Los Angeles and San Diego, the large two-story, Spanish-style home offers two rooms with a shared bath and a patio suite.

Casa de Flores

Casa Crepes

1 21-ounce can cherry, peach, or apple pie filling

🍃 🍃 🍃

2 eggs
1 cup small curd cottage cheese
2 tablespoons oil
¼ cup all-purpose flour

🍃 🍃 🍃

Confectioners' sugar

In a small saucepan heat the pie filling over medium heat. In a blender combine the eggs and cottage cheese. Blend until combined. Add the oil, and then the flour. Blend until smooth. Preheat a frying pan over medium to high heat, and add a small amount of oil. Pour about ⅓ cup of batter into the frying pan and tilt to make a thin crepe. Cook until bubbles rise to the top and the crepe appears dry, and turn. Cook the other side until browned. Continue until all of the batter is used. Spoon the heated pie filling down the middle of each crepe. Fold over and dust with confectioners' sugar.

Serves 5 to 7.

Heritage Breakfast Dumplings

1 9½-ounce can Pillsbury Pastry Pocket
3 ounces raisins
1 21-ounce can apple pie filling

🍃 🍃 🍃

1 cup brown sugar
¾ cup water

Grease a cookie sheet. Separate the pastry into squares. Divide the raisins onto each pastry. Spoon the apples into the middle of each pastry on top of the raisins. Pull the corners together and pinch to seal. With damp fingers smooth the pastry over the filling. Place seam-side down on the cookie sheet. On top of each dumpling, make a ½-inch hole. Bake in a 350° oven for 17 minutes.

In a saucepan combine the brown sugar and water, and bring to a boil. Boil for 5 minutes. When the dumplings are ready, place in individual bowls. Serve the brown sugar syrup in a small pitcher. For each serving, pour the syrup into the holes and on the sides of the dumplings.

Serves 4.

B & B (Breakfast & Brunch) Casserole

½ cup Bisquick
½ cup milk
2 eggs, slightly beaten
3 tablespoons butter, melted
2 teaspoons Dijon mustard
½ pinch nutmeg
2 ounces cooked ham, diced (or Canadian bacon, cut in squares)
1 cup grated Cheddar cheese
2 green onions, finely chopped
1 8-ounce can crushed pineapple, drained

Grease 2 small Pyrex serving dishes. In a medium bowl or blender combine the Bisquick, milk, eggs, butter, mustard, and nutmeg until smooth. Stir in the ham, cheese, onions, and pineapple. Pour into the prepared dishes. Bake in a 350° oven for 30 minutes, or until set.

For brunch, pour into a greased pie plate and bake in a 350° oven for 35 to 40 minutes. This alternative serves 4.

Serves 2.

🐦 🐦 🐦 🐦 🐦

Scrambled Eggs in Potato Boats

2 medium baking potatoes
2 green onions
8 slices bacon
Butter
Salt and pepper

🍃 🍃 🍃

8 eggs
2 to 3 dollops sour cream
Paprika

Wash the potatoes. Bake in a 450° oven for 45 minutes. Slice the green onions. Fry the bacon until crisp. Drain on a paper towel and crumble. Slice the baked potatoes in half and scoop out all but about ¼-inch of potato. (You can save this to make potato pancakes another day.) Brush the inside of the potato boats with butter and sprinkle with salt and pepper. Refrigerate the onions, bacon, and potato boats until morning.

In the morning, bake the buttered potato boats in a 450° oven for 15 minutes. While the potato boats are baking, beat the eggs and add the sliced onions and crumbled bacon. Pour into a lightly oiled skillet and scramble over medium to low heat. When almost set, add the sour cream and turn the heat to low. Blend in the sour cream. Remove the boats from the oven and fill with the egg mixture. Sprinkle with paprika and serve.

Serves 4.

The Cottage

Post Office Box 3292
San Diego, California 92103
(619) 299-1564

Situated in the Hillcrest section of San Diego where old homes and undeveloped canyons offer an unhurried atmosphere, the Cottage evokes the spirit of a bygone era. Victorian-style furniture, a wood-burning stove, and an oak pump organ are provided in the living room. Three people can be accommodated by the king-size bed in the bedroom and the single bed in the living room. The kitchen is fully equipped. The San Diego Zoo and Balboa Park are only five minutes away by car, the beaches fifteen minutes, and Mexico one-half hour.

MB's Almond-Cheese Coffee Cake

1 ¼-ounce package active dry yeast
¼ cup warm water (110° to 115°)
2½ cups all-purpose flour
2 tablespoons sugar

½ teaspoon salt
6 tablespoons cold butter
2 egg yolks
½ cup milk

   🍃 🍃 🍃

1 8-ounce package cream cheese, room temperature
¼ cup sugar
3 tablespoons all-purpose flour
1 egg yolk
1 teaspoon lemon peel
1 teaspoon almond extract
¼ cup sliced almonds

   🍃 🍃 🍃

2 egg whites, lightly beaten

In a measuring cup combine the yeast and water. Let the mixture stand for 5 minutes. In a large mixing bowl combine 2 cups of flour, 2 tablespoons of sugar, and the salt. Using a pastry blender, cut the butter into the flour mixture until it forms large uniform crumbs. Stir in the yeast mixture, 2 egg yolks, and milk. Mix at medium speed to blend well. Stir in ⅓ cup more flour to make a stiff dough. Shape the dough into a ball. Place in a greased bowl, turning to grease the top of the dough. Cover with plastic wrap and chill for 6 hours or overnight.

Punch the dough down and turn onto a floured board. Roll the dough into a 10x13-inch rectangle, adding flour to the board as needed to prevent sticking. Transfer to a 14x17-inch rimless baking sheet.

Combine the cream cheese, ¼ cup sugar, 3 tablespoons of flour, remaining egg yolk, lemon peel, and almond extract. Beat until well blended. Spread the mixture onto the dough to within 1 inch of the outside edges. Sprinkle with almonds. Starting at a long end of the dough, roll up the dough jelly roll fashion just to the center of the rectangle. Repeat with the other long side. This will look like 2 jelly rolls side by side. Using a floured knife, make cuts through one roll at a time, 1½-inches apart, cutting to the center, but leaving attached. Gently lift the slices and turn on their sides to expose the filling. Cover and let rise in a warm place

until doubled in bulk. Brush with egg white. Bake in a 350° oven for 25 minutes or until the top is golden brown.

Serves 6.

Strawberry Bread

½ cup butter or margarine
1 cup sugar
½ teaspoon almond extract
2 eggs, separated
1 cup crushed or chopped fresh strawberries
2 cups all-purpose flour
1 teaspoon baking powder
1 teaspoon baking soda
1 teaspoon salt

Line a 9x5-inch pan with greased wax paper. In a large bowl cream together the butter, sugar, and almond extract. Beat in the egg yolks. Add the strawberries and blend well. In a separate bowl, sift together the flour, baking powder, baking soda, and salt. Set aside. Beat the egg whites until stiff and fold into the strawberry mixture alternately with the flour mixture. Turn the batter into the pan. Bake in a 350° oven for 50 to 60 minutes. Cool for 15 minutes on a rack.

Makes 1 loaf, or 4 servings.

Heritage Park Bed and Breakfast Inn

2470 Heritage Park Row
San Diego, California 92110
(619) 295-7088

Nestled on a quiet 7.8-acre Victorian park in the heart of San Diego's historic Old Town, Heritage Park has been completely restored to its original splendor. Built in 1889, this Queen Anne mansion has several chimneys,

The Cottage

a two-story corner tower, and an en-circling verandah. Guests can choose from nine distinctive accommodations, each furnished in 1890's Victorian style. The homemade breakfast will be served in bed or on the large front verandah. In the evenings the social hour is followed by a classic film. Romantic in-room candlelight dinners or Victorian country suppers are available on request.

Mrs. C's Fabulous Apple Muffins

½ cup margarine
1 cup sugar
2 eggs
1 teaspoon vanilla extract

   ❧ ❧ ❧

2 cups all-purpose flour
1 teaspoon baking powder
1 teaspoon baking soda
1 cup sour cream

   ❧ ❧ ❧

1 7-ounce jar marshmallow creme
1 tablespoon lemon juice
1½ teaspoons cinnamon
2½ cups peeled apple slices
1 cup chopped nuts (optional)
Honey-butter

Grease muffin tins. In a large bowl beat the margarine and sugar until fluffy. Add the eggs one at a time, mixing well. Blend in the vanilla. In a separate bowl combine the flour, baking powder, baking soda, and sour cream. Add the flour mixture to the margarine mixture. Combine the marshmallow creme, lemon juice, cinnamon, apples, and nuts. Fold into the batter and blend well. Pour the batter into muffin cups. Bake in a 350° oven for 30 minutes. Serve with honey-butter.

Makes 18 muffins.

Mrs. C's Fabulous Linzer Torte Muffins

2 cups all-purpose flour
2 teaspoons baking powder
½ teaspoon salt
1 teaspoon cinnamon
⅛ teaspoon cloves
½ cup firmly packed dark brown sugar
¼ cup sugar
½ cup butter or margarine

1 egg
1 teaspoon grated lemon peel
½ teaspoon vanilla extract
1 cup milk
¾ cup ground blanched hazelnuts
¼ cup seedless raspberry jam

Grease 12 muffin cups. In a large bowl stir together the flour, baking powder, salt, cinnamon, and cloves. In another bowl, cream the sugars with the butter until light and fluffy. Beat in the egg, lemon peel, and vanilla. Stir in the milk. Make a well in the center of the dry ingredients and add the butter mixture. Stir just until combined. Stir in the hazelnuts. Spoon half of the batter into the prepared muffin cups. Place 1 teaspoon of jam in the center of each portion of batter. Do not let the jam touch the sides of the muffin cups. Spoon the remaining batter over the jam. Bake in a 400° oven for 15 to 20 minutes, or until lightly browned. Remove to wire racks, and cool for 5 minutes before removing the muffins from the cups.

Serves 12.

Gourmet Apple Strudel

2 Granny Smith apples, peeled, quartered and sliced
¼ cup raisins
¼ cup sugar
1¼ tablespoons cinnamon
1 sheet puff pastry, thawed
½ cup sour cream
1 egg, beaten

In a large bowl add the apples, raisins, sugar, and cinnamon. Mix gently. On a floured surface roll out the puff pastry. Spread the apple mixture over the pastry to within 1 inch of the edge. Spoon the sour cream over the apple mixture. Brush egg along the edges. Fold the pastry together and fold the edges under. Brush the loaf with the remaining egg.

Bake in a 350° oven for 20 minutes or until golden brown.

Serves 10 to 12.

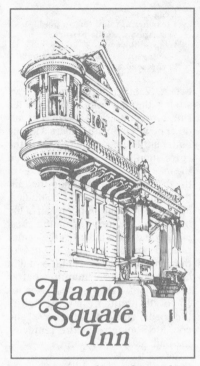

Alamo Square Inn

Berry Patch Filled Squares

¾ cup margarine
½ cup sugar
1 teaspoon vanilla extract
1 egg
2½ cups sifted all-purpose flour
½ teaspoon baking powder
2 cups jam, any flavor

In a large bowl cream the margarine and add the sugar gradually. Add the vanilla and egg, and beat well. Sift the flour with the baking powder and add to the creamed mixture, mixing well after each addition. Press the dough lightly over the bottom and sides of a 9x13-inch baking dish. Bake in a 400° oven for 15 to 20 minutes. In a saucepan heat the jam. Spread the hot jam over the cookie dough. Cool before cutting into squares. Store in the refrigerator.

Makes 40 small squares.

Alamo Square Inn

719 Scott Street
San Francisco, California 94117
(415) 922-2055

At Alamo Square Inn guests relive the grand era when life in San Francisco was elegant and people of vision built homes that became history. Here guests are afforded continental-style accommodations, spectacular city panoramas, and quiet walks in the private garden or in Alamo Square. A variety of rooms and suites are available, from single guest rooms to Oriental-decor suites overlooking the skyline. A continental breakfast may be delivered to one's room or served in the morning room or in the garden. Afternoon tea and wine and evening sherry are also offered. Alamo Square Inn is situated ten blocks west of the San Francisco Civic Center, near Golden Gate Park and the Japan Center.

Zwetschgen Kuchen Mit Streusel
(Prune Streusel)

1 cup all-purpose flour
½ teaspoon baking powder
¼ cup sugar
1 egg
¼ cup butter, cut in pieces
  ❧   ❧   ❧
Prunes (fresh Italian or firm plums)
  ❧   ❧   ❧
1 cup all-purpose flour
⅓ cup sugar
6 tablespoons butter
Dash cinnamon

Butter a springform pan. Sift 1 cup of flour with the baking powder onto a baking board or marble counter. Make a well in the center. Place ¼ cup of sugar and egg in the center, working into ⅔ of the flour until soft. Add the butter pieces and knead until all of the flour is incorporated and a soft ball forms. If sticky, refrigerate for 30 minutes. Roll the dough to ⅛-inch thickness and place in the prepared pan. Press the dough into the form and ½ inch up the sides of the pan. Poke several holes in the base of the dough. Bake in a 350° oven for 10 minutes, until golden brown.

Meanwhile wash the prunes, open out to remove the pits, and partially score each half. Place on the cooled shell. In a small bowl combine 1 cup of flour, ⅓ cup of sugar, 6 tablespoons of butter, and a dash of cinnamon.

Petite Auberge

Work together until the mixture is crumbly. Sprinkle the streusel over the prunes. Bake in a 350° oven for 20 to 30 minutes, or until the streusel is a light golden color.

The kuchen is best when served after standing for 12 to 24 hours to allow the moisture from the prunes to be fully absorbed into the crust.

Serves 8.

Recipe courtesy of Chef Klaus E. May.

Petite Auberge

863 Bush Street
San Francisco, California 94108
(415) 928-6000

Upon entering Petite Auberge, guests are transported into the romantic comfort of a French country inn. An antique carousel horse, burnished woods, and fresh cut flowers provide a warm reception. Its tastefully appointed rooms serve as a relaxing haven away from the hustle and bustle of the city. Turn down service and a flower on the pillow are but a few of the amenities found at Petite Auberge.

French Bread Custard

1 loaf French bread, cut into 1-inch slices
¼ cup unsalted butter, melted

🍃 🍃 🍃

4 eggs
2 egg yolks
½ cup sugar
3 cups milk
1 cup heavy cream
1 tablespoon vanilla extract
¼ teaspoon nutmeg

🍃 🍃 🍃

Confectioners' sugar
Fresh berries

Brush both sides of the bread with the melted butter. Arrange the bread in a 9x13-inch baking pan. In a bowl beat the eggs and yolks together. Add the sugar, milk, cream, vanilla, and nutmeg and beat again. Pour the mixture over the bread. Place the custard dish in a larger pan and pour hot water in the larger pan until it comes halfway up the sides of the dish. Bake in a 350° oven for 35 to 40 minutes, or until lightly browned and puffy. Let the custard rest for about 10 to 15 minutes before serving.

Garnish with confectioners' sugar and fresh berries.

Serves 6 to 8.

Recipe courtesy Wendy Kleinknecht.

The White Swan Inn

845 Bush Street
San Francisco, California 94108
(415) 775-1755

Blending the serenity of an English garden inn with the graceful sophistication of cosmopolitan San Francisco, the White Swan Inn proudly invites the most discriminating traveler to share the superior accom-

The White Swan Inn

modations and personal service. Guests are welcome to enjoy the plush warmth of a romantic garden retreat accented with curved bay windows, fresh flowers, cozy quilts, handsome antiques, comfortable chairs, and fresh fruit. All rooms are tastefully appointed in rich, warm woods.

Chocolate Meringue Cookies

2 large egg whites
½ cup sugar
4 ounces bittersweet chocolate, melted and cooled
1 teaspoon vanilla extract
⅓ cup chopped walnuts, pecans, or toasted almonds

Line a cookie sheet with parchment paper or grease and flour the sheet. In a large bowl beat the egg whites to soft peaks. Continue beating, gradually adding the sugar. Beat until stiff and glossy. Fold in the melted chocolate and then the vanilla and chopped nuts. Drop the meringue by teaspoons onto the prepared sheet. Bake in a 350° oven for 10 minutes.

Makes 2½ dozen.

Recipe courtesy Wendy Kleinknecht.

Blue Quail Inn Bed and Breakfast

1908 Bath Street
Santa Barbara, California 93101
(805) 687-2300

The Blue Quail Inn and cottages welcome guests to relax and enjoy their visit in Santa Barbara. Each guest room and guest cottage is uniquely decorated with antiques and is filled with country charm. Following a leisurely, delicious full breakfast each morning, guests may spend the rest of the day experiencing beautiful Santa Barbara.

Spinach and Cilantro Baked Omelet

1 10-ounce package frozen chopped spinach
1 8-ounce package cream cheese, softened
2 cloves garlic, minced
1 teaspoon salt
Dash pepper
2 tablespoons chopped cilantro
1 cup grated Monterey Jack cheese
20 eggs, beaten

Grease 16 individual 4½-inch baking dishes. Cook the spinach according to the package directions. Drain and squeeze with paper towels. In a bowl combine all of the ingredients using an electric mixer. Spoon or ladle the mixture into each baking dish, filling ¾ full. Bake in a 350° oven for 15 to 25 minutes, until set. Garnish and serve immediately.

Serves 16.

Zucchini and Dill Quiche

1 unbaked 9-inch deep dish pie shell

🌿 🌿

2 cups finely chopped zucchini
1 medium onion, chopped
Oil or butter

🌿 🌿 🌿

3 eggs, beaten
1 cup plain yogurt
1½ cups grated Swiss cheese
2 tablespoons all-purpose flour
½ teaspoon dill
¼ teaspoon salt
Dash pepper

Prick the bottom and sides of the pie shell. Place the pie shell on a cookie sheet. Bake in a 400° oven for 13 minutes. Remove from the oven. Lower the heat to 350°. In a large skillet sauté the zucchini and onions in oil or butter until tender. Drain well. In a large bowl combine the remaining ingredients. Stir in the sautéed vegetables. Pour the mixture into the hot pie shell. Bake in a 350° oven for 25 to 35 minutes, until the center is set.

Serves 6.

Raspberry Cream Cheese Coffee Cake

2¼ cups all-purpose flour
¾ cup sugar
¾ cup butter

🌿 🌿 🌿

½ teaspoon baking powder
½ teaspoon baking soda
¼ teaspoon salt

¾ cup sour cream
1 egg
1 teaspoon almond extract

     ❧ ❧ ❧

1 8-ounce package cream cheese,
    softened
¼ cup sugar
1 egg
½ cup raspberry preserves
½ cup sliced almonds

Grease a 10-inch springform pan. In a large bowl combine the flour and ¾ cup of sugar. Cut in the butter with a pastry cutter until the mixture resembles small crumbs. Reserve 1 cup of the mixture. To the remaining crumb mixture add the next 6 ingredients and mix well. Spread the mixture over the bottom and ½ inch up the sides of the prepared pan. Combine the cream cheese, ¼ cup of sugar, and egg. Spread the cream cheese mixture over the crust mixture. Spoon the preserves over the cream cheese mixture. Add the almonds to the reserved crumb mixture and sprinkle over the top. Bake in a 350° oven for 45 to 55 minutes, until the center is set and the edges are golden brown.
   Serves 8 to 12.

cozy inn features a gourmet breakfast served in guests' rooms on the secluded flower-filled grounds. The inn also boasts a privately used garden hot tub and fireplace suites with canopy beds.

Decadent French Toast

32 slices wheat bread
⅔ cup margarine
4 tablespoons corn syrup
2 cups brown sugar

     ❧ ❧ ❧

2½ cups water
⅔ cup nonfat dry milk
2 teaspoons vanilla extract
10 eggs

     ❧ ❧ ❧

2 cups plain yogurt
2 cups sour cream
Sliced strawberries or peaches

Cut the top and bottom crusts off the bread. In a saucepan bring the margarine, corn syrup, and brown sugar to a boil. Stir until well blended. Pour the liquid into two 9x13-inch pans.

Place the bread in 2 layers in each pan, pressing as needed to fit. In a blender combine 1¼ cups of water, ⅓ cup of dry milk, 1 teaspoon vanilla, and 5 eggs. Blend just until combined. Pour the mixture over one of the pans, all the way to the edges. Repeat with the remaining water, dry milk, vanilla, and eggs. Cover the pans with plastic wrap and refrigerate for 1 hour or overnight. Bake in a 350° oven for 45 minutes. Loosen the sides and invert onto a serving pan.
   Combine the yogurt and sour cream, and place 2 tablespoons of the mixture on each serving. Garnish with sliced strawberries or peaches.
   Serves 16.

Hot Crab Dip

2 3-ounce packages cream cheese,
    softened
½ teaspoon horseradish
1 tablespoon dried onions
1 tablespoon Worcestershire sauce
1 6½-ounce can crab meat, drained
Almonds
Paprika
Triscuits

The Glenborough Inn

1327 Bath Street
Santa Barbara, California 93101
(805) 966-0589

Nestled on the California riviera in the inviting seacoast town of Santa Barbara between mountains and shore, the Glenborough Inn is only a stroll from quaint shops, world class restaurants, and a thriving arts community. A romantic's dream, this

The Glenborough Inn

In a large bowl combine the cream cheese, horseradish, onions, Worcestershire sauce, and crab meat. Spread in a 3-cup baking dish. Sprinkle with almonds and paprika. Bake in a 350° oven for 30 minutes. Serve with Triscuits.

Serves 8.

Buttermilk Coffee Cake

This recipe was featured in *Gourmet Magazine.* It is no regular coffee cake!

2¼ cups all-purpose flour
½ teaspoon cinnamon
1 cup brown sugar
¾ cup sugar
¾ cup oil

    🍃 🍃 🍃

½ cup chopped walnuts
1¼ teaspoons cinnamon
1 teaspoon baking soda
1 teaspoon baking powder
1 egg
1 cup buttermilk

In a large bowl combine the first 5 ingredients. Remove ¾ cup of the mixture to a small bowl and add the walnuts and 1¼ teaspoons cinnamon. Set aside. To the large bowl add the remaining ingredients. Spread the mixture into a 9x13-inch glass pan. Sprinkle the nut mixture over the batter and press in gently. Bake in a 350° oven for 25 to 30 minutes or until a toothpick inserted in the center comes out clean. Watch carefully to prevent the bottom from burning.

Serves 8 to 10.

Ocean View House Bed and Breakfast

Post Office Box 20065
Santa Barbara, California 93102
(805) 966-6659

Enjoy the comfort of a private home in a quiet neighborhood. A continental breakfast is served on a patio while viewing the Channel Islands. Guests can walk to the ocean, and downtown is a short distance away.

Corn Casserole

¼ cup chopped onion
¼ cup chopped red or green bell pepper
1 tablespoon margarine

    🍃 🍃 🍃

2 eggs
1½ cups milk
1 16-ounce package frozen corn
1½ cups shredded sharp Cheddar cheese
2 ounces diced green chilies
Pinch red pepper flakes
Salt and pepper to taste

    🍃 🍃 🍃

¾ cup buttered bread crumbs

Butter a 7x11-inch baking dish. In a small skillet sauté the onion and bell pepper in margarine. Set aside. In a large mixing bowl beat the eggs until foamy. Add the milk, corn, 1 cup of cheese, the chilies, and sautéed onion and pepper. Add the seasonings and stir to blend well. Pour into the prepared baking dish. Bake in a 325° oven for 45 minutes. Combine the bread crumbs and remaining cheese. Spread over the top of the corn mixture and bake an additional

15 minutes. Cut in squares. Individual servings may be frozen.

Serves 6 to 8.

The Old Yacht Club Inn

431 Corona Del Mar
Santa Barbara, California 93103
(805) 962-1277

For turn-of-the-century charm by the sea, the Old Yacht Club Inn is unique. Situated just half a block from the beach, the inn was built in 1912 as a private home and opened as Santa Barbara's first bed and breakfast inn in 1980. Today the home has been furnished with period pieces, European antiques, and Oriental rugs, creating the warm, homey atmosphere of another era. Downstairs, guests are invited to relax and mingle in front of the big brick fireplace with a glass of wine or a cup of tea. Upstairs, four large, sunny guest rooms with private baths have been decorated with an old-fashioned, personal touch. Window seats and balconies provide cozy sitting areas in the larger Castellamare and Portofino rooms.

Next door to the Old Yacht Club Inn, the Hitchcock House offers four guest rooms, each with its own private entry. Each room is named after one of the innkeepers' family and contains family photos, mementos, and furnishings. Dining is a memorable experience. Guests awaken to the smell of freshly brewed coffee, accompanied by juice, fruit, baked breads, and delicious omelets. Five-course gourmet dinners are served in the candlelit dining room, usually during the weekend.

Spanakopitas

I often make these ahead and refrigerate until I'm ready to cook. I usually serve these as an appetizer but a larger serving could be a nutritious entree, too.

1 8-ounce package frozen chopped spinach
6 tablespoons butter, divided
1 tablespoon water
1 3-ounce package cream cheese
4 ounces Feta cheese
¼ teaspoon Nature's Seasonings
Pinch cayenne pepper
1 16-ounce package phyllo dough
2 to 3 ounces Romano cheese

In a covered skillet cook the spinach with 2 tablespoons of butter and about 1 tablespoon of water. Cook over low heat until soft. Add the cream cheese and crumbled Feta cheese to the spinach and turn the heat off. Cover and let sit until the cheese is soft. Stir the mixture to combine the spinach and cheeses. Add the seasonings.

Thaw the phyllo. Melt the remaining butter. Unfold the dough. Work quickly so the dough does not become dry and brittle. Place 3 double sheets side by side on a flat surface and brush with melted butter. Place ⅓ of the spinach mixture on each of the 3 sheets. Fold over the sides and ends, and then wrap into a 4-inch square packet. Place the packets on a baking pan. Pour the remaining butter over the packets. Bake in a 350° oven for 20 to 25 minutes, until the phyllo is browned. Sprinkle Romano cheese over the top. Return to the oven until the cheese melts. Cut each packet into 3 slices. Serve hot.

Makes 9 appetizers.

Italian Cheese Spread with Pesto

2 to 3 large cloves garlic
½ cup packed parsley
2 cups packed basil leaves or 2 tablespoons dried
¾ cup olive oil
¾ cup grated Romano cheese
3 tablespoons pine nuts

&ta; &ta; &ta;

1 8-ounce package cream cheese
6 ounces Provolone cheese
4 tablespoons Romano cheese

In a food processor finely dice the garlic, parsley, and basil. Add the oil and cheese. Mix well. Fold in the pine nuts and remove the mixture from the processor. Cut the cream cheese and Provolone into pieces and cream in the food processor until smooth. Add the Romano and mix well. Put a layer of the cheese mixture in the bottom of a medium-sized ramekin, filling half full. Cover with pesto. Repeat the layers. Serve with crackers or small sliced French bread.

Note: the pesto sauce can be assembled in advance, leaving the Romano cheese and pine nuts out. Store in a covered jar for up to 2 weeks. Add the cheese and pine nuts as the sauce is used. The pesto is delicious on pasta, too.

Serves 4 to 6.

Kielbasa-Cheese Omelet

8 eggs
4 tablespoons water
2 tablespoons butter

&ta; &ta; &ta;

4 ounces sliced Kielbasa sausage
1 tablespoon butter
8 ounces sliced Muenster cheese
Lemon pepper
Chervil

In a large bowl combine the eggs and water, and whisk for 1 to 2 minutes. In a skillet melt 2 tablespoons of butter and pour the eggs into the pan. Allow

the eggs to set on the bottom. Using a spatula, push the cooked part to the middle and allow the liquid to run to the edges and cook through. Repeat until all of the eggs are cooked but not hard. Do not brown the bottom of the eggs.

In a separate skillet sauté the Kielbasa lightly in 1 tablespoon of butter. Place the Kielbasa across the top of the omelet and arrange the Muenster cheese over the sausage. Fold the omelet over. Season with lemon pepper and chervil. Cover and cook over very low heat for 4 to 5 minutes, until the cheese melts.

Serves 4.

Apple-Brie Omelet

8 eggs
4 tablespoons water
2 tablespoons butter

&ta; &ta; &ta;

1 tablespoon butter
2 Green Pippin apples, sliced
2 tablespoons brown sugar
½ teaspoon cinnamon

&ta; &ta; &ta;

4 ounces Brie
Lemon pepper

In a large bowl combine the eggs and water, and whisk for 1 to 2 minutes. In a skillet melt 2 tablespoons of butter and pour the eggs into the pan. Allow the eggs to harden on the bottom. Using a spatula, push the cooked part to the middle and allow the liquid to run to the edges and cook through. Repeat until all of the eggs are cooked but not hard. Do not brown the bottom of the eggs.

In a separate skillet melt 1 tablespoon of butter. Add the apples and sauté for 5 to 6 minutes, until softened. Add the sugar and cinnamon and stir to blend. Cook for 5 minutes more. Unwrap the Brie, leaving the white material on the outside. Cut into slices. Place the apples on top of the omelet. Place the sliced Brie on the apples and fold the omelet over. Cover and cook for 4 to 5 minutes, until the cheese melts. Sprinkle with lemon pepper.

Serves 4.

Conchiglione
(Stuffed Shells)

12 to 16 giant pasta shells
1 pound Ricotta cheese
2 cups grated Mozzarella cheese
1 egg
3 tablespoons grated Romano cheese
2 tablespoons minced parsley
¼ teaspoon salt
½ teaspoon freshly ground pepper

≈   ≈   ≈

Mary's Marinara Sauce
Romano cheese

Cook the pasta shells in boiling water for 10 to 12 minutes or until al dente. Drain and rinse in cold water. Drain again. In a large bowl combine the Ricotta, Mozzarella, egg, Romano cheese, parsley, salt, and pepper. Mix well. Use a tablespoon to stuff the filling into the shells. Spoon 2 to 3 tablespoons of Marinara Sauce into the bottom of a Pyrex baking dish. Place the shells in the dish and cover with sauce. Cover the dish with foil. Bake in a 350° oven for 45 minutes. Serve with additional Marinara Sauce and grated Romano cheese.

Serves 4.

Mary's Marinara Sauce

½ to ¾ cup olive oil
4 to 5 large cloves garlic, diced
1 12-ounce can tomato paste
1 28-ounce can chopped tomatoes
42 ounces water
¼ teaspoon Progresso hot pepper flakes
2 teaspoons salt
4 tablespoons fresh basil, chopped

In a saucepan heat the olive oil over medium heat. Add the garlic and cook, but do not brown, stirring with a wooden spoon. Add the tomato paste and blend well. Stir constantly until the mixture leaves an orange residue on the sides of the pan, 10 to 15 minutes. Be careful not to burn the mixture. Add the tomatoes and blend well. Add 28 to 42 ounces of water to thin the sauce. Sprinkle in the hot pepper sparingly. You can always add more as desired. Add salt and basil. Lower the heat until the sauce barely bubbles and cook for 1 hour to 1 hour and 30 minutes. Adjust the seasonings.

Makes 5 pints.

Stuffed Leg of Lamb

2 tablespoons butter
4 links hot Italian sausage
2 cups chopped spinach
1 cup seasoned bread crumbs
1 6- to 7-pound deboned leg of lamb
Salt and pepper to taste
1 cup red wine
1 cup beef broth
2 tablespoons butter
2 tablespoons all-purpose flour
4 tablespoons fresh mint leaves

In a large skillet melt 2 tablespoons of butter. Slice the Italian sausage and sauté in the melted butter until well cooked but not hard or brown. Add the spinach and cook, covered, for 8 to 10 minutes. Stir in the bread crumbs, mixing well. Cool slightly.

Trim the excess fat from the outside of the lamb. Open underside up on a flat surface. Place the stuffing in the cavity and wrap the leg to cover the stuffing. Secure with turkey stuffing pins. Turn skin side up and season with salt and pepper. Place the lamb in a roasting pan. Bake in a 450° oven for 1 hour.

Add the red wine and beef broth. Cover and reduce the heat to 350°. Cook for another 45 to 60 minutes. Use a meat thermometer for desired doneness. The approximate time for medium is 20 minutes per pound, and for medium well, 25 minutes per pound. Remove the lamb to a heated platter and cover with foil. Degrease the pan juices and return to the pan. Reduce the juice over medium heat for 10 to 15 minutes. Do not burn. Stir in the butter and flour. Add the fresh mint leaves. Cook over medium heat until thickened. Add salt and pepper if desired.

Carve the lamb. Place 1 to 2 tablespoons of stuffing on each serving. Pour 1 to 2 tablespoons of sauce over each serving. Serve with extra mint sauce, or gravy and mint jelly.

Serves 8 to 12.

Potage aux Legumes

1 onion, peeled and chopped
2 carrots, peeled and sliced
4 stalks celery, sliced
4 tablespoons butter
1 zucchini, sliced
3 tablespoons all-purpose flour
1 cup milk, half and half, or cream
1 13½-ounce can chicken broth
Salt and pepper to taste
Dash cayenne pepper
Fresh parsley

Clean and prepare the vegetables. In a heavy saucepan or Dutch oven sauté the onion, carrot, and celery in butter until soft. Add the zucchini and cook for 4 to 5 minutes. Add the flour and stir well. Cook for 5 minutes. Cool slightly. Purée the vegetables in 2 batches. Add a small amount of milk if necessary to make the mixture smooth. Return the vegetable mixture to the pan and add the milk and chicken broth. Cook over low heat until thickened. Add seasonings to taste. Serve with fresh parsley.

Serves 6 to 8.

Simpson House Inn

121 East Arrellaga Street
Santa Barbara, California 93101
(805) 963-7067

When Scotsman Robert Simpson settled in Santa Barbara in the early 1870s, he built a beautiful Eastlake-style Victorian home to remind him of his native land. Honored with a Structure of Merit for its unique architecture, it is secluded in an acre of English gardens. Yet it is just a five-minute walk from Santa Barbara's restaurants, theatres, museums, and shops.

A spacious sitting room with its fireplace and booklined walls adjoins the formal dining room. French doors open onto garden verandas with teak floors and wicker furniture. Each of the guest rooms has a private bathroom with a clawfoot tub and is decorated with antiques, English lace, Oriental rugs, and large beds.

Simpson House Inn

Granola

8 cups rolled oats
1½ cups sunflower seeds
1½ cups coconut shavings
1½ cups lightly chopped almonds
1 cup sesame seeds
2 tablespoons cinnamon
1⅓ cups honey
¾ cup water

In a large bowl combine the dry ingredients. In a separate bowl combine the honey and water, and add to the dry ingredients. Mix well. Spread thinly on cookie sheets. Bake in a 300° oven for 20 minutes, stir, and bake for 10 more minutes.

Serves 20 to 30.

Lemon Curd

1 cup butter
3 cups sugar
Grated rind of 4 lemons
2 cups lemon juice
16 egg yolks
4 egg whites

In the top of a double boiler melt the butter and sugar. Stir in the lemon rind and juice. Beat the egg yolks, and stir into the lemon mixture. Beat the egg whites and fold into the mixture. Cook for about 20 minutes, stirring often, until thickened. Pour into glass jars and refrigerate.

Makes about 6 cups.

Scones

6 cups self-rising flour
4½ tablespoons sugar
1½ cups butter
¾ cup milk
10 beaten eggs

Grease a cookie sheet. In a large bowl combine the flour and sugar, and blend in the butter. Combine the milk and eggs. Add enough of egg-milk mixture to the dry ingredients to make a soft dough, mixing lightly. Turn out onto floured waxed paper. Pat out to 1-inch thickness and cut with a floured cutter. Brush the tops with remaining egg and milk, and place on the prepared cookie sheet. Bake in a 400° oven for 12 minutes.

Makes 18 large scones, 12 servings.

The Madison Street Inn

1390 Madison Street
Santa Clara, California 95050
(408) 249-5541

This inn provides an ideal location for visitors to the San Francisco Bay area. It has five individually decorated guest rooms (three with private baths), a sunny breakfast room, and a parlor decorated with authentic Victorian wallpaper and museum quality furniture. The half-acre landscaped gardens surround the pool and spa. The inn serves elegant breakfasts and gourmet dishes for dinner upon request.

Plum Drink

8 plums, seeded and sliced
2 cups plain lowfat yogurt
1½ teaspoons vanilla extract
½ cup honey
Mint sprigs, crystallized orange or
**   lemon peel for garnish**

In a blender mix the plums, yogurt, and vanilla extract until smooth. Add the honey and blend lightly. Serve garnished with mint sprigs and crystallized orange or lemon peel.
Serves 4.

Peach Fritters

2 cups all-purpose flour
3 teaspoons baking powder
1 teaspoon sugar
⅛ teaspoon salt
1¼ cups milk
3 tablespoons oil
3 egg whites
Oil for deep frying

🐦 🐦 🐦

4 peaches, sliced ½-inch thick
Puréed raspberries

In a mixing bowl sift together the flour, baking powder, sugar, and salt. Combine the milk and oil, and stir into the dry ingredients until smooth. Beat the egg whites until stiff and fold into the mixture. Let the batter stand for 15 minutes. Heat oil in a deep fryer to 375°. Pat the fruit dry and dip into the batter to coat. Let the excess batter drip off. Drop into the heated oil a few at a time and cook until brown. Serve at once with bacon or sausage. Serve with puréed raspberries spooned over the fritters.
Serves 8.

🐦 🐦 🐦 🐦 🐦

Chateau Victorian

118 First Street
Santa Cruz, California 95060
(408) 458-9458

Originally constructed around the turn of the century as a family residence, Chateau Victorian was renovated and opened as an elegant inn in June 1983. All of its accommodations have queen-size beds, fireplaces, and private bathrooms. Breakfast may be served in the lounge dining area or on the secluded deck. In the late afternoon guests can relax in the lounge with beverages, cheese, and crackers. Within one block is the Santa Cruz beach; nearby are the world famous casino and boardwalk and the municipal pier.

Tongue-in-Cheek Chili

This recipe makes a delicious chili that is not too hot or spicy. Additional spices and vegetables can be added to taste.

2 cups dry pinto beans
6 cups water
1 beef tongue
1 pound bacon
1 15¼-ounce can kidney beans
1 15½-ounce can Texas-style
**   barbecue beans**
1 28-ounce can peeled and diced
**   tomatoes**
3 tablespoons chili powder
1 teaspoon paprika
¼ teaspoon cayenne pepper
½ white onion, chopped

Soak the pinto beans overnight in 6 cups of water.
In a 6-quart pot cover the tongue with water, including the water the beans soaked in, and bring to a boil over high heat. Add the pinto beans and lower the heat to a gentle boil. Boil for 1 hour and 30 minutes.
Cook the bacon until lightly browned but still soft. Remove the tongue from the water and peel the skin off. Cut into small pieces and put through a food grinder. Put the bacon through the grinder.
Drain the excess water from the pinto beans and add the ground tongue and bacon. Add the remaining ingredients except the onion. Simmer over low heat for 30 minutes, stirring often so the ingredients are thoroughly mixed. Add the onion just before serving.
Makes approximately 4 quarts.

The Gables

4257 Petaluma Hill Road
Santa Rosa, California 95404
(707) 585-7777

This classic Gothic historical landmark is but one hour from San Francisco. A honeymooners' favorite, the Gables has three sculptured marble fireplaces, spiral stairs, and country elegance. The rooms all have private baths. Santa Rosa is the gateway to the redwoods, Sonoma and Napa valley wineries, and the marvelous California north coast.

The Gables Frittata

8 ounces fresh pork or turkey
**   sausage**

🐦 🐦 🐦

2 cups shredded zucchini
2 green onions, chopped
½ teaspoon dry basil (or 1 teaspoon
**   fresh)**
1 teaspoon Italian seasoning
4 eggs

⅓ cup half and half or cream
4 ounces cream cheese
1 cup shredded Mozzarella cheese
1 cup shredded Cheddar cheese

Spray an 8-inch quiche pan or pie plate with cooking spray. Brown the sausage and drain on paper towels to remove as much grease as possible. Place the sausage in the prepared pan. Spread the zucchini and onions over the sausage, and sprinkle with seasonings. Beat the eggs with the half and half, and pour over the zucchini and sausage. Cut the cream cheese into cubes and sprinkle evenly over the top. Top with the Mozzarella and Cheddar cheeses. Bake in a 325° oven for 45 minutes, or until the middle is set and the top is lightly browned. Do not overcook or the frittata will be rubbery.
Serves 4.

Honey Wheat Bread

2 ¼-ounce packages dry yeast
3 cups warm water (110° to 115°)
⅓ cup oil
½ cup honey
3 teaspoons salt
½ cup nonfat dry milk
4 cups whole wheat flour
4 cups all-purpose flour

Grease 2 baking sheets. In a large bowl dissolve the yeast in the warm water. Add the oil and honey, and let the mixture rest for 15 minutes. Add the salt, dry milk, whole wheat flour, and 1 cup of all-purpose flour. Mix until smooth. (Use an electric mixer at low speed, if possible. If you have a dough hook, use that for the remaining procedure.) Place the dough on a floured board and add up to 3 cups of flour while kneading and mixing. Knead for approximately 7 to 8 minutes, until the dough is springy and smooth. Place the dough in a large greased bowl, turning to grease the top of the dough. Cover with a damp towel and let rise in a warm place until doubled in bulk, about 1 hour. Punch the dough down and divide into 8 small round loaves. Place the loaves on the baking sheets. Let the loaves rise for 30 minutes. Bake in a 325° oven for approximately 30 minutes, or until the loaves sound hollow when tapped on the bottom.
Makes 8 small loaves.

The Gables Special Fudge

3 cups chocolate chips
1 cup butter
1 cup marshmallow creme

&. &. &.

4½ cups sugar
1 12-ounce can evaporated milk

&. &. &.

1 tablespoon vanilla extract
2 cups chopped walnuts or pecans, if desired

Butter a 9x13-inch glass dish. In a large bowl combine the chocolate chips, butter, and marshmallow creme. Set aside. In a large, heavy saucepan combine the sugar and evaporated milk. Cook over medium heat, stirring constantly, until the mixture reaches the soft ball stage, or 238°. This will take 12 to 15 minutes. Reduce heat if the sugar begins to caramelize or scorch. Remove from the heat and pour the mixture in a slow stream into the chocolate chip mixture. Stir constantly until the chocolate is completely melted and the fudge loses its gloss. Stir in the vanilla and walnuts. Spread into the prepared pan. Allow the fudge to cool for several hours.
Makes 5 pounds.

Storybook Inn

28717 Highway 18
Post Office Box 362
Skyforest, California 92385
(714) 336-1483

Storybook Inn is a quiet, refined inn situated on the renowned Rim of the World highway near Lake Arrowhead. Recently restored to its original beauty, the inn offers nine spacious rooms and private baths and extensive amenities. A large bleached mahogany lobby and separate television room are appointed with Chinese furniture. A two-bedroom rustic log cabin is also available. With a complete gourmet breakfast, a daily newspaper, and an evening social hour offering California wines and tasty hot and cold hors d'oeuvres, the Storybook Inn provides a unique country inn experience.

White Sangria

1 750-ml bottle dry white wine
2 kiwis, peeled and sliced
1 large pear, sliced very thin
1 cup seedless green grapes
2 tablespoons superfine sugar
2 tablespoons Calvados, Armagnac, or Tuaca
3 tablespoons Cointreau
1½ cups bottled sparkling water
Sprigs mint or fresh flowers for garnish

Pour the wine into a large glass pitcher. Add the kiwis, pear, grapes, sugar, Calvados, and Cointreau. Cover and refrigerate for 4 to 5 hours. To serve, stir well, add the sparkling water, and pour over ice in tall glasses. Garnish with a sprig of mint or a flower.
Serves 6.

Brie with Apricot Sauce

4 10-ounce cans whole peeled apricots, pitted
¼ cup Grand Marnier (or apricot brandy)
¼ cup slivered almonds
1 10-inch round Brie
Mild crackers

Strain the apricots, reserving the syrup in a saucepan. Boil the syrup over high heat, until reduced by half, 12 to 15 minutes. Cool the syrup. Add the liqueur and 16 of the apricots. On a cookie sheet, lightly brown the almonds in a 275° oven for 10 to 15 minutes. Watch them carefully. To serve, place the Brie on a serving plate, pour the sauce over, and top with almonds. Accompany with crackers.
Serves 24.

Chutney Cheese Spread

2 8-ounce packages cream cheese, room temperature
½ cup chopped chutney
½ cup chopped toasted almonds
½ teaspoon dry mustard (or ½ teaspoon curry powder)

≈ ≈ ≈

½ cup chopped toasted almonds
¼ cup finely snipped parsley
Crackers

In a large bowl whip the cream cheese. Add the chutney, ½ cup of almonds, and mustard. Shape into 2 balls. Roll in the remaining almonds and parsley. Serve with crackers.
Serves 15 to 20.

Kathleen's Piquant Cocktail Meatballs

2 pounds ground round
1 cup corn flakes, crushed
⅓ cup chopped parsley

2 eggs
2 tablespoons soy sauce
¼ teaspoon pepper
½ teaspoon garlic powder

≈ ≈ ≈

½ cup catsup
2 tablespoons grated onions
Lowry's seasoned salt to taste
1 16-ounce can jellied cranberry sauce
1 12-ounce bottle chili sauce
2 tablespoons brown sugar
1 tablespoon lemon juice

In a large bowl mix together the beef, corn flakes, parsley, eggs, soy sauce, pepper, and garlic powder. Form into balls and brown in a skillet.
In a saucepan combine the catsup, grated onion, seasoned salt, cranberry sauce, chili sauce, brown sugar, and lemon juice. Heat, stirring frequently, until well blended and heated through. Place the meatballs in a chafing dish and pour the sauce over all. Bake in a 350° oven until the sauce bubbles and the meatballs are heated through.
Serves 30.

Stuffed Mushrooms

1 3-ounce package cream cheese, softened
1 tablespoon finely minced onion
2 to 3 tablespoons crumbled bleu cheese
¼ cup finely chopped pecans

≈ ≈ ≈

1 pound large mushrooms
3 tablespoons melted butter

In a small bowl combine the cream cheese, onion, bleu cheese, and pecans. Wash and dry the mushrooms, and remove the stems. Brush with melted butter. Stuff the mushrooms with the mixture. Broil for 7 minutes or until bubbly.
Serves 15 to 20.

Bacon and Tomato Dip

9 slices bacon

≈ ≈ ≈

3 small tomatoes, quartered
1 8-ounce package cream cheese, softened and quartered
3 teaspoons prepared mustard
¼ teaspoon Tabasco sauce

≈ ≈ ≈

1½ cups almonds
3 tablespoons green onion
Crackers

In a large skillet fry the bacon until crisp. Drain on paper towels, crumble, and set aside. In a food processor fitted with the steel blade combine the tomatoes, cream cheese, mustard, and Tabasco sauce. Add the almonds, onion, and bacon. Blend until the almonds are chopped. Refrigerate for 2 hours or up to 2 days. Serve with crackers.
Serves 10 to 12.

Balboa Brunch

3 tablespoons butter
3 cups sliced leeks, white part only

≈ ≈ ≈

12 slices white bread
1 pound cooked small shrimp
1 pound Swiss cheese, grated
3 tablespoons chopped fresh dill
5 eggs
2½ cups milk
Salt and pepper to taste

Butter a 9x13-inch glass casserole dish. In a medium skillet melt the butter and sauté the leeks until they are tender. Remove the crusts from the bread and arrange half in the prepared dish. Top with half of the sautéed leeks, half of the shrimp, half of the cheese, and half of the dill. Repeat the layers. In a medium bowl beat together the eggs, milk, salt, and pepper. Pour the eggs over the casserole, cover, and refrigerate overnight.
Bake in a 350° oven for 50 to 60 minutes.
Serves 8.

Josie's Frozen Fruit Salad

This is a great salad to have on hand and serve anytime.

1 8-ounce carton Cool Whip
1 14-ounce can sweetened
   condensed milk

   🍃 🍃 🍃

1 14-ounce can crushed pineapple,
   drained
1 10-ounce package frozen
   strawberries
3 bananas, cut up

In a large bowl fold together the whipped topping and sweetened condensed milk. Add the pineapple, strawberries, and bananas. Pour into a serving dish and freeze until firm. Serves 8 to 10.

Josie's Sour Cream Enchiladas with Ham

1 cup chopped ham
2 cups grated Monterey Jack cheese
½ cup diced green chilies
½ cup sour cream
6 tablespoons chopped fresh
   cilantro

   🍃 🍃 🍃

½ cup butter
½ cup all-purpose flour
4 cups milk
4 cups diced Cheddar cheese
2 teaspoons Dijon mustard
1 teaspoon salt
½ medium onion, grated

   🍃 🍃 🍃

8 small flour tortillas

In a large bowl combine the ham, Monterey Jack cheese, chilies, sour cream, and cilantro. Mix well and set aside.

In a medium saucepan over low heat melt the butter and add the flour, stirring constantly for 3 to 5 minutes. Gradually add the milk and cook, stirring constantly, until the sauce is smooth and thick. Add the cheese and stir until the cheese is melted. Stir in the mustard, salt, and onions. This sauce may be made ahead and refrigerated.

Grease a large baking dish. To assemble, place an equal portion of the ham mixture near the edge of each tortilla and roll tightly. Place seamside down in the prepared pan. Pour the sauce over the enchiladas, covering thoroughly. Bake in a 350° oven for 35 to 40 minutes.

Serves 4 or more.

The Hidden Oak

The Hidden Oak

214 East Napa Street
Sonoma, California 95476
(707) 996-9863

The Hidden Oak is a two-story California craftsman bungalow in the historic neighborhood near the Plaza in old Sonoma. Originally used as a refectory, it is a beautiful, comfortable place for enjoying the lovely Sonoma climate and returning to the place of an earlier time. The three guest rooms are large and airy, each with its private bath. Nearby are wineries, the mission, and many restaurants, shops, and special events.

Banana-Oat Griddle Cakes

¾ cup oatmeal
¾ cup whole wheat flour
1 teaspoon baking soda
1 teaspoon baking powder
1 teaspoon cinnamon

   🍃 🍃 🍃

3 egg whites
2 ripe bananas, mashed
½ cup milk
2 tablespoons oil

In a small bowl combine the dry ingredients. In a large bowl beat the egg whites. Add the bananas and mash to combine with the egg whites. Stir in the milk and oil. Fold the dry ingredients into the wet ingredients, and stir just until blended. Drop the batter by large spoonfuls onto a hot griddle. Spread the mixture with the edge of the spoon. Turn the cakes when bubbles come to the surface. Serve immediately with hot fruit or maple syrup.

Makes 12 3-inch pancakes.

Baked Apples à l'Orange

6 cooking apples (Granny Smith, Pippin, etc.)
½ cup butter, cut into 6 pieces
¾ cup sugar

≈ ≈ ≈

1 cup fresh squeezed orange juice

≈ ≈ ≈

1 tablespoon cornstarch
1 tablespoon cold water
½ cup half and half
½ teaspoon vanilla extract

≈ ≈ ≈

½ teaspoon cinnamon

Core the apples and place in a shallow baking dish just large enough to hold them. Place a butter piece on each apple and sprinkle with sugar. Bake in a 450° oven for 10 minutes. Pour the orange juice into the dish and bake for another 30 minutes or until fork tender, basting occasionally. Remove the apples from the oven and transfer the apples to individual plates or a larger dish.

Pour the juice from the apples into a saucepan. In a small bowl combine the cornstarch with the cold water and stir until blended. Add the half and half and vanilla, and add the mixture to the orange juice. Cook over medium-high heat, stirring constantly, until the sauce thickens. Pour over the apples. Sprinkle with cinnamon and serve.

Serves 6.

Sonoma Scrambled Eggs

½ tablespoon fresh chopped chives
1 tablespoon butter
½ cup half and half or cream

1 8-ounce package cream cheese, cubed
12 eggs

In a large skillet sauté the chives in butter over low heat for 5 minutes. Add the half and half and cream cheese, stirring until the cream cheese melts. In a mixing bowl beat the eggs and pour into a skillet with the cheese mixture. Stir the eggs with sweeping strokes until thick and creamy. Do not overcook. The eggs should still be moist.

Serves 6.

Serenity

15305 Bear Cub Drive
Post Office Box 3484
Sonora, California 95370
(209) 533-1441

Serenity is an elegant nineteenth-century-style home situated on six wooded acres filled with Ponderosa pines, wildflowers, and wildlife. The four guest rooms, all with private baths, provide comfort and beauty. The parlor, library, or verandah are ideal spots for relaxation, as are the beautiful grounds. Nearby are numerous Gold Rush towns, Yosemite National Park, Stanislaus National Forest, and the "big trees." Seasonal recreation abounds, as does the serenity.

Plum Breakfast Pie

½ cup butter
1 cup all-purpose flour
⅓ cup sugar

≈ ≈ ≈

7 to 8 large plums, pitted and sliced
¼ cup water
1 egg, beaten
¾ cup sugar
⅓ cup all-purpose flour

½ teaspoon baking powder
½ teaspoon nutmeg
Dash salt

In a large bowl work the butter, 1 cup of flour, and ⅓ cup of sugar until smooth. Press evenly over the bottom of a 9-inch pie pan. Bake in a 375° oven for 20 minutes or until lightly golden.

Cook the plums and water in a skillet over moderate heat until bubbly and slightly thickened. Stir often. Remove from the heat and cool slightly. Stir in the egg. In a small bowl combine the remaining sugar, flour, baking powder, nutmeg, and salt. Add a small amount of hot plum mixture to make a smooth paste. Combine the paste with the hot plum mixture and stir until well blended. Spread the filling over the baked crust and bake in a 375° oven for 25 minutes. Serve warm.

Serves 8.

Giant Overnight Caramel Rolls

1 ¼-ounce package dry yeast
¼ cup warm water (110° to 115°)
⅓ cup sugar
1 teaspoon salt
⅓ cup oil
3 eggs, beaten
½ cup evaporated milk
½ cup warm water
4 to 4½ cups all-purpose flour

≈ ≈ ≈

1 cup heavy cream
1 cup brown sugar
4 tablespoons butter, melted
Brown sugar
Granulated sugar
Cinnamon

In a large bowl dissolve the yeast in ¼ cup of warm water. Stir in the sugar, salt, oil, eggs, milk, and ½ cup of warm water. Add the flour. The dough will be soft. Turn the dough out onto a floured surface and knead until smooth and elastic, about 5 minutes. Add flour as needed. Place the dough in a greased bowl and turn the dough to grease the top. Cover and let rise in a warm place until doubled in bulk.

Combine the cream and brown sugar and spread in the bottom of two 9-inch square pans. Punch the dough down. Divide the dough in half and roll out to an 8x15-inch rectangle. Brush with half the melted butter, and sprinkle with brown sugar, sugar, and cinnamon. Roll tightly from the 8-inch side. Cut into four 2-inch slices. Place in one prepared pan and press the rolls down. Repeat with the remainder of the dough. Cover and refrigerate overnight. Allow the rolls to come to room temperature before baking. Bake in a 375° oven for 25 minutes.

Serves 8.

Sutter Creek Inn

Post Office Box 385
75 Main Street
Sutter Creek, California 95685
(209) 267-5606

The Sutter Creek Inn is a lovely country inn built over one hundred years ago. It is the oldest bed and breakfast inn west of the Mississippi. It is centrally located in the Mother Lode, two and one-half hours from the Bay area. Each room has a private bath and is decorated uniquely and with flair; many have fireplaces, patios, and secret gardens. Others are furnished with canopied beds and claw-foot bathtubs; some have swinging beds that hang from the ceiling on chains. Lovely gardens surround the inn, providing the perfect setting for relaxing in the hammocks or playing croquet on the lush, green lawns.

Eggs in Cream Sauce

4 tablespoons butter
½ cup chopped or minced onion
4 tablespoons all-purpose flour
3 cups warm milk
1 8-ounce package cream cheese
1 heaping teaspoon Grey Poupon mustard
1 teaspoon garlic salt
½ teaspoon paprika
Tabasco sauce
Chopped parsley

🍃 🍃 🍃

8 to 10 eggs
Parmesan cheese
Paprika
Capers

In a large frying pan melt the butter and sauté the onion until soft. Stir in the flour and slowly add the milk. When the sauce is smooth and boiling, reduce the heat and add the cream cheese. Season with the mustard, garlic salt, paprika, Tabasco sauce, and parsley. Pour the sauce into a 7x11-inch baking dish. Drop the eggs gently into the sauce. Sprinkle with Parmesan cheese and paprika and poach until the desired doneness, about 15 to 20 minutes. Garnish with capers.

Serves 4 to 6.

Zucchini Walnut Pancakes

We serve these pancakes with smoked ham, warm applesauce, maple syrup, and our own homemade blackberry syrup.

5 eggs
6 cups buttermilk
5 tablespoons oil
5 tablespoons sugar
3 cups grated zucchini

🍃 🍃 🍃

5 cups all-purpose flour
1 tablespoon salt
4 teaspoons baking powder
2½ teaspoons baking soda

🍃 🍃 🍃

Chopped walnuts

In a large bowl combine the eggs, buttermilk, oil, and sugar. Add the zucchini. In a separate bowl sift together the flour, salt, baking powder, and baking soda. Stir the dry ingredients into the liquid ingredients, stirring just until blended. Fold in the walnuts. Let the mixture rest. Heat a grill to 375° and cook the pancakes until bubbles rise to the surface and the edges are dry. Turn and lightly brown the other side.

Serves 12 to 15.

Sutter Creek Inn

Creamy Potatoes

1 2-pound package frozen hash
   brown potatoes, thawed
2½ cups grated cheese (Monterey
   Jack and Swiss)
2 cups sour cream
1 10-ounce can cream of mushroom
   soup
½ large onion, chopped
4 cups chopped ham (optional)

&a. &a. &a.

2 cups crushed cornflakes
¼ cup melted butter

Spray two 7x10-inch casserole dishes
with cooking spray. In a large bowl
combine the first 6 ingredients.
Spread the potato mixture in the prepared dishes and sprinkle the corn
flakes over the top. Drizzle with
melted butter. Bake in a 350° oven for
45 minutes.
   Serves 12 to 16.

The Inn at Valley Ford

14395 Highway 1
Post Office Box 439
Valley Ford, California 94972
(707) 876-3182

The Inn at Valley Ford is a Victorian
farmhouse built in the late 1860s. Furnished with antiques, it has four bedroom accommodations that share
two baths. The view from the parlor
window has changed little in the last
120 years: growing crops, a herd of
cows, grazing sheep, and abundant
wildlife. Valley Ford, a focal point for
the many dairy and sheep ranches in
the vicinity, has a population of 126,
the exact number recorded in 1877.

&a. &a. &a. &a. &a.

Old-fashioned Persimmon Cookies

This is an old family recipe for wonderful fruity cookies that last very
well.

1 teaspoon baking soda
1 cup persimmon pulp

&a. &a. &a.

½ cup shortening
1 cup sugar
1 egg

&a. &a. &a.

2 cups all-purpose flour
½ teaspoon salt
1 teaspoon nutmeg
1 teaspoon cinnamon
1 teaspoon cloves
1 cup chopped walnuts
1 to 1½ cups raisins

Grease a cookie sheet. In a small bowl
dissolve the baking soda in the persimmon pulp. In a separate bowl
cream the shortening and sugar. Add
the egg and pulp. In a medium bowl
sift the dry ingredients. Add the dry
ingredients to the creamed mixture.
Fold in the nuts and raisins. Drop by
teaspoonfuls onto the prepared
cookie sheet. Bake in a 350° oven for
15 minutes.
   Makes about 4 dozen cookies.

Grandmother's Oatmeal Cookies

Delicious crisp cookies that are great
with coffee and tea.

1½ cups sugar
¾ to 1 cup oil
2 eggs
1 teaspoon vanilla extract
½ cup milk
1¾ cups all-purpose flour
1 teaspoon salt
1 teaspoon cinnamon
1 teaspoon baking soda
1 teaspoon baking powder
3 cups rolled oats
2 cups cornflakes
1 cup raisins

Grease a cookie sheet. In a large bowl
blend together the sugar, oil, eggs,
and vanilla. Add the milk. In a separate bowl combine the flour, salt, cinnamon, baking soda, and baking
powder. Blend the flour mixture into
the milk mixture. Add the oats, cornflakes, and raisins, blending well.
Drop by teaspoonfuls onto the prepared cookie sheet. Bake in a 350°
oven for 15 minutes, until golden
brown.
   Makes 5 dozen.

Howard Creek Ranch

40501 North Highway One
Post Office Box 121
Westport, California 95488
(707) 964-6725

Howard Creek Ranch is a twenty-
acre valley on the Pacific Ocean affording sweeping views of the ocean,
sandy beaches, and rolling mountains. The historic 1871 farmhouse,
filled with antiques and collectibles,
sits in the middle of the ranch where
horses and cows graze the pastures.
The original fireplace still warms the
parlor. A seventy-five-foot swinging
foot bridge spans Howard Creek as it
flows on its way to the beach 200
yards away.
   Accommodations include suites
and cabins, a wood-heated hot tub,
sauna, pool, massage by reservation,
choice of private or shared baths, and
fireplaces and wood stoves. A full
ranch breakfast is served each morning.

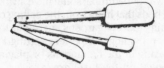

Baked Eggs by Gale

10 eggs, beaten
½ cup melted butter
½ cup all-purpose flour
½ teaspoon salt
Pepper to taste
1 pint small curd cottage cheese

❧ ❧ ❧

½ cup cooked, crumbled bacon
1 cup grated Gruyère cheese
3 green onions, finely chopped

In a large bowl combine the eggs, butter, flour, salt, and pepper, stirring until well blended. Add the cottage cheese. Fold in the remaining ingredients. Pour into a 9x13-inch nonstick pan. Bake in a 325° oven for 35 to 45 minutes or until the eggs are firm and cooked through. Cut into individual pieces and serve immediately.

Variations: Instead of the last 3 ingredients, use one of the following combinations.

1 cup of chopped fresh spinach, ¾ cup shredded Swiss cheese, and ¼ cup grated Parmesan.

1 cup Monterey Jack cheese, 2 to 3 chopped green chilies, and 1 cup cooked, crumbled sage-flavored pork sausage.

1 diced tomato, 1 chopped onion, 3 tablespoons diced pimiento, ½ cup minced parsley, and 2 minced cloves garlic.

2 cooked, crumbled spicy Italian sausages, 1 cup grated Fontina cheese, and 4 tablespoons fresh basil.

Serves 6 to 8.

Macadamia-Banana French Toast

2 bananas
4 eggs
1 cup milk
1 3½-ounce jar macadamia nuts, finely chopped
1 teaspoon vanilla extract
Dash cinnamon or allspice
8 to 10 slices whole wheat bread

Howard Creek Ranch

Butter 2 large baking sheets. In a blender or food processor blend together 1 banana, the eggs, milk, half of the nuts, vanilla, and cinnamon until well blended. Pour into a large shallow dish. Dip the bread slices in the mixture until well absorbed on both sides. Arrange on the prepared baking sheets. Bake in a 475° oven for about 5 minutes, until golden. Remove the toast from the baking sheet and slice each piece diagonally. Dust with confectioners' sugar. Slice the remaining banana and arrange on the toast. Sprinkle with chopped nuts.

Variations: Substitute one 8-ounce can of crushed pineapple for the bananas, using half in the batter and half for topping. Use ½ cup of shredded coconut instead of the macadamia nuts, using half for the batter and half for the topping.

Serves 4 to 5.

Individual Cheese Soufflés

1 teaspoon butter
½ cup chopped fresh mushrooms
2 to 3 teaspoons minced green and red onion
1 tablespoon minced parsley
¼ teaspoon dried basil
¼ teaspoon dried thyme

❧ ❧ ❧

6 eggs, separated
2 teaspoons cognac or brandy
¼ teaspoon dry mustard
¼ teaspoon nutmeg
¼ teaspoon cayenne pepper
1 cup Ricotta cheese
¾ cup grated Parmesan cheese
¾ cup grated Swiss cheese

To prepare the filling, melt the butter in a sauté pan over medium heat. Add the mushrooms, onion, parsley, basil, and thyme. Sauté until the vegetables are tender and the juices almost evaporate. Set aside.

To prepare the soufflé, in a large bowl beat the egg whites until stiff peaks form. In a separate bowl beat the egg yolks, and add the remaining ingredients. Gently fold in the egg whites. Fill four 1-cup soufflé dishes half full with the soufflé mixture. Add ¼ of the filling to each dish, and top with the remaining soufflé mixture. Bake in a 425° oven for 15 to 20 minutes or until puffed and golden. Serve at once.

Serves 4.

Baked Apples with French Cream

4 large apples, halved and cored
2 cups granola
Butter

    ❧ ❧ ❧

1 cup heavy whipping cream
1 teaspoon vanilla extract
3 tablespoons sugar

Butter a shallow baking dish. Place the apple halves in the prepared dish and sprinkle generously with granola. Place a dab of butter on each apple half. Bake in a 350° oven for 45 minutes.

While the apples are baking, whip the cream with the vanilla and sugar until thick and creamy, but still of a pourable consistency. When the apples are done, place each in a serving bowl and pour the cream over the top. Serve immediately.

Serves 6 to 8.

Coleen's California Casa

11715 South Circle Drive
Whittier, California 90601
(213) 699-8427

Situated high above Whittier in a residential area twelve miles east of Los Angeles, this inn provides an ideal setting for late afternoon wine and cheese as the sun sets and the evening lights appear. Accommodations include king- and extra-long twin-size beds, private entrance, and private and shared baths. Tennis and hiking are nearby, and the tourist attractions of the Greater Los Angeles area are within comfortable driving distance.

Tomato Patty Croquettes

16 ounces fresh tomatoes
¾ cup all-purpose flour
¼ cup yellow cornmeal
1 teaspoon baking powder
1 package Italian salad dressing mix
Salt and pepper to taste
Minced onion (optional)
Chopped green pepper (optional)

In a blender chop the tomatoes. In a small bowl combine the flour, cornmeal, and baking powder. Add the mixture to the tomatoes. Add the Italian salad dressing mix and salt and pepper to taste. Add the minced onion and chopped green pepper if desired. Drop the tomato batter by spoonfuls into a hot skillet, keeping the patties separated. Brown on both sides.

Serves 4.

Empañaditas

2 cups sifted all-purpose flour
1 teaspoon seasoned salt
1½ teaspoons chili powder, divided
⅔ cup shortening
5 tablespoons cold water

    ❧ ❧ ❧

1 5-ounce jar chicken (or 5 ounces cooked chicken)
2 tablespoons diced canned green chilies
2 tablespoons diced onions
⅔ cup chopped toasted walnuts
¼ teaspoon salt
¼ cup mayonnaise

In a large bowl sift together the flour, salt, and 1 teaspoon of chili powder. Cut the shortening into the dry ingredients until the mixture resembles coarse meal. Add the water a little at a time, and toss with a fork until the mixture can be formed into a ball, as for pie crust. Chill.

Cut the chicken into small pieces. In a large bowl combine the chicken, chilies, onion, walnuts, salt, remaining chili powder, and mayonnaise. Roll the pastry on a floured surface to ⅛-inch thickness. Cut into rounds, using a 1¾-inch cutter. Spoon filling into each round and fold over, making small turnovers. Press the edges together with the tines of a fork. Prick the top of each turnover. Place on an ungreased cookie sheet. Bake in a 450° oven until golden brown, about 10 to 12 minutes. If these turnovers have been frozen, allow more time when baking.

Makes 5 dozen.

Crustless Quiche

1¼ cups milk
¾ cup all-purpose flour
1 onion, chopped
1 tablespoon melted margarine
1 teaspoon baking powder
2 tablespoons parsley or chives
Salt and pepper to taste
1 cup grated Cheddar cheese
6 slices bacon

Butter a quiche dish. In a food processor combine the first 7 ingredients, processing for 4 minutes. Sprinkle the grated cheese into the prepared dish. Pour the batter over the cheese and arrange the bacon over the batter. Bake in a 350° oven for 40 minutes.

This may be served hot or cold.

Variations: The recipe may be varied by using tuna, salmon, ham, or mushrooms, or a combination of these. Vegetables such as corn, zucchini, or lightly blanched spinach may be used.

Serves 6 to 8.

Country Meadow Inn

11360 Old Redwood Highway
Windsor, California 95492
(707) 431-1276

Country Meadow Inn, built in an elegant Queen Anne Victorian style, is situated atop a lushly landscaped knoll surrounded by rolling hills, vineyard, trees, and meadowlands. In the heart of the Sonoma County wine region, the inn is only an hour's drive from San Francisco and the Pacific Ocean. The country breakfast is served in the dining room or on the deck. Guests may begin their wine tasting a few hundred yards north at Piper Sonoma Cellars or Rodney Strong Wineries; more than fifty award-winning wineries are within a few miles' distance.

Oatmeal and Black Walnut Pancakes
with Orange and Butter Sauce

1 cup unbleached all-purpose flour
1½ cups quick oats
3 teaspoons baking powder
¼ teaspoon salt
2 tablespoons brown sugar
½ cup chopped black walnuts
¼ teaspoon cinnamon

❧ ❧ ❧

1½ cups milk
2 eggs, beaten
2 tablespoons butter, melted

❧ ❧ ❧

1 cup fresh orange juice
4 tablespoons butter
¾ cup brown sugar
1 tablespoon grated orange rind

In a medium bowl combine the first 7 ingredients. Make a well in the center and add the milk, beaten eggs, and melted butter. Mix well. Heat a griddle or large skillet and spray with cooking spray. Spoon the batter onto the griddle to make 4-inch pancakes. Turn the pancakes when bubbles come to the surface.

In a 2-quart saucepan combine the remaining ingredients. Stir until the butter is melted and the brown sugar has dissolved. Simmer slowly for 5 minutes. This sauce will keep in the refrigerator for up to 3 weeks.

Makes 16 to 18 pancakes, and about 2 cups of sauce.

Country Bran Muffins
with Cream Cheese and Preserves

2 cups unbleached all-purpose flour
1 cup oat bran
1 cup wheat bran
1 cup sugar
2 teaspoons baking soda
1 teaspoon salt

❧ ❧ ❧

Country Meadow Inn

2 eggs
2 cups milk
¾ cup oil
2 8-ounce packages cream cheese
Fruit preserves, any flavor

In a large bowl combine the dry ingredients. In a separate bowl combine the eggs, milk, and oil. Make a well in the center of the dry mixture and add the milk mixture. Stir until just combined. This mixture may be stored for up to 3 weeks, making muffins as needed.

Spray muffin cups with cooking spray or fill with paper liners. Fill the cups ⅔ full. Place a 1-inch square of cream cheese in the center of each muffin. Spoon ½ to 1 teaspoon of fruit preserves over the cream cheese. Cover with ⅓ cup of batter. Bake in a 425° oven for 13 to 15 minutes.

Makes 2½ to 3 dozen muffins.

❧ ❧ ❧ ❧ ❧

Fruited Pork Tenderloin

1 2-pound pork tenderloin
2 large cloves garlic, minced
Fresh ground pepper
Thyme to taste
1 cup pitted prunes
1 cup dried apricots
¼ cup sweet butter, softened
1 cup Sauterne

Spray a shallow baking dish with cooking spray. Butterfly the tenderloin and fold open. Sprinkle half the garlic on one side of the loin, and sprinkle with pepper and thyme. Layer the fruits, alternating the two. Fold the top half of the loin over the fruit. Tie with twine. Spread butter over the top of the roast and press the remaining garlic into the butter. Sprinkle with pepper and thyme.

Place the roast in the prepared dish. Pour the Sauterne over the roast. Cover and bake in a 350° oven for 1 hour and 30 minutes, basting every 15 minutes with pan juices. Let the roast sit for about 10 minutes before slicing.

Serves 4.

Fruit Strudel

½ cup butter
1 cup all-purpose flour
½ teaspoon salt
½ cup sour cream

❧ ❧ ❧

3 cups sliced apples, peeled and cored
½ cup raisins
⅓ cup brown sugar
½ teaspoon cinnamon
1 tablespoon lemon juice

❧ ❧ ❧

Confectioners' sugar

In a mixing bowl cut the butter into the flour until thoroughly combined. Add the salt and sour cream, and blend well. Refrigerate for 1 hour, or up to 24 hours.

Spray a cooking sheet with cooking spray. In a medium bowl combine the apples, raisins, brown sugar, cinnamon, and lemon juice. Roll the pastry on a floured surface to a 9x15-inch rectangle. Sprinkle the fruit mixture over the pastry, leaving 1 inch around the edges. Roll the pastry over the fruit and seal the edges. Bake in a 350° oven for 25 to 30 minutes. Cool for 5 minutes, then sprinkle with confectioners' sugar. Serve warm.

Variation: Instead of apples, use 1 cup of apricot, blackberry, strawberry, or peach preserves.

Serves 10.

❧ ❧ ❧ ❧ ❧

Colorado

The Cottonwood Inn

123 San Juan Avenue
Alamosa, Colorado 81101
(719) 589-3882

The Cottonwood is a beautiful turn-of-the-century home in the heart of the San Luis Valley where hospitality is a way of life. Each of the guest rooms is decorated with comfortable antique furniture and artwork by area artists. The family-style breakfast is served in the dining room; guests may enjoy the parlor, relaxing with conversation, reading, or sitting by the fire. Nearby attractions include ski areas, the Cumbres & Toltec Scenic Railroad, and the Great Sand Dunes National Monument.

Raspberry Pancakes

2 eggs
¼ cup sugar
¼ cup oil
2 cups buttermilk

❧ ❧ ❧

¾ cup all-purpose flour
¾ cup whole wheat flour
2 teaspoons baking powder
1 teaspoon salt

3 tablespoons wheat germ
½ pint fresh raspberries

In a medium bowl beat together the eggs, sugar, oil, and buttermilk. In a separate bowl sift together the flours, baking powder, and salt. Stir in the wheat germ. Stir the dry ingredients into the buttermilk mixture until blended. Add the raspberries. Spray a griddle with cooking spray and heat to 350°. Drop ¼ cup of batter onto the griddle at a time. Bake until golden brown, turning when bubbles come to the surface. Serve with butter and maple syrup.
Serves 4.

Queen Anne Inn

2147 Tremont Place
Denver, Colorado 80205
(303) 296-6666

Queen Anne Inn is the first bed and breakfast inn in any of Denver's historic districts and winner of nine awards for excellence. Guests enjoy the grand staircase; quaint rooms; many elegant period furnishings; and the art, music, and greenery found throughout. Just four blocks from the heart of Denver's central business district, it is also within walking distance of many of the city's finest attractions, shops, and restaurants. Ten guest rooms with private baths, afternoon refreshments in the parlor, morning breakfast, an idyllic urban garden, off-street parking, and access to the Rocky Mountains are all part of the pleasure of a stay at the Queen Anne.

Homemade Oat Bran Granola

8 cups rolled oats
1½ cups unprocessed oat bran
½ cup walnut pieces
½ cup raw sunflower seeds
½ cup vegetable oil
¾ cup honey
2 teaspoons vanilla extract
1 cup golden raisins
1 cup raisins
1 to 2 cups millet (puffed)

In a large bowl combine the oats, oat bran, walnuts, and sunflower seeds. In a small saucepan heat the oil, honey, and vanilla, stirring until bubbly. Thoroughly mix the liquids with the oat mixture. Divide between 2 rimmed baking sheets. Bake in a 325° oven for 30 minutes, stirring every 10 minutes to brown evenly. Turn out onto a flat surface to cool. As the mixture cools, stir again to prevent clumping. When completely cool, add the raisins and millet. Store in an airtight container.
Makes about 16 cups of granola.

Strater Hotel

699 Main Avenue
Durango, Colorado 81302
(303) 247-4431
(800) 247-4431

Authentic Victorian elegance with a hint of the Wild West describes the Strater Hotel today, as it has since 1887. Situated in the heart of the historic and entertainment district, this landmark is internationally known for its hospitality, charm, and fine service. Each of the ninety-three rooms is lavishly furnished with authentic American Victorian walnut antiques; all the modern conveniences expected in a great hotel make a stay at the Strater a comfortable experience in Victorian elegance.

The Strater's own Diamond Belle Saloon provides a friendly Old West atmosphere; live rag-time music is performed nightly. Henry's, a Victorian restaurant in the hotel, offers fine dining for breakfast, lunch, and dinner.

Venison Roderick

We use domestic red deer. If you use wild deer, we recommend using meat tenderizer. Venison is naturally low in calories and cholesterol as it has no marbling. Do not use any other type of fat or oil except butter or olive oil, as others ruin the flavor of the meat. This only takes a few minutes to prepare, so have your other dishes well under way.

    1 teaspoon garlic powder
    Salt and pepper to taste
    2 pounds venison saddle or
        tenderloin, sliced ¼-inch thick
    2 tablespoons butter or olive oil
    ¼ cup brandy

Heat a heavy nonstick or cast iron skillet. Sprinkle the garlic powder, salt, and pepper over both sides of the venison medallions. In a hot skillet quickly sauté the venison until done to taste. Remove the venison and deglaze the skillet with brandy. Serve over the venison.

Note: This makes an excellent meal with a light salad, wild rice pilaf, and stuffed crookneck or zucchini squash.

Serves 4.

Roast Russian Boar

    1 3- to 5-pound rolled boar or pork
        roast
    1 pound carrots, cut in 3-inch
        pieces
    2 cups chopped celery
    4 cups diced potatoes
    4 cups chicken stock
    4 cups red wine
    2 cups water
    1 large onion, quartered
    2 cloves crushed garlic
    3 tablespoons dried tarragon

Queen Anne Inn

In a large roast pan with a cover combine the boar and the remaining ingredients. Cover. Bake in a 350° oven for 40 minutes per pound.

Serves 6 to 8.

Durango-style Trout

¼ teaspoon basil
¼ teaspoon oregano
¼ teaspoon minced parsley
½ cup all-purpose flour
4 boned trout fillets
Olive oil or butter

In a shallow bowl combine the herbs and flour. Dredge the trout fillets in the flour mixture. In a nonstick skillet heat a small amount of olive oil over high heat and sauté the fillets until the fish flakes and is golden brown.

Serves 4.

Scotch Steak

1 tablespoon olive oil
¼ cup sliced mushrooms
½ teaspoon salt, or to taste
1 tablespoon cracked peppercorns
1 10-ounce New York strip steak
1½ ounces premium Scotch
Butter

In a heavy skillet combine the first 4 ingredients. Add the steak and cook over medium heat until done to taste. Remove the steak and deglaze with the Scotch. Add butter and stir until melted. Pour the mixture over the steak and serve immediately.

Serves 1.

Stuffed Yellow Crookneck Squash

¼ cup butter
2 cups bread crumbs
2 teaspoons nutmeg
1 teaspoon brown sugar
4 medium yellow squash

Strater Hotel

In a saucepan melt the butter and stir in the bread crumbs, nutmeg, and brown sugar. Set aside. Split the squash lengthwise and remove the seeds. Fill each half with ¼ cup of stuffing. Arrange the stuffed squash on a baking sheet. Bake in a 350° oven for 10 to 15 minutes, depending on the size.

Serves 8.

Brandied Cranberries

1 pound fresh cranberries
2 cups sugar
1 teaspoon cinnamon
½ cup brandy

In a glass ovenproof dish with a cover combine the cranberries, sugar, and cinnamon, and cover. Bake in a 350° oven for 1 hour. Pour the brandy over the hot cranberries, and cool to room temperature. Chill overnight.

Serves 6.

Cottenwood House

Post Office Box 1208
Estes Park, Colorado 80517
(303) 586-5104

Enjoy old-fashioned hospitality in the immaculate circa 1927 mountain home filled with antiques and country furnishings, just minutes from the heart of Estes Park and famous Rocky Mountain National Park. The guest suite consists of two rooms and a private bath; smoking is permitted outside the suite. A full country breakfast is served on a sunny porch. "Soup Kettle Suppers" are offered during winter months with advance notice. Estes Park has quaint shops, excellent restaurants, dinner theaters, and a wide variety of outdoor activities.

Sopa de Albondigas
Mexican Meatball Soup

This is a thick, rich Mexican soup, delicately seasoned with cilantro. It gives a new dimension to Mexican cooking. A meal in itself, we like to serve it with a crisp green salad and corn muffins.

2 slices white bread
Milk
½ pound ground pork
½ pound ground beef
1 tablespoon minced white onion
1 egg
1 clove garlic, minced
2 tablespoons chopped parsley
¼ teaspoon salt
¼ teaspoon fresh ground pepper

&ta; &ta; &ta;

1 tablespoon oil
1 small white onion, minced
1 clove garlic, minced
5 cups homemade beef or chicken
    broth
2 tablespoons tomato paste
1 medium carrot, peeled and diced
1 medium or 2 small zucchini, diced
2 whole tomatoes, seeded and
    cubed
2 tablespoons minced cilantro

Soak the bread in milk until moistened. Squeeze the bread and place in a medium bowl. Stir in the pork, beef, 1 tablespoon of onion, egg, 1 clove of garlic, parsley, salt, and pepper. Shape into bite-sized meatballs. In a nonstick skillet cook the meatballs until lightly browned on all sides. Drain on paper towels. In a large saucepan heat the oil. Add the remaining onion and garlic, and cook until softened. Stir in the broth and tomato paste, and stir until smooth. Simmer for 10 minutes. Add the meatballs and carrot, and simmer for about 20 minutes. Add the zucchini and tomatoes, and simmer for 5 to 10 minutes, until tender. Stir in the cilantro, and adjust the salt and pepper to taste. Serve immediately.
    Serves 6.

Ham and Cheddar Chowder

We serve "Soup Kettle Suppers" in the winter months, and this soup is always a favorite. Serve with a salad, herbed biscuits, and a light dessert (perhaps a chocolate mousse).

¼ cup chopped onion
½ cup diced celery
Butter

&ta; &ta; &ta;

2 cups chicken broth
2 cups diced potatoes
½ cup diced carrots
2 tablespoons dried parsley
1 teaspoon salt
¼ teaspoon pepper

&ta; &ta; &ta;

¼ cup butter
¼ cup all-purpose flour
2 cups milk
2 cups grated Cheddar cheese

&ta; &ta; &ta;

1 cup cubed ham

In a skillet sauté the onions and celery in a small amount of butter. In a large kettle combine the broth, potatoes, carrots, parsley, onion, celery, salt, and pepper. Bring to a boil, reduce the heat, and simmer for 10 to 12 minutes, until the carrots and potatoes are tender. Meanwhile, in a small saucepan melt the butter and add the flour. Stir until smooth, about 1 minute. Slowly add the milk and cook until thickened. Add the grated cheese and stir until melted. Pour the sauce into the soup mixture, and add the ham. Heat through.
    Serves 6.

The Emerald Manor

441 Chiquita Lane
Post Office Box 3592
Estes Park, Colorado 80517
(303) 586-8050

The Emerald Manor is a wee bit of Ireland in the Colorado Rockies, situated within walking distance of downtown Estes Park. Offering warm Irish hospitality, outstanding meals, and cozy accommodations, it has four guest rooms, two having their own private bath. The formal living room lends itself to reading and quiet conversation; the large game room invites guests to relax in front of the fire. Adjacent is an indoor swimming pool with a redwood sauna just off the pool area. Following a delightful breakfast, guests can enjoy the unique beauty of Rocky Mountain National Park and the shops and entertainments of Estes Park.

&ta; &ta; &ta; &ta; &ta;

Barnbrack

6 cups all-purpose flour
1 teaspoon salt
¼ cup butter
½ cup sugar
1½ cups warm milk (110° to 115°)
1½ ounces creamed yeast
3 eggs
2½ cups raisins
4 ounces chopped mixed dried fruit

Grease two 9x5-inch pans. Sift the flour and salt into a bowl. Blend in the butter and sugar until the mixture resembles coarse crumbs. Combine the warm milk and yeast, and set aside for 10 minutes. Add to the batter, and add the eggs. Beat for about 10 minutes. The mixture will become very elastic. Add the raisins and dried fruit. Place the greased pans in a warm oven. When the pans are warmed turn the oven off and place the dough in the warmed pans. Cover and place in the barely warm oven for 1 hour, until the dough doubles in size. Bake in a 500° oven for 5 minutes, reduce the heat to 350°, and bake for 45 minutes. Brush with water and sugar, and brown for 1 minute.
    Serves 20.

The Emerald Manor

Elizabeth Street Guest House Bed and Breakfast

202 East Elizabeth Street
Fort Collins, Colorado 80524
(303) 493-BEDS

Elizabeth Street Guest House is a beautifully restored American four-square brick home. It is lovingly furnished with family antiques, plants, old quilts, and handmade items. The leaded windows and oak woodwork are special features.

Raisin Carrot Muffins

½ cup raisins
½ cup warm water

🌿 🌿 🌿

1 cup all-purpose flour
¾ cup whole wheat flour
1 teaspoon baking soda
½ teaspoon salt
1 teaspoon cinnamon
½ teaspoon nutmeg

🌿 🌿 🌿

1 large egg
½ cup sugar
¼ cup corn oil
⅛ teaspoon vanilla extract
⅛ teaspoon lemon extract
1 cup applesauce
¾ cup grated carrots

Grease 12 muffin cups. In a small bowl combine the raisins with the warm water. Set aside to soak. In a large bowl combine the flours, baking soda, salt, and spices. In a separate bowl beat the egg and sugar with an electric mixer or large whisk until fluffy. Beat in the oil, vanilla, and lemon extract. Stir in the applesauce. Stir the applesauce mixture into the flour mixture until just blended. Fold in the carrots, raisins, and water. Spoon the batter into the prepared muffin cups, filling ¾ full. Bake in a 400° oven for 15 to 18 minutes, until lightly browned and a knife inserted in the center of a muffin comes out clean.
    Makes 12 muffins.

French Muffins

Excellent with honey-butter or jams. These can be made the night before and reheated in a 300° oven for 10 minutes. They are nice instead of rolls with dinner.

1 ¼-ounce package active dry yeast
1½ cups warm water (110° to 115°)
½ cup nonfat dry milk
2½ cups all-purpose flour
1 egg, room temperature
½ teaspoon salt
¼ cup sugar
¼ cup butter, melted

Grease 12 muffin cups. In a large bowl dissolve the yeast in the warm water. Stir in the dry milk. Add the flour ½ cup at a time, until the batter is thick and smooth. Add the egg, blending just until mixed well. Cover with plastic wrap and let rise in a warm place for about 1 hour. Remove the plastic and add the salt and sugar. Stir down to blend, and add the melted butter. The batter will be stringy and elastic. Fill muffin cups ⅔ full. Bake in a 425° oven for 30 to 35 minutes, until golden brown.

Makes 12 muffins.

The Outlook Lodge

Post Office Box 5
Green Mountain Falls, Colorado 80819
(719) 684-2303

Pine and spruce trees surround this 1889 structure. Green Mountain Falls is a heavily wooded little vale with a fishing lake that has a gazebo in the center. Its claim to historical fame comes from being the parsonage for the "Little Brown Church in the Wildwood." Both church and parsonage were built in 1889, and many of the furnishings are the original pieces.

Pumpkin Pecan Muffins

1¼ cups quick or old-fashioned oats
1 cup all-purpose flour
⅓ cup chopped pecans
1 teaspoon baking powder
1 teaspoon cinnamon
½ teaspoon baking soda
½ teaspoon salt
½ teaspoon nutmeg

≈   ≈   ≈

1 cup canned pumpkin
¾ cup firmly packed brown sugar
½ cup oil
¼ cup milk
1 egg
1 teaspoon vanilla extract

≈   ≈   ≈

¼ cup oats
¼ cup all-purpose flour
¼ cup firmly packed brown sugar
3 tablespoons chopped pecans
1 teaspoon cinnamon
¼ cup margarine or butter, softened

Generously grease 18 medium muffin cups or line the cups with paper liners. Combine the first 8 ingredients. Add the pumpkin, brown sugar, oil, milk, egg, and vanilla, stirring until just moistened. Fill the muffin cups ¾ full.

Combine the remaining ingredients. Sprinkle over the muffin batter. Bake in a 400° oven for 15 to 20 minutes or until well done. Remove from the pan and serve warm.

Makes 18 muffins.

Lemon Loaf

6 tablespoons butter
¾ cup sugar
2 eggs
3 tablespoons lemon juice
2 teaspoons grated fresh lemon peel

≈   ≈   ≈

1½ cups sifted flour
1 teaspoon baking soda
1 teaspoon salt
½ cup milk
½ cup chopped walnuts

≈   ≈   ≈

3 tablespoons lemon juice
½ cup sugar

Grease an 8x4-inch loaf pan and line the bottom with wax paper. Cream the butter and sugar until fluffy. Beat in the eggs one at a time. Beat in 3 tablespoons lemon juice and the lemon peel. In a separate bowl combine the flour, baking soda, and salt, and add alternately to the egg mixture with the milk. Fold in the walnuts. Pour the batter into the prepared loaf pan, and tap the pan to settle the batter evenly. Bake in a 350° oven for 1 hour, or until a toothpick inserted in the center comes out clean.

Blend 3 tablespoons of lemon juice with ½ cup of sugar and pour the mixture over the hot bread. Let the bread stand until the mixture is absorbed, at least 15 minutes. Remove the bread from the pan and place on a rack to cool. Remove the wax paper and wrap in plastic. Leave the bread wrapped for 24 hours before slicing.

Makes 1 loaf.

Waunita Hot Springs Ranch

8007 County Road 887
Department 7
Gunnison, Colorado 81230
(303) 641-1266

This 75-year-old lodge has shared warm western hospitality with families, couples, and singles looking for a wholesome, no-alcohol vacation atmosphere. It is secluded amidst beautiful scenery, colorful history, and delightful weather; yet it is easily accessible from Gunnison (thirty minutes) and Colorado Springs (three hours). Activities are as endless as the memories. They include trail rides that go from flowered meadows to snow-ridged mountain tops, and riding instructions are available. Also available are campfire cookouts, fishing, scenic 4x4 trips, river rafting, hay rides, musical shows, and square dancing. Supervised children's activities are provided and a unique crystal clear pool fed by natural hot springs is on the grounds. Accommodations are comfortable and clean, and all have private baths. Meals are delicious and plentiful.

Hot Chocolate Mix

1 2-pound box instant chocolate
    drink mix
12½ cups dry milk
1 pound instant creamer
2 cups powdered sugar
1 teaspoon cinnamon
½ teaspoon nutmeg

In a large bowl combine all of the ingredients. Store in an airtight container. Use ⅛ cup to ¼ cup of mix with every cup of hot water.
Makes about 80 servings.

Corn Chowder

4 slices bacon
1 large onion, chopped
2 cups chopped peeled potatoes
2 cups water
2 17-ounce cans cream-style corn
2 cups light cream or milk
Salt and pepper to taste
1 teaspoon margarine

In a large skillet fry the bacon. Remove the bacon from the pan and sauté the onion in the bacon drippings. Add the potatoes and water. Season to taste with salt and pepper. Simmer for 20 minutes. Add the corn and cream, and simmer for 5 minutes. Just before serving add the bacon and margarine.
Serves 6.

Buttermilk Biscuits

2 cups all-purpose flour
1 tablespoon sugar
1 tablespoon baking powder
½ teaspoon baking soda
¾ teaspoon salt
⅓ cup shortening
1½ cups buttermilk

Lightly grease a cookie sheet or baking pans. In a large bowl mix the dry ingredients well. Cut in the shortening with a pastry blender until the size of coarse meal. Add the buttermilk all at once. Mix lightly and turn onto a floured board. Knead lightly and roll to about ½-inch thickness. Cut dough into biscuits and place on the prepared pans. Bake in a 450° oven for about 15 minutes, or until lightly browned.
Makes 15 to 20 biscuits.

Pizza Loaves

1 pound lean ground beef
1 cup grated Mozzarella cheese
½ cup grated salami
1 teaspoon Italian seasoning
1¼ cups pizza sauce
2 loaves French bread, split
    horizontally
Grated Mozzarella cheese for
    topping

In a large skillet brown the meat. Add the next four ingredients, and simmer until the cheese is melted. Spread the meat mixture on the bread and place on a cookie sheet. Bake in a 400° oven for 15 minutes. Top with additional cheese and bake for 5 minutes, until the cheese is melted.
Serves 10.

Strawberry Pie

1 cup sugar
2 tablespoons cornstarch
1 cup water
¼ cup strawberry gelatin
3 cups hulled strawberries
1 9-inch pie crust, baked
2 cups whipped topping

In a saucepan mix the sugar and cornstarch well. Stirring constantly, add the water. Cook over medium heat until thick. Remove from the heat and add the gelatin. Dissolve. Place the berries in the crust and pour the hot mixture over the berries. Chill for 3 hours. Top with whipped topping.
Serves 6 to 8.

Blue Lake Ranch

16919 State Highway 140
Hesperus, Colorado 81326
(303) 385-4537

Blue Lake Ranch is an elegant country estate with down quilts, family antiques, and flower-filled rooms. Guests may cool off with afternoon tea in the shade of the patio, unwind in the Jacuzzi under the clear night sky, or swim in the spring-fed lake. The majestic LaPlata Mountains are the backdrop.

Piñon Mint Omelet

4 large eggs
1 tablespoon fresh mint
2 large fresh basil leaves
Salt
2 tablespoons piñon nuts

&ep; &ep; &ep;

½ cup Ricotta cheese
½ teaspoon sugar
1 tablespoon cream

&ep; &ep; &ep;

1 tablespoon butter
2 tablespoons piñon nuts
Sugar
Mint leaves and fresh fruit for
    garnish

In a bowl beat the eggs and add the mint, basil, salt, and 2 tablespoons of piñon nuts. In a separate bowl combine the Ricotta, sugar, and cream.
Heat a nonstick skillet until hot. Melt the butter, and quickly pour in the egg mixture. Lift the edge of the omelet, and tilt the pan to let the uncooked eggs run under. Spread with the Ricotta filling and fold the omelet into thirds. Turn onto a plate seamside down. Sprinkle with the remaining piñon nuts and a bit of sugar, and garnish with mint leaves and fresh fruit.
Serves 2.

Basil Yogurt Frittata

This recipe will inspire anyone to grow basil on their windowsill or in a pot by the kitchen door!

1 tablespoon butter
¼ cup thinly sliced scallions
½ cup plain yogurt
6 eggs
Salt and pepper to taste
⅓ cup finely chopped fresh basil leaves
1 tablespoon butter

ès ès ès

⅓ cup freshly grated Parmesan cheese

In a 10-inch skillet with sloping sides melt 1 tablespoon of butter. Add the scallions and cook until soft. In a bowl beat the yogurt with 1 egg. Beat in the remaining eggs one at a time until blended. Add the salt, pepper, and basil. Add the remaining tablespoon of butter to the heated skillet and pour the egg mixture over the scallions. Lift the edge of the omelet, and tilt the pan to let the uncooked eggs run under. Cook until the eggs are softly set but still moist, about 5 minutes. Remove from the heat and sprinkle with Parmesan cheese. Serve immediately.
Serves 3 to 4.

Gingerbread Waffles

For those who don't eat eggs. These have a great flavor and are particularly good garnished with whipped cream cheese and a simple lemon sauce.

⅓ cup packed brown sugar
1 egg, separated
¾ cup buttermilk
¼ cup molasses
3 tablespoons butter, melted

ès ès ès

1 cup all-purpose flour
1½ teaspoons baking powder
1 teaspoon cinnamon
¾ teaspoon allspice
⅜ teaspoon baking soda
¼ teaspoon dry mustard
¼ teaspoon salt
⅓ cup chopped raisins
2 tablespoons minced crystallized ginger
Pinch cream of tartar

Preheat a waffle iron. With an electric mixer, beat the sugar and egg yolk until light and fluffy. Mix in the buttermilk, molasses, and butter. In a large bowl combine the flour, baking powder, spices, baking soda, dry mustard, and salt. Add the liquid ingredients and beat on low speed until blended. Fold in the raisins and ginger. In a separate bowl beat the egg white and cream of tartar until stiff. Fold the egg white into the batter. Spoon the batter into the waffle iron and bake until golden brown.

Makes about 6 waffles.

Warm Fruit Compote
with Sweet Vanilla Cream

1 cup water
1 cup sugar
½ cup orange juice
1 navel orange, halved
2 lemons, halved
2 sticks cinnamon
¼ teaspoon nutmeg
8 whole cloves
1 tablespoon vanilla extract

ès ès ès

2 red Bartlett pears, cored and cut into 1-inch pieces
6 black mission figs, halved
3 navel oranges, peeled and membranes removed, cut into wedges
1 cup hulled strawberries, halved
½ cup Concord grapes, halved and seeded
½ cup Muscat grapes, halved and seeded
½ cup whole seedless grapes

ès ès ès

½ cup cream cheese, softened
¼ cup sugar
1 teaspoon vanilla extract
1 cup heavy cream

ès ès ès

Fresh mint for garnish
4 to 5 sticks cinnamon

In a stainless steel pan combine the water, 1 cup of sugar, orange juice, orange, lemons, cinnamon, nutmeg, cloves, and vanilla. Bring to a boil over high heat, reduce to a simmer, and cook for 5 minutes. In a large serving bowl place the pears, and strain the hot syrup through a fine mesh over the pears. Cool and gently mix in the other fruit.

In a large bowl cream together the cream cheese and ¼ cup of sugar. Blend in the vanilla. Slowly beat in the cream. Strain the mixture. This may be whipped until slightly thickened or served as is.

Serve the compote at room temperature with Sweet Vanilla Cream on the side. Garnish with mint and cinnamon sticks.

Note: If one or more of these fruits are unavailable, add more of another ingredient or use another fresh fruit such as apples or tangerines.
Serves 4 to 5.

The Leadville Country Inn

127 East Eighth Street
Leadville, Colorado 80461
(719) 486-2354
(800) 748-2354

Capturing the romantic spirit of the Victorian era, the Leadville Country Inn invites its guests to discover the comfort and hospitality of a first class Victorian bed and breakfast. Built in 1893, it has been carefully restored to its original splendor. Rich hand rubbed woods, classical music, simmering potpourri, and homemade foods await its guests. Nine of the rooms have private baths. The inn provides candlelight dinners and sleigh rides in the winter and carriage rides in the summer.

Shrimp Dip

1 8-ounce package cream cheese
1 3-ounce package chive cream cheese
1 3-ounce package pimiento cream cheese
Mayonnaise
2 4½-ounce cans shrimp, drained
Dash Worcestershire sauce
Dash Tabasco sauce
1½ tablespoons lemon juice

Cream the cream cheeses with enough mayonnaise to soften. Mash the shrimp with a fork. Add to the cheese with the remaining ingredients. Chill. Serve with crackers.
Serves 8 to 10.

Fireside Drink Mix

2 cups instant coffee creamer
1½ cups instant coffee (decaf is fine)
1½ cups hot cocoa mix
1½ cups sugar (or equivalent Sugar Twin)
1 teaspoon cinnamon
¼ teaspoon nutmeg

In a large bowl combine all of the ingredients. Store the mixture in an airtight container. Use 2 tablespoons of drink mix with each cup of water.
Makes 40 cups of drink.

Cheese Biscuits

1 cup all-purpose flour
½ cup margarine, softened
⅛ teaspoon salt
2 cups grated American cheese

In a large bowl combine the flour, margarine, and salt. Add the cheese and roll into balls. Place the balls on an ungreased baking sheet. Bake in a 350° oven for 10 minutes.
Makes 3 dozen.

Mexican Cornbread

1 small can cream-style corn
1 cup sour cream
½ cup oil
1 cup cornmeal
1 tablespoon baking powder
⅛ teaspoon salt
2 eggs, slightly beaten
1 cup grated Cheddar cheese
3 jalapeños, chopped

Grease an 8-inch square pan. In a large bowl combine the corn, sour cream, and oil. Add the cornmeal, baking powder, and salt. Mix in the eggs, cheese, and jalapeños. Pour the batter into the prepared pan. Bake in a 325° oven for 1 hour.
Serves 6.

Taco Casserole

2 pounds ground beef
1 large onion, chopped

ᔰ ᔰ ᔰ

1 14-ounce can evaporated milk
1 10¾-ounce can cream of chicken soup
1 10¾-ounce can cream of mushroom soup
1 10-ounce can mild enchilada sauce
1 3-ounce can green chilies

ᔰ ᔰ ᔰ

1 11-ounce bag Taco-flavored corn chips, crushed

ᔰ ᔰ ᔰ

4 cups grated Longhorn or Colby cheese

In a skillet brown the ground beef and onion. In a saucepan heat the milk with the soups, enchilada sauce, and chilies until bubbly. Grease a 9x13-inch casserole dish. Layer over the bottom in this order, half of the crushed corn chips, half of the meat mixture, half of the sauce, and half of the cheese. Repeat the layers. Bake in a 350° oven for 30 minutes.
Serves 8.

Hot Fruit Compote

1 16-ounce can peaches
1 16-ounce can pears
1 16-ounce can pineapple chunks
1 medium apple, cored and sliced
1 21-ounce can cherry pie filling
½ cup Granola or Raisin Bran cereal
Vanilla yogurt for topping

Drain the peaches, pears, and pineapple chunks. In a large casserole dish combine the drained fruit, the apple, and the cherry pie filling. Sprinkle with granola or cereal. Bake in a 375° oven for 30 to 40 minutes. Serve in individual bowls with a spoonful of vanilla yogurt.
Serves 6.

Double Chocolate Brownies

1 cup margarine, melted
2 cups sugar
½ cup cocoa
1⅓ cups all-purpose flour
4 eggs
2 tablespoons vanilla extract
1 6-ounce package chocolate chips
1 cup chopped nuts

Grease and flour a 9x13-inch glass pan. In a large bowl combine the margarine, sugar, cocoa, and flour. Add the eggs, one at a time. Add the vanilla, and fold in the chocolate chips and nuts. Bake in a 350° oven for 25 minutes.
Makes 24 brownies.

The Lovelander

217 West Fourth Street
Loveland, Colorado 80537
(303) 669-0798

This turn-of-the-century Victorian residence has served as a boarding house and a country doctor's office before being made into a bed and breakfast inn. The nine-room inn offers easy access to the downtown area; each room offers vintage iron and hardwood beds and tasteful period furniture. Situated just minutes away from Rocky Mountain National Park, the inn is ideally suited as a base for exploring the northern Colorado mountains.

Cinnamon-Raisin Breakfast Pudding

1 loaf whole wheat cinnamon-raisin bread, unsliced
5 eggs
3 egg yolks
¾ cup sugar
3 cups milk
1 cup half and half
1 tablespoon vanilla
1 teaspoon cinnamon
½ teaspoon nutmeg

   🍂   🍂   🍂

½ cup melted butter

   🍂   🍂   🍂

Confectioners' sugar
Fresh berries

Grease a 9x13-inch baking dish and a 9x5-inch loaf pan. Trim the end pieces from the bread and cut into 8 slices. Arrange the bread in the prepared dishes. In a large bowl beat together the whole eggs and the egg yolks. Whisk in the sugar, milk, half and half, vanilla, cinnamon, and nutmeg. Pour the mixture evenly over the bread. Cover the pans with foil and refrigerate overnight. Drizzle with melted butter. Bake in a 350° oven for 45 to 60 minutes. Dust with confectioners' sugar and top with fresh berries.
Serves 8.

Granny's Granola

¾ cup rolled oats
¼ cup wheat germ
¼ cup sunflower seeds
½ cup unsweetened coconut
½ cup bran flakes
½ cup wheat flakes
½ cup rye flakes
6 tablespoons malted milk powder
½ cup toasted cashews
½ cup chopped raw almonds

2½ tablespoons oil
¼ teaspoon vanilla extract
2½ tablespoons honey
2 tablespoons water
½ teaspoon cinnamon
¼ teaspoon salt
1 cup raisins
¼ cup chopped dates

In a large bowl combine the first 10 ingredients. In a separate bowl combine the remaining ingredients except the raisins and dates, and pour over the dry mixture. Mix well and spread in an 11x14-inch pan. Bake in a 325° oven for 15 minutes, stirring every 5 minutes. Cool, add the fruit, and pack in an airtight container.
Makes 8 cups.

Broccoli-Cheese Strata

4 cups fresh whole wheat bread cubes
2 green onions, minced with stems
2 tablespoons chopped fresh parsley
3 cups shredded Cheddar cheese
1 10-ounce package frozen chopped broccoli, thawed
6 to 8 mushrooms, sliced
½ cup chopped red pepper
¼ cup melted margarine
6 eggs, beaten
1 teaspoon dry mustard
½ teaspoon salt
1 tablespoon basil
1 tablespoon tarragon
1 quart milk

Grease a 9x13-inch baking pan. In a large bowl combine the bread, onion, and parsley. Spread the mixture in the bottom of the prepared pan. Sprinkle with 1½ cups of Cheddar cheese. Spread the broccoli, mushrooms, and red pepper over the cheese. Drizzle with margarine. In a small bowl beat the eggs with the mustard, salt, seasonings, and milk, and pour over the vegetable layer. Top with the remaining cheese. Refrigerate overnight. Bake in a 350° oven for 1 hour.
Serves 12.

Spinach-Feta Puff Quiche

1 tablespoon butter
1 small onion, chopped
¼ cup fresh parsley, chopped
1 teaspoon fresh dill
1 teaspoon fresh basil
1 10-ounce package frozen chopped spinach, thawed and squeezed dry
Juice of ½ lemon
3 tablespoons milk
4 ounces Feta cheese, crumbled
1½ cups Swiss cheese, shredded
½ teaspoon ground cumin
Pinch nutmeg
Salt and pepper to taste
3 eggs, separated
1 9-inch unbaked whole wheat pie shell

In a small skillet melt the butter and sauté the onion until translucent. Add the parsley, dill, and basil, and sauté until wilted. In a large bowl combine the onion and herb mixture with the spinach, lemon juice, milk, cheeses, and seasonings. Mix well. Stir the egg yolks into the spinach mixture. Beat the egg whites into stiff peaks and gently fold into the spinach mixture. Pour the mixture into the pie shell. Bake in a 325° oven for 35 to 40 minutes or until the quiche is puffed and lightly browned.

Serves 6.

Cheese and Herb Potatoes

2 pounds frozen hash brown
  potatoes
½ fresh onion, chopped (or ½ cup
  dried onion)
2 teaspoons fresh rosemary,
  tarragon, or basil (or
  combination)
1 tablespoon fresh dill weed
1 teaspoon salt
½ teaspoon pepper
⅓ green pepper, chopped
⅓ red pepper, chopped
4 cups shredded sharp Cheddar
  cheese
1½ cups milk
2 tablespoons margarine, melted
  (optional)

Grease a large casserole dish. Thaw the hash browns. In a large bowl combine the hash browns, seasonings, and chopped peppers. Layer half of the potato mixture in the bottom of the prepared dish. Cover with half of the Cheddar. Top with the remaining hash brown mixture and the remaining Cheddar. Combine the milk and margarine, and pour evenly over the casserole. Bake in a 350° oven for 45 minutes. Serve as a breakfast or dinner side dish.

Serves 12.

Victorian Vinegar Cookies

½ cup butter
½ cup margarine
¾ cup sugar
1 tablespoon white vinegar
1¾ cups all-purpose flour
½ teaspoon baking soda
1 cup finely chopped walnuts

In a large bowl cream the butter and margarine. Add the sugar and vinegar, and beat until fluffy. In a separate bowl sift the flour and baking soda, and add to the creamed mixture. Stir in the nuts. Drop by teaspoonfuls onto an ungreased cookie sheet. Bake in a 300° oven for 30 minutes.

Makes about 4 dozen.

Eagle River Inn

145 North Main Street
Post Office Box 100
Minturn, Colorado 81645
(303) 827-5761
(800) 344-1750

Just around the bend from the world-renowned resorts of Vail and Beaver Creek, the Eagle River Inn dates back to 1894. The 1986 renovation has transformed it into a picturesque landmark at the entrance to Minturn. With a Southwestern style, it features red adobe walls, rambling riverside decks, and a flower-filled back yard. The lobby features Santa Fe furniture, a beehive fireplace, baskets, rugs, and weavings. Twelve guest rooms on two floors above, with private baths, are beautifully appointed. After a hearty breakfast, guests enjoy a full array of summer and winter sports, as well as shops and restaurants.

Eagle River Inn Granola

⅓ cup melted butter
½ cup brown sugar
⅓ cup honey
1 tablespoon cinnamon
1 tablespoon vanilla extract
¼ cup bran (or wheat germ)

ᴥ ᴥ ᴥ

2½ cups oats
½ cup sunflower seeds
⅓ cup whole almonds

ᴥ ᴥ ᴥ

⅓ cup raisins
⅓ cup chopped dried apricots
1 cup dried banana chips

In a small saucepan combine the melted butter, brown sugar, honey, cinnamon, and vanilla. Heat over low heat until the sugar dissolves. Stir in the bran or wheat germ. In a large bowl combine the oats, sunflower seeds, and almonds. Pour the melted mixture over the dried ingredients, and stir until coated well. Pour the melted mixture into a 9x13-inch baking pan. Bake in a 350° oven for 20 to 25 minutes, stirring occasionally. Pour into a large mixing bowl and cool completely. Add the raisins, apricots, and banana chips.

Makes about 6 cups.

Carrot Muffins

3½ cups all-purpose flour
1½ cups sugar
1½ tablespoons baking powder
½ teaspoon salt
1 tablespoon cinnamon
1 teaspoon nutmeg
4 eggs
⅔ cup oil
2 cups grated carrot
Grated rind of 1 orange
1 14-ounce can crushed pineapple,
  drained, reserving juice
1 cup chopped walnuts
Cream Cheese Spread (recipe
  follows)

Grease or line muffin cups with paper liners. In a large bowl combine the flour, sugar, baking powder, salt, and spices. Blend with a fork. In a medium bowl beat the eggs with a fork and add the oil, carrot, orange peel, and pineapple. Stir the liquid ingredients into the dry ingredients just until moistened. If the dough is too dry, add pineapple juice. Fold in the nuts. Spoon into 24 muffin cups. Bake in a 350° oven for 20 minutes. Serve with Cream Cheese Spread.

Makes 24 muffins.

Cream Cheese Spread

    2 8-ounce packages cream cheese,
        softened
    ½ cup honey
    ¼ cup pineapple juice, reserved
        from muffin recipe
    1 tablespoon vanilla extract

In a medium bowl combine all of the ingredients and blend well. Serve at room temperature.

Makes about 3 cups.

Davidson's Country Inn

Highway 160
Post Office Box 87
Pagosa Springs, Colorado 81147
(303) 264-5863

Davidson's Country Inn, a three-story log country inn, is situated on thirty acres of property surrounded by the San Juan Mountains twenty miles from Wolf Creek Ski Area. Each room is tastefully decorated with family heirlooms, valuable antiques, and fine handmade furniture. Many of the ten rooms are large enough to accommodate families or small groups. The inn provides a library, an indoor children's play corner, a game room, a fire pit, horseshoes, picnic table, and outdoor children's play area.

Apple Kringle

    2 cups all-purpose flour
    1 cup margarine
    1 cup sour cream
        ❧ ❧ ❧
    1 teaspoon cinnamon
    1 21-ounce can apple pie filling
        ❧ ❧ ❧
    2 tablespoons melted margarine
    ⅛ cup milk
    1 cup confectioners' sugar
    ½ teaspoon vanilla extract

In a large bowl combine the flour and margarine until crumbly. Add the sour cream and stir until smooth. Cover and refrigerate overnight. In the morning roll the dough into a rectangle. Place the crust on a cookie sheet. Blend the cinnamon into the pie filling. Spread the pie filling in the center of the crust and fold up like an envelope. Bake in a 350° oven for about 30 to 40 minutes, until lightly browned on top.

Combine the melted margarine, milk, confectioners' sugar, and vanilla. Glaze the warm kringle with the mixture.

Serves 12.

Yummy Granola

    10 cups old-fashioned oats
    1 cup wheat germ
    1¼ cups oil
    1¼ cups honey
    1 cup sunflower seeds
    1 cup diced walnuts
    1 10-ounce package flaked coconut

In a large bowl combine all of the ingredients. Spread the mixture into two 9x12-inch cake pans. Bake in a 300° oven for about 30 minutes, stirring every 10 minutes until light golden brown. Remove from the oven and cool for 10 minutes. Store in airtight containers.

Makes fifty ½-cup servings.

Meadow Creek

13438 U.S. Highway 285
Pine, Colorado 80470
(303) 838-4167
(303) 838-4899

As part of the 250-acre Douglass ranch, at one time Meadow Creek was a magnificent private residence. Built in 1929 by Prince Balthasar Odescalchi, a descendant of emperors of the Holy Roman Empire, the stone house is nestled in a secluded meadow surrounded by stone outcroppings, tall pines, and aspens. The six rooms have private baths. The large parlor, dining room, deck, sauna, gazebo, and surrounding land are at guests' disposal. Evening meals are by prior arrangement. Only a 45 minute drive from metro Denver.

Eggs in a Snowbank

    8 slices buttered Texas Toast-sized
        bread
    8 slices Swiss cheese
    8 thin slices breakfast ham
    8 large eggs, separated, yolks intact
    Dash salt
    ½ teaspoon dry mustard
    Paprika

Lightly spray a cookie sheet with cooking spray. Toast the buttered bread for about 5 minutes in a hot oven. Remove and top each with a slice of cheese and a slice of ham. In a mixing bowl beat the egg whites with a dash of salt and the dry mustard until stiff. Using a large spoon, heap the egg whites on top of the prepared bread. Make an indentation in the center of the white and carefully place an egg yolk in each depression. Sprinkle with paprika. Bake in a 400° oven for 10 minutes or until the egg yolks are set.

Serves 8.

Eggs Benedict My Way

4 English muffin halves
4 slices breakfast ham
4 slices Swiss cheese

    ટ ટ ટ

1 10½-ounce can cream of mushroom soup
2 ounces sliced canned mushrooms
½ cup white wine
1 teaspoon dried or fresh snipped chives
1 teaspoon fresh snipped parsley
½ teaspoon garlic powder

    ટ ટ ટ

4 eggs

Arrange the English muffins on a cookie sheet and top each with ham and cheese. Keep the muffins warm in a 375° oven, just until the cheese melts, about 10 minutes.

In a skillet combine the soup, mushrooms, white wine, chives, parsley, and garlic powder. Bring the mixture to a simmer. Break the eggs in the sauce, cover, and poach to the desired doneness, about 5 to 8 minutes. Lift the eggs from the sauce and place on the hot muffins. Top with sauce.

Serves 4.

Colorado Stew

3 to 4 pounds lean round steak, cut into 1-inch pieces
¼ cup oil
2 cups chopped onions
1 tablespoon minced garlic
5 10-ounce cans mild enchilada sauce
1 to 2 cans water (as needed for consistency)
4 to 6 cups diced cooked potatoes
4 cups cooked pinto beans

    ટ ટ ટ

Shredded Cheddar cheese
Flour tortillas or hot cornbread

In a large skillet brown the meat in the oil. Remove the meat to a plate and cook the onions and garlic until softened. Return the meat to the pot, add the enchilada sauce, and 1 can of water. Cover and simmer for at least 1 hour, until the meat is tender. Add the potatoes and pinto beans, and simmer for 30 minutes. Add any additional water needed to achieve the desired consistency. Top with Cheddar cheese and serve with tortillas or hot cornbread.

Serves 10 to 12.

Poppy Seed Dressing

Our house dressing at Meadow Creek.

1 cup oil
⅓ cup white vinegar
1 teaspoon dry mustard
1 tablespoon onion juice
1 teaspoon salt
¼ cup sugar
1 tablespoon poppy seeds

In a blender combine all of the ingredients. Blend on high speed for 30 seconds, until the mixture is a creamy consistency.

This is excellent on spinach salads or any mixed green salads. Refrigerate unused dressing.

Makes about 1½ cups.

Pat's Fresh Garlic Dressing

1 cup safflower oil
⅓ cup cider vinegar
¼ cup sugar

Meadow Creek

½ teaspoon salt
½ teaspoon dry mustard
¼ cup chopped onion
1 tablespoon dry Italian herb
  seasoning
3 to 4 tablespoons minced garlic (or
  to taste)

In a blender combine the oil, vinegar, sugar, salt, mustard, and onion. Blend for 15 to 30 seconds. Add the herb seasoning and garlic, and blend for a few more seconds. Store unused dressing in the refrigerator. This is best if made in advance so the flavors have time to blend.
Makes about 1½ cups.

Mom's Fresh Thousand Island Dressing

5 to 6 tablespoons vinegar
1 cup evaporated milk
3 hard-boiled eggs
1½ cups Miracle Whip salad
  dressing
1 small onion, finely chopped
4 tablespoons sweet pickle relish
3 tablespoons catsup
2 to 3 tablespoons sugar
Dash paprika

In a large bowl combine the vinegar and milk and set aside to thicken. Add the remaining ingredients, blending well. Store unused dressing in the refrigerator, and use within 2 to 3 days.
Makes 1 quart.

Teriyaki Marinade

This is excellent for summer cooking such as shish kebobs, and I use it for London Broil.

1 cup soy sauce
⅓ cup pineapple juice
⅓ cup sherry
½ teaspoon pepper
½ teaspoon ginger
2 tablespoons brown sugar
1 onion, grated or finely chopped
1 clove garlic, minced

In a container with a cover, combine all of the ingredients. Shake or stir well until thoroughly combined. To marinate, in a glass dish pour the marinade over the meat and refrigerate for several hours or overnight. Before grilling, let the meat stand for 1 hour at room temperature. Discard any leftover marinade.
Makes 1⅔ cups.

Pistachio Banana Bread

2½ cups all-purpose flour
1½ cups sugar
2 6-ounce packages pistachio
  pudding mix
½ teaspoon salt
½ teaspoon baking soda
1 teaspoon vanilla extract
1 cup oil
2 cups mashed bananas (about 4)
5 eggs
½ cup chopped pistachio nuts

Line 2 loaf pans with wax paper and grease the sides and the paper, or spray with cooking spray. In a large bowl combine the dry ingredients. Add the remaining ingredients and mix until well blended. Pour the batter into the prepared pans. Bake in a 350° oven for 50 to 60 minutes.
Makes 2 loaves.

Toffee Banana Bread

¾ cup butter-flavored shortening
1½ cups sugar
4 eggs
1½ teaspoons vanilla extract
🐦 🐦 🐦
3 cups all-purpose flour
1½ teaspoons baking soda
1½ teaspoons salt
🐦 🐦 🐦
4 to 5 large ripe bananas, mashed
1 cup toffee bits (such as crumbled
  Heath Bars)

Grease and lightly flour 2 loaf pans. In a mixing bowl cream together the shortening and sugar. Add the eggs and vanilla, and mix until creamy. In a separate bowl combine the flour, baking soda, and salt. Blend the dry ingredients into the creamed mixture. Fold in the mashed bananas and the toffee bits. Pour the mixture into the prepared pans. Bake in a 350° oven for 1 hour.
Makes 2 loaves.

🐦 🐦 🐦 🐦 🐦

Mountain Mudslide

½ cup margarine
1 cup all-purpose flour
1 cup chopped pecans
🐦 🐦 🐦
1 8-ounce package cream cheese,
  softened
1 cup confectioners' sugar
1 cup Cool Whip
🐦 🐦 🐦
1 3-ounce package instant vanilla
  pudding
1 3-ounce package instant chocolate
  pudding
2 cups cold milk
🐦 🐦 🐦
1 cup Cool Whip
Grated chocolate for garnish

In a food processor with a metal blade blend together the margarine, flour, and pecans. Press into a 9x13-inch pan. Bake in a 350° oven for 20 minutes. Cool.

In a medium bowl blend the cream cheese and confectioners' sugar. Fold in 1 cup of Cool Whip. Spread the mixture over the cooled crust. In a large bowl combine the puddings and milk. Refrigerate for a few minutes to thicken slightly. Spread over the cream cheese layer. Spread the remaining Cool Whip over the pudding layer and sprinkle with grated chocolate. Chill for several hours.
Serves 12.

The San Sophia

330 West Pacific Avenue
Post Office Box 1825
Telluride, Colorado 81435
(303) 728-3001
(800) 537-4781

The San Sophia, Telluride's newest luxury inn, is named after a Russian princess. Situated just one block from the Oak Street ski lift, it adjoins the historic downtown. Guests can view the Telluride Valley from the inn's observatory tower. In each of sixteen luxury rooms the San Sophia features period furnishings, brass beds, private baths, cable television, and antique phones. It has covered parking, a gazebo with sunken Jacuzzi, and an English garden. The inn serves full gourmet breakfasts. The Telluride area has a full schedule of recreational and cultural events.

Dianne's High Altitude Coffeecake

This recipe is designed for 8,954 feet, the altitude of Telluride.

6 tablespoons melted butter
1 cup brown sugar
2 teaspoons cinnamon
¼ cup chopped nuts

ᴥ ᴥ ᴥ

½ cup butter, softened
¾ cup sugar
3 eggs
2 cups all-purpose flour
½ teaspoon baking powder
½ teaspoon baking soda
1 cup sour cream
1 teaspoon vanilla extract
Confectioners' sugar frosting

In a small bowl combine the melted butter, brown sugar, cinnamon, and nuts. Grease a 9-inch tube pan and pour some of the brown sugar mixture in the bottom. In a large bowl combine ½ cup of butter, the sugar, eggs, flour, baking powder, baking soda, sour cream, and vanilla. Stir until well blended. Pour the batter over the topping in the tube pan, and top with remaining topping. Swirl through the topping with a knife. Bake in a 350° oven for 45 minutes. Turn out and drizzle with a confectioners' sugar frosting.

Serves 12.

Sophia's Cappuccino Cake

¾ cup oil
½ cup honey
¾ cup plus 2 tablespoons sugar
4 large eggs
½ cup whole milk
½ cup sour cream

ᴥ ᴥ ᴥ

2 cups all-purpose flour
½ cup cocoa
2 teaspoons baking powder
1 teaspoon baking soda

1 tablespoon instant coffee granules
2 teaspoons cinnamon
¼ teaspoon nutmeg
¼ teaspoon cloves

ᴥ ᴥ ᴥ

Confectioners' sugar for topping

Grease a bundt pan. In a mixing bowl combine the first 6 ingredients with an electric mixer until thoroughly blended. In a separate bowl combine the remaining ingredients. Add the dry ingredients to the liquid mixture, beating until just blended. Pour the batter into the prepared pan. Bake in a 350° oven for about 1 hour, or until a toothpick inserted in the center comes out clean. Allow to cool in the pan, then remove to a cake rack to finish cooling. Sprinkle with sifted confectioners' sugar.

Serves 12.

The San Sophia

Dianne's Explosive Almond Cake

¾ cup finely chopped blanched
   almonds
3½ cups unbleached all-purpose
   flour
1 tablespoon plus 1 teaspoon
   baking powder
½ teaspoon salt

   ⁿ⁣ ⁊ ⁊ ⁊

2 cups heavy cream
1 teaspoon vanilla extract
1 teaspoon almond extract
1¾ cups sugar
4 large eggs
¾ cup chopped almonds

Thoroughly butter 2 loaf pans. Coat the bottom and sides of each pan with the finely chopped almonds. In a large bowl sift together the flour, baking powder, and salt. In a separate bowl whip the cream until it holds its shape. Stir in the vanilla, almond extract, and sugar. Beat in the eggs, one at a time. Stir in the dry ingredients until just blended. Pour ¼ of the batter in the bottom of each prepared pan. Sprinkle with half of the chopped almonds, and fill with the remaining batter. Smooth the top and sprinkle with the remaining almonds. (The batter will expand more than you think, so don't panic if the pans don't seem full enough!) Bake in a 350° oven for 1 hour or until a toothpick inserted in the center comes out clean. Cool in the pans before turning onto a cake rack. Cut into ½-inch slices to serve.

Serves 16.

Liz's Vermont in Telluride

¼ cup butter
2 medium onions, minced
5 small apples, cored and diced
2 tablespoons minced parsley
18 slices bacon, cooked and
   crumbled

   ⁊ ⁊ ⁊

¼ cup butter
18 eggs, beaten
¾ cup chopped pecans

In a large skillet melt ¼ cup of butter and sauté the onions, apple, and parsley. Add the crumbled bacon and remove the mixture from the heat. In a separate skillet melt the remaining butter. Add the beaten eggs and cook until they begin to set. Fold in the bacon mixture and scramble to the desired consistency. Sprinkle with pecans.

Note: Seasoning is flexible. Nutmeg or white pepper are good. The most adventuresome choice is to dribble a thin stream of maple syrup over each serving. Crumbled Blue Stilton cheese is excellent, as well.

Serves up to 18.

Connecticut

Sanford/Pond House

20 Main Street North
Bridgewater, Connecticut 06752
(203) 355-4677

A gracious Federal-Greek Revival mansion built in 1845, Sanford/Pond House features stately bedrooms with sitting rooms or sitting areas, all with private baths. A continental breakfast is served.

Apple Pineapple Bread

3 cups all-purpose flour
2 teaspoons baking soda
½ teaspoon salt
½ teaspoon baking powder
¾ cup chopped walnuts
1½ teaspoons cinnamon

ੜ ੜ ੜ

3 eggs
2 cups sugar
¾ cup oil
2 teaspoons vanilla extract
1 8-ounce can crushed pineapple
2 cups shredded apple

Grease and flour two 9x5-inch loaf pans. In a medium bowl combine the flour, baking soda, salt, baking powder, chopped walnuts, and cinnamon. Set aside. In a large mixing bowl beat the eggs lightly and add the sugar, oil, and vanilla. Beat until creamy. Stir in the pineapple with its juice and the apples. Add the dry ingredients, stirring just until moistened. Spoon the batter into the prepared loaf pans. Bake in a 350° oven for 1 hour or until a toothpick inserted in the center comes out clean.

Makes 2 loaves.

Tollgate Hill Inn and Restaurant

Route 202
Litchfield, Connecticut 06759
(203) 482-6116

Find stylish slumber at the Tollgate Hill Inn. An authentic pre-Revolutionary War inn, its twenty rooms, all with private baths, feature queen-size beds and have air conditioning, telephones, and color television. The inn's kitchen has won several culinary awards, and guests enjoy the gracious quiet of two dining areas: the tavern and the formal dining area. A true country inn experience will be enjoyed here.

ੜ ੜ ੜ ੜ ੜ

Pumpkin Pudding
with Orange Sauce

2 cups cooked mashed pumpkin
2 eggs, beaten
1 cup brown sugar
1½ tablespoons butter, softened
1 cup milk
1 teaspoon baking soda
½ teaspoon nutmeg
½ teaspoon cinnamon
½ teaspoon salt
1 cup bread crumbs
½ cup golden raisins
½ cup chopped pecans

ੜ ੜ ੜ

¾ cup sugar
¼ teaspoon salt
1 cup heavy cream
½ cup fresh orange juice
¼ cup butter
4 teaspoons lemon juice
4 teaspoons orange rind

ੜ ੜ ੜ

Whipped cream and mint sprigs for garnish

Grease a 9-inch square baking dish. In a large bowl beat together the pumpkin, eggs, brown sugar, 1½ tablespoons butter, and milk. In a separate bowl combine the baking soda, nutmeg, cinnamon, ½ teaspoon salt, and bread crumbs. Add the dry ingredients to the pumpkin mixture, blending well. Fold in the raisins and pecans. Pour into the prepared dish. Bake in a 400° oven for about 30 minutes, until the pudding comes away from the sides of the pan.

In a medium saucepan combine the sugar and ¼ teaspoon salt, and gradually add the cream. Place the saucepan over low heat and cook until thickened, stirring constantly. Remove from the heat. Blend in the remaining ingredients.

With a 4-inch cookie cutter, cut 4 circles from the pudding. Cut each circle in half. Pour a small amount of sauce on 4 serving plates. Arrange 2 half-circles on a plate with corners touching. Garnish with a small dollop of whipped cream and a mint sprig.

Serves 4.

Highland Farm

Highland Farm

Highland Avenue
New Hartford, Connecticut 06057
(203) 379-6029

Built in 1879, Highland Farm Bed and Breakfast is a grand old Victorian lodging with fourteen gables. With rooms filled with antiques with an Oriental flair, Highland Farm is situated on a secluded hilltop in New Hartford. A hearty breakfast is served each morning. The area offers a variety of year-round activities.

Cranberry Walnut Bread

    2 cups all-purpose flour
    3 teaspoons baking powder
    ½ teaspoon salt
    1 cup sugar
    1 cup cranberries
    1 cup chopped walnuts
    1 egg
    ¾ cup milk
    ¼ cup butter
    1 teaspoon vanilla extract

Grease a 1½-quart loaf pan. In a large bowl stir together the flour, baking powder, and salt. Stir in the sugar, cranberries, and walnuts. In a small bowl lightly beat the egg, and add the milk, butter, and vanilla. Add the milk mixture to the dry ingredients and stir until moistened. Pour the batter into the prepared pan. Bake in a 350° oven for 55 to 60 minutes or until light brown. Cool on a rack for 10 minutes before removing the loaf from the pan. Cool completely. Wrap well and store for several hours before cutting.

Serves 8.

The Palmer Inn

25 Church Street
Noank, Connecticut 06340
(203) 572-9000

The Palmer Inn, built by Palmer Shipyard craftsmen at the turn of the century, is an inn with old traditions. Local artisans assisted in the restoration, which included period wallpaper and brass fixtures. Each guest room has been individually furnished with a collection of antiques and family heirlooms. Guests may enjoy reading in the library, conversing in the parlor, or playing backgammon by the fireplace.

Situated only a short drive from the restaurants and shops of Mystic Village and Seaport, the Palmer Inn provides an elegant continental breakfast and is accessible by car, plane, ferry, train, or boat.

French Toast à la Palmer Inn

8 eggs
1 cup milk
½ teaspoon cinnamon
½ teaspoon nutmeg
½ teaspoon allspice
⅛ teaspoon ginger
1 teaspoon vanilla extract
2 loaves French bread, cut in 1-inch slices

❧ ❧ ❧

1½ cups raisins
¼ cup orange juice
12 slices bacon, cooked and crumbled
1½ cups chopped walnuts
Hot maple syrup

In a shallow bowl combine the eggs, milk, spices and vanilla. Dip the bread in the mixture, coating both sides. In a cast iron skillet melt a small amount of margarine and brown each slice of toast. Keep the cooked slices warm during preparation in a 250° oven. Before serving sprinkle with raisins that have been soaked in the orange juice, crumbled bacon, and chopped walnuts. Pour the maple syrup over the entire platter and serve.
Serves 12.

The Palmer Inn's Apple Pie

This pie was named "Connecticut's Best" at *Yankee* magazine's "Great New England Inns Apple Pie Contest."

2 cups all-purpose flour
⅔ cup shortening
1 teaspoon salt
1 tablespoon cider vinegar
4 to 5 tablespoons ice cold water

❧ ❧ ❧

½ cup sugar
½ cup light brown sugar
¼ cup orange juice
3 tablespoon all-purpose flour
1 tablespoon dark corn syrup
¼ teaspoon nutmeg
½ teaspoon cinnamon
⅛ teaspoon ginger
⅛ teaspoon allspice
6 cups peeled, cored, and thinly sliced Macoun or Cortland apples

In a large bowl stir together 2 cups of flour and salt. Cut in the shortening with a pastry blender. Add the vinegar and sprinkle with the water and stir until the flour is moistened and leaves the side of the bowl. Divide the dough in half and reserve half for the top crust. Roll the remaining dough to ⅛-inch thickness, fold into quarters, and place in a glass pie plate. Unfold and press into the pie plate to form the crust.

In a large bowl combine the sugar, brown sugar, orange juice, 3 tablespoons of flour, corn syrup, and spices. Fold in the apples. Spoon the apple mixture into the pie shell. Roll the remaining crust to ⅛-inch thickness, slit, and place on top of the apple mixture. Bake in a 450° oven for 15 minutes, reduce the heat to 350° and bake for 35 minutes.
Serves 8.

Manor House: The Inn at Norfolk

Post Office Box 447, Maple Avenue
Norfolk, Connecticut 06058
(203) 542-5690

The Manor House is an elegant and romantic Victorian bed and breakfast inn. Guests are surrounded by Old World refinement while they enjoy baronial living and breakfast rooms with Tiffany and leaded glass windows. A six-foot fireplace in the foyer invites relaxing moments for quiet or conversation, and a handsomely carved and cherry-paneled staircase leads to the antique-decorated guest rooms.

❧ ❧ ❧ ❧ ❧

Manor House: The Inn at Norfolk

Orange Waffles

2 cups all-purpose flour
3 teaspoons baking powder
2 tablespoons sugar
½ teaspoon salt
4 eggs, lightly beaten
1 cup milk
4 tablespoons melted butter
3 tablespoons grated orange rind

In a large bowl sift together the dry ingredients. In a separate bowl combine the eggs, milk, butter, and orange rind. Add the milk mixture to the dry ingredients half at a time, beating well after each addition. Heat a waffle iron. Pour about ¾ to 1 cup of batter at a time onto the hot iron and bake until golden brown.

Serves 8.

Lemon Butter Chive Sauce

This sauce is delicious served over poached eggs on English muffins.

⅓ cup butter
2 tablespoons finely chopped chives
1 tablespoon lemon juice
½ teaspoon salt
Dash pepper

In a saucepan melt the butter and add the remaining ingredients. Beat thoroughly. Serve the sauce while hot.

Makes about ½ cup.

Mountain View Inn

Route 272
Norfolk, Connecticut 06058
(203) 542-5595

Nestled high in the Berkshire Hills overlooking Norfolk, the Mountain View Inn is a Victorian house with eleven guest rooms (most with private baths) and loads of hospitality. Guests can choose one- or two-bedroom accommodations, each individually appointed and with their own elegance. Nearby is timeless Norfolk with its village green, bell towers, and post card landscapes, as well as many outdoor sports. At the inn guests can enjoy tea and conversation in the parlor, and delight in bountiful breakfasts, and casual evening fare in the lounge. Gourmet dining may be held at the inn's Maxfield's restaurant.

Strawberry Oat Bread

3 eggs
1 cup sugar
1 cup oil
1 tablespoon vanilla extract
2 cups all-purpose flour
1 cup quick cooking oats
1 tablespoon cinnamon
1 teaspoon salt
1 teaspoon baking soda
½ teaspoon baking powder
2 cups crushed strawberries

Grease and flour two 4x8-inch loaf pans. In a large bowl beat the eggs, sugar, oil, and vanilla. In a separate bowl combine the flour, oats, cinnamon, salt, baking soda, and baking powder. Add the dry ingredients to the egg mixture, blending well. Fold in the strawberries. Pour the batter into the prepared pans. Bake in a 350° oven for 1 hour, or until a toothpick inserted in the center comes out clean.

Makes 2 loaves.

Recipe courtesy Chef James Bain.

Derby Pie

3 cups sugar
½ cup all-purpose flour
6 eggs
1½ cups butter, melted
3 cups chocolate chips
3 cups pecans or walnuts
6 tablespoons bourbon
2 10-inch unbaked pie shells
Whipped cream or ice cream

In a large bowl combine the sugar, flour, eggs, and butter. Add the chocolate chips, pecans, and bourbon. Pour into the pie shells. Bake in a 350° oven for 30 minutes or until done. The pies should be chewy, not runny. Serve warm with whipped cream or ice cream.

Serves 16.

Recipe courtesy Chef James Bain.

The Old Lyme Inn

Lyme Street
Old Lyme, Connecticut 06371
(203) 434-2600

The warm exterior of a fine old nineteenth century home, typifying New England's charming colonial residences, welcomes travelers and diners alike to the elegance of the Old Lyme Inn. Situated on the main street in Old Lyme's historical district, the inn represents the classic traditions of excellence in dining and lodging that is the very heart of a small Connecticut town.

Built in the 1850s, the inn remained a working farm of some 300 acres and a private residence for 100 years. After several grim years as a down-on-its-heels restaurant, it has been restored to its former grandeur. The original ornate iron fence, tree-shaded lawn, and banistered front porch greet each guest. Once inside, the curly maple staircase, hand-painted murals, and antique furnishings remind one of the grace of America's past and the warmth and promise of its future.

Salmon and Sole Crepes

⅛ cup minced shallots
Butter
All-purpose flour
¼ cup white wine
¼ cup fish stock

🍃 🍃 🍃

½ cup heavy cream

🍃 🍃 🍃

½ pound salmon
½ pound sole
1 10-ounce package spinach
1 teaspoon tarragon
Salt and pepper to taste

🍃 🍃 🍃

4 prepared crepes

Sauté half of the shallots in butter and coat with a pinch of flour. Add the wine and fish stock. Reduce by half. Add the cream, and reduce slightly. Sauté the remaining shallots. Add the fish, spinach, seasonings, and sauce. Simmer until the fish is cooked. The mixture should not be runny. Fill the crepes with some of the mixture, roll, and coat with the remaining sauce.
Serves 4.

Cornish Hens with Basil and Walnut Sauce

1 bunch fresh basil (approx. 1 ounce)
½ cup grated Parmesan cheese
1 clove garlic
Salt and pepper to taste
¼ cup shelled walnuts

🍃 🍃 🍃

2 Cornish hens, split and quartered
Butter

🍃 🍃 🍃

½ cup chicken stock
½ cup heavy cream

Basil leaves for garnish
Walnut pieces for garnish

To make pesto combine the first 5 ingredients in a food processor and purée to make a smooth paste.
Cook the hens in butter until tender, cooking legs additional time if needed. Remove to a platter. Drain the grease from the sauté pan and add the chicken stock. Reduce by half. Add the cream, and reduce by half or until of sauce consistency. Swirl in 2 tablespoons of the basil and walnut pesto. Adjust the seasonings. Pour the sauce over the hens. Garnish with basil leaves and walnut pieces.
Serves 4.

Ginger Apple Praline Pie

6 Golden Delicious apples
⅔ to 1 cup sugar
¼ cup King Arthur's flour
½ teaspoon grated lemon peel
½ teaspoon ginger
Dash salt

🍃 🍃 🍃

½ cup packed brown sugar
½ cup flour
¾ cup chopped pecans
¼ cup melted butter

🍃 🍃 🍃

1 9-inch unbaked pie shell (recipe follows)

Core and slice the apples. Toss the apple slices with the sugar, ¼ cup of flour, lemon peel, ginger, and salt.
To make the pecan praline topping, combine the brown sugar, ½ cup of flour, pecans, and melted butter.

The Old Lyme Inn

Sprinkle ¼ of the pecan topping in the bottom of the pie shell. Arrange the apples in a semi-layered fashion. Cover the top with the remaining pecan topping. Bake at 400° for 40 minutes. Serve warm or cold.

Serves 6 to 8.

Pastry

**3 cups sifted all-purpose flour
1 cup Crisco shortening
½ cup cold water
¾ tablespoon salt**

Mix the flour and shortening together until it resembles wet sand. Form a well in the center and add water and salt. Form into a ball as quickly as possible.

Cover and refrigerate for 1 hour. Divide the dough into 3 balls. Reserve 2 for later use. Roll 1 ball out into ⅛ to ¼-inch thickness.

Makes 3 9-inch pie shells.

Yesterday's Yankee

Route 44 East
Salisbury, Connecticut 06068
(203) 435-9539

The first section of Yesterday's Yankee was built in 1744, making it the only original Cape Cod cottage in the village of Salisbury. Much of the house retains its original colonial feeling, with low ceilings, wide board floors, whitewashed walls, and small paned windows. The three bedrooms are air conditioned and share a modern bath. Gourmet or the full breakfast may be enjoyed on the redwood deck on warm mornings. Because of the many recreational, cultural, and shopping opportunities nearby, Yesterday's Yankee is open year-round.

Yankee Granola

This granola is super on ice cream or blended with crumb toppings for cakes, pies, or baked puddings.

**3 cups rolled oats
¼ cup wheat germ
¼ cup dry roasted sunflower seeds
¾ cup slivered almonds**

 🍃 🍃 🍃

**⅓ cup honey
⅓ cup peanut butter
½ teaspoon vanilla extract (or almond extract)
¾ cup raisins**

In a large bowl mix together the oats, wheat germ, sunflower seeds, and almonds. In a saucepan heat the honey and peanut butter until blended, remove from the heat, and add the vanilla. Stir the honey mixture into the dry ingredients until well mixed. Spread in the bottom of a broiler pan. Bake in a 300° oven for 25 minutes, stirring every 5 minutes until evenly browned. Cool completely and add the raisins.

Makes 5 cups, or 20 ¼-cup servings.

Fresh Peach Soup Alexander

**6 ripe peaches, peeled and pitted (plums or nectarines may be added)
¼ cup brown sugar
¼ cup cream sherry
1½ cups lowfat vanilla yogurt
Mint sprigs or fresh blueberries for garnish**

In a food processor purée the fruit. Add the brown sugar and sherry, and blend thoroughly. Cover and store the purée in the refrigerator overnight or until needed. Add the yogurt and stir until smooth. Garnish with a mint sprig or fresh blueberries.

Serves 6.

Yesterday's Yankee

The Inn at Woodstock Hill

94 Plaine Hill Road
South Woodstock, Connecticut

Post Office Box 98
South Woodstock, Connecticut 06267
(203) 928-0528

The Inn at WOODSTOCK HILL

The Inn at Woodstock Hill began life in the early nineteenth century as a gentleman's country estate. Constructed in elegant Christopher Wren style, it rests on its own fourteen acres in restored elegance. The nineteen suites and guest rooms (each with private bath, TV, and telephone) are reminiscent of an English country house. Wood-burning fireplaces add their warmth to six of the rooms.

Tea is served in the afternoon; lunch and dinner are served in the four-star dining room or on the outdoor terrace. This spectacular inn is ideal for business seminars and conferences, weddings, as well as for family travel.

🐚 🐚 🐚 🐚 🐚

Woodstock Swordfish

1 pound center-cut swordfish
   🐚 🐚 🐚
3 tablespoons lemon juice
Dash salt
Pepper to taste
Rose paprika powder
   🐚 🐚 🐚
Olive oil
   🐚 🐚 🐚
2 tablespoons butter
2 green onions, cut up
2 teaspoons chopped garlic
½ teaspoon lemon pepper
1 teaspoon pink peppercorns
4 tablespoons Riesling white wine
1 small bunch dill, chopped

Wash the fish well, remove the skin, and cut into 4 even-sized fillets. In a small bowl combine the lemon juice, salt, pepper, and paprika. Marinate the swordfish in the mixture for about 30 minutes. Brush the fish lightly with olive oil and grill on a hot grill to mark on both sides. Do not cook the fish completely.

In a skillet melt the butter, and add the onions, garlic, lemon pepper, and peppercorns. Sauté for 1 or 2 minutes, then add the wine. Bring the mixture to a boil, and place the swordfish in the sauce. Simmer for 3 minutes, basting the fish constantly. Remove the fish and serve with ½ tablespoon of sauce on each serving. Sprinkle with dill.

Serves 4.

Delaware

The Savannah Inn: Bed and Breakfast

330 Savannah Road
Lewes, Delaware 19958
(302) 645-5592

The Savannah Inn is situated in the town of Lewes, the first town in the first state, in a quiet and relaxing environment near major ocean resorts. Comfortable bedrooms with double beds await guests, and a large screened and glass porch offers comfort for sitting. Breakfast is served buffet style; the cuisine is vegetarian. The menu includes bran muffins or other homemade breads with jams, granola, fresh fruit, juices, and a variety of hot beverages. The Savannah Inn is open during the summer and fall seasons as a bed and breakfast; rooms may be rented without breakfast at other times.

Sunday Morning Breakfast Cake

1 cup milk
1 tablespoon butter
4 eggs
2 cups sugar
2 teaspoons vanilla extract
2 cups all-purpose flour
2 tablespoons baking powder
½ teaspoon salt

🐌 🐌 🐌

½ cup butter
¼ cup cream
1⅓ cups brown sugar
2 teaspoons vanilla extract
2 cups chopped pecans

Grease two 9-inch square cake pans. In a saucepan over low heat combine the milk and 1 tablespoon of butter. Heat thoroughly. In a bowl beat the eggs until thick, and beat in the sugar and 2 teaspoons of vanilla. Sift together the flour, baking powder, and salt, and stir into the egg mixture. Pour the hot milk mixture into the batter and mix quickly. Pour the batter into the prepared pans. Bake in a 350° oven for 25 minutes.

While the cakes are baking, prepare the topping. In a mixing bowl cream together ½ cup of butter and the cream. Add the brown sugar and 2 teaspoons of vanilla. Fold in the pecans. When the cakes are done, spread the topping on the warm cakes. Heat the cakes under the broiler to brown the topping. Serve hot.

Serves 8 to 12.

🐌 🐌 🐌 🐌 🐌

Vintage Pie

Pastry for 2-crust 9-inch pie
1 quart Concord grapes
¾ cup sugar
1½ tablespoons lemon juice
Grated rind of ½ orange
1½ tablespoons instant tapioca
½ cup chopped pecans

Place half of the pastry in a 9-inch pie plate. Reserve the dough for the top crust.

Wash the grapes, and skin them by squeezing over a bowl to pop out the pulp. Reserve the skins. In a saucepan simmer the pulp just until it begins to soften and the seeds start to separate. Rub the pulp through a sieve and discard the seeds. In a food processor with a metal blade, chop the skins (but do not purée them). Combine the skins, pulp, sugar, lemon juice, orange rind, and tapioca. Fold in the pecans. Pour the mixture into the pie shell. Roll the reserved dough out and cut into strips. Arrange the strips in a lattice pattern over the filling. Flute the edges of the crust with 2 fingers or a fork. Bake in a 400° oven for 10 minutes, reduce the heat to 350°, and bake for 20 minutes.

Serves 6 to 8.

Date Pudding

2 tablespoons butter
3 slices good quality white bread
⅔ cup chopped pecans
⅔ cup finely chopped dates
1 egg
¾ cup sugar
¾ cup milk
1 teaspoon baking powder

❧ ❧ ❧

2 eggs, separated
1 cup confectioners' sugar
2 tablespoons bourbon
1 cup whipping cream

In an 8-inch square pan melt the butter in a warm oven. Tear the bread into small bits and spread in the pan. Press the pecans and dates into the bread. Set aside. In a small bowl beat one egg. Beat in the sugar, milk, and baking powder. Pour the mixture over the bread mixture. Bake in a 350° oven for 40 to 50 minutes, until brown.

In a small bowl beat two egg yolks, and add the sugar and bourbon. In a separate bowl beat the egg whites, and fold into the egg yolk mixture. Whip the cream and fold into the mixture. Chill. Serve the chilled topping over the warm pudding.

Serves 6 to 8.

Chutney

4 pounds mangoes or peaches
2 quarts cider vinegar
❧ ❧ ❧
4 cups sugar

❧ ❧ ❧

2 tablespoons white mustard seed
1 tablespoon ground dried chili
    pepper
1½ cups raisins
1 clove garlic, crushed
❧ ❧ ❧
1 pound preserved ginger in syrup,
    chopped

Peel and chop the mangoes. In a stockpot or large saucepan combine the mangoes and 1 quart of vinegar. Boil the mixture for 20 minutes. In a separate pot boil the remaining vinegar with the sugar until it becomes a thick syrup. Pour most of the mango liquid into the syrup and boil until thick. Add the mangoes, mustard seed, chili pepper, raisins, and garlic, and cook for 30 minutes. Add the chopped ginger and its syrup and simmer for 10 minutes. Pour into sterilized jars and seal. Set aside to cool. Place the chutney in a sunny spot in your kitchen for several days.

Makes 4 to 5 pints, or about 70 servings of 2 tablespoons each.

🦆 🦆 🦆 🦆 🦆

Jefferson House

The Strand at the Wharf
New Castle, Delaware 19720
(303) 323-0999
(303) 322-8944

This elegant two-hundred-year-old riverfront inn is packed with charm and history. Situated in the center of the historical district, it is near all the historic buildings, museums, and parks of colonial New Castle. Brick and cobblestone streets, hidden alleys, old churches and graveyards, quaint shops, and wonderful restaurants abound in this scenic area. Guests may wish to watch the impressive ship traffic from the back yard or kayak on the Delaware River themselves. The three charming units feature private baths. The one called the Hearth has its own nineteenth-century fireplace; the Porch has its own screened-in porch; and the Speak-Easy is an efficiency apartment.

The Tastiest, Healthiest Waffle in the World

¼ cup whole wheat pancake mix
¼ cup oat bran
1 teaspoon "egg replacer" (available
    at health food stores)
½ cup apple juice
¼ to ⅓ cup pecans, chopped

In a medium bowl mix all of the ingredients. Heat a waffle iron and spray with cooking spray. Pour the batter onto the hot iron and bake for 30 seconds longer than the waffle iron manufacturer's directions suggest.

Makes 1 waffle.

The Savannah Inn: Bed and Breakfast

Cantwell House

107 High Street
Odessa, Delaware 19730
(302) 378-4179

Built in the 1840s, the Cantwell House was completely refurbished and opened as a bed and breakfast in April 1983. The three-story home has three guest accommodations, two which share a bath. The third-story room affords a view of Odessa from all four sides. An important trading port on the Delaware River until the 1890s, Odessa has fine examples of architecture from several periods. A continental breakfast is served.

Ham & Cheese Crescents

1 8-ounce package crescent rolls
8 slices boiled ham
8 teaspoons orange or lemon
    marmalade (optional)
½ cup coarsely grated Monterey
    Jack cheese

Separate the crescent rolls into 8 triangles, according to the package directions. Place 1 slice of ham on each triangle, folding the ham to fit. Spread with marmalade and sprinkle with grated Monterey Jack cheese. Roll the triangles according to the package directions. Place on an ungreased cookie sheet. Bake in a 400° oven for 10 to 12 minutes.
Serves 4.

Grenadine Fruit Mélange

1 cup cranberries
½ cup water
⅓ cup sugar
¼ cup currants
1 teaspoon lemon juice
1 teaspoon grenadine syrup
4 plums, pitted and cut into thin
    wedges
6 kiwi fruit, sliced and cut into
    halves
Fresh mint

In a saucepan combine the cranberries, water, sugar, currants, lemon juice, and grenadine syrup. Cool and stir over medium heat for 5 to 7 minutes, or until the mixture is the consistency of a thin syrup. Cool the mixture slightly. In a bowl combine the cranberry mixture and plums. Mix well, and refrigerate overnight stirring occasionally. Just before serving, stir in the kiwi and garnish with mint.
Serves 8.

Banana Boats

1 cup pancake mix
1 tablespoon sugar
1 egg
⅔ cup milk

6 medium bananas
Oil
Confectioners' sugar

In a bowl combine the first 4 ingredients. Stir until the mixture is well blended, and set aside.

Heat oil in a deep fryer or deep skillet. Peel the bananas and cut into 1½-inch pieces. Dip each piece into batter and drop into the hot oil. Fry until golden, turning once. Drain on paper towels, and sprinkle with confectioners' sugar.
Serves 4.

Sliced Mangoes
with Candied Ginger

½ cup plus 1 tablespoon water
7½ tablespoons sugar
Peel of 1 lime, cut into thin strips
1 teaspoon chopped crystalized
    ginger
2 tablespoons fresh lime juice

2 mangoes, peeled, pitted and
    sliced ¼-inch thick
1½ tablespoons finely diced
    crystalized ginger

In a saucepan over low heat cook the water, 6½ tablespoons sugar, half of the lime peel, and 1 teaspoon of ginger, stirring until the sugar dissolves. Bring the mixture to a boil. Reduce the heat and simmer for 10 minutes. Cool the syrup completely. Strain the syrup into a bowl, pressing the lime peel and ginger. Add the lime juice. Cover and refrigerate for at least 30 minutes, or up to 2 days.

Toss the remaining lime peel with 1 tablespoon of sugar. Arrange the mangoes in an overlapping pattern on a plate. Drizzle the syrup over the mangoes. Sprinkle with diced ginger and sugared lime peel.
Serves 2.

Sparkling Minted Fruit Mélange

1½ cups unpeeled chopped Golden
    Delicious apples
1½ cups fresh pineapple chunks
1 cup halved seedless red grapes
1 tablespoon chopped fresh mint
1 cup peeled sliced kiwi fruit
    (about 3)
¾ cup sparkling apple juice, chilled
Fresh mint sprigs

In a medium bowl combine the first 4 ingredients and toss gently. Cover and chill for 30 minutes. Line 6 individual compotes with kiwi. Divide the apple mixture evenly among the dishes, and drizzle each with 2 tablespoons of apple juice. Garnish with fresh mint sprigs.
Serves 6.

Banana Splits
with Apricot Cream

2 cups lowfat cottage cheese
3 tablespoons apricot jam
4 bananas
1 cup sliced strawberries
1 cup blueberries
Toasted wheat germ or toasted
    almonds

In a food processor or blender combine the cottage cheese and apricot jam, and blend until completely smooth. Transfer to a bowl and refrigerate, covered, overnight. Peel the bananas and split each lengthwise. Arrange the bananas on 4 serving plates. Spoon some of the apricot cream over each banana. Top with strawberries and blueberries, and sprinkle with wheat germ or almonds.
    Serves 4.

Freezer Strawberry Jam

1 quart ripe strawberries
4 cups sugar
2 tablespoons lemon juice
½ bottle Certo Fruit Pectin

Crush enough of the strawberries to measure 1¾ cups. In a bowl combine the fruit and sugar. In a small bowl combine the lemon juice and Certo, and stir into the fruit. Continue stirring for 3 minutes, until the sugar is dissolved. Pour quickly into jars or plastic containers and cover at once. Allow the jam to sit at room temperature for up to 24 hours. Store in the freezer. For use within 3 days the jam may be kept in the refrigerator.
    Makes about 4 cups.

The Corner Cupboard Inn

50 Park Avenue
Rehoboth Beach, Delaware 19971
(302) 227-8553

The Corner Cupboard Inn, "the inn that was in before inns were in," has been in operation for more than fifty years. The eighteen rooms, all with private baths and air conditioning, are in two houses and an additional small building to the rear of each. While the decor might be termed "early American attic," some very nice antiques are included. The inn is one and one-half blocks from the beach, which is the main attraction. Breakfast and dinner, which are served in the restaurant, are included in the summer rates; and the restaurant is open to the public. During the rest of the year, the rates include breakfast only.

Peach Crisp

4 cups sliced peaches
1 cup brown sugar
1 cup all-purpose flour
½ teaspoon cinnamon
⅓ cup butter

Arrange the peaches in an ovenproof casserole dish. Mix the remaining ingredients together and sprinkle over the peaches. Bake in a 375° oven for 30 to 45 minutes.
    Serves 6.

Lord & Hamilton Seaside Inn

20 Brooklyn Avenue
Rehoboth Beach, Delaware 19971
(302) 227-6960

This nineteenth-century Victorian house, situated on a plot of land purchased by the founder of Rehoboth Methodist Campground, is flanked by porches on three sides. Restored as a bed and breakfast, it is furnished with family heirlooms and antiques. Each of the seven guest rooms, named in honor of a famous literary person, is cheerful and inviting.

Delaware Slippery Dumplings

2 cups all-purpose flour
2 teaspoons baking powder
¼ teaspoon salt
3 tablespoons shortening
½ cup hot water

🌿 🌿 🌿

2 10¾-ounce cans condensed
    chicken broth
1 cup water
1 tablespoon butter

In a large bowl combine the flour, baking powder, and salt. Cut in the shortening with a pastry blender until the mixture forms fine crumbs. Stir enough hot water into the flour mixture to make a firm but manageable dough.
    In a 4-quart saucepan, combine the broth and water and heat to boiling. Add the butter. Let the butter melt and float to the top of the broth.
    On a floured board, roll out the dough to ¹⁄₁₆-inch thickness. Cut into

2-inch squares. Drop the dumplings one at a time into the boiling broth. Reheat the broth to boiling over high heat. Reduce the heat to medium and cook dumplings uncovered until tender; about 15 minutes. Spoon the dumplings into a serving dish with some of the cooking liquid and serve.

Serves 4 to 6.

Sussex Shrimp Dill Dip

¼ cup milk
¼ cup mayonnaise
2 tablespoons lemon juice
1 8-ounce package cream cheese
2 tablespoons finely chopped onion
½ teaspoon salt or to taste
½ teaspoon Tabasco sauce
1 teaspoon dried dill weed
1 cup shrimp, steamed and cleaned, finely chopped
Party crackers

In a large bowl gradually blend together the milk, mayonnaise, and lemon juice with the cream cheese. Beat until smooth. Add the onion, salt, dill weed, and Tabasco. Mix well. Stir in the shrimp and chill for 1 hour before serving. Serve with your favorite party crackers.

Makes about 2½ cups.

Lord and Hamilton Broccoli Salad

3 bunches broccoli
⅔ cup raisins
½ onion finely chopped
10 to 12 slices bacon, cooked and crumbled
½ cup sugar
1 cup mayonnaise
2 tablespoons vinegar

Wash the broccoli thoroughly and separate into small sprigs. In a large bowl mix the broccoli, raisins, finely chopped onion, and the crumbled bacon.

In a separate bowl mix together the sugar, mayonnaise, and vinegar until smooth. Pour over the broccoli mixture and stir until the dressing is thoroughly distributed. Refrigerate for several hours before serving. Arrange on individual salad plates with lettuce or in a large serving bowl.

Serves 6 to 8.

Winterthur Iced Tea

From the Winterthur archives.

1 gallon hot tea (not too strong)
½ cup maple syrup
¼ cup lemon juice
Lemon slices
Mint sprigs
Ice

Combine the tea and maple syrup. Set aside to cool. Refrigerate until thoroughly cold. Add the lemon juice, lemon slices, and ice. Place a mint sprig at the top of each glass.

Serves 10 to 15.

Lord and Hamilton Hot Buttered Rum

½ gallon apple cider
½ cup butter
9 cinnamon sticks
1½ cups rum

Heat the apple cider. Add the butter and 1 cinnamon stick. Heat slowly until the butter is melted. Turn off the heat and add the rum. Stir thoroughly.

Serve in mugs with cinnamon sticks.

Serves 8.

Oysters Delaware

1 pint oysters
3 slices bacon, chopped
4 tablespoons chopped onion
2 tablespoons chopped celery
1 teaspoon lemon juice
½ teaspoon salt
½ teaspoon Worcestershire sauce
⅛ teaspoon pepper
2 drops Tabasco sauce
1 cup Pepperidge Farm stuffing mix
Grated Swiss cheese

LORD & HAMILTON

SEASIDE INN

...a wrinkle in time...

Fry the bacon, onion, and celery until tender. Add the seasonings and mix well. Arrange the well drained oysters on a shallow baking dish. Spread the bacon mixture over the oysters. Sprinkle the dry stuffing mix over the oysters. Sprinkle lightly with the grated cheese. Bake in a 350° oven for 10 minutes or until lightly browned and bubbly.

Serves 4 to 6.

Mother's Cream of Crab Soup

1 small onion, minced
½ carrot, minced
½ stalk celery, minced
2 tablespoons butter
1 tablespoon all-purpose flour
1½ cups chicken stock

🍃 🍃 🍃

1 teaspoon basil
1 teaspoon thyme
1 teaspoon Old Bay Seasoning
1 bay leaf
¼ teaspoon salt
¼ teaspoon white pepper

🍃 🍃 🍃

2 cups cream
1 pound backfin crab meat
Crackers or homemade biscuits

In a 6-quart saucepan sauté the onion, carrot, and celery in the butter. Stir in the flour and gradually add the chicken stock. Stir in the seasonings and cook until slightly thickened. Add the cream and the crab meat and cook until heated. Serve with crackers or homemade biscuits.

Serves 4 to 6.

Small Wonder Bed and Breakfast

Post Office Box 25254
Wilmington, Delaware 19899
(302) 764-0789

At Small Wonder Bed and Breakfast, guests enjoy their stay in a modified Cape Cod home, decorated traditionally in Wedgewood blue with mauve and white highlights. Inn entertainment includes Small Wonder's Baldwin piano or organ, stereo, television, books, shuffleboard, table games, rebounder, exercise gym, and an exhibit of original paintings by Delaware artist Lloyd W. Kline.

Tomato Juice

6 quarts tomatoes, washed and chopped
2 small onions, chopped
2 stalks celery, chopped
2 tablespoons lemon juice
¾ cup sugar
5 teaspoons salt
10 to 12 whole cloves

In a large saucepan or stockpot cook all of the ingredients until the tomatoes are soft. Strain, and discard the skin and seeds. Bring the strained ingredients to a boil, pour into sterilized jars, and seal.

Makes about 6 pints.

Bacon Quiche

½ pound sliced bacon
1 9-inch unbaked pie shell
1½ cups grated Swiss cheese
3 eggs, well beaten
1 cup milk
½ cup cream
¼ teaspoon pepper
Dash cayenne
½ teaspoon powdered mustard

Cook and drain the bacon. Reserve one slice for garnish and crumble the remainder into the pie shell. Sprinkle the Swiss cheese over the bacon. Beat together the eggs, milk, cream, and seasonings. Pour the mixture into the pastry and decorate with the reserved bacon. Bake in a 375° oven for 45 minutes, or until firm and browned. Cool slightly and cut into wedges.

Serves 6 to 8.

District of Columbia

Adams Inn Bed and Breakfast

1744 Lanier Place, N.W.
Washington, D.C. 20009
(202) 745-3600

Adams Inn specializes in hospitable and comfortable surroundings in a personal atmosphere. The rooms are furnished homestyle. Some rooms have a private bath; the rest have a wash basin in the room and share a bath. Guests may relax and socialize in the sitting parlor. A continental breakfast is served in the spacious dining room.

The Adams Inn is just two miles north of the White House in the city's most interesting and diverse neighborhood. The inn is within walking distance of the three major convention hotels: the Shoreham, the Washington Hilton, and the Washington–Sheraton. Many of Washington's top-rated restaurants are only a block or two away, and boutiques, antiques, and international shops abound.

Prune Tea Ring

½ cup warm water (110° to 115°)
1 ¼-ounce package active dry yeast
½ cup warm milk
3 tablespoons shortening
2 tablespoons sugar
1½ teaspoons salt
1 egg
3 cups all-purpose flour

  ❧ ❧ ❧

1 cup chopped prunes
¼ teaspoon cinnamon
1 tablespoon lemon juice
¼ cup sugar
⅛ teaspoon salt

  ❧ ❧ ❧

4 teaspoons warm milk
1 cup sifted confectioners' sugar
¼ teaspoon vanilla extract

In a large bowl combine the water and yeast. Add the milk, shortening, 2 tablespoons of sugar, 1½ teaspoons of salt, egg, and flour. With an electric mixer at low speed beat the mixture just until blended. Let the dough stand for 15 minutes. In a saucepan combine the prunes, cinnamon, lemon juice, ¼ cup of sugar, and ⅛ teaspoon of salt. Simmer until thickened.

Grease a baking sheet. Roll the dough into a 14x12-inch rectangle. Spread the prune mixture over the dough and roll up jelly roll fashion. Arrange in a circle on the prepared baking sheet, joining the ends to form a ring. Cut deep slits almost to the center of the ring about 1 inch apart. Twist the slices cut side up. Let the ring rise for 45 minutes. Bake in a 350° oven for 30 minutes.

In a small bowl combine 4 teaspoons of milk, the confectioners' sugar, and vanilla. Frost the warm tea ring with the mixture.
Serves 6 to 8.

The Embassy Inn

1627 16th Street, N.W.
Washington, DC 20009
(202) 234-7800
(800) 423-9111

The Embassy Inn is a charming thirty-nine-room inn that is reminiscent of the Federal Colonial decor. All rooms have private bathrooms, color television, air conditioning, and telephone. A continental breakfast is served every morning, and in the evening guests are invited to relax with complimentary sherry in the cozy lobby. Situated in the heart of the city and convenient to tourist attractions and a variety of ethnic and traditional restaurants, the Embassy Inn provides its guests a warm atmosphere of book-lined walls, overstuffed armchairs, and a friendly, helpful staff.

Adams Inn

Blueberry Bread

¼ cup shortening
¾ cup sugar
2 teaspoons vanilla extract
1 egg
1½ cups all-purpose flour
1½ teaspoons baking powder
½ cup milk
1 cup blueberries

Grease an 8-inch square pan. In a large bowl cream together the shortening, sugar, and vanilla until fluffy.

Add the egg and beat well. Combine the flour and baking powder. Alternately add the flour and milk, beating well after each addition. Gently fold in the fresh blueberries, adding extra if desired. Pour the batter into the prepared pan. Bake in a 375° oven for 20 minutes. If a glass pan is used, reduce the oven temperature to 350°.

Serves 6 to 8.

The Windsor Inn

1842 16th Street, N.W.
Washington, DC 20009
(202) 667-0300
(800) 423-9111

The Windsor Inn boasts a beautiful art deco lobby complete with striking chandeliers and warm, mauve colors. The thirty-seven rooms and nine suites come with private baths, color television, air conditioning, and telephone. The board room is available for small luncheons, cocktail parties, or meetings. A continental breakfast is served each morning and complimentary sherry in the evening. Situated in the heart of Washington, near restaurants, shops, the Metro, the Adams-Morgan and Dupont Circle areas, the Windsor offers services normally associated with hotels.

Banana Bread

⅓ cup shortening
⅓ cup brown sugar
⅓ cup sugar
2 eggs
3 teaspoons vanilla extract
2 tablespoons milk
1 cup mashed very ripe bananas
1¾ cups all-purpose flour
1¼ teaspoons baking powder
½ teaspoon baking soda
¼ cup honey
¾ cup chopped nuts (walnuts and
    almonds are good)

Grease an 8x4-inch loaf pan. In a large bowl, beat together the shortening and sugars. Add the eggs, vanilla, and milk, mixing well. Alternately add the banana and flour, beating well after each addition. Add the baking powder and baking soda. Beat in the honey and nuts. Pour the batter into the prepared pan. Bake in a 350° oven for 60 to 65 minutes, or until a toothpick inserted in the center comes out clean. Cool in the pan for 10 minutes, and then remove to a wire rack to finish cooling.

Makes 1 loaf.

Florida

Historic Island Hotel

Main Street
Post Office Box 460
Cedar Key, Florida 32625

The Historic Island Hotel is the landmark of Cedar Key. Built in 1849, the hotel provides its guests with a wraparound porch on which to enjoy the sea breezes. The Gourmet-Natural Foods Restaurant has been praised by reviewers nationally and internationally. Known for its uniquely prepared seafood and vegetable specialties, the restaurant is unpretentious and relaxing, with classical background music. A gourmet breakfast is included with the room.

The owner's personal art collection adorns the walls, and fresh flowers brighten the tables. The ten guest rooms, six with private baths, are furnished with antique and "old-attic" furniture and mosquito nets over the beds. The Island Hotel is un-gussied-up Old Florida at its most authentic.

Potato Scallion Soup

4 quarts water
½ cup chicken base
15 medium potatoes, scrubbed and chopped
2 teaspoons pepper
2 tablespoons dill weed
1 tablespoon caraway or fennel seeds
3½ cups chopped scallions
3 tablespoons butter
Milk

In a large stockpot bring the water, base, and potatoes to a boil. Cook until tender. Add the pepper, dill weed, and caraway. In a skillet sauté the scallions in butter until transparent. In a blender purée the scallions, then the potato soup. Return the soup and scallions to the stockpot. Add milk to the desired consistency. Serve very hot or very cold.

Serves 6 to 8.

Island Hotel House Dill Dressing

1 cup mayonnaise (preferably homemade)
3 tablespoons dill weed
2 tablespoons water
3 cloves garlic, crushed and chopped
Dash freshly ground pepper
Sunflower seeds

Blend all of the ingredients except the sunflower seeds. Store the mixture in the refrigerator until needed. To serve, pour the mixture over any mixed green salad, and top with sunflower seeds.

Makes 1 cup.

Energy Muffins

6 cups whole wheat flour
1½ teaspoons salt
¾ cup sugar (optional)
2 tablespoons baking powder
6 eggs
2¼ cups milk
4 cups alfalfa sprouts
1 cup sunflower seeds
2 frozen or fresh bananas, chopped

Grease muffin cups. In a large bowl with a wooden spoon, mix all of the ingredients until just blended. Fill the prepared muffin cups ¾ full. Bake in a 400° oven for 30 minutes.

Makes 2 to 3 dozen muffins.

The Island Hotel Fish and Pastry

3 sheets phyllo dough
1 6- to 8-ounce grouper fillet
¼ cup hot Japanese mustard
¼ cup mayonnaise
¼ teaspoon white pepper
½ cup sparkling mineral water
1 tablespoon butter, melted

Thaw the phyllo dough completely in the refrigerator, keeping it covered to prevent drying. Place the grouper on

Historic Island Hotel

a plate of ice while preparing the other ingredients. Combine the mustard, mayonnaise, and white pepper. Dry the fish and slice into 1x3-inch strips. Dip the fish in the mineral water, then in the mustard sauce. Brush the phyllo leaves with melted butter. Place a strip of fish on each pastry piece and wrap like an envelope. Bake in a 350° oven until the pastry is browned, about 25 minutes. The pastry browns after the fish is cooked.

Serves 1.

Island Hotel Brown Rice

**1 cup brown rice, rinsed and
  drained
1¼ cups boiling water
1 teaspoon chicken base or bouillon
1 tablespoon sherry
1 teaspoon freshly ground pepper**

In a saucepan combine all of the ingredients and reduce the heat. Cover and simmer for 40 minutes. Do not stir or peek.

Serves 4.

Flourless Chocolate Cake

**Butter
3 tablespoons almonds
8 ounces semisweet chocolate
1 cup butter
1 cup sugar
8 eggs, separated
¼ teaspoon Grand Marnier or
  Kahlua**

Generously butter a 9-inch springform pan. Line the bottom with parchment paper, butter again, and flour lightly. Line the outer pan securely with foil, forming a collar. In a food processor chop the almonds until powdery.

In the top of the double boiler over simmering water melt the chocolate and butter, stirring until smooth. Remove from the heat. With an electric mixer beat the sugar and egg yolks until the mixture turns pale and triples in volume, about 8 minutes. Fold into the chocolate mixture. In a separate bowl beat the egg whites until stiff. Stir the nut powder and Grand Marnier into the chocolate mixture. Fold in the egg whites just until blended. Spread the batter in the pre-

pared pan. Set the pan in a hot water bath. Bake in a 350° oven for 55 minutes. Remove from the pan carefully.

Serves 6 to 8.

House on Cherry Street

1844 Cherry Street
Jacksonville, Florida 32205
(904) 384-1999

This colonial house overlooking the St. John's River is decorated with period antiques, Oriental rugs, tall case clocks, a large decoy collection, baskets, pewter, and collectibles. During World War II the Navy leased the residence, converting it into four apartments. The original floor plan was reestablished when it was reconverted to a private home in 1975.

The inn has four air-conditioned rooms, all with private baths. Wine and hors d'oeuvres are served in the evening, and a full breakfast is provided. Nearby are Five Points Shopping Center, Avondale Village, Jacksonville Landing, and various points of interest.

Mom's Hard Candy

You will need a candy thermometer to make this. Oil flavoring may be purchased at the pharmacy.

**1 cup water
3¾ cups sugar
1¼ cups white corn syrup
Oil flavoring (cinnamon, spearmint,
  clove, sassafras, or other)
Food coloring (one color per batch)
❧ ❧ ❧
Confectioners' sugar, about 2
  pounds**

In a large heavy pan bring the water to a boil. Add the sugar and corn syrup, and stir until dissolved. Bring to 300° on a candy thermometer. While the mixture is cooking, cover 3 cookie sheets with confectioners' sugar. Remove the candy from the heat and add the flavoring and coloring. Pour the hot candy onto the confectioners' sugar in ribbons. Cut with scissors as soon *as possible.* Store in airtight containers. The powdered sugar may be stored in the freezer and reused.

Makes about 1½ pounds.

Egg Ramekins for Four

1 12-ounce package Stouffers'
    spinach soufflé, partially cooked
8 eggs
½ cup half and half
6 tablespoons grated Swiss cheese
4 to 6 slices bacon, cooked and
    crumbled
8 teaspoons chopped parsley
Paprika

House on Cherry Street

Spray 4 ramekins with cooking spray. Spoon the soufflé into the ramekins, smoothing to fully cover the bottom. Break 2 eggs into each dish. Spoon half and half on each egg. Top each with one-fourth of the cheese, bacon, and parsley. Sprinkle with paprika. Bake in a 450° oven for 12 to 15 minutes.

Serves 4.

Cheese Straws

Enough for a crowd, and excellent served as an hors d'oeuvre or on the side of a breakfast entree.

1 pound sharp Cheddar cheese
½ teaspoon salt
1¾ cups all-purpose flour
½ cup butter, creamed
¼ teaspoon red pepper

Grate the cheese. In a large bowl combine all of the ingredients and mix thoroughly. Thinly roll into a rectangle and cut into narrow strips 4-inches long. Bake in a 350° oven for 20 to 25 minutes.

Makes 30 to 40 straws.

Merlinn Guesthouse

811 Simonton Street
Key West, Florida 33040
(305) 296-3336

The Merlinn is an island within an island, a private world with an ambiance that captures the many charms of Key West. Its lush Oriental gardens, bridges, sundecks, and fish ponds are in the heart of Old Towne. The bi-level lounge overlooking the terrace features a wall-to-wall bookcase, and its sparkling pool and Jacuzzi are relaxing retreats for the weary traveler. A casual stroll will take guests to Key West's finest shops, restaurants, and night life.

The unique accommodations feature wood-beamed cathedral ceilings, quiet Bahama fans, private baths, air conditioning, and television. Breakfast is served on the tree deck overlooking the gardens and pool, and cocktails and hors d'oeuvres are a popular sunset occasion for meeting guests and the Merlinn staff.

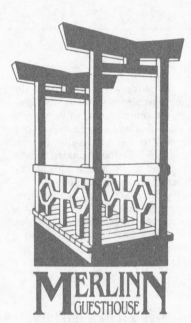

"Keys" Lime Butter Coffee Rolls

1 ¼-ounce package active dry yeast
¼ cup warm water
¼ cup sugar
1 teaspoon salt
6 tablespoons melted butter
2 eggs
½ cup sour cream
2¾ to 3 cups all-purpose flour

¾ cup sugar
¾ cup toasted coconut
2 tablespoons grated lime rind

≈ ≈ ≈

3 tablespoons butter, melted

≈ ≈ ≈

¾ cup sugar
½ cup sour cream
2 tablespoons lime juice (Key lime,
   if available)
¼ cup butter
Grated coconut for garnish

In a large mixing bowl soften the yeast in the warm water. Stir in ¼ cup of sugar, salt, melted butter, eggs, and sour cream. Add the flour gradually, beating well after each addition. Cover and let rise in a warm place until doubled, about 2 hours.

Grease a cookie sheet. To make the coconut-lime filling, in a small bowl combine ¾ cup of sugar, the coconut, and lime rind. When the dough has risen, turn out onto a floured board. Knead about 15 times. Divide the dough into 3 sections, and roll a section into a 9-inch circle. Brush the dough with 1 tablespoon of melted butter. Sprinkle with ⅓ of the coconut-lime filling. Cut into 12 wedges and roll up starting with the wide end, as for a crescent roll. Repeat with the remaining dough sections. Place the rolls point side down on the prepared pan. Cover and let rise until light and doubled in size, about 1 hour. Bake in a 350° oven for 15 to 20 minutes, until golden brown.

In a saucepan combine ¾ cup of sugar, sour cream, lime juice, and butter. Bring to a boil and boil for 3 minutes. Remove the rolls from the oven and pour the hot glaze over the rolls. Top with grated coconut.

Makes 36 rolls.

Hopp-Inn Guest House

Bed & Breakfast Inc. of the Florida Keys
5 Man-o-War Drive
Marathon, Florida 33050
(305) 743-4118

The Hopp-Inn Guest House is on the ocean in Marathon, in the heart of the Florida Keys. It has five guest rooms, each with its private bath and private entrance. Rooms are decorated with bamboo and tropical plants. The surroundings are tropical, with hibiscus, palm trees, poinsettias, banana trees, and many varieties of cactus. A full American breakfast of sausage or bacon, eggs or French toast, and/or cereal and muffins is served. The inn also has three guest apartments, both with an ocean view. These apartments are furnished with a king-sized bed in the master bedroom and have a separate living room/kitchen combination. Activities available include fishing, snorkeling, scuba diving, visiting Key West, John Pennekamp State Park, Bahia Honda State Park, the Dolphin Research Center, and the Theatre of the Sea in Islamorada.

Low Cholesterol Fruity French Toast

6 slices French or Italian bread, cut
   diagonally
¾ cup Egg Beaters
1 cup skim milk
2 tablespoons preserves
   (strawberry, blueberry, or
   peach)
½ teaspoon nutmeg
3 tablespoons margarine
3 cups fruit (strawberry, blueberry,
   or peach)
Confectioners' sugar

In a large baking pan arrange the bread in a single layer. In a large bowl combine the Egg Beaters, milk, preserves, and nutmeg. Beat the mixture until well combined, and pour over the bread slices. Turn the bread over. Refrigerate overnight. In a skillet melt the margarine and fry the toast until light brown on each side. Top with fruit and sugar.

Serves 6.

Fresh Fruit Pie

1 9-inch pie shell, baked
1½ quarts fresh strawberries,
   blueberries, or raspberries
3 tablespoons cornstarch
1 cup sugar
Cool Whip

Wash the berries and place ¾ of them in the pie shell. In a saucepan combine the remaining berries, cornstarch, and sugar. Mash the berries with a potato masher. Simmer the mixture over medium heat until thickened. Pour over the berries in the pie shell and refrigerate for a few hours. Serve with Cool Whip.

Serves 6 to 8.

Doll House Bed and Breakfast

Central Florida Bed & Breakfast
   Reservation Service
719 Southeast 4th Street
Ocala, Florida 32671
(904) 351-1167

The Doll House is an 1899 Victorian house situated in the historic district. It has one large bedroom with double bed and attached private bath and is decorated with antiques, Oriental rugs, and an extensive doll collection. The breakfast specialty is scones, which are served with a complete breakfast. One white cat is in residence. Smoking is permitted on the porch, but not inside the inn.

Catfish with Strawberries

½ cup white wine
½ cup orange juice
2 tablespoons margarine
⅛ teaspoon pepper
1 teaspoon chives
Dash seasoning salt
2 pounds fresh catfish fillets
½ pint frozen strawberries with sugar, thawed
1 pint fresh strawberries
2 tablespoons Key lime juice
1 lime for garnish
2 tablespoons slivered almonds

In a saucepan combine the wine, orange juice, margarine, and spices. Place the fish in the mixture and simmer for about 10 minutes or until opaque. In a food processor, purée the frozen strawberries. Stir in the orange juice. Reserve 4 whole strawberries for garnish, and cut the remainder in half. Add to the puréed mixture. Pour the sauce into a deep platter and arrange the catfish fillets over the sauce. Garnish with whole strawberries and lime slices. Sprinkle with toasted almonds.
Serves 8.

Sweet Veal Bake

4 veal shoulder chops
All-purpose flour
2 tablespoons oil
1 28-ounce can sweet potatoes, reserve liquid
2 large bananas, sliced
1 teaspoon garlic salt
⅛ teaspoon pepper
⅛ teaspoon ginger
2 tablespoons brown sugar
2 tablespoons butter

Dust the veal with flour. In a skillet brown the veal in the oil. Place in a large casserole dish. Arrange the sweet potatoes around the veal, and top with banana slices. Sprinkle with garlic salt, pepper, ginger, and brown sugar. Pour the potato liquid over all and dot with butter. Bake in a 350° oven for 35 minutes.
Serves 4.

Sourdough Scones

2 cups all-purpose flour
2 teaspoons baking powder
1 teaspoon baking soda
½ teaspoon salt
¼ teaspoon turmeric
2 tablespoons sugar
5 tablespoons cold butter or margarine
½ cup raisins, currants, or blueberries
1¼ cups sourdough starter

In a large bowl combine the dry ingredients. Cut in the butter with a pastry blender. Add the fruit, and pour in the sourdough starter. Mix quickly. Turn the dough onto a floured surface and knead lightly. Pat into an 8-inch circle and cut into 8 wedges. Transfer to a greased cookie sheet and bake in a 425° oven for 15 minutes. Cool on a wire rack. Scones may be glazed with egg white and sprinkled with sugar if desired.
Makes 8 scones.

The Spencer Home

313 Spencer Street
Orlando, Florida 32809
(407) 855-5603

The Spencer Home is unique in that it has two front doors, one entering directly into the guest quarters. Accommodations include a roomy suite and two bedrooms. Guests are invited to enjoy the home, including the swimming pool, kitchen, and laundry facilities. Smoking is discouraged.

Fruit Cookies

2 cups butter
1 cup sugar
1 cup brown sugar
3 eggs
1 teaspoon cinnamon
1 teaspoon cloves
2 teaspoons baking soda
3 cups quick cooking oats
5 cups all-purpose flour
1¼ cups chopped dates
½ cup currants
½ cup raisins, halved
1 cup finely chopped candied fruit (pineapple is best)
¾ cup finely chopped candied cherries
1 cup finely chopped pecans or walnuts

In a large bowl combine all of the ingredients. Blend well. Shape the dough into 4 long rolls. Wrap in waxed paper and refrigerate for 24 hours. Cut into small slices and place on an ungreased cookie sheet. Bake in a 350° oven for 10 minutes.
Makes 8 to 9 dozen small cookies.

Five Oaks Inn

1102 Riverside Drive
Palmetto, Florida 34221
(813) 723-1236

This classic Florida home with its old Spanish tiled roof and wraparound porch was built for its view. Situated on the Manatee River with its towering royal palms and moss-covered oaks, the inn features leaded glass china closets, oak colonnades, a fireplace flanked by windowseats, a graceful oak staircase, spacious rooms, and the light and airy enclosed solarium sunporch.

Five Oaks Inn

Carriage Way Bed and Breakfast

70 Cuna Street
St. Augustine, Florida 32084
(904) 829-2467

Carriage Way Bed and Breakfast is situated in the heart of the historic district amid charming shops, museums, and historic sites. Castillo de San Marcos, St. George Street, fine restaurants, carriage tours, and the waterfront are one to four blocks away. Built between 1883 and 1885, the inn has rooms named after prior owners of the house. Accommodations include seven second-floor rooms furnished with antiques, all with private baths. The atmosphere is leisurely and casual, in keeping with Old St. Augustine. Smoking is permitted on the verandah only.

At the Five Oaks Inn there are no traffic jams outside your window to disturb your sleep. While its proximity to Sarasota gives easy access to shopping, Gulf beaches, old Indian burial grounds, orange groves, and the Ringling Brothers facilities, the Five Oaks Inn specializes in privacy and relaxation.

Five Oaks Inn Cheese Pie

1¼ cups all-purpose flour
¾ teaspoon baking powder
¼ teaspoon salt
¼ cup sugar
½ cup butter or margarine
1 egg, beaten

ᨠ ᨠ ᨠ

2 8-ounce packages cream cheese
½ tablespoon all-purpose flour
1 cup sugar
2 eggs, beaten
1½ cups milk
1 teaspoon vanilla extract
Cinnamon

In a large bowl sift together 1¼ cups of flour, baking powder, and salt. Add ¼ cup of sugar. By hand, mix in the butter. Add 1 egg and mix well. Add a little flour if too sticky. Pat the crust into the sides and bottom of a 9-inch pie plate. Flute the edges.

In a separate bowl mix together the cream cheese, ½ tablespoon of flour, and 1 cup of sugar. Add 2 eggs and mix well. Add the milk and vanilla. Pour into the prepared crust and sprinkle with cinnamon. Bake in a 350° oven for 45 minutes, or at 325° for a glass pie plate.

Serves 8 to 10.

Tangy Lemon Bread

¼ cup butter or margarine
¾ cup sugar
2 eggs

ᨠ ᨠ ᨠ

2 cups all-purpose flour
1 tablespoon baking powder
1 teaspoon salt

ᨠ ᨠ ᨠ

½ cup lemon juice
¼ cup milk
2 tablespoons oil
½ cup chopped walnuts

ᨠ ᨠ ᨠ

4 teaspoons lemon juice
4 tablespoons sugar

Grease a 9x5-inch loaf pan. In a large bowl cream together the butter and

¾ cup of sugar until light. Beat in the eggs. In a separate bowl combine the dry ingredients and add to the creamed mixture alternately with ½ cup of lemon juice and the milk. Add the oil and beat until smooth. Fold in the walnuts. Pour the batter in the prepared pan. Bake in a 350° oven for 45 minutes. Watch the loaf carefully and do not overbake.

Combine the remaining lemon juice and sugar. Pour the mixture over the warm loaf and cool for 15 minutes. Cover with a cotton towel until the bread cools to room temperature. Wrap the loaf and store in the freezer. The bread is always best after freezing, but can be stored in the refrigerator. Serve in thin slices.

Makes 1 loaf, 12 servings.

Casa de Solana

21 Aviles Street
St. Augustine, Florida 32084
(904) 824-3555

Casa de Solana is a lovingly renovated colonial home in the heart of St. Augustine's historical area, within walking distance of restaurants, museums, and quaint shops. All four antique-filled guest accommodations are suites, some with fireplaces, some with balconies that overlook the beautiful garden, and others with a breathtaking view of the Matanzas Bay. All have private baths. Tariff includes a full breakfast served in the formal guest dining room, cable TV, chocolates, decanter of sherry, and the use of bicycles for touring the ever-inviting city of St. Augustine.

Banana Nut Loaf

This bread is served in the morning at the Casa de Solana. It is easy to make.

1 cup sugar
¼ cup oil
2 large eggs
½ cup pecans
4 medium-sized bananas
2½ cups Jiffy Baking Mix or any biscuit mix

Grease a 9x5-inch loaf pan. In a large bowl with an electric mixer combine the sugar, oil, eggs, and pecans. Whole nuts may be used because the mixer will chop them. Cut the bananas into the mixture and add the baking mix. Mix well and pour into the prepared pan. Bake in a 350° oven for about 1 hour or until firm in the middle.

Makes 1 loaf, 12 servings.

Bayboro House

1719 Beach Drive S.E.
St. Petersburg, Florida 33701
(813) 823-4955

Bayboro House provides its guests with swimming, sunning, and beachcombing out the front door. Situated away from the bustle of town, it is a place to relax in a setting that expresses the graciousness of the Old South. Each room has its private bath, television, and air conditioning. A continental breakfast is served in the dining room or on the verandah. Nearby are the Salvador Dali Museum, Sunken Gardens, and Bayfront Center.

Casa de Solana

Bayboro House

Tampa Bay Rollups

1 8-ounce package crescent rolls
Cooked sausage or ham

Unroll the crescent roll dough and cut each triangle in half. Place a small amount of crumbled sausage or a small piece of ham on each triangle and roll up into small crescent rolls. Bake in a 425° oven for 15 to 20 minutes.

Makes 16 small rollups.

Gramma's Apple Sunrise Cake

2 cups sugar
2 eggs
½ cup oil
2 teaspoons vanilla extract
2 cups all-purpose flour
2 teaspoons baking soda
2 teaspoons cinnamon
1 teaspoon cloves
4 cups chopped apples

Grease and flour a 9x5-inch cake pan. In a large bowl combine all of the ingredients. Mix well. The mixture will be quite thick. Pour the mixture into the prepared pan. Bake in a 350° oven for 45 minutes or until a toothpick inserted in the center comes out clean.

Makes 18 squares.

Spring Bayou Inn

32 West Tarpon Avenue
Tarpon Springs, Florida 34689
(813) 938-9333

Spring Bayou Inn is a large, comfortable home built around the turn of the century. Unique in architectural detail, it combines the elegance of the past with modern-day conveniences. Guests may relax on the spacious wraparound front porch or in the parlor, where a baby grand piano and complimentary wine provide the opportunity to meet new friends. Conveniently situated near the bayou and local antique shops, the inn is near many excellent restaurants and vacation opportunities. No smoking is permitted within the inn.

Breakfast Sausage Hash

1 medium onion, finely chopped
¼ cup butter, margarine, or
**   vegetable oil**
4 cups peeled and sliced cold baked
**   potatoes**
1 pound bulk sausage, browned,
**   drained and crumbled**
2 teaspoons Worcestershire sauce
1 tablespoon chopped parsley
Salt and pepper to taste
8 beaten eggs
1 cup grated Cheddar cheese

In a large skillet sauté the onions in butter until transparent. Add the potatoes, turning frequently with a spatula, and cook over moderate heat until browned. Add the sausage, Worcestershire sauce, parsley, salt, and pepper. Heat thoroughly. Spread the eggs over the top, and cook until the eggs start to set. Serve with grated cheese over the top.

Serves 8.

Spring Bayou Inn

Old-fashioned Spicy Applesauce

3 pounds tart cooking apples, peeled, cored, and sliced
⅔ cup water
1 cup sugar
Juice of ½ lemon
½ teaspoon cinnamon
⅛ teaspoon nutmeg
1 tablespoon butter or margarine

In a large saucepan combine and simmer all of the ingredients until tender, about 20 minutes. Serve hot or cold.
Serves 6 to 8.

Tropical Baked Bananas

8 slightly underripe bananas
½ cup melted butter or margarine
½ cup grated coconut
Brown sugar

Butter a shallow baking dish. Peel and split the bananas. Arrange in the prepared dish, brush with butter, and sprinkle with coconut. Bake in a 350° oven for 20 minutes, until soft and golden. Sprinkle with brown sugar.
Serves 8 to 12.

The Banyan House

519 South Harbor Drive
Venice, Florida 34285
(813) 484-1385

One of the grand old homes of Venice, the Banyan House has been delightfully restored as a unique vacation residence on the Florida Gulf Coast. The enormous banyan tree that dominates the walled courtyard provides an unusual setting for the garden patio, pool, and spa. A continental breakfast is served in the solarium or on the adjacent courtyard of the garden. The living room features an Italian sculptured fireplace, high-beamed ceiling, and red tile floor, all conducive to conversation or relaxing with a book.

The rooms are individually decorated, providing private baths, color television, fresh towels and maid service daily. Centrally located on the "Island" in Venice, the Banyan House is just a short walk from all the activities of this coastal town.

Sausage and Cheese Tarts

½ pound bulk pork sausage
1¼ cups biscuit mix
½ cup margarine, melted
2 tablespoons boiling water
1 egg, lightly beaten
½ cup half and half
½ cup shredded Cheddar cheese

Grease 12 muffin cups. Cook the sausage over medium heat until browned, stirring to crumble. Drain and set aside. Combine the biscuit mix, margarine, and boiling water, and stir well. Press about 1 tablespoon of dough into the bottom and sides of the prepared muffin cups. Spoon the sausage over the dough. Combine the egg and half and half, blending well. Spoon about 1 tablespoon of egg mixture over each cup. Bake in a 375° oven for 20 minutes. Sprinkle the cheese over the tarts and bake an additional 5 minutes.
Makes 12 tarts.

Apple Pizza

2 cups biscuit mix
½ cup cold water
4 medium apples, sliced very thin
⅓ cup brown sugar
1 teaspoon cinnamon
3 tablespoons margarine, melted
1 cup shredded mild Cheddar cheese

In a small bowl mix the first 2 ingredients. Spread the dough into a pizza pan. Spread the apples over the dough, and sprinkle with brown sugar and cinnamon. Dot with butter. Bake in a 350° oven for 20 minutes, sprinkle with the Cheddar cheese, and bake an additional 10 minutes.
Serves 8.

Baked Fruit Dressing

1 15-ounce can sliced peaches, drained
1 16-ounce can sliced pears, drained
1 15¼-ounce can pineapple chunks, drained
⅓ cup raisins
⅓ cup chopped walnuts
¾ cup light brown sugar, divided
1 teaspoon vanilla extract
1 17-ounce can apricot halves, drained
5 slices white bread, toasted
¾ cup butter or margarine, melted

Lightly oil a 9x13-inch baking dish. Combine the peaches, pears, pineapple, raisins, walnuts, ½ cup of brown sugar, and the vanilla. Stir gently. Spoon into the prepared baking dish, and arrange the apricot halves on top. Cut the bread into ½-inch cubes and sprinkle over the top of the apricots. Combine the remaining ¼ cup of brown sugar and the butter, and pour over the bread cubes. Bake in a 325° oven for 25 to 30 minutes.
Serves 8 to 10.

Georgia

Bellaire House

1234 Bellaire Drive
Atlanta, Georgia 30319
(404) 262-1173
(404) 237-5456

Bellaire House is a small inn situated in the Buckhead area of Atlanta, one of the city's most desirable locations. Near Lenox Square and Phipps Plaza, it is close to some of the best shopping, restaurants, and places to visit in Atlanta. MARTA Rapid Transit is conveniently close.

Stuffed Grape Leaves Southern Style

1¼ pounds ground chuck
2 small onions, finely chopped
3 tablespoons chopped parsley
¼ cup uncooked rice
1 16-ounce can tomatoes, crushed
3 teaspoons dill
Salt and pepper to taste

   🍂 🍂 🍂

1 8-ounce jar grape leaves packed in brine
2 cups water
2 cups beef bouillon
Tomato purée
Yogurt or sour cream

In a large bowl combine the meat, onions, parsley, rice, crushed tomatoes, dill, salt, and pepper. Rinse the grape leaves in warm water, drain, and spread out vein-side up. Cut off the stems. Place a walnut-sized portion of meat mixture on each leaf. Fold over the ends and roll up. Place a few loose leaves in the bottom of a saucepan. Place the rolled leaves in layers in the saucepan. Add the water, bouillon, and the tomato purée. Simmer slowly over low heat for 30 to 45 minutes.
Serves 6.

Bessie's Bed & Breakfast

223 Ponce de Leon Avenue
Atlanta, Georgia 30302
(404) 875-9449

Southern charm and hospitality await guests of this midtown Atlanta inn built in the heart of Atlanta at the turn of the century. A three-story Victorian home, it was originally constructed by a prominent Atlanta physician. A southern or continental breakfast is served in the parlor, where in the evening peanuts, peaches, and Claxton fruitcake are offered.

Guests may choose from deluxe suites, single rooms, and family suites, all with private baths. All accommodations have access to hot-tub facilities, the inn's version of southern hospitality. Nearby are the extensive entertainment traditions of Atlanta such as the Fox Theatre, Piedmont Park, the Carter Presidential Library, and the High Museum.

Super Cheesecake

1½ cups graham cracker crumbs
6 tablespoons butter, melted
2 tablespoons sugar

   🍂 🍂 🍂

2 8-ounce packages cream cheese
2 cups small curd cottage cheese
4 eggs
1½ cups sugar
2 teaspoons vanilla extract
⅓ cup all-purpose flour

   🍂 🍂 🍂

2 cups sour cream
1 teaspoon vanilla extract
½ cup sugar

Combine the graham cracker crumbs, butter, and 2 tablespoons of sugar. Spread the mixture in the bottom and 1 inch up the sides of a 10-inch springform pan.

In a large bowl beat together the cream cheese, cottage cheese, eggs, 1½ cups of sugar, and 2 teaspoons of vanilla. Beat with an electric mixer for 15 minutes. Blend the flour into the cheese mixture and pour over the unbaked crust. Bake in a 350° oven for 1 hour. Combine the remaining ingredients and smooth over the baked cake. Return to the oven for 7 minutes.

Serves 6 to 8.

Shellmont

821 Piedmont Avenue, N.E.
Atlanta, Georgia 30308
(404) 872-9290

This classic Victorian home in historic midtown Atlanta has been made into an exceptional lodging experience. Each guest suite has a private bath and features complimentary beverages in the parlor and chocolates on the pillow at night along with almost one hundred years of history. The lovingly restored Victorian architecture highlights Tiffany windows and magnificent woodwork as backdrop for authentic furnishings. The Carriage House provides an ideal setting for a honeymoon getaway, as the editor of this book can attest.

Cucumber Soup

    3 cucumbers
    ½ onion
    1 10½-ounce can chicken soup
    4 to 5 sprigs fresh dill
    1 teaspoon basil, fresh if available
    1 cup sour cream
    Salt to taste

Peel the cucumbers and cut lengthwise. With a melon scoop remove the seeds. Place the seeded cucumbers in a blender. Add the onion, soup, dill, and basil, and blend well. Add the sour cream and blend. Add the salt. Refrigerate for several hours. Garnish with fresh dill sprigs.

Serves 6.

Mountain Chili

    1 pound ground beef
    1 medium onion, chopped
    1 clove garlic, minced
    1 green pepper, chopped

        ❧ ❧ ❧

    1 28-ounce can tomatoes
    1 16-ounce can dark kidney beans
    1 tablespoon Worcestershire sauce
    1 tablespoon vinegar
    1 teaspoon dry mustard
    1 teaspoon sugar
    1 teaspoon salt
    ⅓ teaspoon black pepper
    ⅔ teaspoon red pepper
    ½ teaspoon chili pepper

In a stock pot brown the ground beef with the onions, garlic, and green pepper. Drain. Add the remaining ingredients. Simmer for several hours.

Serves 6.

❧ ❧ ❧ ❧ ❧

Southern Cornbread Dressing

    4 cups crumbled cornbread
    3 or 4 pieces bread or biscuit, crumbled
    2 13¾-ounce cans Swanson chicken broth
    1 large onion, chopped
    3 ribs celery, chopped
    3 eggs
    1 cup butter, melted

In a large bowl combine the cornbread, bread, and chicken broth, and allow to soak. Add the onions, celery, and eggs, mixing thoroughly. Add the melted buter. Place the mixture in a baking pan. Bake in a 350° oven for 1 hour and 20 minutes.

Serves 6.

Shellmont

Augusta House

Augusta, Georgia

Contact Myriad Properties, Inc.
1936-A North Druid Hills Road N.E.
Atlanta, Georgia 30319
(404) 321-1955

Built in 1928, Augusta House is within walking distance of Augusta College in the most prestigious living area of Augusta. Situated on three and one-half acres of landscaped grounds and formal gardens, the twenty-eight-room house also features a carriage house, cottage, greenhouse, and detached four-car garage. The sixteenth-century stained and leaded glass windows, antique fireplace mantles and carved wall panelings were shipped from England. The oak, white and red walnut, and ash flooring is complemented by beautifully detailed moldings and woodwork.

Sausage & Egg Surprise

9 slices bread, toasted and
  crumbled
1 cup grated Monterey Jack cheese
1 cup grated Cheddar cheese
¼ pound mushrooms, sliced
¼ cup chopped onion
1 pound sausage, cooked and
  crumbled
6 eggs
3 cups milk
½ teaspoon salt

Grease a 9x13-inch baking dish. Arrange the bread on the bottom of the dish buttered side down. In this order add the cheeses, mushrooms, onions, and sausage. In a bowl combine the eggs, milk, and salt with an electric mixer or in a blender. Pour the mixture over the layers. Refriger-

ate overnight. Bake in a 350° oven for 30 to 45 minutes or until the center is set.
Serves 10.

Shrimp and Pasta

This served with a tossed salad and garlic bread makes a complete meal.

8 ounces vermicelli
Salt and pepper to taste
1 cup butter or margarine
2 cloves garlic, minced
12 large shrimp
4 large mushrooms, sliced

🦐 🦐 🦐

Romano cheese
½ cup chopped parsley

Cook the vermicelli in rapidly boiling water for 10 minutes, drain, and rinse in cold water. Toss with salt and pepper to taste. In a large skillet melt the butter. Add the garlic, raw shrimp, and mushrooms. Cook until the shrimp turns pink, about 5 minutes. Add the vermicelli and heat through. Serve on a warmed plate and sprinkle with Romano cheese and chopped parsley.
Serves 2.

Sweet Potato Soufflé

3 pounds sweet potatoes

🦐 🦐 🦐

½ cup margarine
¾ cup sugar
1 teaspoon vanilla extract
¾ cup orange juice
½ teaspoon allspice
½ teaspoon cinnamon
3 eggs, lightly beaten

🦐 🦐 🦐

¼ cup margarine
1½ cups brown sugar
1¼ cups chopped pecans

In a baking pan bake the sweet potatoes in a 350° oven for 1 hour or until soft. Peel the hot potatoes and

mash with ½ cup of margarine. Add the sugar, vanilla, orange juice, allspice, and cinnamon. Mix thoroughly and blend in the eggs. Pour the mixture into a 9x13-inch baking dish. Combine the remaining ingredients and sprinkle over the batter. Bake in a 350° oven for 20 minutes or until a toothpick inserted in the center comes out clean.
Variation: Squash or pumpkin may be substituted for the sweet potatoes.
Serves 8.

The Smith House

202 South Chestatee Street
Dahlonega, Georgia 30533
(404) 864-3566

The story of the Smith House goes back to 1884, when Captain Hall purchased an acre of land east of the town square and began to excavate the land in order to build. When his son discovered a rich vein of gold ore, the city officials would not allow him to mine for gold just one block from the public square. After losing his lawsuit against the city, Hall built his house on top of the vein.

In 1922 Henry and Bessie Smith purchased the property and turned their home into an inn with seven rooms for travelers. Today the Smith House is composed of three establishments: a family-style restaurant, a country inn, and an authentic gift shop. Guests experience true southern hospitality and some of the finest food the South has to offer. The seven rooms have grown to fifteen.

🦐 🦐 🦐 🦐 🦐

Squash Casserole

3 pounds squash, sliced
2 medium onions, chopped
2 medium carrots, grated
1 cup sour cream
2 10½-ounce cans cream of chicken soup
1 8-ounce package herb-seasoned dressing mix
½ cup butter or margarine

In a large stock pot cook the squash, onions, and carrots in salted water until tender. Drain and add the sour cream and soup. Toss the dressing mix with the butter. In a large casserole dish alternate layers of squash mixture and dressing, ending with dressing on top. Bake in a 350° oven for 30 minutes.
Serves 6 to 8.

1842 Inn

353 College Street
Macon, Georgia 31201
(912) 741-1842

The twenty-two guest rooms of this charming inn are within a Greek Revival antebellum house and an adjoining Victorian cottage that share a courtyard and off-street parking. Guests have often commented that the 1842 Inn proves that one does not have to forego the conveniences of the twentieth century to enjoy the elegance of the nineteenth.

The rooms have private baths, central heat and air conditioning, telephones, and television. The sound-insulated walls assure pleasant sleep on the queen- and king-size beds. The business district of Macon, the antebellum heart of the South, is nearby, and fine dining is but a few doors away.

Baked Apples

¾ cup brown sugar
1½ cups orange juice
½ cup raisins
¾ cup chopped pecans
4 large cooking apples, peeled and cored

In a small bowl combine the brown sugar, orange juice, raisins, and pecans. Arrange the apples in an 8-inch square baking dish. Pour the brown sugar mixture over the apples. Bake in a 375° oven for 1 hour, basting the apples frequently with the pan juice.
Serves 4.

1842 Inn

Baked Maple Bananas

2 tablespoons butter or margarine
3 tablespoons maple syrup
4 bananas, cut in half crosswise, then lengthwise
1 tablespoon lemon juice
¼ teaspoon cinnamon (optional)

In a shallow microwave-proof baking dish melt the butter in the microwave oven at high power. Add the maple syrup, blending well. Add the bananas, spooning the mixture over to coat. Cook on high for 1 minute. Turn the bananas over and cook on high for 1 minute and 30 seconds. Sprinkle with lemon juice and cinnamon. Serve warm.
Serves 4.

The Stovall House

Route 1, Box 1476
Sautée, Georgia 30571
(404) 878-3355

The Stovall House, built in 1837, is a Victorian eclectic farmhouse transformed to an inn in 1983. Situated on twenty-eight acres in a valley, the porches and rooms afford the guests views of mountains in all directions. The five guest rooms have private baths and are decorated with family antiques and handiworked stenciling, draperies, net-darned curtains and needlework, which instill the guests with a feeling of being at home. The fifty-seat restaurant provides an intimate, but casual, atmosphere in which patrons can enjoy the unique menu featuring fresh vegetables and herbs. It is a country experience to take home.

Tomato Herb Soup

½ cup olive oil
3 cups chopped celery
2 cups chopped onions
½ cup all-purpose flour
1 46-ounce can V-8 juice
2 quarts water
1 28-ounce can whole peeled tomatoes

❧　❧　❧

1 tablespoon chicken base
2 tablespoons sugar
1 teaspoon thyme
2 bay leaves
2 tablespoons parsley
1 tablespoon basil
½ teaspoon pepper

❧　❧　❧

Parmesan cheese

In a large stockpot heat the oil and sauté the celery and onions. Stir in the flour, blending well. Add the V-8 and water. Purée the tomatoes and add to the soup. Add the chicken base, sugar, herbs, and seasonings, and simmer for 20 minutes. Garnish with Parmesan cheese.

Serves 10 to 12.

Infamous Cheese Muffins

2 cups all-purpose flour
1 tablespoon baking powder
¼ teaspoon pepper
2 tablespoons sugar
½ teaspoon garlic salt
1 cup grated Cheddar cheese
1 egg
1 cup milk
¼ cup oil or melted butter

Grease 12 muffin cups. Combine the dry ingredients. Add liquid ingredients and stir until just moistened. Pour the batter into the prepared muffin cups. Bake in a 400° oven for 20 minutes, or until lightly browned.

Makes 12 muffins.

Herb Marinade for Lamb Chops

4 cloves garlic
½ cup honey
4 teaspoons black pepper
¾ cup olive oil
4 tablespoons soy sauce
1⅓ cups fresh basil leaves

In a food processor mince the garlic well. Add the remaining ingredients. Marinate lamb chops in the mixture for at least 3 hours before grilling or broiling.

Makes about 1½ cups.

Vegetable Casserole

1 pound zucchini, thinly sliced
½ cup onion, chopped
Butter
Dash nutmeg

3 tablespoons all-purpose flour
3 eggs
2 cups grated sharp Cheddar cheese
1 pound Ricotta cheese

🐟 🐟 🐟

Parmesan cheese

In a large skillet sauté the zucchini and onion in the butter. In a large bowl combine the remaining ingredients, except the Parmesan cheese. Add the zucchini and mix well. Place the mixture in a baking dish and sprinkle with Parmesan cheese. Bake in a 375° oven for 35 to 40 minutes.

Serves 4.

Apple Raisin Phyllo

2 tablespoons butter
½ cup sugar
½ teaspoon vanilla extract
Dash salt
4 apples, peeled and sliced
½ cup raisins
1 16-ounce package phyllo dough

🐟 🐟 🐟

¼ cup butter, melted

In a skillet melt 2 tablespoons of butter with the sugar, vanilla, and salt. Stir in the apples and raisins, and simmer until tender. Brush 2 sheets of phyllo with the melted butter. Place about 3 tablespoons of the apple mixture in the center and roll as for an egg roll. Repeat with the remaining phyllo and apple mixture. Place the bundles on a greased baking sheet. Butter the top of each bundle. Bake in a 350° oven for 10 to 15 minutes.

Serves 6.

Ballastone Inn

Fourteen East Oglethorpe Avenue
Savannah, Georgia 31401
(912) 236-1484
(800) 822-4553 (WATS)

The Tiffany of Savannah's small hostelries, the Ballastone Inn nestles in the heart of the historic district within easy walking distance of excellent restaurants, museums, boutiques, and the business district. Built in 1853, it is also known as the "old Anderson House" and has been restored into a showplace for the way Savannahians once lived. Its eighteen guest rooms have their own character and charm. All rooms have private baths, rice poster and canopy beds, marble-top tables and dressers, cheval glass mirrors, comfortable love seats, and wing chairs. Incoming guests are welcomed with a glass of sherry in the parlor, where coffee or tea is always available. Breakfast is served in the parlor, the courtyard, or in one's room, accompanied by fresh flowers and the morning paper. Guests may relax in the beautifully landscaped courtyard; free off-street parking is provided.

Savannah Hash

2 pounds ground sausage
1 medium onion, diced
1 bell pepper, diced
6 medium Idaho potatoes, peeled and diced
Salt and pepper to taste

In a skillet over medium heat crumble and brown the sausage. Drain. Add the remaining ingredients and cook over low heat until tender, about 15 minutes. Stir often during cooking.

Serves 10 to 12.

The Forsyth Park Inn

102 West Hall Street
Savannah, Georgia 31401
(912) 233-6800

The Forsyth Park Inn is a Victorian mansion in the historic district that has been elegantly restored to its earlier splendor. Overlooking Forsyth Park, filled with moss-laden oaks, blooming azaleas, scented magnolias, and lighted monuments, it is convenient to many fine restaurants, antique shops, museums, and the river front.

Rooms feature period furnishings with four-poster king- and queen-size beds, unique fireplaces, antique marble baths or whirlpools, and carefully preserved architectural details. A private carriage cottage in the courtyard is perfect for romantic getaways.

The Forsyth Park Inn

Forsyth Tropical Muffins

    2½ cups unprocessed bran
    1⅓ cups all-purpose flour
    2½ teaspoons baking soda
    ½ teaspoon salt
    1 cup raisins
    1 cup shredded coconut

    🍃 🍃 🍃

    2 eggs
    ½ cup buttermilk
    ½ cup oil
    1 cup mashed ripe bananas
    ½ cup honey

Grease muffin cups. In a large bowl combine the bran, flour, baking soda, salt, raisins, and coconut. Mix well. In a separate bowl beat the eggs, and add the milk, oil, bananas, and honey. Add to the dry ingredients and mix just until blended. Spoon into muffin cups. Bake in a 375° oven for 20 to 25 minutes.

Makes 18 large or 24 small muffins.

The Culpepper House Bed and Breakfast

Broad at Morgan
Post Office Box 462
Senoia, Georgia 30276
(404) 599-8182

The Culpepper House displays many features that were popular during the Victorian period, including matching gingerbread trim on porches and interior staircases, curved wall, stained glass in the stairwell, and pocket sliding doors leading to the parlor. The house is furnished with period furniture, collectibles, and comfortable whimsy. The hostess will prepare some suggestions of activities that should make a stay in "your home away from home" a satisfying adventure.

Gazpacho

    1 16-ounce can tomatoes, drained
    1 clove garlic
    ½ cup sliced green peppers
    ½ cup sliced onions
    1 medium-sized cucumber, sliced

    🍃 🍃 🍃

    2 cups tomato juice
    2 tablespoons oil
    3 tablespoons wine vinegar
    1 tablespoon paprika
    ½ teaspoon salt
    ¼ teaspoon pepper
    ⅛ teaspoon Tabasco sauce

Combine the first 5 ingredients in a blender and blend at high speed until finely chopped, about 5 to 10 seconds. Pour into a large pitcher and add the remaining ingredients. Blend well. Refrigerate until chilled.

Makes 1⅓ quarts, and serves 8 in punch cups.

Oysters Rockefeller

3 tablespoons butter or margarine
½ package frozen chopped spinach
⅓ cup minced onions
1 bay leaf, finely crumbled
1 tablespoon finely snipped parsley
¼ teaspoon celery salt
¼ teaspoon salt
Dash cayenne, Tabasco sauce, or anisette
¼ cup packaged fine bread crumbs

🍃 🍃 🍃

18 large or 24 small oysters on the half shell
2 slices bacon, cut into bits
Grated Parmesan cheese (optional)

Heat the butter in a small saucepan. Add the next 7 ingredients. Cook covered, stirring occasionally, until the spinach is heated through. Add the bread crumbs and mix.

Place the oysters in a large shallow pan. Place a portion of the spinach mixture on each oyster, dot with bacon, and sprinkle with a bit of Parmesan. Bake in a 425° oven for 10 minutes.

Serves 4 to 6.

White Enchiladas

1 10¾-ounce can cream of mushroom soup
1 8-ounce carton sour cream
Water
1 6-ounce can whole green chilies, seeded and mashed

🍃 🍃 🍃

1 pound ground beef
Salt and pepper
1 4-ounce can Old El Paso taco sauce

🍃 🍃 🍃

1 package flour tortillas (8 to 10)

🍃 🍃 🍃

½ cup grated sharp Cheddar cheese

Combine the soup, sour cream, water, and chilies in a saucepan. The mixture should be thin and soupy. Heat, stirring until smooth.

Cook the ground beef in a frying pan until the meat loses its red color. Drain well. Season with salt and pepper. Add the taco sauce and mix well. Steam the tortillas. Roll the meat mixture up in the tortillas and place in a casserole dish in a single layer. Pour the soup mixture over the rolled tortillas. Bake in a 350° oven for 30 minutes. Remove from the oven, sprinkle with grated cheese, and return to the oven until the cheese melts.

The rolled tortillas may be frozen without the soup mixture, thawed, and prepared whenever convenient.

Serves 6 to 8.

Fig Preserves

3 pounds figs
1 cup water
1 pound sugar

Wash the figs, and stem if preferred. Boil the sugar and water. When the syrup comes to a rolling boil, slowly add the figs, keeping the syrup at a boil. Boil for 20 minutes or until syrup is as thick as desired. Pack in sterilized jars and seal.

Makes about 4 pints.

The Veranda

252 Seavy Street
Post Office Box 177
Senoia, Georgia 30276
(404) 599-3905

The Veranda, an elegantly restored turn-of-the-century inn, is the kind of place to visit when you want to leave the cares of the world behind you. Guests relax on the broad rocking

chair verandah that gives the inn its name or play chess and skittles (Victorian pinball) and read in the extensive library. The innkeepers have a kaleidoscope collection, as well as more than 200 walking canes from all over the world. All nine rooms have private baths, central air conditioning, and period antiques. The romantic honeymoon room offers an oversized whirlpool bath. The Veranda is known for its gourmet meals, lavish breakfasts, and shop that sells museum store quality gifts.

Breakfast Mushrooms

Serve these over poached or scrambled eggs, use as an omelet filling, or serve as a spread with toast points.

½ pound fresh mushrooms, sliced
3 tablespoons butter
¾ cup grated sharp Cheddar cheese
¾ cup grated Swiss cheese
2 tablespoons all-purpose flour
1 cup milk
¼ teaspoon salt
¼ teaspoon black pepper
½ cup red wine
¼ cup buttered crumbs

In a skillet sauté the mushrooms in 1 tablespoon of butter. Spread in the bottom of a casserole dish and top with the Cheddar and Swiss cheeses. In a skillet melt 2 tablespoons of butter and stir in the flour. Cook briefly to make a roux. Add the milk and seasonings, and stir or whisk over low heat until smooth and thickened. Add the wine and pour over the mushroom mixture. Top with the buttered crumbs. Bake in a 350° oven for 15 minutes or until bubbly and golden.

Serves 8 to 10 as a topping for eggs.

Bobby's Sweet Georgia Brown Bread

½ cup butter

🍃 🍃 🍃

1 cup graham cracker crumbs
¾ cup cornmeal
½ cup whole wheat flour

½ cup sifted all-purpose flour
¼ cup wheat germ
2 teaspoons baking soda
1½ teaspoons baking powder
¾ teaspoon salt
½ teaspoon cinnamon
½ teaspoon freshly grated nutmeg

🍃 🍃 🍃

¾ cup molasses
2 cups buttermilk

🍃 🍃 🍃

1 cup raisins and/or chopped dates

🍃 🍃 🍃

Butter or softened cream cheese

In the top of a steamer over boiling water melt the butter. In a separate bowl combine the dry ingredients. Mix the molasses and buttermilk together and stir into the dry ingredients, beating well with a spoon. Pour the mixture into the butter in the steamer. Sprinkle the raisins and dates over the batter. Cover and steam for 3 hours, making sure the water doesn't boil dry. Serve hot with butter or cream cheese.

Makes 1 loaf.

Veal Ione

6 tablespoons water
6 tablespoons lemon juice
½ teaspoon coriander
½ teaspoon cardamom
Salt and pepper to taste
6 veal cutlets
⅔ cup all-purpose flour

🍃 🍃 🍃

10 tablespoons butter
2½ cups chicken bouillon

In a shallow dish combine the water, lemon juice, and seasonings. Dip the cutlets in the mixture. Pound the cutlets with a wood mallet or tenderizing tool. Dip each in the lemon mixture again, then in the flour. Dry the cutlets on a cake rack for 10 minutes.

In a nonstick skillet melt the butter. Spread a single layer of cutlets in the butter and cook on one side until golden brown. Turn very carefully and brown the other side. Arrange the cutlets in a single layer. After cooking all of the cutlets, add the remaining flour from coating the cutlets to the skillet to make a roux. Blend well and heat through. Add the remaining lemon water and bouillon. Cook, stirring constantly, until thickened. Pour the mixture over the cutlets and cover tightly. Bake in a 300° oven for 30 to 60 minutes, until very tender. Sprinkle with paprika.

Serves 6.

The Veranda

Mary Ellen's Squash Casserole

2½ pounds yellow squash, sliced
2 medium onions, chopped
½ cup butter
1 4-ounce jar chopped pimientos
1 5-ounce can sliced water chestnuts
1 10½-ounce can cream of chicken soup
1 cup sour cream
4 ounces packaged herb seasoned stuffing mix

Grease a casserole dish. Steam or microwave the squash until tender. Drain well. In a skillet sauté the onion in butter and add to the squash. Stir in the remaining ingredients except the stuffing. Sprinkle half of the stuffing in the bottom of the prepared dish. Cover with the squash mixture, and top with the remaining stuffing mix.

Bake in a 350° oven for 35 to 40 minutes.

Serves 6 to 8.

Veranda Layered Cheesecake

¾ cup graham cracker crumbs
2 tablespoons confectioners' sugar
3 tablespoons melted butter
½ teaspoon cinnamon

❧ ❧ ❧

2 eggs, beaten
½ cup sugar
12 ounces cream cheese, softened
½ teaspoon vanilla extract
Cinnamon to taste

❧ ❧ ❧

1½ cups sour cream
2 tablespoons sugar
½ teaspoon vanilla extract
Fresh unsweetened fruit

In a bowl combine the graham cracker crumbs, confectioners' sugar, melted butter, and ½ teaspoon of cinnamon. Pat the mixture into an 8-inch springform pan. In a large bowl beat the eggs, and add the sugar slowly, beating after each addition. Add the cream cheese and ½ teaspoon of vanilla, and mix well. Pour over the crust and sprinkle with cinnamon. Bake in a 375° oven for 20 to 25 minutes. Chill thoroughly.

Combine the sour cream, sugar, and ½ teaspoon of vanilla. Spread the mixture over the cheesecake. Bake in a 400° oven for 5 to 8 minutes. Chill overnight.

Top with fresh fruit such as sliced ripe strawberries or kiwi fruit just before serving.

Serves 12 to 16.

Hawaii

Kalani Honua

Rural Route 2, Box 4500
Pahoa-Kalapana, Hawaii 96778
(808) 965-7828

Kalani Honua provides an environment in which the "spirit of aloha" flourishes. Situated on twenty secluded acres bordered by lush jungle and a dramatic coastline, the center offers an authentic experience of rural Hawaii. Guests can visit nearby black sand beaches, snorkel in a tide pool, explore a lava tube or warm spring, or bicycle or hike along the coastal road. Close by is Kilauea, an active yet nonthreatening volcano.

The four two-story wooden lodges provide accommodations for individuals and groups. Each has a multipurpose studio/meeting place with an ocean view on the upper level and common kitchen facilities on the ground floor. Delicious meals are available at the Cafe Cashew, where mostly vegetarian foods with occasional fish and chicken entrees are offered.

Coconut Milk Fish

3 pounds fresh island fish fillets
    (tuna, snapper, mahi mahi,
    opakapaka, or local favorite
    catch)
Olive oil
Soy sauce
1 large can frozen coconut milk
Grated ginger
2 tablespoons minced garlic
Handful minced scallions

Clean the fillets and drizzle with olive oil and soy sauce. Place the fillets in a baking dish. Cover with coconut milk and sprinkle with the ginger, garlic, and scallions. Bake in a 350° oven for about 30 minutes, or until the fish flakes easily.
Serves 6.

Tropical Tapioca

1 cup pearl tapioca
4 cups pineapple coconut juice

¾ cup honey
1 teaspoon vanilla extract
Frozen berries, optional
Shredded coconut
Mint sprigs

In a saucepan combine the tapioca and juice, and let the mixture stand for 30 minutes. Bring the mixture to a boil, stirring constantly. Remove from the heat. Add the honey and vanilla. Add frozen berries, if desired. Cool. Garnish with shredded coconut and sprigs of mint.
Serves 12.

Hale Kipa O Kiana

Rural Route 2, Box 4874
Kalapana Shores, Hawaii 96778
(808) 965-8661

This beach house across from the ocean is surrounded by jungle, near an active volcano, and only a short walk from the famous black sand beaches. The house has two guest rooms with private entrances and private baths. Both accommodations have ocean views and use of the guest kitchen. Smoking is permitted outside only.

Honey Pineapple Bread

2 tablespoons oil
1 cup honey
1 egg, lightly beaten
2 cups all-purpose flour
2 teaspoons baking powder
¾ teaspoon salt
1 cup whole bran
1 cup pineapple juice
½ cup finely chopped pineapple
¾ cup chopped Macadamia nuts

Grease a 9x5-inch loaf pan. In a large mixing bowl blend together the oil, honey, and egg. Stir in the flour, baking powder, salt, whole bran, pineapple juice and pineapple. Mix until just blended. Fold in the Macadamia nuts. Pour the batter into the prepared pan. Bake in a 350° oven for 1 hour.

Makes 1 loaf, or 8 servings.

Aloha Papaya Mac Nut Bread

1 cup butter, melted
2 cups sugar
4 eggs, lightly beaten
2 cups fresh papaya pulp

ʔ ʔ ʔ

2 cups sifted all-purpose flour
1 teaspoon salt
2 teaspoons baking soda
2 cups whole wheat flour
½ cup hot water
¾ cup Mauna Loa Macadamia nut
    bits

Grease two 8x4-inch loaf pans. In a large bowl combine the melted butter and sugar. Mix in the eggs and papaya

pulp, blending until smooth. In a separate bowl sift the flour with the salt and baking soda. Stir in the whole wheat flour. Add the dry ingredients to the papaya mixture alternately with the hot water. Fold in the Macadamia nut bits. Pour the batter into the prepared pans. Bake in a 325° oven for 1 hour and 10 minutes.

Makes 2 loaves, or 10 servings.

Nonny's Meatballs

The secret of this recipe is to use 4 eggs per pound of hamburger.

1 pound lean hamburger
1 clove garlic, finely chopped
1 cup fine bread crumbs
2 to 3 tablespoons Romano cheese
1 cup parsley
4 eggs, lightly beaten
Salt and pepper to taste
Fresh basil

ʔ ʔ ʔ

Olive oil for frying

In a large bowl combine all of the ingredients except the oil. Form small balls and fry in olive oil.

Use the meatballs with your favorite pasta sauce.

Makes about 12 meatballs.

Eggplant Parmesano à la Allegra

1 large eggplant
3 tablespoons all-purpose flour
1 egg, beaten
1 tablespoon water
1 cup dried bread crumbs
Parsley
Tomato sauce (your favorite)
1 tablespoon oilve oil
Parmesan cheese
Mozzarella cheese, grated

Remove the skin from the eggplant and cut into ¼-inch slices. Put the flour aside on waxed paper. In a shallow bowl combine the egg and water. Combine the bread crumbs and parsley and place on waxed paper. Dip the eggplant in the flour, then in the egg mixture, and coat in bread crumbs. Refrigerate the eggplant slices for about 1 hour. In a skillet heat the oil and fry the eggplant on both sides until brown. In a 1-quart casserole dish layer ¼ of the tomato sauce, half of the fried eggplant, salt, pepper, Parmesan cheese, and Mozzarella cheese. Repeat the layers, and top with tomato sauce and cheeses. Bake uncovered in a 325° oven for 1 hour.

Serves 6.

Kalani Honua

Poipu Plantation

1792 Pe'e Road
Koloa, Kauai, Hawaii 96756
(808) 742-6757
(800) 733-1632

Centuries of tides and tradewinds have created the beautiful white sand beaches of Poipu, the most appealing resort area on Kauai. Guests of Poipu Plantation will find quiet and seclusion, with exciting ocean and mountain views from each private lanai—1 bedroom, full kitchen, living/dining room, 2 ceiling fans, and tropical decor. Poipu Plantation is a short distance from hotels, restaurants, shopping, a championship golf course, tennis courts, and beach parks. Tropical fish and shells are abundant on nearby beaches and coves. Swimming, snorkeling and diving are good year-round.

Another way to visit and stay in Hawaii is through Bed and Breakfast Hawaii for accommodations in private homes. The bed may be in an extra bedroom, with a private bath, an apartment with a separate entrance, or a free-standing cottage elsewhere on the host's property. Homes are available on the islands of Oahu, Hawaii, Maui, Kauai, Molokai, and Lanai. Write to Post Office Box 449, Kapaa, HI 96746. Call—Kauai phone: (808) 822-7771; or toll free: (800) 733-1632 for reservations.

Queen Emma Brown Bread with Molasses

1 cup whole wheat flour
1 teaspoon baking soda
½ teaspoon salt
1 egg
1 cup Bran Buds cereal
½ cup raisins (or chopped prunes, dates, or figs)
⅓ cup molasses
¾ cup very hot water
2 tablespoons butter, melted

Grease a loaf pan. In a bowl combine the flour, baking soda, and salt. Set aside. In a large bowl mix together the egg, cereal, raisins, and molasses. Add the dry ingredients alternately with the water and butter. Stir until well combined. Spread the batter evenly to fill the prepared pan about ⅔ full. Bake in a 350° oven for about 45 minutes, or until a knife inserted in the center comes out clean.

Makes 1 loaf.

Pineapple Bran Muffins

1 cup bran flakes
1 cup milk
1 cup crushed pineapple
⅓ cup shortening
½ cup sugar
⅓ cup honey
2 eggs, well beaten
1⅓ cups all-purpose flour, sifted
½ teaspoon salt
2 teaspoons baking soda

Grease 12 muffin cups. In a small bowl combine the bran and milk. Set aside. Drain the crushed pineapple and cook in a saucepan until no liquid remains. Cool. Cream together the shortening, sugar, and honey, and add the eggs. Blend in the bran and crushed pineapple. Add the flour, salt, and baking soda, stirring until just blended. Pour the batter into the prepared muffin cups. Bake in a 350° oven for about 15 to 20 minutes.

Makes 12 muffins.

The Plantation Inn

174 Lahainaluna Road
Lahaina, Maui, Hawaii 96761
(808) 667-9225
(800) 433-6815
(808) 667-9293 (FAX)

This unique country inn blends an elegant turn-of-the-century ambiance with the first class amenities of the finest of hotels. Antiques, stained glass, hardwood floors, brass and poster beds, ceiling fans, floral wallcoverings and bedspreads, extensive wood trim, and sprawling verandahs create the charm of old Hawaii. Rooms have private tiled bathrooms with brass fixtures, central air conditioning, television and VCR, refrigerator, and daily maid service. Situated in a quiet country setting and one block from the ocean, it is near unusual shops, quaint bars, and restaurants. Gerard's Restaurant in the inn has been called "one of America's finest restaurants" by Times Books. An elegant French restaurant, it is a favorite fine dining spot for Maui residents and visitors alike.

Calamari
with Lime and Ginger

This recipe was featured in the December, 1989 issue of *Bon Appetit* magazine.

3 limes
🌿 🌿 🌿
3 tablespoons sesame oil

3 tablespoons peanut oil
3 pounds calamari, cleaned, gutted, and sliced ¼-inch thick
Salt and freshly ground pepper
1 scallion, sliced ¼-inch thick
2 ounces fresh ginger, peeled and finely diced

Remove the peel and white pith from the limes. Working over a bowl to catch the juice, cut the small membranes apart and remove the segments. Reserve the lime segments in a separate bowl. In a large heavy skillet heat the oils over medium-high heat. Season the calamari with salt and pepper, and sauté over high heat until opaque, about 1 minute. Remove from the heat and add the scallions, ginger, and lime juice. Transfer to a hot plate, and decorate with lime segments. Serve immediately.

Serves 6 as an appetizer or lunch.
Recipe courtesy Chef Gerard Reversade.

Tarte Tatin with Mango

This recipe was featured in the December, 1989 issue of *Bon Appetit* magazine.

1⅔ cups all-purpose flour
2 tablespoons sugar
Pinch salt
10 tablespoons butter
1 egg
2 tablespoons ice water

 za   za   za

⅔ cup sugar
2 tablespoons water
3 tablespoons butter
7 large mangoes

In a large bowl add the flour, and make a well in the center. Add 2 tablespoons of sugar, salt, 9 tablespoons of butter, the egg, and ice water. Mix well and form into a ball. Wrap in plastic and allow to rest for 1 hour.

In a heavy medium saucepan over medium heat cook the remaining sugar with 2 tablespoons of water, stirring until the sugar dissolves. Boil

until the sugar caramelizes, and blend in the remaining butter. Pour into a 9-inch pie plate. Peel the mangoes and cut into large wedges. Arrange the wedges over the caramelized sugar.

On a floured surface roll the dough into a circle larger than pie plate and ⅛-inch thick. Place the dough over the mangoes and trim the edges. Seal around the edges of the pie plate. Bake in a 450° oven for 30 to 40 minutes. Place a serving platter over the tart and invert. Serve warm.

Serves 8.
Recipe courtesy Chef Gerard Reversade.

Salmis of Pheasant

2 pheasants
Salt and freshly ground pepper to taste
2 tablespoons oil

za   za   za

1 tablespoon butter
1 small carrot, diced
2 shallots, diced
1 ounce prosciutto, diced
1 small stalk celery, diced
4 tablespoons all-purpose flour
2 tablespoons cognac
¼ cup Madeira wine

za   za   za

1 small sprig Italian parsley
1 small sprig thyme
1 small sprig rosemary
1 small sprig sage
1 bay leaf

za   za   za

¼ cup white wine
4 seeds juniper berries, smashed
1 pound wild mushrooms (shiitake, oyster, chanterelle, cepe, or a combination)
1 cup chicken stock
6 tablespoons butter, cut in pieces

za   za   za

2 tablespoons butter
2 truffles

za   za   za

½ pound fresh foie gras, sliced (optional)
2 tablespoons butter

za   za   za

8 slices bread
2 tablespoons butter

Place the giblets inside the pheasants. Season with salt and pepper, and coat with oil. Roast the pheasants on a rotisserie or in a 450° oven to medium-rare, about 30 minutes. Remove the skins and separate the breasts and legs from the carcass. Cut the legs in half and place the thighs and breasts in a covered dish in a warm place. Reserve the livers. Chop the drumsticks, carcass, and skin into coarse chunks. Set aside.

In a skillet melt 1 tablespoon of butter and sauté the diced carrot, shallots, prosciutto, and celery until tender. Add the chopped pheasant, flour, cognac, and Madeira. Ignite and allow the flames to subside. Reduce the mixture for 15 minutes. Make a bouquet garni by combining the Italian parsley, thyme, rosemary, sage, and bay leaf. Tie in a small piece of cheesecloth. Add the bouquet garni, white wine, and berries to the skillet. Remove the stems from the mushrooms and add to the mixture. Add the chicken stock and cook for 30 minutes. Strain the sauce and swirl in 6 tablespoons of butter. Pour the mixture over the pheasant breasts and thighs.

In a skillet melt 2 tablespoons of butter and sauté the mushroom caps and truffles. Add the mixture to the pheasant. In a skillet sauté the foie gras in 2 tablespoons of butter. Set aside. Cut the bread into heart shapes. In a skillet in 2 tablespoons of butter fry the bread until toasted. Spread the foie gras onto the toast and top with the reserved pheasant liver. Transfer the pheasant and sauce to a serving platter, and arrange the toast around the platter.

Serves 8.
Recipe courtesy Chef Gerard Reversade.

Victoria Place

Post Office Box 930
Lawai, Kauai, Hawaii 96765
(808) 332-9300

Perched high on lush hills overlooking thick jungles and the Pacific Ocean, Victoria Place offers an oasis of pampered comfort and privacy. Guest bedrooms in one wing of this home open directly onto a pool surrounded by flowers and plants. The three guest rooms enjoy a constant ocean breeze and private baths. It is located near the resort beaches of Poipu, the National Tropical Botanical Gardens, Old Koloa Town, Lihue, Spouting Horn, and the many recreational facilities in the area.

Banana Lemon Bread

½ cup butter, oil, or margarine
1 cup sugar
2 eggs, beaten
2 cups mashed ripe bananas
6 tablespoons lemon juice

2 cups all-purpose flour
1 tablespoon baking soda
3 tablespoons grated lemon peel

Grease 2 loaf pans or 1 bundt pan. In a large bowl cream together the butter and sugar. Blend in the eggs, bananas, and juice. Stir in the dry ingredients. Add the grated lemon peel. Pour the batter into the prepared pans. Bake in a 350° oven for 1 hour.

Makes 2 loaves, or 12 servings.

Hale 'Aha

3875 Kamehameha Road
Post Office Box 3370
Princeville, Kauai, Hawaii 96722
(808) 826-6733
(800) 826-6733

Situated on a golf course overlooking the Pacific Ocean, Hale 'Aha allows guests to watch golf tournaments from the lanai while checking the waves for an afternoon at the beach. Guests may enjoy breakfast in bed or in the dining room. Each room has its own bath, and private decks

and entrances provide privacy and breathtaking views. There is a wide variety of recreational activities available in the area.

Gelatin Fruit "Breakfast Muffins"

1 6-ounce package strawberry gelatin
2 cups boiling water
1 cup cold water
1 cup cold sweetened condensed milk
Fresh fruit for garnish

Line 18 muffin cups with paper liners. In a bowl combine the gelatin and boiling water, stirring until the gelatin is dissolved. Add the cold water and sweetened condensed milk, stirring until well blended. Pour into the lined muffin cups. Refrigerate until firm. Garnish with fresh fruit.

Serves 18.

Idaho

Idaho Heritage Inn

109 W. Idaho St.
Boise, Idaho 83702
(208) 342-8066

This inn, built in 1904 for one of Boise's early merchants, remained in his family until it was purchased by Governor Chase A. Clark in 1943. Recently restored, it is now on the National Register of Historic Places. Situated in Boise's historic Warm Springs District, it is within walking distance of downtown, 8th Street Marketplace, and Old Boise, all offering excellent restaurants, shops, and theatres. Nearby is Bogus Basin Ski Area; Sun Valley is three hours to the east. All rooms have private baths and period furniture. Breakfast is delivered to guest rooms in the morning; a goblet of wine, a good book, or friendly conversation is never hard to find in the evening.

Chicken Cheese Soup

3 potatoes, peeled and chopped
1 stalk celery, sliced
1 carrot, grated
1 onion, chopped
1 teaspoon parsley
3 tablespoons butter
2 10½-ounce cans cream of chicken soup
1 16-ounce box Velveeta cheese
2 cups chopped cooked chicken
Salt and pepper to taste

In a stock pot boil the potatoes, celery, carrot, and onion in a small amount of water until tender. Add the parsley, butter, and cream of chicken soup. Heat thoroughly. Add the cheese and stir until completely melted. Stir in the chicken, salt, and pepper to taste.
Serves 4 to 6.

Sweet and Sour Meatballs

2 cups plain or Italian bread crumbs
¾ cup milk
2 eggs
2 small onions, minced
½ teaspoon nutmeg
¼ teaspoon dry mustard
1 pound sausage
1 pound hamburger
🍃 🍃 🍃
1 12-ounce bottle beer
2⅓ cups brown sugar (1 pound)
1 12-ounce bottle chili sauce
2 tablespoons cornstarch
2 tablespoons water

In a large bowl blend together the bread crumbs, milk, eggs, onions, nutmeg, dry mustard, sausage, and hamburger. Form the mixture into balls and place on a cookie sheet. Bake in a 375° oven for 15 minutes. Drain any fat.
In a saucepan heat the beer, brown sugar, and chili sauce, stirring until the sugar is dissolved. In a small bowl combine the cornstarch and water, and stir until dissolved. Blend the mixture into the sauce, and stir until thickened. Place the meatballs in the sauce and heat through.
Serves 10.

Whiskey Cake

1 cup raisins
2¼ cups water
½ cup shortening
¾ cup sugar
3 eggs
1 teaspoon baking soda
2 large shots whiskey
2 cups sifted all-purpose flour
1 cup chopped nuts
🍃 🍃 🍃
½ cup butter or margarine
2 cups confectioners' sugar
2 teaspoons vanilla extract
2 tablespoons whiskey

Grease a 9x13-inch baking pan. In a small saucepan boil the raisins in the water until plumped. Cool the raisins. Drain, reserving 1 cup of water. In a large bowl cream together the shortening and sugar. Separate the eggs, and beat 2 egg yolks into the shortening mixture. Reserve 1 egg yolk for the frosting. Add the baking soda to the raisin water, and blend in the shots of whiskey. Add the whiskey mixture to the creamed shortening mixture. Blend in the flour, raisins, and nuts. In a separate bowl beat the egg whites. Fold into the batter. pour the batter into the prepared pan. Bake in a 350° oven for 40 minutes, or until a toothpick inserted in the center comes out clean.

Beat the remaining ingredients, including the reserved egg yolk, until well blended. Frost the warm cake.

Serves 10 to 12.

Idaho Heritage Inn

Cricket on the Hearth

1521 Lakeside Avenue
Coeur d'Alene, Idaho 83814
(208) 664-6926

Cricket on the Hearth's innkeepers have brought the beauty of springtime indoors and have added a touch of country living. The down-home feeling is enhanced by the furnishings that have been selected for comfort and tradition. The living room and game room, each with a warm fireplace, are perfect places to while away the afternoon or evening. Each guest room has been given names reflecting an outstanding feature of the community.

Hot Buttered Beverage Mix

6 cups brown sugar
1 cup butter
2 tablespoons honey
1 tablespoon vanilla extract
1 tablespoon rum extract
1 tablespoon brandy flavoring

1 teaspoon cinnamon
½ teaspoon cloves
½ teaspoon allspice
¼ teaspoon nutmeg

In a bowl combine all of the ingredients with an electric mixer until smooth. Use at room temperature, or store covered and refrigerated for up to 3 months.

To serve, use about 1 tablespoon of beverage mix with 6 to 8 ounces of apple juice, hot milk, coffee, or hot water and rum. Use a cinnamon stick for stirring.

Makes 150 servings.

Al's Bachelor Sweet and Sour Chops

4 to 6 loin-cut pork chops, excess fat trimmed
4 medium potatoes, sliced into ¾-inch slices
2 10-ounce cans cream of mushroom soup
1 small onion, diced
½ clove garlic, diced
3 tablespoons honey
3 tablespoons prepared mustard
3 tablespoons lemon juice
½ teaspoon Worcestershire sauce
½ teaspoon parsley flakes
½ teaspoon sage
½ teaspoon thyme
Salt and pepper to taste

In a large frying pan quickly brown the pork chops on both sides. Place the pork chops in a large baking pan and set aside. Boil the potatoes in salted water until slightly soft. Drain and spread over the pork chops. In a large bowl combine the remaining ingredients and stir until well mixed. Pour the mixture over the potatoes and pork chops. Bake in a 350° oven for 20 to 30 minutes or until the pork chops are well done. Serve with a tossed green salad and garlic toast.

Serves 4 to 6.

Orange Kiss-Me Cake

1 large orange
1 cup raisins
⅓ cup walnut halves

❧ ❧ ❧

2 cups all-purpose flour
1 teaspoon baking soda
½ cup shortening
1 cup sugar
¾ cup milk
2 eggs
¼ cup milk

❧ ❧ ❧

⅓ cup orange juice
⅓ cup sugar
¼ cup chopped walnuts
1 teaspoon cinnamon

Grease the bottom of a 9x13-inch baking pan. In a food processor grind together the orange (including the rind), raisins, and ⅓ cup of walnuts. Set aside.

In a separate bowl combine the flour and baking soda. Cream together the shortening and 1 cup of sugar. Add the dry ingredients and ¾ cup of milk, blending until well combined. Add the eggs and remaining milk, and beat for 1 minute. Fold the ground orange mixture into the batter, and blend well. Pour the batter into the prepared pan. Bake in a 350° oven for 50 minutes or until the cake springs back when touched lightly on the top.

Drizzle the orange juice over the warm cake. Combine the remaining ingredients and sprinkle over the cake.

Serves 10 to 12.

The Greenbriar Inn

315 Wallace
Coeur d'Alene, Idaho 83814
(208) 667-9660

Built in 1908, the Greenbriar is Coeur d'Alene's only nationally registered historic mansion. Situated four blocks from the downtown area, the inn offers a wide range of choices in its seven guest rooms, all furnished with antiques and down comforters imported from Ireland. The light, airy rooms are accentuated by winding mahogany staircases and arched passageways throughout the house.

Guests of the Greenbriar enjoy the year-round outdoor spa, complimentary wine and tea, and early morning coffee. Tandem bike rentals are available for a modest fee. On weekends,

the inn provides a dining room for guests and the public. Private and shared bathrooms are available.

Gingerbread Pancakes

2½ cups all-purpose flour
5 teaspoons baking powder
1½ teaspoons salt
1 teaspoon baking soda
1 teaspoon cinnamon
½ teaspoon ginger
¼ cup molasses
2 cups milk
2 eggs
6 tablespoons butter, melted
1 cup raisins

In a large bowl combine the dry ingredients. Add the remaining ingredients and beat with an electric mixer until well blended. Pour the batter in small amounts onto a 275° griddle. Turn the pancakes when the edges are dry and bubbles rise to the surface.

Serves 6.

Norwegian Toast

1 cup margarine
1½ cups sugar
2 eggs
3¾ cups all-purpose flour
1 teaspoon baking soda
1 teaspoon cardamom

In a large bowl cream together the margarine and sugar. Add the eggs. Blend in the flour, baking soda, and cardamom. Form 10 balls and flatten on 2 ungreased cookie sheets. Bake in a 350° oven for 35 to 40 minutes.

Cut into strips, and spread out. Increase the heat to 375°, and toast for 7 minutes, turning once.

Serves 8 to 10.

Blueberry Pastry

¾ cup sugar
¼ cup butter, softened
1 egg
2 cups all-purpose flour
2 teaspoons baking powder
½ teaspoon salt
½ cup milk
2 cups fresh blueberries

Grease a 9-inch square baking pan. In a large bowl cream together the sugar, butter, and egg. In a separate bowl sift together the flour, baking powder, and salt. Add the dry ingredients to the creamed mixture alternately with the milk. Gently fold in the blueberries. Pour the batter into the prepared pan. Bake in a 350° oven for 40 to 45 minutes.

Serves 6 to 8.

Holmes Retreat

178 North Mink Creek Road
Pocatello, Idaho 83204
(208) 232-5518

Guests of Holmes Retreat, nestled in the mountains alongside scenic Mink Creek, enjoy breakfast in bed, in the dining room, or on a deck where hummingbirds are frequent companions. The inn is known for its hospitality and for the gourmet food that surpasses expectations. Guests may enjoy a walk in nature, where the many hummingbirds and songbirds abound. While turning down your bed at night, the innkeepers tuck in a teddy bear and place a mint on the pillow.

Hot Spiced Apple Cider

1 gallon apple cider or juice
5 cups water
1 cup sugar
1 6-ounce can orange juice concentrate, frozen
2 tablespoons lemon juice
½ ounce cinnamon sticks
1 tablespoon whole cloves
2 teaspoons whole allspice

In a large kettle combine the apple cider, water, and sugar. Heat until dissolved. Reduce the heat to the lowest setting and add the remaining ingredients. Simmer uncovered for 2 hours. The aroma is wonderful.

To store any unused portion, remove the spices and pour into a glass container. Refrigerate, and reheat portions as needed.

Makes 30 6-ounce servings.

The Gourmet Garden

2 tablespoons corn oil margarine
2 tablespoons all-purpose flour
2 cups milk
1 cup grated mild Cheddar cheese
1 4-ounce can sliced mushrooms, drained
1 4-ounce can diced green chilies

🍃 🍃 🍃

½ pound very lean bacon
¼ cup diced scallions, including top
12 large eggs, whisked until frothy
1 cup Whole Grain & Honey bread crumbs
2 tablespoons corn oil margarine, melted
¼ teaspoon paprika

In a saucepan melt 2 tablespoons of margarine. Whisk in the flour, and slowly add the milk. Cook until bubbly, stirring constantly. Add the grated cheese, and remove from the heat. Stir until the cheese melts into the sauce. Add the mushrooms and the entire contents of the can of diced chilies.

In a heavy skillet combine the bacon and scallions, and cook slowly until transparent but not brown. Add the eggs and cook, stirring constantly until softly scrambled but not set. Add the egg mixture to the sauce, stir to combine, and pour into an ungreased 9x13-inch baking dish.

Combine the bread crumbs, 2 tablespoons of margarine, and paprika. Sprinkle over the egg mixture. Cover and refrigerate overnight. Bake uncovered in a 350° oven for 30 minutes. Cut into squares and carefully lift with a spatula. Garnish the plate with fresh mint.

Serves 10.

Clam Chowder

6 to 7 medium Idaho Russet potatoes, peeled and diced
4 to 5 ribs celery, chopped
1 cup chopped onion
½ teaspoon salt
2 6½-ounce cans chopped clams
½ cup corn oil margarine
¾ cup all-purpose flour
1 quart half and half
½ teaspoon garlic salt

In a saucepan add the potatoes, celery, onion, and salt. Add the juice from the clams to the vegetables, reserving the clams. Add water to barely cover the vegetables and cover. Cook until tender. Do not drain.

In a small saucepan melt the margarine. Add the flour, and stir until smooth. Slowly add the half and half, and cook until thickened. Add the garlic salt and the clams. Pour the sauce into the vegetables. Heat the chowder over low heat for 5 mintues. Serve hot.

Serves 6 to 8.

Chicken Pasta Salad

½ cup Miracle Whip
¼ cup freshly grated Parmesan cheese

2 tablespoons milk
½ teaspoon salt
1½ cups chopped cooked chicken
4 ounces corkscrew noodles, cooked
1 tomato, chopped into ¾-inch chunks
½ green pepper, chopped into ½-inch chunks
¼ cup finely chopped onion
5 lettuce leaves

In a large bowl combine the Miracle Whip, cheese, milk, and salt. Mix well. Fold in the remaining ingredients. Cover and chill for 3 to 4 hours. Place the lettuce leaves on 5 serving plates. Spoon some of the salad into a 1-cup measuring cup, pressing firmly, and invert onto a lettuce leaf. Repeat with the remaining salad.

Serves 5.

Idaho Rocky Mountain Ranch

HC64
Box 9934
Stanley, Idaho 83278
(208) 774-3544

Idaho Rocky Mountain Ranch is nestled in one of the most spectacular, least explored regions of America: the Sawtooth and White Cloud mountain ranges of central Idaho. Established in 1930, the ranch remains much as it was sixty years ago; the original log pieces built by the early craftsmen still furnish the lodge and log cabins. Hundreds of miles of trails in the Sawtooth Wilderness lead guests to green meadows, mountain streams, and more than 300 lakes.

After an invigorating day, guests may relax in the natural hot water pool, eat in the restaurant that is open to the public, or visit around the glow of the hearth in the lodge. Log cabin accommodations provide fireplaces and private baths; lodge rooms all are equipped with private baths. Idaho Rocky Mountain Ranch is known to its customers as one of the finest guest ranches in the west.

Raspberry Vinaigrette

1 cup olive oil
½ cup loosely packed fresh mint leaves, finely chopped
¼ cup red raspberry vinegar
½ teaspoon minced garlic
¼ teaspoon freshly ground black pepper
¼ cup fresh or frozen raspberries

In a glass container combine all of the ingredients. Serve with simple salads.
Makes about 2 cups.

Bacon Cheese Muffins

6 to 7 strips bacon
2 cups all-purpose flour
1 tablespoon sugar
1 tablespoon baking powder
1 teaspoon salt
¼ teaspoon pepper or more to taste
1 egg
¾ cup milk
1 medium onion, minced
1 cup grated medium sharp Cheddar cheese

While the bacon is very cold, stack the strips and cut into 4 lengthwise strips, then cut across into ½-inch pieces. In a small heavy saucepan cook the bacon until lightly golden brown but not crisp. Place a strainer over a measuring cup and pour the drippings through the strainer. Add vegetable oil if needed to make ¼ cup. Drain the bacon on paper towels.

Grease 12 muffin cups. In a large bowl combine the flour, sugar, baking powder, salt, and pepper. In a small

bowl whisk the egg, milk, and bacon fat. Add the bacon, onion, and cheese, and pour over the dry ingredients. Fold together with a rubber spatula just until moistened. Spoon the batter into the prepared muffin cups. Bake in a 400° oven for 20 to 25 minutes, or until golden brown and springy to the touch. Cool in the pans for 10 minutes, then turn onto a rack.

Variation: Add a pinch of thyme and oregano, or use plain yogurt or buttermilk instead of milk.

Makes 12 muffins.

Mediterranean Chicken

½ cup Feta cheese
¼ cup minced green onions
Freshly ground pepper to taste
4 6- to 8-ounce boneless chicken breasts, with skin

❧ ❧ ❧

3 tablespoons clarified butter
2 small shallots, minced
¼ teaspoon parsley (or fresh basil)
3 small cloves garlic, minced
1 teaspoon oregano
1 cup sliced mushrooms
1 tablespoon all-purpose flour
⅓ cup white wine
½ cup chicken stock
½ cup diced red tomatoes
1 tablespoon Feta cheese

In a small bowl combine ½ cup of Feta cheese, the green onion, and pepper to taste. Flatten the chicken breasts and lightly pound with a meat mallet. Divide the filling equally between the chicken breasts. Carefully fold the chicken around the filling. Place skin-side up on a shallow baking dish. Bake in a 350° oven for 35 to 40 minutes.

In a small skillet heat the clarified butter until melted. Add the shallots, parsley, garlic, oregano, and mushrooms. Sauté briefly. Add the flour, stirring gently until blended. Slowly add the white wine, stirring constantly until well blended and slightly thickened. Add the chicken stock, stirring until blended. Add the tomatoes and remaining Feta cheese, and simmer for 10 minutes.

Adjust the seasonings to taste and serve over the baked chicken breasts.
Serves 4.

The River Street Inn

The River Street Inn

100 River Street West
Post Office Box 182
Sun Valley, Idaho 83353
(208) 726-3611

The first bed and breakfast in the Sun Valley area, the River Street Inn is situated on Trail Creek in Ketchum. It affords guests a breathtaking view of Bald Mountain. Although it is on a quiet street, it is within walking distance of shops, restaurants, and night life. It is also close to the ski slopes. The rooms are spacious and provide a view of trees and mountains; each has its own bathroom with Japanese soaking tub and separate shower. From the living room, French doors open onto an expansive deck with Trail Creek running below. Breakfast is an event.

Spinach Pie

8 ounces mild Italian sausage
2 10-ounce packages frozen
    chopped spinach, cooked and
    drained

6 eggs, separated
1½ cups grated cheese (Cheddar,
    Swiss, or Monterey Jack)
3 tablespoons dried onions
2 teaspoons Worcestershire sauce
Dash Tabasco sauce
1 sheet puff pastry
1 egg
2 tablespoons water
Sesame seeds

Grease an 8-inch springform pan. Remove the casings from the sausage, and sauté the sausage until browned and crumbly. Thoroughly drain the grease. In a large bowl combine the spinach, 6 egg yolks, grated cheese, dried onions, sausage, Worcestershire sauce, and Tabasco. Mix well. Beat the egg whites until stiff, and fold into the spinach mixture. Add the spinach mixture, and make a lattice with the puff pastry. Beat the egg with

the water. Brush with egg wash, and sprinkle with sesame seeds. Bake in a 350° oven for 30 minutes, or until golden brown.
    Serves 6.

Potato Omelet

¼ cup olive oil
2 medium Idaho potatoes, cut into
    ½-inch cubes
½ cup chopped green onion,
    including tops
¼ cup chopped parsley
1 clove garlic, minced or pressed
6 eggs
¼ cup water
½ teaspoon salt
⅛ teaspoon pepper
Sour cream
4 slices bacon, cooked crisp
Salsa (optional)

In a large frying pan heat the oil over medium-high heat. Add the potatoes and cook until golden brown, stirring very little to let the potatoes become crisp. Add the onion, parsley, and garlic, and cook until the onion is limp. Reduce the heat to medium. In a bowl beat the eggs and water together, and stir in the salt and pepper. Pour the egg mixture over the potato mixture, cover, and cook for 10 minutes. Cut into wedges. Garnish each serving with sour cream and crumbled bacon. Serve with salsa, if desired.
    Serves 6.

Illinois

Holden's Guest House

East Main, Down Sun-Up Lane
Bishop Hill, Illinois 61419
(309) 927-3500

Holden's Guest House provides its guests with a combination of tranquil privacy and rural hospitality in a restored 1869 farmstead. Bishop Hill, an 1846 Swedish commune, is designated a National Historic Landmark and is home to five museums, two dozen shops, and many fine restaurants. Guests of the inn are treated to elegant breakfasts delivered on sterling silver trays, rooms furnished with period antiques, and Bishop Hill collectibles.

Söt Gröt
("Bittered" Sweet Porridge)

5⅓ cups milk
½ teaspoon salt
⅔ cup quick Cream of Wheat
2 firm, ripe pears
2 tablespoons butter
Ground cardamom or mace
Aromatic bitters
Cream and honey
Fresh warm croissants

In a large saucepan bring the milk and salt to nearly boiling. Slowly add the cereal, stirring constantly. Bring to a boil over medium heat, reduce the heat, and stir constantly until thickened. Cover and turn off the heat. Meanwhile, peel, core, and slice the pears. In a sauté pan melt the butter, and add the pears and cardamom to taste. Cover and simmer until tender. As the pears are becoming tender, sprinkle with a generous dash of aromatic bitters. Whip the cereal with a fork, adding milk if too thick. Spoon the fluffed cereal into warmed serving dishes and top with the pear glacé. Serve with cream, honey, and warm croissants.
Serves 4.

Sole Erik

4 pounds garden fresh kale
4 quarts boiling salted water
6 slices bacon, cut into 1-inch
** pieces**
¼ to ½ cup water
3 tablespoons rolled oats

&ta; &ta; &ta;

1 cup dry white vermouth
1 pound fresh fillet of sole

&ta; &ta; &ta;

⅔ cup butter
4 egg yolks
1 tablespoon cream or milk
Salt and white pepper to taste
Dash paprika
Lemon slices to garnish

Wash and strip the fresh kale from the stalks, and chop coarsely. Place the kale in the boiling water and cook just until wilted. Do not overcook. Drain and rinse. In a medium skillet sauté the bacon pieces over medium heat. Add the kale, and ¼ cup of water. Sprinkle the oats over the kale, and stir to blend. Cover and simmer until the oats have thickened, adding more water if necessary. On a large broiler-proof platter or serving plates, form the kale into a bed.

In a medium skillet bring the vermouth to a simmer. Spread the fillets on cheesecloth large enough to span the width of the skillet plus a few inches. Lower the cloth and fillets into the vermouth. Cover and steam for 10 minutes. Place the steamed fillets on the kale and place in a warm oven. Reduce the vermouth to ⅔ cup.

In a medium saucepan melt the butter over very low heat. Whisk the egg yolks, and add to the melted butter. Add the cream, stir, and slowly add the vermouth. Stir constantly until thickened. Add salt and pepper. Remove the fillets from the oven, and increase the heat to broil. Pour the sauce over the fillets, and sprinkle lightly with paprika. Return to the oven and broil until delicately brown. Garnish with lemon slices.
Serves 4.

Veal Cutlet à la Oscar

2 tablespoons butter
2 tablespoons flour
1 cup thin cream
½ cup canned asparagus liquid
1 tablespoon crawfish butter
** (see note)**
12 canned asparagus tips

&ta; &ta; &ta;

3 tablespoons vinegar
1 sprig chervil
1 sprig tarragon
½ teaspoons salt
¼ teaspoon sugar
6 crushed peppercorns
2 tablespoons minced yellow onion
2 egg yolks
½ cup butter
1 tablespoon minced parsley
½ cup cooked or canned lobster

ᔓ ᔓ ᔓ

3 pounds veal cutlets
1½ teaspoon salt
½ teaspoon white pepper
2 to 3 tablespoons butter

Prepare the first sauce. In a saucepan melt 2 tablespoons of butter, and stir in the flour until smooth. Blend in the cream and asparagus liquid. Cook for 2 to 3 minutes, stirring until slightly thickened. Stir in the crawfish butter and mix well. Add the asparagus tips and keep the sauce warm over hot water.

Prepare the second sauce. In the top of a double boiler combine the vinegar, herbs, salt, sugar, peppercorns, and onion. Heat the mixture and reduce to slightly more than 1 tablespoon of liquid remains. Strain and return to the double boiler. Add the egg yolks and 1 tablespoon of butter. Cook, beating briskly, until thickened. Remove from the heat and cool partially, adding dabs of cold butter at intervals. Set aside.

Cut the veal into ½-inch slices. Cut the slices into serving-sized pieces. Season with salt and pepper and pound very thin. In a skillet melt 2 to 3 tablespoons of butter and cook the meat, browning well on both sides. Arrange the meat on a warm platter.

To the second sauce, add some of the juice from the meat and stir in the parsley and lobster. Place 2 asparagus stalks on each serving of veal and top with the first sauce. Pour the second sauce around the veal.

Note: Crawfish butter is made by mixing equal parts of butter and mashed cooked crawfish. Lobster is equally good

Serves 6 to 8.

Holden's Guest House

Uppåkrakakor
(Cookies from Uppakra)

1⅔ cups all-purpose flour
⅓ cup cornstarch
⅓ cup sugar
¾ cup butter
Raspberry jam
1 egg white
3 to 4 tablespoons sugar
3 to 4 tablespoons chopped almonds

Grease a cookie sheet. In a large bowl combine the flour, cornstarch, and sugar. Cut in the butter with a pastry blender. Form a smooth ball and chill until firm. Roll the dough ⅓-inch thick and cut into 2-inch circles. Place 1 teaspoon of jam in the center of each round and fold the cookies off-center, so the bottom edge shows. Brush with egg white, and sprinkle with sugar and almonds. Place on the prepared cookie sheet. Bake in a 350° oven for 8 to 10 minutes.

Makes 4 dozen.

Mormors Hjärtan
(Grandmother's Hearts)

2 cups all-purpose flour
⅓ cup sugar
¾ cup plus 2 tablespoons butter
1 egg yolk (reserve white)
Cinnamon-sugar

Grease a cookie sheet. In a large bowl combine the flour and sugar. Cut in

the butter and add the egg yolk. Gather the dough into a ball and chill until firm. Cut with a heart-shaped cookie cutter and place on the cookie sheet. Brush with lightly beaten egg white. Sprinkle with cinnamon-sugar. Bake in a 350° oven for 8 to 12 minutes.

Makes 4 dozen cookies.

Russinkakor
(Raisin Cookies)

3 tablespoons brandy, rum, or vodka
⅔ cup finely chopped raisins
½ cup butter
¾ cup confectioners' sugar
2 eggs
¾ cup all-purpose flour

Grease a cookie sheet. Pour the brandy over the raisins and marinate for 1 hour. Cream the butter and sugar until the mixture is light and creamy. Add the eggs and flour, blending well. Fold in the raisins and brandy. Place nickel-sized amounts of dough generously spaced on the prepared cookie sheet. Bake in a 375° oven for 8 to 10 minutes. Remove from the cookie sheet while still hot.

Makes 10 dozen.

Avery Guest House

606 South Prospect Street
Galena, Illinois 61036
(815) 777-3883

Built before the Civil War, Avery Guest House was remodeled in the 1920s. Situated within a few blocks of Galena's main shopping area and historical buildings, it is a homey place of refuge after a busy day of exploring.

Four bedrooms with queen-size beds are available, and guests are encouraged to play the piano, watch television, join in a table game, or enjoy the view from the porch swing. Smoking is permitted outdoors.

Hot Cranberry Punch

1 quart cranberries
1 quart water

🐌 🐌 🐌

1 quart water
2 cups sugar
6 ounces red hots
12 cloves

🐌 🐌 🐌

1 6-ounce can frozen orange juice
⅓ cup lemon juice
3 quarts water

In a large saucepan boil the cranberries in 1 quart of water. In a separate pan or stockpot bring 1 quart of water, the sugar, red hots, and cloves to a boil, stirring until dissolved. Add the remaining ingredients, including the cranberries, and heat through.

Serves 20.

Grandma Delzell's Soft Graham Bread

My grandmother gave us this healthy, hearty bread often in the 1930s on the farm in central Michigan—of course, with plenty of butter and honey.

½ cup brown sugar
2 tablespoons fat
2 teaspoons salt
2 teaspoons baking soda
2 cups buttermilk
2 cups graham flour, or more

Grease a 9x13-inch baking pan. In a large bowl combine the first 5 ingredients. Add graham flour to make a stiff dough. Place in the prepared pan. Bake in a 400° oven for 20 minutes.

Serves 12 to 15.

The Comfort Guest House

1000 Third Street
Galena, Illinois 61036
(815) 777-3062

The Comfort Guest House in historic Galena, an authentically restored riverfront town, was built in 1856 by William H. Snyder. It is a leisurely four-block stroll from a downtown brimming with antique shops, galleries, museums, parks, restaurants, and unlimited tranquility. At day's end one can take in the dance of the fireflies from the old porch swing or meander to an antique-furnished room to snuggle under a hand-tied quilt for a peaceful night's rest.

Peach Crisp

4 medium peaches, sliced (or 2 16-
ounce cans, drained)
¾ cup Bisquick
⅔ cup quick-cooking oats
½ cup loosely packed brown sugar

THE COMFORT GUEST HOUSE

3 tablespoons margarine or butter,
softened
½ teaspoon cinnamon
¼ teaspon nutmeg
Frozen yogurt

In an 8-inch square microwave-proof dish arrange the peaches. In a bowl combine the Bisquick, oats, brown sugar, margarine, cinnamon, and nutmeg. Sprinkle over the peaches. Microwave the crisp uncovered on high for 4 minutes. Turn the dish and microwave for 4 to 6 minutes more, until the peaches are tender. Serve with frozen yogurt.

Variation: Use blueberries instead of peaches, or along with the peaches.

Serves 4 to 6.

🐌 🐌 🐌 🐌 🐌

Zucchini Cookies

A soft cookie, great for porch snacks with sun tea.

½ cup oil
1 egg, beaten
½ cup sugar
½ cup brown sugar
1 cup all-purpose flour
½ teaspoon baking soda
¼ teaspoon cinnamon
¼ teaspoon nutmeg
1½ cups rolled oats
1 cup grated zucchini
Nuts, chocolate chips, or dates
(optional)

Grease a cookie sheet. In a large bowl combine the oil, egg, sugar, and brown sugar. In a separate bowl combine the flour, baking soda, cinnamon, and nutmeg. Add the dry ingredients to the egg mixture. Blend in the oats and zucchini. The mixture will be runny. Add nuts, chocolate chips, or dates if desired. Drop by spoonfuls onto the prepared cookie sheet. Bake in a 350° oven for 12 minutes.

Makes 3 dozen cookies.

The Brick House

Box 301
Goodfield, Illinois 61742
(309) 963-2545
(800) 322-2304

The Brick House is a nine-room mansion built by Henry Robinson in 1857. Made with bricks fashioned by Robinson himself, some of its walls measure eighteen inches in width. Boasting most of its original furnishings, the inn is rich in association with Abraham Lincoln. As a circuit court judge, Lincoln frequented the Brick House, not only as a family friend of the Robinsons but also as their lawyer. The four-poster bed Lincoln slept in has been returned to its original resting place in the master bedroom, which bears his name.

Stuffed Mushrooms

150 medium-sized fresh mushrooms
1 pound bacon
½ to ¾ pound shredded Cheddar cheese
1 cup mayonnaise
1 cup dried bread crumbs
1 teaspoon onion salt
1 teaspoon Worcestershire sauce
Small amount of white wine

Remove the stems from the mushrooms. Wash the mushroom caps in cold water. Turn the caps upside down to drain out the water. In a large skillet fry the bacon until crisp. Drain on a paper towel until cooled and crumble. In a bowl combine the bacon, Cheddar, mayonnaise, dried bread crumbs, onion salt, and Worcestershire sauce. Mix well. Mound the mixture onto the mushroom caps. Place the stuffed mushrooms in a shallow baking pan. Drizzle white wine over the mushrooms. Bake in a 350° oven for 10 to 15 minutes. Serve hot.

Makes 35 servings.

Mushrooms Teriyaki

2 6-ounce cans button mushrooms
1 cup bottled teriyaki sauce
½ cup sherry
2 tablespoons grated gingerroot (or 1 tablespoon powdered ginger)
1 clove garlic, minced
2 teaspoons brown sugar

In a serving bowl combine all of the ingredients, tossing to combine. Refrigerate overnight. Serve the mushrooms on toothpicks.

Serves 8 to 10.

Holiday Punch

1 3-ounce package cherry gelatin
1 cup boiling water
1 6-ounce can frozen lemonade concentrate (or pineapple concentrate)
3 cups cold water
1 quart cold cranberry juice
12 ounces ginger ale (or sparkling white wine)
Ice cream (optional)

Dissolve the gelatin in the boiling water. Add the lemonade concentrate, cold water, and the cranberry juice. Chill the mixture. Just before serving, pour the chilled mixture over ice cubes in a large punch bowl. Add ginger ale. Dollops of ice cream can be floated on top of the punch for a frosty effect, if desired.

Serves 25 to 30.

Dillies

A zesty bean salad that can be prepared a day or so ahead.

1 16-ounce can green beans
⅓ cup red wine vinegar
½ teaspoon Beau Monde seasoning
½ teaspoon dill weed
3 tablespoons olive oil
1 tablespoon onion salt

Drain the beans and place in a serving bowl. In a small saucepan heat the vinegar and pour over the beans. When the beans cool add the Beau Monde seasoning, dill weed, and olive oil. Chill well, preferably overnight. Just before serving, sprinkle with onion salt.

Serves 4 to 6.

Maple Leaf Cottage Inn

Post Office Box 156
Historic Elsah, Illinois 62028
(618) 374-1684

Maple Leaf Cottage Inn offers a unique setting, comfortable lodging, and superb dining. The heart of activity takes place in the Garden House where meals are served and crafts, flowers, and personal items are available. Surrounded by a lovely English garden, patio, and verandah, guests enjoy an entire village block of private grounds in a nineteenth-century village. Three cottages provide cozy, private lodging.

Cranapple Frappé

2 cups cranapple juice
1 cup freshly squeezed orange juice
¼ cup whipping cream
1 tablespoon lemon juice

2 bananas
¾ cup crushed ice
Sugar to taste
Fresh mint

In a blender combine all of the ingredients. Blend on high speed for 1 minute. Serve in a frosted stem glass and garnish with mint.

Serves 6.

---

258 Inn

Morton at Church Street
Jacksonville, Illinois 62650
(217) 245-2588
(217) 245-6665 (owner's residence)

This 1845 house, which has been restored to its original state, offers three rooms to its guests. Each room has a private bath, a handmade quilt, and furnishings of the mid-eighteenth century. Situated in the heart of west central Illinois, Jacksonville is noted for its historic landmarks: restored homes and businesses, Illinois College (the state's oldest), the 120-year-old courthouse, and Governor Duncan's Mansion.

258 Inn

Fresh Apple Cinnamon Coffee Cake

1¾ cups sugar
½ cup low cholesterol oil
2 tablespoons water
2 egg whites
2 cups all-purpose flour
1 teaspoon baking soda
2 teaspoons cinnamon
½ teaspoon orange peel
4 cups finely chopped apples
1 cup walnuts or pecans (optional)

&❧ &❧ &❧

¼ cup brown sugar
¼ teaspoon cinnamon

Grease a 10-inch tube pan. In a large bowl combine the sugar, oil, water, and egg whites. In a separate bowl combine the flour, baking soda, and cinnamon. Add the dry ingredients to the liquid mixture, and fold in the orange peel, apples, and walnuts. The batter will be very thick. Transfer the batter to the prepared pan and sprinkle with sugar. Bake in a 350° oven for 55 minutes. Combine the brown sugar and cinnamon, and sprinkle over the warm cake.

Serves 18.

The Standish House

540 West Carroll Street
Lanark, Illinois 61046
(815) 493-2307

Named in honor of Myles Standish, the military leader of the 1620 Plymouth colony and a direct ancestor of inn owner Norman Standish, this 1882 house has been restored to the grandeur it was meant to assume.

Each of the five guest rooms is furnished with eighteenth- and nineteenth-century English antiques and reproductions. Each room has lush carpets and draperies, unique sinks, and queen-size canopied beds.

❧ ❧ ❧ ❧ ❧

Country Pot Roast Dinner

This technique for cooking pot roast has been used in the Standish family for at least 3 generations. As a scoutmaster, I have required all of the Boy Scouts in my troop to cook a pot roast dinner over a campfire to meet the requirements for a Cooking Merit Badge.

3 to 4 pound pot roast
1½ teaspoons salt
1 teaspoon pepper
1½ teaspoons garlic salt
3 tablespoons shortening
1 bay leaf
1 cup water
1½ pounds fresh carrots
4 medium onions
2 pounds potatoes, peeled and
    halved or quartered

&❧ &❧ &❧

3 tablespoons all-purpose flour

Trim away the excess fat from the roast. Season the roast on both sides with salt, pepper and garlic salt to taste. In a heavy skillet or Dutch oven melt the shortening. Place the pot roast in the skillet, add the bay leaf, and simmer over high heat for 5 minutes on each side. Turn periodically to prevent burning. Transfer the roast and pan juice to a small covered roasting pan or covered casserole dish. Save the skillet for making gravy. Add about 1 cup of water. Bake in a 350° oven for about 2 hours and 30 minutes. Check periodically, and add water if needed to maintain the water level.

Wash the carrots and cut to the desired size. Add the carrots to the juice around the roast. Increase the heat to 450° and bake for 30 minutes. Cut the onions in half horizontally, and cut each half into quarters. Lift the roast and place the onions and potatoes underneath. Add water if needed to cover the vegetables, but the roast should be mostly out of the water. Cook for 1 hour.

Pour the juice from the roasting pan into the skillet and add the flour. Season to taste and slowly bring to a boil. Stir constantly until thickened. Separate the carrots, onions, and potatoes, and serve with the roast.

Serves 4 to 6.

Meatless Tamale Pie

**2 cups cooked pinto or kidney
  beans
1 tablespoon tomato paste
3 tablespoons water
½ cup chopped onion
2 tablespoons oil
¼ teaspoon garlic powder
1 teaspoon chili powder
1 teaspoon salt
¼ cup sliced pitted ripe olives
½ cup frozen corn
½ cup green pepper, chopped
¼ cup parsley or cilantro
½ cup chopped celery**

🍂   🍂   🍂

**2½ cups cold water
1½ cups cornmeal
1 teaspoon salt
½ teaspoon chili powder**

🍂   🍂   🍂

¼ cup grated Cheddar cheese

Grease an 8-inch square pan. Mash or grind the cooked beans. In a small bowl combine the tomato paste and water. In a skillet sauté the onions in the oil. Add the mashed beans, tomato mixture, garlic powder, 1 teaspoon of chili powder, salt, olives, corn, green pepper, parsley, and celery. Cook over medium heat, stirring constantly until hot.

In a heavy pan combine the cold water, cornmeal, salt, and ½ teaspoon of chili powder. Cook over medium heat until the mixture thickens and comes to a boil, stirring to prevent scorching. Spread ⅔ of the cornmeal mixture in the bottom of the greased pan. Pour in the bean mixture and top with the remaining cornmeal mixture. Sprinkle with Cheddar cheese. Bake in a 350° oven for 30 minutes.

Serves 6 to 8.

Walnut-Raisin Pie

**1 cup raisins
1 cup walnuts, coarsely chopped
1 9-inch unbaked pie shell
5 eggs
1½ cups sugar
¾ teaspoon cinnamon
¾ teaspoon nutmeg
¾ teaspoon cloves
3 tablespoons lemon juice
3 tablespoons milk**

Soak the raisins in warm water until plump. Drain carefully. Spread the raisins and walnuts evenly in the bottom of the pie shell. In a bowl beat the eggs just until frothy. In a separate bowl combine the sugar and spices. Beat the sugar mixture into the eggs. Add the lemon juice and milk, and beat for a few minutes. Pour the egg mixture over the walnuts and raisins. Bake in a 350° oven for 50 to 55 minutes. Cool completely before serving.

Serves 6 to 8.

Carr Mansion Guesthouse

416 East Broadway
Monmouth, Illinois 61462
(309) 734-3654

This stately mansion built in 1877 was the pride of the Carr family for over sixty years. One of the best surviving examples of late Victorian architecture in western Illinois, it is listed on the National Register of Historic Places. Its twenty rooms have been well preserved. The staircase was designed especially for the home, and the original chandeliers, wall sconces, beveled leaded glass windows, and architectural details are still present. The guesthouse is open year round, with three guest rooms available. Within walking distance of the city square and Monmouth College, the inn is known for the warm hospitality of its hosts. Guests may relax by a cozy fire during the winter months or enjoy the verandah in the summertime.

Harvest Overnight Casserole

**2 pounds bulk sausage
2 apples, cored and sliced
9 slices bread, crusts removed and
  cubed
¾ teaspoon dry mustard
9 eggs, beaten
1½ cups grated sharp Cheddar
  cheese
3 cups milk**

Lightly grease a 9x13-inch baking dish. In a skillet fry the sausage, crumbling it while it cooks. Drain on paper towels, reserving the pan drippings. Place the sausage in the prepared dish. Sauté the apple slices in

Carr Mansion Guesthouse

The Inn on the Square

3 Montgomery Street
Oakland, Illinois 61943
(217) 346-2289
(217) 346-2653

Blending the old with the new, the Inn on the Square offers warm hospitality and simple country pleasures, as well as access to historical sites, recreational activities, and good shopping. The four upstairs bedrooms, furnished for country living, have their own "down the hall" private baths. The library provides opportunity for reading and conversation. The inn has its own gift shop, and the Tea Room offers simple but elegant luncheons.

the sausage drippings. In a bowl combine the apples, bread cubes, mustard, eggs, cheese, and milk. Mix well. Pour the apple mixture over the sausage, cover, and refrigerate overnight. Bake covered in a 350° oven for 30 minutes. Uncover and bake for 30 minutes.

Serves 8.

Aunt Anne's Baked Chili Relleno

2 4-ounce cans green chili peppers, drained
4 cups grated Cheddar cheese
4 cups grated Monterey Jack cheese
5 eggs, beaten
3½ cups milk
½ cup plus 1 teaspoon all-purpose flour
1 teaspoon salt

Dry the peppers on paper towels. Chop the peppers and arrange on the bottom of a 9x13-inch baking dish. In a large bowl combine the remaining ingredients and pour over the peppers. Bake in a 350° oven for 1 hour, or until the custard sets and the top is golden.

Serves 8.

Crab Louis

1 pound crab meat
1 cup chopped celery
¼ cup chopped green onion
½ cup mayonnaise
¼ cup chili sauce
½ cup cream, whipped

In a large bowl combine the crab meat, celery, and onions. In a separate bowl combine the mayonnaise and chili sauce. Blend the mixture into the crab. Fold in the whipped cream and chill. Place each serving on a lettuce leaf and serve with hot croissants.

Serves 10.

Vegetarian Quiche

1 cup Bisquick
2½ cups half and half
4 eggs
½ teaspoon oregano leaves
1 teaspoon salt

The Inn on the Square

Dash pepper
¼ teaspoon garlic powder

   🌢   🌢   🌢

¾ cup grated zucchini
1 cup grated Swiss cheese
1 tablespoon finely chopped onion

Grease a 10-inch pie plate. In a large bowl combine the first 7 ingredients with an electric mixer. Fold in the remaining ingredients, stirring with a spoon. Pour the mixture into the pie plate. Bake in a 375° oven for 50 minutes.

Serves 6.

Cranberry Pudding

2 cups sugar
2 teaspoons vanilla extract
1 cup butter (not margarine)
1 cup half and half

   🌢   🌢   🌢

2 cups all-purpose flour
1 cup sugar
3 teaspoons baking powder
1 cup milk
2 cups cranberries
3 tablespoons butter, melted

Grease a 9x13-inch pan. In the top of a double boiler combine 2 cups of sugar, the vanilla extract, 1 cup of butter, and the half and half. Heat through. Set sauce aside, keeping it warm.

In a bowl combine the flour, 1 cup of sugar, and baking powder. Add the milk and mix well. Fold in the cranberries, and stir in 3 tablespoons of melted butter. Spread the batter into the prepared pan. Bake in a 375° oven for 30 minutes, until done and lightly browned. Cool the cake for 5 minutes. Prick the top with a fork and pour the warm sauce over the top. Serve immediately.

Serves 12.

Yesterday's Memories

303 East Peru
Route 6
Princeton, Illinois 61356
(815) 872-7753

Yesterday's Memories was originally part of the home of Nehemiah Matson, who built his house in the 1850s. After the east wing of the Matson home was moved sometime near the turn of the century, the main house was "modernized" by incorporating newer Queen Anne details that were then in vogue.

Today the homey atmosphere of Yesterday's Memories reflects the interests of its innkeepers. The casual decorating sets the mood for collections of dolls, dollhouses, trains, and other treasures of youth. In summer guests breakfast on the latticed screen porch, then stroll through the organic vegetable garden. In winter the woodstove in the dining room provides warmth.

May Memories Breakfast

Here in our Illinois garden, asparagus and strawberries grow beside each other, and are their best in May. We pick them fresh in the morning and serve with homemade sausage made at our daughter's farm.

1 pound asparagus, cut into 1-inch
   pieces
1 pound bulk sausage
1½ cups milk
2 chicken bouillon cubes
1 10½-ounce can cream of
   mushroom soup
8 slices toast
2 hard-boiled eggs, sliced

**1 pint strawberries
1 8-ounce carton blueberry yogurt**

In a large saucepan over medium-high heat, boil the asparagus in ½ inch of water for 8 minutes. Set aside. In a large skillet crumble and brown the sausage. Drain off the grease. Add the milk and bouillon cubes, and simmer until the bouillon is dissolved. Add the mushroom soup, stirring often until heated through. Add the asparagus.

Arrange 2 slices of toast on each of 4 serving plates. Spoon the sausage mixture over the toast, and arrange sliced egg on the top. Place the strawberries in dessert dishes, and spoon a dollop of yogurt over each serving.

Serves 4.

Yesterday's Memories Pear Pie

This pie is frequently awaiting guests as they arrive in the afternoon.

**2 cups all-purpose flour
1 teaspoon salt
⅔ cup shortening
¼ cup cold water**

**6 cups sliced pears, peeled and cored
¾ cup sugar
1 teaspoon cinnamon
2 tablespoons tapioca
2 tablespoons butter, melted
Milk or egg white**

In a large bowl combine the flour, salt, and shortening, blending with a pastry blender until the mixture resembles small peas. Sprinkle with water and mix only until the flour is moistened. Gather the dough into a ball and divide in half. Roll each piece to fit a 9-inch pie plate. Place one round in the bottom of the pie plate.

In a separate bowl combine the next 5 ingredients. Place the mixture in the pastry shell. Moisten the edges of the pastry, and cover with the remaining pastry, sealing the edges.

Cut slits in the top crust. Brush with milk or egg white and sprinkle with additional sugar. Bake in a 425° oven for 35 to 45 minutes.

Note: The pie may be prepared ahead of time and frozen unbaked. Brush the pastry with milk or butter just before baking. Bake for 1 hour.

Serves 8.

Dumplin' Delights

**1 cup all-purpose flour
½ teaspoon salt
1 teaspoon baking powder
½ cup margarine or butter
¼ cup milk**

**¼ cup sugar
¼ teaspoon cinnamon
Pinch nutmeg
3 large apples, cored, peeled, and halved**

**½ cup firmly packed brown sugar
½ cup sugar
1 cup water**

**½ teaspoon cinnamon
2 tablespoons butter**

In a medium bowl combine the flour, salt, and baking powder. Cut the shortening into the flour mixture with a pastry blender until the mixture resembles small peas. Add milk and mix just until blended. Gather the dough into a ball, wrap in plastic, and chill.

In a small bowl combine the sugar, cinnamon, and nutmeg. Divide the chilled dough into 6 sections. Roll each section into a 6-inch circle on a lightly floured board. Place an apple half on each circle. Spoon 1 teaspoon of cinnamon mixture over the apple. Fold the pastry around the apple, tucking the pastry to fit. Place the dumplings in a 9-inch baking dish, flat-side down.

In a small saucepan combine the remaining ingredients, and heat over low heat until the butter is melted and the sugar is dissolved. Pour the mixture over the dumplings. Bake in a 375° oven for 35 to 40 minutes.

Serves 6.

Yesterday's Memories

Indiana

Maple Leaf Inn Bed and Breakfast

831 North Grand Avenue
Connersville, Indiana 47331
(317) 825-7099

Maple Leaf Inn, built in the mid-1860s, takes its name from the maple trees that surround it. Its four bedrooms, one of which has a private bath, are comfortably furnished with period furniture and paintings by local artists. Area attractions include antique shops, state parks, one of Indiana's largest lakes, and a ride on the Whitewater Valley Railroad to Old Metamora.

Almost-a-Meal Breakfast Drink

- 1 5¼-ounce can pineapple tidbits, undrained
- 1 medium banana
- ¼ cup milk
- 8 ounces pineapple sherbet (or lowfat yogurt)
- 2 tablespoons orange juice

In a food processor combine all of the ingredients. Blend until smooth.
Serves 2.

Warm Breakfast Bananas

- ¼ to ⅓ cup margarine
- 2 to 3 tablespoons lemon juice
- 3 to 4 bananas, peeled
- ¼ cup sugar
- 1 teaspoon cinnamon

In a shallow baking dish melt the butter in a 375° oven. Stir in the lemon juice. Place the bananas in the butter mixture, and brush the mixture onto the bananas until they are well coated. Sprinkle with cinnamon and sugar. Bake in a 375° oven for 15 minutes or until the margarine is bubbly.
Serves 3 to 4.

Kintner House Inn

Capitol and Chestnut
Corydon, Indiana 47112
(812) 738-2020

Opened in July 1873 by Jacob Kintner as Corydon's finest hotel, this three-story brick building contains fifteen guest rooms with private baths. Each room is named after a significant person from Corydon's past.

The first and second floors feature Victorian decor, and the third features a country theme.

Sausage Cheese Grits

- 1 pound sausage, crumbled, browned and drained
- 4 cups water
- 1 cup grits
- 1 teaspoon salt (optional)
- 2 cups shredded Cheddar cheese
- 2 eggs, beaten
- Milk
- 1 teaspoon garlic salt

Arrange the sausage in the bottom of a 2-quart casserole dish. In a saucepan combine the water, grits, and salt, and cook over medium heat until thick. Add the cheese. Place the eggs in a 1 cup measuring cup, and add milk to make 1 cup. Add the egg mixture to the grits mixture. Season with garlic salt. Pour the grits mixture over the sausage. Bake in a 350° oven for 1 hour.
Serves 4.

Cocoa Banana Bread

- ½ cup butter or margarine, softened
- 1 cup sugar
- 1 cup mashed ripe bananas
- ¼ cup milk
- 2 eggs
- 1 teaspoon vanilla extract

❧ ❧ ❧

2 cups all-purpose flour
⅓ cup unsweetened cocoa
1 teaspoon baking soda
½ teaspoon salt
½ cup chopped nuts (optional)

Grease the bottom of a 9x5-inch loaf pan. In a large mixing bowl combine the first 6 ingredients and beat with an electric mixer on medium speed for 1 minute. In a separate bowl combine the flour, cocoa, baking soda, and salt. Stir into the banana mixture until just blended. Add the nuts, if desired. Pour the batter into the prepared pan. Bake in a 350° oven for 50 to 60 minutes. Cool in the pan for 5 minutes, then remove and cool completely.

Makes 1 loaf, 8 servings.

Cragwood Inn

303 North Second Street
Decatur, Indiana 46733
(249) 728-2000

In this graceful Queen Anne home, guests can experience the elegance of Victorian living and old-fashioned hospitality. With five spacious guest rooms, the inn features ornate tin ceilings, four fireplaces, and many original light fixtures. Situated on the edge of downtown Decatur, it is within walking distance of antique shops, specialty stores, good restaurants, and municipal sports facilities.

Connie's Artichoke Dip

2 8-ounce packages cream cheese, softened
1 cup mayonnaise
1 cup Parmesan cheese
1 cup diced marinated artichoke hearts

2 tablespoons liquid from canned artichokes
1 teaspoon dill
1 teaspoon garlic powder

In a large bowl combine all of the ingredients. Transfer the dip to a baking dish and bake uncovered in a 350° oven for 30 minutes or until brown and bubbly.

Serves 10 to 12.

Ham and Swiss Toast

1 loaf French bread
6 slices Swiss cheese
2 ounces thinly sliced ham
4 eggs, beaten
1 cup milk
1 teaspoon vanilla extract

❧ ❧ ❧

½ cup cold water
4 teaspoons cornstarch
½ teaspoon shredded orange peel
1 cup orange juice
2 tablespoons honey

Grease a baking dish. Cut the bread into 12 slices. Cut a pocket into each slice. Fill each pocket with half a slice of cheese and some ham. In a bowl combine the eggs, milk, and vanilla. Dip the bread slices in the mixture, coating both sides. Place on the prepared dish. Bake in a 450° oven for 8 minutes. Turn the slices over and bake for 7 minutes.

In a saucepan blend together the cold water and cornstarch, stirring until dissolved. Add the orange peel, orange juice, and honey. Cook the mixture over medium heat until thick and bubbly. Serve the sauce over the warm toast.

Serves 6.

Cragwood Inn

Fruited Chicken Salad

3 cups cooked chicken chunks
1 5-ounce can sliced water chestnuts
¼ cup chopped pecans
½ cup chopped celery
¼ cup chopped onion
⅔ cup mayonnaise
1 cup halved grapes
1 cup pineapple tidbits
1 11-ounce can mandarin orange
  segments
Lettuce leaves

In a large bowl combine all of the ingredients except the lettuce. Place each serving on a lettuce leaf.
Serves 6 to 8.

De'Coy's Bed and Breakfast

1546 West 100 North
Hartford City, Indiana 47348
(317) 348-2164

Situated just west of Hartford City, De'Coy's offers five attractive bedrooms with extra "Hoosier" touches. Guests enjoy a relaxed rural atmosphere in this restored country home decorated by one of the owners, who is an interior designer.

Individual Ham Puffs

Serve with fresh fruit and muffins.

4 eggs
½ cup milk
½ teaspoon dry mustard
⅛ teaspoon pepper
1 cup shredded cheese
2 3-ounce packages cream cheese,
  cut up

1 cup finely diced cooked ham
½ teaspoon dried parsley flakes

In a blender combine the eggs, milk, mustard, and pepper. Cover and blend until smooth. With the blender running, add the cheeses through the lid opening. Blend until nearly smooth. Stir in the ham and parsley. Pour into 4 ungreased 1-cup soufflé dishes. Bake in a 375° oven for 25 to 30 minutes or until set.
Serves 4.

The Thorpe House

Clayborne Street
Metamora, Indiana 47030
(317) 647-5425
(317) 932-2365

Built in 1840, the Thorpe House still boasts much of its original craftsmanship, from the fancy cast hinges on the front door to the transoms upstairs. Restored in the mid-1980s, the inn has five unique rooms, three with private baths, each named after the owner's paternal Indiana settlers. In Old Metamora, the steam engine still brings passenger cars, the horses still pull the canal boat, and the grist mill still grinds cornmeal. Breakfast is in hearty country style.

Dark French Dressing

This recipe won so many raves that it is now our house dressing.

1 cup oil
⅓ cup ketchup
¼ cup vinegar
1 small onion, quartered

2 teaspoons salt
2 teaspoons paprika
⅔ cup sugar

In a blender combine all of the ingredients. Blend thoroughly. Store the dressing in the refrigerator.
Makes about 2 cups.

Mike's Sweet Potato Casserole

3 cups cooked, mashed sweet
  potatoes
2 eggs
⅓ cup melted butter
½ cup milk
½ cup sugar
1 teaspoon salt
1 teaspoon vanilla extract

✿ ✿ ✿

1 cup brown sugar
½ cup softened butter
⅓ cup all-purpose flour
1 cup chopped pecans

Butter a 9-inch square baking dish. In a large bowl combine the sweet potatoes, eggs, melted butter, milk, sugar, salt, and vanilla extract. Mix well. Spread the mixture into the prepared dish. In a separate bowl combine the brown sugar, softened butter, flour, and pecans. Sprinkle the mixture over the sweet potatoes. Bake in a 350° oven for about 30 minutes.
Serves 6.

Joan's Corn Pudding

2 16-ounce cans cream-style corn
2 17-ounce cans whole kernel corn
Pinch salt
1 cup all-purpose flour
1 cup sugar
2 eggs, beaten
½ cup butter

In a large buttered baking dish combine all of the ingredients except the butter. Place the entire stick of butter on top of the corn mixture. Bake in a 350° oven for about 1 hour.
Serves 6 to 8.

The Thorpe House

The Story Inn

Post Office Box 64
Nashville, Indiana 47448
(812) 988-2273

Once the Story General Store, this landmark from the 1850s is situated on the southern edge of Brown County State Park. It features lodging in the old buggy assembly operation on the second floor and in the surrounding village cottages. All rooms are furnished with period antiques, have private baths, and are air conditioned. The full-service restaurant features expertly prepared meals and imported and domestic beers and wines. Guests may dine indoors or outdoors overlooking the landscaped gardens.

ॐ ॐ ॐ ॐ ॐ

Banana Walnut Pancakes

1 cup unbleached all-purpose flour
1 cup whole wheat flour
¼ cup wheat germ
1 tablespoon baking powder
1½ teaspoons baking soda
Salt (optional)
2 eggs, room temperature
¼ cup safflower oil
2 cups buttermilk, room
    temperature
6 tablespoons honey
2 ripe medium bananas, peeled and
    mashed
½ cup finely chopped walnuts
Maple syrup
Vanilla yogurt, cinnamon, and
    additional bananas

In a large bowl stir together the flours, wheat germ, baking powder, baking soda, and salt to taste. In a separate bowl beat the eggs. Blend in the oil, buttermilk, honey, and bananas, mixing well. Stir in the nuts. Pour the egg mixture into the dry ingredients, and stir just until moistened.

Brush a hot griddle or skillet with oil. Pour about ¼ cup of batter per pancake onto the griddle and spread to make a flat pancake. Cook over medium heat until lightly browned on the bottom and bubbles come to the surface. Turn and brown lightly on the other side, 1 to 2 minutes. Serve with maple syrup or vanilla yogurt flavored with cinnamon and sliced bananas.

Makes about 20 pancakes.

Cyndi's Seafood Lasagna

3 tablespoons olive oil
5 cloves garlic, peeled and minced
1 cup chopped shallots or white
    onions
2 tablespoons dried basil
1 tablespoon dried oregano
Salt and white pepper
4 cups Béchamel sauce (see note)
½ cup freshly grated Parmesan
    cheese
3 tablespoons dry sherry
1 pound medium shrimp, cooked,
    peeled, and deveined
1 pound bay scallops, cooked
2 pounds fresh spinach, rinsed and
    stems removed
2 pounds fresh mushrooms, cleaned
    and chopped
2 tablespoons butter
1 8-ounce package cream cheese
2 pounds cooked lump crab meat,
    drained
2 pounds Mozzarella cheese, grated
1½ pounds lasagna noodles

In a large skillet over medium heat, heat the olive oil. Add the garlic and shallots, and sauté until soft, but not browned, about 5 minutes. Stir in the basil and oregano, and season with salt and pepper to taste. Remove from the heat.

Set aside 1 cup of Béchamel sauce. In a saucepan combine the onion-garlic mixture and the remaining 3 cups of sauce. Stir in the Parmesan and sherry, and heat gently. Fold in the cooked shrimp and scallops. Adjust the seasoning and set aside.

Meanwhile, steam the spinach just until tender and bright green. Drain well and pat dry between paper towels. Chop coarsely.

In a large skillet over medium-high heat, sauté the mushrooms in hot butter until tender and the liquid has evaporated.

Cut the cream cheese into small cubes. Shred the crab meat, removing any shells. Set aside.

Cook the lasagna noodles according to the package directions. Drain well. Grease the bottom of a 9x13x4-inch deep pan. While the noodles are cooking, spread a very thin layer of reserved Béchamel sauce in the bottom of the prepared baking pan. Cover with a layer of cooked noodles, trimming to fit the pan if necessary. Spread half of the seafood sauce over the noodles, top with half of the chopped spinach, half of the cream cheese cubes, a fourth of the Mozzarella, half of the sautéed mushrooms, and half of the shredded crab meat. Repeat the layers, beginning and ending with lasagna noodles. Spread the remaining Béchamel sauce over the noodles, and top with the remaining Mozzarella. Bake uncovered in a 350° oven for 45 minutes to 1 hour, until bubbling and lightly browned. Let the lasagna stand for 10 to 15 minutes before serving.

Note: To make Béchamel sauce, melt ½ cup of butter in a large heavy saucepan over medium heat. Stir in ½ cup of all-purpose flour and cook, stirring constantly, for about 2 minutes. Do not brown. Remove from the heat and gradually stir in 4 cups of milk until smooth. Return to the heat, and stir constantly until thickened. Season to taste with salt and white pepper.

Serves 12 to 16.

Braxtan House Inn

210 North Gospel Street
Paoli, Indiana 47454
(812) 723-4677

Braxtan House Inn is a twenty-one room, three-story Victorian house built in 1893. It first became a hotel in the mid-1920s when bedrooms were opened to wealthy guests who were drawn to Paoli in the summer by the mineral springs. The inn has been restored and refurbished, and the guest rooms offer oak, cherry, and maple woodwork, stained glass windows, and comfortable country style.

Hot German Potato Salad

8 to 10 medium potatoes, boiled
Diced onion
5 hard-boiled eggs, sliced
6 to 10 slices bacon, cooked and crumbled
3 to 4 tablespoons bacon grease
½ cup water
½ cup vinegar
¾ cup sugar
3 tablespoons all-purpose flour
1 tablespoon salt
1 teaspoon celery seed
Egg and bacon for garnish

Peel and slice the potatoes. In a large serving bowl or dish layer the onion, sliced eggs, bacon, and potatoes. In a skillet bring the bacon drippings, water, and vinegar to a boil. In a bowl combine the sugar, flour, salt, and celery seed. Pour the hot liquid into the dry ingredients and stir well. Return the mixture to the skillet and bring to a boil, stirring until thickened. Pour over the layered mixture. Garnish with egg and bacon, if desired.

Serves 10.

Coconut Pound Cake

2 cups sugar
1 cup shortening
5 eggs
2 cups all-purpose flour
1½ teaspoons baking powder
1 teaspoon salt
1 cup buttermilk
1½ teaspoons coconut flavoring
1 cup Angel Flake coconut

🍃 🍃 🍃

1 cup sugar
½ cup hot water
1 teaspoon coconut flavoring

Grease and flour a bundt or tube pan. In a large bowl cream together 2 cups of sugar and shortening. Add the eggs, one at a time, beating well. In a separate bowl combine the flour, baking powder, and salt. Add the flour

Braxtan House Inn

mixture to the creamed mixture alternately with the buttermilk. Add 1½ teaspoons of coconut flavoring and mix well. Fold in the coconut. Pour the batter into the prepared pan. Bake in a 350° oven for 50 to 60 minutes.

In a saucepan combine 1 cup of sugar and the hot water. Stir over low heat until the sugar dissolves. Bring the mixture to a boil, and boil for 1 minute. Remove from the heat and add 1 teaspoon of coconut flavoring. Stir well. While the cake is still hot, prick holes in the top with an ice pick. Pour the hot icing over the cake, letting it run into the holes.

Serves 10 to 12.

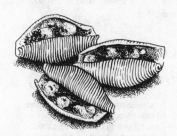

Braxtan House Blend

This is best if the unopened cans of pineapple and mandarin oranges are refrigerated overnight. It should be served immediately so the bananas don't darken.

    1 20-ounce can pineapple chunks,
        drained
    1 11-ounce can mandarin oranges,
        drained
    1 large banana, sliced
    ½ cup flaked coconut
    Whipped cream or nondairy topping
    Maraschino cherries

Mix the pineapple, oranges, banana, and coconut. Divide the mixture among 4 to 6 fruit cups or sherbet dishes. Top with whipped cream and cherries.

Serves 4 to 6.

The Country Homestead Guest Farm

Route 1, Box 353
Richland, Indiana 47634
(812) 359-4870
(812) 359-5229

The Country Homestead is a working cattle and grain farm homesteaded by the innkeepers' great-great-grandparents in 1837. It was refurbished in 1962 and furnished with family heirlooms and country accessories. Three meals a day are served family style. Guests are permitted to fish in the farm pond.

Cream Biscuits

    1 cup heavy cream
    2½ cups biscuit mix
    Cornmeal

Reserve 1 tablespoon of the cream. In a medium bowl combine the biscuit mix and the remaining cream, until blended enough to handle. Knead 6 to 8 times, enough to make the dough smooth. On a baking sheet roll the dough to ½-inch thickness. Cut into 2-inch rounds. Brush with the reserved tablespoon of cream, and sprinkle with cornmeal. Bake in a 400° oven for 12 minutes.

Serves 12 to 15.

Country Waffles

    2 cups biscuit mix
    1 egg
    ½ cup oil
    1½ cups club soda

In a large bowl combine all of the ingredients. Pour the batter onto a 350° to 380° waffle iron and bake until golden. Use all of the batter, wrap leftover waffles in plastic, and freeze. Toast the frozen waffles in a toaster as needed.

Note: The club soda doesn't permit the batter to be stored.

Serves 8 to 10.

Pancake or Waffle Topping

    1 28-ounce can fruit cocktail
    1 orange
    Dash nutmeg
    Dash cinnamon
    1 8-ounce container Cool Whip

Drain the fruit cocktail. Peel and section the orange. In a large bowl combine all of the ingredients. Serve with buttered pancakes or waffles.

Serves 8.

Kartoffels
(German Stuffed Potatoes)

    4 large baking potatoes
    1 pound sausage
    1 small onion, finely diced
    1 10½-ounce can cream of
        mushroom soup
    Dash salt and pepper
    1 tablespoon chopped chives
    8 slices Velveeta cheese

Bake the potatoes until tender. When the potatoes are cool enough to handle, cut in half and spoon out the inside, reserving the skins. In a large skillet sauté the sausage, adding the onions and cooking until the onion is tender. Drain off the excess fat. Add the potatoes, cream of mushroom soup, and seasonings, and mix gently for 1 minute. Place the mixture in the potato skins. Top each with a slice of cheese. Arrange the potato skins on a baking sheet. Bake in a 350° oven for 10 to 15 minutes.

Serves 8.

Iowa

The Shaw House

509 South Oak
Anamosa, Iowa 52205
(319) 462-4485

Enjoy a relaxing step back in time in this three-story, twenty-room Italianate mansion on a hilltop overlooking picturesque Grant Wood country. Modeled after the seacoast homes of Maine, the inn provides a peaceful rural retreat. Guests enjoy iced tea on the front porch swing, "home-grown" breakfasts, and a variety of local attractions including Stone City, the Grant Wood Museum, the reconstructed Ghost Town of Edinburgh, antique stores, and restaurants.

Wapsipinicon Rhubarb Muffins

1½ cups brown sugar
⅔ cup oil
1 egg
1 cup buttermilk or sour milk
1 teaspoon vanilla extract
2½ cups all-purpose flour
1 teaspoon salt
1 teaspoon baking soda
1½ cups diced rhubarb

❧ ❧ ❧

½ cup sugar
½ teaspoon cinnamon
1 tablespoon melted butter

Grease muffin cups. In a large bowl combine the brown sugar, oil, egg, buttermilk, and vanilla. In a separate bowl combine the flour, salt, and baking soda. Add the dry ingredients to the liquid mixture, blending until just moistened. Fold in the rhubarb. Pour the batter into muffin cups. In a small bowl combine the remaining ingredients and sprinkle over the batter. Bake in a 325° oven for 30 minutes.

Makes 15 to 18 muffins.

Victorian Bed and Breakfast Inn

425 Walnut Street
Avoca, Iowa 51521
(712) 343-6336
(800) 397-3914

This 1904 Victorian home was one of the finest residences in this southwest Iowa town, and its restoration has revived the elegance of the time in which it was built. The carefully detailed golden pine woodwork is an outstanding feature, from the pine columns in the dining room and parlor to the large windows in the living area. The four guest rooms share two spacious baths, each complete with a new tile shower and a separate antique tub.

Iowa's Heavenly Pumpkin Muffins

2 cups sifted all-purpose flour
1 tablespoon baking powder
1 teaspoon ground cinnamon
¼ teaspoon ground nutmeg
¼ teaspoon ground ginger
¼ teaspoon salt
½ cup oil
½ cup sugar
2 large eggs
1 cup canned pumpkin
½ cup sour cream

❧ ❧ ❧

2 3-ounce packages cream cheese, each cut into 6 cubes
3 tablespoons apricot preserves
¼ cup sliced almonds
2 tablespoons sugar

Line 12 muffin cups with paper liners. In a large bowl combine the flour, baking powder, cinnamon, nutmeg, ginger, and salt. In another bowl beat the oil and ½ cup of sugar until blended. Add the eggs, pumpkin, and sour cream, and beat thoroughly. Stir the pumpkin mixture into the dry ingredients until just moistened.

Spoon the batter into the prepared muffin cups, filling halfway. Place 1 cube of cream cheese in the center of each cup, and top each cube with preserves. Completely cover the cheese

Victorian Bed and Breakfast Inn

Calmar Guest House

103 North Street
Calmar, Iowa 52132
(319) 562-3851

This 1890 Victorian home was refurbished in 1984 to its original elegance before being opened as a bed and breakfast inn. Its stained glass window depicting the Iowa state flower, the wild rose, inspired the interior color scheme. Its five bedrooms are decorated in modern modes with a few antiques. Nearby attractions include the world's smallest church, Old Fort in Fort Atkinson, the world-famous hand-carved Bily Clocks, the Laura Wilder Museum, and the "Little Brown Church in the Vale."

and preserves with the remaining batter. Sprinkle the muffin tops with almonds and the remaining sugar. Bake in a 400° oven until well browned, about 25 minutes. Remove the muffins from the pan and cool for at least 10 minutes.

Makes 12 muffins.

Bacon, Pepper, and Potato Frittata

4 slices bacon, cut into pieces
2 green onions with tops, chopped
¼ cup chopped green pepper
1 tablespoon chopped red pepper
4 mushrooms, sliced
1 medium cooked potato, grated
Salt and pepper to taste
3 eggs, beaten
⅓ cup milk
¼ cup mixed Swiss and sharp
    Cheddar cheese
Salsa

In a nonstick skillet sauté the bacon until almost crisp. Drain the bacon grease. Add the chopped green onions, green and red peppers, and mushrooms. Sauté and stir for approximately 1 minute. Add the potato and season with salt and pepper. In a separate bowl beat the eggs with the milk. Pour the mixture in the pan and top with grated cheese. Do not stir. Cover with a lid and cook on medium-low heat for approximately 20 minutes. Serve in wedges topped with a teaspoon of your favorite salsa.

Serves 4.

Quiche As You Like It

1 cup shredded cheese
1 cup cooked, cubed meat (or
    chopped vegetables)
1 unbaked 9-inch pie shell
6 eggs
1 cup milk or cream
½ teaspoon salt (optional)
½ teaspoon pepper
1 ounce chopped spinach or chives

Sprinkle the cheese and meat in the bottom of the unbaked pie shell. In a medium bowl beat the eggs, milk, and seasonings until well blended. Pour the egg mixture over the cheese and meat. Sprinkle the spinach or chives over all. Bake in a 350° oven for 35 to 40 minutes or until a knife inserted in the center comes out clean. Let the quiche stand for 1 or 2 minutes before serving.

Serves 6 to 8.

Wine Salad

1 6-ounce package raspberry gelatin
1 cup boiling water
1 16-ounce can crushed pineapple, undrained
1 16-ounce can whole cranberry sauce
¾ cup tawny port wine
1 cup chopped pecans

⋅⋅⋅

1 3-ounce package cream cheese
½ cup sour cream
1 cup chopped nuts

In a small bowl dissolve the gelatin in the boiling water. Pour into a 9x13-inch pan. Add the crushed pineapple, cranberry sauce, wine, and pecans. Refrigerate until firm. In a small bowl combine the cream cheese and sour cream. Spread the mixture over the congealed salad, and sprinkle the remaining nuts over all.

Serves 12.

Paint 'n Primitives

107 East Washington
Centerville, Iowa 52544
(515) 856-8811

This Victorian-style home is situated one block north of Iowa's largest town square. Its three rooms contain antiques, collectibles, television, and sitting space.

Herbed Potatoes

4 medium potatoes, washed and sliced in 8 wedges
½ cup red wine vinegar
3 tablespoons buttery oil
1 teaspoon parsley
1 teaspoon oregano
1 teaspoon rosemary
Salt and pepper to taste

Arrange the potatoes in a baking dish. In a small bowl combine the vinegar and oil. Brush the potatoes with half of this mixture. Bake in a 400° oven for 25 minutes. Brush the potatoes with the remaining vinegar mixture, and bake for 15 more minutes. Sprinkle with the remaining ingredients and bake for 10 minutes. The potatoes should be golden and crisp.

Serves 4.

Dill and Cheese Scones

2½ cups biscuit mix
½ cup grated Cheddar cheese
1 tablespoon sugar
½ teaspoon dill weed
½ cup plain yogurt
1 egg, beaten
2 tablespoons buttery oil

In a large bowl combine the biscuit mix, cheese, sugar, and dill weed. In a separate bowl blend the yogurt and egg, and add to the mixture with the oil. Stir until blended. Turn the dough onto a floured surface and knead 8 to 10 strokes. Pat out into an 8-inch circle, and cut into 12 wedges. Place on a cookie sheet. Bake in a 425° oven for 12 minutes.

Makes 12 scones.

Whole Wheat Bread

This is for cooks venturesome enough to have a kitchen flour mill. It makes super toast, is a welcome change from soft bakery breads, and has a wonderful aroma.

7 cups hard red wheat
¾ cup unpolished rice
¼ cup hulled millet (optional)

⋅⋅⋅

1 cup rolled oats
1 cup yellow cornmeal
½ cup wheat germ
¼ cup millet seed (optional)

1 cup raisins (optional)
1 tablespoon salt
6 cups warm water (110° to 115°)
3 tablespoons active dry yeast
¼ cup oil
6 tablespoons blackstrap molasses

Grease 4 loaf pans. In a flour mill grind the wheat, rice, and millet. In a 6-quart or larger mixing bowl combine the flour, oats, cornmeal, wheat germ, millet seed, raisins, and salt. Mix well and push to the sides of the bowl. In the center add the warm water, yeast, oil, and molasses. Mix until well moistened. Let the dough rise to 1½ times its original volume. Knead and let rise again. Knead the dough again, and divide into 4 sections. Shape into loaves. Place each in a prepared pan. Let the loaves rise to 1½ times their original volume. Bake in a 375° oven for 15 minutes. Reduce the heat to 325° and bake for 30 minutes. Remove the loaves from the pans to a wire rack, and brush the tops with oil or margarine.

Note: The wheat, rice, and millet may be replaced with 11 to 12 cups of whole wheat graham flour.

Makes 4 loaves.

Cklaytonian Bed and Breakfast Inn

Rural Route 2, Box 125A
Clayton, Iowa 52049
(319) 964-2776

Situated in a picturesque village alongside the Mississippi River and protected by colorful bluffs, the Cklaytonian is one mile off the Great River Road. It has five guest accommodations, three with a private bath;

other features include complimentary bicycles for touring the area, cable television, a public boat ramp, ample parking, and areas for cleaning fish and freezers for storing them. The many recreational activities of northeast Iowa are within short driving distances.

Cklaytonian Egg Dish

3 cups dressing cubes (bread)
⅓ pound grated Velveeta cheese
¼ pound bacon, chopped and cooked
2½ cups milk
8 eggs
Salt and pepper to taste
½ cup margarine, melted

In the bottom of an 8x13-inch pan layer in order 2 cups of the bread cubes, the Velveeta cheese, and bacon. In a bowl combine the milk, eggs, and salt and pepper. Pour the mixture over the layers. Arrange the reserved cup of bread cubes over the top, and drizzle melted margarine over all. Cover and refrigerate overnight. Bake in a 350° oven for 1 hour.
Serves 10.

River Oaks Inn

1234 East River Drive
Davenport, Iowa 52803
(319) 326-2629

Situated on scenic River Drive overlooking the Mississippi River, this 1850s home combines Italianate, Victorian, and Prairie architecture. The ornate gazebo near the front of the house is a lovely place to enjoy the river view. Open year round, River Oaks Inn has five bedrooms with private baths.

Family Favorite Turkey Dressing

1½ cups diced onion
2 cups diced celery
1 cup margarine
4 loaves fresh white bread
4 13¾-ounce cans Swanson chicken broth
Salt and pepper to taste
Sage to taste (optional)

In a large skillet sauté the onion and celery in the butter until soft. Tear the bread into pieces and place in a large bowl. Add the sautéed mixture and the remaining ingredients. Stuff the turkey or place in a greased casserole dish. Bake the casserole dish in a 350° oven for 45 minutes, until hot through and crusty on the top.
Serves 16.

Pat's Hot Turkey Salad for Brunch

3 cups diced cooked turkey
4 hard-boiled eggs, chopped
2 cups diced celery
4 ounces mushrooms, sliced
2 tablespoons diced onion
¾ cup Hellman salad dressing
1 tablespoon lemon juice

❧ ❧ ❧

½ cup cornflake crumbs
2 tablespoons melted margarine

In a large bowl combine the turkey, eggs, celery, mushrooms, onion, salad dressing, and lemon juice. Transfer to a 9x13-inch pan. Top with cornflake crumbs and margarine. Bake in a 350° oven for 30 minutes.
Serves 6 to 8.

Cklaytonian Bed and Breakfast Inn

Aunt Tal's Ravioli

Italia Prosperi Torti from Lucca, Italy.
Serve with your favorite pasta sauce
poured over the ravioli.

     1 pound ground pork
     1 pound ground veal
     2 eggs
     2 handfuls bread soaked in water
         and squeezed dry
     ½ to 1 cup Parmesan cheese
     Dash allspice
     Dash nutmeg
     Dash salt and pepper
     Chopped parsley
         ❧   ❧   ❧
     3 eggs
     1 teaspoon salt
     1 tablespoon olive oil
     8 cups all-purpose flour
     2½ cups water
         ❧   ❧   ❧
     Pasta sauce

In a large bowl combine the pork,
veal, 2 eggs, bread, Parmesan, spices,
and seasonings. Set aside. In a separate large bowl beat together 3 eggs,
the salt, and olive oil. Add the flour
and water alternately until the mixture is the consistency of noodle
dough. On a floured board roll the
dough thin. Cut into circles with a
glass. Place a heaping tablespoon of
the meat mixture on each circle. Fold
the circles in half and press the edges
together, sealing with a fork. Boil in
salted water for 20 to 25 minutes.
Drain carefully. Serve with pasta
sauce.
     Serves 16.

The Richards House

1492 Locust Street
Dubuque, Iowa 52001
(319) 557-1492
(319) 557-1002

This elegant four-story, High Victorian home constructed in 1883 is
one of the finest homes of its period in
Dubuque. Featuring a dazzling dis-
play of nearly ninety stained glass
windows, it has seven ornate fireplaces, seven types of woodwork,
hand-painted tiles, and elaborate
built-in cabinets. Rooms are furnished with period antiques, queen-
size beds, and air conditioning. Most
rooms have private baths.

1-2-3 Dressing

     1 teaspoon salt
     2 tablespoons oil
     3 tablespoons vinegar
     3 tablespoons sugar

In a glass container with a cover combine all of the ingredients. Serve with
lettuce or cabbage. Refrigerate any
unused portion.
     Makes about ½ cup.

Don't Peek Stew

     2 pounds round steak
     4 large potatoes, peeled
     4 large carrots, peeled
     1 10½-ounce can cream of
         mushroom soup
     1 soup can water
     ⅓ teaspoon pepper
     ½ package onion soup mix

The Richards House

Cut the steak into cubes, and cut the potatoes and carrots into bite-sized pieces. In a large Dutch oven with a tight fitting cover combine all of the ingredients. Bake in a 325° oven for 3 hours.

Variation: Add any raw vegetables desired.

Serves 8.

Banana Cake

½ cup shortening
2 cups all-purpose flour
1⅓ cups sugar
1 teaspoon baking powder
1 teaspoon baking soda
¼ teaspoon salt
½ cup sour milk or buttermilk
1 cup mashed bananas
2 eggs
½ cup black walnuts
1 teaspoon vanilla extract
Frosting or whipped cream

Grease and flour a 9x13-inch cake pan. Cream the shortening. Stir in the dry ingredients. Add ¼ cup of sour milk and the bananas. Beat with a mixer at low speed until all of the flour is dampened, about 2 minutes. Add the eggs, walnuts, remaining sour milk, and vanilla. Beat at medium speed for 2 minutes. Pour into the prepared cake pan. Bake in a 375° oven for 25 minutes or until a toothpick inserted in the center comes out clean.

Frost or serve with whipped cream.
Serves 8 to 10.

Oatmeal Applesauce Bars

½ cup butter
1 cup brown sugar
1 egg
1 cup fresh applesauce
1 cup oatmeal

&ex; &ex; &ex;

1½ cups all-purpose flour
1 teaspoon baking soda
½ teaspoon nutmeg
1 teaspoon cinnamon
1 teaspoon salt

1 teaspoon vanilla extract
1 cup raisins
Confectioners' sugar frosting

Grease a 9x13-inch baking pan. In a large bowl cream together the butter and sugar. Add the egg and applesauce. Gradually add the oatmeal. Sift together the flour, baking soda, nutmeg, cinnamon, and salt. Add the dry ingredients to the oat mixture. Stir in the vanilla and raisins. Spread the mixture into the prepared pan. Bake in a 350° oven for 20 to 25 minutes.

Frost with confectioners' sugar frosting if desired.

Serves 8 to 10.

FitzGerald's Inn

160 North Third Street
Post Office Box 157
Lansing, Iowa 52151
(319) 538-4872
(319) 538-4263

This newly remodeled 1863 country home retains its tin ceilings, patterned wood floors, and old woodwork. Its terraced grounds rise to a dramatic bluff-top panorama of the Mississippi River at one of its most beautiful stretches. Its accommodations include private and semiprivate baths. Many historical and recreational attractions are within easy driving distance.

Orange Nut Cake

This cake has a refreshing zesty taste and can be served any time, even for breakfast.

1 cup butter
1 cup sugar
3 egg yolks

&ex; &ex;

2 cups all-purpose flour
1 teaspoon baking soda
1 teaspoon baking powder

&ex; &ex; &ex;

1 cup sour cream
Grated rind of 1 orange
½ cup walnuts, chopped
2 tablespoons orange juice
3 egg whites, stiffly beaten

&ex; &ex; &ex;

½ cup orange juice
½ cup sugar
1 tablespoon Cointreau

Butter and flour a 10-inch tube pan. In a large bowl cream together the butter and sugar. Add the egg yolks. In a separate bowl sift together the flour, baking soda, and baking powder. Add the dry ingredients to the creamed mixture alternately with the sour cream. Stir in the orange rind, walnuts, and 2 tablespoons of orange juice. Fold in the egg whites. Pour the batter into the prepared pan. Bake in a 350° oven for 1 hour.

Combine the remaining orange juice, sugar, and Cointreau. Spoon the mixture over the hot cake while still in the pan.

Serves 8 to 10.

Fruit Torte

This dessert takes minutes to prepare and is always a hit.

½ cup butter
1 cup sugar
1 cup all-purpose flour
1 teaspoon baking powder
Salt
2 eggs

&ex; &ex; &ex;

1 pint blueberries
Sugar
Lemon juice
Cinnamon

In a large bowl cream together the butter and sugar. Add the flour, baking powder, salt, and eggs. Spread the mixture evenly in a 9-inch springform pan. Cover the surface with the blueberries and generously sprinkle sugar, lemon juice, and cinnamon over all. Bake in a 350° oven for 1 hour.

Variation: For the topping, use Italian plum halves, sliced apples, or sliced peaches. You may combine any or all of these with the blueberries, as well.

Serves 8.

Apple Orchard Inn

Old Highway 30
Rural Route 3, Box 129
Missouri Valley, Iowa 51555
(712) 642-2418

Guests of the Apple Orchard Inn enjoy the country charm of its hosts and twenty-six acres of orchard, with walking and hiking trails. Overlooking the beautiful Boyer Valley, it affords a view of the western Iowa countryside.

Cider Salad

2 cups apple cider
2 3-ounce packages cherry gelatin
¼ teaspoon cherry flavoring
1 16-ounce can pitted dark cherries
½ cup sliced celery
½ cup chopped walnuts
1 3-ounce package cream cheese, softened
1 cup applesauce
½ teaspoon cinnamon flavoring

In a small saucepan bring the apple cider to a boil. Dissolve the gelatin and cherry flavoring in the hot cider.

Drain the cherries, reserving the liquid. Add enough water to the liquid to make 1½ cups, and stir into the gelatin. Reserve 2 cups of the gelatin mixture and keep at room temperature. Refrigerate the remaining gelatin until partially set. Fold in the cherries, celery, and walnuts. Pour the mixture into a 6½ cup ring mold. Chill until almost firm. In a bowl, gradually add the reserved gelatin to the cream cheese, beating until almost smooth. Stir in the applesauce and the cinnamon flavoring. Spoon over the first layer and chill until firm.

Serves 8.

Cinnamon Apple Raisin Bread

2 eggs
1 cup sugar
½ cup oil
1 teaspoon vanilla extract
1½ cups all-purpose flour
1 teaspoon baking powder
½ teaspoon baking soda
⅛ teaspoon salt
2 teaspoons cinnamon
1 cup chopped peeled apples
½ cup raisins
½ cup walnuts

Grease a 9x5-inch loaf pan. In a large bowl combine all of the ingredients. Pour into the prepared pan. Bake in a 350° oven for 50 to 60 minutes.

Variation: You may add other spices, such as nutmeg and cloves, or add more cinnamon.

Makes 1 loaf, 8 servings.

Grandma Ta's Apple Butter

6 pounds apples, peeled
1 quart apple cider
1¼ cups sugar
2 teaspoons cinnamon
¼ teaspoon salt
¼ teaspoon cloves
¼ teaspoon nutmeg

Quarter or slice the apples. In a large stock pot cook the apples in the apple cider, stirring often until soft. Press through a sieve or food mill. In a large kettle combine the apple pulp, sugar, cinnamon, salt, cloves, and nutmeg. Boil rapidly, stirring constantly to prevent splattering. Cook until thick enough to spread. To test, pour a tablespoon of the hot mixture onto a chilled plate. If no rim of liquid forms around the edge of the apple butter, it is ready. Pour at once into sterilized jars and seal.

Pizza

1 ¼-ounce package active dry yeast
1 cup warm water (110° to 115°)
2 teaspoons sugar
3½ cups all-purpose flour
1 tablespoon oil
1½ teaspoons salt

🍂 🍂 🍂

1 clove garlic
3 tablespoons oil
2 large onions, sliced
1 6-ounce can tomato paste
1 28-ounce can Italian tomatoes
½ teaspoon oregano
1 teaspoon salt
½ teaspoon pepper

🍂 🍂 🍂

⅓ cup Romano cheese (or Parmesan)
2 cups grated Mozzarella cheese

In a large bowl soften the yeast in the warm water, stirring until dissolved. Add the sugar and 1½ cups of flour. Beat until thoroughly blended. Add the oil and salt. Stir in the remaining flour. Turn out onto a lightly floured board and knead until smooth, about

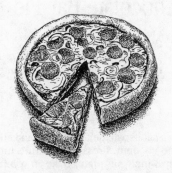

10 minutes. Place the dough in a greased bowl, turning once to grease the top of the dough. Cover with a damp cloth and let rise in a warm place until doubled in size, about 1 hour and 45 minutes. Punch the dough down and refrigerate for 30 minutes.

Grease a 12-inch pizza pan. Roll the dough on a lightly floured surface into a circle ¼-inch thick and about 13 inches in diameter. Place the dough on the prepared pizza pan and crimp the edges. The crust may be frozen at this point if desired.

In a large saucepan sauté the garlic in oil over moderate heat until brown, then discard the garlic. Add the onions and brown lightly. Stir in the tomato paste, and cook for 3 minutes, stirring constantly. Add the tomatoes, oregano, salt, and pepper. Cover tightly, reduce the heat, and simmer gently for 1 hour and 30 minutes.

Spread the sauce over the crust, sprinkle with Romano cheese, and top with Mozzarella cheese. Bake in a 450° oven for 30 minutes. Reduce the heat to 300°, and bake for 15 minutes.

Variations: For pizza with sausage, cut ½ pound of sweet or hot Italian sausage into small pieces and brown in a skillet over moderate heat. Mix with the sauce before spreading on the crust. For pepperoni pizza, add ¼ pound sliced uncooked pepperoni to the sauce. For pizza with mushrooms, sauté 1 cup of sliced mushrooms in oil and add to the sauce.

Serves 4 to 6.

La Corsette Maison

629 First Avenue East
Newton, Iowa 50208
(515) 792-6833

The La Corsette is a turn-of-the-century mission-style mansion with oak woodwork, brass fixtures, art nouveau stained-glass windows, and some original furnishings. Here also is the acclaimed La Corsette restaurant. The bedchambers reflect the French country decor.

Cream of Red and Green Pepper Soup

2 red peppers, finely chopped
2 green peppers, finely chopped
¼ cup finely chopped onion
3 tablespoons butter
1½ cups cream
1½ cups rich chicken stock
Salt to taste
Chopped red and green peppers for garnish

In a large skillet sauté the peppers and onions in butter until semi-soft. Add the cream, chicken stock, and salt. Heat until warm but do not boil. Garnish with finely chopped red and green peppers.

Serves 4.

Salade of Cherry Tomatoes and Fresh Arugula

This is a very simple salad with a great presentation.

10 or more cherry tomatoes per person
Fresh arugula, shredded
Extra virgin olive oil
Freshly ground pepper

Arrange the tomatoes on a salad plate and add the shredded arugula. Drizzle with olive oil. Add a twist of freshly ground pepper. Garnish with a nasturtium blossom and fresh green or purple basil.

Serves 1.

La Corsette Maison

Strawberry Jam

1 cup butter
⅓ cup strawberry jam
3 fresh strawberries
Strawberry or flower for garnish

In a food processor blend the butter, jam, and 3 strawberries until smooth. Transfer to a serving bowl or dish and garnish with a fresh strawberry or flower.

Makes 1½ cups.

Babi's Bed and Breakfast

South Amana, Iowa 52334
(319) 662-4381

Babi is an Old World term for "Grandma," which says much about the atmosphere of this inn. Situated in the heart of the Amana colonies, the inn is on ten acres between South Amana and Homestead. Sleeping accommodations include a suite with a private bath and sitting room or two double rooms that share a bath.

Apricot Chicken

1 10-ounce jar apricot preserves
1 envelope Lipton onion soup mix
1 8-ounce jar Russian salad
    dressing (not creamy)
8 chicken breasts

In a large bowl mix together the apricot jam, onion soup mix, and Russian dressing. Arrange the chicken breasts in a large casserole. Pour the sauce over the chicken and marinate overnight. Bake covered in a 350° oven for 1 hour. Turn the chicken and bake uncovered for 30 minutes. Baste occasionally with sauce.

Serves 4.

Mashed Potato Casserole

10 medium potatoes, peeled
Salt and pepper to taste
1 cup sour cream
1 8-ounce package cream cheese
Chopped onion

&❧ &❧ &❧

Melted butter
Paprika

In a large soup pot boil the potatoes. Drain, season, and mash the potatoes. Add the sour cream, cream cheese, and onion, and mix thoroughly. Place in a 2-quart casserole dish and allow to cool. Cover and refrigerate for 24 hours. Top with melted butter and sprinkle with paprika. Bake in a 350° oven for 30 minutes.

Serves 6 to 8.

Red Cabbage "Bake"

Good with pot roast or Apricot Chicken.

2 tablespoons butter
1 medium onion, chopped
1 medium red cabbage, finely
    chopped
2 tablespoons vinegar
2 teaspoons sugar
2 cloves
2 apples, chopped
Salt and pepper to taste
1 tablespoon all-purpose flour

In a large skillet melt the butter and sauté the onion for 2 to 3 minutes. Add the cabbage, vinegar, sugar, cloves, apples, salt, and pepper. When the cabbage is tender, add flour to thicken.

Serves 6 to 8.

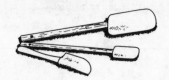

Chocolate Bar Pie

2 tablespoons butter
1⅓ cups coconut

&❧ &❧ &❧

1 tablespoon instant coffee granules
2 tablespoons water
½ pound chocolate bar with
    almonds
4 cups Cool Whip

In a saucepan melt the butter and add the coconut. Press the mixture into an 8-inch pie plate. Bake in a 325° oven for 10 minutes or until golden brown. Set aside.

In a large bowl dissolve the instant coffee in the water. Break the chocolate bar into small pieces and add to the coffee. Fold in the Cool Whip. Spoon the mixture into the coconut crust and refrigerate ovenight.

Serves 6 to 8.

The Hannah Marie Country Inn

Route One
Spencer, Iowa 51301
(712) 262-1286

The Hannah Marie has retained the original character of its ninety-five-year-old farm house. Restored to its first luster, its simplicity reflects the gentle style of long ago days. The marks of many years of living make this house a home: dents in the original doors, sloping ceilings, turn-of-the-century plaster, authentic stairway, and old house noises. Guests are pampered in the Victorian manner; the porch swing and rocking chairs, as well as heirloom table linens, are part of the atmosphere.

Little Cheese Hots

½ cup water
¼ cup butter
½ cup all-purpose flour
¹⁄₁₆ teaspoon cayenne
½ teaspoon vegetable seasoning salt
1 tablespoon dried parsley
2 eggs
12 pieces sharp Cheddar cheese
   (¼x½-inch)

Grease a 12x15-inch baking sheet. In a small saucepan boil the water and butter until the butter melts. Add the flour, cayenne, seasoning salt, and dried parsley all at once. Beat with a spoon until the mixture leaves the sides of the pan and forms a ball. Remove from the heat. Beat in the eggs, one at a time until the dough is glossy. Spoon the dough onto the prepared pan, making 12 mounds. Place a piece of Cheddar cheese in each mound, and cover the cheese completely with the dough. Bake in a 425° oven for 12 minutes. Reduce the heat to 375° and bake for 12 minutes, or until golden brown.
   Makes 12.

Terra Verde Farm

Route #1, Box 86
Swisher, Iowa 52338
(319) 846-2478

At Terra Verde Farm guests are able to see a working Iowa farm up close. Conveniently situated to the Amana colonies, Iowa City, and Cedar Rapids, Terra Verde Farm is an ideal place from which to attend sporting events at the University of Iowa, to participate in duck or pheasant hunting, or to view the Iowa countryside. Accommodations include air-conditioned rooms with private baths and farm-style breakfasts.

Damper

This is a traditional Australian bread made by the swagman in his billy can over the fire.

2 cups self-rising flour
½ teaspoon salt
1¼ cups milk
Butter

Grease a cookie sheet. In a bowl sift together the flour and salt. Add enough milk to make a manageable dough. Shape into a round loaf and place on the prepared cookie sheet. Bake in a 425° oven for 25 to 30 minutes. Baste with milk during cooking. Serve with butter.
   Makes 1 loaf.

One Pan Chicken and Noodles

1 teaspoon minced onion
¼ cup chopped celery
3 tablespoons butter
2 cups cubed, cooked chicken
6 ounces uncooked noodles
1 10½-ounce can cream of chicken
   soup
2¼ cups chicken broth
1 teaspoon lemon juice
¼ teaspoon pepper
3 ounces canned mushrooms with
   juice

In a Dutch oven sauté the onion and celery in butter until tender. Add the chicken and top with the noodles. In a bowl combine the soup, broth, lemon juice, and pepper. Pour over the noodles, moistening all. Scatter the mushrooms on top. Cover and bring to a boil. Reduce the heat to simmer and cook for 15 to 20 minutes, stirring occasionally.
   Serves 6 to 8.

Bran Scones

After a year in Australia, we returned with some recipes we could use at home. This is just one variation of a basic scone recipe.

3 cups whole meal self-rising flour,
   sifted
1 cup bran
2 tablespoons brown sugar
½ cup dates, chopped
1 teaspoon mixed spice
¼ cup butter or margarine
2 tablespoons honey
1 to 1½ cups milk

In a large bowl combine the flour, bran, brown sugar, dates, and spice. In a small saucepan combine the butter, honey, and milk. Heat until the butter is melted, and pour the mixture into the dry ingredients. Turn onto a floured board and knead lightly. Roll the dough to about ½-inch thickness. Cut out the scones using a 2½-inch round cutter. Place the scones on a baking sheet and brush with milk. Bake in a 425° oven for 12 to 14 minutes, or until golden brown.
   Makes 18 scones.

Kansas

Peaceful Acres

Route 5, Box 153
Great Bend, Kansas 67530
(316) 793-7527

Peaceful Acres is a comfortable, sprawling old farm house with two (and possibly three) guest rooms. Guests share a bathroom. A working windmill, small livestock, chickens and guineas, dogs, and cats all share the ten acres.

Caramel Pecan Cinnamon Rolls

1 ¼-ounce package active dry yeast
1 cup warm water (110° to 115°)
¼ cup sugar
1 teaspoon salt
2 tablespoons margarine
1 egg
3¼ to 3½ cups all-purpose flour

🍂 🍂 🍂

⅓ cup margarine
½ cup brown sugar
1 tablespoon corn syrup
⅔ cup pecan halves
½ cup sugar
2 teaspoons cinnamon

In a large mixing bowl dissolve the yeast in the warm water. Stir in ¼ cup of sugar, the salt, 2 tablespoons of margarine, the egg, and 2 cups of flour. Beat until smooth. With a spoon or by hand work in the remaining flour until the dough is easy to handle, and knead. Place the dough in a greased bowl, turning once to grease the top of the dough. Cover and let the dough rise until doubled in bulk.

Melt the remaining margarine with the brown sugar and corn syrup, and place in a 10x14-inch pan. Sprinkle the pecans over the mixture. On a floured surface roll the dough into a rectangle. Combine ½ cup of sugar and the cinnamon. Sprinkle over the dough. Roll up the dough jelly roll fashion and cut into 18 pieces. Place in the pan. Let the rolls rise until doubled in bulk. Bake in a 350° oven for about 25 minutes. Line a tray with waxed paper, and turn the rolls out onto the tray.

Makes 18 large rolls.

Refrigerator Rolls

1¾ cups milk
¼ cup shortening
5 tablespoons sugar
1 ¼-ounce package active dry yeast
3 cups all-purpose flour
½ teaspoon baking soda
1 teaspoon baking powder
1 egg
1 tablespoon salt
5 to 6 cups all-purpose flour

In a saucepan scald the milk and add the shortening and 5 tablespoons of sugar. Cool the mixture to lukewarm and add the yeast. Stir well. Add 3 cups of flour, the baking soda, and baking powder, and beat until the bubbles come. Allow the dough to rise for 30 minutes. Add the beaten egg, salt, and enough flour to make a soft dough. Turn out onto a floured board and knead. Place in a greased bowl, and turn to grease the top of the dough. Let the dough rise until doubled in bulk. Punch down and turn the dough over. Brush the dough with oil, and cover tightly with plastic wrap. Refrigerate until needed, punching the dough down occasionally.

About 2 hours and 30 minutes before serving, grease a baking sheet. Remove the dough from the refrigerator. Cut the dough into 24 pieces and shape into rolls. Place the rolls on the baking sheet, cover, and allow to rise until doubled. Bake in a 350° oven for about 25 minutes, until golden brown.

Makes about 24 rolls.

Three Bean Casserole

½ cup chopped onion
1 pound hamburger
1 16-ounce can pork and beans
1 16-ounce can red beans
1 16-ounce can lima beans
1 tablespoon dry mustard
¾ cup brown sugar
½ cup catsup

In a skillet brown the onion and hamburger. In a casserole dish combine the beef, onion, and remaining ingredients. Cover and bake in a 350° oven for 1 hour.

Serves 6.

Kimble Cliff

6782 Anderson Ave.
Manhattan, Kansas 66502
(913) 539-3816

Kimble Cliff, otherwise known as Cedar Knoll Farm, was built in 1894 of stone quarried nearby, hand fashioned, and decorated. It is a rural bed and breakfast facility with ten rooms and a full attic. The home is well-endowed with antiques collected by the owner, who also owns and operates an antique business. A continental breakfast is served each morning, with the added plus of two or more varieties of coffee cake or sweet rolls and fruit.

Deviled Biscuits

¼ cup margarine
1 4-ounce can deviled ham
1 10-ounce can refrigerator biscuits
Parmesan cheese

Melt the margarine in a 10-inch round cake pan. Add the deviled ham. Roll the biscuits in the mixture, and arrange in the pan. Sprinkle generously with Parmesan cheese. Bake in a 375° oven for 12 to 15 minutes.
Serves 4 to 6.

Almond Coffee Cake

¼ cup margarine
¼ cup brown sugar
½ teaspoon cinnamon
½ cup raspberry preserves
2 10-ounce cans refrigerator
   biscuits

⅓ cup confectioners' sugar
1 teaspoon water
½ teaspoon almond extract
1 teaspoon slivered almonds

In a skillet melt together the margarine, brown sugar, and cinnamon. Remove from the heat. Spoon a teaspoonful of preserves on each biscuit. Fold the biscuits in half. Dip each biscuit in the melted butter mixture and arrange folded edge down in rows in a loaf pan. Bake in a 350° oven for 20 minutes. Cool for 10 minutes.
Combine the confectioners' sugar, water, and almond extract. Drizzle the mixture over the cooled coffee cake and top with slivered almonds.
Serves 12.

Apple Biscuit Ring

¼ cup margarine
¾ cup sugar
1 teaspoon cinnamon
2 10-ounce cans refrigerator
   biscuits
1 apple, cut into 20 slices

1 cup confectioners' sugar
2 to 3 teaspoons milk
¼ teaspoon almond extract

In a small saucepan melt together the margarine, sugar, and cinnamon. Dip each biscuit into the mixture and place an apple slice in each. Fold the biscuits in half and place in a 10-inch round cake pan folded edge down. Bake in a 350° oven for 30 minutes.
Combine the confectioners' sugar, milk, and almond extract and glaze the ring.
Serves 12.

Orange Rolls

2 tablespoons margarine
⅓ cup frozen orange juice
½ cup sugar
1 10-ounce can refrigerator biscuits

Poke a hole all the way through the biscuits. Arrange the biscuits in a 10-inch round cake pan. Melt the margarine with the orange juice and sugar. Pour the mixture over the biscuits. Bake in a 375° oven for 10 to 12 minutes.
Serves 6.

Kimble Cliff

Almeda's Inn

220 South Main
Tonganoxie, Kansas 66086
(913) 845-2295

Formerly known as the Myers Hotel, Almeda's provides an atmosphere of friendly tranquility. Rooms are decorated in a country style. Guests may sip a cup of coffee by the unique stone bar in a room once used as a bus stop in the 1930s, which was the inspiration for the movie *Bus Stop*.

Cranberry Fluff Salad

    1 pound cranberries
    2 cups sugar
    18 large marshmallows, quartered
    1 cup white grapes
    1 cup red grapes
    2 cups heavy whipping cream,
        whipped
    ½ cup toasted almonds

In a food mill or food processor grind the cranberries. Add the sugar and let the mixture stand overnight. Add the marshmallows and grapes. Fold in the whipped cream and almonds. For the best flavor, chill for 12 hours before serving.
Serves 6 to 8.

Thistle Hill

Route 1, Box 93
WaKeeney, Kansas 67672
(913) 743-2644

Thistle Hill is a comfortable two-story inn with a large brick front porch and a screened back porch.

Furnishings are a mixture of antique and early American. The three upstairs rooms share the bath. A visit to Thistle Hill brings fond memories of "Grandma and Grandpa's place." With 320 acres, the farm provides plenty of room to explore.

Mexican Salsa

    8 cups chopped peeled tomatoes
    ⅓ cup canning salt
    1 cup coarsely chopped celery
    ½ cup coarsely chopped onion
    3 sweet green peppers
    3 sweet red peppers
    6 jalapeño peppers
    ⅔ cup sugar
    ½ cup vinegar

In a large glass bowl combine the tomatoes and salt. Mix well and let stand overnight. Drain well but do not rinse. Add the celery and onion. Remove the seeds from the sweet peppers and some of the seeds from the jalapeño peppers, depending on the hotness desired. In a food processor fitted with the coarse blade, chop the peppers. (Be careful not to inhale the fumes of the hot peppers or get the juice in your eyes or on your hands.) In a nonmetallic kettle combine the tomato mixture, sugar, vinegar, and peppers. Bring the mixture to a slow boil. Cook for 15 minutes, stirring frequently.

To preserve, pour into sterilized jars, seal, and place in a hot water bath for 20 minutes.
Makes 4 pints.

Sourdough Buckwheat Pancakes

    ¾ teaspoon active dry yeast
    1 cup sifted all-purpose flour
    1 tablespoon sugar
    1¼ cups warm water (110° to 115°)

    ❧ ❧ ❧

    6 heaping tablespoons all-purpose
        flour

    4 heaping tablespoons buckwheat
        flour
    ¼ teaspoon salt
    2 tablespoons maple syrup

In a large stone crock or bowl combine the yeast, sifted flour, sugar, and warm water. Beat well. Cover with a clean dish towel and let stand in a warm place for 2 days.

The evening before preparing the pancakes, add 6 tablespoons of flour, the buckwheat flour, salt, and enough warm water to form a very thick batter. Beat well. Cover with a dinner plate and set in a warm place. The next morning add the maple syrup and enough warm water to make the consistency of pancake batter. Beat well. Reserve 1 cup of batter for a new starter.

Grease a hot griddle. Pour small amounts of the batter onto the hot griddle and cook until the edges of the cakes are browned and bubbles come to the surface. Turn and bake until the other side is browned.
Serves 4.

Rhubarb Mulberry Pie

    1 cup sugar
    3 tablespoons all-purpose flour
    ⅛ teaspoon salt
    2 cups cut rhubarb
    1½ cups mulberries
    Pastry for a 9-inch 2 crust pie
    2 tablespoons butter

In a small bowl combine the sugar, flour, and salt. Mix well. In a separate bowl combine the rhubarb and mulberries. Sprinkle the sugar mixture over the fruit, and mix lightly. Line a pastry pan with the half of the pastry. Fill the pastry with the rhubarb mixture, dot with butter, and top with the remaining pastry. Cut vents into the top crust and sprinkle with additional sugar. Bake in a 450° oven for 10 minutes, then lower the temperature to 350° for 35 minutes, or until the middle of the pie is bubbly.
Serves 6.

Kentucky

McLean House—the Olde Inn

105 East Stephen Foster
Bardstown, Kentucky 40004
(502) 348-3494

This beautiful Georgian-style building was built in 1812 by Samuel and Hector McLean. The southeast corner housed the U.S. Post Office for many years, and the old nails and pegs upon which public notices were hung exist to this day.

Seven rooms are still used for overnight guests. Every detail has been attended to while appointing the rooms with Colonial furniture. Furnishings range from antique brass fixtures and four-poster canopy beds to fireplaces and footed bathtubs. Some concessions have been made to modern times, such as hidden televisions and air conditioning.

Corn Fritters

2 cups self-rising flour
¼ teaspoon sugar
1 egg
¼ cup whole kernel corn
Milk to moisten
Oil for deep frying
Confectioners' sugar

In a large bowl combine the flour, sugar, egg, corn, and milk. Heat the oil in a deep fryer to 325°. Drop the batter by tablespoons into the hot oil and cook until golden brown. Roll in confectioners' sugar and serve warm.
Serves 4 to 6.

The Old Talbott Tavern

107 West Stephen Foster
Bardstown, Kentucky 40004
(502) 348-3494

Settlers first began arriving in Bardstown about 1775, and in 1782 it was incorporated as a town under the laws of Virginia, of which Kentucky was then a part. The first permanent building erected was a stone, all-purpose public house on the town square, now known as the Talbott Tavern. To this day the tavern still stands as the oldest western stagecoach stop in America. It was licensed when Patrick Henry was governor of Virginia. The original outside stone wall is a rare example of Flemish bond stone construction in which each stone was faced by over two hundred hand-chiseled marks.

Many famous historical characters have visited the inn, including King Louis Philippe of France, Jesse James, Abraham Lincoln, Daniel Boone, George Rogers Clark, John J. Audubon, Theodore O'Hara, and General George Patton. Today's travelers use seven bedrooms furnished with antiques but with all modern conveniences.

Talbott Tavern Chess Pie

2½ cups sugar
½ cup margarine
2 tablespoons self-rising flour
Pinch salt
4 eggs
1½ teaspoons vanilla extract
1 cup milk
2 9-inch unbaked pie shells

In a large bowl cream together the sugar and margarine. Gradually add the flour, salt, and eggs. Add the vanilla and milk, and beat just until combined. Pour the mixture into an unbaked pie shell. Bake in a 375° oven for 1 hour and 25 minutes.
Serves 12.

The Boone Tavern Hotel

CPO 2345
Berea, Kentucky 40404
(606) 986-9358
(606) 986-9559

The fifty-seven guest rooms of the Boone Tavern are filled with elegant handmade furniture, yet they all have modern conveniences. In this inn are blended the quality and tradition of southern hospitality with the youthful vigor of a college town. The staff is made up mostly of Berea College students. No tipping is allowed.

Chicken Flakes in Bird's Nests

4 medium Idaho potatoes
5 cups Chicken Cream Sauce (recipe follows)
4 cups cubed cooked chicken (½-inch cubes or pieces)
Oil for deep frying

Peel and grate or shred the potatoes on a vegetable shredder with ⅜-inch holes. Line the sides of a 4-inch diameter strainer with a thin layer of shredded potatoes and place a 2-inch diameter strainer inside the first to keep the potatoes in place. Heat the oil and fry the potato basket until golden brown. Turn the potato basket out of the strainer, using a knife if necessary to loosen. Allow the potato basket to cool, and reheat in the oven before serving.

In a large bowl combine the cream sauce and chicken, and add seasonings if desired. Serve in the potato basket.

Serves 8.

Chicken Cream Sauce

6 tablespoons chicken fat or margarine
6 tablespoons sifted all-purpose flour
3 cups chicken stock
Salt and pepper to taste

In the top of a double boiler over simmering water melt the fat or margarine and stir in the flour. Cook for 5 minutes. Add the hot chicken stock and stir to dissolve any lumps. Season with salt and pepper.

Makes 3 cups.

Jefferson Davis Pie

2 cups brown sugar
1 tablespoon sifted all-purpose flour
½ teaspoon nutmeg
1 cup cream
4 eggs
1 teaspoon lemon juice
½ teaspoon grated lemon rind
¼ cup melted margarine
1 9-inch unbaked pie shell
Whipped cream

In a large bowl sift together the brown sugar, flour, and nutmeg. Add the cream and mix well. Add the eggs, beating until well blended. Add the lemon juice, rind, and margarine. Beat well. Pour into the unbaked pie shell. Bake in a 375° oven for 45 minutes. Cool and serve with whipped cream.

Serves 8.

P. T. Baker House

406 Highland Avenue
Carrollton, Kentucky 41008
(606) 525-7088 (weekdays)
(502) 732-4210 (weekends)

Built in 1882 as a residence for Paschal Todd Baker, this inn retains its original character and the flavor of the late Victorian era. In addition to the elaborate "gingerbread" that accentuates the exterior, the house boasts a beautiful hand-carved cherry staircase, imposing walnut woodwork, oil lamp chandeliers, seven fireplaces, interior wood shutters, and antique furnishings. The Carrollton area provides antique hunting, golfing, skiing, sightseeing, boating, shopping, and many community events.

Apple Oatmeal Muffins
with Pecan Streusel Topping

1 7-ounce package apple cinnamon muffin mix
1 7-ounce package oatmeal muffin mix
2 eggs
½ cup milk
1 large or 2 medium apples, peeled, cored, and chopped

❧ ❧ ❧

½ cup brown sugar
¼ cup chopped pecans
½ teaspoon pumpkin pie spice

Grease 12 muffin cups. In a large bowl combine the muffin mixes, eggs, and milk, and mix by hand until blended. Fold in the apples. Fill the muffin cups ¾ full. Combine the brown sugar, pecans, and pumpkin pie spice, and sprinkle on top of the batter. Bake in a 400° oven for 15 to 20 minutes, or un-

P. T. Baker House

til a toothpick inserted in the center comes out clean.

Makes 12 muffins.

American Beauty Fruit Compote

1 quart strawberries
4 to 5 medium peaches or
  nectarines
1 cup blueberries, fresh or frozen,
  drained
¼ cup confectioners' sugar
2 cups heavy cream or half and half
6 to 8 Maraschino cherries

Remove the caps and stems from the strawberries, and cut each in half. Quarter any large berries. Place in a bowl, sprinkle 2 tablespoons of sugar on the berries and toss gently to coat. Peel and slice the peaches, and place in a separate bowl. Sprinkle with 1 tablespoon of sugar. Place the blueberries in a third bowl and sprinkle with 1 tablespoon of sugar. In stemmed sherbet or champagne glasses layer the strawberries, peaches, and blueberries. Repeat the layers. Place a cherry on top. Pour the cream down the side of the glass to 1-inch depth.

Serves 6 to 8.

Banana Raisin Bread Pudding

½ small loaf raisin bread
1½ tablespoons butter or margarine
4 bananas, sliced
2 eggs
2½ cups milk
½ cup currant jelly

Grease a 2-quart baking dish. Spread the slices of raisin bread with butter. In the prepared pan alternate layers of raisin bread and sliced bananas, ending with bread. In a bowl beat the eggs. In a separate bowl combine the jelly and milk, stirring until well blended. Combine the eggs and milk mixture and pour over the bread and bananas. Bake in a 350° oven for 1 hour or until a knife inserted in the center comes out clean. Cut into squares.

Variation: Instead of jelly, ¼ cup of sugar and the juice of 1 lemon may be used. Sprinkle the lemon juice over the bananas, and add the sugar to the milk. Proceed as above.

Serves 6 to 8.

Log Cabin Bed and Breakfast

350 North Broadway
Georgetown, Kentucky 40324
(502) 863-3514

Guests can enjoy the best of times in a rustic restored Kentucky log cabin (circa 1809). A shake shingle roof and chinked logs on the outside surround a completely modern interior. The living room is dominated by a huge fieldstone fireplace, and the master bedroom and bath are on the ground floor. A loft bedroom sleeps an additional two people. The dining and kitchen wing is equipped with all new appliances.

Strawberry Tarts

2 cups all-purpose flour
1 cup butter, softened
6 ounces cream cheese, softened

1 teaspoon vanilla extract
2 cups sugar
1 egg
6 ounces cream cheese, softened
Sour cream
Strawberry preserves

In a large bowl combine the flour, butter, and 6 ounces of cream cheese. By hand form the mixture into a large ball. Cut the dough into 4 pieces, and form 48 balls. Flatten and place in tart pans.

In a separate bowl combine the vanilla extract, sugar, egg, and remaining cream cheese, mixing just until well blended. Do not beat. Fill the tart shells ⅔ full. Bake in a 350° oven for 20 minutes. Cool. Lift the tarts from the pan. Place a small amount of sour cream on each tart, and top with a small amount of strawberry preserves. Chill, and serve.

Makes 48 tarts.

Louisiana

The Chimes Cottages

Box 52257
New Orleans, Louisiana 70152-2257
(504) 525-4640
(800) 749-4640

These quaint guest cottages and suites are situated behind an 1876 Uptown home. Stained and leaded glass windows, French doors, cypress staircases, and a brick courtyard enhance the romantic atmosphere of the cottages. Three blocks from St. Charles Avenue, the Chimes Cottages are minutes away from major New Orleans attractions. The historic St. Charles Avenue streetcar line makes the resources of New Orleans accessible without an automobile.

New Orleans Pain Perdu

2 tablespoons corn syrup
1 cup brown sugar
5 tablespoons butter or margarine
1½ loaves French bread, cut into
 ½-inch slices
5 eggs
1½ cups milk
1 teaspoon vanilla extract
Sour cream
Kiwi fruit and strawberries, sliced

In a saucepan combine the corn syrup, brown sugar, and butter. Cook until the butter is melted and the mixture is bubbly. Pour the mixture into a 9x13-inch pan. Arrange the bread in the pan, making 2 layers. In a large bowl combine the eggs, milk, and vanilla. Pour the mixture over the bread. If desired, cover and refrigerate overnight. Bake in a 350° oven for 45 minutes. Lift the edges of the bread with a spatula, and invert onto a serving plate. Spoon the sour cream over the toast, and alternate kiwi and strawberry slices on top. Serve immediately.

Serves 8 to 10.

Easy Creole Delight

An appetizer or light lunch.

¼ teaspoon cayenne
½ teaspoon allspice
½ teaspoon coriander
Salt and pepper to taste

 🍃 🍃 🍃

1 pound whole okra, fresh or frozen
2 tablespoons oil
1 small onion, sliced
2 tablespoons oil
2 cloves garlic, minced
Juice of 1 large or 2 small lemons
2 small tomatoes, sliced
½ cup water

In a small bowl combine the cayenne, allspice, coriander, salt, and pepper. Set aside. Wash and dry the okra, and slice off the stems without exposing the seeds. In a skillet sauté the okra in 2 tablespoons of oil until bright green, about 10 minutes. Remove and drain on paper towels. Sprinkle half of the seasonings over the okra. In a skillet sauté the onion in 2 tablespoons of oil until golden brown, about 10 minutes. Add the garlic. Pour the remaining seasoning mixture over the onions and garlic. Add the okra, and stir to combine. Add the lemon juice. Place the tomato slices on top of the mixture and pour the water over all. Simmer the mixture for 30 minutes over low heat.

Serves 8 to 10.

The Columns

3811 St. Charles Avenue
New Orleans, Louisiana 70115
(504) 899-9308

The Columns Hotel is in the heart of the city's finest residential section, the fashionable, historic garden district on Saint Charles Avenue. Built in 1883 by a wealthy tobacco merchant, the Columns remained a private residence until 1915, when it became an exclusive boarding house. In the 1940s it began its illustrious career as one of the finest small hotels in New Orleans. The St. Charles streetcar passes in front of the hotel and within minutes transports its passengers to the famous old French Quarter, Canal Street, the business district, parks, universities, and elegant shopping.

The Chimes Cottages

Lamothe House

621 Esplanade Avenue
New Orleans, Louisiana 70116
(504) 947-1161

At Lamothe House, the gaiety and gallantry of aristocratic French Louisiana have been preserved with charm and beauty. Each of the individually decorated suites, many overlooking the original flagstone courtyard, has been restored to its nineteenth-century splendor. Period antiques accompany modern conveniences. A "little Creole breakfast" is served each morning in the dining room. Courtesy parking is provided in a private parking area adjoining the courtyard.

A glorious Victorian lounge and beautiful dining room are part of the hotel's assets. Restored period rooms are available for receptions and conferences. The Columns Hotel, with its carved mahogany stairwell, magnificent stained glass panels, skylights, and windows, allows guests to sample those gentler Victorian days of New Orleans in the 1880s. The Victorian Lounge is among the top one-hundred bars in the nation, and The Columns Hotel is listed on the National Register of Historic Places. The inn has eighteen rooms, continental breakfast, and newspaper for the guest. The accommodations are for two persons per room.

Hot Crawfish Dip

1 tablespoon butter
1½ teaspoons Worcestershire sauce
2 tablespoons shallots
2 tablespoons dried parsley
8 ounces crawfish tails, cooked and chopped
4 ounces cream cheese
¼ cup milk
Melba toast rounds

Melt the butter and add the Worcestershire, shallots, parsley, and crawfish. Add the softened cream cheese and milk. Simmer until warm. Serve on toast rounds. Add extra seasonings to taste.
Serves 8.

Buttermilk Pie

3 cups sugar
6 tablespoons all-purpose flour
1½ cups buttermilk
5 eggs, beaten
1 cup butter, melted
2 teaspoons vanilla extract
2 deep dish pie crusts, unbaked

Combine the sugar, flour, and half of the buttermilk. Add the eggs and mix well. Add the remaining buttermilk, blend in the melted butter, and add the vanilla. Pour into the pie crusts. Bake in a 425° oven for ten minutes. Reduce the heat to 350° and bake until a knife inserted in the center comes out clean, about 30 minutes.
Serves 10 to 12.

Mrs. Gertrude Munson's Cafe Brûlot Recipe

20 cubes sugar
2 whole cloves
1 stick cinnamon, broken
¼ orange, peeled
⅛ lemon, peeled

❧ ❧ ❧

¾ cup best domestic brandy
Denatured alcohol
1 pint dark roast coffee

Place the sugar, cloves, cinnamon, orange, and lemon in a brûlot bowl. Pour the brandy over the contents. Into the tray of the brûlot bowl pour the denatured alcohol. Ignite the alcohol and turn out the lights. The brandy will light when it gets hot. After burning the brandy, add the hot coffee. Caution: Don't burn all of the brandy away, it tastes so good.
Serves 8.

Barrow House

524 Royal Street
Post Office Box 1461
St. Francisville, Louisiana 70775
(504) 635-4791

Barrow House is in the heart of the historic district of this picturesque town. The two-story portion of the inn, built in 1809, is in salt-box style; a one-story wing and Greek Revival façade were added in 1855. The one suite and four double rooms, three with private bath and shower, all have television and air conditioning. The inn is furnished with antiques of the 1860s. Guests are warmly welcomed by the innkeepers; a delicious dinner is served in the formal dining room.

ॐ ॐ ॐ ॐ ॐ

Lamothe House

Creole 8-Bean Soup

2 cups dried mixed beans
1 cup chopped onion
½ cup chopped celery
½ cup chopped bell pepper
2 ham hocks or 2 thick slices salt
    pork
3 bay leaves
1 14½-ounce can chopped tomatoes
2 beef bouillon cubes
1 teaspoon thyme
1 teaspoon garlic powder
½ teaspoon oregano
¼ to ½ teaspoon cayenne pepper
½ teaspoon black pepper
10 cups water
1 cup chopped ham
1 cup sliced Andouille or smoked
    sausage
1 10-ounce box frozen sliced okra
    (or green beans)
Salt and Tabasco to taste

In a stock pot add water to a level of 2 inches above the beans and soak overnight. Drain. Add the onion, cel- ery, bell pepper, ham hocks, bay leaves, tomatoes with juice, seasonings, and water. Bring to a boil, cover, and simmer for 1 hour and 30 minutes. Add the ham and Andouille, and simmer for 30 minutes. Add the okra and simmer for 15 minutes. Check the seasonings and add salt and Tabasco to taste.

Serves 8.

Creole Seafood au Gratin

½ cup margarine
2 medium onions, finely chopped
1 bell pepper, finely chopped
2 ribs celery, finely chopped
1 teaspoon paprika
1 teaspoon onion powder

1 teaspoon garlic powder
½ teaspoon dried basil
¼ teaspoon dry mustard
½ teaspoon black pepper
½ teaspoon white pepper
⅛ to ¼ teaspoon red pepper
3 tablespoons all-purpose flour
1 8-ounce package cream cheese
1 10½-ounce can cream of
   mushroom soup
1 8-ounce can sliced mushrooms,
   drained
1 pound peeled shrimp, cooked
1 pound peeled crawfish, cooked
½ pound crab meat
Grated Cheddar cheese
Basmati rice, cooked

In a saucepan melt the butter and sauté the onions, bell pepper, and celery until soft. Add the seasonings and sauté for another 3 minutes. Add the flour and cook for 2 minutes. Cut the cream cheese into pieces and add, stirring until melted. Add the soup and mushrooms. Add the shrimp and heat until barely cooked. Add the crawfish and crab meat and heat through.

This can be made ahead and refrigerated. Reheat over low heat until the mixture comes to a boil, or spoon into 8 to 10 ramekins and heat in a 350° oven for 25 minutes. Sprinkle with grated Cheddar cheese. Serve with Basmati rice, an imported Indian rice found in international grocery stores.

Serves 8 to 10.

Chicken Bayou la Fourche

½ cup margarine
4 cloves garlic, chopped
⅓ cup all-purpose flour
4 cups milk
4 teaspoons chicken broth granules
¼ teaspoon ground bay leaves (or 3
   whole)
½ teaspoon onion powder
¼ teaspoon white pepper
3 tablespoons chopped fresh basil
   (or 1 teaspoon dried)

❧ ❧ ❧

½ cup margarine
½ cup chopped onions
½ cup chopped green onions
¼ cup chopped celery
¼ cup chopped green bell pepper
4 cloves garlic, chopped
2 tablespoons all-purpose flour
1 2-ounce jar chopped pimientos
1 teaspoon Creole mustard
2 tablespoons sherry
1 teaspoon Pernod
Salt and red pepper to taste
1 pound white crab meat, picked
   over

❧ ❧ ❧

12 chicken breast halves
¼ cup margarine
Fresh basil leaves for garnish

Prepare the Basil Cream Sauce. In a saucepan melt ½ cup of margarine and sauté 4 cloves of garlic until golden. Add ⅓ cup of flour and stir until well blended. Cook for 3 minutes. Gradually add the milk, stirring constantly. Bring to a boil. Add the chicken broth granules, bay leaves, onion powder, and white pepper. Reduce the heat to low and cook for 5 minutes. Add the fresh basil. Set aside.

In a large skillet melt ½ cup of butter and sauté the onions, celery, bell pepper, and 4 cloves of garlic for 5 minutes. Add 2 tablespoons flour, and cook for 2 to 3 minutes. Add the pimientos, mustard, sherry, Pernod, 1 cup of Basil Cream Sauce, salt, and red pepper to taste. Cook for 3 minutes. Add the crab meat and stir gently to blend. Remove from the heat.

Flatten the chicken breasts between sheets of plastic wrap with a meat mallet. Spread the flattened chicken on a work surface. Place 2 tablespoons of filling on each breast and roll up, tucking the ends in while rolling. Place the breasts in a baking dish and dot with margarine. Cover. Bake in a 350° oven for 30 minutes. Slice each roll as you would a jelly roll. Place ⅓ cup of heated Basil Cream Sauce on each plate and fan out the chicken slices so the stuffing is exposed. Garnish with fresh basil leaves.

Serves 12.

Louisiana Red Beans

This is an adaptation of the famous New Orleans "wash day" dish, red beans and rice. On Mondays, the lady of the house put a pot of red beans on to simmer for supper while she did the laundry.

1 pound dried red kidney beans
Water to cover
2 ham hocks or 3 slices salt pork
1 cup chopped celery
1 cup chopped onion
½ cup chopped green bell pepper
3 bay leaves
½ teaspoon white pepper
1 teaspoon dried thyme
1 teaspoon garlic powder
¾ teaspoon oregano
¼ teaspoon cayenne pepper
¼ teaspoon black pepper

❧ ❧ ❧

2 tablespoons Worcestershire sauce
1½ tablespoons beef broth granules
Tabasco to taste

Soak the beans overnight in water. In a large stock pot combine the beans and remaining ingredients except the Worcestershire, beef broth granules, and Tabasco. Add water to a level of 1 inch above the bean mixture. Bring to a boil, reduce the heat to low, and cover. Simmer for about 1 hour and 30 minutes, or until the beans are tender but not overcooked. Add the remaining ingredients. Cut the meat from the ham hocks and return the meat to the pot.

Serves 12 to 15.

Barrow House

Mufflatta Bread

An adaptation of a famous New Orleans sandwich.

    1 large or 2 regular loaves French bread

    ❧ ❧ ❧

    ½ cup margarine, softened
    1 cup grated Mozzarella cheese
    ½ cup grated Parmesan cheese
    ¼ cup chopped pimiento-stuffed olives
    2 green onions, chopped
    2 cloves garlic, finely chopped
    ¾ cup finely chopped salami or summer sausage
    ½ teaspoon dried leaf oregano
    ½ cup mayonnaise

Slice the French bread as for a hot dog or poor boy bun, cutting almost through.

In a large bowl combine the remaining ingredients. Spread the mixture onto the French bread. Wrap the sandwich in foil. Bake in a 350° oven for 20 to 25 minutes.

Makes 30 to 40 slices.

❧ ❧ ❧ ❧ ❧

French Silk Chocolate Flower Pots

    1 cup butter, softened
    1½ cups sugar
    2 ounces unsweetened chocolate, melted
    2½ teaspoons vanilla extract
    4 eggs
    1 cup whipping cream
    ¼ cup sugar
    1 ounce shaved or grated semisweet chocolate
    Flowers for garnish

In a large bowl cream together the butter and 1½ cups of sugar with an electric mixer. Blend in the melted chocolate and 2 teaspoons of vanilla. Add the eggs one at a time, beating for 5 minutes after each addition. Divide the mixture among 6 clay or glass flower pots, filling ⅔ full. Whip the cream, adding the remaining sugar gradually. When almost stiff, add ½ teaspoon of vanilla. Spread the cream over the mixture in the flower pots. Sprinkle with grated chocolate and insert a straw in the center of each. Cut the straw just above the whipped cream. Refrigerate the flower pots. Before serving, insert a flower in each straw.

Serves 6.

Maine

Arundel Meadows Inn

Route 1
Arundel, Maine

Post Office Box 1129
Kennebunk, Maine 04043
(207) 985-3770

This 165-year-old farmhouse, situated on the Kennebunk River, is just minutes from Kennebunkport, home of President George Bush. Offering six guest rooms, each uniquely decorated and all with private baths, the inn also provides a suite that accommodates up to four guests. Three of the rooms feature wood burning fireplaces. A full breakfast and afternoon tea are prepared by the innkeeper, who has been chef at several fine Boston restaurants. Only a short drive from beautiful beaches, the inn is surrounded by several towns and villages with a variety of shops, antiques, art galleries, music, theater, excellent restaurants, year-round sporting activities, and many places of historic interest.

Oat Bran Banana Pancakes

1 cup oat bran
1 cup all-purpose flour
2 teaspoons baking soda
1 tablespoon sugar
½ cup mashed banana
2 teaspoons vanilla extract
1½ cups plain yogurt
½ cup chopped pecans
4 egg whites, beaten
2 tablespoons melted butter

In a large bowl combine the bran, flour, baking soda, and sugar. Stir in the banana and vanilla. Add the yogurt and chopped nuts. In a separate bowl beat the egg whites and fold into the bran mixture with the melted butter. Pour a small amount of the batter at a time onto a hot greased griddle. Bake until bubbles rise to the surface and the edges are golden. Turn and bake until done.

Serves 4 to 6.

Triple Fiber Oat Cookies

1 cup butter, softened
½ cup light brown sugar
½ cup sugar
1 egg
½ teaspoon vanilla extract
1 cup oat bran
½ cup all-purpose flour
½ teaspoon baking soda
1 teaspoon cinnamon
3 cups rolled oats
1 cup chopped prunes
½ cup whole almonds, chopped

Grease a baking sheet. In a large bowl beat the butter and sugars together. Add the egg and vanilla. In a separate bowl mix the bran, flour, baking soda, and cinnamon. Add the bran mixture to the butter mixture. Stir in the oats, prunes, and almonds. Roll into 1-inch balls. Flatten slightly onto the prepared baking sheet. Bake in a 375° oven until golden brown.

Makes 3 dozen cookies.

Blueberry Oat Bran Scones

1½ cups oat bran
1½ cups all-purpose flour
⅓ cup light brown sugar
2 teaspoons baking powder
1 teaspoon cream of tartar
½ cup butter
2 eggs
⅓ cup plain yogurt
1 teaspoon vanilla extract
1½ cups blueberries

Grease a baking sheet. In a large bowl mix the bran, flour, sugar, baking powder, and cream of tartar together. Cut in the butter. In a separate bowl mix the eggs, yogurt, and vanilla together. Blend the yogurt mixture into the dry mixture. Fold in the blueberries carefully. Pat into a circle on the prepared baking sheet. Cut into wedges, wiping the knife each time. Bake in a 400° oven for 20 to 25 minutes.

Makes 1 dozen scones.

Katie's Ketch

Post Office Box 105
Bailey Island, Maine 04003
(207) 833-7785

"**W**e were ready to sell our home with so many unused rooms when we read about bed and breakfast. We knew it was for us," say Albert and Katie, grandparents of seven. Albert, a semiretired lobsterman, can tell guests about his colorful military background and his lobstering experiences or recount tales of his family that has fished off the Grand Banks since the 1600s. Katie's plants decorate the house inside and out with a cascade of colors. Being native islanders, Katie and Albert know all the interesting spots within walking distance from the house. Two doubles and a single bedroom are offered for guests, and all rooms are furnished with family heirlooms and feature a panoramic view of the Atlantic Ocean.

Pineapple Delight

1 cup butter or margarine
¼ cup confectioners' sugar
2 cups all-purpose flour

&. &. &.

2 3-ounce packages vanilla instant pudding
1 16-ounce carton sour cream
1 8-ounce carton Cool Whip
1 16-ounce can crushed pineapple

In a large bowl combine the butter, sugar, and flour for a crust. Press the mixture into a 9x13-inch pan. Bake in a 350° oven for 30 minutes or less. Cool.

In a large bowl blend the pudding, sour cream, and Cool Whip. Add the crushed pineapple with juice. Mix well and pour over the cooled crust.

Refrigerate until completely chilled. Delicious!

Lemon Zucchini Muffins

The green of the shredded, unpared zucchini flecks these muffins. Good warm or cold.

2 cups all-purpose flour
½ cup sugar
1 tablespoon baking powder
1 teaspoon salt
1 teaspoon grated lemon peel or 1 teaspoon lemon juice
½ teaspoon nutmeg
½ cup chopped nuts
½ cup raisins
½ cup chopped dates

&. &. &.

2 eggs
½ cup milk
⅓ cup oil
1 cup packed shredded, unpared zucchini (not drained)

Grease 12 muffin cups. In a large bowl combine the flour, sugar, baking powder, salt, lemon peel, and nutmeg. Stir in the nuts, raisins, and dates. In a small bowl, beat the eggs. Beat in the milk and oil. Add the egg mixture to the flour mixture, then sprinkle the zucchini on top. Stir just until blended. Fill the prepared cups ⅔ full. Bake in a 400° oven until a cake tester inserted in the center comes out clean, about 15 to 20 minutes.

Makes 12 regular-sized muffins or 1 coffee cake.

The Lady and the Loon

Post Office Box #98
Bailey Island, Maine 04003
(207) 833-6871

The Lady and the Loon has four rooms available for its guests, who enjoy the privacy of a separate entrance and private baths in one of Bailey Island's original inns. The queen-size beds are covered with handmade quilts, and the rooms provide inspiring island and ocean views. Breakfast may be enjoyed at the picnic table on the backyard bluff overlooking Ragged Island or in the country dining room. Guests may walk the private stairs to the beach, at their own risk, to bask on a large rock and observe the marine environment or to explore one of Maine's tidepools.

Glazed Maple Muffins

¾ cup bran flakes
½ cup milk
½ cup maple syrup
1 egg, beaten
¼ cup oil
1¼ cups all-purpose flour
3 teaspoons baking powder
½ teaspoon salt
⅓ cup sliced almonds

&. &. &.

½ cup (or less) confectioners' sugar
1 tablespoon butter
1 tablespoon maple syrup

Grease 12 muffin cups. In a large bowl combine the bran flakes, milk, and ½ cup of maple syrup. Mix in the egg and oil. In a separate bowl combine the next 4 ingredients. Add the egg mixture to the flour mixture. Stir until just blended, and pour or spoon into the prepared muffin cups. Bake in a 400° oven for 18 to 20 minutes.

In a small bowl mix the sugar, butter, and 1 tablespoon of syrup. Spread over warm muffins.

Makes 12.

Carrot Molasses Muffins

3 cups all-purpose flour
1 teaspoon baking soda
1½ tablespoons baking powder
½ teaspoon salt
1 tablespoon cinnamon
2 cups bran

&a &a &a

4 eggs, beaten
1½ cups oil
1¼ cups brown sugar
¼ cup molasses
3 cups grated carrots
1 cup sliced almonds
Cinnamon-sugar mixture

Grease 20 muffin cups. In a large bowl sift together the flour, baking soda, baking powder, salt, and cinnamon. Add the bran to the flour mixture. In a separate bowl combine the beaten eggs, oil, brown sugar, and molasses. Add the egg mixture to the flour mixture. Add the carrots and almonds. Fill the prepared muffin cups. Sprinkle cinnamon-sugar on top. Bake in a 350° oven for 20 to 25 minutes.

Makes 20 muffins.

Hearthside

early evening get-together, guests feel a special blend of intimacy and Victorian elegance. Built around the turn of the century, the three-story house with its weathered shingles and brightly filled flower boxes is conveniently situated on a side street within easy walking distance of Bar Harbor's fine shops, boutiques, and restaurants. The newly decorated rooms are cozy and warm. Breakfast may be eaten in the dining room or outside on the porch or patio. On chilly evenings evening refreshments and friendly conversation may be enjoyed in front of the parlor fireplace.

Hearthside

7 High Street
Bar Harbor, Maine 04609
(207) 288-4533

At Hearthside Inn warmth, laughter, charm, antiques, and hospitality are combined into one package. From the community breakfast through the

Hearthside's Noodle Kugel

8 ounces broad noodles
2 eggs, well beaten
2 tablespoons sugar
½ teaspoon salt
1 cup sour cream
½ cup creamed cottage cheese
1 3-ounce package cream cheese, softened
2 tablespoons melted butter or margarine

&a &a &a

1 21-ounce can cherry pie filling

Grease a 9-inch square baking dish. Cook the noodles according to the package directions until tender and drain. In a large bowl combine the eggs, sugar, and salt. Stir in the sour cream, cottage cheese, and cream cheese. Add the noodles and butter, and blend well. Place the mixture in the prepared baking dish. Bake in a 375° oven for 45 minutes or until brown and crisp.

Serve hot or cold and top with heated cherry pie filling.

Serves 6 to 8.

Holbrook House

74 Mount Desert Street
Bar Harbor, Maine 04609
(207) 288-4970

Built in 1876, Holbrook House was one of the first cottages to provide lodging for wealthy Easterners who had discovered the fascinating beauty of Mount Desert Island. The inn is one of only a few buildings in Bar Harbor that survived a 1947 forest fire that swept the island. Situated close to restaurants, shops, and the ocean, Holbrook House is a bright, airy Victorian summer cottage decorated with antiques, old-fashioned prints, and period furniture, lace, and chintz. All guest rooms have private baths, and two double-bedroom cottages are available. Smoking is permitted on the front porch only.

Savory Spinach Cheesecake

12 large eggs
1 tablespoon dried onion flakes
2½ cups shredded Cheddar cheese, at room temperature
2 tablespoons prepared mustard
1 teaspoon baking powder
¼ cup butter
1 teaspoon salt
½ teaspoon pepper
½ package chopped spinach, thawed and squeezed dry
3 cups whole milk
1½ cups all-purpose flour

Grease a 9x13-inch glass baking dish. In a blender combine the eggs, onion flakes, cheese, mustard, baking powder, butter, salt, and pepper. Blend to a cream consistency. Add the spinach and blend lightly to mix. Pour into a large mixing bowl. Place the milk in the blender and add the flour while the blender is running. Add the milk and flour mixture to the spinach mixture and mix well. Pour the combined mixture into the prepared baking dish. Set the dish in a metal pan. Do not add water. Bake in a 325° oven until the top is brown and the pudding is set.

Serve with a mild salsa sauce made of 1 can of Old El Paso Mild and Chunky Salsa and 1 16-ounce can of tomato sauce, if desired.

Serves 15.

Blueberry Buckle

1 cup butter
1 cup sugar
4 large eggs
2 cups molasses
4 cups all-purpose flour
1 cup hot water with 2 teaspoons baking soda
1 teaspoon salt
2 teaspoons cinnamon
1 teaspoon allspice
1 teaspoon ginger
½ teaspoon cloves
3 cups fresh or frozen blueberries

Grease an aluminum 12x17-inch baking pan. In a large bowl cream together the butter and sugar until the mixture is almost white. Beat in the eggs one at a time. Slowly stir in molasses. Alternately mix in the flour and water. Add the remaining dry ingredients. Carefully fold in the berries. Pour into the prepared baking pan. Bake in a 325° oven for 1 hour and 15 minutes.

Serves 24.

Chocolate Scones

2¼ cups all-purpose flour
¼ cup whole wheat flour
2 tablespoons sugar
1 tablespoon baking powder
½ teaspoon salt
1 teaspoon cinnamon
½ cup butter
1 large egg
Milk as needed
½ cup Nestle chocolate mini-morsels
Egg whites or heavy cream

In a large mixing bowl combine the flours, sugar, baking powder, salt, and cinnamon. Mix well. Cut the butter into the flour mixture until it resembles small peas. Break the egg into a 1-cup measure and add milk to make ⅔ cup. Add the milk, egg, and chocolate mini-morsels to the flour mixture, and combine lightly until a loose ball is formed (a light hand makes for a light scone). Hand-knead the mixture in the bowl 5 to 10 times and then break into 2 equal balls. Press down each ball on an ungreased cookie sheet to form a 6-inch diameter disc. Score each disc radially into six pieces. Brush with a wash of egg whites or heavy cream. Bake in a 400° oven for 15 to 20 minutes.

Serves 12.

Holbrook House

Fairhaven Inn

North Bath Road
Bath, Maine 04530
(207) 443-4391

Fairhaven is the Maine experience, an inn for all seasons and for all reasons. Nestled into a hillside overlooking the wide Kennebec River, this charming old country inn is surrounded by lush green lawns and bountiful woods and meadows. The Fairhaven welcomes guests for a night or two or for a vacation of a week or more to enjoy the atmosphere of old Maine.

Northport House Bed & Breakfast

Chilled Blueberry Soup

   2 cups fresh or frozen Maine
      blueberries
   1 cup cranberry juice
   ½ cup lemon juice
   ½ cup sugar
   2 cups whipped cream (not
      prepared topping, whip your
      own)
   Mint leaves and blueberries for
      garnish

Purée the blueberries. In a saucepan combine the blueberries, cranberry juice, lemon juice, and sugar. Simmer covered for 10 minutes. When cool, fold in the whipped cream. Chill for several hours.
   Serve in dessert dishes and garnish with a mint leaf from the garden with a few berries by its side.
   Serves 4 to 6.

Northport House Bed and Breakfast

City One, Mounted Route
U.S. Route 1
Belfast, Maine 04915
(207) 338-1422

This restored Victorian house (circa 1873) is in a coastal community near Camden and Searsport. At one time it was an overnight stop on the Portland/Bar Harbor Road. In the morning guests enjoy a full breakfast served in the large common room or on the deck. The eight guest rooms are spacious and tastefully decorated, featuring period pieces reflecting traditional New England charm.

Northport House Basic Pancake Mix

   5 cups all-purpose flour
   1 cup nonfat dry milk
   ¼ cup sugar
   3 tablespoons baking powder
   2 teaspoons salt

In a large bowl mix all of the ingredients by hand until thoroughly incorporated. Store in a plastic container in a cool dry place until needed.
   (See the following pancake recipe.)
   Makes about 6½ cups.

Northport House Plain Pancakes

   3 cups Northport House Basic
      Pancake Mix
   ½ teaspoon oil
   3 medium eggs
   2 cups milk or water

In a large bowl mix all of the ingredients until totally incorporated. Let the batter stand 5 minutes before using. Cook on a 375° griddle approximately 2½ minutes per side.

Note: To the above recipe you can add your favorite fruit.

Variation: For buttermilk pancakes, replace 2 cups of milk or water used in plain pancakes with 1 cup of buttermilk and 1 cup of milk or water.

For sourdough pancakes, replace 2 cups of milk or water used in plain pancakes with 1 cup of sour cream or plain yogurt and 1 cup of milk or water.

Makes 4 to 6 medium-sized pancakes.

Beer Bread with Caraway Seeds

3 cups all-purpose flour
3 tablespoons baking powder
3 tablespoons sugar
1 12-ounce can beer, room temperature
3 tablespoons caraway seeds

❧ ❧ ❧

3 tablespoons melted butter

Grease and flour a 9x5-inch loaf pan. In a large bowl mix together the flour, baking powder, and sugar until incorporated. Gradually add the beer until the dough is very wet and sticky. Add the caraway seeds. Pour into the prepared pan. Bake in a 350° oven for 45 to 55 minutes. Remove the loaf from the pan immediately and swab with melted butter. Cover with foil.

Great for toast with your favorite jam or jelly.

Makes 1 loaf.

The Blue Hill Inn

Union Street
Post Office Box 403
Blue Hill, Maine 04614
(207) 374-2844

The Blue Hill Inn has earned high marks as one of mid-coast Maine's most distinguished country inns. It has been in operation for 150 consecutive years. Situated at the head of Blue Hill Bay, it overlooks the Blue Hill Mountains. The inn has two common rooms, a dining room, and eleven guest rooms, each with a private bath. Furnishings are from the nineteenth century, and working fireplaces are in several of the rooms. The chef specializes in contemporary food presentation based on classical French techniques. Six-course meals are offered in the evenings. A nightly innkeepers' reception with cocktails and hors d'oeuvres provides opportunity for socializing.

Gratiné of Local Berries and Citrus Fruit

2 cups light cream
½ cup sugar
1 vanilla bean, split lengthwise
5 egg yolks

❧ ❧ ❧

1 pink grapefruit cut into segments
1 navel orange cut into segments
1 kiwi fruit, peeled and cut into 6 slices
Fresh blueberries (approximately ½ cup)
Fresh strawberries (halved) or raspberries
Confectioners' sugar

In a saucepan bring the cream, sugar, and vanilla bean to a simmer over low heat. Pour ⅛ of the cream mixture into the egg yolks and mix well. Slowly pour the mixture back into the remaining cream mixture, stirring constantly over low heat until thickened enough to coat the back of a wooden spoon. Strain, cover with plastic film. Cool in an ice bath, and refrigerate. This Anglaise sauce will keep for 2 days in the refrigerator.

To serve, pour the Anglaise sauce completely over the bottom of 2 dinner-sized plates (use broiler-proof ware). Make an alternating spoke pattern of grapefruit and orange segments on outer portion of each plate. Place 3 of the kiwi slices in center of each plate and mound the slices with half of the blueberries. Place the raspberries or strawberry halves around the kiwi slices. Sprinkle all liberally with confectioners' sugar and place under a hot broiler until glazed, approximately 4 minutes.

Serves 2.

Mussels with Cilantro and Curry

5 pounds fresh mussels
2 medium-sized Spanish onions, finely diced
5 cloves garlic, finely minced
2 tablespoons unsalted butter
2 tablespoons coriander
2 tablepoons curry powder
2 tablespoons crushed white peppercorns
1½ cups good dry white wine
½ cup water
3 bay leaves
1 bunch cilantro, coarsely chopped

❧ ❧ ❧

8 thin slices French bread
2 tablespoons olive oil
1 teaspoon paprika

Thoroughly wash and debeard the mussels. Soak in ice water for 1 hour before using. In a large non-reactive pot cook the onions and garlic in butter over low heat until the onions are translucent and soft. Add the cor-

The Blue Hill Inn

iander, curry powder, white peppercorns, and drained mussels. Stir to coat the shells. Pour in the wine and water, and add the bay leaves and cilantro. Cover and steam over high heat for about 7 minutes until the mussels open, shaking the pot from time to time. Arrange the cooked mussels in a circular pattern inside heated soup bowls, and pour the strained stock liberally over all. Garnish with toasted French bread slices dredged in olive oil and sprinkled with paprika.

Serves 8.

Roasted Duck
with Cinnamon, Vanilla, and Pears

1 5- to 5½-pound duck (cleaned and trimmed of excess fat)
2 shallots, sliced
1 garlic clove, crushed
1 carrot, sliced
1 celery rib, cut into pieces
Coarse salt
1 tablespoon olive oil

🙚 🙚 🙚

1 ripe Bartlett pear
1½ cups good dry red wine
2 whole cinnamon sticks
1 vanilla bean, split lengthwise
2 tablespoons unsalted butter

Place the duck, shallots, garlic, carrot, and celery in an uncovered roasting pan. Rub the duck with salt and olive oil. Bake in a 450 to 500° oven for 15 to 18 minutes, keeping the breast meat rare. Remove the duck, pour off the excess fat, and keep the duck warm.

While the duck is cooking, peel and halve the pear. In a saucepan combine the wine, cinnamon sticks, and vanilla bean. Add the pear and poach over moderate heat until done. Remove the pear and keep warm. Add the poaching liquid to the roasting pan and reduce over high heat until slightly thickened and a syrup-like consistency. While reducing the pan liquids, carve off the breast meat (whole) and legs, returning the legs to the oven to finish cooking, about 5 minutes. Slice the breasts and fan out on 2 heated plates. Keep warm. Whip the 2 tablespoons butter into the re-

duced liquid, strain, and pour over the breast slices. Slice the pear halves and arrange on plates, along with the leg portions. Sprinkle coarse salt sparsely over all.

Serves 2.

Stewed Halibut
with Fresh Vegetable Ratatouille

1 red pepper
1 green pepper
6 ripe Italian plum tomatoes
1 eggplant
1 zucchini
1 yellow (summer) squash
1 onion
1 leek
2 cloves garlic
2 tablespoons olive oil
¼ cup water
Coarse salt, black peppercorns
Fresh basil, chopped
4 boned fresh halibut fillets
Coarse salt

Roast the peppers in a 450° oven until skin is blackened. Remove and cover with a damp cloth. When cooled, remove the skin and cut into julienne strips, saving all juices. Plunge the tomatoes into boiling water, count to ten, remove, and plunge into ice water until cooled. Peel and remove the seeds. Dice into medium pieces, saving all liquid. Wash the eggplant, zucchini, and yellow squash. Dice into medium pieces. Finely dice the onion, leek, and garlic.

In a large sauté pan, heat the olive oil over low heat. Add the onion, leek, and garlic, and cook until translucent. Add the eggplant, squashes, tomatoes, peppers, reserved juices, water, salt, and freshly ground peppercorns to taste. Cover with a lid or foil and simmer over low heat for 45 minutes. Remove from the heat, add the basil, and place the halibut fillets on top. Sprinkle with additional coarse salt and rub with a little olive oil. Cover again and bake in a 450°

oven for approximately 5 minutes. Place the halibut on heated plates, surrounded by the ratatouille, and liberally pour the cooking juices over all.

Serves 4.

Flourless Chocolate Torte
with Coffee Cream

2 cups light cream
½ cup sugar
⅓ cup freshly ground coffee beans (finely ground)
½ vanilla bean, split lengthwise
5 egg yolks, at room temperature, beaten

&. &. &.

10 ounces bittersweet chocolate
½ cup unsalted butter
6 eggs, separated
1 cup sugar
2 teaspoons Kahlua
½ teaspoon vanilla extract

&. &. &.

1 cup heavy cream
¼ cup confectioners' sugar
1 tablespoon Kahlua

&. &. &.

1 cup shaved bittersweet chocolate curls

Bring 2 cups of cream, ½ cup of sugar, coffee grounds, and vanilla bean to a simmer over low heat (do not boil). Pour ⅛ of the liquid into the yolks, and mix well. Slowly pour the yolk mixture into the cream mixture, stirring constantly over low heat until the back of a wooden spoon remains coated when wiped with a finger. Strain, cover with plastic film, cool in an ice bath, and refrigerate.

Butter and flour ten 4-ounce soufflé cups. In the top of a double boiler over low heat (do not let water boil) melt the chocolate and butter. Stir until smooth. Keep the mixture warm.

Whip the egg whites with ½ cup sugar until stiff peaks form; reserve. In a separate bowl whip the egg yolks with the remaining ½ cup of sugar until pale yellow and tripled in volume.

Gently fold the melted chocolate, vanilla, and 2 teaspoons of Kahlua into the yolks. Gently fold the egg whites into the chocolate-yolk mixture. Pour the batter into the prepared soufflé cups, filling ¾ full. Bake in a 350° oven for 25 to 30 minutes, until a cake tester inserted in the center comes out clean. Cool and remove the tortes from the molds.

Place 1 cup of cream in a mixing bowl, and add the confectioners' sugar and 1 tablespoon of Kahlua while beating at high speed. Beat until soft peaks form.

To assemble, cover the bottoms of 10 chilled dessert plates with the coffee cream sauce. Place a torte in the center of each plate. Garnish with a dollop of Kahlua whipped cream, and cover with chocolate curls.

Serves 10.

Frozen Whiskey Soufflé

2 cups heavy cream
6 egg whites
1 cup sugar
12 egg yolks
¾ cup good quality whiskey
¼ cup confectioners' sugar

Form 1-inch collars with aluminum foil around twelve 4-ounce soufflé cups. Whip the heavy cream to soft peaks and reserve in the refrigerator. Whisk the egg whites with ½ cup of sugar until glossy stiff peaks form. Set aside. Whip the egg yolks with ½ cup sugar until pale yellow and tripled in volume. Fold all three together, adding the whiskey. Pour into the prepared soufflé cups, bringing the mixture completely to the top of each collar. Freeze for 6 hours or until hard set.

To serve, remove the foil collars and sprinkle liberally with confectioners' sugar.

Serves 12.

Kenniston Hill Inn

Route 27
Boothbay, Maine 04537
(207) 633-2159

Kenniston Hill Inn perpetuates the name of the original owner, a member of a prominent Boothbay family. This 200-year-old house has been transformed into a cozy, inviting home with rooms each having its own personality. Most have a queen or king bed, private bath, and fireplace. A bountiful family breakfast is served in the dining area overlooking gardens and fields, or by a roaring fire on a cool morning. Because the host was a chef/restaurateur in Vermont before opening the inn, tantalizing specialties are always on the menu. A public golf course borders the property, and cycles are available. The harbor is but minutes down the road, as are a dinner theater, shops, galleries, cruise boats, and the ferry to Monhegan Island. Children over ten are allowed, but no pets.

Zucchini and Walnut Sour Cream Pancakes

1⅓ cups milk
1 cup sour cream
2 eggs
2 tablespoons melted butter
2 cups pancake mix
1 cup grated zucchini, squeezed dry
¼ cup chopped walnuts

&. &. &.

Butter and warm maple syrup

Kenniston Hill Inn

In a large bowl combine the milk, sour cream, eggs, and melted butter. Mix thoroughly. Add the pancake mix and stir until just combined. The batter will be lumpy. Add the zucchini and walnuts. Pour onto a hot, lightly greased 400° griddle or frying pan. Cook until bubbles appear on the surface and the underside is golden. Turn once.

Serve with plenty of butter and warm maple syrup.

Serves 6 to 8 (makes 30 medium-sized pancakes).

Fresh Vegetable Frittata

6 eggs
½ teaspoon salt
½ teaspoon pepper
3 tablespoons butter
3 small zucchini, sliced
1 large onion, sliced
1 clove garlic, minced
1 cup fresh mushrooms, sliced
2 cups fresh spinach, washed and cut into 1-inch strips
1 tablespoon chopped parsley
1 teaspoon Italian herb seasoning

1 cup grated Parmesan or Swiss cheese
3 tablespoons butter

In a large bowl beat the eggs and add the salt and pepper. In a large skillet melt 3 tablespoons of butter over medium heat. Sauté the zucchini, onion, garlic, and mushrooms in the butter until limp. Add the spinach and toss until wilted. Sprinkle with parsley and Italian seasoning. Remove the pan from the heat. Stir about ¾ cup of cheese into the eggs. Fold the cooked vegetable mixture into the egg and cheese mixture, and blend well.

Wipe the skillet and add the remaining 3 tablespoons of butter. Place over medium heat. When the butter begins to foam, add the egg and vegetable mixture and turn the heat to low. Cook the eggs without stirring until thickened and set. When only the top is still moist, sprinkle with the remaining ¼ cup of cheese. Place the skillet under a preheated broiler until the top is light golden brown. Slide the loosened frittata onto a warm serving plate. Cut into wedges.

Serves 4 to 6.

Blackberry Inn

82 Elm Street
Camden, Maine 04843
(207) 236-6060

Blackberry Inn, a stately 1860 Italianate Victorian home, provides sunny, spacious bedrooms comfortably furnished in antiques. From the original tin ceilings framed by delicate moldings to the intricate plasterwork to the polished parquet floors, ornate mantles, and original brass fixtures, the inn's beauty has been enhanced by period furnishings and Oriental rugs. Breakfast is served in the sunny morning parlor or dining room. Most rooms have a private half-bath and queen-size bed; nearly all have a fine view of nearby Mount Battie.

Blueberry Blintzes
with Blueberry Sauce

These blintzes can be prepared ahead of time, then cooked along with the sauce the next morning for an elegant breakfast.

1½ cups all-purpose flour
1½ cups milk
2 eggs
2 tablespoons oil
1 teaspoon margarine

🍂 🍂 🍂

1 cup cottage cheese
½ cup sour cream
⅓ cup sugar
1 teaspoon cinnamon
½ cup wild blueberries, fresh or frozen
3 tablespoons butter

🍂 🍂 🍂

4 teaspoons cornstarch
2 tablespoons water
2 cups wild blueberries, fresh or frozen
½ cup sugar
½ cup Grand Marnier

Blackberry Inn

In a blender combine the flour, milk, eggs, and oil, blending until smooth. In a 6 to 7-inch crepe pan melt the butter over medium heat. Make thin pancakes, cooking only on one side. Allow each to cool on wire rack, then stack between sheets of waxed paper.

In a medium bowl beat the cottage cheese until very smooth. Beat in the sour cream, ½ cup of sugar, and cinnamon. Fold in ½ cup of blueberries. Place about 2 tablespoons of the mixture in the center of the cooked side of each crepe. Fold in opposite edges about 1 inch, then fold in the remaining edges to enclose, making a rectangular envelope. Heat 3 tablespoons of butter in a large frying pan. Place the blintzes in the pan, seam side down. Fry carefully, turning once, until golden brown.

Mix the cornstarch and water until smooth. In a medium saucepan heat ½ cup of blueberries and ½ cup of sugar, lightly crushing one quarter or so of the berries with a spoon. Add the cornstarch mixture and Grand Marnier. Cook over medium heat, stirring frequently. Watch carefully, as the sauce will thicken rapidly. (If it becomes too thick, thin with a little water.) Top the blintzes with the sauce.

Serves 4 to 6.

Blue Chip Cookies

These spicy cookies offer a healthful alternative to chocolate.

> 2¼ cups all-purpose flour
> 2 teaspoons baking powder
> ½ teaspoon salt
> 1½ teaspoons cinnamon
> 1½ teaspoons nutmeg
> ½ cup butter
> ¾ cup sugar
> 1 cup brown sugar
> 2 eggs
> 1 cup oatmeal
> 1 cup chopped walnuts
> 1 cup fresh or frozen wild
>   blueberries

Grease cookie sheets. In a medium bowl combine the flour, baking powder, salt, and spices. In a large mixing bowl cream the butter with an electric mixer until fluffy. Add the sugar and brown sugar, and beat until light in color. Beat in the eggs. Stir in the flour mixture, oatmeal, and walnuts. Gently stir in the blueberries. Drop by rounded spoonfuls onto the cookie sheets. Bake in a 350° oven for 8 to 10 minutes or until the cookies are lightly browned. Cool on the racks.

Makes 3 dozen cookies.

Chilled Blueberry Soup

A refreshing summer appetizer.

> 1 cup fresh or frozen thawed
>   blueberries
> ½ cup water
> ¼ cup sugar
> ½ cup lemon juice
> 1 teaspoon coriander
> ¼ teaspoon cinnamon
> ½ cup plain yogurt
> ½ cup sour cream
> ½ cup dry red wine

In a blender purée the blueberries until smooth. In a medium saucepan, combine the puréed blueberries, water, sugar, lemon juice, and spices. Cover and simmer over low heat for 10 minutes. Whisk in the remaining ingredients, blending until smooth. Chill for several hours before serving.

Serves 6 (in ½-cup bowls).

Blue Harbor House

67 Elm Street
U.S. Route 1
Camden, Maine 04843
(207) 236-3196

Blue Harbor House is a classic New England Cape structure built before 1835. Completely restored and renovated, it provides modern comfort while capturing the essence of a time that has passed forever. Each room is tastefully decorated with country antiques, quilts, and stenciled walls. Sit-

Blue Harbor House

uated within walking distance of Camden's harbor, fine shops, and restaurants, the inn is an ideal place from which to explore the area. Acadia State Park, Tenants Harbor, Bar Harbor, and Boothbay are nearby.

Meaty Lentil Soup

This is a meaty soup, light in color.

    1 package smoked ham bones
    2 quarts water
    1 flank steak
    2 large carrots, shredded
    1 large onion
    2 stalks celery, with leaves
    Dash soy sauce
    Bay leaf
    2 to 3 garlic cloves, peeled and
        quartered
    6 good grinds fresh pepper
    1 teaspoon salt
    2 cups dried lentils, washed,
        drained, and picked over

    ❧ ❧ ❧

    Sour cream and shredded cheese
        for garnish
    Lemon, lime, or fresh onions for
        garnish

In a saucepan boil ham bones in water for 20 to 30 minutes. Let cool. Skim the fat and remove the meat. Reserve the water, meat, and bones. Cube the flank steak and brown in a large soup pot. Remove the meat and drain the grease from pot. Place all of the vegetables and spices in the pot and cook until well browned but not overcooked. Add the meat, ham bones, and water to the soup pot. Add the lentils. Cover with water and bring to a boil. Reduce the heat and simmer for 2 to 4 hours. Let the mixture cool and skim the fat from the pot. Remove the ham bones and bay leaf. Reheat and add water to make the desired amount of liquid. Serve garnished with sour cream, cheese, a squeeze of lemon or lime, or fresh onions.

Serves 8 to 12.

Hawthorn Inn

9 High Street
Camden, Maine 04843
(207) 236-8842

This stately, turreted Victorian mansion, completed in 1894, was built by a prosperous coal merchant for his family. The inn has the original stained glass panels in the front parlor windows and a magnificent three-story staircase in the foyer. Upstairs are five rooms, most with private baths. Downstairs are two garden rooms with private baths. Most of the rooms overlook Camden Harbor or the Camden Hills. Accommodations are also available in the adjacent carriage house, which offers two luxury townhouse apartments and a large one-bedroom getaway with private balcony and whirlpool Jacuzzi.

After a delicious breakfast laid out by the dining room fireplace or on the outdoor deck, guests may stroll down the back lawn and through the amphitheater to Camden's waterfront shops and restaurants.

Eggs Continental

    5 cups sour cream
    ¼ cup milk (or enough to cream
        with sour cream)
    ½ teaspoon parsley
    ½ teaspoon basil
    ½ teaspoon oregano
    1 bay leaf
    ½ teaspoon thyme
    12 slices bacon, cooked and
        crumbled
    10 frozen toaster potato pancakes
        (or ready-cooked hash browns)
    12 hard-boiled eggs, sliced
    2 cups grated Cheddar cheese

In a large bowl mix the sour cream, milk, seasonings, and bacon together, and set aside. In a 9x13-inch serving dish, layer the hash browns, hard-boiled eggs, and sour cream mixture. Sprinkle with grated cheese. Bake uncovered in a 325° oven for 30 minutes.

Serves 14 for breakfast.

Raisin Scones

    2 cups all-purpose flour
    2 tablespoons sugar
    2 teaspoons baking powder
    ½ teaspoon baking soda
    ½ teaspoon salt
    Finely grated peel of 1 lemon
    ½ cup chilled butter
    1 cup chopped walnuts
    ½ cup raisins
    ¾ cup buttermilk
    Additional buttermilk and sugar for
        topping

Grease a cookie sheet. In a large bowl mix the flour, sugar, baking powder, soda, salt, and lemon peel. Using a pastry blender, cut in the butter until the mixture resembles coarse meal. Mix in all but 2 tablespoons of nuts and add the raisins. Mix in the buttermilk with a fork. Gather the dough into a ball and knead for 2 minutes on a floured board. Pat out into a ¾-inch thick piece and with a 2-inch cookie cutter, cut out scones. Place 1 inch apart on the prepared cookie sheet. Brush with buttermilk; sprinkle with the reserved nuts and sugar. Bake in a 425° oven for 12 minutes. Serve warm with clotted cream and jam, or butter if clotted cream is unavailable.

Makes about 12 scones.

Windward House

6 High Street
Camden, Maine 04843
(207) 236-9656

Windward House, built by a prominent local lumberman and ship builder in 1854, is a fine example of Greek Revival architecture. Completely restored, it is situated above Camden Harbor at the base of Mount Battie in the heart of the High Street Historic District. Each guest room has period antiques, discriminating wallpapers, color-coordinated linens, and a private bath. Guests are encouraged to relax in the warmth of the beautiful soapstone fireplace in the living room or lounge in the library. On warm afternoons, guests can sit on the deck that overlooks the orchard. Nearby are hiking, horseback riding, museums, lighthouses, and the many Camden attractions.

Windward House Ham and Cheese Quiche

4 cups all-purpose flour
1¾ cups Crisco shortening
1 tablespoon sugar
2 teaspoons salt
1 tablespoon vinegar
1 egg
½ cup water

❧ ❧ ❧

2 cups grated Swiss cheese
2 cups grated Cheddar cheese
2 tablespoons all-purpose flour
2 cups diced ham
9 eggs, well beaten
3 cups half and half (or 1½ cups milk plus 1½ cups half and half)
1 to 1½ teaspoons salt
Pepper to taste

In a large bowl cut together 4 cups of flour, shortening, sugar, and 2 teaspoons of salt with a fork. In a separate bowl, beat the vinegar, egg, and water. Combine the mixtures, stirring with a fork until all ingredients are moistened. Mold dough into a ball with hands. Divide the dough into 4 balls. Chill for 15 minutes before rolling. Dough can be refrigerated up to 3 days or can be frozen. Roll out 2 balls of dough and place in two 10-inch quiche pans. Freeze the remaining dough for later use.

In a bowl combine the cheeses and dredge with 2 tablespoons of flour. Arrange the cheese evenly in the bottom of the prepared unbaked pastry shells. Sprinkle the diced ham over the cheeses. Combine the eggs, half and half, salt, and pepper. Pour over the cheeses and ham.

Bake in a 400° oven for 15 minutes. Reduce the heat to 325° and bake 30 more minutes or until a knife inserted in the center comes out clean.

Serves 12 generously.

❧ ❧ ❧ ❧ ❧

The Cape Neddick House

1300 Route 1, Box 70
Cape Neddick, Maine 03902
(207) 363-2500

This late 1880s Victorian farmhouse with slate roof and connected outbuildings has remained in the Goodwin family since it was built. It features high ceilings, bull's eye moldings, Christian doors, two fireplaces, and side-by-side staircases. Its six airy, antique-filled bedrooms are named for the New England states. Guests gather in the dining room or on the deck for breakfast, which is sprinkled with tales of days past and mixed with generous old-fashioned hospitality. Cape Neddick Park and Gallery is but a short, pleasant walk along the river. Historic York Village and Harbor, the Nubble Lighthouse, and Long and Short Sands beaches are nearby.

Zucchini Parmesan

May use as appetizer or quiche for breakfast or brunch.

4 eggs, well beaten
½ cup vegetable oil

❧ ❧ ❧

1 cup Bisquick
½ teaspoon seasoned salt
1½ teaspoons oregano
Dash garlic powder

❧ ❧ ❧

½ cup chopped onions
½ cup grated Parmesan cheese
2 tablespoons chopped parsley
3 cups thinly sliced zucchini, unpeeled

Grease a 9x13-inch baking dish. Beat the eggs and oil together with an electric mixer or food processor. In a separate bowl combine the dry ingredients. Fold the dry ingredients into the egg mixture. Add the remaining ingredients. Pour into the prepared pan or pie plate. Bake in a 350° oven for 30 minutes.

Freezes well.

Serves 48 appetizer pieces.

Apple Fritters

1½ cups all-purpose flour
2 tablespoons baking powder
2 tablespoons sugar
1 cup milk
1 egg
4 to 6 apples, peeled, cored, and chopped in approximately 1-inch pieces
1½ cups oil
Cinnamon and sugar

In a medium bowl mix together the dry ingredients. Add the milk and egg, and beat until well blended. Add chopped apples and mix. Heat the oil in a deep-sided pan or fryer. Drop batter-covered apple pieces in the hot oil. Cook until golden. Drain on a paper towel and sprinkle with cinnamon and sugar.

Note: This recipe batter can be used to make fried onion rings, zucchini, etc. (omit the sugar).

Serves 6 to 8.

Apple Jacks

1 cup light brown sugar
½ cup shortening
1 egg
1½ cups sifted all-purpose flour
½ teaspoon baking soda
½ teaspoon salt
1 teaspoon nutmeg
1 teaspoon cinnamon
1 cup chopped, unpeeled apples

Grease a cookie sheet. In a large bowl cream together the sugar and shortening. Beat in the egg. Sift together the dry ingredients and add to the moist ingredients, beating until well blended. Stir in the apples. Drop in the shape of balls onto the prepared cookie sheet. Bake in a 375° oven for 12 to 15 minutes.

Makes about 2 dozen.

Center Lovell Inn

Route 5
Center Lovell, Maine 04016
(207) 925-1575

The Center Lovell Inn boasts ten guest rooms, two cozy parlors, and a gracious wraparound porch for dining and relaxing. It has been restored according to a philosophy that says "We are all caretakers of our world." The beautifully prepared gourmet dishes are served in front of the huge fireplace in its small, homey dining room.

Apple Spice Coffee Cake

½ cup oil
2 eggs
1 teaspoon vanilla extract
1¾ cups sugar
2 cups all-purpose flour
2 teaspoons cinnamon
1 teaspoon salt
2 teaspoons baking soda
4 cups apples, diced

French vanilla ice cream or sorbet

Grease and flour a 10-inch tube pan. In a large mixing bowl mix all of the ingredients except the ice cream and pour into the prepared pan. Bake in a 350° oven for 45 to 50 minutes, until a knife inserted in the center comes out clean. Cool in the pan for 10 minutes before inverting on a cooling rack.

Serve warm with French vanilla ice cream or a sorbet.

Serves 16.

Center Lovell Inn

Quick and Easy Ricotta Gnocchi

1 pound Ricotta
1 egg
2 cups all-purpose flour

🍂 🍂 🍂

Butter and Parmesan cheese
Pesto sauce or Marinara sauce and
   Romano cheese

In a large bowl combine the first 3 ingredients. Mix well and roll out little balls into finger-sized rolls. With well-floured hands, pinch into ¾-inch lengths. Lay on a flour sprinkled cookie sheet, freeze, and pack into plastic containers until ready to use.

Drop into 1 gallon of boiling, salted water and skim off when they rise to the top. Serve with butter and Parmesan cheese, pesto sauce, or simple Marinara sauce (plum tomatoes) and Romano cheese.

Serves 4 to 6.

The Brannon-Bunker Inn

H.C.R. 64, #045
Route 129
Damariscotta, Maine 04543
(207) 563-5941

Situated in Maine's rural mid-coast region, the Brannon-Bunker Inn is close to all Damariscotta, Boothbay, Wiscasset, Bath, and Camden activities. Built in the 1820s, it has been home to many generations of Mainers. Made into a dance hall known as La Hacienda in the 1920s, it was later converted into sleeping rooms and then opened in the 1950s as the area's first bed and breakfast. Its eight sleeping rooms feature stenciled walls and floors, quaint wallpapers, homemade quilts, tieback curtains,

and country crafts. The upstairs sitting area is a gallery of Americana reflecting the innkeeper's interest in World War I memorabilia.

Upside-down Plum Muffins

¼ cup margarine, melted
3 tablespoons sugar
¼ teaspoon cinnamon
4 small plums, cut in thirds

🍂 🍂 🍂

1 egg
1 cup milk
¼ cup vegetable oil
2 cups all-purpose flour
1 tablespoon baking powder
¼ cup sugar
¼ teaspoon salt

Grease 12 muffin cups. Spoon 1 teaspoon of melted margarine into each muffin cup. In a small bowl combine 3 tablespoons of sugar with the cinnamon, and sprinkle over the margarine in the muffin cups. Place a plum third in each muffin cup.

In a medium-sized bowl beat the egg. Add the milk and oil. Stir in the flour, baking powder, ¼ cup of sugar, and salt until the flour is moistened. Do not overmix. Spoon the batter over the plums. Bake in a 400° oven for 20 to 25 minutes or until golden brown. Immediately invert the pan on a cooling rack. Cool for one minute, and remove from the pan. Serve warm.

Serves 12.

Elderberry Delight Muffins

2 cups all-purpose flour
1 tablespoon baking powder
½ teaspoon salt
1 cup sugar
1 egg, beaten
⅓ cup butter, melted
½ cup sour cream
½ cup milk
1½ cups elderberries

Line 12 muffin cups with paper liners. In a large bowl sift the flour, baking powder, salt, and sugar together. Stir in the egg, butter, sour cream, and milk until blended. Fold in the elderberries. Fill the lined muffin tins full. Bake in a 400° oven for 20 minutes.

Variation: You can also use raspberries or wineberries.

Makes 12 muffins.

Lincoln House

Dennysville, Maine 04628
(207) 726-3953

Built in 1787 by Judge Theodore Lincoln, Lincoln House offers dining and lodging to all who seek hospitality and elegance in a quiet, secluded setting. The ninety-five wooded acres surrounding it provide a diversity of wildlife. Bald eagles and ospreys are seen frequently, seals swim in the river with North Atlantic salmon, and deer are plentiful. Each evening full meals are offered, as are breakfasts in the mornings. Guests enjoy the use of the living room with its Steinway grand piano, the library, and the unique "back hall." Nearby attractions include the Roosevelt Cottage on Campobello Island, Cobscook State Park, Quoddy Head Lighthouse, and Moosehorn National Wildlife Refuge.

Crab Bisque

1 onion, chopped
2 tablespoons butter
1 tablespoon all-purpose flour
1 10½-ounce can tomato soup
1 quart half and half
1 pound fresh crab meat
¼ cup sherry
Salt and pepper

In a saucepan cook the onion in butter until clear. Add the flour and bubble a minute or so. Add the tomato soup and half and half. Cook for 10 minutes, being careful not to scorch. Add the crab meat, sherry, salt, and plenty of freshly ground pepper. Heat thoroughly but do not boil.

Serves 6 to 8.

Green Beans with Basil

3 tablespoons butter
½ cup chopped onion
¼ cup chopped celery
1 clove garlic, minced
½ teaspoon dried rosemary
½ teaspoon dried basil (if fresh, use 2 teaspoons)

&ambr; &ambr; &ambr;

1 pound green beans

In a saucepan melt the butter. Add all of the remaining ingredients except the beans, and cook until the onions and celery are clear.

Cook the beans until crunchy, about 15 minutes. Drain. Toss in onion mixture and serve.

Serves 5 to 6.

Cranberry Pecan Pie

1 cup sugar
1½ tablespoons all-purpose flour
¼ cup softened butter
2 eggs
¾ cup light corn syrup
¼ teaspooon salt
1 teaspoon vanilla extract
1 teaspoon grated orange peel
½ teaspoon nutmeg
1 cup pecans (or walnuts), chopped
1 cup fresh or frozen cranberries
1 9-inch unbaked pastry shell

&ambr; &ambr; &ambr;

Whipped cream, optional

In a large bowl cream together the sugar, flour, and butter. Add eggs, corn syrup, salt, vanilla, orange peel, and nutmeg; beat until well blended. Stir in nuts and cranberries. Pour into the pastry shell. Bake in a 350° oven for 60 to 70 minutes or until a knife inserted in center comes out clean.

If desired, serve with dollop of whipped cream.

Serves 6 to 8.

Five Gables Inn

Murray Hill Road
East Boothbay, Maine 04544
(207) 633-4551

One of coastal Maine's most exciting restoration projects in recent years, the Five Gables Inn overlooks the expanse of Linekin Bay. This 125-year-old inn is the only summer hotel remaining where years ago several existed. All fifteen rooms, each with a private bath, have a lovely view of the bay; five have working fireplaces. A spacious wraparound verandah provides a comfortable place to retreat on warm days. In cooler weather the large common room with a cozy fireplace provides comfort.

Paul's Bacon and Potato Pie

1 pound bacon, cut in 1-inch pieces
8 eggs, whisked until foamy
2 cups grated Cheddar cheese
1 medium onion, chopped
1 pound potatoes, peeled and grated
½ teaspoon seasoned pepper

Grease a 9x13-inch baking dish. In a frying pan, brown the bacon until crisp. Drain and blot on paper toweling. Combine the bacon and the remaining ingredients. Spread the mixture evenly in the prepared baking dish. Bake in a 350° oven for 45 minutes. Cut into squares.

Note: Grate the potatoes into a bowl of cold water, then pour into a colander and rinse with fresh water when ready to mix with other ingredients. Lightly press them with a wooden spoon against the colander to remove excess moisture.

Serves 8 to 10.

High Meadows

Route 101
Eliot, Maine 03903
(207) 439-0590

Situated on the side of a hill in the town of Eliot, this colonial house was built in 1736 by a merchant ship builder and sea captain. Today it has all the modern conveniences while retaining the charm of the past. High Meadows offers a quiet atmosphere in a country setting, just four and one-half miles from shopping and six miles from historic Portsmouth and York. The port area is well known for its outstanding restaurants, theatre, and arts events. Guests can enjoy a pleasure cruise or whale watching; local beaches or golf courses are nearby.

Spinach Squares

¼ cup butter
3 eggs
1 cup all-purpose flour
1 cup milk
1 tablespoon baking powder
1 pound Monterey Jack cheese, shredded
2 10-ounce packages frozen chopped spinach (thawed, drained, and squeezed)
1 small onion, chopped
Dash garlic

Melt the butter and grease all sides of a 9x13-inch baking dish. In a large bowl beat the eggs, and add the flour, milk, and baking powder. Mix well. Add the cheese, spinach, onion, and garlic. Pour into the prepared baking dish. Bake in a 350° oven for 35 minutes.
Serves 8.

Kuchen with Peaches

½ cup butter, melted
¾ cup sugar
1 egg
1 cup sour cream
1½ cups all-purpose flour
¾ teaspoon baking powder

ใช ใช ใช

¼ cup butter
¼ cup sugar
¼ cup brown sugar
¼ cup all-purpose flour
¼ teaspoon cloves
¼ teaspoon cinnamon
3 large sliced peaches (3 cups), or blueberries

Grease a 9x13-inch pan. In a large bowl cream together ½ cup of butter and ¾ cup of sugar. Blend in the eggs and sour cream. Mix in 1½ cups of flour and the baking powder. Spread the dough in the prepared pan.

In a small bowl mix ¼ cup of butter, ¼ cup of sugar, ¼ cup of brown sugar, ¼ cup of flour, the cloves, and cinnamon.

Sprinkle half of the topping over the dough, top with fruit, and sprinkle with the remaining topping. Bake in a 350° oven for 35 to 40 minutes.
Serves 8.

The Bagley House

Rural Route 3, Box 269C
Freeport, Maine 04032
(207) 865-6566

The Bagley House, built in 1772, is ten minutes away from downtown Freeport. Situated on six acres of fields and woods, it offers a comfortable retreat from the bustle of commerce in a peaceful country setting. Five guest rooms, each furnished with antiques or custom pieces, feature handsewn quilts, stenciled rugs, electric blankets, individually controlled heat, fresh flowers, and private baths. Breakfast is served in the kitchen, where guests gather around an eight-foot antique baker's table. No smoking is permitted.

Bagley House Crab Meat Strata

7 slices white bread
1½ cups grated Swiss cheese
¼ cup finely chopped onion
¼ cup finely diced sweet red pepper
¼ cup finely diced celery
8 ounces fresh crab meat

ใช ใช ใช

5 large eggs
2½ cups milk
2 tablespoons mayonnaise
¼ teaspoon dry mustard

Butter an 8x12-inch glass baking dish. Trim the crust off the bread slices and discard. Cut the bread into cubes and place in bottom of the prepared baking dish. Layer the cheese, vegetables, and crab meat on top of the bread cubes. In a large bowl beat the remaining ingredients together, and pour over the layered ingredients. Cover with plastic wrap and refrigerate overnight. Bake in a 350° oven for 50 minutes, or until a knife inserted in the center comes out clean.
Serves 6.

The Isaac Randall House

Independence Drive
Freeport, Maine 04032
(207) 865-9295

This 1823 farmhouse is situated on a five-acre wooded lot just a few blocks from L.L. Bean and downtown Freeport. The ten rooms, eight with private baths, are charming and comfortable, furnished with antiques, Oriental rugs, and lovely old quilts. A hearty breakfast is served, and snacks are provided in the evening. Smoking is discouraged.

Maine Blueberry Pancakes

8 cups unbleached all-purpose flour
1 cup sugar
⅓ cup baking powder
1 teaspoon salt

ใช ใช ใช

2 tablespoons margarine
1 egg
1 cup milk
¼ to ⅓ cup small, low-bush Maine blueberries

The Bagley House

Lookout Point House

141 Lookout Point Road
Harpswell, Maine 04079
(207) 833-5509

Lookout Point House has fifteen guest rooms overlooking the ocean. The inn offers swimming, boating, bicycling, or relaxing on the porch as part of a stay. The immediate area offers the finest in summer theaters, gourmet restaurants, and antique shops. The innkeepers' hospitality makes a stay as relaxing as a visit to yesterday's world. Each morning's meal is a country breakfast.

In a large bowl combine the flour, sugar, baking powder, and salt. Store in a large covered crock. Stir thoroughly and use as needed.

Melt the margarine. In a medium bowl combine 1 cup of dry mix, the egg, milk, and blueberries. Add the margarine. Turn with a whisk and rubber spatula into a very, very stiff batter. (The batter should be barely stirrable but thoroughly mixed. It shouldn't pour.) Drop ⅓-cup portions of batter onto a hot greased griddle. Turn when brown and cook until done.

Makes about 8 pancakes.

Southwestern Polish Strata

2 tablespoons margarine
1 loaf white bread
1 pound Kielbasa, thinly sliced
2½ to 3 cups coarsely grated extra sharp Cheddar cheese (or Argentine Sardo cheese, if available)
2 4-ounce cans chopped green chilies
2 4-ounce cans mushrooms, chopped (or ½ pound fresh)
1 small red onion, finely chopped
12 eggs
1 cup milk
Sliced pimiento (optional)
Hot Taco sauce (optional)

Grease a 9x14-inch Pyrex baking dish with the margarine. Remove the crust from enough bread slices to completely line the baking dish, filling in all cracks. Cover the bread with Kielbasa slices. Sprinkle half of the cheese over the Kielbasa. Remove the crust from enough bread slices to make another complete layer of bread, covering the cheese and Kielbasa, and filling in the cracks. Spread the chilies, mushrooms, onions, and remaining cheese over the second bread layer. Whip the eggs and milk together and pour evenly over the layers until the eggs soak through the entire dish. (If the batter isn't sufficient to soak the entire dish, make more to taste.) Add the pimientos or Taco sauce if desired. Refrigerate for at least 8 hours. Bake in a 350° oven for 1 hour to 1 hour and 15 minutes.

Serves 12 to 16.

Corn-Squash Casserole

Excellent fall dish.

½ cup chopped onion
½ cup chopped green pepper
2 tablespoons margarine
2 cups cooked, mashed winter squash
1 16-ounce can cream-style corn
1 cup crushed saltine crackers
1 cup shredded Cheddar cheese
2 tablespoons chopped pimento
2 tablespoons coarsely crushed saltine crackers
1 teaspoon butter or margarine, melted

In a 1½-quart saucepan, cook the onion and peppers in 2 tablespoons of margarine until tender but not brown. Stir in the squash, corn, 1 cup of crushed crackers, cheese, and pimento. Place in a 1½-quart casserole. Combine the remaining 2 tablespoons of crackers with 1 teaspoon of butter. Sprinkle over the casserole. Bake in a 350° oven for 40 to 45 minutes.

Serves 6.

1761

Raspberry Muffins

Given us by a guest named Harold Noreen and much enjoyed by our guests.

1½ cups all-purpose flour
½ teaspoon baking soda
½ teaspoon salt
1½ teaspoon cinnamon
1 cup sugar
1 12-ounce package frozen raspberries, thawed
2 eggs, well beaten
⅔ cup oil
½ cup chopped pecans

Grease 12 muffin cups. In a large bowl mix the flour, baking soda, salt, cinnamon, and sugar together. Make a well in the center and stir in the undrained raspberries and eggs. Thoroughly mix in the oil and pecans. Spoon the batter into the prepared muffin cups, filling to the top. Bake in a 400° oven for 15 to 20 minutes.

(Batter may be poured into a 9x5-inch loaf pan and baked in a 350° oven for 1 hour.)

Makes 12 muffins.

The Keeper's House

Post Office Box 26
Isle au Haut, Maine 04645
(207) 367-2261

The Keeper's House sits atop ragged ledges overlooking the Atlantic Ocean, surrounded by dense spruce forests and island panoramas. Built in 1907 by the U.S. Lighthouse Service and now on the National Register of Historic Places, this restored lighthouse station is a living museum where guests can take a step back in time. Guests depart from the coastal port of Stonington on the mailboat that serves the island fishing village of Isle au Haut. The inn is down the remote shoreline from the village, inaccessible to telephone, automobile,

The Keeper's House

and power lines. The Acadia National Park system includes over one-half of the island, which is a naturalist's delight.

The four guest rooms in the main house are large and cheerful; all have exceptional views, and the wind and waves provide the only night sounds. A separate tiny building is available, too. Dinners by candlelight feature native seafood and chicken with a gourmet touch. No red meat is served, and vegetarian and special diet requests are accommodated by advance requests. It is open May 1 through October 31.

Lemon Yogurt Muffins

These muffins are light and yummy and are often served with a Keeper's House meal.

¼ cup butter
5 tablespoons honey
1 cup yogurt
1 egg
¼ cup fresh lemon juice
½ teaspoon grated lemon rind
1 cup all-purpose flour
1 cup whole wheat flour
1½ teaspoons baking soda
⅛ teaspoon salt

Grease 12 muffin cups. In a small saucepan melt the butter and honey together. In a bowl beat together the yogurt, egg, lemon juice, and rind. Add the butter and honey, and beat well. Sift together the dry ingredients. Add the lemon mixture and stir briefly, until just moistened. Fill the prepared cups ⅔ full. Bake in a 350° oven for 25 minutes.

Makes 12 muffins.

Dilled Cucumber Salad

2 large cucumbers, pared and thinly sliced
1 teaspoon salt
1 cup plain yogurt
1 tablespoon finely chopped onions
½ teaspoon sugar
Dash Tabasco sauce
1 tablespoon finely chopped fresh dill or 1 teaspoon dried dill
Lettuce leaves, washed and crisped
2 tomatoes, peeled and cut into wedges

Toss the cucumbers with salt and place in a colander for 1 hour. Rinse well and drain thoroughly. In a medium-sized bowl combine the yogurt, onion, sugar, Tabasco sauce, and dill. Pat the cucumbers dry with paper towels and add to the yogurt dressing. Toss well. Serve on lettuce leaves and garnish with tomato wedges.

Serves 4.

Crab Imperial

Another Keeper's House favorite.

½ cup milk
1½ teaspoons butter
1 tablespoon all-purpose flour
1 egg yolk
1½ teaspoons lemon juice
½ teaspoon Worcestershire sauce
1 tablespoon mayonnaise
½ teaspoon dry mustard
⅛ teaspoon cayenne pepper
¼ teaspoon white pepper
¼ teaspoon salt
¼ teaspoon pepper
1 pound crab meat

🍃 🍃 🍃

¼ cup butter
3 cloves garlic, crushed
1½ cups bread crumbs
2 teaspoons lemon juice
½ teaspoon pepper
Paprika

Butter 6 ramekins. Heat the milk to the boiling point. In a skillet, melt the margarine and whisk in the flour. Add the milk, whisking until smooth. Whisk a small amount of the heated

mixture into the egg yolk. Add the egg yolk, 1½ teaspoons of lemon juice, Worcestershire sauce, mayonnaise, and seasonings. Blend well. Add the crab meat. Fill the buttered dishes.

Melt ¼ cup of butter. Add the garlic and sauté. Add the bread crumbs, 2 teaspoons of lemon juice, and ½ teaspoon of pepper.

Cover the crab meat mixture with the crumb mixture. Sprinkle with paprika. Bake in a 350° oven for 15 minutes.

Serves 6.

Raspberry Chicken

2 whole boneless, skinless chicken breasts
2 tablespoons butter
¼ cup finely chopped onions
¼ cup raspberry vinegar
¼ cup chicken broth
¼ cup heavy cream
1 tablespoon canned crushed tomatoes
¼ cup frozen raspberries

Split and flatten the breasts. In a large skillet melt the butter. Add the chicken and cook for 3 minutes on each side. Remove and reserve. Add the onion to the fat in the pan and cook for 15 minutes. Add the vinegar and cook uncovered until the syrup is reduced to 1 tablespoon. Whisk in the chicken broth, heavy cream, and crushed tomatoes. Simmer for 1 minute. Return the chicken to the skillet and simmer gently in the sauce, basting often until done, about 5 minutes. Remove the chicken. Add the raspberries to the sauce and cook over low heat for 1 minute. Pour the sauce over the chicken and serve immediately.

Serves 4.

Healthy Brownies

⅓ cup butter or margarine
1 6-ounce package chocolate bits

❧ ❧ ❧

1 cup rolled oats
¼ cup wheat germ
⅓ cup nonfat dry milk
½ teaspoon baking powder
¼ teaspoon salt
½ cup chopped walnuts

❧ ❧ ❧

2 eggs
¼ cup brown sugar
2 tablespoons sugar
1 teaspoon vanilla extract

Grease an 8-inch square pan. In a small saucepan melt the butter and chocolate bits. In a medium bowl combine the oats, wheat germ, dry milk, baking powder, salt, and nuts. In a large bowl beat the eggs, and mix in the sugars and vanilla until the mixture is thick. Stir in the melted chocolate mixture. Fold in the oat mixture until it is just blended. Pour the batter into the prepared pan. Bake in a 350° oven for 20 to 25 minutes.

Makes 9 squares.

ental flavor is evident upon entering the foyer, which is dominated by a carved shrine door. Three spacious rooms with private baths and a luxurious suite are available for guests. Breakfast is in the treetops in the second floor kitchen with a view of the Kennebunk River. Featured on the menu are homemade breads and jams, colorful and tasty combinations of fresh fruits, and egg dishes, served on blue and white china. The garden offers a secluded area for rest and relaxation.

Flan de Tres Leches

½ cup sugar

❧ ❧ ❧

1 12-ounce can evaporated milk
1 14-ounce can sweetened
    condensed milk
Pinch salt
2 cups hot milk
6 eggs
1 teaspoon vanilla extract or orange
    extract
½ cup brandy

Place the sugar in a small saucepan over low heat. Stir constantly until melted. Pour into the bottom of a 2-quart glass casserole. Swirl to cover the bottom and sides. Set aside to cool.

Mix together the remaining ingredients and pour into the casserole. Place the casserole in a pan of hot water. Water should come halfway up the side of the bowl. Bake in a 325° oven for 45 minutes to 1 hour. The custard is done when a knife inserted in the center comes out clean. Cool. Unmold by inverting on a large plate. Cut into wedges and serve. Also good with blackberry or raspberry sauce on top.

Serves 4 to 6.

Spinach and Mushroom Quiche

1½ cups chopped green peppers
1½ cups chopped onion
3 cups sliced mushrooms
¼ cup chopped parsley
3 tablespoons oil

The Inn on South Street

Post Office Box 478A, South Street
Kennebunkport, Maine 04046
(207) 967-4639
(207) 967-5151

The Inn on South Street is situated on a quiet, tree-lined street in the historic part of the village. It is within easy walking distance to shops, restaurants, and beaches. The inn is open year round. The decor of this nineteenth century Greek Revival home is strongly reminiscent of Kennebunkport's maritime past. The Ori-

The Inn on South Street

12 eggs
2 pounds Ricotta cheese
1 tablespoon minced garlic
1½ teaspoons salt
Dash Tabasco sauce
2 10-ounce packages frozen
   chopped spinach
2 cups grated Cheddar cheese

   🍂 🍂 🍂

4 unbaked 9-inch pie shells

In a skillet sauté the vegetables in oil until crisp tender. Cool. Beat the eggs with the Ricotta cheese. Add the garlic, salt, and Tabasco sauce. Defrost the spinach and squeeze out as much moisture as possible. Add to the egg mixture along with the cheese and sautéed vegetables. Mix until well blended. Spoon the mixture into the pie shells and spread evenly. Bake in a 325° oven for 45 minutes or until set in the center. These quiches freeze well.

Serves 24.

🍂 🍂 🍂 🍂 🍂

Chocolate Applesauce Bread

¾ cup butter
2 cups sugar
3 eggs
1 25-ounce jar unsweetened
   applesauce
4 cups all-purpose flour
2½ teaspoons baking soda
¾ teaspoon salt
¾ teaspoon cinnamon
4 tablespoons cocoa
Chocolate chips

Grease three 4x7-inch loaf pans. In a large bowl cream the butter and sugar together. Add the eggs, mixing well. Add the applesauce. Sift the flour, soda, salt, cinnamon, and cocoa together. Add to the applesauce mixture. Pour into the prepared pans. Sprinkle with chocolate chips. Bake in a 350° oven for 1 hour.

Makes 3 loaves.

Kylemere House

South Street
Post Office Box 1333
Kennebunkport, Maine 04046
(207) 967-2780

The Kylemere House is a charming historic Federal home built in 1818 by Daniel Walker, a descendant of an original Kennebunkport family. A quiet haven, it is just a few minutes' walk from the ocean, shops, and restaurants. The rooms are warm and inviting, with colors that enhance the charm and New England decor of this delightful seaport inn. A leisurely gourmet breakfast is served in the formal dining room overlooking the gardens. Afternoons may find guests sipping English tea, drinking lemonade, or enjoying a glass of wine.

Orange Muffins

½ cup unsalted butter
1 cup sugar
2 eggs
1 teaspoon baking soda
1 cup buttermilk
2 cups all-purpose flour
½ teaspoon salt
Zest of 1 orange
1 cup raisins

   🍂 🍂 🍂

Juice of 1 orange
½ cup sugar

Grease 18 muffin cups. In a large bowl cream the butter and 1 cup of sugar together. Add the eggs and beat well. Add the baking soda to the buttermilk. Sift the flour and salt together. Alternately add the buttermilk and flour to the sugar mixture. Grind the orange zest and raisins in a food processor, and add to the batter. Pour the batter into the prepared muffin tins.

Bake in a 400° oven for 15 minutes.

Combine the orange juice and ½ cup of sugar, and brush on top of the warm muffins.

Serves 18.

Fruit Crisp

1 cup butter, softened
1½ cups rolled oats
¾ cup light brown sugar
¾ cup all-purpose flour
2 teaspoons cinnamon
6 medium apples
6 medium pears
1 fresh pineapple, peeled and cored

In a medium bowl mix the butter, oats, brown sugar, flour, and cinnamon together until blended. Pare, core, and thinly slice the apples and pears. Cut the pineapple in chunks. Place all fruits in a 9x13-inch baking dish and sprinkle the topping evenly over the mixture. Bake in a 400° oven for 35 minutes.

Serves 12.

The Newcastle Inn

Newcastle, Maine 04553
(207) 563-5685

The Newcastle Inn, beautifully situated on the banks of the Damariscotta River, is the oldest operating inn in the area. Its fifteen guest rooms all have private baths. Guests begin the day by indulging in the acclaimed multicourse gourmet breakfast in the sunlit dining room. The inn places emphasis on gourmet dining, good conversation, comfortable and romantic surroundings, and quiet seclusion.

Blueberry Lemon Bread

6 tablespoons butter, softened
1 cup sugar
2 eggs
1½ cups all-purpose flour
1 tablespoon baking powder
1 teaspoon salt
½ cup milk
1 cup fresh blueberries
1½ tablespoons grated lemon rind
1 teaspoon lemon juice

Grease and flour a 7½x3¼-inch loaf pan. In a large bowl cream the butter and sugar together. Add the eggs and mix. In a separate bowl sift together the flour, baking powder, and salt. Add the milk and sifted ingredients alternately to the creamed mixture. Stir in the blueberries, lemon rind, and juice. Pour the batter into the prepared pan. Bake in a 350° oven for 50 to 60 minutes or until a toothpick inserted in the center comes out clean.
Makes 1 loaf.

The Island House

Box 1006
Southwest Harbor, Maine 04679
(207) 244-5180

The Island House, which opened in 1832, was the first summer hotel on Mount Desert Island, and it still retains the charm of that period. Notable guests have included Ralph Waldo Emerson and John Greenleaf Whittier. Much of the pine woodwork, the double living rooms with their two fireplaces, and the front door are from the original hotel. Now it is a gracious, restful seacoast home with pumpkin board floors and cheerful,

The Island House

spacious rooms. The main house has four double rooms with shared baths, and the old carriage house has a charming loft apartment with its own bath. A full, varied breakfast is offered, with such favorites as home-baked blueberry coffee cakes and muffins and hot cheese and sausage casseroles. Situated on the quiet side of the island, the Island House is within comfortable walking distance of the center of the village and a 5-minute drive to Acadia National Park.

Blueberry Sour Cream Coffee Cake

½ cup margarine
1 cup sugar
2 eggs
2 cups sifted all-purpose flour
1 teaspoon baking soda
½ teaspoon salt
1 cup sour cream

🍃 🍃 🍃

¼ cup sugar
1 teaspoon cinnamon
1 teaspoon vanilla extract

🍃 🍃 🍃

1 cup fresh or frozen blueberries
½ cup walnuts

Grease a bundt pan. In a large bowl cream the margarine with 1 cup of sugar. Add the eggs. Sift the dry ingredients together and add to the egg mixture alternately with the sour cream. Pour half of the batter into the prepared pan and spread evenly. Combine ¼ cup of sugar, the cinnamon, and vanilla. Spread half of the mixture onto the batter. Sprinkle with ½ cup of blueberries and ¼ cup of walnuts. Spread on the remaining batter, cinnamon mixture, and fruit and nuts. Bake in a 350° oven for 50 to 60 minutes or until a toothpick inserted in the center comes out clean.
Serves 8 to 10.

Eggs Florentine à la Island House

3 tablespoons butter or margarine
3 tablespoons all-purpose flour
1 teaspoon salt
¼ teaspoon white pepper
¼ teaspoon marjoram
1½ cups evaporated milk

🍃 🍃 🍃

1 10-ounce package frozen, chopped spinach
4 poached eggs
¼ cup grated Parmesan cheese

Grease 4 ramekins or individual souf-flé dishes. In a saucepan or double boiler over low heat melt the butter or margarine. Blend in the flour, salt, pepper, and marjoram. Add the milk all at once, stirring constantly until thickened and bubbly. Set aside.

Cook the spinach according to the package directions. Drain well. Spread in the bottom of the prepared dishes. Top with 1 poached egg in each dish. Pour the sauce liberally over each egg-spinach combination. Sprinkle with cheese. Place under the broiler until lightly browned and bubbly. Serve immediately with warm muffins or home-baked toasted bread.

Serves 4.

Broad Bay Inn and Gallery

Main Street
Post Office Box 607
Waldoboro, Maine 04572
(207) 832-6668

Built in classical colonial style, the Broad Bay Inn and Gallery has been restored to its 1830s grandeur. Situated within walking distance of restaurants, tennis, river, shops, antiques, and the Waldo Theatre, it has an art gallery that displays works by well known artists and sells limited edition prints, crafts, and gift items. The inn's five rooms are appointed with Victorian furnishings, canopy beds, and handmade bedspreads. The attractive grounds feature a sun deck and herb garden. Candlelight dinners on Saturday night are available with prior arrangement. The inn is centrally located on the Maine coast, close to Camden, Damariscotta, Pemaquid, and ferries to Monhegan Island.

Curried Spinach Soup

Everyone will ask you for this recipe and will be so surprised by the ingredients and also how easy it is to make.

5 to 6 tablespoons butter
3 large onions, thinly sliced
2 large potatoes, thinly sliced
4 10½-ounce cans chicken broth
2½ cups milk
Salt to taste
1 small bay leaf
½ teaspoon tarragon
1 10-ounce package frozen spinach
2 teaspoons soy sauce
¼ teaspoon curry powder

❧ ❧ ❧

1 cup heavy cream
Fresh mint

In a heavy pan melt the butter. Sauté the onions in the butter until wilted. Add the potatoes, broth, milk, salt, bay leaf, and tarragon. Simmer covered until the potatoes are tender, about 10 minutes. Add the spinach and continue to simmer until the spinach defrosts. Purée in a blender. Rinse the pan and return the puréed

mixture to the pan. Add the soy sauce and curry powder. Taste and adjust the seasonings. Chill. Add the heavy cream, and blend well. Garnish with fresh mint. Yummy!

Serves 10 to 12.

Candlelight Spicy Roast Lamb

1½ tablespoons fresh rosemary
    leaves
½ cup fresh mint leaves
4 garlic cloves, crushed
½ cup raspberry vinegar
¼ cup soy sauce
½ cup wine, red preferred
3 tablespoons crushed peppercorns
1 5 to 6-pound boned leg of lamb
2 tablespoons Dijon mustard

In a shallow bowl combine the rosemary, mint, garlic, vinegar, soy sauce, red wine, and 1 tablespoon of crushed pepper. Marinate the lamb in the refrigerator for 8 to 9 hours. Turn occasionally.

Remove the lamb, drain, and reserve the marinade. Roll the roast

Broad Bay Inn and Gallery

and tie with string. Spread mustard over the meat and add the remaining pepper. Bake in a 350° oven for 1 hour and 30 minutes for medium rare. Bake an additional 15 minutes for well done. Baste occasionally. Let the roast stand for 15 minutes before carving. Serve with the juices as gravy. Delicious!

Serves 6 to 8.

Broad Bay Herb Bread

If you are a bread "lover," you will just adore this bread, and so will your guests.

        1 cup scalded milk
        2 tablespoons sugar
        2½ teaspoons salt
        ¼ cup shortening
        1 cup lukewarm water (110° to 115°)
        2 ¼-ounce packages active dry yeast
        7 cups sifted all-purpose flour

        ❧ ❧ ❧

        2 cups finely chopped parsley
        2 cups finely chopped scallions
        1 large clove garlic, minced
        2 tablespoons butter
        2 eggs, beaten
        Salt and pepper to taste

        ❧ ❧ ❧

        Melted butter or salad oil

In a saucepan scald the milk. Add the sugar, salt, and shortening. Cool to lukewarm. Pour the water into a bowl, add the yeast and stir. Add the milk to the dissolved mixture. Add 4 cups of flour and beat. Add the remaining flour, stir, and let stand for 10 minutes. On a floured surface, knead the dough until smooth. Place in a greased bowl and turn to grease the surface. Cover and let rise in a warm place until double. Punch down, turn out, and let rest for 10 minutes.

Grease two 9x5-inch bread pans. Cut the dough in half and shape into 2 balls. Roll each into a rectangle about ¼-inch thick and 9 inches wide.

In a sauté pan cook the parsley, scallions, and garlic in 2 tablespoons of butter until wilted. Cool. Reserve 2 tablespoons of beaten egg, and add the remaining egg to the vegetables. Season with salt and pepper.

Brush the dough with the reserved egg. Spread the filling over the dough to within 1 inch of the edge and roll jelly-roll fashion. Pinch the edges to seal. Place in the prepared bread pans seam side down.

Brush the tops with melted butter or oil, cover with waxed paper, and let rise in a warm place until slightly higher in the middle than the edge (about 50 to 60 minutes). Cut gashes in the top of the loaves. Bake in a 400° oven for 1 hour. Turn out and cool on a rack.

Makes 2 loaves.

Timbale de Fruits de Mer
(Fish Casserole)

Elegant and delicious.

        1 pound scallops
        1 pound shrimp, peeled
        3 shallots, minced
        ¼ cup dry vermouth or sherry
        2 cups water
        Thyme
        Bay leaf
        Parsley
        1 onion
        Salt and pepper
        1 pound fillet of flounder or sole
        3 tablespoons all-purpose flour
        3 tablespoons butter
        Lemon juice
        ½ cup heavy cream

Marinate the scallops and shrimp with the vermouth and minced shallots. In a casserole dish, prepare a "fumet" with water, thyme, bay leaf, parsley, onion, salt, and pepper. Bring to a boil and simmer a few minutes. Poach the scallops and shrimp (adding the "marinade" to the casserole), and the fillet of flounder for 6 to 7 minutes; then turn off the heat.

In a pan prepare a "roux" with the flour and butter, and start a sauce with the liquid from the casserole. Beat the lemon juice and cream into the sauce. Transfer the fish from the casserole into the sauce. Bring to a boil. Serve right away as is or as a sauce on a cheese soufflé. Bon Appetit!

Serves 4 to 6.

Divine Apple Tarte

This recipe is so beautiful, our guests run to get a camera. Oh, yes, and it is delicious, too.

        8 ounces thawed pastry (pastry sheets)
        4 firm apples (Cortland, Winesap, Golden Delicious)
        ¼ cup sugar
        3 tablespoons unsalted butter
        Confectioners' sugar

Place the pastry dough on a floured surface. Trace the circumference of the tarte or pie pan. Cut, and place the trimmings on top of the circle. Press down, turn the dough over, and roll evenly in all directions to keep the dough circular. Lift often to keep from sticking. Relax the dough when it reaches 10 inches in diameter for about 15 minutes.

Wet a 12-inch tarte pan (do not dry). Roll out the relaxed dough to a 14-inch diameter circle. Transfer to the wet pan. Pat in place and trim to fit the pan. Cover and chill.

Peel, core, and thinly slice the apples. Prick the chilled pastry with the tines of a fork. Sprinkle the dough with 2 tablespoons of sugar. Place the apple slices slightly overlapping in rows of concentric circles. Sprinkle with the remaining 2 tablespoons of sugar and dot with the butter. Cover and refrigerate until ready to bake.

Bake the tarte in a 475° oven for 20 minutes on the lowest rack. Dust with confectioners' sugar. Transfer to the uppermost rack and bake for 5 more minutes until browned. Serve immediately! Absolutely delicious!

Serves 8.

The Roaring Lion

Post Office Box 756
75 Main Street
Waldoboro, Maine 04572
(207) 832-4038

The Roaring Lion is a country Victorian bed and breakfast facility that is open all year round. Situated just off Route 1, it was built in 1905 and features classic oak woodwork, tin ceilings, two fireplaces, and a screened porch. A visit to the Roaring Lion provides guests a quiet atmosphere conducive to rest and refreshment. Of its four guest rooms, one has a private bath. A full homemade breakfast, featuring such special dishes as "lion eggs," includes homemade breads, muffins, coffee cakes, jams, and jellies. The inn also provides vegetarian and macrobiotic diets on request.

Custard Cornbread

½ cup all-purpose flour
¾ cup cornmeal (freshly ground)
2⅓ tablespoons brown sugar
1 teaspoon baking powder
½ teaspoon salt
1 egg
1½ cups milk
2 tablespoons butter, melted and cooled

In a medium bowl mix the dry ingredients together well. Add the egg, 1 cup of milk, and the cooled butter. Mix well. Place in an 8-inch square pan. Pour the remaining ½ cup of milk on top of the batter. Bake in a 400° oven for 20 minutes until set but not dry (should be soft).
Serves 6.

Vegetarian or Macrobiotic Cornbread

2 cups cornmeal (freshly ground)
1 cup whole wheat pastry flour
1 teaspoon sea salt
1 tablespoon baking powder

❧ ❧ ❧

2 to 3 tablespoons corn oil
2 to 3 tablespoons rice syrup (optional)
½ cup soy milk
½ to ¾ cup apple or pear juice
1 cup cooked brown rice

Oil an 8-inch square baking pan. In a large bowl combine the cornmeal, flour, salt, and baking powder. Mix together well. Set aside 1½ cups of the mixture, and store the remainder in an airtight container.

Add the corn oil and rice syrup to 1½ cups of the dry mixture. Mix well until crumbly. Add the soy milk and fruit juice and mix well to make a thin batter. Add the cooked rice and mix well. Turn out into the prepared pan. Bake in a 400° oven for 20 minutes until set but not dry.
Serves 4 to 6.

Kawanhee Inn

Weld, Maine 04285
(207) 585-2243

Winter address:
7 Broadway
Farmington, Maine 04938
(207) 778-4306
(207) 778-3809

Situated on a high knoll, Kawanhee Inn commands a beautiful view of the lake and mountains. On entering the lodge, one can see the rustic appointments, including a stone fireplace, comfortable chairs, and reading lamps. Its fourteen bedrooms provide a homey, friendly atmosphere. The eleven housekeeping cabins face the lake and mountains; some are close to the water's edge.

Kawanhee Inn is noted for its delicious home cooked food for family dining. Attractive lunches are prepared at any time for picnics. A white sand beach on the grounds is safe for small children and nonswimmers. Lake Webb, five miles long and two miles wide, is surrounded by mountains and is ideal for bathing, boating, and bass fishing.

Apricot-Sesame Dressing (Lite)

1 teaspoon cornstarch
⅛ teaspoon garlic powder
⅛ teaspoon ginger
1 5½-ounce can apricot nectar
¼ cup red wine vinegar
1 tablespoon honey
1 teaspoon sesame oil
1 teaspoon toasted sesame seeds

In a small saucepan combine the cornstarch, garlic powder, and ginger. Stir in the apricot nectar, vinegar, honey, oil, and sesame seeds. Cook, stirring constantly until thickened and bubbly. Cook for 2 more minutes. Chill.

Makes ⅔ cup (22 calories per tablespoon).

Minted Baby Carrots

3 12-ounce bags baby carrots, cleaned
¼ cup mint jelly
2 tablespoons butter
1 tablespoon chopped fresh mint or 1 teaspoon dried mint leaves

In 1 inch of boiling water heat the carrots to boiling. Reduce the heat to low, cover, and simmer for approximately 15 minutes, until tender. Drain and stir in the mint jelly, butter, and mint. Cook over medium heat, stirring gently, until the jelly and butter melt.

Serves 10.

The Stacked Arms

RFD #2, Box 420
Wiscasset, Maine 04578
(207) 882-5436

The Stacked Arms Bed and Breakfast has five bedrooms available for guests, four with shared baths and one with twin-sized beds and a private bath. Each bedroom has been decorated in its own color scheme and style. A large, light, and airy dining room with individual tables and family-style dining table are available. The Stacked Arms also has a large lounge with a floor-to-ceiling bookcase filled with a variety of reading material. Seven acres of land surround the house, and a path goes to the top of a hill that overlooks Wiscasset Harbor and part of the village. Guests may prefer to relax in the shade of a spreading pine or oak tree where there is always a breeze, or stroll through the grounds where there are many different trees and flowers to admire.

Moussaka
(Eggplant Pâté)

3 tablespoons chopped onion
3 tablespoons butter or lard
1 pound ground lamb
1 cup tomato sauce
1 cup white wine
1 cup water
Salt and pepper
2 tablespoons chopped parsley
Nutmeg

🍃 🍃 🍃

3 or 4 medium-sized eggplants
Salt
Oil or lard for deep-frying

🍃 🍃 🍃

3 or 4 tablespoons butter
1 cup all-purpose flour
Salt, white pepper, and grated nutmeg
1 quart milk
2 eggs, beaten

🍃 🍃 🍃

½ cup dry bread crumbs
1 cup grated cheese
Butter, melted

In a large skillet brown the onions in butter or lard. Add the ground lamb mixing constantly until the mixture becomes crumbly. Add the tomato sauce, wine, water, salt, pepper, parsley, and nutmeg. Cover the pan and cook for 1 hour over low heat, until the gravy is reduced by one half.

Cut the eggplants lengthwise in slices about ¼-inch thick. Salt, drain in a colander, and fry in deep fat.

In a saucepan melt the butter. Add the flour and a small amount of milk. Stir until smooth. Add the salt, pepper, nutmeg, and remaining milk. Cook until thickened. Pour a small amount of the heated mixture into the eggs and blend well. Pour the egg mixture into the sauce and blend well.

Arrange the eggplants in a shallow pan with a few bread crumbs.

Remove the lamb from the heat, add ½ cup of grated cheese and ¼ cup of bread crumbs. Spread evenly over the eggplants. Top evenly with the white sauce, and add the remaining cheese and bread crumbs. Pour some melted butter over the top. Bake in a 375° oven for 15 minutes until golden brown. Cool slightly and cut in squares as you would macaroni au gratin.

Note: You may substitute potatoes for the eggplant.

Serves 6 to 8.

Barley Casserole

This may be a substitute for a potato or rice dish.

> 1 cup barley
> 5 tablespoons butter
> 1 large onion
> ¾ cup sliced mushrooms
> 2½ cups chicken broth
> ½ cup toasted, slivered almonds

In a small skillet sauté the barley in 2 tablespoons of butter until golden brown. Transfer to a 2-quart casserole dish. Sauté the onion in 2 tablespoons butter until golden brown. Add to the barley. Add the mushrooms and 1 tablespoon of butter. Add 1 cup of broth. Bake in a 350° oven for 40 minutes. Add 1 more cup of broth and bake an additional 40 minutes. Add the remaining ½ cup of broth and bake for 25 more minutes. Mix in the almonds.
Serves 4.

Rhubarb Dessert

> 6 cups rhubarb, cut in ½-inch
>   lengths
> 1 3-ounce package strawberry
>   gelatin
> 1 cup miniature marshmallows
> 1 cup sugar
>
> ❧ ❧ ❧
>
> 2 tablespoons butter, softened
> 1 cup sugar
> 1 egg
> 1½ cups all-purpose flour
> 2 teaspoons baking powder
> ½ teaspoon salt
> ⅔ cup milk
>
> ❧ ❧ ❧
>
> Ice cream or whipped cream

Grease a 9x13-inch baking pan. Place the rhubarb in the prepared pan. Sprinkle with dry gelatin, add the marshmallows, and 1 cup of sugar.

In a mixing bowl cream the butter with 1 cup of sugar. Add the egg, beating thoroughly. Sift together the flour, baking powder, and salt. Add to the creamed mixture with enough milk to make a cake batter.

Pour over the rhubarb mixture. Bake in a 375° oven for 45 minutes or until the topping is golden brown. Serve hot or cold with ice cream or whipped cream.
Serves 12.

Dockside Guest Quarters

On the Harbor
Post Office Box 205
York, Maine 03909
(207) 363-2868

Dockside Guest Quarters is a gracious nineteenth century house with five guest rooms, three with private baths and all with views of the harbor. Also available are seventeen modern units along the shoreline. The continental-plus breakfast buffet offers fruits and fresh-baked breads. The varied menu features Maine lobster and other seafood; a bar is in the restaurant building. Available in York are five beaches, golf, tennis, fishing, the Ogunquit Playhouse, shops, historic York, and bicycling.

Duck Liver Pâté

> 2 cups margarine
> 2½ pounds duck livers
> 1 tablespoon freshly crushed garlic
> ½ cup chopped celery
> ½ cup chopped onion
> 1½ teaspoons whole cloves, in a
>   gauze bag

In a skillet cover and simmer all of the ingredients for about 1 hour and 15 minutes. Remove the cloves. Drain off the liquid and set aside. Purée the livers. Slowly pour the liquid back into the puréed livers, beating with a wire whip until smooth. Place in a serving dish or terrine. Refrigerate until firm. Serve on crackers.
Serves about 32.

Maine Shrimp and Gruyère Casserole

> 6 slices whole grain bread
> 8 slices Gruyère cheese, ½-inch
>   thick
> ½ pound shrimp (or more if
>   desired)
> 4 eggs
> 2 cups milk
> 1 teaspoon dry mustard
> 1 tablespoon fresh chives, minced
> ¼ teaspoon cayenne pepper
> 2 tablespoons chopped parsley

Butter a large shallow casserole and place the bread slices on the bottom. Top the bread with cheese and cover with shrimp. In a separate bowl, mix the eggs, milk, and seasonings with a wire whip. Pour over the bread, cheese, and shrimp. Refrigerate for 1 hour and 30 minutes, until the bread has absorbed most of the liquid. Bake in a 350° oven for 25 to 30 minutes.
Serves 4 to 6.

Lobster Thermidor

> 4 2-pound lobsters
> ½ cup butter
> 4 ounces brandy
> Juice of 1 lemon
> 1 onion, finely chopped
> 2 tablespoons butter
> 12 mushrooms, sliced
> 1 tablespoon dry mustard
> 2 tablespoons tomato paste
> 1 tablespoon paprika
> 1 teaspoon tarragon
> 1 cup fish or chicken stock
> 2 tablespoons all-purpose flour
> ¾ cup heavy cream
> 1 cup Hollandaise sauce
> Chopped parsley

Boil the lobsters until cooked. Cool and remove the meat. Cut up the lobster meat and sauté in ½ cup of butter, the brandy, and lemon juice. In a separate pan sauté the onion in 2 tablespoons of butter until lightly brown. Add the mushrooms and sauté lightly. Add the dry mustard, tomato paste, paprika, tarragon, and stock. Bring to a boil. Mix the flour and cream until smooth. Reduce the heat under the sauce and add the flour and cream mixture. Stir constantly until thick. Add the lobster and transfer to a casserole. Cover with Hollandaise sauce and parsley, and brown under the broiler.

Serves 4.

Coconut Cloud Pie

3½ cups Rice Chex, crushed to 1¼
 cups
¼ cup brown sugar
⅓ cup margarine, melted
¼ teaspoon almond extract

   🍃 🍃 🍃

¾ cup milk
½ teaspoon vanilla extract
1 3-ounce package instant vanilla
 pudding

   🍃 🍃 🍃

1 cup sour cream
1 cup cream, whipped stiff
¾ cup flaked coconut

   🍃 🍃 🍃

Whipped cream and toasted coconut
 for garnish

In a large bowl combine the Rice Chex, brown sugar, margarine, and almond extract. Press into a 9-inch pie plate.

In a large bowl combine milk, vanilla, and pudding. In a separate bowl combine the sour cream, whipped cream, and coconut. Fold the cream mixture into the pudding mixture.

Pour into the prepared crust and refrigerate. Garnish with whipped cream and toasted coconut.

Serves 6 to 8.

Scotland Bridge Inn

One Scotland Bridge Road
York, Maine 03909
(207) 363-4432

Scotland Bridge Inn is a nineteenth-century home off U.S. Highway 1. Offering comfortable rooms with shared bath and a two-room suite with private bath, the inn also provides its guests a full breakfast. Patrons are welcome to relax on the tree-shaded porch or enjoy the living room in all seasons. The inn is within minutes of popular restaurants, clambakes, golfing, auctions, hunting, ocean boating, and swimming.

My Mother's Biscuits

3 tablespoons shortening
2 cups all-purpose flour
½ teaspoon salt
3 teaspoons baking powder
1 cup milk

Grease a 9-inch square pan. In a large bowl cut the shortening into the dry ingredients. Add the milk all at once, being careful not to handle too much when put on floured board. Flatten and cut with a small biscuit cutter. Arrange in the prepared pan. Bake in a 400° oven (after preheating to 450°) for 12 minutes.

Serves 6 to 8.

Apple Cake

4 medium apples
8 teaspoons sugar
2 teaspoons cinnamon
4 eggs
2 cups sugar
1 cup plus 1 tablespoon oil

3 cups sifted all-purpose flour
3 teaspoons baking powder
½ teaspoon salt
½ cup orange juice
1 teaspoon vanilla extract
Confectioners' sugar (optional)

Grease and flour a 9-inch tube pan. Quarter, core, peel, and slice the apples. In a small bowl mix 8 teaspoons of sugar and the cinnamon.

In a large bowl beat the eggs until thickened. Gradually beat in 2 cups of sugar and the oil. In a separate bowl sift the flour, baking powder, and salt together. Add the dry ingredients to the beaten egg mixture alternately with the orange juice. Beat in the vanilla.

Pour about a fourth of the batter into the prepared pan. Arrange half of the sliced apples on top and sprinkle with a third of the sugar-cinnamon mixture. Then add another fourth of the batter, half of the remaining apple slices, and sprinkle with half of the remaining sugar-cinnamon mixture. Add half of the remaining dough, the remaining apple slices, and sugar-cinnamon mixture. Top with the last of the batter. Bake in a 350° oven for 1 hour. Sprinkle with confectioners' sugar.

Serves 12.

The Wild Rose of York

78 Long Sands Road
York, Maine 03909
(207) 363-2532

The Wild Rose of York is a new replica of an 1814 captain's house. Boasting fireplaces in most rooms, its cozy decor includes braided rugs, four poster and high back beds, wallpapers with tiny flowers, and, in one room, stenciling that matches a hand-

The Wild Rose of York

made green, white, and red quilt. Rooms are named for wildflowers. Breakfast and tea are served on the large porch, which is also a great place to sun, play cards, have cookouts, or relax and read a good book. The house sits high on a hill with a view of the rolling lawn where children can sled in winter. The Wild Rose is open all year.

Mrs. Kmiec's Polish Easter Bapka

1 or 2 yeast cakes
½ cup warm milk (85°)
5 eggs, beaten
½ teaspoon vanilla extract
½ teaspoon salt
2 tablespoons cream cheese
1 cup sugar
5 cups all-purpose flour
½ cup butter, melted

&ampersand; &ampersand; &ampersand;

4 tablespoons cream cheese
1 egg yolk
¾ cup sugar

&ampersand; &ampersand; &ampersand;

1 egg, beaten

&ampersand; &ampersand; &ampersand;

3 tablespoons butter
¼ cup sugar
2 tablespoons all-purpose flour

Dissolve the yeast in the milk. In a large bowl beat the 5 eggs, vanilla, salt, 2 tablespoons of cream cheese, and 1 cup of sugar until foamy. Add 5 cups of flour and blend well. Add ½ cup of butter, the milk, and yeast. Work well by hand until doughy. Add more flour if needed. Knead until well mixed. Place the dough in a greased bowl, cover, and let rise until doubled. Turn the dough onto a floured board and knead slightly. Pat or roll to ½-inch thickness. Cut into 4 pieces.

In a small bowl cream 4 tablespoons of cream cheese, the egg yolk, and ¾ cup of sugar together. Spread on the dough and form into 4 long rolls. Grease 2 deep round pans or dishes. Twist 2 rolls together and shape into a circle. Repeat with the remaining dough. Place in the pans and tuck in the ends.

Brush the dough with the beaten egg. Combine 3 tablespoons of butter, ¼ cup of sugar, and 2 tablespoons of flour until crumbly. Sprinkle over the dough. Let the dough rise again. Bake in a 350° oven for 45 minutes. Serve warm or cold.

Note: A hard-boiled, colored egg can be baked into the center, and it is traditionally served with butter carved in the shape of a lamb.

Makes 2 loaves.

Coffee Cake

1 cup biscuit mix
2 tablespoons sugar
2 tablespoons brown sugar
¼ cup butter or margarine, softened
2 tablespoons milk
¼ cup chopped nuts (optional)

&ampersand; &ampersand; &ampersand;

1 3-ounce package vanilla instant pudding
1 cup plus 2 tablespoons cold milk
½ teaspoon vanilla extract (optional)

&ampersand; &ampersand; &ampersand;

1 8¾-ounce can peach halves
1 8¾-ounce can apricots
1 8¾-ounce can pears
1 11-ounce can mandarin oranges
½ banana
1 kiwi fruit
Several fresh purple grapes, halved
2 to 3 Maraschino cherries
Cinnamon sugar (optional)

Grease a 9-inch cake or flan pan. In a medium bowl combine the biscuit mix, sugar, brown sugar, butter, ⅛ cup of milk, and nuts with a fork. Spread onto the prepared pan. Press out to thinly cover the bottom and build up the sides. Bake in a 350° oven for 15 to 20 minutes, until crunchy. Cool.

In a small bowl mix the pudding, 1 cup plus 2 tablespoons cold milk, and vanilla well with a wire whisk. Pour over the crust and cool. (Or cool the crust before adding the pudding.)

Place the fruits on double paper towels and pat dry. Thinly slice the peaches, apricots, pears, bananas, kiwi, and cherries, and arrange in close rows on top of the pudding. Use the mandarin oranges and thinly sliced cherries for vertical lines between rows of fruit. Be creative with your designs! Lightly sprinkle with cinnamon sugar.

Serves 6 to 8.

Homestead Inn

Post Office Box 15
Route 1A
York Beach, Maine 03910
(207) 363-8952

Built in the early 1900s, the Homestead Inn is a turn-of-the-century boarding house that was converted to a home in the 1960s. Upon entering the inn, guests will be in the living room, with its fireplace, picturesque window seat, and family library. The interior woodwork remains the old hard pine, including the stairway banisters. Homestead Inn offers four large rooms, individually decorated and with panoramic views of the Atlantic Ocean and Mount Agamenticus. In the evening guests are lulled to sleep by the rhythm of the surf; in the morning they are awakened by the calling of seagulls and the aroma of freshly brewed coffee.

New England Maple Bread

A favorite of our guests in the fall.

> 1 cup mlk
> ¼ cup butter
> 1 cup maple syrup
> 1½ cups all-purpose flour
> 1 cup whole wheat flour
> ½ teaspoon salt
> 1 tablespoon baking powder
> 2 eggs, beaten
> ¾ cup chopped walnuts

Grease and flour a 9x5-inch loaf pan. In a small saucepan heat the milk and butter until the butter is completely melted. Stir in the maple syrup and remove from the heat. In a medium bowl sift together the flours, salt, and baking powder. When the milk mixture has cooled slightly, pour it into a large mixing bowl and beat in the eggs. Beat in the dry ingredients until well blended. Fold in the nuts. Pour into the prepared pan. Bake in a 325°

oven for approximately 1 hour. Cool on a wire rack for 15 minutes before removing from the pan.
　　Makes 1 loaf.

✓ good!

Homestead Cranberry Fruit Bread

Cranberries are a New England staple often appreciated by visitors.

> 2 cups all-purpose flour
> 1 cup sugar
> 1½ teaspoons baking powder
> ½ teaspoon baking soda
> 1 teaspoon salt
> ¼ cup shortening
> ¾ cup orange juice
> 1 tablespoon grated orange rind
> 1 egg, well beaten
> ½ cup chopped nuts
> 2 cups chopped cranberries

Grease two 9x5-inch loaf pans. In a large bowl combine the first 5 ingredients. Cut in the shortening. Combine the orange juice, rind, and egg, and pour all at once into the dry ingredients. Mix until just moistened. Carefully fold in the cranberries and nuts. Spoon into the prepared pans, and spread the corners and sides higher than the center. Bake in a 350° oven for 40 minutes to 1 hour.
　　Makes 2 loaves.

Maryland

Shaw's Fancy

161 Green Street
Annapolis, Maryland 21401
(301) 268-9750

Originally built for a Maryland judge in 1902, Shaw's Fancy showcases tiger oak woodwork, Georgia pine floors, brass and tile fireplaces, and a green leather foyer. Decorated in Victorian comfort and luxury, the inn features two suites (each with queen-size bed and private bath) and two rooms. The continental breakfast includes freshly baked goods, fruits, cheeses, and homemade granola. Smoking is allowed on the porch only.

Buckwheat Granola Scones

1⅓ cups all-purpose flour
⅔ cup buckwheat flour
¼ cup brown sugar
2¼ teaspoons baking powder
⅓ cup butter, chilled and cut up
⅓ cup milk
1 large egg
1 teaspoon vanilla extract or maple extract
1½ cups crunchy granola (homemade is best, if you have it!)

Lightly butter a cookie sheet. In a large bowl stir together the flours, brown sugar, and baking powder. Add the butter. Using a pastry cutter, cut in the butter until the mixture is the texture of cornmeal. In a separate bowl mix the milk, egg, and vanilla. Stir the liquids into the flour mixture. The dough will be sticky. With lightly floured hands, knead in the granola. Use an ice cream scoop or ⅓ cup measure to spoon the dough onto the cookie sheet, spacing 2½ to 3 inches apart. Bake in a 375° oven for 20 to 25 mintues, until a toothpick comes out clean. Remove from the oven and place on wire racks. Serve warm or cold.

Makes 8 scones.

Shaw's Fancy Bread Pudding

8 to 10 cups leftover muffin or bread chunks
2 cups milk
1 29-ounce can "juice packed" peaches, apricots, or pears (drain and reserve juice)
1 cup nuts or raisins (optional)
⅓ cup brown sugar
3 eggs, separated
1½ teaspoons vanilla extract

ta ta ta

Fruit
Freshly whipped cream
Grated nutmeg

Shaw's Fancy

Grease 12 to 16 individual custard cups. In a large bowl soak the bread crumbs in the milk and juice reserved from the canned fruit for 15 minutes. Chop the canned fruit into small pieces. Gently stir the fruit into the pudding mixture. Stir in the nuts or raisins if desired.

In a separate bowl stir together the sugar, egg yolks, and vanilla. Gently stir into the muffin mixture. Beat the egg whites until stiff and fold into the muffin mixture. Spoon the mixture into the prepared custard cups. Place a pan of water in the bottom of the oven to "steam" the puddings. Bake in a preheated 350° oven for approximately 1 hour. Test for doneness using a toothpick. Remove and cool in the dishes on a baking rack. The individual puddings may be stored in the freezer, thawed overnight in the refrigerator, then microwaved for 1 to 2 minutes before serving.

Serve warm topped with fruit, freshly whipped cream, and grated numeg.

Healthy variation: Add ¾ cup of oat bran and ¾ cup of prune juice, apple juice, or apricot nectar. Use honey in place of the brown sugar.

Serves 12 to 16.

The Inn at Mitchell House

Rural Route 2, Box 329
Tolchester Estates
Chestertown, Maryland 21620
(301) 778-6500

Nestled on ten rolling acres, surrounded by woods and stream, and overlooking a pond, this historic, eighteenth-century manor house with seven fireplaces offers a touch of tranquility to those who yearn for a retreat from the mundane. The five bedrooms, authentically furnished with period antique appointments, greet guests with warmth and invite them to take a restful step back in time.

Crab Omelet

3 eggs
1 tablespoon water
1 tablespoon butter
⅓ to ½ cup lump crab meat
1 ounce cream cheese, in small
    pieces
½ teaspoon Old Bay Seasoning
Watercress

Heat an omelet pan. In a small bowl beat the eggs and add the water. Place the butter in the heated pan and heat until bubbly. Add the egg mixture. Top with the crab meat and cream cheese. Sprinkle with seasoning. When slightly set (about 1½ minutes), place under the broiler until firm. Fold the omelet, and garnish with watercress.

Serves 1.

Wonderful English Muffins

Excellent compliment to chicken salad or basic scrambled eggs.

6 English muffins
Butter, softened
Curry powder
3 cups shredded Cheddar or Colby
    cheese

Split the muffins and spread with butter. Sprinkle with curry powder to taste. Top each half with ¼ cup of cheese. Place under a broiler and toast.

Serves 6.

The Inn at Mitchell House

Fried Tomatoes

½ cup bacon drippings
½ cup all-purpose flour
1 tablespoon sugar
Salt and pepper to taste
4 ripe, but firm, tomatoes, cut into
    ½-inch slices
Fresh chives

In a large skillet heat the bacon fat. In a shallow bowl mix the flour, sugar, salt, and pepper. Cover each tomato slice with the flour mixture. Place in the hot fat and cook over medium heat until very crisp, about 10 minutes. Turn to cook both sides. Top with fresh chives.

Serves 2 to 4.

Bed and Breakfast at Lewrene Farm

Rural Route 3, Box 150
Hagerstown, Maryland 21740
(301) 582-1735

This colonial style home is situated on a quiet 125-acre farm and woodland. Guests may relax in the large living room and visit with the hosts and other guests by the fireplace. The deluxe, comfortable bedrooms provide private or shared baths. The hostess speaks Spanish and limited German. Nearby points of interest include Antietam Battlefield, Harpers Ferry, Fort Frederick, and the Appalachian Trail.

Homemade Applesauce

4 pounds apples (Red Delicious are prettiest)
2 cups water
2 tablespoons cinnamon hearts

Wash the apples, but do not peel. Core and cut into wedges directly into a cooking pan. Add water to make 1 to 2 inches in the bottom of the pan. Cook until the apples are soft. Force through a food mill or sieve. Add cinnamon hearts while the apple mixture is still hot. Stir well to color and give a good sweet, cinnamon flavor.

Makes 1 quart of sauce.

Apple Crunch

Can be served hot or cold and is a winner either way. My guests enjoy this very much.

1 quart pared, cored and sliced apples
1 cup sugar
⅛ teaspoon salt
1 teaspoon cinnamon
1 tablespoon all-purpose flour

᠅ ᠅ ᠅

¾ cup oatmeal flakes
¾ cup brown sugar
¼ teaspoon baking soda
¼ cup butter, melted

᠅ ᠅ ᠅

Rich milk or whipped cream

Grease a 2-quart baking dish. In a small bowl combine the sugar, salt, cinnamon, and flour. Sprinkle over the apples. Place the apples in the bottom of the prepared baking dish.

In a small bowl combine the oatmeal, brown sugar, and baking soda. Add the melted butter and rub into the oatmeal mixture to make crumbs. Place the crumbs on top of the apples, patting them down evenly. Bake in a 375° oven for approximately 40 minutes. After baking, serve with rich milk or whipped cream.

Serves 6 to 8.

National Pike Inn

9-11 West Main Street
Post Office Box 299
New Market, Maryland 21774
(301) 865-5055

National Pike Inn was built in the late 1700s and early 1800s. Named for the first federally funded highway in the nation, this Federal house has been completely restored. It has five air conditioned guest rooms with private baths. There is a large colonial sitting room and private courtyard. New Market has over thirty antique shops, and the inn across the street is known for dining excellence. The town of New Market is registered on the National Register of Historic Places.

Barbecue String Beans

4 slices bacon
¼ cup chopped onion
½ cup ketchup
¼ cup brown sugar
1 tablespoon Worcestershire sauce
2 16-ounce cans French-cut green beans, drained

In a skillet cook the bacon until crisp. Brown the onion in the bacon fat. Add the ketchup, brown sugar, and Wor-

cestershire sauce. Place the green beans in a casserole dish. Pour the sauce over the top. Do not stir. Bake in a 350° oven for 20 minutes.

Serves 6.

Apple Slices

2½ cups all-purpose flour
1 tablespoon sugar
1 teaspoon salt
1 cup shortening
1 egg, separated
Milk
⅔ cup crushed corn flakes
5 cups sliced apples
1½ cups sugar
1 teaspoon cinnamon

᠅ ᠅ ᠅

1 cup sifted confectioners' sugar
2 tablespoons fresh lemon juice

In a large bowl sift together the flour, sugar, and salt. Cut in the shortening with a pastry blender. Put the egg yolk into the measuring cup and add enough milk to make ⅔ cup. Mix the dough just enough to shape into a ball. Roll out half of the dough and place in a 15x11-inch pan. Cover the dough with the crushed corn flakes, apples, sugar, and cinnamon. Top with the remaining dough and pinch around the edge. Cut vent holes. Beat the egg white until stiff. Spread on the crust. Bake in a 400° oven for 40 minutes.

In a small bowl combine the confectioners' sugar and lemon juice. Pour over the top of the entire dish while it is hot from the oven.

Serves 8 to 10.

Hazel's Shoe Fly Cake

4 cups all-purpose flour
2 cups sugar
1 teaspoon salt
1 cup shortening

🌤 🌤 🌤

2 cups warm water
1 cup green label baking molasses
1 tablespoon baking soda

🌤 🌤 🌤

½ cup all-purpose flour
½ cup sugar
¼ cup margarine
1 teaspoon cinnamon

Grease a 10x13-inch pan. In a large bowl blend together 4 cups of flour, 2 cups of sugar, the salt, and shortening. When blended, remove one cup of the mixture and set aside. In a separate bowl mix the water, molasses, and baking soda. Stir the liquid ingredients into the dry ingredients. Pour the batter into the prepared pan.

Prepare a crumb topping with ½ cup of flour, ½ cup of sugar, the margarine, and cinnamon. Add the reserved dry mixture. Sprinkle the crumbs on top of the batter. Bake in a 350° oven for 50 to 60 minutes.

Serves 15.

porch overlooking a beautifully landscaped yard. For fine dining, Mealey's (across the street) has served New Market since the early 1800s.

Crab Soufflé

4 slices firm bread, crust off, cubed
1 pound fresh crab meat
1 small red or green pepper, chopped
1 medium onion, chopped
1 cup chopped celery
1½ cups mayonnaise
1 teaspoon Old Bay Seasoning
4 slices firm bread, crust off, cut in triangles
3 cups milk
4 eggs

🌤 🌤 🌤

1 10½-ounce can cream of mushroom soup
1 cup grated Cheddar cheese
Paprika

Layer the bottom of a casserole dish with the cubed bread. Mix the next 6 ingredients together and spoon over the bread. Arrange the triangle bread pieces over the crab meat mixture. Beat together the milk and eggs until well blended. Pour over the crab meat and bread mixture. Cover tightly and refrigerate overnight. Bake uncovered in a 325° oven for 15 minutes. Remove from the oven. Spread the soup over mixture. Sprinkle grated Cheddar and paprika on top. Bake for 1 hour.

Serves 12.

The Robert Morris Inn

Box 70
On the Tred Avon
Oxford, Maryland 21654
(301) 226-5111

It has been said that the Robert Morris Inn is one of the most relaxed places on the eastern shore of Maryland. Situated by the scenic Tred Avon River, it offers quiet walks along the beach, peaceful spots to read a book, breathtaking sunsets, and good eastern shore food.

Strawberry Inn

17 Main Street
Post Office Box 237
New Market, Maryland 21774
(301) 865-3318

Strawberry Inn is a completely restored inn furnished in period and antique pieces. Each of its five guest rooms has a private bath and air conditioning. The continental breakfast is served on butler's trays outside guests' doors in the morning, in the cheerful dining room, or on the back

The Robert Morris Inn

Scalloped Oysters

½ cup dry bread crumbs
½ cup coarse cracker crumbs
5 tablespoons melted butter
1 pint oysters
½ teaspoon salt
½ teaspoon pepper
⅛ teaspoon nutmeg
2 tablespoons chopped parsley
1 10½-ounce can cream of
   mushroom soup

Grease a casserole dish. In a small bowl combine the bread crumbs, cracker crumbs, and butter. Place half of the mixture in the prepared casserole. Arrange the oysters in layers, sprinkling each layer with seasonings. Pour the mushroom soup over the oysters, and top with the remaining crumbs. Bake in a 350° oven for 1 hour.
Serves 4.

Davis House

Charles and Maltby Streets
Post Office Box 759
Solomon's Island, Maryland 20688
(301) 326-4811

This charming Victorian house commands a striking frontal view of the harbor and overlooks the mouth of the Patuxent River. In this restored inn, the living room and library provide pleasant relaxing places for conversation or rest; they open onto a large, sunny verandah. Six air conditioned guest rooms with queen-size beds share three bathrooms. The innkeepers speak Spanish and Finnish in addition to English.

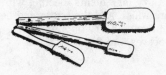

Chocolate Rolle

1½ cups sugar
6 eggs
¾ cup potato flour
1½ teaspoons baking powder
¼ cup cocoa

🍃 🍃 🍃

¾ cup margarine or butter
⅔ cup confectioners' sugar
1 egg yolk
1 teaspoon vanilla extract

Line a 20x13-inch rimmed cookie sheet with buttered waxed paper. In a large bowl cream the sugar and eggs together until very light. Add the flour, baking powder, and cocoa. Pour the batter onto the prepared cookie sheet and spread evenly. Bake in a 350° oven for 20 minutes.

In a medium bowl cream the margarine, confectioners' sugar, egg yolk, and vanilla together. Dampen a dish towel and spread on a table. Cover with waxed paper and sprinkle with confectioners' sugar. When the cake is done, turn onto waxed paper and let cool. Spread the filling on the cake and roll up. Refrigerate in the towel.
Serves 14 to 16.

The Newel Post

3428 Uniontown Road
Uniontown, Maryland 21157
(301) 775-2655

The Newel Post is a Queen Anne-style Victorian house built at the turn of the century by Dr. Luther Kemp. The inn, with its fine handcrafted wood, has been carefully restored to its original elegance. Beautiful stained glass windows, chestnut shutters, period wallcoverings, and original lighting fixtures are some of the unique features of this house. At this inn guests find cozy rooms filled with Victorian furniture. Down pillows, freshly cut flowers, and an ample breakfast bespeak a time when comfort and style were the way of life.

Date-Orange Muffins

1 cup chopped dates
2 teaspoons grated orange rind
2 cups all-purpose flour
½ cup sugar
2 teaspoons baking powder
½ teaspoon salt
½ cup oil
½ cup orange juice
2 eggs
½ cup chopped walnuts

Grease 6 large muffin cups. In a small bowl combine the dates and grated rind, and set aside. In a large bowl combine the flour, sugar, baking powder, and salt. In a separate bowl mix the oil, juice, and eggs. Pour all at once into the dry ingredients and stir until just moistened. Add the dates, rind, and nuts. Pour into the prepared muffin cups. Bake in a 375° oven for 25 minutes.
Makes 6 large muffins.

Davis House

Lemon Crumb Squares

1 14-ounce can sweetened
    condensed milk
½ cup lemon juice
1 teaspoon grated lemon rind
1½ cups sifted all-purpose flour
1 teaspoon baking powder
½ teaspoon salt
⅔ cup butter
1 cup dark brown sugar
1 cup uncooked oatmeal

Butter an 8x12-inch baking pan. In a small bowl blend together the milk, juice, and lemon rind. Set aside. In a large bowl sift the flour, baking powder, and salt together. In a separate bowl cream the butter and blend in the sugar. Add the oatmeal and flour mixture, and mix until crumbly. Spread half of the mixture in the prepared pan and pat down. Spread the condensed milk mixture over the batter and cover with the remaining crumb mixture. Bake in a 350° oven for 25 minutes or until brown around the edges. Cool for 15 minutes before cutting.
    Serves 24.

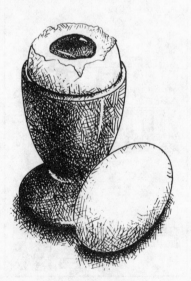

Winchester Country Inn

430 South Bishop Street
Westminster, Maryland 21157
(301) 876-7373

Built in the 1760s by the founder of Westminster, the Winchester Country Inn is one of Carroll County's oldest buildings. Refurbished with antiques and period furnishings, it includes many pieces from prominent local families. Beautifully restored pine flooring, original moldings, hand-blown window panes, and period fixtures make this a uniquely attractive inn. Of the five guest rooms, three have private baths and two have shared baths. Recreational facilities and historic points of interest abound nearby, including the Historic Union Mills Homestead, Carroll County Farm Museum, wine vineyards, and antique shops.

Sherried French Toast

1 egg
1 cup milk
½ cup sherry
8 to 10 slices dry bread

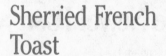

Jam or syrup

Butter a cookie sheet. In a shallow bowl beat the egg and milk together, and add the sherry. Dip the slices of bread in the mixture and place on the prepared cookie sheet. Bake in a 350° oven for 30 minutes, turning once. Serve warm with jam or syrup.
    Serves 6 to 8.

Old-fashioned Biscuits

2 cups all-purpose flour
1 teaspoon baking soda
3 teaspoons baking powder
¼ cup lard or shortening
Buttermilk

In a large bowl combine the dry ingredients. Cut in the lard with a fork. Add the buttermilk to form a soft ball. Turn out onto a floured board and roll ½-inch thick. Cut with a cutter or drinking glass. Arrange on a baking sheet. Bake in a 350° oven for 30 minutes.
    Serves 6 to 8.

Fluffy Pancakes

1 cup Maypo cereal
¼ teaspoon salt
1 tablespoon sugar
1 tablespoon baking powder
1 egg
1 cup milk
2 rounded tablespoons sour cream
2 tablespoons butter, melted

In a large bowl sift the dry ingredients. In a separate bowl, beat the egg, milk, and sour cream. Pour into the dry ingredients, beating with a wire whisk. Add the butter and beat until smooth. Fry on a griddle.
    Serves 6 to 8.

Massachusetts

The Old Cape House

108 Old Main Street
Bass River, Massachusetts 02664
(508) 398-1068

The Old Cape House, situated on historic Old Main Street, was built in the early 1800s by the Bakers, a farming and seafaring family who owned most of the land in Bass River. The inn is a fine example of the Greek Revival architecture of the nineteenth century and is eligible for the National Register of Historic Places. In keeping with the English motif, the guest rooms are named after London streets. All suites and guest rooms feature beamed ceilings and are comfortably furnished in New England style with handmade quilts for the cooler evenings. Breakfast is served in the colonial dining room, featuring a sumptuous table of homemade muffins, coffee cakes, breads, cereals, fresh fruits, and homemade preserves with lots of good conversation.

ཙ ཙ ཙ ཙ ཙ

Boston Brown Bread

2 cups buttermilk
1 cup all-purpose flour
1 cup cornmeal
1 cup whole wheat flour
1 cup raisins
¾ cup dark molasses
2 teaspoons baking soda
1 teaspoon salt

Grease 4 16-ounce vegetable cans or 2 1-pound coffee cans. In a large mixing bowl mix together all of the ingredients for 2 minutes, until well blended and moist. Fill the cans about ⅔ full and cover tightly with foil. Place the cans in a large saucepan on a rack and add water until it just comes to the bottom of the cans. Boil for approximately 3 hours, adding water as necessary. Immediately unmold by removing the bottom of the cans and pushing the bread through the top.

To bake, grease a 2-quart casserole. Pour the batter into the prepared pan. Bake in a 325° oven for about 1 hour.

Cranberry Butter

1 cup cranberries (thawed, if frozen)
1 cup sugar
½ cup butter
1 tablespoon lemon juice

In a blender or food processor purée the cranberries and sugar until fine. Add the butter and lemon juice and purée in a blender until smooth. Place the mixture in a saucepan and heat until the butter is melted. Transfer to a serving dish and chill. Delicious on toast, pancakes, waffles, or as a spread with cranberry muffins or English muffins.

Makes 2½ cups.

Lemon Curd

4 medium lemons
1½ cups sugar
½ cup butter
4 lightly beaten eggs

Grate the lemon rind and squeeze the juice. In a large bowl combine the rind, juice, and sugar. Cut the butter into small pieces and add to the eggs. Mix with the lemon juice and sugar. Place in the top of a double boiler and stir over simmering water until the sugar has dissolved and butter has melted. Continue to cook until thick enough to coat the back of a wooden spoon. Pour into jars and store in the refrigerator for up to 2 months.

Makes about 3 cups.

Microwave Cheese Onion Omelet

> 2 slices white bread, crusts removed
>   and diced
> 4 eggs
> 1 cup milk
> ½ cup grated Cheddar cheese
> 1 onion, chopped
> Pinch salt and pepper

Place the bread cubes in a microwaveable pie plate. In a medium bowl beat the eggs and milk, adding the cheese and mixing well. Sprinkle the chopped onions over the bread and add the egg mixture, stirring to combine. Season to taste with salt and pepper. Cover the plate with vented plastic wrap. Microwave on high for approximately 1 to 2 minutes, until the eggs are set. (Be careful not to overcook.)

Variation: Use chopped green peppers instead of onions or a combination of chopped fresh herbs such as chives, parsley, basil, oregano, sage, etc.

Serves 4.

Isaiah Clark House

1187 Old King's Highway
Route 6A
Brewster, Massachusetts 02631
(508) 896-2223

The Isaiah Clark House is a charming eighteenth-century sea captain's home near the shores of Cape Cod Bay. Today it retains many reminders of the Clark family, among them the signature of Captain Clark's thirteen-year-old son Jeremy on the back of a bedroom door. On the lawn a giant spruce brought as a seedling from Norway by Captain Clark on his ship still flourishes. Set on five acres of lush gardens and fruit trees, it provides guest rooms with private baths, handmade quilts, and evening chocolates. Several fireplaces, handsome antiques, predinner get-togethers, and hearty New England breakfasts make for a memorable stay.

Summer Herb Frittata

> 3 large eggs
> Pinch salt and white pepper
> 1 teaspoon melted butter
> ¼ cup grated Pecorino

> ½ teaspoon fresh chopped sage
> ½ teaspoon fresh chopped chives
> ½ teaspoon fresh chopped basil
> 1 medium-size tomato

> 1 tablespoon extra virgin olive oil
> 1 sprig fresh mint, for garnish

In a medium bowl mix all of the ingredients together except the oil and mint. Mix well. In an 8-inch nonstick pan, heat 1 tablespoon extra virgin olive oil. Pour the frittata mixture and cook on medium heat approximately 4 minutes. Turn once. Cut in pie fashion. Serve with a sprig of mint.

Serve with toasted Italian bread! Serves 2 to 3.

Cobbs Cove

Post Office Box 208
Route 6A
Barnstable Village
Cape Cod, Massachusetts 02630
(617) 362-9356

This colonial-timbered manor on a site in use since 1643, commands a 360-degree view overlooking Barnstable Village, the harbor and the ocean. Centrally located on Route 6A, it is convenient to Hyannis and its airport. Cobbs Cove offers six spacious suites providing gracious accommodations for guests who enjoy an intimate atmosphere. Each room includes a full bath with a whirlpool tub, a dressing room, and a picture window view. The tradition of Cobbs Cove is in the oldtime manner of good food and conversation to warm the heart and delight the spirit. Guests share the unspoiled, historical north shore of Cape Cod, a pleasure in all seasons. They may walk the winding paths and then return to a warm winter's fire or the peaceful garden patio.

Lemon Almond Madeleines

4 large eggs at room temperature
⅔ cup sugar
½ teaspoon almond extract
1½ teaspoons lemon zest
1 cup all-purpose flour
½ cup almonds, ground coarse
½ cup butter melted and cooled
   slightly

Butter madeleine molds. In a large bowl beat the eggs with the sugar until thick and pale and forms a ribbon. Beat in the almond extract and zest. Stir in the flour in 4 batches, folding in gently after each addition. Add the almonds and the butter, folding in gently and thoroughly. Spoon the batter into the prepared molds. Bake in the lower-third of a preheated 375° oven for 10 minutes. Turn out on racks and cool.
Makes 24.

Tomato Pie

1¾ cups all-purpose flour
1 teaspoon nonfat dry milk
¼ teaspoon salt
½ cup butter
1 large egg
   ❧ ❧ ❧
¼ cup Dijon-style mustard
¼ pound Gruyère, coarsely grated
3 large (1½ pounds) tomatoes,
   sliced ⅓-inch thick
2 tablespoons minced fresh parsley
   leaves
1 tablespoon minced fresh oregano
   or thyme
1 teaspoon minced garlic
¼ cup olive oil

Stir together the flour, milk, and salt. Add the butter and blend to meal consistency. Add the egg. Press the dough into 11-inch pie plate or tart pan. Chill for 30 minutes.
Spread the mustard over the chilled shell and sprinkle with cheese. Arrange the tomato slices over the cheese. Sprinkle with parsley, oregano, garlic, and oil. Bake in a 400° oven for 40 minutes.
Serves 8.

Fish Cakes

6 tablespoons butter
⅓ cup chopped scallions (white
   part)
1⅔ cups mashed potatoes
1 tablespoon sour cream
6 ounces flaked cooked fish
1 egg
¼ teaspoon dry mustard
Salt and pepper to taste
3 tablespoons minced parsley
Dried bread crumbs
1 tablespoon olive oil

In a skillet heat 2 tablespoons of butter and sauté scallions for 5 minutes. Blend the potatoes with 1 tablespoon of butter and the sour cream. Combine with the fish. Beat the egg with the mustard, salt, and pepper. Stir in the scallions and parsley. Using a spatula, combine with the potatoes and fish. Form into 8 cakes. Dip each cake into the bread crumbs. Heat the remaining butter and the olive oil, and sauté the cakes slowly about 3 minutes on each side.
Makes 8.

The Prindle House

Charlton, Massachusetts 01507
(508) 248-3134

The Prindle House, a 1734 farmhouse, offers the tranquil atmosphere developed through centuries of care and generations of preservation. The dining, living, and keeping rooms have working fireplaces, and the large porch is a pleasant place for relaxation and breakfast. The two double and one twin bedrooms share a bathroom. Smoking is in restricted areas only.

Prindle House Oven Baked Oatmeal

2 cups oatmeal (or 4 packages of
   flavored instant oatmeal)
1½ teaspoons baking powder
½ teaspoon salt
   ❧ ❧ ❧
1 cup milk
2 eggs
¼ cup oil
½ cup brown sugar
   ❧ ❧ ❧
Vanilla yogurt or milk for serving

Butter a 1-quart baking dish. In a large bowl combine the dry ingredients. Set aside. In a blender combine the milk, eggs, oil, and brown sugar. Blend for 30 seconds, or until well mixed. Pour the moist ingredients into the dry ingredients, stirring to mix. Set aside for 5 minutes. Stir once again and pour into the prepared dish. Bake in a 325° oven for 45 minutes. Top with vanilla yogurt or milk.
Serves 4.

Prindle House Holiday Cheese Ring

4 cups grated sharp Cheddar cheese
1 cup finely chopped nuts
1 cup mayonnaise
1 small onion, finely chopped
Dash black pepper
Dash cayenne
Dash Worcestershire sauce
   ❧ ❧ ❧
Strawberry or raspberry preserves

Spray a gelatin ring mold with cooking spray. Combine all of the ingredients except the preserves in a bowl. Turn the combined ingredients into the prepared mold and refrigerate for 3 to 4 hours. Remove the cheese ring from the mold and place on a serving dish with preserves in the middle of the ring.

Serve with your favorite crackers! Serves 12 to 15.

The Anderson-Wheeler Homestead

154 Fitchburg Turnpike
Concord, Massachusetts 01742
(508) 369-3756

When Fitchburg Turnpike was the main road between Boston and Fitchburg, the Lee family ran a stagecoach stop on this site, where they provided room and board and a change of horses, as well as a leather and blacksmith shop. In 1890 the buildings burned and were rebuilt by Frank Wheeler, grandfather of the present owner.

This charming Victorian home has a wraparound verandah and five bedrooms decorated with antiques and accentuated with fireplaces and window seats. Overlooking the Sudbury River, the inn also has an extensive lawn area and is conveniently situated near restaurants and shops. It is only three miles to historic Concord, Walden Pond, and the Audubon Center.

Oatmeal Scones
with "Clotted" Cream

1¼ cups all-purpose flour
⅓ cup sugar
2 teaspoons baking powder
½ teaspoon salt
½ cup butter
1 cup quick cooking oats
¼ cup raisins
1 egg
⅓ cup milk
1 tablespoon butter, melted

🍂 🍂 🍂

1 3-ounce package cream cheese, softened
1 cup heavy cream
1 teaspoon confectioners' sugar
Pinch salt

🍂 🍂 🍂

Raspberry jam

In a large bowl combine the dry ingredients. Cut in the butter until the mixture resembles coarse crumbs. Mix in the oats and raisins. Slowly add the egg mixed with milk, stirring just until the dry ingredients are moistened. Turn the dough out on a floured surface and knead gently 5 or 6 times. Roll to a circle ½-inch thick. Place on an ungreased baking sheet. Cut in wedges and brush with melted butter. Bake in a 375° oven for 15 minutes or until golden brown.

In a small bowl beat the cream cheese, heavy cream, confectioners' sugar, and salt together until thick. Serve scones warm with a dollop of "clotted" cream and raspberry jam.
Serves 8.

Finnish Coffee Bread

1 ¼-ounce package dry yeast
½ cup warm water (110° to 115°)
2 cups milk, scalded and cooled to lukewarm
1 cup sugar
1 teaspoon salt
7 or 8 cardamom pods, seeded and crushed
4 eggs, beaten
8 to 9 cups sifted all-purpose flour
½ cup plus 1 tablespoon melted butter

Grease a large baking sheet. In a large bowl dissolve the yeast in the warm water. Stir in the next 5 ingredients and enough flour (about 2 cups) to make a batter. Beat until smooth and elastic. Add about 3 more cups of flour and beat until smooth. Add the butter and stir in well. Knead in the remaining flour gradually until stiff. Let rise in a warm place for 1 hour. Punch down. Let the dough rise again until double.

Divide into 3 parts and shape into 3 long ropes. Braid the ropes together and place on the prepared sheet. Let the braid rise for 1 hour. Brush with 1 tablespoon of melted butter. Sprinkle with sugar. Bake in a 400° oven for 25 to 30 minutes.
Serves 10.

Breakfast Pudding

Children love this.

3¾ cups milk
⅔ cup quick Cream of Wheat
2 eggs, beaten
1 teaspoon vanilla extract
¼ cup sugar (or to taste)
½ teaspoon salt (optional)

🍂 🍂 🍂

Vanilla ice cream
Heated berry jam or sauce

In a large saucepan heat the milk to almost boiling. Add the cream of wheat slowly, stirring constantly. Reduce the heat and cook for 2½ minutes or until thickened. In a large bowl beat together the eggs, vanilla, sugar, and salt. Add the cream of wheat mixture slowly to the egg mixture and beat well. Serve hot with a dollop of vanilla ice cream and hot berry jam or sauce.
Serves 4.

Hawthorne Inn

462 Lexington Road
Concord, Massachusetts 01742
(508) 369-5610

Situated in the historic area of Concord, the Hawthorne Inn was built in the 1870s on land that once belonged to Ralph Waldo Emerson, the Alcotts, and Nathaniel Hawthorne. The seven rooms—named Emerson, Alcott, Musketequid, Walden, Sleepy Hollow, Punkatasset, and Concord—contain antique furnishings, handmade quilts, wooden floors, and original art. In the common room are numerous books and magazines, along with a warm fire on chilly evenings. Within walking distance are many historic homes and Old North Bridge where the "shot heard round the world" was fired.

Morning Delight

6 eggs
1 cup milk (or ½ cup milk and ½ cup sour cream)
2 cups butter
2 cups sugar
1 teaspoon vanilla extract
1¼ teaspoons baking powder
4 cups all-purpose flour

ᴥ ᴥ ᴥ

3 bananas, mashed
⅓ cup coconut
⅓ cup almonds

Butter and flour 1 large and 1 small bundt pan. In a food processor blend the eggs, milk, butter, sugar, vanilla, and baking powder. Pour the mixture into a large bowl and add the flour, mixing well. Add the bananas, coconut, and almonds. Pour the batter into the prepared pans. Bake in a 350° oven for 1 hour and 15 minutes, or until a toothpick inserted in the center of the large cake comes out clean.

Variations: Instead of bananas, coconut, and almonds, use 3 chopped apples, 1 cup of walnuts, and ½ cup of raisins, or 3 chopped oranges or lemons, or 1½ cups berries.

Serves 16 to 18.

Salty Dog Inn

451 Main Street
Cotuit, Massachusetts 02635
(508) 428-5228

The Salty Dog Inn is a place to escape the stress of the city and step back to the simple pleasures of life. *Yankee* magazine has reported that Main Street is "one of the most beautiful in America."

Originally owned by a sea captain and his family, the inn has spacious and comfortable guest rooms with double, queen- or king-size beds. Guests can experience Cape Cod's attractions in any season, enjoying fine dining, theatre, and shopping at Hyannis and Falmouth, as well as boutiques, artists' colonies, antique shops, or relaxing on the spacious lawn under a 300-year-old oak tree.

Pineapple Noodle Pudding

Can be used as a side dish or luncheon dish.

3 quarts water
1 tablespoon salt
8 ounces medium width egg noodles

ᴥ ᴥ ᴥ

1 pound (2 cups) Ricotta or creamed cottage cheese
1 egg
⅓ cup light brown sugar
½ teaspoon cinnamon
Dash salt
3 tablespoons chopped toasted almonds
1 20-ounce can crushed pineapple, undrained

Grease a 1½-quart casserole dish. In a saucepan bring the water to a boil. Add the salt. Gradually add the noodles so that the water continues to boil. Cook uncovered, stirring occasionally for 5 minutes. (Noodles will still be hard.) Drain. In a large bowl beat together the Ricotta, egg, brown

Hawthorne Inn

sugar, cinnamon, and salt. Add the almonds and noodles, and toss lightly. Turn into the prepared casserole, spreading evenly. Top with the undrained pineapple. Bake in a 350° oven for 40 minutes. Serve warm.

Serves 8.

New England Sole with Chilies

1½ cups stone ground cornmeal
1 cup buttermilk
2 large eggs
3 tablespoons oil
1 4-ounce can chopped green chilies, drained
1 tablespoon sugar
½ teaspoon chili powder
¼ teaspoon salt
1 teaspoon baking soda

🍃 🍃 🍃

1 pound thin skinless sole or flounder fillets, cut into 2 to 3-inch squares
1 16-ounce can tomatoes, drained and chopped
¼ cup chopped fresh parsley
1 teaspoon dried basil leaves
⅛ teaspoon salt
⅛ teaspoon black pepper

Grease a 9x13-inch baking pan. In a large bowl stir together the cornmeal, buttermilk, eggs, oil, chilies, sugar, chili powder, and salt. Stir in the baking soda and mix well. Pour the batter into the prepared pan and spread evenly. Arrange the fillet pieces on top of the batter. Try not to let the fish overlap. Spread chopped tomato over the casserole. Mix the seasonings together and sprinkle over the casserole. Bake in a 425° oven for 18 to 23 minutes. Cut into squares.

Serves 4 to 5.

Cheese Puffs

½ cup butter or margarine, softened
½ teaspoon curry powder
1 teaspoon dry mustard
½ teaspoon salt
1 teaspoon grated onion
2 cups grated Mozzarella cheese
½ cup finely chopped walnuts, toasted
1¼ cups sifted all-purpose flour

In a large bowl cream the butter or margarine together with the curry, mustard, salt, onion, and cheese until well blended. Stir in the walnuts and flour. Roll level tablespoons of dough into balls and place on an ungreased cookie sheet. Bake in a 350° oven for 10 to 15 minutes, until lightly browned. Remove to wire racks. Serve warm or cold.

Makes 2½ dozen.

Lentil Spaghetti Sauce

(Meatless Main Dish)

Serve with spaghetti, Parmesan cheese, and a green salad.

2 cups chopped onion
2 cloves garlic, minced
12 ounces fresh mushrooms, coarsely chopped
2 tablespoons olive oil
1 cup dried lentils, rinsed and picked over
2 cups beef broth or vegetable broth
1 6-ounce can unsalted tomato paste
½ teaspoon oregano
¼ teaspoon basil
¼ teaspoon cayenne pepper
1 teaspoon salt

In a large saucepan sauté the onion, garlic, and mushrooms in oil until tender. Stir in the lentils and broth, and bring to a boil. Reduce the heat, cover, and simmer for 20 to 30 minutes or until the lentils are tender. Stir in the tomato paste and seasonings. Simmer another 10 minutes. Stir occasionally.

Serves 4 to 5.

Cumworth Farm

Rural Route 1, Box 110
Cummington, Massachusetts 01026
(413) 634-5529

A working farm on which sheep are raised and maple syrup and berries are produced in season, 200-year-old Cumworth Farm offers six bedrooms with a choice of continental or American breakfasts. Situated in a lovely country setting, it is close to skiing in the winter and hiking trails in the summer.

Coconut Drops

1 cup sweetened condensed milk
½ pound shredded coconut
Dash salt
1 teaspoon vanilla extract

Grease muffin cups or custard cups. In a large bowl combine all of the ingredients and mix well. Let the mixture sit for the coconut to absorb the milk. Drop from a teaspoon into the prepared baking cups. Bake in a 350° oven for 10 minutes.

Makes 2 dozen.

Deerfield Inn

The Street
Deerfield, Massachusetts 01342
(413) 774-5587

Deerfield Inn, a one-hundred-year-old inn in Old New England style, is in the center of historic Deerfield with its twelve museum houses. It has twenty-three guest rooms, all with private bathrooms. Furnished with many antiques, the inn has two living rooms, one with a fireplace, a fine restaurant, a seasonal coffee shop, and a private dining room for groups. Louis Wynne, Jr., is executive chef of this inn.

Applesauce Walnut Bread

1 cup applesauce
1 cup sugar
¼ cup melted butter
3 egg whites
3 tablespoons milk
2 cups sifted all-purpose flour
1 teaspoon baking soda
1 teaspoon baking powder
½ teaspoon cinnamon
½ teaspoon salt
¼ teaspoon nutmeg
¾ cup chopped walnuts

Grease and flour a 9x5-inch loaf pan. In a large bowl combine the applesauce, sugar, butter, egg whites, and milk. Mix thoroughly. Add the flour, baking soda, baking powder, cinnamon, salt, and nutmeg. Mix until well blended. Fold in the nuts. Pour the batter into the prepared pan. Bake in a 350° oven for 60 to 70 minutes.
Makes 1 loaf.

New England Apple Cheddar Bread

⅔ cup sugar
2 cups self-rising flour
1 teaspoon cinnamon
½ cup chopped cashews, walnuts, or pecans
2 eggs, slightly beaten
½ cup melted butter
½ cup finely chopped and peeled Cortland or Rome apples
½ cup grated Vermont sharp Cheddar cheese
¼ cup milk

Grease a 9x5-inch loaf pan. In a large bowl combine the sugar, flour, cinnamon, and nuts. In a separate bowl combine eggs, butter, apples, cheese, and milk. Add to sugar mixture. Pour into the prepared pan. Bake in a 350° oven for 1 hour. Cover with foil if it gets brown too quickly.
Makes 1 loaf.

Graham Griddle Cakes

1¼ cups milk
1 cup graham flour
½ cup all-purpose flour
1 tablespoon molasses
2 teaspoons baking powder
2 eggs

Scald the milk and pour onto the graham flour. Chill the mixture slightly and add the remaining ingredients. Beat well. Heat and grease a griddle or skillet. Pour the mixture in small amounts onto the hot griddle. Bake until bubbles appear on the surface and the edges are browned. Turn and brown the other side.
Serves 4.

Chocolate Potato Cake

1 medium potato
1½ ounces semi-sweet chocolate
⅔ cup butter
6 tablespoons sugar
2 eggs
1 teaspoon vanilla extract
1½ cups all-purpose flour
1 teaspoon baking powder
½ teaspoon cinnamon
¼ teaspoon nutmeg
⅛ teaspoon salt
½ cup milk
½ cup finely chopped hazelnuts (or almonds, walnuts, or pecans)

❧ ❧ ❧

1 tablespoon egg white
1 cup confectioners' sugar
1 tablespoon cocoa
1½ tablespoons rum

Grease and flour a 9x5-inch loaf pan. Peel the potato, grate coarsely, place in tea towel, and squeeze dry. Set aside. Grate the chocolate, and set aside. Cream the butter and sugar until light. Add the eggs and vanilla. Beat well. Sift together the flour, baking powder, spices, and salt. Add alternately with the milk to the creamed mixture. Add the potato, chocolate,

Deerfield Inn

and nuts, and mix well. Turn into the prepared loaf pan. Bake in a 350° oven for 55 minutes or until a toothpick inserted in the center comes out clean. Cool the cake in the pan for 30 minutes. Turn out onto a wire rack. Beat the egg white with a fork until foamy. Add the confectioners' sugar, cocoa, and rum, and stir until smooth. Spread over the warm cake.

Serves 8.

Raisin and Cottage Cheese Buns

Roll the dough up tightly so the filling inside will not spill out when the cylinder of dough is cut into pieces. Serve these nutritious buns warm with a white icing.

1 cup cottage cheese
3 tablespoons milk
1 egg, separated
⅓ cup oil
⅓ cup sugar
1 cup whole wheat flour
½ cup all-purpose flour
2 teaspoons baking powder

ɗ ɗ ɗ

½ cup raisins
½ cup chopped nuts
5 tablespoons sugar
1 tablespoon cinnamon

Grease a large baking sheet. In a large bowl mix together the cottage cheese, milk, egg yolk, oil, and sugar. Mix the flours and baking powder together and add to the cottage cheese mixture. The mixture will be sticky. Knead on a lightly floured board for only a short time and roll into a 17x8-inch rectangle. Brush with the egg white. Sprinkle with raisins, nuts, sugar, and cinnamon. Roll up to make a long cylinder and cut into 12 pieces. Place in the prepared pan. Bake in a 350° oven for about 25 minutes.

Makes 12 rolls.

Deerfield Inn Caviar Pie

12 eggs, hard boiled
½ cup butter
3 teaspoons prepared mustard
½ teaspoon salt
¼ teaspoon pepper
2 teaspoons cider vinegar

ɗ ɗ ɗ

1 cup chopped green onions

ɗ ɗ ɗ

¾ cup sour cream
10 ounces cream cheese
4 tablespoons chopped pimiento

ɗ ɗ ɗ

Red caviar
Black caviar
Pumpernickel toast

In a food processor combine the eggs, butter, mustard, salt, pepper, and vinegar until smooth. Spread on the bottom of a buttered 8-inch springform pan. Sprinkle with onions. Refrigerate at least 1 hour. Combine the sour cream, cream cheese, and pimiento in the food processor until smooth. Layer on top. Refrigerate for at least 1 hour. When ready to serve, cut into 16 wedges and top with 1 teaspoon each of red and black caviar. Serve with pumpernickel toast slices.

Makes 16 slices.

Isaiah Hall B & B Inn

152 Whig Street
Dennis, Massachusetts 02638
(508) 385-9928

Tucked away on a quiet, historic street, this lovely 1857 farmhouse was originally the home of Isaiah B. Hall, a builder and cooper (barrel maker). A short distance behind the

house, Isaiah's brother Henry cultivated the first cranberry bogs in America.

This house has served as an inn since 1948, with guest rooms in the main house and the carriage house. In this romantic country refuge, guests may choose to relax on a porch rocker, in front of a Victorian parlor stove, or in a converted carriage house with white wicker furniture and knotty pine. Featured in many bed and breakfast books, this inn was chosen as one of the best bed and breakfasts on Cape Cod by *Cape Cod Life* magazine.

Cape Cod Cranberry Bread

¾ cup orange juice
1 beaten egg
2 tablespoons cooking oil
2 cups all-purpose flour
¾ cup sugar
1½ teaspoons baking powder
1 teaspoon salt
½ teaspoon baking soda
1 cup chopped fresh or frozen cranberries
½ cup walnuts

Grease and flour an 8x4-inch loaf pan. In a small bowl combine the juice, egg, and oil. In a large bowl stir together the flour, sugar, baking powder, salt, and baking soda. Add the orange juice mixture, stirring until just moistened. Fold in the cranberries and walnuts. Turn into the prepared pan. Bake in a 350° oven for 50 to 60 minutes or until a wooden pick inserted in the center comes out clean. Cool for 10 minutes and remove from the pan.

Makes 1 loaf, 11 to 12 slices.

The Over Look Inn

3085 County Road
Route 6
Eastham, Cape Cod, Massachusetts 02642
(508) 255-1886
(800) 699-5782 (Massachusetts only)

The Over Look Inn is a restored Victorian sea captain's house in the heart of historic Eastham, the oldest town on Cape Cod. Surrounded by one and one-half acres of tree-filled grounds, the inn has ten bedrooms with private baths, queen-size brass beds, claw-foot bathtubs, wicker, lace, and Victorian furnishings. Guests enjoy tea in the parlor and may play cards or relax with a good book in the "Churchill" library overlooking the front gardens. The Hemingway Room boasts a fine Victorian billiard table for guests' enjoyment.

Hemingway's Spanish Delight

5 eggs
¼ cup all-purpose flour
½ teaspoon baking powder
2 cups cottage cheese
¼ cup butter, melted
2 cups shredded Monterey Jack cheese
1 yellow onion, peeled and chopped
1 tablespoon butter

4 green onions, chopped
½ green pepper, chopped
½ red pepper, chopped
½ cup chopped parsley (or any fresh vegetable)

Lightly grease a 6x9-inch baking dish. In a large bowl whip the eggs until fluffy. Add the flour and baking powder, blending well. Add the cottage cheese, melted butter, and half of the Monterey Jack. In a frying pan sauté the yellow onions in 1 tablespoon of butter until slightly brown. Add the onions to the cottage cheese mixture. Add the green onions, peppers, and parsley. Place the mixture in the prepared baking dish. Top with the remaining cheese. Bake in a 350° oven for 25 minutes, until lightly browned. Cool and cut into squares. Serves 4 to 6.

Brittany Pie

3 eggs
½ teaspoon dry mustard
Few grains cayenne pepper
1½ cups half and half
1 unbaked 9-inch pastry shell
1 6½-ounce can tuna, drained and flaked
2 cups shredded Swiss cheese
1 teaspoon all-purpose flour

In a medium bowl beat the eggs, dry mustard, and cayenne pepper together until foamy. Beat in the half and half. Cover the bottom of the pastry shell with a layer of tuna. Sprinkle half of the cheese over the tuna. Repeat layering. Sprinkle flour over the cheese. Pour the egg mixture over all. Bake in a 400° oven for 35 minutes. Serves 6 to 8.

Lemon Bars

1 cup all-purpose flour
½ cup butter
¼ cup confectioners' sugar

ᴥ ᴥ ᴥ

1 cup sugar
½ teaspoon baking powder
2 tablespoons lemon juice
2 eggs, beaten
½ tablespoon all-purpose flour

Grease a 9-inch square pan. In a small bowl blend 1 cup of flour, the butter, and confectioners' sugar together. Press into the prepared pan. Bake in a 350° oven for 20 minutes.

Combine 1 cup of sugar, the baking powder, lemon juice, eggs, and ½ tablespoon of flour. Pour over the baked crust. Bake in a 350° oven for 25 minutes. Cool and cut into bars.

Makes 9 to 12 squares.

Chili

1 pound minced beef
1 green pepper, diced
2 onions, chopped
1 10½-ounce can tomato soup
1 16-ounce can kidney beans
3 tablespoons vinegar
1 teaspoon sugar
½ teaspoon ginger
1½ teaspoons chili powder
1½ teaspoons cinnamon
1½ teaspoons nutmeg
1½ teaspoons curry powder

ᴥ ᴥ ᴥ

1 apple, diced

In a frying pan brown the beef. Drain the meat and set aside. In the same pan sauté the peppers and onions until soft. Remove the grease from the pan and add the remaining ingredients, except the apples. Simmer over medium heat for 45 minutes. Add the apples and continue to simmer for 15 more minutes. Best if made ahead and reheated.

Serves 4.

The Nauset House Inn

Beach Road
Post Office Box 774
East Orleans, Massachusetts 02643
(617) 255-2195

The Nauset House Inn is a place where the gentle amenities of life are still observed. It is a quiet place removed from the cares of the workaday world, where sea and shore, orchard and field all combine to create a perfect setting for tranquil relaxation. Family-owned and operated, the Nauset House Inn, near one of the world's great ocean beaches, is also close to all those things for which Cape Cod is famous: quaint antique and craft shops, sophisticated restaurants and remarkable art galleries, scenic paths, and remote places for sunning, swimming, and picnicking.

The inn has fourteen cozy guest rooms (most with private bath), old-fashioned country breakfasts, and, among other surprises, a unique turn-of-the-century conservatory filled with plants and flowers and comfortable wicker furniture. Most important is the inn's warm and intimate atmosphere that is sure to delight and make the time spent there truly memorable.

Oatmeal Butterscotch Muffins

1 18-ounce box regular rolled oats
1 quart buttermilk
1 pound dark brown sugar
1½ cups margarine, melted and
    cooled
6 eggs, slightly beaten

3 cups all-purpose flour
4 teaspoons baking powder
1 teaspoon salt
1½ teaspoons baking soda
1½ cups butterscotch chips

Grease muffin cups. In a large bowl combine the oats and buttermilk. Mix well. Crumble the brown sugar over the top. Let stand for 1 hour. Combine the margarine and eggs, and set aside. Sift together the flour, baking powder, salt, and baking soda. Add the margarine and eggs to the oats, mixing well. Stir in the flour mixture and butterscotch chips. Spoon the batter into the prepared muffin cups, filling ⅔ full. Bake in a 400° oven for 15 to 20 minutes. Freezes well.

Makes 3 dozen.

Point Way Inn

Main Street and Pease's Point Way
Box 128
Edgartown, Massachusetts 02539
(508) 627-8633

This charming 150-year-old sea captain's house on Martha's Vineyard boasts fifteen guest rooms and eleven fireplaces. As a seaport inn it reflects the innkeepers' sailing experiences, with the walls of the reception area papered with charts previously used on family cruises and pictures of family boats throughout and sailing trophies in the breakfast room. All the guest rooms have private baths and full-length mirrors; some of the rooms have canopied four-poster beds, working fireplaces, and French doors opening onto private balconies. In the evening guests find a decanter of sherry in their rooms and their beds turned down when they return from dinner. Many guests have been challenged by the five-hundred-piece custom-made wooden jigsaw puzzle. Croquet is set up at all times on the large lawn, and lemonade and cookies are served every summer afternoon in the garden gazebo. The innkeepers' zest for their work makes this an unusual inn indeed.

Orange-Caraway Bread

4¼ cups all-purpose flour
4 teaspoons baking powder
1 teaspoon salt
½ cup butter
½ cup grated orange peel
2 eggs
3 tablespoons caraway seeds
1 cup orange juice
1½ cups milk
1 cup sugar

Grease 3 small loaf pans. In a large bowl combine the flour, baking powder, and salt. Cut in the butter. In a separate bowl combine the orange peel, eggs, caraway seeds, orange juice, milk, and sugar. Blend into the dry ingredients. Pour the batter into the prepared pans. Bake in a 350° oven for 55 to 60 minutes.

Makes 3 small loaves.

Oatmeal Cookies

1⅓ cups all-purpose flour
½ teaspoon salt
1 teaspoon baking soda
1 cup butter, melted
1 cup brown sugar
½ cup sugar
1 egg
2 teaspoons vanilla extract
¼ cup water
3 cups oats
½ cup raisins

Heavily grease a large cookie sheet. In a large bowl combine the flour, salt, and baking soda. In a separate bowl combine the butter and sugars. Add the egg and vanilla. Mix until light and fluffy. Add the dry ingredients alternately with water. Stir in the oats and raisins. Drop by rounded teaspoons onto the greased cookie sheet. Bake in a 375° oven for 10 to 11 minutes. Cool on paper towels.

Makes about 5 dozen.

Point Way Inn

Village Green Inn

40 West Main Street
Falmouth, Massachusetts 02540
(508) 548-5621

Elegant accommodations, nineteenth century charm, and warm hospitality await guests at this gracious old Victorian inn. The tastefully appointed guest rooms offer private baths and uniquely designed fireplaces. Afternoon sherry or lemonade may be enjoyed on the two large open porches overlooking the wellgroomed lawns that surround the inn and carriage house. The full breakfasts include such specialties as a hot spiced fruit dish, apple-plum crumble, or a fresh ambrosia.

Village Green Inn Frittata

1 16-ounce can sliced potatoes, drained
1 cup chopped ham
3 tablespoons minced onion
¼ teaspoon crushed thyme
2 tablespoons oil
8 eggs
⅓ cup milk
1 teaspoon parsley
¼ teaspoon pepper
¼ cup shredded Cheddar cheese

In a 10-inch skillet toss together the potatoes, ham, onion, thyme, and oil. Spread evenly over the bottom of pan and cook 10 minutes on low. In a small bowl beat together the eggs, milk, parsley, and pepper. Pour over the hot potato mixture. Cover and cook over low heat for 8 to 10 minutes, until set but glossy and moist. Sprinkle the cheese over the top and broil until the cheese is melted and bubbly. Cut into wedges and serve.

Serves 6.

Ham and Egg Roll

5 eggs, separated
2 tablespoons butter
2 tablespoons Parmesan cheese
4 tablespoons all-purpose flour
6 tablespoons sour cream
Pinch nutmeg
Salt and pepper to taste

෨ ෨ ෨

3 tablespoons sour cream
½ pound finely ground ham
2 tablespoons Parmesan cheese

෨ ෨ ෨

6 tablespoons butter
¼ cup all-purpose flour
½ teaspoon dry mustard
½ teaspoon salt
¼ teaspoon pepper
2 cups milk
1 cup shredded Cheddar cheese
1½ to 2 teaspoons dill

Butter and flour a jelly-roll pan. In a medium bowl beat the egg whites until stiff and set aside. Cream 2 tablespoons of butter with the egg yolks, 2 tablespoons of Parmesan cheese, 4 tablespoons of flour, 6 tablespoons of sour cream, the nutmeg, salt, and

Village Green Inn

pepper. Fold into the beaten whites. Spread the egg mixture in the prepared pan. Bake in a 350° oven for 12 to 15 minutes.

Place the cooked egg mixture on a damp kitchen towel. While still hot, spread with 3 tablespoons of sour cream. Sprinkle with ham and 2 tablespoons of Parmesan cheese. Roll like a jelly roll. Bake in a 350° oven for 5 more minutes.

Melt 6 tablespoons of butter and stir in 4 tablespoons of flour, the mustard, salt, and pepper. Bubble and stir for 1 minute. Remove from the heat and slowly stir in the milk. Return to the stove and stir constantly until the mixture begins to boil. Add the Cheddar cheese and dill, and stir over low heat until melted.

Slice the roll into 6 pieces and serve with the cheese-dill sauce.

Serves 6.

Nutmeg Muffins

2 cups all-purpose flour
1½ cups brown sugar
¾ cup butter
1 cup all-purpose flour
2 teaspoons baking powder
2 teaspoons nutmeg
½ teaspoon baking soda
½ teaspoon salt
2 eggs, slightly beaten
1 cup buttermilk

Grease or line muffin cups with paper liners. In a large bowl mix 2 cups of flour and the brown sugar. Cut in the butter until the mixture resembles cornmeal. Reserve ¾ cup for topping. Add the remaining ingredients and stir until just moistened. Spoon into the prepared muffin tins, filling ⅔ full. Top each muffin with 1½ teaspoons of topping. Bake in a 350° oven for 20 minutes.

Makes 18.

🐦 🐦 🐦 🐦 🐦

Seekonk Pines Inn

142 Seekonk Cross Road
Great Barrington, Massachusetts 01230
(413) 528-4192

Seekonk Pines began its life in 1832 when a man named Horace Church built a frame farmhouse, which was later enlarged to accommodate a growing family. Today it consists of seven guest rooms, two with private baths, decorated with period furnishings and antique quilts. The commons room has a large fireplace, piano, color television, and library. A large swimming pool is available for guests' use. The full country breakfast, which changes daily, includes such specialties as puffed German pancakes, corn pudding, quiche, whole grain pancakes, and French toast.

Seekonk Pines Corn Pudding

3 cups corn scraped off cob
6 egg yolks
1½ cups lowfat milk
1½ tablespoons all-purpose flour
1 tablespoon maple syrup
1 teaspoon salt
½ teaspoon pepper
6 stiffly beaten egg whites
½ cup grated Cheddar cheese

In a blender or food processor combine the first 7 ingredients and blend thoroughly. Transfer to a large bowl and gently fold in the egg whites and grated cheese. Pour the batter into a large soufflé dish or 2 smaller ones. Bake in a 350° oven for 35 to 45 minutes until set and golden.

Serves 9 to 10.

Multi-grain Nut Pancakes

2 cups brown rice flour
2 cups oat flour
2 cups rye flour
1 cup ground hazelnuts
8 teaspoons baking powder

🍂 🍂 🍂

6 eggs, separated
¼ cup oil (we use canola, a mono-unsaturated oil)
1 tablespoon vanilla extract
6 tablespoons maple syrup
1 quart nonfat buttermilk
1 pint lowfat milk

In a large bowl combine all of the dry ingredients. In a separate bowl beat the egg whites until stiff. Add the yolks, oil, vanilla, and maple syrup. Pour the egg mixture and the buttermilk into the dry mixture. Add some or all of the milk to adjust the consistency of the batter so it will just "run" when dropped on the griddle. Blend the batter with as few strokes as possible. (I use a large egg whisk which blends quickly without whipping.) Heat a griddle and lightly coat with oil (for the first batch only). Drop the batter onto the hot griddle. Turn when the edges began to look dry.

Makes approximately 60 pancakes.

Seekonk Pines Inn

The Larches

97 Chatham Road
Harwich, Massachusetts 02645
(508) 432-0150

The Larches is a charming 1835 Greek Revival house with an added contemporary wing. Surrounded by large flower and vegetable gardens, the house is close to swimming, bike trails, art galleries, theater, and summer stock. A continental breakfast is served in gracious surroundings, on the patio if preferred.

Ham Loaf

2 pounds ground ham
2 pounds ground pork
2 cups graham cracker crumbs
3 eggs
1½ cups milk

🍂 🍂 🍂

1 10½-ounce can tomato soup
½ cup water
1 tablespoon dry mustard
½ cup vinegar
1 cup brown sugar

In a large bowl combine the first 5 ingredients and mix well. Form into 2 loaves and place in 2 loaf pans. Combine the remaining ingredients to make a sauce. Baste the loaves with sauce. Bake in a 325° oven for 45 minutes or until done. Serve the remaining sauce as a gravy.

Serves 10 to 12.

The Inn on Bank Street

88 Bank Street
Harwich Port, Massachusetts 02646
(508) 432-3206

The Inn on Bank Street is a bed and breakfast facility in the center of Harwich Port on Cape Cod, a five-minute walk from the ocean and also close to restaurants, stores, galleries, and antique shops. Its six sunny guest rooms have private entrances; all have private baths. A peaceful atmosphere prevails, with gulls the only sound heard in the mornings. The cozy living room and library with piano, television, and fireplace are for guests' enjoyment. A leisurely breakfast is served on the sun porch: fresh-ground coffee, fruit, juice, granola, homemade bread or muffins (served with cheerful stories and jokes).

The Big Chocolate Cookie

½ cup butter
1½ cups sugar
2 eggs
2 ounces unsweetened chocolate, melted
1 cup sour cream
1 teaspoon vanilla extract

2¾ cups all-purpose flour
½ teaspoon baking soda
½ teaspoon baking powder
½ teaspoon salt

🐚 🐚 🐚

2 tablespoons butter
2 ounces unsweetened chocolate, melted
3 cups sifted confectioners' sugar
1 teaspoon (or more) milk

Grease a baking sheet. In a large bowl cream together ½ cup of butter and the sugar. Add the eggs and beat well. Add 2 ounces of chocolate, the sour cream, and vanilla and beat well. Mix in the flour, baking soda, baking powder, and salt. Chill for 1 hour. Drop on a greased baking sheet by big rounded teaspoons. Bake in a 425° oven for 8 minutes. Combine the remaining ingredients and frost the cookies.

Makes 55 cookies.

The Inn on Sea Street

358 Sea Street
Hyannis, Massachusetts 02601
(508) 775-8030

The Inn on Sea Street is a small, elegant Victorian inn situated a few steps from the beach on Nantucket Sound. This 1850 home has been restored and furnished with period pieces selected for comfort and utility. Situated near shops, churches, night life, outdoor sports, restaurants, the ferry to the islands, and other facilities, it is an ideal spot from which to launch one's exploration of Cape Cod.

🐚 🐚 🐚 🐚 🐚

Crab Scramble

¼ cup butter
9 eggs, beaten
½ cup milk
1 8-ounce package cream cheese, cubed
1 6½-ounce can crab meat
½ teaspoon salt
¼ teaspoon pepper
1 tablespoon chopped fresh baby dill

In a 7x12-inch pan melt the butter. In a large bowl combine the eggs, milk, cream cheese, crab meat, salt, and pepper. Pour the mixture over the melted butter and sprinkle with dill. Bake in a 350° oven for 30 minutes.

Serves 6 to 8.

The Harbor Light Inn

58 Washington Street
Marblehead, Massachusetts 01945
(617) 631-2186

The Harbor Light Inn is an elegant four-star inn situated in the heart of the historic district. Each room is furnished with eighteenth-century antiques, many featuring canopy beds, fireplaces, or Jacuzzis and all with private baths and air conditioning. The continental breakfast features homemade breads, muffins, and sweet rolls. Situated one block from Marblehead's bustling yacht harbor, the inn is within easy walking distance of many fine shops, restaurants, and art galleries.

Tootsie's Fluffy Rolls

1 ¼-ounce package active dry yeast
⅓ cup warm water (110° to 115°)
Pinch sugar
1 cup mik, scalded
⅓ cup sugar
⅓ cup margarine or butter
1 egg, beaten
4 cups all-purpose flour
½ cup margarine or butter, melted

Dissolve the yeast in the water and add a pinch of sugar. In a separate bowl mix together the hot milk, sugar, and ⅓ cup of margarine. When warm, add the yeast and beaten egg. Stir in the flour and mix until blended. The dough will be wet. Let the dough rise 1 hour or until double. Knead the dough for 5 minutes and then roll to ½-inch thickness. Cut into rolls with a drinking glass. Dip the rolls in ½ cup of melted butter. Let the rolls rise again for 1 hour or until double. Bake in a 350° oven for 20 to 25 minutes until golden brown.

Makes about 1 dozen rolls.

Great-Grandmother's Fruit Cake

2 cups sugar
2 cups cold water
1 pound raisins with seeds
1 pound seedless raisins
1 6-ounce jar mixed candied fruit
1 10-ounce jar grape jelly
½ cup nuts
3 tablespoons butter

🐚 🐚 🐚

3½ cups sifted all-purpose flour
½ teaspoon baking powder
1 teaspoon cloves
1 teaspoon allspice
1 teaspoon cinnamon
½ teaspoon salt
2 eggs, beaten

Grease 2 large or 4 small loaf pans. In a large kettle combine the sugar, cold

The Harbor Light Inn

The Carlisle House Inn

26 North Water Street
Nantucket, Massachusetts 02554
(508) 228-0720

This beautiful 220-year-old sea captain's home has been carefully restored with great attention to detail. It now boasts working fireplaces, authentic pine flooring, antiques, private baths, cozy rooms, and canopy beds. A complimentary continental breakfast is served on the verandah, which features white wicker furniture.

water, raisins, candied fruit, grape jelly, nuts, and butter. Bring the mixture to a boil and boil for 5 minutes, stirring constantly. Allow the mixture to cool.

Sift the flour with the baking powder, cloves, allspice, cinnamon, and salt. Add the dry ingredients and the eggs to the fruit mixture, blending well. Pour the batter into the prepared pans. Bake in a 300° oven for 2 hours or until done.

Serves 16.

Rijstpap
(Flemish style "Rice Milk")

1 cup water
1 teaspoon salt
½ cup rice (not instant)
1 quart milk
1 teaspoon cinnamon
⅓ stick vanilla (or 2 teaspoons vanilla extract)
⅛ teaspoon saffron powder
3 tablespoons sugar

Wash the rice thoroughly. Bring the water and salt to a rolling boil. Add the rice and boil for 5 minutes. Add ½ quart of milk, the cinnamon, and vanilla stick (if using vanilla flavoring, it will be added later). Reduce heat and bring to a slow boil. Add the remaining milk and saffron. Simmer for 1 hour, stirring constantly (rice milk will stick and burn very easily) until the mixture thickens and the rice is soft (consistency should be that of cooked pudding). Add the sugar and vanilla extract, if used, during the last 3 minutes of cooking. Pour the rice milk into custard cups and chill. Serve with brown sugar.

Serves 6.

English Plum Pudding with Hard Sauce

1 cup all-purpose flour
½ cup sugar
1 teaspoon baking powder
1 teaspoon cinnamon
½ teaspoon allspice
1 teaspoon salt
½ teaspoon cloves

❰ ❰ ❰

1 cup suet, finely chopped
3 eggs, well beaten
1 cup molasses
1 cup Drambuie

❰ ❰ ❰

3½ cups seedless raisins
½ cup orange or lemon peel, finely chopped
½ cup chopped almonds
1½ cups bread crumbs

❰ ❰ ❰

5 tablespoons butter
1 cup confectioners' sugar
⅛ teaspoon salt
1 teaspoon vanilla extract (or 1 tablespoon rum or brandy)
¼ cup heavy cream

Butter a 1-quart pudding mold. In a large bowl mix the dry ingredients. In a separate large bowl combine the suet, eggs, molasses, and Drambuie. Combine the fruit and nuts and sift the flour, spices, and baking powder over them. Add the floured fruits and nuts and bread crumbs to the liquid ingredients. Pour the mixture into the prepared mold. Cover the mold with foil and tie with string. Place the mold on a rack in a deep kettle. Add 1 inch of boiling water. Cover and steam for 4 to 6 hours, adding water if necessary. Cool for 10 minutes. Unmold and serve warm with Hard Sauce (see below).

In a small bowl cream the butter until soft. Gradually beat in the sugar until well blended. Add the salt and vanilla, blending well. Beat in the cream until smooth. Chill thoroughly. Serve over the warm pudding.

If desired, pour slightly heated Drambuie over the pudding, ignite, and bring flaming to the table.

Serves 4 to 6.

The
CARLISLE
HOUSE
INN

1765

Carrot Nut Loaf

1⅓ cups cold water
1⅓ cups sugar
1 cup grated carrots
1 cup raisins
1 teaspoon cinnamon
1 teaspoon nutmeg
¼ teaspoon cloves
¼ cup butter
2 cups all-purpose flour
1 teaspoon baking powder
1 teaspoon baking soda
½ teaspoon salt
½ cup walnuts

Grease a 9x5-inch loaf pan. In a large saucepan combine the cold water, sugar, carrots, raisins, cinnamon, nutmeg, cloves, and melted butter. Bring the mixture to a boil and boil for 5 minutes. Allow the mixture to cool.

In a large bowl combine the flour, baking powder, baking soda, salt, and walnuts. Fold the dry ingredients into the carrot mixture and blend well. Pour the batter into the prepared pan. Bake in a 350° oven for 1 hour.

Makes 1 loaf, or 8 servings.

Century House

10 Cliff Road
Post Office Box 603
Nantucket, Massachusetts 02554
(617) 228-0530

This restored 1833 Late Federal-style sea captain's mansion in the historic district is but a short walk to Jetties Beach, Steamboat Wharf, and Main Street. Most of the rooms have private bathrooms, and six enjoy the charm of old fireplaces. Each features its own distinctive view of the town. The parlor is the visual and social focal point of the inn. The overall decor is in the Laura Ashley style. In addition to the main house, there are two guest cottages with kitchen facilities, ample amenities, and outstanding views.

Mom's Nantucket Cranberry Tea Bread

Peel of 1 orange, grated
½ cup orange juice
3 tablespoons oil (Wesson oil is fine)
Water
2 eggs, well beaten
1 cup sugar
  ❧ ❧ ❧
2 cups all-purpose flour
½ teaspoon salt
1½ teaspoons baking powder
½ teaspoon baking soda
  ❧ ❧ ❧
1 cup nuts, chopped
1 cup cranberries, chopped

Grease and flour a 9x5-inch loaf pan. In a 1-cup measuring cup combine the grated peel, orange juice and oil. Add enough water to measure ¾ cup of liquid. In a large mixing bowl combine the eggs and sugar. Add the liquid. Sift the dry ingredients and blend with the liquid mixture. Add the nuts and cranberries. Pour the batter into the prepared pan. Bake in a 325° oven for 1 hour.

Makes 1 loaf.

The Four Chimneys

38 Orange Street
Nantucket Island, Massachusetts 02554
(508) 228-1912

In the heart of Nantucket Island's unique historic district, the Four Chimneys is on famed Orange Street, where 126 sea captains built their mansions and is just a short, picturesque walk from cobblestoned Main Street. Five original "master rooms" have been authentically restored and furnished with period antiques, canopy beds, and Oriental rugs. Each of these traditional four-square rooms has its original fireplace, and one has its own porch. Other rooms are done in a more casual, country style.

The Four Chimneys

Pumpkin Walnut Loaf

1¼ cups brown sugar
¾ cup walnut oil
2 cups pumpkin purée
4 eggs

🍃 🍃 🍃

4 cups wheat or rye flour
4 teaspoons baking powder
1 teaspoon baking soda
1 teaspoon cinnamon
½ teaspoon ginger
1 teaspoon nutmeg or mace

🍃 🍃 🍃

3 apples, shredded
1½ cups walnuts
Dates (optional)

Grease two 9x5-inch loaf pans. In a large bowl blend the sugar, oil, pumpkin, and eggs together. In a separate bowl mix the dry ingredients. Add ⅓ of the flour mixture at a time into the pumpkin mixture, beating well after each addition. Add the apples, walnuts, and dates. Fill the prepared pans ½ full. Bake in a 350° oven for 45 minutes.

Makes 2 loaves.

The Farmhouse at Nauset Beach

163 Beach Road
Orleans, Massachusetts 02653
(508) 255-6654

The Farmhouse at Nauset Beach is a nineteenth-century farmhouse that has been carefully restored and furnished. Guests enjoy a blend of country life in a seashore setting. Some rooms have an ocean view, and it is just a short walk to the Nauset Beach.

Banana-Cherry Peaches Marmalade

10 peaches
4 bananas
1 cup red Maraschino cherries, chopped
2 1¾-ounce packages Sure Jell
8 cups sugar

Mash the fruit well and place in a saucepan. Add the Sure Jell and sugar. Bring to a boil and boil for 4 minutes. Skim. Pour into 16 small jars and seal.

Makes 16 small (8-ounce) jars.

Grandmother Standish's Grape Nut Pudding

1 quart milk, scalded
1 cup Grape Nuts
1 cup sugar

4 eggs, beaten
Salt
Vanilla extract or lemon flavoring

Butter a casserole dish. In a large bowl combine the hot milk and Grape Nuts. Cool. Add the sugar, eggs, salt, and flavoring. Pour the mixture into the buttered dish. Bake in a 350° oven for 20 minutes or until set, like a custard.

Serves 6 to 8.

Chalet d'Alicia

East Windsor Road
Peru, Massachusetts 01235
(413) 655-8292

Situated high in the Berkshire Hills, Chalet d'Alicia offers a majestic view of the surrounding countryside. Open year-round, the inn offers three rooms, one with a private bath, and guests enjoy a full breakfast in a comfortable country kitchen. Ponds for swimming, hiking and cross country skiing trails, and a hot tub for relaxing are just part of the experience. During the Berkshire seasons accommodations in the area can be difficult to find, so call early.

Chalet d'Alicia Strata

8 slices white bread, crust trimmed
off, cut into triangles
8 ounces Cheddar cheese, sliced
½ cup diced ham
¼ cup diced onion
6 eggs
3 cups milk
Salt
½ cup butter or margarine, melted
1 teaspoon prepared mustard

Grease a 9-inch square baking dish. Set the triangles of bread aside. Fit the remaining scraps in the greased dish. Lay the slices of cheese on top of the bread. Sprinkle the ham and onions on top. Place the bread triangles on top of everything. Whip the remaining ingredients together and pour over all. Refrigerate overnight. Bake in a 350° oven for 1 hour. Allow to stand 5 minutes before serving.

Serves 8.

Winterwood at Petersham

North Main Street
Petersham, Massachusetts 01366
(508) 724-8885

Just off the Common in the historical district of Petersham is Winterwood, a lovely Greek Revival mansion that was built as a summer home in 1842 and is now on the National Register of Historic Homes. Radiating a hospitable, congenial atmosphere, it is a good place to relax, enjoy a good book, or perhaps indulge in a luxurious bubblebath. Every effort is made to make the guest as comfortable and as pampered as possible.

A lovely staircase leads overnight guests to their accommodations on the second floor, where there are five guest rooms, one a two-room suite with twin fireplaces. Each bedchamber is furnished with antiques. All have maintained their distinctive personalities and include a private bath. Most have working fireplaces.

French Raspberry Bread Pudding

10 cups cubed French (not
sourdough) bread (1-inch
squares)
1 tablespoon cinnamon
1½ cups butter, melted
10 eggs
2 pints whipping cream
1 cup sugar
2½ teaspoons vanilla extract

❧ ❧ ❧

1 cup seedless raspberry jam
2 tablespoons Chambord

❧ ❧ ❧

2 cups whipping cream
4 tablespoons sugar

Butter a 9x13-inch glass baking dish. Place the bread on a cookie sheet. Bake in a 300° oven for 40 minutes or until dry. In a large bowl toss the bread, cinnamon, and butter. Transfer to the prepared baking dish. In a large bowl beat the eggs, 2 pints of whipping cream, 1 cup of sugar, and the vanilla thoroughly. Pour over the bread. Bake in a 375° oven for about 50 minutes until a toothpick inserted in the center comes out clean.

In a small pan over medium-low heat melt the jam. Stir in the Chambord. Cool. Remove the pudding from the oven and set on a cooling rack. Using a pastry brush, spread the raspberry jam mixture over the top of the pudding. Cool to room temperature.

In a large bowl beat 2 cups of whipping cream and 4 tablespoons sugar to soft peaks. Serve over the pudding.

Variation: Serve the pudding slightly warm in glass bowls. Pour Chambord over the pudding, top with whipped cream, and garnish with raspberries.

Serves 10.

❧ ❧ ❧ ❧ ❧

Bed 'n B'fast

44 Commercial Street
Provincetown, Massachusetts 02657
(508) 487-9555

This Greek Revival house of the 1850s was built as a duplex with a common front door and front stairway. Today it is an intimate small bed and breakfast with rooms and apartments, a common room with television, VCR, records, tapes, and a small library.

Situated between Provincetown and the beach, Bed 'n B'fast has more or less staked out its portion of Herring Cove Beach along the sand dunes. Here guests can walk hand in hand, watching seals popping up out of the surf, whales blowing in the distance, and the fleet returning at sunset. In town are more than seventy restaurants catering to every taste, as well as shops, galleries, and museums.

Linguica Cheese Omelet

4 jumbo eggs
2 tablespoons water
2 tablespoons chopped onion
2 tablespoons green pepper
1 tablespoon butter
2 tablespoons chopped Linguica
(Portuguese sweet sausage)
1 tablespoon chopped Swiss cheese
1 tablespoon chopped sharp
Cheddar cheese

In a small bowl combine the eggs and water and beat well. In a sauté pan sauté the onion and pepper in butter. Add the Linguica and cook a few moments until the sausage is heated through. Pour the beaten eggs over the mixture. Add the chopped cheese mixture to ½ of the omelet. Lift that side with a spatula and let the uncooked egg run under, continuing until nearly done. Fold over half of the omelet and transfer to a warm plate.
Serves 2.

Bed 'n B'fast Clam Puffs

1 8-ounce package cream cheese, softened
1 teaspoon parsley flakes
1 tablespoon finely chopped onion (optional)
Few drops Tabasco (optional)
½ pint chopped clams, or more to taste, drained
1 package Old-Fashioned Common crackers
Paprika

In a medium bowl blend the cream cheese, parsley, onion, Tabasco, and clams. Split the Common crackers with your fingers, and top each half with generous amount of puff mixture. Place on a cookie sheet and sprinkle with paprika. Broil until the mixture browns. Serve immediately.
Serves 12.

Eden Pines Inn

Eden Road
Rockport, Massachusetts 01966
(508) 546-2505

Eden Pines Inn is directly on the ocean, one mile from the picturesque town of Rockport. Built around the turn of the century, it has been an inn for nearly forty-five years. It has six bedrooms, all with private baths, decorated in pale, restful shades. All have sitting areas, and some have private decks overlooking the ocean. The scene of Thacher's Island and Loblolly Cove is especially delightful in the morning when the lobstermen haul their traps. A large brick deck ablaze with flowers frames the view. Breakfast is served on the enclosed porch overlooking the ocean. Provisions are made for enjoying coffee and tea throughout the day and drinks before dinner. During cooler weather, a large granite fireplace that graces the comfortably appointed living room is lighted.

Eden Pines Apple Cake

¾ cup sugar
1½ cups unbleached all-purpose flour
½ teaspoon baking powder
1 teaspoon baking soda
½ cup butter
½ cup milk, divided
1 egg
2 cups coarsely chopped apples

≈ ≈ ≈

½ cup light brown sugar
¾ teaspoon cinnamon
1 tablespoon butter, softened
¼ cup chopped nuts

Lightly grease an 8-inch square baking pan. In a large mixing bowl sift the dry ingredients together. Add the butter and ¼ cup of milk and beat at low speed for 2 minutes. Add the egg and beat 1 minute. Add the remaining ¼ cup milk and beat 1 minute more. Fold in the apples. Spread in the prepared pan. Combine the remaining ingredients and sprinkle over the batter. Bake in a 350° oven for 35 to 40 minutes.
Serves 6.

The Inn on Cove Hill

37 Mount Pleasant Street
Rockport, Massachusetts 01966
(508) 546-2701

Rockport is a small New England seaport town with stately colonial homes, a dramatic rocky coastline, and white picket fences festooned with pastel beach roses. Behind one of those fences is the Inn on Cove Hill, a gracious Federal-style home, just one block from one of the most picturesque harbors in New England. The inn was built in 1791 from the proceeds of pirates' gold found at nearby Gully Point. Many of the decorative and architectural features of this authentic colonial home have been carefully preserved or restored, providing guests the opportunity to stay in one of the few truly historical inns of Rockport.

Orange Buttermilk Muffins

6 tablespoons shortening
½ cup sugar
1 egg
2 cups all-purpose flour
1 teaspoon baking powder
1 teaspoon baking soda
Dash salt
½ orange with peel
1 cup buttermilk

Grease 8 large or 12 small muffin tins. In a large bowl cream together the shortening and sugar. Add the egg and beat well. Combine the dry ingredients and add to the creamed mixture. In a blender combine the orange and buttermilk. Process and add to the batter, mixing only until all ingredients are just moistened. Pour the batter into the prepared muffin tins. Bake in a 400° oven for 20 to 25 minutes.

Makes 8 large or 12 small muffins.

Pumpkin Muffins

¾ cup sugar
¼ cup vegetable oil
2 eggs
¾ cup canned or fresh cooked pumpkin
¼ cup water
1½ cups all-purpose flour
¾ teaspoon baking powder
½ teaspoon baking soda
¼ teaspoon cloves
½ teaspoon cinnamon
¼ teaspoon nutmeg
½ teaspoon salt

Grease 8 large or 12 small muffin tins. In a large bowl combine the sugar and oil. Add the eggs and beat well. Blend in the pumpkin and water. Combine the dry ingredients and add to the creamed mixture. Mix only until all ingredients are just moistened. Pour the batter into the prepared muffin tins. Bake in a 400° oven for 20 to 25 minutes.

Makes 8 large or 12 small muffins.

Moist Bran Muffins

1 cup buttermilk
¼ fresh lemon with peel
1 cup bran
½ cup oatmeal
⅓ cup oil
1 egg
⅔ cup brown sugar
½ teaspoon vanilla extract
½ cup raisins or dates
1 cup all-purpose flour
1 teaspoon baking soda
1 teaspoon baking powder
½ teaspoon salt

Grease 8 large or 12 small muffin tins. In a blender combine the buttermilk and lemon and process. In a large bowl combine the buttermilk mixture, bran, oatmeal, oil, and egg. Add

The Inn on Cove Hill

the sugar, vanilla, and raisins. Combine the dry ingredients and add to creamed mixture. Mix only until all ingredients are just moistened. Pour the batter into the prepared muffin tins. Bake in a 400° oven for 20 to 25 minutes.

Makes 8 large or 12 small muffins.

Old Farm Inn

291 Granite Street
Rockport, Massachusetts 01966
(508) 546-3237

Situated at the northernmost tip of Cape Ann, the Old Farm Inn is thought to have been constructed in 1799. In 1936 Naomi Babson's novel *The Yankee Bodleys* was based on the lives of people who lived here in the 1830s. Today it is a cozy country inn set in peaceful surroundings that provides the amenities of modern living. The innkeepers say, "We are not a museum filled with delicate antiques, so we encourage you to kick off your shoes and relax for a moment" with other guests in the sitting room. Halibut Point, only a few minutes' walk from the inn, has been called one of the most beautiful places in the world. From there, on a clear day you can see all the way to Maine while viewing the spectacular rock shelves and wild oceanfront that make the point a nature lover's paradise.

Creamy Garlic Soup

When we had our restaurant, this was one of our most popular soups. It was printed in *Bon Appetit's* reader request column, and my friends beg me to make it when I invite them to dinner.

¼ cup butter
1½ cups chopped white onion
½ cup chopped garlic
½ cup all-purpose flour
7 cups strong beef broth
1 cup dry white wine or vermouth
½ cup sour cream
½ teaspoon fresh grated nutmeg
Seasoned croutons and chives for garnish

In a saucepan melt the butter and sauté the onion and garlic until soft. Stir in the flour and cook for 3 minutes stirring constantly. Add the broth and wine. Bring to a boil, then reduce the heat and simmer for 20 minutes. Remove and cool to lukewarm. Purée in batches and return to the pan. Stir in the sour cream and nutmeg, and reheat but do not boil. Garnish with seasoned croutons and/ or chives if you prefer.

Serves 8 to 10.

Shoofly Coffeecake

I grew up in Pennsylvania where it is common to have Amish Shoofly Pie for breakfast. This is a wonderful variation.

4 cups all-purpose flour
2 cups brown sugar
¾ cup Crisco shortening
1 teaspoon salt
1 teaspoon vanilla extract
2 cups boiling water
1 heaping cup molasses
1 tablespoon baking soda

Grease and flour a 9x13-inch pan. In a large bowl combine the flour, brown sugar, shortening, salt, and vanilla, using a pastry blender until well blended. Remove 1 cup of crumbs and

reserve. In a separate bowl stir together the boiling water, molasses, and baking soda (this will foam up when baking soda is added). Pour into the dry mixture and stir well until smooth (I use a whisk to blend). Pour into the prepared pan. Sprinkle with the reserved crumbs. Bake in a 350° oven for 45 minutes.

Serves 18 to 24.

Old-fashioned Fried Mush

Serve with butter and maple syrup.

1½ cups yellow cornmeal
1½ teaspoons salt
3 tablespoons all-purpose flour
Shortening

Butter a 9x5-inch loaf pan. Heat 4½ cups water to boiling and hold. In a medium bowl combine the cornmeal and salt. Quickly stir 1½ cups of cold water into the dry mixture until smooth. Immediately mix the cold batter into the boiling water and return to boiling. Stir and cook until the mush thickens. Cover the pan, lower the heat to simmer, and cook for 10 minutes. Turn into the prepared pan and cover with a loose piece of waxed paper (to allow the excess moisture to escape). Let cool and store in the refrigerator overnight. In the morning, slice thin and flour each piece on both sides. Fry in a skillet with shortening until brown and crisp.

Serves 12.

Old Farm Inn Oatmeal

½ cup dried fruits, or more to taste
2 cups water
2 cups apple or prune juice
2 cups quick rolled oats

❧ ❧ ❧

2 teaspoons cinnamon
½ cup brown sugar
¼ cup butter

In a large bowl soak the dried chopped fruits in the combined water and juice (use any or a combination of dried apricots, apples, pears, prunes, dates, or raisins). In the morning, bring the mixture to a boil. Add the oatmeal and stir for 1 minute. Cover and remove from the heat. Let sit a few minutes. Before serving, stir in the cinnamon, brown sugar, and butter.

Variations: Peel and dice apples and substitute for dried fruits.

Reduce liquid by ½ cup and add evaporated milk (5-ounce can) or condensed milk (5-ounce can), stirring in before covering and removing from heat.

Stir in or sprinkle with chopped walnuts, pecans, or sautéed almonds.

Stir in ½ cup coconut before removing from heat.

Serves 8 to 10.

Peach-Oatmeal Bread

This tastes so healthy, you know it's good for you.

2 cups whole wheat flour
1 cup quick rolled oats
⅔ cup brown sugar
2½ teaspoons baking powder
1 teaspoon baking soda
½ teaspoon salt
1 teaspoon cinnamon
½ teaspoon nutmeg

  ❧   ❧   ❧

2 eggs
1 cup milk
¼ cup melted margarine or oil
2 medium-ripe peaches, chopped or
 1 8¾-ounce can sliced peaches,
 drained with syrup reserved
2 tablespoons sesame seeds

Grease a 9-inch square pan. In a large bowl mix the flour, oats, sugar, baking powder, baking soda, salt, cinnamon, and nutmeg together. Lightly beat the eggs. Add the milk (if using canned peaches, use reserved peach syrup and fill to 1 cup with milk). Add the oil or melted margarine. Stir the liquid

mixture into the dry mixture, leaving some streaks of flour. Chop the peaches and fold into the batter. Toast the sesame seeds and stir in 1 tablespoon. Turn into the prepared pan. Sprinkle the remaining 1 tablespoon of sesame seeds on top. Bake in a 350° oven for 35 minutes or until toothpick inserted in the center comes out clean.

Serves 12.

Pleasant Street Inn

17 Pleasant Street
Rockport, Massachusetts 01966
(508) 546-3915

This Victorian inn overlooking the village of Rockport on Cape Ann has been renovated recently, keeping the house's architectural integrity while providing modern conveniences. Guests are invited to enjoy the living room, relax on the front verandah, and eat the continental breakfast in the dining room. The seven large rooms all have private baths, and ample parking is available. From this inn guests are only steps away from nearby restaurants and gift shops. The artists' colony has numerous studios and galleries; other leisure opportunities are deep-sea fishing, golfing, tennis, and whale watch cruises.

Pecan Corn Bread

⅔ cup all-purpose flour
⅔ cup yellow cornmeal
⅔ cup ground pecans
½ cup sugar
¾ teaspoon baking powder
½ teaspoon baking soda

  ❧   ❧   ❧

2 eggs, beaten
½ cup buttermilk
⅓ cup butter, melted

Grease and flour a 9-inch round baking pan. In a medium bowl stir together the flour, cornmeal, ground pecans, sugar, baking powder, and baking soda. Make a well in the center. In a small bowl combine the eggs, buttermilk, and butter. Add all at once to the flour mixture. Stir until the flour mixture is moistened. Pour into the prepared baking pan. Bake in a 400° oven for 20 to 25 minutes.

Makes 12 wedges.

Blueberry Coconut Muffins

1¾ cups flour
½ teaspoon salt
3 teaspoons baking powder
⅔ cup sugar

  ❧   ❧   ❧

1 egg
⅔ cup milk
¼ cup oil
1 teaspoon vanilla extract

  ❧   ❧   ❧

1 cup blueberries
½ cup flaked coconut

Grease muffin tins. In a large bowl mix the flour, salt, baking powder, and sugar. In a separate bowl beat the egg. Add the milk, oil, and vanilla. Add the liquid ingredients to the flour mixture. Stir just until the flour mixture is moistened. Carefully stir in the blueberries and coconut. Pour into the prepared muffin tins. Bake in a 375° oven for 20 to 25 minutes.

Makes 9 to 12 muffins.

Captain Ezra Nye Guest House

152 Main Street
Sandwich, Massachusetts 02563
(800) 388-2278

This restored captain's house is situated in the heart of historical Sandwich village. Open year round, it provides comfortable rooms, most with private baths, and breakfast, which is served in the dining room between eight and ten each morning and includes fresh fruit and homemade pastries. Earlier breakfasts may be arranged upon request. Guests are invited to watch television or play the piano in the parlor, enjoy a cup of tea, or choose from an assortment of games and books in the cozy den. The Captain Ezra Nye Guest House is within walking distance of the Thornton Burgess Doll and Glass Museums, Hoxie House, Heritage Plantation, Cape Cod Scenic Railroad, Dexter Grist Mill on Shawme Pond, public tennis courts, beaches, fine restaurants, churches, and antique and artisan shops.

Captain Ezra Nye Guest House

Bread Pudding with Blueberry Sauce

    5 cups leftover muffins, diced
    3 cups warm milk
    Pinch salt
    ⅓ cup sugar
    1 teaspoon almond extract
    ¼ cup raisins, currants, or nuts
       (optional)
    1 teaspoon anise (optional)

       🍃 🍃 🍃

    2 cups sugar
    1½ cups water
    4 cups blueberries, picked over and
       washed

       🍃 🍃 🍃

    2 tablespoons brandy

Grease a 9x13-inch baking pan. In a large bowl pour the warm milk over bread. In a separate bowl combine the salt, ⅓ cup of sugar, almond extract, raisins, and anise, and add to the first mixture, stirring gently with a fork. Pour the batter into the prepared pan set in a pan of water. Bake in a 350° oven for 45 minutes.

Bring 2 cups of sugar and the water to a boil, and boil for 10 minutes. Add the blueberries and cook about 15 minutes. Skim off any froth. Cool and add the brandy. Serve as a topping on the pudding.

Serves 12.

Lemon Poppy Seed Bread

    1 cup sugar
    6 tablespoons shortening
    Grated rind of 1 lemon
    2 eggs
    1½ cups all-purpose flour
    Pinch salt
    1 teaspoon baking powder
    ½ cup poppy seeds
    ½ cup milk

       🍃 🍃 🍃

    Juice of 1 lemon
    ½ cup sugar

Grease a 9x5-inch loaf pan. In a large bowl cream 1 cup of sugar and the shortening together, and add the rind and eggs. In a separate bowl sift the dry ingredients and add the poppy seeds. Blend into the liquid ingredients alternately with milk. Pour the batter into the prepared pan. Bake in a 325° oven for 1 hour. Remove from oven.

Combine the lemon juice and ½ cup of sugar. Pour over the hot bread while still in the pan. Turn out and cool for about 20 minutes. This is very moist and delicious.

Makes 1 loaf, or 8 servings.

The Dan'l Webster Inn

149 Main Street
Sandwich, Massachusetts 02563
(508) 888-3622

The Dan'l Webster is an award-winning inn located in Cape Cod's oldest town of Sandwich. This four-star country inn offers fine dining, charming accommodations including 39 lovely rooms and 8 suites. Experience the Dan'l Webster Inn's charm and history in the quaint village of Sandwich.

Fillet of Sole Webster

    6 5 to 6-ounce grey sole fillets
    1 cup light cream
    Flour
    Clarified butter

       🍃 🍃 🍃

    1 cup unsalted butter, softened
    ¼ cup chopped parsley
    ¼ cup white wine
    2 tablespoons lemon juice
    1 tablespoon minced shallots

🍂 🍂 🍂

4 artichoke bottoms, sliced
3 ounces shrimp (raw, peeled, and deveined)
3 ounces button mushrooms, blanched
1 ounce almonds, slivered and blanched
1 tablespoon fresh tarragon

In a shallow bowl soak the fillets in the light cream for 5 minutes. Drain off the excess. Dredge lightly in flour. Shake off the excess and sauté flesh-side down in hot clarified butter until golden brown. This should be done very quickly; it is important that the butter is very hot. Turn the fillets and sauté for 30 seconds. Remove to a platter.

In a blender or food processor combine the softened butter, parsley, wine, lemon juice, and shallots. Transfer to a heated skillet. Sauté the artichoke bottoms, shrimp, mushrooms, almonds, and tarragon in the lemon butter until hot. Spoon over the fillets and serve.

Serves 6.

Pumpkin Apple Soup

1 21-ounce can pumpkin purée
¼ pound applesauce
2½ teaspoons nutmeg
2½ teaspoons ginger
¼ teaspoon cloves
2½ cups butter
3 quarts chicken stock
1½ cups brown sugar
2 quarts light cream, hot

In a large saucepan or soup pot cook all ingredients except the cream until smooth and hot. Simmer 15 minutes. Fold in the cream and blend well.

Makes 1¼ gallons.

The Dan'l Webster Inn

Ye Olde Nantucket House

2647 Main Street
Post Office Box 468
South Chatham, Massachusetts 02659
(508) 432-5641

Originally built on Nantucket Sound before its whaling industry began to fail, this classic Greek Revival-style home was brought to its present location around 1867. In this historic house in the historic district, guests find a friendly and informal atmosphere. Stenciled walls, pine floors, antiques, and attractive window and wall coverings provide a unique Victorian ambiance, and each of the five guest rooms has its own bath. The inn is but a short walk to Nantucket Sound beach and is convenient to dining, shopping, golfing, and fishing.

Chocolate Chip Orange Scones

2 cups all-purpose flour
⅓ cup sugar
2 teaspoons baking powder
½ teaspoon salt
½ cup unsalted butter, chilled

🍂 🍂 🍂

2 large eggs
¼ cup orange juice
1 teaspoon vanilla extract
½ teaspoon grated orange peel

🍂 🍂 🍂

¾ cup miniature semisweet chocolate chips

🍂 🍂 🍂

1 egg white mixed with ½ teaspoon water for glaze (optional)

In a large bowl stir together the flour, sugar, baking powder, and salt. Cut the butter into ½-inch cubes and distribute them over the flour mixture. With a pastry blender or two knives used scissors fashion, cut in the butter until the mixture resembles coarse crumbs. In a small bowl stir together the eggs, orange juice, vanilla, and orange peel. Add the egg mixture to the flour mixture and stir to combine. The dough will be sticky.

With lightly floured hands knead in the chocolate chips until they are evenly distributed.

Butter a 9-inch circle in the center of a baking sheet. With lightly floured hands pat the dough into an 8-inch circle in the center of the prepared baking sheet. If desired, brush the egg white mixture over the tops and sides of the dough. With a serrated knife cut into 8 wedges. Bake in a preheated 400° oven for 20 to 25 minutes or until a cake tester or toothpick inserted into the center of a scone comes out clean. Remove the baking sheet to a wire rack and cool for 10 minutes. With a spatula, transfer the scones to a wire rack to cool. Recut into wedges if necessary. Serve warm or cool completely and store in an air-tight container. These scones freeze well.

Makes 8 scones.

Westview Landing

4 Westview Avenue
Post Office Box 4141
South Chelmsford, Massachusetts 01824
(508) 256-0074

Westview Landing is a large, contemporary home set on a tranquil pond where guests can enjoy a relaxed country atmosphere. A private beach, swimming, boating, and fishing provide opportunity to relax and unwind during the summer. Breakfast is served on the spacious patio overlooking the large sundeck. The multilevel house includes three guest rooms and a large bath.

Lavosh
(Cracker Bread)

1 cup all-purpose flour
1½ teaspoons sugar
⅛ teaspoon baking soda
½ teaspoon salt
2 tablespoons butter, softened
6 tablespoons buttermilk (or sour milk)
1 egg white, lightly beaten
1 tablespoon sesame seeds

In a medium bowl combine the flour, sugar, baking soda, and salt. With a pastry blender cut in the butter until finely blended. Add the buttermilk to form a ball. On a floured surface, knead the dough lightly. Divide in half and roll each half out to a 10-inch circle. Place on a baking sheet. Brush with egg white and sprinkle with sesame seeds. Bake in a 450° oven for 10 to 12 minutes. When using 2 baking sheets, switch after 5 minutes, so they brown evenly.

Serves 2.

Historic Merrell Tavern Inn

Main Street, Route 102
South Lee, Massachusetts 01260
(413) 243-1794

The authenticity and charm of this inn is enhanced by the natural beauty of its quaint New England setting. The Historic Merrell Tavern Inn is less than a mile from Norman Rockwell's beloved Stockbridge, in the heart of the beautiful Berkshire region.

Built about 1800, it retains its antique woodwork, fixtures, and original colonial bar, one of the few remaining in America. Rooms are furnished with a canopy or four-poster bed and antiques collected by the innkeepers over the past twenty-five years. Guests may roam the grounds, with the old stone walls and foundations, or stroll down to the shore of the Housatonic River, which borders the inn's property. Guests are able to rest, relax, and take advantage of the many cultural and natural pleasures that the area provides.

Baked French Toast Cockaigne

I came across this idea when making bread pudding. Rum could be used as a flavoring instead of vanilla, especially at holiday time. Coconut, almonds, or chopped walnuts could be used instead of the crumble topping.

4 eggs
½ teaspoon salt
1 cup milk
½ teaspoon vanilla extract

ℰ ℰ ℰ

¼ cup all-purpose flour
¼ cup brown sugar
¼ teaspoon cinnamon
1 tablespoon butter

ℰ ℰ ℰ

16 slices Italian or French bread cut about ¾-inch thick
Choice of cherry, blueberry, or apple pie filling

In a pan large enough for dipping bread slices combine the eggs, salt, milk, and vanilla.

Combine (for the topping) the flour, brown sugar, cinnamon, and butter. Mix with a fork or pastry mixer until crumbly.

Arrange on each of 4 well-buttered ovenproof plates, 4 overlapping slices of bread already thoroughly dipped in the batter. Spread topping of pie filling in a line across the center of the overlapping bread slices. Sprinkle with crumble topping and cinnamon.

Brown and serve sausage links may also be added at this point to each plate. Bake in a 400° oven for 10 to 15 minutes or until brown and crispy. May be served with maple syrup and butter.

Serves 4.

Historic Merrell Tavern Inn

The Red Lion Inn

Stockbridge, Massachusetts 01262
(413) 298-5545

In a lovely Berkshire Hills town that once was an Indian village, on a street that once was a stagecoach road, the gracious old Red Lion Inn bids its guests a warm welcome. Here one enters a world of courtesy and hospitality amidst the charm of Staffordshire china, colonial pewter, eighteenth-century furniture, and almost every contemporary comfort one might want. Guests may dine on traditional New England fare, or on continental specialties with vintage wines; and they sleep in spacious rooms overlooking historic Stockbridge and the rolling Berkshires.

Stockbridge and the Berkshires are rich in fall foliage, golf courses, ski areas, and woodland trails. Within easy strolling distance of the Red Lion are antique shops, boutiques, galleries, and museums. A bit farther away are the Berkshire Theater Festival, the Tanglewood summer concerts, the Jacob's Pillow Dance Festival, and Chesterwood. And all around is the beautiful Berkshire countryside.

Chocolate Chip Pie

2⅔ cups all-purpose flour
2½ teaspoons baking powder
½ teaspoon salt
1 1-pound box light brown sugar
1 teaspoon vanilla extract
¾ cup butter
3 eggs
1 6-ounce package chocolate chips
1 cup chopped nuts

🍂 🍂 🍂

Melted butter

In a large bowl combine all of the ingredients except the melted butter.

Pour the mixture into a 9-inch pie pan. Bake in a 350° oven for 35 minutes. Top with melted butter.
Serves 6 to 8.

Indian Pudding

4 cups milk
¼ cup butter
½ cup cornmeal
½ cup molasses
¼ cup sugar
1 cup chopped apples
½ cup raisins
4½ teaspoons cinnamon
1½ teaspoons ginger
½ teaspoon salt
1 egg

In a saucepan combine 2½ cups of milk with the butter and scald. Combine ½ cup of milk and the cornmeal, and add to the scalded milk and butter. Cook for 20 minutes, stirring slowly so the mixture does not burn. Add the molasses, sugar, apples, and raisins. Stir in the cinnamon, ginger, salt, and egg. Cook for 5 more minutes. Pour into a well-greased shallow pan. Pour the remaining cup of milk over this. Bake in a 325° oven for 1½ hours or until the pudding is set. Serve warm with ice cream or whipped cream.
Serves 8 to 10.

Autumn Bisque Soup

1 small butternut squash (1 pound), unpeeled, cut in half and seeded
2 green apples, peeled, cored, and chopped
1 medium onion, chopped
Pinch rosemary
Pinch marjoram
1 quart chicken stock
2 slices white bread, trimmed and cubed
1½ teaspoons salt
¼ teaspoon pepper

🍂 🍂 🍂

2 egg yolks
¼ cup heavy cream

In a heavy saucepan combine the squash, apples, onion, herbs, stock, bread cubes, salt, and pepper. Bring to a boil and simmer uncovered for 30 to 45 minutes. Scoop out the flesh of the squash, discard the skins and return the pulp to the soup. Purée the soup in a blender till smooth. Return the puréed soup to the saucepan.

In a small bowl, beat the egg yolks and cream together. Beat in a little of the hot soup, then stir back into the saucepan. Heat, do not boil, and serve.

Serves 4 to 6.

The Red Lion Inn

Chicken Pot Pie

4 chicken breasts with bones
1½ quarts water
¼ cup white wine
½ teaspoon rosemary
1 clove garlic, crushed
2 small bay leaves
½ teaspoon leaf thyme
¼ teaspoon leaf tarragon
4 whole black peppercorns

🍂 🍂 🍂

¼ cup clarified butter
¼ cup all-purpose flour

🍂 🍂 🍂

2 carrots, peeled and diced
24 pearled onions
1 cup peas

🍂 🍂 🍂

6 buttermilk biscuits (recipe follows)

In a saucepan combine the chicken, water, wine, and spices. Bring to a boil. Skim. Reduce the heat, and simmer for 20 to 30 minutes or until the chicken is tender.

Remove the chicken from the pot. Cool. Skin and remove the meat from the bone, reserving the meat. Add the bones back to the stock. Simmer the stock until reduced by half. Strain, and bring back to a boil. In a small saucepan make a roux by melting the butter over low heat and stirring in the flour. Cook for 5 minutes, but do not brown. Stir the roux into the boiling liquid and simmer for 10 minutes, until thickened. Adjust the seasonings to taste.

Cook the carrots in boiling salted water, and in another small pot cook the onions in the same manner.

Dice the chicken, and combine all ingredients in individual crocks. Add warm sauce. Top each with a buttermilk biscuit (recipe follows). Serve piping hot.

Serves 6.

Buttermilk Biscuits

4 cups plus 6 tablespoons all-purpose flour
1 tablespoon plus 1 teaspoon baking powder
⅛ teaspoon salt
7 tablespoons butter
1¼ cups buttermilk

🍂 🍂 🍂

1 egg
1 tablespoon water

🍂 🍂 🍂

Melted butter

In a large bowl combine the dry ingredients. Cut in the butter until the mixture resembles small peas. Add the buttermilk. Turn onto a floured board, and roll out the dough. Cut with a biscuit cutter. Combine the egg and water, and beat until frothy. Brush the mixture over the biscuits. Bake in a 400° oven for 25 to 30 minutes or until golden brown. When the biscuits are removed from the oven, brush with melted butter.

Makes 12 biscuits.

Publick House on the Common

Post Office Box 187
Sturbridge, Massachusetts 01566
(508) 347-3313

The Publick House is three minutes and two centuries from I-91 and the Massachusetts Turnpike. Publick House Historic Inn serves hearty Yankee breakfasts, lunches, dinners, and suppers every day of the year, and the guest rooms are indulgently comfortable.

New England Clam Chowder

¼ pound salt pork
1 large onion, finely diced
1½ cups water
3 medium-size potatoes, peeled and cubed
1 quart chopped clams
3 cups light cream
¼ cup butter
Salt and pepper
Crackers

Cut the salt pork into small dices and render in a saucepan. Reserve the cracklings. In the fat cook the onion until golden. In a 2-quart pan add the water and potatoes and cook for 10 minutes. Drain the liquor from the potatoes into a 4-quart pan. Add the clams and cook for 25 minutes. Add the cream, cracklings, potatoes, onion, butter, and salt and pepper to taste. Serve in soup bowls with crackers.

Serves 8.

Publick House
Historic Inn & Country Motor Lodge
On the Common — Sturbridge, Mass. 01566

Deep Dish Apple Pie à la Mode

Sliced apples, fresh or frozen
1¼ cups sugar
Juice of ½ lemon
1 teaspoon cinnamon
½ teaspoon nutmeg
Pinch salt
1 tablespoon butter
Pastry for 1 crust
Ice cream

Fill a deep dish baking pan with apples (quantity depends on the size of the pan). Add the sugar and lemon juice. Sprinkle with cinnamon, nutmeg, and salt. Dot with chips of butter. Cover with flaky pastry, making sure the pastry is well over the edge of the pan. Brush with melted butter and prick with a fork. Bake in a 350° oven for approximately 1 hour. Serve with ice cream.

Serves 6 to 8.

Chocolate Chip Cookies

2½ cups sifted all-purpose flour
1 teaspoon baking soda
1 teaspoon salt

☙ ☙ ☙

1 cup softened butter or shortening
¾ cup sugar
¾ cup brown sugar
1 teaspoon vanilla extract
½ teaspoon water

☙ ☙ ☙

2 eggs
1 12-ounce package (2 cups) chocolate morsels
1 cup coarsely chopped nuts

In a large bowl sift together the dry ingredients. In a separate bowl combine the butter, sugars, vanilla, and water, and beat until creamy. Add the eggs and the flour mixture, mixing well. Stir in the chocolate morsels and nuts. Drop onto greased cookie sheets in the size desired. Bake in a 375° oven for 10 to 12 minutes.

Makes about 100 2-inch cookies.

The Rose Cottage

Honeysuckle Hill

591 Old Kings Highway
West Barnstable, Massachusetts 02668
(508) 362-8418

Honeysuckle Hill was built in the early 1800s as a farm house near the great salt marshes of Cape Cod. Completely restored, the inn is now a comfortable, rambling place decorated in a Cape Cod version of the English Country style. Guests discover chintz, antiques, cushions, comfortable chairs, feather beds and down comforters, two shaggy dogs, and at every bedside a tin of homemade cookies. The hearty country breakfasts feature such specialties as sausage soufflés or blueberry pancakes, and traditional afternoon teas are served in the dining room. The wraparound screen porch is a place to relax after a busy day. From the beautiful great room, French doors lead to the garden.

Chocolate Cookie Cream Cheese "Indulgences"

20 Oreo cookies, or similar cookies
2 8-ounce packages cream cheese, room temperature
¾ cup sugar
2 tablespoons all-purpose flour
3 eggs
🍂 🍂 🍂
¾ cup sour cream
3 tablespoons sugar

Line 16 muffin cups with paper liners. Separate the cookies into two wafers. Put one in each liner and set the others aside.

In a bowl combine the cream cheese, sugar, flour, and eggs with an electric mixer. Beat for 4 minutes. Put 1 tablespoon of the mixture on the top of each cookie half in the liners. Make crumbs out of 4 Oreo cookies and put a sprinkle on top of the cheese mixture in each liner. Divide the remaining cheese mixture on top of the crumbs. Bake in a 350° oven for 20 to 25 minutes. Remove from the oven.

Combine the sour cream and sugar. Spread each cake with the mixture. Return to the oven for 4 minutes. Remove from the oven and place remaining wafers on top of each cheesecake. Chill before serving. Store in the refrigerator.

P.S. While waiting for them to cool, sit down with a glass of milk and eat the rest of the package of Oreos!

Serves 8 to 16, at tea time.

The Rose Cottage

24 Worcester Street
Routes 12 and 140
West Boylston, Massachusetts 01583
(508) 835-4034

Built in 1850, the Rose Cottage, with its wide board floors, white marble fireplaces, gaslight hanging lamps, and floor-to-ceiling windows, is a classic example of Gothic Revival architecture. All five guest rooms are furnished with antique patchwork quilts, interior shutters, and New England decorations. Rose Cottage also has an executive apartment for guests who come for a longer stay and a conference facility. A variety of delicious foods are served at breakfast. The inn also has an antique shop featuring two floors of quality American and European furniture, gold and costume jewelry, toys, games, cut glass, collectibles, and more.

Sour Cream Stuffed Boneless Chicken

4 heaping cups cooked, cubed chicken
1 10½-ounce can cream of chicken soup
1 10½-ounce can cream of celery soup
1 pint sour cream
1 8-ounce package herb stuffing mix
Dash black pepper

In a 9x13-inch oven pan layer the chicken, soups, and sour cream. Don't mix. Prepare the stuffing according to the package directions (extra special if sautéed celery, onions, and/or mushrooms are added), adding pepper to taste. Spread over the sour cream. Bake in a 350° oven for 45 minutes. Serve like lasagna.

This can be made a day ahead.
Makes 9 generous servings.

My Own Cheese Spread or Cheese Ball

Serve with crackers, celery, or any vegetables.

2 8-ounce packages cream cheese, room temperature
1 8½-ounce can crushed pineapple, drained
¼ cup finely chopped green pepper
1½ teaspoons finely chopped onion
1 teaspoon seasoned salt (celery is best)
1 cup finely chopped nuts

In a large bowl blend the softened cream cheese with the remaining ingredients. Transfer to a serving dish.

For a cheese ball, combine all of the ingredients except the nuts. Roll into a ball and wrap in plastic. Refrigerate. Before serving, roll in the chopped nuts. Keeps well and can be made ahead.

Makes 1 ball or about 4 cups of spread.

The Elms

495 West Falmouth Highway
Post Office Box 895
West Falmouth, Massachusetts 02574
(508) 540-7232

A refurbished Victorian home built in 1739 and added onto in 1850, the Elms features nine double rooms, seven with private baths. Each room has its own style. A four-course gourmet breakfast is served in the sun-lit dining room; in late afternoon guests are invited to mingle in the living room over complimentary sherry. Ideally situated for the theatre and many fine restaurants, the Elms is near Woods Hole, the boat for Martha's Vineyard, and Nantucket Sound.

Artichoke Canapé

2 6-ounce jars marinated artichoke
   hearts
1 small onion, finely chopped
1 clove garlic, minced

⩖ ⩖ ⩖

4 eggs
¼ cup dry bread crumbs
¼ teaspoon salt
⅛ teaspoon pepper
⅛ teaspoon oregano
⅛ teaspoon hot sauce
½ pound shredded Cheddar cheese
2 tablespoons minced parsley

Butter a 7x11-inch baking pan. Drain the juice from 1 jar of artichoke hearts into a frying pan. Discard the juice from the other jar. Chop the artichokes and set aside. Sauté the onion and garlic in liquid until transparent.

In a large bowl beat the eggs until frothy. Add the bread crumbs and seasonings. Stir in the cheese, parsley, artichoke hearts, and onion mixture. Place the ingredients in the prepared pan. Bake in a 350° oven for 30 minutes. Cool and cut into 1-inch squares. Serve cold or hot.

Makes 40 squares.

Cape Cod Sunny Pines

77 Main Street
Post Office Box 667
West Harwich, Massachusetts 02671
(508) 432-9628

Reminiscent of a small Irish manor, this inn provides Irish hospitality in a Victorian ambience and six private suites, each individually climate controlled. Guests may relax by the pool or Jacuzzi, or by the roaring fireplace with complimentary wine and appetizers each evening. The gourmet Irish breakfast is served family style by candlelight in the formal dining room on bone china and crystal to the lilt of Irish music.

Curney Cake or Irish Soda Bread

6 cups all-purpose flour
2 teaspoons baking soda
2 tablespoons baking powder
1 teaspoon salt
½ cup sugar

⩖ ⩖ ⩖

1 quart buttermilk
4 eggs, beaten
2 tablespoons butter, melted

⩖ ⩖ ⩖

1 cup currants
½ cup raisins
¼ cup caraway seeds

In a large bowl combine the dry ingredients. In a separate bowl combine the liquid ingredients. Add the liquid mixture to the dry ingredients, mixing well. Stir in the fruit and seeds.

Pour the batter into 3 large or 5 small loaf pans. Bake in a 375° oven for 45 minutes to 1 hour. Freezes beautifully.

Makes 3 large or 5 small loaves.

Country Cricket Village Inn

Huntington Road, Route 112
Worthington, Massachusetts 01098
(413) 238-5366

This colonial-style inn is on twenty-three acres near the town common. Each of its five bedrooms, with private bath, has its own quality. A common room provides opportunity for visiting, reading, viewing television, or gazing into the fire. The full breakfast features such delights as Belgium waffles with pure maple syrup, hot breads or muffins, and French beignets. Luncheon and dinner menus change frequently to provide the most seasonal foods available. Situated centrally, the inn makes it easy for guests to enjoy the many cultural activities of the Berkshires and the Hampshire Hills.

Hampshire Hills Corn Chowder

¼ pound bacon
1½ cups butter or margarine
6 large onions, finely chopped

⩖ ⩖ ⩖

6 large potatoes
1½ cups all-purpose flour
1 quart half and half (milk and
   cream)
16 ounces whole kernel corn,
   canned or fresh
16 ounces creamed corn, canned or
   fresh
Salt and pepper
Chopped fresh parsley for garnish

Select a cast iron or heavy cooking pot. Cook the bacon until crisp, remove from the pot, and chop in small bits. Leave 1 tablespoon of bacon grease in pot. Add ½ cup of butter and the onions, and sauté until the onions are soft.

Peel the potatoes and chop in ½-inch cubes. Cover with water in a separate pot and simmer until cooked but firm. Remove the onions from the pot and add 1 cup of butter. Cook over medium heat until melted and add the flour to form a roux. Add the half and half, stirring continually with a whisk until the mixture boils. Drain the whole corn and potatoes, reserving the liquid. Add the creamed corn to the white sauce, and slowly add the reserved corn-potato water until the white sauce reaches the desired soup consistency. Add the bacon bits, drained whole corn, potato cubes, and onions. Season to taste. Simmer over low heat for 30 minutes, being careful to stir frequently to prevent scorching. This chowder is better the second day. Garnish with fresh chopped parsley.

Serves 8 to 10.

Maple Cheesecake

1 cup graham cracker crumbs
2 tablespoons butter, melted
3 8-ounce packages cream cheese
3 large eggs
1½ teaspoons vanilla extract
¼ teaspoon salt
1¼ cups pure maple syrup

≈ ≈ ≈

1 cup sour cream
2 tablespoons honey
1 teaspoon vanilla extract

≈ ≈ ≈

2 tablespoons maple syrup per serving

In a small bowl combine the crumbs and melted butter. Lightly butter a 9-inch springform pan, dust the sides with crumbs, and press the remainder into the bottom of the pan.

Chill. In a large bowl beat the cream cheese well, adding the eggs one at a time and beating after each addition. Add 1½ teaspoons of vanilla, the salt, and maple syrup. Beat well. Pour into the chilled crust. Bake in a 350° oven until firm, about 45 to 50 minutes. Remove from the oven.

Combine the sour cream, honey, and 1 teaspoon of vanilla. Pour over the top of the cheesecake. Increase the oven temperature to 400° and bake 5 more minutes. Cool overnight. Pour 2 tablespoons of syrup over each serving.

Serves 12.

Michigan

The Old Lamp-Lighter's Homestay

276 Capital Avenue, N.E.
Battle Creek, Michigan 49017
(616) 963-2603

This magnificent historic home has been featured in *Innsider* and *Country Inns* magazine. It boasts fifteen-inch walls, a clear clay French tile roof, a quarry tile porch floor, an elegant open oak staircase, and a large stained glass window on the first floor. The dining room is entered through stained glass French doors that complement the hand-painted muraled walls. The living room features stained glass windows, imported Dutch lace curtains, and a French Aubusson rug. Magnificent chandeliers containing signature Steuben globes adorn the first floor. The seven rooms on the second and third floors, all with private baths, are individually decorated. Smoking is not permitted.

Strawberry Muffins

2 cups quartered strawberries
¼ cup sugar
1½ cups all-purpose flour
½ teaspoon baking soda
1 teaspoon cinnamon
½ teaspoon nutmeg
2 eggs, beaten
¾ cup oil
1 cup sugar
1 teaspoon vanilla extract
¾ cup chopped walnuts

In a medium bowl toss the berries with ¼ cup of sugar and let stand at room temperature for 1 hour. In a large bowl combine the flour, baking soda, and spices. In a separate bowl mix the beaten eggs and oil, add 1 cup sugar, and beat. Add the berries, vanilla, and nuts to the egg mixture and gently stir. Fold this mixture into the dry ingredients. Fill muffin cups ¾ full. Bake in a 350° oven about 25 minutes. Best made ahead, even frozen and served cold.

Serves 12 to 14.

Silver Creek Lodge

4361 US 23 South
Black River, Michigan 48721
(517) 471-2198
(517) 724-6430

This unique home and antique shop is set on eighty tranquil wooded acres that adjoin a 5,200-acre national forest. There are five guest rooms, one with private bath. Hiking, cross-country skiing, hay and sleigh rides, and the opportunity to observe wild birds and animals in their natural surroundings are part of what guests at Silver Creek Lodge experience.

Fantastic Brownies

This is an old family recipe.

½ cup butter
1 cup sugar
2 eggs
1 teaspoon vanilla extract
1 ounce unsweetened chocolate, melted
½ cup all-purpose flour
⅛ teaspoon baking powder
1 cup walnuts or pecans, chopped

Confectioners' sugar for topping

Grease an 8-inch square pan. In a large bowl cream together the butter, sugar, eggs, vanilla, and chocolate. Add the flour, baking powder, and walnuts. Pour into the prepared pan. Bake in a 325° oven for 30 minutes. Cool and sprinkle with confectioners' sugar.

Serves 10.

Ladyfingers

3 eggs, separated
⅓ cup confectioners' sugar
⅓ cup all-purpose flour, sifted
½ teaspoon vanilla extract
Sugar

Grease and line a cookie sheet with brown paper. In a large bowl beat the yolks with an electric mixer for 5 minutes on medium speed. Set aside, and wash the mixer beaters. In a separate bowl beat the whites until soft. Gradually add the sugar and slowly beat till stiff. Fold the yolks and the flour into the egg white mixture. Add the vanilla. Shape into thin fingers with a spoon on the prepared cookie sheet. Bake in a 350° oven for 10 to 12 minutes. Cool on a cake rack and sprinkle with sugar.
Serves 14.

Featherlight Puffs

1 cup all-purpose flour, sifted
1 tablespoon sugar
1 cup water
⅓ cup butter
4 eggs
1 teaspoon vanilla extract
Fat for deep frying, heated to 350°
Confectioners' sugar

In a medium bowl sift the flour and sugar. Set aside. Heat the water and butter together until the butter melts. Add the flour mixture all at once, stirring rapidly with a spoon until the dough leaves the sides of the pan and forms a lump. Remove from the heat and beat in the eggs one at a time, beating hard after each addition. When the dough is no longer slippery looking, stir in the vanilla. Preheat the shortening to 350° on a deep fat thermometer or until a cube of bread browns in 60 seconds. Scoop a heaping teaspoon of dough and with a second teaspoon push it off into the heated fat. When puffed and golden brown, remove and drain on a paper towel. Sprinkle with confectioners' sugar and serve warm.
Makes 6 dozen.

Michigan Fruit Cup

1 melon (any kind), scooped into balls
2 cups strawberries, washed and halved
2 cups blueberries, washed
Other fruit of choice to equal 2 more cups

❧ ❧ ❧

½ cup sour cream or yogurt
¼ cup confectioners' sugar or honey
¼ cup orange juice
⅓ cup chopped pecans

In a large bowl combine the fruits. In a separate bowl mix the ingredients for the sauce, pour it over the fruit, and refrigerate for at least 1 hour. Serve in parfait glasses.
Serves 12.

Pecan Waffles

3 eggs, separated
1½ cups buttermilk
1 teaspoon baking powder
½ cup butter or margarine, melted
1 teaspoon baking soda
1 teaspoon vanilla extract
1 cup sour cream
¼ cup sugar
½ cup chopped pecans
2 cups all-purpose flour

❧ ❧ ❧

Maple syrup
Sausages
Apple cider

In a medium bowl beat the egg whites until stiff. Set aside. In a large bowl beat the remaining waffle ingredients together. Fold in the egg whites. Pour into a hot waffle iron that has been greased and bake.
Serve with hot maple syrup and sausages that have been steamed in apple cider and then browned.
Serves 8.

Cheddar Popovers

3 eggs, at room temperature
1 cup milk
1 cup all-purpose flour
3 tablespoons oil
½ cup shredded Cheddar cheese

Preheat cast iron muffin tins for 10 minutes in a 400° oven. In a large bowl mix the eggs, milk, flour, and oil. Fold in the cheese. Grease the hot muffin tins. Pour in the popover batter. Bake in a 400° oven for 30 to 40 minutes, until puffed and golden brown. Serve with jam and eggs.
Makes 10 to 12, depending on the size of the muffin pan.

Heart Smart Eggs Mornay

2 tablespoons cholesterol-free margarine
¼ cup chopped red peppers
¼ cup chopped green peppers
¼ cup diced onion
½ cup diced fresh or canned mushrooms
½ cup diced potatoes
1 carton Egg Beaters

❧ ❧ ❧

¼ cup Parmesan cheese
1 cup soft bread crumbs

❧ ❧ ❧

3 egg whites

❧ ❧ ❧

2 tablespoons cholesterol-free margarine
2 tablespoons all-purpose flour
1 teaspoon low-sodium chicken bouillon
1½ cups Coffee Rich (or any cholesterol-free milk or cream product)
½ cup grated lowfat Swiss cheese

❧ ❧ ❧

Parsley for garnish

In a small skillet melt 2 tablespoons of margarine and sauté all of the vegetables until crisp-tender.
Spray a baking dish with cooking spray. Transfer the vegetables to the sprayed baking dish. Add the eggs to the heated skillet and softly scramble. Add to the vegetables in the baking dish and mix together.
In a small bowl mix the Parmesan cheese and bread crumbs. Set aside. Beat the egg whites until stiff. Set aside.

In a small pan over medium heat combine the margarine, flour, and bouillon. Cook until smooth and bubbly. Add the Coffee Rich, stir, and watch carefully until smooth. Remove from the heat and add the cheese, stirring until melted. Reserve ½ cup of sauce to drizzle on the dish before serving.

Fold the egg whites into the remaining sauce, and gently fold into the egg mixture. Sprinkle with bread crumbs. Bake in a 400° oven for 20 to 25 minutes or until puffy and golden. Top each serving with a tablespoon of sauce and sprinkle with a bit of parsley.

Serves 6.

The Chicago Street Inn

219 Chicago Street
Brooklyn, Michigan 49230
(517) 592-3888

The four guest rooms in this Victorian home offer a nostalgic retreat into the past. Downstairs, the entry, sitting, and dining rooms all have oak

The Chicago Street Inn

moldings, fretwork, and cherry wood trim. These rooms, lit by original electric chandeliers and European stained glass windows, are furnished with local and family antiques. The deluxe continental breakfast is ample.

Ilene and Irene's Special Potato Dish

This dish is excellent for all meals and pot luck dinners.

> 8 cups cooked, diced potatoes
> 6 slices uncooked bacon, diced
> 1 large onion, diced
> ¼ pound Velveeta cheese, diced
> ¼ cup chopped green olives
> 1 cup mayonnaise

In a 9x12-inch baking dish mix all ingredients together. Chill overnight. Bake in a 350° oven for 1 hour.

Serves 10.

Country Charm Farm

5048 Conkey Road
Caseville, Michigan 48725
(517) 856-3110

This lovely country home overlooking a duck pond and a forty-acre meadow is part of a whimsical working farm with several kinds of animals on it. The newly decorated house features all the modern conveniences along with the warmth of the past. Each of the four rooms is individually decorated. Nearby facilities include Sleepers' State Park, several antique shops, great hunting and fishing, cross-country skiing, and snowmobiling.

Golden Cream Soup

> 3 cups chopped potatoes
> 2 cups water
> ½ cup chopped celery
> ½ cup chopped carrots
> ½ cup chopped onions
> 1 teaspoon parsley flakes
> 1 chicken bouillon cube
> ½ teaspoon salt
> Pepper, to taste
> 1½ cups milk
> 1 to 2 tablespoons all-purpose flour
> ½ cup butter, melted
> ½ pound Velveeta cheese, cubed
> 1 cup chopped ham or cooked bacon

In a saucepan or crock pot combine the potatoes, water, celery, carrots, onion, parsley, bouillon cube, and seasonings. Cover and simmer for 15 minutes or until the vegetables are tender. Add the milk and heat. Mix the flour with the melted butter and add to the soup mixture, stirring slowly until thickened. Add the cheese and stir until melted. Add the ham or bacon. Cook another 10 minutes on low heat and enjoy.

Serves 4.

Rhubarb Crunch

> 2 cups all-purpose flour
> 2 cups brown sugar
> ½ cup margarine
> 2 cups oatmeal
> 2 teaspoons cinnamon
>
> ❧ ❧ ❧
>
> 8 cups rhubarb
>
> ❧ ❧ ❧
>
> 2 cups sugar
> ¼ cup cornstarch
> 2 cups water

In a large bowl combine the flour, brown sugar, margarine, oatmeal, and cinnamon. Press half of the mixture into a 9x13-inch baking pan. Arrange the rhubarb over the crumb mixture.

In a saucepan combine the sugar, cornstarch, and water. Heat over medium heat, stirring often, until thickened and clear. Pour the mixture over the rhubarb. Top with the remaining crumb mixture. Bake in a 350° oven for 1 hour or until done.

Serves 6.

Bed and Breakfast at the Pines

327 Ardussi Street
Frankenmuth, Michigan 48734
(517) 652-9019

Bed and Breakfast at the Pines provides its guests with a Bavarian atmosphere. Situated in a quiet residential area, it is within walking distance of famous restaurants and main tourist attractions in Frankenmuth. The bedrooms are decorated with heirloom quilts, ceiling fans, and fresh flowers. No smoking is permitted.

Sour Cream Cinnamon Twists

1 cup sour cream
3 tablespoons sugar
⅛ teaspoon baking soda
1 teaspoon salt
1 1-ounce cake compressed yeast
1 large egg
2 tablespoons soft shortening
3 cups sifted all-purpose flour

&ea; &ea; &ea;

2 tablespoons butter, softened
⅓ cup brown sugar
1 teaspoon cinnamon

&ea; &ea; &ea;

1 cup confectioners' sugar
1 to 2 tablespoons milk, water, or cream (use amount for desired thickness)
½ teaspoon vanilla extract or other flavor

Grease 2 baking sheets. In a large saucepan heat the sour cream to lukewarm. Remove from the heat and stir in the sugar, baking soda, and salt. Crumble the yeast cake into the mixture and stir until dissolved. Add the egg, shortening, and flour. Mix well (use hands if necessary). Turn the dough onto a floured surface and fold over several times until the dough is smooth. Then roll into a 24x6-inch oblong.

Spread with soft butter. Combine the brown sugar and cinnamon and sprinkle half of the dough with the mixture. Fold the other half over. Cut into 24 strips 1-inch wide. Hold a strip at both ends and twist (in opposite directions). Place the twisted strips on the baking sheet 2 inches apart. Press both ends of the twists to the baking sheet. Cover and let rise until light, approximately 1 hour. Bake in a 375° oven for 12 to 15 minutes.

Combine the confectioners' sugar, milk, and flavoring and frost the twists while warm. Serve with butter.

Makes 24 twists.

"No Crumble" Whole Wheat Bread

1 tablespoon active dry yeast
2 cups warm water (110° to 115°)
⅓ cup molasses or honey
2 tablespoons salad oil
2 teaspoons salt
5 to 6 cups whole wheat flour

Dissolve the yeast in the warm water. Add the molasses, oil, and salt. Slowly add the flour, mixing well, and knead until smooth and elastic. Place in an oiled bowl and let rise until double. Punch down and let rise again in the same bowl. Shape into 2 loaves and place in 2 loaf pans. Let rise in the pans until almost double. (Care should be taken not to let the dough get too light before baking or a crumbly loaf will result. If the dough does get too light, just punch down and re-shape the loaves.) Bake in a 350° oven for 45 to 50 minutes.

Makes 2 loaves.

Golden Squash-Raisin Bread

This bread is excellent toasted, and wonderful for ham sandwiches.

1 cup milk
1 cup cooked mashed winter squash (Buttercup or Hubbard)
¼ cup oil
¼ cup honey
2 teaspoons salt
1 teaspoon cinnamon
1 teaspoon nutmeg or other spices (like pumpkin pie)
2 ¼-ounce packages active dry yeast
½ cup warm water (110° to 115°)
2 eggs
1½ cups raisins
6 to 6½ cups all-purpose flour

Grease two 9x5-inch loaf pans. In a saucepan scald the milk. Add the squash, oil, honey, salt, and spices. Cool to lukewarm. Sprinkle the yeast on the warm water. Stir to dissolve. When the milk mixture is lukewarm, add the yeast mixture. Add the eggs, raisins, and half of the flour. Beat until the batter is smooth. Mix in the remaining flour, a little at a time, until the dough leaves the sides of the bowl. Turn onto a floured board and knead for about 10 minutes or until the dough is elastic. Place in a greased bowl. Cover and allow to rise until doubled, about 1 hour.

Punch down and turn onto a board. Divide in half and shape into loaves. Place in the prepared pans. Brush the tops with melted margarine. Cover and let rise until doubled, about 1 hour. Bake in a 375° oven for 40 minutes or until golden in color. Remove from the pans and cool.

Makes 2 standard-sized loaves.

Caraway-Rye Bread

    2 tablespoons brown sugar
    1 tablespoon salt
    2½ cups lukewarm water (100° to
        115°)
    2 tablespoons molasses
    2 tablespoons caraway seeds
    2 cakes compressed yeast (or 2
        packages active dry)
    2 tablespoons soft shortening
    1 cup rye flour
    6 to 6½ cups all-purpose flour

Grease two 9x5-inch loaf pans. In a large bowl mix the sugar and salt together. Add the liquid, molasses, and caraway. Add the yeast, stirring until dissolved. Stir in the shortening and rye flour. Add the all-purpose flour in 2 additions, using the amount necessary to make it easy to handle. Knead on a floured board until the dough is smooth and elastic. Place in a greased bowl, turning the dough once to grease the top. Cover and let rise in a warm place until double. Punch down and let rise again.

Punch down and divide the dough to form 2 loaves. Place the loaves in the prepared pans. Let rise again. Bake in a 375° oven for 30 to 40 minutes, browning the loaves to taste.

Makes 2 standard-sized loaves.

Old-fashioned Sour Cream Sugar Cookies

    1 cup shortening
    1⅔ cups sugar
    2 eggs
    1 teaspoon vanilla extract
    4½ cups sifted all-purpose flour
    ½ teaspoon baking powder
    1 teaspoon baking soda

    1 teaspoon salt
    1 teaspoon nutmeg
    1 cup sour cream
    1 tablespoon lemon juice
    ❧ ❧ ❧
    Raisins
    Sugar

Grease a baking sheet. In a large bowl cream the shortening and sugar together; add eggs and vanilla. Beat until fluffy. In a separate bowl sift the dry ingredients. Add to the liquid ingredients alternately with the sour cream and lemon juice. Chill the dough. Roll out thick on floured surface. Cut with a 3-inch cutter. Place on the prepared baking sheet. Place a single raisin in the center of each cookie and sprinkle with sugar. Bake in a 375° oven for 12 minutes.

Makes between 2½ and 3 dozen, depending on the size of cutter.

The Chafins Balmoral Farm

1245 West Washington Road
Ithaca, Michigan 48847
(517) 875-3410

This turn-of-the-century home offers two bedrooms that can accommodate up to six people. The house and the hip-roofed barn are all part of a working, cash crop farm. The remodeled home is furnished with family antiques, and its kitchen has been featured in *Country Woman*. Alma College and Central Michigan University are nearby.

Quick Croissants

    1 ¼-ounce package active dry yeast
    1 cup warm water (110° to 115°)
    ¾ cup evaporated milk, undiluted

    1½ teaspoons salt
    ⅓ cup sugar
    1 egg
    5 cups sifted all-purpose flour
    ¼ cup butter or margarine, melted
        and cooled
    ❧ ❧ ❧
    1 cup butter or margarine
    ❧ ❧ ❧
    1 egg, beaten with 1 tablespoon
        water

In a medium bowl soften the yeast in water. Add the milk, salt, sugar, egg, 1 cup of flour, and ¼ cup of melted butter. Set aside.

In a large bowl cut 1 cup of firm butter into the remaining 4 cups of flour until the butter particles are the size of dried kidney beans. Pour the yeast batter over the top and carefully turn the mixture over with a spatula, blending until all of the flour is moistened. Cover and refrigerate for 4 hours, or up to 4 days. Remove the dough to a floured board, press into a compact ball, and knead about 6 turns to release the air bubbles. Divide the dough into 2, 3, or 4 parts, depending on the size of rolls desired. Shape 1 section at a time, keeping the remaining dough refrigerated. Roll the dough on a floured board into a 17- to 22-inch circle. Cut into 8 pie-shaped wedges. Roll each starting with the wider edge and ending with the point, and place on an ungreased sheet.

Brush the tops with the egg and water mixture. Let the croissants rise. When double, bake in a 325° oven for 35 minutes.

Makes 16 to 32 croissants.

Marina Guest House

230 Arbutus
Post Office Box 344
Manistique, Michigan 49854
(906) 341-5147

Situated one block from the business district, this inn faces the city marina. Built in 1905 and rebuilt in 1922, it was a bed and breakfast for fourteen years during the Great Depression. Open year-round, it serves a hearty breakfast to its guests.

Breakfast Sausage Ring

2 pounds lean pork sausage
1½ to 2 cups diced apples
2 cups plain dry bread cubes
¼ cup minced onion
2 eggs

In a large mixing bowl mix all of the ingredients. Press into a bundt or large ring mold pan. Place in a 400° oven and reduce the temperature to 350°. Bake for 1 hour. Before serving drain off the grease and turn out on a serving dish.
Serves 8 to 12.

The Mayflower Bed and Breakfast Hotel

Main and Ann Arbor Trail
Plymouth, Michigan 48170
(313) 453-1620

The family-operated Mayflower Bed and Breakfast Hotel is a Michigan landmark. This 100-room English-style inn features a full complimentary breakfast for overnight guests, elegant but comfortable surroundings, and a reputation for good food and hospitality. Situated in the heart of beautiful Plymouth, the Mayflower is within walking distance of 150 charming shops. Kellogg Park, with its brick walks and lovely shade trees—the center of this colonial New England-style town—is directly across the street from the hotel. This town square is the site for many of Plymouth's events and festivals, including band concerts, street dances, art fairs, the popular fall festival, farmer's market, and the renowned Plymouth ice sculpture spectacular in January.

Chargrilled Pork Tenderloin
with Orange Brandy Marinade and Mango Chutney Cream Sauce

1 ounce brandy
½ cup orange juice
¼ teaspoon fresh grated ginger

❧ ❧ ❧

2 1-pound pork tenderloins, trimmed and cleaned

❧ ❧ ❧

½ cup mango chutney
1 ounce brandy
¼ teaspoon minced garlic
¾ cup veal or beef stock
¼ cup heavy cream
¼ teaspoon salt
¼ teaspoon white pepper

To prepare the Orange Brandy Marinade, in a shallow dish combine 1 ounce of brandy with the orange juice and ginger, blending well. Marinate the pork tenderloins in the mixture for 4 hours.

To prepare the Mango Chutney Cream Sauce, in a saucepan combine the chutney and garlic. Heat slightly. Remove the pan from the heat and add the brandy. Return to the heat and allow the alcohol to dissipate. Add the stock and reduce by half. Add the cream and reduce by ¼. Season with salt and pepper. Keep warm.

Chargrill the marinated pork tenderloin over medium heat for about 6 minutes on each side. Slice the pork and fan onto 4 serving plates. Top with the warm Mango Chutney Sauce.

Serve the pork with Poached Pears with Fruit Nut Compote and Potato Pancakes with Applesauce and sour cream (recipes follow).
Serves 4.

Poached Pears
with Fruit Nut Compote

2 pears, peeled, cored and halved
4 cups apple juice
1 stick cinnamon
3 whole cloves
½ teaspoon fresh lemon juice

❧ ❧ ❧

3 cups chilled apple juice

❧ ❧ ❧

4 tablespoons butter
2 tablespoons brown sugar
⅛ cup diced Granny Smith apples
¼ cup honey
½ teaspoon allspice
½ teaspoon cloves
½ teaspoon nutmeg

❧ ❧ ❧

⅛ cup chopped dried apricots
⅛ cup diced pitted prunes
⅛ cup diced dried cherries
⅛ cup golden raisins
⅛ cup roasted walnut pieces
⅛ cup diced pecans

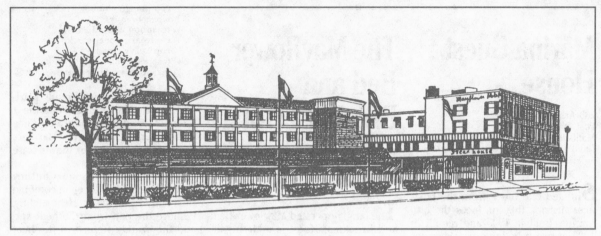

The Mayflower

In a saucepan combine the pears, apple juice, cinnamon stick, cloves, and lemon juice. Simmer for 5 to 6 minutes. Remove the pears from the simmering liquid. Strain and reserve the liquid. Place the pears in the chilled apple juice.

To prepare the Fruit Nut Compote, in a small saucepan melt the butter. Add the brown sugar and apples, and sauté until the apples become tender. Add the honey, allspice, cloves, and nutmeg, stirring to blend well. Combine the fruits and nuts in a large mixing bowl and pour the warm apple mixture over the fruit and nuts. Toss well to coat.

Slice the pear halves and fan onto the serving plates with the Chargrilled Pork Tenderloin (see recipe). Top the fanned pears with the Fruit Nut Compote. Keep the plates warm while preparing the Potato Pancakes with Applesauce and Sour Cream.

Serves 4.

Potato Pancakes
with Applesauce and Sour Cream

3 Idaho potatoes
1 cup minced Spanish onions
1 cup cracker crumbs

2 eggs
2 tablespoons all-purpose flour
¼ teaspoon nutmeg
1 teaspoon chopped parsley
¼ teaspoon salt
¼ teaspoon white pepper

❧ ❧ ❧

6 Granny Smith apples, peeled, seeded, and diced
Poaching liquid from Poached Pears
1 teaspoon cinnamon

❧ ❧ ❧

2 tablespoons oil

❧ ❧ ❧

Sour cream

Grate the potatoes with a box grater and squeeze the grated potatoes until they are dry. In a large bowl combine the potatoes and the onions, cracker crumbs, eggs, flour, nutmeg, parsley, salt, and pepper. Toss to mix well. Cover tightly with plastic wrap and refrigerate until well chilled.

In a saucepan combine the apples and the poaching liquid from the pears. Add the cinnamon. Simmer the apples until most of the liquid has been absorbed. Mix with a spoon to break up any remaining large pieces of apple. Transfer the mixture to a small bowl and refrigerate.

In a skillet heat the oil. Sauté ⅛ of the potato mixture at a time in the heated oil, until all of the potato mixture has been used. Place 2 Potato

Pancakes on each serving plate with the Chargrilled Pork Tenderloin and the Poached Pears. Top the pancakes with the Applesauce and a dollop of sour cream. Serve immediately.

Serves 4.

The Victorian Inn

1229 Seventh Street
Port Huron, Michigan 48060
(313) 984-1437

Built in 1896 as a residence for the family of James A. Davidson, a Port Huron business leader, the Victorian Inn has been restored to its original elegance by its present owners. Here guests will enjoy the charm of the Victorian era in the elegant dining and gracious guest room accommodations. The restaurant and pub are open to guests and residents of the community.

Hazelnut Chicken
with Orange Thyme Cream

We serve this entree with a bed of wild rice pilaf, vegetable, and garnish of orange butterflies or segments and chive blossoms.

1 whole boneless chicken breast, skinned and halved
⅓ cup finely chopped husked hazelnuts
⅓ cup fine fresh bread crumbs or cracker crumbs
¼ teaspoon dried crumbled thyme
All-purpose flour
1 egg, beaten to blend with 1 tablespoon milk

🙢 🙢 🙢

3 tablespoons unsalted butter
1 cup whipping cream
½ cup fresh orange juice
1 tablespoon Frangelico liqueur
⅛ teaspoon dried thyme
Salt and freshly ground pepper

Using a flat mallet or rolling pin, pound the chicken between 2 sheeets of waxed paper or plastic wrap to a thickness of ¼ inch. Combine the hazelnuts, crumbs, and ¼ teaspoon of thyme. Dredge the chicken in the flour, shaking off the excess. Dip into the egg mixture, then into the hazelnut mixture.

In a large heavy skillet over medium heat, melt the butter. Add the chicken and cook until golden brown and springy to the touch, about 3 minutes per side. Transfer to plates and keep warm. Stir the cream, orange juice, liqueur, and ⅛ teaspoon of thyme into the skillet and bring to a boil. Reduce the heat and simmer until reduced to ⅔ cup and slightly thickened. Season with salt and pepper. Spoon the sauce over the chicken just before serving.

The orange thyme cream can be made ahead of time and held in the refrigerator. It must be warmed carefully because if it gets too hot it will separate. If that happens just cook it down again and whisk it back together.

Serves 2.

Pumpkin Cheesecake

¾ cup graham cracker crumbs
½ cup ground pecans
2 tablespoons sugar
2 tablespoons brown sugar
¼ cup butter or margarine, melted

🙢 🙢 🙢

¾ cup sugar
¾ cup pumpkin (canned)
3 egg yolks
1½ teaspoons cinnamon
½ teaspoon mace
½ teaspoon ginger
¼ teaspoon salt
3 8-ounce packages of cream cheese (softened)
¼ cup plus 2 tablespoons sugar
1 egg plus one egg yolk
2 tablespoons whipping cream
1 tablespoon cornstarch
½ teaspoon vanilla extract
½ teaspoon lemon extract

🙢 🙢 🙢

Whipped cream (optional)
Pecans (optional)

Combine the first 5 ingredients and mix well. Firmly press mixture into a 9-inch springform pan. In a medium bowl, combine ¾ cup of sugar, the pumpkin, 3 egg yolks, spices, and salt. Mix well and set aside.

Beat the cream cheese with an electric mixer until light and fluffy. Gradually add ¼ cup plus 2 tablespoons of sugar, mixing well. Add the egg, egg yolk, and whipping cream, beating well. Add the cornstarch and extracts and beat until smooth. Add the pumpkin mixture. Pour into the prepared pan. Bake in a 350° oven for 50 to 55 minutes (the center will be soft but will firm up when chilled). Cool on a wire rack. Chill thoroughly. Garnish with whipped cream and pecan halves if desired.

Serves 6 to 8.

The Victorian Inn

Country Heritage Bed and Breakfast

64707 Mound Road
Romeo, Michigan 48065
(313) 752-2879

This Greek Revival-style home built in 1840 is furnished with antiques, country accessories, and family heirlooms. Situated on six acres, on which the old farm buildings remain, the inn offers a suite with a fireplace in the sitting room and bedroom. An outdoor pool is available for guests' use, and Arthur the peacock may welcome your arrival. A continental breakfast is served.

Apple Coffee Cake

1½ cups chopped apples
1 8-ounce can Hungry Jack biscuits
1 tablespoon margarine
⅓ cup brown sugar
¼ teaspoon cinnamon
⅓ cup light corn syrup
1 egg
½ cup chopped pecans

🌢 🌢 🌢

⅓ cup confectioners' sugar
¼ teaspoon vanilla extract
2 teaspoons milk

Grease an 8-inch pan. Spread 1 cup of apples in the pan. Separate the biscuits and cut in fourths, arranging point side up over the apples. Top with the remaining ½ cup of apples. Combine the margarine, brown sugar, cinnamon, syrup, and egg. Beat for 2 to 3 minutes, until the sugar is partially dissolved. Stir in the pecans. Spoon over the biscuits and apples. Bake in a 350° oven for 35 to 45 minutes. Cool for 5 minutes. Combine the

remaining ingredients and glaze the coffee cake.
Serves 6.

Peaches with Cinnamon Cream

1 8-ounce carton vanilla yogurt
¼ teaspoon cinnamon
1 teaspoon honey
1 fresh peach, sliced
Cinnamon or granola for garnish

In a medium bowl combine the yogurt, cinnamon, and honey. Blend well. Arrange the peach slices in 2 individual serving dishes. Spoon the yogurt mixture evenly over the peaches. Sprinkle each with a little cinnamon or 2 tablespoons of granola.
Serves 2.

Jumbo Banana Muffins

These muffins took a first-prize blue ribbon at the 1989 Michigan State Fair.

1¼ cups whole wheat flour
1 cup all-purpose flour
½ cup sugar
2 teaspoons baking powder
2 teaspoons cinnamon
½ teaspoon nutmeg
½ teaspoon baking soda

🌢 🌢 🌢

½ cup buttermilk
½ cup oil
1 egg
½ cup mashed banana

Grease 8 muffin tins. In a large bowl combine the dry ingredients. In a separate bowl combine the buttermilk, oil, egg, and mashed banana. Add to the dry ingredients and stir. Pour the batter into muffin tins. Bake in a 375° oven for 18 to 20 minutes.
Makes 8 muffins.

Spicy Pear Muffins

2 cups all-purpose flour
1 tablespoon baking powder
½ teaspoon salt
¼ cup sugar
1 egg, beaten
1 cup milk
3 tablespoons oil
1 cup chopped pears

🌢 🌢 🌢

½ cup brown sugar
⅓ cup chopped nuts
½ teaspoon cinnamon
Pinch ginger

Grease 9 large muffin tins. In a large bowl combine the flour, baking powder, salt, and sugar. In a separate bowl combine the egg and milk, and add the oil and pears. Pour the liquid mixture into the dry ingredients, stirring just until moistened.

In a small bowl combine the brown sugar, nuts, and spices. Fill muffin cups ⅓ full with batter and sprinkle with half of the brown sugar mixture. Top with more batter and the remaining brown sugar mixture. Bake in a 400° oven for 15 minutes.
Makes 9 large muffins.

The Ross

229 Michigan Avenue
South Haven, Michigan 49090
(616) 637-2256

The Ross was built in 1886 for Volney Ross, a prominent member of the South Haven business community. This delightful inn has a country flavor, with television and comfortable chairs in the lounge offering a place to relax at the end of the day. The Ross retains much of its original charm. Guests are served the continental breakfast of freshly baked goods.

The Ross

A Bed & Breakfast House

Crab Soufflé

An elegant "make-ahead" brunch favorite.

12 slices bread, crusts removed
Butter, melted

&ч &ч &ч

1 pound cooked crab meat
1 cup chopped celery
2 teaspoons onion juice or 1 small onion, grated
2 teaspoons prepared mustard
½ cup mayonnaise
Dash Tabasco sauce
Dash lemon juice
Sharp Cheddar cheese, grated
5 eggs
2 cups milk

Dip the bread in melted butter. Line a 9x13-inch baking dish with a layer of bread.

In a large bowl combine the next 7 ingredients. Spread over the layer of bread. Next place another layer of bread over the spread. Top with the cheese. Beat the eggs, add the milk, and pour over the layer of "sandwiches." Cover and refrigerate for at least 2 to 4 hours, preferably overnight. Set the dish in a pan of hot water. Bake in a 325° oven for 1 hour.
Variation: Substitute the equivalent amount of chicken for crab and create a chicken soufflé.
Serves 10 to 12.

Seascape Bed and Breakfast

20009 Breton
Spring Lake, Michigan 49456
(616) 842-8409

The word *Seascape* evokes thoughts of majestic sunsets, seagulls swooping over sparkling water, seaport harbors with their quaint old lighthouses, and sugar sand beaches cultivated with sea oats. All this and more is the view guests enjoy every day at Seascape. Seascape is an all-season inn that offers a kaleidoscope of scenes with the changing of the seasons. Guests rekindle the half-forgotten pleasures of hospitality and feel as if they are staying with friends.

Blueberries and Cheese Coffee Cake

1¼ cups sugar
½ cup margarine
2 eggs

&ч &ч &ч

2¼ cups all-purpose flour
1 tablespoon baking powder
1 teaspoon salt

&ч &ч &ч

¾ cup milk
¼ cup water
1 8-ounce package cream cheese, softened
1 teaspoon lemon rind
2 cups blueberries
¼ cup all-purpose flour

&ч &ч &ч

¼ cup sugar
¼ cup all-purpose flour
1 teaspoon lemon rind
2 tablespoons margarine

Grease a 9x13-inch pan. In a large bowl cream together 1¼ cups of sugar and ½ cup of margarine. Add the eggs. In a separate bowl combine the dry ingredients. Add to the creamed mixture, alternating with milk and water. Mix well after each addition. Beat in the cream cheese, mixing well. Stir in 1 teaspoon of lemon rind. Toss the blueberries with ¼ cup of flour and gently fold into the batter. Pour into the prepared pan.

Combine the remaining ingredients and sprinkle over the batter. Bake in a 350° oven for 45 to 50 minutes.
Serves 18.

Warwickshire Inn

5037 Barney Road
Traverse City, Michigan 49684
(616) 946-7176

The Warwickshire Inn is an antique-filled country farmhouse built about 1900 atop a long hill that gives a panoramic view of Traverse City and East and West bays. Traverse City's first bed and breakfast home, it is situated two miles west of town in a location easily accessible to Devonshire antiques, ski resorts, and cross country skiing, downtown, shopping, and beaches. All the Warwickshire's rooms are spacious and comfortable.

&ч &ч &ч &ч &ч

French Toast

This is our favorite recipe and is a great hit with our guests.

6 eggs
1½ cups milk
1 teaspoon vanilla extract
½ teaspoon cinnamon
1 loaf French bread
1 8-ounce package cream cheese, softened
Jam or jelly (any flavor)
2 cups dry cereal, crushed
Butter

In a large bowl beat the eggs and blend in the milk, vanilla, and cinnamon. Slice the French bread nearly in half sideways. Spread cream cheese on each side and then spread jam or jelly on top of the cream cheese. Put the loaf back together and make 1-inch slices on a diagonal. Soak in the egg batter on both sides. Dip in crushed cereal and fry in butter on a heated griddle. Serve with your favorite syrup.

Serves 6 to 8.

Creamed Eggs à la Asparagus

3 tablespoons butter
¼ cup minced onion
1 cup cubed ham
3 tablespoons all-purpose flour
1¾ cups milk
½ cup shredded sharp Cheddar cheese
5 hard-boiled eggs, sliced

❧ ❧ ❧

½ pound fresh or frozen asparagus
English muffins

In a skillet melt the butter and sauté the onion and ham. Blend in the flour. Add the milk, cooking and stirring until the sauce is thick. Add the cheese, stirring until melted. Fold in the egg slices.

Gently boil the asparagus. When the spears are tender cut some into thirds and add to the cheese sauce. Arrange the remainder on top of sauce. Serve on toasted muffins.

Serves 4 to 6.

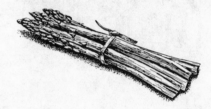

Minnesota

Quill & Quilt

615 West Hoffman Street
Cannon Falls, Minnesota 55009
(507) 263-5507

From its oak and Italian marble fireplace to its quilt-covered four-poster beds, the Quill and Quilt offers a unique blend of Colonial Revival elegance and country comfort. Guests enjoy this home's six bay windows, well-stocked library, and array of porches and decks. From the tea and wine social to the dainty chocolates guests find on their pillows, guests are treated to cheery hospitality and country comfort. Each of the four guest rooms has its individual atmosphere to add to the inn's charm. Carefully restored to its original elegance, the Quill and Quilt continues to mirror the diverse talents of the many craftsmen who took part in its construction.

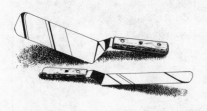

Raspberry Champagne Punch

We serve this for our holiday open house and on Christmas Eve and New Years' Eve.

> 750 ml dry white wine
> 750 ml champagne
> 750 ml 7-Up (white soda)
> 2 shots raspberry liqueur
> 1 pint fresh or frozen raspberries

Combine all ingredients in a punch bowl just prior to serving.
Serves 10 to 12.

Blue Cheese Stuffed Pork Chops

> 3 tablespoons butter
> 2 teaspoons minced onion
> ½ cup finely sliced mushrooms
> 1 cup seasoned bread crumbs
> ½ cup crumbled blue cheese
> ½ cup grated Parmesan cheese
> 8 thick pork chops with pockets cut

In a skillet melt butter. Add the onion and mushrooms, and cook for 5 minutes. Remove from the heat and stir in the bread crumbs, blue cheese, and Parmesan. Stuff the pork pockets with the mixture, secure with toothpicks, and place in a glass baking dish. Sprinkle any remaining stuffing over the chops. Bake uncovered in a 325° oven for 1 hour.
Serves 8.

Orange French Toast

> 2 eggs, lightly beaten
> ¼ cup orange liqueur or orange juice
> ½ cup half and half or milk
> 1 tablespoon sugar
> Dash salt
> 8 slices English muffin bread
> Confectioners' sugar

Spray 2 baking sheets with nonstick cooking spray.

In a shallow bowl mix the eggs, orange liqueur or juice, half and half, sugar, and salt. Dip bread in egg mixture and place on cookie sheet. Spoon 1 or 2 teaspoons of remaining batter on each slice. Bake in a 500° oven for 6 to 8 minutes on one side; then turn and bake for 4 to 6 minutes on the other side, watching closely. Cut the toast diagonally and sprinkle with confectioners' sugar before serving.
Serves 4.

Bluff Creek Inn

1161 Bluff Creek Drive
Chaska, Minnesota 55318
(612) 445-2735

Bluff Creek Inn is a historical Victorian folk home in the Minnesota River valley. Built on a land grant from Abraham Lincoln to Joseph Vogel, a German immigrant, the inn offers nineteenth-century hospitality in a country bed and breakfast setting. It is ten minutes from Canterbury Downs, Murphy's Landing, Chanhassen Dinner Theater, Minnesota Landscape Arboretum, the Renaissance Festival, and the "494" strip. It has four guest rooms, one with private bath. Three of the rooms have "water closets" and share a Victorian shower room.

Eggs Celant

½ pound Gruyère cheese, grated
4 tablespoons butter
1 cup heavy cream
½ teaspoon salt
Dash pepper
1½ teaspoons dry mustard
12 eggs, slightly beaten
Blanched asparagus spears, cut into
1-inch pieces (optional)

Butter a 13x9-inch baking dish. Spread the cheese in the prepared dish. Dot with butter. Mix the cream with the seasonings and mustard. Pour half over the cheese. Add the slightly beaten eggs to the dish, then add the remaining cream mixture. Sprinkle the asparagus pieces over all, if desired. Bake in a 325° oven for 35 minutes until set.
Serves 12.

The Hutchinson House

305 N.W. Second Street
Faribault, Minnesota 55021
(507) 332-7519

The Hutchinson House is a restored three-level Queen Anne Victorian home built in 1892 for one of Faribault's leading citizens. Each of the four elegant bedrooms has a private bath. Embellishments include unique light fixtures, comforters, Oriental rugs, handmade lace, and stained glass. The home-cooked breakfast is served on the wraparound porch, in the parlor, or in one's bedroom, depending on weather or personal preference.

Banana Wild Rice Crepes

1 cup whole wheat flour
1 cup all-purpose flour
1 cup Bisquick
2 tablespoons cinnamon-sugar
mixture
2 teaspoons baking powder
1 teaspoon cardamom

☙ ☙ ☙

2 eggs, lightly beaten
1 large ripe banana, lightly mashed
1 cup half-and-half

☙ ☙ ☙

1 cup buttermilk
2¼ cups 2% milk
1½ cups cooked wild rice

☙ ☙ ☙

Sour cream
Warmed pure maple syrup

In a large bowl combine the flours, Bisquick, cinnamon sugar, baking powder, and cardamom.

In another bowl combine the eggs,

Bluff Creek Inn

banana, and half-and-half, carefully mixing until all lumps are incorporated. Combine the egg mixture with the flour mixture and mix until no lumps appear.

Add the buttermilk and milk. Mix well, add the rice, and let set for 15 minutes.

Gently stir the mixture to distribute the rice. Using a scant ⅓-cup measuring scoop measure the batter to make crepes and cook as for any standard crepe recipe. Be careful not to overcook, or they will become too dry.

Before serving, spread a thin coat of sour cream over the top of each crepe, then roll into a cigar shape. Serve topped with syrup.

Note: Crepes can be frozen after they're cooked and cooled. To serve, bring to room temperature so they can be separated easily. Add sour cream, roll and then heat in a microwave oven until just warmed through.

Makes 40 thin 6-inch crepes.

East Bay Hotel

Grand Marais, Minnesota 55604
(218) 387-2800

The East Bay Hotel was built in the early 1900s, when it was known as the Lake Side Hotel. The old hotel has been carefully restored, retaining its character while modernizing it to today's expectations of comfort. Some of the twenty guest rooms have private baths and each room has its own style of decor. The hotel overlooks Lake Superior at the start of the Boundry Waters Canoe Area and is near cross-country ski trails.

Raspberry Dessert

2½ cups pretzels, crumbled coarsely (not sticks)
¾ cup melted butter
3 tablespoons sugar

🍃 🍃 🍃

1 8-ounce package cream cheese
1 cup sugar
1 package Dream Whip

🍃 🍃 🍃

2 3-ounce packages raspberry gelatin
2 cups boiling water
2 10-ounce packages frozen raspberries
Whipped cream for topping

Mix the pretzels, melted butter, and 3 tablespoons of sugar. Press into a 13x9-inch pan. Bake in a 375° oven for 10 minutes. Let cool.

Mix the cream cheese and 1 cup of sugar with an electric beater. Prepare the Dream Whip according to the package directions, and fold into the cream cheese mixture. Spread on the cooled crust.

Dissolve the raspberry gelatin in boiling water. Add the frozen raspberries and stir until thawed, being careful to preserve the whole berries. Cool the mixture. When the mixture is slightly thickened, spread over the cream cheese mixture and refrigerate until set. Serve with whipped topping.

Serves 12.

Ham Balls in Sweet and Sour Sauce

1½ pounds ground ham
½ pound ground pork
1 cup fine dry bread crumbs
1 cup evaporated milk
2 eggs

🍃 🍃 🍃

1 cup brown sugar
½ cup water
¼ cup vinegar
½ teaspoon dry mustard

In a large bowl mix the ham, pork, bread crumbs, milk, and eggs together. Shape into balls.

In a separate bowl combine the brown sugar, water, vinegar, and dry mustard. Place the balls in a single layer in a baking dish and cover with the sauce. Bake in a 350° oven for 1½ hours, basting every 30 minutes.

Serves 6.

The American House

410 East Third Street
Morris, Minnesota 56267
(612) 589-4054

This lovely old home, built in 1900, is named for the first hotel established in Morris, which supplied horses and guides for hunters who came from great distances. The inn offers country charm with an original stencil design and parquet hardwood flooring in the dining room, stained glass windows, beaded woodwork, unique brass doorknobs, and family heirlooms and antiques. The three guest rooms are individually decorated.

Grandma's Old-fashioned Chocolate Pie

¾ cup sugar
½ cup butter, room temperature
1 teaspoon vanilla extract
1 ounce Baker's chocolate, melted
2 eggs, room temperature
1 8-inch baked pie shell

Beat together the sugar, butter, vanilla, and chocolate. Add the eggs one at a time, beating after each addition.

Continue beating for 10 minutes or until the mixture is fluffy. Spoon into the pie shell. Place in a freezer for at least 12 hours before serving.

Serves 6 to 8.

Pratt-Taber Inn

706 West Fourth
Red Wing, Minnesota 55066
(612) 388-5945

This thirteen-room, Italianate-style inn, restored to its original glory, offers its guests a taste of nineteenth-century atmosphere. Its builder included such fine details as feather-painted slate fireplaces, "gingerbread" woodwork, and star-studded porch detail. Butternut and walnut woods were used throughout the inn. Each of the six bedrooms is furnished with early Renaissance Revival and country Victorian antiques. Guests enjoy playing the old-time Victrola, looking at stereographic cards, or relaxing on the screened porch or in front of the fireplaces. Pratt-Taber Inn is within walking distance of downtown and the Mississippi River. Nearby is the Cannon Valley Trail, which is groomed for biking, nature walks, and cross country skiing, as well as trolley car rides, riverboat excursions with dinners, and the Amtrack train depot. Bikes are available at the inn.

Pratt-Taber Inn

Easy Surprise Cornbread Muffins

Totally delights the guests.

1 8½-ounce box Jiffy cornbread
  muffin mix
5 extra small eggs

Grease 5 extra large muffin tins. Prepare the cornbread muffin batter according to the package directions and pour into the muffin tins. Drop an egg into each ½ filled cup. Bake according to package directions.

Makes 5 muffins.

Wood Stove Potpourri

¼ cup whole cloves
¼ cup whole allspice
¼ cup broken cinnamon pieces
¼ cup dried orange peel
¼ cup dried lemon peel
¼ cup dried peppermint leaves

Combine all of the ingredients in a simmering pot, fill with water, and simmer for that welcoming aroma of country cooking.

🦆 🦆 🦆 🦆 🦆

Canterbury Inn

723 Second Street, Southwest
Rochester, Minnesota 55902
(507) 289-5553

Canterbury Inn, Rochester's first bed and breakfast, spoils its guests in the gracious surroundings of a restored Victorian home within three blocks of the Mayo Clinic and St. Mary's Hospital. The inn's informal, comfortable living room provides reading and writing materials, games and music, plus hors d'oeuvres and libations each day from 5:30 to 7:00. Full breakfasts feature a variety of specialties and the innkeepers conform to dietary needs and schedules. The inn offers central air conditioning, a cozy fireplace in the winter, and a shady porch in the summer. King, queen, and twin beds are available, and each of the four double rooms has a private bath with both shower and tub. Private, offstreet parking is provided. No pets are allowed.

Layered Nacho Dip

1 8-ounce package cream cheese
½ fresh jalapeño pepper, seeded and chopped
2 cups grated sharp Cheddar cheese
8 ounces medium-hot Mexican salsa
3 ounces ripe olives, chopped

🌶 🌶 🌶

Corn tostados

Soften the cream cheese and spread over the bottom of a serving casserole. Sprinkle jalapeño bits evenly over the cheese. Spread with grated Cheddar. Pour on the salsa and sprinkle with olives. Bake uncovered in a 350° oven for 30 minutes.

Serve with chips.

Serves 4 to 6.

Canterbury Eggs Benedict

12 green tomato slices, ½-inch thick
Cornmeal
Salt and pepper
Bacon drippings

🌶 🌶 🌶

3 egg yolks
2 tablespoons fresh lemon juice
½ teaspoon salt
Dash hot pepper sauce
½ cup butter, melted and hot

🌶 🌶 🌶

1 dozen eggs, poached
6 English muffins (Bay or Thomas preferred)
12 very thin slices ham

Dredge the green tomato slices in cornmeal, salt, and pepper. Fry slowly in bacon drippings (at least 15 minutes).

Prepare a Hollandaise sauce by combining the next four ingredients into a blender and blending briefly.

CANTERBURY INN
BED & BREAKFAST

Add the melted butter to the blender contents while the butter is still bubbling and the blender is running. (Leftover Hollandaise may be stored several days. Warm only to room temperature when using later. It will bake easily!)

For poaching eggs, put a small quantity of milk into the poaching water, and it will keep the eggs from splattering apart.

Assemble on each toasted, buttered English muffin half, 1 fried green tomato slice, 1 slice of warmed ham, and 1 poached egg topped with 1 tablespoon of Hollandaise sauce.

Serves 6.

Chase's Bed and Breakfast

508 North Huron Avenue
Spring Valley, Minnesota 55975
(507) 346-2850

This romantic French Renaissance mansion provides comfort and solitude for its guests. The five guest rooms, with private bath, also have overhead fans and unique accommodations. Nearby are the Laura Ingalls Wilder site, Mystery Cave, and an Amish settlement.

Corn Pancakes

Serve with syrup or jam. My guests like wild plum jam.

2 eggs
1¼ cups liquid (corn juice and water)
⅓ cup nonfat dry milk
½ teaspoon baking soda
1¼ cups all-purpose flour
1 teaspoon sugar
2 tablespoons oil
1 teaspoon baking powder
½ teaspoon salt (optional)
1 16-ounce can whole kernel corn, drained

In a large bowl stir all of the ingredients together. Bake on a greased heated griddle.

Makes 16 4-inch pancakes.

Grape Nuts Muffins

1¼ cups all-purpose flour
3 teaspoons baking powder
½ teaspoon salt (optional)
½ cup sugar
1¼ cups milk
1½ cups Grape Nuts cereal
1 egg
⅓ cup oil

Grease 12 muffin cups. In a large bowl stir together all of the ingredients. Fill the prepared muffin cups. Bake in a 400° oven for 25 minutes.

Makes 12 muffins.

Mississippi

Edgewood

412 Storm Avenue
Brookhaven, Mississippi 39601
(601) 833-2001

Edgewood, built in 1908, took four years to complete. With its many beautiful details, it is considered an architectural gem in the Greek Revival style. It has been completely restored over a thirty-year period by David Lovell, an architectural designer, who furnished it with fine antiques and beautiful chandeliers. Edgewood has recently been opened for tours, parties, and weddings. Eight rooms are available for overnight guests in the main house and the carriage house. Dinner is served by reservation.

Sausage Rice Casserole

1 cup rice
3 stalks celery, chopped
1 small onion, chopped
1 bell pepper, chopped
1 6-ounce can mushroom stems
½ cup butter or margarine
6 ounces hot pork sausage
1 can beef consommé
Salt and pepper
1½ teaspoons curry powder

Cook, rinse, and drain the rice. Transfer the rice to a casserole dish. In a skillet sauté the celery, onions, bell pepper, and mushrooms in butter or margarine. In a separate skillet cook the sausage, and drain on paper towels. Mix the sausage, consommé, and sautéed vegetables with the rice. Add the salt, pepper, and curry powder. Bake in a 325° oven until bubbly. This can be refrigerated up to a week before cooking.

Serves 4.

🐦 🐦 🐦 🐦 🐦

Salmon Mousse

1 8-ounce can feta salmon
1¼ tablespoons lemon juice
3 tablespoons minced onions
2 8-ounce packages cream cheese
¼ teaspoon salt
1½ tablespoons horseradish

In a serving bowl combine all of the ingredients. Chill in the refrigerator for several hours. It can be used as a mousse or as a spread on melba toast rounds, and can be topped with caviar.

Makes about 3¼ cups.

Edgewood

Hamilton Place

105 East Mason
Holly Springs, Mississippi 38635
(601) 252-4368

Hamilton Place was built in 1838 by William F. Mason, treasurer of the Illinois Central Railroad. The home is a typical Louisiana raised cottage; it is listed on the National Register of Historic Places and is filled with eighteenth- and nineteenth-century antiques. Guests may relax by the swimming pool or the year-round hot tub. Bikes are also available. The carriage house is now an antique shop. Holly Springs has an abundance of antebellum homes, an art gallery museum, and a Green Line historical driving tour.

Orange Frosty

    1 6-ounce can frozen orange juice
        concentrate, thawed and
        undiluted
    ¼ cup sifted confectioners' sugar
    8 pineapple chunks
    1 ripe banana, cut into chunks
    3 cups crushed ice

Combine all of the ingredients except the ice in the container of an electric blender. Process until smooth. Add the ice and process until frothy. Serve immediately.
    Makes about 4 cups.

Honey Blueberry Butter Spread

    ½ cup fresh or frozen blueberries,
        thawed
    ¼ cup honey
    ½ cup butter or margarine, softened
        to room temperature

In a saucepan bring the blueberries and 2 tablespoons of the honey to a boil over medium-high heat, stirring constantly for about 3 to 4 minutes, until mixture thickens and is reduced by half. Cool and blend in the remaining honey. Beat in the butter.
    Makes about ⅔ cups.

Red Creek Colonial Inn

7416 Red Creek Road
Long Beach, Mississippi 39560
(601) 452-3080
(800) 729-9670

Situated on the beautiful Mississippi Gulf Coast, Red Creek Colonial Inn was built as a "raised French cottage"

circa 1899. One of the innkeepers' favorite "places" is the sixty-four-foot front porch with its two swings and room for reading and relaxation. The rooms in this seven bedroom, five bath inn are tastefully appointed; a variety of usable antiques, six fireplaces, old-fashioned wooden radios, a Victorian organ, and a breakfast porch all add to the relaxing atmosphere.

Big Shrimp Omelet

    6 eggs
    1 tablespoon butter, melted
    1 tablespoon finely chopped green
        onion
    1 teaspoon finely chopped parsley
    ⅓ cup butter
    ¼ pound peeled, cleaned, freshly
        boiled small shrimp
    Pepper
    Green onions, finely chopped
    Salt
    Garlic salt
    American cheese (optional)

Hamilton Place

In a medium bowl beat the eggs thoroughly and add 1 tablespoon of melted butter and the onions. Add the parsley and mix lightly. In a warmed cast iron frying pan combine ⅓ cup of butter and the egg mixture. Increase the heat slightly and roll the mixture as it cooks. Roll mixture over, decrease the heat, and continue to cook. As the softness disappears, add the shrimp, pepper, another sprinkle of green onions, and season lightly with salt and garlic salt. If cheese is added, omit most of the garlic salt. Serve with home-grown, sliced tomatoes and freshly baked bread, rolls, and home-made jams.

Serves 2.

Potatoes, Ah, Crab!

    4 large potatoes
    ⅓ cup butter
    ½ cup light cream
    1 teaspoon salt
    1 tablespoon grated onion (Vidalia, if possible)
    1 cup shredded sharp Cheddar cheese
    1 cup cooked crab meat (fresh, if possible)

Bake the potatoes in a 400° oven until tender. Cut completely in half lengthwise, and scoop out most of the pulp. Add the butter to the potato pulp and mash. Beat in the light cream, salt, onion, and cheese. Fold in the crab meat and pile back into the potato shells. Refrigerate until mealtime. Sprinkle with a little more cheese and reheat in a 450° oven for about 15 minutes.

Serves 4.

Bayou Chicken Surprise

    4 medium chicken breasts
    ½ medium bell pepper, chopped
    1 onion, chopped
    1 16-ounce package mild pork sausage

    ¼ teaspoon salt
    Oil
    2 cups chicken broth
    1 cup Uncle Ben's rice

Cut the chicken breasts into bite-sized pieces. In a frying pan combine the chicken with the bell pepper and onion. Add the sausage and salt and sauté until golden brown in enough oil to keep from sticking. Add the chicken broth and rice. Cover the pan and cook slowly for 45 minutes.

Serves 8.

Pecan Divinity

    3 cups sugar
    ½ cup light Karo syrup
    ¾ cup water
    ½ teaspoon salt
    ½ teaspoon vanilla extract
    ¼ cup egg whites
    1 cup pecan pieces

In a saucepan combine the sugar, Karo, and water. Cook over low heat, stirring until dissolved. Increase the heat until the mixture boils, then cover the boiling mixture, without stirring, for 3 minutes. Cook evenly until the temperature of the mixture is 265° or firms up. In a bowl combine the salt, vanilla, and egg whites, whipping until stiff. Slowly pour this mixture into the hot syrup. Continue cooking until the mixture will almost hold its shape, then stir in the pecan pieces. Drop the divinity by teaspoons onto waxed paper and cool at room temperature until set.

Serves 30.

Red Creek Remoulade Sauce

    1 cup mayonnaise
    4 hard-boiled eggs, finely chopped
    1 teaspoon dry mustard
    2 tablespoons finely chopped parsley
    1 tablespoon finely chopped green pepper
    1 teaspoon finely chopped garlic
    1 tablespoon anchovy paste
    1 teaspoon Worcestershire sauce
    6 finely chopped olives
    White pepper
    1 tablespoon finely chopped gherkins
    1 tablespoon finely chopped capers
    1 tablespoon finely chopped chervil
    1 tablespoon finely chopped tarragon

In a mixing bowl combine the mayonnaise and eggs, and thoroughly blend by hand. Mix in the dry mustard, parsley, green pepper, garlic, anchovy paste, Worcestershire sauce, olives, and white pepper to taste. Add the gherkins, capers, chervil, and tarragon. Add more white pepper, to taste, if necessary.

Makes about 1½ cups.

Anchuca

1010 First East
Vicksburg, Mississippi 39180
(601) 636-4931
(800) 262-4822 (Outside Mississippi)

Anchuca was built in 1830 in Greek Revival style in the center of the historic section of Vicksburg. It is magnificently furnished with period antiques and gas-burning chandeliers. Overnight guests are accommodated in the original slave quarters, the turn-of-the century guest cottage, or in the main house. Bedrooms are all furnished with period antiques and have private baths, color televisions, telephones, heating, and air conditioning. The price of the room includes a big southern breakfast, a tour of the house, and use of the swimming pool and Jacuzzi hot tub.

Chocolate Sheet Cake

2 cups all-purpose flour
2 cups sugar
½ teaspoon salt
½ cup margarine
½ cup shortening
3 tablespoons cocoa
1 cup water

   🙚 🙚 🙚

½ cup buttermilk
1 teaspoon baking soda
2 eggs, slightly beaten
1 teaspoon vanilla extract

   🙚 🙚 🙚

½ cup margarine
6 tablespoons milk
3 tablespoons cocoa
1 1-pound package confectioners'
   sugar
1 teaspoon vanilla extract
1 cup pecans, chopped

Grease and flour a 9x13-inch pan. In a mixing bowl combine the flour, sugar, and salt. In a saucepan combine ½ cup of margarine, the shortening, 3 tablespoons of cocoa, and the water. Bring the mixture to a boil, pour over the flour mixture, and beat.

In a separate bowl combine the buttermilk and the baking soda. Add the milk mixture to the flour mixture and beat well. Add the eggs and 1 teaspoon of vanilla, and continue to beat the mixture. Pour batter into the prepared pan. Bake in a 375° oven for 30 to 35 minutes.

In a saucepan combine ½ cup of margarine, the milk, and 3 tablespoons of cocoa, and bring to a boil. Remove from the heat and add the confectioners' sugar, 1 teaspoon of vanilla, and the pecans. Spread icing over the cooled cake.

Serves 10 to 15.

Anchuca

Bourbon Pie

½ package Famous chocolate wafers
3 tablespoons butter, melted

   🙚 🙚 🙚

1 12-ounce can Pet evaporated milk
21 marshmallows
½ pint whipping cream
3 tablespoons bourbon

Roll the wafers into crumbs and mix with the melted butter. Reserve ½ cup of the crumbs for a topping. Spread the remaining crumbs evenly in a 9-inch pie pan. Bake in a 350° oven for 5 minutes. Cool the pie shell.

In a double boiler over hot water combine the Pet milk with the marshmallows, stirring until smooth. Cool the mixture. In a mixing bowl whip the cream and add the bourbon. Fold the cream mixture into the cooled marshmallow mixture and pour into the pie shell. Sprinkle the reserved crumbs over the pie filling. Chill thoroughly.

Serves 6 to 8.

Cedar Grove Estate

2300 Washington Street
Vicksburg, Mississippi 39180
(601) 636-2800
(800) 862-1300
(800) 448-2820 (Mississippi)

Cedar Grove Estate is one of the South's largest and loveliest historic mansions. Built by John Klein as a wedding present for his bride in 1848, it is exquisitely furnished with many original antiques, including gaslit chandeliers, gold leaf mirrors, and Italian marble mantels. During the Civil War, it survived the ravages of the Battle of Vicksburg, but a Union cannonball remains lodged in the parlor wall. Guests of this luxurious inn enjoy the beauty of formal gardens, gazebos, fountains, a court- yard, pool, and spa. Its eighteen accommodations for overnight guests make it the largest bed and breakfast inn in Mississippi. The breakfast is strictly southern.

Bourbon Ribs

Try these for one of the best bar- becues you have ever tasted.

4 pounds beef or pork ribs

&ea; &ea; &ea;

**1 medium onion, chopped
    (approximately ½ cup)**
½ cup light molasses
½ cup catsup
**2 teaspoons finely shredded orange
    peel**
⅓ cup orange juice
2 tablespoons cooking oil
1 tablespoon vinegar
1 tablespoon steak sauce
½ teaspoon prepared mustard
½ teaspoon Worcestershire sauce
¼ teaspoon garlic powder
¼ teaspoon salt
¼ teaspoon pepper
¼ teaspoon hot pepper sauce
⅛ teaspoon cloves
¼ cup bourbon

In a large Dutch oven or saucepan combine the ribs with enough water to cover and bring to a boil. Reduce the heat, cover, and simmer for 40 to 55 minutes, until the ribs are tender. Remove from the heat and drain thor- oughly.

In a medium saucepan combine the remaining ingredients. Bring the sauce to a boil and gently simmer un- covered for 15 to 20 minutes.

Grill the ribs over slow coals for about 45 minutes, turning every 15 minutes and basting with the sauce. Extra sauce can be served with the meat.

Serves 4.

Missouri

Borgman's Bed and Breakfast

Arrow Rock, Missouri 65320
(816) 837-3350

When guests arrive, they are shown to one of four spacious rooms where they can relax. They may prefer to enjoy the sitting room or porches, stop by the kitchen to visit with the cooks, wind up an old Victrola for a song, choose a game or puzzle, read a book, or just sit a spell and listen to the sounds of Arrow Rock. Grandma's Trunk may reveal a home-crafted item to purchase. In the morning, a family-style breakfast of freshly baked breads, juice or fruit, and coffee or tea begins the day.

Pecan Mini-muffins

⅓ cup butter or margarine, melted
1 cup brown sugar
2 eggs
½ cup all-purpose flour
1 cup chopped pecans
1 teaspoon vanilla extract

In a large bowl combine all of the ingredients. Fill mini-muffin pans ¾ full and bake in a 350° oven for 10 to 15 minutes.
 Makes 30 mini-muffins.

Garth Woodside Mansion

Rural Route #1
Hannibal, Missouri 63401
(314) 221-2789

Mark Twain slept here at the home of his friends, John and Helen Garth, in what is now called the Clemens Room. Situated on thirty-nine acres of meadows and woodlands, this magnificent Victorian mansion still retains many of the furnishings of the Garth family. The eight guest rooms are reached by a magnificent "flying staircase," one with no visible means of support. Six of the rooms have private baths, and there is a two-bedroom suite. Fresh pastries, juices, and coffee are standard fare for the home-cooked breakfast, and the French toast with warm peach sauce is a gourmet's delight. Among the many nearby attractions are Mark Twain's boyhood home and museum and courtroom that provided the setting for the trial of Muff Potter in *Tom Sawyer*.

Borgman's Bed and Breakfast

Garth Woodside Mansion

Garth Peach French Toast

1 cup brown sugar
½ cup butter or margarine
2 tablespoons water
1 29-ounce can sliced peaches
1 loaf French bread, sliced

&ac &ac &ac

5 eggs
1½ cups milk
1 teaspoon vanilla extract

In a medium saucepan combine the sugar and butter and heat over medium-low heat until the mixture bubbles. Add the water and continue cooking until sauce becomes thick and foamy. Pour into a 9x13-inch baking dish. Drain the peaches well and reserve the syrup. Place the peaches on the cooled caramel sauce. Cover the fruit with the slices of bread. In a blender combine the eggs, milk, and vanilla, and blend thoroughly. Pour the liquid mixture over the bread, cover, and refrigerate overnight.

Bake in a 350° oven for 40 minutes, loosely covering with foil the last 10 to 15 minutes. Heat the reserved peach syrup and pour over the toast.
Serves 12 to 14.

Crepes

4 eggs
¼ teaspoon salt
2 cups all-purpose flour
2¼ cups milk
¼ cup butter, melted

In a blender container combine all of the ingredients. Blend for 1 minute. Scrape down the sides and continue to blend for 15 more seconds or until smooth. Refrigerate the batter for 1 hour. Cook the crepes in a greased skillet until brown on both sides.
Makes 32 to 36 crepes.

Sausage Crepe Flowers

½ pound bulk sausage
¼ cup chopped onions

&ac &ac &ac

½ cup milk
3 eggs
½ cup mayonnaise
2 cups shredded Cheddar cheese

&ac &ac &ac

12 crepes

Grease 12 muffin tins. In a skillet brown the sausage with the onions and drain. Combine the remaining ingredients and add to the sausage mixture. Line the muffin tins with the crepes and fill ¾ full with the sausage mixture. Bake in a 350° oven for 15 minutes. Cover loosely with foil and bake 15 more minutes until set.
Serves 12.

Elegant Oranges

4 medium navel oranges
1 tablespoon sugar
¼ teaspoon cinnamon
2 tablespoons orange-flavored liqueur (Triple Sec)
Coconut, grapes, chopped nuts, or mint leaves for garnish

Peel the oranges close to the fruit, cutting away the bitter white inner peel. Thinly slice the oranges crosswise. Sprinkle the sugar and cinnamon evenly over the orange slices and cover with the liqueur. Let the orange slices stand uncovered at room temperature for 30 minutes to 1 hour. Garnish with coconut, grapes, chopped nuts, or mint leaves.
Serves 4.

Cream Topping
(for any fresh fruit)

1 cup sour cream
½ cup sifted confectioners' sugar
4 tablespoons lemon juice

In a small bowl combine all the ingredients. Cover and chilll.
Serves 4.

Lady Fingers Supreme

1 8-ounce package cream cheese
1 cup sugar
½ teaspoon vanilla extract
1 pint heavy cream
3 packages unfilled lady fingers
1 21-ounce can fruit pie filling
   (cherry, blueberry, etc.)

In a medium mixing bowl mix together the cream cheese, sugar, and vanilla. In a separate bowl beat the heavy cream until stiff. Add the cream mixture to the cheese mixture. Line the sides and bottom of a 9-inch springform pan with the lady fingers (brown side toward pan). Alternately layer the cheese mixture and the remaining lady fingers, ending with the cheese. Refrigerate overnight. Release from the pan and top with the fruit topping. Keep refrigerated until served.
Serves 10 to 12.

Birk's Goethe Street Gasthaus

700 Goethe Street
Hermann, Missouri 65041
(314) 486-2911
(800) 748-7883

Birk's Goethe Street Gasthaus is a 104-year-old Victorian mansion built by the owner of the third largest winery in the world. Furnished in period furniture, it has brass beds, six-foot tubs with gold eagle claw feet, and ten-foot doors with transoms. Here hospitality is not a business, it's a way of life. On the first two full weekends of every month *The Goethe Street Mansion Mystery* is performed

at the inn, with the help of Hermann's small theatre group. The scene of the mystery begins to be unveiled at this time, and the next day is spent scurrying to investigate, interrogate, report, and attempt to unmask the villain. Nine charming accommodations are available.

Birk's Goethe Street Gasthaus

Buffalo Fire Flings

5 pounds chicken wings

1 cup margarine
1 to 1½ cups hot sauce
1 teaspoon Tabasco sauce
4 0.6-ounce packages dry Italian
   Salad Dressing Mix
¼ cup lemon juice
1 teaspoon dry basil

Bake the chicken wings in a 350° oven for 45 minutes to 1 hour until fully cooked. In a medium saucepan melt the margarine. Stir in the remaining ingredients and baste the cooked chicken. Cook the chicken 10 more minutes.
Serves 8 to 10.

Copper Penny Salad

1 medium onion
1 small green pepper
5 cups sliced, cooked carrots
1 10½-ounce can tomato soup
½ cup salad oil
1 cup sugar
¾ cup vinegar
1 teaspoon prepared mustard
1 teaspoon Worcestershire sauce
1 teaspoon salt
Pepper to taste

Thinly slice the onion and green pepper and combine in a large bowl with the carrots. In a medium bowl combine the remaining ingredients and add to the vegetables. Marinate for 12 hours.
Serves 8.

Lakeview Bed and Breakfast

3609 Basswood Drive
Lee's Summit, Missouri 64064
(816) 478-2154

This traditional-style three-level house overlooking a lake provides three guest bedrooms with two and one-half private baths. The family room is on the lower level, as well as the kitchen decorated in ice cream parlor ambience; the library is on the third level. The full breakfast is served in the kitchen or in one of the two sunrooms. Within one-half hour's travel are the amenities of beautiful Kansas City, the Truman library and home, Worlds of Fun, and many other points of interest. Smoking is not permitted.

Cheddar Apple Breakfast Lasagna

1 cup sour cream
⅓ cup brown sugar
2 9-ounce packages frozen French toast (or 12 slices homemade)
8 ounces sliced, boiled ham
2½ cups shredded Cheddar cheese, divided
1 20-ounce can apple pie filling
1 cup granola with raisins

Grease a 9x13-inch baking pan. In a small bowl blend together the sour cream and sugar. Chill. Prepare the French toast according to the package directions and place 6 slices in the bottom of the prepared pan. Top with a layer of the ham, 2 cups of cheese, and the remaining French toast. Spread the pie filling over the toast and sprinkle with the granola. Bake in a 350° oven for 25 minutes. Top with the remaining ½ cup of cheese and return to the oven until the cheese melts. Serve with the sour cream mixture.
Serves 6.

Down to Earth Lifestyles

Route 22
Parkville, Missouri 64152
(816) 891-1018

Down to Earth Lifestyles offers a quiet country setting near Parkville, between the Kansas City International Airport and downtown Kansas City. The private rooms are cozy, each with a private bath, color television, telephone, and radio, and the living areas are spacious. This new, earth-integrated home is surrounded by eighty-five acres of grounds that provide many opportunities for exercise. The indoor heated swimming pool, wildlife and farm animals, piano, jogging and walking areas, and ponds for fishing are popular with guests. Breakfast is by special order, served at the time and place of guests' choice.

Easy Dip for Fruit

1 12-ounce carton sour cream
1 3-ounce package strawberry gelatin

Several hours before serving, in a small bowl combine the sour cream and gelatin. Blend the mixture until smooth. Serve as a dip with chunks of fruit or cheese.
Makes about 1½ cups.

Hot Spiced Tea

12 tea bags
12 cups water

❧ ❧ ❧

2 cups water
2 cups sugar
1 6-ounce can frozen lemonade concentrate
1 6-ounce can frozen orange juice concentrate
1 6-ounce can frozen pineapple juice concentrate
4 sticks cinnamon

Boil the tea bags in the 12 cups of water for 5 minutes. Discard the bags. Add 2 cups of water, the sugar, juices, and cinnamon sticks. Heat through.
Serves 35.

Russian Sandwich

Swiss cheese, sliced
Ham, sliced
Chicken breast, sliced
Lettuce
Rye bread
1000 Island dressing
Cucumber, sliced tomato, sliced hard-boiled egg, and bacon strips for garnish

For each serving layer the cheese, ham, chicken, and lettuce on a slice of bread. Cover with the dressing. Garnish with cucumber, tomato, hard-boiled egg, and bacon strips.
Serves 1.

Banana Pineapple Nut Bread

½ cup shortening
1½ cups sugar
2 eggs
1 teaspoon salt
¼ teaspoon baking powder
¾ teaspoon baking soda
2 cups all-purpose flour
10 to 12 Maraschino cherries, chopped
½ cup chopped nuts
1 cup crushed pineapple, drained
1 large banana, mashed

Grease two 8x4-inch loaf pans. In a large bowl cream together the shortening and sugar. Add the eggs and mix well. In a separate bowl combine the salt, baking powder, baking soda, and flour. Stir the dry ingredients into the creamed mixture. Add the cherries, nuts, pineapple, and banana. Pour the batter into the prepared pans. Bake in a 350° oven for 40 to 50 minutes until done.
Freezes well.
Makes 2 loaves.

Harding House Bed and Breakfast

219 North 20th Street
St. Joseph, Missouri 64501
(816) 232-7020

A gracious turn-of-the-century home with beveled glass windows, beautiful oak woodwork, and many antiques, Harding House offers four guest rooms and warm hospitality. Tea or sherry is served by the fire in cool weather and on the porch during warm months. A full American breakfast is served. The inn is centrally located in St. Joseph. The Pony Express Stables, Jesse James Home, St. Joseph Museum, the Doll Museum, Psychiatric Museum, Robidoux Row, and many antique shops, parks and fine restaurants are nearby.

Toast Blintzes

16 slices bread
3 tablespoons milk
1 cup large curd cottage cheese, drained
3 tablespoons butter, melted

🍃 🍃 🍃

2 cups strawberries

Cut 3-inch rounds from each bread slice. Brush one side of each bread round with the milk. Place 2 tablespoons of cottage cheese in the center of 8 bread rounds. Place the remaining bread rounds milk side down over the cheese. Press the edges together and brush the tops with the butter. Toast on a baking sheet in a 400° oven for about 10 minutes.

Serve hot with strawberries that have been sliced, sweetened, and chilled.
Makes 8 blintzes.

Cinnamon Nut Twirls

6 cups all-purpose flour
1½ teaspoons baking soda
1½ teaspoons salt
¾ cup shortening

🍃 🍃 🍃

1 tablespoon sugar
¾ cup buttermilk
Butter, melted

🍃 🍃 🍃

2 tablespoons butter, melted
½ cup brown sugar
½ teaspoon cinnamon (or orange rind)
½ cup chopped nuts

🍃 🍃 🍃

½ cup confectioners' sugar
2 to 3 tablespoons water
¼ cup chopped nuts

Grease a shallow baking pan. In a large bowl combine the flour, baking soda, and salt. Cut in the shortening until the mixture resembles coarse corn meal. Unused basic mixture may be stored in the refrigerator for several weeks. This is enough for 3 recipes of Twirls.

Combine 2¼ cups of basic mixture with the sugar. Add enough buttermilk to make a soft dough. Turn the dough onto a lightly floured board and knead slightly. Roll ¼-inch thick and brush with melted butter.

In a small bowl combine the 2 tablespoons of melted butter, brown sugar, cinnamon, and nuts. Spread the mixture onto the dough and press in firmly. Cut the dough into 1x6-inch strips. Using 2 strips of dough, place together sugared side up and twist, bringing the ends together to make a circle. Place in a greased shallow pan. Bake in a 475° oven for 10 minutes.

In a small bowl combine the confectioners' sugar and water. While the twists are hot, glaze them with the thin icing. Sprinkle with ¼ cup of nuts.
Serves 6 to 8.

Lafayette House

2156 Lafayette Avenue
St. Louis, Missouri 63104
(314) 772-4429

An 1876 brick Queen Anne mansion overlooking Lafayette Park "in the center of things to do in St. Louis," Lafayette house is tastefully furnished with antiques. The extensive library is available for browsing, and soft drinks, wine, cheese, and crackers are provided. The third-floor suite has a kitchen and private bath; second floor rooms have shared and private baths. Smoking is permitted.

Lafayette House Brunch Casserole

4 cups cubed cooked white meat chicken
2 10-ounce packages medium-wide noodles, cooked
3 10½-ounce cans cream of chicken soup, undiluted
1½ to 2 cups warm water
1 large green pepper, finely chopped

2 pounds Velveeta cheese, diced
2 large cans sliced or chopped
  mushrooms, drained
2 small jars pimento, finely
  chopped

Butter 1 large or 2 small casserole dishes. In a large bowl combine all of the ingredients and fill the prepared dishes ⅔ full. Bake in a 350° oven for 1 to 1½ hours until brown on top and bubbly.

Serves 10 to 12.

Banana Butterscotch Loaf

3½ cups all-purpose flour
4 teaspoons baking powder
1 teaspoon baking soda
1 teaspoon cinnamon
1 teaspoon nutmeg
1 teaspoon salt

&a   &a   &a

2 cups ripe mashed bananas
1½ cups sugar
2 eggs
½ cup butter, melted
½ cup evaporated milk
2 cups chopped pecans
1 12-ounce package butterscotch
  morsels

Grease and flour two 9x5-inch loaf pans. In a small bowl combine the dry ingredients and set aside.

In a large bowl combine the banana, sugar, eggs, and melted butter, beating until creamy. Add the dry ingredients alternately with the milk, mixing until well blended. Stir in the nuts and butterscotch morsels. Pour the batter into the prepared pans. Bake in a 350° oven for 1 hour, or until a toothpick inserted in the center comes out clean.

Makes 2 loaves.

Montana

O'Duach'ain Country Inn

675 Ferndale Drive
Bigfork, Montana 59911
(406) 837-6851

A gracious three-level authentic log home set on five acres, O'Duach'ain Country Inn is a charming home decorated with antique furniture, artifacts, and artistry. With a charming "lodge" atmosphere, this inn provides solitude in which to enjoy the Big Sky country. Guests enjoy the recreation room, parlor, outdoor hot-tub spa, and the full gourmet breakfast served elegantly in the dining room. The two rock fireplaces give cozy warmth for peaceful, discreet, luxurious solitude. Nearby, boating, fishing, swimming, walking, and riding trails are easily accessible. Guests who have stayed at O'Duach'ain describe it as "hard to find and difficult to leave." It is hard to find a more charming place.

Irish Stuffed Toast

1 8-ounce package cream cheese
1 teaspoon vanilla extract
½ cup chopped almonds

⁊ ⁊ ⁊

1 loaf unsliced French bread
4 eggs

1 cup whipping cream
½ teaspoon vanilla extract

⁊ ⁊ ⁊

½ teaspoon nutmeg
1 12-ounce jar apricot preserves
1 16-ounce can apricots, drained

In a small bowl combine the cream cheese and 1 teaspoon of vanilla until fluffy. Stir in the nuts.

Cut the bread into ½-inch slices, then slice again halfway through to form a pocket. Fill the pocket with a tablespoon of the cream cheese mixture.

In a medium bowl beat together the eggs, whipping cream, and ½ teaspoon of vanilla. Dip the bread pockets into the egg mixture, but do not soak. Cook the bread on a lightly greased griddle until golden brown.

Heat the preserves, apricots and nutmeg together and drizzle over the cooked toast.

Makes 10 to 12 pieces of toast.

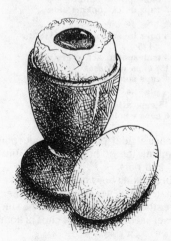

Lone Mountain Ranch

Box 69
Big Sky, Montana 59716

The Lone Mountain Ranch is known as one of the finest Nordic skiing centers in America, and the innkeepers pledge to make it better every year. Capacity is about fifty guests. The Old West atmosphere creates a warmth and ambience that adds greatly to the enjoyment of visiting the ranch.

An ideal destination for vacationing Nordic skiers, it has forty miles of expertly groomed cross-country trails in deep, dry snow to make track skiing delightful. Available are a complete rental and retail shop, certified instruction, and guided all-day trips into the wilderness of Yellowstone and the Spanish Peaks. Snow coach trips to Old Faithful, gourmet on-the-snow luncheons, horse-drawn sleigh rides, the new dining lodge, evening entertainment, and the outdoor hot tub are some of the reasons guests return year after year.

⁊ ⁊ ⁊ ⁊ ⁊

Cowboy Coffee Cake

20 cups all-purpose flour
16 cups brown sugar
4 teaspoons salt
5¼ cups margarine
4 teaspoons baking soda
2 tablespoons baking powder

❧ ❧ ❧

16 eggs, beaten
1 gallon milk
4 teaspoons cinnamon
4 teaspoons nutmeg

Grease and flour eight to ten 9-inch square baking pans. In a large bowl combine all the dry ingredients until crumbly. Reserve 4 cups.

In a separate bowl combine the eggs, milk, cinnamon, and nutmeg. Add the liquid mixture to the dry ingredients and mix well. Spread the batter into the prepared pans and sprinkle the reserved dry mixture over batter. Bake in a 375° oven until golden brown. Serve warm.

Makes 8 to 10 cakes.

Orange Knots

6 cups warm water
4 tablespoons active dry yeast
2 cups nonfat dry milk
1 cup sugar
½ cup molasses
3 tablespoons grated orange rind
3 tablespoons butter, melted

❧ ❧ ❧

15 cups all-purpose flour
2 tablespoons salt

❧ ❧ ❧

1 egg, beaten
2 tablespoons water

In a large bowl combine the water, yeast, milk, sugar, molasses, orange rind, and butter. Let soak for 5 minutes.

In a separate bowl combine the flour and salt and add to the liquid ingredients. Mix well for approximately 3 minutes. Place the dough in a well-greased bowl, cover, and let rise for 1 hour. Punch down and cut

LONE MOUNTAIN RANCH

into 1-ounce pieces. Roll into small tube shapes and tie into half knots.

Combine the egg and 2 tablespoons of water and brush the knots with the mixture. Bake in a 375° oven. Glaze with an orange honey glaze after baking.

Makes 12 dozen.

Sunflower Seed Bread

4½ cups boiling water
3 tablespoons salt
3 tablespoons butter
3 cups quick-cooking oats

❧ ❧ ❧

6 cups lukewarm water (110° to 115°)
3 tablespoons active dry yeast
1½ cups molasses
4 cups sunflower seeds

❧ ❧ ❧

18 cups all-purpose flour
6 cups whole wheat flour

Grease 9 loaf pans. In a saucepan combine the boiling water, salt, butter, and oats.

In a mixing bowl combine the lukewarm water, yeast, and molasses. After the yeast activates, add the sunflower seeds and about 4 cups of flour.

Mix well. Add the remaining flour, mixing well. Knead until a soft dough forms. Place the dough in a greased bowl and let rise until doubled in bulk. Punch down and shape into 9 loaves. Place the loaves in the prepared pans and let rise until doubled. Bake in a 375° oven for 25 to 30 minutes.

Makes 9 loaves.

Camp Creek Inn

7674 Highway 93 South
Sula, Montana 59871
(406) 821-3508

Camp Creek Inn is an early twentieth century ranch house that has been converted to a bed and breakfast and horse motel. Nestled in the Bitterroot Valley, it is known to old-timers as Old Pine Knot Ranch. Extending into the mountains surrounding the ranch are miles of trails for horseback riding, hiking, Alpine and cross-country skiing, and snowmobiling. This area is known for its great hunting and wonderful fishing. The Camp Creek Inn truly offers the comfort and excitement of ranch life.

Camp Creek Inn Brunch Enchiladas

2 cups cooked, ground ham
½ cup sliced green onions
½ cup chopped green peppers
2½ cups shredded Cheddar cheese
8 7-inch flour tortilla shells
4 eggs, beaten
2 cups light cream or milk
1 tablespoon all-purpose flour
Salt to taste
¼ teaspoon garlic powder
Dash Tabasco sauce

Grease a 12x7-inch baking dish. In a bowl combine the ham, onion, and green peppers. Place ⅓-cup of the mixture and 3 tablespoons of the cheese on the edge of each tortilla. Roll up. Arrange tortillas seam side down in prepared dish. In a separate bowl combine the eggs, cream, flour, salt, garlic powder, and Tabasco. Pour sauce over the tortillas. Cover and refrigerate several hours or overnight. Bake uncovered in a 350° oven for 45 to 50 minutes. Sprinkle with the remaining cheese and bake 3 more minutes or until the cheese is melted. Let stand 10 minutes before serving.
Serves 8.

The Stonehouse Inn

306 East Idaho Street
Post Office Box 202
Virginia City, Montana 59755
(406) 843-5504
(406) 682-7153

Built in 1884 by a blacksmith who came to Virginia City by wagon train, the Stonehouse Inn is a large, two-story home listed on the National Historical Registry. Twelve-foot ceilings, antique brass beds, stenciling, and lots of antiques give the inn an authentic, romantic feel. A wood cookstove in the kitchen and period dress by the hostess add to the homey, old-time atmosphere. Breakfast, with its sourdough bread, scones, muffins, and fruit, is another warm, homey experience in this charming inn.

Miso-Carrot Soup

2½ cups sliced, fresh carrots
4 cups water
6 tablespoons miso
1½ teaspoons curry powder
1½ teaspoons lemon juice
Pepper to taste
Chopped green onion or parsley to
garnish

In a saucepan simmer the carrots in 2 cups of water over medium heat for 18 to 20 minutes, until tender. Set aside and cool. Purée in a blender or food processor. Return to the saucepan and stir in the miso, remaining 2 cups of water, and curry powder. Bring to a boil, stirring constantly. Reduce the heat and let simmer, covered, for 10 minutes. Stir in the lemon juice and add pepper to taste. Garnish with chopped green onion or parsley.
Serves 4.

Caraway Cheese Muffins

1 cup rye flour
¾ cup whole wheat flour
2½ teaspoons baking powder
1 egg
¾ cup skim milk
⅓ cup oil
1 cup shredded Cheddar cheese
2 teaspoons caraway seeds

Grease 12 muffin tins. In a large bowl combine the dry ingredients. In a separate bowl combine the egg, milk, and the oil, mixing well. Add the liquid mixture to the dry ingredients and add the cheese and caraway seeds. Pour the batter into the prepared tins. Bake in a 400° oven for 20 to 25 minutes.
Makes 12 muffins.

ᘓ ᘓ ᘓ ᘓ ᘓ

Happy Angler Bread

1 cup whole wheat flour
½ cup wheat germ
2½ teaspoons baking powder
3 cups bran flakes
½ cup honey
1 egg
1 cup lowfat yogurt
1 cup skim milk
1½ cups raisins

Grease a loaf pan. In a bowl combine the flour, wheat germ, baking powder and bran flakes. In a separate bowl combine the honey and egg. Add the yogurt and milk to the egg mixture, mixing well. Stir the liquid mixture into the dry ingredients and add the raisins, mixing thoroughly. Pour the batter into the prepared pan. Bake in a 350° oven for 1 hour.
Makes 1 loaf.

Pear-Mince Pie

⅔ cup margarine, softened
2 cups whole wheat pastry flour
2 teaspoons salt
7 to 8 tablespoons water

❧ ❧ ❧

6 cups pears, cubed
1½ cups raisins
¾ cup brown sugar
1½ teaspoons cinnamon
1 teaspoon cloves
1½ teaspoons nutmeg
1 cup apple cider or juice

In a medium bowl cut the margarine into the flour and salt, and add the water to moisten. Shape the dough into 2 balls. Roll out half the dough and place the bottom crust in a pie pan.

In a large saucepan combine the remaining ingredients. Stir occasionally over medium heat for 1 hour, until the pears are tender and the sauce is syrupy. Water may be added to prevent the sauce from becoming too dry. Spoon the filling into the unbaked pie shell and add the top layer of pastry. Bake in a 375° oven for 1 hour.

Serves 6 to 8.

Virginia City Country Inn

115 East Idaho
Post Office Box 61
Virginia City, Montana 59755

Built in 1879 in Virginia City in the heart of the Alder Gulch mining district, this inn has been restored to its original charm. The rooms are cozy and bright with homemade quilts adorning antique beds, Victorian wallpaper, and lace curtains. Rooms feature double and queen-size beds; two baths, with claw-foot tubs and antique pull-chain water closets, are shared by the guests. Breakfasts are the occasion of good food and warm conversation.

❧ ❧ ❧ ❧ ❧

Raised Waffles

½ cup warm water
1 ¼-ounce package active dry yeast
2 cups milk, warmed
½ cup butter, melted
1 teaspoon salt
1 teaspoon sugar
2 cups all-purpose flour

❧ ❧ ❧

2 eggs
¼ teaspoon baking soda

In a large bowl combine the water and the yeast. Let stand for 5 minutes to dissolve. In a separate bowl combine the milk, butter, salt, sugar, and flour. Add the flour mixture to the yeast mixture and beat until smooth and blended. A hand-rotary mixer works great to get rid of the lumps. Cover the bowl with plastic wrap and let the dough stand overnight at room temperature.

Just before cooking beat in the eggs and add the baking soda, mixing well. Pour the thin batter onto a hot greased waffle iron and cook until golden brown.

Makes 8 waffles.

Grandma Witzels Rye Bread

1 ¼-ounce package active dry yeast
1½ cups warm water (110° to 115°)
2 cups all-purpose flour
2 cups rye flour

Soak the yeast in warm water. Add the flours and beat until spongy, then let set until double in bulk, about 1 hour. Add enough flour to make a stiff dough. Shape the dough into a round loaf, turn onto a baking sheet, and let rise until double in size, about 1 more hour. Bake in a 350° oven until golden brown.

Makes 1 loaf.

❧ ❧ ❧ ❧ ❧

Zucchini Casserole

1 cup water
1 tablespoon dehydrated onion flakes
4 cups cubed zucchini

❧ ❧ ❧

2 medium eggs
½ cup evaporated skim milk
½ cup grated Monterey Jack cheese
2 tablespoons margarine
1 teaspoon salt
½ teaspoon pepper
½ teaspoon garlic powder
Paprika

In a saucepan mix the water, onions, and zucchini. Cook the vegetables until tender and drain. In a bowl beat the eggs and add the milk, cheese, margarine, salt, pepper, and garlic powder. Add the vegetables. Place in a casserole dish and sprinkle with paprika. Bake in a 375° oven for 45 minutes.

Note: This is like a quiche when it is finished. It would be a great dish for breakfast, especially for vegetable lovers.

Serves 2.

Nebraska

Fort Robinson Inn

Fort Robinson State Park
Post Office Box 392
Crawford, Nebraska 69339
(308) 665-2660

Established as a post-Civil War Indian Agency protective post, Fort Robinson remained active through World War II. In nearly 22,000 acres of wide open country, history and beauty are blended with many recreational opportunities. The 1874, 1887, and 1909 officers' quarters are now housekeeping cabins, and individual rooms in the lodge (1909 enlisted men's barracks) are also available. Three hearty meals a day are served in the inn.

Buffalo Stew

30 pounds cooked buffalo stew
  meat with broth
2 large cabbage heads, chopped
  small
5 tablespoons basil
3 large onions, chopped small
10 bay leaves

❧ ❧ ❧

3 to 4 gallons vegetable stew mix,
  drained
1½ quarts tomato soup

In a large pot combine the stew meat and broth, cabbage, basil, onions, and bay leaves and cook at a temperature of 375° for 2 hours. Reduce the heat to 250° and add the vegetables and tomato soup. Simmer for approximately 1 hour.
Serves 60.

Corn Bread

4 cups all-purpose flour
4 cups corn meal
1 cup sugar
2 teaspoons salt
⅓ cup baking powder
1 cup oil
4 cups milk
8 eggs

Grease and flour a 13x17-inch baking pan. In a large bowl combine the flour, corn meal, sugar, salt, and baking powder. In a separate bowl combine the oil, milk, and eggs. Add the liquid mixture to the dry ingredients, mixing well. Pour the batter into the prepared pan. Bake in a 350° oven for 45 minutes or until golden brown.
Serves 15 to 20.

The Offutt House

140 North 39th Street
Omaha, Nebraska 68131
(402) 553-0951

This comfortable mansion, built in 1894, is part of Omaha's Historic Gold Coast. The architectural style is chateauxesque. The two-and-one-half-story, fourteen-room mansion is furnished with antiques and period furniture. Conveniently situated near downtown Omaha, it is also close to the Old Market area, which has many attractive shops and excellent restaurants.

My Favorite Stew

2 tablespoons lard
2 pounds beef, cut into pieces
2 tablespoons paprika
¾ cup all-purpose flour
1 pound onions, chopped
3 to 4 cloves garlic
2 tablespoons tomato paste, diluted
  in a little water
Salt and pepper
Bouquet Garni
Red wine
1 lump sugar

In a skillet heat the lard and brown the meat on all sides. Sprinkle the meat

The Offutt House

Crab Puffs

1 jar Kraft Sharp English Cheese
1½ teaspoons garlic powder
½ cup butter, softened
1 6½-ounce can crab meat
1 package English Muffins

Combine the English cheese, garlic powder, and softened butter, beating well. Fold in the crabmeat. Spread on the muffin halves. Broil 6 inches from the heat for 5 to 10 minutes.

Makes 48 canapes, with each muffin half cut in quarters.

Raspberry Cheesecake

1 package chocolate wafers, ground
**   in food processor**
½ cup sugar
½ cup butter, melted
❧ ❧ ❧
2 8-ounce packages cream cheese,
**   softened**
3 eggs
1¼ cups sugar
⅓ cup juice from raspberries
Dash salt
3 cups sour cream
2 12-ounce packages frozen
**   raspberries, thawed and drained**

Make a crust by combining the chocolate wafers, ½ cup of sugar, and melted butter. Press onto the bottom and sides of a 10-inch springform pan.

In a medium bowl combine the cream cheese, eggs, 1¼ cups of sugar, juice, and salt, beating well. Fold in the sour cream and raspberries. Pour the filling into the crust. Bake in a 350° oven for 1 hour to 1 hour and 30 minutes, until a toothpick inserted in the center comes out clean.

Serves 16.

with paprika and flour, coating well. Transfer the meat to a stewing pan and add the onions, garlic, tomato paste, salt, pepper, and Bouquet Garni. Cover with red wine and water (¾ wine to ¼ water), and add the sugar. Cover the pan and bake in a 350° oven for 3 hours, or until tender.

Serves 8.

In a bowl combine the corn and egg. Add the flour, baking powder, salt, and nutmeg, mixing well. In a medium-sized skillet over medium-high heat melt the butter. Drop the batter by tablespoons into the skillet and fry until brown on one side. Turn and fry on the other side. Serve hot with butter and your favorite syrup.

Serves 2.

Corn Fritters

½ cup cream-style corn
1 egg, lightly beaten
3 tablespoons all-purpose flour
½ teaspoon baking powder
Pinch salt
Pinch nutmeg
3 tablespoons unsalted butter
Syrup

Nevada

The Edwards House

204 North Minnesota Street
Carson City, Nevada 89703
(702) 882-4884

This traditional bed and breakfast inn is situated on a tree-lined street just off the main avenue. Built in 1886 by prisoners who cut the eighteen-inch sandstone blocks from the prison quarry, the house maintains a moderate temperature, no matter what the season. Throughout the inn there are elegant high ceilings, wallpapered walls, shining hardwood floors, window seats, and numerous nooks and crannies. Guests may relax on the large tree-covered patio with its grape arbor and gazebo. Inside the gazebo is a hot tub for relaxing. A full gourmet breakfast typically includes fresh fruit, strata, vegetable frittata, or eggs benedict in pastry. In the evening a decanter of cream sherry or wine is served in each guest room.

Broo's Brew

2 cups French vanilla coffee beans
1 cup Vienna coffee beans

Grind the coffee beans fresh each morning into a bowl and mix together well. This is very rich, so use 3 scoops instead of 4 for a 10-cup coffee maker. Brew coffee for 1 regular cycle.

Rick's Strata

12 slices of bread, crust removed
1 cup chopped ham
1 8-ounce package chopped broccoli
1 cup shredded Cheddar cheese

❦ ❦ ❦

2 cups milk
6 medium eggs
1 teaspoon minced onion

Grease a 9x12-inch casserole dish. Layer 6 slices of bread in the bottom of the dish. Top with a layer of ham, broccoli, and cheese. Cover with another layer of 6 slices of bread. In a mixing bowl combine the milk, eggs, and onion to make a sauce and pour evenly over the casserole layers. Refrigerate overnight. Bake in a 350° oven for 35 to 45 minutes.

Serves 6.

Bed and Breakfast of South Reno

136 Andrew Lane
Reno, Nevada 89511
(702) 849-0772

Situated ten miles south of Reno just off Highway 395, this bed and breakfast features poster beds and beamed ceilings in its rooms. Landscaped lawns, patios, and decks surround the summer heated swimming pool. Facing the inn are ranch lands, Mount Rose and Slide Mountain, places to hike, sleigh riding, and Alpine skiing. Nearby attractions include Virginia City, Reno, Lake Tahoe, sightseeing, and fishing.

Caroline's Egg Soufflé

1 large onion, finely chopped
1 green pepper, finely chopped (optional)
Butter
1½ pounds bulk sausage
3 cups cubed sourdough French bread
2 cups grated Cheddar cheese

❦ ❦ ❦

293

8 eggs
2 to 3 cups milk
Salt and pepper to taste
Potato chip crumbs

Butter a 9x13-inch baking dish. In a large skillet sauté the onions and green pepper in butter. Remove and reserve. Brown the sausage in the skillet, then remove and drain. Using the same skillet toast the bread cubes in a small amount of butter and the remaining pan drippings. Layer in the buttered pan the bread cubes, onions and peppers, and the sausage. Top with 1 cup of cheese.

In a large bowl beat the eggs, and add the milk and seasonings. Pour over the layers. Sprinkle with the remaining cheese. Top with potato chip crumbs. Bake in a 350° oven for 30 minutes. Then turn the oven to 400° and allow the soufflé to brown for 5 to 10 minutes.

Serves 10 to 12.

Old Pioneer Garden

Unionville, Nevada 89418
(702) 538-7585

Originally settled during the 1860s as a mining camp, this quiet, tree-shaded canyon is home to about twenty people and the Old Pioneer Garden. The inn consists of the Hadley House, built in 1861; the Ross House, built in 1868 as a wagon-master's cabin; and the Talcott House, built in 1865. Evenings can be spent in front of the fireplace in winter or in the gazebo during warm weather. There is a large library available for guests. In this canyon guests can fish the cold streams, swim, ride horses, or bicycle.

Applesauce Pancakes

1 cup corn flour
1 cup all-purpose flour
2 teaspoons baking powder
1 teaspoon baking soda
½ teaspoon salt
¾ cup buttermilk
2 tablespoons butter, melted
½ cup applesauce
Dash of cinnamon
1 egg

In a mixing bowl combine the dry ingredients. Add the buttermilk, melted butter, applesauce, and cinnamon. Add the egg and beat quickly. Sauté in a pan or on a griddle in oil or butter or a combination of both until golden on both sides.

Serves 4.

🐦 🐦 🐦 🐦 🐦

Corn Flour Fritters

We stone grind corn kernels to make our own fresh corn flour. This is our most popular breakfast item.

2 cups corn flour
1 teaspoon baking powder
½ teaspoon baking soda
1 egg
Buttermilk
1½ cups sliced peaches, pears, apples, or apricots (fresh, or canned from our own orchards)
Oil and butter
Maple syrup and yogurt

In a large bowl combine the flour, baking powder, baking soda, and egg. Quickly mix in enough buttermilk to make a thick soupy batter. Add the fruit. Heat a combination of oil (we use safflower) and butter in a skillet. Drop the batter by tablespoons into the oil and sauté until golden brown on both sides. Serve with maple syrup and yogurt.

Serves 4.

Marinated Lamb or Goat

1 cup oil (olive or safflower)
¼ cup lemon juice
¼ cup lime juice
¼ cup vinegar
1 teaspoon salt
½ teaspoon paprika
½ teaspoon dry mustard
3 cloves crushed garlic
Dash oregano, rosemary, thyme, parsley, and pepper
1 pound meat, cut in 1-inch pieces (some with bone in for flavor)

In a medium bowl combine the oil, lemon juice, lime juice, vinegar, salt, paprika, dry mustard, garlic, and seasonings as a marinade. Pour over the meat in a porcelain or stainless steel container and refrigerate overnight. Simmer the meat in the marinade for 1 hour and 30 minutes or until the meat is tender, or skewer the meat, brush with the marinade, and bake in a 350° oven for 15 minutes or until browned and tender.

Serves 4.

Chicken or Duck with Orange Sauce

2 tablespoons red wine
2 tablespoons butter
2 tablespoons orange peel
½ cup orange juice
⅛ teaspoon salt
⅛ teaspoon dry mustard
¼ teaspoon tarragon
2 tablespoons chopped onion
¼ cup currant jelly (we grow our own currants)
🐦 🐦 🐦
1 young duck or chicken, whole or in pieces
🐦 🐦 🐦
1½ teaspoons cornstarch

In a saucepan combine the wine, butter, orange peel, orange juice, salt, dry mustard, tarragon, onion, and jelly. Heat and continue to stir until the jelly melts.

Place the meat in a roasting pan breast up and baste with half the sauce. Bake in a 325° oven for approximately 2 to 2½ hours, pricking the skin with a fork and basting often.

Add the cornstarch to the remaining half of the sauce in the saucepan. Cook over medium heat, stirring until the mixture thickens. Boil for 1 minute and pour over the meat to serve.

Serves 6.

Romanoff Noodles

- 1 10-ounce package wide egg noodles
- 1½ cups sour cream
- ¼ cup grated sharp cheese
- 1 teaspoon salt
- ½ teaspoon pepper
- 2 cloves garlic, crushed
- 2 tablespoons butter
- Chopped parsley

Cook the noodles, drain, and set aside. In a medium bowl combine the sour cream, cheese, salt, pepper, and garlic. Stir the butter into the hot noodles and add the sour cream mixture. Sprinkle with the parsley.

Serves 4.

The Gold Hill Hotel

Post Office Box 304
Virginia City, Nevada 89440
(702) 847-0111

Guests of the Gold Hill Hotel, Nevada's oldest, recapture the opulence of the 1800s in the fifteen charming, luxurious rooms furnished with period antiques. Four of the rooms have fireplaces; most have private baths. Guests can eat in the Crown Point Restaurant, which features gourmet French and American cuisine.

Chef Geoff's Grand Marnier Chocolate Mousse

- 5 eggs, room temperature
- 10 tablespoons sugar
- 2 cups heavy cream
- 6 ounces Belgian semi-sweet chocolate
- 2 ounces Grand Marnier

Separate the eggs and whip the egg whites until stiff, adding 5 tablespoons of the sugar. In a separate bowl whip the egg yolks with the remaining sugar. Combine the egg mixtures. In a separate bowl whip the heavy cream to soft peaks. In a saucepan over very low heat melt the chocolate, remove from the heat, and then fold in half of the cream mixture. Cool slightly, add the Grand Marnier, and fold in the egg mixture and the remaining cream mixture. Ladle into 12 dessert glasses and refrigerate at least 2 hours.

Note: You may top the mousse with additional whipped cream stars and shaved chocolate, a fresh mint leaf, and a candied orange slice.

Serves 12.

Gold Hill Hot Fudge

- 2 cups cream
- 1 cup butter
- 1½ cups sugar
- 1½ cups brown sugar
- 2 cups cocoa
- ¼ cup coffee
- Dash vanilla extract

In a saucepan combine the cream and butter. Bring to a boil. In a medium bowl combine the sugars and cocoa and add to the cream mixture, stirring constantly with a whip. Add the coffee and vanilla. Serve hot.

Serves 12.

Amaretto Cheesecake

- 3 cups graham cracker crumbs
- ½ cup sugar
- 1 teaspoon nutmeg
- ½ cup cocoa
- ¾ cup butter, melted

❧ ❧ ❧

- 4 pounds cream cheese, at room temperature
- 1½ cups sugar
- 4 eggs
- 5 tablespoons cornstarch
- 2 cups sour cream
- 2 teaspoons almond extract
- 3 ounces Amaretto

❧ ❧ ❧

- 2 cups sour cream
- ½ cup sugar
- Juice of 2 lemons
- Sautéed chopped almonds

Grease two 10-inch springform pans. In a blender container combine the graham cracker crumbs, ½ cup of sugar, nutmeg, cocoa, and melted butter, and purée. Spread the crust into the prepared pans and chill for 10 minutes.

In a large bowl combine the cream cheese, 1½ cups of sugar, the eggs, cornstarch, 2 cups of sour cream, almond extract, and Amaretto, mixing together well. Pour the filling into the crumb-lined pans. Bake in a 400° oven for 15 minutes. Reduce the heat to 325° and continue baking for 1 more hour. Remove from the oven.

In a medium bowl combine 2 cups of sour cream, ½ cup of sugar, the lemon juice, and almonds. Spread the topping over the cheesecakes and bake for 10 more minutes. Chill overnight.

Serves 24.

New Hampshire

English House

Route 4 and 11
Post Office Box 162
Andover, New Hampshire 03216
(603) 735-5987

Situated in the center of the village adjacent to Proctor Academy, the English House offers seven guest rooms with private baths, a lovely view, and a homey atmosphere. The hosts, who are from England, share in cooking the hearty breakfasts, which include freshly baked breads or muffins and a specialty dish. Guests of English House can enjoy cross-country skiing from the premises and downhill skiing just minutes away. In summer there are boating, swimming, fishing, golf, and tennis. Fine dining, shopping, theater, and museums are nearby.

Oyster Frittata

6 slices bacon, cut in half
¼ cup butter
1 10-ounce jar oysters
6 eggs
Flour
⅓ cup fine bread crumbs

ᵃᵃ ᵃᵃ ᵃᵃ

1 tablespoon water
½ tablespoon salt
Pinch of pepper
2 tablespoons chopped parsley
1 tablespoon butter

In a 10-inch skillet fry the bacon until crisp. Drain the bacon and discard the drippings. Add 3 tablespoons of the butter to the pan and melt. Drain the oysters and pat dry on a paper towel. In a medium bowl beat 1 egg. Coat the oysters in the flour, then dip in the egg and roll in the bread crumbs. Add the oysters to the skillet and cook over medium heat, turning to brown on both sides.

Add the remaining eggs to the beaten egg, along with the water, salt, and pepper. Beat until frothy. Sprinkle the oysters in the pan with parsley and pour in the beaten eggs. Cook until the bottom and sides are set. Invert the frittata onto a large flat plate. Add 1 tablespoon of butter to the pan,

melt, and then slide the frittata back into the pan to cook the second side.

Decorate with the bacon strips and cut into wedges.
Serves 4.

Kedgeree

¼ cup butter
1 small onion, chopped
1 teaspoon curry powder
1 cup long-grain rice
Salt and pepper
2 cups water

ᵃᵃ ᵃᵃ ᵃᵃ

¾ pound smoked haddock (Finnan haddock is best)
2 tablespoons all-purpose flour
½ teaspoon cayenne pepper

English House

1½ cups chicken stock
3 hard-boiled eggs
Chopped parsley
Paprika

In a large skillet melt 2 tablespoons of butter. Sauté the onions until soft. Stir in the curry powder and rice. Sprinkle with salt and pepper. Add the water, cover, and cook over low heat about 20 minutes, until the rice is tender and the liquid is absorbed. Keep the rice warm.

Steam the fish or poach it in milk and water. Flake the fish and keep it warm. In a medium saucepan melt 2 tablespoons of butter. Add the flour and pepper, mixing well. Blend in the chicken stock, stirring while cooking until the mixture thickens. Keep boiling until reduced to about 1 cup.

Chop the egg whites and set aside. Hand press the egg yolks through a sieve and set aside. In a medium bowl combine the rice, fish, egg whites, parsley, and sauce. Turn onto a warm dish. Garnish with the sieved yolks and paprika. Serve hot.

Serves 4.

The Steele Homestead Inn

Rural Route 1, Box 78
Antrim, New Hampshire 03440
(603) 588-6772

The Steele Homestead Inn has been renovated to conform to the time when it was built, 1810. Located in Antrim, which was named for its first inhabitant's native county in Ireland, the inn sits back from the main road on four acres of land. The expansive front lawn, flower-filled gardens, and small fruit orchard welcome guests, while the inn is bordered by a small forest of deciduous trees and evergreens. There are four large guest rooms, two with their own fireplaces and private baths. The price of lodging includes a hearty breakfast of favorite homemade specialties prepared by the innkeepers. A roomy, comfortable parlor, complete with fireplace, on the lower floor is available to guests for reading and relaxation.

The Kids' Favorite

Our guests have loved this for breakfast. I serve it with homemade biscuits or corn bread. My Mom served this when I was young and I in turn served it to our children (sometimes for supper). It always was and still is "The Kids' Favorite."

6 pork sausage patties (hamburger size)
6 slices thin white bread (or large biscuit halves)
12 thick slices firm tomatoes
Butter
Mrs. Dash or herb mixture

   ∾ ∾ ∾

5 to 6 tablespoons butter or margarine
5 to 6 tablespoons all-purpose flour
3 cups milk
Lawry's salt and pepper to taste

Brown and cook the sausage patties in an iron skillet. Set aside in foil in a warm oven. Pour the grease from the pan and set pan aside for gravy. Toast the bread slices and keep warm. On a broiler pan place the tomato slices, dot with butter, and sprinkle with Mrs. Dash or herb mixture of your choice. Broil tomato slices until bubbly but not mushy.

In the skillet melt the butter over low heat, scraping up the cracklings from the sausage. Add the flour and cook over low heat, stirring constantly until the mixture is smooth and bubbly. Add the milk slowly, stirring constantly with a whisk. Bring to a boil for 1 minute and cook until the desired thickness, stirring constantly. Add the salt and pepper to taste.

To serve, place a toasted bread slice on each plate. Top with a small amount of gravy, then the sausage, and top with 1 slice of broiled tomato. Spoon generous portions of gravy over the serving and place second slice of tomato on side of plate. Serve piping hot.

Serves 6.

Pecan Coffee Cake

The wonderful part of this recipe for innkeepers is that the uncooked coffee cake can be frozen to be baked fresh in the morning, right from the freezer. If you're going to freeze it before baking, let it rise for half the time and place it immediately into the freezer uncovered.

Pecan halves
¼ cup butter, melted
¼ cup brown sugar

   ∾ ∾ ∾

½ cup milk
1 teaspoon salt
1 tablespoon sugar
1 tablespoon active dry yeast
1 egg
2 tablespoons soft shortening
2 to 2¼ cups sifted all-purpose flour

   ∾ ∾ ∾

1 tablespoon butter, softened
¼ cup sugar
1 teaspoon cinnamon

Spread pecan halves over the bottom of a 9x13-inch baking pan. Cover with ¼ cup of melted butter and brown sugar.

In a medium saucepan heat the milk to lukewarm. Remove from the heat and stir in the salt, 1 tablespoon of sugar, and yeast to dissolve. Stir in the egg and shortening. Mix in enough of the flour to just handle the dough. Mix the dough by hand until it is moderately stiff. Turn it onto a floured board and fold it over several times until smooth.

Roll the dough into a 12x7-inch oblong and spread with 1 tablespoon

The Bradford Inn

The Bradford Inn

Main Street
Bradford, New Hampshire 03221
(603) 938-5309

Opened in 1898 as a small country hotel, the Bradford Inn continues to provide its guests with warmth, hospitality, and good food. J. Albert's Restaurant, named after the inn's founder and located at the inn, serves a menu of regional favorite "suppers." The inn's location in southwest New Hampshire provides guests the opportunity to enjoy New England's many pleasures.

of softened butter. Sprinkle with ¼ cup of sugar and the cinnamon. Roll up the dough from the long side, press down at the seam, and cut into 12 slices. Place the slices in the prepared pan and let rise until light, about 25 to 30 minutes. Bake in a 400° oven for 20 to 25 minutes. Invert onto a plate.

Serves 12.

Lemon Surprise

Cake is on top, pudding on bottom. Invert with a spatula so the pudding side is up when serving.

    1½ cups sugar
    4½ tablespoons all-purpose flour
    3 tablespoons butter, softened
    3 eggs, separated
    Juice of 2½ lemons (½ cup)
    1 cup milk
    Grated rind of orange

In a medium bowl blend the sugar and flour together with the softened butter. Add the egg yolks, beating well.

Add the lemon juice and milk, beating well. In a small bowl whip the egg whites until stiff and fold into the batter. Add the orange rind. Pour the batter into a casserole dish and set the dish in a pan of water. Bake in a 350° oven for 35 to 40 minutes, or until the top is brown, separating from the sides of the pan, and "spongy" to the touch.

Serve with whipped cream or other cream topping.

Serves 4 to 6.

Deviled Clams

    24 littleneck clams, shucked on the
        half shell
    6 tablespoons butter
    3 tablespoons minced onion
    1 clove garlic, minced
    1 tablespoon minced parsley
    ¼ cup beer
    4 slices crisp bacon, crumbled
    4 tablespoons bread crumbs
    Parsley leaves and lemon wedges
        for garnish

Coarsley chop the clams. In a medium bowl cream together the butter, onion, garlic, and parsley. Blend in the beer. Mix in the bacon and clams. Fill the clam shells with the mixture and sprinkle with the bread crumbs. Place on baking sheets and bake in a 375° oven for 10 minutes. Garnish with parsley leaves and lemon wedges.

Serves 4.

๛ ๛ ๛ ๛ ๛

Shrimp on the Half Shell

12 jumbo shrimp (unit size 12, 1 pound)
3 tablespoons sesame oil
1 clove garlic, finely minced
1 teaspoon minced ginger
3 tablespoons minced scallions
2 tablespoons soy sauce
2 tablespoons whiskey
¼ cup chicken stock

🍃 🍃 🍃

Hot cooked rice

Split the shrimp in half lengthwise, shells and all. Wash out the veins but let the shrimp remain in the halved shells. In a heavy skillet heat the oil, arrange the shrimp shell-side down, and cook gently for 5 minutes. Add the garlic, ginger, scallions, soy sauce, whiskey, and chicken stock, and let the shrimp simmer gently until tender, about 10 minutes. Serve in the shells on a bed of rice. Top the shrimp with the sauce.
Serves 4.

Breakfast Casserole

1 6-ounce package herb croutons
12 ounces mushrooms, sautéed in butter
1 pound cooked ham, cubed
3 cups shredded Cheddar cheese
12 eggs
1 10½-ounce can cream of mushroom soup
⅓ cup vermouth
½ cup light cream

🍃 🍃 🍃

1 15-ounce can tomato sauce
2 tablespoons brown sugar
1 teaspoon dried basil
½ teaspoon dried oregano

Grease a 10x18-inch glass baking dish. Layer the croutons, mushrooms, ham, and cheese in the prepared dish. In a large bowl combine the eggs, soup, vermouth, and cream, mixing well. Pour over the layered ingredients and cover with plastic wrap. Refrigerate overnight. Remove from the refrigerator 30 minutes before baking. Bake uncovered in a 375° oven for 1 hour.

In a medium bowl combine the tomato sauce, brown sugar, basil, and oregano, and heat. Serve the sauce with the casserole.
Serves 15.

Granola Bars

1½ cups oatmeal
1½ cups all-purpose flour
1 cup brown sugar
1 teaspoon cinnamon
¼ teaspoon nutmeg
2 teaspoons baking powder
½ cup chopped pecans
½ cup chopped dried apricots
½ cup raisins
2 eggs
½ cup milk
1 teaspoon vanilla extract
½ cup margarine, melted

Grease a 9x13-inch baking pan. In a large bowl combine the oatmeal, flour, brown sugar, cinnamon, nutmeg, baking powder, pecans, and fruit. Stir in the eggs, milk, vanilla, and margarine. Pour into the prepared pan and spread evenly. Bake in a 375° oven for 25 to 30 minutes.
Serves 24.

Mountain Lake Inn

Post Office Box 443
Bradford, New Hampshire 03221
(603) 938-2136
(800) 662-6005

Mountain Lake Inn, built in 1760 on the shores of Lake Massasecum, offers its guests a private sandy beach and 165 acres of woods and trails on which they can walk in summer and snowshoe in winter. Tastefully furnished with American and English period antiques, the rooms and suites have private baths. A full country breakfast is served.

Mountain Lake Inn

Quick Method Oatmeal Bread

2 cups boiling water
1 cup quick cooking oatmeal
⅓ cup shortening
½ cup molasses
4 teaspoons salt
2 ¼-ounce packages active dry yeast
2 eggs, beaten
4½ cups all-purpose flour

Grease two 9x4-inch glass loaf pans. In a large bowl combine boiling water, oatmeal, shortening, molasses, and salt. Cool to lukewarm. Add the yeast and mix well. Blend in the eggs. Add the flour and mix well. Place the dough in a greased bowl and cover. Refrigerate at least 3 hours. Shape into 2 loaves on a well-floured board or counter top. Place in the prepared pans and let rise for 2 hours. Bake in a 375° oven for 45 to 55 minutes.

Makes 2 loaves.

Helga's Bed and Breakfast

92 Packers Falls Road
Durham, New Hampshire

Mailing Address:
92 Packers Falls Road
Newmarket, New Hampshire 03857
(603) 659-6856

Situated on seven and one-half acres of lawn, gardens, and woods, this inn provides a friendly, homey atmosphere in which guests are made to feel comfortable. The four guest rooms, two with private balconies and two with sky lights and picture windows, share two bathrooms. The host cooks American, German, Austrian, and Czech specialties (the inn includes a bakery), and the breakfast is a very satisfying experience.

Salzburger Nockerle (Austrian Specialty)

"Nockerle" is pronounced nocker-le, meaning dumpling. If done right Nockerle are really delicious, but it takes a little practice to do it right.

2 tablespoons fresh unsalted butter
5 eggs, separated
5 tablespoons sugar
1 teaspoon vanilla extract
¼ cup all-purpose flour
1 tablespoon rum
Confectioners' sugar

Place the butter in a glass baking dish and heat in the oven until the butter melts but does not brown. In a medium bowl beat the egg whites, gradually adding the sugar, until very stiff. In a separate bowl beat the egg yolks and the vanilla together, gradually adding some of the beaten egg white. Add the remaining egg white to the top of the egg yolk mixture and cover with the sifted flour. Mix together lightly but thoroughly, and add the rum. With a large spoon or dough scraper scoop a portion of the dough into the hot baking dish, 1 scoop for each nockerle. Bake in a 350° oven for approximately 8 to 10 minutes. When finished baking the nockerle should be doubled in size. Sprinkle liberally with confectioners' sugar. Serve hot.

Makes 3 or 4 nockerle.

The Stonebridge Inn

Route 9
Star Route 3, Box 82
Hillsborough, New Hampshire 03244
(603) 464-3155

The Stonebridge Inn is a dream-come-true for the innkeepers, Nelson and Lynne Adame. A mid-1800s farmhouse, it has been restored and redecorated (much by their own hands) to create the kind of small country inn everyone has always hoped to find. The inn has four guestrooms, each with its own private bath. Whatever the season, there always is plenty to do at Stonebridge.

Seafood Streudel

1 16-ounce package phyllo sheets
   🍃   🍃   🍃
1 cup clam broth
2 pounds seafood (shrimp, scallops, crab, fish, or surimi)
¼ cup white wine
¼ teaspoon Old Bay Seasoning or a dash of nutmeg
3 tablespoons butter, melted
3 tablespoons all-purpose flour
1 cup sour cream
1 cup butter or margarine, melted

Let the phyllo thaw overnight in the refrigerator, then let it stand at room temperature for 2 hours.

In a medium saucepan bring the clam broth to a boil. Coarsely chop the seafood and poach it in the broth. (If you are using surimi as part of the mixture, you don't have to poach it.) Remove the seafood to a large bowl, reserving the broth. Add the white wine and seasonings to the broth. Boil until it is reduced by half. In a small saucepan cook 3 tablespoons of

The Stonebridge Inn

grounds. In cool weather one can curl up by a crackling fire in the sitting room and enjoy a good book or games and puzzles. In warmer weather the sixty-foot-long screened-in porch is the perfect spot to pass a few relaxed hours. Each morning guests are treated to a full breakfast featuring homemade breads and muffins.

Poppy Seed Bread

1 18¼-ounce package yellow cake mix
1 3¾-ounce lemon instant pudding mix
4 eggs
1 cup hot water
½ cup oil
¼ cup poppy seeds

Grease a 9x13-inch baking pan. In a large mixing bowl combine the cake mix, pudding mix, eggs, water, oil, and poppy seeds. Beat 4 minutes at medium speed with an electric mixer or 400 strokes by hand. Pour the batter into the prepared pan and bake in a 350° oven for 45 minutes, or until a toothpick inserted in the center comes out clean.

Serves 10 to 12.

melted butter with the flour until a thick paste forms. Add this roux to the broth and continue boiling until it is thickened. Cool, then mix in the sour cream and pour the sauce into the seafood.

Butter a baking sheet. Carefully unwrap the phyllo. Cover with a damp kitchen towel. Beginning with 3 sheets of phyllo, brush the top one with melted butter, and put about ½ cup of the seafood mixture vertically down the right side of the dough about 1½ inches from the edge. Fold the top of the dough about 1½ inches and then the bottom. Starting at the right, roll up the streudel. place on the baking sheet and brush with more butter. Repeat with the remaining dough and seafood mixture. Bake in a 400° oven for 20 to 25 minutes.

Makes 8 streudels.

The Inn on Golden Pond

Route 3
Post Office Box 680
Holderness, New Hampshire 03245
(603) 968-7269

Across the street from the Inn on Golden Pond is Squam Lake, the setting for the movie starring Katharine Hepburn and Henry Fonda. The inn itself is a gracious country home built in 1879 amid some of New England's most picturesque countryside. It sits on fifty-five acres of land, mostly wooded, with trails circling the property to provide an ideal setting for hikers, strollers, and cross country skiers. The grounds immediately surrounding the inn are spotted with meandering stone walls, old split rail fences, and a variety of flowers, shrubs, and shade trees. Each room is individually decorated; most have private baths, and all overlook the

Apple Muffins

1 egg
½ cup milk
¼ cup oil
1½ cups all-purpose flour
½ cup sugar
1 teaspoon cinnamon
2 teaspoons baking powder
½ teaspoon salt
3 small apples, peeled and diced

Grease 12 muffin tins. In a medium bowl beat together the eggs, milk, and oil. Add the flour, sugar, cinnamon, baking powder, and salt, mixing well. Stir in the apples. Fill the prepared tins ⅔ full. Bake in a 400° oven for 20 to 30 minutes.
Makes 12 muffins.

The Inn at Jackson

The Inn at Jackson

Main Street at Thorn Hill Road
Post Office Box H
Jackson, New Hampshire 03846
(603) 383-4321
(800) 289-8600

Guests of the Inn at Jackson discover a six-room country mansion with a comfortable and relaxed atmosphere. Designed by Stanford White as a private home at the turn of the century, it now offers its guests beautiful views of the surrounding mountains. Varied activities such as cross-country skiing and golf are popular. Many other familiy activities are available in the surrounding valley.

🦆 🦆 🦆 🦆 🦆

Mom's German Potato Salad

½ cup water
½ cup vinegar
½ teaspoon yellow mustard
2 eggs, beaten
Dash salt and pepper

🦆 🦆 🦆

4 slices bacon
1 cup sugar
5 pounds potatoes, peeled and cooked
2 stalks celery, chopped
½ cup chopped onion
Chopped olives
2 hard-boiled eggs
Celery salt to taste

In a medium bowl mix the water, vinegar, mustard, eggs, salt, and pepper. Set aside. Fry the bacon, and reserve some bacon fat in the skillet. Chop the bacon. Pour the water and vinegar mixture into the skillet and cook until it begins to thicken. Slowly add the sugar, stirring constantly to thicken. Cut up the potatoes and mix in a large bowl with the bacon, celery, onion, olives, and hard-boiled eggs. Pour the thickened sauce into the bowl and stir well. Sprinkle with celery salt. Refrigerate overnight.
Serves 12.

Gram's Potato Filling

2 medium onions
4 to 5 stalks celery
½ cup butter
2½ pounds potatoes, peeled
1 6-ounce package bread croutons

🦆 🦆 🦆

3 eggs
1 teaspoon parsley
½ teaspoon poultry seasoning
Dash salt and pepper
Chicken broth (or turkey broth)

Butter a 9x13-inch baking pan. In a skillet sauté the onions and celery in the butter. Dice the potatoes and add to the onions and celery, cooking until done. In a large bowl combine the potatoes, onions, and celery with the bread croutons.

In a separate bowl beat the eggs, parsley, poultry seasoning, salt, and pepper. Pour over the potato mixture. Add enough broth to moisten the mixture. Pour into a buttered pan and bake in a 350° oven for 1 hour.

If stuffing a turkey, add 1 hour and 30 minutes to the cooking time for the turkey.
Serves 8 to 10.

Inn at Thorn Hill

Thorn Hill Road, Box A
Jackson Village, New Hampshire 03846
(603) 383-4242
(603) 383-6448

Designed in 1895 by Stanford White, this 1895 yellow clapboard inn affords its guests spectacular views of Mount Washington and the White Mountains area. Rooms are decorated with antiques, including canopied beds and handmade quilts. The main inn includes a forty-two-seat dining room with fireplace, a cozy pub with fireplace, a parlor with the inn's only television, and a spacious drawing room. The Carriage House next door has a twenty-by-forty-foot great room, fireplace, and seven guest rooms. Three additional cottages are available at this extraordinary "getaway" inn.

Poppy Seed Dressing

½ gallon mayonnaise
1 cup sugar
2 to 3 tablespoons Dijon mustard
1 cup poppy seeds
1½ cups white vinegar

Combine all of the ingredients in a mixer or food processor.
Makes about 3 quarts.

Lobster Pie Thorn Hill

1 puff pastry, cut in strips 1¼" wide
  and 13" long
4 1½ pound fresh lobsters, cooked
Newburg sauce

🍂 🍂 🍂

Parsley
Lemon wedges

Using four four-inch casseroles (the kind scampi is served in) line the insides (not the bottom) with the pastry, overlapping the ends a little. Bake in 350° oven until lightly browned. Remove from oven.

Remove the lobster from the shells and pull apart into large chunks. Into the center of the casseroles add 3 tablespoons of sauce, then the lobster chunks, then enough sauce to cover the lobster well. Bake in a 350° oven until bubbly. Remove from the oven and loosen edges with a knife, and with stainless spatula slide onto serving plates so that the ring of pastry stays together and the lobster is in the middle. Garnish with parsley and lemon wedges.

Recipe courtesy of Chef Ken Beaudion.
Serves 4.

Edencroft Manor

Rural Delivery No. 1, Route 135
Littleton, New Hampshire 03561
(603) 444-6766

The Edencroft is a charming country inn with comfortable lodging, good food, and friendly hospitality. Six guest rooms, one with a fireplace, provide guests with firm beds and freedom from television. Most rooms have private baths. Beside the fireplace in the common room or in the full-service lounge overlooking the White Mountains one can meet other guests, browse through the selection of books and magazines, or play games. A soundproof children's corner is a plus. Trails for hiking, cross-country skiing, or snowmobiling leave from the inn. Canoeing, swimming, or fishing are just two miles away at Moor Lake and major ski areas are fifteen minutes distant.

Edencroft Manor

New England Bread Pudding
at Edencroft Manor

3½ cups milk
¼ cup butter
2 cups dry bread cubes (we combine white bread and cinnamon raisin bread)
2 eggs, slightly beaten
½ cup sugar
½ cup sherry
1 teaspoon cinnamon
1 teaspoon mace
1 teaspoon nutmeg
¾ cup raisins
Whipped cream

Scald the milk, add the butter, and pour over the bread cubes. Let the bread cubes soak about 5 mintues. In a medium bowl combine the eggs, sugar, sherry, spices, and raisins, mixing well. Pour over the bread cubes. Pour the mixture into a buttered baking dish and set the dish in a pan of water. Bake in a 375° oven for 1 hour, or until a knife inserted in the center comes out clean. Serve with whipped cream.
Serves 6.

Peep-Willow Farm

Bixby Street
Marlborough, New Hampshire 03455
(603) 876-3807

Peep-Willow Farm is a Thoroughbred horse farm that also caters to humans. Guests are invited to "help out" around the farm that contains twenty acres in the Marlborough hills, but riding is not permitted. Breakfast "New Hampshire" style is included.

Seafood Soufflé

1 pound seafood, chunked (ham is good, too)
2 cups shredded Cheddar cheese
6 slices bread, cubed
½ cup butter or margarine, melted
3 eggs
½ teaspoon dry mustard
⅓ teaspoon salt
2 cups milk

Grease a casserole or soufflé dish. Arrange the seafood, cheese, and bread into layers in the prepared dish. Pour melted butter over the mixture. In a medium bowl beat the eggs. Add the mustard, salt, and milk, mixing well. Pour over the casserole and let sit for 3 hours or overnight. Bake in a 350° oven for 1 hour.
Serves 4 to 6.

Peep-Willow Chicken Salad Supreme

4 cups chunked chicken
1 cup mayonnaise
2 cups white grapes
2 cups chopped celery

❧ ❧ ❧

2 teaspoons curry powder
¾ cup mayonnaise
¼ cup sour cream
1 teaspoon lemon juice
Salt and pepper to taste
Chutney

In a large bowl combine the chicken and 1 cup of mayonnaise. Stir in the grapes and celery. In a separate bowl combine the curry powder with ¾ cup of mayonnaise, sour cream, and lemon juice. Add the mixture to the chicken, and season with the salt and pepper. Serve with chutney.
Serves 6.

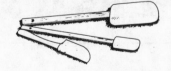

Pleasant Lake Inn

Pleasant Street
Post Office Box 1030
New London, New Hampshire 03257
(603) 526-6271

Built as a Cape farmhouse in 1790, Pleasant Lake Inn was converted in 1878 to a summer resort and became Pleasant Lake Inn in 1978. All twelve guest rooms have been renovated and equipped with private baths. From each room one can view the mountains and think of Kate Smith singing "When the Moon Comes over the Mountain," which was about Mount Kearsage. Pleasant Lake Inn prides itself on cleanliness, hearty country breakfasts, and gourmet dinners. Smoking is permitted only in common rooms. Five acres of woods, pastures, and gardens surround the inn.

Fresh Apple Walnut Cake

1 cup butter or margarine
2 cups sugar
3 eggs
3 cups sifted all-purpose flour
1½ teaspoons baking soda
½ teaspoon salt
1 teaspoon cinnamon
¼ teaspoon mace
1 teaspoon vanilla extract
3 cups chopped peeled apples
2 cups chopped walnuts

Grease and flour a 10-inch tube pan. In a medium bowl cream together the butter and sugar. Add the eggs one at a time, beating well after each addition. In a separate bowl mix and sift together the flour, baking soda, salt, cinnamon, and mace. Add the dry ingredients gradually to the cream mix-

Pleasant Lake Inn

ture. Stir in the vanilla, apples, and walnuts to form a stiff batter. Spoon into the prepared pan. Bake in a 325° oven for 1 hour and 30 minutes. Cool in the pan for 20 minutes, then remove to a rack. A macaroon-type crust forms on the top of the cake.

Makes 16 to 20 slices.

The Inn at Coit Mountain

HCR 63, Box 3
Newport, New Hampshire 03773
(603) 863-3583
(800) 367-2364

Nature's four seasons provide the backdrop to this gracious and historic Georgian home. Whether guests prefer the greening spring, languid summer afternoons, colorful autumn foliage, or winter-white mornings, they will delight in a stay at this inn. The library, with its oak paneling and massive granite fireplace, offers year-round charm and warmth to accom-

pany a good book, needlework, or a puzzle. Morning comes alive with the smell of freshly baked breads for the country breakfast before a corner fireplace. Dinners are available *by prior arrangements*. The bedrooms are spacious and comfortable, and some have fireplaces. A luxury suite with two rooms, bath, and king-size bed is also available. The Lake Sunapee area provides a variety of recreation, including cross-country and Alpine skiing in winter.

Eggs à la Suisse

2 eggs
2 slices bacon, fried crisp
1 tablespoon light cream
1 tablespoon sherry
1 teaspoon Worcestershire sauce
Cayenne pepper
2 tablespoons grated Swiss cheese

Break the eggs into a ramekin and surround with bacon, keeping the yolks centered in the dish. Top with cream, sherry, and Worcestershire sauce. Sprinkle with pepper and top with cheese. Bake in a 400° oven for 10 minutes.

Serves 1.

Swedish-style Lamb

4 to 4½-pound lamb roast
Salt and pepper to taste
1 cup strong coffee with cream and sugar

&. &. &.

2 tablespoons currant jelly
2 tablespoons all-purpose flour
1½ cups milk

Place the lamb in a roasting pan and add salt and pepper to taste. Roast in a 325° oven uncovered for 1 hour and 30 minutes. Add the coffee and roast 1 more hour. Remove the roast from the pan and carve.

Add the jelly and flour to the pan juices, stirring until smooth. Blend in the milk and heat until thickened.

Serves 8 to 10.

Lime Sour Cream Pie

A guaranteed refreshing summertime dessert.

¾ cup sugar
3 tablespoons cornstarch
Freshly grated peel and juice of 2 large limes
1 cup half and half
¼ cup butter, cut up
1 cup sour cream
1 baked 9-inch pie shell
1 cup whipping cream
1 or 2 tablespoons sugar

In a medium saucepan combine ¾ cup of sugar, the cornstarch, and lime peel, mixing well. Add the lime juice and stir until smooth. Blend in the half and half and the butter. Place over medium heat and stir until the mixture thickens and starts to boil. Remove from the heat and let cool. Fold in the sour cream and turn into the baked pie shell. Beat the whipping cream with 1 or 2 tablespoons of sugar and spread over the pie as a topping.

Serves 6 to 8.

The Buttonwood Inn

Mount Surprise Road
Post Office Box 1817
North Conway, New Hampshire 03860
(603) 356-2625

Tucked away on Mount Surprise, the Buttonwood Inn will bring you "home" to traditional New England. Situated on five wooded acres, it provides private and semiprivate baths, television rooms, lawn sports, an outdoor pool, and easy access to nearby recreational activities. The innkeepers have modeled the Buttonwood after the best they have found in other inns.

Chocolate Chip Sour Cream Coffee Cake

½ cup margarine
1 cup sugar
2 eggs, beaten
1 cup sour cream
2 tablespoons milk
2 cups all-purpose flour
1 teaspoon baking soda
1 teaspoon baking powder
1 6-ounce package chocolate chips

ðə ðə ðə

2 teaspoons cinnamon
½ cup sugar

Grease and flour a 10-inch tube baking pan. In a medium bowl cream together the margarine and 1 cup of sugar. Beat in the eggs until the mixture is light and fluffy. In a separate bowl combine the sour cream and milk and set aside. Sift together the flour, baking soda, and baking powder and add alternately with the sour cream mixture until well blended. Fold in the chocolate chips. Spoon half of the batter into the prepared pan. Combine the cinnamon and ½ cup of sugar and sprinkle half of the mixture over the batter. Spoon in the remaining batter and sprinkle with the remaining cinnamon mixture. Bake in a 350° oven for 45 minutes. Cool on a wire rack.
Serves 14.

The Buttonwood Inn

Thin New Hampshire Maple Syrup Pancakes

1 cup all-purpose flour
1½ teaspoons baking powder
1 tablespoon real New Hampshire maple syrup
1 egg, beaten
1¼ cups milk
3 tablespoons margarine or butter, melted

In a large bowl sift together the flour and baking powder. In a separate bowl combine the syrup, egg, and milk. Add the liquid mixture gradually to the dry ingredients, stirring until moistened. Add the margarine. The batter should be fairly thin (add more milk if necessary). Bake on a hot griddle until bubbles come to the surface and the edges are done. Turn and brown the other side. The pancakes should be the thickness of a crepe.
Makes 8 to 10 pancakes.

The Buttonwood's Chicken Supreme

4 boned and skinned chicken breasts
½ pound fresh mushrooms, sliced
1 10½-ounce can cream of mushroom soup
½ soup can sherry (red vermouth can also be used)
1 cup sour cream
Paprika
Hot cooked rice

In a shallow baking dish arrange the chicken so the pieces do not overlap. Cover with the mushrooms. Combine the soup, sherry, and sour cream, stirring until blended. Pour over the chicken until completely covered. Dust with paprika. Bake in a 350° oven for 35 to 40 minutes. Serve over rice.
Serves 4.

Sunny Side Inn

Seavey Street
North Conway, New Hampshire 03860
(603) 356-6239

This small, affordable inn provides guests with a quiet residential setting within a short walk of North Conway village with its many fine shops and restaurants. Guest rooms with private or shared baths are available. One room has a private entrance and porch with Adirondack chairs. Miles of hiking and ski trails for all levels of ability and technical rock climbing are nearby, along with other manmade and natural mountain attractions.

ðə ðə ðə ðə ðə

Spiced Pancakes

Excellent on cold New England mornings.

1¼ cups all-purpose flour
2 tablespoons sugar
1 teaspoon baking powder
½ teaspoon baking soda
½ teaspoon salt
½ teaspoon cinnamon
¼ teaspoon nutmeg
1 large egg
1¼ cups buttermilk
2 tablespoons oil

❧ ❧ ❧

Confectioners' sugar
Sliced bananas (optional)
Hot maple syrup

In a large bowl sift together the flour, sugar, baking powder, baking soda, salt, and spices. In a separate bowl beat together the egg, buttermilk, and oil. Add to the dry ingredients and stir until the batter is just moistened. On a medium to hot greased griddle or skillet pour ¼ cup of batter for each pancake. Turn when the edges are dry and the top is bubbly.

Sprinkle with confectioners' sugar and top with sliced bananas, if desired, and serve with hot maple syrup and bacon or sausage.

Makes eight 4-inch pancakes.

Follansbee Inn

Post Office Box 92
North Sutton, New Hampshire 03260
(603) 927-4221

The Follansbee Inn is an authentic nineteenth-century New England farmhouse with a porch, comfortable meeting room, and twenty-three quaint bedrooms. The inn is on the shore of peaceful Kazar Lake with a private pier for swimming, fishing, and boating, as well as cross-country skiing right from the front door.

Downhill skiing is only minutes away. A full country breakfast comes with the price of the room. Since this is a completely no smoking inn, guests enjoy clean New Hampshire air inside and out.

Cranberry Mousse Salad

Great with turkey!

1 20-ounce can crushed pineapple
1 6-ounce package strawberry
   gelatin
1 cup water
1 16-ounce can whole cranberry
   sauce
3 tablespoons fresh lemon juice
1 teaspoon grated lemon peel
¼ teaspoon ground nutmeg

❧ ❧ ❧

2 cups sour cream
½ cup chopped pecans

Drain the pineapple juice into a medium saucepan and reserve the pineapple. In the saucepan combine the pineapple juice, gelatin, and water. Heat to boiling, stirring constantly. Remove from the heat and blend in the cranberry sauce, lemon juice, peel, and nutmeg. Chill until slightly thick. Blend in the sour cream, pineapple, and nuts. Pour into a 2-quart mold and chill until firm, preferably overnight. Unmold and serve. Very tasty!

Serves 10.

Snowvillage Inn

Snowville, New Hampshire 03849
(603) 447-2818

Built circa 1900, Snowvillage Inn originally was a summer retreat for Frank Simonds, a writer who valued its peace, seclusion, and spectacular setting, qualities retained to this day. The nineteen guest rooms, each with private bath and some with fireplaces, are comfortably furnished with country antiques. Each guest room is named after a writer. Activities are suggested by the setting: cross-country skiing, hiking up Foss Mountain, sledding, and tennis on the clay court. After a busy day guests can relax in the sauna or find refreshments and company in the cozy lounge.

Artichoke Spread

1 14-ounce can artichoke hearts
   packed in water
1 clove garlic, crushed
3 tablespoons mayonnaise
Pinch paprika

Drain the artichokes and chop finely. In a small saucepan combine the artichokes, garlic, and mayonnaise. Stir over medium heat until warm (do not boil). Transfer the spread to a serving bowl, sprinkle with paprika, and surround with crackers.

Serves 10.

Jaeger Rouladen (Hunter's Beef Rolls)

Piquant stuffed beef rolls in a wine sauce.

6 slices bacon
1 large onion, minced
2 tablespoons minced parsley
4 tablespoons bread crumbs
   (preferably pumpernickel)
2 dill pickles, minced
6 anchovy fillets, chopped
1 tablespoon drained, chopped
   capers

❧ ❧ ❧

12 ¼-inch slices bottom round beef
   (have your butcher cut this)
2 to 3 tablespoons mustard
Pepper
Flour
4 tablespoons butter

๑ ๑ ๑
1 cup Burgundy wine
1 cup beef stock
๑ ๑ ๑
½ cup sour cream
Salt and pepper to taste
1 tablespoon sugar or splash of
    Curaçao
1 tablespoon lemon juice

In a large skillet sauté the bacon until almost crisp. Remove, reserving the fat in the skillet. Cool, then dice the bacon. Set aside. In the same fat (adding 1 to 2 tablespoons of butter if needed), sauté the onion for 10 minutes. Add the parsley and bread crumbs and sauté for another 5 minutes. Remove the skillet from the heat and add the pickles, anchovies, capers, and diced bacon. Mix well and let cool.

Between 2 layers of waxed paper pound the beef slices as thin as possible without tearing. The slices should be paper thin and rectangular or oval in shape. Spread the slices on a flat surface, narrow side up, brush with mustard, and sprinkle with freshly ground pepper. Spread the filling on the slices, leaving ½ inch on the sides and the top bare. Fold in the sides and tightly roll up each slice, securing the seam with a toothpick. Dredge the beef rolls in the flour and brown in the hot butter, a few at a time, removing them to a warm covered dish as they are done.

Pour the excess fat from skillet and add the wine and beek stock. Over high heat, quickly stir loose with a whisk the solid particles in the pan. Reduce the heat and place the beef rouladen back into the pan and simmer covered for 1 to 1½ hours, or until the rouladen are tender.

Move the rouladen to a covered dish and keep warm. Reduce the liquid in the pan to about 2 cups, stir in the sour cream, season with salt and pepper, and add the sugar and lemon juice. The sauce should be a robust sweet-and-sour.

To serve remove the toothpicks from the rouladen, place 2 rouladen on a serving dish and cover with some of the sauce. Great with spaetzle, mashed potatoes, or raw potato pancakes.

Serves 6.

The Hilltop Inn

Main Street, Route 117
Sugar Hill, New Hampshire 03585
(603) 823-5695

The Hilltop Inn is an 1895 Victorian home close to all Franconia Notch attractions: Alpine and Nordic skiing, swimming, canoeing, fishing, biking, hiking, horseback riding, wind surfing, glider rides, Cannon Mountain, the Tram-Way, the Old Man of the Mountain, and the flume. After a day in Franconia Notch, guests can escape up to Sugar Hill, where they can enjoy New Hampshire's scenery and slow pace. The sunsets from the inn's kitchen window are spectacular. In the morning breakfast is cooked in the kitchen, which is the heart of the home. The Hilltop Inn is on Route 117 between Franconia and Lisbon.

Applesauce Maple Spice Squares

1 cup butter or margarine, softened
2 cups brown sugar
2 eggs
½ cup cold coffee
3 tablespoons maple syrup
3½ cups sifted all-purpose flour
1½ teaspoons baking soda
1 teaspoon salt
1 teaspoon nutmeg
1 teaspoon cloves
2 teaspoons cinnamon
2 cups thick applesauce
½ cup nuts
1 cup raisins

Lightly grease and flour a 9x13-inch pan. In a large bowl cream together the butter, sugar, and eggs. Mix in the coffee and maple syrup. In a separate bowl mix together the dry ingredients. Blend the dry ingredients into the creamed mixture. Add the applesauce, nuts, and raisins, mixing well. Spread evenly in the prepared pan. Bake in a 350° oven for 25 to 35 minutes. Cut into squares.

Makes 2 dozen squares.

Zabaglione for Fresh Fruit and Pastries

2 8-ounce packages cream cheese
4 egg yolks
2 tablespoons dry white wine
½ cup sugar

In a medium bowl beat together all the ingredients, until thick and creamy. Serve with sliced fruit or berries, or use as a filling for cream puff pastries.

Makes about 3 cups.

Wholegrain Jam Squares

2 cups uncooked oats
1¾ cups all-purpose flour
1 cup butter or margarine, softened
1 cup brown sugar
½ cup chopped nuts
½ cup chopped raisins or currants
1 teaspoon cinnamon
¾ teaspoon baking soda
¾ teaspoon salt
1 cup jam or fruit preserves of your
    choice

In a large bowl combine all of the ingredients except the jam, until well mixed and crumbly. Reserve 2 cups of the mixture. Press the remaining crumb mixture into a 9x13-inch pan. Spread the jam over the crumb crust.

The Hilltop Inn

Sprinkle the reserved crumb mixture as a topping over the jam. Bake in a 350° oven for 25 to 30 minutes, or until golden brown.

Makes 2 dozen squares.

The Birchwood Inn

Route 45
Temple, New Hampshire 03084
(603) 878-3285

While the Birchwood Inn was opened about 1775, the present brick structure was probably built circa 1800. The present barns were added in 1848, and the inn has remained in much the same form since that time. It is listed on the National Register of Historic Places. Two centuries have seen "the old hotel" entertain many overnight guests, Henry David Thoreau among them. In addition to the tavern, dining, and guest room operations, the inn has housed the Temple Post Office, a small general store, the town meeting hall, and, most recently, an antique shop. One of the most notable features of the inn is the dining room mural painted by the New England itinerant painter Rufus Porter. His works can also be found at Old Sturbridge Village in Massachusetts.

Whole Grain Muffins

2 cups all-purpose flour
½ cup brown sugar
½ cup sugar
1 tablespoon baking powder
½ teaspoon salt
1 cup Mueslix (whole grain cereal)

🌿 🌿 🌿

2 eggs
½ cup milk
½ cup butter or margarine, melted
1 teaspoon vanilla extract

Grease 12 muffin tins. In a large bowl combine the dry ingredients. In a separate bowl combine the eggs, milk, butter, and vanilla. Add to the dry ingredients, mixing together well. Pour the batter into the prepared muffin tins. Bake in a 375° oven for 20 to 25 minutes.

Makes 12.

Braised Cucumbers

¼ cup butter or margarine
1 tablespoon sugar
½ teaspoon salt
2 large cucumbers, peeled and cut into 2-inch pieces
1 medium onion, chopped
2 tomatoes, quartered

¼ cup water
1 teaspoon lemon juice
¼ teaspoon fresh dill weed
½ cup sour cream

In a large skillet melt the butter and add the sugar and salt. Cook until lightly browned. Add the cucumbers and onions, stirring until the onions are transparent. Add the tomatoes, water, lemon juice, and dill weed. Cook for 10 to 12 minutes. Stir in the sour cream. Serve immediately.

Serves 6.

Eggplant Caponata

¼ cup olive oil
2 cups chopped celery
¾ cup chopped onion

🌿 🌿

2 pounds eggplant, peeled and cut into ½-inch cubes
¼ cup red wine vinegar
2 teaspoons sugar
2 cups drained plum tomatoes
Salt
Ground pepper
2 tablespoons capers

Heat 2 tablespoons of the oil in a large skillet. Add the celery and cook over medium heat for 10 minutes. Stir in the onions and sauté until soft. Transfer the vegetables to a bowl.

Add 2 tablespoons of the oil to the skillet and sauté the eggplant on high heat until browned, adding more oil as needed. Return the celery and onion to the skillet. Stir in the vinegar, sugar, tomatoes, salt, pepper, and capers. Bring to a boil, then reduce heat and simmer uncovered for 15 to 20

minutes. Check the seasonings and add more vinegar if needed. Chill.

Keeps for 2 weeks in the refrigerator.

Serves 6 to 8.

Figgy Pudding

2 cups sugar
2 eggs
1½ cups all-purpose flour
1½ teaspoons baking powder
1 teaspoon salt
1 teaspoon vanilla extract
¼ cup milk
½ pound dates
1 cup nuts

    🍂   🍂   🍂

½ cup butter
1½ cups brown sugar
2 cups boiling water

Grease a 9x13-inch pan. In a large bowl cream together the sugar and eggs. Add the flour, baking powder, salt, and vanilla, alternately with the milk. Stir in the dates and nuts. Pour the batter into the prepared pan.

Combine the butter, brown sugar, and boiling water. Pour over the batter. Bake in a 350° oven for 45 minutes to 1 hour.

Serves 12.

Stepping Stones

Bennington Battle Trail
Wilton Center, New Hampshire 03086
(603) 654-9048

This small bed and breakfast is in the picturebook village of Wilton Center, a quiet, rural retreat just sixty miles from downtown Boston. The gracious old house overlooks a sunny terrace and extensive gardens. Handwoven rugs and throws, down comforters, and fresh flowers brighten the three bedrooms. The cozy living room offers good reading, stereo, and a warm fire; the solar breakfast room is bright with flowering plants and pottery. Throughout the house, handwoven fabrics contribute to the warm and friendly atmosphere. Included in the cost of the room is a home-cooked breakfast and afternoon tea. The cookie jar is always full of ginger cookies, a specialty; and a small refrigerator is available for guests' use.

Angel-light Gingerbread

½ cup butter
1 cup sugar
½ cup molasses

    🍂   🍂   🍂

2 cups all-purpose flour
2 teaspoons baking powder
½ teaspoon salt
½ teaspoon nutmeg
½ teaspoon cinnamon
½ teaspoon ginger
¼ teaspoon cloves

    🍂   🍂   🍂

1 cup boiling water
Confectioners' sugar

Grease a 9x13-inch or two 8-inch square baking pans. In a large bowl cream together the butter and sugar. Add the molasses, beating thoroughly. Sift the dry ingredients and stir into the batter until just moistened. Add the boiling water, then quickly pour into the prepared pan. Bake in a 400° oven for 30 to 35 minutes, or until a toothpick inserted in the center comes out clean. When cooled, dust with the confectioners' sugar.

Serves 12.

New Jersey

Conover's Bay Head Inn

646 Main Avenue
Bay Head, New Jersey 08742
(201) 892-4664

Built in 1912 as a summer cottage, Conover's Bay Head Inn has been rated a "ten" by *Good Housekeeping* magazine. Each of the air-conditioned bedrooms has its own personality. Views from the inn are as impressive as the rooms, with the ocean, bay, marina, and yacht club nearby, as well as the many other spectacular old houses. The massive cut-stone fireplace greets guests as they enter. Smoking is permitted on the porches.

Tomato Breakfast Quiche

¾ cup Hungry Jack Mashed Potato
    Flakes
¾ cup all-purpose flour
¼ cup grated Parmesan cheese
¼ teaspoon salt
⅓ cup margarine, softened
¼ cup water

   ❧ ❧ ❧

1½ cups grated Cheddar cheese
¼ cup Hungry Jack Mashed Potato
    Flakes

1 medium tomato, chopped
5 eggs
¼ cup sour cream
1 teaspoon chopped chives
1 teaspoon fresh chopped basil
½ teaspoon salt
2 tablespoons corn flake crumbs

In a medium bowl combine ¾ cup of potato flakes, flour, Parmesan cheese, and salt. Cut in the margarine until crumbly. Add the water, stirring just until the dough forms. Press into a 9-inch pie pan, flute the edges, and prick the crust with a fork. Bake in a 350° oven for 10 minutes.

Sprinkle 1 cup of the Cheddar cheese over the partially baked crust. Add ¼ cup of potato flakes. Spoon on the tomato and top with the remaining Cheddar cheese. In a separate bowl combine the eggs, sour cream, chives, basil, and salt, beating until well blended. Pour the egg mixture over the cheese. Sprinkle with the corn flake crumbs. Bake for another 25 to 30 minutes, or until lightly browned and a knife inserted near the center comes out clean. Let stand 5 minutes before cutting.

Serves 6.

Green Tomato Bread

3 eggs
1½ cups sugar
1 cup corn oil
1 teaspoon salt
1 tablespoon vanilla extract
2 cups grated, well drained, green
    tomatoes

   ❧ ❧ ❧

3 cups all-purpose flour
1¼ teaspoons baking soda
½ teaspoon baking powder
½ teaspoon cinnamon
½ teaspoon nutmeg

   ❧ ❧ ❧

¾ cup raisins
1 cup chopped nuts

Grease and flour two 9x5-inch bread pans. In a large bowl thoroughly beat the eggs. Add the sugar, oil, salt, vanilla, and tomatoes, beating well.

In a separate bowl sift together the dry ingredients. Gradually add the dry ingredients to the tomato mixture. Stir in the raisins and nuts. Pour the batter into the prepared pans. Bake in a 350° oven for 45 to 50 minutes or until a toothpick inserted in the center comes out clean.

Makes 2 loaves.

Miracle Squares

Equally popular at breakfast or tea time.

1 cup packed brown sugar
1 cup margarine, softened
1 teaspoon vanilla extract

1 egg
1 cup all-purpose flour
½ cup whole wheat flour
1 cup chopped pecans or walnuts

🍃 🍃 🍃

1 10-ounce jar orange marmalade or
apricot preserves

🍃 🍃 🍃

½ cup confectioners' sugar
2 or 3 teaspoons milk

Lightly grease a 9x13-inch pan. In a medium bowl cream the brown sugar and margarine together until light and fluffy. Add the vanilla and egg, beating well. Add the flours and nuts to the sugar mixture, blending well. Press half of the dough into the prepared pan and spread with the marmalade. Drop the remaining dough by teaspoonfuls over the marmalade. Bake in a 350° oven for 25 to 30 minutes.

In a small bowl combine the confectioners' sugar and enough milk to make a glaze. Drizzle the glaze over the top of the cake. When the glaze is set cut into squares.

Makes 26 squares.

The Barnard— Good House

238 Perry Street
Cape May, New Jersey 08204
(609) 884-5381

Originally a fifteen-room summer cottage, this bed and breakfast was built in the French Second Empire architectural style with mansard roof and a full verandah. The three-story home contains five guest rooms. An antique pump organ often serves as a catalyst for impromptu songfests. Complete gourmet breakfasts are served every morning.

Eggs in Purgatory

6 tablespoons virgin olive oil
1 large onion, minced
7 pounds fresh ripe tomatoes, peeled, seeded, and chopped
6 tablespoons torn fresh basil leaves
6 tablespoons minced fresh parsley
Salt and freshly ground pepper

🍃 🍃 🍃

10 to 12 eggs
10 to 12 ⅓-inch thick slices Italian bread (I use homemade)
Olive oil
3 ounces freshly grated Parmesan cheese

In a large heavy skillet heat the olive oil over medium heat. Add the onion and sauté until softened, stirring occasionally, about 6 minutes. Add the tomatoes and bring to a simmer. Mix in the herbs and spices. Increase the heat to high and cook until almost all of the liquid is eliminated, stirring frequently, about 15 minutes. (This can be made ahead and refrigerated.)

Press the back of a large spoon into the heated tomato mixture in 10 to 12 places, forming well-like shapes. Carefully break 1 egg into each well, and season the eggs with salt and pepper. Cover and cook over low heat until the eggs are soft poached, about 6 minutes.

Brush both sides of the bread with oil and place on a baking sheet. Broil the bread until golden brown on both sides. Place the toast in shallow serving bowls and gently spoon the eggs and sauce over the toast. Sprinkle the eggs with the cheese.

Note: If this is made with all the right ingredients the taste is wonderful. Very well received by the guests and usually accompanied with corn pudding as a side dish.

Serves 8 to 10.

Lobster Frittata

3 tablespoons olive oil
1 medium red onion, thinly sliced
2 cloves garlic, minced
3 summer squash, sliced ¼-inch thick
1 yellow bell pepper, seeded and cut into ¼-inch strips
2 red bell peppers, seeded and cut into ¼-inch strips

🍃 🍃 🍃

6 large eggs
¼ cup heavy or whipping cream
1 teaspoon saffron threads
3 tablespoons chopped fresh basil
Salt and freshly ground pepper to taste
2 5-ounce packages Boursin cheese
1 pound cooked fresh lobster meat cut into bite-sized chunks
2 cups freshly grated Gruyère cheese

Butter the bottom and sides of a 10-inch springform pan. In a large pot heat the oil over medium-high heat. Sauté the onions, garlic, squash, and peppers, stirring frequently until crisp-tender, about 10 to 15 minutes.

In a large bowl beat the eggs and cream together with a whisk. Add the saffron, basil, salt, and pepper, and blend thoroughly. Crumble the Boursin into small pieces and stir into the egg mixture. Stir in the lobster chunks and sautéed vegetables. Add the Gruyère, stirring well to combine. Pour the mixture into the prepared pan and place the pan on a baking sheet. Bake in a 350° oven for 45 to 60 minutes until just firm throughout. Let cool for 10 minutes and cut into wedges.

Serves 6 to 8.

Cold Cranberry Soup

6 cups fresh cranberries
4 cups water
2 whole cloves (tied in cheesecloth bag)

🍃 🍃 🍃

1½ cups sugar
4½ teaspoons all-purpose flour
2¼ cups sour cream (or plain yogurt)
1½ cups dry red wine (white Zinfandel works, too)
1½ cups freshly squeezed orange juice

🍃 🍃 🍃

Cream or yogurt and fresh fruit for garnish

In a large saucepan simmer the cranberries, water, and cloves for 10 minutes. Drain the cranberries, reserving 1 cup of the cooking liquid. Discard the cloves. Purée the cranberries in a blender or food processor. Press through the fine mesh of a food mill or a strainer into a large heavy saucepan. Mix in the reserved cooking liquid.

In a medium bowl combine the sugar and flour. Stir in the sour cream, wine, and orange juice. Mix into the cranberry mixture. Slowly bring to a boil, stirring constantly. Reduce the heat and simmer for 2 minutes, stirring constantly. Cool. Refrigerate until the soup is well chilled. (This can be prepared 1 day ahead.) Garnish with a dollop of cream or yogurt and fresh fruit and serve in a pretty champagne shell.

Makes about 3 quarts, serving 10 to 12.

Cold Peach Soup

   10 to 12 fresh ripe peaches
   1 cup sugar
   6 tablespoons fresh lemon juice
   2 tablespoons frozen orange juice
       concentrate
   ¼ cup sweet sherry
   2 cups sour cream

In a food processor purée the peaches and sugar together. Blend in the lemon juice, orange juice concentrate, sherry, and sour cream. Chill at least 2 hours.
Serves 12.

Built Circa 1890

The Captain Mey's

The Captain Mey's

202 Ocean Street
Cape May, New Jersey 08204
(609) 884-7793

The Dutch heritage at Captain Mey's Inn is truly evident in the Persian rugs on table tops, the Delft Blue collection, and the Dutch artifacts throughout. Guests are surrounded by rich, warm oak and Tiffany stained glass in this authentically restored inn. Rooms are spacious, with antiques, walnut bedsteads, marble-topped dressers, hand-made quilts, and fresh flowers. The chestnut oak Eastlake paneling in the dining room, leaded glass window seat, and fireplace with its intricately carved mantel all contribute to the Victorian elegance of this inn. During the summer months guests can enjoy a leisurely breakfast or a refreshing glass of iced tea in the afternoon on the wraparound verandah with wicker furniture. The full country breakfast consists of homemade breads, cakes, egg dishes, breakfast meats, cheese imported from Holland, fresh fruit, and jelly made from beach plums.

Double Dutch Eggs

   12 eggs
   Salt to taste
   ½ can evaporated milk
   1 8-ounce package cream cheese
   2 tablespoons freshly chopped
       chives

   ❧ ❧ ❧

   12 slices white bread
   Butter

   ❧ ❧ ❧

   Melon

Lightly grease 12 muffin tins. In a mixing bowl combine the eggs with the salt and milk. Pour the egg mixture into a buttered frying pan and scramble lightly. Add the cream cheese and chopped chives.

Butter both sides of the bread and place 1 slice into each muffin tin. Toast in the oven. Pour the egg mixture into the toast cups and sprinkle with chives. Garnish with a slice of melon.
Serves 6.

The Chalfonte

301 Howard Street
Cape May, New Jersey 08204
(609) 884-8409

The Chalfonte, a 110-year-old Victorian hotel in the heart of the historic district, is the oldest hotel in continual operation in Cape May. The rooms are simple, with no telephones, television, or air conditioning. Although the hotel is very basic (only eleven of the 108 rooms have a private bath), its guests return year after year. The dining room was originally built as a ballroom and seats 175 comfortably. Meals are served family-style at the long tables. Breakfast and dinner are included in the rates, but the dining room is open to the public as well. The long porches filled with rocking chairs and the quiet King Edward Room bar make relaxing a necessary part of the day.

Spoonbread

1 cup Indian Head white cornmeal
2 tablespoons butter
3 cups milk
3 eggs, well beaten
1½ teaspoons salt
3 teaspoons baking powder

Grease a 1½ to 2-quart casserole. In a saucepan combine the cornmeal, butter, and 2 cups of the milk. Cook slowly over medium heat, bringing the mixture just to a boil and continue to stir constantly. In a medium bowl blend together the eggs, salt, and the remaining 1 cup of milk. Add to the cornmeal mixture, mixing well. Stir in the baking powder. Pour the batter into the prepared casserole. Bake in a 450° oven for 25 to 35 minutes.

Serves 6 to 8.

Chalfonte Fried Chicken

3 pounds chicken, cut-up
1 cup all-purpose flour
Salt and pepper to taste
2 tablespoons paprika
2 cups Crisco oil or corn oil
Half an onion, thickly sliced

Soak the chicken in salted water (1 tablespoon per quart of water) for 1 hour. Pat dry. In a medium bowl combine the flour, salt, pepper, and paprika. Roll the chicken pieces (2 at a time) in the mixture, covering well. Pour the Crisco into a large skillet and heat to medium-high temperature. Add the onion rings. Fry the chicken for 10 minutes, turn over and continue frying until tender, crisp, and brown, approximately 10 more minutes. Test for doneness with a fork.

Serves 4.

The Chalfonte

Colvmns by the Sea

1513 Beach Drive
Cape May, New Jersey 08204
(609) 884-2228

This turn-of-the-century mansion is filled with the charm and grace of an era when a summer "cottage" had twenty rooms, twelve-foot ceilings, and hand-carved woodwork. Inside are two fireplaces, a three-story staircase, large rooms, and plenty of windows. All rooms at this inn have private baths and ocean views. A gourmet breakfast and afternoon refreshments are served, and guests can use the inn's bikes, beach badges, towels, and chairs. Smoking is limited to the seaside verandah.

Colvmns Hash

1 cup chopped green pepper
1 cup chopped red pepper
2 tablespoons butter
1 cup chopped scallions, including
   green ends
1½ pounds frozen hash brown
   potatoes

18 eggs
2 cups half and half
Parsley
Salt and pepper to taste

2 pounds ham, cubed

In a large skillet sauté the peppers and onion in the butter. Add the potatoes and brown lightly.

In a large bowl combine the eggs, half and half, and seasonings. Place the potato mixture in a 9x13-inch glass baking dish. Pour the egg mixture over the potatoes.

Sprinkle the top with the cubed ham. Bake in a 400° oven for 30 to 40 minutes, or until set.
Serves 12.

Barry's Broccoli

This salad is better the longer it sits. Great with seafood or for a covered-dish party. It is also good as a side dish with egg casseroles.

1 head broccoli, broken in florets
1 medium red onion, diced
8 ounces Cheddar, Mozzarella, or
   Swiss cheese, grated
½ pound crisp bacon, crumbled
Slivered almonds, toasted

1 cup mayonnaise
½ cup sugar
2 or 3 tablespoons cider vinegar

In a large serving bowl combine the broccoli, onion, Cheddar cheese, bacon, and almonds.

In a small bowl combine the mayonnaise, sugar, and vinegar. Pour the dressing into the salad, tossing until well combined.
Serves 6 to 8.

The Gingerbread House

28 Gurney Street
Cape May, New Jersey 08204
(609) 884-0211

The Gingerbread House is one of eight identical cottages, known as the Stockton Row Cottages, designed and built in 1869 by Stephen Button. Tastefully restored and decorated with period furnishings, lace curtains, and many plants and fresh flowers, the inn is one-half block from the ocean and within walking distance of Cape May's finest restaurants and historic homes. Its six guest rooms, most with private baths, are large and comfortably decorated.

Crème de Menthe Squares

1 cup sugar
½ cup butter or margarine
4 eggs, beaten
1 16-ounce can chocolate syrup
1 cup all-purpose flour
½ teaspoon salt
1 teaspoon vanilla extract

2 cups confectioners' sugar
½ cup butter or margarine
3 tablespoons crème de menthe
   (green)

1 6-ounce package chocolate chips
6 tablespoons butter or margarine

Grease a 9x13-inch baking pan. In a large bowl combine the sugar, ½ cup of butter, eggs, chocolate syrup, flour, salt, and vanilla, mixing together with an electric mixer. Pour the batter into the prepared pan. Bake in a 350° oven for 30 minutes. Cool in the pan.

In a medium bowl combine the confectioners' sugar, ½ cup of butter, and the crème de menthe, mixing with an electric mixer until smooth. Spread over the cake and refrigerate to harden.

In a small saucepan combine the chocolate chips and 6 tablespoons of butter, stirring until melted. Spread over the mint layer and chill for 10 to 30 minutes. Cut into squares.

This freezes well. Great for afternoon tea!
Makes 60 to 80 squares.

Chocolate Dream Bars

These are rich and perfect with tea!

    1 cup brown sugar
    1½ cups oatmeal
    Pinch salt
    1½ cups all-purpose flour
    1 teaspoon baking soda
    ¾ cup butter or margarine

    🍃 🍃 🍃

    1 14-ounce can sweetened
      condensed milk
    1 12-ounce package chocolate chips
    2 tablespoons water
    1 teaspoon vanilla extract

Grease a 9x13-inch baking pan. In a large bowl combine the brown sugar, oatmeal, salt, flour, and baking soda. Cut in the butter until the mixture is crumbly. Pat half of the mixture into the prepared pan.

In a medium saucepan combine the sweetened condensed milk, chocolate chips, water, and vanilla, stirring until melted. Pour over the crumb mixture. Sprinkle the remaining crumb mixture over the filling. Bake in a 350° oven for 20 minutes. Let cool completely before cutting. This may be frozen.

Makes 48 squares.

The Humphrey Hughes House

29 Ocean Street
Cape May, New Jersey 08204
(609) 884-4428

Built in 1903, the Humphrey Hughes House is nestled in the heart of Cape May's historic section. Sea breezes whisper through the guest rooms and the large, wraparound verandah on which guests sit in wicker armchairs.

In the evening guests can relax in front of two crackling fireplaces or marvel at the inn's outstanding features. Nearby attractions, in addition to the surf and beach, are museum tours, botanical gardens, Cape May State Park, birdwatching, and much more.

24-Hour Wine and Cheese Strata

    1 loaf French bread, cut into small
      pieces
    6 tablespoons butter, melted
    3 cups grated Swiss cheese
    2 cups grated Monterey Jack cheese
    ¼ pound Virginia baked ham,
      chopped

    🍃 🍃 🍃

    16 eggs
    3¼ cups milk
    1 cup dry white or red wine
    1 tablespoon dry mustard
    ¼ teaspoon black pepper
    ⅔ cup Parmesan cheese
    ½ teaspoon red pepper

    🍃 🍃 🍃

    1½ cups sour cream

Butter two 9x13-inch glass dishes. Place the bread on the bottom of the dishes and drizzle with the butter.

Layer the cheeses and the ham over the bread.

In a large bowl combine the eggs, milk, wine, dry mustard, black pepper, Parmesan cheese, and red pepper. Pour the liquid mixture over the layers and refrigerate overnight. Bake covered in a 325° oven for 1 hour. Spread the top with sour cream and bake uncovered for 10 more minutes. Cool 5 minutes and cut into squares.

Serves 12.

Mainstay Inn

635 Columbia Avenue
Cape May, New Jersey 08204
(609) 884-8690

The Mainstay, built in 1872 as an elegant, exclusive clubhouse where friends could devote themselves to gambling and other gentlemanly amusements, is a grand villa with fourteen-foot ceilings, ornate plaster mouldings, elaborate chandeliers, a sweeping verandah, and a cupola to top it off. Luxuriously furnished, it has twelve-foot mirrors, marble-topped sideboards, and graceful loveseats. Called "by far the most lavishly and faithfully restored" of Cape May's inns by *Travel and Leisure* magazine, it has twelve guest rooms named for famous Americans who have visited Cape May.

Corn Quiche

    3 eggs
    1 ¼-inch thick slice onion
    1 tablespoon all-purpose flour
    1 tablespoon sugar
    1 teaspoon salt
    3 tablespoons butter, melted
    1⅓ cups light cream, scalded
    2 cups corn, fresh or frozen
      (defrosted)
    1 9-inch unbaked pie shell

Mainstay Inn

In a blender combine the eggs, onion, flour, sugar, and salt. Add the butter and cream, blending well. Add the corn and blend only slightly. Pour into the unbaked pie shell. Bake in a 375° oven for 45 minutes.

Serves 6 to 8.

Chicken Pecan Quiche

2 cups finely chopped cooked
   chicken
1 cup grated Monterey Jack cheese
¼ cup scallions
1 tablespoon chopped parsley
1 tablespoon all-purpose flour
1 unbaked 9-inch pie shell

  🐦 🐦 🐦

3 eggs, beaten
1¼ cups half and half
½ teaspoon brown mustard
½ cup chopped pecans

In a large bowl combine the chicken, cheese, scallions, parsley, and flour. Sprinkle into the pie shell.

In a medium bowl combine the eggs, half and half, and mustard. Pour over the chicken mixture and top with the pecans. Bake in a 325° oven for 60 minutes.

Serves 6.

🐦 🐦 🐦 🐦 🐦

Cranberry Date Bars

1 12-ounce package cranberries
1 8-ounce package chopped pitted
   dates
1 teaspoon vanilla extract

  🐦 🐦 🐦

2 cups all-purpose flour
2 cups rolled oats
1½ cups packed brown sugar
½ teaspoon baking soda
¼ teaspoon salt
1 cup butter, melted

  🐦 🐦 🐦

2 cups sifted confectioners' sugar
½ teaspoon vanilla extract
2 to 3 tablespoons orange juice

In a medium saucepan combine the cranberries and dates. Cook over low heat, stirring constantly, for 10 to 15 minutes or until the cranberries pop. Stir in 1 teaspoon of vanilla. Set aside.

In a large bowl stir together the flour, oats, brown sugar, baking soda, and salt. Stir in the butter until well blended. Pat half of the oat mixture on the bottom of a 9x13-inch baking pan. Bake in a 350° oven for 8 minutes. Carefully spread the filling over the oat mixture. Sprinkle the remaining oat mixture on top. Pat gently and bake for 20 to 25 more minutes or until golden. Cool on a wire rack.

In a medium bowl stir together the confectioners' sugar, ½ teaspoon of vanilla, and enough orange juice to make a drizzling consistency. Glaze the bars.

Makes 32 bars.

🐦 🐦 🐦 🐦 🐦

Ham and Apple Pie

3 tablespoons all-purpose flour
¾ cup brown sugar
½ teaspoon cinnamon
½ teaspoon mace
Dash pepper
6 cups tart apples, peeled and
   sliced
¼ to ½ pound cooked ham, in
   small pieces
1 unbaked 9-inch pie crust
Cheddar, Monterey Jack, or Gouda
   cheese

Grease a 1½-quart oblong baking dish. In a medium bowl combine the flour, brown sugar, cinnamon, mace, and pepper. Put 2 cups of apples and half of the ham in the prepared dish. Sprinkle with half of the flour mixture. Layer with another 2 cups of apples and the remaining ham and flour mixture. Top with the remaining apples, and cover with the pie crust. Seal the edges. Bake in a 325° oven for 1 hour and 30 minutes. Cut into squares and serve warm with cheese.

Serves 6.

Banana-Pineapple Crisp

3 ripe bananas, sliced in ½-inch
  rounds (2 cups)
1 20-ounce can pineapple chunks,
  drained (reserve ¼ cup juice)
2 tablespoons apricot preserves

❧ ❧ ❧

½ cup old-fashioned oats
½ cup light brown sugar
¼ cup all-purpose flour
¼ cup coconut
¼ cup butter, cut into small pieces

In a shallow 1½-quart baking dish combine the bananas and pineapple, mixing gently. Stir the preserves into the pineapple juice and pour over the fruit mixture.

In a medium bowl combine the oats, sugar, flour, and coconut. Cut in the butter with a pastry blender until mixture resembles crumbs. Sprinkle over the fruit mixture. Bake in a 400° oven for 15 to 20 minutes, until the topping is lightly browned and the juices bubble.

Serves 6.

Perry Street Inn

20 Perry Street
Cape May, New Jersey 08204
(609) 884-4590 or
(201) 689-3940

Facing the Atlantic Ocean, the Perry Street Inn is not only near the beach but is also close to the mall and the historic district. Parking is provided. The rooms are nicely decorated with antiques, and rocking on the porch is a relaxing way to spend a few hours. A continental breakfast is served.

Honey Muffins

¼ cup cream
2 tablespoons oil
3 tablespoons honey
1 teaspoon vanilla extract
2 eggs, beaten
½ cup dark brown sugar

❧ ❧ ❧

2 cups all-purpose flour
2 teaspoons baking powder
1 teaspoon baking soda
½ teaspoon salt
¼ cup seedless raisins, dates, or
  coconut

Grease 12 muffin cups. In a medium bowl combine the cream, oil, honey, and vanilla. Add the eggs and sugar, mixing well.

In a separate bowl sift together the dry ingredients and add the raisins, tossing to coat well. Add the dry ingredients to the liquid mixture. The batter will be stiff. Spoon into the prepared muffin cups. Bake in a 400° oven for 20 minutes.

Makes 12 muffins.

Boiled Scallops

2 cups water
2 bay leaves
2 cloves garlic
¼ teaspoon salt
¼ teaspoon celery salt
½ cup lemon juice
½ cup olive oil
1 small onion

❧ ❧ ❧

1 pound scallops

In an enamel saucepan combine all the ingredients except the scallops and boil for 15 to 20 minutes. Add the scallops and cook until the scallops are opaque. Serve hot with a fresh vegetable or cold in a salad.

Serves 4.

Apple Wedges with Brandied Cheese

1 8-ounce package cream cheese,
  softened
4 ounces Bleu cheese
2 tablespoons brandy
½ cup ground pecans
2 tablespoons finely chopped green
  onions
Chopped pecans

❧ ❧ ❧

1 tablespoon lemon juice
2 cups water
3 apples, cup into wedges

❧ ❧ ❧

Watercress

In a medium bowl combine the cheeses. Add the brandy, ground pecans, and onions. Cover and refrigerate for a few hours to mellow. Shape into a ball and roll in chopped pecans.

In a small bowl combine the lemon juice and water. Dip the apple wedges in the mixture to prevent discoloration. Arrange the apple wedges and watercress around the cheese ball.

Serves 4 to 6.

The Queen Victoria

102 Ocean Street
Cape May, New Jersey 08204
(609) 884-8702

Named in honor of the British monarch who loved the sea, the Queen Victoria was restored to its original elegance in celebration of the building's 1981 centennial. At the Queen Victoria guests can enjoy the personal service, comfort, and charm of a country inn and one of the innkeepers is always on hand. It is furnished

The Queen Victoria

The Queen's Bath Salts

3 cups epsom salts
¾ cup baking soda
¾ cup Calgon water softener

Combine all of the ingredients and store in an attractive airtight container. Sprinkle about 1 cup of the bath salts in your tub for a refreshing bath.

Makes about 4½ cups.

Windward House

24 Jackson Street
Cape May, New Jersey 08204
(609) 884-3368

with authentic Victorian pieces of walnut, wicker, oak, and pine. Bedrooms have quilts on antique bedsteads and fresh flowers on the tables. In the morning a hearty country breakfast awaits guests in the dining room.

Mincemeat Brunch Cake

Adapted from a recipe in *Sunset* magazine.

1½ cups sugar
1 cup butter or margarine, softened
1½ teaspoons baking powder
1½ teaspoons vanilla extract
½ teaspoon grated orange peel
4 eggs
3 cups all-purpose flour
2 cups mincemeat
⅔ cup chopped nuts

🍂 🍂 🍂

1 cup confectioners' sugar
2 tablespoons orange juice

Grease a 10x15-inch rimmed baking pan or two 7x9-inch glass baking dishes. In a large bowl combine the sugar and butter, beating together until creamy. Beat in the baking powder, vanilla, and orange peel. Add the eggs one at a time, beating well after each addition. Gradually mix in the flour. Spread ⅔ of the batter in the prepared pans. Spread the mincemeat evenly on top and drop the remaining batter by tablespoons onto the mincemeat. Sprinkle the nuts evenly over the batter. Bake in a 350° oven for 30 to 35 minutes, until lightly browned.

In a small bowl combine the confectioners' sugar and orange juice. Drizzle over the warm cake and cut into squares.

Serves 15 to 20.

Windward House, in the heart of Cape May's historic district, is an Edwardian shingle-style cottage, a late Victorian design used mostly in coastal regions. The inn has upper and lower porches, a long central hall, large and airy rooms, and one of Cape May's finest collections of stained and beveled glass. Windward House has six rooms and two suites, all with private baths, air conditioning, and small refrigerators. The suites have television. The inn is close to the beach, the mall, and most of Cape May's restaurants.

Windward House

cheese. Layer the remaining bread, dried beef, and cheese on top. In a separate bowl combine the eggs and milk. Pour over the bread mixture and refrigerate overnight. Bake in a 300° oven for 1 hour. Let stand a few minutes before serving.

Serves 8 to 10.

Chicken-Broccoli Crepes

¼ cup butter or margarine
¼ cup baking mix
½ teaspoon salt
¼ teaspoon pepper
2 cups milk
2 cups cut-up cooked chicken
1 2-ounce jar diced pimiento, drained
1 tablespoon chives
1 pound broccoli, cooked and drained

❧ ❧ ❧

12 prepared crepes

In a saucepan heat the butter over medium-high heat until melted. Stir in the baking mix, salt, and pepper. Cook over low heat, stirring constantly, until smooth and bubbly. Remove from the heat and stir in the milk. Heat to boiling, stirring constantly, and boil for 1 minute. Stir in the chicken, pimiento, and chives, and heat until hot. Place 1 stalk of broccoli on each warm crepe and roll up. Place 2 crepes, seam sides down on each plate, and top with ½ cup of the chicken mixture.

Serves 6.

Pineapple Cheese Tarts

½ cup butter or margarine
1 3-ounce package cream cheese
Pinch salt
1 cup all-purpose flour
¼ cup pineapple jam

In a medium bowl combine the butter and cream cheese until creamy. Add the salt and flour, mixing with a fork. Chill the dough. Roll out and cut into 12 squares, filling each with a teaspoon of jam. Fold over, press edges together, and prick with a fork. Bake on a cookie sheet in a 375° oven for 12 to 15 minutes.

Makes 12.

Apricot Pancakes

3 eggs
1½ cups low-fat milk
¾ cup all-purpose flour
2 tablespoons rum
½ teaspoon vanilla extract
¼ teaspoon salt

❧ ❧ ❧

1 16-ounce can apricot halves, drained
3 pieces crystallized ginger, finely chopped
2 tablespoons sifted confectioners' sugar

In a blender combine the eggs, milk, flour, rum, vanilla, and salt, blending until smooth. Pour half of the batter into a deep 8-inch baking dish. Bake in a 375° oven for 20 minutes. Arrange the apricot halves and ginger on top of the partially set batter. Pour the remaining batter over the top. Bake an additional 25 minutes. Sprinkle with the confectioners' sugar.

Serves 4.

Dried Beef Brunch Bake

16 slices white bread, buttered
5 to 8 ounces dried beef
4 cups grated sharp cheese
8 eggs
1 quart milk

Place 8 slices of the bread, buttered side down, in a 9x13-inch casserole. Cover with half of the dried beef and

Ice Cream Muffins

1 cup vanilla ice cream, or your favorite flavor
1 cup self-rising flour

Grease 6 muffin tins or line with paper liners. Let the ice cream soften slightly, then mix in the flour. Fill the prepared muffin cups ¾ full. Bake in a 425° oven for 12 to 15 minutes. Leftovers will reheat well.

Serves 6.

Maple Walnut Blue Corn Bread

¼ cup corn oil
2 cups blue cornmeal (available at health food and gourmet stores)
2 cups yellow cornmeal
2 tablespoons salt
2 tablespoons baking soda

🍂 🍂 🍂

6 to 7 eggs
4 cups buttermilk

🍂 🍂 🍂

⅔ cup coarsely chopped walnuts
½ cup maple syrup

Pour the oil into a 9x13-inch casserole and warm in a 425° oven. In a large bowl combine the cornmeals, salt, and baking soda.

In a separate bowl beat the eggs and buttermilk together. Add the liquid mixture to the cornmeal mixture. Pour into the prepared casserole and bake for 25 to 30 minutes. Pierce the warm bread evenly with a fork.

In a saucepan combine the walnuts and maple syrup, and heat over medium heat. Carefully pour the mixture over the warm bread.

Serves 6 to 8.

Heath Bar Crunch

1 cup butter, melted
1 cup sugar
Saltine crackers
1 12-ounce package chocolate chips

Line a cookie sheet with foil. In a small saucepan combine the butter and sugar until syrupy. Coat the prepared cookie sheet with the syrup. Cover with 1 layer of saltine crackers. Heat in a 400° oven. Sprinkle the chocolate chips over the hot crackers. Heat in the oven for a few more minutes. Spread the softened chips over the crackers like an icing. Refrigerate to cool and harden. Break into squares and store in refrigerator.

Serves 6 to 8.

Christmas Sugar Plums

1 egg white
¼ cup cold water
1 teaspoon cream of tartar
1 teaspoon vanilla extract
6 cups sifted confectioners' sugar
¼ cup butter, softened
½ cup unsweetened grated coconut
¼ cup chopped candied cherries
¼ cup chopped candied pineapple

🍂 🍂 🍂

1½ pounds large pitted prunes
Sugar
Candied cherries

In a large bowl combine the egg white, water, cream of tartar, and vanilla, beating until the mixture is frothy. Add the confectioners' sugar ¼ of a cup at a time, continuing to beat the mixture until it is thick and smooth. Add the butter, mixing well. Stir in the coconut, cherries, and pineapple. Cover and refrigerate for at least 48 hours.

Split the prunes lengthwise and stuff each prune with 1½ teaspoons of the filling, then roll the prunes in sugar. Garnish each sugar plum with a sliver of candied cherry and store in an airtight container.

Serves 8 to 10.

Ashling Cottage: A Victorian Seaside Inn

106 Sussex Avenue
Spring Lake, New Jersey 07762
(201) 449-3553

Sitting beneath sentinel sycamores, Ashling Cottage has served as a seaside haven for over 100 years. Its bedrooms are tastefully decorated and some have private porches or sunken bathrooms. Guests join the innkeepers in the solarium for a sumptuous buffet breakfast as they watch the sun rise over the ocean.

Basic Muffin Mix

7 cups all-purpose flour
1½ cups sugar
2½ tablespoons baking powder
3 teaspoons salt

Combine all of the ingredients and store in an airtight container.

This mix can be made ahead and used for endless varieties of fruit and sweet muffins.

Makes about 8¾ cups.

Peach Melba Muffins

3 cups Basic Muffin Mix (see recipe)
2 tablespoons brown sugar
1 teaspoon cinnamon

🍂 🍂 🍂

¼ cup butter, melted
½ cup milk

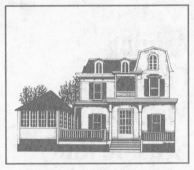

Ashling Cottage

½ cup dry sherry
1 teaspoon vanilla extract
½ cup chopped peaches
½ cup raspberries

Grease 12 muffin tins. In a large bowl combine the Basic Muffin Mix, brown sugar, and cinnamon. Add the remaining ingredients and spoon into the prepared muffin tins. Bake in a 375° oven for 15 to 20 minutes.

Makes 1 dozen muffins.

Pineapple Zucchini Bread

3 eggs
1 cup oil
2 cups sugar
2 cups grated zucchini
3 teaspoons vanilla extract

3 cups all-purpose flour
1 teaspoon salt
1 teaspoon baking soda
3 teaspoons cinnamon

1 cup chopped nuts
1 8-ounce can crushed pineapple
   with juice

Grease 2 loaf pans. In a large bowl combine the eggs, oil, sugar, zucchini, and vanilla.

In a separate bowl combine the dry ingredients. Add the dry mixture to the zucchini mixture, stirring until blended. Add the nuts and pineapple, stirring until just blended. Spread the batter into the prepared pans. Bake in a 350° oven for 40 to 60 minutes.

Freezes well and tastes great with cream cheese spread.

Makes 2 loaves.

Normandy Inn

21 Tuttle Avenue
Spring Lake, New Jersey 07762
(201) 449-7172

Built as a private residence in 1888, this Italianate villa with Queen Anne modifications is filled with prized possessions. An 1860 signed Hertner bed, woven Brussels carpet, Robert Lincoln's bedroom wallpaper, an antique English tall clock case, a rococo damask parlor seat, and marble sculptures are among them. All the inn's rooms have private baths and air conditioning. Situated one-half block from the ocean, several of its rooms have ocean views.

Broccoli and Ham Omelet

1 cup diced cooked ham
1 cup very small broccoli florets,
   steamed until tender

3 tablespoons butter
3 tablespoons all-purpose flour
1½ cups milk
½ cup shredded sharp white
   Cheddar cheese
1 tablespoon sherry (optional)

1 tablespoon clarified butter
3 eggs, well beaten
Salt and pepper to taste

⅓ cup sautéed onion (or
   mushrooms)
Cherry tomato halves
Sprigs of fresh herbs

In a small bowl combine the ham and broccoli. Set aside.

In a small saucepan melt the butter. Stir in the flour to make a paste. Blend in a small amount of the milk. Gradually add the remaining milk, stirring constantly until the sauce starts to thicken. Add the cheese, sherry if desired, ham, broccoli, and the sautéed onions.

Heat an omelet pan over a high flame. Add the clarified butter and heat until hot but not smoking. Pour the eggs into the pan. Pull the eggs away from the sides of the pan with a rubber scraper while moving the pan constantly to prevent sticking. Just before the eggs are completely set, spoon the ham and broccoli into the center of the omelet. Top with some of the sauce. Gently slide the omelet out of the pan onto a plate allowing the omelet to fold in half. Garnish with cherry tomato halves and sprigs of fresh herbs.

Note: Our hint for getting the center of the omelet cooked before the underside gets too brown is to add the filling and place the omelet pan under the broiler for just a few seconds until the desired dryness is reached.

Serves 6.

New Mexico

La Posada de Chimayo

Post Office Box 463
Chimayo, New Mexico 87522

Known for its historic old church and a tradition of fine Spanish weaving, Chimayo is a favorite northern New Mexico destination. This small inn is a typical New Mexico adobe, with brick floors, corner fireplaces, Mexican rugs, and hand-woven bedspreads. Each of the two suites has a sitting room, bedroom with a double bed, and private bath. The substantial breakfast varies from day to day. In the vicinity are Indian pueblos, archaeological sites, desert country, Alpine forests, skiing, and hiking.

Sofia Trujillo's Red Chile

A real northern New Mexico breakfast will consist of fried eggs, home-fried potatoes, bacon or sausage, and flour tortillas. Red chile would be ladled over the eggs and potatoes.

    ½ pound pork, ground or chopped
    2 to 3 cloves garlic
    2 cups water
    ✿   ✿   ✿

    2 tablespoons pork fat or margarine
    2 tablespoons quick-mixing flour
    1 heaping tablespoon ground red
        chile (Chimayo Chile is the best)

In a medium saucepan stew the pork and garlic in the water about 15 minutes, until the pork is thoroughly cooked.

In a heavy saucepan melt the fat. Add the flour and cook over medium heat until bubbly. Add the red chile and stir constantly until you can smell it. Do not burn! Gradually add the liquid from the stewed pork and the pork meat, simmering for a few minutes. If mixture is too thin, add a small amount of the flour.

Serves 4.

The Galisteo Inn

Box 4
Galisteo, New Mexico 87540
(505) 982-1506

The Galisteo Inn offers a unique environment designed with its guests' comfort and enjoyment in mind. The main house is over 240 years old and sits on eight picturesque acres with a pond, pastures, and huge cottonwood trees spreading over green lawns. Guest accommodations are priced to fit a variety of budgets and tastes. The Galisteo Inn combines a homey atmosphere with the best in a modern facility. The cedar sauna, heated pool, mountain bikes and horseback rides provide pleasant relaxation. Therapeutic massage is available at additional cost. The restaurant serves fresh, innovative American cuisine; local produce and regional dishes are emphasized. Breakfast is included in the price of an overnight stay.

Yellow Cornmeal Scones

    2 cups unbleached white flour
    1 cup yellow cornmeal
    ⅓ cup sugar
    1 tablespoon baking powder
    ½ teaspoon salt
    1 teaspoon cinnamon
    ¾ cup unsalted butter, cut into
        small pieces
    ¾ cup currants or raisins (optional)
    1 cup buttermilk

Grease a cookie sheet. In a food processor bowl combine the flour, cornmeal, sugar, baking powder, salt, and cinnamon. Cut the butter into the dry ingredients. Add the currants or raisins, if desired. Slowly add the buttermilk, using the pulse button to combine the mixture. Mix only until just moistened. It is important not to overmix.

Turn the dough onto a lightly floured board. Pat the dough by hand into a 1-inch thick square. Cut into small, even squares and place on the prepared cookie sheet. Bake for 10 to 15 minutes, or until golden brown.

Makes 16 scones.

Bluecornsticks

2¼ cups blue cornmeal
1½ cups unbleached white flour
⅓ cup sugar
2 teaspoons salt
4 teaspoons baking powder
3 eggs, separated
2¾ cups cream, room temperature
¾ cup plus 2 tablespoons butter, melted

Grease 16 cornstick mold cups. In a large bowl combine the meal, flour, sugar, salt, and baking powder. In a separate bowl combine the slightly beaten egg yolks with the cream and butter. Add the cream mixture to the dry ingredients, mixing just until moistened. In a small bowl beat the egg whites until soft peaks form and fold into the batter.

Spoon the batter into cast iron cornstick molds. Bake in a 400° oven for 10 to 15 minutes, or until golden brown. Remove from the molds and repeat until all the batter is used.

Makes approximately 16 cornsticks.

Butternut Squash Gratin

1 small butternut squash, peeled, seeded, and sliced into ⅛-inch slices
1 small red onion, peeled, quartered, and thinly sliced
1 leek, cleaned, halved, and thinly sliced
½ cup grated Parmesan cheese
Salt and pepper
¾ cup heavy cream

Butter an 8x11-inch baking dish. Place half of the squash slices in the prepared dish, overlapping the slices to make an even layer. Add a layer of red onion and leek slices. Sprinkle with half of the Parmesan cheese, salt, and pepper. Top with a layer of squash, the remaining Parmesan cheese, salt, and pepper. Pour the cream over the squash and cover with aluminum foil. Bake in a 350° oven for 1 hour, or until the squash is tender and the cream is reduced. Do not overbake or the cream will separate.

Serves 12.

Inn of the Arts

618 South Alameda Boulevard
Las Cruces, New Mexico 88005
(505) 526-3327

Inn of the Arts is a combination art gallery and bed and breakfast inn. Made up of two homes connected by a large common room with enormous arched windows and an eighteen-foot ceiling, it provides its guests with alcoves, a sunken sitting room, tropical garden, circular staircase, a 250-year-old German Neubrandenburg rosewood piano, and sparkling Mexican fountain. Each of the inn's fourteen guest rooms is dedicated to a well-known Western artist and is decorated to reflect its namesake's style. Breakfast is continental; on weekends waffles, popovers, and scrambled eggs are added. An afternoon social hour, complete with wine and southwestern hors d'oeuvres, is popular with guests.

Southwestern Breakfast Casserole

5 slices bread, buttered and cubed
¾ pound Longhorn cheese, grated
4 ounces frozen green chili, thawed and drained
🌭 🌭 🌭
4 eggs, beaten
2 cups milk
1 teaspoon dry mustard
1 teaspoon salt
Dash cayenne pepper

Inn of the Arts

The Grant Corner Inn

Grease and heat a waffle iron. In a medium bowl beat the 4 egg whites until stiff but not dry, and set aside.

In a medium mixing bowl beat the 4 egg yolks with 3 tablespoons of sugar and the salt. Blend in 2 teaspoons of lemon juice, the lemon rind, and butter, beating well. Sift in the flour, and fold in the egg whites. Bake in the prepared waffle iron until golden brown.

In the top pan of a double boiler combine the egg yolks and ½ cup of sugar. Beat until thick and lemon-colored. Blend in the milk and set over simmering water. Cook, stirring constantly, until the custard thickens and coats a spoon, about 8 minutes. Transfer the custard to a medium porcelain or glass bowl. Stir in 5 tablespoons of lemon juice, and chill for at least 3 hours. Just before serving, fold in the whipped cream.

Serves 4 to 5.

Alternate the layers of bread, cheese, and chili in a 1-quart casserole.

In a blender combine the remaining ingredients and pour over the bread mixture. Refrigerate overnight. Bake in a 350° oven for 1 hour.

Serves 6 to 8.

The Grant Corner Inn

122 Grant Avenue
Santa Fe, New Mexico 87501
(505) 983-6678

Grant Corner Inn, a colonial manor home, is near the old plaza, among intriguing shops, restaurants, and galleries with ample guest parking on the premises. Built in the early 1900s as a private home, the recently renovated inn has nine charming guest rooms, each appointed with antiques and treasures from around the world. Antique quilts, brass and four-poster beds, armoires, and art work make each room special. Each room is modernized with private phones, cable television, and ceiling fans. Breakfast is served daily in front of a crackling fire in the dining room or on the front verandah in summer months. A varied menu includes such treats as banana waffles, eggs Florentine, and New Mexican soufflé. Complimentary wine is served in the evening.

Lemon Waffles

4 eggs, separated
3 tablespoons sugar
½ teaspoon salt
1 cup milk
2 teaspoons fresh lemon juice
2 tablespoons grated lemon rind
¼ cup butter, melted and cooled
1 cup all-purpose flour

   🌿 🌿 🌿

5 egg yolks
½ cup sugar
1 cup milk, scalded
5 tablespoons fresh lemon juice
½ cup heavy cream, whipped

Peachy Corn Bread

½ cup oil
¾ cup sugar
2 eggs, beaten
1½ cups all-purpose flour
1 tablespoon baking powder
¼ teaspoon salt
1½ cups yellow cornmeal
1 cup milk
4 ripe peaches, peeled and chopped

   🌿 🌿 🌿

¾ cup unsalted butter
¾ cup mild honey

Grease and flour a 9x13-inch baking pan. In a medium bowl blend the oil and sugar. Beat in the eggs and set aside. In a small mixing bowl sift the flour, baking powder, salt, and cornmeal. Add the dry ingredients to the egg mixture alternately with the milk. Stir in the peaches. Pour the batter into the prepared pan. Bake in a 400° oven for 25 to 30 minutes, or until golden brown.

In a small bowl beat the butter with an electric mixer until light and fluffy. Gradually add the honey, scraping down the sides of the bowl. Beat until the mixture is smooth and creamy.

Serve with the warm corn bread. This makes about 1½ cups of whipped honey butter.

Serves 12.

Dutch Honey Spice Bread

3 eggs
¾ cup dark brown sugar
¼ cup butter, melted
¾ cup mild honey

&a   &a   &a

2¼ cups all-purpose flour
1 teaspoon baking powder
¾ teaspoon baking soda
½ teaspoon salt
1½ teaspoons cinnamon
½ teaspoon allspice
1 cup chopped walnuts
¾ cup very strong brewed coffee, cooled
Grated rind of 2 oranges

Grease and flour a 9x5-inch loaf pan. In a medium bowl beat the eggs and sugar with an electric mixer until just blended. Add the butter and honey, beating just until combined. Set aside.

In a medium bowl sift together the flour, baking powder, baking soda, salt, cinnamon, and allspice. In a small bowl toss the walnuts with 1 tablespoon of the flour mixture. Set the walnuts aside. Add the flour mixture to the creamed ingredients alternately with the coffee. Stir in the walnuts and orange rind. Smooth the batter into the prepared pan (it will be full). Bake in a 350° oven for 1 hour and 10 to 15 minutes, or until the top springs back when touched. If the loaf is browning too quickly, cover with foil for the last 30 minutes of baking time. Cool in the pan for 10 minutes, then invert onto a rack to cool.

Makes 1 large loaf.

Pimiento Shrimp Timbales

1 tablespoon butter
1 shallot, minced
1 8-ounce package peeled frozen small cooked shrimp, thawed and drained
3 tablespoons julienned pimiento, drained
¼ teaspoon chervil
½ teaspoon salt
1¼ cups milk
¼ cup whipping cream
4 eggs, lightly beaten

&a   &a   &a

4 eggs yolks
1½ tablespoons lemon juice
¼ teaspoon salt
Pinch white pepper
4 tablespoons cream
1 tablespoon chopped chives

Generously grease 4 large custard cups or 4 individual ovenproof ramekins. In a medium sauté pan melt the butter over medium heat. Add the shallot and sauté for 1 minute. Add the shrimp, pimiento, and chervil, and sauté just until heated through. Set aside to drain in a colander.

In a small bowl beat together the salt, milk, cream, and eggs. Divide the shrimp mixture among the prepared custard cups. Divide the milk-egg mixture among the cups. Place the cups in a 2-inch deep baking pan and fill with water to within 1 inch of the top of the cups. Bake in a 325° oven for 20 to 30 minutes, or until a knife inserted in the center of a timbale comes out clean.

In a double boiler over barely simmering water whisk 4 egg yolks until thickened. Beat in the lemon juice, salt, pepper, and cream, and continue whisking until the sauce thickens again, and coats the back of a spoon. Add the chives.

Remove the timbales from the water bath and allow to set for 3 minutes, then unmold onto serving plates. Serve with warm lemon-chive sauce.

Serves 4.

Savory Ham Loaf
with Creamed Eggs

1 pound ham, coarsely ground
½ pound fresh lean pork, coarsely ground
2 teaspoons Dijon mustard
1 teaspoon brown sugar
2 eggs
1 small onion, finely chopped
¾ cup fresh bread crumbs
½ cup tomato sauce
½ teaspoon pepper

&a   &a   &a

Creamed Eggs (recipe follows)
Paprika

Grease an 8x4-inch loaf pan. In a large bowl combine the ham, pork, mustard, brown sugar, eggs, onion, bread crumbs, tomato sauce, and pepper. Press into the prepared pan. Place the pan in a shallow pan and add 1 inch of water to the outer pan. Bake in a 350° oven for 1 hour. Drain off any grease, and let the loaf cool in the pan for 30 minutes before unmolding. Cut into 1-inch thick slices and serve warm with Creamed Eggs. Garnish with a sprinkle of paprika.

Serves 8.

Creamed Eggs

2 cups basic white sauce
1 teaspoon Dijon mustard
¼ teaspoon cayenne
½ teaspoon paprika
6 hard-cooked eggs, shelled and sliced

In a serving bowl combine the white sauce, mustard, and seasonings. Gently fold the sliced eggs into the sauce. Serve warm with Savory Ham Loaf.

Serves 8.

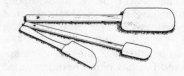

Preston House Bed and Breakfast

106 Faithway Street
Santa Fe, New Mexico 87501
(505) 982-3465

Preston House is the elegant recreation of noted artist/designer Signe Bergman, who moved to Santa Fe in 1974 to pursue her painting career. When she was commissioned by the Santa Barbara Biltmore Hotel to paint its murals in 1978, Signe began to think about a hotel of her own. She is now able to bring her taste and sense of the good life to Preston House in Old Santa Fe. At Preston House a living memory stands gracefully between two centuries.

Mandelbrof— Almond Toasts

1 cup whole almonds

❧ ❧ ❧

2 cups all-purpose flour
2½ teaspoons baking powder
½ teaspoon salt
¼ teaspoon nutmeg

❧ ❧ ❧

6 tablespoons butter, softened
⅔ cup sugar
1 teaspoon almond extract
½ teaspoon vanilla extract
2 eggs

Spread the almonds on a baking sheet and toast in a 300° oven for 15 minutes. Set aside.

In a medium bowl sift together the flour, baking powder, salt, and nutmeg.

In a separate bowl combine the butter and sugar until creamy. Add the almond and vanilla extracts. Beat in the eggs one at a time and stir in the flour mixture. Mix in the almonds. Form the dough into two 9½x3½-inch strips on foil-lined baking sheets. Bake in a 375° oven for 15 to 20 minutes, or until golden. Let cool 20 minutes. Cut the logs into ¾-inch slices with a serrated knife. Lay the slices flat on the baking sheets and return to a 300° oven and bake 20 or more minutes on one side, turn and bake 10 more minutes. Cool.

Makes 25 cookies.

Challah

1 ¼-ounce package active dry yeast
1¼ cups warm water (110° to 115°)

❧ ❧ ❧

¼ cup sugar
2 eggs
¼ cup oil
1 teaspoon salt
5 to 5½ cups all-purpose flour

❧ ❧ ❧

1 egg yolk, beaten with 1 tablespoon water
Poppy seeds

In a large bowl dissolve the yeast in the water. Stir in the sugar, eggs, oil, and salt. Gradually beat in 4½ cups of flour. Turn dough onto a floured board and knead in as much of the remaining flour as needed to make a smooth, soft dough. Place in a greased bowl and let rise until doubled, about 1 hour and 30 minutes. Punch down and divide dough in half. Separate each dough half into thirds and braid, pinching the ends together. Let rise until doubled. Brush with the egg glaze and sprinkle with poppy seeds. Bake in a 350° oven for 35 minutes.

Makes 2 loaves.

Pear Raspberry Cobbler

½ cup frozen butter
1½ cups all-purpose flour
Pinch salt
2 tablespoons sugar
3 tablespoons water

❧ ❧ ❧

6 cups peeled, cored, sliced pears
1¼ cups raspberries, fresh or frozen
¾ cup sugar
4 tablespoons butter

❧ ❧ ❧

1 egg white, combined with 1 teaspoon water

Grease a 9-inch square pan. In a food processor combine ½ cup of butter, flour, salt, and 2 tablespoons of sugar. Turn the processor on and off until the mixture resembles coarse meal. Add the water and process until the dough has come together.

In a large bowl combine the pears, raspberries, and ¾ cup of sugar. Pour into the prepared pan and dot with 4 tablespoons of butter. Roll the dough into a square and fit on top of the fruit mixture. Cut decorative slits and holes in the dough. Glaze with the egg white mixture and sprinkle with sugar, if desired. Bake in a 425° oven for 45 minutes.

Serves 6 to 10.

Whistling Waters

Taos, New Mexico

Mailing Address:
Talpa Route, Box 9
Ranchos de Taos, New Mexico 87557
(505) 758-7798

Soft pink adobe walls, dark green trim, low doorways, dark beams, six fireplaces, old hand-crafted painted cupboards, clay pots, homespun yarns, woven rugs, quiet courtyards with rustling cottonwoods, and whistling waters make up this unusual adobe inn. In the sales gallery are watercolors, pottery, jewelry, eclectic clothing, woven shawls, and much more. A delicious breakfast is served to guests at this relaxing getaway.

Jam and Cheese Loaf

1 ¼-ounce package active dry yeast
½ cup warm water (110° to 115°)
2½ cups Bisquick
1 egg, beaten
1 tablespoon sugar

❧ ❧ ❧

1 8-ounce package cream cheese, softened
½ cup sugar
1 tablespoon lemon juice

❧ ❧ ❧

¼ cup jam or preserves

Grease a 15½x12-inch baking sheet. In a medium bowl dissolve the yeast in the water. Stir in the Bisquick, egg, and 1 tablespoon of sugar. Turn dough onto a surface dusted with Bisquick. Knead gently for 20 strokes. Place the dough in the center of the prepared baking sheet and roll to a 14x9-inch rectangle.

In a medium bowl combine the cream cheese, ½ cup of sugar, and lemon juice. Spread the mixture lengthwise down the center one-third of the dough. Make 3-inch long cuts at 1-inch intervals on both of the long sides of the dough. Fold the strips at an angle over the filling. Cover and chill overnight. Bake in a 350° oven for 20 minutes. Spoon the jam down the center of the loaf. Bake 5 more minutes.

Serves 6 to 8.

The Gregory House

Country Inn and Restaurant
Averill Park, New York 12018
(518) 674-3774

Built in 1830 as a private residence, the Gregory House is now an intimate country inn with twelve comfortably furnished guest rooms and a three-star restaurant. Located near the Berkshire and Green mountains in upstate New York, the inn provides its visitors many natural, cultural, and historic attractions. For the less adventuresome, the solitude of lounging in front of the fire in the inn's common room or around the pool in the summer is enough reward.

Apple Bavarian Torte

1 cup all-purpose flour
⅓ cup sugar
½ teaspoon vanilla extract
½ cup butter, cut in pieces

🍂 🍂 🍂

2 8-ounce packages cream cheese
½ cup sugar
1 teaspoon vanilla extract
2 eggs, at room temperature

🍂 🍂 🍂

Apples, peeled, cored and sliced
¼ cup sugar
½ teaspoon cinnamon
½ teaspoon vanilla extract
⅓ cup chopped walnuts

In a medium bowl combine the first 4 ingredients for a crust and press onto the bottom and sides of a 10-inch springform pan. Bake in a 350° oven until golden. Cool.

In a medium bowl combine the cream cheese, ½ cup of sugar, and 1 teaspoon vanilla, beating until smooth. Beat in the eggs one at a time. Spoon the filling into the crust.

In a medium bowl combine the apples, ¼ cup of sugar, cinnamon, ½ teaspoon vanilla, and walnuts. Arrange as a topping in a spoke-like design. Bake in a 450° oven for 15 minutes. Reduce temperature to 350° and continue baking for 45 minutes, or until a cake tester inserted in the center comes out clean.

Serves 8.

Gregory House Bread Pudding

6 cups French bread, cubed
1½ cups chocolate chips

🍂 🍂 🍂

6 cups milk
¾ cup sugar

The Gregory House

9 tablespoons butter
6 eggs
Dash salt
1½ teaspoons vanilla extract

Butter an ovenproof 2-quart casserole. Place the bread cubes in the prepared casserole and sprinkle with the chocolate chips.

In a large saucepan combine the milk, sugar, and butter, heating until the sugar dissolves. In a separate bowl combine the eggs and salt, beating slightly. Add the egg mixture to the milk mixture. Stir in the vanilla. Pour the liquid mixture over the bread and chocolate. Bake in a 350° oven for 1 hour, or until a knife inserted in the center comes out clean.

Serves 6 to 8.

Bailey's Chocolate Chip Cheesecake

Graham cracker crumbs
Melted butter

❧ ❧ ❧

36 ounces cream cheese, softened
1⅔ cups sugar
5 eggs
1 cup Bailey's Irish Cream
1 tablespoon vanilla extract
½ cup chocolate chips

❧ ❧ ❧

½ cup chocolate chips
Whipped cream
Chocolate sprinkles

Combine the graham cracker crumbs and melted butter, and press into the bottom and sides of a 10-inch springform pan. Bake in a 325° oven for 10 minutes. Remove and cool.

In a large bowl beat the cream cheese until smooth. Gradually add the sugar, beating until well blended. Beat in the eggs one at a time. Blend in the Bailey's Irish Cream and vanilla. Sprinkle ½ cup of chocolate chips over the bottom of the baked crust and pour in the filling.

Sprinkle ½ cup of chocolate chips over the filling. Bake in a 325° oven for about 1 hour and 20 minutes, until

puffed. Serve with whipped cream and chocolate sprinkles.

Serves 8.

The Portico

3741 Lake Road
Brockport, New York 14420
(716) 637-0220

The Portico is a unique example of Greek Revival architecture, with three porticos, massive columns, pediments, and a cupola. Situated in the historic district of Clarkson, it showcases leaded glass foyer panels, ten-foot ceilings, large windows, and three working fireplaces. The full breakfast may include such unusual offerings as mandarin oranges, bananas and kiwi topped with a cream cheese rose, chicken crepes with spinach, croissants, or rum-raisin French toast with warmed maple syrup. Inn activities include afternoon tea, croquet, horseshoes, or Dutch shuffleboard. Nearby attractions include the barge canal, antique shops, the George Eastman House, Strasenburgh Planetarium, and Batavia Downs.

Mushroom Caps Supreme

As an hors d'oeuvre we serve these with small glasses of hot Japanese plum wine. They are equally good to serve as an accompaniment at breakfast with French toast and bacon.

8 slices bacon
⅓ cup Major Grey chutney
12 ounces fresh mushrooms, stems removed and cleaned
⅓ cup bread crumbs
2 tablespoons butter

Lightly butter a cake pan. In a skillet fry the bacon, drain, and chop into bits. In a bowl combine the chutney and bacon bits, chopping up any large pieces of the chutney. Stuff the mushroom caps with the mixture and arrange in the prepared pan. Sprinkle with the bread crumbs and top each with a dot of butter. Broil and serve hot.

Serves 6.

The Portico's Christmas Wine Punch

1 cup lemon juice
2 cups sugar
1 12-ounce can frozen orange juice concentrate, thawed
1 quart Port wine
2 quarts Burgundy
2 quarts club soda
Ice ring

In a large punch bowl stir the lemon juice, sugar, and orange juice concentrate together. Slowly add the Port and Burgundy, stirring to dissolve the sugar. Add the club soda and ice ring. (The punch base can be made ahead of time. Add the club soda and ice ring just before serving.)

Makes 50 punch-sized cups.

Spinach Strawberry Salad
with Creamy Cashew Dressing

½ cup oil
⅓ cup cashews
¼ cup warm water
3 tablespoons honey
1 tablespoon freshly squeezed
    lemon juice
2 teaspoons white vinegar
1½ teaspoons dill
¾ teaspoon soy sauce
2 cloves garlic

⁂

Torn spinach leaves
Sliced strawberries
Mushroom slices
Alfalfa sprouts

In a blender mix the 9 dressing ingredients until smooth and creamy. Chill.

On 6 salad plates arrange the spinach leaves, strawberries, mushrooms, and alfalfa sprouts. Spoon the chilled dressing over the salads.

The leftover dressing will keep in the refrigerator for up to 2 weeks.

Serves 6.

Chicken Crepes Florentine

4 eggs
¼ teaspoon salt
2 cups all-purpose flour
2¼ cups milk
¼ cup butter, melted

⁂

1 cup diced, cooked chicken
½ cup cooked chopped spinach,
    drained
¼ cup saltine cracker crumbs
¼ cup grated Parmesan cheese
1 tablespoon minced onion
1 can cream of chicken soup,
    divided in half

⁂

½ cup half and half
¼ cup slivered toasted almonds

In a large bowl beat the eggs and salt together. Gradually add the flour and milk alternately. Beat in the melted butter. Chill the batter at least 1 hour. Heat oil in a crepe pan and cook each crepe until lightly colored. Cool. Crepes can be frozen and used as needed. (Makes 32 to 36 crepes.)

In a large bowl combine the chicken, spinach, cracker crumbs, cheese, onion, and half of the can of soup. Fill the crepes with the mixture and roll up. Arrange in the prepared dish, folded side down. (Crepes can be assembled to this point up to 10 hours before baking.)

In a small bowl combine the half and half with the remaining soup. Pour over the crepes and sprinkle with almonds. Bake in a 350° oven for 20 to 25 minutes.

Makes filling for 8 to 10 crepes, serving 4 to 5 allowing 2 crepes each.

Quigley's Parsnips and Pineapple

¼ cup butter
1½ cups coarse dry bread crumbs

⁂

3 cups cooked parsnips, cut up
1½ cups diced pineapple, drained,
    reserving juice
½ cup brown sugar
Dash salt
⅛ teaspoon nutmeg
⅛ teaspoon cloves
1 cup pineapple juice (add water to
    reserved juice to make 1 cup)

Butter a 2-quart casserole dish. In a skillet melt the butter. Add the bread crumbs and brown lightly. Set aside some of the crumbs for a topping.

In the casserole place alternate layers of the crumbs, parsnips, and pineapple. Sprinkle with sugar, salt, and spices. Pour the juice over the top and sprinkle with the remaining crumbs. Bake in a 350° oven for 30 minutes.

Serves 6.

The Edge of Thyme

6 Main Street
Candor, New York 13743
(607) 659-5155

At this well-maintained formal home, the summer home of John D. Rockefeller's private secretary, guests can turn back the clock to the turn of the century. With its leaded-glass-windowed porch, marble fireplaces, parquet floors, beautiful stairway, gardens, arbor, and gracious atmosphere, this inn exemplifies Victorian elegance. Private and semiprivate rooms are available.

Blueberry Sour Cream Pancakes with Lemon Sauce

2 cups all-purpose flour
2 teaspoons baking powder
1 teaspoon baking soda
2 tablespoons sugar
2 cups sour cream (or yogurt)
2 eggs
⅓ cup oil
2 cups blueberries, dusted with
    nutmeg

In a medium bowl combine the flour, baking powder, baking soda, and sugar. In a separate bowl combine the sour cream, eggs, and oil. Stir the liquid ingredients into the dry ingredients. Use 5 tablespoons of batter for each pancake and sprinkle the blueberries on top. Turn the pancake.

Serves 4 to 6.

⁂

Lemon Sauce for Pancakes

1 cup sugar
2 cups hot water
2 tablespoons cornstarch
¼ cup butter
1 teaspoon lemon rind

In a medium saucepan combine the sugar, hot water, and cornstarch. Add the butter and lemon rind. Cook until the mixture thickens to a syrup consistency.

Makes about 3 cups.

The Edge of Thyme Fruit Tart

1¼ cups all-purpose flour
¼ cup sugar
½ cup butter
1 egg yolk
1 teaspoon vanilla extract

   ᴥ ᴥ ᴥ

Fresh fruit (apricots, apples, grapes, peaches, or cherries)
2 tablespoons orange marmalade (or apricot preserves)
Kiwi

In a medium bowl combine the first 5 ingredients and pat into a tart pan. Arrange the fresh fruit on top. Bake in a 350° oven for 30 minutes. Top with the orange marmalade while warm. Decorate with kiwi.

Serves 8.

The Brae Loch Inn

5 Albany Street
U.S. Route 20
Cazenovia, New York
(315) 655-3431

Family owned and operated since 1946, Brae Loch Inn is as close to a Scottish Inn as you will find this far west of Edinburgh. The innkeeper dresses in a Scottish kilt as he greets diners, who are served by attendants in kilts and traditional Glengarrie hats. Guests are encouraged to explore the lounge and Scottish gift shop at their leisure. The twelve guest rooms, all with private baths, feature the old-time charm of antiques and the luxury of Stickley furniture. Guests are permitted at a nearby golf course and the town beach.

Scottish Salmon Soufflé

3 tablespoons butter
6 tablespoons all-purpose flour
2 cups milk
3 eggs, separated
Salt and pepper

   ᴥ ᴥ ᴥ

2 ¼-ounce packages powdered gelatin
3 tablespoons lemon juice
1 pound cooked salmon (or two 7¾-ounce cans)
¼ cup single cream
1 tablespoon Drambuie
Dash Tabasco sauce
Pinch ground mace

   ᴥ ᴥ ᴥ

Sliced cucumbers

Encircle a 1½-pint soufflé dish with a 2-inch collar of foil and fasten with tape. In a medium saucepan melt the butter. Add the flour, then gradually stir in the milk to make a smooth sauce. Bring the sauce to a boil, stirring constantly until the sauce thickens. Stir in the egg yolks and cook for 1 minute. Season the sauce with salt and pepper and set aside to cool slightly.

In a small bowl dissolve the gelatin in the lemon juice. Stir the mixture into the sauce. Flake the salmon, removing any bones and skin, and stir into the sauce. Add the cream, Drambuie, Tabasco sauce, mace, and additional salt and pepper. Set the soufflé mixture aside until it is almost set.

In a medium bowl whisk the egg whites until stiff. Fold a tablespoon of the whites into the soufflé mixture, then lightly fold in the remaining whites. Pour the mixture into the prepared dish. It should come at least 1 inch above the edge. Let set overnight. The next day carefully peel off the collar and serve the soufflé garnished with sliced cucumbers.

Serves 4.

Scottish Whole Wheat Scones

½ cup all-purpose flour
1 teaspoon baking soda
2 teaspoons cream of tartar
Pinch salt
1½ cups whole wheat flour
¼ cup butter
¼ cup milk

In a large bowl combine the flour, baking soda, cream of tartar, and salt. Stir in the whole wheat flour. Cut in the butter until evenly distributed, then stir in enough milk to make a soft but not sticky dough. Turn the dough onto a floured surface and knead lightly until smooth. Roll the dough to a ½-inch thickness and cut into 2½-inch rounds. Place on a baking tray and brush the tops with milk. Bake in a 425° oven for 10 minutes, or until golden brown.

Makes 8 scones.

The Friends Lake Inn

Friends Lake Road
Chestertown, New York 12817
(518) 494-4751

Located in the Adirondacks overlooking Friends Lake, the Friends Lake Inn is conveniently situated just twenty minutes north of Lake George, one and one-half hours north of Albany, and one hour south of Lake Placid. Gore Mountain Ski Center is only fifteen minutes away. Formerly called the Murphy's, it was built in the 1860s as a boarding house to accommodate the tanners who worked in the major industry of early Chestertown. The inn has been completely restored and refurbished and now provides a pleasant, relaxed atmosphere for individuals, couples, or families. Downhill skiers, cross-country skiers, trail hikers, anglers, hunters, boaters, or loafers will appreciate the beauty of the Adirondacks and the Friends Lake Inn. Individually decorated with a warm country flair, each guest room is comfortable and relaxing. Many of the rooms have brass and iron beds and provide their occupants with magnificent lake views.

Saffron Seafood Chowder

1 large onion, diced
4 stalks celery, diced
3 bay leaves
1 teaspoon thyme
¼ cup unsalted butter
1 pound Boston Bluefish fillets
12 jumbo shrimp
4 ounces salmon
8 ounces scallops
2 pinches saffron
2 quarts water
Salt and pepper to taste

In a skillet sauté the onion, celery, and spices in the butter until the vegetables are soft. Add the seafood, saffron, and water, and let simmer for 45 minutes. Season with the salt and pepper.
Variation: Add 2 to 3 cups of heavy cream after the chowder has simmered for 45 minutes. Don't boil it again.
Serves 4 to 6.

Sautéed Cutlets of Veal
with a Sweet Bell Pepper Compote

¼ cup unsalted butter or oil
12 ounces veal cutlets
All-purpose flour
¼ cup diced red pepper
¼ cup diced yellow pepper
¼ cup diced green pepper
¼ teaspoon chopped shallots
¼ teaspoon minced garlic
¼ cup Burgundy or Port wine
¼ cup chicken stock or water
Salt and pepper to taste

In a heavy frying pan melt the butter. Lightly dredge the veal in the flour and quickly sauté in the butter. Remove the veal from the pan, reserving the butter. Add the peppers, shallots, and garlic. Add the wine, stock, and seasonings, and simmer until the liquid is reduced to half. Place the mixture on 2 serving plates. Serve the veal over the warm compote and garnish with crisp pepper slices.
Serves 2.

Fresh Fruit Sabayon

5 egg yolks
3 drops vanilla extract
¾ cup sugar
¼ cup white wine
½ cup Marsala
❧ ❧ ❧
20 fresh strawberries
1 cup fresh blueberries
1 cup fresh red raspberries
Grated lemon and lime zest

Chill 4 serving plates. In the top of a double boiler pan whisk the egg yolks, vanilla, and sugar together until thick and pale. Place the pan over the simmering water of the double boiler. Slowly add the white wine and Marsala. When the Sabayon is thick and frothy, remove the pan and pour evenly onto the chilled plates. Arrange the berries on the Sabayon and garnish with grated lemon and lime zest.
Serves 4.

All-Purpose Seafood Marinade

2 cups olive oil
3 cups soy sauce
1½ cups pineapple juice
1 lemon
1 lime
1 orange
⅛ cup minced garlic
⅛ cup chopped shallots

In a large container mix the oil, soy sauce, and pineapple juice. Halve and squeeze the lime, lemon, and orange juice into the mixture. Add the squeezed citrus shells. Mix in the garlic and shallots. This may be used to marinate any seafood: tuna, swordfish, shrimp, or other.
Makes about 7 cups.

🦆 🦆 🦆 🦆 🦆

Back of the Beyond

7233 Lower East Hill Road
Colden, New York 14033
(716) 652-0427

This charming country mini-estate is in the Boston hills and ski area of western New York, about twenty-five miles from Buffalo and fifty miles from Niagara Falls. Accommodations are in a separate chalet with three available bedrooms, one and one-half baths, and a fully furnished kitchen. The dining/living room, piano, pool table, and fireplaces are available to guests. A rustic post-beam cabin in the woods will accommodate two more. A full country herbal breakfast is served daily, and the organic herb, flower, and vegetable gardens are for the delight of guests who want to stroll and relax on the grounds. A greenhouse and Herbtique Gift Shop is part of the complex, as are a large pond for swimming and lovely woods for hiking. Lawn games are provided for the summer and autumn visitors, and cross-country skiing is free on the inn's own trails.

Vegetable Frittata

We use our own organic vegetables in this recipe.

6 eggs, lightly beaten

&ea; &ea; &ea;

⅓ cup thinly sliced onion
⅓ cup diced green and red peppers
⅓ cup sliced mushrooms
⅓ cup diced zucchini
3 to 4 drops low salt soy sauce
8 ounces plain tomato sauce
½ cup shredded part-skim Mozzarella cheese

1 teaspoon dried basil
(or 1 tablespoon fresh)
1 teaspoon dried oregano
(or 1 tablespoon fresh)

In a non-stick, broil-proof pan scramble the eggs. Do not overcook! Set aside.

In a separate pan lightly sauté the vegetables in soy sauce, just until slightly tender, about 3 to 5 minutes. Spread the vegetables on top of the eggs, cover with the tomato sauce, and sprinkle with the cheese and herbs. Broil until the tomato sauce bubbles and the cheese melts.

Note: This dish may be made ahead and reheated. You may also substitute the vegetables of your choice. Garnish with fresh basil if available.

Serves 6.

Mandarin Mint Muffins

1 cup unbleached all-purpose flour
½ cup wheat germ
½ cup oat bran
½ teaspoon baking powder
1 teaspoon baking soda
¼ teaspoon salt
¾ cup flaked coconut

&ea; &ea; &ea;

1 large egg
½ cup oil
½ cup brown sugar, lightly packed
½ cup orange juice
1 11-ounce can mandarin oranges, drained
1 teaspoon dried mint
(or 1 tablespoon fresh)

Grease muffin tins. In a large bowl combine the dry ingredients.

In a separate bowl combine the egg, oil, sugar, and juice. Add the oranges and mint. Add the liquid ingredients to the dry mixture, gently stirring until just moistened. Pour batter into the prepared tins and bake in a 400° oven for 15 to 20 minutes.

Makes 12 muffins.

Margaret Thacher's Spruce Haven Bed and Breakfast

9 James Street
Post Office Box 119
Dryden, New York 13053
(607) 844-8052

Spruce Haven is a log home set in pine trees near downtown Dryden. Built by the hostess and her husband, it offers two guest rooms that share a bath. No smoking is permitted. Nearby attractions include Cornell University, Ithaca College, and Finger Lake vacation area.

Porridge DeLite

This is a real favorite with my guests. Some say it is good enough for dessert.

2½ cups apple cider or apple juice
⅓ cup cream of buckwheat cereal
(I use Pocona from Penn Yann, NY)
¼ cup rolled oats
1 apple, cored, peeled and chopped
1 teaspoon margarine
⅓ cup chopped walnuts
1 teaspoon vanilla extract

In a saucepan bring the cider to a boil. Slowly stir in the cream of buckwheat, oats, apple, margarine, and walnuts. Continue to boil for 10 to 12 minutes, or until desired consistency, stirring constantly. Add the vanilla just before serving. (More cider or cereal may be added during cooking as needed for consistency.) Serve hot or cold with milk or cream.

Serves 4.

Raised Doughnuts

1 cup milk
1 0.6-ounce cake compressed yeast
4 cups bread flour

ಜ ಜ ಜ

½ cup shortening
1 teaspoon salt
⅓ cup sugar
3 eggs

ಜ ಜ ಜ

2 cups confectioners' sugar, sifted
2 tablespoons hot milk
1 teaspoon vanilla extract or maple
    flavoring

In a saucepan heat the milk to luke-warm (80° to 90°). Add the yeast, stirring to dissolve. Add 1½ cups of the flour and beat until smooth.

In a bowl combine the shortening, salt, and sugar. Add the eggs, blending well. Add to the yeast mixture. Add the remaining flour and beat well. Let rise at a temperature of 80° to 86°, until doubled. Roll the dough to ½-inch thickness and cut with a doughnut cutter. Let stand 15 to 20 minutes before frying.

In a deep fat fryer heated to 365° to 375°, drop the raised side of dough and fry about 2 to 3 minutes. Turn to brown. Drain on absorbent paper.

In a bowl combine 2 cups of confectioners' sugar with enough hot milk to make a thin frosting. Add the flavoring. Dip the doughnuts into the frosting and drain on a wire rack.

Serves 10 to 12.

Nonwheat Date Muffins

Many people are allergic to wheat, and it is nice to have baked goods for them.

¼ cup mashed tofu
2 tablespoons oil
1 egg
¾ to 1 cup apricot juice
½ teaspoon vanilla extract

ಜ ಜ ಜ

1½ cups brown rice flour
¼ cup soy flour
¼ cup tapioca flour
2½ teaspoons baking powder
¼ teaspoon cream of tartar
2 teaspoons cinnamon
¾ cup soft chopped dates

Oil small muffin tins. In a blender combine the tofu, oil, egg, juice, and vanilla.

In a large bowl sift together the flours, baking powder, cream of tartar, and cinnamon. Add the blended mixture and fold in the dates. Pour batter into the prepared tins. Bake in a 350° oven for 20 to 25 minutes, or until the muffins spring back when lightly pressed.

Makes about 18 small muffins.

Tutti Fruitti Nutty Bread

¾ cup shortening
½ cup honey
3 eggs, beaten
3½ cups all-purpose flour
¼ teaspoon salt
1½ teaspoons baking powder
1½ teaspoons baking soda
2¼ tablespoons sour milk
⅓ cup ground orange with rind
¼ cup ground apple with peel
½ cup mashed banana
1½ teaspoons vanilla extract
½ cup chopped pecans

Grease a 9x5-inch loaf pan. In a large bowl cream together the shortening and honey until light and fluffy. Add the eggs and mix well.

In a separate bowl sift together the flour, salt, baking powder, and baking soda. Add to the creamed mixture. Stir in the milk, fruits, vanilla, and pecans. Spread the batter in the prepared loaf pan. Bake in a 350° oven for 1 hour.

Makes 1 loaf.

Mill House Inn

33 North Main Street
East Hampton, New York 11937
(516) 324-9766

This charming old colonial inn is opposite Old Hook Windmill and the village green. Offering guests European-style bed and breakfast accommodations, its location allows them easy access to shopping, restaurants, movies, theater, and beaches. Most of the guest rooms offer private baths, and there is a two-bedroom suite with a sitting area. A full breakfast is served in the dining room or on the sun porch. Guests are invited to relax on the sun porch, in the yard, or in the living room with a wood-burning fireplace.

Baked Brie in Phyllo

¼ cup apricot preserves
1 2-pound wheel Brie (or
    Camembert) cheese
½ pound frozen phyllo dough (ten
    to twelve 18x14-inch sheets),
    thawed
½ cup butter or margarine, melted
Fresh dill (optional)
Red and green grapes (optional)
Apples or pears (optional)

Spread the preserves on top of the Brie. Brushing each sheet of phyllo dough with melted butter, wrap the Brie, turning the cheese over after applying a sheet of dough for even distribution. Brush the wrapped Brie with butter. Cover and refrigerate. Before serving place the phyllo-wrapped cheese in a shallow baking pan and bake in a 425° oven for 8 to 12 minutes or until golden. Let stand 10 minutes and garnish with dill, grapes, apples, or pears.

Serves 24 to 30.

Summer Garden Salad

1 pound fresh peas, shelled
1 teaspoon sugar

🍃 🍃 🍃

½ cup olive oil
½ cup fresh grapefruit juice
1 tablespoon plus 1 teaspoon white wine vinegar
2 garlic cloves, crushed through a press
½ teaspoon Dijon mustard
½ teaspoon salt
¼ teaspoon freshly ground pepper

🍃 🍃 🍃

1 head Romaine lettuce
1 head Bibb lettuce
1 bunch spinach, stemmed
¼ pound Chinese snow peas, strings removed
8 scallions, cut into 2-inch sections
1 large grapefruit, peeled and sectioned

In a large saucepan of boiling water add the peas and sugar and cook until the peas are tender but still firm, about 10 minutes. Rinse the peas under cold water and drain well.

In a small bowl whisk together the oil, grapefruit juice, vinegar, garlic, mustard, salt, and pepper to make a dressing.

Wash and dry the lettuce and spinach. Tear the leaves into bite-sized pieces and place in a large salad bowl. Add the peas, snow peas, scallions, and grapefruit. About 30 minutes before serving, pour the dressing over the salad and toss to coat.

Serves 8 to 10.

Peas à la Française

3 10-ounce packages frozen small peas
½ pound tiny white onions (about 24 count)
¼ cup butter
¼ cup boiling water
1 tablespoon sugar
¼ teaspoon chervil
¼ teaspoon thyme
1½ teaspoons salt
Freshly ground black pepper
2 cups shredded lettuce

Remove the peas from the freezer and thaw for 1 hour. Peel the onions. If the onions are not the tiniest ones, remove 1 or 2 layers to reduce them to cocktail size. In a small saucepan cook the onions in boiling salted water for 5 minutes and drain. In a large heavy saucepan melt the butter. Add the onions, ¼ cup of boiling water, sugar, herbs, salt, and pepper. Add the peas and toss to blend them with the seasonings. Gently stir in the lettuce. Cover the pan and cook over medium heat just until the peas are tender, about 5 minutes.

Serves 10 to 12.

Inn at Lake Joseph

Rural Delivery 5 Box 85
Forestburgh, New York 12777
(914) 791-9506

This country Victorian mansion, dating from the 1880s, was once the summer home of Cardinals Hayes and Spellman of New York. Its seven rooms, three with private bath, are beautifully furnished; and a full breakfast and dinner are served daily. Meals can be served on the porch, in the formal dining room, or around the kitchen table. From the three window seats in the three living rooms, guests can look across the well-kept lawn to the woods.

Penne Armitriciana

This pasta dish is often served as a first course, but makes a wonderful buffet or picnic dish as well. Line the serving dish with seasonal greens for a colorful presentation.

1 pound Penne pasta
2 tablespoons virgin olive oil

🍃 🍃 🍃

3 cups tomato sauce
¼ pound bacon, chopped
1 medium onion, thinly sliced
¼ cup balsamic vinegar

In a large pot of salted boiling water cook the pasta until al dente, about 6 to 7 minutes.

In a saucepan heat the tomato sauce. In a large sauté pan heat the olive oil and add the bacon, cooking it until lightly crisp. Add the onions and sauté until golden brown. Drain all the fat from the pan. Add the tomato sauce and reduce by one-third over low heat. Add the vinegar. Mix sauce with the pasta.

Serves 4.

Insalata di Rucola

2 bunches arrugula
3 ounces fresh Parmesan cheese, shaved
Black olives and radishes to garnish

🍃 🍃 🍃

Tarragon Vinaigrette

Wash the arrugula leaves in cold water until all the sand is removed. Drain or spin. Place on salad plates and sprinkle with Parmesan and garnish with sliced olives and radishes. Before serving, sprinkle with Tarragon Vinaigrette.

Serves 4.

Inn at Lake Joseph

Tarragon Vinaigrette

This dressing keeps well when refrigerated for about 2 weeks.

3 tablespoons tarragon wine vinegar
3 tablespoons fresh lemon juice
¼ teaspoon salt
⅛ teaspoon freshly ground black pepper
¼ teaspoon sugar
½ clove garlic, minced
¾ cup vegetable oil
½ cup virgin olive oil

In a small bowl combine all the ingredients except the oils, mixing well. Slowly add the vegetable oil in a slow stream, beating continuously with a whisk until emulsified. Add the olive oil. Mix well and refrigerate at least 1 hour before serving.

Makes about 1½ cups.

Grilled Swordfish with Salsa Piquante

At the Inn, we serve this dish with a rice pilaf and Insalata di Rucola (a wonderful green salad).

1 cup virgin olive oil
Freshly ground black pepper
3 tablespoons fresh oregano sprigs (or 3 teaspoons dried)
¼ cup lemon juice
Salt to taste

❦ ❦ ❦

4 8-ounce swordfish fillets

❦ ❦ ❦

2 cups virgin olive oil
¼ cup imported capers
¼ cup chopped parsley
¼ cup finely chopped red pepper
¼ cup finely chopped scallions
2 tablespoons lemon juice
Salt and pepper to taste

In a bowl combine 1 cup of oil, black pepper, oregano, lemon juice, and salt for a marinade. Marinate the fillets at least 2 hours, turning once.

In a medium saucepan combine 2 cups of oil, capers, parsley, red pepper, scallions, lemon juice, salt, and pepper. Cook the piquante sauce for 5 minutes over medium heat, and keep at room temperature until serving.

Grill the fillets over a very hot fire for 3 minutes on each side. Serve with the piquante sauce as a garnish.

Serves 4.

Grilled Lamb Brochettes (Kabobs)

2 cups olive oil
3 sprigs fresh rosemary
Juice of 1 lemon
Juice of 1 lime
Salt and pepper to taste
½ teaspoon sugar
1 pound lamb shoulder, cut into 1-inch cubes

❦ ❦ ❦

1 red pepper, quartered
1 large onion, quartered
1 green pepper, quartered
½ pound large mushrooms, cleaned and stems removed

In a medium bowl combine the oil, rosemary, juices, salt, pepper, and sugar. Add the lamb. Stir once, cover bowl, and refrigerate overnight.

Using skewers at least 10-inches long, alternate cubes of lamb, red pepper, onion, green pepper, and mushrooms. Repeat until the skewer is full. Grill over a hot fire for 5 minutes on each side. Serve with rice and salad.

Serves 4.

Chocolate Mousse Grand Marnier

This is a very special mousse. You've got to try it! An elegant way to serve this or a fruit mousse is in "Chocolate Sacks."

12 ounces semisweet chocolate
2 tablespoons Grand Marnier
1 egg, beaten

❦ ❦ ❦

1 cup heavy cream, whipped
2 egg whites, beaten until soft peaks form

❦ ❦ ❦

Whipped cream, shaved chocolate, fresh mint leaves

In a double boiler melt the chocolate and allow to cool. In a small bowl combine the Grand Marnier and egg. Add to the chocolate and mix.

In a separate bowl fold the chocolate into the whipped cream. Gently fold the chocolate mixture into the egg whites. Pour mixture into individual serving cups and refrigerate.

Before serving garnish with whipped cream, shaved chocolate, and a fresh mint leaf.

Serves 6.

Chocolate Sacks (for mousse)

7 ounces semisweet chocolate
Small #6 paper bags (6x4x11-inch)
Vegetable oil

In a double boiler melt the chocolate and set aside. Cut 2 inches off the top of the bag and cut a semicircular indentation in the center top of the bag. Completely coat the exterior of the bag with the oil. Rub excess off with a paper towel. Stack 1 or 2 large cans on a tray, place the bag over them, upside down. The bag should not touch the tray. Using a pastry brush, coat the bag heavily with melted chocolate, using extra at the creases and bottom. Refrigerate until hard. Repeat the process. Carefully peel the paper away from the chocolate and fill with mousse!

Serves 6.

The Bowman House

61 Lake Street
Post Office Box 586
Hammondsport, New York 14840
(607) 569-2516

The Bowman House is a large, 1880s restored home in the heart of wine-making country. The four guest rooms have the finest in comfort and privacy. In the afternoon there is wine and cheese; in the evening, good conversation and mints on the pillows. Breakfast is served with style.

Jessie's Old-fashioned Crumb Cake

Great as a wintertime breakfast coffee cake.

3 cups brown sugar
4 cups all-purpose flour
2 teaspoons cinnamon
2 teaspoons salt
1 cup margarine

&ate; &ate; &ate;

2 teaspoons baking soda
2 cups sour milk
2 eggs
1 teaspoon vanilla extract

Grease a 9x13-inch baking dish. In a large bowl combine the sugar, flour, cinnamon, and salt. Cut in the butter until the mixture is crumbly. Set aside 2 cups of the mixture for a topping.

In a separate bowl dissolve the baking soda in the milk. Add the eggs and vanilla. Add the liquid mixture to the crumb mixture and mix. Pour batter into the prepared dish and sprinkle with the reserved crumbs. Bake in a 350° oven for 35 to 40 minutes.

Serves 10 to 12.

Aileen's Pumpkin Bread

Great sliced and spread with softened cream cheese.

1 cup pumpkin
1 cup sugar
¾ cup oil
2 eggs
1½ cups all-purpose flour
1 teaspoon baking soda
1 teaspoon baking powder
1 teaspoon nutmeg
1 teaspoon cinnamon
¼ teaspoon salt
½ cup chopped nuts

Grease three #2 tin cans. In a large bowl combine the ingredients. Pour batter into the prepared cans and bake in a 350° oven for 50 minutes.

Makes 3 round loaves.

&ate; &ate; &ate; &ate; &ate;

Sunrise Inn

Hancock, New York

Mailing Address:
Rural Delivery 1, Box 232 B
Walton, New York 13856
(607) 865-7254

The Sunrise Inn is a small farmhouse overlooking Read Creek and nearby mountains. Open as an inn since the 1920s, it brings to its guests all the warmth of the "good old days." The two guest rooms share a bath, and the parlor is available for relaxing, reading, chatting, or playing checkers. A private cabin for two is also available. An antique shop is located adjacent to the inn.

Sunrise Soda Bread

2 cups sifted all-purpose flour
1½ teaspoons baking powder
¾ teaspoon baking soda
1 teaspoon salt
3 tablespoons sugar
1½ teaspoons caraway seeds
3 tablespoons shortening
1 cup buttermilk
½ cup raisins
1½ tablespoons butter, melted

Grease a baking sheet. In a large bowl sift together the flour, baking powder, baking soda, salt, and sugar. Add the caraway seeds and cut in the shortening until it is in fine pieces. Make a well in the center. Pour in the buttermilk and add the raisins. Mix lightly to form a soft dough. Knead gently a few strokes and shape the dough into a round loaf. Place on the prepared baking sheet. Baste the top of the loaf with the melted butter. Bake in a 350° oven for approximately 45 minutes until golden brown.

Makes 1 loaf.

Cranberry Scones

2¼ cups all-purpose flour
½ cup sugar
2 teaspoons baking powder
½ teaspoon salt (optional)
½ teaspoon cloves
¼ cup margarine
1 cup sour cream
¾ cup cranberries

Grease a baking sheet. In a large bowl combine the flour, sugar, baking powder, salt, and cloves. Cut in the margarine until the mixture resembles coarse crumbs. Reserve 2 teaspoons of the sour cream. Stir the remaining sour cream and the cranberries into the dry ingredients. Mix lightly with a fork until a soft dough forms. Knead about 5 times and roll the dough into a 7-inch circle. Cut into wedges and place 1-inch apart on the prepared baking sheet. Pierce the tops of each wedge with a fork and brush with the reserved sour cream.

Bake in a 425° oven for approximately 18 minutes, or until golden brown.

Makes 4 to 8 wedges.

Apple-Pumpkin Pie

1 uncooked 9-inch pie shell
2 tablespoons all-purpose flour
¼ cup brown sugar
½ teaspoon cinnamon
2½ cups peeled, thinly sliced apples

🍂 🍂 🍂

1 cup canned pumpkin
⅔ cup evaporated milk
1 egg
½ cup sugar
½ teaspoon ginger
¼ teaspoon salt
⅛ teaspoon cloves

In a medium bowl combine the flour, brown sugar, and cinnamon. Stir in the apples. Place mixture in the uncooked pie shell and set aside.

In a large bowl combine the remaining ingredients, mixing thoroughly. Pour this mixture over the apple mixture in the pie shell. Bake in a 425° oven for 15 minutes. Reduce the oven temperature to 350° and bake for an additional 30 minutes, or until the filling is set. Cool on a rack. Refrigerate leftovers.

Serves 6 to 8.

Bed and Breakfast at the Duvalls

237 Cathedral Avenue
Hempstead, New York 11550
(on the Garden City Line)
(516) 292-9219

This charming old Dutch Colonial house offers its guests three air-conditioned rooms with private baths and color television. One room has twin four-poster beds, another a king-size bed and dressing room. Families usually prefer the adjoining parlor and porch. Breakfast is served on the patio or in the plant-filled breakfast room. Smoking is not permitted.

Bed and Breakfast at the Duvalls

Cheese Roll with Pecans

1 pound sharp Cheddar cheese, grated
½ pound cream cheese
1 teaspoon garlic powder
1 cup finely ground pecans

🌿 🌿 🌿

½ teaspoon curry powder
½ teaspoon paprika

In a large bowl soften cheeses at room temperature. Beat together until fluffy. Beat in the garlic powder and pecans. Divide the mixture and roll into 4-inch rolls. Let stand until dry.

Cover the cheese roll with a mixture of the curry powder and paprika. Serve with crackers. Can be frozen.

Makes 6 to 8 rolls.

Appetizer

⅓ cup plus 1 tablespoon olive oil
2 teaspoons chopped garlic
1 cup thinly sliced fresh mushrooms
⅓ cup chopped anchovy fillets (2 small tins)
Juice of 1 lemon
Freshly ground black pepper
½ cup chopped pitted black olives
¼ teaspoon crushed hot red pepper flakes

🌿 🌿 🌿

1 pound thin spaghetti
Olive oil

In a small skillet heat the olive oil. Add the garlic and stir, but don't brown. Add the mushrooms and cook until wilted. Add the anchovies, stir, and remove from the heat. Add the lemon juice and black pepper to taste. Add the olives and pepper flakes. Set sauce aside.

Cook the spaghetti, drain, and toss with olive oil. Add the sauce and toss. Let stand to room temperature.

Serves 4 as a main dish or 8 as an appetizer.

The Rose Inn

813 Auburn Road, Route 34
Post Office Box 6576
Ithaca, New York 14851-6576
(607) 533-4202

This large Italianate mansion was built in the 1850s on twenty acres in the hills north of Ithaca. The inn offers sixteen guest rooms with private baths, including three honeymoon suites with Jacuzzis and fireplaces. Each room is luxurious, with lace curtains, ceiling fans, terry robes, fresh flowers, and more. Great care is taken to provide an unusual breakfast, which is served in the dining room, parlor, or foyer. An elegant dinner, which must be reserved in advance, is also served. The Rose Inn is situated in the center of the Finger Lakes region of upstate New York, which boasts several fine vineyards and wineries well worth the effort to visit.

The Rose Inn

Scampi Mediterranean

Cognac flambéed large shrimp with a touch of curry, tomato, and cream.

½ teaspoon minced garlic
1 tablespoon Italian dressing
10 large shrimp (U 15 size) shelled, deveined, tails on
1 cup cooked pasta, Acini di Pepe or herbed rice, lightly buttered and seasoned with garlic salt, pepper, and fresh parsley flakes
2 tablespoons olive oil
20 pine nuts
Chopped parsley

❧ ❧ ❧

1 ounce Cognac or brandy
1 tablespoon chopped shallots
¼ teaspoon curry powder
¼ teaspoon chicken base
2 tablespoons tomato paste
½ cup white wine
½ cup whole cream

In a bowl combine the garlic and Italian dressing for a marinade. Add the shrimp and marinate for 1 hour. Arrange ½ cup of the Acini di Pepe on each of 2 warmed plates, making a semicircle inside of each plate. Cover and place in a warm oven. In a 7-inch sauté pan heat the olive oil and brown the pine nuts. Remove the nuts with a slotted spoon and drain on paper towel. Garnish with the parsley and set aside.

In the same hot pan sauté the shrimp for 1 minute on one side and turn. Add the cognac and flambé for 1 minute. Remove the shrimp to the prepared plates, arranging in a fan with the tails to the center of the plate. Cover again and return to the warming oven.

To the sauté pan add the shallots and curry powder, stirring constantly with the wooden spoon for 30 seconds. Stir in the tomato paste, chicken base, and white wine, boiling rapidly to reduce the wine. When the oil begins to separate from the sauce, stir in the cream and continue boiling until the center of the pan boils and the sauce thickens, approximately 3 minutes. Spoon the sauce over the shrimp. Garnish with the toasted pine nuts and chopped parsley.

Serves 2.

The Lamplight Inn

2129 Lake Avenue
Post Office Box 70
Lake Luzerne, New York 12846-0070
(518) 696-4294

No expense was spared when Howard Conkling, a wealthy lumberman and summer resident of Lake Luzerne, built this Victorian Gothic estate. Five doors off the parlor lead out to the spacious wrap-around verandah and lawns. On the first floor, twelve-foot beamed ceilings and a chestnut keyhole staircase were crafted in England.

Guests at the Lamplight Inn experience a warm, welcoming atmosphere. A wood burning fireplace, comfortable Victorian furnishings, the verandah, and a garden contribute to this feeling. Each of the guest rooms is unique, with five having fireplaces. The rooms have private bathrooms and antique furnishings. The full breakfast adds to the warm, homey atmosphere.

Chocolate Mini-chip Streusel Coffeecake

6 tablespoons butter or margarine
½ cup sugar
2 eggs
½ teaspoon vanilla extract
¼ cup sour cream
1½ cups all-purpose flour
1 teaspoon baking powder
½ teaspoon baking soda
½ cup orange juice
2 teaspoons grated orange peel

❧ ❧ ❧

⅔ cup light brown sugar
½ cup chopped walnuts
½ cup semisweet chocolate mini-chips

Grease a 9-inch square pan. In a large bowl cream together the butter and sugar. Add the eggs and vanilla, beating well. Blend in the sour cream. In a separate bowl combine the flour, baking powder, and baking soda. Add the dry ingredients to the butter mixture alternately with the orange juice, blending well. Stir in the orange peel. Pour half of the batter into the prepared pan.

In a medium bowl combine the brown sugar and walnuts. Divide in half and add the mini-chips to one portion. Sprinkle the streusel mixture containing the mini-chips evenly over the batter. Spoon the remaining batter over the streusel and spread evenly to cover. Sprinkle the remaining streusel topping over the top. Bake in a 350° oven for 30 minutes. Sprinkle with additional mini-chips. Serve warm or cold.

Serves 9.

Harvest Apple Cake
with Apple Frosting

2 cups all-purpose flour
1 cup sugar
1½ teaspoons baking soda
1 teaspoon salt
1 teaspoon cinnamon
¼ teaspoon nutmeg
¼ cup light brown sugar

❧ ❧ ❧

½ cup butter or margarine
1 cup apple juice
2 eggs
1½ cups finely chopped pared apples
½ cup raisins
½ cup chopped walnuts

❧ ❧ ❧

2 tablespoons butter or margarine
1 cup confectioners' sugar
½ teaspoon vanilla extract
1 to 2 tablespoons apple juice

The Lamplight Inn

Plumbush

Route 33
Rural Delivery 2, Box 332
Mayville, New York 14757
(716) 789-5309

This inn is set on 125 acres atop a ridge near Chautauqua Lake. A beautifully restored Italian villa-style country home built about 1865, it is painted in the Plumbush theme of mauve, pinks, burgundy, and greens, and boasts a tower with a commanding view of countryside. The four guest rooms, all with private baths, are furnished with quality antiques. Homemade cookies, coffee, tea, and hot chocolate are available throughout the day. Plumbush is one mile from Chautauqua Institution with its summer arts and religious programs, restaurants, and shops. Plumbush was featured recently in *Innsider* magazine.

Grease a bundt pan. In a large bowl combine the 7 dry ingredients. Add ½ cup of butter and 1 cup of apple juice, beating with an electric mixer for 2 minutes. Beat in the eggs. Stir in the chopped apple, raisins, and walnuts. Pour the batter into the prepared pan. Bake in a 350° oven for 30 to 35 minutes, or until done.

In a medium bowl combine 2 tablespoons of butter, the confectioners' sugar, and vanilla. Add 1 to 2 tablespoons of apple juice, beating until the frosting is a spreading consistency. Spread the frosting over the cake.

Serves 12.

Spinach Pie

1 frozen 9-inch pie crust
6 slices bacon, chopped
1 onion, chopped
1 10-ounce package frozen chopped spinach, thawed and drained well
15 ounces Ricotta or pot cheese
1 cup grated Parmesan cheese
3 eggs
Pinch nutmeg
Dash pepper
Dash Tabasco
Sliced tomato for garnish

In a 375° oven prebake the pie crust for 10 minutes until firm. In a skillet sauté the bacon and drain. Sauté the onion in the bacon fat and drain. In a medium bowl mix the spinach with the Ricotta and add the bacon, onion, and Parmesan. Add the eggs, mixing well. Stir in the nutmeg, pepper, and Tabasco. Spread the filling in the pie crust and bake for 30 more minutes, or until done.

Serves 4 to 6.

Oatmeal Muffins

1 cup quick oats
1 cup sour milk or buttermilk
1 egg
½ cup brown sugar
½ cup shortening, melted
1 cup all-purpose flour
½ teaspoon salt
1 teaspoon baking powder
½ teaspoon baking soda

Line 12 muffin cups with paper liners. In a large bowl combine all the ingredients. Cover and refrigerate until ready to bake. Pour batter into prepared muffin tins and bake in a 400° oven for 20 to 25 minutes. Great with strawberry jam.

Note: Batter can be refrigerated up to 4 days.

Makes 12 muffins.

Chocolate Chip Cookies

1 cup margarine
¾ cup sugar
¾ cup brown sugar
1 teaspoon vanilla extract
2 eggs
½ cup old-fashioned oat flakes
2 cups all-purpose flour
1 teaspoon baking soda
1 teaspoon salt
2 cups chocolate chips
1 cup chopped nuts

In a large bowl cream together the margarine, sugars, and vanilla. Add the eggs. Stir in the oat flakes. In a separate bowl sift together the flour, baking soda, and salt. Add to the creamed mixture. Stir in the chocolate chips and nuts. Drop by spoonfuls on a baking sheet and bake in a 350° oven for 10 minutes.

Makes 50 to 60 cookies.

Peach Cobbler

3 cups fresh or frozen sliced peaches, thawed with any juice there might be
⅔ to 1 cup sugar
1 tablespoon cornstarch
1 cup water
Butter

🦢 🦢 🦢

1 cup all-purpose flour
1 tablespoon sugar
1½ teaspoons baking powder
½ teaspoon salt
3 tablespoons shortening
½ cup milk
1 teaspoon sugar and cinnamon

In a large saucepan combine the peaches, ⅔ cup of sugar, cornstarch, and water. Bring to a boil and boil for 1 minute, stirring constantly. Pour into a 1½-quart baking dish and dot with butter.

In a medium bowl combine the flour, 1 tablespoon of sugar, baking powder, and salt. Cut in the shortening until the mixture is in fine crumbs. Stir in the milk. Drop by spoonfuls onto the hot fruit and sprinkle with the sugar and cinnamon. Bake in a 400° oven for 25 to 30 minutes until golden brown. Serve warm with cream.

Note: If using No. 2 size of canned fruit, decrease sugar to ½ cup and omit the water. Berries and cherries are also good.

Serves 6 to 8.

Genesee Country Inn

948 George Street
Mumford, New York 14511
(716) 538-2500

The Genesee Country Inn and Conference Center is just twenty-five minutes from Rochester, New York, and less than a mile from the Genesee village and museum. Six acres of grounds include creeks, fully stocked trout ponds, gardens, and a sixteen-foot waterfall. Guests awaken to the soothing sounds of Allens Creek, which flows beneath the inn foundation, and enjoy an ample breakfast in a splendid room overlooking the creek. Fall color tours, cross-country skiing, antiquing, biking, and hiking are available and inn guests may enjoy year-round trout fishing.

Cinnamon-Nutmeg Pancake Sauce

1 cup sugar
3 tablespoons all-purpose flour
1 teaspoon cinnamon
½ teaspoon nutmeg
2 cups water
1 teaspoon vanilla extract
2 tablespoons butter

In a medium saucepan combine the sugar, flour, cinnamon, nutmeg, and water. Simmer for 2 minutes or until thickened. Remove from the heat and whisk in the vanilla and butter. Serve warm with pancakes.

Makes about 2 cups.

🦢 🦢 🦢 🦢 🦢

Genesee Country Inn Three-Cheese Breakfast Bake

1 large loaf white bread
12 large eggs, room temperature
2 tablespoons Dijon mustard
3 cups milk

🦢 🦢 🦢

1 pound bacon or sausage
½ cup Parmesan cheese
1 cup Mozzarella cheese, grated
1 cup Cheddar cheese, grated

Butter a 10x14-inch casserole. Trim the crusts from the bread and line the bottom of the prepared casserole. In a large bowl combine the eggs, mustard, and milk, mixing thoroughly. Pour on top of the bread.

In a skillet sauté the meat, drain, and crumble on top of the casserole. Sprinkle with the 3 cheeses. Cover with plastic wrap and refrigerate overnight. Bake in a 350° oven for 30 minutes or until nicely browned.

Serves 12.

Linen 'n Lace

659 Chilton Avenue
Niagara Falls, New York 14301
(716) 285-3935

This restored 1906 home features stained glass windows, beautiful oak woodwork, and many original light fixtures. The four rooms offer private or shared baths. Situated on a quiet residential street, the inn is close to bridges leading to the Canadian border, the convention center, Rainbow Shopping Mall, Wintergarden, and the Niagara Reservation State Park. Ample off-street parking is available. Breakfast is served family style.

ぉ ぉ ぉ ぉ ぉ

Linen 'n Lace

Night Before French Toast

1 thin loaf of French or Italian
  bread
8 large eggs
¾ teaspoon salt
3 cups milk
4 teaspoons sugar
1 tablespoon vanilla extract (or
  almond)
Cinnamon
Allspice
2 tablespoons butter, cut into small
  slices

Butter a 9x13-inch deep baking pan. Cut the bread into 1-inch thick slices and arrange in a single layer in the pan. In a large bowl, combine the eggs, salt, milk, sugar, and vanilla, beating with an electric mixer. Pour the mixture over the bread. Sprinkle with the cinnamon and allspice. Cover with foil and refrigerate 6 to 24 hours. Dot with butter and bake uncovered in a 350° oven for 45 to 50 minutes until the bread is lightly browned. Remove from the oven and let stand for 5 minutes. Serve with warm maple syrup or confectioners' sugar, yogurt, or fresh fruit.
  Serves 4.

Breakfast Casserole

10 large eggs
2½ cups milk
1 teaspoon salt
1 teaspoon dry mustard
8 slices thick bread, cut into cubes
1 cup shredded sharp Cheddar
  cheese
1 pound cooked pork sausage,
  broken up (Jimmy Dean's
  original flavor is excellent)

Butter a 9x13-inch baking pan. In a large bowl beat the eggs with an electric mixer. Add the milk, salt, and dry mustard. Stir in the bread, cheese, and cooked sausage, mixing thoroughly. Spread mixture in the prepared pan. Cover with foil and refrigerate at least 12 hours before baking. Bake in a 350° oven for 35 to 40 minutes. Cut into large squares and serve with toast or English muffins.
  Serves 6 to 8 people.

Zucchini Appetizer

3 cups thinly sliced unpared
  zucchini
1 cup Bisquick
½ cup finely chopped onions
½ cup grated Parmesan cheese
2 tablespoons chopped parsley
½ teaspoon salt
½ teaspoon oregano
Dash pepper
1 clove garlic, finely chopped
½ cup oil
4 eggs, slightly beaten

Grease a 9x13-inch pan. In a large bowl combine all the ingredients. Spread the batter in the prepared pan. Bake in a 350° oven for 25 minutes, until golden brown. Cut into small squares and serve warm.
  Makes 24 squares.

Butternut Bed and Breakfast

44 East Street
Box 728
Nunda, New York 14517
(716) 468-5074

A Colonial Revival home with spacious, comfortable rooms, fireplaces, and screened porches, the Butternut offers gracious turn-of-the-century hospitality to its guests. Named after the magnificent butternut tree in the back yard, the inn boasts natural oak woodwork, parquet floors, original hand painting on many of the walls, and a Franklin stove in the cozy kitchen. Tea is served in the afternoon, after which guests are shown up the curving staircase to one of four guest rooms with private or shared baths. Ten- and twelve-speed bikes are available for guests' use.

French Breakfast Puffs

⅓ cup shortening, softened
½ cup sugar
1 egg
1½ cups all-purpose flour
2 teaspoons baking powder
½ teaspoon salt
½ teaspoon nutmeg
½ cup milk

🐦 🐦 🐦

½ cup sugar
1 teaspoon cinnamon
6 tablespoons butter, melted

Grease muffin cups. In a large bowl cream together the shortening, sugar, and egg. In a separate bowl sift together the flour, baking powder, salt, and nutmeg. Stir into the sugar mixture, alternately with the milk. Fill the prepared muffin cups ⅔ full. Bake in a 350° oven for 20 to 25 minutes, until golden brown.

In a small bowl combine the sugar and cinnamon. Roll the warm muffins in melted butter, then in the cinnamon and sugar mixture. Serve hot. Delicious!

Makes 12 muffins.

Creole Pork Chops

6 pork chops
Salt and pepper to taste
Oil
½ green pepper, chopped into large pieces
½ red pepper, chopped into large pieces
1 stalk celery, chopped into large pieces
6 fresh mushrooms, sliced
½ sweet onion, chopped into large pieces
1 14½-ounce can whole peeled tomatoes
Rice or linguine

Season the pork chops with salt and pepper. In a large frying pan brown the chops in hot oil. Remove the chops from the pan and sauté the vegetables in the oil until soft but not browned. Cut the tomatoes into quarters, add to the pan, and heat through. Return the chops to the pan and cover. Simmer for 30 minutes. Remove the cover and continue to simmer for 30 more minutes to thicken the sauce. Serve hot with rice or linguine, along with the sauce on the side.

Serves 6.

Chicken Casserole

3 large chicken breasts
Bay leaf, celery, and seasonings (optional)
Margarine
Water
1 8-ounce package stuffing mix
1 onion, chopped
1 pint sour cream
1 10½-ounce can cream of mushroom soup
1 can sliced mushrooms

Grease a casserole dish. In a large saucepan cover the chicken with water and cook for 45 minutes. A bay leaf, celery, and seasonings may be added to the water. Bone and cut up the chicken into bite-sized pieces. Add the margarine and water to the stuffing mix, following the package instructions for the amounts. Stir in the onion. In a large bowl combine half of the stuffing with the chicken, sour cream, soup, and mushrooms. Spread into the prepared casserole. Cover with the remaining stuffing mix. Bake in a 325° oven for 1 hour.

Serves 6 to 8.

Broccoli Casserole

1½ pounds fresh broccoli, cut up
1 10½-ounce can cream of mushroom soup
¼ cup mayonnaise
¼ cup shredded sharp Cheddar cheese
1 tablespoon chopped pimiento
1 can mushrooms, drained
1½ teaspoons lemon juice
½ cup rich round cracker crumbs

In a covered saucepan cook the broccoli in a small amount of boiling, salted water for 10 to 15 minutes. Drain and place into a 1½-quart casserole. In a medium bowl combine the soup, mayonnaise, cheese, pimiento, mushrooms, and lemon juice. Pour the mixture over the broccoli. Top with the cracker crumbs. Bake in a 350° oven for 35 minutes.

Serves 6 to 8.

Strawberry Castle Bed and Breakfast

1883 Penfield Road (Route 441)
Penfield, New York 14526
(716) 385-3266

A warm welcome awaits the guests of Strawberry Castle. They can wander the lawns and gardens, sit beneath the huge maple tree, and enjoy the birds singing. Strawberry Castle's rooms are large, comfortable, and pleasant, and are virtually unaltered from the original design. Sunning on the patio and swimming in the pool are among guests' most enjoyed experiences.

Strawberry Castle

Frozen Fruit Salad

A great make-ahead breakfast fruit plate or can be used as a salad or dessert.

> 2 cups sour cream or sour cream substitute
> 1 cup crushed pineapple, drained
> 2 bananas, mashed
> ½ cup fresh berries or grapes (optional)
> ½ cup chopped pecans or walnuts
> ¾ cup sugar
> ½ teaspoon salt (optional)
> 2 tablespoons chopped maraschino cherries

In a large bowl combine all the ingredients. Pour into ramekins or individual molds and freeze. Serve on lettuce, top with sour cream and a few fresh grapes or strawberries.
  Serves 4.

The Village Victorian Inn at Rhinebeck

31 Center Street
Rhinebeck, New York 12572
(914) 876-8345

The Village Victorian Inn is a rare and wonderful combination of an elegant Victorian inn and a casual bed and breakfast. The parlor is for guest use, providing an ideal setting for socializing, relaxing with a book, playing chess, or watching television. A porch with wicker chairs waits outside. All guest rooms have full private baths, firm mattresses, and ceiling fans. Breakfast is a sumptuous treat of eggs benedict, cheese blintzes, pecan French toast, omelets, quiches, breads, muffins with jam, and more.

Fresh Apple Cinnamon Muffins

> 1½ cups all-purpose flour
> ½ cup nonfat dry milk
> ⅓ cup sugar
> 2 teaspoons baking powder
> ½ teaspoon cinnamon
> ½ teaspoon salt
> 1 egg
> ½ cup water
> 1 cup finely chopped peeled apple
> ¼ cup butter, melted
>
> ⅓ cup chopped nuts
> ¼ cup brown sugar
> ½ teaspoon cinnamon

Butter 2½-inch muffin cups. In a large bowl combine the flour, dry milk, sugar, baking powder, ½ teaspoon of cinnamon, and salt. In a separate bowl beat the egg with the water. Stir the apple and butter into the egg mixture. Add the egg mixture all at once to the dry mixture. Stir until just moistened. Fill the prepared muffin cups ⅔ full.
  In a small bowl combine the nuts, brown sugar, and ½ teaspoon of cinnamon. Sprinkle over each muffin. Bake in a 375° oven for 15 to 20 minutes. Remove from pan immediately and serve warm.
  Makes 12 muffins.

Village Victorian Inn Butter Cookies

> 3 cups butter or margarine, softened
> 4½ cups all-purpose flour
> 1½ cups sugar
> 3 egg yolks
> 1 teaspoon vanilla extract
> 1 tablespoon butter extract
> 1 teaspoon another flavoring, if desired
> ½ teaspoon salt

In a large bowl combine all the ingredients at once and mix thoroughly by hand. Fill a cookie press and dispense onto an ungreased cookie sheet. Bake in a 350° oven for 10 to 12 minutes or until brown on the edges.

Makes about 5 dozen cookies.

The Village Victorian Inn

Huff House

Rural Delivery 2
Roscoe, New York 12776
(914) 482-4579
(607) 498-9953

Huff House is a family run resort with 180 acres of unspoiled mountain top beauty, including wooded nature trails, a Par 3 golf course, two tennis courts, heated pool, two spring-fed lakes, indoor and outdoor shuffleboard, playground, game and card rooms, cocktail lounge, and horseback riding nearby. Every room affords a clear view of the Catskills. The owners pride themselves on quiet, comfortable accommodations, excellent cuisine, and a happy, relaxed atmosphere. Three meals are served daily. Meeting rooms are available, too.

🐋 🐋 🐋 🐋 🐋

Tuna Mold

1 10¾-ounce can tomato soup
1 cup mayonnaise
1 8-ounce package cream cheese
2 envelopes Knox unflavored gelatin
¼ cup cold water
2 7-ounce cans water packed tuna, flaked
Pinch sugar
Pepper to taste
1 tablespoon lemon juice
1 medium onion, finely chopped
½ cup finely chopped celery

Grease a 5½-cup fish mold. In a saucepan combine the tomato soup, mayonnaise, and cream cheese and cook until melted. Soften the gelatin in the cold water. Remove the soup mixture from the heat and add the gelatin, mixing well. Add the remaining ingredients and continue to mix well. Pour into the prepared mold and congeal.

Serves 12.

Blonde Brownies

⅓ cup margarine, melted
1 cup light brown sugar
1 unbeaten egg, plus 1 yolk
1 teaspoon vanilla extract
1 cup all-purpose flour
½ teaspoon baking powder
½ teaspoon salt
½ cup walnuts

Grease an 8-inch square pan. In a saucepan melt the margarine. Add the brown sugar and mix thoroughly. Stir in the egg, egg yolk, and vanilla, beating well. In a separate bowl combine the flour, baking powder, and salt. Stir into the egg mixture. Batter will be stiff. Add the nuts. Pour the batter into the prepared pan and bake in a 350° oven for 25 to 30 minutes. Cut into squares while still warm.

Makes 9 brownies.

Westchester House

102 Lincoln Avenue
Saratoga Springs, New York 12866
(518) 587-7613

This Queen Anne Victorian inn dating from the 1880s boasts two elaborate fireplaces, distinctive wainscoting, fanciful combinations of exterior shingles, and a whimsical roofline. Charming shops and restaurants are within an easy walk. After a busy day of sampling the delights of Saratoga, guests relax on the wraparound porch, in the garden, or in the parlors as they enjoy a glass of lemonade.

Zesty Cheese Spread

This spread is excellent on crackers or for dipping fresh vegetables. It also freezes well.

2 cloves mashed garlic
2 8-ounce packages reduced calorie cream cheese, softened
1 cup margarine, softened
¼ teaspoon pepper
¼ teaspoon salt
½ teaspoon oregano
¼ teaspoon thyme
¼ teaspoon basil
¼ teaspoon marjoram
¼ teaspoon dill

In a food processor combine all the ingredients until well blended. Chill for 24 hours. Remove from the refrigerator 30 minutes before serving.

Makes about 3 cups.

🐋 🐋 🐋 🐋 🐋

Westchester House

Asparagus Topped with Crab

1 pound fresh asparagus, parboiled
2 tablespoons chopped green
   pepper
1 tablespoon chopped onion
¼ cup margarine
2 cups lowfat plain yogurt
1 teaspoon Worcestershire sauce
1 teaspoon tarragon
1 teaspoon lemon juice
12 ounces crab meat
½ cup grated Parmesan cheese

Place the asparagus in a 1½-quart shallow baking dish. In a frying pan sauté the green pepper and onion in the margarine. In a mixing bowl combine the yogurt, Worcestershire sauce, tarragon, and lemon juice. Add the green pepper, onion, and crab meat. Pour mixture over the asparagus and sprinkle with Parmesan. Bake in a 400° oven for 20 minutes.
Serves 4 to 6.

Chilled Tomato Soup

2 16-ounce cans tomatoes,
   undrained
4 green onions with tops, minced
1 teaspoon sugar
1 tablespoon fresh parsley
¼ teaspoon dried basil
2 cups lowfat plain yogurt

In a food processor or blender purée the tomatoes. Add the remaining ingredients and blend well. Chill for 3 to 4 hours.
Serves 6.

Chicken Tetrazzini

½ pound mushrooms, sliced
3 tablespoons margarine
3 cups lowfat plain yogurt
¼ cup sherry
4 cups cooked chicken, cubed
½ pound thin spaghetti, cooked &
   drained
½ cup grated Parmesan cheese

Grease a shallow 2-quart casserole. In a frying pan sauté the mushrooms in the margarine. In a mixing bowl combine the mushrooms with the yogurt, sherry, chicken, and spaghetti. Place into the prepared casserole and sprinkle with Parmesan. Bake in a 350° oven for 30 minutes.
Serves 6 to 8.

Veal Vermouth

1½ pounds veal medallions
¼ cup margarine
1 clove garlic, minced
½ pound mushrooms, sliced
1 tablespoon lemon juice
½ cup dry vermouth
2 tablespoons snipped parsley

In a frying pan sauté the veal in the margarine. Add the garlic. Cover with the mushrooms and sprinkle with the lemon juice. Pour in the vermouth and cover. Cook over low heat for 20 minutes. Just before serving sprinkle with the parsley.
Serves 4.

Sherwood Inn

26 West Genesee Street
Skaneateles, New York 13152
(315) 685-3405

Sherwood Inn transports its visitors into the gracious comfort that is the tradition of a good country inn. The handsome lobby with fireplace, Stickley furniture, baby grand piano, and Oriental carpets offers a warm reception. Each of the guest rooms has been meticulously restored with softly shaded floral prints, pegged wooden floors, authentic antique furniture and brass, and fine wood detailing. Many of the guest rooms overlook Skaneateles Lake; all have telephones and private baths. Breakfast is in the lobby, where guests plan the day's activities.

Such notable magazines as *Bon Appetit, Country Living, Harper's Bazaar,* and *New York* have recognized the inn's dining as exceptional. Dining is in the friendly, casual tavern or in one of the inn's formal dining rooms. In summer guests can relax with their meal on the screened-in porch while watching sailboats on the lake. Ample conference space is available for business groups or parties.

Peanut Butter Soup

½ cup diced onions
½ cup diced celery
¼ cup diced green bell pepper
1 teaspoon minced garlic
3 tablespoons butter
3 tablespoons all-purpose flour
2½ cups water
6 cups milk
1 cup creamy peanut butter
2 tablespoons tomato paste
3 tablespoons soy sauce
Chopped peanuts to garnish

In a frying pan sauté the onions, celery, green pepper, and garlic in the butter until soft. Add the flour and cook for 2 to 3 minutes. Stir in the water and milk, and bring to a boil. Add the peanut butter, tomato paste, and soy sauce, and simmer for 15 minutes. Serve garnished with chopped peanuts.

Serves 8 to 10.

Recipe courtesy of Keith Brown and Chef Elon Wagoner.

Grilled Salmon

Juice of 1 lemon
½ cup olive oil
½ teaspoon freshly ground pepper
1 teaspoon fresh chives (or ½ teaspoon dried)
1 teaspoon minced parsley
7 ounces salmon, skinned, deboned, and divided in half

🍂 🍂 🍂

2 grape leaves
Compound Butter (recipe follows)

In a mixing bowl combine the lemon juice, oil, pepper, chives, and parsley. Marinate the salmon in the mixture for 1 hour.

Wrap the salmon in the grape leaves and grill for about 2 minutes on each side and serve with Compound Butter.

Serves 2.

Recipe courtesy of Chef Elon Wagoner.

Compound Butter

4 ounces Feta cheese
½ cup unsalted butter, softened
1 teaspoon freshly ground black pepper
½ teaspoon oregano
2 tablespoons parsley
½ cup lemon juice
¼ cup capers

In a food processor combine the cheese, butter, pepper, oregano, parsley, and lemon juice. Stir in the capers by hand.

Makes about 1½ cups.

Recipe courtesy of Chef Elon Wagoner.

Mill House Inn

Route 43
Stephentown, New York 12168

Post Office Box 1079
Hancock, Massachusetts 01237
(518) 733-5606

Once a sawmill, Mill House Inn is now a country inn with Old World charm. The warmth of the rough-sawn paneling and beams contributes to the feeling of friendliness, as does the common room where guests can meet for conversation or reading. The Mill House is a place to relax and enjoy the quiet of the Berkshires. The guest rooms have private baths, individual heat control, and air conditioning. Breakfast is served in the Europa room or on the garden deck. Afternoon tea is served compliments of the inn.

Stone-ground Wheat Cakes

These pancakes are delightfully light and flavorful and have been a Stephentown breakfast favorite for many years. Romana Tallet at the inn recommends Hodgson Mill brand wheat flour. For a variation add fresh blueberries after spooning the batter onto the griddle.

½ cup stone-ground wheat flour
1 cup all-purpose flour
½ teaspoon salt
3½ teaspoons baking powder
2 tablespoons sugar
1 egg
2 cups milk
2 tablespoons corn oil
Butter

In a large bowl combine the flours, salt, baking powder, and sugar. In a smaller bowl mix together the egg, milk, and oil. Pour the liquid ingredients into the dry, stirring gently until thoroughly mixed. Do not overmix. Spoon the batter onto a hot well-buttered griddle. Cook until bubbles appear, then flip and brown the other side of each pancake.

Serves 4.

Three Village Inn

150 Main Street
Stony Brook, New York 11790
(516) 751-0555

Three Village Inn has thirty-two rooms, several in the original 1751 wing. Six country cottages are nestled under tall shade trees with views of Stony Brook Harbor; all have private baths and several have bricked patios and working fireplaces. Guests have three dining rooms to choose from, serving such favorites as cold plum soup, baked Indian pudding, medallions of veal with wild mushrooms and chestnuts. Later, guests can relax in the cozy atmosphere of the Sand Bar Tap Room. The inn has been refurbished, which the innkeepers point out involves more than a fresh coat of paint. New fabrics, wallpapers, and furnishings complement the inn's large brick fireplaces, colonial cooking cranes and pots, and wide plank floors. Even the grounds have been newly landscaped.

Cold Plum Soup

1 29-ounce can purple plums
1 cup water
⅔ cup sugar
1 cinnamon stick
¼ teaspoon white pepper
Pinch salt
½ cup heavy cream
½ cup dry red wine
1 tablespoon cornstarch
2 tablespoons lemon juice
1 teaspoon grated lemon rind

🍂 🍂 🍂

1 cup sour cream
3 tablespoons brandy
Cinnamon

Drain the plums, reserving the syrup. Pit and chop the plums. In a medium saucepan combine the plums with the reserved syrup, water, sugar, cinnamon stick, white pepper, and salt. Bring the liquid to a boil over moderately high heat. Reduce the heat to medium and cook the mixture for 5 minutes, stirring occasionally. Stir in the heavy cream. In a separate bowl combine the wine with the cornstarch, and stir into the mixture. Cook, stirring constantly, until the mixture is thickened. Stir in the lemon juice and rind. Remove the pan from the heat.

Measure ½ cup of the soup mixture into a small bowl. Whisk in the sour cream, then the brandy. Stir the mixture into the soup, stirring until it is smooth. Let the soup cool. Chill, covered, for at least 4 hours. Ladle the soup into cups and garnish each serving with a dollop of sour cream and a sprinkling of cinnamon.

Serves 8.

Pot Roast

4 to 5 pounds eye round roast, with all fat removed
2 bay leaves
3 carrots
2 large onions
2 stalks celery
1 teaspoon salt
1 teaspoon black pepper
8 peppercorns
3 cups red wine
3 cups red wine vinegar
3 cups water
1 clove garlic
½ cup sugar

🍂 🍂 🍂

1 cup tomato purée
1 cup chili sauce

🍂 🍂 🍂

½ cup butter, melted
½ cup all-purpose flour

In a large baking pan combine the meat with the bay leaves, vegetables, seasonings, wine, vinegar, water, garlic, and sugar. (Meat should be completely covered with the liquid.) Marinate in the refrigerator for 15 hours. Bake uncovered in a 350° oven, turning occasionally until the meat is brown.

Remove from the oven and add the tomato purée and chili sauce. Boil, covered, until the meat is tender. Remove the meat and vegetables.

In a small bowl combine the butter and flour as a roux and add to the baking pan to thicken the gravy.

Serves 6 to 8.

Medallions of Veal
with Shiitake Mushrooms

5 ounces veal medallions
½ cup all-purpose flour
2 tablespoons clarified butter
2 ounces shiitake mushroom caps, sliced
4 whole chestnuts, peeled
¼ cup medium dry sherry
¼ cup brown gravy
Salt and pepper to taste

Lightly flour the medallions of veal. In a frying pan sauté the veal in the clarified butter approximately 45 seconds on each side. Add the mushrooms, chestnuts, and sherry. Reduce the liquid for approximately 1 minute. Add the brown gravy and season with salt and pepper. Remove from the heat and serve immediately.

Serves 2.

Sage Cottage

112 East Main Street
Box 626
Trumansburg, New York 14886
(607) 387-6449

Sage Cottage, just north of Ithaca and minutes from Taughannock Falls, is situated in a rejuvenated Gothic Revival home built about 1855. There are four guest rooms. Breakfast always includes fresh herb breads, biscuits, and jams made with herbs from the gardens.

Sunflower-Squash Salad

⅓ cup sunflower seeds
1 tablespoon corn or sunflower oil
3 tablespoons cider vinegar
1 large clove garlic, minced
Black pepper
2 small yellow summer squash, sliced into ⅛-inch rounds
2 small zucchini, cut in matchstick-sized pieces
½ medium red pepper, diced

Toast the sunflower seeds in a 250° oven for 15 minutes. In a blender combine half of the seeds with the oil, vinegar, garlic, and black pepper as a dressing. Set aside remaining seeds for garnish.

In the center of a high-sided platter, arrange the yellow squash slices. Place the zucchini around the edge of the platter and add the red pepper around the center. Pour the dressing over the vegetables and sprinkle with the reserved sunflower seeds. Cover and refrigerate for at least 1 hour to improve the flavor.
Serves 4.

Green Thursday Pasta

2 large cloves garlic, minced
¾ cup finely minced parsley
1½ teaspoons dried marjoram (or 1 tablespoon fresh)
1 teaspoon dried basil (or 1 tablespoon fresh)
1 teaspoon brown sugar
¼ cup red wine vinegar
¾ teaspoon dry mustard
½ teaspoon celery seeds, crushed
1 egg
2 tablespoons lemon juice
Freshly ground pepper
½ cup freshly grated Romano cheese

🌰 🌰 🌰

1 pound spiral pasta, rotelli, etc.

In a food processor or on a cutting board with a sharp knife mince the garlic with the minced parsley. Place in a small bowl and beat in the herbs, brown sugar, vinegar, mustard, celery seeds, egg, lemon juice, and pepper. Add the cheese and mix thoroughly. Allow to stand at room temperature.

Cook the pasta according to the package directions, drain, and return to the cooking pot. Toss with the parsley and cheese mixture. Serve immediately with extra freshly grated cheese.
Serves 6.

T-Burg Grape Tart

4 rounded cups stemmed Concord grapes
5 sprigs fresh thyme
⅓ cup honey

🌰 🌰 🌰

1 tablespoon lemon juice
1 tablespoon water
1½ tablespoons cornstarch

🌰 🌰 🌰

1 pie crust
1 teaspoon grated orange peel

Lightly oil a large, shallow soufflé dish or 8 individual ramekins. Squeeze the grapes out of the skins and set skins aside. In a saucepan combine the grapes, thyme, and honey. Bring just to a boil and simmer for 5 minutes. Pour into a Foley Food Mill and process to remove the seeds.

In a medium bowl combine the skins and grape mixture. In a separate bowl combine the lemon juice and water, and stir in the cornstarch. Add to the grape mixture. Pour into the prepared dish.

Prepare a pie crust with orange peel added. Top the grape mixture with rounds of the pie crust mixture. Bake in a 350° oven for 30 minutes (20 minutes for ramekins).
Serves 8.

The Merrill Magee House

2 Hudson Street
Warrensburg, New York 12885
(518) 623-2449

A country inn for all seasons, Merrill Magee House is listed on the National Register of Historic Places. A Greek Revival house, it has changed little since 1850 (the original wallpaper lines the entrance hall). From the inviting wicker chairs on the porch to the elegant candlelit dining rooms, the inn offers the romance of a visit to an English country estate. Guest rooms abound with nineteenth-century charm and twentieth-century comforts. An intimate dinner at the inn's dining room means a choice of several sumptuous dishes. A typical breakfast includes fruit, country ham and eggs, or apple-raisin nut pancakes. Situated in the Adirondack State Park, it can offer outdoor activities for everyone.

Zucchini Soup

1 pound sweet Italian sausage
2 cups chopped celery
1 cup chopped onions

ﷺ ﷺ ﷺ

2 pounds zucchini, cubed
2 28-ounce cans diced tomatoes
2 teaspoons salt
1 teaspoons oregano
½ teaspoon basil
1 teaspoon Italian seasoning
1 teaspoon sugar
¼ teaspoon garlic powder

ﷺ ﷺ ﷺ

1 green pepper, chopped

Cut the sausages into bite-sized pieces and sauté in a frying pan until brown. Add the celery and onions, and sauté until tender.

In a large pot place the sausages, celery, and onions. Add the zucchini, tomatoes, and seasonings. Cook covered for 20 minutes. Add the green pepper and cook uncovered for 10 more minutes.

Serve with a salad and hot garlic bread for a great main dish.

Serves 6 to 8 people.

Orange Nut Bread

2 eggs
2½ cups sugar
¼ cup oil
1 grated orange rind
1 teaspoon vanilla extract
6 cups all-purpose flour
3 teaspoons salt
7 teaspoons baking powder
3 cups milk
1½ cups chopped walnuts

Grease 2 loaf pans. In a large bowl combine the eggs, sugar, oil, orange rind, and vanilla with an electric mixer. In a separate bowl combine the flour, salt, and baking powder, mixing well. Add the flour mixture alternately with the milk to the egg mixture. Add the nuts. Divide the batter between the prepared pans. Bake in a 350° oven for 45 minutes.

Makes 2 loaves.

Sweet Potato Pudding

3 pounds sweet potatoes, cooked
    and peeled
¼ cup butter
½ cup brown sugar
1 cup milk
½ teaspoon cinnamon
½ teaspoon nutmeg

ﷺ ﷺ ﷺ

¼ cup brown sugar
¼ cup chopped walnuts

Butter a 1½-quart casserole dish. In a large bowl mash the potatoes. Stir in the butter, ½ cup of brown sugar, milk, cinnamon, and nutmeg. Place the mixture into the prepared casserole.

In a small bowl combine ¼ cup of brown sugar and the walnuts. Sprinkle over the mixture as a topping. Bake in a 350° oven for 30 minutes.

Serves 4 to 6.

James Russell Webster Mansion Inn

115 East Main Street
Waterloo, New York 13165
(315) 539-3032

A New Age inn, the James Russell Webster Mansion Inn is a special place for people who want to enjoy a haute cuisine experience in a European palace. Two palatial air-conditioned suites, marble bathrooms and fireplaces, private entrances, slipper footwear, no telephones or televisions to disturb privacy, and seventeenth-, eighteenth-, and nineteenth-century antiques are among the things that make this inn special. Elegant breakfasts and haute cuisine candlelight dining (advance dinner notice required) are available for guests and the public. Staying here is like living and dining "behind the velvet ropes of a major museum."

Grande Cuisine Quiche Lorraine
with Baked Tomato Garni

2 large onions, thinly sliced
2 tablespoons butter
1 9-inch unbaked pie shell, chilled
½ pound natural Swiss cheese,
    grated
1 tablespoon all-purpose flour
10 sausage links, small breakfast
    size, cooked until brown,
    drained and cut into ¼-inch
    pieces
6 spinach leaves, finely chopped
3 eggs
1 cup heavy cream
¼ teaspoon salt
⅛ teaspoon pepper
¼-inch ring sliced from a whole
    sweet red pepper

In a small skillet sauté the onions in the butter until tender. Turn into the pie shell. Toss the grated cheese with the flour and sprinkle over the onions. Add the sausages and chopped spinach. In a separate bowl beat the eggs well. Stir in the cream, salt, and pepper, and pour over the pie filling. Place the red pepper ring in the center. Bake in a 400° oven for 20 minutes. Reduce the temperature to 300° and bake for 25 more minutes or until a knife inserted in the center comes out clean. Serve hot, cut in wedges.

Serves 6 to 8.

Baked Tomato Garni

24 cherry tomatoes, uniform in size
3 tablespoons butter, melted
Fines herbs, to taste
Salt and pepper, to taste
Parmesan cheese, to taste
Endive

Prick the tomatoes all over with a fork. Brush with the melted butter. Sprinkle with the fines herbes, salt, pepper, and cheese. Place in a small pan. Bake in a 300° oven for 15 to 20 minutes.

Use as a garnish next to the Quiche Lorraine atop a bed of endive.

Makes 24 garni.

Woven Waters

Cincinnatus Lake Route 41
HC-73, Box 193E
Willet, New York 13863
(607) 656-8672

Woven Waters, a completely renovated bank barn, invites its guests to relax in the warmth of the stone fireplace under the beamed cathedral ceiling. The continental-plus breakfast is enjoyed in the dining room or, weather permitting, on the porches. Situated on the border between the Fingers Lakes and historic Leatherstocking regions of New York, the inn is only minutes away from diverse recreational activities.

Viennese Crescent Ring

1 cup finely ground almonds
⅓ cup confectioners' sugar
2 tablespoons margarine, softened
1 teaspoon almond extract
1 egg, separated
2 8-ounce cans crescent dinner rolls

🌿 🌿 🌿

⅔ cup peach or apricot preserves
¼ cup sliced almonds
1 tablespoon sugar

In a medium bowl combine the ground almonds, confectioners' sugar, margarine, almond extract, and egg yolk, mixing well. Set aside. Separate 1 can of dough into 8 triangles. Place the dough on a 12-inch pizza pan and press over the bottom to form a crust, sealing the perforations.

Separate the remaining can of dough into 8 triangles. Spread 1 rounded tablespoon of the almond filling on each triangle. Roll up the dough starting at the shortest side and roll to the opposite point. Arrange the filled crescents point side down evenly around the edge of the dough-lined pan. Spoon the preserves evenly over the center of the dough, spreading just to the filled rolls. Beat the egg white until frothy and brush on the tops of the filled crescents. Sprinkle the almonds and sugar on top. Bake in a 350° oven for 25 to 30 minutes until golden brown.

Serves 6 to 8.

Woven Waters Orange Bread

3 cups all-purpose flour
4 teaspoons baking powder
1 teaspoon salt
⅓ cup sugar
2 tablespoons shortening
⅔ cup milk
⅓ cup orange juice
Grated rind of 1 orange
½ cup orange marmalade
1 egg

Grease a bread pan. In a large bowl sift together the flour, baking powder, salt, and sugar. Cut in the shortening. Add the milk and orange juice, then the marmalade and the egg. Beat together well and pour into the prepared pan. Bake in a 375° oven for 55 minutes.

Makes 1 loaf.

Fruit Teabread Woven Waters

1 cup currants
1 cup golden raisins
1 cup brown sugar
Finely grated rind of 2 oranges
1¼ cups hot tea

🌿 🌿 🌿

2 generous cups self-rising flour
1 egg

In a large bowl combine the fruit, brown sugar, and orange rind. Pour in the hot tea and stir well. Cover and let stand overnight.

Grease and line with waxed-paper an 8-inch round cake pan. Stir the flour and egg into the fruit mixture and mix thoroughly. Place the mixture in the prepared pan. Bake in a 300° oven for 1 hour and 30 minutes.

Serves 6.

AppleWood Manor

62 Cumberland Circle
Asheville, North Carolina 28801
(704) 254-2244

AppleWood Manor is situated on one and one-half acres of country living in the historic Montford district of Asheville surrounded by giant oaks, pines, maples, and wildflower gardens. At check-in a cup of tea or glass of sherry is served on one of the porches; breakfast is served in the formal dining room or one of the porches, or in the privacy of one's own room.

Alberto's Capellini

½ **pound bacon, reserve drippings**
3 **ounces toasted pine nuts**
5 **cloves garlic, finely minced**
⅓ **cup olive oil**
3 **tablespoons sugar**
1 **lemon**

❧ ❧ ❧

1 **pound Capellini (Angel hair pasta)**
⅓ **cup finely chopped fresh parsley**
½ **cup grated Romano cheese**

Cook the bacon until crisp. Crumble and set aside. Retain 3 tablespoons of the drippings. Toast the pine nuts and set aside. In a large skillet over medium heat sauté the garlic in the olive oil until light brown. Add the bacon drippings, sugar, and lemon zest. Remove from the heat and add the bacon bits.

Prepare the Capellini according to the package instructions. Pour the sauce over the freshly cooked pasta. Sprinkle generously with the parsley and grated cheese.

Serves 4 as an entrée, 8 as an appetizer.

Recipe courtesy owner Albert James LoPresti.

Pumante Puffs

8 **ounces smoked Mozzarella cheese, shredded**
½ **cup butter, softened**
¼ **cup chopped dried tomatoes**
1 **cup unbleached flour**
½ **tablespoon basil**
½ **tablespoon garlic powder**
½ **tablespoon black pepper**

In a medium bowl blend the Mozzarella and butter until creamy. Stir in the tomatoes, flour, basil, garlic, and pepper. Mix well. Shape the dough into 1-inch balls and place on an ungreased cookie pan. Bake in a 350° oven for 15 minutes, or until golden.

Note: Freezes well, cooked or uncooked.

Makes 2 to 3 dozen puffs.

❧ ❧ ❧ ❧ ❧

Banana Maple Soufflé

3 **very ripe bananas**
1 **tablespoon maple syrup**
1 **teaspoon vanilla extract**
2 **egg yolks**
4 **egg whites**
2 **tablespoons fructose**

Lightly grease four ½ cup-size soufflé cups. Purée the bananas, syrup, vanilla, and yolks until smooth. Set aside. In a medium bowl beat the egg whites until they form stiff peaks. Add the fructose and continue beating. Stir into the banana mixture. Spoon the batter into the prepared soufflé cups. Bake in a 400° oven for 12 to 15 minutes, until lightly browned on top.

Serves 4.

Corner Oak Manor

53 St. Dunstans Road
Asheville, North Carolina 28803
(704) 253-3525

Corner Oak Manor

Corner Oak Manor is a lovely English Tudor home, surrounded by oak, maple, and pine trees. The rooms have queen-size beds and private baths. The full breakfast may include such entrees as blueberry ricotta pancakes, four cheese and herb quiche, and orange French toast. Other amenities include flowers and chocolates in each room, afternoon refreshments, outdoor deck with Jacuzzi, and a reading and game room.

Corner Oak Garden Fresh Omelets

¼ cup grated Cheddar cheese
¼ cup grated Swiss cheese
¼ cup grated Monterey Jack cheese
¼ cup grated Parmesan cheese
1 tablespoon freshly chopped chives
1 tablespoon freshly chopped thyme
1 tablespoon freshly chopped parsley
1 tablespoon freshly chopped basil

🌺 🌺 🌺

1 small bunch green onions, chopped
2 tomatoes, peeled and chopped

🌺 🌺 🌺

2 tablespoons butter
8 eggs, room temperature

In a medium bowl combine the cheese and herbs. Set aside. In a separate bowl combine the green onions and tomatoes. Set aside.

For each omelet melt ½ tablespoon butter in an omelet pan. Beat 2 eggs and pour into the pan. Lift the edges and let the uncooked eggs flow underneath. When the omelet is nearly done, top half with ¼ of the cheese mixture and ¼ of the tomato mixture. When cooked through slide the filled omelet half onto a plate and flip the unfilled half on top. Garnish with additional cheese and fresh herbs. Repeat for the remaining omelets.

Serves 4.

Cream of Broccoli-Cheddar Soup

4 cups chopped broccoli
4 cups chicken broth

🌺 🌺 🌺

¼ cup butter
¼ cup all-purpose flour
1½ cups cream
1 cup grated sharp Cheddar cheese
Freshly ground pepper
Pinch cayenne
Pinch nutmeg

In a large saucepan cook the broccoli in the chicken broth until tender. Purée in a food processor or blender.

In a large pot melt the butter. Whisk in the flour and cook for 2 to 3 minutes. Whisk in the broccoli purée. Cook 5 minutes, or until thickened and bubbly. Whisk in the cream cheese, pepper, cayenne, and nutmeg. Continue cooking until the cream is heated through and the cheese is melted.

Serves 4 to 6.

Cranberries in Red Wine

1 12-ounce package cranberries
1½ cups sugar
1 cup red wine (Zinfandel or Cabernet Sauvignon)
1 3-inch cinnamon stick
1 7-inch strip orange peel, no white part, julienned crossways

Pick over the cranberries, rinse, and drain. In a large saucepan combine the sugar and wine, and bring to a boil, stirring until the sugar is dissolved. Add the cinnamon stick, orange peel and cranberries. Return the mixture to a boil and reduce heat to a vigorous simmer. Partially cover and cook for 15 minutes. Remove the mixture from the heat and cool to room temperature. Remove and discard the cinnamon stick. Spoon the mixture into a jar with tight-fitting lid and chill in the refrigerator up to 2 months.

Makes 1½ cups.

The Grove Park Inn and Country Club

290 Macon Avenue
Asheville, North Carolina 28804
(704) 252-2711

The Grove Park Inn is a grand hotel. In 1913 this meant the daily polishing of coins so that guests, such as Thomas Edison, never received a tarnished silver dollar. In 1984 it meant the construction of a premier conference center capable of handling meetings of up to 1000. Today it means both returning to the early years in such ways as a leisurely horse-and-carriage ride through the pines and the enjoyment of an indoor sports complex to serve the most active guest any time of the year. Full amenities, combined with championship golf; an incomparable collection of restaurants, lounges, and shops; classic service and rare atmosphere make the Grove Park Inn the most complete year-round resort hotel in the Carolinas. Sitting on the western slope of Sunset Mountain, the inn looks toward the glorious Blue Ridge Mountains.

Grilled Lemon Duck Breast

4 8- to 10-ounce duck breasts
4 scallions, finely chopped
1 teaspoon freshly grated ginger
2 teaspoons turmeric
2 teaspoons dark soy sauce
½ tablespoon freshly minced garlic
½ teaspoon grated lemon rind
1 cup white wine
Salt
Freshly cracked pepper
1 teaspoon brown sugar
Lemon wedges

Make criss-cross cuts through the skin of the duck breasts and trim off the excess fat. In a medium bowl combine the scallions, ginger, turmeric, soy sauce, garlic, lemon rind, white wine, salt, pepper, and brown sugar. Pour the mixture over the duck breasts and marinate for a minimum of 4 hours.

Prepare a charcoal grill. Place the duck breasts skin side down on the grill. Cook for 15 to 18 minutes, turning frequently. Remove the duck, slice paper thin, and arrange on a plate. Garnish with lemon wedges and serve with Shanghai Dipping Sauce.

Serves 4.

Shanghai Dipping Sauce

1 cup Fish Sauce
1 tablespoon finely chopped ginger
2 cloves finely chopped garlic
1 teaspoon hot red pepper flakes or cayenne pepper to taste
3 tablespoons lemon juice
1 cup white wine
2 tablespoons brown sugar

In a medium bowl combine all the ingredients, blending well. Leftover sauce keeps well in the refrigerator for a week.

Note: Fish Sauce is widely found in Chinese, Vietnamese, and Korean

The Grove Park Inn and Country Club

grocery and specialty stores.
Makes about 2¼ cups.

Frozen Raspberry Soufflé

12 egg yolks
2 cups sugar
1 cup raspberry liqueur
1 cup freshly puréed raspberries
Grated rind of 1 lemon

≈ ≈ ≈

½ cup heavy cream

≈ ≈ ≈

6 egg whites
Whipped cream and fresh
  raspberries for garnish

Prepare a 5-cup soufflé dish with a waxed paper collar that has been folded into thirds and secured with string. Prepare a saucepan with enough water to come up around the sides of a 2-quart dish without overflowing, remove the bowl, and bring the water to a boil.

Place the 2-quart bowl in the pan of boiling water and combine the egg yolks with 1½ cups of sugar, beating with a whisk or electric mixer until fluffy and lemon colored. Add the raspberry liqueur, raspberries, and lemon rind, continuing to beat the mixture until it has a custard-like consistency and keeping the temperature between 120° to 140°. Scrape the bowl down with a rubber spatula and let the mixture cool on ice or in the refrigerator.

In a separate bowl whip the heavy cream with 2 tablespoons of sugar until peaks form. Fold into the egg mixture.

In a separate bowl, combine the egg whites and the remaining sugar, and beat until stiff. Fold into the soufflé mixture. Pour the mixture into the prepared soufflé dish and place in the freezer overnight. Remove the waxed paper and clean the outside of the dish with hot water. Decorate the top of the soufflé with rosettes of whipped cream and fresh raspberries.
Serves 8.

Delamar Inn

217 Turner Street
Beaufort, North Carolina 28516
(919) 728-4300

Guests of Delmar Inn enjoy the Scottish hospitality of a Civil War home in the heart of Beaufort's historic district. Three antique furnished bedrooms, each with private bath, are offered. After a breakfast, a second cup of coffee and newspaper may be enjoyed on the upper porch, or an easy stroll may be taken to the waterfront, shops, and historic sites.

Holiday Rice Bread

1½ cups orange juice
2 cups sugar
2 eggs
2 teaspoons grated orange peel
¼ cup margarine, melted

≈ ≈ ≈

3½ cups all-purpose flour
2 teaspoons baking powder
1 teaspoon baking soda
1 teaspoon salt
1 cup cooked rice
¼ cup finely chopped pecans

≈ ≈ ≈

½ cup confectioners' sugar
3 tablespoons orange juice
½ teaspoon grated orange peel

Grease and flour two 9x5-inch loaf pans. In a medium bowl combine the 1½ cups of orange juice, sugar, eggs, 2 teaspoons of orange peel, and margarine.

In a separate bowl combine the flour, baking powder, baking soda and salt. Add the orange juice mixture to the dry ingredients and mix well. Fold in the rice and pecans. Pour the batter into the prepared pans. Bake in a 350° oven for 1 hour, or until a knife inserted in the center comes out clean. Cool in the pans for 5 minutes.

In a small bowl combine the powdered sugar, 3 tablespoons of orange juice, and ½ teaspoon of orange peel. Drizzle the sauce over the loaves when cool.
Makes 2 loaves.

Langdon House

135 Craven Street
Beaufort, North Carolina 28516
(919) 728-5499

Langdon House (circa 1732) represents building techniques and materials spanning 250 years, from the time of hand-forged nails and hand-wrought timbers to the twentieth century with central heating and cooling. The house has survived Indians, revolution, pirates, and the Civil War; and today it is in the heart of Beaufort's historic district. Restoration grounds, waterfront boardwalks, shops, restaurants, museums, churches, and the library are all just a block distant. Wild ponies on the banks across the creek, sailboats on the Intracoastal Waterway, blazing sunsets, and salt air breezes touch the senses. The first floor hall, parlor, and four bedrooms are reserved for visitors. Each guest room has a queen-size bed and a private bath. A full gourmet breakfast of fresh fruit, gourmet cheese, select breads, and imported coffee and tea is served in guest rooms or in the parlor.

Fruit Filled French Toast

6 eggs
¼ teaspoon cinnamon
2 teaspoons sugar
2 teaspoons almond or vanilla extract
¼ cup Triple-Sec
¼ cup light cream
Pinch salt

🍃 🍃 🍃

1 loaf French bread
Ricotta cheese
12 tablespoons blueberry jam
Peanut oil
Grated nutmeg
Confectioners' sugar

In a medium bowl combine the first 7 ingredients and whisk until well blended.

Slice the bread into ⅜-inch slices, cutting completely through only on every other slice so that you create a "book" of two bread slices joined together by the crust. Gently open the "pages" of the bread "book" and spread one lightly with the ricotta cheese and the other liberally with a tablespoon of jam. Soak the jam/ricotta sandwiches in the egg mixture at least 1 hour or overnight, turning the sandwiches to evenly coat both sides of the sandwiches with the egg mixture.

In a skillet heat the peanut oil enough so the moist French toast sizzles when it hits the pan. When the first side has browned, turn and brown the other side. Reduce the pan's temperature to very low and cook the toast gently until the egg has set completely through the sandwich. Dust with the nutmeg and confectioners' sugar. Serve with a nice garnish.

Note: After dipping the sandwiches in the egg mixture, they can be frozen separately on a sheet of waxed paper, then separated, wrapped, and stored in the freezer for later use.

Serves 6.

Better Than Life Itself Bran Muffins

1 cup all-purpose flour
½ cup sugar
2½ teaspoons baking powder
½ teaspoon baking soda
½ teaspoon salt

🍃 🍃 🍃

1¼ cups Nabisco 100% Bran cereal
1 cup milk
1 egg
¼ cup corn oil
Ripe bananas, minced pear, grated apple, raisins, and nuts (optional)

Grease muffin cups. In a medium bowl combine the flour, sugar, baking powder, baking soda, and salt.

In a medium bowl combine the bran and milk, and let stand for 5 minutes. Add the egg and oil to the mixture, beating until well blended. Stir in any combination of fruit or nuts. Stir in the dry ingredients until well blended. Fill the prepared muffin cups ⅔ full. Bake in a 400° oven for 20 minutes.

Makes 12 to 14 muffins.

Crab Cakes

1 pound backfin crab meat
4 ounces (½ small package) Pepperidge Farm stuffing mix
1 cup butter
1 large onion, finely chopped
1 stalk celery, finely chopped
1 green pepper, finely chopped
1 red bell pepper, finely chopped
2 tablespoons mayonnaise
3 tablespoons French-style mustard
3 eggs
2 tablespoons Worcestershire sauce
Freshly ground black pepper to taste

🍃 🍃 🍃

Oil

"Sift" through the crab meat with your fingers to remove the "fins" and shell. In a large bowl combine all the ingredients except the oil. Form into 2½x¾-inch patties. In a skillet fry the

patties in the hot oil until brown, then drain on paper towels.

Serves 6 to 8.

Ragged Garden Bed and Breakfast

Sunset Drive
Post Office Box 1927
Blowing Rock, North Carolina 28605
(704) 295-9703

A touch of the past has come alive in this grandiose old home. Named Ragged Garden when it was built at the turn of the century, it sits on an attractive one-acre setting, surrounded by roses, rhododendrons, and majestic trees. Situated one block off Main Street, it is close to shops, art galleries, boutiques, and parks. The inn has three different dining areas, including one for private dining.

Minestrone

The Chef's mother's recipe.

¼ cup butter or margarine
¼ cup olive oil
1 large onion, coarsely chopped

Freshly minced parsley
4 to 5 large garlic cloves, finely
    chopped
3 cups homemade chicken broth
2 cups water
¾ cup dried beans, Northern or
    pinto
1 cup string beans
3 stalks celery, diced
3 carrots, diced
⅓ head cabbage, chopped
2 medium zucchini, chopped
Pasta, small or cut up
6 tablespoons (½ small can) tomato
    paste
6 to 7 leaves fresh basil or ½
    teaspoon dry basil
Salt and pepper
Pinch freshly grated nutmeg
Parmesan cheese

In a saucepan melt the butter and oil together over medium-low heat. Add the onion and parsley, and cook for 5 minutes. Add the garlic and continue to simmer until the onion is translucent. Add the broth, water, and dry beans, bringing to a gentle boil and cooking for 2 minutes. Add the string beans, celery, and cabbage, cooking for 10 more minutes. Add the zucchini and cook for 30 more minutes. Add the pasta, tomato paste, basil, salt, pepper, and nutmeg, and continue to cook for 1 hour and 30 minutes. Serve hot with the freshly grated Parmesan cheese.

Serves 6 to 8.

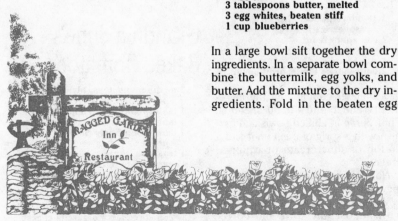

Folkestone Inn

767 West Deep Creek Road
Bryson City, North Carolina 28713
(704) 488-2730

The traveler who enjoys a peaceful, rural setting and a homecooked breakfast should delight in Folkestone Inn. Nearby activities include river rafting on the Nantahala River; exploring the Great Smoky Mountains National Park; the Cherokee Indian Reservation with its museum, craft shops, and outdoor drama *Unto These Hills*; the Biltmore House in Asheville; tubing; and fishing. All nine rooms have private baths.

Blueberry Cornmeal Pancakes

1¼ cups all-purpose flour
1½ teaspoons baking powder
¼ cup sugar
½ teaspoon baking soda
½ teaspoon salt
1 cup yellow cornmeal

❧ ❧ ❧

2 cups buttermilk
3 egg yolks
3 tablespoons butter, melted
3 egg whites, beaten stiff
1 cup blueberries

In a large bowl sift together the dry ingredients. In a separate bowl combine the buttermilk, egg yolks, and butter. Add the mixture to the dry ingredients. Fold in the beaten egg whites. Pour ¼ cup of batter onto the griddle and sprinkle with the blueberries. Cook the pancakes until bubbles form and start popping. Turn only once and cook until done.

Makes 18 to 20 pancakes.

Grand Marnier Syrup

This is used with blueberry pancakes and garnished with orange slices.

2 cups orange juice
2 cups sugar
2 tablespoons lemon juice
2 tablespoons orange marmalade
3 tablespoons Grand Marnier

In a medium saucepan combine the orange juice and sugar and bring to a boil, stirring constantly. Skim off the foam with a metal spoon and add the remaining ingredients.

Makes about 2½ cups.

Pumpkin Biscuits

2 cups all-purpose flour
1 tablespoon baking powder
1 teaspoon salt
Pinch ginger
Pinch allspice

❧ ❧ ❧

3 tablespoons butter
3 tablespoons shortening
½ cup pumpkin purée
½ cup milk
Molasses

Grease a cookie sheet. In a medium bowl combine the dry ingredients.

Cut in the butter and shortening until the mixture has the consistency of cornmeal. Add the pumpkin and milk alternately, stirring after each addition. Turn the dough onto a floured board and knead for 30 seconds. Pat out the dough to ½-inch thickness, cut with a small cutter, and place on the prepared cookie sheet. Bake in a 425° oven for 15 to 18 minutes. Serve with molasses.

Makes about 18 biscuits.

Scones

2 cups all-purpose flour
½ cup sugar
2 teaspoons baking powder
½ teaspoon salt
5½ tablespoons butter, chilled
1 egg
1 egg yolk
⅓ to ½ cup milk

🌝 🌝 🌝

1 egg white
Sugar

In a large bowl combine the flour, ½ cup of sugar, baking powder, and salt. Cut in the butter with a pastry blender until the mixture resembles coarse crumbs. In a separate bowl combine the egg, egg yolk, and ⅓ cup of milk. Add the egg mixture to the flour mixture, stirring until the flour is just moistened. Add more milk to make a soft dough. Turn the dough onto a floured surface and knead gently about 10 times. Roll to ½-inch thickness and cut into 2-inch circles. Place 1-inch apart on an ungreased baking sheet.

In a small bowl beat the egg white until frothy. Brush over the circles and sprinkle lightly with the sugar. Bake in a 425° oven for 12 to 14 minutes. Transfer to a wire rack and cool for 5 to 10 minutes.

Variation: Add raisins or dried fruit.

Makes 18 scones.

The Fryemont Inn

Post Office Box 459
Bryson City, North Carolina 28713
(704) 488-2159

Near the Great Smoky Mountains National Park, the Fryemont thus is close to one of the world's finest wildlife sanctuaries. The park has more than 800 miles of streams, mountain peaks over 6000 feet high, endless biking trails, and abundant flora and fauna. Other attractions near the inn include whitewater rafting, horseback riding, the Blue Ridge Parkway, Fontana Dam and Reservoir, Cherokee Indian Reservation, the Biltmore House and Gardens, the Thomas Wolfe home, and Gatlinburg, Tennessee. The dining room is open for breakfast and dinner seven days a week. Dress is casual and comfortable. A modified American plan is available.

Chilled Raspberry Soup

1 10-ounce package frozen
    raspberries in syrup
1 cup sour cream
¼ cup sugar
1 cup Chablis
2 tablespoons Chambord liqueur

In a blender combine all the ingredients and blend for 30 seconds. Chill. Serve in chilled bowls and garnish with a sprig of fresh mint and a dollop of sour cream or whipped cream.

Note: If fresh raspberries are used, increase the sugar to taste.

Variation: This recipe can be used with almost any fruit and corresponding liqueur combination (for example, fresh peaches and Peach Schnapps). Cantaloupe Soup or Honeydew Soup is made the same way, with or without melon liqueur. Serves 6.

Mashed Potatoes Supreme

6 potatoes, peeled and cubed

🌝 🌝 🌝

⅓ cup butter, melted
½ cup milk
½ cup sour cream
2 teaspoons salt
Dash pepper
1 teaspoon chopped chives
½ cup grated Cheddar cheese

Grease a 1½-quart casserole dish. In a saucepan cover the potatoes with lightly salted water and bring to a boil, then simmer until tender and drain.

In a large bowl mash the potatoes with an electric mixer until most of the lumps are gone. Add the butter and continue mixing until smooth. Add the milk, sour cream, salt, pepper, and chives, mixing until well blended. Place in the prepared casserole and cover with the cheese. Bake in a 350° oven for 5 minutes, or until the cheese melts.

Serves 8.

Grandma June's Baked Tomatoes

3 medium tomatoes, blanched,
    peeled and quartered
1 tablespoon finely chopped onion
1 tablespoon finely chopped celery
1 tablespoon finely chopped green
    pepper
1 teaspoon sugar
½ cup tomato juice
1 cup seasoned salad croutons
¼ cup freshly grated Parmesan
    cheese
Salt and pepper to taste
½ cup shredded Mozzarella cheese

The Fryemont Inn

Butter a 1-quart casserole dish. In a large saucepan combine the tomatoes, onion, celery, green pepper, sugar, tomato juice, salt, and pepper. Cook over low heat until the tomatoes break up. Place in the prepared casserole and mix in ¾ cup of croutons. Crush the remaining croutons and combine with the Parmesan cheese. Sprinkle over the top of the casserole. Bake in a 350° oven for 20 minutes. Sprinkle Mozzarella cheese over the top. Bake an additional 10 minutes.

Note: You can substitute a good quality canned stewed tomato for the fresh tomatoes.

Serves 6.

High Hampton Inn and Country Club

Cashiers, North Carolina 28717
(704) 743-2411

High in the Blue Ridge Mountains, High Hampton Inn is a rustic but comfortable retreat. A huge stone chimney with four fireplaces is the focal point of the lobby. Bedrooms have walls of sawmill-finished pine and sturdy mountain-crafted furniture. Country ham, homemade breads, and vegetables from the kitchen garden grace the table while dahlias in the flower garden lift the soul. While all seasons are beautiful in Cashiers Valley with its caves, streams, and surrounding craggy

peaks, spring and fall are spectacular when the rhododendrons and dogwoods blossom and the leaves turn fiery colors. (Lower rates are in effect, too.)

High Hampton Rainbow Trout

A true gourmet never removes the heads of delicious High Hampton Trout. Happy Eating!

High Hampton Trout
Salt
Coarse Pepper
Pancake flour

&. &. &.

Oil
Parsley and lemon wedges for garnish

Clean and thoroughly dry the trout and sprinkle with the salt and pepper. Dust the outside of the trout with the flour.

In an electric skillet heat enough oil to half cover the fish to a temperature of 385°. Cook the trout covered for 6 to 8 minutes. Turn with a spatula, being careful not to break the whole fish, and finish cooking uncovered. Arrange on a hot platter and garnish with parsley and lemon wedges.

Note: Applesauce served with fried fish brings out the delicacy of the fish flavor.

Spanish Eggplant

2 eggplants, pared and cubed
Butter
1 cup chopped onions
1 cup chopped green peppers

&. &. &.

2 14½-ounce cans stewed tomatoes
½ cup brown sugar
2 tablespoons Parmesan cheese
Salt
White pepper
1 teaspoon garlic powder
Buttered bread crumbs
Parmesan cheese

In a saucepan parboil the eggplants in salted water, then drain. In a skillet melt the butter and sauté the onions and peppers.

Add the tomatoes to the eggplant and season with the brown sugar, 2 tablespoons Parmesan cheese, salt, pepper, and garlic powder. Add the onions and peppers. Place in a 2-quart casserole and sprinkle with the bread crumbs and additional cheese. Bake until brown.

Note: This casserole reheats beautifully and is even better the second day. I have also had good luck freezing it.

It is always served at High Hampton with roast beef.

Serves 4.

Black Bottom Pie

1½ cups crushed zwieback
¼ cup confectioners' sugar
6 tablespoons butter, melted
1 teaspoon cinnamon

ã ã ã

1 tablespoon unflavored gelatin
½ cup cold water
2 cups rich milk
4 egg yolks, beaten lightly
1 cup sugar
4 teaspoons cornstarch
1½ ounces chocolate, melted
½ teaspoon vanilla extract
1 teaspoon almond flavoring

ã ã ã

3 egg whites
¼ teaspoon salt
¼ teaspoon cream of tartar
¼ cup sugar

ã ã ã

1 cup heavy cream
2 tablespoons confectioners' sugar

In a medium bowl combine the zwieback, confectioners' sugar, butter, and cinnamon. Place in a 9-inch pie pan and pat along the sides and bottom to form a crust. Bake in a 350° oven for 15 minutes.

In a small bowl soak the gelatin in the water. In a saucepan scald the milk. In the top of a double boiler combine the egg yolks, 1 cup of sugar, and cornstarch. Gradually stir in the

milk and cook over hot water until the custard will coat a spoon.

Take out 1 cup of the custard and add the chocolate to it, beating until well blended and cool. Add the vanilla and pour into the pie shell. Dissolve the gelatin in the remaining custard and cool, but do not permit the custard to stiffen. Stir in the almond flavoring.

In a medium bowl combine the egg whites and salt, beating until blended. Add the cream of tartar and beat until stiff, gradually adding the ¼ cup of sugar. Fold in the remaining custard and cover the chocolate custard with the almond-flavored custard. Chill and set.

In a medium bowl whip the heavy cream with the confectioners' sugar and spread over the pie. Enjoy!

Serves 6 to 8.

The Homeplace

5901 Sardis Road
Charlotte, North Carolina 28226
(704) 365-1936

At the Homeplace the warm, friendly atmosphere hasn't changed since 1902. Situated on two and one-half wooded acres in southeast Charlotte, the Homeplace is conveniently located near shopping malls and downtown. The completely restored home has the original hand-crafted staircase, ten-foot beaded ceilings, heart-of-pine floors, and a formal parlor. The three bedrooms with queen beds and private baths are decorated with Victorian elegance and old-fashioned charm. Mornings are welcomed with a complete breakfast of eggs, homemade breads, pastries, jellies, and fresh fruit, coffee and tea served in the main dining

area or on the screened porch when weather permits. Evenings can be enjoyed by gathering in the parlor for appetizers or desserts and southern hospitality.

Cream Waffles

2 eggs
1¾ cups milk
½ cup butter, melted
2 cups all-purpose flour
4 teaspoons baking powder
½ teaspoon salt
1 tablespoon sugar

In a large bowl beat the eggs. Add the remaining ingredients and beat until smooth. Do not stir the batter between bakings.

Makes 6 round waffles.

Cinnamon Cream Syrup

1 cup sugar
½ cup light corn syrup
¼ cup water
½ to ¾ teaspoon cinnamon
½ cup evaporated milk

In a saucepan combine the sugar, corn syrup, water, and cinnamon. Bring to a boil over medium heat, stirring constantly. Cook and stir for 1 minute. Cool for 5 minutes and stir in the evaporated milk. Serve warm.

Note: Syrup can be kept tightly covered in the refrigerator for weeks. To reheat, warm slowly or it will overcook and become stringy.

Makes about 1¼ cups.

The Homeplace

The Inn on Providence

6700 Providence Road
Charlotte, North Carolina 28226
(704) 366-6700

The atmosphere of this three-story southern homestead with its warm, gracious hospitality creates a uniquely restful experience. The inn has a large reception foyer, walnut-paneled library, formal sitting room with fireplace, elegant oak-floored dining room, screened verandah, spacious lawns, and an outdoor swimming pool. The five guest rooms, three with private baths, are uniquely furnished and decorated by theme, including the Master's Quarters, the Plantation Room, Scarlett's Room, and Library Room. The southern breakfast is full and inviting.

Yankee Spoiler Casserole

1 cup hot cooked grits
1 8½-ounce box Jiffy corn muffin mix
4 eggs, beaten
1¾ cups hot milk
½ cup butter
Salt and pepper

🍃 🍃 🍃

1 pound hot bulk sausage, cooked and drained
1 cup grated cheese

In a large bowl combine the grits, muffin mix, eggs, milk, butter, salt, and pepper. In a 1½-quart casserole layer the sausage and grits mixture. Top with the cheese. Bake in a 325° oven for 45 minutes.
Serves 8.

Sausage Breakfast Casserole

7 to 8 slices bread, crusts removed, spread with margarine and cubed
1 pound bulk cooked sausage, crumbled and drained
2 cups shredded sharp Cheddar cheese

🍃 🍃 🍃

7 to 8 eggs
2½ cups milk
1 teaspoon salt
1 teaspoon dry mustard

In a 3-quart casserole dish place the bread, and top with the sausage and cheese.

In a medium bowl combine the eggs, milk, salt, and dry mustard, beating well. Pour the mixture over the casserole and refrigerate for 8 to 12 hours. Bake in a 350° oven for 40 to 45 minutes.
Serves 12.

Oven Pancake— Pannekoeken

½ cup all-purpose flour
½ cup milk
2 eggs, slightly beaten
¼ teaspoon salt
Pinch nutmeg
1 cup fruit, such as blueberries, apples, etc. (optional)

🍃 🍃 🍃

¼ cup butter
Confectioners' sugar
Maple syrup, jam, jelly, or marmalade

In a medium bowl blend together the first 5 ingredients. Fold in the fruit, if desired.

In a 12-inch ovenproof skillet melt the butter. When the butter is very hot, pour in the batter. Bake in a 450° oven for 15 minutes, or until golden brown. Sprinkle generously with confectioners' sugar and serve immediately from the skillet with maple syrup, jam, jelly, or marmalade.

Note: This recipe doubles nicely. Serves 4.

Sausage and Apricot-Topped French Toast

1 pound sausage links
1 1-pound 14-ounce can apricot halves, drained
3 tablespoons brown sugar, firmly packed

🍂 🍂 🍂

6 eggs
½ cup biscuit mix
2 tablespoons sugar
½ teaspoon cinnamon
1½ cups milk

🍂 🍂 🍂

1 loaf day-old French bread
Oil
Sour cream

In a skillet brown the sausage links. Push the sausage to one side of the skillet and drain, reserving 2 tablespoons of the drippings. Add the apricots and brown sugar to the reserved drippings, stirring until the sugar dissolves. Mix sauce with the sausages and keep warm while making the French toast.

In a blender combine the eggs, biscuit mix, sugar, cinnamon, and milk, mixing until smooth. Cut the bread into 1-inch thick slices and soak in the batter, turning until saturated.

In a frying pan over medium heat add about ¼-inch of oil. When the oil is hot, add a few bread slices at a time. Cover and cook for 5 minutes, or until browned and slightly puffy. Turn and cook the other side. Drain on a paper towel and keep warm while frying the remaining slices of bread. Serve with the glazed apricots, sausages, and sour cream. Delicious!

Serves 6.

Banana Muffins

½ cup butter
½ cup sugar
1 egg
1 cup mashed bananas
1 teaspoon baking soda dissolved in 1 tablespoon hot water

🍂 🍂 🍂

1½ cups all-purpose flour
¼ teaspoon salt
1 teaspoon nutmeg
½ cup chopped walnuts

Grease 12 muffin cups. In a large bowl cream together the butter and sugar with an electric mixer. Add the egg, bananas, and dissolved baking soda, mixing well. Stir in the flour, salt, nutmeg, and walnuts, blending well. Pour the batter in muffin cups and bake in a 375° oven for 20 minutes.

Variation: Add coconut or chocolate chips.

Makes 12 muffins.

Curried Fruit Compote

½ cup butter or margarine
1 tablespoon cornstarch
1 teaspoon curry powder
¾ cup brown sugar

🍂 🍂 🍂

1 16-ounce can chunk pineapple, drained
1 16-ounce can sliced pears, drained
1 16-ounce can sliced peaches, drained
1 6-ounce small jar sliced candied apples, cut in halves, drained
Handful of raisins

Butter a casserole dish. In a saucepan melt the butter and add the cornstarch, curry powder, and brown sugar, heating over medium heat.

Mix the fruit in the prepared casserole and pour the hot sugar mixture over the top, mixing well. Bake in a 350° oven until piping hot.

Serves 8 to 10.

The Gingerbread Inn

Post Office Box 187
Chimney Rock, North Carolina 28720
(704) 625-4038

Spicy, hot gingerbread to take the chill off cool mountain nights is served to guests at the Gingerbread Inn as they relax in rocking chairs on decks overlooking the Rocky Broad River. Later they retire to rooms furnished with country furniture, home-sewn quilts, and ruffled curtains. The warm atmosphere of wicker, chintz, and cross-stitch is enhanced by ceiling fans, grapevine wreaths, and authentic antique toys. Breakfast usually features homemade raisin bread and specially prepared jams.

Added attractions are nearby Chimney Rock Park, Hickory Nut Gorge, and beautiful Lake Lure. Within easy driving distance are the Biltmore Estate and Flat Rock Playhouse. Trout fishing, hiking, and wading in icy mountain streams are other popular activities.

Sour Cream Muffins

2 cups Bisquick
½ cup butter, melted
1 8-ounce carton sour cream

Grease 12 small muffin cups. In a medium bowl combine the ingredients, mixing well. Pour batter into muffin tins and bake in a 350° oven for 15 to 20 minutes.

Makes 12 small muffins.

🦆 🦆 🦆 🦆 🦆

The Jarrett House

Jere's Muffins

2 cups all-purpose flour
2 teaspoons baking soda
½ teaspoon salt
1¼ cups sugar
2 teaspoons cinnamon

🍃 🍃 🍃

2 cups grated carrots
½ cup nuts
1 apple, grated
½ cup raisins
3 eggs
1 cup oil
2 teaspoons vanilla extract

Grease muffin cups. In a large bowl combine the flour, baking soda, salt, sugar, and cinnamon.

In a separate bowl combine the remaining ingredients. Stir the mixture into the dry ingredients. Pour batter in muffin cups and bake in a 350° oven for 20 minutes.

Makes 18 large muffins.

The Jarrett House

Post Office Box 219
Dillsboro, North Carolina 28725
(704) 586-9964

One of the oldest inns in western North Carolina, the Jarrett House is a throw-back to the days of the horse and buggy and the wood-burning passenger train. First opened in 1884, the inn has provided food and lodging for over one hundred years. Featured in *Southern Living,* the *Miami Herald,* the *New York Times,* the *Chicago Tribune,* and many others, this inn continues to maintain a reputation unsurpassed. Food is served family-style with all the trimmings.

Jarrett House Vinegar Pie

½ cup margarine, melted and cooled
1½ cups sugar
2 tablespoons all-purpose flour

1 tablespoon vanilla extract
2 tablespoons apple cider vinegar
3 eggs

🍃 🍃 🍃

1 9-inch unbaked pie shell

In a large bowl combine the first 6 ingredients. Pour into the pie shell. Bake in a 300° oven for 45 minutes.
  Serves 6.

La Grange Plantation Inn

Route 3, Box 610
Henderson, North Carolina 27536
(919) 438-2421

La Grange Plantation Inn is an elegant twentieth-century bed and breakfast inn set in a gracious eighteenth-century plantation house. Situated at the edge of Kerr Lake, the inn was begun in 1770 and remodeled and later enlarged to its present size. It is furnished with American and English antiques. Guests can enjoy as much privacy or socializing as they prefer. The delicious full breakfast is served in the dining room addition.

Cashew-Cheddar Roll

Paprika

🍃 🍃 🍃

1 pound sharp Cheddar cheese
1 cup cashews
1 8-ounce package cream cheese
2 cloves garlic, minced

Dust a sheet of waxed paper with paprika.

In a food processor finely grate the Cheddar. Grind the cashews. Process the cream cheese until soft. In a large bowl mix the cheese, cashews, and cream cheese together, and stir in the garlic. Shape the mixture into two 1½-inch rolls. Roll on the waxed paper until thoroughly coated with the paprika. Wrap the rolls in fresh waxed paper and refrigerate. Thinly slice to serve on round crackers.

Note: These rolls may be frozen, or they keep well in the refrigerator.

Makes 2 rolls, each roll serves 10 to 15 people.

La Grange Plantation Inn

Baked Chicken Brunch Casserole

Butter
12 slices day-old white bread, crusts removed
3 cups cooked chicken, roughly chopped
½ cup chopped onion
1½ cups grated Cheddar cheese

🐦 🐦 🐦

6 eggs, beaten
2½ cups milk
Paprika

🐦 🐦 🐦

Sour Cream-Onion Sauce
Parsley or cherry tomatoes to garnish

Butter a 9x13-inch pyrex dish. Butter one side of each bread slice and place 6 slices in the prepared dish, buttered side down. Layer the chicken, onion, and cheese over the bread. Cover the layers with the remaining bread slices, buttered side up.

In a medium bowl combine the eggs and milk. Pour over the casserole and sprinkle with paprika. Refrigerate overnight. Bake in a 325° oven for 1 to 1¼ hours.

Top the cooked casserole with the Sour Cream-Onion Sauce and garnish with parsley or cherry tomatoes.

Serves 8 to 10.

🐦 🐦 🐦 🐦 🐦

Ham Puff

12 ounces ham, cubed
3 cups grated extra-sharp Cheddar cheese
25 soda crackers, crumbled
½ cup chopped onion
½ medium red pepper, chopped
½ medium green pepper, chopped
Salt and pepper

🐦 🐦 🐦

3 eggs, beaten
2 cups milk
Parsley

In a 9x13-inch pyrex dish randomly sprinkle the ham, cheese, crackers, onion, and peppers. Sprinkle with salt and pepper.

In a separate bowl combine the eggs and milk. Pour over the casserole. Garnish with parsley. Bake in a 325° oven for 1 hour.

Serves 8 to 10.

Sour Cream-Onion Sauce

This sauce is intended to be served with Baked Chicken Brunch Casserole, but it is excellent also for napping savory-filled crepes.

½ cup chopped onion
½ cup butter or margarine
2 tablespoons all-purpose flour
1 cup light cream
1 teaspoon salt
½ teaspoon white pepper
¾ cup sour cream

In a medium saucepan cook the onion in the butter until soft, but not browned. Stir in the flour, cream, salt, and pepper. Bring mixture to a boil, stirring constantly until blended. Stir in the sour cream until heated thoroughly, but do not boil.

Serves 8 to 10.

Spiced Fruit with Port

1 8-ounce can sliced peaches
1 16-ounce can pear halves
1 8-ounce can apricot halves
1 16-ounce can pitted sour cherries
4 slices lemon
2 cinnamon sticks
3 whole cloves
3 whole allspice
½ teaspoon ginger

🐦 🐦 🐦

⅓ cup Port wine

In a large saucepan combine the drained syrup from the peaches, pears, and apricots. Add half of the drained cherry syrup. Set the fruit aside in a large bowl. Add the lemon slices and spices to the syrups and boil for 20 minutes.

Add the Port and pour over the fruits. Return the fruits and sauce to the saucepan and let the flavors blend for 2 hours or more. Serve warm.

Serves 8 to 10.

The Waverly Inn

783 North Main Street
Hendersonville, North Carolina 28739
(704) 693-9193
(800) 537-8195

The Waverly Inn combines Victorian stateliness with the charm of the Colonial Revival period. The rooms are graciously furnished, some with claw-footed tubs, king and queen four-poster canopy beds, or turn-of-the-century spindle beds. On the front verandah guests chat while sitting on the rocking chairs. A complete "all you can eat" southern breakfast is served in the dining room. Special weekends include Murder Mystery, golf, Charles Dickens, and storytelling. Since before the Civil War Hendersonville has welcomed guests who wished to escape the heat. Travelers still come for cool summer evenings and romantic winter getaways.

Moravian Sugar Cake

1 cup sugar
½ cup Crisco or margarine
1 cup unseasoned hot mashed potatoes
2 eggs, beaten
1½ packages active dry yeast, dissolved in 1 cup potato water
1½ teaspoons salt
4 cups all-purpose flour

🍂 🍂 🍂

1 cup butter
1 16-ounce box light brown sugar
2 teaspoons cinnamon
¼ pint whipping cream

Grease two 9-inch square baking pans. In a large bowl cream together the sugar and Crisco. Add the mashed potatoes, mixing well. Add the eggs, dissolved yeast, and salt. Mix in enough of the flour to make a soft dough, stirring the last portion in by hand. Turn onto a lightly floured surface and knead until smooth and elastic. Spread evenly onto the prepared pans. Let rise until doubled in bulk, then make indentations in the dough with a thumb and forefinger. Fill the indentations with pieces of butter and cover the cake with the brown sugar. Dust with the cinnamon and drizzle the cream over the surface. Bake in a 350° oven for 15 to 20 minutes, until golden brown.
Serves 10 to 12.

Colonial Pines Inn

Hickory Street
Box 2309
Highlands, North Carolina 28741
(704) 526-2060

A quiet country guest house, Colonial Pines Inn is on a secluded hillside half a mile from Main Street. Surrounded by the spruce, hemlock, pine, and rhododendron of Nantahala Forest, it has wide porches and a lovely mountain view. Rooms in the main house include private baths, breakfast, and the use of a comfortable living room with antique furnishings, fireplace, television, and a grand piano. Two separate cottages with kitchens are also available, one with a fireplace and view.

Corn-for-breakfast Quiche

A crustless New England dish which we serve for breakfast with ham, fresh fruit, and homemade breads.

16 ounces fresh or frozen corn niblets
1 pound grated Cheddar cheese

🍂 🍂 🍂

8 eggs
2 cups half and half
1 teaspoon salt
½ teaspoon pepper
½ teaspoon nutmeg
Dash cayenne
¼ cup Parmesan cheese

Grease a 9x13-inch baking dish. Layer the corn and Cheddar cheese in the prepared dish.

In a large bowl combine the butter, eggs, half and half, and seasonings. Pour over the corn and cheese. Sprinkle with the Parmesan cheese. Bake in a 350° oven for 45 minutes, until lightly browned. Cool slightly before cutting.
Serves 8.

Fresh Fruit Bread

A wonderfully versatile bread adaptable to any season of the year. Freezes well.

1½ cups butter
2½ cups sugar
6 eggs
1 16-ounce carton sour cream
1 tablespoon vanilla extract

🍂 🍂 🍂

Colonial Pines Inn

6 cups all-purpose flour
1½ teaspoons baking powder
1 teaspoon baking soda
1½ teaspoons salt
1 teaspoon cinnamon
4 cups coarsely chopped strawberries, blueberries, or peaches

Grease and flour 4 bread pans. In a large bowl cream together the butter and sugar. Add the eggs, sour cream, and vanilla.

In a separate bowl sift together the flour, baking powder, baking soda, salt, and cinnamon. Add to the cream mixture. Carefully fold in the fruit. Pour the batter into the prepared pans. Bake in a 350° oven for 1 hour.

Variations: For prune bread use 1½ pounds chopped pitted prunes, 1½ teaspoons cardamon, 1 teaspoon nutmeg, and 2 tablespoons grated orange peel.

For cranberry bread use 4 cups whole cranberries, eliminate the cinnamon, and add 2 tablespoons grated orange peel and 2 teaspoons orange extract.

Makes 4 loaves.

Oat Bran Bread

Our guests' favorite breakfast bread and also great for sandwiches.

2 ¼-ounce packages active dry yeast
¾ cup warm water (110° to 115°)

🍃 🍃 🍃

3 cups old-fashioned oats
1 cup oat bran
½ cup brown sugar
1½ tablespoons salt
½ cup oil
3 cups scalded milk
6 to 7 cups bread flour

🍃 🍃 🍃

1 egg white
1 tablespoon water

Grease and flour 4 bread pans. In a small bowl dissolve the yeast in ¾ cup of warm water. Set aside.

In a large bowl combine the oats, oat bran, brown sugar, salt, and oil. Cover with the scalded milk. Mix and

cool slightly. When warm to the touch, add the yeast. Add the flour and knead the dough until smooth and elastic. Place in a greased bowl, cover, and let rise until doubled. Punch down and let rise again until doubled. Shape the loaves and place in the prepared pans. Let rise again. Glaze the risen loaves with the egg white mixed with 1 tablespoon of water. Sprinkle the tops with oats. Bake in a 375° oven for 25 to 30 minutes.

Makes 4 loaves.

Cataloochee Ranch

Route 1, Box 500
Maggie Valley, North Carolina 28751
(704) 926-0285 (winter)
(704) 926-1401

Cataloochee Ranch spreads across a thousand acres in the Great Smoky Mountains and has catered to its guests for over fifty years. Refreshing mountain breezes from the peaks share the sunshine, while warm fires welcome the cool nights. At Cataloochee guests can stay in their own cabin with an open fireplace and a private bath, or in the stone and hewn-log main ranch house. In both cases they will be surrounded with the rustic beauty and charm of handmade quilts, antiques, and furniture carved from native cherry and walnut. The ranch's varied, bountiful meals feature seasonal garden vegetables and homemade jams.

Lazy Man's Bread

Just what it says—good bread for those who don't like to knead and roll out biscuits and clean up the mess.

¼ cup shortening
2 cups self-rising flour
1½ cups milk

In an 8-inch iron skillet place 1 tablespoon of shortening and put in a 450° oven. In a medium bowl combine the remaining shortening, flour, and milk, mixing well. Pour batter into the hot skillet and bake about 15 minutes, until crusty brown.

Serves 4 to 6.

Cornmeal Gravy

1 cup cornmeal
4 tablespoons bacon fat
Milk
Salt and pepper

In a skillet mix the cornmeal into the bacon fat and cook a few minutes, stirring constantly. Gradually add enough milk to desired consistency and season with salt and pepper.

Makes about 3 cups, depending on consistency desired.

Candy Roaster Puff

A candy roaster is a member of the pumpkin family, but has a much more delicate flavor and does not have the stringy texture. It is indigenous to these mountains and comes in all colors, shapes, and sizes, from ugly warty green to a gorgeous orange hue. Cut up into chunks it freezes very well, and no blanching is necessary.

1½ cups candy roaster
Butter
⅓ cup sugar
2 eggs
1½ cups milk
½ teaspoon vanilla extract
Dash nutmeg
Dash cinnamon

Butter a quart casserole. Cook the candy roaster, mash, and add a little butter. Add the remaining ingredients and place the mixture in the prepared casserole. Bake in a 325° oven for 45 minutes, until set.

Variation: Sweet potatoes or butternut squash can also be used.

Serves 4.

Steamed Snow Peas

1 pound snow peas
Sugar
Butter or margarine

Into rapidly boiling salted water (just barely enough to cover the peas), drop the snow peas and add a touch of sugar. Return the water to a boil and turn off the heat. Drain and season with a generous amount of butter.

Variation: If snow peas are not available, sugar snap pea pods can be used, but boil about 5 minutes.

Note: When cooking any fresh or frozen vegetable, always have your water boiling before putting in the vegetable. This will keep the color brilliant.

Serves 4.

Zucchini Creole

1 onion, diced
1 green pepper, diced
1 stalk celery, diced
3 tablespoons margarine
1 14½-ounce can tomatoes
4 medium zucchini, cut in ¼-inch
   pieces, cooked
½ teaspoon sugar
Salt and pepper
½ teaspoon garlic powder
½ cup catsup

In a skillet sauté the onions, green pepper, and celery in the margarine until the onion is transparent. Add the tomatoes, zucchini, sugar, salt, pepper, garlic, and catsup. Simmer about 15 minutes.

Variation: Cabbage, lima beans, or eggplant can also be used.

Serves 4 to 6.

Apple or Rhubarb Float

3 cups applesauce or cooked
   rhubarb, sweetened to taste
3 egg whites

In a saucepan bring the applesauce or rhubarb to a boil. In a large bowl beat the egg whites until stiff. Fold the boiling applesauce into the egg whites and serve.

Serves 6.

Old-fashioned Stack Cake

This was the traditional Christmas cake of the mountains and oh, so good. Not too sweet, but sweet enough. The thinner the layers and the more of them, the better the cook. It is also said that this cake was used at wedding receptions. Each family was to bring a layer of cake of any kind. These were spread with stewed dried apples and stacked one on the other. The more layers on the cake the more popular the bride.

3 cups all-purpose flour
½ teaspoon baking powder
½ teaspoon cream of tartar
1 cup brown sugar, firmly packed
½ cup shortening
½ cup butter
2 eggs
1 teaspoon vanilla extract

🍃 🍃 🍃

2 8-ounce packs dried apples
5 cups water
1 cup water
1 teaspoon cinnamon
1 teaspoon nutmeg
¼ teaspoon cloves
¼ teaspoon salt

🍃 🍃 🍃

Whipped cream (optional)

Line seven 8-inch cake pans with waxed paper. In a large bowl combine the first 8 ingredients. Pat about ½ cup of the dough into each of the pre-

pared pans. Bake in a 350° oven for 8 to 10 minutes.

In a saucepan simmer the apples in the water for 45 to 50 minutes, until very soft. Stir in the sugar, spices, and salt. Spread on the cake layers while still hot and stack, leaving the top layer plain. Slice thin and serve with whipped cream, if desired.

Serves 8 to 10.

Marshall House

5 Hill Street
Post Office Box 865
Marshall, North Carolina 28753
(704) 649-9205
(800) 562-9258

Marshall House is nestled on a hill overlooking the town of Marshall. Its large verandah offers a view of the village, which is situated on the banks of the French Broad River. Designed as a private residence in 1903, the Marshall House is constructed of pebbledash, a masonry material introduced to the area by George Vanderbilt when he built the Biltmore House. The nine guest rooms, two with private baths, are decorated with period furniture. The house is decorated with many porcelain antiques, a German stein collection, tea cups and pots, and furniture and mirrors of the 1920s to 1940s. The house has four fireplaces.

Chicken 'n Broccoli
with Cheddar Cheese Sauce

2 large bunches broccoli, steamed crisp
2 chickens, steamed and deboned
4 cups medium cream sauce with cheese
1 cup bread crumbs, browned in butter

In a casserole dish layer the broccoli and chicken. Cover with the cheese sauce and sprinkle with the bread crumbs. Bake in a 350° oven for 40 minutes.
Serves 8 to 10.

Bread Pudding à la Boylan

This makes a great breakfast dessert.

3½ cups milk
1 cup sugar
4 eggs
1 teaspoon cinnamon
1 teaspoon nutmeg

  ❧ ❧ ❧

12 slices white bread
Sweet butter
3 large apples, peeled, cored, and sliced
1½-ounce package Sun Maid raisins

  ❧ ❧ ❧

Sugar
Cinnamon

Butter a large, deep 2-quart teflon or Corning Ware bowl. In a large bowl combine the milk, sugar, eggs, cinnamon, and nutmeg, mixing well with a wooden spoon.
Toast the bread and generously spread with butter. Break the bread into small pieces and add to the mixture. Mix in the apples and raisins. Place the mixture in the prepared bowl and sprinkle with sugar and cinnamon. Bake in a 350° oven for 1 hour and 10 minutes, until browned. Serve warm or cold, either plain, with a whipped cream topping or ice cream.
Serves 8.

Pine Ridge Inn

2893 West Pine Street
Mount Airy, North Carolina 27030
(919) 789-5034

At Pine Ridge Inn, surrounded by the Blue Ridge Mountains, guests are treated to the luxury of the past. Built in 1948, Pine Ridge Inn has private bedroom suites, a swimming pool with sun deck, a large indoor hot tub, an exercise room, and many amenities of a grand hotel. A continental breakfast is served each morning. Pine Ridge offers bed and breakfast for the traveling executive, the executive spouse, the visiting relative accustomed to traveling first class, or to a couple looking for a truly luxurious weekend away from home. Golf privileges at Cross Creek Country Club are available to guests.

Dinner Party Menu for 6

Hot Avocado with Seafood
  ❧ ❧ ❧
Veal with Mushrooms
  ❧ ❧ ❧
Vegetable Risotto, Broccoli
  ❧ ❧ ❧
Chocolate Soufflés with Marsala Ice Cream

The first course is an unusual hot avocado with a creamy seafood filling. To follow, tender veal with a rich mushroom sauce and a colorful vegetable accompaniment. Dessert is delicious—hot chocolate soufflé served with Marsala Ice Cream. You take some of the hot soufflé on a spoon and eat it together with some of the ice cream.

To do ahead: The first course sauce can be made in advance. The seafood can be prepared and refrigerated.
The veal can be cooked in its sauce for 1 hour, removed from the oven, cooled, covered, and refrigerated. When reheating turn the veal over, put into a 350° oven for the remaining 30 minutes of cooking time, or until tender.
The rice can be cooked the day before. To reheat spread into a greased baking dish, dot with 1 ounce of butter, cover, and bake in a 350° oven for about 10 minutes, until heated through, stirring occasionally.
The soufflé can be prepared on the morning of the party up to where the egg whites are folded in. The mixture will thicken slightly on standing, thus making it difficult to fold in the egg whites. Let the basin stand over simmering water for a few minutes (don't let the water touch the basin), to warm very slightly, then quickly and lightly fold in the beaten egg whites as directed in the recipe, put into the soufflé dishes, and bake at once.
The ice cream can be made several

days ahead. On the morning of the party, spoon the ice cream into small serving dishes and return them to the freezer.

Hot Avocado with Seafood

12 shelled oysters or 1 cup lobster, cooked
12 ounces shrimp, cooked and drained
7½-ounce can crab meat, flaked
3 teaspoons capers

ew   ew   ew

½ cup mayonnaise
4 sprigs parsley
1 tablespoon chopped chives
½ teaspoon French mustard
2 teaspoons lemon juice
Salt and pepper
1 egg yolk

ew   ew   ew

3 avocados
Paprika

In a large bowl combine the oysters, shrimp, crab meat, and capers.

In a blender or food processor combine the mayonnaise, parsley, chives, mustard, and lemon juice. Process or blend for 15 seconds. Season with salt and pepper, add the egg yolk, and process or blend for 5 more seconds. Combine ⅓ of the sauce with the seafood.

Cut the avocados in half and remove the stones. Place a teaspoon of the sauce in each avocado half and fill evenly with the seafood. Top the filling with additional sauce and sprinkle with paprika. Place the avocados in a small baking dish with ½-inch of hot water. Bake in a 350° oven for 10 minutes, until the tops are lightly browned and set. Do not overcook or reheat avocados, or they will turn bitter.

Serves 6.

Veal with Mushrooms

3 pounds nut of veal (fillet from the end of the leg)
½ cup dry white wine
¼ cup dry sherry

ew   ew   ew

3 tablespoons oil
2 tablespoons butter
1 onion, chopped
1 tablespoon all-purpose flour
½ cup cream
1 chicken stock cube, crumbled
½ cup water
1 teaspoon Worcestershire sauce
½ teaspoon thyme
½ teaspoon tarragon

ew   ew   ew

Butter
8 ounces mushrooms, thinly sliced

ew   ew   ew

1 teaspoon cornflour
1 teaspoon water
Salt and pepper

Cut the sinew from the veal and place in a large bowl. Cover with the wine and sherry and marinate for 4 hours, turning occasionally. Remove the veal and pat dry. Reserve the marinade.

In a large pan heat the oil and 2 tablespoons of butter. Brown the veal on all sides, then remove and place in an ovenproof dish. Pour off the pan juices, reserving 1 tablespoon in the pan. Add the onion and cook for 2 minutes. Add the flour, stirring for 1 minute. Add the strained marinade, cream, stock cube, water, Worcestershire sauce, thyme, and tarragon, stirring until boiling. Pour the sauce over the veal, cover, and bake in a 350° oven for 1½ hours, or until tender.

Melt additional butter in a pan, add the mushrooms, and cook over high heat for 2 minutes.

Remove the veal from the cooking sauce and keep warm. In a saucepan combine the sauce and mushrooms. Add the cornflour and water, stirring constantly until boiling. Season with salt and pepper. Pour over the sliced veal.

Serves 6.

Vegetable Risotto

¼ cup butter
1 onion, finely chopped
1 clove garlic, crushed
1 cup long grain rice
½ cup dry white wine
2½ cups hot water
½ 2-gram packet saffron threads
1 chicken stock cube

ew   ew   ew

½ red pepper, finely chopped
½ green pepper, finely chopped
1 stalk celery, finely chopped
2 tablespoons butter
2 tablespoons grated Parmesan cheese
Salt and pepper

In a pan melt ¼ cup of butter, adding the onion and garlic and cooking until the onion is tender. Add the rice and stir until well coated with the butter mixture. Add the wine, 1 cup of hot water, saffron, and stock cube, stirring constantly and bringing to a boil. Cover. When the water has almost evaporated, add the remaining 1½ cups of hot water, and reduce the heat, cooking about 20 minutes until this water has been evaporated. Add the peppers and celery, mixing well. Stir in 2 tablespoons of butter, Parmesan cheese, and salt and pepper. Stir gently until the butter melts.

Serves 6.

Chocolate Soufflé

3 tablespoons butter
2 tablespoons all-purpose flour
½ cup milk
4 ounces dark chocolate
3 tablespoons sugar
4 eggs, separated

ew   ew   ew

Sugar
1 tablespoon confectioners' sugar

Lightly grease six ½-cup soufflé dishes. In a saucepan melt the butter, add the flour, and cook for 1 minute, stirring constantly. Add the milk, stirring until combined. Add the chocolate broken into small pieces, stirring until melted and the mixture thickens. Remove from the heat, and add the sugar and egg yolks, mixing well.

In a medium bowl beat the egg whites until soft peaks form. Fold ⅓ of the egg whites into the chocolate mixture. Then pour the chocolate mixture into the remaining egg whites and gently fold together.

Sprinkle sugar in the bottom and on the sides of the prepared dishes, shaking out excess. Divide the soufflé mixture evenly among the dishes and place on a baking tray. Bake in a 375° oven for 12 minutes. Sift confectioners' sugar over the top and serve immediately.

Serves 6.

❧ ❧ ❧ ❧ ❧

Marsala Ice Cream

3 eggs, separated
½ cup sugar
2 tablespoons Marsala
2 tablespoons water

❧ ❧ ❧

½ pint whipping cream
Chocolate curls or grated chocolate (optional)

In a heatproof bowl combine the egg yolks, sugar, Marsala, and water. Beat over simmering water until the mixture is lukewarm. Remove from the heat and continue beating about 10 minutes until the mixture is fluffy and cool.

In a bowl whip the cream until firm peaks form and fold into the Marsala mixture. In a separate bowl whip the egg whites until soft peaks form and fold into the Marsala mixture. Spoon the mixture into an ice cream container or cake tin and cover with aluminum foil. Stir occasionally with a fork while freezing. Spoon into individual dishes to serve and top with chocolate curls or grated chocolate, if desired.

Serves 6.

Winborne House

Bed and Breakfast in Historic
  Murfreesboro
333 Jay Trail
Murfreesboro, North Carolina 27855
(919) 398-5224

Guests spend the night with a warm and friendly couple in the restored Winborne House. They may relax on the front porch, take a walk in a quiet place, and enjoy a continental breakfast. Town tours are available.

Cinnamon Twists

A hit with guests—nothing beats the smell of baking bread. These can be made ahead and baked in time for breakfast.

1 cup sour cream (or plain yogurt)
6 tablespoons shortening
3 tablespoons sugar
⅛ teaspoon baking soda
1 teaspoon salt
1 ¼-ounce package active dry yeast
¼ cup lukewarm water (110° to 115°)
3 cups all-purpose flour

❧ ❧ ❧

Margarine, melted
½ cup brown sugar
1½ teaspoons cinnamon

In a saucepan bring the sour cream to a boil. Add the shortening, sugar, baking soda, and salt. Mix and let cool to lukewarm. In a small bowl dissolve the yeast in the warm water. Add to the cooled sour cream mixture. Add the flour, kneading until smooth. Cover the dough with a damp cloth and let rest for 5 minutes. Roll into a ¼-inch thick rectangle.

Spread the entire dough with the melted margarine. In a small bowl combine the brown sugar and cinnamon. Sprinkle over half of the dough. Fold the dough in half and press together. Cut into 1-inch strips, twist, and place on a baking sheet. Let rise about 45 minutes until double. Bake in a 375° oven for 12 to 15 minutes, then spread with a thin confectioners' sugar glaze. Do not overbake.

Makes about 18 twists.

Winborne House

Pigs-in-a-Blanket

Our tour groups love them with coffee and they're always a hit with grandchildren or visiting little people.

1 8-ounce can refrigerator biscuits
20 Oscar Mayer Little Smokies
Sausages

Cut the biscuits in half and wrap each half around a sausage. Place on a cookie sheet. Bake in a 400° oven for 8 to 10 minutes, or until the biscuits are lightly browned.
Makes 20.

Poor Man's Crab Cakes

2 cups grated zucchini, drained
2 eggs
1 cup bread crumbs
1 tablespoon mayonnaise
1 tablespoon Old Bay seasoning
2 tablespoons grated onion

❧ ❧ ❧

Flour

In a large bowl combine all the ingredients, mixing well. Form into cakes and roll in the flour. Fry the cakes in hot oil.
Serves 4 to 6.

Eggplant Casserole

1 eggplant, peeled and cubed

❧ ❧ ❧

3 tablespoons butter
3 tablespoons all-purpose flour
2 cups tomatoes (fresh, if possible)
1 small onion, chopped
½ green pepper, chopped
1 tablespoon brown sugar

❧ ❧ ❧

Grated cheese
Cracker crumbs

Grease a casserole. In a saucepan cook the eggplant in boiling water for 10 minutes and drain. Place in the prepared casserole.

In a saucepan heat the margarine and stir in the flour. Add the tomatoes, onion, green pepper, and sugar, cooking until the sauce thickens. Pour over the eggplant and top with grated cheese and crumbs. Bake in a 350° oven for 30 minutes.
Serves 6.

The Aerie

509 Pollock Street
New Bern, North Carolina 28560
(919) 636-5553

Situated just one block from Tryon Palace, The Aerie is nestled in the heart of New Bern's historic district. Built by Samuel Street in the early 1880s, the Victorian house was a private residence until it was restored as a bed and breakfast inn in the mid-1980s. The seven guest rooms, all with private baths, television, and telephones, are individually decorated. Complimentary beverages and light refreshments are available in the afternoons and evenings. A generous country breakfast is served in the morning. Because of the inn's central location, it is within a short walk of many historic homes, gardens, museums, churches, and fine downtown shops.

Wheat Germ Muffins

⅔ cup Bisquick
⅓ cup wheat germ
¼ cup sugar

❧ ❧ ❧

1 egg
⅓ cup water
2 tablespoons peanut butter
½ teaspoon vanilla extract

Grease or line muffin tins. In a large bowl sift together the Bisquick, wheat germ, and sugar.

In a separate bowl beat the egg and water together lightly. Stir in the peanut butter and vanilla. Add the mixture to the dry ingredients, just until moistened. Don't overmix. Spoon the batter into the prepared tins. Bake in a 375° oven for 20 to 25 minutes.
Makes 6 muffins.

Pumpkin Muffins

1½ cups all-purpose flour
¾ cup sugar
¾ teaspoon baking powder
½ teaspoon baking soda
¼ teaspoon cloves
½ teaspoon cinnamon
¼ teaspoon nutmeg
½ teaspoon salt

❧ ❧ ❧

¼ cup oil
¼ cup water
2 eggs, slightly beaten
¾ cup canned pumpkin

Grease or line muffin tins. In a large bowl combine the flour, sugar, baking powder, baking soda, and seasonings.

In a separate bowl combine the oil, water, eggs, and pumpkin. Add the mixture to the dry ingredients, stirring just until moistened. Spoon the batter into the prepared tins. Bake in a 400° oven for 20 to 25 minutes.
Makes 12 muffins.

Cinnamon Bread

1 cup sugar
½ cup shortening
2 eggs
1 teaspoon vanilla extract
1 cup buttermilk
2 cups all-purpose flour
½ teaspoon salt
1 teaspoon baking powder
1 teaspoon baking soda

❧ ❧ ❧

⅓ cup sugar
½ teaspoon cinnamon

Grease 2 medium-sized loaf pans. In a large bowl cream together 1 cup of sugar and shortening thoroughly. Beat in the eggs, vanilla, and buttermilk. Add the flour, salt, baking powder, and baking soda and blend well. Pour the batter into the prepared pans.

In a separate bowl combine ⅓ cup of sugar and the cinnamon. Swirl into the batter. Bake in a 350° oven for 40 minutes.

Note: For a wonderful drop cookie, simply substitute sour cream for the buttermilk. Drop the batter onto an ungreased cookie sheet, sprinkle with cinnamon and sugar, and bake in a 400° oven for 8 to 10 minutes.

Makes 2 loaves.

Pineapple Spoonbread

¾ cup sugar
½ cup butter
4 eggs, beaten
5 slices white bread, decrusted and cubed
1 20-ounce can crushed pineapple, drained

Grease a quiche dish or a large pie plate. In a large bowl cream together the sugar and butter thoroughly. Stir in the eggs, bread cubes, and pineapple. Pour mixture into the prepared dish. Bake in a 350° oven for 40 to 45 minutes.

Serves 12.

New Berne House

709 Broad Street
New Bern, North Carolina 28560
(919) 636-2250
(800) 842-7688

This splendidly restored Colonial Revival home is the epitome of southern charm. With its charming porch and garden, accentuated with an old swing and oversized hammocks shaded by magnolia, pecan, and camelia trees, it reminds guests of the hospitality for which the South has long been known. Centrally located, it is within a comfortable walk to historic sights, highlighted by the Tryon Palace and its formal gardens. Quaint shops, fine restaurants, and historic buildings are all "in the neighborhood." New Berne Inn is seasoned with antiques and treasures, including the "notorious" brass bed reportedly rescued from a burning brothel in 1897. Each of the six guest rooms radiates charm and character, with a private bath, telephone, and (if you must) television.

Pralines 'n Cream Waffles

The praline sauce is also excellent over ice cream or pound cake!

Belgian Waffles for 6

❧ ❧ ❧

2 tablespoons butter
⅔ cup Domino brown sugar

The Aerie

New Berne House

In a medium bowl combine the cream cheese and ⅓ cup of milk, mixing with a fork until the consistency of sour cream. Add the confectioners' sugar to taste. Spread as a topping on the crepes and garnish with sliced strawberries.

Serves 8 (2 crepes each).

White Chocolate Mousse with Raspberry Sauce

Makes a beautiful addition to a dessert buffet. Also good in a chocolate no-bake pie crust.

> 2 cups heavy cream
> 1 envelope unflavored gelatin
> 6 ounces white baking chocolate
>
> ❧ ❧ ❧
>
> 2 teaspoons vanilla extract
> 2 egg whites
> 4 tablespoons sugar
>
> ❧ ❧ ❧
>
> Melba sauce or seedless raspberry jam
> Brandy (optional)

In a heavy saucepan pour 1 cup of cream. Sprinkle the gelatin over the surface and let it stand for 5 minutes to soften (no heat). Begin to heat the cream over a low heat, stirring until the gelatin dissolves. Add the chocolate, stirring occasionally until it melts and mixture is smooth. Remove from the heat and let stand covered for 15 minutes to cool.

In a separate bowl whip the remaining 1 cup of cream with the vanilla until light and fluffy. In a separate bowl beat the egg whites until stiff. Add the sugar 1 tablespoon at a time, beating after each addition. Combine the chocolate mixture, cream mixture, and egg whites, and fold gently to blend well. Pour into a small trifle or decorative bowl and let stand for a few minutes.

Thin the sauce or jam with brandy and drizzle over the top of mousse in

---

> 1⅓ cups cream or half and half
> ½ cup pecan pieces
>
> ❧ ❧ ❧
>
> Whipped cream, strawberries, and kiwi to garnish

In a saucepan melt the butter. Add the sugar, stirring until the sauce is bubbly and the consistency of caramel. Gradually add the cream, stirring constantly. Continue heating until the sauce thickens, then stir in the pecans. Spoon over the warm waffles and top with a dollop of whipped cream. Garnish with strawberries or kiwi.

Serves 6.

Spiced Apple Crepes

These may sound complicated, but they are really fast and easy!

> 1½ cups sifted all-purpose flour
> ¼ cup confectioners' sugar
> 2 teaspoons baking powder
> 1 teaspoon salt
> 4 eggs
> 1½ cups milk
> ½ cup water
> 2 tablespoons vanilla extract
>
> ❧ ❧ ❧

> 2 tablespoons butter
> 6 to 8 Granny Smith apples, cored and sliced ¼-inch thick
> 1 to 2 tablespoons sugar
> 2 teaspoons cinnamon
> ½ cup walnut pieces
>
> ❧ ❧ ❧
>
> 1 8-ounce package cream cheese, softened
> ⅓ cup milk
> 3 tablespoons confectioners' sugar or honey
> Sliced strawberries to garnish

In a medium bowl sift together the flour, ¼ cup of confectioners' sugar, baking powder, and salt. In a separate bowl beat the eggs and add 1½ cups of milk, water, and vanilla, beating well. Add to the dry ingredients. Let rest for 15 minutes to overnight. Pour ¼-cup of the crepe batter into a heated 7-inch non-stick crepe skillet, swirling to coat evenly. Turn crepe when the edges brown, about 2 minutes, and cook the other side about 1 minute. (I keep 3 pans going, make them ahead, refrigerate or freeze, and reheat in the microwave.)

In a large skillet melt the butter and add the apples, tossing to coat evenly. Add the sugar and cinnamon. Cover and simmer for 10 to 15 minutes until tender. Add the walnuts during the last few minutes. Generously fill the warm crepes and roll.

straight, narrow, parallel lines. Use a knife to pull cross-parallel lines through to create a pattern.

Serves 4 to 6.

Blush Wine Jelly

This is a beautiful jelly—so popular we often serve it with breakfast, but prefer it on scones for afternoon tea. Virtually any wine could be substituted. We've done gift paks with a variety of white, blush, and red.

> 2 cups white Zinfandel or good blush wine
> 3 cups sugar
> 1 pouch pectin

Sterilize containers. In a saucepan over medium heat combine the wine and sugar, stirring until sugar is dissolved. Bring just to a simmer, don't boil. Remove from the heat and stir in the pectin. Pour immediately into prepared containers.

Makes 1 pint.

The Tar Heel Inn

Post Office Box 176
Oriental, North Carolina 28571
(919) 249-1078

Built at the turn of the century and restored in detail, the Tar Heel Inn captures the atmosphere of an English country inn. Its six bedrooms are individually decorated and feature king- or queen-size four-poster beds, ample closets, and private baths. Situated at the confluence of the Neuse River and Pamlico Sound, Oriental, known as the sailing capital of North Carolina, provides a serene setting for year-round enjoyment.

Down East Blintzes

> 2 tablespoons butter
>
> ❧ ❧ ❧
>
> 1 8-ounce package cream cheese
> 1 4-ounce carton cottage cheese
> 1 cup grated Cheddar cheese
> ¼ cup sugar
> 1 teaspoon vanilla extract (or flavor of fruit)
> ¼ teaspoon salt
> ½ cup fresh or canned fruit, drained
>
> ❧ ❧ ❧
>
> 1 Recipe Crepes à la Tar Heel

Brush a 9x13-inch baking dish with 2 tablespoons butter. In a medium bowl combine the cheeses, sugar, vanilla, and salt. Beat at medium speed with an electric mixer for 3 minutes, until smooth. Cover and chill.

Fold the 2 opposite sides of the crepe over 2 rounded tablespoons of the filling, then fold over the open ends to form a square. Place the folded blintzes seam side down in the prepared dish. Brush with melted butter. Bake in a 325° oven for 15 minutes. Garnish with fresh fruit or Tar Heel Fruit Sauce. A teaspoon of sour cream and chopped walnuts or pecans are also delicious!

Serves 5, with 3 blintzes each.

Crepes à la Tar Heel

> ¾ cup milk
> ¾ cup cold water
> 3 eggs
> 1 tablespoon sugar
> 3 teaspoons flavoring (banana, vanilla, etc.)
> 1½ cups sifted all-purpose flour
> 5 tablespoons butter, melted
>
> ❧ ❧ ❧
>
> 1 8-ounce package cream cheese, softened
> ½ cup fresh or canned fruit, drained
> 3 tablespoons confectioners' sugar
>
> ❧ ❧ ❧
>
> Tar Heel Fruit Sauce
> Sour cream and chopped walnuts or pecans for garnish

In a blender combine the milk, water, and eggs. Add the sugar, flavoring, flour, and butter. Pour ¼ cup of batter into a lightly-oiled 8-inch skillet heated over medium heat, rotating to form a thin layer. When the crepe looks dry and brown on the edges, turn and cook a few more seconds.

In a bowl whip together the cream cheese, fruit, and confectioners'

The Tar Heel Inn

sugar. Put a dollop on the crepe and roll. Top with 3 tablespoons of Tar Heel Fruit Sauce and a teaspoon of sour cream, along with a teaspoon of chopped walnuts or pecans for garnish.

Note: The cooked crepes may be kept in a 200° oven between paper towels or cloths until ready to fill.

Makes 16 crepes, or 5 servings.

Tar Heel Fruit Sauce

½ to ¾ cup sugar
1 tablespoon cornstarch (or 2 tablespoons all-purpose flour)
1 cup unsweetened fruit juice
2 teaspoons lemon or lime juice
2 tablespoons butter
1 cup fresh or canned fruit of any kind (blueberries or strawberries are especially good—use apple or orange-type juices in base)
Flavoring

In the top of a double boiler combine the sugar and cornstarch. Add the fruit juice and cook until thick and clear. Add the lemon juice and butter and cool slightly. Stir in the fruit and flavoring as desired. Serve hot or cold.

Makes 5 servings, ½ cup each.

Overnight Spiced French Toast

3 eggs
½ cup milk
2 tablespoons sugar
½ teaspoon baking powder
¼ teaspoon cinnamon
¼ teaspoon nutmeg
1 teaspoon vanilla extract
6 slices egg, French, or sourdough bread, sliced ¾-inch thick

❧ ❧ ❧

4 tablespoons butter or margarine
Sour cream, pecans, and confectioners' sugar to garnish
Dave's Special Cinnamon Syrup, warmed

In a medium bowl whisk together the eggs, milk, sugar, baking powder, cinnamon, nutmeg, and vanilla until blended. Place the bread slices on a rimmed baking sheet and slowly pour the batter over the bread. Turn the bread until it is well coated with the batter. Cover the bread with waxed paper and refrigerate overnight.

In a skillet melt the butter. Slowly fry the bread over moderate heat until golden on both sides. Do not crowd the pieces. Garnish with a dollop of sour cream and a sprinkling of pecans, and dust with confectioners' sugar. Serve warm with Cinnamon Syrup.

Note: These can be covered on a baking sheet and kept overnight in the refrigerator, or stored for 2 days in plastic bags. The end results will be light, moist, spongy-on-the-inside, crispy-on-the-outside.

Serves 6.

Dave's Special Syrup

This creamy, fragrant cinnamon syrup is the perfect topping for spiced French toast, pancakes, or waffles.

1 cup sugar
½ cup honey (or white Karo)
¼ cup water
½ teaspoon cinnamon
½ cup whipping cream

In a saucepan stir together the sugar, honey, water, and cinnamon. Bring to a boil over moderate heat, stirring constantly. Boil for 2 minutes. Remove from the heat and stir in the cream. Cool for at least 30 minutes. Syrup will thicken as it cools. Serve warm or at room temperature.

Note: Can be refrigerated for several months.

Makes 1½ cups, serving 12.

❧ ❧ ❧ ❧ ❧

Pilot Knob

Post Office Box 1280
Pilot Mountain, North Carolina 27041
(919) 325-2502

Pilot Knob is situated in a wooded landscape on the eastern slope of Pilot Mountain. Massive timbers and stone fireplaces recall a time when life was hard and simple, while comfortable furnishings and whirlpools built for two belie the fact that the inn's five cabins were converted from hundred-year-old tobacco barns. The secluded setting of each cabin allows guests to enjoy privacy, and at breakfast they can get to know one another in the dining room. The inn has a swimming pool and day sauna. The nearby Blue Ridge Parkway provides easy access to such tourist favorites as Mabry Mill and Old Salem.

Pilot Knob Breakfast Bars

½ cup margarine
½ cup brown sugar
3 tablespoons corn syrup
3 cups oatmeal

In a saucepan melt the margarine. Add the brown sugar and syrup. Stir in the oatmeal, mixing well. Spread the batter in a 11x7-inch pan. Bake in a 350° oven for 20 to 25 minutes.

Serves 8.

Monkey Bread

Chopped pecans
❧ ❧ ❧
½ cup butter or margarine
1 cup brown sugar
2 tablespoons water
½ cup chopped pecans
❧ ❧ ❧
2 cans flaky canned biscuits

Grease a tube pan. Sprinkle the bottom with pecans.

In a saucepan melt the butter and add the sugar, water, and pecans.

Cut the biscuit dough in halves and ball up (you should have 40 balls). Place 20 balls in the bottom of the prepared pan and drizzle with half of the melted mixture. Place the remaining 20 balls in the pan and top with the remaining mixture. Bake in a 350° oven for 20 to 25 minutes.

Serves 10 to 12.

Wheat Berry Bread

1 cup wheat berries
3 cups water
❧ ❧ ❧
1 ¼-ounce package active dry yeast
2 teaspoons sugar
¼ cup nonfat dry milk
3 ounces honey
3 ounces molasses
⅓ cup wheat germ
¼ teaspoon salt
6 to 8 cups all-purpose flour
1 egg, beaten
½ teaspoon coarse salt

Grease a baking sheet. In a saucepan combine the wheat berries with 3 cups of water and bring to a boil. Reduce the heat and simmer for 1½ to 2 hours until the berries are tender. Let cool in the liquid, then drain, reserving the liquid.

In a large bowl combine the yeast, sugar, dry milk, honey, molasses, wheat germ, and salt with the drained berries. Add 6 cups of flour. Measure the reserved liquid and add enough water to make about 2¼ cups, then heat until it is hot to the touch. Pour the liquid into the flour mixture and stir with a wooden spoon. Knead the dough by hand, incorporating as much of the remaining flour as needed, then turn the dough out on a floured surface and knead for 5 to 10 minutes.

Place the dough in a greased bowl, turning to cover with oil. Cover the bowl and let the dough rise until doubled, about 45 minutes. Punch down and divide the dough into 3 round loaves and let rise about 30 minutes on the prepared baking sheet. Bake in a 350° oven for about 25 minutes. Remove from the oven and brush with the beaten egg and sprinkle with the coarse salt. Return to the oven and bake an additional 25 to 30 minutes.

Makes 3 loaves.

Pilot Knob Brown Bread

2 ¼-ounce packages active dry yeast
½ cup warm water (110° to 115°)
1 cup molasses
¼ cup shortening, melted
½ cup brown sugar
1½ tablespoons salt
10 to 12 cups all-purpose flour

Grease 4 bread pans. In a large bowl dissolve the yeast in the warm water. Add the remaining ingredients, adding just enough of the flour to form a dough the texture of white bread. Knead until smooth and elastic. Place in a greased bowl and cover. Let rise until doubled in bulk. Beat down and form dough into 4 loaves. Place in the prepared pans, cover, and let rise again until doubled in bulk. Bake in a 365° oven for 15 minutes, then reduce the temperature to 350° and bake for 30 more minutes until the loaves are brown and sound hollow when tapped. Remove from the pans and brush with melted butter.

Makes 4 loaves.

Fearrington House Inn

Chapel Hill, North Carolina

Fearrington Village Center
Pittsboro, North Carolina 27312
(919) 542-2121

Reminiscent of a small European inn, Fearrington House Inn is a fourteen-room inn that maintains membership in Relais and Chateaux, an association of 350 deluxe hotels and gourmet restaurants in thirty-seven countries. Guests enjoy attentive service unsurpassed. Each room is a unique blend of architecture, antiques, artwork, and fabrics. The inn is the result of a decade-long search for original artwork, English antiques, and hand-picked appointments. Even the beautiful pine plank flooring came from an old English workhouse. Guests may wish to wander in the beautifully landscaped grounds, curl up with a good book in the courtyard, or relax with others with wine and cheese in the garden house.

Fearrington House Cooler

2 peaches
1 bottle (750 ml) white wine
Handful assorted mints: orange, spearmint

Place the peaches in boiling water a few seconds so that the skin can be easily removed. Remove the skin and place the whole fruit in a pitcher with the wine and mints. Let steep 4 hours before serving. Pour over ice in stemmed goblets and garnish each with a sprig of mint or a peach slice.

Serves 6.

Chilled Tomato Soup with Basil Sorbet

2 tablespoons butter
1 onion, chopped
1 leek, chopped
2 carrots, chopped
3 to 3½ pounds fresh tomatoes,
    peeled, seeded, and chopped
1 orange rind, grated
1 to 2 drops Tabasco
½ teaspoon salt
Freshly ground pepper
2 cups water
1 cup chicken stock
1 bouquet garni (basil, thyme,
    parsley, chives, summer savory,
    and dill)
1½ cups heavy cream
1 recipe Basil Sorbet

In a large saucepan melt the butter. Add the onion, leek, and carrots. Cook over medium heat about 8 minutes or until soft and translucent but not browned. Add the tomatoes, orange rind, Tabasco, salt, pepper, water, and chicken stock. Make a bouquet garni by tying the herbs in a square piece of cheesecloth. Place in the pot. Cover and simmer 30 to 40 minutes over a low flame. Remove the bouquet garni and set the soup aside to cool. Purée in a blender or food processor. Cool to room temperature and add the heavy cream. Chill. Serve the soup in individual bowls with a scoop of basil sorbet in the center of each. Garnish with fresh basil.

Serves 6.

Basil Sorbet

½ cup sugar
1½ cups water
Juice of 2 lemons
2 lemon rinds, grated
½ cup finely minced parsley
1½ cups finely minced basil
Fresh basil leaves for garnish

In a large saucepan dissolve the sugar in the water and bring to a boil to make a syrup. Cool and combine the remaining ingredients with the syrup. Freeze.

Makes approximately 2 cups.

Shrimp and Scallops
in Scallop Pastry Shells

Prepare the pastry shells and shrimp a day ahead. The actual cooking takes only minutes, since the seafood needs to be cooked quickly.

3 tablespoons butter
1 tablespoon olive oil
2 large shallots, minced
2 large cloves garlic, minced
⅓ cup minced green pepper
⅓ cup minced red bell pepper (if
    available)
3 ounces mushrooms, minced
1 medium-size carrot, minced
1 sprig fresh thyme
¾ cup dry white wine
¼ teaspoon salt
Freshly ground pepper
1 pound scallops, cleaned and with
    beards removed
½ pound shrimp, cleaned and
    cooked
6 to 8 cherry tomatoes, halved and
    seeded
1 recipe Scallop Pastry Shells
1 tablespoon minced mixed herbs
    (tarragon, parsley, chervil,
    chives)

In a skillet melt the butter, add the olive oil, and sauté the shallots and garlic over medium heat for 2 minutes. Add the peppers, mushrooms, carrots, and thyme. Cook about 10 minutes or until crispy tender. Incorporate the wine and raise the heat to reduce the liquid slightly. Blend in the salt and pepper. Add the scallops and cook over low heat for 1 to 2 minutes. Mix in the shrimp and tomatoes and heat through. Divide the mixture among the scallop pastry shells and garnish with minced herbs.

Serves 6.

Fearrington House Inn

Scallop Pastry Shells

Natural scallop shells (which are used as molds in this recipe) are available at most kitchen supply stores, since they are commonly used for Coquilles St. Jacques.

> 1 recipe Never-Fail Pastry
> 12 scallop shells

Roll the pastry to ⅛-inch thickness. Cut into 6 circles roughly 2 inches larger in diameter than the scallop shells. Ease the circle into the shell, shaping it to the exact dimensions of the shell. Trim off the excess pastry. Prick the shell and weight it (to keep from shrinking) by placing an empty scallop shell on top. Bake in a 425° oven for 10 minutes. Remove the top shell and continue baking until the pastry is golden brown. Carefully remove the pastry from the shell and cool on a rack.

Makes 6 shells.

Never-Fail Pastry

This dough may be kept in the refrigerator for 3 days or frozen. No matter how much it is handled, it will always be flaky and tender. When it is rolled, it behaves exactly as desired.

> 2 cups unbleached flour
> 1½ teaspoons sugar
> 1 teaspoon salt
> ¾ cup shortening
>
> ❧ ❧ ❧
>
> 1 egg
> ¼ cup water
> 1½ teaspoons vinegar

In a large bowl mix the flour, sugar, and salt together with a pastry blender. Cut the shortening into the mixture until the pieces resemble coarse meal.

In a separate bowl beat the egg with the water and vinegar. Combine the two mixtures by tossing with two forks until all the ingredients are moistened and may be gathered into a ball. Chill before rolling.

Yields two 9-inch pie crusts.

Snow Peas and Sugar Snaps
in Lemon Thyme Butter

> 2 tablespoons butter, softened
> ½ teaspoon lemon juice
> ½ teaspoon finely minced parsley
> 1½ teaspoons finely minced lemon thyme
> 6 ounces snow peas
> 12 ounces sugar snap peas

In a medium bowl mix the butter with the lemon juice, parsley, and lemon thyme. Set aside. String both the snow peas and the sugar snaps on both ends. Cook the snow peas in boiling water for 1 minute, drain in a colander, and refresh under cold water briefly to stop the cooking process. Cook the sugar snaps for 2 minutes, drain, and refresh briefly under cold water. Mix the snow peas and the sugar snaps together while still warm and toss with the herbed butter.

Serves 6.

Squash Gratin
with White Cheddar Cheese

> 1 medium-sized onion, thinly sliced
> 2 pounds yellow squash, thinly sliced
> 1 teaspoon salt
> Freshly ground pepper
>
> ❧ ❧ ❧
>
> 2 eggs
> 2 tablespoons sugar
> ½ cup milk
> ½ pound Vermont or New York white Cheddar cheese, grated
> 1 to 2 tablespoons butter

In a saucepan cook the onions and squash in a small amount of boiling water for 10 to 15 minutes or until fork tender. Drain well. Arrange in a 2-quart baking dish. Add the salt and pepper.

In a medium bowl combine the eggs, sugar, milk, and cheese. Pour over the squash mixture and dot with thin slices of butter. Bake in a 350° oven for 45 minutes. Cut into squares and then into diamonds to make a prettier shape on the plate.

Serves 6 to 8.

❧ ❧ ❧ ❧ ❧

Shortbread
with Lemon Curd and Blackberry Sauce

Each component of this special dessert is simple to prepare. The result is something available only during the summertime.

> 1 cup butter, softened
> ⅔ cup confectioners' sugar
> 2 cups unbleached flour
> Pinch salt
> ¼ teaspoon almond extract
>
> ❧ ❧ ❧
>
> 1 recipe Blackberry Sauce
> 1 recipe Lemon Curd
> 24 fresh blackberries

Line a 9x13-inch pan with parchment paper. In a large bowl cream together the butter and sugar until light and fluffy. In a separate bowl sift the flour and salt together and add to the creamed mixture. Mix in the almond extract. Pat the dough into the prepared pan. Bake in a 325° oven for 35 to 40 minutes or until the center feels firm when gently pressed. The shortbread should not brown. Remove from the pan and cut into 8 squares, and then cut each square into 2 triangles while still warm. Cool on a rack.

Ladle ¼ cup of the blackberry sauce into a dessert plate. Top with 2 shortbread triangles, 2 tablespoons of lemon curd, and 3 fresh blackberries. Garnish with a white or yellow marigold.

Serves 8.

Lemon Curd

5 egg yolks
¾ cup sugar
Juice and grated rind of 2 large
lemons
¼ cup unsalted butter

In the top of a double boiler over simmering water combine the egg yolks and sugar over low heat. Gradually add the lemon juice, stirring constantly for 12 to 15 minutes until the mixture coats the back of a spoon and is thickened. Do not let the mixture boil. Remove from the heat and continue stirring until slightly cool. Cut the butter into small pieces and blend into the lemon mixture with the grated lemon rind. Cool and refrigerate.

Makes 1 to 1¼ cups.

Blackberry Sauce

⅔ cup sugar
1 tablespoon cornstarch
Pinch salt
⅔ cup water
1 lemon rind, grated

🥢 🥢 🥢

2 cups fresh blackberries

In a saucepan combine the sugar with the cornstarch and salt, mixing until completely blended with no lumps. Add the water and grated lemon rind. Cook and stir until the mixture comes to a boil and is thick.

Push the blackberries through a strainer to remove the seeds. Add to the mixture and return to the boiling point. Remove from the heat and cool. Chill.

Makes 2 cups.

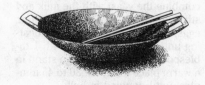

Pine Needles Resort

Post Office Box 88
Southern Pines, North Carolina 28387
(919) 692-7111

Pine Needles is a small, intimate resort for those who desire a private club away from home that offers the finest in accommodations, recreation, and dining. The rustic club house overlooks one of the most popular golf courses in the area and includes a spa with weight room, sauna and whirlpool, a heated swimming pool, and lighted tennis courts. Dining at Pine Needles is always a delightful experience, and relaxing at the "In the Rough" bar is a pleasant way to unwind after a day of golfing. The inn limits itself to 140 guests.

Pollo à la Pine Needles

This is a splendid dish. Serve with a white Cabernet.

1 teaspoon minced garlic
1 teaspoon minced shallots
½ cup butter
½ cup chopped red and green
peppers

🥢 🥢 🥢

1 8-ounce boneless split chicken
breast
1 cup all-purpose flour
½ cup butter
¾ pound mushrooms, sliced
Salt and pepper to taste
1 cup white wine
Phyllo dough
1 egg
1 tablespoon water

In a 2½-quart skillet sauté the garlic and shallots in ½ cup of butter. Add the peppers and cook until soft. Re-

move the pepper mixture from the skillet. In the same skillet melt the remaining butter. Flour the chicken breast and sauté until each side is glazed. Add the mushrooms and white wine, and season to taste. Simmer for 2 to 3 minutes. Place the chicken breast on the phyllo dough. Top with the pepper mixture and the mushrooms. Fold the dough over the chicken and vegetables, leaving no holes. Beat the egg with the water and brush the mixture over the dough. Place on a cookie sheet. Bake in a 350° oven for 10 minutes. Garnish as desired.

Serves 2.

Recipe courtesy Executive Chef Donato Sassano.

Mill Farm Inn

Post Office Box 1251
Tryon, North Carolina 28782
(704) 859-6992

Guests at Mill Farm Inn enjoy a true home-like atmosphere. Most of the attractive bedrooms with private baths have king-size beds; the spacious living room has a glowing fireplace; and the Pacolet River flows past the rear boundary of the large yard in which the inn sits. Bird-watching is a favorite pastime here. A complimentary continental breakfast of specialty breads that vary daily, English muffins, cereal, juice, preserves and jelly, coffee, tea and milk is served each morning.

Pumpkin Bread

12 cups sugar
4 cups oil or margarine
16 eggs
4 16-ounce cans pumpkin
14 cups self-rising flour
2 tablespoons plus 2 teaspoons
   baking soda
2 tablespoons plus 2 teaspoons salt
4 teaspoons baking powder
4 teaspoons nutmeg
4 teaspoons allspice
4 teaspoons cinnamon
2⅔ cups water

Grease and flour 9 loaf pans. In a large bowl cream together the sugar and oil. Add the eggs and pumpkin, mixing well. In a separate bowl sift together the dry ingredients and add alternately with the water to the creamed mixture. Pour the batter into the prepared pans. Bake in a 350° oven for 1 hour and 30 minutes. Let stand for 10 minutes.
Makes 9 loaves.

Banana Bread

30 overripe bananas
8 cups sugar
8 eggs
12 cups self-rising flour
2 cups margarine, melted
8 teaspoons baking soda
4 teaspoons salt
4 teaspoons baking powder

Grease 8 loaf pans. In a large bowl mash the bananas with a fork. Stir in the other ingredients. Pour the batter into the prepared pans. Bake in a 350° oven for 1 hour and 30 minutes. Let stand for 10 minutes.
Makes 8 loaves.

Brown Breakfast Bread

3 cups honey
3 cups molasses
14 cups wheat flour
8 teaspoons baking soda
5½ teaspoons baking powder
8 teaspoons ginger
8 teaspoons cinnamon
8 teaspoons allspice
4 dashes salt
8 cups milk
4 cups raisins
Small jar marmalade

Grease 8 loaf pans. In a large bowl beat together the honey and molasses. Add the dry ingredients and stir in the milk, raisins, and marmalade. Pour the batter into the prepared pans. Bake in a 350° oven for 2 hours.
Makes 8 loaves.

Oatmeal Applesauce Bread

10 cups sifted self-rising flour
6 cups sugar
8 teaspoons salt
8 teaspoons baking powder
8 teaspoons baking soda
4 teaspoons cinnamon
4 teaspoons nutmeg
8 cups oatmeal
4 cups raisins
8 cups applesauce
2⅔ cups oil or margarine
16 large eggs
3 cups milk

Grease and flour 8 loaf pans. In a large bowl sift together the dry ingredients. Stir in the oatmeal and raisins. In a separate bowl beat together the applesauce, oil, eggs, and milk. Make a well in the center of the dry ingredients and pour in the applesauce mixture. Stir only until moistened. Pour the batter into the prepared pans. Bake in a 350° oven for 55 to 60 minutes. Let cool before removing from the pans.
Makes 8 loaves.

Stone Hedge Inn

Post Office Box 366
Tryon, North Carolina 28782
(704) 859-9114

Situated in a spectacular setting at the base of Tryon Mountain, the Stone Hedge Inn provides a restful haven for the weary traveler and a retreat for couples looking for a cozy getaway weekend. Each guest room has a private bath, color television, air conditioning, and a beautiful mountain view. The dining room serves the finest of foods, and the service is what one expects from a fine country inn.

Christmas Stollen

2 ¼-ounce packages active dry yeast
1 cup lukewarm milk (110° to 115°)
5 to 5½ cups all-purpose flour
2 eggs
½ teaspoon salt
½ teaspoon almond or vanilla
   extract
1 cup butter, softened
½ cup sugar
¼ cup chopped lemon or orange
   peel
⅔ cup seedless raisins
⅔ cup dried currants
½ cup slivered, blanched almonds
      ❧ ❧ ❧
½ cup butter, melted
⅔ cup confectioners' sugar

Grease a baking sheet. In a large bowl combine the yeast with the milk and stir to dissolve. Add 4 cups of flour, eggs, salt, and almond extract, beating until smooth. Sprinkle with 1 tablespoon of flour. Let dough stand in a warm place for about 30 to 45 minutes, until doubled in bulk.

Punch down and place on a lightly floured surface. Knead in 1 cup of softened butter, sugar, and remaining flour, until smooth and well blended. Knead in the orange peel, raisins, currants, and almonds. Divide the dough in half and roll each portion to a 9x6-inch oval shape ¾-inch thick. Fold one long side ¾ over to the other side. Gently press the edges together to make a 3x9-inch loaf. Place on the prepared baking sheet and cover. Let rise in a warm place for 30 to 45 minutes, until doubled in bulk.

Brush the loaves with ¼ cup of melted butter. Bake in a 400° oven for 25 to 35 minutes or until golden brown. Brush with the remaining ¼ cup of melted butter and sprinkle with the confectioners' sugar. Return to the oven for 1 minute. Remove and cool on racks.

Makes 2 loaves.

Zucchini Nut Muffins

    4 cups sugar
    6 cups all-purpose flour
    2 teaspoons cinnamon
    2 teaspoons salt
    2 teaspoons baking powder
    2 teaspoons baking soda
       ⦂ã ⦂ã ⦂ã
    8 eggs
    2 cups oil
    4 cups shredded zucchini
    1 cup golden raisins
    1 cup chopped pecans
    2 teaspoons vanilla extract

Grease 48 muffin cups. In a large bowl mix together the dry ingredients and set aside.

In a separate bowl beat the eggs with a whisk and slowly incorporate the oil. Stir in the zucchini, raisins, pecans, and vanilla. Stir the liquid ingredients into the dry ingredients, mixing well. Pour the batter into the prepared muffin cups. Bake in a 350° oven for 25 to 30 minutes. Let cool in the pan for 10 minutes, then remove to a rack.

Makes 48 muffins.

Hallcrest Inn, Inc.

299 Halltop Circle
Waynesville, North Carolina 28786
(704) 456-6457

Overlooking the Waynesville Valley in beautiful western North Carolina sits a 110-year-old farmhouse now known as Hallcrest Inn. This small country inn features home-style cooking served around the large lazy-susan tables. The charm of the old house is enhanced by the many family treasures and keepsakes throughout. Its warm hospitality bespeaks the genuine pleasure its owners, Russell and Margaret Burson, take in catering to their guests.

Apple Cheese Casserole

This is delicious and could be used as a side dish or dessert.

    1 can sweetened apples, undrained
       (not pie filling)
       ⦂ã ⦂ã ⦂ã
    ½ cup butter, softened
    8 ounces Velveeta cheese, room
       temperature
    ¾ cup all-purpose flour
    1 cup sugar

Place the apples in a casserole dish.

In a medium bowl combine the butter, cheese, flour, and sugar, blending until smooth. Spread topping over the apples. Bake in a 325° oven for 30 to 45 minutes until brown.

Serves 6.

Hallcrest Inn

Beet Salad

2 jars pickled beets, diced
1 cup chopped celery
1 medium onion, chopped
1 10-ounce package green peas,
**   thawed**
Dash salt
Mayonnaise

In a large bowl combine all the ingredients, blending in enough mayonnaise to moisten. Chill.
Serves 6.

Cornbread Casserole

1 17-ounce can cream-style corn
1 cup sour cream
½ cup oil
3 eggs
1 cup self-rising cornmeal

In a large bowl combine all the ingredients. Pour into a casserole dish. Bake in a 400° oven for 45 minutes.
Serves 6.

Garden Muffins

This is extra good in the summer when friends' gardens are overflowing with vegetables and they share them with you!

3 cups all-purpose flour
1½ cups sugar
1 teaspoon cinnamon
1 teaspoon salt
¾ teaspoon baking soda
1 teaspoon baking powder
2 cups combination of shredded
**   yellow squash, zucchini, and**
**   carrots**

    ❧ ❧ ❧

3 eggs
1 cup oil
1 teaspoon vanilla extract

Grease 24 muffin tins. In a large bowl stir together the dry ingredients and vegetables.

In a separate bowl beat together the eggs, oil, and vanilla. Pour over the dry ingredients, stirring just until moistened. Pour batter into muffin tins. Bake in a 350° oven for 15 minutes.

Makes 24 muffins.

Anderson Guest House

520 Orange Street
Wilmington, North Carolina 28401
(919) 343-8128

Guests of the Anderson Guest House enjoy the charm and privacy of guest house accommodations in historic downtown Wilmington. Each room has a bath, fireplace, and air conditioner, and overlooks a private garden.

Anderson Guest House Crepes

1 cup milk
2 eggs
¾ cup all-purpose flour

    ❧ ❧ ❧

Dry Ridge Inn

26 Brown Street
Weaverville, North Carolina 28787
(704) 658-3899

Built in 1849 as a parsonage for what then was the Salem Campground, the Dry Ridge Inn is but a ten-minute drive from downtown Asheville. During the Civil War it was used as a camp hospital for Confederate soldiers suffering from pneumonia. Today it is a pleasant inn with comfortable accommodations. A full country breakfast is served.

    ❧ ❧ ❧ ❧ ❧

Dry Ridge Inn
ca. 1849

1 pint whipping cream
1 egg
1 tablespoon sugar
Fresh fruit such as bananas,
    blueberries, peaches, or
    strawberries

In a blender combine the milk, 2 eggs, and flour. Prepare the crepes (makes 10), reserving 4 and freezing the rest.

In a small saucepan combine the whipping cream, 1 egg, and sugar. Over low heat stir the mixture with a whisk for 5 minutes, until slightly thickened. Do not heat fast or the eggs will curdle. Add the fruit and pour over the crepes. Very delicious!

Serves 2.

Baked Eggs Florentine Piquante

⅔ cup mayonnaise
¼ teaspoon salt
⅛ teaspoon pepper
1 teaspoon Worcestershire sauce
½ teaspoon grated onion
¼ cup milk
1 cup grated sharp Cheddar cheese

&a   &a   &a

1 10-ounce package frozen spinach,
    cooked and well drained
6 eggs

Butter 6 custard cups. In a saucepan combine the mayonnaise, salt, pepper, Worcestershire sauce, and onion. Add the milk gradually, blending until smooth. Add the cheese and cook over low heat, stirring constantly for 5 minutes, until the cheese melts and the mixture is thick and smooth. Place a small amount of the sauce in the bottom of each of the prepared custard cups and cover with the spinach. Break an egg into each cup and cover with 2 tablespoons of the sauce and add additional cheese, if desired. Bake in a 350° oven for 15 to 30 minutes, until the eggs are the desired consistency.

Serves 6.

The Colonel Ludlow House

Summit and West Fifth
Winston-Salem, North Carolina 27101
(919) 777-1887

This charming Victorian house built by Jacob Lott Ludlow in 1887 has been restored and converted into a luxurious bed and breakfast inn. The formal parlor, dining room, and unique guest rooms (each with a private bath and some with a two-person whirlpool tub) are furnished with beautiful period antiques. In the historic west end community of Winston-Salem, it is within walking distance of restaurants, cafés, shops, and parks.

Only slightly farther away, but also within walking distance, is the downtown business district.

Bacon-Cheddar Muffins

1¾ cups all-purpose flour
½ cup shredded sharp Cheddar
    cheese
¼ cup sugar
2 teaspoons baking powder
¼ teaspoon salt
¼ teaspoon ground red pepper

&a   &a   &a

1 egg, beaten
¾ cup milk
⅓ cup oil
6 strips bacon, crisp-cooked and
    crumbled

Line or grease 8 muffin cups and top of pan, and sprinkle with cornmeal. In a large bowl stir together the flour, cheese, sugar, baking powder, salt, and red pepper.

The Colonel Ludlow House

In a separate bowl combine the egg, milk, and oil. Make a well in the center of the dry ingredients and add the liquid mixture, stirring just until moistened. Batter should be lumpy. Fold in the crumbled bacon. Fill the prepared muffin cups to the top. Bake in a 400° oven for 20 to 25 minutes.

Makes 8 muffins.

Grasshopper Cheesecake

1½ cups chocolate wafer crumbs
   (about 26 wafers)
¼ cup butter, melted

☙ ☙ ☙

1½ cups sugar
4 eggs
1 egg yolk
¼ cup plus 2 tablespoons white or
   green crème de menthe
3 tablespoons white crème de cacao
3 8-ounce packages cream cheese,
   softened

☙ ☙ ☙

4 1-ounce squares semi-sweet
   chocolate
½ cup sour cream

In a medium bowl combine the wafer crumbs and butter. Press into the bottom of an 8-inch springform pan.

In a large bowl mix the sugar with the eggs, adding one egg at a time and beating after each addition. Add the egg yolk, beating in well. Stir in the crème de menthe and crème de cacao. Beat in the cream cheese. Spoon the mixture into the crust. Bake in a 350° oven for 1 hour or until set.

In the top of a double boiler or in the microwave melt the chocolate. Allow to cool and stir in the sour cream. Spread the mixture over the top of the cool cheesecake. Chill well before cutting.

Serves 8.

Lowe-Alston House

204 Cascade Avenue
Winston-Salem, North Carolina 27127
(919) 727-1211

Built in 1912, this Greek Revival residence is listed on the National Register of Historic Places. Convenient to Old Salem, the North Carolina School of the Arts, and downtown Winston-Salem, the inn provides guest rooms with queen-size poster beds, footed bathtubs, and shared baths. Breakfast is served in the formal dining room or in the privacy of one's own room.

English Muffin Spread

1 cup shredded Cheddar cheese
½ cup mayonnaise
½ cup black olives, drained
½ teaspoon paprika
½ teaspoon black pepper
Dash Tabasco (optional)

In a food processor blend all the ingredients. Spread on English muffin halves and broil until toasted. Serve hot.

Note: The spread can be prepared and kept in the refrigerator.

Makes about 2 cups.

North Dakota

Eva's Bed and Breakfast

Star Route, Box 10
Wing, North Dakota 58494

Eva's Bed and Breakfast is in the rolling hills three miles west of Wing on Highway 36, two miles north, and one-fourth mile west. The home is a ranch style, built in 1983. It has two bedrooms, an office, kitchen, dining room, living room, and a utility room on the main floor, and two bedrooms, bath, and large family room with fireplace, hot tub, and television in the basement. The innkeepers are semi-retired and help with their son's 3,500-acre ranch and farm. Pony rides are available and a tour of the farm/ranch operation can be arranged. Area interests include Michel Lake for good fishing, picnics, and boating. Other attractions are the zoo, Heritage Center, museums, and libraries.

Oriental Salad

10 ounces macaroni rings
¾ cup mayonnaise
2 tablespoons soy sauce
2 tablespoons oyster sauce
1 teaspoon hot mustard
1 teaspoon salt
¼ teaspoon garlic salt
Dash white pepper

≈ ≈ ≈

1 6-ounce can bean sprouts, drained
1 cup frozen peas, thawed
½ cup diced celery
⅓ cup diced green pepper
⅓ cup chopped onion
1 6-ounce can water chestnuts, drained
1 2-ounce can mushrooms, drained
Carrots for color

Prepare the macaroni according to the package directions. Drain. In a large bowl combine the mayonnaise, soy sauce, oyster sauce, hot mustard, salt, garlic salt, and white pepper. Add the macaroni and remaining ingredients and mix well.

Serves 4.

Popovers

4 eggs
2 cups milk
2 cups all-purpose flour
1 teaspoon salt

Grease 12 muffin cups. In a medium bowl lightly beat the eggs. Add the milk, flour, and salt. Fill popover pan cups ¾ full. Bake in a 450° oven for 25 minutes. Reduce the oven temperature to 350° and bake for 15 to 20 more minutes. Remove.

Makes 12 popovers.

Ohio

The Frederick Fitting House

A Bed and Breakfast Country Inn
72 Fitting Avenue
Bellville, Ohio 44813
(419) 886-2863

Frederick Fitting was a prominent Bellville citizen who built this home in 1863. A contractor, farmer, and financier, he brought the railroad to Bellville. His home reflects the grand mid-western tradition of rural hospitality in a village setting. It has three rooms for guests: the Colonial Room, the Shaker Room, and the Victorian Room. Each is decorated as its name suggests. The semi-private bath is newly remodeled with hand-painted Italian tile and matching wallpaper. The village of Bellville offers visitors a highly regarded smorgasbord restaurant named The San-Dar, a fine golf course, hard surface tennis courts, an abundance of Victorian homes with intricate nineteenth-century gingerbread trim, pleasant walks, jogging trails in all directions, and a collection of little shops along Main Street. Canoeing and skiing (both downhill and cross-country) are available within a few minutes' drive.

๒ล ๒ล ๒ล ๒ล ๒ล

Baked Omelette

½ cup unsalted butter
12 eggs
Salt and pepper
Tabasco sauce
½ cup all-purpose flour
1 teaspoon baking powder
2 cups sautéed sausage
1 cup fresh mushrooms, sautéed
1 pound Monterey Jack cheese, shredded
1 pint small curd cottage cheese

In a 9x13-inch baking dish melt the butter. In a large bowl beat the eggs with the salt and pepper. Add 5 to 6 drops of Tabasco. Stir in the flour, baking powder, sausage, mushrooms, and the cheeses. Add half of the melted butter from the baking dish. Pour batter into the baking dish. Bake in a 400° oven for 15 minutes. Reduce the temperature to 350° and bake for 20 more minutes, or until browned on top. Let set for at least 10 minutes before cutting into squares.

Serves 8 to 12.

Breakfast Strudels

10½ tablespoons unsalted butter, melted
1½ tablespoons all-purpose flour
¾ cup milk
6 tablespoons grated cheese (Swiss, Muenster, Monterey Jack, or Mozzarella)
2 tablespoons freshly grated Parmesan cheese
½ teaspoon salt
Pinch paprika
Nutmeg to taste

๒ล ๒ล ๒ล

¼ pound seasoned bulk pork sausage (or crumbled fried bacon, diced ham, or Canadian bacon)
5 eggs
1 teaspoon thyme
1 teaspoon basil
Freshly ground black pepper

๒ล ๒ล ๒ล

6 sheets phyllo dough

Brush a rimmed baking sheet with melted butter. In a saucepan over medium-high heat combine 1½ tablespoons of the butter with the flour, stirring for 3 minutes. Whisk in the milk, constantly stirring for 2 to 3 minutes until the mixture comes to a boil and thickens. Remove from the heat and stir in the cheeses a little at a time. Add ¼ teaspoon of salt and the paprika. Season with the nutmeg. Pour mixture into a medium bowl.

In a skillet cook the sausage until no longer pink, breaking the meat into small pieces. Drain on paper towels. In a separate bowl combine the eggs, thyme, basil, ¼ teaspoon of salt, and pepper. Add the sausage.

In a large heavy skillet melt 1 tablespoon of the butter. Add the egg mixture and stir until just set and scrambled. Mix the eggs into the cheese sauce and cool completely.

Arrange 1 phyllo sheet of dough on a work surface (keep the remaining sheets covered with a damp towel). Brush the sheet with melted butter, fold in half, and brush again with the butter. Spoon ⅓ cup of filling onto the end of the dough. Spread the filling in a strip, leaving a border on the edges.

Fold the edges over the filling. Starting at the end with the filling, fold the dough up to form a package. Place the package seam side down on the baking sheet. Brush the top with butter. Repeat with the remaining pastry. Bake in a 375° oven for 15 minutes, until golden brown. Allow to cool 5 minutes before serving.

Note: Dough can be prepared with filling ahead of time, wrapped tightly in plastic wrap and refrigerated. Let stand at room temperature before baking.

Serves 6.

Brunch Eggs with Spanish Sauce

    1 loaf sliced white bread
    ½ cup butter
    6 eggs
    3 cups milk
    ¾ teaspoon dry mustard
    ¾ teaspoon white pepper
    4 cups grated Cheddar cheese

    ❧ ❧ ❧

    ⅓ cup chopped onion
    ¼ cup chopped green pepper
    ¾ cup sliced fresh mushrooms
    3 tablespoons oil
    1 tablespoon cornstarch
    1 16-ounce can tomatoes, undrained
    1 teaspoon salt
    Dash pepper
    2 teaspoons sugar
    Dash cayenne

Butter a 9x13-inch casserole. Butter both sides of the bread and cut in cubes. Set aside. In a medium bowl combine the eggs, milk, mustard, and pepper. Layer the cheese and bread cubes in the prepared casserole. Pour the egg mixture over the cheese and bread, cover, and refrigerate for 8 to 12 hours or overnight. Bake uncovered in at 350° oven for 30 to 45 minutes, or until the eggs are set.

In a large skillet brown the onion, green pepper, and mushrooms in the oil. In a small bowl combine the cornstarch with 2 tablespoons of the liquid from the tomatoes and add to the vegetable mixture. Add the tomatoes, remaining liquid, salt, pepper, sugar, and cayenne. Cook over low heat, stirring often, for 15 to 20 minutes, until the vegetables are tender and the sauce is slightly thickened. Serve with the Brunch Eggs.

Serves 8.

Andrews' German Village Bed and Breakfast

1058 Jaeger Street
Columbus, Ohio 43206
(614) 444-7222

This German-style brick home built in the 1880s is situated across from lovely Schiller Park, where guests can enjoy theater under the stars or open-air concerts all summer or a brisk walk among its three hundred trees year-round. Rooms have twin or queen beds, televison, and a shared bath. The inn is in German Village with its brick streets and sidewalks, quaint brick homes with wrought iron fences, shops, and restaurants.

Lauren's Scallops

    1 pound bay scallops
    1 large green pepper, diced
    ½ small Bermuda onion, diced
    ½ can (3 ounces) whole water
        chestnuts
    ¼ teaspoon cracked pepper seed
    ¼ teaspoon ground black pepper
    ¼ teaspoon coriander
    ½ teaspoon sweet basil
    ¾ 15-ounce can tomato sauce
    Cornstarch

    ❧ ❧ ❧

    Rice or noodles

In a large skillet combine the scallops, green pepper, onion, and water chestnuts. Season with the pepper seed, black pepper, coriander, and basil. Stir in the tomato sauce,

The Frederick Fitting House

thicken with the cornstarch, and simmer for 30 minutes. Serve over rice or noodles.

Serves 2 to 3.

Lyle House Bed and Breakfast

825 Ebner Street
Columbus, Ohio 43206
(614) 443-9859

This one hundred-year-old brick home is furnished with antiques and eighteenth century reproductions. For the music lover, there are dulcimers, banjos, recorders, and piano; for animal lovers, there is the innkeeper's collie: Highland. Two guest rooms, one in country farmhouse motif and the other in Colonial, are offered. Lyle House is within walking distance of the shops and restaurants of German Village.

Hot Spiced Wassail

A good drink for any cold, winter night or day. Guests enjoy a cup when they first arrive.

    2 tablespoons whole cloves
    1 tablespoon whole allspice
    6 cinnamon sticks
    1 cup brown sugar
    4 cups water
        ❧ ❧ ❧
    ½ teaspoon salt (optional)
    5 cups pineapple juice
    4 cups cranberry juice
    2 cups grape juice
        ❧ ❧ ❧
    Orange slices and whole cloves

In a saucepan combine the spices with the brown sugar and water. Simmer together for 15 minutes. Strain through several layers of cheesecloth (or place the spices in a tea steeper).

In a large saucepan combine the salt and fruit juices. Add the strained spice mixture and simmer for 20 to 30 minutes. Serve from a warmed punch bowl or electric coffee pot. Float a clove-studded orange slice in each cup, if desired.

Makes 1 gallon.

The Inn on Kelleys Island

Box 11
Kelleys Island, Ohio 43438
(419) 746-2258

Guests of the Inn on Kelleys Island may relax on the Victorian porch overlooking Lake Erie, chat with other guests in front of a crackling fire in the marble fireplace, or cast a line off the private beach. Built in 1876, the home became an inn about 1905. It is the former home of Captain Frank Hamilton, a marine historian of the Great Lakes and Kelleys Island. In the National Historic District of Kelleys Island, the inn is conveniently near the ferry dock and only minutes from the island's restaurants. Its beautiful surroundings, relaxing atmosphere, and old-fashioned charm make this a delightful place to visit.

Spinach Cheese Appetizers

    ⅓ cup butter or margarine
    3 eggs
    1 cup all-purpose flour
    1 cup milk
    1 teaspoon salt
    1 teaspoon baking powder
    1 10-ounce package frozen chopped
        spinach
    ½ pound Monterey Jack cheese,
        grated
    ½ pound jalapeño pepper cheese,
        grated

In a 9x13-inch glass baking dish melt the butter. In a large bowl beat the eggs. Add the flour, milk, salt, and baking powder, blending with a beater until smooth. Thaw the spinach and squeeze dry. Add the spinach and the grated cheeses to the egg mixture, mixing well. Spoon the mixture into the prepared dish. Bake in a 350° oven for 35 minutes. Cool slightly before cutting into small squares.

Note: Freezes well.

Serves 60.

Pumpkin Pie Dessert

    1 18½-ounce package yellow cake
        mix, with 1 cup reserved
    ½ cup butter or margarine, melted
    1 egg, slightly beaten
        ❧ ❧ ❧
    1 1-pound, 13-ounce can pumpkin
    ⅔ cup milk
    ½ cup brown sugar
    3 eggs
    1½ teaspoons cinnamon
    ¼ cup sugar
        ❧ ❧ ❧
    ¼ cup butter, softened
    ½ cup brown sugar
    ⅔ cup whole walnuts
        ❧ ❧ ❧
    8 ounces whipped cream

Grease and flour a 9x13-inch pan. In a medium bowl mix together the cake mix, ½ cup of melted butter, and 1 egg. Press into the prepared pan.

In a large bowl combine the pumpkin, milk, ½ cup of brown sugar, 3 eggs, cinnamon, and sugar. Mix thoroughly and pour over the cake mix in the pan.

In a medium bowl combine the reserved cake mix, ¼ cup of softened butter, and ½ cup of brown sugar, mixing until crumbly. Sprinkle on top of the filling.

Top with the walnuts. Bake in a 350° oven for 55 minutes. Cool and serve with whipped cream.

Serves 15 to 18.

Country Manor

6315 Zoar Road
Morrow, Ohio 45152
(513) 899-2440

Country Manor, circa 1868, is situated on fifty-five rolling acres overlooking the Little Miami River valley. The house has a large center hall, hardwood floors, high ceilings, original woodwork, and central air conditioning. The full country breakfast varies from day to day. Guests can walk in the woods, feed the fish in the pond, ride the wagon pulled by the Belgian draft horse team, swing on the front porch while sipping cold lemonade, or enjoy hot tea in front of a crackling fire in the family room.

Country Manor Scrambled Egg Bake

Great served with salsa!

¼ cup margarine
1 medium onion, chopped
½ large green pepper, chopped
1 tablespoon minced garlic
1 4-ounce can mushroom pieces and stems, drained
12 eggs, scrambled with a little water
½ cup chopped ham
2 cups frozen hash browns
1 cup shredded cheese (your favorite)

In a skillet melt the margarine and cook the onion, green pepper, and garlic together until transparent. Add the mushrooms and eggs, cooking just until done. In a baking dish layer the potatoes, scrambled eggs, ham, and cheese. Bake in a 350° oven for 10 minutes until set.

Note: If using hash browns, brown and cook for 15 minutes before adding to baking dish.

Serves 6 to 8.

Strawberry-Pecan Bread

1½ cups all-purpose flour
1 cup sugar
½ teaspoon salt
½ teaspoon baking soda
1½ teaspoons cinnamon
½ cup oil
¼ cup margarine, melted
2 eggs
1 10-ounce package frozen strawberries, syrup pack
½ cup chopped pecans

Grease and flour 2 small loaf pans or 4 mini loaf pans. In a large bowl combine the flour, sugar, salt, baking soda, and cinnamon. Blend in the oil and margarine. Add the eggs, beating well. Crush the strawberries in the

juice and add to the batter. Stir in the pecans, blending well. Pour batter into the prepared pans. Bake in a 350° oven for 60 minutes for the small pans or 30 to 40 minutes for the mini pans.

Makes 2 small or 4 mini loaves.

The Russell-Cooper House

115 East Gambier Street
Mount Vernon, Ohio 43050
(614) 397-8638

This Victorian Gothic house has received the Association of American Historic Inns' 1989 Outstanding Achievement Award for its meticulous restoration work. All six guest rooms, decorated in period antiques, have private baths. A full, delightful country breakfast is served in the dining room. A smoking area is provided.

Russell-Cooper House Cheese Rugula

1 large loaf Pepperidge Farm bread
2 8-ounce packages cream cheese, softened

≈ ≈ ≈

5 cups sugar
2 tablespoons cinnamon
1 to 1½ cups butter or margarine, melted

Trim the crusts from the bread and roll each slice very thin. Spread with softened cream cheese and roll into logs.

In a small bowl combine the sugar and cinnamon. Dip the logs into the butter and then into the sugar and cinnamon mixture. Place close together on a large cookie sheet and freeze. When ready to use, remove the logs to another cookie sheet and bake in a 350° oven for 5 minutes. Slice logs into thirds and continue baking for 10 more minutes. Serve hot.

Serves 30.

Wind's Way

3851 Edwards Road
Newtown, Ohio 45244
(513) 561-1933

This 1840 house built by Welsh natives on property obtained through a Revolutionary War land grant also houses Wind's Way Antiques, a shop that specializes in eighteenth-century antiques. The inn's spacious rooms are furnished with antiques.

Each room has a private bath (one with a whirlpool), air conditioning, color television, and queen-size beds. The fifty-foot front porch and comfortable sitting areas are ideal for rest and relaxation. The complimentary breakfast can best be described as gourmet continental.

Pears in Zinfandel

1¾ cups sugar
2½ cups Zinfandel
1 lemon slice
2 whole cloves
6 very firm pears, peeled, cored, and halved

In a large flat-bottomed pan combine the sugar, Zinfandel, lemon slice, and cloves. Bring to a boil over high heat, stirring constantly to dissolve the sugar. Turn the heat down to simmer and add the pears. Simmer until the pears are tender, turning occasionally as the fruit turns red. Remove the pears and serve the sauce separately.

Serves 6.

Broccoli/Cheddar Quiche

4 eggs
3 tablespoons all-purpose flour
½ teaspoon oregano
½ teaspoon favorite herb seasoning mix
1½ cups light cream
2 cups shredded Cheddar cheese
¼ cup chopped scallions

᨞ ᨞ ᨞

1 10-ounce package frozen broccoli spears
1 tablespoon butter
Parsley for garnish

Butter a 9-inch pie plate. In a large bowl combine the eggs, flour, oregano, and herb seasoning, blending well. Stir in the cream, cheese, and scallions, mixing well. Pour into the prepared pie plate. Bake in a 350° oven for 50 minutes, or until set. Let cool for 10 minutes.

While the quiche is baking, cook the broccoli and drain. Toss with the butter and keep warm. To serve, arrange the broccoli in spokes on top of the quiche. Garnish with parsley.

Serves 8.

Griddle Cakes with Almonds

3 eggs
1 cup light cream
¼ cup oil
2 cups buttermilk baking mix
¼ cup wheat germ
1 tablespoon sugar
1 tablespoon grated orange peel
¾ teaspoon cinnamon
¾ cup chopped almonds

Lightly grease a griddle or skillet. In a small bowl beat the eggs with an electric mixer until light and lemon colored. Gradually stir in the cream, oil, baking mix, wheat germ, sugar, orange peel, and cinnamon, mixing just enough to blend. Spoon the batter in ¼-cup amounts onto the prepared griddle. Sprinkle each batch with

The Russell-Cooper House

Wind's Way

about 1 tablespoon of almonds. Cook until golden brown on both sides, turning once. Serve with fresh fruit or syrup.

Makes 12 cakes.

The Oberlin College Inn

Route 58 and College Street
Oberlin, Ohio 44074

Situated on the historic campus of one of America's most respected colleges, the Oberlin College Inn has been known for its gracious hospitality since 1833. Today the inn serves a wide variety of functions, from providing a room for the night, to an elegant dinner for two, to a wedding reception for two hundred guests. Its quiet, relaxed atmosphere and excellent facilities have made it a favorite setting for meetings, seminars, conferences, receptions, and banquets.

Breast of Duck Framboise

2 tablespoons clarified butter
1 boneless duck breast with skin (from a 5-pound duckling, reserving remainder of duck)
¼ cup Framboise
¼ cup Burgundy
¼ cup brown sauce (or Heinz bottled beef gravy)

Heat a heavy sauté pan over high heat. Add the butter. Cut slits on the skin side of the duck breast, not cutting the meat. Place skin side down in the prepared pan and render at medium to medium-high temperature pouring off the excess grease. The breast should be very dark brown to insure that it will not be greasy. Turn the breast after the skin has been rendered and cook on the meat side about 2 minutes (meat should be medium rare to medium). Remove the breast of duck and keep warm.

Add the Framboise and ignite to burn off the alcohol content. Add the Burgundy and reduce by half. Add the brown sauce and heat, reducing by half. With the breast meat side up, slice very thin, keeping slices in order. Place on a plate slightly fanned out. Lace the sauce over the inside half of the duck breast (center of plate half). Garnish with fresh mint sprig and serve with a vegetable and potato.

Serves 2.

Pumpkin Cheesecake

2½ cups graham crackers
½ cup clarified butter
Pinch cinnamon

❧ ❧ ❧

1 cup sugar
¾ cup pumpkin
3 egg yolks, lightly beaten
1 tablespoon cinnamon
½ teaspoon ginger
½ teaspoon salt
½ teaspoon mace

❧ ❧ ❧

1½ cups sugar
3 8-ounce packages cream cheese, softened
2 eggs
2 egg yolks
2 tablespoons heavy cream
1 tablespoon cornstarch
½ teaspoon lemon extract
½ teaspoon vanilla extract

In a medium bowl combine the cracker crumbs, butter, and a pinch of cinnamon. Press into the bottom of a 9-inch springform pan. Bake in a 350° oven until golden and slightly set.

In a medium bowl combine 1 cup sugar, pumpkin, 3 egg yolks, 1 tablespoon cinnamon, ginger, salt, and mace, mixing well. Set aside.

In a separate bowl cream together 1½ cups sugar, cream cheese, and 2 eggs until smooth and fluffy. Add the 2 egg yolks one at a time to the cream mixture, beating well after each addition. Add in the cream, cornstarch, lemon extract, and vanilla. Fold in the pumpkin mixture. Pour into the prepared crust and bake in a 475° oven for 10 minutes. Reduce the temperature to 250° and bake approximately 1 hour and 30 minutes. Cake will still be soft in the middle. Chill at least 5 hours.

Serves 6 to 8.

Zane Trace Bed and Breakfast

Box 115, Main Street
Old Washington, Ohio 43768
(614) 489-5970
(614) 489-5734

Built in 1859, this Italianate Victorian home on the Old National Trail and in Zane Grey territory has historical charm aplenty. A feeling of spaciousness abounds in this nineteenth-century home with its three guest rooms. Two rooms are spacious with queen-size beds and fireplaces; one of the two has an adjoining single bedroom-sitting room available. An elegant parlor for conversation is furnished as parlors of yesteryear were. A card and reading room is available for entertainment, along with a large, screened porch overlooking the heated swimming pool. Many historical sites and museums as well as three major lakes for boating and recreation are nearby. The Zane Grey Museum, depicting the great Western novelist, is in nearby Zanesville. Continental breakfast is provided.

ಶಿ ಶಿ ಶಿ ಶಿ ಶಿ

Eggs In Snow

2 slices bread
Butter
Salt and pepper
Nutmeg
2 eggs, separated
Grated cheese

Toast the bread on 1 side; turn and toast other side very lightly. Butter this side and keep toast warm. Add the salt, pepper, and nutmeg to the egg whites and beat until stiff. Spread over the buttered toast. Make a slight indentation in the middle and drop in the egg yolk. Sprinkle with cheese. Place under the broiler for a few minutes or until the egg yolk is set.

Serves 2.

Corn Casserole

8 ears fresh corn on cob
2 eggs, well beaten
2 tablespoons grated onion
¼ cup butter, melted
¾ teaspoon salt
Dash pepper
¾ cup milk

Scrape the corn off the cobs in a large bowl. Add the eggs and onion, mixing well. Stir in the butter, salt, pepper, and milk. Place in a baking dish. Bake in a 350° oven for 40 minutes, or until set in the center.

Serves 8.

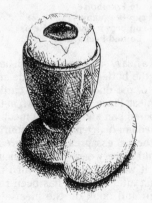

Central House Country Inn

27 West Columbus Street
Pickerington, Ohio 43147
(614) 837-0932

Simple and unpretentious, Central House Country Inn is typical of small hotels. Built before 1860, it operated through 1938 as the Central Hotel. Recently restored using original woodwork, doors, and windows, it has made two concessions to the twentieth century: central heating and air conditioning and private baths for each bedroom. The upstairs rooms are small and cozy just as they were 130 years ago; the downstairs bedroom is large and elegant. The delicious complimentary breakfast features ample baked goods served in the dining room.

Golden Cheese and Sausage Puff

1 pound mild sausage, bulk or roll
6 eggs
4 cups milk
½ teaspoon salt
½ teaspoon dried or prepared mustard
1 tablespoon dried parsley flakes
1 loaf French bread
2 cups shredded medium Cheddar cheese
Paprika

Lightly grease a 9x13-inch baking pan or large casserole. In a skillet cook, drain, and crumble the sausage. In a medium bowl combine the eggs, milk, salt, mustard, and parsley, beating well. Cube the bread and place in the bottom of the prepared pan. Mix in the sausage with a fork or by hand and sprinkle with the cheese. Pour the milk mixture over the casserole and sprinkle with paprika for a little color. Casserole can be refrigerated up to 24 hours before baking. Bake in a 350° oven for 45 to 60 minutes, until puffed and golden brown and the center is set.

Serves 8 to 10.

Uncle Jim's Favorite Cinnamon Rolls

½ cup butter, melted
2 cups very hot water
½ cup brown sugar
2 large eggs
½ teaspoon salt
2 ¼-ounce packages active dry yeast
7 cups flour (white, unbleached or part whole wheat)

🌿 🌿 🌿

½ cup butter, melted
Brown sugar, cinnamon, and chopped nuts

🌿 🌿 🌿

¼ cup butter, melted
¼ cup milk or cream
1 teaspoon vanilla extract
Confectioners' sugar

Lightly grease baking sheets. In a large bowl combine ½ cup melted butter, hot water, brown sugar, eggs, salt, and yeast. Whisk or mix together with a fork until well blended. Add 4 cups of flour, mixing well. Add about ½ cup of flour at a time, mixing well by hand, until the dough is smooth and not sticky. Let dough rise in a warm place about 45 to 60 minutes until doubled in bulk, then divide in half. Roll each portion into a ½-inch thick rectangle.

Spread ¼ cup of melted butter over each half and sprinkle liberally with brown sugar, cinnamon, and chopped nuts. Roll up and pinch long edge closed. Slice each roll into 8 to 12 slices. Place on the prepared baking sheets and let rise until doubled in size. Bake in a 375° oven for 18 to 20 minutes.

In a medium bowl combine ¼ cup melted butter, milk, vanilla, and con-

fectioners' sugar. Frost rolls when they have cooled.

Note: These rolls freeze well. (Keep frosting in the refrigerator.) Just warm rolls in the microwave and spread with the buttercream frosting.

Serves 16 to 24.

Yoders Spring Lake Bed and Breakfast

8144 Cemetery Pike
Plain City, Ohio 43064
(614) 873-4489

Yoders overlooks a five-acre, spring-fed lake in the middle of a 107-acre farm. Those who wish to try their hand at fishing are invited to bring a pole. Three rooms are available for single or double occupancy.

Scrapple

2 quarts water
1 cup cornmeal
½ cup all-purpose flour
1 teaspoon salt
¼ teaspoon pepper
½ teaspoon onion powder
½ pound fresh sausage
Flour and oil for frying

Butter bread pans. In a heavy saucepan combine all the ingredients. Cook over low heat for 1 hour, stirring often. Pour cooked mixture into prepared bread pans and cool. Run a knife around the sides to loosen and remove from the pans. Wrap in Saran Wrap and refrigerate overnight. Slice, roll in flour, brown in hot oil, and serve with warm syrup.

Serves 6 to 8.

Cauliflower Salad

1 head cauliflower, chopped
1 head lettuce, chopped
1 medium onion, chopped
1 pound bacon, fried and crumbled
1 cup mayonnaise
⅔ cup sugar
1 cup grated Mozzarella cheese
1 cup grated Cheddar cheese

In a large bowl layer the cauliflower, lettuce, onion, and bacon. Spread the mayonnaise over the top. Sprinkle with the sugar and cover with the cheeses. Store in the refrigerator at least 5 hours. Toss before serving.

Serves 15 to 20.

The Baird House

201 North Second Street
Mulberry and Highway 52W
Ripley, Ohio 45167

This elegantly restored home overlooking the Ohio River was built in 1825 and is listed on the National Register. The wrought-iron-lace porch and balcony along the front façade were shipped by boat from Cincinnati; the eleven marble fireplaces were shipped from Italy; and the enormous chandelier in the parlor was manufactured in France. Guests who enjoy casual country relaxation will enjoy a cup of espresso on the upper deck or an "everything omelette" that is the specialty of the inn. Within walking distance are many antique shops.

Spinach Quiche

3 eggs, lightly beaten
1 cup sour cream
Salt, pepper, sugar
½ cup minced onion
½ cup finely chopped pimento
1 cup shredded Swiss cheese
1 10-ounce package chopped
** spinach, drained**
1 9-inch unbaked pie shell
6 slices bacon, crisply fried and
** crumbled**

In a large bowl combine the eggs, sour cream, seasonings, onion, and pimento, mixing well. Add the cheese and spinach. Pour into the pie shell and sprinkle with the bacon. Bake in a 425° oven for 15 minutes. Reduce the temperature to 300° and bake 30 more minutes.

Note: This can be prepared in a baked crust, but be sure the sides do not shrink.

Serves 6 to 8.

Lemony Pound Cake

We serve tea at 4:00 P.M. to our guests and have an assortment of sweets available, one of which is this cake.

2 cups butter
2 cups sugar
9 eggs, separated
2 teaspoons lemon extract
½ teaspoon mace
2 tablespoons grated lemon peel

   ая ая ая

4 cups cake flour, sifted
½ teaspoon salt
½ teaspoon cream of tartar
2 tablespoons caraway (or poppy
** seed)**
Confectioners' sugar

Grease a tube pan or 2 loaf pans. In a large bowl cream together the butter, sugar, and egg yolks. Add the lemon extract, mace, and lemon peel.

In a separate bowl sift together the flour, salt, and cream of tartar. Stir in the seeds. Add to the creamed mix-

ture. In a separate large bowl beat all the egg whites until stiff but not dry. Gently fold into the batter. Pour the batter into the prepared pan. Bake in a 325° oven for 1 hour. Dust with confectioners' sugar and thinly slice.

Makes 2 large loaves, or 10 to 12 servings each.

Homemade Apricot Brandy

Available in our guest rooms and used as an optional "nightcap."

3 cups sugar
1 fifth vodka
6 ounces dried apricots, chopped

Dissolve the sugar in the vodka (takes 2 to 3 days). Add the apricots and pour into a glass container to brew for 6 weeks.

Note: Nice to prepare in time for Christmas. The drained apricots may be used in a fruit cake.

Serves 6.

The Signal House

234 North Front Street
Ripley, Ohio 45167
(513) 392-1640

This stately home on the Ohio River left its mark in history through its involvement in the Underground Railroad. Built in the 1830s, the Greek Italianate-style home features ornate plaster mouldings that surround the twelve-foot ceilings, spacious rooms, and three relaxing porches from which to enjoy the splendid view of the Ohio River. Nearby points of inter-

est include museums, restaurants, and a wide array of antique and craft shops.

Scalloped Pineapple

½ cup margarine
2 eggs
1 20-ounce can crushed pineapple
¾ cup sugar
1 tablespoon all-purpose flour
5 slices bread, diced

In a skillet brown the margarine. Remove from the heat and cool. In a medium bowl beat the eggs and add the pineapple, sugar, and flour. Add to the margarine. Place half of the bread in the bottom of a 9-inch square pan. Cover with the pineapple mixture and top with the remaining bread. Bake in a 350° oven for 35 minutes.

Note: Recipe can be doubled and baked in a 9x13-inch pan.

Serves 4 to 6.

The Signal House

Chicken Peach Almondine

¼ cup butter
4 chicken breasts
½ teaspoon salt
3 green onions with tops, sliced
½ cup slivered almonds

½ teaspoon tarragon
½ cup chopped parsley
1 29-ounce can cling peach halves,
    drained
½ cup grated Parmesan cheese

In a skillet melt the butter. Add the chicken, brown lightly, and remove from the skillet to a baking dish. Add the salt, onions, almonds, tarragon, and parsley to the melted butter in the skillet. Stir to mix well and pour over the chicken in the baking dish. Cover and bake in a 350° oven for 45 minutes. Uncover and add the peaches. Sprinkle with the cheese and bake uncovered 15 more minutes.
Serves 4.

Holiday Pastries

2 14-ounce packages hot roll mix
1 10¾-ounce can Cheddar cheese
    soup, undiluted
2 eggs, slightly beaten
½ cup sugar
½ teaspoon almond extract

ₐ ₐ ₐ

1 21-ounce can fruit pie filling (or
    jam or jelly or pineapple cream
    cheese for filling)
Glaze, if desired

Lightly grease cookie sheets. In a large bowl dissolve the yeast packages from the hot roll mix as directed, using only ¾ cup water. Continue to follow the mix directions and add the soup, eggs, sugar, and almond extract in the flour mixture. Let rise as directed and shape dough in 48 small balls. Flatten dough to form circles and place on the prepared cookie sheets. Let rise again until doubled.
Press the center of each roll to make a dent and fill with about 1 tablespoon of the filling. Bake in a 375° oven for 20 minutes, or until brown. Cool and glaze if desired.
Note: To make ahead, quick-freeze the baked pastries in a single layer on a cookie sheet for 1½ hours, then place in airtight plastic bags.
Serves 8.

"Somer Tea"

200 South Columbus Street
Box 308
Somerset, Ohio 43783
(614) 743-2909

This bed and breakfast is named for the collection of more than 250 small teapots and the friendly village of Somerset. On the National Register of Historic Homes, "Somer Tea" was once occupied by two of Civil War General Phillip Sheridan's nieces. The two large guest rooms, which share a bath, are furnished with furniture that has sentimental value to the innkeepers. A full country breakfast is served. Tea is always available in the kitchen, on the porch swing, or on the deck.

Gingery Apricot-Banana Compote

1 17-ounce can unpeeled apricot
    halves
¾ cup orange juice
1 tablespoon finely chopped
    crystallized ginger

ₐ ₐ ₐ

1 medium banana, bias-sliced
¼ cup toasted coconut

Drain the apricots, reserving ½ cup syrup. In a medium saucepan combine the reserved apricot syrup, orange juice, and ginger. Bring to boil, reduce heat, and simmer uncovered for 5 minutes. Stir in the apricots, return to a boil, then simmer uncovered for 3 minutes. Remove from the heat.
Transfer the fruit and syrup to a bowl and cool slightly. Gently stir in the banana, spoon in dessert dishes, and sprinkle with coconut.
Note: Compote may be chilled for several hours or overnight before adding the banana.
Serves 5.

Banana-Praline Muffins

A neighbor shared this recipe with me and it has made a big hit with our guests.

3 tablespoons brown sugar
1 tablespoon sour cream
⅓ cup broken pecans

ₐ ₐ ₐ

3 small bananas
1 egg, slightly beaten
½ cup sugar
¼ cup oil
1½ cups pancake mix

Grease or line muffin cups with paper liners. In a small bowl combine the brown sugar and sour cream. Stir in the pecans and set aside.
In a medium bowl mash the bananas. In a separate bowl combine the egg, sugar, oil, and the mashed bananas, stirring until blended. Add the pancake mix, stirring just until moistened. Fill the prepared muffin cups ⅔ full. Top each muffin with 1 teaspoon of the pecan mix. Bake in a 400° oven for 10 to 15 minutes, or until brown.
Makes 12 muffins.

Holiday Mashed Potatoes

3 pounds potatoes, peeled, cooked,
    and hot
1 8-ounce package cream cheese, at
    room temperature
¼ cup butter or margarine
½ cup sour cream

ₐ ₐ ₐ

½ cup milk
2 eggs, lightly beaten
¼ cup finely chopped onions
    (optional)
1 teaspoon salt
Dash pepper

In a large bowl mash the hot potatoes with an electric mixer or by hand until smooth. Add the cream cheese in small pieces and the butter. Beat well until the cheese and butter are both melted and completely mixed in. Stir in the sour cream.

In a separate bowl add the milk to the eggs and onions. Stir in the potato mixture, salt, and pepper. Beat well until light and fluffy. Place in a 9-inch round casserole and refrigerate several hours or overnight. Bake in a 350° oven for 45 minutes until the top is lightly browned.

Serves 8 to 12.

Locust Lane Farm Bed and Breakfast

5590 Kessler Cowlesville Road
West Milton, Ohio 45383
(513) 698-4743

This inn is a delightful old Cape Cod home in a rural setting. Guests are invited to relax in the library or in front of the fireplace. Both guest rooms are air-conditioned, and a full breakfast is served on the screened porch in warm weather. Nearby activities include antique shops, restaurants, golf, tennis, canoeing, and the nature center.

Dried Fruit Cream Scones

    2 cups all-purpose flour
    1 tablespoon baking powder
    ½ teaspoon salt
    ¼ cup sugar
    ¾ cup finely chopped dried fruit
        (apricots, prunes, peaches, etc.)
    ½ cup golden raisins
    1¼ cups heavy cream
        ❧   ❧   ❧
    3 tablespoons butter, melted
    2 tablespoons sugar

In a large bowl combine the flour, baking powder, salt, and ¼ cup of sugar, stirring with a fork to mix well. Add the dried fruit and raisins. Stir in the cream and mix lightly until the dough holds together. Dough will be sticky. Transfer the dough to a lightly floured board and knead 8 or 9 times. Pat the dough into a 10-inch circle.

Spread the melted butter over the dough and sprinkle with 2 tablespoons of sugar. Cut the circle into 12 wedges and place each piece on a baking sheet, allowing 1 inch between each piece. Bake in a 350° oven for 15 minutes or until lightly browned.

Serves 12.

Orange Bran Muffins

    3 cups All-Bran cereal
    ¾ cup boiling water
    2 heaping tablespoons frozen
        orange juice concentrate
    ½ cup oil
    2 eggs, slightly beaten
        ❧   ❧   ❧
    2½ cups all-purpose flour
    1 cup sugar
    3¼ teaspoons baking soda
    1 teaspoon baking powder
    2 cups buttermilk
        ❧   ❧   ❧
    Orange Butter (recipe follows)

Grease muffin tins. In a large bowl combine 1 cup of cereal, boiling water, orange juice, and oil. Beat in the eggs and set aside.

In a separate bowl combine the flour, sugar, baking soda, and baking powder. Stir in the buttermilk and the cereal mixture. Add the remaining 2 cups of cereal, mixing well. Fill the prepared muffin tins ⅔ full. Bake in a 350° oven for 15 to 20 minutes.

Serve with Orange Butter.

Makes 18 muffins.

❧ ❧ ❧ ❧ ❧

Orange Butter

    ½ cup butter, softened
    1 3-ounce package cream cheese,
        softened
    ⅓ cup confectioners' sugar
    2 tablespoons grated orange rind
    2 tablespoons frozen orange juice
        concentrate

In a medium bowl combine all the ingredients and beat with an electric mixer or vigorously by hand until smooth. Store in the refrigerator, but serve at room temperature.

Note: If butter is crumbly, beat again at room temperature.

Makes about 1 cup.

Spanish Sauce
for Scrambled Eggs

    1 teaspoon olive oil
    1 tablespoon chopped onion
    ½ clove garlic, minced
    2 tablespoons chopped green
        pepper
    2 cups chopped ripe or frozen
        tomatoes
    1 teaspoon basil
    1 tablespoon chopped parsley
    Salt and pepper

In a skillet heat the oil and sauté the onion, garlic, and green pepper. Add the tomatoes, basil, parsley, salt, and pepper. Cook over medium heat until thickened.

Note: This sauce can be frozen and also used in omelets.

Serves 8.

Minted Fruit Juice Sauce

1 cup sugar
⅔ cup water
½ cup chopped peppermint or
   spearmint leaves
¼ cup lemon juice
¼ cup orange juice

In a saucepan combine the sugar and water. Boil for 3 minutes. Add the mint, cool, and strain. Add the juices and chill. Pour over fresh melon and fruit.
Serves 12.

The Cider Mill

Post Office Box 441, Second Street
Zoar, Ohio 44697
(216) 874-3133

Zoar Village, founded in 1817 by a group of Germans seeking freedom from religious persecution, was a successful commune when the pioneers built their steam-operated mill in 1863. To increase efficiency, they used the building as a cabinet shop during the off season. Now renovated, it is a bed and breakfast called the Cider Mill. Somehow the serenity of these early settlers lingers in the atmosphere to provide a tranquil stay for modern travelers. A delicious breakfast is served from the country kitchen each morning.

Hot Spiced Cider

On frosty weekends in the fall and winter we use an old percolator to keep the cider hot and ready for all our visitors. On extra cold nights, each serving can be fortified with a shot of rum.

2 teaspoons whole cloves
2 teaspoons whole allspice
2 3-inch cinnamon sticks
1 gallon sweet apple cider
⅔ cup sugar
2 whole oranges

Tie the spices in cheesecloth or place in a tea ball. In a large cooking pot combine the spices with the cider, sugar, and whole oranges. Heat to boiling, cover, and simmer for 20 minutes.
Serves 12.

The Inn at Cowger House

Fourth Street
Zoar, Ohio 44697
(216) 874-3542

At Cowger House guests meet "a little bit of Williamsburg" in Ohio. Guests may choose from rooms at the manor with its tasteful colonial decor or the 1817 cabin with its rustic, charming ambience. A full country breakfast is served.

A full menu is served at the restaurant, which is open for the public. Guests are greeted by Mary, who arrived in Zoar in 1840 and is still doing the cooking, or Edward of Virginia, a recuperating Civil War soldier who has just witnessed the dastardly deed of John Wilkes Booth (provided he's not at the grog shop!).

Stroganoff Crepes

1 pound ground beef
½ cup chopped onions
1 garlic clove, minced
2 tablespoons all-purpose flour
Pinch salt and pepper
¼ teaspoon paprika
1 10½-ounce can of mushroom soup
1 cup sour cream

❧ ❧ ❧
16 crepes
Butter, melted

In a skillet brown the beef, onions, and garlic, and drain. Stir in the flour until smooth. Stir in the salt, pepper, paprika, and soup. Simmer for 5 minutes. Remove from the heat, and stir in the sour cream.

Spoon the mixture into each crepe. Place in an ungreased baking dish and brush with melted butter. Bake in a 350° oven for 15 minutes, until heated through. Top with more sour cream, if desired.
Fills 16 crepes.

Grandma Ray's Christmas Pudding

My grandmother always made this pudding for Christmas, and the tradition still lives on. Hope it begins a tradition for someone else.

1 cup brown sugar
2 cups water
1 tablespoon butter
½ cup sugar
½ cup raisins
½ cup dates
❧ ❧ ❧
1 tablespoon shortening
½ teaspoon nutmeg
½ teaspoon cinnamon
½ cup buttermilk
1 teaspoon baking soda
1 cup all-purpose flour

In a saucepan combine the brown sugar, water, and butter. Heat and cook slowly. In a separate bowl soak the raisins and dates until soft and drain, or add to the saucepan mixture and cook until softened. Pour the mixture into an 8-inch baking pan.

In a medium bowl combine the shortening, nutmeg, cinnamon, buttermilk, baking soda, and flour. Mix thoroughly to form a dough. Drop into the hot syrup and cover. Bake in a 350° oven for 45 minutes.
Serves 6 to 8.

Oklahoma

Clayton Country Inn

Route 1, Box 08
Clayton, Oklahoma 74536
(918) 569-4165

Clayton Country Inn is in the heart of Oklahoma's beautiful Kiamichi Mountain Country, easily accessible from Tulsa, Oklahoma City, and Dallas. The inn has six large, comfortable guest rooms and the nearby cottage has two complete apartments, each with living room, bedroom, equipped kitchenette, and fireplace. The great room in the inn is for guests' use; its high, log-beamed ceiling, natural rock fireplace, easy chairs and big sofas, television, and wide windows with a view of the mountains and river create a restful setting for games, reading, or loafing. The knotty pine and fireplace theme is carried from the great room into the dining room where guests enjoy excellent food prepared with the utmost care.

Bran Muffins

5 cups all-purpose flour
3 cups sugar
1 12-ounce box Raisin Bran cereal
5 teaspoons baking soda
2 teaspoons salt
1 teaspoon cinnamon
½ teaspoon allspice

🍂 🍂 🍂

4 eggs, beaten
1 quart buttermilk
1 cup oil
1 14-ounce can crushed pineapple

Grease muffin cups. In a large bowl combine the flour, sugar, cereal, baking soda, salt, cinnamon, and allspice. Add the eggs, buttermilk, oil, and pineapple. Pour batter into muffin tins. Bake in a 400° oven for 15 to 20 minutes.

Note: Batter keeps for 6 weeks in the refrigerator.

Makes 5 dozen muffins.

Corn Casserole

4 3-ounce packages cream cheese
½ cup milk
¼ cup butter
1 teaspoon garlic salt
4 cups white corn
2 4-ounce cans green chilies

🍂 🍂 🍂

Clayton Country Inn

400

Butter
Grated cheese
Paprika

In a saucepan heat together the cream cheese, milk, butter, and garlic salt, stirring until smooth. Remove from the heat and stir in the corn and green chilies. Pour into a 1½-quart baking dish and dot with butter. Sprinkle with grated cheese and paprika. Bake in a 350° oven for 30 minutes.

Serves 6.

Stone Lion Inn

1016 West Warner
Guthrie, Oklahoma 73044
(405) 282-0012

This beautiful Victorian home, which was built in 1907 by a successful Guthrie businessman, still retains its original oak floors, three fireplaces, leaded glass doors, formal parlors, library, and third-floor ballroom. Named the Stone Lion Inn for the two stone lions that guard the front door, it has been painstakingly restored to its early grandeur with period antiques, polished woodwork, gleaming hardwood floors, and replica wallpaper. Guests are invited to enjoy a glass of wine and cheese by the fire on cold winter evenings or eat strawberries and cream while sitting on the front porch swing during the summer. The six guest rooms vary in size, from a quaint single room to the elegant suite.

Stuffed Acorn Squash

    2 large acorn squash
    1 tablespoon oil
    ¾ pound ground beef
    ½ cup chopped onion
    ½ cup chopped celery
    1 cup cooked rice
    ¼ cup sunflower seeds
    1 tart apple, unpeeled and chopped
    1 teaspoon curry powder
    1½ teaspoons salt
    5 teaspoons brown sugar
    1 egg
    4 teaspoons butter

Cut the squash in half and scoop out the seeds. Place cut-side down in a baking dish. Add ½ inch of boiling water. Bake in a 375° oven for about 25 minutes, or until the squash is tender.

In a skillet heat the oil over low heat and brown the ground beef with the onion. Add the celery and simmer for 3 minutes. Stir in the apple, rice, sunflower seeds, and curry powder. Simmer for about 3 minutes or until the apple is tender. Add 1 teaspoon of salt and 1 teaspoon of brown sugar. Stir in the egg. Remove from the heat and set aside.

Turn the squash over and place 1 teaspoon of brown sugar into each half. Sprinkle with the remaining salt. Divide the beef mixture among the squash halves. Press the filling down firmly, mounding in the center. Heat in a 375° oven for about 10 to 15 minutes before serving.

Serves 4.

Veal Cutlets

    2 veal cutlets
    1 clove garlic, cut
    1 tablespoon olive oil
    Salt
    Paprika
    ¼ cup dry sherry
    ⅓ cup thick cream
    1½ tablespoons currant jelly
    2 tablespoons butter

Rub the cutlets with the garlic. In a skillet heat the olive oil and sauté the cutlets quickly on both sides until brown. Season the steaks with salt and paprika. Add the sherry and deglaze the pan. Add the cream, currant jelly, and butter. Cook, stirring constantly, until heated through. Add additional seasoning if needed.

Serves 2.

Stone Lion Inn

The Grandison Inn

1841 NW 15th Street
Oklahoma City, Oklahoma 73106
(405) 521-0011

This 1896 Victorian three-story home convenient to downtown Oklahoma City is furnished with Victorian-era antiques, and its five guest rooms all have private baths. An attractive house with lots of windows, the Grandison also features fruit bearing trees and a garden gazebo. Smoking is permitted.

Grandison Potatoes

4 to 5 medium potatoes
½ cup butter, melted
Onion flakes
Parsley flakes
Dill

Scrub the potatoes and slice into ¼-inch slices, leaving the skin on. Layer the slices in a 9x13-inch pan. Drizzle with melted butter and sprinkle heavily with onion flakes, parsley flakes, and dill. Bake in a 350° oven for 45 minutes.

Serves 6.

Beef Stroganoff

This dish is excellent served with broccoli spears drizzled with melted butter and grated Parmesan cheese.

2 tablespoons olive oil
1 pound ground or cubed beef
1 medium onion, sliced
1 10-ounce can cream of mushroom soup
1 4-ounce can mushrooms, drained
1 clove garlic, minced
2 tablespoons Worcestershire sauce
Salt and pepper to taste
Paprika and nutmeg to taste
¼ cup red wine
1 cup sour cream
Cooked noodles, rice, or chow mein noodles

In a skillet heat the oil and brown the beef, onion, and garlic. Stir in the soup, mushrooms, and wine. Add the seasonings. Simmer for 15 to 20 minutes. Just before serving, add the sour cream and heat through. Serve over noodles, rice, or chow mein noodles.

Serves 4.

Cornish Hens
Baked in Champagne

2 Cornish game hens
Salt
¼ cup melted butter
Freshly ground pepper
¼ cup champagne
Cooked rice

Clean the hens and remove the organs. Lightly salt the cavities. Brush with melted butter and lay in a baking pan, breast side up. Pepper the hens to taste. Bake in a 425° oven for 10 minutes to brown. Reduce the heat to 350°, pour the champagne over the hens, and return to the oven for 30 to 45 minutes. Baste every 5 minutes.

Serve the hens whole or split over a bed of cooked rice.

Serves 2, or 4 if split.

Oregon

Chanticleer Bed and Breakfast Inn

120 Gresham Street
Ashland, Oregon 97520
(503) 482-1919

In Chaucer's *Canterbury Tales* "Chanticleer and the Fox" is a barnyard fable whose origin comes from the heart of Europe. Chanticleer Bed and Breakfast Inn reflects the same European country feeling. This snug and cozy six-room guest house is situated in a quiet residential neighborhood, a short walk from the Oregon Shakespearean Festival, Lithia Park, and the shops and restaurants of Ashland's Plaza. The Rogue River's white water rafting and Mount Ashland's ski slopes are in close driving distance. Some of the inn's rooms overlook the Bear Creek Valley and Cascade foothills; others open onto a peaceful brick patio. Guest rooms are furnished with antiques, fluffy comforters, and fresh flowers, and each room has a private bath and is air-conditioned. The spacious living room offers books and magazines to curl up with while warming one's toes by the open hearth fireplace. A full breakfast is served in the sunny din-

ing room; by request, guests may have breakfast in bed.

Rhubarb Sour Cream Cake

¼ cup butter, softened
1½ cups light brown sugar
1 large egg, lightly beaten
1 teaspoon vanilla extract

    🍂 🍂 🍂

2⅓ cups all-purpose flour
1 teaspoon baking soda
4 generous cups rhubarb, cut in
    chunks
1 cup sour cream
Freshly grated nutmeg

    🍂 🍂 🍂

Whipped cream

Grease a 9x13-inch pan. In a large bowl cream together the butter and brown sugar. Beat in the eggs and vanilla.

In a separate bowl combine the flour and baking soda. Stir into the butter mixture. Add the rhubarb and sour cream. The batter will be stiff and can be mixed by hand. Pat into the prepared pan and sprinkle lightly with nutmeg. Bake in a 350° oven for 40 minutes. Serve warm with whipped cream.

Serves 8.

Orange Omelet Soufflé

12 eggs, separated
3 tablespoons sugar
3 tablespoons all-purpose flour
1 tablespoon grated orange rind

    🍂 🍂 🍂

3 cups fresh orange juice
½ cup butter
Brown sugar

    🍂 🍂 🍂

Sliced strawberries

In a large bowl combine the egg whites and sugar. In a separate bowl combine the flour, orange rind, and egg yolks, beating together well. Refrigerate both mixtures. Before baking, whip the egg white mixture until stiff. Gently fold into the egg yolk mixture.

In a saucepan combine the orange juice and butter, and sweeten to taste with the brown sugar. Heat the sauce until warm. Place a small amount of the orange sauce in the bottom of 8 ramekins. Gently mound spoonfuls of the soufflé mixture into the ramekins. Bake in a 375° oven for 10 minutes, or until lightly browned and set. Garnish with sliced strawberries and smother with orange sauce.

Serves 8.

Cowslip's Belle

159 North Main Street
Ashland, Oregon 97520
(503) 488-2901

This craftsman's home and newly renovated carriage house were built in 1913 and remain essentially as they were then, with original woodwork and beveled glass. Vintage furniture adds to the comfortable surroundings. The four guest rooms, each with a private bath, have queen beds, air conditioning, and down comforters. A delightful breakfast is served in the sunny dining room. Conveniently situated three blocks from the Shakespearean theaters, shops, restaurants, and Lithia Park, Cowslip's Belle provides a warm welcome in any season.

Chocolate Mousse Truffles

12 ounces semi-sweet chocolate, chopped into small pieces
¼ cup unsalted butter, quartered
¾ cup heavy cream, scalded and strained

1 egg white, beaten stiff

❧ ❧ ❧

8 ounces semi-sweet chocolate, chopped into small pieces
Confectioners' sugar

Line a cookie sheet with waxed paper. In a microwave on high at 1-minute intervals melt the 12 ounces of chocolate and butter together until smooth, stirring occasionally. Mix in the heated cream until completely blended with the chocolate mixture. Gradually stir in the egg white. Mixture should be frothy. Cover and refrigerate until firm. Spoon 1-inch rounds onto the prepared cookie sheet and refrigerate until firm. Rub the palms of your hands with confectioners' sugar. Roll each mound into a ball and refrigerate.

Melt the 8 ounces of chocolate to a temperature of 110°, stirring occasionally. Bring the temperature of the chocolate down to 89° by stirring occasionally in a bowl for about 30 minutes. Quickly dip each ball in the melted chocolate, wiping excess chocolate on the edge of the bowl as you dip. Place the truffle on waxed paper. When all the truffles have been dipped, refrigerate for 1 hour. Place in paper candy cups and store in an airtight container. Truffles may be refrigerated for up to 2 weeks.

Makes 25 truffles.

Pandowdy

Serve warm with cream on top for breakfast, or with an ice cream topping for a dinner dessert.

¾ cup unsalted butter
6 cups sliced peaches or apples
3 cups sugar
1½ cups all-purpose flour
1½ teaspoons baking powder
½ teaspoon salt
¾ teaspoon cinnamon
1½ cups milk
¾ teaspoon vanilla extract

In a 9x13-inch glass dish melt the butter. In a large bowl combine the fruit and 1½ cups of sugar. In a separate bowl sift together the flour, baking powder, salt, and cinnamon. Add the remaining milk, 1½ cups sugar, and vanilla to the dry ingredients, mixing well. Stir the batter into the butter in the prepared dish. Top with the fruit mixture. Bake in a 350° oven for 35 minutes. Increase temperature to 400° and bake until golden around the edges.

Serves 8.

Hersey House

451 North Main Street
Ashland, Oregon 97520
(503) 482-4563

A spacious front porch beckons guests into this turn-of-the-century Victorian home, now fully restored. Inside, the L-shaped staircase leads to the four guest rooms, one of which has a private balcony overlooking the Cascade foothills and the Rouge Valley. Another has a pleasing view of Mount Ashland. Each room has a private bath. Breakfast is set each morning overlooking the colorful English country garden. House specialties include gingerbread pancakes, Eggs

Cowslip's Belle

Hersey, sourdough pancakes, and avocado omelets. In the late afternoon a social hour in the main parlor gives guests a chance to exchange news of the day's pleasures. Ashland's Plaza, Lithia Park, and the Oregon Shakespearean Festival theaters are all a short walk from the inn.

Danish Omelet

16 eggs
½ cup half and half

🍃 🍃 🍃

1½ cups whipping cream
2 3-ounce packages cream cheese
½ cup blue cheese, very veined
¼ cup herbal cheese
Butter

Butter ramekin dishes. In a large bowl combine the eggs and half and half. Prepare omelets and flip into prepared ramekin dishes.

In a medium saucepan over very low heat combine the whipping cream and the cheeses with a whisk. Blend and cook for 20 to 30 minutes. Cover each omelet with ¼ cup of the sauce. Bake the omelets in a 400° oven for 8 to 10 minutes until puffy.

Serves 8.

Lynn's Sausage Egg Crepe Cups

4 eggs
¼ cup butter, melted
2 cups all-purpose flour
1 teaspoon salt
2⅔ cups milk

🍃 🍃 🍃

8 ounces spicy ground sausage
½ cup chopped green pepper
½ cup chopped red pepper
¼ cup chopped onion
8 eggs
¼ cup milk
1 teaspoon celery salt

🍃 🍃 🍃

Sour cream

Hershey House

Grease muffin tins. In a large bowl combine the 4 eggs, butter, flour, salt, and 2⅔ cups of milk. Pour 1½ tablespoons of the batter into a 5-inch crepe pan. Cook over medium-high heat until brown. Turn over and cook for a few seconds, then remove from the pan. Prepare all the crepes and place in the prepared muffin tins so the edges ruffle.

In a medium skillet over medium-high heat brown the sausage, stirring occasionally. Drain. Sauté the peppers and onion in the skillet and mix with the sausage. In a medium bowl combine the 8 eggs, ¼ cup of milk, and celery salt. Sprinkle 3 tablespoons of the sausage mixture into the bottom of each cup and cover with 3 tablespoons of the egg mixture. Bake in a 350° oven for 25 to 30 minutes, until a knife inserted in the center comes out clean.

Makes 16 cups to serve 8.

The Morical House

668 North Main Street
Ashland, Oregon 97520
(503) 482-2254

A restored 1880s farmhouse, the Morical House offers twentieth century comfort and nineteenth century beauty, leaded and stained glass windows, finely crafted woodwork, and antique furniture. The five guest rooms, all having private baths with brass fixtures, are uniquely decorated with period furniture and offer beautiful mountain views. The generous breakfast is served in the dining room and enclosed sun porch overlooking an acre of attractively landscaped grounds. In the afternoon refreshments are served in the parlor or garden, and guests may stroll the grounds, enjoy a game of croquet, or perfect their golfing skills on the putting green.

Fresh Pear Cake

4 cups fresh Bartlett pears, peeled,
**   cored, and chopped**
2 cups sugar
1 cup chopped pecans
3 cups all-purpose flour
1 teaspoon cinnamon
½ teaspoon nutmeg
2 teaspoons baking soda

🍃 🍃 🍃

2 eggs
1 cup oil
1 teaspoon vanilla extract
Confectioners' sugar

Spray a bundt pan with non-stick cooking spray. In a large bowl combine the pears, sugar, and pecans. Let stand for 1 hour, stirring occasionally. In a separate bowl combine the flour, cinnamon, nutmeg, and baking soda. Stir into the pear mixture.

In a small bowl combine the eggs, oil, and vanilla with a wire whisk. Stir into the pear mixture. Pour the batter into the prepared pan. Bake in a 350° oven for 50 to 60 minutes. Cool on a wire rack. Invert onto a plate and dust with confectioners' sugar.

Serves 10 to 12.

The Morical House

Salsa Fresca

We use this salsa to accompany chili and cheese strata, huevos rancheros, or cheese omelets.

    2 pounds fresh tomatoes, peeled
        and chopped
    1 cup finely chopped onion
    2 cloves garlic, smashed and
        chopped
    2 tablespoons olive oil
    2 cans chopped green chilies
    ½ teaspoon cumin
    Tabasco sauce

    🍃 🍃 🍃

    ½ cup finely chopped fresh cilantro
    ½ cup finely chopped green onions
    ½ cup finely chopped fresh parsley

In a large bowl combine the tomatoes, 1 cup of chopped onion, garlic, oil, green chilies, and cumin. Add the Tabasco sauce to taste. Refrigerate until ready to use, up to 4 days. Just before serving add the fresh cilantro, green onions, and parsley. Taste and adjust for additional seasoning.

Makes 1 quart (8 ½-cup servings).

Marinated Antipasto

We provide complimentary refreshments in the afternoon and this has always been a winner.

    ¾ to 1 pound fresh mushrooms,
        cleaned
    1 can plain artichoke hearts,
        washed well, drained, and
        quartered
    2 cups pitted olives
    1 basket cherry tomatoes
    1 cup roasted red peppers

    🍃 🍃 🍃

    1½ cups white wine vinegar
    1½ cups olive oil
    ½ cup minced onion
    5 cloves garlic, crushed
    2 teaspoons sugar
    1 tablespoon dried crushed basil
    1 tablespoon dried crushed oregano
    1 tablespoon freshly ground black
        pepper

    🍃 🍃 🍃

    Sliced hard salami, garlic Monterey
        Jack cheese, and sliced baguette
        French bread to accompany

In a shallow 9x11-inch dish arrange the mushrooms, artichoke hearts, olives, cherry tomatoes, and red peppers in rows.

In a saucepan combine the remaining ingredients, bring to a boil, and simmer for 5 minutes. Cool for 10 minutes. Pour over the vegetables and gently turn the vegetables so they are well coated. Refrigerate for 12 hours, turning vegetables at least once. Drain and serve at room temperature on a platter with sliced hard salami and garlic cheese. Accompany with sliced baguette French bread.

Serves 10 to 12.

Mount Ashland Inn

550 Mount Ashland Road
Post Office Box 944
Ashland, Oregon 97520
(503) 482-8707

Mount Ashland Inn is no ordinary bed and breakfast. Crafted of cedar logs cut on the surrounding property, it blends with its wooded setting. Inside, a large stone fireplace dominates the main room, and a bookcase filled with games, books, and memorabilia invites guests to browse and relax. The guest rooms have private baths, a queen or king bed, an individually controlled thermostat, and handmade quilts. Breakfast is a hearty affair of home-baked breads, fresh fruits, and other tempting dishes. In the evening guests can enjoy complimentary beverages served by a cozy fire or on the deck.

Apple Walnut Whole Wheat Pancakes

    ⅔ cup milk
    2 tablespoons butter or margarine,
        melted
    2 tablespoons molasses
    1 egg
    ⅔ cup all-purpose flour
    ⅓ cup whole wheat flour
    2 teaspoons baking powder
    ¼ teaspoon salt
    ¼ cup chopped walnuts
    ½ medium green apple, peeled and
        diced

In a medium bowl combine the milk, butter, molasses, and egg. Beat together lightly. In a separate bowl sift together the flour, baking powder, and salt. Add the walnuts and apple to the flour mixture. Add the flour mixture all at once to the milk mixture, stirring just enough to moisten. Add more milk, if necessary, to make the batter the consistency of heavy cream. Cook the pancakes on a hot griddle.

Makes 10 4-inch pancakes.

Brandied-Candied Yams

1 29-ounce can yams, reserving drained liquid
2 tablespoons butter, melted
¼ cup brown sugar
¼ cup chopped walnuts or pecans
1½ tablespoons brandy

Place the yams in an ungreased baking dish. In a medium bowl combine the butter, brown sugar, walnuts, brandy, and ¼ cup of the reserved liquid from the yams. Drizzle sauce over the yams. Bake in a 350° oven for 35 to 40 minutes until bubbly.

Serves 6.

Date and Nut Pinwheel Cookies

1 cup margarine
1 cup brown sugar
2 eggs
1 teaspoon vanilla extract
3½ cups all-purpose flour
1 teaspoon baking soda

   🍂 🍂 🍂

1 pound chopped dates
¼ cup sugar
⅔ cup hot water
1 cup chopped nuts

In a large bowl cream together the margarine and brown sugar. Add the eggs and vanilla, mixing well. In a separate bowl sift together the flour and baking soda. Gradually stir the dry ingredients into the creamed mixture. Form the dough into a ball and chill for several hours.

In a saucepan combine the dates, sugar, and hot water. Boil for 5 minutes and add the nuts. Divide the dough into 2 balls and roll each portion into a 9x15-inch rectangle ⅛-inch thick. Spread half of the filling on each rectangle. Roll the dough along the long side to form a log and chill for at least 1 hour. Slice logs into ½-inch pinwheels and place on ungreased cookie sheets. Bake in a 400° oven for 10 to 12 minutes.

Note: The logs may be frozen before baking.

Makes 5 dozen cookies.

Romeo Inn

295 Idaho Street
Ashland, Oregon 97520
(503) 488-0884

Romeo Inn is set in a quiet residential area eight blocks from the nationally acclaimed Oregon Shakespearean Festival. Built in the early 1930s, this classic Cape Cod house sits amid towering 200- to 300-year-old Ponderosa pines overlooking the Rogue Valley and Cascade Mountains. On the back side of the property is a large patio with a swimming pool, spa, flower garden, and sitting areas. The inn's four spacious guest rooms and two luxurious suites are decorated with hand-stitched Amish quilts, and they have king-size beds and private baths. Breakfasts are served in the dining room, where guests can meet one another around a table set with fine china. The delicious menu changes daily.

Romeo Inn Baked Chili Rellenos

1½ pounds lean ground beef
1 cup chopped onion
Salt and pepper
3 4-ounce cans chopped green chilies
4½ cups shredded Cheddar cheese

   🍂 🍂 🍂

3¾ cups milk
10 eggs, beaten
1¼ cups all-purpose flour
1 teaspoon salt
Dash pepper
Tabasco sauce

Grease a 10x13-inch baking pan. In a skillet brown the beef and onion, and drain well. Season the meat with salt and pepper. Place half of the chilies in the prepared pan. Cover with a layer of cheese and meat and top with the remaining chilies.

Romeo Inn

In a large bowl combine the milk, eggs, flour, 1 teaspoon of salt, pepper, and several dashes of Tabasco sauce. Beat until smooth and pour over the chilies. Bake in a 350° oven for 45 to 50 minutes.

Serves 12.

Romeo Inn Lemon Cheese Braid

1 tablespoon active dry yeast
¼ cup very warm water (110° to 115°)
⅓ cup milk
¼ cup butter
4 cups bread flour
¼ cup sugar
½ teaspoon salt
2 eggs

🥄 🥄 🥄

2 8-ounce packages cream cheese, softened
½ cup sugar
1 egg
Grated peel of 1 lemon
½ cup currants or raisins

🥄 🥄 🥄

1 tablespoon butter, melted
½ cup confectioners' sugar
2 tablespoons fresh lemon juice

Grease 2 baking sheets. In a small bowl dissolve the yeast in the warm water. Microwave the milk and butter together on high for 1 minute and set aside. In a food processor combine the flour, sugar, and salt, and pulse a few times to mix the dry ingredients together. Place 2 eggs on top of the flour mixture and pour the yeast mixture over the eggs. With the processor running, pour the milk and butter into the flour mixture. Process about 1 minute until the dough forms a ball. Place the dough in a greased bowl, cover, and let rise about 1 hour, until doubled. Punch down and divide in half. Roll each portion into a 12-inch square. Place on the prepared baking sheets.

In a medium bowl cream together the cream cheese and sugar. Add 1 egg and the lemon peel, blending thoroughly. Stir in the raisins. Spread the filling down the center third of each piece of dough. Cut the sides into 1-inch strips. Fold the strips over the filling, alternating from side to side, to form a braid. Cover and let rise in a warm place about 30 to 45 minutes until doubled. Bake in a 375° oven for 30 minutes, until nicely browned. Cool slightly on a baking rack.

In a small bowl combine 1 tablespoon melted butter, confectioners' sugar, and lemon juice, beating together for a smooth icing. Drizzle over the cooled bread.

Makes 2 coffee cakes.

Romeo Inn Peach Delight

1 large fresh peach, seeded, peeled and cut into chunks
4 cups freshly squeezed orange juice
⅓ cup milk
Dash vanilla extract

In a blender combine all the ingredients, mixing until smooth. Serve in fruit juice glasses.

Serves 6 to 8.

Sandlake Country Inn

8505 Galloway Road
Cloverdale, Oregon 97112
(503) 965-6745

Built from red fir bridge timbers that were lost when a Norwegian sailing vessel shipwrecked in the vicinity in 1890, this two-story 1894 farmhouse is a secret hideaway nestled on the awesome Oregon coast. Offering the gracious service of a fine hotel, the inn offers the romance and seclusion of a country inn and the gracious service of a fine hotel. The rooms are fresh, immaculate, and comfortable, with plants, fresh flowers, antiques, and art treasures. The full gourmet breakfast can be enjoyed in the privacy of one's room or with other guests in the parlor.

Wake-up Parfaits

3 tablespoons orange juice
2 cups sliced bananas or peaches
2 cups fresh blackberries, raspberries, or blueberries
1 cup vanilla yogurt
1 cup homemade granola

In a large bowl combine the juice and fruit. In 6 wine goblets layer half the fruit, half the granola, and half the yogurt. Repeat the layers. Garnish with a sprig of fresh mint and an edible flower, such as johnnie-jump-up or nasturtium. Chill until served.

Serves 6.

Cilantro Spice Bread

1 ¼-ounce package active dry yeast
¼ cup warm water (110° to 115°)
1 egg
½ cup honey
½ cup chopped fresh cilantro
½ teaspoon cinnamon
¼ teaspoon cloves
1 teaspoon salt
1 cup milk, at room temperature
½ cup butter, melted and cooled
4 to 4¾ cups all-purpose flour

Grease a loaf pan. In a large bowl combine the yeast and water. Let stand for 5 minutes. Add the egg, honey, cilantro, cinnamon, cloves, salt, milk, and butter, mixing well. Stir in the flour and knead for 10 minutes. Shape and place in a loaf pan. Let rise until doubled. Bake in a 325° oven for 50 to 60 minutes, until crusty and it sounds hollow when tapped. Cool on a wire rack before removing from the pan.

Makes 1 loaf.

Sandlake Country Inn

Ringo's Make-ahead Kielbasa and Eggs

5 potatoes, chunked
2 large cloves garlic, minced
½ medium onion, diced
Butter
1 pound Kielbasa, chunked

🍃 🍃 🍃

4 eggs, beaten
1¼ cups cream
1 tablespoon dry mustard
¼ cup shredded cheese

In a cooking pot cover the potatoes with water and bring to a boil, then simmer for 12 minutes. In a skillet sauté the garlic and onions in butter until limp. Add the Kielbasa and sauté. Cut the potatoes into bite-size chunks and add to the Kielbasa. Continue to cook for 5 more minutes. Pour the mixture into a casserole dish.

In a medium bowl combine the eggs, cream, and mustard. Pour over the Kielbasa mixture and sprinkle with the cheese. Bake uncovered in a 375° oven for 35 minutes. Let sit for 5 minutes before serving.

Serves 4.

Madison Inn Bed and Breakfast

660 Madison Avenue
Corvallis, Oregon 97333
(503) 757-1274

The Madison Inn is a well-maintained historical home facing Central Park on a quiet street in downtown Corvallis. Oregon State University is within walking distance, a feature especially convenient for visiting professors from throughout the world. The five-story home offers comfortable guest rooms and varied breakfasts that may include fruit-studded scones and individual puffed pancakes, served with fresh fruit or juice and custom-blended coffee or tea. For quiet comfort, pleasant sur-roundings and conversation, the Madison Inn is a good choice.

Laurel's Stuffed Mushrooms

80 mushrooms
½ cup butter, melted

🍃 🍃 🍃

¾ cup Parmesan cheese
½ cup mushroom stems
½ teaspoon garlic salt
1 8-ounce package cream cheese, softened

Line baking trays with foil. Wash and remove the caps from the mushrooms. Brush with the butter and place on the prepared trays.

In a medium bowl combine the Parmesan, mushroom stems, garlic salt, and cream cheese, blending together well. Fill the caps with the mixture. Bake in a 350° oven for 15 minutes. May be frozen. Bake an additional 5 minutes.

Makes 80 stuffed mushrooms.

Kjaer's House in the Woods

814 Lorane Highway
Eugene, Oregon 97405
(503) 343-3234

The House in the Woods is a turn-of-the-century Craftsman-style home set in two acres of fir and oak trees, rhododendron, and azaleas. The interior is highlighted by hardwood floors, Oriental rugs, and a square grand piano. The three guest rooms are individually decorated; the downstairs garden room looks out onto a small garden and has a private bathroom. Breakfast shows Danish and German influences in the dishes offered.

Oatmeal Filbert Pancakes

1½ cups regular oatmeal
2 cups buttermilk
½ cup sifted all-purpose flour
1 tablespoon sugar
1 teaspoon baking soda
½ teaspoon salt
2 eggs, beaten
½ cup chopped filberts

🍂 🍂 🍂

Corn oil

In a large bowl combine the oatmeal and buttermilk. In a separate bowl combine the flour, sugar, baking soda, and salt. Beat the dry ingredients, egg, and filberts into the oatmeal mixture to make a thin batter. Fry the pancakes in corn oil in an electric frying pan at 340° until lightly browned.

Serves 4.

Katy's Raspberry Sherbet

Oregon has excellent berries in the Willamette Valley and this is a favorite recipe. I serve it in a cantaloupe half, garnished with a frozen raspberry dipped in granulated sugar and a sprig of fresh mint. It makes a very pretty first course, but it is also an easy dessert or a refreshing snack for a hot and tired guest on a hot summer afternoon.

4 cups water
4 cups sugar
Juice of 4 lemons
Juice of 4 oranges
4 mashed bananas
2 14-ounce cans crushed pineapple,
  with juice
1 20-ounce package frozen
  unsweetened red raspberries,
  thawed

In a saucepan boil the water and sugar together and cook until clear. In a large bowl combine the juices and fruits. Add to the cooked syrup and mash together. Freeze overnight. Thaw slightly, beat, and refreeze. Keeps well in a freezer container for 6 months.

Serves 20.

Willowbrook Inn

628 Foots Creek Road
Gold Hill, Oregon 97525
(503) 582-0075

Built in 1905, the Willowbrook Inn is nestled in the rolling hills of scenic Southern Oregon. Here guests can watch deer grazing in the meadow, enjoy a bicycle ride through the countryside, sip lemonade on the porch, watch the stars on clear country nights, or splash in the swimming pool. The rooms feature queen-size beds, private baths, and fresh flowers. The hearty breakfast includes various specialties of the inn. White water rafting or fishing on the Rogue River are available nearby.

Herb Garden Frittata

This is served surrounded by purple and green basil for a stunning presentation.

1 medium onion, thinly sliced
¼ cup olive oil
3 small zucchini, thinly sliced
6 large eggs
½ teaspoon salt
½ teaspoon pepper
5 tablespoons grated Parmesan
  cheese
¼ cup butter
1 tablespoon chopped parsley
4 to 5 basil leaves, cut in thin strips
1 tablespoon chopped oregano
  leaves

In a skillet cook the onion in the olive oil until transparent. Add the zucchini and brown lightly. Reduce the heat and let the zucchini cook down for 4 to 5 minutes, drain, and cool.

In a medium bowl beat the eggs with the salt and pepper. Add the zucchini and onion mixture and 4 tablespoons of the Parmesan cheese. Heat the butter in a heavy 10-inch black iron skillet until it foams. Pour the mixture into the pan and sprinkle with the parsley, basil, and oregano. Cook the eggs over very low heat for about 20 minutes until barely set. Sprinkle with the remaining tablespoon of cheese and put under a hot broiler for 30 to 60 seconds. Run a sharp knife around the edge of the frittata to loosen it and slide it onto a plate. Cut into wedges and serve at room temperature.

Note: This recipe can be halved and cooked in a 7-inch skillet to serve 2 to 3.

Serves 6.

Sausage Pie

½ pound sweet Italian sausage
½ onion, chopped
1 small potato, peeled and cut into
  ½-inch cubes
2 tablespoons golden raisins
½ teaspoon anise seed
½ teaspoons dry sage
Pinch cinnamon
½ cup water
1 Golden Delicious apple, peeled,
  cored, and sliced
¼ cup apple juice
Cornstarch

🍂 🍂 🍂

½ sheet frozen puff pastry, thawed
1 egg, beaten

In a skillet over medium heat brown the sausage and set aside. In 1 tablespoon of fat cook the onion, potato, raisins, anise, sage, and cinnamon until the onion is limp. Add ¼ cup of water, the apple, and juice. Cover and simmer about 5 minutes until the potato is tender. Mix cornstarch with the remaining ¼ cup of water and add to the pan, stirring over high heat until the sauce boils and thickens. Stir in the sausage. Spoon the mixture into a 1-pint au gratin dish.

Roll the puff pastry about 2 inches longer and wider than the dish. Brush the edge of the dish with the egg. Fit the pastry over the filling and press against the dish, then trim. Brush the pastry with the egg and set the dish on a baking tray. Bake in a 375° oven for 40 minutes, until well browned. Garnish with sage blossoms or other fresh herbs. Cut through the crust with a spoon to serve.

Note: This may be made ahead, covered, and chilled overnight before baking. The recipe can be doubled or quadrupled to serve up to 8, and baked in a 1 or 2-quart baking dish.

Serves 2 to 3.

Hot Vanilla

This is an old family Christmas morning favorite and preferred by our children to the more usual hot chocolate. We now offer it to our guests as a treat after skiing the slopes of Mt. Ashland.

1 cup milk
1 teaspoon honey
1 drop vanilla extract
Pinch cinnamon

Willowbrook Inn

In a saucepan heat the milk until very hot but not boiling. Pour into a mug and add the honey, vanilla, and cinnamon.

Serves 1.

Gold Nugget Cakes

Being in an historic gold mining area, it seems only natural that we should serve these pancakes highlighted with discoveries of bits of golden crystallized ginger in them. Serve with maple syrup or peach sauce.

5 tablespoons butter or margarine
1 cup milk
2 eggs
1¼ cups all-purpose flour
4 teaspoons baking powder
¾ teaspoon salt
1 tablespoon (powdered) ginger
6 ounces crystallized ginger, cut in ¼-inch cubes

Grease a griddle. In a saucepan combine the butter and milk, heating until the butter melts, then cool. In a small bowl beat the eggs, then stir into the milk mixture, mixing well. In a separate bowl combine the flour, baking powder, salt, and powdered ginger. Add the dry ingredients to the liquid mixture and stir until incorporated. Pour about 3 tablespoons of the batter for each pancake onto the griddle and sprinkle each with 1 teaspoon of the crystallized ginger. Cook until little bubbles appear, flip, and cook another 30 seconds.

Makes twenty-four 4-inch pancakes.

Peach Sauce

¼ cup sugar
1 tablespoon cornstarch
2 cups sliced fresh or frozen peaches
2 tablespoons lemon juice
⅓ cup water

In a saucepan combine the sugar and cornstarch. Add the peaches, lemon juice, and water, and cook over me-

dium heat, stirring until the mixture is thickened. Serve warm with the Gold Nugget Cakes.

Makes 2 cups.

McCully House Inn

240 East California Street
Post Office Box 13
Jacksonville, Oregon 97530
(503) 899-1942

When newly constructed in 1861, Dr. J. W. McCully's mansion was one of the most palatial residences in this booming gold rush town. Today visitors can continue to enjoy the elegance of this historic home, one of six original dwellings of the town. European and American antiques, polished hardwood floors, lace curtains, and a magnificent square grand piano help create an atmosphere of quiet elegance. Every room and its private bath have been decorated to capture the historic heritage of the home.

Peach and Sesame Glazed Duckling

2 ducklings

🍃 🍃 🍃

½ gallon apple cider vinegar
2½ cups sugar
1 tablespoon freshly grated ginger
3 ripe peaches, puréed
Salt and pepper

🍃 🍃 🍃

½ cup toasted sesame seeds

Remove the legs, breasts, and excess fat from the ducklings. In an electric skillet over low heat render the fat, then add the legs. Cook at 275° for 2½ to 3 hours until tender. Cook the breasts at 450° for 30 minutes until rare.

In a large saucepan combine the vinegar, sugar, and ginger. Heat until mixture is reduced and syrupy. Add the puréed peaches, and season with salt and pepper. Cook for 10 to 15 minutes and strain. Brush the legs and breasts with the glaze and sprinkle with the sesame seeds. Garnish with more sauce and fresh peach slices to serve.

Serves 4, with 1 quart of glaze.

Hot and Sweet Pepper Soup

2 red peppers, julienned
2 yellow peppers, julienned
2 green peppers, julienned
1 large yellow onion, julienned
3 cloves garlic, minced
1 large Anaheim chili pepper, roasted and finely chopped
1 jalapeño pepper, roasted and finely chopped
2 ripe tomatoes, finely diced
2½ quarts chicken stock
Salt and pepper

In a large skillet sauté the peppers and onion with the garlic. Add the Anaheim and jalapeño peppers and the tomatoes, and sauté for 1 minute. Add the chicken stock and bring to a boil. Lower heat and simmer for 10 to 15 minutes. Season with salt and pepper. Serve with a dollop of sour cream and a cilantro sprig.

Serves 10 to 12.

Chocolate Almond Tart

3 cups all-purpose flour
½ teaspoon salt
1 tablespoon sugar
1 lemon
1½ cups butter
¼ cup water
½ teaspoon vanilla extract

ଛ ଛ ଛ

1 cup toasted slivered almonds
1 cup heavy cream
3 ounces dark chocolate
2 tablespoons brown sugar
2 egg yolks
1 teaspoon vanilla extract
½ teaspoon almond extract

ଛ ଛ ଛ

1 cup heavy cream
½ cup confectioners' sugar
1 teaspoon vanilla extract

In a bowl combine the flour, salt, and sugar. Grate the lemon zest and add to the flour mixture. Cut the butter into cubes and cut into flour. In a separate bowl combine the water and ½ teaspoon of vanilla and add to the flour mixture just until the dough holds together. Divide the dough into 3 balls, wrap, and refrigerate until chilled. Roll out 1 ball and place in a 10-inch fluted tart pan. Freeze the remaining dough for future use. Weigh down the pastry with dried beans. Bake in a 350° oven for 20 minutes, until golden brown. Remove and cool.

Place the almonds in the bottom of the tart shell. In a saucepan scald the 1 cup of heavy cream. Lower the heat and add the chocolate and brown sugar, stirring with a whisk for 5 minutes until melted. Add the chocolate to the egg yolks. Stir in 1 teaspoon of vanilla and the almond extract and pour into the tart shell. Bake in a 350° oven for 10 minutes, then cool.

In a bowl whip the heavy cream with the confectioners' sugar and 1 teaspoon of vanilla. Fill a pastry bag with a star tip and cover the tart shell with whipped cream. Garnish with shaved chocolate.

Serves 8.

McCully House Inn

Marjon Bed and Breakfast Inn

44975 Leaburg Dam Road
Leaburg, Oregon 97489
(503) 896-3145

This elegant bed and breakfast offers luxury along the McKenzie River, twenty-four miles east of Eugene. A garden containing 2,000 azaleas and 700 rhododendrons and a natural fern bed that slopes to the river contribute to the charming atmosphere of this inn. Breakfast is served on a covered terrace, weather permitting. Accommodations for two couples are available at this beautiful inn with an Oriental atmosphere.

Baked Egg Surprise

1½ tablespoons cream
1 extra large egg
Salt and pepper
Sugar
Havarti cheese, frozen and grated
Caraway seeds

    ❧   ❧   ❧

3 small frozen sausage links
1 tablespoon raw baby green peas, fresh or frozen

Spray an individual baking dish with non-stick cooking spray and add the cream. Break the egg into the dish being careful not to break the yolk. Sprinkle with salt, pepper, and sugar. Generously cover with the grated cheese. Sprinkle with 8 caraway seeds. Bake in a 425° oven for 8 to 10 minutes, until the white is firm but the yolk still jiggles. Do not overcook.

Slice the sausage links crosswise in ¼-inch slices. Fry sausage and drain. Sprinkle the cooked egg with the sausage slices and green peas.

Serves 1.

The Pringle House

Seventh and Locust Streets
Post Office Box 578
Oakland, Oregon 97462
(503) 459-5038

Standing on a rise overlooking downtown Oakland, the Pringle House offers unique accommodations to its guests. Constructed in 1893 and returned to its Victorian design by Jim and Demay Pringle, it is one of many homes and businesses on the National Historic Register in this quaint city of 850 people. Guests may relax in the comfort of the parlor, in winged-backed chairs in front of the sitting room fireplace, in the privacy of the garden, or in their rooms. Many like to view Demay's doll collection or Jim's memorabilia of his life in music. Breakfast, served in the dining room, is a gourmet affair, with such delights as fresh fruit compote, freshly baked croissants, quiches, and more. Oakland activities include a fine museum, antique and craft shops, and one of Oregon's finest ice cream parlors and dinner houses.

Eggnog French Toast Almondine

4 eggs
¼ cup sugar
¾ cup light cream
1 tablespoon brandy
½ teaspoon vanilla extract
¼ teaspoon nutmeg
8 slices French bread, ¾-inch thick

    ❧   ❧   ❧

1 cup sliced natural almonds
6 tablespoons butter
Strawberry Sauce (recipe follows)

In a bowl whisk together the eggs and sugar. Stir in the cream, brandy, vanilla, and nutmeg. Place the bread slices in a shallow baking dish and

The Pringle House

cover with the egg mixture. Turn bread to coat all sides. Cover and refrigerate overnight.

Remove the bread from the dish and coat the flat sides with the almonds. In a skillet melt the butter and cook the toast over medium heat until golden brown on both sides. Serve with Strawberry Sauce.

Serves 6.

Strawberry Sauce

1 12-ounce package frozen strawberries
1 tablespoon sugar
1 tablespoon water

In a medium saucepan combine the strawberries, sugar, and water. Simmer for 5 minutes, crushing the berries with a spoon. Remove from the heat and cool slightly before serving. Spoon over hot Eggnog French Toast Almondine.

Makes 1¼ cups.

Hostess House

5758 Northeast Emerson
Portland, Oregon 97218-2406
(503) 282-7892

Hostess House offers warmth and hospitality in a well-kept contemporary home in a quiet residential neighborhood. Five miles from Portland's airport and within a ten-minute drive from famous Lloyd Center, it provides easy access to major interstate highways. The three guest rooms, decorated in oak furniture, share a bath. The deep, terraced backyard is beautifully maintained; a deck and patio add to guests' enjoyment. Breakfast is according to guest preferences. Smoking is permitted outside. Tennis, golf, and skiing are nearby.

Cream of Broccoli Soup

1½ tablespoons margarine
1 cup chopped carrots
¾ cup chopped onion (or 3
    tablespoons instant minced
    onion)
2 cups chicken broth
⅓ cup brown rice
¼ teaspoon mace
¼ teaspoon basil
¼ teaspoon marjoram
¼ teaspoon summer savory
1 tablespoon lemon juice

🎗 🎗 🎗

2 medium stalks broccoli (or 1 10-
    ounce package frozen broccoli)
⅛ teaspoon black pepper
1 cup nonfat dry milk
Lemon slices

In a large skillet over medium heat melt the margarine. Sauté the carrots and onion until the onion is softened. Add the chicken broth, rice, mace, herbs, and lemon juice. Bring the mixture to a boil, then reduce heat to simmer. Cook covered for 45 minutes.

Pare and steam the broccoli spears until tender-crisp. Cut the stems from the broccoli flowerettes and reserve both parts. If desired, pour the broth mixture into a blender container, add the broccoli stems, and liquify. Add the broccoli flowerettes, pepper, and milk. Reheat over low heat. Serve garnished with a thin lemon slice floating in the soup.

Serves 4.

Hamburger Soup

1 pound hamburger
½ teaspoon salt
¼ teaspoon pepper
¼ teaspoon oregano
¼ teaspoon basil
⅛ teaspoon savory salt
1 tablespoon soy sauce
6 cups chicken broth
1 16-ounce can tomato sauce
1 cup diced celery
¼ cup diced carrots
⅓ cup dried split peas
1 cup elbow macaroni

In a skillet sauté the ground beef until browned, then drain. Add the salt, pepper, oregano, basil, savory salt, soy sauce, broth, and tomato sauce. Simmer for 15 minutes. Add the celery, carrots, split peas, and macaroni. Simmer for 30 more minutes.

Serves 4.

Italian Spaghetti

2 pounds hamburger
1 cup chopped onion
½ teaspoon salt
⅛ teaspoon pepper
3 6-ounce cans tomato paste
3 8-ounce cans tomato sauce
1 quart canned tomatoes, chopped

🎗 🎗 🎗

¾ teaspoon oregano
½ teaspoon chopped rosemary
½ teaspoon sweet basil
1 bay leaf
3 cloves garlic (or ½ teaspoon
    garlic powder)
1 tablespoon honey or sugar

🎗 🎗 🎗

1 pound spaghetti
Parmesan cheese

In a skillet brown the hamburger, leaving chunky, then drain. Brown the onion slightly, then drain. In a large cooking pot combine the hamburger and onion, adding the salt, pepper, tomato paste, tomato sauce, and tomatoes. Simmer for 1 hour. Add the oregano, rosemary, basil, bay leaf, garlic, and honey. Simmer for at least 1 more hour. Remove the bay leaf.

Cook the spaghetti according to the package directions.

Serve with sauce and Parmesan cheese.

Serves 12.

Swedish Meatballs

These are excellent served over cooked rice or Chinese noodles.

1½ pounds hamburger
1 egg
¼ cup milk
¼ cup cracker crumbs
⅛ to ¼ teaspoon ginger
1 tablespoon onion flakes
1 teaspoon salt

🎗 🎗 🎗

2 tablespoons vinegar
2 tablespoons cornstarch
2 tablespoons brown sugar or honey
1 to 2 tablespoons soy sauce
1 20-ounce can pineapple chunks,
    with juice

In a large bowl combine the hamburger, egg, milk, cracker crumbs, ginger, onion flakes, and salt. Form into meatballs. Brown lightly in a skillet and drain.

In a saucepan combine the vinegar, cornstarch, brown sugar, soy sauce and pineapple juice. Cook the sauce over low heat until thickened and pour over the meatballs. In the skillet, heat for 2 to 3 minutes. Stir in the pineapple chunks.

Serves 6.

Coq au Vin

This French dish is almost a meal in itself. Add crusty bread, green salad dressed with oil and vinegar, and a dessert of miniature cream puffs drizzled with chocolate syrup.

½ teaspoon crushed thyme leaves
1 bay leaf
2 large sprigs parsley

🎗 🎗 🎗

3 to 3½-pound broiler fryer
    chicken, cut up (prefer to
    debone)
½ cup all-purpose flour
1 teaspoon salt
¼ teaspoon pepper
6 slices bacon

🎗 🎗 🎗

6 small onions (or 6 tablespoons
    instant minced onion)
½ pound mushrooms, sliced
4 carrots, halved
1 cup chicken broth
1 cup Burgundy (or grape juice)
1 clove garlic, crushed
½ teaspoon salt

Prepare a Bouquet Garni by tying the thyme leaves, bay leaf, and parsley sprigs in a cheesecloth bag or placing in a tea bag.

Wash the chicken and pat dry. In a bowl combine the flour, 1 teaspoon of salt, and pepper. Coat the chicken with the flour mixture. In a large skillet fry the bacon until crisp, then drain, crumble, and set aside. Brown the chicken in the hot bacon drippings. Set chicken aside.

Sauté the onions and mushrooms in the bacon drippings until the onions are tender, then drain. In a large skillet combine the chicken with the Bouquet Garni, bacon, onions, and mushrooms. Stir in the carrots, chicken broth, Burgundy, garlic, and ½ teaspoon of salt. Simmer covered for 1 hour until tender. Remove the Bouquet Garni before serving and skim off the excess fat. Sprinkle with snipped parsley, if desired.

Serves 6.

Fresh Citrus Compote Dessert

3 oranges, peeled and sectioned (1½ cups)
2 grapefruit, peeled and sectioned (1½ cups)

🍃 🍃 🍃

⅓ cup Sauterne or light wine (or white grape juice)
¼ cup honey
¼ cup fresh orange juice (or concentrated)
⅛ to ¼ teaspoon cinnamon
¼ cup finely chopped toasted almonds

Section the oranges and grapefruit by using a sharp knife and cutting a slice from the top of the fruit. Cut off the peel, round and round, spiral fashion. Go over the fruit again, removing any remaining white membrane. Cut along the side of each dividing membrane from the outside to the middle of the core and remove section by section over a bowl to retain the juice.

In a saucepan combine the wine, honey, orange juice, and cinnamon. Cook over medium heat until the sugar is dissolved. Add the citrus fruit sections and heat for 1 minute. Pour into a serving dish and sprinkle with the almonds. Serve hot or cold.

Serves 4 to 5.

The John Palmer House

4314 North Mississippi Avenue
Portland, Oregon 97217
(503) 284-5893

Guests at this Victorian house erected in 1890 are privileged to "live the romance of the Victorian Era" in an elegant, antique-filled setting. The walls are covered with 1880 wallpapers, and the gas-electric light fixtures gleam softly, reflecting the colors in the magnificent Povey windows. Such touches as gardenias on the pillows, chilled champagne in silver coolers, fruit baskets, Victorian sleepwear, horse and carriage rides, five- and seven-course gourmet meals, and all the privacy anybody could want are the specialties of this inn.

Baton Rouge Omelette

1 12-ounce can stewed tomatoes
1 12-ounce can tomato sauce
1 green pepper, diced
3 stalks celery, diced
1 onion, diced
2 green onions, diced

🍃 🍃 🍃

1 teaspoon salt
1 teaspoon basil
1 teaspoon oregano
½ teaspoon thyme
1 teaspoon paprika
½ teaspoon red pepper
½ teaspoon black pepper
½ teaspoon white pepper
½ teaspoon garlic powder
12 eggs
1 avocado, quartered
4 ounces cream cheese
4 ounces bay shrimp

In a large saucepan combine the tomatoes, tomato sauce, pepper, cel-

ery, and onions. Stir in the seasonings. Simmer for 30 minutes until thickened. Set aside and keep warm.

Beat 3 eggs at a time and pour into an omelette pan. Cook until desired doneness and add ¼ of the avocado, 1 ounce of cream cheese, and 1 ounce of bay shrimp as a filling for each omelette. Fold over and place on a warmed plate. Top with the creole sauce.

Serves 4.

The Umpqua House

7338 Oak Hill Road
Roseburg, Oregon 97470
(503) 459-4700

Situated on a hillside in a rural setting overlooking the beautiful Umpqua Valley, this inn offers privacy, quiet, and a little pampering to the traveler looking for a rest. This two-story home offers two rooms with private entrances. Breakfasts cater to guests' dietary needs and eating preferences; the innkeeper is a health educator with training in nutritional counseling, and she makes her expertise available to guests.

Pumpkin Muffins

½ cup oil or butter
1 cup canned or freshly cooked pumpkin
2 eggs, slightly beaten
1 teaspoon vanilla extract
½ cup honey or fruit concentrate
½ cup unsweetened applesauce
1 scant cup whole wheat flour
1 scant cup oat flour
1 teaspoon cinnamon
½ teaspoon nutmeg
½ teaspoon allspice

¼ teaspoon ginger
1 teaspoon baking soda
1 cup raisins soaked in ¼ cup apple juice, water, or whiskey
¾ cup walnuts

Line muffin tins with paper cups. In a large bowl combine the oil, pumpkin, eggs, vanilla, honey, and applesauce.

In a separate bowl combine the flour with the spices and baking soda. Add to the pumpkin mixture, blending well. Add the raisins with the liquid. Stir in the nuts and mix thoroughly. Pour the batter into the prepared muffin tins. Bake in a 325° oven for 25 to 30 minutes.

Makes 12 muffins.

Cranberry Crunch

1 cup rolled oat flakes
½ cup oat flour, wheat flour, or rice flour
½ to ¾ cup brown sugar or honey
½ cup butter, softened

   ❧ ❧ ❧

1 pound cranberries
1 tablespoon honey

Grease an 8-inch square pan. In a medium bowl combine the oats, flour, and sugar. Cut the butter into small particles and cut into the flour mixture with a pastry blender.

In a cooking pot combine the cranberries with 1 to 1½ cups of water. Cook uncovered for 5 minutes until the berries begin to pop. Pour off the liquid and add the honey. Pour half of the flour mixture into the prepared pan. Spoon the cranberry mixture over the flour mixture and cover with the remaining flour mixture. Bake in a 350° oven for 40 minutes. Cool and cut into squares.

Serves 6.

Eggplant Relish

This is my mother-in-law's mother's recipe from Russia.

1 large eggplant
½ large onion, finely chopped
1 large sweet green or red pepper, chopped (preferably red)
2 or 3 large ripe red tomatoes, chopped
2 tablespoons oil
2 tablespoons freshly squeezed lemon juice
Salt and pepper

Pierce the eggplant with a fork. Bake in a 425° oven for 20 minutes. Cool, peel, and coarsely chop. Combine with the onion, sweet pepper, and tomatoes. Add the oil, lemon juice, and seasonings. Refrigerate until chilled and serve on crackers as an appetizer.

Serves 8.

Eggplant-Sweet Potato Casserole

Butter
1 large eggplant
1 large sweet potato
1 large carrot
1 large onion, thinly sliced
1 large ripe red tomato, sliced
1 medium zucchini, sliced
½ cup finely chopped parsley
Italian herb seasoning
Salt and pepper
½ cup wheat germ or bread crumbs
½ to 2 cups grated Cheddar or Jack cheese
½ cup tomato juice or V-8 juice

Butter a large pyrex rectangular baking dish. Steam the eggplant until tender and thinly slice. Steam the sweet potato and carrot until barely tender and thinly slice. Place a layer of onion slices in the prepared dish and cover with 1 layer each of the sliced sweet potato, eggplant, carrot, and tomato. Sprinkle with the parsley. Season sparingly with the Italian herb seasoning, salt, and pepper. Sprinkle with the wheat germ or crumbs. Cover with half of the cheese. Layer again in the same order ending with the grated cheese. Add the tomato juice and cover with tin foil. Bake in a 325° oven for 1 hour. Serve with freshly baked corn bread.

Note: If you are watching calories or cholesterol, reduce the cheese to ½ cup and dot with butter.

Serves 8.

Pennsylvania

The Pine Knob Inn

Route 447
Canadensis, Pennsylvania 18325
(717) 595-2532

At this historic inn in the heart of the Pocono Mountains the traditions of yesteryear have not been forgotten. The atmosphere is friendly and informal. Guests may swim in the oversized pool, play a set of tennis, or try archery, badminton, shuffleboard, or other lawn games. Fishing in Broadhead Creek or hiking to the top of Pine Knob are other favorite activities.

The hearty country breakfast provides a satisfying beginning to a busy day. Dinner is also served in the charming country dining room, with the diversified menu offering a variety of cuisines. The cocktail lounge provides an attractive gathering spot for a friendly chat with old and new acquaintances.

Colonial Innkeeper Pie

4 ounces unsweetened chocolate
½ cup water
⅔ cup sugar
¼ cup butter, melted
1½ teaspoons vanilla extract

🍂 🍂 🍂

1 cup sifted all-purpose flour
¾ cup sugar
1 teaspoon baking powder
¼ cup shortening or margarine
½ cup milk
½ teaspoon vanilla extract
1 egg
1 8-inch unbaked pie shell

🍂 🍂 🍂

½ cup sliced almonds

In a saucepan melt the chocolate with the water and ⅔ cup of sugar. Bring to a boil, stirring constantly. Remove from the heat and stir in the butter and 1½ teaspoons of vanilla. Cool for 20 minutes.

In a large mixing bowl sift together the flour, ¾ cup of sugar, and baking powder. Cut in the shortening. Add the milk and ½ teaspoon of vanilla, beating for 2 minutes. Add the egg and beat for 2 more minutes. Pour the batter into the pie shell.

Pour the chocolate sauce over the batter. Sprinkle with the almonds. Bake in a 350° oven for 55 to 60 minutes. Serve warm with vanilla ice cream or bourbon-spiked whipped cream.

Note: During the baking the chocolate sauce will drizzle through the cake batter adding to its moistness and forming a thick layer of gooey chocolate under the cake layer.

Serves 8.

The Pine Knob Inn

Churchtown Inn

Route 23
Churchtown, Pennsylvania 17555
(215) 445-7794

The most prominent landmark in this Pennsylvania Dutch hamlet, the Churchtown Inn is a splendid fieldstone mansion overlooking picture-postcard fields and farms. Built in 1735, the house resonates with the solid comforts and grace that distinguish a home built for gentry. The inn features a full breakfast, lovely Victorian parlors, elegant but cozy bedrooms, private and shared baths, queen and single beds, air conditioning and television, dinner at a nearby Amish home by prior arrangement, carriage rides, barbecues, mystery weekends, and special holiday packages. Smoking is in designated areas only.

Stu's Granola-Oatmeal Pancakes

2 cups milk
1 cup granola
1 cup old fashioned rolled oats

   🍃 🍃 🍃

½ cup butter, melted and cooled
½ cup all purpose flour
2 eggs, slightly beaten
2 tablespoons sugar
2 teaspoons baking powder
¼ teaspoon nutmeg
¼ teaspoon cinnamon
⅛ teaspoon salt
1 teaspoon vanilla extract

In a medium bowl combine the milk, granola, and oats. Cover and refrigerate overnight.

In a small bowl combine the remaining ingredients. Gradually add the mixture to the granola mixture, stirring until smooth. Pour ⅓ cup portions of the batter on a hot buttered griddle and cook until golden brown. Makes 10 5-inch pancakes.

Churchtown Inn's Oatmeal Custard

A wonderful winter morning start!

½ cup milk
½ cup heavy cream (or 1 cup milk or 1 cup half and half)
4 eggs
Salt
5 teaspoons sugar
1 teaspoon vanilla extract
½ cup quick oatmeal
½ teaspoon nutmeg
3 tablespoons chopped raisins (or 4 teaspoons chopped nuts)
Cinnamon

Butter 4 custard cups and set in a shallow baking dish half filled with hot water. In a large bowl combine the milk, cream, eggs, and salt. Add the sugar, vanilla, oatmeal, and nutmeg. Add the raisins if desired. Fill the prepared custard cups to ½-inch of the top. Sprinkle with a pinch of cinnamon. Bake in a 375° oven for 20 to 25 minutes until set. Remove from the oven and let stand for 5 minutes.

Note: This may be prepared the night before and baked in the morning.
Serves 4.

Conifer Ridge Farm

Rural Delivery 2, Box 202A
Clearville, Pennsylvania 15535
(814) 784-3342

The main house on this 126-acre farm is a contemporary passive solar home with rustic exterior and exceptional interior beauty. The antique brick indoor walls and ancient oak beams combine with an open contemporary design for elegance and comfort. The large country breakfast is served in the sunroom. Also available is a rustic, cozy cabin in the woods. The seasonal Barn Christmas Shop, in a portion of the barn, specializes in local crafts.

Churchtown Inn

Chicken Parisienne

2 to 4 whole chicken breasts, halved
Salt and pepper
3 tablespoons butter
1 small onion, sliced
1 cup freshly sliced mushrooms

🍃 🍃 🍃

1 cup sour cream
1 10½-ounce can cream of chicken
   soup
½ to ¾ cup sherry cooking wine

Season the chicken breasts with salt and pepper. In a skillet brown the chicken on both sides in the butter. Arrange the chicken, onions, and mushrooms in a casserole.

Combine the sour cream, chicken soup, and wine. Pour over the chicken. Bake in a 400° oven for 40 to 50 minutes.

Serves 4.

French Apple Cream Pie

¾ cup sugar
2 tablespoons all-purpose flour
¾ teaspoon cinnamon
½ teaspoon salt
1 8-inch unbaked pie shell
4 or 5 medium apples, pared and
   sliced
½ cup heavy cream

In a small bowl combine the sugar, flour, cinnamon, and salt. Sprinkle half of the mixture in the bottom of the pie shell. Add the apple slices and top with the remaining sugar mixture. Top with the cream. Bake in a 450° oven for 15 minutes. Reduce the temperature to 350° and bake 45 minutes.

Note: Be sure to use a firm, tart pie apple. I use Stayman apples.

Serves 8.

Gateway Lodge

Route 36, Box 125
Cooksburg, Pennsylvania 16217
(814) 744-8017
(800) 843-6862 (Pennsylvania only)

Gateway Lodge is a rustic log cabin country inn in the original Black Forest given to Willam Penn in 1681 by King Charles II of England. Built in this wonderful setting in 1934, it utilizes pine and hemlock logs, wormy pine walls and trim, and oak flooring, all suggesting pioneer ruggedness. Except for an added staircase, front porch, and indoor pool, the lodge stands as it was originally built. Recreational activities are abundant year-round: bird watching, hiking, summer theater-going, bicycling, canoeing, skiing, fishing, golf, and much more. Bedrooms are furnished with hand-hewn wormy chestnut beds, calico-printed antique quilts, antique furnishings, and Early American oval braided rugs.

Mushroom-Broccoli Chowder

1 14½-ounce can chicken broth
½ 10-ounce package frozen broccoli

🍃 🍃 🍃

1½ cups sliced fresh mushrooms
½ cup chopped onion
2 tablespoons butter
2 tablespoons all-purpose flour
½ teaspoon salt
⅛ teaspoon pepper
1¼ cups milk
1 8-ounce package corn
1 tablespoon pimento

In a saucepan combine the broth and broccoli, and cook for 5 miutes. Set aside.

In a saucepan cook the mushrooms and onion in the butter. Blend in the flour, salt, pepper, and milk. Cook until thickened. Add the broccoli and broth. Stir in the corn and pimento, and heat through.

Serves 4.

Cream of Onion Soup

4 cups lengthwise-sliced onions
¼ cup butter
2 to 3 quarts water
4 cups nonfat dry milk
2 tablespoons cornstarch
2 tablespoons chicken base
¼ teaspoon salt (optional)
Pepper

In a large cooking pot sauté the onions in the butter. Cover and cook until tender. Add most of the water and dry milk. Mix the remaining water with the cornstarch. Add the cornstarch mixture, chicken base, salt, and pepper, stirring until thickened.

Serves 6.

The Inn at Fordhook Farm

105 New Britain Road
Doylestown, Pennsylvania 18901
(215) 345-1766

Friendly, comfortable, and quietly elegant, the Inn at Fordhook Farm, still the Burpee (seed company) family home, offers the tranquility and beauty of a 200-year-old house and sixty acres of meadows, woodlands, gardens, and historic buildings. Guests will enjoy the large bedrooms furnished with family antiques and mementos, the full traditional breakfast in the beamed dining room, and afternoon tea by the fire or on the terrace in the shade of giant old linden trees. The inn is near Valley Forge, New Hope, and Philadelphia.

Company Eggs

Hot-deviled eggs.

8 hard-boiled eggs

ɐ ɐ ɐ

¼ cup butter, melted
½ teaspoon Worcestershire sauce
¼ teaspoon dry mustard
1 tablespoon chopped parsley
1 teaspoon chopped chives
⅓ cup diced ham

ɐ ɐ ɐ

3 tablespoons butter
3 tablespoons all-purpose flour
1 cup chicken broth
¾ cup milk

ɐ ɐ ɐ

1 cup shredded cheese (American, Cheddar, Monterey Jack, or Swiss)
Paprika
Salt and pepper

Butter a shallow baking dish. Cut the hard-boiled eggs in half lengthwise and scoop out the yolks. In a food processor or blender combine the egg yolks with ¼ cup of melted butter, Worcestershire, mustard powder, parsley, chives, and ham. Blend until well mixed. Stuff the egg halves with the filling and place in a single layer in the prepared dish.

In a saucepan or frying pan combine 3 tablespoons of butter with the flour for a roux. Slowly add the chicken broth. When the sauce is thick and bubbling, slowly add the milk. Pour the sauce over the stuffed eggs.

Sprinkle with the cheese, paprika, salt, and pepper. Bake in a 350° oven for 30 minutes until hot and bubbly.

Serves 6 to 8.

Cranberry Scones

3 cups all-purpose flour
½ cup sugar
¼ teaspoon cinnamon
⅛ teaspoon allspice
1 tablespoon baking powder
½ teaspoon baking soda
½ teaspoon salt
1½ teaspoons grated orange peel
¾ cup butter or margarine
1 cup fresh or frozen cranberries
½ cup chopped pecans
1 cup buttermilk

Grease a baking sheet. In a large bowl sift together the flour, sugar, spices, baking powder, baking soda, and salt. Add the orange peel and mix. Cut the butter into small chunks and cut or rub into the flour mixture until coarse crumbs form. Stir in the cranberries and pecans. Add the buttermilk. Mix the dough until it is evenly moist, then gather into a ball. On a floured board roll or pat the dough into a ¾-inch thick circle. Cut into 2½-inch rounds and place on the prepared baking sheet, leaving plenty of space between the scones. Reroll the scraps and cut. Bake on the lower shelf of a 400° oven for 10 to 15 minutes.

Makes 12 scones.

Shady Lane Lodge—A Bed and Breakfast Inn

Allegheny Avenue
Eagles Mere, Pennsylvania 17731
(717) 525-3394

The Shady Lane Lodge is a quiet bed and breakfast inn in the picturesque mountain-top village of Eagles Mere, known as "The Town Time Forgot." It provides visitors a lovely step into the past.

The lodge has seven guest rooms, all with private baths; it also has two sitting rooms and a dining room. Guests enjoy a quiet wooded setting within walking distance of the lake; gift and antique shops are nearby, too. Winter sports include cross-country skiing, tobogganing, and ice skating.

Lemon Blueberry Brunch Cake

1 18-ounce package lemon cake mix
¼ cup margarine or butter, softened
1 3-ounce package cream cheese, softened
⅓ cup water
2 eggs
1 21-ounce can blueberry pie filling
½ cup finely chopped almonds or pecans

ɐ ɐ ɐ

½ cup confectioners' sugar
1 tablespoon margarine or butter, softened
2 to 3 teaspoons milk
¼ teaspoon lemon extract

Grease and flour a 9x13-inch pan. In a large mixing bowl combine the cake mix, ¼ cup of margarine, and cream cheese. Mix with an electric mixer at low speed until fine crumbs form. Set aside 1 cup of the crumbs. Add the water and eggs to the remaining crumb mixture, and beat for 2 minutes at high speed. Pour into the prepared pan. Spoon the pie filling over the batter, gently spreading to cover. Combine the reserved crumbs with the almonds, and sprinkle over the pie filling. Bake in a 350° oven for 35 to 45 minutes or until set in the center and the edges are golden brown. Cool for 25 minutes.

In a small bowl blend the confectioners' sugar, 1 tablespoon of margarine, milk, and lemon extract until the glaze is smooth. Drizzle over the warm cake. Store in the refrigerator.

Serves 12.

Custard Coffee Cake

A delicious and moist coffee cake.

1 18-ounce package yellow cake mix
1½ cups Ricotta cheese (or 1
15-ounce container)
4 eggs, beaten
⅓ cup sugar
1 teaspoon vanilla extract
Confectioners' sugar

Grease and flour a 9x13-inch pan. Prepare the cake mix according to the package directions. Pour the mixture into the prepared pan. In a medium bowl combine the cheese, eggs, sugar, and vanilla. Gently pour the cheese mixture over the cake batter. Bake in a 350° oven for 40 to 45 minutes. Sift confectioners' sugar over the top of the warm cake.
Serves 8 to 10.

The Bechtel Mansion Inn

400 West King Street
East Berlin, Pennsylvania 17316
(717) 259-7760

This charming 1897 Victorian home has been carefully preserved to retain its original beauty. The parlor retains the original Brussels carpet and wallpaper and exhibits part of the family's Chinese Celedon collection of porcelain. The dining room has etched glass windows, a large window seat, built-in oak windows, and an unusual brass chandelier. The living room has vertical oak sliding shutters, a bay window, a red Bokhara rug, an early nineteenth-century oak with mahogany inlay secretary, and a hand-carved chair. This attention to

detail continues in the six bedrooms and suites available for guests on the first and second floors, as well as the five third-floor rooms. The Victorian carriage house also serves as an antique shop and unique guest quarters. A deluxe continental breakfast is served.

Pennsylvania Dutch Crunchy Apple Muffins

2 cups all-purpose flour
½ cup nonfat dry milk
⅓ cup sugar
4 teaspoons baking powder
1 teaspoon salt
1 teaspoon cinnamon
1 cup finely cut peeled apples or
applesauce
¾ cup water
¼ cup oil
1 egg

  🍂 🍂 🍂

½ cup brown sugar
½ cup chopped nuts
½ teaspoon cinnamon

Grease 12 muffin tins. In a large bowl sift together the flour, dry milk, sugar, baking powder, salt, and 1 teaspoon of cinnamon. Mix in the apples. Stir in the water, oil, and egg. Pour into the prepared muffin tins.
In a small bowl combine the brown sugar, nuts, and ½ teaspoon of cinnamon. Sprinkle over the top of the batter. Bake in a 400° oven for 20 minutes.
Makes 12 muffins.

The Guesthouse and 1777 House at Doneckers

318-324 North State Street
Ephrata, Pennsylvania 17522
(717) 733-8696

Pampering guests is the aim of the innkeepers of the Guesthouse at Doneckers. Refreshing coolers or pots of iced tea on request, chocolates by the bed at night, a balcony deck for sunning, a cozy parlor for relaxing, good food in the restaurant—all these and more add up to a feeling of elegance and well being. The Guesthouse has twenty-nine rooms, each individually decorated with cherry wood vanities, folk art, designer linens, and fine crystal. Several suites have Jacuzzis and fireplaces. The restaurant specializes in French cuisine. More than fifty art studios and galleries, markets, antiques, and the Ephrata Cloister Museum are nearby.

Upside Down Orange Cake

4 oranges
4 cups water
2¾ cups sugar

  🍂 🍂 🍂

½ cup sugar
½ cup water
Grand Marnier
Juice of ½ orange

  🍂 🍂 🍂

1 generous cup Chantilly Cream
(recipe follows)
1¼ cups Vanilla Pastry Cream
(recipe follows)
1 Genoise

Thinly slice the oranges. In a saucepan combine 4 cups of water and 2¾ cups of sugar and bring to a boil. Add the orange slices and summer slowly for 2 hours. Pour the oranges and syrup into a bowl and set aside for 1 day.

Butter an 8½-inch cake pan and dust with sugar. In a saucepan combine ½ cup of sugar and ½ cup water. Simmer for 5 minutes. Flavor with Grand Marnier and the juice.

In a medium bowl whip the Chantilly Cream. Reserve half of the orange slices for decorating the cake and cut the remaining slices into small pieces. Mix the pieces with the Vanilla Pastry Cream, then fold the cream and oranges very delicately into the whipped Chantilly Cream.

Line the prepared pan with the orange slices. Fill half the pan with the orange-flavored pastry cream. Cut the Genoise into 2 layers with a serrated knife and brush both layers with the syrup. Place 1 layer on top of the pastry cream, trimming if necessary to fit the pan. Cover the layer with the remaining orange-flavored pastry cream and place another layer of Genoise on top. Press the cake with a weighted dinner plate and refrigerate for 2 hours. Dip the cake pan into hot water and unmold onto a plate. Serve within 48 hours and keep refrigerated until ready to serve.

Serves 6.

Recipe courtesy Chef Jean-Maurice Jugé.

Chantilly Cream

1 cup créme fraîche, very cold (or heavy cream)
3 tablespoons cold milk
1 tablespoon sugar (or ¾ teaspoon vanilla sugar)
1½ tablespoons shaved ice or ice water

In a chilled mixing bowl combine the créme fraîche with the milk. Add the sugar and shaved ice. Whip at low speed for 1 minute, then whip at high speed for 1 to 3 minutes until soft peaks form.

Note: This may be used as is or added to other pastry creams to make them lighter. Be sure to have all your ingredients very cold before you start, or you will run the risk of turning the cream into butter. The cream keeps for 24 hours if refrigerated in a tightly closed container.

Makes 2 cups.

Recipe courtesy Chef Jean-Maurice Jugé.

Vanilla Pastry Cream

2 cups milk
½ vanilla bean, split in half lengthwise

Ꮬ Ꮬ Ꮬ

⅔ cup sugar
6 egg yolks
¼ cup all-purpose flour or cornstarch

In a saucepan combine the milk and vanilla bean, and bring to a boil. Cover and keep hot.

In a medium mixing bowl combine the sugar and egg yolks. Beat with a wire whisk or an electric mixer on medium speed until the mixture whitens and forms a ribbon. Gently stir in the flour. Strain out the vanilla bean and pour the hot milk into the egg mixture, beating constantly with the whisk. Pour the mixture back into the saucepan and bring to a boil, stirring constantly with the whisk so the mixture does not stick. Boil for 1 minute, stirring vigorously. Pour into a bowl and lightly rub the surface of the cream with a lump of butter to keep a skin from forming as it cools.

Makes 2⅓ cups.

Recipe courtesy Chef Jean-Maurice Jugé.

Ꮬ Ꮬ Ꮬ Ꮬ Ꮬ

Stuffed Salmon
with Yellow Pepper Sauce

2 to 2¼ pounds salmon fillet
3 1-pound lobsters

Ꮬ Ꮬ Ꮬ

3 tablespoons unsalted butter
2 shallots, finely diced
3 cups heavy cream
¾ cup dry vermouth
¾ cup fish stock
2 bay leaves
1 teaspoon black peppercorns

Ꮬ Ꮬ Ꮬ

7 ounces fresh sea scallops
3 bunches basil

Ꮬ Ꮬ Ꮬ

2 yellow bell peppers
½ cup unsalted butter
2 shallots, finely minced
1 cup dry white wine
1 cup fish stock
Salt and freshly ground pepper

Ꮬ Ꮬ Ꮬ

2 tomatoes and caviar for garnish

Butter six 8-inch squares of foil. Remove the bones from the salmon fillet with tweezers or small pliers. Trim about ½ inch from the belly portion and 2 inches off the tail portion. Remove the skin, and cut into 6 portions. Place a salmon fillet in the center of each prepared foil square. Cover each piece with plastic wrap and pound the salmon lightly to a ¼-inch thickness. Cover and refrigerate.

Remove the meat from the lobsters and dice into ½-inch pieces. Cover and refrigerate.

In a saucepan melt 1 tablespoon of butter and sauté the 2 diced shallots over medium heat for 5 minutes until translucent. Add 2 cups of the cream, vermouth, ¾ cup of fish stock, bay leaves, and peppercorns. Reduce the mixture over low heat until 1 cup of liquid remains. Strain and refrigerate.

Chill the bowl and blade of a food processor. Clean the scallops and put them through a fine meat grinder and refrigerate. Clean the basil and blanch the leaves in boiling salted water for 30 seconds, then drain and drop into ice water. Squeeze dry in a linen tea towel and finely chop. In the chilled bowl combine the basil and scallops, and blend for 1 minute. Slowly add the reduced cream, then the remaining 1 cup of heavy cream, scraping down the sides of the bowl as necessary. Gently fold the lobster meat into the mousse. Divide the mousse mixture evenly onto the surface of each salmon fillet and roll into a tube. Twist the foil tightly so the rolls remain firm. Place the rolls in a baking dish with ½ inch of water. Bake in a 350° oven for 20 minutes. Remove from the oven and allow to rest for 5 minutes. Carve each roll into 5 medallions.

Remove the ribs and seeds from the peppers and dice into ½-inch pieces. In a saucepan melt 2 tablespoons of butter over medium heat, and sauté the 2 minced shallots for 3 minutes. Add the peppers and sauté until soft. Add the wine and reduce by half, then add 1 cup of fish stock and simmer for 15 minutes.

In a blender or food processor purée the sauce, and add the remaining 6 tablespoons of butter, bit by bit. Strain and season with the salt and pepper. Place a bed of sauce on a plate and arrange the medallions of salmon. Garnish with leaves made from skinless tomatoes and caviar.

Serves 6.

Recipe courtesy Chef Jean-Maurice Jugé.

Napoleon of Scallops and Truffles

2 large Idaho potatoes
2 tablespoons clarified butter
Salt and pepper

❧ ❧ ❧

4 ears yellow corn
6 tablespoons unsalted butter
1½ cups half and half
½ cup heavy cream

❧ ❧ ❧

1½ pounds large sea scallops
Salt and pepper
3 tablespoons clarified butter
42 thin slices of black truffle

Brush a Teflon-coated frying pan with butter. Peel, slice, and julienne the potatoes as fine as angel hair pasta. Mix with 2 tablespoons of the butter, and season with the salt and pepper.

Place a 4-inch round cookie form onto the prepared pan and pack the potato into the cookie round until you form a ⅛-inch thick pancake. Fry the potato disks until golden brown, then remove the form, turn the potato disk over and brown the other side. Continue until 18 potato disks are formed. Bake in a 350° oven and cook until crisp. Drain on paper towels and keep warm.

Cut the kernels from the corn. In a saucepan melt 6 tablespoons of butter and sauté the corn until tender. Add the half and half, and cook until very tender. Purée the corn, pass through a fine sieve, and return to the heat with the cream. Season and keep warm.

Slice the scallops horizontally into thirds and season with salt and pepper. In a sauté pan heat the remaining 3 tablespoons of clarified butter. Cook the scallops until golden brown on both sides. Remove with a slotted spoon and set aside.

Assemble each Napoleon by placing scallop slices and 3 slices of truffle on 2 potato disks. Stack them, and top with a third disk, garnishing the top with another slice of truffle. Serve on a hot plate and spoon the corn sauce around.

Serves 6.

Recipe courtesy Chef Jean-Maurice Jugé.

Trio of Chocolate Mousses

2 eggs, separated
2½ tablespoons sugar
1 tablespoon mocha paste
3 ounces good quality dark
**   chocolate, melted**
¼ cup heavy cream, whipped

❧ ❧ ❧

1 egg
1 egg yolk
4 ounces milk chocolate, melted
2 tablespoons dark rum
1 tablespoon unflavored gelatin
2 tablespoons cold water
¾ cup heavy cream, whipped

The 1777 House at Doneckers

❧ ❧ ❧

1 egg
1 egg yolk
4 ounces white chocolate, melted
2 tablespoons cherry liqueur
1 teaspoon unflavored gelatin
2 tablespoons cold water
¾ cup heavy cream, whipped

❧ ❧ ❧

2 cups sauce anglaise (recipe is in any classic French cookbook)
Fresh mint sprigs

In a medium bowl combine 2 egg yolks and ½ tablespoon of sugar, and beat until light and lemon-colored. Beat in the mocha paste and the dark chocolate. Gently fold in ¼ cup of heavy cream that has been whipped. Beat the 2 egg whites with 2 tablespoons of sugar until stiff peaks form. Gently fold into the chocolate mixture. Pour into a 2-inch deep flat dish, cover with plastic wrap, and refrigerate for at least 8 hours.

In a medium bowl combine 1 egg and 1 egg yolk and whip until lemon colored and thick. Slowly add the milk chocolate and rum. In a saucepan sprinkle 1 tablespoon of gelatin over 2 tablespoons of cold water. Allow to soften for 10 minutes, then heat until the gelatin is dissolved and no granules remain. Stir the gelatin into the mousse, then gently fold in ¾ cup of heavy cream that has been whipped. Pour into a 2-inch deep flat dish, cover with plastic wrap, and refrigerate for at least 8 hours.

Repeat the procedure with the remaining eggs, white chocolate, cherry liqueur, gelatin, cold water, and heavy cream. Pour the mousse into a 2-inch deep flat dish, cover, and refrigerate for at least 8 hours.

To serve place a pool of sauce anglaise on chilled serving plates. Dip a serving spoon into hot water and place 2 scoops of each mousse on the sauce. Garnish with fresh mint.

Serves 8.

Recipe courtesy Chef Jean-Maurice Jugé.

❧ ❧ ❧ ❧ ❧

Mushroom Soup

2 quarts veal stock
1 quart mushroom stock
1 quart chicken stock
2 ounces dry morrels
2 cups warm water
2 ounces clarified butter or olive oil
1 ounce peeled chopped shallots
1 ounce peeled chopped garlic
4 ounces sliced Pennsylvania white mushrooms
1 tablespoon freshly chopped tarragon
1 tablespoon freshly chopped marjoram
2 tablespoons tomato paste

❧ ❧ ❧

1 pound shiitake mushrooms, sliced
1 ounce cepes powder
6 ounces cornstarch
1 cup heavy cream
1 cup soy sauce
Salt and pepper
2 cups white port wine

In a large cooking pot combine the veal stock, mushroom stock, and chicken stock, and heat. In a bowl combine the morrels in the water and set aside.

In a marmite heat the oil until hot. Add the shallots and garlic, and sauté until translucent. Do not burn the garlic. Add the white mushrooms and sauté until the mushrooms have released their water. Add the herbs and tomato paste. Cover and sweat the pot for 5 minutes. Add the stock and bring to a boil.

Remove the morrels from their juice and squeeze excess moisture from them and reserve. Add the juice to the soup. Slice the morrels into strips so they are still identifiable. Combine with the shiitake mushrooms and sauté. Add the cepes powder. Dilute the cornstarch in enough water to soak up the starch. Whisk into the boiling soup and simmer for 20 minutes. Lower the heat and add the heavy cream, soy sauce, salt, pepper, and port wine. Heat through.

Serves 8.

Recipe courtesy Chef Jean-Maurice Jugé.

The Brafferton Inn

44-46 York Street
Gettysburg, Pennsylvania 17325
(717) 337-3423

Guests of the Brafferton Inn, built in 1787, are able to experience historic Gettysburg in the home where its history began. Featured in *Country Living* magazine and *Early American Life,* it is one of Pennsylvania's most unique and historic homes. In the center hallway the canvas floor cloth was designed to mirror the vine and pineapple stencil on the walls. The woodwork throughout has been colored with Williamsburg paint, and the walls were toned with simulated whitewash. The large living room retains its original fireplace, dark hardwood floors, and player piano. The dining room, the "new addition" from the mid-eighteen-hundreds, features a primitive mural depicting eighteen historic Gettysburg area structures. Guest rooms, all furnished with coverlets that match the stenciling, are air conditioned for summer comfort.

Peaches and Cream French Toast

3 eggs
3 tablespoons peach preserves
¾ cup half and half
6 slices French bread, ½-inch thick

❧ ❧ ❧

⅓ cup peach preserves
½ cup butter or margarine
2 fresh peaches, peeled and sliced
Confectioners' sugar
Toasted almonds

In a small bowl combine the eggs and 3 tablespoons of peach preserves,

The Brafferton Inn

blending together with a fork or wire whisk. Beat in the half and half. Place a single layer of bread slices in a 7x11-inch baking dish. Pour the egg mixture over the bread. Cover and refrigerate for several hours or overnight.

In a blender combine ⅓ cup of peach preserves and the softened butter, blending on high speed until fluffy. Set aside.

In a large skillet melt 2 tablespoons of margarine and add 3 bread slices. Cook over medium-high heat until golden brown, turning once. Remove from the skillet and keep warm. Repeat with the remaining bread and butter. Serve with 1 tablespoon of peach butter and peach slices. Sprinkle with confectioners' sugar and almonds.

Serves 4 to 6.

Beechmont

315 Broadway
Hanover, Pennsylvania 17331
(717) 632-3013

Andrew Jackson was president when this house was built. Thirty years later it was a silent witness to the Civil War's first major battle on northern soil. Now restored to its Federal period elegance, it offers its guests a bridge across time. A winding staircase ascends to guest rooms on the second floor, each decorated in period furniture. The formal, landscaped courtyard reflects the constantly changing seasons. Breakfast begins with Beechmont's prize-winning granola and continues through a fresh fruit course, an elegant entree, and breads and rolls. Guests may relax in comfort in the parlor or beneath the canopy of the century-old magnolia tree.

🐌 🐌 🐌 🐌 🐌

Fruit Compote

Serve as a soup or as a topping for rice pudding or granola.

    4 cups chopped pitted prunes
    2 cups unpeeled thinly-sliced citrus
        fruits (oranges, lemons, or
        limes)
    2 cups fresh or frozen blueberries
    2 cups fresh or frozen pitted
        cherries
    2 cups hulled fresh or frozen
        strawberries
    4 cinnamon sticks
    1 teaspoon cloves
    ½ teaspoon ginger
    ½ teaspoon nutmeg
    Water

In a large kettle combine the prunes, citrus fruits, blueberries, cherries, strawberries, and spices in a large kettle. Cover with water, bring to a boil, reduce heat, and simmer for 2 hours. Remove the cinnamon sticks and rinds from the citrus fruits. Serve warm or chilled.

Serves 6, if served as a soup.

Rice Pudding

    1⅓ cups Uncle Ben's Converted Rice
    3 cups water
    3 tablespoons cornstarch
    ½ gallon milk
    1 12-ounce can evaporated milk
    1 cup sugar
    1½ tablespoons vanilla extract

In a saucepan boil the rice and water until the water is absorbed. Dissolve the cornstarch in a small amount of cold milk. Add the cornstarch, milks, and sugar to the rice, and simmer until reduced to proper consistency. Add the vanilla.

Serves 10.

Corn Custard Cups

    1 16-ounce can cream-style corn
    1 13-ounce can evaporated milk
    3 tablespoons cornstarch
    1 tablespoon confectioners' sugar
    ½ teaspoon nutmeg
    3 eggs
    Butter, melted

Grease 12 muffin cups. In a blender purée the corn for 1 minute. Add the milk and blend for 1 minute. Add the cornstarch, confectioners' sugar, and nutmeg, and blend for 1 minute. Add the eggs and blend for 15 seconds. Fill 12 muffin tins full. Bake in a 325° oven for 40 minutes. After the crust forms brush with butter and continue baking.

Serves 12.

Florentine Tarts

1 onion, minced
½ cup butter, melted
½ 10-ounce package frozen spinach
½ teaspoon celery seed
½ teaspoon dry mustard
½ teaspoon Beaumonde
½ teaspoon nutmeg
1 cup diced ham or smoked turkey
2 tablespoons all-purpose flour

🍃 🍃 🍃

12 eggs
½ cup all-purpose flour
2 tablespoons confectioners' sugar
1 teaspoon baking powder
1 pound shredded cheese
1 pound large curd cottage cheese

Grease muffin cups. In a saucepan sauté the onion in the butter. Add the spinach, spices, meat, and 2 tablespoons of flour.

In a bowl whisk together the eggs, ½ cup of flour, confectioners' sugar, and baking powder. Add the cheeses, then the spinach mixture. Fill muffin tins full. Bake in a 350° oven for 15 minutes.

Serves 18.

Pumpkin Soufflé

¼ cup all-purpose flour
¼ cup confectioners' sugar
1 12-ounce can evaporated milk
4 eggs, separated
Allspice
Nutmeg
Cinnamon
1 16-ounce can prepared pumpkin

In a bowl combine the flour and confectioners' sugar. In a separate bowl beat the mixture into the milk. Add the egg yolks and beat. Add the spices to taste, along with the pumpkin. In a separate bowl beat the egg whites and fold into the pumpkin mixture. Pour batter into muffin tins. Bake in a 350° oven for 30 minutes.

Serves 12.

Pineapple Soufflé

¼ cup butter, softened
¾ cup sugar
4 eggs
Nutmeg
2 tablespoons lemon juice
1 30-ounce can crushed pineapple in juice, slightly drained
5 slices bread, cubed
Maraschino cherries for garnish

Grease 12 muffin cups. In a bowl blend together the butter and sugar. Whisk in the eggs. Whisk in the nutmeg, lemon juice, pineapple, and bread. Pour the batter into the prepared muffin cups. Bake in a 325° oven for 30 minutes or until golden brown. Garnish with a maraschino cherry.

Serves 12.

The Bucksville House

Route 412 and Buck Drive
Rural Delivery 2, Box 146
Kintnersville, Pennsylvania 18930
(215) 847-8948

Bucksville House provides the visitor with country charm and almost two hundred years of history. From its beginning in 1795 the inn became a common rest stop for travelers and stagecoaches between Philadelphia and Easton or Allentown. Expanded several times, it has now been fully restored. All the rooms are tastefully decorated with a mixture of antiques and country reproductions. Some of the rooms have fireplaces, and all have private baths. Breakfast is served in the garden gazebo or in the dining room with its Mercer tile floor and walk-in fireplace. Guests are also invited to relax in the parlor or cozy den with its coal stove, television, and game boards.

Beechmont

The Bucksville House

Nutty Raisin Bran Waffles

1½ cups all-purpose flour
4 teaspoons baking powder
¾ teaspoon salt
1½ tablespoons sugar
2 cups bran cereal
3 eggs
2¼ cups milk
⅓ cup oil
½ cup chopped pecans
¾ cup raisins

In a bowl combine the flour, baking powder, salt, sugar, and cereal. Set aside. In a separate bowl combine the eggs, milk, and oil. Add the liquid ingredients to the dry ingredients, beating until smooth. Fold in the pecans and raisins. Bake on a waffle iron until golden.

Serves 6.

Hot Spiced Cranberry Punch

¾ cup brown sugar
1 cup water
¼ teaspoon salt
½ teaspoon allspice

½ teaspoon cinnamon
1 quart pineapple juice

ᕦ ᕦ ᕦ

2 16-ounce jellied cranberry sauce
3 cups water

ᕦ ᕦ ᕦ

Peppermint sticks

In a large saucepan combine the brown sugar, 1 cup of water, spices, and pineapple juice. In a bowl whip the cranberry sauce with the 3 cups of water, and add to the spicy mixture. Bring to a boil. Serve with peppermint sticks.

Makes 10 cups.

White Rock Farm

154 White Rock Road
Kirkwood, Pennsylvania 17536
(717) 529-6744

White Rock Farm is a 150-acre beef and crop farm in southern Lancaster County. Overlooking the scenic Octorara Creek and historic White Rock covered bridge, it offers nature trails, wildlife, and true country living. Fall asleep in a large antique bed listening to the crickets sing. Wake up to the morning crowing of a rooster or the clip-clop of an Amish horse and buggy passing by. Enjoy a "real" farmer's breakfast. The three rooms in the stone farmhouse share a modern bath and a separate guest entrance.

Crustless Bacon and Egg Quiche

8 strips bacon, diced
3 eggs
1½ cups milk
½ cup Bisquick
¼ cup butter, melted
Dash pepper
1 cup shredded Cheddar cheese

Grease a 9-inch pie pan. In a skillet fry the bacon until crisp. In a blender combine the eggs, milk, Bisquick, butter, and pepper. Blend for 15 seconds until well mixed. Pour the egg mixture into the prepared pan. Sprinkle with diced bacon and cheese and gently press below the surface with a fork. Bake in a 350° oven for 30 minutes or until a knife inserted halfway between the center and the edge comes out clean. Let stand for 10 minutes.

Serves 4 to 6.

The Golden Plough Inn

Peddler's Village
Route 202 and Street Road
Lahaska, Bucks County, Pennsylvania
  18931
(215) 794-4000

The Golden Plough Inn is situated in Bucks County's most picturesque area. Each of its rooms is individually decorated to convey the style and warmth of eighteenth-century Bucks County, with cherry woods, four-poster beds, and window seats. All are air conditioned, with private bath, television, and telephone. Just ouside the inn is Peddler's Village, with its winding brick paths, flower gardens, restaurants and specialty shops. The inn's three award-winning restaurants—the Cock 'n Bull, Jenny's, and the Spotted Hog—serve a variety of cuisines.

French Toast
Stuffed with Apricots and Pecans

½ cup finely chopped dried apricots
¼ cup orange juice
8 ounces cream cheese
¼ cup coarsely chopped pecans
16 slices sourdough bread or
  challah (egg bread), ¾-inch
  thick

  ❧ ❧ ❧

2 cups milk
1 cup half and half
6 eggs
5 tablespoons sugar
4 teaspoons grated orange rind
1 teaspoon vanilla extract
1 teaspoon salt
½ cup butter, or as needed

  ❧ ❧ ❧

18 ounces apricot preserves
¾ cup orange juice

In a saucepan combine the apricots and ¼ cup of orange juice and bring to a boil. Simmer for 10 minutes or until the apricots are tender, then cool to room temperature. In a small bowl combine the cream cheese, pecans, and apricot mixture. Spread over 8 slices of bread, forming 8 sandwiches.

In a bowl combine the milk, half and half, eggs, sugar, orange rind, vanilla, and salt. Dip the sandwiches into the egg mixture to completely coat. In a skillet melt 2 tablespoons of the butter. Add the sandwiches and cook until golden brown, adding more butter to the skillet as necessary.

In a heavy saucepan combine the preserves and ¾ cup of orange juice. Bring to a boil, stirring occasionally. Serve syrup hot with the French Toast.

Serves 8.

Best Irish Soda Bread

4 cups all-purpose flour
4 teaspoons baking powder
½ teaspoon baking soda
1 teaspoon salt
3 tablespoons sugar
1 cup currants and/or dark seedless
  raisins
2 cups buttermilk
1 teaspoon cinnamon
Butter, melted
Sugar

Grease and flour a cookie sheet. In a large bowl combine the flour, baking powder, baking soda, salt, and sugar. Stir in the currants making sure they are separated. Add the buttermilk, mixing until it forms a dough ball. Add the cinnamon, mixing slightly. Knead by machine or hand for 5 minutes. Form the dough into smooth 10-ounce balls and place on the prepared cookie sheet. Bake in a 350° oven for 35 to 40 minutes until the loaves are lightly browned and sound hollow when tapped on the bottom. Remove to a wire rack, rub with the butter, and dust with sugar.

Makes 4 to 5 loaves.

Mushrooms Pennsylvania

4 slices bias-cut French bread,
  ¾-inch thick
½ cup butter, melted
2 to 3 garlic cloves, finely chopped
Chopped parsley
Grated Parmesan cheese
Paprika

  ❧ ❧ ❧

6 tablespoons butter
1 pound fresh mushrooms, cleaned
  and quartered
2 ounces sundried tomatoes, sliced
  and soaked in white wine
  overnight
1 cup Madeira
1 tablespoon finely chopped
  shallots
¾ cup heavy cream
Ground white pepper
2 scallions, cleaned and sliced

Using ½ cup of melted butter, butter 1 side of each bread slice. Top each slice with the garlic and sprinkle with parsley, cheese, and paprika. Bake in a 400° oven until golden brown.

In a heavy skillet melt 6 tablespoons of butter. When butter sizzles add the mushrooms and sauté until cooked through. Drain the tomatoes and add to the pan. Add the Madeira and shallots, reducing the wine by two-thirds. Pour in the cream and add the pepper to taste. Allow the sauce to reduce to a slightly thick consistency. Place one bread slice on each serving plate and divide the mushrooms evenly over the bread. Top each dish with a few of the scallion slices.

Serves 4.

Filet Dijon

½ cup Dijon mustard
6 tablespoons white wine
¼ cup soy sauce
½ cup dark brown sugar
2 teaspoons Worcestershire sauce
⅓ cup minced scallions
4 8-ounce beef tenderloin steaks
   (filet mignon)

❀ ❀ ❀

2 cups Dijon mustard
2 cups brown sugar
1 cup white wine

In a small bowl combine ½ cup Dijon mustard, 6 tablespoons white wine, soy sauce, ½ cup brown sugar, Worcestershire sauce, and scallions, stirring until well blended. Marinate four 8-ounce filets in the sauce. Cover and refrigerate overnight.

Before preparation, in a small bowl combine 2 cups Dijon mustard, 2 cups brown sugar, and 1 cup white wine. Stir until well blended. Set glaze aside.

Broil the filets until desired doneness. Pat with Dijon sugar glaze. Return the filets to the broiler until the glaze bubbles.

Serves 4.

Creamy Vinaigrette

1 8-ounce package cream cheese,
   softened
1 cup oil
⅓ cup wine vinegar

❀ ❀ ❀

1 tablespoon finely chopped
   Spanish onion
1 teaspoon crumbled dry parsley
Pinch basil leaves
Pinch marjoram leaves
2 pinches oregano
¾ teaspoon black pepper
Pinch rosemary
Pinch rubbed sage
2 pinches thyme
1½ teaspoons salt
1¼ teaspoons dry mustard

In a medium bowl with an electric mixer blend the cream cheese until smooth. Gradually add the oil and vinegar, mixing until well blended.

Add the remaining ingredients, mixing thoroughly until a creamy consistency.

Makes about 2½ cups.

The King's Cottage

1049 East King Street
Lancaster, Pennsylvania 17602
(717) 397-1017

The King's Cottage is an elegant Spanish mansion beautifully restored for the discriminating traveler. Oriental and handmade wool rugs accent the polished hardwood floors. Each guest room has a king- or queen-size bed, private bath, and a comfortable sitting area. Many of the baths have original stained glass windows and turn-of-the-century fixtures. The art deco fireplace in the living room is complemented by matched sets of French doors. A sweeping staircase leads to the second floor, and the library has a magnificent marble fireplace. Nearby restaurants reflect a variety of preferences, from country to French.

The King's French Toast

1 cup butter, softened
⅓ cup orange marmalade

❀ ❀ ❀

6 eggs
⅓ cup orange juice
2 tablespoons Triple Sec
⅓ cup half and half
3 tablespoons sugar
¼ teaspoon vanilla extract
Pinch salt
Finely grated peel of ½ an orange
8 slices French bread, ¾-inch thick

❀ ❀ ❀

3 to 4 tablespoons butter
Confectioners' sugar and mandarin
   oranges for garnish

In a small bowl whip 1 cup of butter until light. Mix in the orange marmalade.

In a medium bowl beat the eggs. Add the orange juice, Triple Sec, half and half, sugar, vanilla, salt, and grated orange peel. Dip the bread into the egg mixture, coating all the surfaces. Transfer to a baking dish. Pour any remaining batter over the bread. Cover and refrigerate overnight.

In a large skillet melt 3 tablespoons of butter over medium-high heat. Add the bread slices and cook until browned on both sides. Spread the orange butter over one side of the French toast and transfer to a serving platter. Sprinkle with confectioners' sugar and garnish with mandarin oranges. Serve with maple syrup.

Serves 3 to 4.

Strawberry Poached Pears

1 10-ounce package frozen
   strawberries, thawed
1 tablespoon lemon juice
⅓ cup sugar
6 large pears

❀ ❀ ❀

1 tablespoon cornstarch
2 tablespoons water
¼ cup semi-sweet chocolate chips
Whipped cream for garnish

In a blender combine the strawberries, lemon juice, and sugar, blending until smooth. Peel pears, leaving stems intact and core from the blossom end. Arrange the pears in a baking dish with the stems toward the center and pour the strawberry mixture over the pears. Cover with waxed paper and microwave on high for 4 minutes.

In a cup combine the cornstarch and water, then mix into the pears and strawberry sauce. Turn the pears over and spoon the strawberry sauce over them. Cover and microwave on high another 4 minutes or until fork tender. Remove from the microwave and let cool. Refrigerate for at least 3 hours.

Remove 1 cup of the strawberry sauce and heat in the microwave until boiling. Remove from the microwave and add the chocolate chips. Let stand until the chips have melted. Stir the sauce until smooth. Reheat the pears in the microwave on medium heat. Transfer the pears to individual serving dishes, spoon the remaining strawberry sauce over the pears, then spoon 1 to 2 tablespoons of the chocolate sauce on top. Garnish with a dollup of whipped cream.

Serves 6.

Witmer's Tavern

Witmer's Tavern-Historic 1725 Inn

2014 Old Philadelphia Pike
Lancaster, Pennsylvania 17602
(717) 299-5305

Witmer's Tavern is the most intact and authentic eighteenth-century inn in south-central Pennsylvania. The sole survivor of some sixty-two inns that once lined the nation's first turnpike between Lancaster and Philadelphia, it has been modernized with air conditioning and modern baths. Guests are served breakfast in the sitting room. In the east end of the building, Pandora's Antique/Quilt Shop is internationally known for its fine antiques and quilts. Several fine restaurants and shops are nearby.

Lafayette's Rice Cake

General Lafayette acquired his taste for this cake while recuperating in Bethlehem, Pennsylvania, at the Sun Inn during the Valley Forge winter encampment. Wherever he traveled and found Mennonite cooks, he requested it. At Historic 1725 Witmer's Tavern, this dessert is now served on special occasions.

1 cup butter, softened
2 cups sugar
4 egg yolks
2 cups rice flour
1 cup wheat flour
1 teaspoon baking powder
¼ teaspoon nutmeg
2 tablespoons rum or brandy
1 cup milk
4 egg whites, stiffly beaten
Confectioners' sugar (optional)

Butter Turk's-head mold (or loaf tin) and lightly dust with flour. In a medium bowl cream together the butter and sugar. Add the egg yolks one at a time, beating until creamy. In a separate bowl sift together the rice and wheat flours with the baking powder and nutmeg. In a cup combine the rum with the milk. Blend the flour mixture into the butter mixture and gently beat in the milk mixture until smooth. Fold in the beaten egg whites. Transfer the mixture to the prepared mold. Bake in a 350° oven for 1 hour. Cool for 15 minutes before removing from the pan. Sprinkle the cooled cake with confectioners' sugar, if desired.

Serves 8 to 10.

The Alden House

62 East Main Street
Lititz, Pennsylvania 17543
(717) 627-3363

A part of the Main Street life since the 1850s, the Alden House has been painstakingly restored to its original Civil War-era elegance and charm. Here guests enjoy private rooms and baths and are welcomed to a morning breakfast buffet served in the breakfast nook or on one of three porches.

Shoofly Cake

2 cups warm water
1 teaspoon baking soda
1 cup molasses
 ❧ ❧ ❧
4 cups all-purpose flour
2 cups sugar
1 cup shortening

Grease a 9x13-inch pan. In a large bowl combine the water, baking soda, and molasses. Stir once and set aside.

In a separate bowl combine the flour, sugar, and shortening. Mix thoroughly by hand until the mixture makes crumbs. Reserve 1 cup of the crumbs. Pour the dry ingredients into the liquid ingredients, folding in lightly. Pour the batter into the prepared pan. Sprinkle the reserved crumbs over the top. Bake in a 340° oven for 45 to 60 minutes until done.

Serves 8 to 10.

Country Spun Sheep Farm

Post Office Box 117
Loganville, Pennsylvania 17342
(717) 428-1162

Country decor, plenty of hospitality, and a delicious breakfast are just a few of the ingredients that create a memorable experience for guests of Country Spun Farm. Guests may relax in spacious, air-conditioned rooms with private baths, walk in the woods and fields, watch birds, drink iced tea while reading a good book under the mulberry tree, or enjoy one of the nearby restaurants offering country dining at its best. No smoking is permitted indoors.

Cheddar Creamed Eggs on Toast

4 slices bacon
1 medium onion, chopped
1½ cups grated Cheddar cheese
3 tablespoons all-purpose flour
1½ cups milk
6 hard-boiled eggs, sliced
Toast or English muffins
Chopped parsley for garnish

In a skillet fry the bacon, drain, and crumble. Brown the onion in a small amount of the fat. In a medium bowl combine the cheese and flour. Add to the onion in the skillet, and slowly stir in the milk while heating. Stir often until the mixture thickens. Fold in the bacon and sliced eggs. Serve on toast or English muffins and garnish with parsley.

Serves 4 to 6.

Easy Skillet Sticky Buns

2 loaves frozen white bread dough
½ cup butter
¾ pound light brown sugar
¼ cup Gold Label molasses
½ cup water
½ teaspoon cinnamon
Butter, melted

Allow the bread dough to thaw covered for at least 4 hours. In a 12-inch iron skillet combine the butter, brown sugar, molasses, water, and cinnamon. Pour half of the mixture into another 12-inch skillet. Bring to a boil and cook for 5 minutes. Roll out the bread dough to an 8x12-inch rectangle. Brush with the melted butter and sprinkle with more cinnamon. Roll up widthwise and slice in 1-inch thick slices. Arrange in the skillet, placing crumpled foil in the center to hold in place until the buns rise and fill the pan. Cover and refrigerate overnight. Bake in a 350° oven until the buns are well browned.

Serves 6 to 8.

Herr Farmhouse Inn

2256 Huber Drive
Manheim, Pennsylvania 17545
(717) 653-9852

Dating back to 1738, the Farmhouse Inn receives its ambience from the fan lights adorning the main entrance, six working fireplaces, original pine floors, carefully restored elegance, and tranquility. Equally enjoyable are spending a cozy winter's night by the fireplace or sipping tea in the sun room on a bright summer morning. Nestled on eleven and one-half acres of rolling farmland, it provides views of pastoral horizons broken only by an occasional barn or silo.

Lemon Bread

½ cup butter
1 cup sugar
2 eggs
Grated rind of 1 lemon
1½ cups all-purpose flour
1 teaspoon baking soda
½ teaspoon salt
½ cup milk

🍂 🍂 🍂

Juice of 1 lemon
½ cup sugar

Grease a loaf pan. In a bowl cream together the butter and 1 cup of sugar. Add the eggs and beat well. Add the rind. In a separate bowl combine the flour, baking soda, and salt. Add alternately with the milk. Pour the batter into the prepared pan. Bake in a 350° oven for 1 hour.

In a bowl combine the juice with ½ cup of sugar. Spoon over the warm bread. Let cool in the pan overnight.

Serves 12 to 18.

Coffee Muffins

1½ cups all-purpose flour
2¼ teaspoons baking powder
¼ teaspoon salt
¾ cup chopped walnuts or pecans
3 tablespoons butter
⅔ cup strong coffee
¼ cup brown sugar
1 egg

Grease or line muffin pans. In a large bowl combine the flour, baking powder, and salt. Add the walnuts. In a small saucepan melt the butter with the coffee and brown sugar. Cool slightly, then add to the flour mixture. Beat well and stir in the egg. Fill the prepared muffin pans half full. Bake in a 375° oven for 20 minutes until firm. Serve with butter and marmalade.

Makes 9 to 12 muffins.

Apple-Orange Coffee Cake

2 to 2½ cups thinly sliced apples
2 tablespoons brown sugar
1 tablespoon butter, melted
1 teaspoon cinnamon

🍂 🍂 🍂

1 18½-ounce box orange cake mix
1 cup milk
⅔ cup quick-cooking oats
1 egg

🍂 🍂 🍂

1 cup sifted confectioners' sugar
1 tablespoon milk

Grease a 9x13-inch cake pan. In a bowl combine the apples, brown sugar, butter, and cinnamon. Set aside.

Prepare the orange cake mix according to directions on the package, reducing the milk to 1 cup. Add the oats and egg. Pour batter in a 9x13-inch cake pan and sprinkle with the apple topping. Bake in a 375° oven for 30 minutes.

In a small bowl combine the confectioners' sugar and 1 tablespoon of milk for a glaze. Drizzle over the warm cake.

Serves 12 to 18.

The Stranahan House

117 East Market Street
Mercer, Pennsylvania 16137
(412) 662-4516

A 150-year-old building, the Stranahan House provides a peaceful night's rest and a delicious breakfast amidst antique furnishings rich in the area's heritage. This classic red brick home is near the center of town just a few steps from stately Mercer County Courthouse and conveniently close to an array of historical and recreational sites. The two guestrooms are on the second floor. One is furnished with Victorian furniture that was made in Philadelphia; it has a double bed, ceiling paddle fan, mauve carpeting, and blue and mauve floral stripe wallpaper. The other room has two double beds in cherry—1830 spool rope beds that are roped, but supported, to give guests a firm, comfortable night's rest. It has a working fireplace, and its walls are stenciled in an old-fashioned border.

Continental Chicken

1 5-ounce package dried beef, chopped and rinsed
6 boned chicken breasts, skinned
Pepper
6 pieces partially cooked bacon
6 whole mushrooms
1 10¾-ounce can cream of mushroom soup
1 cup sour cream
1 4-ounce can mushrooms, drained
1 teaspoon dill weed (optional)

Line a 9x13-inch pan with the dried beef. Sprinkle the chicken with pepper and wrap in the bacon. Place a mushroom on the top of each chicken breast and secure with a toothpick. In a medium bowl combine the mushroom soup, sour cream, mushrooms, and dill weed. Pour over the chicken. Bake uncovered in a 350° oven for 30 minutes. Cover and bake an additional 30 minutes.

Serves 6.

Vegetable Lasagna Roll-ups

1 16-ounce package lasagna noodles
8 ounces Mozzarella cheese, shredded
2 pounds Ricotta cheese

2 cups finely chopped mushrooms
4 broccoli stalks with florets,
    cooked for 5 minutes, drained,
    and chopped
4 finely chopped scallions
2 tablespoons chopped dried
    oregano
1½ teaspoons dried basil
½ cup chopped parsley
Black pepper
3 cups spaghetti sauce

In a large pot cook the lasagna noodles in boiling water for 12 to 15 minutes and drain. In a medium bowl combine the cheeses, vegetables, herbs, and pepper. Spoon about ⅓-cup portion of the mixture onto each lasagna noodle and roll up. Spread some of the spaghetti sauce on the bottom of a 9x13-inch baking dish and place the lasagna rolls seam-side down in the dish. Pour the remaining sauce over the lasagna rolls and cover with aluminum foil. Bake in a 350° oven for 35 minutes.

Serves 6 to 8.

The Stranahan House

Curried Chicken Salad

¼ cup honey
¼ cup chutney
¼ cup water
⅓ cup mayonnaise
1 cup whipped cream
4 cups bite-sized cooked chicken
Salt and pepper
1 tablespoon curry powder

In a saucepan combine the honey, chutney, and water, and simmer gently for 15 minutes. Cool and set aside. In a small bowl combine the mayonnaise and whipped cream. Fold into the chutney mixture, then into the chicken. Season with salt, pepper, and curry powder.

Serves 8.

Marinated Garden Vegetables

2 cups broccoli flowerets
2 cups cauliflower flowerets
2 cups sliced carrots
1 medium zucchini, sliced
1 medium cucumber, sliced
½ cup chopped sweet red pepper
½ cup chopped green pepper
½ cup sliced celery
½ cup sliced black olives

🍃 🍃 🍃

1¼ cups oil
⅔ cup vinegar
½ cup sugar
2 cloves garlic, crushed
1 teaspoon salt
1 teaspoon white pepper

🍃 🍃 🍃

8 cherry tomatoes, halved
1 cup halved mushrooms

In a large bowl combine the 9 vegetables.

In a jar combine the oil, vinegar, sugar, garlic, salt, and pepper. Cover tightly and shake vigorously. Pour over the vegetables and toss gently. Cover and chill at least 12 hours.

Add the tomatoes and mushrooms just before serving.

Serves 12 (makes 1¾ cups of dressing).

Gingerbread Men

½ cup sugar
½ cup shortening
½ cup light molasses
2 cups all-purpose flour
½ teaspoon baking powder
½ teaspoon baking soda
½ teaspoon salt
1½ teaspoons cinnamon
1 teaspoon cloves
1 teaspoon ginger
½ teaspoon nutmeg
1 egg yolk

In a large bowl with an electric mixer beat together the sugar, shortening, and molasses, until light and fluffy. Add the flour, baking powder, baking soda, salt, spices, and egg yolk. Beat at low speed until blended, occasionally scraping the bowl with a rubber spatula. Shape the dough into a ball and wrap with plastic wrap. Refrigerate at least 2 hours or place in the freezer for 40 minutes. Roll the cookie dough out thin and cut cookies with a gingerbread man cutter. Place on cookie sheets and decorate. Bake in a 350° oven for 10 minutes.

Serves 8 to 10.

Taco Dip

> 1 8-ounce package cream cheese, softened
> 8 ounces sour cream
> 1 package taco seasoning mix
> Chopped onion
> Chopped lettuce
> Chopped tomatoes
> Chopped black olives
> Tortilla chips

In a medium bowl cream together the cream cheese, sour cream, and taco seasoning mix. Spread mixture in a very shallow dish. Top with the onion, lettuce, tomatoes, and olives. Serve with tortilla chips.

Serves 6.

Tulpehocken Manor Inn and Plantation

650 West Lincoln Avenue
Myerstown, Pennsylvania 17067
(717) 866-4926
(717) 392-2311

Tulpehocken Manor Plantation is a 150-acre working farm on which grain crops are raised and Black Angus beef cattle are bred. With the multiple building complex the Michael Ley mansion offers individual rooms with shared hall baths. Antiques abound throughout.

The Cyrus Sherk Haus has three guest rooms and accommodates six people; it also has a kitchen and one bath. The Christopher Ley Spring House has group facilities for up to twelve people, with five bedrooms, one and one-half baths, kitchen, and dining-living room combination. The attic apartment in the Michael Spangler Spring House is a large one-room efficiency guest apartment with kitchen and bath for up to four people.

Each of the five guest apartments in the George Spangler Apartment House has its own kitchen and private bath. These apartments accommodate from two to five people.

Corn Omelet

> 2 ears fresh corn
> 2 eggs
> Salt and pepper
> 1 teaspoon chow-chow (optional)
> Promise Light Vegetable Spread
> Sliced tomatoes for garnish

Cut the corn from the corn cobs. In a medium bowl combine the corn, eggs, salt, pepper, and chow-chow, mixing with a fork. In a 7-inch skillet melt the vegetable spread. Pour the egg mixture into the skillet and cook until the edges of the omelet are brown and the center sets. Top with a little additional vegetable spread, cut in the center, and lift from the pan with a spatula onto 2 serving plates. Serve with freshly sliced tomatoes.

Serves 2.

Pineapple Hill

Rural Route 3
Box 34C
New Hope, Pennsylvania 18938
(215) 862-9608

Pineapple Hill is a spacious Bucks County farmhouse built about 1780. Nestled on five acres overlooking a bend along scenic River Road beside the Delaware River, the inn beckons invitingly to guests. Inside, the central hall leads to a parlor displaying country and primitive furniture, old quilts, folk art, and Persian carpets. On the other side of the hallway is a second sitting room with a big bay window. The guest rooms upstairs are furnished similarly and have either brass, spindle, or rope beds; blanket chests; and chests of drawers.

Guests can enjoy the many attractions of New Hope and the surrounding area, including many fine restaurants, important historical sites, parks, rafting or tubing on the Delaware, antiquing, arts and crafts galleries, and beautiful scenery. They also may enjoy the parlor fireplace with a good book or play a game of backgammon. In the summer they can lounge beside the pool located within the stone ruins of the farm's original barn. Breakfast includes a fresh fruit salad and croissants with homemade jams and jellies. Afternoon refreshments are also included in the rates, as are complimentary after-dinner beverages.

Pineapple Bread Pudding

> 4 eggs
> 1 cup sugar
> 2 20-ounce cans crushed pineapple

Pineapple Hill

¾ cup sour cream
1 teaspoon vanilla extract

Grease 12 muffin cups. In a medium bowl stir together the flour, poppy seed, salt, and baking powder. In a large mixing bowl beat together the sugar and butter with an electric mixer for 2 minutes. Beat in the eggs one at a time until blended. Beat in the sour cream and vanilla. Gradually beat in the flour mixture until well combined. Spoon the batter into muffin cups. Bake in a 375° oven for 15 to 20 minutes.

Makes 12 muffins.

Jewish Apple Cake

My grandmother's recipe.

5 to 6 apples
3 teaspoons cinnamon

🐦 🐦 🐦

3 cups all-purpose flour
2 cups sugar
1 cup oil
4 eggs
½ cup orange juice
3 teaspoons baking powder
2½ teaspoons vanilla extract
1 teaspoon salt

🐦 🐦 🐦

½ cup walnuts
6 tablespoons honey

Grease and flour a tube pan. Pare, core, and slice the apples. Sprinkle them with the cinnamon. Set aside.

In a large bowl combine the flour, sugar, oil, eggs, orange juice, baking powder, vanilla, and salt. Beat to make a smooth batter. Pour half the batter into the prepared pan. Arrange half of the apples over the batter, and top with the walnuts and honey. Cover with the remaining batter and apples arranged evenly over the top. Add a few more walnuts and honey. Bake in a 350° oven for 1½ hours until cake is golden brown.

Serves 15 to 18.

🐦 🐦 🐦 🐦 🐦

¼ cup all-purpose flour
½ cup butter
10 slices white bread, cubed

Butter a 9x13-inch pan. In a medium bowl beat together the eggs and sugar. Add the pineapple and flour. In a skillet melt the butter and brown the bread cubes. Cover the bottom of the prepared pan with the bread cubes and pour in the egg mixture. Bake in a 350° oven for 35 to 40 minutes until browned and set.

Serves 6 to 8.

The Wedgwood Inn

111 West Bridge Street
New Hope, Pennsylvania 18938
(215) 862-2570

Voted Inn of the Year in 1989 by readers of *The Complete Guide to Bed and Breakfasts, Inns and Guesthouses in the United States and Canada,* this gracious two-and-one-half story structure with a gabled hip roof is surrounded by manicured landscaping. The inn is only steps away from the village center of New Hope, a historic artist's colony. Its large verandah has scrolled wood brackets, turned posts, a porte-cochere, and a gazebo. Hardwood floors, lofty windows, and antique furnishings create a comfortable nineteenth-century feeling in each of the twelve bedrooms. The innkeepers have filled their inn with Wedgwood pottery, original art, handmade quilts, and fresh flowers. The continental-plus breakfast is served in the sunporch or gazebo, or in one's private bedroom. Days end with a tot of almond liqueur at bedside and mints waiting on the pillows of turned-down beds. The Wedgwood is also a place where innkeepers-to-be are trained.

Poppyseed Muffins

2 cups all-purpose flour
¼ cup poppy seed
½ teaspoon salt
¼ teaspoon baking powder
½ cup sugar
½ cup butter, softened
2 eggs

Cappuccino Chip Muffins

    2 cups all-purpose flour
    ½ cup sugar
    2½ teaspoons baking powder
    2 teaspoons instant espresso coffee
        powder
    ½ teaspoon salt
    ½ teaspoon cinnamon
    1 cup milk, scalded and cooled
    ½ cup butter, melted and cooled
    1 egg, slightly beaten
    1 teaspoon vanilla extract
    ¾ cup semi-sweet chocolate mini-
        chips

Grease muffin cups. In a large bowl stir together the flour, sugar, baking powder, espresso coffee powder, salt, and cinnamon. In a separate bowl stir together the milk, butter, egg, and vanilla, until blended. Make a well in the center of the dry ingredients and add the milk mixture, stirring just to combine. Stir in the chocolate mini-chips. Spoon the batter into the prepared muffin cups. Bake in a 375° oven for 15 to 20 minutes.

    Makes 12 muffins or 24 mini-muffins.

Lemon Raspberry Muffins

    2 cups all-purpose flour
    ½ cup sugar
    1 teaspoon baking powder
    1 teaspoon baking soda
    ½ teaspoon salt
    1 cup lemon yogurt
    ¼ cup butter, melted and cooled
    1 egg, lightly beaten
    2 teaspoons grated lemon peel
    1 teaspoon vanilla extract
    2 cups fresh or frozen raspberries,
        drained

Grease muffin cups. In a large bowl stir together the flour, sugar, baking powder, baking soda, and salt. In a separate bowl stir together the yogurt, butter, egg, lemon peel, and vanilla, until blended. Make a well in the center of the dry ingredients. Add

the yogurt mixture and stir just to combine. Stir in the raspberries. Spoon the batter into prepared muffin cups. Bake in a 400° oven for 20 to 25 minutes.

Variation: You can substitute blueberries.

    Makes 12 muffins.

Chocolate-Strawberry-Banana Bombe

A sumptuous delight for afternoon tea!

    4 layers chocolate cake, cooled
    6 to 8 bananas, ripe but firm
    2 tablespoons sugar
    2 to 3 pints strawberries, reserve
        several for garnish
    3 cups whipping cream, whipped to
        stiff peaks

In a small bowl mash 2 large bananas with 1 tablespoon sugar. Spread half of the mixture on the first layer of cake and cover with banana slices. Place the second layer of cake on top.

    In a small bowl mash ½ pint of the strawberries with 1 tablespoon of sugar. Spread on the second layer and cover with sliced strawberries. Place the third layer of the cake on top. Spread the layer with the remaining banana mixture and banana slices. Place the fourth layer on top. Cover the top and sides of the cake with the whipped cream and decorate with strawberries.

    Serves 15 to 18.

Southern Style Banana Pudding

This is a favorite afternoon tea recipe of guests and staff. We serve this at afternoon tea in one of our gazebos and play croquet!

    2 boxes vanilla wafers
    6 to 8 bananas, ripe but firm
    3 large boxes vanilla pudding
    9 cups milk

In a large bowl beginning with the vanilla wafers alternate layers of vanilla wafers and banana slices, reserving a handful of the wafers for the top. Prepare the pudding one box at a time according to the package directions. Pour the pudding slowly over the wafers and bananas before it sets. Crumble the reserved wafers over the top. Chill at least 2 hours before serving.

    Serves 18 to 20.

Hickory Bridge Farm

Orrtanna, Pennsylvania 17353
(717) 642-5261

Situated in the foothills of the Appalachian Mountains in south-central Pennsylvania, Hickory Bridge Farm provides a beautiful setting in all seasons. Dining is offered in a charming century-old barn decorated with many farm antiques. Home-cooked dinners are served farm-style on Friday, Saturday, and Sunday. The country cottages are located in the woods and overlook a well-stocked mountain trout stream. The farmhouse, also located on the stream, is decorated with antiques and has several guest rooms.

Adams County Apple Dip

8 red apples
¼ cup lemon juice
1 large container Cool Whip or 1 recipe Dream Whip
1 8-ounce package Philadelphia cream cheese
1 cup strawberry jam
Few drops red food coloring

Core and cut each apple into 16 wedges. Drop into a bowl with the lemon juice. In a small bowl combine the cream cheese, jam, and food coloring, blending well. Fold in the Cool Whip lightly. To serve, place the apple wedges around the plate and place the bowl of dip in the center.

Serves 50.

Hickory Bridge Farm's Spiced Peaches

1 16-ounce can peach halves, reserve juice
1½ cups sugar
½ cup vinegar
1 tablespoon whole cloves
1 stick cinnamon
½ cup fruity brandy (optional)

In a saucepan combine the peach juice, sugar, vinegar, cloves, and cinnamon, and bring to a boil. Allow to cool. Add the peaches to the juice and let set overnight. Add the brandy, if desired.

Note: Peaches can be placed in jars and processed in a canner according to directions.

Serves 4.

Pleasant Grove Farm

368 Pilottown Road
Peach Bottom, Pennsylvania 17563
(717) 548-3100

Situated in beautiful, historic Lancaster County, this 160-acre dairy farm has been a family-run operation for 108 years, earning it the title of "Century Farm" by the Pennsylvania Department of Agriculture. As a working farm, it provides guests the opportunity to experience daily life in a rural setting. Four rooms and shared baths, plus one loft for children, are available, as well as a motor home that is equipped for four persons. Tenting in the yard, an above-ground swimming pool, sand for children to play in, a pond for fishing, and hiking in the meadow are among the facilities and activities on the farm.

Pleasant Grove is also an excellent starting point for day trips to such attractions as Longwood Gardens, the Gettysburg Battlefield, Hershey Park, Dutch Wonderland, the birthplace of Robert Fulton, Washington, D.C., and Amish farms.

Angel Flake Biscuits

5 cups all-purpose flour
3 teaspoons baking powder
1 teaspoon salt
1 teaspoon baking soda
3 tablespoons sugar
¾ cup shortening
1 0.6-ounce cake compressed yeast
½ cup warm water (85°)
2 cups buttermilk

In a large bowl sift together the flour, baking powder, salt, baking soda, and sugar. Cut in the shortening until thoroughly mixed. Dissolve the yeast in the warm water. Add the dissolved yeast and buttermilk. Work the dough together with a large spoon until all the flour mixture is moistened. Cover the bowl and refrigerate until ready to

Pleasant Grove Farm

use. Roll out the dough to 1-inch thickness and cut with a biscuit cutter. Place on an ungreased cookie sheet. Bake in a 400° oven for 15 minutes until golden brown.

Note: This dough will keep fresh for several weeks in the refrigerator. Makes 30 biscuits.

Bishop's Bread

2¾ cups sifted all-purpose flour
3 teaspoons baking powder
1 teaspoon salt
½ cup butter or margarine, softened
1 cup light brown sugar
2 eggs
1 cup milk

   🍃 🍃 🍃

½ cup sugar
½ cup all-purpose flour
¼ cup butter
1 teaspoon cinnamon

Grease a 9x13-inch pan. In a medium bowl sift together 2¾ cups of flour, baking powder, and salt. In a separate bowl with an electric mixer at medium speed beat ½ cup of butter with the brown sugar and eggs until light and fluffy. At low speed blend in the milk, then the flour mixture, beating just to combine. Spread the batter evenly in the prepared pan.

In a small bowl combine the sugar, ½ cup flour, ¼ cup butter, and cinnamon until crumbly. Sprinkle the streusel topping over the batter. Bake in a 375° oven for 25 minutes. Let cool on a wire rack.

Serves 16.

Shoofly Pie

1 cup molasses
2 egg yolks, well beaten
1 tablespoon baking soda dissolved in 1½ cups boiling water

   🍃 🍃 🍃

1½ cups all-purpose flour
1 cup brown sugar
¼ cup shortening
½ teaspoon salt
1 teaspoon cinnamon
½ teaspoon cloves
¼ teaspoon nutmeg
1 9-inch unbaked pie shell

In a medium bowl combine the molasses, egg yolks, and dissolved baking soda. In a separate bowl combine the flour, brown sugar, shortening, salt, and spices until crumbly. Alternate the liquid mixture and the crumbs into the pie crust. Bake in a 425° oven until the crust is browned, then reduce the temperature to 350° and bake for 10 more minutes.

Serves 6 to 8.

Monte Cristo

Very pretty.

½ cup butter, softened
2 teaspoons prepared mustard
12 slices white bread
6 slices Swiss cheese, cut in half
6 slices cooked ham

   🍃 🍃 🍃

3 eggs, beaten
⅓ cup milk
Confectioners' sugar and cherry preserves

In a small bowl beat together the butter and mustard until well blended. Spread on one side of each slice of bread. For each sandwich, top one slice of bread with half a slice of cheese, one slice of ham, half a slice of cheese, and a second slice of bread, butter-side down.

In a medium bowl beat together the eggs and milk. Dip each sandwich into the egg mixture. Brown both sides of the sandwich on a lightly buttered griddle. Place on a cookie sheet

and bake in a 425° oven for 8 to 10 minutes. Slice each sandwich in half, sprinkle with confectioners' sugar, and top with preserves.

Serves 6.

The Inn at Starlight Lake

Starlight, Pennsylvania 18461
(717) 798-2519

"**O**ne morning long ago in the quiet of the world when there was less noise and more green . . . " the Inn at Starlight Lake welcomed its first guests. Since 1909 it has been a place where visitors have come to relax and renew themselves. Situated beside Starlight Lake, the inn is surrounded by acres of untouched forests and farmland meadows. Fern banks, moss-covered boulders, shady dells, and woodlands greet the eye at every turn. There are activities here for every season.

The Mainhouse provides twenty comfortable rooms; there are also ten cottage rooms and a family house. Baby sitting is available, as is a playground and a shallow swimming area. Guests are offered a full breakfast and dinner with the price of their room. Wines, spirits, and late night snacks are served in the congenial setting of the Stovepipe Bar.

Sour Cream Apple Pie

2 cups all-purpose flour
½ teaspoon baking powder
Scant ¾ teaspoon salt
½ cup lard
½ cup butter
6 tablespoons cold water

   🍃 🍃 🍃

2 tablespoons all-purpose flour
⅛ teaspoon salt
⅔ cup sugar
1 egg, unbeaten
1 cup sour cream
1 teaspoon vanilla extract
¼ teaspoon nutmeg
2 cups diced apples

🌿 🌿 🌿

⅓ cup brown sugar
⅓ cup all-purpose flour
1 teaspoon cinnamon
¼ cup butter

In a medium bowl combine 2 cups of flour, baking powder, and a scant ¾ teaspoon of salt. Cut in the lard and ½ cup of butter until the mixture is in small pieces. Add enough of the water to hold the dough together. Turn onto a floured board and knead gently for a few seconds. Divide the dough in half and roll each portion for a 9-inch pie crust. Place one crust into a pie pan. Freeze the remaining crust for future use.

In a medium bowl combine 2 tablespoons of flour, ⅛ teaspoon of salt, and sugar. Add the egg, sour cream, vanilla, and nutmeg, beating to a smooth thin batter. Stir in the apples. Pour filling into the prepared pie crust. Bake in a 400° oven for 15 minutes, then reduce the temperature to 350° and bake for 30 more minutes. Remove from the oven.

In a small bowl combine the brown sugar, ⅓ cup of flour, cinnamon, and ¼ cup of butter. Sprinkle topping over pie. Return to a 400° oven and bake an additional 10 minutes.

Serves 6 to 8.

Raised Dough Waffle Batter

1 cup lukewarm water (110° to 115°)
1 tablespoon active dry yeast
1½ cups nonfat dry milk
4 cups lukewarm water (110° to 115°)
1 cup oil
2 teaspoons salt
2 teaspoons sugar
3 cups all-purpose flour

1 cup whole wheat flour
½ cup wheat germ

🌿 🌿 🌿

4 eggs, well-beaten
2 pinches baking soda

In a small bowl combine 1 cup water with the yeast. Set aside to dissolve for 5 minutes.

In a large bowl combine the milk, 4 cups water, oil, salt, sugar, flours, and wheat germ. Add the yeast mixture and cover. Set the bowl in a warm place to allow the dough to rise.

The next morning beat together the eggs and baking soda. Add to the dough, mixing well. Bake on a greased waffle iron.

Serves 4.

Whole Wheat Buttermilk Pancakes

3 cups all-purpose flour
3 cups whole wheat flour
1 tablespoon wheat germ
1 tablespoon salt
3 tablespoons sugar
3 tablespoons cornmeal
1 tablespoon baking soda
2¼ tablespoons baking powder
6 eggs
5½ cups buttermilk or sour milk
3 tablespoons melted shortening or oil

In a large bowl combine the flours, wheat germ, salt, sugar, cornmeal, baking soda, and baking powder. In a separate bowl combine the eggs, milk, and shortening. Blend the two mixtures together, adjusting the consistency of the batter by increasing or decreasing the amount of milk. Bake on a greased griddle until the edges are golden and bubbles rise to the surface.

Variation: Fruit such as blueberries may be added.

Serves 8.

Jefferson Inn

Route 171
Rural Delivery 2, Box 36
Thompson, Pennsylvania 18465
(717) 727-2625

Built in 1871, Jefferson Inn offers accommodations and a full-service restaurant in the rolling hills of northeastern Pennsylvania. Thousands of acres are available nearby for fishing, boating, and some of the best deer and turkey hunting around. The six guest rooms, with private or shared baths, are furnished in period style. The innkeeper is a professional chef and offers "hunger-size" meals in the restaurant.

Country Chocolate Cake

1 cup sugar
1½ cups all-purpose flour
Dash salt
5 tablespoons cocoa
1 teaspoon baking soda
1 tablespoon vinegar
¼ teaspoon red food coloring
¼ cup oil
1 cup cold water
1½ teaspoons vanilla extract

In a large bowl combine all the ingredients, mixing until smooth. Pour the batter into an ungreased 8-inch pan. Bake in a 350° oven for 35 minutes.

Serves 6.

Pace One Restaurant and Country Inn

Thornton Road
Thornton, Pennsylvania 19373
(215) 459-3702

Pace One has that breath of fresh air for which city people search and Ted Pace's famous country cooking is served with an extra helping of friendly service in an eighteenth-century restored stone barn. The country inn, with rooms for overnight accommodations, is newly opened. Its rooms all have private baths or showers. A continental breakfast is available every morning, consisting of coffee, juice, Danish, and fresh fruit. Lunch, dinner, and Sunday brunch are available in the restaurant. Meeting and banquet facilities for up to eighty people are available.

Strawberry Soup

> **6 pints strawberries**
>
>   🍓 🍓 🍓
>
> **4 cups water**
> **2½ cups rosé wine**
> **½ cup lemon juice**
> **1½ sticks cinnamon**
> **1 cup sugar**
>
>   🍓 🍓 🍓
>
> **1½ cups heavy cream**
> **¾ cup sour cream**
>
>   🍓 🍓 🍓
>
> **Strawberries and whipped cream**
> **for garnish**

Pull the stems from the strawberries, wash, and purée. Set aside.

In a large pot combine the water, wine, lemon juice, and cinnamon. Bring to a boil and simmer for 10 minutes. Add the strawberry purée and boil another 5 minutes, stirring occasionally.

Remove the cinnamon sticks and add the sugar. Chill. In a small bowl whip the cream until it begins to thicken. Add the sour cream and whip for another 2 minutes. Stir into the soup.

Garnish each bowl with a fresh strawberry and whipped cream.

Serves 6 to 8.

The Victorian Guest House

118 York Avenue, Route 6
Towanda, Pennsylvania 18848
(717) 265-6972

Situated in the midst of the Endless Mountains, this 1897 inn is a classic Victorian structure with porches, arches, and a host of period architectural splendors. It is filled with antiques. The eleven spacious rooms, all furnished in antiques, include air conditioning, television, and telephones. There are one single and ten double rooms; five have private baths, two have semibaths, and four share two baths.

The Guest House is only six blocks from the center of town with its restaurants and shops. Many outdoor activities are available nearby. Off-street parking is provided.

Cream Cheese and Raspberry Coffee Cake

> **1 8-ounce package cream cheese,**
>   **softened**
> **1 cup sugar**
> **½ cup margarine or butter**
> **1¾ cups all-purpose flour**
> **2 eggs**
> **¼ cup milk**
> **1 teaspoon baking powder**
> **½ teaspoon baking soda**
> **½ teaspoon vanilla extract**
> **¼ teaspoon salt**
> **½ cup raspberry preserves**
> **Confectioners' sugar**

Grease and flour a 9x13-inch baking pan. In a large mixing bowl beat the cream cheese, sugar, and margarine with an electric mixer on medium speed until fluffy. Add half the flour, eggs, milk, baking powder, baking soda, vanilla, and salt. Beat 2 more minutes until well blended. Beat in the remaining flour on low speed until well mixed. Spread evenly in the prepared pan. Spoon the raspberry preserves in 8 to 10 dollops on top of the batter. With a knife swirl the preserves into the batter to marbleize. Bake in a 350° oven for 30 to 35 minutes until a toothpick inserted in the center comes out clean. Cool slightly on a wire rack. Sprinkle lightly with sifted confectioners' sugar.

Serves 24.

The Victorian Guest House

Cheddar Chicken Delight

12 deboned chicken breast halves
1 10½-ounce can mushroom soup
2 cups grated Monterey Jack or
yellow Cheddar cheese
Salt and pepper

Grease a 9x13-inch glass baking dish. Cut the chicken breasts into thirds and place in the prepared dish. Pour the mushroom soup over the chicken. Season with salt and pepper and spread the cheese on top of the casserole. Bake in a 350° oven for 1 hour.
Serves 6 to 8.

Stir Fry Chicken Almond

6 whole chicken breasts
Accent
Soy sauce

Peanut oil
1 6-ounce package slivered almonds
3 green peppers, thinly sliced
2 4-ounce cans mushroom pieces,
reserving drained juice
Cornstarch

Rice, cooked
2 to 3 eggs, beaten

Debone and skin the chicken breasts and dice into small pieces. Sprinkle the chicken with Accent and a generous amount of soy sauce. Cover and allow to marinate 1 to 2 hours before cooking.

Pour the peanut oil in a wok, adding the almonds and browning slightly. Remove the almonds from the wok with a slotted spoon. Add the green pepper and cook 5 minutes until slightly tender. Remove from the wok with a slotted spoon. Add the chicken and cook until chicken turns white and is done. Return the almonds and peppers to the wok.

In a saucepan heat the drained juice from the mushrooms until boiling. Add enough cornstarch to thicken and 2 teaspoons of soy sauce. Pour over the chicken. Remove and keep warm.

Heat additional peanut oil in the wok. Add the cooked rice, stirring until heated. Add the eggs to the rice, stirring constantly until the eggs are fully cooked. Place the chicken almond on a platter and serve with the fried rice.
Serves 8 to 10.

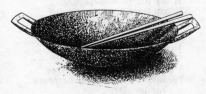

Bed and Breakfast of Valley Forge

Post Office Box 562
Valley Forge, Pennsylvania 19481
(215) 783-7838
FAX: (215) 783-7783

A bed and breakfast reservation service with more than one hundred diverse selections, Bed and Breakfast of Valley Forge offers locations in Philadelphia, the Main Line, Valley Forge, Reading, West Chester, the Brandywine Valley, Bucks County, Lancaster County, and the Poconos.

Facilities include garden townhouses, historically restored homes and barns, carriage houses, guest cottages, country farms, country inns, and ski locations. A wide range of prices and amenities are available.

Ham/Potato O'Brien Casserole

4 baking potatoes, baked
12 to 16 ounces ham steak, diced
into large pieces
¼ cup chopped pimento
¼ cup chopped scallions
¼ cup chopped green pepper
1 cup mayonnaise
½ cup grated Cheddar cheese
(optional)

Scoop the baked potato from the shells and toss with the ham, pimento, scallions, green pepper, cheese, and mayonnaise. Spread the mixture into a casserole and top with the cheese, if desired. Bake in a 375° oven for 30 to 45 minutes until the top is crispy brown.

Serves 4 to 6.

Croissants
with Scrambled Eggs and Smoked Salmon

7 eggs
3 tablespoons heavy cream
¼ teaspoon Kosher salt (optional)
Freshly ground pepper
4 ounces shredded smoked salmon
3 tablespoons unsalted butter or
margarine
6 warm bakery croissants, split
lengthwise halfway through
Hollandaise sauce (I use Knorr's)
Chopped scallions, parsley, or
chives

In a large bowl whisk the eggs. Stir in the cream, salt, pepper, and salmon. In a heavy skillet melt the butter over medium heat. Reduce the heat to low and add the egg mixture. Cook for 12 to 15 minutes, stirring gently until the eggs form creamy curds. Remove from the heat. Spoon the egg mixture onto the bottom half of the croissants and close. Top each croissant with a spoonful of Hollandaise and sprinkle with the scallions, parsley, or chives.

Serves 6.

Ham Steak and Pineapple Strata

1 ham steak
Ground cloves
¼ cup liquid brown sugar

🌿 🌿 🌿

½ cup butter
1 cup sugar
4 eggs
1 20-ounce can crushed pineapple,
drained
5 slices white bread, crusts removed
and cubed

Butter a casserole. In a medium bowl cream together the butter and sugar. Add the eggs, one at a time, beating 30 seconds after each egg. Add the pineapple to the creamed mixture. Place the bread cubes in the prepared casserole. Pour the egg mixture over the bread cubes. Cover with plastic wrap and refrigerate overnight. Bake in a 350° oven for 1 hour. Serve the Strata with the Ham Steak.

Lightly sprinkle each side of the ham steak with the cloves and rub into the steak. In a fry pan heat the brown sugar and fry the ham steak on both sides until the brown sugar is absorbed.

Serves 4.

Sticky Buns

1 0.6-ounce cake compressed yeast
¼ cup lukewarm water (85°)
1 cup scalded milk
¼ cup shortening
¼ cup sugar
1 teaspoon salt
3¼ to 3½ cups sifted all-purpose
flour
1 egg, beaten

🌿 🌿 🌿

¼ cup butter, melted
½ cup brown sugar
2 teaspoons cinnamon

🌿 🌿 🌿

1 cup brown sugar
½ cup butter
1 tablespoon light corn syrup
Pecans, raisins, and/or currants
(optional)
2 teaspoons water

Grease two 9x13-inch pans. Soften the yeast in the water. In a medium saucepan combine the milk, shortening, sugar, and salt. Cool to lukewarm. In a large bowl combine 1 cup of flour, the yeast mixture and egg, beating in with an electric mixer. Change to 1 beater and add remaining flour, beating to form a soft dough. Cover and let rise 1½ to 2 hours, until doubled. Punch down and turn onto a well-floured surface. Divide the dough in half and roll each portion into an 8x13-inch rectangle.

Brush each rectangle with 2 tablespoons of melted butter. In a small bowl combine ½ cup of brown sugar and cinnamon. Spread half of the mixture on each portion of dough. Roll each rectangle into a jelly roll and press ends closed. Cut each roll into 9 slices.

In a small saucepan combine 1 cup of brown sugar, ½ cup butter, and corn syrup. Add the pecans, raisins, and/or currants, if desired. Divide the mixture between the pans and add 1 teaspoon of water. Put the dough slices cut-side down in the pans on top of the sugar mixture. Let rise 35 to 45 minutes until doubled. Bake in a 375° oven for 25 minutes. Cool for 1 to 2 minutes. Invert the pan on a plate or foil. Cool and freeze if desired.

Note: The secret of preventing the topping from sticking to the pan is the teaspoon of water.

Makes 18 buns.

Woodhill Farms Inn

150 Glenwood Drive
Washington Crossing, Pennsylvania 18977
(215) 493-1974

Ideally situated on ten secluded, wooded acres, this modern six-bedroom inn offers cozy guest rooms equipped with private bath, color television, and individual temperature controls. In the afternoon, complimentary wine and snacks are served by the fireplace. Breakfast each morning is a delicious, lingering event. Afterward, visitors can explore the banks of the Delaware River, visit the state park, paddle a canoe, or bicycle along a towpath. Fine restaurants and bistros, art galleries, antique shops, theaters, and boutiques are all nearby.

Vermont Oatmeal Shortbread

1 cup butter or margarine
½ cup brown sugar
1 teaspoon coffee brandy, or rum
1 cup sifted all-purpose flour
½ teaspoon baking soda
2 cups rolled oats

In a medium bowl mix the butter, brown sugar, and brandy together with an electric mixer or by hand until fluffy. In a separate bowl combine the flour, baking soda, and oats. Blend into the butter mixture. Chill for 1 to 2 hours. On a lightly floured board roll the dough ¼-inch thick. Cut into squares, rounds, or triangles. Place on an ungreased cookie sheet. Bake in a 350° oven for 10 to 12 minutes.

Makes 3 to 4 dozen pieces.

Kaltenbach's

Stony Fork Road (Kelsey Avenue)
Rural Delivery 6, Box 106A
Wellsboro, Pennsylvania 16901
(717) 724-4954

This sprawling country home with room for thirty-two guests offers visitors comfortable lodging, home-style breakfasts, and warm hospitality. Set on a seventy-two-acre farm, Kaltenbach's provides ample opportunity for walks through meadows, pastures, and forests, picnicking, and watching the sheep, pigs, rabbits, and wildlife. All-you-can-eat country style breakfasts are served. A honeymoon suite with a tub for two, and hunting and golf packages are available.

Pumpkin Roll

3 eggs
1 cup sugar
⅔ cup pumpkin
1 teaspoon baking soda
1 teaspoon cinnamon
¾ cup all-purpose flour

   🍂   🍂   🍂

Confectioners' sugar
1 8-ounce package cream cheese, softened
¼ cup butter, softened
1 cup confectioners' sugar
1 teaspoon vanilla extract

Grease a rimmed cookie sheet and line with greased and floured waxed paper. In a medium bowl combine the eggs and sugar. Add the pumpkin, baking soda, cinnamon, and flour. Spread the batter onto the prepared cookie sheet. Bake in a 350° oven for 15 minutes.

Remove the warm cake from the cookie sheet onto a dishtowel covered with confectioners' sugar. Roll up and let cool. In a medium bowl blend together the cream cheese, butter, 1 cup of confectioners' sugar, and vanilla. Unwrap the jelly roll and spread with the filling. Reroll, wrap in aluminum foil, and refrigerate.

Serves 8.

Blueberry Muffins

½ cup butter
¾ cup sugar
1 egg
2 cups sifted all-purpose flour
2 teaspoons baking powder
½ teaspoon salt
½ cup milk
2 cups blueberries

   🍂   🍂   🍂

½ cup sugar
¼ cup butter, softened
⅓ cup all-purpose flour
½ teaspoon cinnamon

Oil muffin tins. In a large bowl cream together ½ cup of butter and ¾ cup of sugar. Add the egg, beating well. In a separate bowl combine 2 cups of flour, baking powder, and salt. Add to the creamed mixture alternately with the milk. Fold in the blueberries. Fill the prepared muffin tins two-thirds full.

In a small bowl combine ½ cup of sugar, ¼ cup of butter, ⅓ cup of flour, and cinnamon until crumbly. Sprinkle the topping over the muffin batter. Bake in a 400° oven for 20 to 25 minutes.

Makes 1 dozen.

Rhode Island

Hotel Manisses

Post Office Box 1
Block Island, Rhode Island 02807
(401) 466-2836

This 1872 Victorian hotel has been fully restored to its original state, including the elegant lobby and sitting room. The seventeen rooms, all with private bath and some with Jacuzzis, are decorated in period furniture. The restaurant serves gourmet meals, in addition to the full breakfast, and afternoon tea is served daily.

Sautéed Scallops
with Nectarines

Oil
1¾ pounds sea scallops
1 small red pepper, diced
1 small green pepper, diced
2 cloves garlic, finely diced
6 nectarines, split, cored, and sliced
¼ teaspoon cayenne pepper
1 teaspoon basil
¼ cup white wine
Juice of 2 lemons
½ cup heavy cream
½ cup plus 2 tablespoons butter

In a sauté pan heat a small amount of oil. Add the scallops and brown slightly. Add the peppers, garlic, nectarines, cayenne pepper, basil, and white wine. Cook for about 1 minute, stirring frequently. Add the lemon juice and cream, and bring to a boil. Boil for 1 to 2 minutes. Slowly whip in the butter. Serve immediately.
    Serves 4.

The 1661 Inn and The 1661 Inn Guest House

Spring Street
Block Island, Rhode Island 02807
(401) 466-2421
(401) 466-2063

Taking its name from the year in which Block Island was settled by colonists from New England, the 1661 Inn is decorated in authentic New England antiques and early American paintings. Rooms have been named after the original settlers; each has colonial furniture and wallpaper, and some have private baths and Jacuzzis, refrigerators, and private decks overlooking the ocean and Old Harbor. A full buffet breakfast is served daily. Other meals are served at the nearby Hotel Manisses.

Baked Bluefish

1 5 to 7-pound whole bluefish, cleaned and scaled
¼ cup soy sauce
Oil
4 stalks celery, chopped
4 large carrots, chopped
1 large onion, chopped
½ cup fresh basil leaves
¼ cup melted butter

Wash the bluefish inside and out in cold water. Pat dry. Rub the inside and outside with soy sauce.
    In a skillet heat a small amount of oil and sauté the celery, carrots, and onion. Cool slightly and fill the bluefish body cavity with some of the vegetable mixture and basil. Stand the fish upright on a buttered baking pan. Surround the fish with the remaining vegetable mixture and brush with butter. Bake in a 375° oven for 8 to 10 minutes per pound.
    Serves 6 to 8.

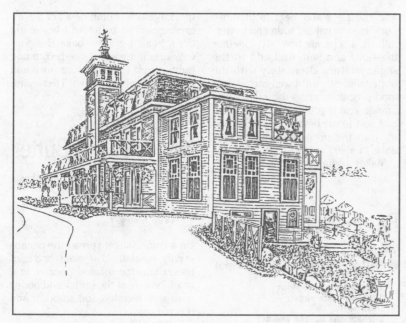

Hotel Manisses

around the edges, about 3 hours. Transfer to a large bowl and whip until smooth and creamy. Freeze again until firm, about 2 hours.

Serves 4 to 6.

Shortbread
(D's Secret Recipe)

Great with coffee or tea, and always a hit with our guests.

> 1 cup butter
> ½ cup sugar
> 2½ cups all-purpose flour
> Confectioners' sugar (optional)
> Almond essence

Grease two 8-inch square baking pans. In a large bowl cream the butter until soft. Add the sugar gradually, and stir in the flour. Add several drops of almond essence. Knead the dough by hand until well blended. Divide the dough in half and press into the prepared pans. The dough should be ½ inch thick. Score into finger-sized portions for easy cutting later. Bake in a 300° to 350° oven for 25 to 30 minutes or until golden brown. Don't overbake. Cut while warm. Cool on wire racks. If desired, sprinkle with confectioners' sugar.

Serves 6 to 8.

One Willow by the Sea Bed and Breakfast

1 Willow Road, Ocean Ridge
Charlestown, Rhode Island 02813
(401) 364-0802

One Willow welcomes its guests to warm hospitality in charming rural surroundings. After freshly ground coffee or tea (English teapot style) and a delicious breakfast, guests may relax on the sundeck or in the garden, or make tracks for the ocean. The area is famous for its beautiful white sandy beaches and shoreline attractions. Biking and hiking trails are everywhere, and the area is a paradise for birdwatchers. Open year-round, One Willow provides opportunities to unwind in every season.

Old-Fashioned Peach Ice Cream

This is delicious. It is also wonderful with strawberries and other fruits.

> 2 pounds peaches (about 6)
> 1½ cups sugar
> 3 tablespoons lemon juice
> 2 eggs, separated
> 2 tablespoons confectioners' sugar
> 1 cup heavy cream

Peel and halve the peaches, and remove the pits. In a food processor combine the peaches, sugar, and lemon juice. Do not overblend. In a large bowl beat the egg whites with the confectioners' sugar until soft peaks form. In a small bowl beat the egg yolks until creamy. In a separate bowl beat the cream until fluffy. Fold the egg yolks into the egg whites, and then whisk in the cream and peaches. Pour the mixture into a one-quart freezer container. Freeze until firm

Bed and Breakfast at the Richards'

144 Gibson Avenue
Narragansett, Rhode Island 02882
(401) 789-7746

In this historic 1884 home, guests enjoy a relaxed atmosphere that encourages relaxing by the fire in the library or by the fireplace in one's own room. Down comforters, canopy beds, private and semiprivate baths, wicker, and antiques all lend a country air. Nearby attractions include the Matunuck Theatre-by-the-Sea, summer concerts on the Village Green, shopping, good restaurants, tennis, fishing, great beaches, and Newport. Breakfast includes such delights as Johnnycakes, cheese blintzes, blueberry muffins, and freshly ground coffee or tea.

Orange Muffins

¾ cup sugar
½ cup butter
2 eggs
1 teaspoon baking soda
1 cup buttermilk
2 cups all-purpose flour
½ teaspoon salt
1 cup raisins
Zest of 1 orange

Grease 12 muffin cups. In a large bowl cream together the sugar and butter with an electric mixer until smooth.

Add the eggs and beat until fluffy. Combine the baking soda and buttermilk. In a separate bowl sift together the flour and salt, and add to the sugar mixture alternately with the buttermilk. Stir until well mixed. In a food processor chop the raisins and orange zest together. Add the raisins and zest to the batter. Spoon the batter into the prepared muffin cups. Bake in a 400° oven for 20 minutes.

Makes 12 large muffins.

Pumpkin Pancakes

These pancakes are excellent served with Honey Pecan Butter (see recipe).

1 cup all-purpose flour
2 tablespoons sugar
Dash salt
2 teaspoons baking powder
1 cup milk
2 tablespoons oil
1 egg
½ teaspoon cinnamon
½ cup canned pumpkin
½ cup sour cream

In a large bowl combine all of the ingredients. The batter will be lumpy. On a heated griddle bake the pancakes until the edges are brown and bubbles rise to the surface. Turn and bake until golden brown. These pancakes are very light.

Serves 2.

Honey Pecan Butter

Serve this with Pumpkin Pancakes.

⅓ cup pecans
½ cup butter
¼ cup honey

On a baking sheet spread the pecans evenly. Toast in a 350° oven for 8 minutes. Chop the toasted pecans. In a small bowl beat the butter and honey until well blended and smooth. Add the pecans.

Makes about 1 cup.

The House of Snee

191 Ocean Road
Narragansett, Rhode Island 02882
(401) 783-9494

In this Dutch Colonial turn-of-the-century home that overlooks the Atlantic Ocean, guests can relax on the porch in the evening as they watch the lights of boats heading in and out of the bay. Double, twin, and single bedrooms are available, all of which share a bath and tub or shower. The full breakfast includes home-baked goodies.

Bed and Breakfast at the Richards'

Coffee Can Bread

4 cups all-purpose flour
1 ¼-ounce package active dry yeast
¼ cup sugar
1 teaspoon salt
½ cup water
½ cup milk
½ cup butter or margarine
Chopped pecans
Chopped raisins or currants
2 eggs, lightly beaten

Grease two 1-pound coffee cans. In a medium bowl combine 2 cups of flour and the yeast. In a large saucepan combine the sugar, salt, water, milk, and butter. Cook over low heat, stirring until the sugar is dissolved and the butter is melted. Cool for 5 minutes. Add the flour-yeast mixture, stirring until well blended. Add the remaining flour, the nuts, raisins, and eggs. Turn the dough onto a floured board and knead until the dough is smooth and the raisins are well-distributed. Divide the dough in half and place each half in a prepared coffee can. Grease the plastic tops that go with the coffee cans, and cover the dough. Let the dough rise until it reaches the plastic tops. Remove the tops. Bake in a 375° oven for 35 to 40 minutes.

Serves 6.

French Breakfast Puffs

⅓ cup shortening, softened
½ cup sugar
1 egg
1½ cups sifted all-purpose flour
1½ teaspoons baking powder
½ teaspoon salt
¼ teaspoon nutmeg
½ cup milk
3 tablespoons melted butter
2 tablespoons sugar
1 teaspoon cinnamon

Grease 12 muffin cups. In a large bowl mix together the first 3 ingredients until well blended. In a separate bowl sift the flour with the baking powder, salt, and nutmeg. Add the flour mixture to the shortening mixture alternately with the milk. Spoon the batter into the prepared muffin cups. Bake in a 350° oven for 20 to 25 minutes.

Roll the hot muffins in the melted butter. Combine the sugar and cinnamon, and sprinkle over the muffins.

Makes 12 muffins.

The Brinley Victorian Inn

23 Brinley Street
Newport, Rhode Island 02840
(401) 849-7645

The Brinley Victorian Inn rewards its guests with Victorian wallpapers, satin and lace window curtains, platform rockers and settees, mints on the pillow, current magazines by the bed, and antique miniature lamps on the mantle. Nestled on a quiet street just off famed Bellevue Avenue, it is but a walk down cobblestone streets to the lavish mansions of the Gilded Age, the Tennis Hall of Fame, quaint shops, Cliff Walk, and more. The oldest continuously used library and the Newport Art Museum are just around the corner. Some guests prefer to cozy up on the old-fashioned porch swing or sunbathe in the courtyard. The seventeen guest rooms offer private and shared baths.

Eye of the Storm Rhode Island Apple Pie

Rhode Island's own Sakonnet Vineyard created "Eye of the Storm" blush wine to celebrate the quiet passing of hurricane Gloria over their vines. Little did they know that the pale pink wine would inspire this recipe for Brinley's Rhode Island Apple Pie!

⅓ cup golden raisins
Sakonnet Vineyard Eye of the Storm
blush wine (or any rosé)
5 cups tart baking apples
½ teaspoon cinnamon
¼ teaspoon cloves
¼ teaspoon nutmeg

The House of Snee

½ cup light brown sugar
2 tablespoons honey
1 tablespoon cornstarch
Pastry for one 9-inch 2-crust pie
1 tablespoon butter

In a small bowl soak the raisins in wine to cover. Set aside. Peel, core, and slice the apples. In a large bowl combine the apples, cinnamon, cloves, nutmeg, brown sugar, honey, raisin mixture, and cornstarch. Toss well to combine. Pour the mixture into the pie shell. Dot with butter. Bake in a 350° oven for 30 minutes. Reduce the heat to 300°, and bake for 20 minutes.

Serves 6 to 8.

Cliffside Inn

Two Seaview Avenue
Newport, Rhode Island 02840
(401) 847-1811

Originally a summer home called Villa du Cote, Cliffside was built in 1880 by Governor Thomas Swann of Maryland. Near the Atlantic Ocean and Newport's famed Cliff Walk, it is in a residential neighborhood away from traffic and noise, yet within walking distance of the mansions, restaurants, boutiques, and other attractions of Newport. The ten guest accommodations, all with private baths, are individually decorated. The cozy bay windows and comfortable porch provide wonderful spots for relaxing, reading a book, or enjoying good conversation.

Yankee Pleaser Casserole

2 pounds bulk sausage, cooked and
    drained
2 cups grated cheese

4 eggs
1 cup cooked grits
1 8½-ounce package Jiffy corn
    muffin mix
1¾ cups hot milk
½ cup butter, melted

Grease a 2-quart casserole dish. Layer the sausage and 1 cup of cheese in the bottom of the casserole. In a medium bowl combine the eggs, grits, muffin mix, milk, and butter, and pour over the sausage and cheese. Top with the remaining cheese. At this point, if desired the uncooked mixture may be refrigerated overnight. Bake in a 325° oven for 45 minutes.

Serves 8 to 10.

Fruit Bits Coffee Cake

¾ cup butter
1½ cups sugar
4 eggs
1 cup sour cream
1½ teaspoons vanilla extract
3 cups all-purpose flour

1½ teaspoons baking powder
¾ teaspoon salt
¾ teaspoon baking soda
2 6-ounce packages chopped dried
    mixed fruit

❧ ❧ ❧

½ cup brown sugar
2 tablespoons butter
2 tablespoons all-purpose flour
1 teaspoon cinnamon

Grease a ring mold. In a large bowl cream together ¾ cup of butter, sugar, eggs, sour cream, and vanilla. In a separate bowl combine 3 cups of flour, baking powder, salt, baking soda, and fruit bits. Toss until well combined. Add the dry ingredients to the creamed mixture, blending until just moistened. In a separate bowl combine the brown sugar, 2 tablespoons of butter, 2 tablespoons of flour, and the cinnamon. Blend until the mixture forms a crumbly streusel. Pour half of the batter into the prepared mold and sprinkle with half of the streusel. Add the remaining batter and top with the remaining streusel. Bake in a 350° oven for 50 to 60 minutes.

Serves 8 to 10.

The Brinley Victorian Inn

Pear Bread

½ cup butter
1 cup sugar
2 eggs
2 cups all-purpose flour
½ teaspoon baking powder
1 teaspoon baking soda
½ teaspoon salt
⅛ teaspoon nutmeg
¼ cup yogurt or buttermilk
1 teaspoon vanilla extract
2 medium pears, chopped

Grease a large loaf pan or 2 small loaf pans. In a large bowl cream together the butter, sugar, and eggs. Add the dry ingredients alternately with the yogurt and buttermilk. Fold in the vanilla and pears. Pour the batter into the prepared loaf pan or pans. Bake in a 350° oven for 1 hour.

Makes 1 large or 2 small loaves.

Sausage Balls

2 pounds bulk sausage, cooked and drained
1 cup Pepperidge Farm Seasoned Stuffing Mix
½ cup milk
¼ cup chopped onion
1 cup chopped apple
2 eggs

Grease 12 muffin cups, a ring mold, or a loaf pan. In a large bowl combine all of the ingredients. Shape the mixture into balls and place in the prepared pan. Bake in a 350° oven for 45 minutes.

Makes 12 to 14 balls.

Cran-Apple Muffins

5 to 6 baking apples
2 tablespoons cinnamon
5 tablespoons sugar

❧ ❧ ❧

2 cups sugar
3 cups all-purpose flour
1 cup oil
4 extra large eggs
½ cup cranberry juice
3 teaspoons baking powder
3 teaspoons vanilla extract
1 teaspoon salt
4 ounces whole fresh cranberries

Grease 18 muffin cups. Peel, core, and cut the apples into small pieces. In a bowl combine the apples, cinnamon, and 5 tablespoons of sugar. Set aside.

In a separate bowl combine the remaining ingredients until just moistened. Spoon batter into the muffin tins, filling half full. Place 1 tablespoon of apple mixture in each muffin cup and top with the remaining batter. Bake in a 375° oven for about 20 to 30 minutes. Cool the muffins for 10 minutes before removing from the pan. Serve warm.

Makes 18 muffins.

"Almost Heaven"

49 West Street
Snug Harbor
Wakefield, Rhode Island 02879
(401) 783-9272

Situated "around the corner" from Rhode Island's beautiful beaches, marinas, and famous seafood restaurants, "Almost Heaven" offers the traveler easy access to all the tourist and entertainment facilities of the area. All its rooms are on the first floor reached by a private entrance. Breakfast is served on the screened deck when the weather permits.

Super Cinnamon Rolls

⅔ cup finely chopped pecans
⅓ cup brown sugar
⅓ cup confectioners' sugar
1 teaspoon cinnamon
¼ cup butter or margarine, softened
2 8-ounce cans refrigerated crescent dinner rolls

❧ ❧ ❧

1 cup confectioners' sugar
1 tablespoon butter or margarine, softened
2 to 3 tablespoons milk

In a small bowl combine the first 5 ingredients. Unroll 1 can of crescent roll dough into a large rectangle, pressing the perforations to seal. Spread with the nut mixture. Unroll the second can of dough and press the perforations to seal. Place the dough over the nut mixture, pressing the edges to seal. Cut into 8 strips. (The strips can be cut in half to make small rolls.) Seal the edges of each strip, twist, and roll into a coil. Place the rolls on a cookie sheet. Bake in a 375° oven for 15 to 20 minutes, until golden brown. Combine the remaining ingredients and drizzle over the warm rolls.

Makes 8 large or 16 small rolls.

Iowa Corn Cakes

1 egg
1¼ cups buttermilk
½ teaspoon baking soda
1¼ cups sifted all-purpose flour
1 teaspoon sugar
2 tablespoons Puritan oil
1 teaspoon baking powder
½ teaspoon salt
1 large or 2 small ears fresh cooked corn

In a large bowl beat the egg thoroughly. Beat in the buttermilk and baking soda. Add the flour, sugar, oil, baking powder, and salt. Remove the kernels from the corn with a knife. Add the corn kernels to the batter. On a hot griddle spoon the batter in quantities slightly larger than a silver dollar. Bake until the edges are golden, turn and bake until done. Serve with maple syrup.

Variation: ¾ cup of sifted flour and ½ cup of cornmeal may be used in place of 1¼ cups sifted flour.

Serves 6.

Strawberry-Rhubarb Coffeecake

1½ pounds rhubarb
1 16-ounce package frozen,
  sweetened strawberries
2 tablespoons lemon juice
2¾ cups sugar
⅓ cup cornstarch

❧ ❧ ❧

3¾ cups all-purpose flour
1 teaspoon baking powder
1 teaspoon baking soda
½ teaspoon salt
1¼ cups butter or margarine
1½ cups buttermilk
2 large eggs
1 teaspoon vanilla extract

Clean the rhubarb and cut into 1-inch pieces. This should make about 3 cups. In a 3-quart saucepan combine the rhubarb, strawberries, and lemon juice. Cover and cook over medium heat for 5 minutes. In a small bowl stir together 1 cup of sugar and the cornstarch. Gradually stir the cornstarch mixture into the rhubarb mixture and heat to boiling. Cook, stirring constantly, for 4 minutes. Cool slightly.

Grease a 9x13-inch baking pan. In a large bowl combine 3 cups of flour, 1 cup of sugar, the baking powder, baking soda, and salt. Cut 1 cup of butter into the flour mixture with a pastry blender or 2 knives until the mixture resembles coarse crumbs. In a small bowl beat together the buttermilk, eggs, and vanilla. Stir the buttermilk mixture into the crumbled mixture until just combined. Spread half of the batter evenly in the greased pan. Spread the rhubarb filling over the batter. Drop the remaining batter by heaping tablespoonfuls over the rhubarb filling.

In a small saucepan over low heat melt the remaining ¼ cup of butter. Stir in the remaining ¾ cup of flour and ¾ cup of sugar until the mixture resembles coarse crumbs. Sprinkle the crumbs over the top of the batter. Bake in a 350° oven for 40 to 45 minutes, or until golden brown and bubbly. Cool in the pan for 10 min-utes. Cut into squares and serve warm.
Serves 12.

Bed and Breakfast at Highland Farm

4145 Tower Hill Road
Wakefield, Rhode Island 02879
(401) 783-2408

In this old New England farmhouse built in the early 1800s, three bedrooms with double beds are available. Highland Farm covers twenty-eight acres and is ten minutes from the ocean. Nearby points of interest include shopping, the famous Narragansett Pier, Galilee Fishing Village, charter boats, the Village of Kingston, the University of Rhode Island and Newport (30 minutes away). In addition to the full cookie can, guests enjoy eggs, pancakes, cereal, juice, coffee, tea, hot muffins, fruit, and wonderful conversation.

Zucchini Quiche

4 eggs
½ cup oil
1 cup biscuit mix
1 medium onion, chopped
3 cups grated or thinly sliced
  zucchini
½ cup Parmesan cheese

Grease a 9-inch pie plate. In a large bowl combine all of the ingredients. Mix well. Pour the mixture into the prepared pie plate. Bake in a 400° oven for 35 minutes or until a knife inserted in the center comes out clean.
Serves 6.

Seafood Casserole

3 tablespoons butter
3 tablespoons all-purpose flour
2 cups milk

❧ ❧ ❧

1 tablespoon butter
1 medium onion, diced
2 stalks celery, diced
1 large carrot, grated
1½ pounds seafood (imitation crab,
  scallops, haddock)
4 hard boiled eggs, chopped
Parmesan cheese

In a skillet melt 3 tablespoons of butter and blend in the flour. Simmer a couple of minutes. Gradually add the milk, stirring until thickened. Set aside.

In a saucepan with a cover melt 1 tablespoon of butter and sauté the onion, celery, and carrots. Cover and simmer, stirring occasionally for about 7 minutes. Add the seafood and chopped eggs. Place the mixture in a casserole dish and cover with the white sauce. Sprinkle with Parmesan cheese, and place pieces of butter on top. Bake in a 350° oven until browned.
Serves 6.

Candy

1 pound white chocolate
½ cup chunky peanut butter
1½ cups mini marshmallows
1 cup unsalted peanuts
1½ cups Rice Krispies cereal

In a microwave-safe bowl melt the chocolate. Add the remaining ingredients and stir until combined. Drop by spoonfuls onto waxed paper or a cookie sheet. Refrigerate until firm.
Serves 6.

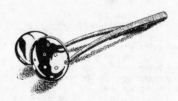

Orange Pineapple Salad

- 1 24-ounce carton cottage cheese
- 1 8-ounce carton Cool Whip
- 2 3-ounce packages orange gelatin
- 1 15-ounce can pineapple tidbits (or crushed), drained
- 1 11-ounce can mandarin oranges, drained

In a large bowl combine the cottage cheese and Cool Whip. Add the dry gelatin and mix well. Fold in the pineapple and mandarin oranges. Refrigerate.

Serves 6 to 8.

Buckeyes

- ½ cup margarine
- 1 1-pound box confectioners' sugar
- 1½ cups peanut butter
- 1 teaspoon vanilla extract
- 1 6-ounce package chocolate chips
- ¼ block paraffin

In a medium bowl cream together the butter, sugar, peanut butter, and vanilla by hand. Roll the mixture into small balls. Chill for 4 hours.

In the top of a double boiler over simmering water melt the chocolate and paraffin. Dip the balls in the chocolate mixture and place on waxed paper to set.

Makes 5 dozen.

Woody Hill Guest House

330 Woody Hill Road
Westerly, Rhode Island 02891
(401) 322-0452

Close to the beaten path and yet not on it, the Woody Hill Guest House of-

fers quiet country living in a convenient location just two miles from the ocean. Situated on a hilltop and surrounded by rolling fields and informal gardens, the house provides a pleasant change from the usual tourist accommodations. Antiques, wideboard floors, and handmade quilts lend an Early American atmosphere, and guests are welcome to rock contentedly on the porch or read in the library.

Wonderful Chicken Salad

- 2½ cups diced cooked chicken
- 1 cup finely cut celery
- 1 cup seedless grapes
- 1 cup finely chopped nuts
- 1 teaspoon minced onion
- 1 teaspoon salt
- ¾ to 1 cup mayonnaise or salad dressing
- ½ cup heavy cream, whipped

🍃 🍃 🍃

Crisp lettuce or other greens
Olives, sweet pickle gherkins for garnish

In a large bowl combine the first 8 ingredients. Chill. Serve on lettuce or greens, garnished with olives and pickles or any garnish you wish.

Serves 6.

Herb and Butter Bread

- 7½ to 8 cups all-purpose flour
- ⅓ cup brown sugar
- 3 teaspoons salt
- 1 teaspoon basil
- 1 teaspoon caraway seed
- ½ teaspoon thyme
- 2 ¼-ounce packages active dry yeast
- 2½ cups milk
- ½ cup butter or margarine

In a large bowl combine 3 cups of flour, the brown sugar, salt, basil, caraway seed, thyme, and dry yeast.

In a saucepan heat the milk and butter until the milk is warm (110° to 115°). The butter does not need to melt. Add the milk to the flour mixture with an electric mixer on low speed until moistened. Beat at medium speed for 3 minutes. By hand, stir in the remaining flour until a stiff dough is formed. Turn the dough onto a floured board and knead for 5 minutes, until smooth and elastic. Place the dough in a greased bowl, turning to grease the top. Cover and let rise for 1 hour to 1 hour and 30 minutes, until doubled.

Grease 2 loaf pans. Punch down and divide into 2 portions. Shape into loaves and place in the prepared loaf pans. Let the loaves rise for 45 to 60 minutes. Bake in a 375° oven for 35 to 50 minutes, until golden brown. Remove from the pans immediately. Cool.

Makes 2 loaves.

Mulled Orange-Apple Punch

- 1½ quarts unsweetened orange juice
- 1 quart apple juice
- ⅓ cup light corn syrup
- 24 whole cloves
- 6 sticks cinnamon
- 1 lemon, thinly sliced (optional)

In a large saucepan combine the orange juice, apple juice, corn syrup, cloves, and cinnamon. Bring to a boil. Reduce the heat and simmer for 5 to 10 minutes or as long as desired, to blend the flavors. Serve steaming hot with a lemon slice in each mug.

Makes 3½ quarts, or 12 servings.

South Carolina

The Evergreen Inn and 1109 South Main Restaurant

1109 South Main
Anderson, South Carolina 29621
(803) 225-1109

The Evergreen Inn and 1109 South Main Restaurant is two buildings, a Greek Revival-style mansion, built in 1906, that serves as the restaurant and the Evergreen Inn, which dates from 1834, next door. Offering eight guest rooms, five with private baths, this is a beautiful, gracious inn that combines southern hospitality with gourmet dining in an elegant setting. The chef, co-owner Peter Ryter, is a member of La Chaine des Rotisseurs, a worldwide French gourmet society founded in 1234. Rooms include a complimentary cocktail or wine in the evening; breakfast is served continental-style. For privacy, no television or telephone are provided in rooms. The restaurant is closed Sunday and Monday.

🐚 🐚 🐚 🐚 🐚

Cream Caramel Custard

1 cup sugar
3 tablespoons water

🐚 🐚 🐚

4 eggs
3 egg yolks
2 tablespoons vanilla extract
¼ cup sugar
4 cups milk

In a saucepan over low heat combine the sugar and water. Over low heat cook the mixture until golden brown, stirring frequently. Pour into 6 ramekins.

In a large bowl combine the eggs, egg yolks, vanilla, and sugar. Add the milk to the egg mixture. Pour the mixture into the ramekins. Set the ramekins in a large pan and add water to the pan half the depth of the ramekins. Bake in a 375° oven for 30 minutes or until set.

Serves 6.

Oyster Bienville

1 tablespoon oil
1 pound shredded crab
2 teaspoons minced fresh garlic
1 tablespoon Pernod
½ cup white wine
2 teaspoons all-purpose flour
1 cup fresh cream

In a skillet heat the oil and sauté the crab with the garlic over low heat for 1 minute. Add the Pernod and the wine, and reduce the liquid to about ¼ cup. Add the flour, then the cream. In a food processor blend the mixture until well mixed.

Shuck about 20 oysters and place on a flat pan. Bake in a 375° oven for 4 minutes. Spoon the crab mixture onto the oysters and broil until the top is golden brown.

Variation: Top with Hollandaise sauce.

Serves 4.

Escargot 1109

4 Pepperidge Farm pastry shells

🐚 🐚 🐚

½ cup butter
28 canned escargots, rinsed well
1 tablespoon fresh minced garlic
2 tablespoons chopped parsley
2 tablespoons cognac
½ cup Reisling wine
1 cup demi glace (brown stock)
1 cup fresh cream

Bake the pastry shells according to the package directions.

In a sauté pan over medium heat melt the butter and add the escargots, garlic, and parsley, stirring constantly. Add the cognac. Ignite the cognac and let it burn off. Add the white wine and reduce, cooking for 3 to 4 minutes. Add the demi glace and cream, and bring to a boil. Pour the mixture into the hot shells. Serve as an appetizer.

Serves 4.

🐚 🐚 🐚 🐚 🐚

The Evergreen Inn

Emincée de Veau Zurchoise

¼ cup butter
½ onion, finely chopped
2 pounds finely sliced trimmed veal
  strips
1 pound fresh mushrooms, sliced
¼ cup white wine
1 cup brown stock
1 pint cream
Salt and pepper to taste

In a sauté pan melt the butter over medium heat. Add the onions, and cook until soft. Add the veal and sauté quickly. Add the mushrooms and cook, stirring constantly, for about 1 minute. Do not overcook. Spoon out the meat mixture into a side dish. Add the wine to the remaining juices and reduce, cooking for about 1 to 2 minutes. Add the brown stock, stirring constantly, and bring to a boil. Add enough cream to produce a light cream texture. Add the meat mixture and bring to a boil. Serve at once.
  Serves 6.

Roesti Potatoes
Swiss Style Grated and Sautéed Potatoes

2 boiled baking potatoes, chilled
½ cup butter
Salt and pepper to taste

Peel the potatoes and discard the skin. Coarsely grate the potatoes.
  In a cast iron skillet melt the butter, and sprinkle the grated potatoes over the butter. Do not stir. Add salt and pepper to taste, and brown completely on one side. Turn and form into oval shaped individual portions. Cook until golden brown.
  Serves 6.

The Cedars Bed and Breakfast

1325 Williston Road
Post Office Box 117
Beech Island, South Carolina 29841
(803) 827-0248

The moment guests enter the drive, they know this is a special place. Tucked away on twelve park-like acres, the Cedars is a step back in time to a more genteel way of life. The completely renovated house is furnished in the traditional manner and accented with antiques. The guest bedrooms feature queen-size poster beds, ceiling fans, fireplaces, and modern private baths. Guests are welcome to fully enjoy the house and its amenities, to read and relax in the upstairs parlor, have afternoon tea, and stroll the grounds. Dogwood, wisteria, redbud, and crape myrtle bloom in profusion, while mockingbirds sing their greetings. A continental breakfast is served each morning by the fireplace in the country kitchen or in the formal dining room. Within easy access are Aiken and its famed Thoroughbred country and Augusta, home of the Masters Golf Tournament, many fine restaurants, antique shops, restored historic "Old Towne," and Riverwalk Park.

Sauerbraten

1 large onion, sliced
1 carrot, sliced
1 stalk celery, sliced
6 large sprigs parsley
1 cup vinegar
1 cup good dry red wine
1 large bay leaf
¼ teaspoon thyme
2 cups water

The Cedars

Peel the bananas and cut lengthwise into quarters. Melt the butter in a large skillet, and stir in the brown sugar, brandy, and pecans. Cook, stirring constantly, until the mixture bubbles. Add the bananas and cook, basting with sauce, until heated through. Serve with ice cream.

Serves 6.

The Fripp House Inn

Post Office Box 857
Bluffton, South Carolina 29910
(803) 757-2139

3 pounds boneless chuck
Salt and pepper to taste
2 beef bouillon cubes
3 tablespoons all-purpose flour
¼ teaspoon ginger
¼ cup water

In a saucepan combine the onion, carrot, celery, parsley, vinegar, wine, bay leaf, thyme, and 2 cups of water. Bring to a boil and simmer for 5 minutes. Cool to room temperature.

In a large crock or enameled pan (nonmetallic) pour the liquid and vegetables over the meat. Let the meat marinate for 2 to 3 days, turning occasionally. Remove the meat and save the liquid. Sprinkle the meat with salt and pepper. Bake in a 450° oven until browned. Transfer the meat to a Dutch oven, and add the marinating liquid and vegetables. Simmer slowly until tender, about 2 hours.

Remove the meat and add the bouillon to the liquid. In a small bowl combine the flour, ginger, and ¼ cup of water. Slowly pour the flour mixture into the liquid, stirring with a wire whisk. Simmer for 10 minutes. Slice the meat and reheat in the gravy.

Serves 6.

Ritzy Chicken Casserole

4 whole chicken breasts
1 8-ounce carton sour cream
2 10½-ounce cans cream of chicken soup
Ritz crackers, crumbled for topping
Butter

In a large saucepan boil the chicken in water to cover until the chicken is tender. Remove the skin and bone, and cut into chunks. Place the chicken in a casserole dish. In a bowl combine the sour cream and soup. Pour the mixture over the chicken. Sprinkle with cracker crumbs and dot with butter. Bake in a 350° oven for about 1 hour, until light brown and bubbly.

Serves 6.

Bananas Praline

6 bananas
¼ cup butter
¼ cup brown sugar
¼ cup brandy
½ cup chopped pecans

❧ ❧

Vanilla ice cream

Azaleas and camellias line the garden pathways beneath ancient oaks and magnolias on the grounds of the Fripp House Inn. Built in the early 1800s when families of rice and cotton planters came to Bluffton's May River to escape the summer heat, the inn has retained the charm of its earlier era. There are comfortable rockers on the front porch, canopy beds, clawfoot tubs, ten fireplaces, and period antiques throughout the inn. Modern conveniences, such as air conditioning, cable television, VCR, and a twenty-by-forty-foot swimming pool, have been added. Breakfast is served on the garden porch or in front of a crackling fire. A set-up bar and snacks are provided in the evening.

Low Country Clam Dip

- 1 8-ounce package cream cheese, room temperature
- 1 6½-ounce can minced clams
- 2 tablespoons mayonnaise
- 2 tablespoons minced onion
- 1 teaspoon Worcestershire sauce
- 3 tablespoons finely chopped parsley
- 1 to 2 teaspoons lemon juice

  ❧ ❧ ❧

Fritos corn chips

Combine the cream cheese, clams, mayonnaise, onion, Worcestershire sauce, and parsley. Add enough lemon juice to achieve the desired consistency. Serve with corn chips.

Serves 6.

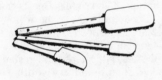

Holiday Wassail

- 1 tablespoon whole cloves
- 2 cinnamon sticks
- 2 quarts apple cider or juice
- 1 quart cranapple juice
- 1 46-ounce can pineapple juice
- 1 12-ounce can frozen orange juice concentrate
- 1 6-ounce can frozen lemonade concentrate
- 1 cup water
- ½ cup honey
- ½ cup brown sugar
- ½ teaspoon nutmeg
- 1 lemon, sliced
- 1 orange, sliced

Tie the cloves and cinnamon in a cheesecloth bag. In a large kettle combine all of the ingredients and stir. Bring the mixture to a boil and simmer for 15 minutes. Remove the cheesecloth bag.

Makes 1½ gallons.

1837 Bed and Breakfast

126 Wentworth Street
Charleston, South Carolina 29401
(803) 723-7166

This circa 1800 home and brick carriage house were originally owned by a cotton planter. Now owned and restored by two artists, the inn provides rooms individually furnished and decorated with antiques and period pieces. The formal parlor has the original red cypress wainscotting, cornice moulding, and wide heart pine floors. The carriage house with its pine beamed ceilings and exposed Charleston red brick walls shows evidence of the slaves' cooking stoves. A hearty breakfast offers opportunity to meet other guests while enjoying excellent food.

Mexican Frittata

- ¼ cup butter
- ½ cup onion, chopped
- 1 17-ounce can corn, drained
- 2 8-ounce cans chopped mild green chilies, drained
- 1¼ teaspoons chili powder
- 18 large eggs
- 1 cup sour cream
- ½ teaspoon salt
- Dash red pepper
- ⅓ cup all-purpose flour
- 3 cups shredded sharp Cheddar cheese
- 2½ cups shredded Monterey Jack

  ❧ ❧ ❧

Medium salsa
Sour cream

Grease 2 9-inch pie plates. In a skillet over medium heat melt the butter and sauté the onion, corn, and chilies until the flavors blend. In a bowl whisk the eggs and sour cream together.

Add the sautéed mixture and the remaining ingredients. Pour into the prepared pans. Bake in a 350° oven for about 1 hour.

Cut the frittatas into wedges and serve with salsa and sour cream on each wedge.

Serves 16.

Ham and Cheese Puffs

- 1½ pounds chopped ham
- 4 cups shredded Monterey Jack cheese
- 2 8-ounce packages cream cheese
- 2 8-ounce cans chopped mushrooms
- 16 puff pastry shells

  ❧ ❧ ❧

Sour cream
Chives
Paprika

In a large bowl combine the ham, Monterey Jack cheese, cream cheese, and mushrooms.

Bake the puff pastry in a 350° oven for 20 minutes, until light and golden brown. Heat the ham mixture (in the oven or microwave). Fill the puffs with the heated ham mixture. Garnish with a dollop of sour cream and sprinkle with chives and paprika.

Serves 16.

The Lodge Alley Inn

195 East Bay Street
Charleston, South Carolina 29401
(803) 722-1611

The Lodge Alley Inn takes its name from the Marine Lodge of Freemasons established in the alley in 1773, where Charleston defied the British-imposed tax by holding her own tea party in 1774. It is in Charleston's historic district, offering thirty-four inn rooms, each with a fireplace, fifty-eight one- and two-bedroom suites, each with a kitchen, and a two-bedroom penthouse. The inn also has facilities for private meetings and functions, dining in the French Quarter Restaurant, and relaxation in the Charleston Tea Party Lounge, eighteenth-century parlor, courtyard, and gardens. Lodge Alley Inn is within easy strolling distance of historic homes, fine restaurants, and shops.

Tuna Loin "au Poivre"
with Tomato Relish

1 8-ounce tuna loin
Salt and cayenne pepper to taste
1 cup olive oil, divided
Cracked black pepper

   ❧ ❧ ❧

3 fresh plum tomatoes
½ cup olive oil
2 fresh shallots, chopped
1 clove garlic, chopped
1 branch fresh thyme
1 tablespoon chopped fresh basil
½ tablespoon chopped chives
Salt and pepper to taste

   ❧ ❧ ❧

Fresh basil leaves for garnish

Clean and skin the tuna loin, and season with salt and cayenne pepper. Dip the tuna in ½ cup of olive oil and roll in the black pepper, covering well.

In a heavy sauté pan heat the ½ cup of olive oil. Sauté the tuna for 30 seconds on each side or until medium rare (pink inside). Remove and keep warm.

Plunge the tomatoes into boiling water and hold for 1 minute. Plunge into ice water and hold for a few seconds. Peel the tomatoes, halve, and squeeze out the seeds and juice. Chop the tomato pulp. In a heavy sauté pan heat ½ cup of olive oil and add the chopped tomatoes, shallots, and garlic. Cook for 2 minutes. During the last minute add the herbs, salt, and pepper to taste.

To serve, divide the tomato relish between 2 serving plates. Slice the tuna loin and place on top of the relish. Garnish with fresh basil leaves.
Serves 2.

Veal la Louisiane

4 2½-ounce slices boneless veal
Salt and freshly ground white
   pepper
All-purpose flour
2 tablespoons oil
½ pound mushrooms, sliced
2 cups whipping cream
¼ cup Madeira
¼ cup butter, cut into 12 pieces
4 ounces cooked crab meat
8 jumbo shrimp, peeled, deveined
   and cooked
4 poached crayfish (optional)

Pound the veal to ¼-inch thickness. Season with salt and pepper. Dredge the veal in flour, shaking off the excess. In a large skillet heat the oil over medium heat. Add the veal and brown for 45 seconds on each side. Transfer the veal to a platter and keep warm.

Add the mushrooms to the skillet and sauté for 5 minutes. Add the cream and Madeira, and reduce until thickened, about 15 minutes. Season with salt and pepper. Stir in the butter 1 piece at a time, incorporating each piece completely before adding another. Add the crab meat and shrimp, and cook for about 1 minute, until heated through. Pour over the veal. Top each slice with 1 poached crayfish if desired. Serve immediately.
Serves 4.

The Shaw House

8 Cyprus Court
Georgetown, South Carolina 29440
(803) 546-9663

The Shaw House is a spacious home with antique-filled rooms. Guests can enjoy a beautiful view of the Willowbank Marsh. The hostess has intimate knowledge of the area, including historical sites, gift shops, and restaurants. A complimentary southern home-cooked breakfast is included, with fresh hot bread and individual pots of coffee. The Shaw House is near Myrtle Beach, Pawley Island, and Charleston.

Kisses

3 egg whites
1 cup sugar
1 teaspoon vinegar
1¼ cups chopped nuts

Grease a cookie sheet. Preheat the oven to 350°. In a large bowl combine the egg whites, sugar, and vinegar. Beat with an electric mixer at high speed for 10 minutes. Fold in the nuts. Drop by teaspoonfuls onto the prepared cookie sheet. Place the cookie sheet in the oven and turn the oven off. Leave the cookies in the oven until the oven is cooled, or leave overnight.
Makes about 2½ dozen.

Sausage Quiche

1 pound sausage, cooked
2 tablespoons sausage drippings
½ cup green peppers
½ cup chopped onions
1 tablespoon all-purpose flour
1½ cups grated sharp Cheddar
    cheese
1 unbaked 9-inch pie shell
2 eggs, beaten
1 cup evaporated milk
1 teaspoon salt
1 teaspoon pepper

In a skillet heat the sausage drippings and sauté the peppers and onions until tender. In a small bowl combine the flour and cheese. In the bottom of the pie shell place the sausage and sautéed mixture, and top with the cheese mixture. Beat together the remaining ingredients and pour over the cheese. Bake in a 350° oven for 35 minutes.
    Serves 6 to 8.

the Shaw House

Baked Eggs
on Corned Beef Hash

1 12-ounce can corned beef hash
2 eggs
2 tablespoons shredded Cheddar
    cheese
Salt and pepper to taste

Divide the corned beef hash between 2 custard cups. Make a hollow in the center of the hash and break an egg

into each cup. Pierce the egg yolks. Sprinkle each with 1 tablespoon of cheese. Season to taste. Cover each with a paper towel. Bake in a 350° oven for 5 minutes. Let stand covered for 1 minute.
    Serves 2.

Carrot Lemon Squares

1 cup melted margarine
1¼ cups sugar
4 eggs
1 cup cooked mashed carrots
2 cups all-purpose flour
1 teaspoon baking powder
1½ teaspoons vanilla extract
¾ teaspoon lemon extract

🌿 🌿 🌿

2¼ cups confectioners' sugar
¼ cup water
1½ tablespoons lemon extract

Grease a 10x15-inch pan. In a large mixing bowl cream together the margarine and sugar. Add the eggs one at a time, beating well after each addition. Add the carrots, flour, and baking powder. Beat for 1 minute. Stir in the vanilla and ¾ teaspoon of lemon extract. Spoon the batter into the pan. Bake in a 350° oven for 25 minutes. Cool.
    In a small bowl combine the confectioners' sugar, water, and lemon extract. Stir until smooth. Pour the mixture over the cooled cake. Cut into squares.
    Makes 5 dozen.

Windsong—A Bed and Breakfast

Route 1, Box 300
Mayesville, South Carolina 29104

Windsong is a spacious house in an excellent location for people wanting a rural setting for their vacation or needing a place to stop on their travels north and south. Its comfortable guest rooms have a separate entrance, and the house's balconies and porches provide ample opportunity for relaxation and conversation. The miles of private, isolated country trails surrounding Windsong invite long, quiet walks.

Crab-Potato Casserole

4 large white potatoes, peeled
¾ cup butter or margarine
¾ cup whipping or light cream
Cayenne pepper to taste
½ teaspoon garlic powder
2 tablespoons grated onion
¼ cup chopped parsley
¼ cup chopped green onions
½ teaspoon salt
1 to 1½ cups grated sharp Cheddar
    cheese
1 pound white crab meat
Paprika

Boil the potatoes until soft. Whip the potatoes with the butter, cream, cayenne pepper, garlic powder, onion, parsley, green onion, salt, and cheese. Gently fold in the crab meat. Place the mixture in a casserole dish and sprinkle with paprika. Bake in a 400° oven for 20 to 25 minutes.
    Serves 8.

Windsong

Fruit Salad

4 bananas, sliced
1 21-ounce can cherry pie filling
1 15¼-ounce can pineapple tidbits,
   drained

Combine all of the ingredients and refrigerate.
   Serves 10 to 12.

Clam Dip

1 8-ounce package cream cheese
1 3-ounce package cream cheese
1 6½-ounce can minced clams with
   juice
1 small onion, grated
Garlic salt and pepper to taste

In a serving bowl combine all of the ingredients.
   Makes about 2 cups.

Laurel Hill Plantation

1031 Tall Pine Road
Mount Pleasant, South Carolina 29464
(803) 884-8208

Laurel Hill Plantation faces the intracoastal waterway and the Atlantic Ocean. The house is furnished in country antiques and has four guest rooms, each with a private bath. A full country breakfast is provided.

Grits Casserole

1 cup grits
1½ cups grated sharp Cheddar
   cheese
2 tablespoons butter
5 eggs
1½ cups milk
Salt and pepper to taste
2 pounds ground sausage, cooked
   and drained

In a saucepan cook the grits according to the package directions. Cool. Add the cheese and butter. In a medium bowl beat the eggs, and add the milk, salt, and pepper. Add to the cooled grits mixture. Place the sausage in the bottom of a casserole dish and pour the grits mixture over the sausage. Bake in a 350° oven for 1 hour.
   Serves 10 to 12.

Bed and Breakfast at Summerville

304 South Hampton Street
Summerville, South Carolina 29483
(803) 871-5275

The primary unit offered for bed and breakfast is the restored servants' quarters dating from 1865. A large room with beamed ceilings, it has a fireplace in the sitting area and a double bed in the sleeping area. A bath with a shower, fully equipped kitchen, heat and air conditioning, two bikes and a grill are part of the facilities. Accommodations are also available in the main house (listed on the National Register of Historic Places) in a large upstairs room furnished with antiques, including a canopy bed.

The bath is private but not connected. The room opens to the upstairs porch. Breakfast can be served by the pool or gazebo or in the greenhouse as weather permits. Complimentary wine and soft drinks, fruit, and flowers are provided for guests. The pool, open late-May to mid-September is available to guests at most hours. During winter months and for stays longer than three days, breakfast is placed in the cottage refrigerator.

Puffed Peach Pancakes

3 tablespoons dark brown sugar
⅛ teaspoon cinnamon
1 tablespoon fresh lemon juice
1 peach, sliced
2 tablespoons butter or margarine
2 large eggs, beaten
6 tablespoons all-purpose flour
⅛ teaspoon salt
⅓ cup milk

🍂 🍂 🍂

Syrup

In a medium bowl stir together 1 tablespoon of brown sugar, the cinnamon, lemon juice, and peaches. Toss to cover. Divide the margarine between 2 shallow 1-cup ovenproof dishes. Heat in a 425° oven for about 1 minute or until melted. In a medium bowl combine the eggs, flour, 2 tablespoons of brown sugar, salt, and milk. Whisk until blended. The batter will be lumpy. Divide most of the batter between the dishes, reserving a small amount. Arrange the drained peach slices in spoke fashion on top. Pour the reserved sugar mixture over

each. Bake in a 425° oven for 16 to 18 minutes or until puffed and golden. Serve with syrup.
Serves 2.

Sour Cream Biscuits

½ cup self-rising flour
⅛ teaspoon baking soda
⅓ cup plus 1 tablespoon sour cream

In a small bowl combine all of the ingredients and stir until smooth. Turn out onto a floured board and roll to ½-inch thickness. Cut with a biscuit cutter and place on a baking sheet. Bake in a 425° oven for 10 to 15 minutes.
Serves 2.

Orange Spread

Serve on biscuits or muffins.

1 8-ounce package cream cheese
½ cup orange marmalade
¼ teaspoon ginger

Combine all of the ingredients and mix until fluffy.
Makes 1½ cups.

Zucchini Muffins
with Citrus Glaze

2 eggs
1 cup sugar
½ cup oil
1 tablespoon vanilla extract
2 cups unpeeled shredded zucchini

🍂 🍂 🍂

2 cups all-purpose flour
1 teaspoon baking soda
¼ teaspoon baking powder
½ teaspoon salt
1½ teaspoons cinnamon
1 cup raisins
½ cup chopped pecans

🍂 🍂 🍂

1¼ cups sifted confectioners' sugar
1 teaspoon grated orange rind
¼ cup orange juice
1 teaspoon vanilla extract

Grease 24 muffin cups. In a medium bowl combine the eggs, sugar, oil, and 1 tablespoon of vanilla. Stir in the zucchini. In a large bowl combine the flour, baking soda, baking powder, salt, and cinnamon. In a small bowl toss the raisins and pecans with ¼ cup of the flour mixture.

Make a well in the center of the dry ingredients. Pour the zucchini mixture into the well and stir into the dry ingredients until just moistened. Stir in the raisins and pecans. Spoon into the prepared muffin cups, filling ⅔ full. Bake in a 350° oven for 20 minutes.

Combine the remaining ingredients, stirring until well blended. Remove the muffins from the pans and spoon the glaze over all.
Makes 24.

🍂 🍂 🍂 🍂 🍂

South Dakota

Bed and Breakfast at Skoglund Farm

Route #1, Box 45
Canova, South Dakota 57321
(605) 247-3445

The Skoglund Farm is a farmhouse that brings back memories of Grandpa's home. Decorated in country style, with antiques and collectibles, it expresses the personality of the innkeepers. It has four rooms for guest use and provides guests with a continental breakfast served country-style and the evening meal.

Horseback riding is available on the premises. Nearby attractions are the Corn Palace, the Doll Palace, and the "Little House on the Prairie."

South Dakota Pheasant Delight

2 pheasants
Cornmeal
Oil

🐦 🐦 🐦

2 cups white and wild rice
1 teaspoon salt
½ cup chopped parsley
½ cup butter, melted
1 teaspoon curry powder

🐦 🐦 🐦

1 cup cream

Cut up the pheasants. Roll the pheasant pieces in cornmeal. In a skillet heat enough oil to cover the bottom. Cook the pheasant until brown.

Cook the rice until almost done. Drain and rinse several times with cold water. In a bowl combine the rice, salt, parsley, butter, and curry powder. Place the mixture in the bottom of a 2-quart casserole dish. Arrange the pheasant over the rice mixture and pour the cream over the top. Bake in a 350° oven for 1 hour or until done. Serve on a large meat platter garnished with fresh parsley leaves.

Serves 4 to 6.

🐦 🐦 🐦 🐦 🐦

Audrie's Cranbury Corner Bed and Breakfast

Rural Route 8
Box 2400
Rapid City, South Dakota 57702
(605) 342-7788

The ultimate in charm and Old World hospitality, Audrie's provides spacious rooms furnished in comfortable European antiques. Each room has a private entrance, private bath, fireplace, patio, and hot tub. A full Black Hills-style breakfast is served.

Fruited Iced Tea

5 teaspoons Lipton Iced Tea Mix (lemon flavor)
1½ teaspoons Nestea Ice Teasers (orange flavor)
1 gallon water

Combine all of the ingredients. Serve over ice.

Variation: Add any fruit juice desired to change the flavor a bit. We use cranberry, of course.

Makes 1 gallon.

Cranbury Corner Muffins

2 cups all-purpose flour
2 teaspoons baking powder
½ teaspoon salt
½ cup margarine
1 cup sugar
2 large eggs
1 teaspoon vanilla extract
1 teaspoon butter vanilla extract
1 heaping tablespoon cream cheese
½ cup milk
½ can (16-ounce can) whole
    cranberry sauce
½ cup chopped nuts

❧ ❧ ❧

⅓ cup sugar
½ teaspoon nutmeg
½ teaspoon cinnamon

Grease 12 muffin cups. In a medium bowl sift together the flour, baking powder, and salt. In a large bowl cream the butter and 1 cup of sugar until fluffy. Beat in the eggs and add the vanillas and cream cheese. Stir in the flour mixture and the milk. Fold in the cranberry sauce and nuts. Spoon the batter into the tins, filling to the top. In a small bowl combine ⅓ cup of sugar, the nutmeg, and cinnamon. Sprinkle over the batter. Bake in a 375° oven for 25 to 30 minutes, until golden. Let the muffins cool in the pan for 15 minutes.
Makes 12 to 14.

Orange Rolls

These rolls are so tender that they melt in your mouth.

1 ¼-ounce package active dry yeast
¼ cup warm water (115°)
1 cup sugar, divided
1 teaspoon salt
2 eggs
½ cup sour cream
½ cup melted butter or margarine
3½ cups sifted all-purpose flour
2 tablespoons grated orange rind

❧ ❧ ❧

¾ cup sugar
½ cup sour cream
2 tablespoons orange juice
½ cup butter or margarine

In a large mixing bowl dissolve the yeast in warm water. With an electric mixer beat in ¼ cup of the sugar, the salt, eggs, sour cream, and 6 tablespoons of melted butter. Gradually add 2 cups of flour. Beat until smooth. Knead the remaining flour into the dough. Place the dough in a bowl and let rise in a warm place until doubled in bulk, about 2 hours.

Grease a 9x13-inch pan. Turn the dough out onto a floured surface and knead about 15 times. Divide the dough in half and roll half into a 12-inch circle. In a small bowl combine ¾ cup of sugar and the orange rind. Brush the dough with 1 tablespoon of melted butter and sprinkle with half of the orange-sugar mixture. Cut into 12 wedges. Roll up, starting with the wide end. Repeat with the remaining dough. Place point side down in the prepared pan. Cover and let rise in a warm place for about 1 hour. Bake in a 350° oven for about 20 minutes or until golden.

In a saucepan combine the remaining ingredients and bring to a boil. Boil for 3 minutes, stirring constantly. Pour over the hot rolls.
Makes 24.

Lake Side Farm

Rural Route 2, Box 52
Webster, South Dakota 57274
(605) 486-4430

This farm home is situated in the northeast lake region of South Dakota. Fishing, boating, and water recreation are nearby. Guests may tour the farm. Children are welcome, but smoking and alcoholic beverages are not. Pets are allowed by appointment only.

Scandinavian Almond Butter Cake

¾ cup butter
1 cup sugar
3 egg yolks
1 teaspoon almond extract
2¼ cups sifted cake flour
2 teaspoons baking powder
¼ teaspoon salt
¾ cup milk
3 egg whites

❧ ❧ ❧

1 tablespoon grated orange rind
½ cup orange juice
½ cup sugar
½ cup butter
2 eggs, slightly beaten

Grease and flour a bundt pan. In a large mixing bowl cream ¾ cup butter. Gradually add 1 cup of sugar and beat until light and fluffy. Beat in the egg yolks, one at a time. Add the extract. In a separate bowl sift together the flour, baking powder, and salt. Add the flour mixture to the creamed mixture alternately with the milk, beginning and ending with the dry ingredients. Beat the egg whites until soft peaks form, and fold into the batter. Turn into the prepared pan. Bake in a 325° oven for 45 to 50 minutes. Do not overbake.

In a saucepan combine the orange rind, orange juice, ½ cup of sugar, and ½ cup of butter. Cook over low heat until the butter is melted and the sugar is dissolved. Remove from the heat. Stirring vigorously, blend the 2 remaining eggs into the orange mixture. Cook over low heat, stirring until slightly thickened. Do not boil. Makes 1¾ cups.

To serve, slice the cake and top with orange butter sauce.
Serves 8 to 10.

🦆 🦆 🦆 🦆 🦆

Easy Croissants

5 cups all-purpose flour
2 ¼-ounce packages active dry yeast
¼ cup sugar
2 teaspoons salt
1 cup water
¾ cup evaporated milk
¼ cup butter or margarine
2 eggs
1 cup butter or margarine, cut into pieces
1 tablespoon water

In a large mixing bowl combine 1 cup of flour, the yeast, sugar, and salt. Mix well. In a saucepan heat 1 cup of water, the milk, and ¼ cup of butter until warm (120° to 130°, the butter does not need to melt). Add to the flour mixture. Add 1 egg. Blend with an electric mixer on low speed until moistened, then beat for 3 minutes at medium speed. Set aside.

In a large bowl cut 1 cup of firm butter into the remaining 4 cups of flour until the mixture resembles small peas. Pour the yeast mixture over the crumbled mixture and fold in until all of the flour is moistened. Cover and refrigerate for 2 hours.

Turn the dough onto a floured surface and knead about 6 times to release air bubbles. Divide into 4 parts. Roll each fourth into a 14-inch circle. With a sharp knife cut each circle into 10 pie-shaped wedges. Starting with a wide edge, roll each wedge toward the point. Place on ungreased baking sheets point side down, curving into croissants. Cover and let rise in a warm place until almost doubled, about 30 to 45 minutes.

In a small bowl slightly beat the remaining egg. Add the water, blending well. Brush the rolls with the egg mixture. Bake in a 350° oven for 15 to 18 minutes, until golden brown. Remove from the baking sheets and cool.

Variation: For a larger roll that can be split and spread with your favorite filling, divide each circle into 4 or 6 wedges. Makes 16 to 24 rolls.

Makes 40 rolls.

The Mulberry Inn

The Mulberry Inn

512 Mulberry Street
Yankton, South Dakota 57078
(605) 665-7116

Built in 1873, the Mulberry Inn is listed on the National Register of Historic Places. The eighteen-room inn boasts a red brick exterior, high ceilings, shutters, a beautifully carved, massive front door, walnut paneling, and parquet floors. The six guest rooms are furnished with attractive antiques, Laura Ashley wallpapers, and fresh flowers. Complimentary wine and cheese and coffee are served in the parlors each evening; both contain marble fireplaces, and a cheery bay window. The dining room opens onto a large porch.

Ham Brunch Casserole

12 slices day-old white bread
1 pound cubed ham
2 cups shredded Cheddar cheese
2 cups shredded Monterey Jack cheese
12 eggs
3 cups milk
½ teaspoon salt and pepper

Grease a 9x13-inch pan. Remove the crusts from the bread and cut into ½-inch strips. Line the bottom of the pan with half of the bread slices. Scatter the ham cubes over the bread and top with the cheeses. Top with the remaining bread. In a large bowl combine the eggs, milk, salt, and pepper. Pour over the casserole. Cover and refrigerate overnight.

Bake in a 350° oven for 1 hour. Cool the casserole before serving.

Variation: Substitute Velveeta Mexican Shredded Hot Cheese for the cheeses.

Serves 12.

Tennessee

Hachland Vineyard

Hachland Hill Dining Inn and Catering Service
1601 Madison Street
Clarksville, Tennessee 37040
(615) 255-1727—Hachland Vineyard (in Joelton)
(615) 647-4084—Hachland Hill Dining Inn

Hachland Vineyard, in the Nashville area, offers fine fare in a restored cedar log house built around 1805. Those who love old things will revel in the wide pine board floors and hand-rubbed logs that only time-mellowed wood can have. The Vineyard, with its private guest rooms, is the ideal spot for corporate retreats, business meetings, seminars, as well as private family gatherings. The Vineyard sleeps twenty-five.

Hachland Hill Inn in Clarksville is forty-five minutes northwest of downtown Nashville. The grand ballroom can seat 300 people for a private dinner. The adjoining terrace and garden rooms overlook wildflower gardens and a bird sanctuary. Roaring fires burn throughout the mansion from late September until May. Three of Clarksville's oldest log houses have been reconstructed in the garden area where old-fashioned barbecue suppers with square dancers are held. Hachland Hill sleeps fifteen.

At both settings, Hachland Properties provide unlimited menu selection from such international cuisine as chateaubriand to "down-on-the-farm" country suppers of southern fried chicken, Tennessee country ham, and biscuits.

Phila's Famous Pancakes

1 cup sour cream
1 cup cottage cheese
¾ cup all-purpose flour
4 eggs, separated
¼ teaspoon salt
1 tablespoon sugar

Syrup

In a large bowl combine the sour cream and cottage cheese. Stir in the flour and well beaten egg yolks. Beat until smooth and add the salt and sugar. In a separate bowl beat the egg whites until stiff. Fold the egg whites into the batter. Heat a greased griddle and fry the pancakes in small amounts until the edges are golden and bubbles rise to the surface. Turn and cook until golden. Serve with syrup.

Serves 4 to 6.

Phila's Frozen Fruit Salad

1 14-ounce can sweetened condensed milk
¼ cup lemon juice
1 cup cream, whipped
1 21-ounce can cherry pie filling
1 14-ounce can crushed pineapple
2 bananas, sliced
½ cup chopped pecans
½ cup sliced pears
½ cup sliced peaches
Mayonnaise

In a large bowl combine the sweetened condensed milk and the lemon juice. Stir until thickened. Fold in the remaining ingredients except the mayonnaise. Spread the mixture in a 9x13-inch dish. Freeze until firm.

Cut into squares while still frozen and serve at once with a dollop of mayonnaise on each serving.

Serves 12.

Hachland Hill Inn

Buckhorn Inn

Tudor Mountain Road
Gatlinburg, Tennessee 37738
(615) 436-4668

The Buckhorn Inn sits on thirty acres atop a peaceful hilltop less than one mile from the entrance to the Great Smoky Mountains National Park. Built in 1938, the inn, with its guest cottages and main lodge, provides all the comforts desired in a mountain retreat. The guest rooms are spacious and have private baths. The dining room invites guests to the evening meal served in country surroundings.

Mud Pie

    1 pound Oreo cookies
    1 cup butter, melted
    ½ gallon double vanilla ice cream
    ½ gallon coffee ice cream
    1 pint chocolate fudge suace
    Sliced almonds

In a food processor with a metal blade process the cookies until finely crumbled. In a small mixing bowl combine the crumbs and melted butter. Line the bottom and sides of a 12-inch springform pan with the crumb mixture. Place in the freezer for 30 minutes.

In a large mixing bowl combine the ice creams and allow to soften. Blend until smooth. Fill the cookie-lined pan with the ice cream and freeze for at least 2 hours.

Remove the pie from the freezer. Cover the top with fudge sauce and sprinkle with almonds. Refreeze for at least 1 hour before serving.

Serves 8.

Farmer's Omelet

    2 tablespoons butter or margarine
    2 tablespoons diced onion
    1 tablespoon diced green pepper
    1 tablespoon diced red pepper
    ¼ cup sliced medium mushrooms
    2 small red potatoes, boiled and
        diced
    ¼ cup diced dill pickle
    3 eggs, beaten
    2 slices Farmer's cheese

In an omelet pan melt the butter over low heat. Add the next 6 ingredients. Sauté over low heat for 5 minutes, or until the vegetables are crisp and tender. Add the eggs. With a rubber spatula lift the eggs to allow the uncooked eggs to run under. When most of the omelet is cooked, flip or place under the broiler to cook the top. Place the cheese on half of the omelet. Fold and serve.

Serves 2.

Summer Vegetable Soup

    2 quarts beef stock
    2 pounds mushrooms, sliced
    1 medium eggplant, peeled and
        diced in ½-inch squares
    2 medium yellow squash, diced
    1 medium onion, diced

        ❧ ❧ ❧

    1 medium zucchini, shredded
    2 tablespoons all-purpose flour
    2 tablespoons lemon juice
    1 tablespoon oregano
    1 teaspoon white pepper

In a 4-quart soup pot combine the beef stock and the next 4 ingredients. Bring to a boil, and boil for 5 minutes. In a large bowl combine the zucchini and the remaining ingredients. Add the mixture to the soup and simmer for 1 hour. Water may have to be added. Taste and adjust the seasonings, and serve.

Serves 6 to 8.

Marinated Beef Tenderloin

    1 5 to 6-pound beef tenderloin,
        trimmed
    1 cup soy sauce
    1 cup red wine
    ½ cup olive oil
    3 large cloves garlic
    1 tablespoon cracked black pepper
    2 teaspoons hot sauce
    1 teaspoon thyme
    3 bay leaves

Place the tenderloin in a baking pan. In a large bowl combine the remaining ingredients. Pour the mixture over the tenderloin. Cover and marinate in the refrigerator for 6 to 10 hours.

Drain and reserve the marinade. Bake the tenderloin in a 350° oven for 1 hour and 15 minutes or until a meat thermometer registers 140° for medium rare. Slice and serve with heated marinade spooned over the meat.

Serves 8 to 10.

Stuffed Chicken Breast in Puff Pastry

    4 boneless chicken breasts
    ½ avocado, sliced
    1 ounce prosciutto, thinly sliced
    4 ounces cream cheese
    4 5x5-inch puff pastry squares (your
        recipe or commercial)
    2 tablespoons butter, melted
    Chicken sauce (your favorite)

Grease a shallow baking dish. Remove the skins from the chicken breasts. Stuff each breast with a slice of avocado, ¼ of the prosciutto, and 1 ounce of cream cheese. Wrap each stuffed chicken breast with a square of puff pastry. Place in the prepared baking dish. Brush the tops with butter. Bake in a 350° oven for 1 hour or until golden brown. Serve immediately with your favorite chicken sauce.

Serves 4.

Big Spring Inn

315 North Main Street
Greeneville, Tennessee 37743
(615) 638-2917

Big Spring Inn is a three-story brick Victorian home with leaded and stained glass windows, spacious porches, and a rolled dormer. The house is decorated in a charming mix of antiques and reproductions with the accent on comfort and privacy. Upon arrival, the tired traveler is treated to a cozy chair in the guest parlor, a refreshing beverage, and the afternoon paper. Each of the five guest rooms is different, and all have the thoughtful touches of fresh flowers, a small snack, and thick terrycloth robes. Also available for guests is a quiet upstairs library and a tree-filled yard large enough for an afternoon stroll. Breakfast, included in the room rate, consists of homemade bread or muffins, along with a variety of breakfast specialties, including such delights as walnut glazed bacon and French toast with ginger peaches. Early or late risers will find hot coffee, homemade muffins, and assorted cold cereals.

🍃 🍃 🍃 🍃 🍃

Orange Pancakes
with Orange Sauce

1¼ cups baking mix
1 tablespoon sugar
Grated rind of 1 orange
¾ cup plain yogurt
⅓ cup orange juice
1 egg

🍃 🍃 🍃

½ cup sugar
1 tablespoon cornstarch
⅛ teaspoon cinnamon
⅛ teaspoon nutmeg
1 cup orange juice
1 tablespoon lemon juice
2 tablespoons butter

In a medium bowl combine the baking mix, sugar, and grated orange rind. In a large bowl combine the yogurt, ⅓ cup of orange juice, and the egg. Stir dry ingredients into the yogurt mixture, stirring just until moistened. Pour the batter onto a greased hot griddle and bake until the edges are browned and bubbles rise to the surface. Turn and cook the other side until golden.

In a saucepan combine ½ cup of sugar, the cornstarch, cinnamon, and nutmeg. Slowly add 1 cup of orange juice and the lemon juice. Bring the mixture to a boil, and boil for 1 minute. Remove from the heat and stir in the butter. Serve with the pancakes.

Makes 10 4-inch pancakes and 1¼ cups of sauce.

Individual Cheese Soufflés

These cheese soufflés are frozen ahead to be taken out as needed for guests. A very elegant breakfast with croissants and fruit, and the hard part is done ahead of time.

2 tablespoons butter
¼ cup all-purpose flour
½ teaspoon salt
¼ teaspoon pepper
¼ teaspoon dry mustard
1 cup milk
1½ cups shredded sharp Cheddar
    cheese
6 eggs, separated

Butter six 1-cup soufflé dishes. In a heavy saucepan over low heat melt the butter. Blend in the flour, salt, pepper, and dry mustard. Cook for 1 minute. Gradually add the milk, and cook over medium heat, stirring constantly until thickened. Add the cheese, stirring until melted. Remove from the heat and cool slightly.

In a medium bowl beat the egg yolks until thick and lemon colored. Add a small amount of cheese sauce to the yolks and mix well. Stir the yolk mixture into the remaining cheese mixture.

Beat the egg whites until stiff but not dry. Fold into the cheese mixture. Pour into the prepared soufflé dishes and cover with plastic wrap. Freeze.

To bake, place the frozen soufflés on a baking sheet. Bake in a 350° oven for 40 minutes.

Serves 6.

Peas Sautéed with Toasted Walnuts

½ cup coarsely chopped walnuts,
    toasted

🍃 🍃 🍃

1 tablespoon unsalted butter
4 scallions, sliced
¼ cup chicken stock
2 teaspoons honey

2 cups fresh or frozen peas
⅛ to ¼ teaspoon Tabasco sauce
Salt and pepper to taste

Spread the walnuts in a single layer on a cookie sheet. Bake in a 400° oven for 5 minutes. Set aside.

In a large skillet over medium heat melt the butter. Add the scallions, and cook for 2 to 3 minutes. Add the chicken stock and honey. Increase the heat to high, and stir in the peas. Cook, stirring constantly, until the liquid has evaporated and the peas are tender, about 3 minutes. Add the Tabasco sauce, salt, and pepper. Stir in the walnuts.

Serves 4.

Golden Parmesan Potatoes

2 tablespoons all-purpose flour
2 tablespoons grated Parmesan cheese
¼ teaspoon salt
Dash pepper
4 potatoes, cut into quarters or eighths
3 to 4 tablespoons butter, melted
Chopped parsley for garnish

In a sealable plastic sandwich bag combine the flour, cheese, salt, and pepper. Toss the potatoes in the flour mixture.

In a large shallow baking dish melt the butter. Put the potatoes in a single layer in the dish. Bake in a 375° oven for 1 hour, turning once after 30 minutes. Garnish with chopped parsley.

Serves 4.

Snapp Inn

Route 3, Box 102
Limestone, Tennessee 37681
(615) 257-2482

At this 1815 Federal brick home furnished with antiques, guests can experience country living in a friendly, family atmosphere. From here guests can relax, enjoy the view of mountains, and hike to Davy Crockett Birthplace State Park. The two guest rooms have private baths.

Large Applesauce Cake

3 cups thick applesauce
1 cup shortening
2½ cups brown sugar

🍎 🍎 🍎

4 cups all-purpose flour
2 teaspoons cinnamon
2 teaspoons nutmeg
1 teaspoon cloves
1 teaspoon salt
4 teaspoons baking soda

2 teaspoons baking powder

🍎 🍎 🍎

1½ cups raisins
1 cup nuts, chopped
Confectioners' sugar icing

Grease and flour an 11x14-inch baking pan. In a saucepan heat the applesauce. Add the shortening, stirring until melted. Remove the saucepan from the heat and cool. Add the brown sugar.

In a large bowl sift together the dry ingredients. Add the dry ingredients to the applesauce mixture. Add the raisins and nuts. Pour the batter into the prepared baking pan. Bake in a 325° oven for 1 hour and 15 minutes, or until a toothpick inserted in the center comes out clean. Frost with confectioners' sugar icing.

Serves 30.

Breakfast Cookies

1 cup raisins
1 cup shredded coconut
1 cup Wheaties
1 cup oatmeal
2 cups all-purpose flour
½ teaspoon baking powder
½ teaspoon baking soda
½ teaspoon salt

🍎 🍎 🍎

Snapp Inn

¾ cup shortening
¾ cup brown sugar
¾ cup sugar
2 eggs
1 teaspoon vanilla extract

Grease a cookie sheet. In a large bowl combine the first 8 ingredients. In a separate bowl combine the shortening, brown sugar, and sugar. Add the eggs and vanilla to the shortening mixture. Add the dry ingredients to the shortening mixture, stirring until a firm dough forms. Divide the dough into 12 balls. Flatten the balls on the prepared cookie sheet. Bake in a 375° oven for 15 minutes.

Makes 12 large cookies.

Lynchburg Bed and Breakfast

Lynchburg, Tennessee 37352
(615) 759-7158

At this nineteenth-century home within walking distance of the Jack Daniel's Distillery, guests enjoy spacious rooms with private baths and carefully selected antiques. After a continental breakfast, guests may relax on the shady front porch while enjoying the hills and hollows of southern Middle Tennessee.

Country Sausage Muffins

½ pound bulk pork sausage
1 cup all-purpose flour
1 cup self-rising cornmeal
1 2-ounce jar chopped pimiento, drained
1 8-ounce carton French onion dip
½ cup milk

Grease muffin cups. In a skillet brown the sausage, stirring to crumble. Drain well, reserving 2 tablespoons of the drippings. In a large bowl combine the flour, cornmeal, sausage, pimiento, reserved drippings, onion dip, and milk. Fill the prepared muffin cups ⅔ full. Bake in a 425° oven for 20 to 25 minutes.

Makes 24.

Lockeland Springs Bed and Breakfast

1414 Stratton Avenue
Nashville, Tennessee 37206
(615) 320-7914
(615) 227-5323

Lockeland Springs is a charming old house built at the turn of the century near downtown Nashville. Recently restored to its original elegance, the home is decorated with a mixture of antique furniture, century-old Persian carpets, and the owner's collection of European and American art. Two high-ceiling guest rooms with private baths are available. Breakfast in the dining room is served with china, silver, and gracious hospitality; and the meal often includes homemade shortbread or scones

along with gourmet teas and coffees. Fresh flowers and vegetables come straight from the garden in season.

Praline Candy

1 pound light brown sugar
¼ cup water
1½ cups pecans
¼ cup butter

In a saucepan combine the brown sugar and water. Cook until the mixture sugars on the side of the pan, stirring constantly. Add the pecans and butter. Beat until thick and cloudy. Drop from a spoon onto waxed paper.

Makes about 1½ pounds.

Mrs. Buerschaper's Molasses Crinkles

¼ cup melted butter
¼ cup molasses
1 cup sugar
1 egg
¼ teaspoon salt
2 teaspoons baking soda
1 teaspoon cinnamon
1 teaspoon allspice
1 teaspoon ginger
2 cups unbleached all-purpose flour

 ❧ ❧ ❧

Sugar

Lightly grease a cookie sheet. In a large bowl combine all of the ingredients. Shape into 1-inch balls and roll in sugar. Place on the prepared cookie sheet. Bake in a 350° oven for 12 to 15 minutes.

Makes about 3 dozen.

Lockeland Springs Bed and Breakfast

remaining cheese and bake for 10 more minutes or until the cheese is browned.

Serves 4.

Ledford Mill and Museum

Route 2, Box 152
Wartrace, Tennessee 37183
(615) 455-2546

Ledford Mill was built by Sanford Ledford at the headwaters of Shippmans Creek in Moore County, Tennessee, in the early 1880s and continued to be operated by his family until 1942. The forty-two-inch grindstones, powered by a water turbine, ground wheat and corn for the local population and several whiskey stills in the area.

The first renovation was completed in the early 1970s by a local businessman, and further restoration is being done by its present owners. The building is on the National and Tennessee historic registers. A small apartment suitable for a couple or a family of four is available for bed and breakfast accommodations.

Arroz con Chiles

2 to 3 cups sour cream
2 cups green chiles, peeled and chopped
3 to 4 cups cooked rice
Salt and pepper to taste
Butter
¾ pound Monterey Jack cheese, cut into strips
½ cup grated Cheddar cheese

Butter a 2½-quart baking dish. Thoroughly mix the sour cream and green chiles. Season the rice with salt and pepper. In the prepared dish layer half of the rice, sour cream, and Monterey Jack cheese strips. Repeat the layers, ending with cheese strips. Bake in a 350° oven or 30 minutes. Sprinkle with Cheddar cheese and return to the oven until the cheese is melted.

Variation: Macaroni, noodles, or hominy may be used instead of rice.

Serves 6 to 8.

Stuffed Peppers

4 large green peppers
1 tablespoon butter or margarine
1 small onion, chopped
1 clove garlic, pressed
1 pound ground beef (or chuck, round, or sirloin)
1 cup rice, cooked
1 teaspoon salt
1 8-ounce can tomato sauce
¼ cup sherry
1 teaspoon basil
1 tablespoon Worcestershire sauce
¾ cup grated Cheddar cheese

Butter a baking dish. Cut the green peppers in half lengthwise. Remove the stems, membranes, and seeds. In a saucepan boil the peppers in water to cover for 5 minutes. Drain. Place in the prepared baking dish.

In a skillet melt the butter and sauté the onion and garlic until tender. Add the ground beef and brown lightly. Add the rice, salt, tomato sauce, sherry, basil, Worcestershire sauce, and ½ cup of cheese. Mix well. Fill the peppers with the mixture. Bake in a 350° oven for 30 minutes. Top with the

Pumpkin Corn Bread

1½ cups all-purpose flour
1¼ cups cornmeal
1 teaspoon cinnamon
½ teaspoon mace (optional)
1½ teaspoons salt
½ teaspoon baking soda
1 tablespoon baking powder

🍂 🍂 🍂

⅓ cup butter or margarine
3 eggs
1 cup cooked pumpkin
8 ounces (½ can) whole berry cranberry sauce

🍂 🍂 🍂

⅔ cup chopped pecans

Grease and flour a 10-inch round or 9x5-inch loaf pan. In a medium bowl sift the flour and add the cornmeal, cinnamon, mace, salt, baking soda, and baking powder. Set aside.

In a large bowl cream the butter and eggs with an electric mixer. Add the pumpkin and cranberry sauce. Blend in the dry ingredients and the pecans, mixing just until moistened. Do not overmix. Pour the batter into the prepared pan. Bake in a 350° to 375° oven for about 1 hour.

Serves 8.

Cheddar Chili Pie

1 pound lean ground beef
1 large onion, chopped
2 cloves garlic, finely chopped
1 28-ounce can tomatoes
1 15-ounce can kidney beans, undrained
1¼ cups cornmeal
1 cup grated Cheddar cheese
2 tablespoons chili powder
1 teaspoon cumin
¼ teaspoon cayenne
½ teaspoon crushed red pepper
½ teaspoon black pepper
Dash Tabasco sauce
1¼ cups skim milk
Salt and pepper to taste
2 eggs, lightly beaten

In a saucepan sauté the beef, onion, and garlic until browned. Drain off the fat. Add the tomatoes, kidney beans with liquid, ¾ cup cornmeal, ½ cup Cheddar cheese, seasonings, and Tabasco sauce. Cook over low heat, stirring occasionally, for about 15 minutes. Pour into a 2½-quart casserole dish.

In the same saucepan combine the milk, remaining cornmeal, and salt and pepper to taste. Stir over low heat until the mixture thickens slightly. Add the remaining cheese and the eggs, stirring until smooth. Pour the batter over the ground beef mixture. Bake uncovered in a 375° oven for 30 minutes or until the crust is lightly browned.

Serves 6.

Cornmeal Waffles

2 large eggs
1¾ cups milk
1 cup cornmeal
1 cup all-purpose flour
¼ cup sugar (optional)
1 tablespoon baking powder
1 teaspoon salt
6 tablespoons melted butter or margarine

In a large bowl beat the eggs and add the milk. In a separate bowl combine the dry ingredients and stir into the egg mixture. Gradually add the melted butter. Spoon into a greased hot waffle iron, and bake according to the manufacturers' directions.

Makes about 2 dozen waffles.

Heart Healthy Corn Muffins

½ cup honey
2 eggs
3 egg whites
1¾ cups skim milk
¼ cup oil
⅓ cup sugar
2 tablespoons baking powder
3½ cups all-purpose flour
1 cup cornmeal
¼ teaspoon salt

Spray muffin cups with baking spray or line with paper liners. In a large bowl whisk together the honey, eggs, egg whites, milk, and oil. Add the dry ingredients and mix with an electric mixer at medium speed for 2 minutes. Spoon the batter into the prepared muffin cups, filling ¾ full. Bake in a 400° oven for about 15 minutes, or until the tops are golden grown.

Makes 24 muffins.

Cornmeal Cookies

1 cup butter or margarine, room temperature
1 cup sugar
2 egg yolks
1 teaspoon grated lemon peel

1½ cups all-purpose flour
1 cup yellow cornmeal
Additional sugar for topping

In a medium bowl combine the butter and sugar. Beat with an electric mixer until lighter in color and well blended. Add the egg yolks and mix well. Stir in the lemon peel, flour, and cornmeal to mix well. Wrap the dough in a plastic bag and chill for 3 to 4 hours, until firm.

Turn the dough onto a floured surface and roll to ¼-inch thickness. Cut into 2½-inch heart shapes. Place on an ungreased baking sheet and sprinkle with additional sugar. Bake in a 350° oven for 8 to 10 minutes, until the edges are browned.

Variation: The dough may be rolled into a 2-inch cylinder before chilling and sliced into ¼-inch thick rounds before baking.

Makes about 3 dozen cookies.

Fried Corn Bread

1 cup cornmeal
⅔ cup unbleached all-purpose flour
1½ teaspoons baking powder
½ teaspoon salt
¾ cup milk
¼ cup margarine, melted
1 egg, beaten
1 cup shredded sharp natural Cheddar cheese

In a large bowl combine the dry ingredients. In a separate bowl combine the milk, margarine, and egg, mixing until just moistened. Stir in the cheese. For each serving, spoon about ¼ cup of batter onto a lightly greased hot griddle or skillet and flatten slightly. Cook until lightly browned on both sides. If the batter becomes too thick, add a small amount of milk. Serve with margarine.

Variation: For spicy corn bread, add 2 tablespoons chopped drained jalapeño peppers to the batter.

Serves 10.

Carrington's Bluff

1900 David Street
Austin, Texas 78705
(512) 479-0638

Situated in the heart of Austin on a one-acre, tree-covered bluff, this turn-of-the-century Texas classic has been transformed into a country inn in the city. The front porch lined with wooden rockers and blooming plants invites guests to sit among the gentle breezes. A stenciled, cloth-covered table beckons guests to enjoy morning coffee and afternoon tea. The innkeepers bring experience in two previous inns to Carrington's Bluff, and they have combined Texas hospitality with English charm to make this a unique, delightful place.

Fresh Fruit Dip

1 16-ounce carton sour cream
¼ cup brown sugar
1 teaspoon vanilla extract
¼ cup white rum
1 teaspoon cinnamon
¼ cup chopped pecans (optional)

In a serving bowl combine all of the ingredients and blend well. Chill for 1 hour become serving. Great as a dip for fresh fruit or fruit salad.
Makes about 2½ cups.

Baked Havarti Egg

1 teaspoon butter
1 tablespoon half and half
1 large egg
1 heaping tablespoon grated Havarti cheese (do not substitute)
⅛ teaspoon dill

Melt the butter in a custard cup. Add the half and half. Crack the egg into the cup and cover with Havarti. Sprinkle with dill. Bake in a 450° oven for 10 to 12 minutes.
Serves 1.

Grandma's Chicken and Tortilla Dumplings

1 whole chicken
5 cups water
5 chicken bouillon cubes
3 to 4 stalks celery with tops
1 onion, sliced
1 package (1 dozen) flour tortillas
½ to 1 cup milk
Flour, if needed
Salt and pepper to taste

In a large saucepan cook the chicken with the water, bouillon cubes, celery, and onion to give the broth flavor. Simmer until tender. Remove the chicken to cool, and discard the vegetables.

Cut the flour tortillas into short strips. Cook covered in broth for about 20 minutes over low heat. Meanwhile, remove the chicken meat from the bones and add to the pot. Add the milk and heat thoroughly. Thicken with flour if necessary. Season with salt and pepper to taste.
Serves 6.

Chilies and Sausage Quiche

2 unbaked 8-inch pie shells
1 7-ounce can whole green chilies
1 pound hot bulk sausage, cooked, drained and crumbled
4 eggs, lightly beaten
2 cups half and half
½ cup grated Parmesan cheese
½ cup grated Swiss cheese
Salt and pepper to taste

Line the bottom of the pie shells with split and seeded whole chilies. Sprinkle the sausage over the chilies. In a medium bowl combine the eggs, half and half, cheeses, and seasonings. Pour over the sausage. Bake in a 350° oven for 30 to 40 minutes, or until the top is golden brown. Remove from the oven and allow to set for 5 minutes before serving.
Serves 8.

Carrington's Bluff

The McCallum House

613 West 32nd
Austin, Texas 78705
(512) 451-6744

Built in 1907 by A. N. McCallum, school superintendent for the Austin city schools, and his wife, Jane, this historic two-story Princess Anne Victorian house is situated eight blocks north of the University of Texas. The inn has been fully renovated and furnished with antiques by its current resident owners. Three guest rooms are on the second floor, each with private bath; a fourth suite is on the third floor. A garden apartment is located in another building on the property.

❧ ❧ ❧ ❧ ❧

Calico Coffee Cake

2 cups all-purpose flour
1 cup sugar
1 teaspoon baking powder
1¼ cups yogurt
½ cup oil
2 eggs, beaten
2 teaspoons vanilla extract
1 6-ounce package chocolate chips, melted
½ cup brown sugar
¼ cup margarine
½ cup chopped pecans
Confectioners' sugar icing

Grease 1 large or 2 small bundt pans. In a large bowl combine the flour, sugar, and baking powder. Add the yogurt, oil, eggs, and vanilla. In a separate bowl combine ¾ cup of the batter with the melted chocolate chips. In a small bowl combine the brown sugar, margarine, and pecans. Sprinkle half of the brown sugar mixture in the prepared pan. Pour in half of the batter, and add all of the chocolate mixture. Top with the remaining batter and then the remaining brown sugar mixture. Bake in a 350° oven for 45 to 60 minutes for a large pan, or 20 to 30 minutes for 2 small pans. Drizzle with confectioners' sugar icing, if desired.
Serves 10 to 12.

Tropical Muffins

1 cup all-purpose flour
1 cup ground rolled oats
1 cup sugar
1 teaspoon cinnamon
2 teaspoons baking powder
½ teaspoon baking soda
1 egg, beaten
1 8-ounce can crushed pineapple
½ cup milk
¼ cup oil
⅓ cup brown sugar
⅓ cup shredded coconut
⅓ cup chopped nuts

Grease mini muffin cups. In a large bowl combine and blend the dry ingredients. Add the egg, pineapple, milk, and oil, and blend well. In a separate bowl combine the brown sugar, coconut, and nuts. Pour the batter into the prepared muffin cups and top with the coconut mixture. Bake in a 400° oven for 10 minutes.
Note: 18 regular muffin cups may be used. Bake in a 375° oven for 20 minutes.
Makes 36 mini muffins.

Lemon Muffins

1 cup all-purpose flour
1 cup ground rolled oats
⅔ cup sugar
2 teaspoons baking powder
1 egg, beaten
⅔ cup milk
1 teaspoon lemon or lime zest
1 tablespoon lemon juice
⅓ cup oil

❧ ❧ ❧

¼ cup lemon juice
½ cup sugar

Grease mini muffin cups. In a large bowl combine the dry ingredients. Add the egg, milk, zest, 1 tablespoon lemon juice, and the oil. Pour the batter into the prepared muffin cups. Bake in a 400° oven for about 10 minutes, until a toothpick inserted in the center comes out clean.

The McCallum House

Small Inn

4815 West Bayshore
Bacliff, Texas 77518
(713) 339-3489

With a panoramic view of Galveston Bay through its living room windows, Small Inn provides guests with the entertainment of watching ocean freighters, sailboats, pelicans, and sea gulls all at work. Guests may also swim in the pool, fish from the pier, or take advantage of the many recreational opportunities nearby. When the weather permits, breakfast is served by the pool.

Combine ¼ cup of lemon juice and ½ cup of sugar. Drizzle the mixture over the hot muffins.

Makes 24 mini muffins.

Jalapeño Cornbread

½ cup milk
2 eggs
1½ cups shredded Cheddar cheese
1 cup cream-style corn
¼ cup salsa (picante)
1 cup cornmeal
½ cup all-purpose flour
1 tablespoon baking powder

Oil an 8-inch square baking pan. In a large bowl combine the milk, eggs, Cheddar, corn, and salsa. In a separate bowl combine the dry ingredients. Add the dry ingredients to the liquid ingredients, blending well. Pour the batter into the prepared pans. Bake in a 375° oven for 40 to 45 minutes.

Note: Preheated "corn pone" pans may be used. Bake in a 425° oven for 10 to 15 minutes.

Serves 8 to 9.

Migas

This is wonderful served with Jalapeño Cornbread.

3 eggs
1 cup broken tortilla chips
¼ cup salsa (picante)
1 cup shredded Monterey Jack cheese
1 cup shredded Cheddar cheese
2 to 3 green onions, chopped
2 to 3 strips red pepper
2 small tomatoes, chopped

In a large bowl combine the eggs, tortilla chips, salsa, Monterey Jack, and Cheddar. In a skillet sauté the onions, peppers, and tomatoes. Add the egg mixture, and scramble briefly. Serve soft.

Serves 6.

"Hand-Held" Breakfast

I often have guests who get up early to go beach combing and birding. I send them off with this nutritious "cookie."

1¼ cups all-purpose flour
⅔ cup sugar
½ cup Grape Nuts
1 teaspoon baking powder
½ pound bacon, cooked and crumbled
½ cup margarine, softened
1 egg
4 tablespoons frozen orange juice concentrate
2 tablespoons orange peel

In a large bowl combine the flour, sugar, Grape Nuts, and baking powder. Add the remaining ingredients and blend well. Drop by tablespoonfuls onto an ungreased baking sheet about 2 inches apart. Bake in a 350° oven for 10 to 12 minutes.

Makes about 18 "cookies."

Potato Bacon Pie

I serve this with a poached egg on each slice and cheese sauce on the side.

**4 cups cooked potatoes, mashed but
    not whipped
½ cup milk
12 slices bacon, cooked and
    crumbled**

Grease an 8-inch pie plate. In a large bowl combine all of the ingredients. Spread into the prepared pie plate. Bake in a 350° oven for 35 minutes, until the top is lightly browned.
Serves 6.

Bananas Baked in Orange Juice

**6 to 8 bananas
3 tablespoons orange juice
½ cup brown sugar
1 orange, peeled and cut into
    chunks
2 tablespoons honey
1 tablespoon lemon juice
¼ teaspoon pumpkin pie spice**

Peel the bananas and arrange in a shallow dish. In a small bowl combine the remaining ingredients and pour over the bananas. Bake in a 325° oven for 25 minutes. Serve hot or cold.
Serves 6.

The Gilded Thistle

1805 Broadway
Galveston Island, Texas 77550
(409) 763-0194

The Gilded Thistle is a well-appointed historical home that has stood the test of time in this sandy place. Beautifully decorated, it has been featured in *Texas Monthly* magazine, *New York Times, House Beautiful,* and in "PM Magazine." The three guest accommodations are complemented by a wine and cheese tray in the evening and a complete breakfast in the morning. Coffee and juice are served at the door in the morning.

Cheesecake

**2 cups graham cracker crumbs
¼ cup butter, melted
Finely chopped walnuts
1 tablespoon cinnamon**

🦆 🦆 🦆

**3 8-ounce packages Philadelphia
    cream cheese, room temperature
1 cup sugar
6 large eggs
1 teaspoon vanilla extract
1 teaspoon almond extract
1 8-ounce carton Daisy Brand sour
    cream**

Combine the graham cracker crumbs, melted butter, walnuts, and cinnamon. Press the mixture into the bottom and sides of a 9-inch springform pan.

In a large bowl beat 1 package of cream cheese with 1 cup of sugar and 2 eggs until smooth. Add a second package of cream cheese and 2 eggs, and beat until well blended. Add the remaining cream cheese and eggs, the vanilla, almond extract, and sour cream. Beat until well blended. Pour the mixture into the graham cracker crust. Bake in a 325° oven for 1 hour.
Serves 16.

Wise Manor

312 Houston Street
Jefferson, Texas 75657
(214) 665-2386

Wise Manor is a quiet retreat in a Victorian home that houses family antiques of three generations. Rates are reasonable. Breakfast is continental (at a modest extra charge), or reservations can be made at the second oldest hotel in Texas, the Excelsior House, for a sumptuous plantation breakfast.

Hurry-Up Butterhorn Rolls

**1 ¼-ounce package active dry yeast
¾ cup warm water (110° to 115°)
2½ cups baking mix**

Grease a large baking sheet. In a large bowl dissolve the yeast in the warm water. Stir in the baking mix and beat vigorously. Turn the dough onto a surface lightly dusted with baking mix. Knead until smooth, about 30 strokes. Cover and let rest for 10 minutes.

Roll the dough into a 12-inch circle. Cut into 16 wedges. Beginning at the wide end, roll each wedge toward the point. Place point side down on the prepared baking sheet. Cover with a damp cloth and let rise for 1 hour, until doubled in bulk. Bake in a 400° oven for 10 to 15 minutes. Brush with butter or margarine while warm.
Makes 16 rolls.

🦆 🦆 🦆 🦆 🦆

Mexican Cornbread

1½ cups yellow cornmeal
½ cup all-purpose flour
1 teaspoon salt
⅔ cup milk
1 20-ounce can cream-style corn
2 cups grated Cheddar cheese
2 eggs
1 medium onion, chopped
3 jalapeño peppers, chopped
½ cup bacon drippings

Grease a 9x13-inch pan. In a large bowl combine all of the ingredients. Pour the batter into the prepared pan. Bake in a 325° oven for 50 to 60 minutes. Do not undercook. Cool before cutting.
Serves 12.

Wood-Boone Norrell House

215 East Rusk
Marshall, Texas 75670
(214) 935-1800
(800) 423-1356

This 1884 home makes it possible to step back in time and imagine life as it was when verandahs, stained glass, and grand staircases were commonplace. Situated in downtown Marshall, two blocks from the old courthouse and the historic district, it is minutes away from antique shopping, golfing, and fishing. Each room, with private bath, is decorated with turn-of-the-century antiques. In the morning a full country breakfast, just like Grandma used to make, is served.

Raisin Pie

This is my favorite pie recipe. It is very old-fashioned.

1 cup raisins
Water
½ cup butter
3 eggs, separated
3 tablespoons all-purpose flour
1 cup sugar
½ cup pecans (optional)
1 baked 9-inch pie crust (I use Pillsbury)

In a small saucepan cook the raisins in water to cover until slightly plumped. Drain most of the water, and add the butter. Beat the egg yolks and add some of the hot raisin mixture to the yolks. Stir well. Add the yolk mixture to the raisins. In a small bowl combine the flour and sugar, and add to the raisin mixture. Cook until thick, and add the pecans. Pour the mixture into the pie crust. Beat the egg whites and spread them over the raisin mixture. Bake in a 350° oven for about 8 minutes, until the meringue is golden.
Serves 8.

Buttermilk Biscuits

2 cups all-purpose flour
2½ teaspoons baking powder
½ teaspoon baking soda
1 teaspoon salt
2 tablespoons lard (I use butter-flavored Crisco)
1 cup buttermilk (or more if needed)

Grease a cookie sheet or baking pan. In a large bowl sift together the dry ingredients. Cut in the lard with a pastry blender or 2 knives. Add the milk and stir until a soft dough is formed, about 25 strokes. Turn the dough onto a floured board and knead until smooth. Roll to ½-inch thickness for fluffy biscuits, or ¼-inch thickness for thin, crusty

Wood-Boone Norrell House

biscuits. Cut with a floured biscuit cutter. Place the biscuits on the prepared cookie sheet. Bake in a 450° oven for 13 to 15 minutes.

Makes 12 to 15 biscuits.

Banana Pudding

This is a wonderfully rich, quick recipe.

- 1 14-ounce can sweetened condensed milk
- 1½ cups water
- 1 3-ounce box banana instant pudding mix
- 1 pint whipped cream
- 3 to 4 bananas
- Vanilla wafers

In a large bowl combine the sweetened condensed milk and the water. Add the instant pudding, and refrigerate for about 5 minutes.

Fold the whipped cream into the pudding mixture. In a serving dish layer the wafers, bananas, and pudding, ending with wafers.

Serves 6.

Rio Frio Bed 'n Breakfast

Rural Route 1120
Rio Frio, Texas 78879
(512) 232-6633

Rio Frio Bed 'n Breakfast is situated in the beautiful Frio Canyon in the Texas hill country. Accommodations include a Spanish-style home on the river, a log home in the country, and several cabins and homes. Each is unique and perfect for a week or weekend get-away. All accommodations have heating and air conditioning, fully equipped kitchens, picnic tables, and barbecue pits; most have woodburning fireplaces.

Quick Ham and Swiss Quiche

- 2 cups chopped cooked ham
- 1 cup shredded Swiss cheese
- ⅓ cup chopped green onions
- 4 eggs
- 2 cups milk
- 1 cup baking mix
- ¼ teaspoon salt
- ⅛ teaspoon pepper
- 1 tablespoon chopped parsley

Butter a 10-inch pie plate. Sprinkle the ham, cheese, and onion in the bottom of the pie plate. In a blender beat the remaining ingredients until smooth, about 15 seconds. Pour into the pie plate. Bake in a 400° oven for 35 to 45 minutes, until a knife inserted in the center comes out clean. Cool for 5 minutes.

Serves 8.

Sausage Cheese Balls

- 3 cups baking mix
- 1 pound hot sausage, uncooked
- 1½-pound stick Coon Cheese (black rind), grated (or Cheddar)
- 2 tablespoons water

In a large bowl combine all of the ingredients. Form into balls the size of large walnuts. Bake in a 350° oven until browned.

Makes about 50 balls.

Fruit Cobbler

- ½ cup butter, melted
- 1 cup all-purpose flour
- 1 teaspoon salt
- 1 teaspoon baking powder
- 1 cup sugar
- 1 cup milk
- 1 quart fruit

In the bottom of a 2-quart dish melt the butter. In a large bowl combine the remaining ingredients. Pour the batter into the dish. Add the fruit. Bake in a 325° oven for about 1 hour.

Serves 16.

Bluebird Hill

Indian Blanket Ranch
Box 206, Highway 1050
Utopia, Texas 78884
(512) 966-3525
(512) 966-2320

Bluebird Hill is a hill country home with two guestrooms, five patios, an extensive library, satellite television, a blazing fireplace, a tree-shaded hammock, and Texas and American flags flapping in the wind. Also available is the hideaway cabin, with its open-beamed ceiling, tin roof, and sleeping loft. Hiking and mountain climbing can be enjoyed in the area, as well as swimming in the Sabinal or Frio rivers. In the summertime rodeos, tennis, horseback riding, and outdoor theater are popular area activities.

Ham Crepes

- 1 10½-ounce can mushroom soup
- 1¼ cups milk
- 1 egg, slightly beaten
- 1 cup pancake mix
- 1 tablespoon butter
- 12 slices boiled ham
- 3 cups grated sharp Cheddar cheese

Grease a 9x13-inch baking dish. In a medium bowl combine half of the soup, ¾ cup of milk, and the egg. Add the pancake mix and blend well. Stir in the butter. Pour a small amount of batter on a greased griddle and bake until browned on both sides. Place 1 slice of ham on each crepe and sprinkle with cheese, reserving some of the cheese for the topping. Roll up the crepes and place in the prepared dish. Cover with the remaining cheese. Combine the remaining soup and ½ cup of milk, and pour over the crepes. Place under the broiler until bubbly.

Serves 6.

Pig Licking Cake

1 18-ounce box yellow cake mix
4 eggs
¼ cup oil
½ cup butter
1 11-ounce can mandarin oranges
    with juice

&ear; &ear; &ear;

1 12-ounce carton Cool Whip
1 3-ounce box instant vanilla
    pudding
1 20-ounce can crushed pineapple,
    drained

In a large bowl mix together the cake mix, eggs, oil, and butter. Add the mandarin oranges and juice, and beat well by hand. Pour the batter into three 9-inch round cake pans. Bake in a 350° oven for 20 minutes.

In a large bowl combine the Cool Whip and instant pudding mix. Add the drained crushed pineapple. Refrigerate until the cake is cooled. Spread between the layers and frost the top and sides of the cake. Store the cake in the refrigerator.

Serves 8 to 10.

Texan Vinegar Cobbler

2 cups water
⅓ cup apple cider vinegar
1½ cups sugar
1 tablespoon butter, melted

&ear; &ear; &ear;

2 cups all-purpose flour
⅔ cup shortening (or margarine)
¼ teaspoon salt
¼ teaspoon baking powder
Water

&ear; &ear; &ear;

Butter, softened
⅔ cup sugar
Cinnamon

In a 9x13-inch pan combine the water, vinegar, sugar, and 1 tablespoon of butter. In a bowl combine the flour, shortening, salt, baking powder, and enough water to make a stiff dough.

Roll the dough to ¼-inch thickness. Spread with soft butter and sprinkle with ⅔ cup of sugar and cinnamon. Roll up jelly-roll fashion and slice into 1-inch slices. Place in the sauce and spoon sauce over the rolls. Bake in a 350° oven until slightly browned.

Serves 6.

Weimar Country Inn

101 Jackson
Post Office Box 782
Weimar, Texas 78962
(409) 725-8888

For over 100 years, Weimar Country Inn has provided comfortable lodging and country cooking for travelers. Located midway between Houston and San Antonio, it is ideal for honeymoons, historic excursions, corporate meetings, or relaxing. Nine rooms with authentic Texas decor welcome the inn's guests. The rooms boast Texas names, Victorian antiques, and handmade quilts. Guests awaken to a complimentary continental breakfast of coffee, juice, and home-baked kolaches served in the upstairs parlor.

Broiled Catfish
with Jalapeño Pecan Sauce

6 7-ounce catfish fillets
½ cup melted butter
2 jalapeño peppers, cleaned and
    seeded
2 cloves garlic
½ cup pecans
¼ cup fresh parsley

&ear; &ear; &ear;

Lemon wedges and parsley for
    garnish

Butter a broiler pan. Place the catfish on the prepared pan. Brush the tops of the fillets with butter. Broil for 10 minutes.

In a food processor combine the peppers, garlic, pecans, remaining melted butter, and parsley. Process until smooth. The sauce should be thick, and well blended. Spoon some of the sauce over the catfish and place under the broiler. Broil for 5 to 8 minutes or until the fish flakes easily. Place the fillets on a heated platter. Heat the sauce and pour over the fillets. Garnish with lemon wedges and parsley.

Serves 6.

Weimar Country Inn

Utah

Peterson's Bed and Breakfast

95 North 300 West
Post Office Box 142
Monroe, Utah 84754
(801) 527-4830

Situated in the Little Green Valley in rural south-central Utah, this inn is close to five national parks and four national forests. A one-hundred-year-old restored farmhouse, it offers three guest rooms and is near fishing, tennis, golfing, and hunting. A full country breakfast is served.

Company Carrots

2 pounds carrots
½ cup mayonnaise
1 tablespoon minced onion
1 tablespoon prepared horseradish
Salt and pepper to taste
¼ cup cracker crumbs
2 tablespoons butter (or more to taste)
Chopped parsley

Cut the carrots lengthwise into narrow strips. Cook in salted water until tender.

In a small bowl combine ¼ cup of liquid from the carrots, the mayonnaise, onion, and horseradish. Add salt and pepper to taste. Arrange the carrots in a 1½-quart baking dish. Top with the mayonnaise mixture. Sprinkle with cracker crumbs and dot with butter. Sprinkle parsley over the top. Bake in a 375° oven for 20 minutes.

Serves 6 to 8.

The Old Miners' Lodge

615 Woodside Avenue
Post Office Box 2639
Park City, Utah 84060-2639
(801) 645-8068

The Old Miners' Lodge is a restored 1893 building in the National Historic District of the colorful resort town of Park City. It was built as housing for local miners seeking their fortunes from the surrounding ore-rich hills. Now its rooms have been named after some of these colorful personalities and restored to the furnishings of their time. Guests begin each morning with a hearty country-style breakfast. In the evening the large living room becomes a gathering place for guests, and complimentary refreshments are served. A revitalizing outdoor hot tub welcomes everyone back after a satisfying day outdoors. The area provides year-round recreation to its visitors, such as skiing, snowmobiling, hot air ballooning, golf, tennis, hiking, and horseback riding.

Peterson's Bed and Breakfast

477

The Old Miners' Inn

Susan's Chicken Fajitas

8 chicken breast halves, skinned and boned

❧ ❧ ❧

**1 4-ounce jar picante sauce or salsa
1 bunch cilantro, finely chopped
1 tomato, cubed
1 teaspoon garlic salt
2 tablespoons oil
1 teaspoon coarsely ground pepper**

❧ ❧ ❧

**Flour or corn tortillas
Chopped tomatoes
Salsa
Chopped onions
Sliced olives
Grated cheese
Guacamole
Sour cream**

In a shallow pan arrange the chicken. In a medium bowl combine the picante sauce, cilantro, tomato, garlic salt, oil, and pepper. Pour the mixture over the chicken and marinate for at least 3 hours (but not more than 6 hours).

Barbecue the chicken over a medium flame for about 7 minutes per side, until just cooked through. Do not overcook. Slice into thin strips, place in the tortillas, and serve with the remaining ingredients as garnishes.

Serves 4.

Red Cabbage Salad

**1 medium head red cabbage
1 cup vinegar
½ cup oil
1 tablespoon sugar
1 teaspoon dried or freshly chopped basil
½ teaspoon dry mustard
2 tablespoons lemon juice
Garlic salt and pepper to taste**

Grate or finely chop the cabbage. In a small bowl combine the remaining ingredients. Pour the mixture over the cabbage, and toss well. Serve with a slotted spoon.

Serves 6.

Barbequed Flank Steak

1 1½-pound flank steak

❧ ❧ ❧

**½ teaspoon salt
¼ teaspoon coarsely ground pepper**

**1 teaspoon basil
1 teaspoon rosemary
2 cloves garlic, minced
1 medium onion, chopped
½ cup wine vinegar
1 cup oil**

Place the flank steak in a shallow pan. In a medium bowl combine the remaining ingredients. Pour the marinade mixture over the steak. Cover and refrigerate for at least 2 hours, preferably 4 to 6 hours. Turn the steak occasionally.

Barbecue the steak over high heat for about 10 minutes per side for medium.

Strain the onions from the marinade. In a small skillet sauté the onions until tender. Slice the steak on the diagonal, and serve with the onions as a garnish.

Serves 4.

Daniel's Oven Chicken

**8 chicken breast halves
Garlic salt
Pepper
Lemon juice**

Place the chicken in a single layer in a shallow baking dish, bone-side down. Sprinkle generously with garlic salt and pepper. Pour lemon juice over the top, ¼ inch deep in the pan. Bake in a 350° oven for 1 hour or until done.

Serves 8.

The Washington School Inn

543 Park Avenue
Park City, Utah 84060
(801) 649-3800
(800) 824-1672

Open year round, the Washington School Inn was built in 1889 and is on the National Register of Historic Places. It has twelve guest rooms, all with private baths, and three suites. On the first level are a whirlpool spa, dry sauna, and ski lockers and changing rooms. A large living room with fireplace and an elegant dining room are attractive to guests year round.

Ginger Snaps

We often double this recipe and store it in the refrigerator. We bake a few on demand.

¾ cup shortening
½ cup sugar
½ cup brown sugar
¼ cup molasses
1 egg
2 cups all-purpose flour
1 teaspoon baking soda
1 teaspoon cinnamon
½ teaspoon cloves
½ teaspoon ginger
½ teaspoon salt

In a large bowl cream the shortening, sugar, and brown sugar. Add the molasses and egg, and beat well. In a separate bowl combine the dry ingredients. Add the dry mixture to the molasses mixture, blending well. Chill the dough for 1 hour.

Shape the dough into small balls and roll in sugar. Place on a cookie sheet. Bake in a 375° oven for 9 minutes.

Makes about 4 dozen.

Whole Wheat Muffins

1 cup margarine
2 cups brown sugar
2 eggs
2 cups milk
4 cups whole wheat flour
2 teaspoons baking soda
1 teaspoon salt

Spray muffin cups with cooking spray. In a large bowl combine the margarine and brown sugar. Add the eggs and beat well. In a separate bowl mix the dry ingredients. Add the dry ingredients to the margarine mixture. Pour the batter into the prepared muffin cups, filling ⅔ full. Bake in a 400° oven for 20 minutes.

Makes 2 dozen muffins.

Peanut Butter Squares

¼ cup margarine
¾ cup sugar
1 cup crunchy peanut butter
1 egg
1¼ cups all-purpose flour
1 teaspoon baking soda
½ teaspoon salt
½ teaspoon cinnamon
¼ teaspoon nutmeg
¼ teaspoon cloves
1½ cups applesauce (or drained crushed pineapple)
Confectioners' sugar

Grease an 8-inch square pan. In a large bowl cream the margarine. Add the sugar and beat well. Add the peanut butter and beat well. In a separate bowl combine the flour, baking soda, salt, and spices. Add to the creamed mixture alternately with the applesauce, beginning and ending with the flour mixture. Bake in a 375° oven for 40 to 50 minutes. Sprinkle with confectioners' sugar just before serving.

Serves 16.

Seven Wives Inn

217 North 100 West
St. George, Utah 84770
(801) 628-3737

Along the walking tour of St. George, just across from the Brigham Young home and two blocks from the historic Washington County Court House, lies Seven Wives Inn, southern Utah's first bed and breakfast inn. Each bedroom in the original inn is named after one of the seven wives of the late B. F. Johnson, who spent considerable time in the St. George area. Six more guest rooms are in the home next door. All thirteen rooms have private baths. A gourmet breakfast is served each morning in the dining room. A swimming pool on the premises is for guest use.

Chicken Veronica

2 cups whipping cream
2 teaspoons buttermilk

   🍃 🍃 🍃

2 whole chicken breasts, halved and boned
Salt and pepper to taste
2 teaspoons paprika
2 tablespoons olive oil
2 cloves garlic, chopped
1½ cups green or red seedless grapes, halved
½ jalapeño pepper, thinly sliced
2 cups cooked rice
2 tablespoons toasted sesame seeds

In a large glass jar combine the whipping cream and buttermilk. Shake for 1 minute. Let the mixture stand in a warm place until thickened, about 12 hours. Stir well and refrigerate for at least 24 hours. The crème fraîche will keep for about 7 to 10 days.

Seven Wives Inn

Pound the chicken breasts to ⅜-inch thickness. Sprinkle with salt and pepper. Sprinkle generously with paprika. In a skillet heat the olive oil and add the garlic. Brown the chicken breasts skin-side first, turning to brown the other side. Place the browned chicken in a shallow pan and keep warm in a warm oven. In the skillet with the olive oil combine the grapes and jalapeño pepper, and warm through.

For each serving, arrange ½ cup of rice on each of 4 plates. Surround the rice with toasted sesame seeds. Place the chicken breasts on the rice. Top with grapes, a few slices of jalapeño pepper, and a little of the pan juices. Top with crème fraîche.

Serves 4.

Breakfast Bread Pudding

We use raspberries, blueberries, peaches, strawberries, blackberries, or a combination of 2 or 3 for the topping.

⅓ cup butter, melted
12 slices raisin bread
4 eggs
2 egg yolks
¾ cup sugar
1 cup whipping cream
3 cups milk
1 teaspoon vanilla extract
Confectioners' sugar
Fresh or frozen fruit, slightly
**   sweetened**

With a pastry brush spread melted butter on both sides of the bread. In a 7x11-inch dish place the bread in 2 layers.

In a medium bowl beat the eggs and egg yolks with a wire whisk. Continue to beat while gradually adding the sugar. Add the cream, milk, and vanilla. Mix well. Pour the custard over the bread. Place the dish in a larger pan and pour warm water into the large pan halfway up the side of the dish. Bake in a 350° oven for 45 minutes to 1 hour, until puffy and brown and a knife inserted in the center comes out clean. Cut into 6 or 8

pieces. Sprinkle each serving with confectioners' sugar and top with fruit.

Serves 6 to 8.

Quail Hills

3744 East North Little Cottonwood Road
Sandy, Utah 84092
(801) 942-2858

Nestled at the base of the spectacular Wasatch Mountains, Quail Hills is surrounded with acres of beautiful canyon land. In the summer, the swimming pool and hot spa make for relaxing enjoyment. In the winter skiing is the main attraction. Each guest room has its own personality, with private or shared baths.

Festive Fruit Salad

½ cup sugar
2 tablespoons cornstarch
Pinch salt
1 cup boiling water
1 cup whipping cream

ও   ও   ও

3 cups cubed apples
4 bananas, sliced
Juice of ½ lemon
1 cup frozen raspberries

In a saucepan combine the sugar, cornstarch, salt, and 1 cup of boiling water. Cook until clear, stirring constantly. Cool, and add the whipping cream. Whip until stiff. In a bowl combine the apples and bananas, and add the lemon juice. Add the raspberries. Stir the fruit into the creamed mixture and serve.

Variations: Add a few walnuts, or use ½ cup maraschino cherries instead of the raspberries.

Serves 4 to 6.

Vermont

The Arlington Inn

Historic Route 7A
Post Office Box 369
Arlington, Vermont 05250
(802) 375-6532

The Arlington Inn, a stately Greek Revival mansion, was built as the private home of Martin Deming, a railroad magnate and Vermont politician. Today its elegantly appointed guest rooms, each named after a Deming family member, create an atmosphere of an age long since past. Faithfully restored to capture the charm of the mid-nineteenth century, it provides an idyllic place to sit in front of a roaring fireplace in winter or to rock away the hours on the front porch in the summer. In addition to the varied activities the seasons suggest, antique shops, boutiques, restaurants, and museums abound in the area.

Vermont Breast of Pheasant
Sauce of Green Peppercorns and Red Currants with Cranberry Chutney

3 2½ to 3-pound pheasants (whole or breasts only)
Flour
Salt and pepper
Clarified butter

❧ ❧ ❧

2 cups pheasant stock (use bones from pheasant or chicken stock)
2 cups beef stock
1 tablespoon green peppercorn purée
½ cup red currant jelly
Cornstarch and water
Salt and pepper

❧ ❧ ❧

¼ onion, puréed
1 tablespoon puréed ginger
1 clove garlic
½ cup raspberry vinegar
1 lemon
1 orange
1 pound cranberries
1 apple
1 cup sugar
Cornstarch and water

Bone the pheasant breasts and roll in flour seasoned with salt and pepper. In hot clarified butter sauté the pheasant breasts on each side until brown. Finish by baking in a 425° oven for 5 to 7 minutes.

In a medium pot combine the pheasant stock, beef stock, green peppercorns, and red currant jelly. Bring to a boil and reduce by half. Thicken with the cornstarch and water solution. Season with salt and pepper.

In a medium saucepan cook the onion, ginger, and garlic in the vinegar. In a blender purée the lemon and orange. Add to the vinegar along with the cranberries, apple, and sugar. Bring to a boil and thicken with the cornstarch and water. Cool. Use 2 tablespoons per serving.
Serves 6.

Grilled New Skete Sausage Pizza

1 pound pizza dough
4 tablespoons olive oil
2 freshly chopped tomatoes
8 ounces New Skete sausage links, poached, chilled, and sliced on the bias
4 cups grated jalapeño Monterey Jack cheese
Salt and pepper
Parsley or fresh herbs

Cut the pizza dough into 4 equal pieces. Roll with flour into balls and let the dough warm to room temperature for approximately 15 minutes. Work the dough to the desired shape by hand on a well-floured board. Oil the grill and cook the pizza on each side. Place on a pan and brush the top side with olive oil. Top the pizza with the tomatoes, sausage, and cheese. Salt and pepper to taste. Bake in a 450° to 500° oven for 6 minutes until crisp. Slice and sprinkle the top with parsley or fresh herbs.
Serves 4.

The Arlington Inn

Lobster and Scallops, Squid Ink Pasta

with White Zinfandel Oregano Butter Sauce

4 1¼-pound lobsters
12 ounces sea scallops

🖎 🖎 🖎

1 shallot, chopped
4 ounces white Zinfandel wine
2 ounces heavy cream
1 cup unsalted butter
2 to 3 sprigs freshly chopped
  oregano
Salt and white pepper

🖎 🖎 🖎

6 ounces squid ink pasta
Carrots and zucchini, julienned

Boil the lobsters for 5 minutes and cool. Take out the lobster meat carefully to keep the tail and claws intact. Clean the sea scallops.

In a stainless steel pan combine the shallots and wine. Reduce to almost dry. Add the heavy cream and reduce the cream by half. Remove from the heat for 2 minutes. Place on low heat and slowly whisk in the cold butter. Season with the oregano, salt, and pepper. Lightly poach the lobster and scallops in the wine sauce.

Cook the pasta in boiling water according to the package directions. Serve the seafood and sauce over the pasta. Garnish the plate with julienne slices of carrots and zucchini.

Serves 4.

Veal and Strawberries

20 ounces veal scaloppini
Flour, salt, and pepper
Clarified butter

🖎 🖎 🖎

1 shallot, chopped
4 ounces white wine
2 ounces heavy cream
1 cup unsalted butter
Salt and white pepper
4 sprigs freshly chopped dill

🖎 🖎 🖎

1 pint strawberries

Pound the veal into scaloppinis. Dredge in seasoned flour and sauté in clarified butter in a hot pan. Keep warm.

In a stainless steel pan combine the shallot and white wine. Reduce to almost dry. Add the heavy cream and reduce until the cream starts to turn light brown. Take off the heat for 2 minutes. Place on low heat and slowly whisk in the cold butter. Season with

the salt, pepper, and dill. Pour the sauce over the veal and garnish with the strawberries.

Serves 4.

Hill Farm Inn

Rural Route 2, Box 2015
Arlington, Vermont 05250
(802) 375-2269
(800) 882-2545

Hill Farm Inn is a country inn in the true sense of the word. Surrounded by neighboring farms, it is set on fifty acres. Spectacular views in every direction make the setting unsurpassed for artists and photographers, as well as for those just seeking a tranquil, scenic vacation spot. The main inn has seven guest rooms on the second floor, and the 1790 guest house next door has six guest rooms. Eight of the thirteen rooms have private baths. All rooms are spacious and comfortable, and many have beautiful views of the mountains. During the summer and fall months, several cabins are available, each with full bath. The common rooms are used by guests, whether visiting with new friends around the living room fireplace, doing puzzles and playing table games in the dining room, or dining in front of its antique fireplace.

Hill Farm Inn Granola

1 cup raw rolled oats
⅓ cup chopped walnuts
⅓ cup raw wheat germ
⅓ cup sesame seeds
⅓ cup sunflower seeds
⅓ cup shredded coconut
⅓ cup chopped banana chips
¼ cup brown sugar

In a large, heavy skillet, combine the oats and walnuts. Roast over medium-low heat for 5 minutes, stirring often. Add the wheat germ, sesame seeds, sunflower seeds, coconut, and banana chips. Continue stirring and dry roast for 10 minutes. Add the brown sugar, stirring and roasting for 2 more minutes. Cool and store in an airtight container.

Makes 3 cups.

Blue Cheese Appetizer

- **2 8-ounce packages cream cheese, softened**
- **1 4-ounce package blue cheese, crumbled**
- **1 cup shredded sharp Cheddar cheese**
- **¼ cup minced onion**
- **1 tablespoon Worcestershire sauce**

In a large bowl combine all the ingredients, blending thoroughly. Pack in crocks and store in the refrigerator.

Makes 2½ cups.

Spicy Tomato Soup

- **1½ cups chopped onion**
- **3 cloves minced garlic**
- **1 tablespoon butter, melted**
- **1 tablespoon oil**

- **1 teaspoon dill weed**
- **⅛ teaspoon black pepper**
- **6 cups tomato juice**
- **1 tablespoon honey**
- **1 medium fresh tomato, chopped**

In a saucepan sauté the onions and garlic in the butter and oil for 5 minutes. Add the dill weed, pepper, tomato juice, and honey. Cover and simmer for 1 hour. Whisk in the tomato 5 minutes before serving.

Serves 6.

Roast Sage Potatoes

- **2 pounds all-purpose potatoes**
- **½ clove garlic**
- **⅓ cup oil**
- **1 teaspoon dried sage leaves**
- **½ teaspoon dried thyme leaves**
- **Salt and pepper**

Scrub the potatoes and cut into bite-sized chunks (do not peel). Place in a 9x13-inch baking pan. Peel and chop the garlic. In a small bowl combine the oil, garlic, sage, thyme, salt, and pepper, mixing thoroughly. Pour over the potatoes, stirring until the potatoes are coated with the oil mixture. Bake in a 350° oven for 1 hour, stirring occasionally until the potatoes are tender and golden.

Serves 6.

Baked Scallops and Mushrooms

- **½ cup butter**
- **2 cups thinly sliced mushrooms**
- **1 medium onion, finely chopped**
- **4 cloves garlic, minced**

- **2 pounds bay scallops**
- **1 cup soft bread crumbs**
- **1 cup finely chopped parsley**

In a large skillet melt ¼ cup of butter and sauté the mushrooms until tender. Add the onion and garlic, cooking briefly. Remove from the heat.

In a large bowl combine the scallops, bread crumbs, parsley, and mushroom mixture, mixing well. Spoon into a 9x13-inch dish. Melt the remaining ¼ cup of butter and drizzle over the mixture in the dish. Bake in a 450° oven for 10 minutes.

Serves 6.

Rhubarb Crisp

- **4 cups cut-up fresh rhubarb**
- **½ teaspoon salt**
- **1⅔ cups sugar**
- **¾ cup all-purpose flour**
- **1 teaspoon cinnamon**
- **⅓ cup butter, softened**

Vanilla ice cream

Place the rhubarb in an ungreased 8-inch square baking dish. Sprinkle with the salt. In a small bowl combine the sugar, flour, and cinnamon. Add the butter and mix thoroughly until the mixture is crumbly. Spread over the rhubarb. Bake in a 350° oven for 45 minutes. Serve warm with vanilla ice cream.

Serves 6.

Hill Farm Inn

The Leslie Place

Box 62
Belmont, Vermont 05730
(802) 259-2903

Peacefully set on one hundred acres, this 1840s New England farmhouse has been lovingly restored, and the spacious accommodations and picturesque setting create a welcome retreat in any season. The bedroom and three-bedroom suite provide a relaxing, comfortable environment.

Peach-Apricot Cobbler

1 1-pound 13-ounce can sliced peaches
1 8¾-ounce can apricot halves
½ cup sugar
1 tablespoon cornstarch
1 tablespoon butter
¼ teaspoon cinnamon

&a &a &a

1 cup sifted all-purpose flour
1 tablespoon sugar
1½ teaspoons baking powder
½ teaspoon salt
3 tablespoons shortening
½ cup milk

&a &a &a

Cream

Drain the peaches and apricots, reserving 1 cup of juice. In a saucepan combine ½ cup of sugar and cornstarch. Blend in the 1 cup of juice and cook over medium heat, stirring constantly until the mixture comes to a boil. Cook for 1 minute. Remove from the heat and stir in the butter and cinnamon. Add the peaches and apricots to the thickened mixture and pour into a 1½-quart casserole. Place in a 400° oven.

In a medium bowl sift together the flour, 1 tablespoon of sugar, baking powder, and salt. Cut in the shortening until the mixture resembles coarse crumbs. Stir in the milk to make a soft dough. Drop by spoonfuls over the hot fruit and continue baking for a total of 30 minutes until browned. Serve with cream.

Serves 6.

The Leslie Place

Easy Maple Granola

2 cups regular rolled oats
¼ cup maple syrup
⅓ cup oil
¼ teaspoon salt
½ teaspoon vanilla extract

&a &a &a

Raisins (optional)

In a medium bowl combine the oats, maple syrup, oil, salt, and vanilla. Spread thinly on a cookie sheet. Bake in a 350° oven for 20 to 25 minutes until lightly brown.

In a large bowl combine the baked granola and raisins, if desired. Allow to cool before storing.

Note: The recipe can be increased 4 to 8 times and the extra granola stored in the freezer.

Makes about 2 cups.

&a &a &a &a &a

Blueberry Drop Biscuits

1 cup fresh blueberries
3 tablespoons sugar
2 cups sifted all-purpose flour
3 teaspoons baking powder
¾ teaspoon salt
2 tablespoons shortening, cold
1 cup milk, cold

Butter a baking sheet. Wash, drain, and dry the blueberries between paper towels. In a medium bowl combine the blueberries with 2 tablespoons of sugar. In a separate bowl sift together the flour, baking powder, and salt. With a pastry blender cut the shortening into the dry ingredients. Add the milk all at once, stirring with a fork. Add the blueberries. Drop by spoonfuls 1-inch apart on the prepared baking sheet. Sprinkle the biscuits with the remaining tablespoon of sugar. Bake in a 450° oven for 12 minutes. Serve hot with butter.

Serves 8 to 10.

Rosy Applesauce

Red Delicious eating apples and a food blender make this easy applesauce in no time. With no cooking!

¼ cup fresh lemon juice
½ cup light corn syrup
2 tablespoons sugar
6 medium red eating apples
Freshly ground nutmeg, optional

In a blender combine the lemon juice, corn syrup, and sugar. Purée on medium speed for 30 seconds and pour into a 1½-quart bowl. Core and slice unpeeled apples into the liquid and stir as they are added to prevent discoloration. Fill the blender half full with the apples and liquid. Cover and blend on high speed until the peeling is puréed. Repeat until all the apples are blended. Pour the applesauce into an airtight container and refrigerate. Serve sprinkled with nutmeg, if desired.
Serves 4.

The Churchill House Inn

Route 73 East
Brandon, Vermont 05733
(802) 247-3300

From the beginning, this century-old farmhouse has offered hospitality to the traveler. Built by the Churchill family in 1871, it was a halfway house for patrons of the adjoining mill and store. That spirit of hospitality remains, and a blend of original furnishings, antique pieces, and modern bedding provides a homelike atmosphere. The inn has nine guest rooms and eight baths. Recent additions include a pool, sauna, and screened-in porch. The inn is known for its intimate atmosphere and its good food, especially its homemade breads, soups, and desserts. The inn's location in the Green Mountain National Forest offers ideal surroundings for the active person. Excellent hiking, biking, fishing, or cross-country skiing await the guest at the door.

Green Salad
with Chevre and Hot Bacon Dressing

5 slices bacon
1 egg, beaten
⅓ cup vinegar
¼ cup minced onion
¼ teaspoon salt
2 tablespoons sugar
2 tablespoons water
2 cups torn leaf lettuce
2 ounces chevre

In a 400° oven cook the bacon for 10 minutes until crisp. Drain, reserve the drippings, and set the bacon aside. In a small saucepan combine the bacon drippings with the egg, vinegar, minced onion, salt, sugar, and water. Whisk together over medium heat until thickened. Remove from the heat. Arrange the lettuce on 6 plates and dress with the hot dressing. Garnish with the bacon and room temperature chevre.
Serves 6.

Lemon Soufflé Pudding

1 cup sugar
¼ cup all-purpose flour
⅛ teaspoon salt
2 tablespoons butter
5 tablespoons lemon juice
Grated rind of 1 lemon
1½ cups milk
3 eggs, separated

Grease a baking dish and place it in a baking pan with water. In a small bowl combine the sugar, flour, and salt. In a small saucepan melt the butter and add the sugar mixture. Add the lemon juice and lemon rind, blending well. Add the milk and the beaten egg yolks. In a separate bowl beat the egg whites until stiff, then fold into the mixture in the saucepan. Pour the mixture into the prepared dish. Bake in a 350° oven for 45 minutes.
Serves 4 to 6.

Churchill Chocolate Pie

1¼ cups sugar
¼ teaspoon salt
¼ cup cornstarch
2 cups milk
2 egg yolks, beaten
2 squares chocolate, melted
1 teaspoon vanilla extract
1 baked 9-inch pie shell

In the top of a double boiler combine the sugar, salt, and cornstarch. Add the milk and cook for 15 minutes, stirring frequently. Combine a small amount of the hot liquid into the egg yolks, then add back to the double boiler. Add the chocolate and cook for 5 minutes. Remove from the heat and add the vanilla. Pour into a baked pie shell.
Serves 6.

The Churchill House Inn

Bread and Butter Pickles

**4 quarts medium cucumbers,
    unpeeled and sliced
6 medium onions, thinly sliced
½ cup canning salt**

  🖙 🖙 🖙

**4 cups sugar
5 cups vinegar
2 teaspoons mustard seed
1 teaspoon celery seed
1½ teaspoons turmeric
1 teaspoon cinnamon
1 teaspoon cloves**

In a large container alternately layer the cucumbers, onion, salt, and ice cubes. Put a weight on top for 3 hours and then drain.

In a large kettle combine the sugar, vinegar, mustard seed, celery seed, and turmeric. Bring to a boil. In a cheesecloth bag combine the cinnamon and cloves. Attach the bag to the side of the kettle so that it hangs into the boiling syrup. Add the cucumber mixture to the boiling syrup, stirring as they heat, and return the temperature to low. Place into canning jars.

Note: Do not boil the cucumbers or they will get soft.

Makes about 12 pints.

Hot Mulled Wine

**1½ cups boiling water
½ cup sugar
½ lemon, sliced
3 sticks cinnamon
3 whole cloves
1 large bottle California Burgundy
    or other red dinner wine
Nutmeg**

In a large saucepan combine the boiling water, sugar, lemon, cinnamon, and cloves, stirring until the sugar dissolves. Add the wine and simmer for 20 minutes. (DO NOT BOIL!) Strain. Serve hot with a sprinkling of nutmeg.

Serves 8 to 10.

Churchill House Cheesecake

**1½ cups graham or zwieback
    crumbs
3 tablespoons sugar
¼ cup butter, melted**

  🖙 🖙 🖙

**3 8-ounce packages cream cheese,
    softened
1¼ cups sugar
4 eggs
1 teaspoon vanilla extract
¾ teaspoon grated lemon rind**

  🖙 🖙 🖙

**1 pint sour cream
1 teaspoon vanilla extract
2 tablespoons sugar
Cinnamon**

Butter the sides of a 10-inch spring-form pan. In a medium bowl combine the crumbs and sugar. Coat the sides of the prepared pan. Mix the remaining crumbs with the butter, reserving 2 tablespoons for a topping. Pat the crumb mixture into the bottom of the pan and set aside.

In a medium bowl blend together the cream cheese and sugar. Add the eggs one at a time, beating well after each addition. Add 1 teaspoon of vanilla and the lemon rind, beating for 5 minutes. Pour the cake batter into the prepared pan. Bake in a 350° oven for 35 minutes. Open the oven door slightly and cool for 1 hour.

Combine the sour cream and 1 teaspoon of vanilla. Spread the sour cream on the cake. Sprinkle with 2 tablespoons of sugar, cinnamon, and the reserved 2 tablespoons of crumb mixture. Bake in a 425° oven for 5 to 10 minutes to set the topping.

Serves 8.

Rack of Lamb

3 cloves garlic, minced
¼ cup Dijon mustard
¼ cup white wine
¼ cup olive oil
3 tablespoons rosemary, crushed
1 8-rib rack of lamb, trimmed

In a small bowl combine the garlic, mustard, wine, oil, and rosemary. Brush on the lamb and let sit for at least 1 hour. Roast the lamb in a 450° oven for 30 minutes for medium-rare.
Serves 4.

Barbecued Butterflied Lamb

2 cloves garlic, minced
¼ cup soy sauce
6 ounces pineapple juice
¼ cup sherry
1 tablespoon brown sugar
1 6-pound butterflied leg of lamb

In a small bowl combine the garlic, soy sauce, pineapple juice, sherry, and brown sugar. Marinate the lamb in the sauce for several hours. Grill the lamb about 20 minutes per side for medium.
Serves 12.

Orange Whole Wheat Pancakes

2 eggs, beaten
¼ cup oil
1 tablespoon vanilla extract
1 teaspoon almond extract
2 cups orange juice
2 cups whole wheat flour
½ teaspoon salt
½ teaspoon baking soda
Blueberries, banana slices, apple chunks or ½ cup granola (optional)

In a medium bowl combine the eggs, oil, vanilla, and almond extract. Add 1¾ cups of orange juice. In a separate bowl sift together the flour, salt, and baking soda. Slowly blend the dry ingredients into the liquid ingredients, adding the remaining ¼ cup of orange juice until the mixture is the desired consistency. Blend just until the mixture is moistened. Fold in the fruit or granola, if desired. Bake on a hot greased griddle until bubbles come to the surface. Turn and bake until golden.
Serves 4.

Mill Brook

Route 44
Post Office Box 410
Brownsville, Vermont 05037
(802) 484-7283

The Mill Brook is a charming getaway that once served as a boarding house for loggers in the 1800s. Eight New England-style guest rooms, some with antiques and a rich assortment of Fraktur paintings on the woodwork, are offered. Both private and shared bathrooms are available. A gourmet breakfast is served. There are also four cozy sitting rooms, one with a glass front woodburning stove, for relaxing, reading, writing, or planning one's activities.

Catamount Burgers

Named for the lynx-like wild cat that legend has it roams the hills of Vermont. Serve at breakfast with waffles or Lost Bread (French toast), or pancakes on our breakfast buffet.

1 pound maple glazed baked ham, thinly sliced
½ pound Vermont Cheddar cheese, thinly sliced
¼ cup Vermont maple syrup
1 tablespoon Tabasco hot sauce

Lightly oil the bottom of a 9x13-inch microwave-proof baking pan. Alternate the slices of ham and cheese, overlapping slightly, starting and ending with the ham (simulating the stripes of a cat). Pour the maple syrup evenly over the ham and cheese and drizzle with the Tabasco. Cover tightly with plastic wrap and microwave at high for 3 minutes. Turn the dish and microwave for 1½ more minutes to melt the cheese and heat the ham.
Note: This can also be grilled, but do not bake in a regular oven. The ham becomes tough and too dry.
Serves 4 to 6.

The Shire Inn

Main Street
Post Office Box 37
Chelsea, Vermont 05038
(802) 685-3031

The Shire Inn, built in 1832, is a warm place that offers comfortable, elegant accommodations. Set on a twenty-acre site, it features a variety of flowers and herbs in the large gardens. With cross-country skis and bicycles available at the inn, the Shire truly is an inn for all seasons. All the rooms are distinctive, with private baths and most with working fireplaces. A gourmet dinner by candlelight is served in the evening and a full breakfast each morning. Guests find the food excellent, the rooms lovely, the fireplaces cozy, and the hospitality warm.

Amaretto Chicken

¼ cup butter
6 chicken breast halves, skinned
    and boned
Flour
1 clove garlic, chopped
3 tablespoons sliced almonds
¼ cup Amaretto
1 cup heavy cream

In a large skillet melt the butter. Coat the chicken breasts in the flour and sauté in the butter, turning until cooked through. Add the garlic. Remove the chicken to the platter and keep warm. Add the almonds and Amaretto to the skillet and cook for 1 minute. Add the cream and heat. Pour the sauce over the chicken.
Serves 6.

The Shire Inn

Zucchini Madeleines

This recipe was the winner of the Shire Inn's 1989 Great Recipe Race. Our guests submitted recipes from all over the country. This recipe comes from Darrie Hinson of Dallas, Texas. We serve it with a shrimp sauce as an appetizer.

1 cup shredded zucchini, salted and
    drained (drain at least 1 hour in
    a colander)
1 large onion, chopped
1 clove garlic, chopped
10 eggs, beaten
¾ cup oil
½ cup fresh Parmesan cheese
1½ teaspoons pepper
2 cups biscuit mix

Grease and flour madeleine pans. In a large bowl combine all the ingredients. Spoon the mixture into the prepared pan. Bake in a 350° oven for 20 to 25 minutes.
Serves 30.

Boiled Cider Pie

This recipe was given to us by Marion Gilman, who lives in town and makes these pies for the inn.

1 gallon apple cider

    ❧ ❧ ❧

½ cup brown sugar
½ cup sugar
1½ tablespoons all-purpose flour
1 tablespoon water
1 egg
Pastry for 2-crust 9-inch pie
1 tablespoon butter

In a large saucepan boil the cider at a soft boil temperature until it has the consistency of molasses. Reserve ⅓ cup, and pour the rest into a jar. Refrigerate or seal for later use.

In a medium bowl combine ⅓ cup of boiled cider, sugars, flour, water, and egg. Pour into the pie shell. Dot the top with the butter. Put on the top crust. Bake in a 350° oven for 40 minutes.

Note: One gallon of cider makes approximately 1 pint. Any extra can be canned in a glass jar. It keeps for a long time.
Serves 6.

Maple-Cream Apple Tart

1½ cups all-purpose flour
3 tablespoons sugar
¼ teaspoon salt
⅓ cup butter or margarine

    ❧ ❧ ❧

3 McIntosh apples or green apples,
    peeled, cored, and sliced
¾ cup sugar
1 teaspoon cinnamon
¼ teaspoon nutmeg

    ❧ ❧ ❧

2 egg yolks
1 cup heavy cream
⅓ cup Vermont maple syrup

    ❧ ❧ ❧

Vanilla ice cream

In a large bowl stir together the flour, 3 tablespoons of sugar, and salt. Cut in the butter until the mixture is the consistency of cornmeal. Press the crumbs firmly into the bottom and 1 inch up the sides of a 9-inch springform pan.

Arrange the apple slices on the crust in rows or groupings that suggest cutting portions. In a small bowl combine ¾ cup of sugar, cinnamon, and nutmeg, and sprinkle over the apples. Bake in a 400° oven for 15 minutes.

In a small bowl beat the egg yolks and stir in the cream and syrup. Pour evenly over the apples and continue baking for an additional 30 minutes. Serve with vanilla ice cream.

Serves 8 to 10.

Lemon Poppy Veal

6 veal cutlets
Flour
Butter
1½ tablespoons poppy seeds
¼ cup brandy
½ cup lemon juice
1 cup heavy cream

Coat the veal with flour. In a skillet melt the butter and sauté the veal, turning to cook through. Remove the cutlets to a platter and keep warm. Add the poppy seeds and brandy, and cook for 1 minute. Add the lemon juice and cream, heating through.

Serve the sauce over the veal.
Serves 6.

Cheese Bundles

1 sheet puff pastry
1 teaspoon cream cheese
6 teaspoons Feta cheese
6 teaspoons Blue cheese
3 tablespoons butter, melted

Cut the puff pastry in half lengthwise, and then into 3 equal strips to make 6 squares. Spoon equal portions of each cheese into the center of each pastry square. Fold to make a triangle. With a fork press the edges together to seal. Fold the upper corners under and brush with the butter. Place on an ungreased cookie sheet. Bake in a 375° oven for 18 to 20 minutes.

Serves 6.

Cranberry-Cider Chops

6 lamb chops or 6 pork chops
1 teaspoon salt
Flour
4 apples, sliced
2 cups cranberries
1 cup brown sugar
1½ cups apple cider

Butter a 2-quart casserole dish. Sprinkle the chops with the salt and dredge in the flour. In a skillet sauté the chops until brown (do not cook the lamb long). In a medium bowl combine the apples, cranberries, and brown sugar. Spread the fruit mixture in the bottom of the prepared dish and top with the chops and cider. Bake in a 350° oven 15 to 20 minutes for the lamb chops or 1 hour and 30 minutes for the pork chops, until tender.

Note: Turn the chops during cooking so both sides are flavored with the fruit.

Serves 6.

Pineapple Sage Chicken

¼ cup butter
6 chicken breast halves, skinned and boned
Flour
¼ cup dry sherry
1 tablespoon chopped fresh sage
1 20-ounce can pineapple chunks in juice
1 cup heavy cream

In a skillet melt the butter. Coat the chicken breasts with the flour and sauté in the butter, turning until cooked through. Remove the chicken to a platter and keep warm. Add the sherry to the skillet with the sage and reduce. Add the pineapple and juice, cooking for 3 minutes to reduce. Add the cream and heat through. Serve the sauce over the chicken.

Serves 6.

Lamb en Croûte

1 to 1½ pounds lamb loin, cubed
Olive oil
2 sheets puff pastry
2 cloves fresh garlic, chopped
Salt and pepper
Oregano
1 cup fresh spinach, cooked and chopped
1 tomato, sliced
Butter, melted

In a skillet sauté the lamb in hot olive oil until browned (do not cook through). Cut each pastry sheet in half. Divide the lamb among the sheets of pastry. Sprinkle with the garlic and season with salt, pepper, and oregano. Place the spinach and tomato slices on top. Fold the pastry over to make a rectangle. Press the edges together with a fork to seal. Brush with the melted butter and place on a cookie sheet. Bake in a 400° oven for 20 mintes until brown.

Serves 4.

Pasta with Roasted Red Pepper Sauce

4 to 5 large roasted red peppers
2 cloves garlic
¼ cup Italian salad dressing
½ cup heavy cream
2 tablespoons freshly chopped basil
¼ teaspoon cayenne pepper
Salt and pepper

🐟 🐟 🐟

1 pound fettuccini

🐟 🐟 🐟

Grated Parmesan cheese for garnish

In a food processor fitted with a metal blade process the peppers, garlic, and salad dressing until smooth. Add the cream, basil, cayenne pepper, salt, and pepper, blending well.

Cook the fettuccini according to the package directions. Toss with the sauce and serve. Garnish with the Parmesan cheese and/or strips of red pepper.

Serves 6.

Praline Custard Pie

4 eggs
1 cup milk
2 cups heavy cream
½ cup biscuit mix
½ cup butter
1 cup sugar
1 teaspoon nutmeg
1 teaspoon cinnamon
1 teaspoon vanilla extract

&a &a &a

⅓ cup brown sugar
⅓ cup chopped pecans
1 tablespoon butter, softened

Grease a 9-inch pie plate. In a blender at high speed blend the eggs, milk, cream, biscuit mix, butter, sugar, nutmeg, cinnamon, and vanilla. Pour into the prepared pie plate. Bake in a 350° oven for 45 minutes.

In a small bowl combine the brown sugar, pecans, and 1 tablespoon of butter. Spread the topping on the custard and cook for 10 more minutes.

Serves 8.

Eierkuchen with Apricot Sauce

¼ cup butter

&a &a &a

½ cup all-purpose flour
½ cup milk
2 eggs
2 teaspoons vanilla extract
2 tablespoons sugar
Dash salt

&a &a &a

3 tablespoons apricot preserves
1 heaping teaspoon allspice

In a 350° oven melt the butter in a 9-inch pie plate until it sizzles, but do not burn.

In a blender combine the flour, milk, eggs, vanilla, sugar, and salt, blending until smooth. Pour mixture into the pie plate over the sizzling butter. Bake in a 350° oven for 20 minutes.

In a saucepan over low heat combine the preserves and allspice, stirring until warm. Spread the sauce on top of the pie and continue to bake for 5 more minutes. Serve immediately while hot.

Serves 3 to 4.

Baked Pears

2 Anjou pears
1 cup sugar
4 tablespoons vanilla extract
1 teaspoon almond extract
1 cup heavy cream

&a &a &a

Sliced almonds for garnish

Halve the pears, core, and peel. Sprinkle ¼ cup of sugar in each of 4 ramekin cups. Place a pear half on top of the sugar and pour 1 tablespoon of vanilla and ¼ teaspoon of almond extract over each pear. Bake in a 350° oven for 20 to 30 minutes. Pour ¼ cup of cream over each pear and continue baking for 20 to 30 more minutes. Remove from the oven and cool for 5 minutes before serving. Garnish with sliced almonds.

Note: If ramekins are not available, use a casserole dish.

Serves 4.

Broccoli-Cashew Pasta Salad

1 pound rainbow rotini

&a &a &a

1 head broccoli, chopped
1 red onion, chopped
½ cup raisins
1 cup mayonnaise
⅓ cup sugar
3 tablespoons vinegar
½ cup cashews

Cook the rotini according to the package directions.

In a large bowl combine the broccoli, onion, and raisins. Set aside. In a small bowl combine the mayonnaise, sugar, and vinegar. Toss the sauce with the broccoli mixture and add the cashews. Toss with the pasta.

Serves 6.

Swordfish with Lime Mayonnaise

4 6-ounce Swordfish fillets

&a &a &a

3 egg yolks
1½ teaspoons mustard
Salt
White pepper
3 tablespoons lime juice, or to taste
1 cup olive oil or ½ cup olive oil
    and ½ cup vegetable oil

Grill or broil the swordfish.

In a food processor fitted with a metal blade combine the egg yolks, mustard, salt, pepper, and lime juice, blending well. While the processor is running add the oil through the hole in the lid drop by drop, increasing to a steady trickle until the sauce is the desired consistency. This makes 1 cup of Lime Mayonnaise.

Note: Overbeating will result in the mayonnaise being too thick.

Serves 4.

Confetti Bread

⅔ cup butter, softened
1⅓ cups sugar
4 eggs
2 cups applesauce
½ cup milk
4 cups sifted all-purpose flour
2 teaspoons baking powder
1 teaspoon baking soda
1 teaspoon salt
1 tablespoon grated lemon rind
1 tablespoon grated orange rind
1½ cups chopped nuts

Grease and flour two 5x9-inch loaf pans. In a bowl cream together the butter and sugar. Beat in the eggs one at a time. Stir in the applesauce and milk. In a separate bowl sift together the flour, baking powder, baking soda, and salt. Add to the creamed mixture, mixing well. Add the lemon rind, orange rind, and nuts. Pour into the prepared pans. Bake in a 350° oven for 1 hour.

Makes 2 loaves.

Henry Farm Inn

Green Mountain Turnpike
Post Office Box 636
Chester, Vermont 05143
(802) 875-2674

Henry Farm Inn

The Henry Farm Inn provides an ideal location for the visitor seeking the many outdoor activities available in the Chester area. Nestled between a sloping meadow and a pond, with fifty acres of forested foothills near a sparkling river, it is a haven of tranquility. Seven spacious bedrooms with private baths are offered. Also available are a country dining room and two cozy sitting rooms. In its earlier days, Henry Farm Inn served as a stagecoach stop and tavern. It retains its original charm, with wide pine floors, hand-hewn sheathing, eight fireplaces, a beehive oven, and Early American ambiance.

Broiled Stuffed Shrimp

1½ cups Ritz crackers, crumbled
½ cup butter, melted
1 small stalk celery, chopped
1 small garlic clove, chopped
2 ounces lobster meat

🍤 🍤 🍤

16 large shrimp
White pepper

In a large bowl combine together the crackers, butter, celery, and garlic. Mix in the lobster meat.

Butterfly the shrimp, brush with butter, and broil for 3 to 5 minutes until slightly pink. Stuff the shrimp with the butter mixture and top with the white pepper. Continue to broil the shrimp until golden brown.

Serves 4.

Mountain Top Inn

Mountain Top Road
Chittenden, Vermont 05737
(802) 483-2311 (in Vermont and Canada)
(800) 445-2100 (outside Vermont)

The altitude of Mountain Top Inn is 2000 feet, so it commands a spectacular view of the Green Mountains, which also are reflected in the lake. The inn's post-and-beam construction, combined with many fireplaces and polished furniture, creates a warm retreat. The maple sugar house on the premises produces the fine maple syrup served in the dining room. There are thirty-five guest rooms in addition to fifteen cottage and chalet units. Other amenities include a cocktail lounge; a well-outfitted gamesroom; whirlpool and sauna; heated outdoor pool; and a lighted outdoor skating rink. Depending on the season, guests have recreational choices of horse-drawn sleigh rides or hay rides, skiing, tobogganing, and sledding; lake-oriented sports such as boating, wind surfing, fishing, and swimming; pitch 'n putt golfing; and hiking or horseback riding throughout the 1000-acre grounds or adjacent national forest.

Baked Brie

1 cup brown sugar
1 cup almonds
3 ounces Scotch

🍤 🍤 🍤

4 ounce wedge Brie
2 slices French bread, toasted
1 leaf lettuce
¼ MacIntosh apple

Mountain Top Inn

In a food processor combine the sugar, almonds, and Scotch. Finely grind.

In a casserole dish place the Brie and top with 2 ounces of the brown sugar topping. Broil until it is melted. Place the melted Brie on top of the toast and garnish with lettuce and apples.

Serves 1.

Sautéed Chicken Breast

    6 ounces boneless chicken breast,
        skinned
    Flour
    ¼ cup butter
    2 tablespoons lemon juice
    1½ ounces white wine
    1½ ounces sherry
    ½ ounce chopped scallions
    2 sprigs rosemary
    ¼ cup heavy cream

Dredge the chicken in the flour. In a hot skillet melt the butter and add the chicken, lemon juice, white wine, sherry, scallions, and rosemary. Sauté the chicken until it is firm to the touch, then add the cream. Let cream reduce.

Serves 1.

Native Lamb

    1⅓ ounces Roquefort cheese
    2 scallions, chopped
    2 teaspoons chives
    ½ teaspoon salt
    ¼ teaspoon thyme
    ½ teaspoon black pepper
    1 cup bread crumbs
    2 tablespoons butter

        🍃 🍃 🍃

    6 ounces split hotel rack of lamb
        (3 pieces)
    Tomato sauce

In a medium bowl combine the Roquefort, scallions, chives, seasonings, bread crumbs, and butter.

Broil the lamb for approximately 1 minute on each side, then top each piece with 1 tablespoon of the Roquefort dressing. Continue to broil until the topping is browned or until the lamb is the desired temperature. On a dinner plate place 2 ounces of tomato sauce, then the rack of lamb.

Serves 1.

Medallions of Pork Loin

    1 pound pork loin
    Flour
    ¼ cup butter
    ½ ounce chopped scallions
    Juice from ½ lemon
    ½ Granny Smith apple, sliced
    2 ounces Apple Jack brandy
    Garlic

Trim the fat off the pork loin and slice into four 4-ounce pieces. Tenderize the meat by pounding, then dredge in the flour. In a hot skillet melt the butter, then add the pork, scallions, and lemon juice. Sauté for approximately 2 to 3 minutes. Add the apple and flavor with the brandy and garlic. Cook for 2 more minutes.

Serves 2.

Tulip Tree Inn

Chittenden Dam Road
Chittenden, Vermont 05737
(802) 483-6213

This is the way you have always pictured a country inn. Its eight warm, charming guest rooms all have private baths, and many have their own Jacuzzi. Secluded in the Green Mountain National Forest, the inn offers a bit of backwoods luxury. The fine candlelight dinners, an extensive wine list, warmth, and charm are unsurpassed.

Tomato Soup
with Cream and Gin

    1 28-ounce can crushed tomatoes
    2 cups canned chicken broth
    1 tablespoon garlic powder
    1 teaspoon sage
    1 teaspoon sweet basil
    2 tablespoons sugar
    Heavy cream
    Gin

In a large saucepan combine the tomatoes, broth, garlic powder, sage, basil, and sugar. Simmer for 30 minutes. Pour into individual serving bowls and dribble 1 tablespoon of heavy cream over the top, followed by a jigger of gin.

Serves 6.

🐦 🐦 🐦 🐦 🐦

Carrot Soup

This is our most requested recipe. After reading it, all have been surprised—it's so easy to make with such unorthodox ingredients.

1 16-ounce bag frozen sliced carrots
2 tablespoons dehydrated minced onion
1 13-ounce can chicken broth
1 teaspoon white pepper
1 teaspoon curry powder
1 teaspoon salt
12 ounces heavy cream
1 8-ounce container plain yogurt

In a medium soup pot cook the carrots and onion in the broth until tender. Purée in a blender and return to the pot. Add the white pepper, curry powder, salt, and heavy cream, heating through. Serve with a dollop of yogurt.
Serves 8.

❧ ❧ ❧ ❧ ❧

Medallions of Pork
with Apricot Orange Sauce

2 1-pound pork tenderloins
3 tablespoons apricot preserves
½ cup orange juice
2 cloves garlic
2 tablespoons soy sauce
1 teaspoon Dijon mustard

Place the pork in a glass baking dish. In a blender combine the preserves, orange juice, garlic, soy sauce, and mustard, blending until smooth. Pour over the pork and marinate at least 6 hours.

Reserve the marinade. Bake the pork in a 450° oven for 20 minutes. Slice into ¼-inch slices. Heat the marinade and pour over the pork to serve.
Serves 4.

Peach Cheesecake

Butter, melted
1½ pounds cream cheese
6 large eggs
1½ cups sugar
2 16-ounce cans peaches, drained

Brush the bottom and sides of a 10-inch springform pan with melted butter. In a food processor combine the cream cheese, eggs, and sugar. Blend until smooth, then add the peaches. Continue processing until smooth. Pour mixture into the prepared pan. Bake in a 325° oven for 1 hour. Turn off the oven and let the cake cool in the oven for 20 minutes.
Serves 12 to 16.

The Craftsbury Inn

Craftsbury, Vermont 05826
(802) 586-2848

Built in 1850 as a private home in northeast Vermont, the Craftsbury Inn offers warm hospitality and superb food to its guests. The ten guest rooms contain custom-made quilts, best sellers, and paintings by local artists. Called "Vermont's most remarkable hill town" by the *Boston Globe,* Craftsbury offers many charming local events, endless natural beauty, and ample opportunity for hiking, biking, and day car trips.

Breast of Chicken
with Maple Mustard Sauce

4 6-ounce boneless breasts of chicken, skinned
1 cup clarified butter
Flour

❧ ❧ ❧
1 shallot, finely diced
⅓ cup brandy
⅓ cup white wine
1 tablespoon Worcestershire sauce
1 tablespoon Dijon mustard
3 tablespoons Pommery mustard
3 tablespoons maple syrup
2 chicken bouillon cubes dissolved in 1 cup warm water
1 cup heavy cream
❧ ❧ ❧
4 scallions, chopped

Place the chicken skin side down, cover with plastic wrap, and pound firmly to a ¼-inch thickness. Cut each piece of chicken into 3 strips. Cover the bottom of a large sauté pan with clarified butter and heat over medium-high heat. Lightly coat the chicken pieces with flour, then sauté the meat in the hot butter until golden brown. Place the browned chicken on a small sheet pan. Bake in a 300° oven for 8 minutes until done.

Measure 2 tablespoons of clarified butter back into the sauté pan. Add 1 diced shallot and heat over medium heat, stirring for 30 seconds. Remove the pan from the heat and add the brandy, white wine, Worcestershire sauce, mustards, maple syrup, and chicken stock. Place the pan back on the heat and reduce the liquids to half. Add the heavy cream and reduce to half again, until the sauce is the consistency of gravy.

Remove the chicken from the oven and place in the sauce. Garnish with the chopped scallions.
Serves 4.

The Little Lodge at Dorset

Route 30
Box 673
Dorset, Vermont 05251
(802) 867-4040

This attractive old house, listed in the National Registry of Historic Places, offers five bedrooms decorated with the country look. They have crocheted or quilted bed covers, lots of calico, stenciling, wide floorboards, braided rugs, and private baths. There are several comfortable sitting areas for relaxing, including a hexagonal porch that is screened in during the summer and glassed in during the winter. In the barnboard den with a view of the pond and the mountains, a cheery fireplace, many books, and a refrigerator are popular with guests.

Orange Coriander Bread

The most frequently requested recipe by our guests.

¼ cup butter
1 cup sugar
1 cup orange juice
1 cup golden raisins
2 eggs, well beaten
½ cup crushed or powdered
    coriander (yes! ½ cup!)
½ cup chopped nuts
2 cups all-purpose flour
1 teaspoon baking powder
1 teaspoon baking soda

Grease 2 small loaf pans with cooking spray. In a large bowl combine the butter and sugar. Add the orange juice, raisins, eggs, and coriander, mixing well. Blend in the nuts, flour, baking powder, and baking soda. Pour the batter into the prepared pans. Bake in a 350° oven for 45 minutes.

Note: Recipe can be doubled to make 3 regular-sized loaves.
Makes 2 small loaves.

Cooper Hill Inn

Cooper Hill Road
Post Office Box 146
East Dover, Vermont 05341
(802) 348-6333

A thirteen-bedroom country inn, Cooper Hill Inn is in the Green Mountains of southern Vermont. On a quiet country road at an elevation of 2,400 feet, the inn commands a one hundred-mile view of Vermont, New Hampshire, and Massachusetts. The atmosphere is homey and relaxed, and the home-cooked meals with freshly baked breads and desserts are a treat. Children are welcome.

Cabbage Carrot Soup

1 small head cabbage
1 onion
1 quart water

3 to 4 potatoes
3 to 4 carrots
1 quart water
1 teaspoon dill weed
1 cup sour cream

In a large saucepan cook the cabbage and onion in 1 quart of water.

In a separate pan cook the potatoes and carrots in 1 quart of water. Mash some of the potatoes and carrots for a thicker texture. Add the cabbage mixture to the carrot mixture. Add the dill and sour cream just before serving. Do not boil.

Makes 3 to 4 quarts.

Fruited Spinach Salad

¼ cup white wine vinegar
3 tablespoons oil
2 tablespoons honey
1 teaspoon poppy seed
½ teaspoon dry mustard

8 cups spinach, torn (or use half lettuce)

Cooper Hill Inn

1 papaya, seeded, peeled, and
    cubed (or 2 medium pears)
1½ cups seedless grapes, halved

In a small jar combine the vinegar, oil, honey, poppy seed, and dry mustard for the dressing. Refrigerate.

In a large bowl prepare the spinach, papaya, and grapes. Toss with the dressing just before serving.

Serves 10.

Chicken and Green Peppers in Wine Sauce

1½ cut-up broilers
Salt and pepper
Garlic powder

❧ ❧ ❧

1 green pepper, chopped
1 large onion, chopped
2 stalks celery, chopped
2 tablespoons shortening

❧ ❧ ❧

½ cup catsup
Juice of 1 orange
Juice of 1 lemon
⅓ cup sugar (or less)
1 cup port wine

In a greased baking pan arrange the chicken in one layer. Season with the salt, pepper, and garlic powder.

In a skillet sauté the green pepper, onions, and celery in the shortening.

In a small bowl combine the catsup, juices, sugar, and wine. Add the sauce to the sautéed vegetables and bring to a boil. Pour over the chicken. Bake uncovered in a 325° oven for 1½ to 2 hours, basting occasionally.

Note: This is especially good with brown rice.

Serves 8 to 9.

Berkson Farms

Enosburg Falls, Vermont 05450
(802) 933-2522

Situated on 600 acres in the Missisquoi River valley, Berkson Farms is a century-old farmhouse with eight newly renovated rooms offering a beautiful Vermont view. Guests enjoy a spacious living room and library, as well as a comfortable family and game room. The Berkson can easily accommodate twelve to fourteen guests. The innkeepers serve a Vermont-style breakfast of farm fresh eggs, milk from the dairy, fresh creamery butter, and maple syrup made on the farm. In the evening, a country-style dinner is served in the dining room around the old wooden dining table. Berkson Farms offers four seasons of country living.

Apple Dumplings

Apples, peeled and sliced
½ cup sugar
½ cup brown sugar
1 tablespoon nutmeg
1 tablespoon cinnamon

❧ ❧ ❧

Bisquick recipe for shortcake,
    doubled

❧ ❧ ❧

1½ cups sugar
¾ cup water
1 teaspoon vanilla extract

Fill a 9x12-inch cake pan half full with the apples. In a small bowl combine ½ cup of sugar, brown sugar, nutmeg, and cinnamon. Sprinkle over the apples.

Prepare the shortcake recipe using a little more water. Pour over the apples. Bake in a 350° oven for 15 to 20 minutes until golden brown.

In a small bowl combine 1½ cups of sugar, water, and vanilla. Poke holes in the shortcake and pour the sauce over the top. Serve upside down.

Serves 20.

Maplewood Inn

Route 22-A South
Fair Haven, Vermont 05743
(802) 265-8039

Maplewood Inn is a beautifully restored Greek Revival-style home built circa 1843. Affording the traveler magnificent country views from every window, it offers elegant guest rooms and suites, with four-poster or brass beds and the "little touches," from chocolate treats to wine. The inn shines with handsome and varied woodwork, and several rooms are provided for relaxation. It even has a collection of ingenious nineteenth-century hand-forged iron tavern puzzles to challenge the curious. Many activities are nearby, from skiing in the winter to boating or golfing in the summer. A leisurely game of croquet can be played on the south lawn.

Amaretto-Almond French Toast

2 cups Butter Almond ice cream
5 eggs
3 tablespoons Amaretto liqueur
12 slices French bread, ¾-inch
    thickness
Sliced or slivered almonds

❧ ❧ ❧

Butter
Confectioners' sugar
Vermont maple syrup

Melt the ice cream at room temperature or in a microwave on high for 1 to 2 minutes. Add the eggs and beat

Maplewood Inn

until blended. Beat in the Amaretto until mixed well. Dip the bread slices into the mixture, coating well, and pressing the almonds from the ice cream into the slices. Add extra almonds as necessary.

In an electric skillet, grill, or fry pan melt the butter at 350°. Fry the bread until golden brown. Slightly overlap 3 slices per serving and dust with confectioners' sugar. Sprinkle with almonds. Serve with maple syrup.

Serves 4.

Foolproof Quiche

1 deep-dish 9-inch baked pie shell
4 ounces sharp Cheddar cheese, coarsely grated
4 ounces Swiss cheese, coarsely grated
3 eggs, beaten
1 cup heavy cream
¼ teaspoon white or black pepper
¼ teaspoon nutmeg
Paprika

Arrange the cheeses in the pie shell.

In a saucepan heat the eggs, cream, pepper, and nutmeg, stirring constantly until hot. Pour the egg mixture over the cheeses, stirring to mix evenly. Sprinkle with the paprika. Bake in a 350° oven for 30 minutes or until a knife inserted in the center comes out clean. Cool for 5 to 10 minutes, then slice.

Note: Ham bits, bacon, or diced vegetables can be added to the cheeses.

Serves 6 to 8 (or 4 to 6 if using a standard pie shell).

Silver Maple Lodge

Rural Route 1, Box 8
Fairlee, Vermont 05045
(802) 333-4326
(800) 666-1946

Situated in the upper Connecticut River valley just south of Fairlee village, Silver Maple Lodge was built as a farmhouse in 1855. Converted in 1925 to a seven-bedroom inn, it was expanded to ten bedrooms. Later five cottages were added, with knotty pine walls and wide board floors.

On the wraparound porch, guests gather to relax and visit; on the side lawn they can play horseshoes, croquet, badminton, or shuffleboard. The Appalachian Trail passes within nine miles of the lodge, and hot air balloon flights, gliding, and flying rides and lessons are available at nearby Post Mills Airport.

Strawberry Swirl Coffee Cake

¾ cup butter or margarine, softened
1½ cups sugar
3 eggs
1½ teaspoons vanilla extract

❧ ❧ ❧

3 cups all-purpose flour
1½ teaspoons baking powder
1½ teaspoons baking soda
¼ teaspoon salt
1½ cups sour cream

❧ ❧ ❧

Strawberry preserves
Sugar

Grease two 9x5-inch loaf pans. In a large mixer bowl combine the butter, sugar, eggs, and vanilla, beating on medium speed for 2 minutes or 300 vigorous strokes by hand.

Alternately mix in the flour, baking powder, baking soda, and salt with the sour cream. Spoon most of the batter into the prepared pans, reserving just enough to cover the tops. Spread a thin layer of preserves onto the batter and swirl with a fork. Do not blend into the batter. Cover with the reserved batter and dust tops lightly with sugar. Bake in a 350° oven for 1 hour or until a toothpick inserted in the center comes out clean. Cool in the pans.

Note: If using self-rising flour, omit the baking powder, baking soda, and salt.

Serves 14 to 16.

Silver Maple Lodge

Spicy Orange Nut Bread

- 1 cup ground orange rind (2 to 3 oranges chopped or ground in a blender)
- ½ cup water
- 2 tablespoons sugar

&ampamp; &ampamp; &ampamp;

- 2¼ cups all-purpose flour
- 1 cup sugar
- 2½ teaspoons baking powder
- ¾ teaspoon salt
- ½ teaspoon cinnamon
- ⅔ cup milk
- 3 tablespoons oil or melted shortening
- 2 eggs
- ½ teaspoon orange extract
- ¼ teaspoon vanilla extract
- 2 drops almond extract
- 2 drops lemon extract
- ¾ cup coarsely chopped walnuts

&ampamp; &ampamp; &ampamp;

- ½ teaspoon cinnamon
- 2 tablespoons sugar

Grease two 8x4-inch loaf pans. In a small saucepan combine the orange rind, water, and 2 tablespoons of sugar. Heat to boiling, then simmer for 10 to 15 minutes until the rind is tender and the water has almost been absorbed. Cool.

In a mixing bowl sift together the flour, 1 cup of sugar, baking powder, salt, and ½ teaspoon of cinnamon. Add the milk, oil, eggs, and flavorings. Beat at low speed just until well mixed. Stir in the orange peel and walnuts. Divide the batter evenly into the prepared pans.

In a small bowl combine ½ teaspoon of cinnamon and 2 tablespoons of sugar. Sprinkle the batter generously with the topping. Bake in a 350° oven for 45 to 50 minutes. Turn out and cool on a rack.

Serves 14 to 16.

Fair Meadows Farm Bed and Breakfast

Box 430
Franklin, Vermont 05457
(802) 285-2132

At this inn nestled in the northwest corner of Vermont guests are offered peace, quiet, and comfort. The century-old farmhouse that is surrounded by meadows and woods contains four large bedrooms. Guests are invited to make themselves at home, visiting, watching television, or playing the piano. Bicycling, hiking, and swimming are accessible nearby.

Rhubarb and Raisin Muffins

- ⅓ cup Crisco or margarine
- ⅔ cup sugar
- 2 eggs, well beaten
- 1¾ cups all-purpose flour
- ¾ teaspoon baking soda
- 1¼ teaspoons cream of tartar
- 1 cup rhubarb sauce
- ½ cup raisins

In a large bowl cream together the Crisco and sugar until fluffy. Beat in the eggs. In a separate bowl combine the flour, baking soda, and cream of tartar. Add the flour mixture to the creamed mixture alternately with the rhubarb sauce. Stir in the raisins. Pour the batter in muffin tins. Bake in a 350° oven for 20 minutes.

Makes 12 muffins.

&ampamp; &ampamp; &ampamp; &ampamp; &ampamp;

Blueberry Hill

Goshen, Vermont 05733
(802) 247-6735
(802) 247-6535
(800) 448-0707

Nestled at the foot of Romance Mountain in Green Mountain National Forest, Blueberry Hill is a restored 1813 farmhouse. Its guest rooms, each with private bath, are filled with antiques, warm quilts, and homey atmosphere. At dinner, guests are seated in the candlelit communal dining room. The four sumptuous courses are served in an unhurried, Old-World style. After dinner, guests lounge away the cool mountain evenings before the sitting room fire or snuggle under a handmade quilt to read their favorite book. There are no radios, televisions, or bedside telephones to disturb the tranquility of the inn.

Mussel Soup

1 onion, diced
2 shallots, minced
3 cloves garlic, minced
2 carrots, diced
3 stalks celery, diced
2 red bell peppers, diced
¼ to ½ cup all-purpose flour
Reduction of crayfish or duck stock with white wine
Thyme, basil, sorrel to taste
Salt
Freshly ground pepper
1 peck steamed mussels, removed from shells
Heavy cream
Worcestershire sauce (optional)

In a soup pot sauté the onion, shallots, garlic, carrots, celery, and bell pepper until translucent. Add the flour, stirring to incorporate with the vegetables. Cook until there is no longer a flour taste. Gradually whisk in the stock, bring to a boil, and sim-

mer for 30 minutes. Add the herbs, salt, and pepper to taste. In a blender combine the mixture with ¼ of the mussels and purée. Return the purée to the soup pot and add more stock or heavy cream to the desired consistency. Bring to a boil and add the Worcestershire sauce, if desired. Stir in the remaining mussels.
Serves 10.

Canard en Croute

½ cup butter
1 garlic clove
2 shallots, minced
1 red bell pepper, seeded and minced
4 ounces wild mushrooms, chopped
4 boned duck legs
4 ounces duck liver
¼ cup brandy
Basil
Thyme
Salt
Freshly ground pepper
White pepper (optional)
2 eggs
¼ cup heavy cream

&a &a &a

Puff pastry
Egg wash

In a sauté pan melt the butter. Add the garlic, shallots, red bell pepper, and mushrooms, cooking a few minutes. Add the duck meat and livers. Sauté until the meats are just cooked. Add the brandy and ignite. Add the basil, thyme, salt, and pepper to taste. Remove from heat and cool for several minutes. In a food processor purée the mixture. Add the eggs and heavy cream, then cool completely.

Cut four 6-inch circles of pastry. Divide the mixture into 4 portions, placing each portion in half of a circle. Fold over and crimp the edges with a fork. Brush with an egg wash and place a decorative design on the top with extra pastry. Brush again with the egg wash. Place on a baking sheet. Bake in a 425° oven for 20 minutes or until golden brown.
Serves 4.

Stuffed Saddle of Rabbit
with Pistachios and Apricots

1 rabbit

&a &a &a

1 shallot, minced
2 cloves garlic, minced
Sprigs of fresh thyme
1 tablespoon green peppercorns
Freshly ground nutmeg, to taste
Salt
Freshly ground pepper
3 tablespoons Madeira
2 tablespoons brandy or cognac
1 egg
3 tablespoons heavy cream
⅛ cup julienned dried apricots
2 tablespoons pistachios
Pernod Beurre Blanc (recipe follows)

Bone the rabbit and remove the front and hind legs. Carefully cut from the legs any usable meat, trimming the tendons and silver skin as necessary. In a food processor grind the meat a few portions at a time. In a large bowl combine the ground meat with the remaining ingredients. Refrigerate for 30 minutes.

Lay the saddle of the rabbit on a flat surface. Mound the meat stuffing in a cylinder down the center. Wrap with the side pieces. Secure with several pieces of butcher twine and wrap in aluminum foil. Place in a roasting pan. Bake in a 350° oven for 20 to 30 minutes until the center is done. Let rest for a few minutes before slicing. Serve with Pernod Beurre Blanc sauce.
Serves 4.

Pernod Beurre Blanc

Serve with Stuffed Saddle of Rabbit.

**Rabbit bones
2 carrots, chopped
2 stalks celery, chopped
1 onion, chopped
1 teaspoon juniper berries
Fresh thyme
1 teaspoon white peppercorns
2 cloves garlic, minced
1 shallot, minced
4 cups white wine
¼ cup Pernod
½ cup unsalted butter
Salt
Freshly ground white pepper**

The Inn at Woodchuck Hill Farm

Brown the rabbit bones in the oven. In a stock pot combine the browned bones with the carrots, celery, onions, juniper berries, thyme, peppercorns, garlic, and shallots. Cover with water and the wine. Bring to a boil and simmer for 2 hours. Strain and reduce to ½ cup. Add the Pernod and reduce to a glaze. Whisk in the butter, a little at a time, until all of it is incorporated. Season with salt and white pepper.

Makes about 1 cup.

The Inn at Woodchuck Hill Farm

Middletown Road
Grafton, Vermont 05146
(802) 843-2398

A fully restored circa 1790 farmhouse, this inn caters to those who enjoy the peace and quiet of rural New England. Situated on a hilltop, it is surrounded by two hundred acres of fields and woodlands, lawns and shrubbery. A large pond provides an area for swimming, and the gazebo is perfect for reading or contemplation. In addition to the six rooms upstairs in the main house, the inn has a studio room with a kitchen and bath and a fully restored barn that can accommodate as many as four persons. Guests are served a gourmet dinner by prior reservation.

Banana Orange Muffins

A "good for you" breakfast muffin.

**1½ cups all-purpose flour
½ cup sugar
3 teaspoons baking powder
¼ teaspoon salt
1 cup regular wheat germ
1 cup mashed bananas (2 small)
½ cup orange juice
¼ cup oil
2 eggs**

Grease muffin tins. In a medium bowl sift together the flour, sugar, baking powder, and salt. Stir in the wheat germ. In a separate bowl combine the bananas, orange juice, oil, and eggs. Make a well in the center of the dry ingredients and add the liquid mixture all at once. Stir just enough to blend. Fill the prepared muffin tins ¾ full. Bake in a 400° oven for 20 to 25 minutes.

Makes 18 muffins.

Pavlova

This was given to me by an Australian lady who had us to tea and served this wonderful and very impressive looking sweet.

**4 egg whites
1 cup superfine dessert sugar
1 tablespoon white vinegar
1 tablespoon cornstarch**

❧   ❧   ❧

**Whipped cream
Fresh fruit**

Line a cookie sheet with aluminum foil. In a medium bowl beat the egg whites until very stiff. Add ½ cup of the sugar, beating until completely dissolved. Add the remaining sugar and beat well for 3 minutes. Fold in the vinegar and cornstarch. On the prepared cookie sheet form the mixture into an 8-inch circle with the sides slightly higher. Bake in a 325° oven for 10 minutes. Reduce the oven temperature to 220° and bake for 20 to 30 more minutes until the outside is crisp and sounds hollow when tapped. Turn off the oven and open door. Let the dessert cool in the oven. (The center will crack when cool.) Fill with whipped cream and fruit, decorating the edge with fresh flowers. Serve with extra fruit.

Note: This freezes well.

Serves 6 to 8.

Carrot Soup

    5 tablespoons butter or margarine
    1 large leek, cleaned and chopped
       (or 2 onions)
    2 medium potatoes, peeled and
       cubed
    2 pounds carrots, peeled and sliced
    6 cups chicken stock
    Pinch thyme
    3 teaspoons curry powder
    Salt
    Freshly ground pepper
    Chives, parsley, or coriander to
       garnish

In a soup pot melt 2 tablespoons of butter. Cook the leek for 10 minutes, stirring often until it is soft but not brown. Add the potatoes, carrots, and chicken stock. Cover and simmer for 45 minutes. In a blender or food processor purée the mixture until smooth. Add the remaining butter and seasonings. Sprinkle with chopped chives, parsley, or coriander to serve.

Serves 6 to 8.

The Vermont Inn

Route 4
Killington, Vermont 05751
(802) 775-0708

Nestled in the beautiful Green Mountains and surrounded by spectacular mountain views, the Vermont Inn has a country sophistication of its own. This area of the mountains offers the East's best skiing, as well as year-round activities and outdoor sports. The guest rooms have the look of warm country charm; most have private baths and a few share facilities. Built as a farmhouse in the 1840s, the Vermont Inn is known for its fine dining and lodging. The original wood beams are exposed in the living room where guests may enjoy congenial company by the warmth of the fire. The lounge also provides a cozy atmosphere where guests can gather. Recipes courtesy of Chef Stephen Hatch.

Veal Marie

    3 1-ounce slices veal leg
    Flour
    Olive oil
    1 clove garlic, minced
    1 shallot, diced
    ¼ cup sliced mushrooms
    2 artichoke hearts, quartered
    2 ounces Madeira wine
    ½ cup demi glace or veal stock
    Salt and pepper
    ¼ cup shredded Monterey Jack
       cheese

Pound the veal slices, dredge in flour, and sauté in the oil until brown on one side. Turn over and add the garlic, shallots, mushrooms, and artichoke hearts. Add the wine, flambé, and add the demi glace. Season with the salt and pepper. Top with the cheese and finish cooking under a broiler until the cheese is browned.

Serves 1.

Tenderloin of Pork Champignons

    4 1-ounce slices pork tenderloin
    Flour
    Butter
    ½ cup sliced mushrooms
    2 sprigs fresh thyme, chopped
    1 teaspoon chopped fresh parsley
    2 ounces Harvey's Bristol Cream
    1 teaspoon finely chopped leek
    ½ cup heavy cream
    Salt and pepper

Pound the pork tenderloin slices and dredge in flour. In a skillet sauté in a small amount of butter until the pork is browned on both sides. Add the mushrooms, thyme, parsley, Harvey's Bristol Cream, and flambé. When the alcohol has burned off, add the leek and heavy cream, simmering until the cream is reduced to a shiny sauce. Season with the salt and pepper.

Serves 1.

The Highland House: A Country Inn

Route 100
Londonderry, Vermont 05148
(802) 824-3019

The Highland House is an 1842 white colonial inn, with swimming pool and tennis court, set on thirty-two acres. It has seventeen rooms, fifteen with private baths and four with private sitting rooms. Rates include a full breakfast. Special features include the expansive maple-shaded lawn, the fisherman's net hammock, croquet, and horseshoes. The Highland House is open to the public for dinner Wednesday through Sunday by reservation. It provides classic dining with homemade soups, breads, and desserts.

Kentucky Derby Pie

¾ cup sugar
½ cup butter, melted
½ cup all-purpose flour
2 eggs, slightly beaten
¾ cup semi-sweet chocolate chips
1 cup chopped walnuts
1 tablespoon bourbon

❧ ❧ ❧

1 9-inch unbaked pie shell

In a medium bowl combine all the ingredients and pour into the pie shell. Bake in a 350° oven for 30 minutes.
Serves 8.

Corn Chowder Soup

3 or 4 strips bacon (cut into ½-inch pieces)
2 medium onions, thinly sliced or chopped
2 to 3 medium potatoes, diced
½ teaspoon salt
1 17-ounce can cream-style corn
½ to 1 cup heavy cream
Pepper

In a skillet fry the bacon until brown. Crumble into bits and set aside. Sauté the onions in the bacon drippings until soft, but do not burn. Add the potatoes, salt, and just enough water to cover. Simmer until the potatoes are tender. Add the corn and bacon bits, continuing to simmer about 10 minutes. Add the heavy cream and additional salt and pepper to taste. Heat thoroughly, but do not boil.
Serves 6.

Pesto

Serve over spaghetti or tortellini.

2 cups fresh basil
½ cup oil
⅓ cup pine nuts
1 large clove garlic
1 teaspoon salt
½ teaspoon pepper
3 ounces Parmesan cheese

In a food processor combine the basil, oil, pine nuts, garlic, salt, and pepper. Pour into a bowl and stir in the cheese. Cover and refrigerate.
Makes 2 cups.

The Governor's Inn

86 Main Street
Ludlow, Vermont 05149
(802) 228-8830

Built originally by William Wallace Stickney, a governor of Vermont, as his private dwelling, the Governor's Inn stands as a classic example of the fine craftsmanship of the late Victorian period (circa 1890). As a stylish, romantic, intimate village inn, it now has become a haven for enjoying life's pleasures and a base for exploring Vermont. The Governor's Inn is less than one mile from Okemo Mountain, popular for its skiing facilities. At this inn guests find excellent food, a cozy room, friendliness, and warm, generous hospitality.

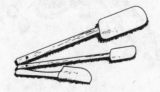

Apricot Victorian

The Governor's Inn has won a very special award for this recipe—1984 Smuckers: Best In New England Country Inn Cooking. Enjoy!

1 20-ounce can apricots in heavy syrup, drained
1 12-ounce jar apricot preserves
Juice of ½ lemon, seeds removed
½ pint heavy whipping cream for garnish

In a food processor purée the drained fruit. In a saucepan heat the preserves until melted and very liquid, then strain out the solids. In a medium bowl combine the preserves, fruit, and lemon juice, stirring until completely blended. Pour the mixture into a 9-inch metal cake pan and freeze overnight. Scoop the dessert into stemmed glasses and top with the heavy cream.
Note: The cream will freeze and glaze the Victorian. This recipe keeps well in the freezer.
Serves 4 to 8.

The Governor's Inn Potato Confetti

Winner of the 1988 Uncle Ben's Potato Division Contest. Serve as a side dish with lamb, roast beef, baked chicken, or at a brunch with scrambled eggs and pan-fried trout.

Thick peeling of 1 large zucchini
6 new carrots
1 to 2 leeks (yellow and white part only)
2 to 3 tablespoons butter

❧ ❧ ❧

6 eggs, slightly beaten
½ teaspoon nutmeg
¼ teaspoon white pepper
Salt (optional)
8 cups dry mashed potato
Heavy cream (optional)
½ cup sour cream for garnish (optional)

Butter twelve ½-cup straight-sided baking cups and place in a roasting pan half full of water. Peel the skin from the zucchini, cut it into julienne strips, and cut it crosswise to make an even dice. Set aside. Wash and scrub the carrots, cut into julienne strips, and cut crosswise to make an even dice. Set aside. Wash the leek pieces and julienne into ½-inch long strips. Set aside. In a sauté pan melt the butter and sauté the carrots over low-medium heat for 5 minutes until they shine and seem a little limp. Add the zucchini and leeks, continuing to sauté for 3 minutes and stirring often. Remove the vegetables with a slotted spoon and set aside.

In a medium bowl combine the eggs, nutmeg, white pepper, and salt, whipping with a whisk to blend well. Add the mixture to the mashed potato, mixing well to blend. If the mashed potato mixture is too stiff, add the heavy cream by the tablespoon until it is the consistency of softly whipped cream. Fold in the sautéed vegetables. Divide the mixture into the prepared custard cups, smoothing the surface with a knife. Bake in a 350° oven for 35 minutes until the potato custard is set. Remove from the oven and allow the custard cups to rest in the water bath for about 15 minutes. Invert and remove from the baking cups to serve. Garnish with a dollop of sour cream, a few reserved sautéed vegetables, parsley, and a bright orange nasturtium flower.

Note: This side-dish is designed to add height to the plate and add an interesting touch of color. It combines both potato and vegetable into one very creative presentation. Prepare enough mashed potato to equal 8 cups. If using packaged instant potato, follow the manufacturer's instructions using ½ to ¾ cup less water and use heavy cream instead of milk. If preparing your own mashed potatoes, bake Idaho potatoes and use heavy cream in the mashing. In either case, use less liquid than usual to produce a rather dry mashed potato. The confetti cups can be frozen after baking and reheated.
Serves 12.

Rice Salad Village Inn

1986 Winner Uncle Ben's Salad Division.

2 cups long-grain white rice
½ cup butter
Salt and pepper
½ cup toasted slivered almonds
1 jar marinated artichoke hearts, drained and cut lengthwise into quarters
½ cup cooked fresh peas (do not use canned)
¼ cup chopped pimento
1 bunch scallions, thinly sliced
½ pound marinated mushrooms, sliced
½ cup sliced black olives
½ pound salami, diced
½ cup freshly chopped parsley

🌿 🌿 🌿

1½ teaspoons dried basil
1½ teaspoons dried tarragon
1 teaspoon Dijon mustard
¼ cup red wine vinegar
¼ cup salad oil
Salt and pepper

Oil a ring mold or a bundt pan. In a large pot of boiling salted water add the rice. Cook on low heat for 18 minutes. Drain and rinse with warm

water. Add the butter, salt, and pepper. Dry in a 250° oven for 30 minutes, stirring occasionally with a fork. In a large bowl combine the rice with the almonds, artichoke hearts, peas, pimento, scallions, mushrooms, olives, salami, and parsley.

In a separate bowl combine the basil, tarragon, Dijon mustard, wine vinegar, oil, salt, and pepper for a vinaigrette dressing. Add to the rice mixture, mixing well. Pack the mixture tightly into the prepared ring mold and refrigerate overnight. Unmold and garnish with watercress and cherry tomatoes.

Note: This recipe can be doubled.
Serves 12.

Gram's Graham Bread

1987 Yankee Cook-Off Quick Breads Winner.

1½ cups graham flour (or King Arthur whole wheat flour)
2 cups King Arthur flour
½ cup brown sugar
½ cup Grandma's molasses
2 cups soured milk (to sour, place 2 tablespoons cider vinegar in a 2-cup measure, fill with whole milk, and let stand for 5 minutes)
2 teaspoons baking soda
1 teaspoon salt

Grease a large loaf pan, 3 or 4 small loaf pans, or 40 miniature muffin tins. In a large bowl combine all the ingredients and beat on medium speed with an electric mixer until just blended. Pour the batter into the prepared pans. Bake in a 350° oven for 45 minutes for a large loaf, 30 minutes for small loaves, or 20 minutes for miniature muffins, until a toothpick inserted in the center comes out clean. Cool in the pan for 5 minutes, then turn out on a wire rack.

Note: This recipe doubles well.
Makes 1 large loaf, 3 or 4 small loaves, or 40 miniature muffins.

Scallops, Crabmeat, and Shrimp
in a Brandied Cream Sauce

1988 Domaines OTT International Chefs Challenge Winner, from Chef Deedy Marble.

- **1½ pounds fresh sea scallops**
- **½ pound crabmeat (carefully picked over)**

  🐚 🐚 🐚

- **½ cup unsalted butter**
- **6 shallots, sliced**
- **½ teaspoon mild curry powder**
- **¼ teaspoon red cayenne pepper**
- **½ cup all-purpose flour**
- **½ cup dry white wine**
- **½ cup dry sherry**
- **1 ounce brandy**
- **¼ teaspoon white pepper (or to taste)**
- **Nutmeg**
- **¾ teaspoon salt or chicken bouillon granules (or 1 tablespoon moist chicken base)**
- **2 cups sour cream**

  🐚 🐚 🐚

- **1 sleeve buttery crackers, crumbled**
- **¼ cup butter, melted**
- **12 large cooked shrimp**
- **Paprika for garnish**

In a medium bowl combine the scallops and crabmeat. Using the back of a fork mash the scallops and break up the crabmeat. Set aside.

In a heavy saucepan melt ½ cup of butter and sauté the shallots until just lightly browned. Add the curry powder and red pepper, stirring to cook slightly. Add the flour and stir well to create a roux. Add the white wine, sherry, and brandy. Sprinkle with the white pepper, nutmeg, and salt. Stir in the sour cream, mixing well. Simmer for 30 minutes over low heat, stirring occasionally. Pour over the scallop-crabmeat mixture and ladle into scallop shells.

In a small bowl combine the cracker crumbs with ¼ cup of melted butter. Place two shrimp on the top of each scallop mixture, and sprinkle liberally with the buttered crumbs and paprika. Bake in a 400° oven for 20 minutes.

Serves 6.

The Governor's Inn Tea Dates

1987 Presentation of Afternoon Tea, First Prize Winner.

- **1 pound pitted dates**
- **1 cup chopped almonds**
- **Salt**
- **2 teaspoons unsalted butter**
- **1 tablespoon honey**

Stuff the dates with the almonds and roll lightly in the salt. In a small heavy-bottomed saucepan melt the butter. Add the honey and gently bring to a boil. Fry the dates in the mixture and serve at once.

Serves 6 to 8.

Orange Nut Bread

October 1989 Yankee Food Festival, Great New England Cook Winner. Lovely for a leisurely breakfast or brunch.

- **2 cups sifted all-purpose flour**
- **½ teaspoon salt**
- **1 teaspoon baking powder**
- **¼ teaspoon baking soda**
- **⅔ cup sugar**
- **⅓ cup unsalted butter or margarine, room temperature**
- **2 eggs**
- **½ cup freshly squeezed orange juice, with pulp**
- **½ cup water**
- **½ teaspoon vanilla extract**
- **½ teaspoon orange extract**
- **1 cup chopped walnuts**

  🐚 🐚 🐚

- **Orange Cream Cheese Spread (see recipe)**

Grease three 3½x6-inch loaf pans. In a medium bowl sift together the flour, salt, baking powder, and baking soda. In a large bowl cream together the sugar and butter. Beat in the eggs, one at a time. Stir in the orange juice and water alternately with the flour mixture. Add the extracts and walnuts. Pour the batter into the prepared loaf pans. Bake in a 350° oven for 40 to 45 minutes. Remove from the pans, cool, and wrap. Chill well before thinly slicing. Serve with Orange Cream Cheese Spread.

Makes 3 small loaves.

Orange Cream Cheese Spread

- **3 8-ounce packages cream cheese, room temperature (or Tofutti cream cheese)**
- **1 navel orange, cut in chunks with peel**
- **3 to 4 tablespoons confectioners' sugar**

In a food processor with a steel blade combine the cream cheese, orange, and confectioners' sugar. Refrigerate for several hours to blend the flavors. Spread on thinly sliced Orange Nut Bread and make little sandwiches. Arrange on a doily-lined serving plate and garnish with orange nasturtiums and sprigs of fresh mint.

Makes about 4 cups.

The Wildflower Inn

Star Route
Lyndonville, Vermont 05851
(802) 626-8310

Situated in Vermont's secluded northeast area, the Wildflower Inn is part of a 500-acre farm. The inn has fifteen bedrooms and five suites with a scenic view from every window. The cross-country ski trails that run throughout the property are connected to the inn. Downhill skiing at Burke Mountain is just four miles away. Whether served in the dining room or on the dining porch, full country breakfasts are hearty and delicious, with fresh eggs, homemade breads, and fresh fruits. A specialty of the house is the pancakes; made from a mixture of several grains, they are surprisingly light and fluffy.

Maple Wheat Germ Bread

2 cups all-purpose flour
¾ cup wheat germ
1½ teaspoons baking powder
½ teaspoon baking soda
2 eggs
1 cup milk
⅔ cup maple syrup
⅓ cup oil

Grease a 9x5-inch loaf pan. In a medium bowl combine the flour, wheat germ, baking powder, and baking soda. In a separate bowl combine the eggs, milk, syrup, and oil. Combine the dry and liquid ingredients, mixing well. Pour the batter into the prepared pan. Bake in a 350° oven for 45 minutes.

Makes 1 loaf.

The Inn at Manchester

Box 41
Manchester, Vermont 05254
(802) 362-1793

Four beautiful acres surround the Inn at Manchester. Enhanced by a grove of birch trees, a brook (home of two resident trout), and mountains in the background, this restored Victorian mansion has nineteen bedrooms, thirteen with private baths. The three sitting areas for guests include a television and game room. In winter guests sip their wine and munch on crackers and cheese by the fireplaces. A full country breakfast is served, including cottage cakes, omelets, apple or blueberry pancakes, homemade breads and granola, fresh juice or fruit, and Vermont maple syrup.

Vegetable Pancakes

Great for a breakfast or dinner as a side dish.

1 medium potato
3 small summer squash
2 small zucchini
1 small onion
2 eggs
¼ cup all-purpose flour
Salt and pepper

Peel the potato, summer squash, zucchini, and onion, and grate all the vegetables into a bowl. Add the egg, flour, salt, and pepper. Fry on a griddle over medium heat until golden brown.

Serves 4 to 6.

Aunt Rose's Lemon Chiffon Pie

2¼ teaspoons unflavored gelatin
½ cup cold water
6 eggs, separated
7 to 8 tablespoons fresh lemon
 juice
¾ cup sugar
Grated rind of 1 lemon
  ❧ ❧ ❧
½ cup sugar
¼ teaspoon salt
  ❧ ❧ ❧
1 10-inch baked pie crust
1 pint heavy cream

Soften the gelatin in the water. In a double boiler beat the egg yolks slightly and add the lemon juice, ¾ cup of sugar, and rind, stirring constantly until thickened. Add the gelatin mixture and refrigerate until cool.

Beat the egg whites until stiff. When the gelatin mixture begins to thicken fold in the egg whites, ½ cup of sugar, and salt. Pile the chiffon mixture into the prepared pie crust, chill, and top with whipped cream.

Serves 8.

Cheese Ball

½ green pepper
1 small onion
16 stuffed olives
1 8-ounce package cream cheese, softened
Chopped walnuts

In a food processor chop the green pepper, onion, and olives. Mix in the cream cheese. Shape into a ball, roll in the walnuts, and chill.

Serves 10 to 12.

Swift House Inn

25 Stewart Lane
Middlebury, Vermont 05753
(802) 388-9925

The Swift House is a village inn in a Federal-style home with eight elaborately carved fireplaces, all working, and some of them in the guest rooms. Furnished with Queen Anne and Chippendale antiques, it also has four-poster beds and Oriental rugs. Dinner by candlelight is served in front of the fireplace on white linen tablecloths, with real silver. Spacious lawns and formal gardens form the view from the terraces. Recreational opportunities include miles of hiking trails, trout fishing in Otter Creek, and swimming and sailing at nearby lakes. Golf and skiing are nearby. Guests enjoy a dinner menu that changes nightly, offering the finest selections.

Veal Medallions
with Country Ham, Havarti, and Artichoke Purée

8 veal scallops (about 1 pound), pounded thin between sheets of waxed paper
½ teaspoon salt
¼ teaspoon freshly ground black pepper
1½ tablespoons unsalted butter
1½ tablespoons extra virgin olive oil
1 6-ounce jar marinated artichoke hearts, drained and puréed
4 thin slices smoked country ham, halved crosswise
4 ounces Havarti or Provolone cheese, grated (1 cup)

Sprinkle the veal scallops with the salt and pepper. In a large sauté pan heat the butter and olive oil. Add the veal and sauté for 3 minutes until browned on both sides. Transfer the scallops to a large baking pan. Spread a thin layer of the artichoke purée on each scallop, top with a piece of ham, and sprinkle with cheese. Broil for 3 to 4 minutes until the cheese is golden.

Serves 4.

Swift House Inn

Grilled Norwegian Salmon Fillet
with Golden Chantrelle Mushroom Beurre Blanc

4 5- to 7-ounce salmon fillets, deboned
Extra virgin olive oil
Salt
Freshly ground pepper
1 pound Golden Chantrelle mushrooms, thinly sliced
6 large shallots, peeled and finely diced
6 ounces dry white wine
½ cup unsalted butter, softened

Baste the salmon fillets with the olive oil and sprinkle with salt and pepper. Grill about 3 to 5 minutes per side for medium-rare, or continue grilling to the desired doneness. In a sauté pan heat 1 tablespoon of olive oil. Add the mushrooms, shallots, and additional salt and pepper to taste. When the mushrooms are translucent, add the white wine and reduce by 75%. Remove the pan from the heat and slowly whisk in the butter, stirring constantly until the butter is incorporated. Serve the sauce with the salmon.
Serves 4.

Poppy Seed Bread

2½ cups sugar
2 cups butter, melted and cooled
½ cup maple syrup
2 cups half and half
5 large eggs
2 teaspoons vanilla extract

&ã &ã &ã

¾ cup poppy seeds
4½ cups all-purpose flour
4½ teaspoons baking powder

Grease 3 loaf pans. In a large bowl combine the sugar, butter, syrup, half and half, eggs, and vanilla. Mix together well.
Gently stir in the poppy seeds, flour, and baking powder just until

moistened. Do not overmix. Divide the batter between the prepared pans. Bake in a 350° oven for 60 minutes until done.
Makes 3 loaves.

Apple Cranberry Tart
with Rum Raisins

¾ cup fresh cranberries
⅓ cup sugar

&ã &ã &ã

¼ cup raisins
¼ cup Myers Rum

&ã &ã &ã

2 teaspoons lemon peel
⅓ cup blanched almonds
⅔ cup sugar
8 apples
1 tablespoon all-purpose flour
1 teaspoon cornstarch
½ teaspoon cinnamon
1 tablespoon lemon juice
2 10-inch unbaked pie shells
Lattice crust for two 10-inch pies

&ã &ã &ã

1 egg
1 tablespoon milk
½ teaspoon cinnamon
1 tablespoon sugar

In a food processor with a metal blade chop the cranberries, on-off 2 times. In a small bowl combine the cranberries with ⅓ cup of sugar and let stand for 1 hour.
Plump the raisins in the rum. In a food processor with a metal blade chop the lemon peel and almonds with ⅔ cup of sugar. Slice the apples. In a large bowl combine the lemon peel mixture, flour, cornstarch, and ½ teaspoon of cinnamon. Add the apples, cranberries, raisins, rum, and lemon juice. Fill the prepared pie shells and top with a lattice crust.
Combine the egg and milk and brush over the crust. Combine ½ teaspoon of cinnamon and 1 tablespoon of sugar, and sprinkle over the crust. Bake in a 425° oven for 20 minutes, then reduce the temperature to 350° and bake an additional 40 minutes.
Makes 2 pies.

The Hortonville Inn

Rural Delivery 1, Box 14
Mount Holly, Vermont 05758
(802) 259-2587

The Hortonville Inn, a short distance from the Okemo Mountain ski area, enjoys a picturesque setting and boasts thirteen landscaped and wooded acres for its guests. Trails abound for cross-country skiing. The rooms in the 150-year-old home are large, airy, and homey. Each has a radio, television, and VCR, and the inn has an entertainment area with a video machine and a library of over 200 movies, games, and many books. The fireplace is an ideal place to warm oneself with a cup of hot chocolate or tea and a few chocolate chip cookies. A full three-course breakfast is served.

Hot Mulled Cider à la Hortonville

Warm and soothing after a cold day on the slopes.

1 gallon cider
1 cup brown sugar
½ cup butter
1 stick cinnamon, broken
2 teaspoons whole cloves

In a large pot bring the cider to a boil. Add the remaining ingredients and simmer over low heat, stirring until the sugar dissolves.
Makes about 1 gallon.

&ã &ã &ã &ã &ã

maining raspberries, sugar, egg whites, lemon juice, and salt, beating for 15 minutes or until stiff. Fold in the whipped cream and almonds. Mound in the prepared pie shell and freeze until firm. Garnish with the reserved raspberries and sprigs of mint.

Serves 6 to 8.

The Hortonville Inn

Polynesian Crab Spread

A fancy cracker spread.

    2 cups sour cream
    2 teaspoons curry powder
    1 teaspoon onion powder
    ⅛ teaspoon black pepper
    ½ teaspoon salt
    1 cup shredded coconut
    ½ pound cooked crabmeat, flaked

In a large bowl combine all the ingredients, mixing well. Chill. Serve on crackers or Melba toast.

Makes about 3 cups.

Royal Granola

Granola fit for a king.

    2 cups shredded coconut
    7 cups rolled oats
    1 cup sesame seeds
    1 cup wheat germ
    1 cup sunflower seeds
    1 cup cashews
    1 teaspoon cinnamon
    ¼ cup carob powder
    1 cup sliced dates
        ❧ ❧ ❧
    4 cups honey
    1 tablespoon vanilla extract
    1 cup pure oil
        ❧ ❧ ❧
    1 cup raisins

Oil shallow baking pans. In a large bowl combine the dry ingredients and dried fruits, except the raisins. In a small bowl combine the honey, vanilla, and oil, and pour over the dry mixture. Spread no more than ½-inch thick into the prepared pans. Bake in a 350° oven for 20 minutes or until evenly browned, stirring after 10 minutes. Do not overbake. Add the raisins and cool.

Note: Recipe can be divided in half. Makes about 20 cups.

Frozen Raspberry Pie

    ½ teaspoon almond extract
    Pastry for 1 9-inch pie shell
        ❧ ❧ ❧
    1 10-ounce package frozen
        raspberries, thawed
    1 cup sugar
    2 egg whites, at room temperature
    1 tablespoon lemon juice
    Dash salt
    1 cup whipping cream, whipped
    ¼ cup chopped roasted almonds
    Mint sprigs for garnish

Add the almond extract to the pastry dough and bake the pie shell.

Reserve a few raspberries for garnish. In a large bowl combine the re-

Brookside Farms

Highway 22A
Orwell, Vermont 05760
(802) 948-2727

Shimmering white Ionic columns grace the front of this stately mansion that dates back to the eighteenth century. Meticulously restored and maintained, this fabulous showplace offers a combination of yesterday's elegance and today's convenience. A three-hundred-acre working farm, it has many animals, maple syrup production, well manicured grounds, and spectacular views. In the main house, guests have access to a ten-thousand-volume library, a comfortable den with television and game tables, and classically decorated rooms. Nearby are several miles of cross-country skiing and hiking trails.

Chicken Grenadine

A fabulous party dish!

    1 cup all-purpose flour
    1 teaspoon chopped garlic
    1 teaspoon savory salt
    1 whole chicken, cut into serving
        pieces
    ½ cup butter

    🍃 🍃 🍃

    1 large onion, chopped
    1 large can sliced mushrooms,
        drained
    1½ to 2 cups grenadine syrup
    1 cup brandy
    2 tablespoons turmeric

    🍃 🍃 🍃

    Flat noodles

In a large shaking bag combine the flour, garlic, and salt. Coat each piece of chicken thoroughly with the seasoned flour. In a heavy skillet melt the butter and brown the chicken on both sides.

In a deep ovenproof baking dish place a layer of chicken and half the onions and mushrooms. In a small bowl combine the grenadine and brandy. Pour half the mixture over the chicken. Repeat the layers of chicken, onions, mushrooms, and liquid. Bake covered in a 350° oven for 1 to 1½ hours, basting every 30 minutes with the liquid. Serve over flat noodles.

Serves 4 to 6.

Yankees' Northview Bed and Breakfast

Rural Delivery 2, Box 1000
Plainfield, Vermont 05667
(802) 454-7191

Northview is a nine-room colonial home set on a hill and surrounded by stone walls and white fences. The location assures guests of enough quiet to enjoy the sounds of the seasons, while being close to Montpelier, the state capital, and to Barre, the home of the world's largest granite quarry. Excellent sports and recreational opportunities, as well as many unique points of interest (including historic Kent Corner and Museum) are within easy reach. The rooms, many with hand-stenciled walls, are furnished with antiques and reproductions. Three guest rooms share a full bath. One double-bedded corner room has a canopied rope bed; another boasts a hand-crocheted bedspread and quilts. The third room with twin beds has a large hooked rug done in dusty roses. Guests are greeted with fresh flowers and begin each morning with a hearty breakfast complete with homemade pastries, muffins, and jams. Often breakfast is served outside on the garden patio overlooking the meadows and mountains; in cooler weather it is served close to the pot-belly stove in the large kitchen or in the stenciled dining room.

Raspberry Orange Muffins

    2 cups all-purpose flour
    ¼ cup sugar
    3 teaspoons baking powder
    1 egg
    ¾ cup milk
    ⅓ cup oil
    ½ cup frozen whole raspberries
    1 teaspoon grated orange rind

Grease muffin tins. In a large bowl combine all the ingredients, stirring just until well blended. Pour the batter into the prepared muffin tins and freeze until needed. Bake in a 375° oven for 25 to 30 minutes.

Note: This "make ahead and freeze" method is great!

Serves 12.

Placidia Farm Bed and Breakfast

Rural Delivery 1, Box 275
Randolph, Vermont 05060
(802) 728-9883

This hand-hewn log house was used as a weekend retreat by the hosts before they decided to open it to travelers. Its large bedroom has a double bed and private bath; rollaway cots and room fans are available as requested. The living room, with its television, stereo, and radio, provides a place for socializing. Breakfast is served on the sun porch, with the hosts joining guests for coffee and conversation once the meal is served. Local activities include hiking and cross-country skiing on the property. Pets are not welcome; nonsmokers are preferred.

Chicken Breasts Supreme

    3 chicken breasts, halved and
        skinned
    Salt and pepper
    Paprika
    3 tablespoons butter

    🍃 🍃 🍃

    1 can cream of mushroom soup
    1 4-ounce can mushrooms, drained
    ⅓ cup milk
    ½ cup grated Cheddar cheese
    2 tablespoons minced onion
    2 tablespoons Worcestershire sauce
    ⅔ cup sour cream

    🍃 🍃 🍃

    Rice

Season the chicken with the salt, pepper, and paprika. In a large skillet melt the butter and brown the chicken. Place the chicken in a baking dish.

In a saucepan combine the mushroom soup, mushrooms, milk, cheese, onion, and Worcestershire sauce. Cook over low heat until the cheese melts. Remove from the heat and stir in the sour cream, blending well. Pour over the chicken and cover tightly with foil. Bake in a 350° oven for 45 minutes. Uncover and bake an additional 30 minutes, basting occasionally with the sauce.

Serve with rice, using the sauce as a gravy.

Serves 4 to 6.

The Chipman Inn

Route 125
Ripton, Vermont 05766
(802) 388-2390

Built in 1828 by Daniel Chipman, a founder of Middlebury College, this inn is small, informal, and very comfortable. All nine guest rooms have private baths and attractive antiques. Public rooms include a lounge/bar where guests relax before a large Franklin fireplace. The dining room is lit by candles, warmed by a fireplace, and decorated with colonial stenciling. For guests who wish for more than relaxation, the immediate area offers year-round recreational sports and cultural events.

ಜಾ ಜಾ ಜಾ ಜಾ ಜಾ

Red Lentil Soup

1 medium onion, chopped
1 red pepper, chopped
2 cloves garlic, minced (or put through garlic press)
¼ cup margarine or butter
1 quart chicken stock
1 tomato, peeled, seeded, and chopped
3 slices bacon, cooked crisp and crumbled (optional)
1 cup red lentils (green or brown will do, but the color isn't as pretty)
Lemon juice
Salt and pepper
Paprika
Cumin (optional)

In a large saucepan sauté the onion, pepper, and garlic in the margarine until quite soft. Add the chicken stock, tomato, and bacon, and bring to a boil. Pick over and rinse the lentils, and add to the soup. Simmer at least 1 hour, adding water if necessary and stirring frequently. Season with lemon juice, salt, pepper, and cumin.

Note: The recipe can be tripled, and it freezes well.

Serves 5 to 6.

Cranapple Blue Ribbon Pie

Pastry for 9-inch double crust pie
1¾ to 2 cups sugar
⅓ cup all-purpose flour
3 cups sliced, pared apples
2 cups fresh or frozen cranberries
2 tablespoons butter

Prepare the pie crust. In a small bowl combine the sugar and flour. Beginning and ending with the apples, alternate layers of the apples, cranberries, and sugar mixture in the pie shell. Dot with the butter and cover with the top crust, seal, and flute the edges. Bake in a 425° oven for 40 to 50 minutes or until nicely browned.

Serves 6.

The Chipman Inn

Liberty Hill Farm

Rochester, Vermont 05767
(802) 767-3926

Liberty Hill is a 100-acre farm nestled between the White River and the Green Mountains. The house is 150 years old and contains five guest bedrooms and three shared baths. It has three living room areas, so there is plenty of space for guests to read, work jigsaw puzzles, compete in board games, or relax and watch the fire in the fireplace stove. Breakfast is served between 8:00 and 9:00 A.M. and consists of fruit, juice, coffee, tea, bacon, eggs, pancakes, sausage, and homemade coffee cakes. Dinner is served family-style at 6:00 P.M. and usually consists of a roast, three vegetables, salad, homemade breads, and homemade desserts.

This is a beautiful area providing plentiful diversion for the outdoor enthusiast, with many museums and cultural events that take place during the year. Sleigh rides are fun in the winter, and in the summer guests enjoy lighting bonfires on the beach. The White River is known for trout fishing, and the Green Mountain National Forest, stretching for miles behind the farm, has many old logging roads and country roads for hiking and cross-country skiing. Five major downhill ski areas are within thirty minutes of the farm.

Pumpkin Crescents

1 ¼-ounce package active dry yeast
1 cup warm water (110° to 115°)
1 cup canned pumpkin
⅓ cup sugar
½ cup shortening
1 egg
1½ teaspoons salt
5 to 6 cups all-purpose flour

🍂 🍂 🍂

Margarine or butter, softened

Grease a cookie sheet. In a large bowl dissolve the yeast in the warm water. Stir in the pumpkin, sugar, shortening, egg, salt, and 3 cups of flour. Beat until smooth. Mix in enough of the remaining flour to make the dough easy to handle. Turn the dough onto a lightly floured surface and knead about 5 minutes, until smooth and elastic. Place in a greased bowl, then turn greased-side up and cover. Let rise in a warm place for about 1 hour, until doubled.

Punch down dough and divide into 3 equal portions. On a floured surface roll each portion into a 12-inch circle. Spread with margarine and cut into 12 wedges. Beginning at the rounded edges tightly roll each wedge into a crescent. Place rolls with the points underneath and slightly curved on the prepared cookie sheet. Let rise 30 to 45 minutes until doubled. Bake in a 400° oven for 14 to 20 minutes until golden brown.

Makes 3 dozen rolls.

Apple Caramel Rolls

½ cup brown sugar, firmly packed
½ cup margarine or butter
36 pecan halves

🍂 🍂 🍂

2 cups Bisquick baking mix
½ cup cold water

🍂 🍂 🍂

2 tablespoons margarine or butter, softened
¼ cup brown sugar, firmly packed
1 cup finely chopped apple

Place 2 teaspoons of brown sugar, 2 teaspoons margarine, and 3 pecan halves in each of 12 muffin cups. Heat in a 450° oven until melted.

In a medium bowl combine the Bisquick and water until a soft dough forms. Beat vigorously for 20 strokes. On a floured cloth-covered board gently smooth the dough into a ball, and knead 5 times. Roll the dough into a 14x9-inch rectangle. Spread the dough with 2 tablespoons of margarine. Sprinkle with ¼ cup of brown sugar and the apple. Beginning on the longer side tightly roll the dough, sealing well by pinching the edge of the dough into the roll. Cut into twelve 1¼-inch slices. Place the slices cut-side down in the muffin cups. Bake in a 450° oven for 10 minutes. Immediately invert the pan onto a heatproof serving plate. Leave pan over the rolls for 1 minute before removing. Refrigerate any leftover rolls.

Makes 12 rolls.

California Casserole

2 10-ounce boxes frozen broccoli
2 10-ounce boxes frozen Brussel sprouts
2 10-ounce boxes frozen cauliflower

🍂 🍂 🍂

2 10½-ounce cans cream of mushroom soup
½ cup slivered almonds
1 cup sliced water chestnuts
2 cups shredded Velveeta cheese
1 cup French-fried onion rings

Cook the broccoli, Brussel sprouts, and cauliflower as directed on the package. Place vegetables in a baking dish.

In a large saucepan combine the mushroom soup, almonds, water chestnuts, and cheese. Heat until the cheese melts. Pour the sauce over the vegetables and sprinkle with the onion rings. Bake in a 350° oven for 30 minutes.

Serves 10 to 12.

Maple Pudding Cake

A pudding-like sauce forms as the cake bakes.

1½ cups all-purpose flour
¾ cup sugar
2 teaspoons baking powder
½ teaspoon salt
¾ cup milk
½ cup chopped walnuts

🍂 🍂 🍂

1½ cups maple syrup
¾ cup water
2 tablespoons butter

🍂 🍂 🍂

Whipped cream or ice cream

Grease an 8-inch square pan. In a medium bowl combine the flour, sugar, baking powder, salt, milk, and walnuts. Pour into the prepared pan.

In a small saucepan combine the syrup, water, and butter. Heat just until the butter melts. Pour the sauce over the cake batter, but do not stir. Bake in a 350° oven for 45 minutes. Serve warm with whipped cream or ice cream.

Serves 6.

the dining room, enhanced by Audubon prints and soft candlelight. The breakfast buffet is hearty enough for the big eater, yet tempting to those who rarely partake of this meal. The dinner menu changes nightly and includes traditional American fare, continental specialties, and some creative surprises. Southern Vermont's vast recreational opportunities are easily accessible to guests of the Londonderry.

Raspberry Vinaigrette Salad Dressing

1 cup yogurt
2 cups raspberry syrup
¼ cup oil
¼ cup red wine vinegar
1 tablespoon poppy seeds
¼ teaspoon mint leaves

In a container with a cover combine all of the ingredients. Blend or shake until well blended.

Makes about 2½ cups.

Veal Baltimore

25 oysters, drained
2 tablespoons bacon fat
2 teaspoons chopped chives
1 teaspoon thyme
1 tablespoon chopped parsley
1 teaspoon salt
Freshly ground black pepper
1 quart stale bread cubes

🍂 🍂 🍂

4 6-ounce veal cutlets
Flour
3 eggs, beaten
Oil
¼ cup Parmesan cheese
⅛ cup chopped chives
¼ cup oil or clarified butter
Marsala, Tarragon, or Madeira
    sauce

In a large skillet sauté the oysters in the bacon fat with 2 teaspoons of chives, thyme, parsley, and salt. Cook until the oysters are hot, but not overcooked. Add the black pepper and lightly toss with the bread crumbs to make a stuffing. If too dry, add a little of the liquor from the oysters.

Place the veal between 2 pieces of waxed paper and pound thin, then dredge in the flour. In a shallow bowl beat together the eggs, cheese, and

The Londonderry Inn

Route 100
South Londonderry, Vermont 05155
(802) 824-5226

The Londonderry Inn's twenty-five comfortable guest rooms are part of what was the Melendy Dairy Farm 150 years ago. A former woodshed is now

The Londonderry Inn

chives. Dip the veal in the egg batter and sauté on both sides in heated oil until golden brown. Drain the excess oil off the cutlets and cut each in half. Divide the stuffing between 6 of the cutlets and cover with the remaining pieces of veal. Place in a baking dish and cover each portion with either a Marsala, Tarragon, or Madeira sauce. Bake covered in a 350° oven for 20 minutes.

Serves 4.

Kedron Valley Inn

Route 106
South Woodstock, Vermont 05071
(802) 457-1473

Kedron Valley is one of the oldest inns in Vermont, operating since the early 1800s. Today all rooms have private baths. The food is mouth-watering contemporary American cuisine prepared by our Parisian-trained chef, who is also a lifetime Vermonter, and featuring unique combinations of local products. Golf, indoor and outdoor tennis, and athletic facilities for swimming, squash, and aerobics are only five minutes up the road. Activities available in the area include skiing, horse-drawn sleigh rides, swimming in the springfed pond, or trail rides at the nearby stables.

Mushroom Pâté

2 pounds mushrooms
4 cups water

&a. &a. &a.

2 8-ounce packages cream cheese, softened
½ cup butter, softened
1 tablespoon fresh rosemary
1 teaspoon white pepper
½ teaspoon salt
1 teaspoon minced garlic
1 ounce Marsala wine (optional)

Wash the mushrooms and cut into halves. In a blender or food processor purée the mushrooms with the water. In a large saucepan bring the mixture to a boil, then simmer for 30 minutes. Strain the mixture, separating the thicker mushroom portion from the liquid. Reserve the mushroom portion. Simmer the liquid again until it is reduced to about ½ cup. Set aside the glaze.

In a mixing bowl combine the remaining ingredients, blending thoroughly. Add the thicker mushroom purée and the cooled glaze to the blended ingredients to make the pâté. Serve with crackers.

Note: The pâté can be refrigerated for up to 7 days.

Serves 10 to 12.

Grilled Swordfish
with Pineapple and Cilantro Salsa

6 1-inch thick swordfish steaks
¼ cup oil
1 teaspoon minced ginger
1 teaspoon minced garlic

&a. &a. &a.

1 medium fresh pineapple (or 1 16-ounce can diced pineapple)
½ cup pineapple juice
1 tablespoon minced garlic
2 teaspoons minced ginger
1 tablespoon fresh chopped cilantro
½ teaspoon hot chili oil (or 1 teaspoon diced red chilies)

In a small bowl combine the oil, 1 teaspoon of ginger, and 1 teaspoon of

garlic for a marinade. Pour over the steaks and let sit for at least 6 hours or overnight.

Peel, core, and dice the pineapple. In a medium bowl combine the diced pineapple with the pineapple juice, 1 tablespoon minced garlic, 2 teaspoons minced ginger, cilantro, and hot chili oil. Refrigerate the salsa for at least 1 hour. Grill the swordfish steaks for 2 minutes on each side. Top with the salsa.

Note: The salsa can be refrigerated for up to a week before using.

Serves 6.

Green Mountain Inn

Post Office Box 1379
Stowe, Vermont 05672
(802) 253-4400

The Green Mountain Inn is a beautifully restored 1833 inn listed on the National Register of Historic Places. Fifty-six antique-furnished rooms and suites, two superb restaurants and bars, meeting facilities, heated outdoor pool, Stowe's finest health club, gift shop, and beauty salon are on the premises. Green Mountain Inn is conveniently situated in picturesque Stowe Village. It is close to alpine and cross-country skiing, golf, tennis, hiking, and Stowe's eleven-mile recreation path.

Roast Duck
with Peach and Pink Peppercorn Sauce

1 4-pound duck
1 onion
1 stalk celery

Green Mountain Inn

❧ ❧ ❧

2 tablespoons sugar
1 pound peaches, peeled, pitted,
  and thinly sliced
1 teaspoon pink peppercorns
Salt and pepper

Roast the duck in a 375° oven for 2½ to 3 hours. Remove and cool. Cut the duck in half along either side of the backbone. Remove the chest bones, leaving in the leg and wing bones. In a small pot cover the bones with water and simmer with the onion and celery for 30 minutes. Strain and reserve ½ cup of duck stock.

In a shallow saucepan melt the sugar over low heat. Add the duck stock, stirring until the caramelized sugar is dissolved. Add the peaches, peppercorns, salt, and pepper. Bring to a boil, then simmer until reduced by half. Reheat the duck in a 450° oven until heated through and the skin is nicely crisped. Lightly spoon the sauce over the duck to serve.

Serves 2.

Annie Pie

1 to 2 tablespoons graham cracker
  crumbs
3 egg whites
¼ teaspoon salt
1 teaspoon vanilla extract
1 cup sugar

❧ ❧ ❧

½ cup graham cracker crumbs
½ cup coconut flakes
¼ cup chopped walnuts
½ teaspoon baking powder
1½ pints Ben & Jerry's Heath Bar
  Crunch Ice Cream, softened (or
  your favorite butter brickle)

❧ ❧ ❧

1½ cups heavy cream
2 tablespoons sugar
Vanilla extract

Grease a 10-inch pie plate and dust with graham crumbs. In a medium bowl beat the egg whites until foamy. Add the salt and 1 teaspoon of vanilla, beating on high speed. Slowly add 1 cup of sugar to make a thick meringue.

In a medium bowl combine the graham crumbs, coconut, walnuts, and baking powder. Stir the mixture into the meringue. Spread into the prepared pie plate. Bake in a 350° oven for 20 to 30 minutes. Turn off the oven and let the pie shell cool. Fill the shell with the ice ceram.

In a medium bowl whip the heavy cream with 2 tablespoons of sugar and a drop of vanilla. Spread and smooth over the pie and freeze for at least 4 hours.

Serves 8 to 10.

Note: We serve this with hot fudge sauce.

❧ ❧ ❧ ❧ ❧

Creamy Garlic Salad Dressing

6 cloves garlic
1 teaspoon celery salt
¼ teaspoon black pepper
⅛ teaspoon salt

❧ ❧ ❧

¼ cup red wine vinegar
1 quart Hellmann's mayonnaise
1 cup buttermilk
¼ cup freshly chopped parsley

In a food processor combine the garlic, celery salt, pepper, and salt.

In a small bowl combine the vinegar, mayonnaise, buttermilk, and parsley. Blend with the garlic mixture, stirring well.

Makes about 1 quart.

Two Potato Soup

2 large onions, peeled and sliced
¼ cup butter
3 large sweet potatoes, peeled and diced
3 large white potatoes, peeled and diced
Chicken stock
1½ cups heavy cream
1 tablespoon curry powder
Salt and pepper

In a large saucepan sauté the onions in the butter until very soft and slightly glazed. Add both potatoes with enough chicken stock to cover. Simmer for 30 to 40 minutes until the potatoes are very done, almost mushy. In a food processor or blender purée the potato mixture and return to the saucepan. Stir in the heavy cream, being careful not to boil the soup. Combine a little water with the curry powder and stir into the soup. Add more chicken stock if necessary to desired consistency. Season with the salt and pepper.
Serves 8 to 12.

Grey Fox Inn

Route 108
Mountain Road
Stowe, Vermont 05672
(802) 253-8921

The Grey Fox Inn offers a variety of accommodations, all with private bath and/or shower. The scenery and year-round activities make this one of the top resorts in the northeast in all seasons. It is within walking distance of the playhouse and Stowe's famous nightspots, and one and one-half miles from the scenic village.

Curry Dip

2 teaspoons curry powder
1 cup plain yogurt
3 tablespoons ketchup
3 tablespoons grated onion
1 cup mayonnaise
¼ cup honey

In a small bowl combine all the ingredients, mixing well. Chill. Serve with crudités or as a salad dressing.
Makes about 3 cups.

Spinach Soufflé

Unflavored dry bread crumbs
2 tablespoons butter
1 tablespoon all-purpose flour
¼ teaspoon salt
¼ teaspoon pepper
Dash nutmeg
1 cup milk
1 10-ounce package frozen spinach, cooked and pressed dry
½ cup Swiss or Gruyère cheese

❧ ❧ ❧

4 egg whites

Grease a 4-cup soufflé dish and coat with bread crumbs, shaking out the excess. In a saucepan melt the butter. Add the flour, stirring and bubbling for 1 minute. Add the salt, pepper, nutmeg, and milk, stirring with a wire whisk over medium heat until slightly thickened. Add the spinach and cheese. Cook for 5 minutes.

In a mixing bowl beat the egg whites until soft peaks form. Fold into the spinach mixture. Pour into the prepared dish. Bake in a 375° oven for 25 to 30 minutes, until golden and firm to the touch.

Note: This recipe can be multiplied easily and is great for a crowd! I make up big pans of it to serve up to 60 people!
Serves 4.

Hungarian Noodles

¼ cup diced onions
1 clove garlic
1 tablespoon butter
4 ounces noodles, cooked
12 ounces cottage cheese
1 cup sour cream
1 teaspoon Worcestershire sauce
2 teaspoons poppy seeds
Paprika

In a small saucepan sauté the onion and garlic in the butter. In a casserole dish combine the sautéed onion and garlic with the noodles, cottage cheese, sour cream, Worcestershire sauce, and poppy seeds, stirring gently. Sprinkle with the paprika. Bake in a 350° oven for 25 minutes.
Serves 6.

Ski Inn

Stowe, Vermont 05672
(802) 253-4050

Set back from the highway amid the evergreens, the Ski Inn is a traditional New England inn made comfortably modern. This quiet, restful place provides a flat hiking road, trout stream, and cookout facilities on the twenty-eight acres of woodlands adjacent to the Mount Mansfield ski area. Ski trails on Mount Mansfield offer some of the most challenging descents in the East, complemented by many intermediate and beginning trails. In addition, there are miles of cross-country trails.

❧ ❧ ❧ ❧ ❧

Mocha Chiffon Pie

    1 envelope unflavored gelatin
    ¼ cup cold water
    3 tablespoons cocoa
    ¾ cup sugar
    ¾ cup water
    2 teaspoons instant coffee

        ❧ ❧ ❧

    3 eggs, separated
    1 teaspoon vanilla extract
    ½ teaspoon imitation rum extract

        ❧ ❧ ❧

    ¼ teaspoon salt
    ¼ cup sugar
    1 9-inch baked pie shell
    Whipped cream for garnish

Soften the gelatin in ¼ cup of cold water. In a heavy saucepan combine the cocoa, ¾ cup of sugar, ¾ cup of water, and instant coffee, stirring to dissolve the sugar. Bring to a boil and cook gently for 4 to 5 minutes, stirring constantly.

In a medium bowl beat the egg yolks slightly. Slowly pour the hot mixture over the egg yolks, stirring constantly. Return the mixture to the saucepan, stirring until thickened. Remove from the heat. Add the gelatin, vanilla, and rum extract, stirring until the gelatin dissolves. Chill the mixture until it mounds slightly when dropped from a spoon.

In a medium bowl beat the egg whites and salt together until foamy. Beat in ¼ cup of sugar by single teaspoons, beating constantly until stiff peaks form. Fold into the gelatin mixture and turn into the prepared pie shell. Chill until set. Garnish with whipped cream.

Serves 6 to 8.

Mushroom Ragoût

An easy vegetarian main dish or vegetable side dish.

    1 large onion
    2 large garlic cloves, minced
    ½ cup butter
    1½ pounds mushrooms, thinly
        sliced

        ❧ ❧ ❧

    4 eggs
    1 cup milk
    6 slices bread, crusts trimmed and
        cut into small cubes
    Pinch nutmeg
    Pinch ground red pepper
    Salt and pepper

Grease a 2-quart baking dish. In a saucepan sauté the onion and garlic in the butter for 5 minutes. Add the mushrooms and cook for 5 more minutes. Remove from the heat.

In a medium bowl combine the eggs and milk, beating well. Stir in the bread cubes and seasonings, and add the mushroom mixture, blending gently. Spoon into the prepared dish. Bake in a 350° oven for 1 hour, or until set.

Serves 6 to 8.

Herb Marinated Pork Tenderloin
with Maple Mustard Sauce

    5 bay leaves
    1 teaspoon cloves
    ½ teaspoon cayenne pepper
    1 teaspoon nutmeg
    1 teaspoon ground thyme
    ½ teaspoon allspice
    ½ teaspoon cinnamon
    ½ teaspoon basil
    ½ teaspoon freshly ground black
        pepper
    ½ teaspoon salt

        ❧ ❧ ❧

    2 pork tenderloins (2¾ pounds
        total)
    Olive oil

        ❧ ❧ ❧

    ¾ cup pure Vermont maple syrup
    ½ cup Dijon mustard

Combine the spices and rub into the meat. Cover and refrigerate for several hours. Bring meat to room temperature and rub generously with olive oil. Roast in a 375° oven for 1 hour, or until the internal temperature reaches 150°.

In a small bowl whisk together the maple syrup and mustard. Slice the tenderloin and serve with the sauce at room temperature.

Serves 4.

Steamed Cranberry Pudding

    ⅓ cup hot water
    ½ cup dark molasses
    1½ cups all-purpose flour
    2 teaspoons baking soda
    2 cups cranberries

        ❧ ❧ ❧

    ½ cup sugar
    1 cup light cream
    ½ cup unsalted butter
    1 teaspoon vanilla extract
    Candied cherries for garnish

Grease two 1-pound coffee cans. In a medium bowl combine the water, molasses, flour, baking soda, and cranberries for a thick batter. Put the batter into the prepared cans and cover securely with foil. Place on a rack in a large pot containing 4 to 5 inches of simmering water. Simmer for 2 hours, adding water to the pot as necessary. Cool, remove from the cans, wrap in foil, and refrigerate. Slice to serve.

In a saucepan combine the sugar, cream, butter, and vanilla, simmering until blended. Cover the sliced pudding with a generous amount of the sauce. Garnish with a candied cherry.

Serves 10 to 12.

Thatcher Brook Inn

Scenic Route 100
Waterbury, Vermont 05676
(802) 244-5911
(800) 292-5911

Thatcher Brook Inn is a faithfully restored Victorian Mansion listed on the Vermont Register of Historic Buildings. Many details show how no expense was spared in building the house, from the hand-carved fireplace and stairway, pocket doors between the two front rooms, the window seat in the lobby, and the beautiful oak cabinets. One of the most striking features is the gazebo-type front porch. The rooms provide canopy beds, whirlpool tub, or fireplaces. The gourmet restaurant and Bailey's Fireside Tavern provide excellent food and hospitality.

Thatcher Brook Inn

Thatcher Brook Inn's Roast Pork Tenderloin

with Amaretto Sauce

Pork tenderloin
Cracked black pepper
Maple syrup
Granny Smith apples, diced
Vermont Cheddar cheese, diced
Bacon

≈ ≈ ≈

3 tablespoons apple jelly
½ shot Amaretto

Pound out the pork tenderloin with a mallet until ¼-inch thick. Lightly sprinkle with the pepper, then brush with maple syrup. Sprinkle with the apples and cheese. Tightly roll up the tenderloin and wrap with the bacon. Roast in a 450° oven for 20 to 25 minutes for well done.

In a saucepan melt the apple jelly. Add the Amaretto and simmer, watching carefully. Pour the sauce onto a plate and place the tenderloin on top.

Serves 1.

The Colonial House

Route 100
Weston, Vermont 05161
(802) 824-6286

Colonial House is an inn in which guests can enjoy the hospitality of the innkeepers and partake of the many recreational activities in the area. Its large living room and attached solarium provide a place to visit, relax, or enjoy the view. Over 150 miles of hiking and cross-country skiing trails are immediately accessible, and several alpine ski mountains are in the area. Guests awaken to the aroma of cinnamon-raisin bread fresh from the oven, mingled with the smell of fresh coffee. The leisurely country breakfasts include pancakes and farm fresh eggs. Nearby is the town of Weston, nestled in the Green Mountains, with its country stores, intriguing shops, small museums, craft center, town green, and beautiful churches. Weston Priory is just north of town. Hiking, swimming, golf, tennis, and canoeing are available nearby.

Hungarian Mushroom Soup

An old favorite at the Colonial House, rich and filling, but not too hard on the diets. A great appetizer, or can be used for a main course, accompanied with a salad and fresh bread, piping hot from the oven.

    4 cups chopped onion
    ½ cup margarine
    4 cups freshly sliced mushrooms
    1½ tablespoons dill weed
    2½ tablespoons soy sauce
    2½ tablespoons Hungarian paprika
    4 cups beef or chicken stock

    ❧ ❧ ❧

    6 tablespoons all-purpose flour
    2½ cups milk
    Salt
    Freshly ground black pepper
    1½ to 2 tablespoons lemon juice
    1¼ cups sour cream or yogurt
    Parsley or fresh dill for garnish

In a large saucepan sauté the onions in the margarine for 3 to 4 minutes until transparent. Add the mushrooms, dill, soy sauce, paprika, and stock, simmering for 15 minutes.

In a small bowl combine the flour and milk, whisking until smooth. Gradually add to the stock mixture, stirring until slightly thickened. Just before serving add the salt, pepper, lemon juice, and sour cream. Garnish individual servings with parsley or fresh dill.

Serves 8 to 10.

Colonial House Oatmeal Bread

This bread was originally known as "Can't Do It Again" bread because it was made with our leftover cooked cereals from breakfast. Betty decided a few years ago that she would standardize the recipe to make a consistent bread. The result was a bread that is delicious freshly sliced out of the oven, and it can't be beat toasted.

    2 tablespoons margarine
    1 cup cooked Scottish oatmeal
    1½ teaspoons salt
    2 tablespoons water
    1 egg, slightly beaten
    2 tablespoons molasses
    2 tablespoons cooked wheat berries
        (optional)
    1 ¼-ounce package active dry yeast
    ½ cup lukewarm water
    1 teaspoon sugar
    5 to 6 cups unbleached all-purpose
        flour

Grease 2 loaf pans or Todd Pottery bread pans. In a saucepan melt the margarine and add the oatmeal, salt, 2 tablespoons of water, egg, molasses, and wheat berries. Heat to lukewarm. In a separate bowl proof the yeast for 10 minutes in ½ cup of lukewarm water and sugar. Stir the yeast mixture into the oatmeal and add 2½ cups of flour, stirring until mixed. Knead in the remaining flour by hand or with a dough hook until the dough is smooth and elastic, but not dry. Place the dough in a greased bowl, turn to grease the top, cover, and let rise until doubled.

Punch down and shape into 2 loaves. Put into the prepared pans, cover, and let rise until dough reaches the top of the pans. Sprinkle the tops with rolled oats. Bake in a 375° oven for 35 to 40 minutes or until the top is browned. Remove from the pans and cool on a wire rack.

Makes 2 loaves.

The Colonial House

The Silver Fox Inn

Route 133
Post Office Box 1222
West Rutland, Vermont 05777
(802) 438-5555

Once part of a thousand-acre dairy farm, the Silver Fox remains a gracious country farmhouse. The living room dates back to 1768 and is still a comfortable place to enjoy a good book, converse with inn guests, or appreciate the warmth of a wood-burning stove on a chilly evening. The seven guest bedrooms, all with private baths, are decorated with charming country furnishings. Hearty country breakfasts and elegant dinners are served in two intimate dining rooms that accommodate thirty guests. A full service bar, as well as fine wines, is available to complement the diners.

The Silver Fox Inn

Salmon Florentine en Croute

4 salmon fillets, boned and skinned
1 10-ounce package chopped frozen spinach, cooked and well drained
4 ounces cream cheese, softened
¼ teaspoon tarragon
¼ teaspoon thyme
1 16-ounce box phyllo pastry leaves
Butter, melted
1 large banana, peeled, cut in half lengthwise and quartered

&a &a &a

Basic white sauce
¼ cup white wine
Nutmeg

Rinse the salmon in cold water. Reserve ¼ cup of the spinach. In a medium bowl combine the remaining spinach with the cream cheese, tarragon, and thyme. Brush one sheet of the pastry with melted butter and top with another sheet. Brush the second pastry sheet with melted butter and top with one salmon fillet. Add ¼ of the banana and cream cheese mixture. Fold in the sides of the pastry over the filling, then fold over the top and bottom making a square package. Place each pastry package on a large ungreased baking sheet. Bake in a 425° oven for 15 to 25 minutes.

In a small saucepan prepare the white sauce, adding the wine, nutmeg, and the reserved spinach. Spoon over the baked salmon packages.

Serves 4.

Rack of Lamb
with Apricot and Mint Jelly Glaze

4 French-cut racks of lamb
Garlic powder
1 10-ounce jar apricot jelly or preserves
1 10-ounce jar mint jelly

&a &a &a

1 13¾-ounce can chicken broth
Flour
Water
¼ cup brandy to taste

Lightly score the lamb and sprinkle each rack with garlic powder. Frost each rack with ¼ of the apricot and mint jellies. Bake in a 325° oven for 1 hour for medium doneness.

Deglaze the roasting pan with the chicken broth. Thicken the juices with the flour and water, adding the brandy to taste. Spoon the gravy over the lamb.

Serves 4.

&a &a &a &a &a

Windham Hill Inn

West Townshend, Vermont 05359
(802) 874-4080

Since its beginning as a nineteenth-century Vermont family farm, Windham Hill Inn has enjoyed a history of comfortable living. Each of the rooms in the restored farmhouse and barn has a view of the mountains. They are filled with antiques, Oriental rugs, handmade quilts, old photographs, and paintings that will attract those who love the feeling of stepping into the charm of the past but in the comfort of the present. Days at Windham Hill begin with a hearty country breakfast and end with the evening's candlelight dinner and relaxation in the common rooms. In between, the surrounding countryside beckons with a diversity of summer and winter sports activities, historic villages with antique shops, summer theatre and festivals, and brilliant fall foliage.

Windham Hill Inn

Spinach Mushroom Pie

½ pound fresh mushrooms, minced
3 tablespoons butter
½ cup dry bread crumbs

🍂 🍂 🍂

1½ cups grated Swiss cheese
6 slices fried bacon, crumbled
3 tablespoons all-purpose flour
3 eggs, slightly beaten
⅔ cup mayonnaise
1 10-ounce package frozen chopped spinach, drained well and squeezed dry

In a saucepan sauté the mushrooms in the butter. Add the bread crumbs, tossing together lightly. Press into a 9-inch pie pan.

In a medium bowl combine the remaining ingredients and pour into the prepared crust. Bake in a 350° oven for 40 minutes. Let sit for 10 minutes before cutting.
Serves 8 to 10.

Maple Poppy Seed Dressing

¾ cup maple syrup
1¼ teaspoons salt
½ cup apple cider vinegar
1⅓ cups oil
1½ teaspoons dry mustard
1 tablespoon poppy seeds

In a medium bowl combine all the ingredients, mixing thoroughly. Store in a jar at room temperature. Best served on fruit or a spinach salad.
Makes about 2½ cups.

Sweet Pea Soup

1 10-ounce package frozen peas
½ cup chopped leeks
10 spinach leaves
10 lettuce leaves
1 10¾-ounce can chicken broth
½ teaspoon chervil
Salt
Pepper
¾ cup light cream
Chopped parsley for garnish

In a large pot combine the peas, leeks, spinach and lettuce leaves, chicken broth, chervil, salt, and pepper. Cover and simmer for 20 minutes, or until all the vegetables are soft. In a blender purée together well and add the cream. Garnish with chopped parsley.
Serves 6.

Misty Mountain Lodge

Stowe Hill Road, Box 114
Wilmington, Vermont 05363
(802) 464-3961

A farmhouse inn with nine guest rooms, Misty Mountain (built in 1803) is in a rural area near the Mount Snow Haystack Ski Area. It is the only inn in the Mount Snow valley owned and operated by a native Vermonter. Delicious home-cooked meals are served family style. The country breakfast is complemented by the homemade jams and jellies. The wide lawn and winding trails make for outdoor relaxation. The host loves music and plays the guitar and banjo to entertain the guests. Winter skiing and summer relaxation, lakes, tennis, and Marlboro music await every guest.

Dandelion Jelly

This is our most popular jelly, because it is so different. I think it tastes like honey. Since I make all the jellies we serve, this is wonderful because I have no trouble finding enough dandelions to make the jelly.

Dandelions
1 quart water

❧ ❧ ❧

3 cups liquid
1 teaspoon lemon or orange extract
1 1¾-ounce package Sure-Jell
4½ cups sugar

Pick and wash the blossoms and put as many as you can into 1 quart of water. Boil for 3 minutes, stirring the flowers. Boil only for 3 minutes or it will turn green. Reserve 3 cups of the liquid.

In a medium saucepan boil the 3 cups of dandelion liquid and extract with the Sure-Jell. Add the sugar. Boil for 3 minutes, stirring constantly. Remove from the flame and put into jars, sealing as for jelly.

Makes about four 8-ounce jars.

Trail's End

Smith Road
Wilmington, Vermont 05363
(802) 464-2727

Just five miles from Mount Snow, Trail's End is a secluded country inn offering warm hospitality and charm. Rooms are individually decorated and have private baths. Fireplace suites have canopy beds and whirlpool tubs. A dramatic lounge with two-story fireplace and loft is a favorite of guests; the game room is also a popular place. Hearty country breakfasts and home-cooked dinners are served family style. The inn offers an outdoor swimming pool, a clay tennis court, a fully stocked trout pond, and lovely English flower gardens.

Westport Salad

1 cup mayonnaise
2 tablespoons Parmesan cheese
1 tablespoon lemon juice
⅛ teaspoon garlic powder
¼ teaspoon salt
¼ teaspoon freshly ground pepper
Dash Accent

❧ ❧ ❧

Iceberg lettuce
Romaine lettuce or spinach
¾ cup grated cauliflower
¾ cup toasted bread crumbs

In a medium bowl combine the mayonnaise, Parmesan, lemon juice, garlic powder, salt, pepper, and Accent to make a dressing. Refrigerate

for 2 hours or more for the flavors to develop.

Toss the greens with the dressing and half of the grated cauliflower. Top each serving with the remaining cauliflower and toasted bread crumbs.

Serves 6.

Carbonnade of Beef

Our skiers love this dish. It's hearty and it's cooked with beer instead of wine. We serve it with Noodle-Carrot Toss.

½ cup all-purpose flour
2½ tablespoons salt
1 teaspoon pepper
1 6-pound boneless beef chuck roast, sliced
5 tablespoons oil
5 tablespoons butter or margarine
8 cups onions, thickly sliced
2 garlic cloves, crushed

❧ ❧ ❧

6 sprigs parsley
2 bay leaves
1 teaspoon crushed thyme

❧ ❧ ❧

2 cups beef broth
2 12-ounce cans ale or beer
¼ cup light brown sugar
2 tablespoons white vinegar

In a large bowl combine the flour, 1 tablespoon of salt, and ½ teaspoon of pepper. Add the beef and toss lightly, coating well. In a large skillet heat 4 tablespoons of oil and 4 tablespoons of butter over medium heat. Cook the beef, a few slices at a time, until browned. Remove the beef with a slotted spoon. Add the remaining oil and butter, heating until melted. Add the onions and garlic, and sauté 5 minutes until tender. Remove from the skillet.

Make a bouquet garni by placing the parsley, bay leaves, and thyme in a piece of cheesecloth. Tie to form a bag. In a 4½-quart casserole alternate layers of the beef and onions. Place the bouquet garni in the center of the mixture.

In a skillet combine the beef broth, ale, sugar, vinegar, and remaining salt and pepper. Heat to boiling, stirring frequently. Pour over the beef and onions, cover the casserole, and bake in a 325° oven for 2½ hours. The meat should be fork tender. Discard the bouquet garni and skim off the fat.

Serves 12.

Inn Chicken

Inn Chicken is our house specialty. It is so moist and tasty it requires no additional sauce.

    4 boneless, skinless chicken breasts
    2 garlic cloves, minced
    1 cup sour cream
    2 tablespoons lemon juice
    ½ teaspoon paprika
    1 teaspoon Tabasco sauce
    1 cup bread crumbs
    ½ cup butter, melted

Butter a baking dish. Combine the garlic, sour cream, lemon juice, paprika, and Tabasco. Marinate the chicken in this mixture overnight in the refrigerator. Roll the chicken in the bread crumbs and place in the prepared baking dish. Drizzle with the melted butter. Bake in a 350° oven for 1 hour.

Serves 4.

Noodle Carrot Toss

A colorful accompaniment to Carbonnade of Beef.

    2 12-ounce packages medium egg
        noodles
    ¾ cup butter or margarine, melted
        ❧ ❧ ❧
    1 tablespoon salt
    6 cups shredded carrots
    ¾ cup finely chopped parsley
        ❧ ❧ ❧
    4 eggs, slightly beaten
    1¼ cups milk
    ¾ teaspoon pepper

Butter an oven casserole. In a large saucepan cook the noodles according to the package directions, boiling only 4 minutes. Drain and return to the saucepan. Add the butter and set aside.

In a large saucepan heat 1 inch of water with 1 tablespoon of salt to boiling. Add the carrots and cook for 2 to 3 minutes, stirring occasionally. Drain well and add the carrots and parsley to the noodles.

In a medium bowl combine the remaining ingredients, beating until smooth. Pour over the noodle mixture and toss well. Pour into the prepared casserole and cover. Bake in a 375° oven for 40 minutes, stirring occasionally.

Serves 12.

Raspberry Clafouti

A simple French dessert.

    3 eggs
    1¼ cups milk
    ⅔ cup all-purpose flour
    ⅓ cup sugar
    2 teaspoons vanilla extract
    ¼ teaspoon nutmeg
    ⅛ teaspoon salt
        ❧ ❧ ❧
    1½ cups raspberries
        ❧ ❧ ❧
    Confectioners' sugar

Butter a 9-inch pie plate. In a small bowl beat the eggs with an electric mixer until foamy. Add the remaining ingredients except the raspberries and confectioners' sugar. Beat on low speed until smooth. Pour the batter into the prepared pie plate. Sprinkle the berries on top. Bake in a 350° oven for 45 minutes. Sprinkle with confectioners' sugar before serving.

Serves 8.

Juniper Hill Inn

Rural Route 1, Box 79 Juniper Hill Road
Windsor, Vermont 05089
(802) 674-5273

Atop Juniper Hill, the Juniper Hill Inn has a commanding view of Mount Ascutney and the valley below. The winding drive, lined with a fieldstone wall and tall, whispering pines, offers an ideal setting for walking. This three-story mansion has fifteen guestrooms, all with private baths and nine with working fireplaces. The library wing, with its elegant Palladian window and oak stairway, leads to two special, large guestrooms, one with a canopy bed ideal for honeymoons or anniversaries, the other with its own screened porch. Full country breakfasts are served daily. Breakfast in bed will be brought if arranged in advance, and candlelight dinners are served in the elegant dining room. Dining is also open to the public on Friday, Saturday, holidays, and between December 26 and January 1 by reservation.

Vermont Cheddar Cheese Soup

    3 tablespoons butter
    3 scallions
    1 small onion, chopped
    1 stalk celery, chopped
    3 tablespoons all-purpose flour
    ⅛ teaspoon nutmeg
    ⅛ teaspoon pepper
    2 cups chicken broth
    1 quart milk
    2 cups shredded Cheddar cheese
    Salt

In a large soup pot melt the butter. Add the scallions, onions, and celery, cooking until tender. Sift in the flour, nutmeg, and pepper, cooking for 2 to

Juniper Hill Inn

3 minutes. Gradually stir in the broth. Bring the mixture to a boil, cover, reduce the heat, and simmer for 15 minutes. Cool the mixture, then strain it into a bowl and return to the pot. Add the milk and bring the soup just to a boil. Gradually add the cheese, stirring until melted. Return the soup to a boil, stirring often. Add the salt to taste.

Serves 6 to 8.

Chicken Lombardi

6 6-ounce boneless chicken breasts, skinned
3 tablespoons oil
1 cup dry white wine
2 cups freshly sliced mushrooms
8 ounces Mozzarella cheese, grated

In a skillet sauté the chicken breasts in the oil. Set aside. Deglaze the pan with the wine and add the mushrooms, simmering for 1 minute. Arrange the chicken in a baking dish. Pour the mushrooms and wine over the chicken and top with the cheese. Bake in a 350° oven for 30 to 45 minutes, until the cheese is golden brown.

Serves 6.

Jaeger Schnitzel

6 4-ounce veal cutlets
3 tablespoons oil
2 cups freshly sliced mushrooms
½ cup white wine
3 tablespoons all-purpose flour
1 16-ounce carton sour cream

🍃 🍃 🍃

Noodles or spaetzle

In a skillet sauté the veal in the oil for 2 minutes per side. Set aside. Sauté the mushrooms with the wine until tender. In a small bowl blend the flour into the sour cream, then add to the mushrooms and wine. Add the veal and simmer for 20 minutes. Serve with noodles or homemade spaetzle.

Serves 6.

Pork Loin
with Mustard Sauce

2 pounds boneless pork loin
Salt, pepper, oregano, and rosemary to taste

🍃 🍃 🍃

1 egg yolk
1 tablespoon Dijon mustard or brown mustard
¼ cup heavy cream
½ cup dry white wine

1 clove garlic, crushed
1 teaspoon tarragon
½ teaspoon brandy
Salt and pepper

Sprinkle the herbs on the pork loin. Set on a rack and roast in a 400° oven for 10 minutes, then reduce the temperature to 325° and roast for 25 minutes per pound. The temperature of the meat will be between 165° and 170°.

In a small bowl beat together the egg yolk and mustard. Stir in the cream and set aside. Pour the pan juices from the pork loin roasting pan into a skillet and add the wine. Add the garlic, tarragon, brandy, salt, and pepper. Boil for 1 minute. Remove the skillet from the heat and stir in the cream mixture. Return to the heat, stirring until thickened. Do not boil. Slice the pork and serve with the mustard sauce.

Serves 6 to 8.

Very Berry Lemon Cake

4 eggs
1 cup plain yogurt or dairy sour cream
1 18½-ounce box Pillsbury Plus Lemon Cake Mix
1 cup frozen blueberries
Lemon frosting

Grease a 10-inch Bundt pan. In a large mixing bowl combine the eggs, yogurt, and cake mix. Mix with an electric mixer on low until blended, then beat for 2 more minutes. Reduce the speed and stir in the blueberries. Pour the batter into the prepared pan. Bake in a 350° oven for 35 to 45 minutes. Cool for 15 minutes and remove from the pan to cool completely. Frost with the lemon frosting.

Serves 16.

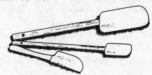

The Jackson House at Woodstock

Route 4 West
Woodstock, Vermont 05091
(802) 457-2065

In 1890 Wales Johnson set out to build "the finest house in Woodstock." The three-story Victorian mansion he created became a guest house in 1940, then called "Seven Maples" for the stately trees that lined the front lawn. Today it is an inn for discerning individuals who appreciate fine things like Chinese porcelains and rugs, French cut crystal, and the polished cherry staircase. The ten guest rooms, all with private baths, are furnished with antiques of different periods, including the Josephine Tasher Bonaparte, lavishly furnished in French Empire decor; the Mary Todd Lincoln, with an ornate, high-back Victorian double bed of the Lincoln period; Thorn Birds, with brass and bamboo reminiscent of the King George IV pavilion at Brighton; and two luxurious suites, Nicholas I and Francesca.

Fresh Smoked Salmon in Scrambled Eggs

We like to complement with a cheese blintz, sausage, scone, and muffins.

1 tablespoon butter
2 tablespoons chopped shallots
Cream cheese (about the size of a large walnut)
3 eggs, beaten
Scant ¼ cup heavy cream
2 tablespoons chopped parsley
¾ ounce fresh Norwegian or Nova Scotia smoked salmon, diced
Salt, pepper, and oregano to taste

In an omelet pan melt the butter. Sauté the shallots until opaque, then add the cream cheese until softened. In a small bowl combine the eggs, cream, parsley, salmon, salt, pepper, and oregano. Add to the pan and cook over low heat, stirring frequently. Serve in a warm ramekin.
Serves 2.

🐚 🐚 🐚 🐚 🐚

The Woodstock Inn

Fourteen the Green
Woodstock, Vermont 05091
(802) 457-1100

Built in 1969, the Woodstock Inn radiates the Colonial New England style, enhanced by up-to-date luxury. The inn is three stories on the front and four on the garden side. Its 143 guest rooms are air conditioned and appointed with specially designed furniture and handmade quilts. Other facilities include a coffee shop, dining room, lounges, gift shop, a complete indoor sports facility, and country club. Downhill and cross-country skiing are nearby.

Shrimp Obregon à l'Absinthe

1 pound shrimp (cleaned, peeled, and deveined)
2 thin zests of lemon skin
2 whole garlic cloves, peeled
2 tablespoons butter
Salt and pepper to taste
1 cup heavy whipping cream
1 to 2 ounces Pernod liquor

In a skillet sauté the shrimp with the lemon and garlic in the butter, but do not overcook. Salt and pepper to taste. Remove the shrimp from the pan and discard the lemon zest and garlic. Reduce the shrimp juice until the pan is almost dry, then add the cream and Pernod, cooking until the sauce is reduced to half. Return the shrimp to the sauce.
Note: Optional additions are Vermont Cheddar cheese, wild mushrooms, leeks, Parisienne vegetables, Galliano, or fresh herbs.
Serves 4.

Broiled Seafood Brochette Woodstock Inn

16 shrimp, shelled and deveined
1 pound sea scallops
1 pound swordfish meat, skinned, and diced into 1 to 1½-inch cubes
1 pound salmon fillet, skinned, and diced into 1 to 1½-inch cubes
8 mushroom caps

🐚 🐚 🐚

2 limes
Olive oil
Salt, pepper, fresh thyme or favorite herbs

🐚 🐚 🐚

Cooked rice
1 carrot, peeled and finely julienned
1 pound fresh assorted wild mushrooms, sautéed
½ pound fresh pea pods
3 cups fennel sauce

The Woodstock Inn

Alternate the shrimp, scallops, swordfish, and salmon on 8 skewers and repeat. Top with a mushroom cap.

Rub lightly with the fresh lime juice and olive oil. Sprinkle with herbs. Broil the brochette until done, approximately 3 minutes on each side.

Arrange on a bed of rice and garnish with carrots, sautéed mushrooms, and pea pods. Serve with fresh fennel sauce on the side.

Serves 8.

Galantine of Duck and Chanterelles

Appetizer.

4 duck breasts, boned and skinned
3 tablespoons oil
¼ cup sherry wine
1 cup milk

🍃 🍃 🍃

1 can chanterelles (or ¾ pound fresh chanterelles, chopped)
1 tablespoon chopped shallots
1 tablespoon chopped parsley
2 tablespoons sherry vinegar
Salt and pepper
3 egg yolks

🍃 🍃 🍃

6 grape leaves

🍃 🍃 🍃

4 ounces Vermont Cheddar cheese, grated

Marinate the duck breasts overnight in the oil, sherry wine, and milk.

In a skillet sauté the chanterelles with the shallots. Add the parsley and deglaze with the vinegar. Season with the salt and pepper. Let cool and add the egg yolks.

Pound the duck breasts slightly and place on the prepared grape leaves. Spread the chanterelle mixture on the duck, top with the cheese, and roll. Cover with aluminum foil and seal. Cook in a steamer for 12 minutes.

Serve with chervil herb sauce.

Note: If a steamer is not available, lay the grape leaves on buttered or sprayed parchment paper and roll. Tie in cheesecloth, drop into hot chicken stock, and cook for approximately 20 minutes. Cool in the broth.

Serves 8.

Roast Duck and Spiral à l'Orange

2 whole ducklings, oven ready

🍃 🍃 🍃

2 ripe mangoes
1 banana
1 lemon or lime
½ cup chutney
Raisins
Chopped nuts (walnuts, butternuts, or your favorite)

🍃 🍃 🍃

1 cup heavy cream
¼ cup Grand Marnier
Cornstarch and water
10 ounces spiral noodles, blanched
    for 6 minutes in boiling salted
    water
1 cup orange sauce (optional)
Fresh mint

Cook the ducklings, separate, and bone out, until one leg bone and one wing bone remain. Set aside and keep warm.

Separate the mangoes, leaving the skin on. Top each quarter with sliced banana and sprinkle with lemon juice. Top with chutney, raisins, and nuts. Place in a pie tin. Bake in a 350° oven.

In a saucepan reduce the heavy cream with the Grand Marnier. Tighten slightly with cornstarch and water, letting the sauce cook out. Add

the spinach, reduce slightly, and serve with the hot duck, baked mango, spirals, and orange sauce. Garnish with fresh mint.

Serves 4.

Escargot Fettucini Vermont Style

10 ounces fettuccini, blanched
2 tablespoons olive oil
2 tablespoons tomato paste
2 teaspoons pesto
6 ounces fiddleheads, blanched

    🌿 🌿 🌿

24 escargots (or scallops or shrimp,
    all optional)
Butter
Fresh garlic to taste
Galliano or brandy
½ cup cream

8 ounces Vermont Cheddar cheese,
    grated
Paprika

In a skillet sauté the fettuccini in the olive oil. Add the tomato paste and pesto. Place in 4 individual casserole dishes. Top with the fiddleheads.

In a skillet slightly sauté the fish in butter, and add the garlic. Flame with the Galliano. Remove and place on top of the fiddleheads. Divide the cream among the dishes, then top with the cheese and paprika. Bake in a 400° oven until done.

Serves 4.

Virginia

Morrison House

116 South Alfred Street
Alexandria, Virginia 22314
(703) 838-0800
(800) 367-8000
(800) 533-1808 (Virginia only)
FAX: (703) 684-6283

Centrally located in Alexandria's Old Town, Morrison House is but a stroll from historic landmarks, picturesque cobblestone streets, and the beautiful waterfront. It offers forty-four custom-furnished guest rooms and three luxurious suites, all featuring Federal period furnishings, queen- or king-size beds, two telephones, climate control, television, and private Italian marbled baths. Twenty-four-hour butler, concierge, and room services, indoor valet parking, turndown service, English tea in the parlor every afternoon, and a staff that speaks Spanish, French, Italian, German, Chinese, Japanese, and Farsi are some of the services offered.

The Grill restaurant, four-diamond rated by AAA, specializes in New American cuisine in a clublike setting.

Mexican Corn Soup

> 3½ cups fresh corn kernels
> 1 cup chicken broth
> ½ cup butter
> 2 cups milk
> 1 clove garlic, minced
> 2 teaspoons fresh oregano
> Salt and pepper to taste
> 2 tablespoons chili pepper
> 1 chicken breast, cooked, boned
>   and chopped
> 1 cup cubed Monterey Jack cheese
> 1 tablespoon minced parsley
> Tortilla chips

In a food processor purée the corn and chicken broth. In a saucepan combine the butter and the corn mixture, and simmer for 5 minutes. Add the milk, garlic, oregano, salt, and pepper, and bring to a boil. Reduce the heat, add the chili peppers, and simmer for 5 minutes. Remove the soup from the heat and add the cheese. Stir until smooth. Ladle into bowls and serve with tortilla chips.
Serves 6.
Recipe courtesy Chef John Walsh.

Warm Banana Split

> 6 ripe bananas
> Chocolate and vanilla ice cream
> Chocolate Sauce (recipe follows)
> Caramel Sauce (recipe follows)
> Sweetened whipped cream
> Fresh berries or sliced fruit

Bake the unpeeled bananas in a 400° oven until lightly blackened. Cut the bananas in half lengthwise with a wire. Remove the peel and place on a plate. Place a scoop of vanilla ice cream topped with Chocolate Sauce on one side, and a scoop of chocolate ice cream with Caramel Sauce on the other. Top with whipped cream and garnish with fruit.
Serves 6.
Recipe courtesy Chef John Walsh.

Chocolate Sauce

> 1 pound semisweet chocolate,
>   chopped
> ½ cup chopped pecans
> ½ cup chopped walnuts
> ½ cup almonds

Melt the chocolate in the top of a double boiler over simmering water. Add the pecans, walnuts, and almonds. Serve over ice cream.
Makes about 3½ cups.
Recipe courtesy Chef John Walsh.

Caramel Sauce

> 1 cup sugar
> 1½ cups water
> 1½ cups heavy cream
> 4 tablespoons butter

In a small saucepan combine the sugar and water. Cook over moderate heat until dark brown, about 8 to 10 minutes. Remove from the heat and slowly stir in the cream and butter. Serve warm over ice cream.
Makes about 3 cups.
Recipe courtesy Chef John Walsh.

Olive Mill Bed and Breakfast

Route 231, General Delivery
Banco, Madison County, Virginia 22711
(703) 923-4664

Following the traditions of Virginia hospitality, Olive Mill is a private home in the foothills of the Blue Ridge Mountains. Attesting to the prosperity of the milling trade until the mid-twentieth century, the miller's house is of generous size and offers three large guest rooms. Spacious porches front and back provide for relaxation and a view of the forty-foot swimming pool. A full country breakfast is served in the dining room, with a fire in the fireplace in cool weather.

Next door is the historic Olive Mill, which features gifts and crafts from Virginia and Scandinavia. A visitor center provides information on area surroundings.

Piquant Pepper Jelly

1½ cups chopped green, red, or
  yellow bell peppers
1½ cups cider vinegar
6½ cups sugar
25 shakes Tabasco sauce
1 6-ounce bottle liquid pectin
Food coloring (optional)

In a saucepan combine the peppers, vinegar, sugar, and Tabasco sauce. Bring to a high boil, and boil for about 2 minutes. Set aside for 20 minutes. Return to the heat and bring to a boil again. Boil for about 2 minutes. Remove from the heat. Add the pectin, and food coloring if desired. Pour the mixture into sterilized jars and seal.

Makes about 6 8-ounce glasses.

Elmo's Rest

Route 2, Box 198
Bedford, Virginia 24523
(703) 586-3707

Elmo's Rest is a farmhouse dating from the 1890s on a 250-acre fruit and cattle farm that is made available weekly, April through November, to one family or group at a time. While no meals are furnished, the kitchen is fully equipped. Parts of the house date back to the late eighteenth century. Antique furnishings enhance the house's authenticity.

On this working farm guests can observe and participate in many activities. There are horses for riding, creeks for wading, and trails for hiking, as well as hammocks and chairs for relaxing in comfort.

Nectarine Carrot Cake

1½ cups chopped nectarines
1½ cups grated carrots
2 cups all-purpose flour
¾ cup brown sugar
½ cup chopped walnuts
2½ teaspoons baking powder
1½ teaspoons cinnamon
¾ teaspoon salt
½ teaspoon nutmeg
½ cup oil
2 eggs
1 teaspoon vanilla extract

Grease and flour a 9-inch ring mold. In a large bowl combine all of the ingredients. Pour the batter into the prepared mold. Bake in a 350° oven for 45 minutes or until a toothpick inserted in the center comes out clean. Cool in the pan for 10 minutes. Invert onto a wire rack to cool completely. Dust with confectioners' sugar.

Serves 8 to 10.

Baked Pumpkin
with Apple-Raisin Filling

1 4 to 5-pound pumpkin
1 tablespoon margarine or butter,
  melted
2 tablespoons brown sugar
4 to 5 cups sliced, peeled apples
½ cup raisins
⅓ cup brown sugar
4 teaspoons all-purpose flour
¾ teaspoon cinnamon
¼ teaspoon nutmeg

Cut out the top of the pumpkin. Reserve the lid. Scrape out the seeds and strings. Brush the inside of the pumpkin with melted margarine and sprinkle with 2 tablespoons of brown sugar. Replace the lid and place the pumpkin in a shallow roasting pan. Bake in a 375° oven for 20 minutes.

In a medium bowl mix together the apples and remaining ingredients. Spoon into the pumpkin and replace the lid. Return to the oven and bake for 1 hour and 30 minutes. Remove the lid and bake for 15 minutes, or until the pumpkin and apples are tender. Serve hot, scooping out pumpkin flesh with apple filling.

Serves 10.

Bourbon Apple Pie

1 cup sweet apples, peeled, sliced,
  stewed and mashed
1 cup sugar
¼ cup softened butter
¾ cup bourbon
1 cup heavy cream
½ teaspoon nutmeg
3 eggs, separated
1 unbaked 9-inch pie shell
Whipped cream

In a large bowl beat the warm apples with sugar and butter. When the apple mixture has cooled, add the bourbon, cream, nutmeg, and egg yolks. Beat the egg whites, and fold into the mixture. Pour the filling into the pie shell. Bake in a 425° oven for 10 minutes. Reduce the heat to 325°, and bake for 30 to 40 minutes. The top will puff up in the oven and fall while cooling. This is delicious served hot or cold. Serve with whipped cream.

Serves 6 to 8.

Sauerkraut
with Apples and Tomato

1 pound sauerkraut
2 tablespoons butter or bacon
  drippings
1 cup chopped peeled tomatoes (or
  1 8-ounce can, drained)
2 tart apples, peeled, cored and
  sliced

In a strainer or colander drain the sauerkraut well. Rinse in cold water and drain again. In a large skillet heat the butter. Add the sauerkraut, tomatoes, and apples. Cover and simmer for 20 minutes, stirring once or twice. Uncover and boil rapidly to reduce any excess liquid. Serve hot.

Serves 4.

Waldorf Salad

3 to 4 tart red apples
2 teaspoons sugar
Juice of ½ lemon
2 stalks celery, finely chopped
¾ cup coarsely chopped walnuts or
  pecans
¼ cup mayonnaise
¼ cup heavy cream, whipped
4 lettuce leaves

Core and dice the apples, leaving the peel on 1 or 2 for color. In a medium bowl toss the apples with the sugar and lemon juice. Add the celery and nuts, and mix carefully with a wooden spoon. In a separate bowl fold the mayonnaise and whipped cream together. Add the mayonnaise mixture to the apple mixture and toss thoroughly. Place the lettuce leaves on individual plates and mound salad in the center of each. Chill for 1 hour before serving.

Serves 4.

Turkey and Curry Salad

4 cups cubed cooked turkey
1 15¼-ounce can crushed
  pineapple, drained
1 large apple, peeled and cubed
2 oranges, peeled and cubed
½ cup Maraschino cherries, halved
¾ cup mayonnaise
1 tablespoon fresh lemon juice
½ teaspoon curry powder
Lettuce or pita bread

In a large bowl combine all of the ingredients except the lettuce and pita. Chill until serving time. Serve on a large bed of lettuce or in pita bread.

Serves 4 to 6.

North Bend Plantation

Route 1, Box 13A
Charles City, Virginia 23030
(804) 829-5176

North Bend is rich in Civil War and Charles City County history. Here General Sheridan headquartered as he directed his armies, and the plantation desk he used still has labels pasted on the pigeon holes showing the names of different companies' papers and orders. Restored to its earlier beauty, North Bend boasts Federal-style mantels and stair carvings and a fine collection of old and rare books.

Each room at North Bend is large and filled with family antiques and collectibles. The billiard room is available for guests' pleasure.

🐦 🐦 🐦 🐦 🐦

Southern Cold Oven Pound Cake

1 cup butter
½ cup Wesson oil
4 eggs
3 cups all-purpose flour
3 cups sugar
¼ teaspoon salt
1 cup milk
1 teaspoon vanilla extract
1 teaspoon lemon extract

Grease and flour an angel food cake pan. In a large bowl beat the butter and oil until smooth. Add the eggs 1 at a time, and beat well. In a separate bowl combine the flour, sugar, and salt. Add the dry ingredients to the butter mixture alternately with the milk. Add the vanilla and lemon extracts. Pour the batter into the prepared pan and place in a cold oven. Turn the oven temperature to 350° and bake for 1 hour and 30 minutes, or until a toothpick inserted in the center comes out clean.

Serves 8 to 10.

Southern Spoon Bread
or Batter Bread

1½ tablespoons butter
2 eggs
1 cup buttermilk
1½ cups yellow cornmeal
1½ teaspoons salt
1½ heaping teaspoons baking
  powder
3 cups boiling water

In an 8-inch square pan melt the butter in a 450° oven. Do not burn the butter.

In a large bowl beat the eggs and add the buttermilk. Mix well. Into the egg mixture sift the cornmeal, salt, and baking powder. Add the boiling water and beat thoroughly. Pour the mixture into the hot pan. Bake in a 450° oven for 20 to 30 minutes, until very brown.

Serves 9.

La Vista Plantation

4420 Guinea Station Road
Fredericksburg, Virginia 22401
(703) 898-8444

Situated in historic Spotsylvania County, La Vista was built in 1838 and is rich in Civil War history. The plantation house reflects the Classical Revival style, with high ceilings, heart of pine floors, acorn and oak leaf moldings, and a two-story front portico. The ten-acre grounds present a fine balance of mature trees, shrubs, pastures, woods, gardens, and a pond.

Guest lodgings are in an English basement blessed with sunny exposures. The spacious air-conditioned suite offers a large living room with fireplace, fully equipped kitchen, sitting room, and bedroom. A large room with private bath is also available. A healthy country breakfast is served.

Creamed Virginia Country Ham

3 tablespoons butter
3 tablespoons onion
2 tablespoons chopped red pepper
2 tablespoons chopped green pepper

2 cups chopped leftover country ham
2 tablespoons all-purpose flour
2 cups milk, or more if needed
1 teaspoon sherry
Coarsely ground black pepper to taste
Biscuits, toast, or toasted English muffins

In a heavy saucepan over medium heat melt the butter. Sauté the onion and peppers until just soft. Add the ham and stir until coated. Sprinkle the flour over the ham and stir until dissolved. Add the milk and sherry, and stir until thickened. Add more milk if needed. Serve at once over biscuits, toast, or toasted English muffins.

Serves 4.

Sleepy Hollow Farm

Route 3, Box 43
Gordonsville, Virginia 22942
(703) 832-5555

Sleepy Hollow is situated in the historical district of western Orange County on Route 231, an old toll road

between Gordonsville and Somerset. Generations have left their mark on the old brick house that was built around the eighteenth-century structure. The main house and the chestnut cottage out back, once a slave cabin, are furnished in antiques and family mementos. They contain wood stoves, fireplaces, porches, and terraces. Wildlife, a pond, a gazebo, and delicious spring water are on the grounds, and black Angus cattle graze in the pasture. Sixteen guests can be accommodated in both houses. Hearty country breakfasts are served in one of the dining areas, and refreshments are served at teatime.

Blackberry Cobbler

2 cups sifted unbleached all-purpose flour
¼ teaspoon salt
½ teaspoon baking soda
2 teaspoons baking powder
5 tablespoons butter
½ cup sugar
⅔ cup sour milk or buttermilk
6 tablespoons butter

ow ow ow

¾ cup sugar
5 cups blackberries
2 teaspoons cornstarch
¼ cup butter, cut into small pieces

ow ow ow

Cream
Sugar

ow ow ow

⅔ cup sugar
¼ teaspoon freshly grated nutmeg
2 teaspoons cornstarch
Pinch salt
1 cup boiling water
3 tablespoons orange juice or peach brandy

In a large mixing bowl sift together the flour, ¼ teaspoon of salt, the baking soda, and baking powder. Cut 5 tablespoons of butter into the flour mixture with a pastry blender or 2 knives. Add ½ cup of sugar. Blend the mixture until coarse. Sprinkle in the milk and mix with a spatula or wooden spoon. Shape the dough into

Sleepy Hollow Farm

a ball and turn onto a lightly floured surface. Knead for 1 to 2 minutes, quickly punching the dough. Divide the ball in half. Roll out half to ¼-inch thickness and place in an 8-inch square pan. Cover with waxed paper and refrigerate until chilled.

Sprinkle the chilled pastry with ¼ cup of sugar and the blackberries. Add 2 teaspoons of cornstarch to ½ cup of sugar, and sprinkle the mixture over the blackberries. Dot with small pieces of butter. Roll out the remaining dough and place over the berries. Make steam holes in the top. Brush the top with cream and sprinkle with a small amount of sugar. Place the cobbler in a 450° oven, and reduce the heat immediately to 425°. Bake for 45 minutes. Remove from the oven and cool on a wire rack before serving.

In a 1-quart saucepan combine ⅔ cup of sugar, the nutmeg, 2 teaspoons of cornstarch, and a pinch of salt. Pour in the boiling water, stirring constantly. Bring the mixture to a boil over medium heat. Boil gently for 10 minutes. Set aside until ready to serve. Reheat without boiling and add the orange juice or brandy. Serve over the cobbler.

Serves 9.

Poulet à L'Orange

1 chicken, cut into 4 or 8 parts
1 tablespoon Hungarian paprika
1 tablespoon fresh ginger
1½ teaspoons salt
1 tablespoon dry mustard
½ cup vermouth
1 6-ounce can frozen orange juice
**   concentrate**
Rice

In a shallow dish or plastic bag combine the paprika, ginger, salt, and dry mustard. Roll the chicken in the mixture until well covered. Arrange the chicken in a baking pan. In a small bowl combine the vermouth and orange juice concentrate. Pour the mixture over the chicken. Bake in a 375° oven for 1 hour, basting at least every 15 minutes. Serve with rice.

Serves 4.

Fried Tomatoes

½ cup all-purpose flour
½ teaspoon salt
¼ teaspoon pepper
¼ cup sugar
5 to 6 green or firm red tomatoes
2 to 3 tablespoons butter or bacon
**   drippings**

In a shallow bowl sift together the flour, salt, pepper, and sugar. Slice the tomatoes into ¼-inch slices. Coat both sides of the tomato slices in the flour mixture and place on waxed paper. Let the slices sit for a few minutes.

In a skillet heat the butter or bacon drippings until melted and hot. Sauté the tomatoes on each side until golden. Serve hot.

Serves 6 to 8.

Shenandoah Springs Country Inn

Box 122
Haywood, Virginia 22722
(703) 923-4300

This pre-Civil War home is situated on one thousand acres of forest land, meadows, shady lanes, bridle trails, and scenic views. Offering single and family rooms with private and semi-private baths, it offers horseback riding, swimming, and fishing for its guests' pleasure.

Shenandoah Springs Country Inn

Stuffed Shells Shenandoah

1 cup Ricotta cheese
¼ cup shredded Mozzarella cheese
¼ cup Parmesan cheese
1 egg, slightly beaten
1 10-ounce package frozen chopped spinach, cooked and drained
½ teaspoon oregano
¼ teaspoon salt
12 jumbo pasta shells, cooked, drained and cooled
1¾ cups spaghetti sauce (your favorite recipe)
Chopped parsley

In a large bowl combine the Ricotta, Mozzarella, Parmesan, egg, spinach, oregano, and salt. Spoon 3 tablespoons of the mixture into each shell. Arrange the shells in an 8x12-inch baking dish. Spoon the sauce over the shells. Cover with foil. Bake in a 350° oven for 35 minutes. Sprinkle with chopped parsley.
Serves 6.

🐦 🐦 🐦 🐦 🐦

The Inn at Levelfields

State Route 3
Post Office Box 216
Lancaster, Virginia 22503
(804) 435-6887

The manor house has been an architectural landmark since before the Civil War. The second homestead to be built on this site, it once was the center of a plantation of over 1,200 acres. Characterized by an impressive double-tiered portico on the south front and four massive chimneys, Levelfields is one of the last antebellum mansions to be built in Virginia. Situated on fifty-four acres, it is notable for its lofty proportions, spacious dining and guest rooms, each with a working fireplace, and beautiful rooms.

A hearty breakfast is served in the dining room; refreshments are offered in the afternoon; and dinner is available in one of the two dining rooms Thursday through Monday.

Imperial Crab

1 pound backfin or lump crab meat
½ teaspoon salt
⅛ teaspoon pepper
Dash cayenne pepper
1 tablespoon capers
½ cup mayonnaise
½ cup bread crumbs
Dash paprika
2 tablespoons melted butter

Grease 4 crab shells or individual casserole dishes. In a large bowl carefully mix the crab, seasonings, capers, and mayonnaise. Heap into the prepared shells or dishes. Sprinkle with bread crumbs and paprika. Drizzle melted butter over the top. Bake in a 350° oven for 25 minutes.
Serves 4.

🐦 🐦 🐦 🐦 🐦

Mushroom-Mustard Soup

½ cup butter
2 pounds mushrooms, thinly sliced
4 cups chicken stock
½ cup dry sherry
1 tablespoon Dijon mustard
Salt and freshly ground pepper
1 cup whipping cream

In a large heavy saucepan over medium high heat melt the butter. Heat the butter until browned. Add the mushrooms and cook until the moisture evaporates, stirring frequently, about 10 minutes. Add the chicken stock, sherry, and mustard, and simmer briskly for 10 minutes. Season with salt and pepper. Add the cream and warm through. Serve immediately.
Serves 4 to 6.

Shenandoah Countryside

Route #2, Box 370
Luray, Virginia 22835
(703) 743-6434

This brick farmhouse, set on forty-five acres provides a panoramic view of the Shenandoah Valley and Blue Ridge mountains. Guests are invited to relax in the Finnish sauna or outside on one of three porches. Breakfast is served outdoors when weather permits, and at the harvest table on other occasions. Nearby attractions include the Shenandoah National Park, Luray Caverns, and country roads.

Upside Down Lemon Pie

4 eggs, separated
Pinch cream of tartar
1½ cups sugar
1 cup finely chopped pecans
Juice of 2 lemons
Rind of 1 lemon
½ teaspoon unflavored gelatin
1 tablespoon cold water
1½ cups whipping cream, whipped

Butter a 9-inch pie plate. In a large bowl with an electric mixer beat the egg whites with cream of tartar until foamy. Gradually add 1 cup of sugar and beat until stiff. Fold in the nuts. Line the bottom and sides of the prepared pie plate with meringue. Bake in a 325° oven for 25 minutes. Push down to form the shape of a crust, leaving a 1-inch rim. Bake for 25 minutes more. Cool the meringue completely.

In a medium bowl beat the egg yolks until slightly thickened. Add the lemon juice, rind, and ½ cup of sugar. In the top of a double boiler over simmering water cook the lemon mixture, stirring constantly until thick enough to coat the back of a wooden spoon. Soften the gelatin in the water. Add the gelatin to the lemon mixture. Stir to dissolve. Cool completely. Fold ⅔ of the whipped cream into the lemon mixture. Pour the lemon filling into the meringue. Garnish with the remaining cream.
Serves 8.

Walnut Onion Hearth Bread

3½ to 4 cups unbleached all-purpose flour
½ cup whole wheat flour
1 ¼-ounce package active dry yeast
1 tablespoon salt
1 cup warm milk (120° to 130°)
1 cup warm water (120° to 130°)
1 cup coarsely chopped walnuts
¾ cup finely chopped onion
½ cup margarine
2 tablespoons cornmeal

In a large mixing bowl combine 1¾ cups of unbleached flour, the whole wheat flour, yeast, and salt. Add the milk and water, and beat for 2 minutes. Stir in the walnuts, onion, and margarine. Mix well. Blend and knead in the remaining flour to make a stiff dough. Place the dough in a greased bowl. Cover with plastic wrap and a hot damp towel. Let the dough rise until doubled in bulk.

Sprinkle a baking sheet with cornmeal. Turn the dough onto a floured board and knead for 3 to 4 minutes. Shape into 2 balls and place on the baking sheet. Let the dough rise uncovered for 15 minutes. Bake in a 425° oven for 30 minutes. Reduce the heat to 300° and bake for 30 minutes more.
Makes 2 loaves.

🐦 🐦 🐦 🐦 🐦

Micajah Davis House Inn

1101 Jackson Street
Lynchburg, Virginia 24504
(804) 846-5622

Situated in a district listed on the National Register of Historic Places, the Micajah Davis House Inn is comprised of an 1817 Federal-style house; the Weaver's Cottage that was originally built as the kitchen dependency (the only one of its kind left in Lynchburg); and The Rose and Thistle, an 1890s Victorian-style house. Each is completely restored, decorated, and furnished with objects appropriate to its era. Lynchburg offers a rich variety of recreational activities year-round.

Creamy Scrambled Eggs
in Buttery Croustades

8 hard rolls (about 3 inches in diameter)
½ cup plus 2 tablespoons butter
16 eggs
¼ cup milk
4 ounces (½ package) cream cheese, softened
2 teaspoons salt
2 teaspoons pepper
1 pound bulk sausage, browned and drained
6 green onions, chopped
3 Roma tomatoes, chopped
1 tablespoon basil
Chopped parsley or chives

Slice the top from each roll. Pinch out the centers, leaving ¼-inch thick shells. Melt ½ cup of butter. Generously brush each roll with melted butter and place the rolls on a baking sheet. Bake in a 350° oven until crisp and lightly browned.

Meanwhile beat the eggs, and add the milk, cream cheese, 1 teaspoon of salt, and 1 teaspoon of pepper. Place the remaining 2 tablespoons of butter in a 2-quart pyrex dish and cover with waxed paper. Microwave at high heat for 2 minutes. Pour the egg mixture into the melted butter. Microwave at medium heat for 8 to 10 minutes, stirring the eggs at 1 minute intervals.

While the eggs are cooking combine the sausage, green onions, tomatoes, 1 teaspoon of salt, 1 teaspoon of pepper, and the basil. Mix thoroughly. Add the sausage mixture to the cooked egg mixture, mixing well. Spoon the egg-sausage mixture into the toasted croustades and sprinkle with chopped parsley or fresh chives. Serve immediately.

Serves 8.

Brown Cream and Fruit

½ teaspoon vanilla extract
3 tablespoons light brown sugar
¾ cup sour cream
1 tablespoon Grand Marnier
　(optional)
2 oranges
2 firm apples
2 bananas
2 to 3 tablespoons berries
1 kiwi fruit, sliced

In a small container combine the vanilla, brown sugar, sour cream, and Grand Marnier. Mix thoroughly and refrigerate. Peel the oranges and remove as much of the pith as possible. Cut each orange section into bite-sized pieces. Wash, core, and cut the apple into bite-sized pieces. Peel the bananas and cut in half lengthwise. Cut the halves into pieces. Combine the fruit in a large bowl and toss gently so the juice from the oranges will stop the bananas and apples from discoloring. Add the brown cream sauce and toss gently. Top the fruit with the berries and kiwi slices. Refrigerate until ready to serve.

Serves 8.

Hot Cheese Crisps

2 slices cooked ham, chopped
2 cups shredded sharp Cheddar
　cheese
1 4 to 6-ounce jar pitted ripe olives,
　chopped
1 cup mayonnaise
2 tablespoons mustard
2 tablespoons chopped green
　onions (optional)
2 packages Sesame Rye Crisps

In a medium bowl combine all of the ingredients except the crackers. Spread about 1 tablespoon of the mixture on each cracker. Place the topped crackers on a baking sheet. Broil until the cheese is hot and bubbly. Serve hot.

Makes 24 appetizers.

Fancy Baked Eggs

1½ cups canned shoestring potatoes
4 eggs
6 tablespoons chopped green
　onions
2 cups shredded sharp Cheddar
　cheese
6 slices bacon, cooked and finely
　chopped
2 tablespoons finely chopped
　parsley
¼ cup chopped tomatoes
Dash basil

Butter a 10-inch glass pie plate. Spread the shoestring potatoes evenly in the bottom of the pie plate. Make 4 holes in the potatoes down to the bottom of the dish. The holes should be about 1½ to 2 inches wide. Carefully break an egg into each hole. Bake in a 350° oven for 10 to 12 minutes, until the egg whites are almost set. Sprinkle the green onions, cheese, bacon, and parsley over the potatoes. Return to the oven for 3 to 4 minutes, or until the eggs are set to the desired doneness. Cut into 4 wedges, sprinkle the tomatoes on each wedge, and garnish with basil. Serve immediately.

Serves 4.

The Red Fox Inn and Tavern

Post Office Box 385
Middleburg, Virginia 22117
(703) 687-6301
(703) 471-4455 (D.C. Metro)

An inspired blend of period furnishings with modern conveniences makes a night's stay at the Red Fox Inn and Tavern a special occasion. The traditional character of the inn has been preserved with period-style furniture, area rugs, writing tables, original wooden mantel pieces, and hand-stenciled details. Guest rooms have been furnished with fabrics, furniture, wallcoverings, and accessories in the eighteenth-century style. Each of the centrally air-conditioned bedrooms has a four-poster bed (most with canopies), private bath, direct-dial telephone, and color television. Some have fireplaces. Fresh cut flowers, cotton bathrobes, and bedside sweets are a few of the many extra touches that make an overnight visit at this historic country inn memorable. In the morning, guests may enjoy the paper with a complimentary continental breakfast in their rooms. Country breakfasts, hearty lunches, and elegant dinners are served in the main dining rooms. Room service is also available.

Smoked Salmon Waffle
with Sour Cream and Caviar

- 4 cups all-purpose flour
- 2 tablespoons baking soda
- 1 teaspoon salt
- 6 eggs, separated
- 3 cups milk
- ½ cup melted butter
- 4 ounces smoked salmon
- ¼ cup minced green onions

In a large bowl sift together the dry ingredients. In a separate bowl whip the egg yolks and add the milk. Fold the dry ingredients into the egg yolk mixture. Add the melted butter and mix well. Beat the egg whites until stiff and fold into the batter. Carefully fold in the salmon and green onions. Bake in a heated waffle iron according to the manufacturers' directions. Top with caviar and sour cream.

Serves 8.

Recipe courtesy Chef Thomas S. Hepner.

Venison Stew

- ½ cup butter
- 3 pounds venison leg or shoulder, cut into 1-inch cubes
- 2 large onions, cut into 1-inch cubes
- 3 stalks celery, cut into ½-inch slices
- 2 large carrots, cut into ½-inch slices
- 3 turnips, cut into ½-inch cubes
- 2 medium potatoes, peeled and cut into ½-inch cubes
- 1 tomato, puréed
- 2 tablespoons leaf thyme
- 4 bay leaves
- 2 tablespoons basil
- Salt to taste
- ½ cup all-purpose flour
- 1 pint port wine
- ½ gallon venison or beef stock
- 10 juniper berries
- 2 teaspoons marjoram
- 1 teaspoon allspice
- 1 teaspoon coriander
- ¼ teaspoon cloves
- 1 teaspoon black pepper
- ¼ teaspoon ginger
- 1 tablespoon minced garlic
- ½ teaspoon cinnamon
- Wild rice or noodles

In a large stew pot melt the butter. When hot, brown the meat. As the meat browns, add the onions and celery and brown together. In a separate pot combine the remaining vegetables and add water to cover. Add 1 tablespoon of thyme, 2 bay leaves, 1 tablespoon of basil, and salt to taste. Cook over low heat until the vegetables are half cooked. Drain, reserving the stock.

When the meat, onions, and celery are brown, dust with flour and stir until the flour coats the meat and begins to brown. Add the port and mix until a paste is formed, scraping the bottom of the saucepan. Reduce the heat to medium and add the stock slowly, stirring rapidly. Add all of the remaining seasonings and the par-cooked vegetables. Cook for about 1 hour, until the meat is tender. Correct the seasonings with salt to taste.

Serve with wild rice or over noodles.

Serves 6 to 8.

Recipe courtesy Chef Thomas S. Hepner.

Southwestern Style Catfish

- ½ cup lime juice
- ½ cup lemon juice
- 1 red onion, finely diced
- 1 clove garlic, finely minced
- ¼ bunch finely chopped cilantro
- 2 tablespoons paprika
- ¼ to 1 teaspoon cayenne pepper (to taste)
- 1 tablespoon chili powder
- ½ teaspoon cuminos
- Salt and pepper to taste
- Olive oil (about 1 cup)
- 6 8-ounce catfish fillets

&. &. &.

- 3 tomatillos, finely diced
- 1 large tomato, finely diced
- 1 large green pepper, finely diced
- 1 medium red onion, finely diced
- 1 serrano chili, finely diced
- Juice of 3 limes
- ½ bunch cilantro, chopped
- 1 teaspoon chili powder
- Salt and black pepper to taste
- 1 teaspoon red wine vinegar (optional)

&. &. &.

- All-purpose flour
- 1 cup fish stock
- 2 avocados, sliced into 24 wedges

In a shallow dish combine ½ cup of lime juice, the lemon juice, 1 diced red onion, garlic, ¼ bunch cilantro, paprika, cayenne pepper, 1 tablespoon of chili powder, cuminos, salt, pepper, and olive oil to cover. Blend well. Add the catfish and marinate for at least 6 hours.

In a medium bowl combine the tomatillos, tomato, green pepper, 1 diced red onion, the serrano chili, juice of 3 limes, ½ bunch chopped cilantro, 1 teaspoon of chili powder, salt, pepper, and red wine vinegar. Blend well. Set the salsa aside.

In a large skillet add enough olive oil to cover the bottom of the pan. Dredge the catfish in flour and place flesh-side down in the heated oil. Fry until well browned, about 2 minutes. Turn and brown the other side. Add the fish stock and place in a 400° oven for 6 to 10 minutes, until the fish is done.

Remove the fish to a serving platter. Fan 4 wedges of avocado on each fillet and spread a line of salsa over the avocado wedges.

Serves 6.

Recipe courtesy Chef Thomas S. Hepner.

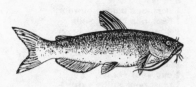

Medallions of Beef
with Sauce Beurre Rouge

¼ cup clarified butter
3 pounds center-cut beef tenderloin, trimmed and cut into 12 medallions
Salt and pepper

ᴈ ᴈ ᴈ

2 tablespoons minced shallots
1 cup red wine
¼ cup raspberry vinegar
1 tablespoon seedless raspberry jam
¼ cup demi glace (reduced beef stock)
Juice of 1 lemon
Dash Worcestershire sauce
¼ teaspoon black pepper
1 cup heavy cream
1 cup butter, chilled and cut into pieces

In a large sauté pan melt 2 tablespoons of clarified butter. Season the meat with salt and pepper. Sauté the medallions in the butter for about 3 to 4 minutes on each side. Transfer to a warm plate and keep warm in a 170° oven.

Add the shallots to the sauté pan and cook for 1 minute. Add the wine, vinegar, jam, demi glace, lemon juice, Worcestershire sauce, and pepper. Cook until most of the liquid has evaporated and it looks gelatinous and sticky. Add the cream and bring to a boil, cooking until dense and the mixture coats the back of a spoon. Whip in the pieces of butter, a small amount at a time. Season to taste with salt.

Arrange the meat on plates and top with sauce.

Serves 4.

Recipe courtesy Chef Thomas S. Hepner.

Medallions of Roast Pork Tenderloin
with Black Currant Sauce

¼ cup honey
1 teaspoon cumin
1 teaspoon coriander
2 pork tenderloins, cleaned

ᴈ ᴈ ᴈ

1 cup sugar
1 cup currant or balsamic vinegar
1 cup black currants
2 shallots, peeled and chopped
1 teaspoon fresh thyme
3 cups demi glace (reduced beef stock)
Salt to taste
Whole butter to taste

In a skillet heat the honey and spices until foaming. Place the pork in the skillet and cook, turning occasionally. Transfer to a baking dish. Bake in a 350° oven until the desired doneness.

In a saucepan caramelize the sugar and vinegar. Add ½ cup of the currants, all of the shallots, and ½ teaspoon of thyme. Add the demi glace and reduce by ⅓. Strain and add the remaining currants and thyme. Season to taste. Swirl in whole butter to enrich the sauce if desired.

Serves 2.

Recipe courtesy Chef Thomas S. Hepner.

Greenvale Manor

Route 354
Post Office Box 70
Mollusk, Virginia 22517
(804) 462-5995

Beautifully situated on the Rappahannock River and Greenvale Creek, Greenvale Manor is a classic example of the many large waterfront plantations of Lancaster County. At Greenvale guests can fish and crab off the dock, swim in the pool, rent a boat at the marina across the creek, ride bikes, play croquet or badminton, read in the game room, or lounge on the verandah and enjoy the views. All the rooms have private baths.

Horseradish and Corned Beef Dip

1 12-ounce can corned beef
1 5-ounce jar horseradish
1 cup mayonnaise
1 medium onion, minced
Pepper to taste
Worcestershire sauce to taste
Fresh parsley for garnish
Crackers or thinly sliced rye bread

Finely chop the corned beef. In a medium bowl combine the chopped corned beef, horseradish, mayonnaise, corned beef, onion, pepper, and Worcestershire sauce. Mix well and chill for at least a few hours, or overnight. Place in a serving bowl and garnish with fresh parsley. Serve with crackers or thin slices of rye bread. This keeps well if refrigerated.

Makes about 3 cups.

ᴈ ᴈ ᴈ ᴈ ᴈ

Marmalade Muffins

¼ cup butter or margarine
1 cup sour cream
¼ cup milk
1 egg
½ teaspoon vanilla extract
1½ cups all-purpose flour
¼ cup sugar
2 teaspoons baking powder
½ teaspoon baking soda
½ teaspoon salt
1 cup sweet marmalade

Grease 12 muffin cups. In a saucepan melt the butter. Remove from the heat and add the sour cream and milk. Blend well. Beat in the egg and vanilla. In a separate bowl combine the dry ingredients. Add the butter mixture to the dry ingredients and stir until just moistened. Add the marmalade and mix again. Spoon the batter into the prepared muffin cups. Bake in a 350° oven for 15 to 20 minutes.

Makes 12 muffins.

Highland Inn

Post Office Box 40
Monterey, Virginia 24465
(703) 468-2143

This three-story white Victorian clapboard hotel, now known as the Highland Inn, was known as the "Pride of the Mountains" when it was built as a resort hotel. Its outstanding architectural feature is an elaborate Eastlake-style, two-level porch. The Highland Inn is one of the few hotels of its size to continue operation. Henry Ford and Field Marshal Rommel have visited the Highland Inn in the past.

❧ ❧ ❧ ❧ ❧

Ham and Apple Pie

Pastry for 1 10-inch 2-crust pie
6 to 8 tart apples, cored, peeled and thinly sliced
½ pound cooked ham, diced
¾ cup brown sugar
2 tablespoons all-purpose flour
½ teaspoon salt
½ teaspoon pepper

In the bottom of the pastry place ⅓ of the apple slices and half of the ham. In a small bowl combine the sugar, flour, salt, and pepper. Sprinkle half of the mixture over the apples and ham. Add another ⅓ of the apples, the remaining ham, and the remaining flour mixture. Top with the remaining apples and cover with pastry. Seal the edges and pierce with a fork for the steam to escape. Bake in a 325° oven for 1 hour and 30 minutes, until the apples are tender and the top lightly browned.

Serves 6 to 8.

Cranberry Coffee Cake

½ cup butter or margarine
1 cup sugar
2 eggs
1 teaspoon baking powder
1 teaspoon baking soda
1 8-ounce can whole berry cranberry sauce
2 cups all-purpose flour
½ teaspoon salt
1 cup sour cream
1 teaspoon vanilla extract
½ cup chopped nuts

❧ ❧ ❧

½ cup confectioners' sugar
1 tablespoon milk
¼ teaspoon almond extract

Grease and flour a tube pan. In a large bowl cream together the butter and sugar. Add the eggs one at a time, blending well after each addition. In a separate bowl combine the dry ingredients. Add the dry ingredients to the creamed mixture alternately with the sour cream, ending with the flour. Add the vanilla.

Pour half of the batter into the prepared tube pan. Top with half of the cranberry sauce. Add the remaining batter and top with the remaining cranberry sauce. Top with nuts. Bake in a 350° oven for 1 hour.

In a medium bowl combine the confectioners' sugar, milk, and almond extract. Ice the cooled cake.

Serves 10.

Highland Inn

The Inn at Montross

Post Office Box 908
Montross, Virginia 22520
(804) 493-9097

The Inn at Montross was built prior to 1683, and parts of the structure have been in continuous use for over three hundred years. The six guest rooms, each with private bath and individual heat and air conditioning, are furnished with four-poster beds, some with canopies. All rooms have cable television and telephones, as well as in-room coffee makers. The main floor boasts a small lounge with television and a grand piano that guests (and occasionally guest artists) are invited to use. Background music is played through one of the finest sound systems in the area. Chef Jeffrey Keane serves gourmet continental meals featuring homemade pastries and desserts in the two dining rooms, which are open to the public for luncheons and dinner daily. John Minor's Ordinary, an English-style tavern downstairs from the inn, is a popular place to gather.

The Inn at Montross

Swedish Gravlax
with Mustard-Dill Sauce

This can be served as an appetizer or an hors d'oeuvre. The salmon without the sauce makes a wonderful sandwich filling, or an interesting alternative to the traditional "Lox on a bagel."

1 9 to 11-pound Norwegian salmon
1 cup sugar
1 cup salt
1 cup cracked black pepper
2 heads fresh dill, finely chopped

ᴥ ᴥ ᴥ

4 large eggs
½ cup Dijon mustard
1 tablespoon dry mustard
½ cup sugar
1 cup oil
½ bunch fresh dill, finely chopped
¼ cup red vinegar

ᴥ ᴥ ᴥ

Lettuce and red onion rings for garnish

Fillet the salmon, leaving the skin on. Using needle-nosed pliers remove all bones from both fillets. In a medium bowl combine 1 cup of sugar and the salt. Coat the flesh side of each fillet with the mixture, then coat each fillet with black pepper. Lay 2 heads of dill over one of the fillets and top with the other fillet (flesh side to flesh side).

Press between 2 baking sheets and weigh with any suitable heavy object. Keep refrigerated for 6 days or until all of the sugar-salt mixture has been absorbed.

In a large bowl combine the eggs, Dijon mustard, dry mustard, and ½ cup of sugar. Slowly add the oil. When the mixture is blended, add ½ bunch of fresh dill and red vinegar.

To serve, scrape the dill and black pepper mixture from the salmon. Slice the salmon diagonally into paper-thin slices. Place on serving plates. Garnish serving plates with the sauce, and add lettuce and red onion rings.

Serves 24.

Recipe courtesy Chef Jeffrey Keane.

Praline Ice Cream

1 quart heavy cream
1 cup Frangelica (almond-flavored liqueur)
1½ cups praline paste
6 whole eggs
16 egg yolks
1 cup plus 5 tablespoons sugar

ᴥ ᴥ ᴥ

1 pint heavy cream
1½ pounds Belgian chocolate

In a large bowl whip 1 quart of cream with the Frangelica and praline paste until smooth. Refrigerate.

In the top of a double boiler over simmering water combine the eggs, egg yolks, and sugar. Heat until lukewarm, stirring constantly. Do not boil. Beat the mixture with an electric mixer until the mixture triples in volume and forms ribbons. Remove from the heat and fold into the chilled praline cream mixture. Freeze overnight.

In a saucepan bring 1 pint of cream to a boil. Remove from the heat and add the chocolate, stirring until the chocolate has melted. Strain through a fine sieve. Serve with the ice cream.

Makes about 2 quarts of ice cream, and about 5 cups of sauce.

Recipe courtesy Chef Jeffrey Keane.

Lobster Gratinee

2 1½-pound Maine lobsters, cooked

❧ ❧ ❧

½ cup olive oil
1 carrot, chopped
2 stalks celery, chopped
1 large onion, chopped
2 unpeeled cloves garlic, chopped
Pinch salt
Pinch cayenne pepper
Pinch paprika
1 cup tomato paste
2 cups domestic brandy
1 cup white wine (dry vermouth preferred)
2 gallons water

❧ ❧ ❧

½ cup butter
½ cup all-purpose flour

❧ ❧ ❧

½ cup unsweetened whipping cream
½ cup tomato concasee (diced, seeded and peeled tomatoes)
½ cup julienned scallions
½ cup sliced mushrooms
½ cup Hollandaise sauce

Clean the lobsters and remove all meat from the lobster shells. Reserve the shells and heads for the sauce. Dice the meat into ½-inch pieces and refrigerate until needed.

Purée the lobster carcasses with the paddle attachment on a food mixer (the use of a food processor is not recommended). Heat a large saucepot. Add the olive oil and sauté the puréed shells for 5 minutes. Add the chopped vegetables and sauté for 4 minutes more. Add the seasonings. Add the tomato paste and cook for 3 minutes. Deglaze the pan with brandy and white wine. Add the water and cook until the mixture is reduced by half. Strain through a cheesecloth into another pot. Reheat to a boil. In a skillet make a roux by melting the butter and adding the flour. Stir until well blended. Add the roux to the boiling sauce. Simmer for 2 hours to remove the starchy flavor. Strain the sauce through a fine sieve and keep warm until needed.

Whip the cream until stiff. Reduce 1 cup of the lobster sauce by ⅓, and add the tomatoes, scallions, mushrooms, and lobster meat. Bring to a boil and remove from the heat. Quickly fold in the whipped cream followed by the Hollandaise sauce. Pour the mixture into a serving dish and then gratinee (form a light crust) under the broiler. Serve immediately.

Serves 2.

Recipe courtesy Chef Jeffrey Keane.

Chicken Morel

½ pound bacon, diced
½ cup diced shallots
Pinch fresh thyme
Pinch fresh sage
1 cup morel mushrooms, chopped
½ cup port wine
3 8-ounce boneless chicken breasts (1 skinless, 2 with skins)
Salt to taste
½ cup egg whites
½ cup heavy cream
Butter, melted

❧ ❧ ❧

1 tablespoon chopped shallots
1 cup port wine
¼ cup demi glace (reduced brown stock)
1 tablespoon butter

In a large skillet sauté the bacon until crisp. Add the shallots, thyme, sage, and morels. Deglaze the pan with ½ cup of port wine and cook until all of the liquid has evaporated.

In a food processor purée the skinless chicken breast, and add a pinch of salt, the egg whites, and heavy cream. Blend the ingredients and fold in the mushroom mixture.

Loosen the skin on the remaining chicken breasts to form a pocket. Stuff with the mushroom mixture. If desired, the breasts may be frozen at this point, or refrigerated for up to 24 hours.

Place the chicken in a baking pan and brush with melted butter. Bake in a 375° oven for 20 minutes.

In a small saucepan cook the shallots in 1 cup of port wine until the liquid is reduced by half. Add the demi glace and bring to a boil for 1 minute. Stir in the whole butter.

To serve, make a pool of the sauce on a portion of the plate, and neatly fan slices of chicken on top of the sauce.

Serves 2.

Recipe courtesy Chef Jeffrey Keane.

Warm Duck Salad

¼ cup sesame oil
1 cup cooked julienned duck meat
1 cup sliced mushrooms
½ red pepper, finely julienned
½ yellow pepper, finely julienned
½ green pepper, finely julienned
¼ cup raspberry vinegar
½ pound cleaned spinach

Heat a sauté pan until extremely hot. Add the sesame oil and quickly sauté the duck, mushrooms, and peppers. Deglaze with raspberry vinegar, and remove from the heat. Add the spinach and fold rapidly. The spinach should be slightly warm but not wilted or soggy.

Serves 2.

Recipe courtesy Chef Jeffrey Keane.

Escargot Montross Inn

1 12x16-inch sheet puff pastry
10 imported helix snails
½ cup garlic butter
1 egg
½ cup water

🐌 🐌 🐌

2 cloves finely chopped garlic
Pinch chopped shallots
½ cup white wine (or dry vermouth)
1 cup chicken stock
1 cup heavy cream
½ cup lightly salted butter
½ cup tomato concasee (chopped,
**   seeded and peeled tomatoes)**

Cut ten 1½-inch squares and ten 2½-inch squares of puff pastry. Place a snail on each small square and top with a piece of garlic butter. Place a larger square over each of the snails. Trim the edges and crimp decoratively. Refrigerate until needed.

Combine the egg and water. Brush the pastry with the mixture. Bake in a 400° oven for about 6 minutes, until golden brown.

In a skillet sauté the garlic and shallots for about 1 minute. Deglaze the pan with white wine, bring to a boil, and reduce by half. Add the chicken stock and reduce by half. Add the cream and reduce by half. Remove from the heat and quickly whisk in the butter. Strain the sauce.

To serve, pour the sauce onto serving plates. On each plate arrange five baked snails in a circle, and place the tomato concasee in the center.

Serves 2.

Recipe courtesy Chef Jeffrey Keane.

Holly Point

Box 64
Morattico, Virginia 22523
(804) 462-7759

Holly Point is situated on more than 120 acres of pine forest and looks out over a lovely view of the Rappahanock River. In addition to the many interesting historical sites nearby, there are numerous land and water activities, such as hiking, biking, swimming, boating, water skiing, fishing, and crabbing. Holly Point has three guest rooms.

🐌 🐌 🐌 🐌 🐌

Cherry Black Walnut Bread

Cherries and walnuts are grown at Holly Point.

1 cup pie cherries
1 cup sugar
¼ cup oil
2 eggs
¼ cup milk
2 cups all-purpose flour
1 teaspoon baking soda
1 teaspoon baking powder
½ cup black walnuts

Grease a 9x5-inch loaf pan. In a large bowl combine the cherries, sugar, oil, eggs, and milk. In a separate bowl sift together the dry ingredients. Stir the dry ingredients into the cherry mixture. Add the walnuts and beat well. Pour into the prepared pan. Bake in a 350° oven for about 1 hour.

Makes 1 loaf.

Hoe Cakes

From the kitchen of George Washington.

1 cup water-ground cornmeal
1 cup cold water
1 teaspoon salt
Maple syrup, honey, or molasses

In a medium bowl combine the cornmeal, water, and salt. Fry on a hot hoe (griddle), turning to brown on both sides. Serve with maple syrup, honey, or molasses.

Serves 4.

Trillium House: A Country Inn at Wintergreen

Post Office Box 280
Nellysford, Virginia 22958
(804) 325-9126

Trillium House is one of a few country inns in America designed and built to meet today's travel standards while retaining the charm and friendliness of bygone days. This inn has twelve guest rooms (including two suites), each with private bath and controlled temperature. Guests will find all they need for a relaxing getaway: a large family library, woodstove, leisurely breakfasts, and Wintergreen's 10,000 acres of space. However, nearby is a rich tradition of American history, including Monticello, Ash Lawn, and the Woodrow Wilson Birthplace. A full breakfast each morning is included in the price of the room. Dinner is served on Fridays, Saturdays, and special occasions. Luncheons and banquets are available by prior arrangement.

Corn Blini
with Salsa Shrimp

1 tablespoon vegetable juice
1 large ripe tomato, chopped
1 jalapeño pepper, seeded and
  finely chopped
1 tablespoon finely chopped red
  bell pepper
1 tomatillo, chopped
Fresh ground black pepper
1 small clove garlic, minced
1 tablespoon chopped red onion
1 teaspoon fresh lemon and lime
  juice
2 teaspoons finely chopped fresh
  cilantro

   🍃 🍃 🍃

½ teaspoon cumin
1 cup yellow cornmeal
⅔ cup unbleached all-purpose flour
1 teaspoon baking powder
¼ teaspoon salt
1 teaspoon sugar
¼ cup corn kernels (canned or
  steamed fresh)
1 egg, slightly beaten
⅓ cup melted butter
1¼ cups milk

   🍃 🍃 🍃

3 to 4 tablespoons olive oil
2 dozen raw large shrimp, peeled
  and deveined

   🍃 🍃 🍃

3 tablespoons sour cream
3 tablespoons sharp Cheddar
  cheese

In a small bowl combine the vegetable juice, chopped tomato, jalapeño pepper, red bell pepper, tomatillo, black pepper, garlic, red onion, lemon juice, lime juice, and cilantro. Set aside. The salsa mixture may be made 24 hours in advance if desired.

In a medium bowl combine the cumin, cornmeal, flour, baking powder, salt, sugar, and corn. In a small bowl combine the egg, butter, and milk. Stir the wet ingredients into the dry ingredients just until moistened.

In a nonstick skillet heat 1 tablespoon of olive oil over medium heat. Using half the batter, make 3 pancakes in the hot oil. Bake until bubbles rise to the surface and the edges are golden. Turn and bake until browned. Repeat with the remaining batter, adding oil if needed. Set aside on 6 heated plates.

In a separate skillet heat the remaining olive oil. Sauté the shrimp until almost done, covering if needed. Add the salsa and heat through, 1 to 2 minutes over medium high heat. Place 4 shrimp on each corn blini and top with a teaspoon each of sour cream and Cheddar.

Serves 6.

Orange Ham Pasta

12 ounces linguine pasta
6 tablespoons unsalted butter,
  softened

2 shallots, finely chopped
½ pound smoked ham, julienned
½ cup orange juice concentrate,
  thawed
¼ teaspoon coriander
½ teaspoon white pepper
1 tablespoon chopped parsley
1 tablespoon chopped natural
  pistachios

In a large stockpot cook the linguine in water until al dente. Drain. In a skillet heat 2 tablespoons of butter and sauté the shallots and ham over medium heat for 2 to 3 minutes. Add 2 tablespoons of orange juice concentrate and heat through. In a large bowl combine the linguine, remaining butter, orange concentrate, coriander, and white pepper. Divide among plates and top with ham, chopped parsley, and nuts.

Serves 4 as a light lunch, or 6 as an appetizer.

Vineyard Salad

6 ounces Brie (or Saga, Edam,
  Gouda, cream cheese)
1 sheet phyllo dough
2 tablespoons butter, melted
2 tablespoons chopped almonds

   🍃 🍃 🍃

2 teaspoons sherry or champagne
  mustard
⅓ cup white wine vinegar
1 tablespoon honey
¼ teaspoon salt
⅛ teaspoon cardamom
Fresh ground black or white pepper
  to taste
1 cup olive oil
½ cup safflower oil, grapeseed oil,
  or other light oil

   🍃 🍃 🍃

Mixed greens, rinsed and drained
  (Boston, Belgian Endive,
  Arugula, spinach, or watercress)
1 cup rinsed, drained and halved
  seedless red and/or green
  grapes

Cut the cheese into 6 equal portions. Cut the phyllo sheet in half widthwise. Brush half with a little of the melted butter. Place the second half over the buttered half and cut into 6 squares. Wrap each piece of cheese

Trillium House

with a square of phyllo, brushing with the remaining butter to seal. Work quickly to prevent the phyllo from drying out. Sprinkle with almonds. Bake on the top shelf in a 400° oven for about 8 to 10 minutes, just until the pastry is golden brown.

In a bowl or blender combine the sherry or champagne mustard, white wine vinegar, honey, salt, cardamom, and pepper. Dribble the oils into the vinegar mixture in a slow, steady stream. This makes about 2 cups of wine vinaigrette.

To serve, divide the greens among 6 salad plates. Top with grapes and baked cheese. Drizzle with wine vinaigrette. Serve immediately.

Serves 6.

BLT Salad

> Mixed greens (romaine, radicchio, Boston)
> 3 medium-sized ripe tomatoes, rinsed and sliced
> 6 slices bacon, cooked, drained and chopped
>
>   ❧   ❧   ❧
>
> ⅓ cup balsamic vinegar
> 1 teaspoon Dijon mustard
> 3 tablespoons fresh basil leaves, washed and patted dry
> 1 tablespoon chopped green onion
> 1 cup olive oil
> Salt and freshly ground pepper to taste
>
>   ❧   ❧   ❧
>
> Wheat Croutons (recipe follows)
> Pesto Mayonnaise (recipe follows)

Divide the greens among 6 salad plates. Top with sliced tomatoes and chopped bacon.

In a blender combine the vinegar, Dijon mustard, basil leaves, and onion. Slowly add the oil to blend. Season to taste. This makes about 1½ cups of dressing.

To serve the salad, drizzle with basil dressing. Sprinkle on the Whole Wheat Croutons and pipe a small rosette of Pesto Mayonnaise on top.

Serves 6.

Wheat Croutons

> 4 slices multigrain bread
> 3 tablespoons butter, melted
> Salt and freshly ground pepper

Cube the bread and place in a small roasting pan. Drizzle with melted butter and season with salt and pepper. Bake in a 350° oven for 15 to 20 minutes, stirring once.

Makes 6 salad garnishes.

Pesto Mayonnaise

> 1 cup fresh basil leaves, washed and patted dry
> 2 large cloves fresh garlic, peeled and chopped
> ½ cup pine nuts
> ½ cup olive oil
> ½ cup freshly grated Parmesan cheese
> 2 tablespoons freshly grated Romano cheese
> 1 cup mayonnaise
> Salt and freshly ground pepper to taste

In a blender combine the basil, garlic, and pine nuts. Slowly add the oil. Add the cheeses, mayonnaise, and seasonings. Blend just until combined.

Makes about 3 cups.

Salmon with Horseradish Crust

> 6 fresh salmon fillets
> ¾ cup dry white wine
> 4 ounces softened cream cheese
> 1 tablespoon Dijon mustard
> ½ teaspoon salt
> ½ cup finely chopped smoked salmon
> 2½ tablespoons finely grated fresh horseradish
> 2 teaspoons grated lemon peel
> 6 tablespoons butter, melted
> 1¼ cups fine bread crumbs
> Fresh chives

Butter a baking pan. Place the salmon in the pan and pour the wine over the top. In a small bowl beat the cream cheese until fluffy, and add the mustard, salt, smoked salmon, horseradish, and lemon peel, blending well. Spread the mixture over the fillets. Combine the butter and bread crumbs and sprinkle evenly over the fillets. Bake in a 425° oven for about 15 minutes. Garnish with a cross of fresh chives and serve immediately.

Serves 6.

Grilled Veal Chops with Pecan Butter

> ½ cup olive oil
> 3 tablespoons balsamic vinegar
> 3 tablespoons white wine
> 2 tablespoons Dijon mustard
> 1 teaspoon dried thyme (or 2 teaspoons chopped fresh)
> Salt and freshly ground black pepper to taste
> 6 Frenched veal rib chops
>
>   ❧   ❧   ❧
>
> ⅓ cup chopped pecans
> 6 tablespoons butter, softened
> 1 tablespoon minced chives
> ¼ teaspoon curry powder
> 1 teaspoon lemon juice

In a small bowl whisk together the olive oil, vinegar, wine, mustard, thyme, salt, and pepper. Place the veal chops in a glass baking dish and marinate for 3 to 4 hours.

Place the pecans on a baking sheet. Roast in a 375° oven for 8 to 10 minutes. Cool, finely chop, and combine with the softened butter, chives, curry powder, and lemon juice. Pipe the mixture into 6 decorative "S" swirls on a baking sheet or plate and chill.

Grill the marinated veal chops over medium hot coals for 3 to 5 minutes per side, depending on the desired doneness. Serve with pecan butter.

Serves 6.

  ❧   ❧   ❧   ❧   ❧

Hazelnut Potatoes

18 small red-skinned potatoes
2 tablespoons olive oil
Coarse salt and freshly ground
**   pepper**
2 tablespoons butter
1 medium onion, halved and thinly
**   sliced**
½ cup chopped hazelnuts
¼ cup Frangelica (hazelnut liqueur)
½ cup sour cream
1½ tablespoons coarse ground
**   Dijon mustard**
1 tablespoon chopped fresh parsley

Oil the potatoes and season with salt and pepper. Place the potatoes in a baking pan. Roast in a 400° oven until tender, about 45 minutes to 1 hour, shaking the pan occasionally.

In a sauté pan over medium heat melt the butter and sauté the onions for 3 to 4 minutes. Add the nuts and sauté for another 1 to 2 minutes. Add the Frangelica and reduce to a thin syrup. Remove from the heat and add the sour cream and mustard. Place the roasted potatoes in a large bowl and pour the hazelnut sauce over the top. Toss to coat. Sprinkle parsley over all before serving.

Serves 6 as an appetizer or side dish.

White Chocolate & Mint Brownie Ice Cream

3 cups whipping cream
1 cup milk
1 vanilla bean, split lengthwise (or
**   1 tablespoon vanilla extract)**
¼ cup fresh mint leaves, coarsely
**   chopped**
5 large egg yolks
1 pound white chocolate, finely
**   chopped**

🍂 🍂 🍂

2 cups crumbled brownie pieces
½ cup mint chocolate chips
White and dark chocolate curls or
**   leaves**

In a heavy 2-quart saucepan heat the cream, milk, vanilla bean, and mint, stirring constantly until hot but not boiling. In a bowl whisk the egg yolks until light and lemon colored. Slowly pour about 1 cup of the hot cream mixture into the egg yolks, mixing until smooth. Pour the egg yolk mixture into the saucepan. Whisk constantly over low heat until the mixture thickens and coats the back of a spoon, 4 to 5 minutes. Strain to remove the mint leaves and vanilla bean. Whisk in the white chocolate until melted. Cool at room temperature. Freeze in an ice cream maker according to the manufacturer's instructions. When set, quickly stir in the brownie pieces and chocolate chips. Top with white and dark chocolate curls or leaves.

Makes about 2 quarts.

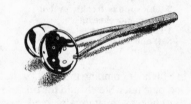

Bensonhouse

"The Emmanuel Hutzer House"
2036 Monument Avenue
Richmond, Virginia 23220
(804) 353-6900

This 8,000-square-foot inn has undergone an almost total renovation. It was designed in Italian Renaissance style, with a slightly French accent, but the leaded glass windows with coffered ceilings with dropped beams and mahogany panelling add a medieval flavor. An elevator leads to the second floor guest rooms, all with private baths and two with fireplaces. A special honeymoon package is available on request.

Raisin, Sunflower Seed, and Oatmeal Bread

1 cup quick oats
½ cup brown sugar
½ cup raisins
½ cup whole wheat flour
1 tablespoon salt
2 tablespoons margarine
2 cups boiling water
1 ¼-ounce package active dry yeast
1 teaspoon honey
½ cup warm water (110° to 115°)
½ cup sunflower seeds
5 cups all-purpose flour

In a large bowl combine the oats, brown sugar, raisins, whole wheat flour, salt, and margarine. Add the boiling water and allow the mixture to cool to lukewarm.

In a separate bowl combine the yeast, honey, and warm water and set aside to proof. Add the proofed yeast mixture to the lukewarm batter. Add the sunflower seeds and flour. When the dough is firm and easily handled, turn onto a floured board. Knead until smooth and blistery, about 5 to 8 minutes. Place in a greased bowl and cover. Let rise until doubled in bulk.

Grease two 9x5-inch loaf pans. Punch down and divide in half. Form into 2 loaves and place in the prepared pans. Let the loaves rise to the top of the pan. Bake in a 350° oven for 30 to 40 minutes. The loaves will be done when they sound hollow when tapped on the bottom of the pans. Remove the loaves from the pans and cool on a wire rack. Brush the loaves with margarine for a soft crust.

Makes 2 loaves.

Bensonhouse

L'Auberge Provençale

Route 341, Box 119
White Post, Virginia 22663
(703) 837-1375

In this beautiful 1753 stone farmhouse in the farming country of the Shenandoah Valley, Celeste and Alain Borel have created a French country inn and restaurant. Alain has become well known for his "cuisine moderne," and the inn frequently has diners who drive from the Washington, D.C., area. The entrees are truly impressive and the desserts wonderful. Guest rooms in the main house and nearby cottage are furnished with antique and wicker furniture, four-poster and white iron beds, and, in two rooms in the main house, fireplaces.

Les Crevettes à la Russe

Shrimp sautéed with fresh ginger and scallions, and deglazed with vodka. We recommend serving this dish with a fresh herb or spinach pasta.

> **24 large shrimp, shelled and**
>   **deveined**
> **All-purpose flour**
> **Oil**
> **3 tablespoons butter**
> **1 lemon**
> **1 large shallot, chopped**
> **2 large cloves garlic, chopped**
> **1 teaspoon grated fresh ginger**
> **3 ounces vodka**
> **1 tablespoon chopped parsley**
> **½ bunch julienned scallions**
> **Salt and pepper to taste**
> **1 cup shrimp stock (recipe follows)**

Dust the shrimp with flour. In a skillet over high heat add the oil. Sauté the shrimp on one side for 3 minutes. Reduce the heat to medium, turn the shrimp, and cook for 2 minutes more. Add 1 tablespoon of butter and the juice of ½ lemon. Cook for 2 minutes. Remove the shrimp and drain on a rack or paper towel.

Wipe the skillet, and add the remaining butter, shallots, garlic, and ginger. Cook until the ingredients sweat but do not brown, about 20 seconds. Add 4 tablespoons of the vodka over high heat and ignite. When the flame subsides add the shrimp stock, juice of ½ lemon, and remaining vodka. Reduce by half. Add the parsley and scallions, and cook until the scallions are al dente. Salt and pepper to taste.

Arrange the shrimp on 4 serving plates. Pour the sauce over the shrimp and serve.

Serves 4.

Shrimp Stock

Shells of 24 large shrimp
1 carrot, cut up
1 onion, chopped
1 stalk celery, cut up
Fresh herbs (such as thyme,
 marjoram, parsley)
Water
Dry white wine

In a medium saucepan combine the shrimp shells, carrot, onion, celery, and herbs. Cover with a mixture of half water and half wine. Bring to a boil and simmer for 30 to 45 minutes to extract the flavor from the shells, herbs, and vegetables. Skim off any foam that collects during cooking.

Makes about 1 pint.

Les Ris de Veau
au Porto et aux Capers

Sweetbreads with vintage port and capers.

2 pounds sweetbreads
2 quarts water
1 teaspoon salt
½ teaspoon pepper
6 bay leaves
3 ounces red wine vinegar
All-purpose flour
Salt and pepper to taste
½ cup butter, unsalted
Juice of ½ lemon
2 medium shallots, chopped
1 cup port wine, vintage or ruby
1 cup concentrated veal stock
2 teaspoons baby capers
Salt and pepper to taste

Rinse the sweetbreads in a bowl with slow running water for 4 hours. Clean and devein.

In a large saucepan boil 2 quarts of water with 1 teaspoon of salt, ½ teaspoon of pepper, the bay leaves, and red wine vinegar. Plunge the sweetbreads into the water, reduce the heat and simmer for 20 minutes. Drain and cool the sweetbreads. Using a heavy skillet as a weight, press the sweetbreads with the skillet for 30 minutes, until slightly flattened. Dust the sweetbreads with flour, salt, and pepper.

In a heavy skillet heat ¼ cup of butter and sauté the sweetbreads until slightly golden. Squeeze lemon juice over all. Remove from the heat. Place the sweetbreads on a warm plate.

With a clean towel wipe the residue from the skillet. Add 2 tablespoons of butter and the shallots, and cook until soft. Add the port and veal stock, and reduce by half over medium heat. Add the capers, and season with salt and pepper. Remove the pan from the heat and add the remaining butter. Pour the sauce with the capers around and over the sweetbreads. Serve.

Serves 4.

Le Saumon de
Norvege au Pernod

We recommend serving this dish with fresh spinach pasta or a light curried balsamic rice.

1 quart fish stock
1 small bunch rosemary
2 lemons
4 bay leaves
6 6 to 7-ounce Norwegian salmon
 fillets, bones removed
6 tablespoons butter
2 large whole shallots, peeled and
 finely chopped
1 large clove garlic, peeled and
 finely chopped
1 tablespoon chopped rosemary
½ cup Pernod

In a fish poacher combine ¾ of the fish stock, sprigs of rosemary, juice of ½ lemon, and the bay leaves. Bring to a boil over high heat.

Squeeze the remaining lemon juice over both sides of the salmon fillets. Place the fillets on the rack of the poacher, making sure the liquid does not touch the fish. Cover and let the stock boil for 2 minutes. Remove the poacher from the heat and let steam for about 6 minutes without removing the lid. If the fillets are thin, the steaming time may be reduced.

In a medium skillet over high heat melt 2 tablespoons of butter. Do not brown the butter. Add the shallots and cook until transparent. Add the garlic and chopped rosemary, and sauté for 10 seconds. Add ¾ of the Pernod, and cook for 1 minute. Reduce the heat to medium and add the remaining fish stock. Reduce the liquid by ¼. Cut the remaining butter into small pieces and incorporate into the liquid a small amount at a time, moving the skillet back and forth over the heat until it has a nice glaze. The sauce should coat the back of a wooden spoon. Salt and pepper to taste. Add the remaining Pernod. Remove from the heat.

Place 1 fillet of salmon on each of 6 warmed plates. Pour the sauce over the fish and garnish with sprigs of fresh rosemary.

Serves 6.

Les Escargots à la Crème de Roquefort

1 pint whipping cream
1 large shallot, finely chopped
2 cloves garlic, finely chopped
3 tablespoons veal stock
4 tablespoons Roquefort cheese
2 tablespoons chopped parsley
24 extra-large French escargots
Pepper to taste
1 cup wild rice, cooked

In a saucepan combine the cream, shallots, garlic, veal stock, and Roquefort cheese. Reduce by ⅓ over medium heat, whisking constantly so that the mixture does not curdle. Add the chopped parsley and escargots. Add pepper. Simmer for 2 minutes and remove from the heat.

Divide the rice among 4 serving plates. Make a well in the center and place 6 escargots in the center of each well. Pour sauce around the wells and serve immediately.

Note: Do not add salt, as most Roquefort imported into this country has salt added as a preservative.

Serves 4.

Les Moules aux Herbes de Provence

Mussels with fresh herbs of Provence. Provence is the garden of France where traditionally herbs are used with a heavy hand in most recipes. Alain Borel created this recipe while vacationing at the seaside. Dried herbs are not recommended.

1½ cups dry vermouth
1 teaspoon chopped shallots
½ teaspoon chopped garlic
¼ teaspoon white pepper
Juice of ½ lemon
1 teaspoon tarragon
1 tablespoon mint
½ teaspoon parsley
1 teaspoon oregano
½ teaspoon thyme
½ teaspoon fennel

&ta; &ta; &ta;

5 pounds fresh mussels, washed and debearded

In a large stainless steel pot combine all of the ingredients except the mussels and bring to a boil. Add the mussels and cover the pot. When the mussels open up, immediately remove the pot from the heat. Do not overcook the mussels or they will become rubbery. Arrange the mussels in serving dishes, discarding any unopened ones. Ladle some of the broth and herbs on top of each serving. Serve immediately.

Serves 4 to 6.

Timbale de Crabe au Mais

Crab Timbale with Corn Sauce

1 ear fresh corn
¼ cup butter
1 white leek, chopped
1 shallot, chopped
½ teaspoon summer savory
Dash cayenne pepper
Pinch salt and white pepper
1½ cups milk
2 tablespoons butter
½ cup heavy cream

&ta; &ta; &ta;

2 tablespoons unsalted butter
1 teaspoon chopped shallots
½ pound jumbo lump crab meat, picked over
2 tablespoons chopped tarragon
1 cup milk
3 whole eggs and 1 egg yolk
¾ cup cream
Salt and white pepper to taste
2 pinches freshly grated nutmeg

Remove the kernels from the corn. In a skillet melt 2 tablespoons of butter. Add the corn, leek, 1 chopped shallot, savory, cayenne, salt, and pepper. Sweat over low heat for 2 minutes. Add 1½ cups of milk. Cook covered over medium low heat until the corn is tender, about 15 minutes. Place the mixture in a blender, and blend until liquified. The consistency should just coat a spoon. Cut 2 tablespoons of butter into chunks, and add a small amount at a time, incorporating well after each addition. Add the heavy cream. Strain into a small saucepan and set aside.

In a non-corrosive skillet melt the remaining 2 tablespoons of butter. Add 1 teaspoon of chopped shallots and sweat for 1 minute. Carefully add the crab and tarragon, and cook for 1 minute. Add 1 cup of milk, and gently heat until just warm.

In a stainless steel bowl beat the eggs and egg yolk lightly. Stir in ¾ cup of cream. Add the milk mixture to the cream mixture and add the salt, pepper, and nutmeg. Stir gently to combine.

Oil six 4-ounce molds or ramekins. Place the ramekins in a deep baking dish. Ladle equal amounts of crab mixture into each mold. Pour hot water into the baking dish halfway up the sides of the molds. Bake in a 350° oven for 35 minutes or until the timbales are slightly firm when gently prodded.

Turn the timbales out onto warm plates. Heat the corn sauce until warmed through, adding a little milk if necessary for the proper consistency. Pour hot sauce around the timbales and serve.

Serves 6.

Gateau au Chocolat Formidable

Double-rich chocolate cake with white chocolate sauce and fresh sage. We serve this with fresh coconut ice cream, giving a good contrast of texture, temperature, and flavor. You may experiment with other ice creams to suit your taste.

        1¾ cups all-purpose flour
        2 cups sugar
        ¾ cup cocoa
        1½ teaspoons baking powder
        1½ teaspoons baking soda
        1 teaspoon salt
        2 eggs
        2 cups hot coffee
        3 tablespoons oil
        1 tablespoon vanilla extract

        ❧ ❧ ❧

        4 ounces bittersweet chocolate,
            chopped
        1 ounce semisweet chocolate,
            chopped
        ¼ cup coffee
        3 tablespoons unsalted butter
        Optional liqueur to taste (cognac,
            chartreuse, etc.)

        ❧ ❧ ❧

        4 ounces white Belgian chocolate
        ⅓ cup heavy cream or crème
            fraîche
        1 small bunch fresh sage, chopped

Butter and flour a 10-inch springform pan. In a large bowl combine the first 6 ingredients, mixing until well blended. While continuing to mix, add the eggs, hot coffee, oil, and vanilla. Blend until smooth. Pour the batter into the prepared pan. Bake in a 375° oven for 30 minutes or until a knife inserted in the center comes out clean.

In the top of a double boiler over simmering water melt the bittersweet and semisweet chocolate with ¼ cup of coffee until very smooth and glossy. Remove from the heat and stir in the butter a piece at a time, incorporating well after each addition. Stir in the liqueur if desired, and cool at room temperature until ready to use. Frost the cooled cake.

In the top of a double boiler over simmering water melt the chocolate with the heavy cream. Add the chopped sage and keep warm until ready to use. For best flavor, make the sauce ahead of time so the sage has time to flavor the sauce.

To serve, spoon white chocolate and sage around each slice of cake. Serves 8.

Newport House Bed and Breakfast

710 South Henry Street
Williamsburg, Virginia 23186-4113
(804) 229-1775

Newport House was built in 1988 from a 1756 design for a now-lost house in Newport, Rhode Island. Furnished totally in period with English and American antiques, it offers spacious bedrooms with four-poster canopy beds and private baths. The inn is five minutes' walk from Colonial Williamsburg with the many restaurants, shops, and colonial taverns.

Newport House

Colonial Bread

This recipe will make 2 loaves, but we prefer to make round loaves the way they did in colonial days. We use a large wedding cake pan whose sides have been augmented with a strip of aluminum flashing, available from any building supply store.

        3 cups whole wheat flour
        2 tablespoons active dry yeast
        3 cups warm water (110° to 115°)

        ❧ ❧ ❧

        3 cups bread flour
        3 cups unbleached all-purpose flour
        2 tablespoons salt
        Water

In a medium bowl combine the whole wheat flour, yeast, and warm water. Cover with a damp tea towel and leave in a warm place for 8 to 12 hours, or overnight.

Grease a large cake pan or spray with cooking spray. In a large bowl combine the remaining dry ingredients. Add the starter mixture to the dry ingredients. Add enough water to make a stiff dough. Turn the dough onto a floured surface and knead well. Place the dough in a bowl and cover with a damp towel. Let the dough rise in a warm place for 2 hours. Punch down and place in a large baking pan. Cover with a damp towel and let rise in a warm place for 1 hour.

Bake in a 450° oven for 30 minutes. Remove the bread from the pan, reduce the heat to 300°, and bake for 30 minutes more.

Makes 1 large or 2 regular loaves.

Blue Bird Haven Bed and Breakfast

8691 Barhamsville Road
Williamsburg-Toano, Virginia 23168
(804) 566-0177

In this Tidewater area ranch-style home with comfortable rooms, guests enjoy plenty of good food and the relaxed atmosphere of home. The innkeeper says, "If you don't feel at home here, you should be there." Its three guest rooms offer queen- and double-size four-poster beds and wicker beds, equipped with hand-made quilts, afghans, pictures, and rugs. Amenities include private baths, air conditioning, a working fireplace, bedtime desserts, and fresh flowers.

One Way to Cook a Whole Country Ham

1 12 to 15-pound country ham (bone-in)
5 cups cold water or apple juice

Have the butcher cut off the ham hock and save it for later use. Wash and scrub the ham with a stiff brush or pot scrubber to remove any mold or excess salt and pepper. Place the ham in a large, deep soaking pot and fill with cold water to cover the ham. Cover and soak for up to 12 hours. Drain.

Place the ham on a rack in a roaster or a large roasting pan. Add 5 cups of cold water. Cover with a roaster lid or a sheet of heavy duty foil tightly sealed around the edges of the pan. Bake the ham in a 500° oven for 15 minutes. Turn the heat off, leaving the ham in the oven. Do not open the oven door.

After 3 hours, turn the oven on again to 500°. Bake for 20 minutes more, and turn the oven off. Allow the ham to stay in the oven overnight. The ham will be done the next morning.

Remove the skin, fat, and bone while still warm, if desired. Refrigerate, and slice as needed. This is best very thinly sliced.

Note: The ham keeps well for weeks, if covered securely and refrigerated. The ham may also be sliced and frozen in Zip-Lock bags. The ham hock and bone add a delicious flavor to soups or dried beans and peas.

Makes filling for 150 to 175 cocktail-sized biscuits, or 50 to 60 entrée servings.

Frozen Cranberry Salad

1 8-ounce package cream cheese, softened
1 14-ounce can sweetened condensed milk
1 teaspoon horseradish
1 16-ounce can whole berry cranberry sauce
1 14-ounce can pineapple tidbits
½ cup chopped pecans or walnuts
1 8-ounce carton Cool Whip

🍃 🍃 🍃

Lettuce leaves
Mayonnaise

In a food processor or blender combine the first 3 ingredients. Blend until smooth. Pour into a large bowl. Add the next 4 ingredients and stir until smooth. Pour into an 8-inch square pyrex dish and freeze for at least 24 hours. This will keep almost indefinitely when covered and frozen solid.

To serve, cut into squares and place on lettuce leaves. Top with real mayonnaise (homemade is best).

Serves 8 to 10.

Moist Sweet Potato-Bran Muffins

1½ cups dark raisins
1½ cups all-purpose flour
1 cup bran (shredded type, such as Fiber 1)
1 teaspoon baking powder
1 teaspoon baking soda
2 tablespoons cinnamon
½ teaspoon pumpkin pie spice
1 cup plain nonfat yogurt
½ cup honey
¾ cup fresh orange juice
2 cups peeled, grated raw sweet potatoes (about 2 small potatoes)
2 tablespoons oil

Soak the raisins in boiling water for 15 minutes. Drain and squeeze dry with a paper towel. Line 3-inch muffin cups with paper baking cups or spray with cooking spray.

In a large mixing bowl combine the flour, bran, baking powder, baking soda, cinnamon, mace, and pumpkin pie spice. Make a well in the center of the mixture. Set aside.

In a separate bowl combine the yogurt, honey, orange juice, grated potatoes, plumped raisins, and oil. Mix well and pour into the center of the dry ingredients. Stir gently and quickly until just blended. Do not overbeat.

Spoon the batter into the prepared muffin cups, filling ¾ full. Bake in a 350° oven for 20 to 22 minutes, or until a toothpick inserted in the center comes out clean.

Makes 18 3-inch muffins.

Tex Mex Dip

This is an attractive, delicious dip that most people enjoy. I have seen 8 people eat an entire dish of this.

    1 cup sour cream
    ½ cup real mayonnaise
    1 1¼-ounce package taco seasoning
        mix
    3 medium ripe avocados
    3 tablespoons freshly squeezed
        lemon juice
    ½ teaspoon salt
    ¼ teaspoon black pepper
    1 15-ounce can refried beans
    2 cups cored, seeded and chopped
        fresh tomatoes, drained
    3 bunches small green onions and
        tops, sliced
    2 3½-ounce cans black olives,
        chopped
    2 cups grated sharp Cheddar cheese
    1 1-pound bag tortilla chips

In a small bowl combine the sour cream, mayonnaise, and taco seasoning. Set aside.

Peel, pit, and mash the avocados. Add the lemon juice, salt, and pepper. Spread the beans on the bottom of a 10-inch flat dish or in a 3-quart oblong pyrex baking dish. Cover the beans with sour cream mixture. Spread the avocado mixture over the sour cream mixture. Sprinkle in order the chopped tomatoes, green onions, black olives, and grated cheese. Serve with tortilla chips.

This may be made up to 6 hours in advance and kept refrigerated.

Makes about 3 quarts.

Cinnamon Candy Salad

    1 3-ounce package cherry gelatin
    ¼ cup red cinnamon candies
    2 cups boiling water
    1 cup chopped celery
    1 cup chopped pared apples
    ½ cup chopped walnuts

In a saucepan dissolve the cinnamon candies in the boiling water, stirring frequently. Remove from the heat and add the gelatin. Stir until dissolved. Cool slightly and refrigerate until the consistency of egg whites. Add the remaining ingredients and mix well. Pour into a mold or 8-inch square pan. Chill until firm, about 3 to 4 hours.

Serves 6.

Tidewater Crab Meat Pâté

    1 10¾-ounce can cream of
        mushroom soup
    1 package unflavored gelatin
    3 tablespoons cold water
    ¾ cup mayonnaise
    1 8-ounce package cream cheese,
        softened
    ½ pound fresh crab meat, flaked
    1 small onion, grated
    1 cup finely chopped celery
    Parsley for garnish

Oil a 4-cup mold. In a saucepan over low heat warm the soup. Soften the gelatin in cold water and add to the soup, mixing well to dissolve. Add the next 5 ingredients and blend well. Spoon the mixture into the prepared mold and chill overnight. Unmold onto a platter and garnish with parsley. Serve with assorted crackers.

Makes about 4 cups.

Ed's Easy Spaghetti Sauce

    2 pounds ground beef
    1 medium onion, chopped
    1 15½-ounce jar spaghetti sauce
        with mushrooms
    1 12-ounce can tomato juice
    2 cups water
    Salt and pepper to taste

In a large skillet brown the beef with the chopped onion. Drain. Add the spaghetti sauce, tomato juice, and water. Simmer for 1 hour. Season with salt and pepper. Serve over hot spaghetti.

Serves 6 to 8.

Oriental Cole Slaw

    2 tablespoons sunflower seeds
    ½ cup slivered almonds
    1 3-ounce package Ramen soup mix
        (chicken or pork)
    1 medium head fresh cabbage,
        shredded
    6 green onions, diced
    ❧ ❧ ❧
    3 tablespoons brown sugar
    1 teaspoon salt
    2 tablespoons cider vinegar
    ½ cup oil
    ½ teaspoon whole oregano
    1 packet soup seasoning (in Ramen
        soup package)

Toast the sunflower seeds and almonds. Cool. Break the Ramen noodles into small pieces. In a large bowl combine the cabbage, onions, noodles, sunflower seeds, and almonds.

In a small bowl combine the remaining ingredients. Pour over the cabbage mixture about 30 minutes before serving.

Serves 8 to 10.

Cottle & Kempin Salad

A guest named Kempin gave me this recipe. It is so good!

    Iceburg and romaine lettuce,
        washed, drained and torn
    1 6-ounce can artichoke hearts,
        drained
    1 6-ounce can hearts of palm,
        drained
    1 4-ounce jar sliced pimento,
        drained
    1 large red onion, cut into rings
    ½ cup grated Parmesan cheese
    ½ cup good vinegar
    ½ cup oil

In a large bowl combine the torn iceburg and romaine lettuce. Add the next 4 ingredients. In a small bowl combine the remaining ingredients. About 30 minutes before serving, pour the dressing mixture over the lettuce mixture.

Serves 12 to 15.

Washington

Ashford Mansion

Box G
Ashford, Washington 98304
(206) 569-2739

This country-style home, listed on the National Register for Historic Places, was built by the Ashford family at the turn of the century about six miles from the entrance to Mount Rainier National Park. The setting is delightful. Against a background of giant evergreens, it has a lower porch that extends three-quarters of the way around the house, a verandah on both ends of the second floor, and a bubbling stream but a few feet away. The outward appearance has remained the same since 1903. Accommodations include the parlor with its fireplace where guests can relax, sip a hot or cold drink, play the grand piano or have a game of checkers.

Rhubarb Conserve

This conserve has been a big hit at the Ashford Mansion, even with guests who say they don't like rhubarb. Rhubarb grows prolifically in

ASHFORD MANSION 1903

the Great Northwest, as do all plants and vegetation. This recipe is from a local lady, Mrs. Falch.

4 cups prepared rhubarb
¼ cup lemon juice
½ cup raisins
½ cup nuts
7 cups sugar
½ bottle (3-ounce bottle) Certo

In a large saucepan bring the rhubarb to a boil in water to cover. Simmer until tender. Measure 4 cups into a large saucepan. Add the juice, raisins, and nuts. Add the sugar and bring to a boil. Boil for 1 minute, stirring constantly. Remove from the heat and stir in the Certo. Pour into sterilized jars and seal with paraffin.
    Makes 2 pints.

Mountain Meadows Inn

28912 Surface Road 706E
Ashford, Washington 98304
(206) 569-2788

Built in 1910 as the home of a mill superintendent, Mountain Meadows Inn provides a view from its spacious porch that overlooks a natural wildlife habitat. Here it is easy to feel at home and slip into the slower pace of a peaceful setting. Guests might choose to walk the trails through the remains of the old logging village or go out early to watch nature wake up. The rooms are furnished with antiques and contain private baths. Among the friendly farm animals is Oscar the llama.

Tanna's Best Manicotti

- 1 pound ground beef
- 1 medium onion, chopped
- 1 clove garlic, minced
- 2 cups creamed cottage cheese
- 2 cups shredded Mozzarella cheese
- 1 teaspoon salt
- 1 cup real mayonnaise
- 1 teaspoon dried oregano
- ½ teaspoon thyme
- 16 manicotti, cooked and drained
- 1 16-ounce jar spaghetti sauce (or homemade)
- Parmesan cheese

Grease a 9x13-inch pan. In a large skillet brown the meat with the onion and garlic. Drain and cool. In a large bowl combine the cottage cheese, 1 cup of the Mozzarella, salt, mayonnaise, oregano, thyme, and the meat. Fill each manicotti with ¼ cup of filling. Arrange in a single layer in the prepared pan. Pour spaghetti sauce over the top. Sprinkle any remaining filling over the manicotti, and top with the remaining Mozzarella cheese and the Parmesan cheese. Cover with foil. Bake in a 325° oven for 15 minutes. Remove the foil and bake for 10 minutes more.

Serves 6 to 8.

North Garden Inn

1014 North Garden
Bellingham, Washington 98225
(206) 671-7828
(800) 922-6414

Set in an enchanting environment, the North Garden Inn is an 1897 Queen Anne Victorian home that provides ten comfortable guest rooms with five full baths. Many of the guest rooms have a splendid view of Bellingham Bay with its islands. The inn has two studio grand pianos in performance condition, and guests are encouraged to enjoy them. Breakfast is continental in the European tradition.

Apple Dapple French Toast Cobbler

- 1 8-ounce baguette French Bread
- 4 eggs
- 1 cup milk
- ¼ teaspoon baking powder
- 1 teaspoon vanilla extract
- 6 apples, peeled, cored and sliced
- ½ cup brown sugar
- 1 teaspoon cinnamon
- 2 tablespoons melted butter

Slice the bread into 1-inch slices. In a bowl whisk together the eggs, milk, baking powder, and vanilla. Pour over the bread, turning to coat completely. Cover with plastic wrap and let the bread stand until all of the liquid has been absorbed.

Grease a 9x13-inch pan. Place the sliced apples in the bottom of the pan. Sprinkle brown sugar and cinnamon over the apples. Arrange the soaked bread over the top. Brush with melted butter. Bake in a 450° oven for 25 minutes.

Serves 8.

Award Winning Clam Chowder

- ¼ cup butter
- 1 tablespoon olive oil
- 3 yellow onions, peeled and diced
- 4 cloves garlic, pressed
- 3 stalks celery, diced
- 6 carrots, peeled and diced
- 8 small potatoes, peeled and diced
- 1 pound bacon
- 4 10½-ounce cans tomato soup
- 2 teaspoons salt

North Garden Inn

White pepper
4 teaspoons sweet basil
4 large tomatoes, seeded and
  chopped
1 10-ounce package frozen corn
1 pint half and half
8 6½-ounce cans chopped clams (or
  fresh clams, if possible)

In a large skillet melt the butter and add the olive oil. Sauté the onions and garlic. Add the celery, carrots, and potatoes. Set aside. Fry the bacon until crisp. Drain and break into small pieces.

In a stock pot combine the tomato soup and enough water to make 1 gallon. Add the sautéed vegetables and seasonings. When the vegetables are tender, add the tomatoes and corn. Cook until the corn is heated through. Add the half and half and the clams. Add enough water to make 2 gallons. Heat and adjust the seasonings. Serve with bacon bits sprinkled over each serving.

Makes 2 gallons.

Little Cape Horn

4 Little Cape Horn
Cathlamet, Washington 98612
(206) 425-7395

Situated on the scenic Ocean Beach Highway amid waterfalls, tall cedars and firs, and fruit and holly trees, this modern house is set near the water and the sandy beach overlooking the Columbia River. In view of guests who relax on the sun decks, seals frolic, gulls soar, and tug boats and ships glide by. Breakfast is ample and inviting. Smoking is permitted outside the house only.

Fresh Pear Tart

1¼ cups all-purpose flour
Salt to taste (about ½ teaspoon)
½ cup butter
2 tablespoons sour cream

    ❧ ❧ ❧

3 egg yolks
1 cup sugar
2 tablespoons all-purpose flour
⅓ cup sour cream
2 to 3 fresh ripe pears

Grease a 9-inch pie plate or tart pan. In a food processor combine 1¼ cups of flour, salt, butter, and 2 tablespoons of sour cream. Blend until the mixture forms a ball. Pat out into the prepared pie plate and flute the edges. Bake in a 425° for 10 minutes.

In a medium bowl combine the egg yolks, sugar, 2 tablespoons of flour, and ⅓ cup of sour cream. Peel and slice the pears. Arrange the pears in the bottom of the baked pie shell. Cover with the sour cream mixture. Cover the pie plate with foil. Bake in a 365° oven for 35 minutes. Remove the foil and bake until set.

Serves 6 to 8.

Danish Ableskivers

3 eggs, separated
2 tablespoons sugar
½ teaspoon salt
2 cups buttermilk
2 cups all-purpose flour
1 teaspoon baking powder
1 teaspoon baking soda
Butter
Applesauce
Lemon wedges
Confectioners' sugar
Maple syrup, jams, or jellies

In a food processor beat the egg yolks. Add the sugar, salt, and buttermilk. In a bowl combine the flour, baking powder, and baking soda. Add the dry ingredients to the egg yolk mixture. In a separate bowl beat the egg whites. Fold the egg whites into the batter.

Heat an ableskiver iron and add a small amount of butter to each depression. Fill each depression about ⅔ full. Place ½ to ¾ teaspoon of applesauce on each. Cover with a small amount of batter. Cook until bubbly and carefully turn with a fork. Bake until brown. Serve immediately with lemon wedges, confectioners' sugar, butter, maple syrup, or jams and jellies.

Serves 6.

The Victorian Bed and Breakfast

602 North Main
Coupeville, Washington 98239
(206) 678-5305

It has been one hundred years since Washington pioneer Jacob Jenne built this Italianate Victorian home on beautiful Whidbey Island. Today it provides gracious accommodations to guests who choose from among the upstairs bedrooms, which have private baths, or the guest cottage hideaway. The full breakfast is served buffet style. Coupeville, called the City of Sea Captains because of its many seafaring settlers, has many stately Victorian homes, quaint wharf and waterfront shops, and the distinctive character of the surrounding Eby's Landing National Historic Reserve.

Hot Chicken Sandwiches

12 slices white bread

≈ ≈ ≈

**2 cups cubed cooked chicken breast
  or turkey**
½ cup finely chopped onion
½ cup chopped green pepper
½ cup chopped celery
½ cup mayonnaise
Salt and pepper

≈ ≈ ≈

2 eggs
1½ cups milk
1 cup grated American cheese
**2 10¾-ounce cans cream of
  mushroom soup**

Grease a 9x13-inch casserole. Trim the crusts from the bread. Place 6 slices of the bread in the bottom of the casserole dish.

In a large bowl combine the chicken, onion, green pepper, celery, mayonnaise, salt, and pepper. Spread the mixture over the bread. Top with the remaining slices of bread. In a small bowl beat the eggs with the milk. Pour the mixture over the bread. Refrigerate overnight.

Spread the mushroom soup over the sandwiches. Bake in a 375° oven for 45 minutes. Remove from the oven and sprinkle the cheese over the top. Bake 15 minutes more. Let the sandwiches sit for 10 minutes, until firm.

Serves 6.

Quiche

½ cup butter
½ cup all-purpose flour

≈ ≈ ≈

6 eggs
1 cup milk
4 cups grated Monterey Jack cheese
1 3-ounce package cream cheese
2 cups cottage cheese
1 teaspoon baking powder
1 teaspoon salt
1 teaspoon sugar
Cubed ham (or shrimp or crab)

Grease a 9x13-inch pan. In a skillet melt the butter. Add the flour and cook until a smooth roux. In a large bowl beat the eggs. Add the milk, roux, and remaining ingredients. Mix well. Pour into the prepared pan. Bake in a 350° oven for 45 minutes.

Note: The quiche can be poured into the prepared pan and frozen before baking.

Serves 8.

Kangaroo House

Post Office Box 334
Eastsound, Washington 98245
(206) 376-2175

Built in 1907, this 6,700-square-foot home is named after the kangaroo that Captain Harold Ferris brought to live with him here in 1953. Old-time islanders still delight in telling stories about this colorful pet, Josie. Within walking distance of village shops and restaurants, Kangaroo House is ideally situated for a bed and breakfast. Guest accommodations include five bedrooms, a large sitting room with a fieldstone fireplace, a study, and a delightful breakfast room. All are furnished in turn-of-the-century style. The house is surrounded by large decks with flowering plants and vines, a large yard with flower and herb gardens, and a wooded area with shady paths.

Lemon Zucchini Muffins

1½ cups all-purpose flour
½ cup oat bran flour
1 tablespoon baking powder
½ teaspoon salt
1 teaspoon grated lemon peel
½ teaspoon nutmeg
½ cup chopped nuts
½ cup golden raisins
2 eggs
½ cup milk
⅓ cup oil
1 cup shredded zucchini, packed

≈ ≈ ≈

3 tablespoons all-purpose flour
3 tablespoons sugar
3 tablespoons wheat germ
2 tablespoons butter
1 teaspoon grated lemon peel

Grease 12 muffin cups. In a large bowl combine the first 6 ingredients. Stir in the nuts and raisins. In a small bowl beat the eggs with a fork, and beat in the milk and oil. Add the egg mixture to the dry ingredients. Fold in the zucchini, stirring until just blended. Fill the prepared muffin cups ⅔ full. In a small bowl combine the remaining ingredients and sprinkle over the batter. Bake in a 400° oven for 20 minutes.

Makes 12 muffins.

Breakfast Peach Fritters

1½ cups all-purpose flour
½ cup oat bran flour
4 teaspoons baking powder
Dash salt
¼ cup sugar
2 eggs
¼ cup melted butter
1 cup milk (approximately)
1 teaspoon almond flavoring
**1 quart peeled, sliced peaches
  (fresh or frozen)**
Raspberry sauce and yogurt

In a large bowl combine the dry ingredients. In a small bowl beat the eggs well with a fork. Add the melted butter, milk, and almond flavoring, and beat until well blended. Add the egg mixture to the dry ingredients and beat gently. Fold in the peaches. Let the mixture sit for at least 10 minutes.

Bake on a hot greased griddle as for pancakes, turning when the edges are browned and bubbles rise to the surface. This will take longer than for regular pancakes.

Serve with raspberry sauce and a dollop of yogurt.

Makes 20 4-inch pancakes.

Apple Buckwheat Pancakes
with Rumrunner Apple Butter

1 cup all-purpose flour
½ cup buckwheat flour
½ teaspoon salt
3 tablespoons sugar
2 teaspoons baking powder
2 eggs
3 tablespoons melted butter
1 to 1½ cups buttermilk
2 cups peeled, shredded apple
½ teaspoon cinnamon

    ❧ ❧ ❧

1 quart commercial apple butter
Juice of 1 lime
⅓ cup rum
⅓ cup water
½ teaspoon allspice
½ teaspoon cloves

In a medium bowl combine the flour, buckwheat flour, salt, sugar, and baking powder. In a small bowl beat the eggs with a fork. Add the melted butter and milk, and beat well. Pour over the dry ingredients, and add the shredded apples and cinnamon. Stir until just blended. Cook on a hot greased griddle until the edges are golden and bubbles rise to the surface. Serve with warm Rumrunner Apple Butter sauce.

In a saucepan combine all of the remaining ingredients. Simmer for 10 minutes. Adjust the spices and rum to taste. Serve with Apple Buckwheat Pancakes. Refrigerate any leftover sauce.

Serves 6.

Turtleback Farm Inn

Route 1, Box 650
Eastsound, Washington 98245
(206) 376-4914

Situated on Orcas Island, considered by most to be the loveliest of the islands that dot the San Juan archipelago in Puget Sound, this charming inn overlooks eighty acres of forest and farmland. Mount Constitution provides the backdrop to the east. Renovated and expanded in 1985, the inn boasts of a Rumford fireplace, seven guest rooms with private baths, and fine antique and contemporary furnishings. Breakfast is served in the dining room or on the large deck overlooking the valley. In the evening, guests are offered a glass of sherry, a cheery fire, a game of chess, cards, or Scrabble, and the chance to step back in time and capture moments of good fellowship.

Cornmeal Waffles

½ cup all-purpose flour
½ cup whole wheat flour
¾ cup cornmeal
¼ cup wheat germ
2 teaspoons baking powder
1 teaspoon baking soda
½ teaspoon salt
2 tablespoons sugar
2 eggs, separated
6 tablespoons melted butter, cooled
2 cups buttermilk
Butter and maple syrup

In a medium bowl combine the dry ingredients. In a large bowl combine the egg yolks, melted butter, and buttermilk. Beat until well blended. Add the flour mixture to the egg yolk mixture, stirring until smooth. In a separate bowl beat the egg whites until stiff. Fold the egg whites into the batter until just blended. Bake in a hot waffle iron according to the manufacturer's directions until golden. Serve with butter and maple syrup.

Serves 4.

Turtleback Farm Inn

Yogurt Pancakes
with Fresh Berries

½ cup unbleached all-purpose flour
½ cup whole wheat flour
1 tablespoon sugar
1 teaspoon baking powder
½ teaspoon baking soda
¼ teaspoon salt
½ teaspoon nutmeg
1 egg
½ cup milk
½ cup plain yogurt
2 tablespoons oil
¾ cup fresh blackberries (or
    raspberries, peaches, sliced
    bananas, or nectarines)
Butter and maple syrup

In a large bowl combine the flours, sugar, baking powder, baking soda, salt, and nutmeg. In a separate bowl beat the egg with the milk and yogurt. Beat in the oil, and add the mixture to the dry ingredients. Stir until just moistened. Do not overmix. Gently fold in the fruit. Bake on a hot greased griddle until the edges are golden and bubbles rise to the surface. Turn and bake until golden. Serve at once with butter and pure maple syrup.
Serves 3 to 4.

Soufflé Roll

¼ cup butter
½ cup all-purpose flour
1 teaspoon salt
Pepper to taste
2 cups milk
5 eggs, separated
❧ ❧ ❧
2 tablespoons butter
1 10-ounce package frozen spinach
    (or 1 large bunch, cleaned)
1 pound sliced mushrooms
1 8-ounce package cream cheese
Salt and pepper to taste

In a saucepan melt ¼ cup of butter. Blend in the flour, salt, and pepper. Stir in the milk and bring to a boil, stirring constantly until thickened. Cool. Add the beaten egg yolks. Beat the egg whites until stiff and fold into the cooled sauce.

Line a jelly roll pan with waxed paper. Butter and flour the pan. Pour in the soufflé mixture, spreading lightly to form an even layer. Bake in a 400° oven for 30 minutes or until lightly browned. Invert immediately onto a towel.

In a skillet melt 2 tablespoons of butter. Add the spinach and mushrooms to the butter. Add the cream cheese and mix well. Be certain that the filling is well heated. Season well with salt and pepper.

Remove the waxed paper from the soufflé. Spread the warm filling evenly over the soufflé mixture, and roll up with the help of the towel.

The Hill Top Bed and Breakfast

5832 Church Road
Ferndale, Washington 98248
(206) 384-3619

Situated high on a hill in Ferndale, Hill Top Bed and Breakfast overlooks the farmland of the Nooksack Valley and provides a beautiful view of the rugged Cascade Mountains. Decorated with Early American charm, the three guest rooms have four-poster beds and homemade quilts. The homemade breakfast is hearty. Hill Top is convenient to Birch Bay, Lynden, and Mount Baker. No smoking is permitted.

Hamburger Steak, Saucy Style

1 pound ground beef
½ cup soft bread crumbs (1 slice,
    crumbled)
½ teaspoon salt
¼ teaspoon pepper
❧ ❧ ❧
1 8-ounce can tomato sauce
1 tablespoon chopped green onion
2 tablespoons brown sugar
1 teaspoon Worcestershire sauce
1 teaspoon prepared mustard

In a medium bowl combine the beef, bread crumbs, salt, and pepper. Form into 4 patties. In a skillet brown the patties and pour off the excess fat. In a medium bowl combine the remaining ingredients. Pour over the patties in the skillet. Simmer for 10 minutes.
Serve over rice.
Serves 2 to 4.

Pacific Northwest Blueberry Sauce

Serve over plain yogurt, ice cream, pancakes, or waffles, topped with whipped cream.

2 cups fresh or frozen blueberries
1 teaspoon pumpkin pie spice
½ cup sugar (or ¼ cup Sprinkle
    Sweet sugar substitute)
2 tablespoons brandy or orange
    juice

In a medium saucepan combine all of the ingredients. Bring to a boil over medium heat, stirring until the sugar dissolves. Reduce the heat and simmer uncovered for 5 minutes.
Serves 8.

Apple Cider Syrup

1 cup sugar
2 tablespoons cornstarch
½ teaspoon pumpkin pie spice
2 cups apple cider or apple juice
¼ cup butter
2 teaspoons lemon juice

In a saucepan combine the sugar, cornstarch, and pumpkin pie spice. Add the cider, butter, and lemon juice. Cook for about 5 minutes, until thickened. Serve generously over pancakes.

Makes about 2 cups.

Moon and Sixpence

3021 Beaverton Valley Road
Friday Harbor, Washington 98250
(206) 378-4138

A classic country bed and breakfast in the middle of San Juan Island, Moon and Sixpence provides its guests with views of Mount Dallas, marshes, meadows, pasture, and a pond. Accommodations in this remodeled dairy farm built in the early 1900s are in the farmhouse and in the outbuildings. The five guest facilities are unique; one is a one-room cabin, and another a tower with a reading loft. Nearby are walking and hiking trails, seaside picnic sites, whale watching sites, fishing, boating, or swimming.

Bread Pudding
with Blackberry Sauce

8 ounces day-old sourdough French bread
½ cup raisins
2 eggs
½ cup sugar
3 cups 1% milk
2 teaspoons vanilla extract
1 teaspoon nutmeg
Confectioners' sugar

    🍃 🍃 🍃

2 cups fresh blackberries
⅓ cup sugar
½ cup orange juice

In a 9x13-inch baking dish arrange the bread slices to cover the bottom. Sprinkle the raisins over the bread. In a medium bowl combine the eggs, ½ cup of sugar, milk, and vanilla, whisking until thoroughly mixed. Pour the egg mixture over the bread slices. Sprinkle with nutmeg. Cover with plastic wrap and store in the refrigerator overnight.

Bake in a 350° oven for 50 minutes. Let the pudding sit for 15 minutes before serving. Sprinkle with confectioners' sugar.

While the pudding is in the oven, prepare the sauce. In a saucepan combine the blackberries, ⅓ cup of sugar, and the orange juice. Bring to a boil. Reduce the heat to low immediately. Cook, stirring constantly, for 15 minutes. Serve warm in a side dish with the pudding.

Serves 8.

Tucker House

260 B Street
Friday Harbor, Washington 98250
(206) 378-2783

Tucker House is a turn-of-the-century home that has been updated to offer a variety of accommodations in six rooms and cottages. The inn offers decks for conversation, a hot tub for relaxing, and a picket-fenced yard for children. A full breakfast is served in the solarium. Situated two blocks from the ferry landing, the inn is within walking distance of shops, restaurants, galleries, marinas, the Whale Museum, and other places of interest.

  🦆 🦆 🦆 🦆 🦆

Tucker House Baked Egg

1 egg
1½ tablespoons grated Cheddar cheese
Chopped dried parsley

Spray a 4-ounce soufflé ramekin with cooking spray. Break the egg into the ramekin. Sprinkle with cheese. Bake in a 350° oven for 15 minutes. Sprinkle with chopped parsley. Serve immediately.

Variation: Slice a cherry tomato and place on top of the cheese before baking.

Serves 1.

Cinnamon Bread

1 ¼-ounce package active dry yeast
¼ cup warm water (110° to 115°)
⅔ cup warm milk (110° to 115°)
1 teaspoon salt
½ cup sugar
½ cup butter, melted and cooled
2 eggs
3 to 3½ cups all-purpose flour
1½ teaspoons cinnamon

    🍃 🍃 🍃

½ cup confectioners' sugar
½ teaspoon vanilla extract
1 tablespoon milk

In a large bowl combine the yeast and warm water. Let the mixture stand until bubbly. Stir in the warm milk, salt, ¼ cup of sugar, and ¼ cup of butter. Add the eggs and 1½ cups of flour. Beat in the remaining flour until smooth. Place the dough in a greased bowl and turn to coat the top. Cover and let rise in a warm place until doubled, about 1 hour. Turn the dough onto a floured board and knead lightly, adding more flour as needed.

Grease a 9x5-inch loaf pan. Roll the dough into a 9x18-inch rectangle. Brush with 2 tablespoons of the remaining butter. Mix the remaining sugar with cinnamon. Sprinkle the mixture over the dough. Roll up tightly, beginning with a long edge.

Turn the loaf over and pinch a seam down the center. Place the shaped loaf in the prepared loaf pan. Brush the top with the remaining butter. Cover and let rise in a warm place until almost doubled, about 45 minutes. Bake in a 350° oven for about 30 to 35 minutes, or until the loaf is nicely browned and sounds hollow when tapped on the bottom.

In a small bowl stir together the confectioners' sugar, vanilla, and 1 tablespoon of milk. While the bread is still warm, drizzle the icing over the top. Let it run down the sides. Cool before slicing.

Makes 1 loaf.

Country Cottage of Langley

Country Cottage of Langley

215 6th Street
Langley, Washington 98260
(206) 221-8709

Country Cottage provides any guest to Whidbey Island in Puget Sound a lovely retreat reminiscent of a fine country home. Situated on three scenic acres with a sweeping view of the village of Langley, the Cascades, and the Saratoga Passage, it has a decor of country elegance that relaxes guests and makes them feel at home. Guests can rest in one of the inn's four country suites with private baths or stroll the country roads while gazing at mountains and sea. A full gourmet breakfast is served in the sun room or in the scenic dining room.

Cocoa Buttermilk Bars

¼ cup cocoa
1 cup margarine
1 cup water
2 cups sifted all-purpose flour
2 cups sugar
1 teaspoon baking soda
1 teaspoon cinnamon
2 eggs
⅓ cup buttermilk
1 teaspoon vanilla extract

🍃 🍃 🍃

½ cup margarine
5 tablespoons buttermilk
¼ cup cocoa
1 1-pound box confectioners' sugar
1 teaspoon vanilla extract
1 cup chopped nuts
1 cup miniature marshmallows

Grease and flour an 11x17-inch jelly roll pan. In a saucepan combine ¼ cup of cocoa, 1 cup of margarine, and water. Bring the mixture to a boil. In a large bowl combine the flour, sugar, baking soda, and cinnamon. Pour the heated mixture over the dry ingredients and blend well. Add the eggs, buttermilk, and vanilla. Pour into the prepared pan. Bake in a 400° oven for 10 minutes or until done.

In a saucepan combine ½ cup of margarine, 5 tablespoons of buttermilk, and ¼ cup of cocoa. Bring the mixture to a boil. Add the remaining ingredients. Frost the cake with the hot frosting, a small section at a time, so the marshmallows do not melt.

Serves 12.

Log Castle Bed and Breakfast

3273 East Saratoga Road
Langley, Washington 98260
(206) 321-5483

The Log Castle Bed and Breakfast is a charming country inn that provides gracious accommodations for those who wish to experience the quiet of island life. The four guest rooms, all with spectactular views, are named after the owners' grown daughters. All have private baths. Guests find the lodge warm and inviting as they relax before the large stone fireplace after a walk on a secluded beach. From the inn guests can listen to the sound of gulls as they watch for bald eagles and sea lions. The food is a legend. Homemade bread and warm cinnamon rolls direct from the oven are included in the full breakfast served on the large, round log table.

Cottage Cheese Hotcakes

3 eggs, separated
¾ cup cottage cheese
¼ cup all-purpose flour
¼ teaspoon salt
Sour cream
Jam

In a medium bowl beat the egg yolks until thick. Add the cottage cheese and beat well. Stir in the flour and salt. In a separate bowl beat the egg whites until stiff. Fold the egg whites into the batter. Pour the batter onto a 380° griddle into 3-inch pancakes, and bake for about 2 minutes. Turn and bake until the edges are dry to the touch. Serve immediately with 1 teaspoon each of sour cream and jam.
    Serves 3.

Log Castle Bed and Breakfast

Maple Nut Bread

1 egg
1 cup sugar
1 teaspoon mapleine
1 cup milk
1¾ cups all-purpose flour
2 teaspoons baking powder
¼ teaspoon salt
1 cup chopped walnuts

Grease a 9x5-inch loaf pan. In a medium bowl combine the egg, sugar, and mapleine. Add the milk, flour, baking powder, and salt. Beat lightly. Add the walnuts and blend. Pour into the prepared loaf pan and let the batter sit for 20 minutes in a warm place. Bake in a 325° oven for 1 hour.
    Makes 1 loaf.

Haus Rohrbach Pension

12882 Ranger Road
Leavenworth, Washington 98826
(509) 548-7024

A European-style country inn overlooking the beautiful Leavenworth Valley, Haus Rohrbach Pension is a little bit of the Austrian Alps in the Washington Cascades. Ten cozy rooms and a chalet are available to guests. Breakfast is served on the deck, where guests can watch cows, goats, and ducks. Guests can be as busy or as lazy as they wish, sunbathing by the pool, floating the river, hiking into the high country, or sitting in the shade.

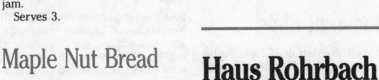

Haus Salsa

6 cups peeled and chopped
    tomatoes
2½ cups finely chopped seeded
    jalapeño or hot peppers
3½ cups chopped seeded mild
    peppers
1½ cups chopped onions
1 tablespoon salt
6 cloves garlic, minced
3 cups vinegar

In a saucepan combine all of the ingredients. Bring the mixture to a boil. Cover and simmer for 5 minutes. Pack in hot clean jars and seal. Process in a hot water bath for 30 minutes.
    Makes about 8 pints.

Bartlett Pear Nut Bread

6 to 9 fresh Bartlett pears (6 cups
    coarsely grated)
9 eggs
3 cups oil
4½ cups sugar
1½ teaspoons grated lemon peel
1 tablespoon vanilla extract
9 cups sifted all-purpose flour

1 tablespoon salt
1 tablespoon baking soda
¾ teaspoon baking powder
4½ teaspoons cinnamon
2 cups chopped nuts

Grease four 3x7-inch loaf pans. Coarsely grate the pears to make 6 cups. In a large bowl beat the eggs until light and fluffy. Add the oil, sugar, lemon peel, vanilla, and grated pear. Mix thoroughly. Sift together the dry ingredients and add to the pear mixture, mixing until blended. Stir in the nuts. Pour the batter into the prepared pans. Bake in a 325° oven for 50 to 60 minutes or until the bread tests done.

Makes 4 loaves.

Haus Rohrbach Pension

Sylvan Haus

417 Wilder Hill Drive
Post Office Box 416
Montesano, Washington 98563
(206) 249-3453

Sylvan Haus is a gracious three-story family home surrounded by towering evergreens. A cozy fireplace greets all who step into the family kitchen; antique pharmaceutical memorabilia and drugstore medical bottles line the rustic walls of the two-story dining room; and large decks with a private hot tub offer relaxation. There are three guest rooms, with private and semiprivate baths. Smoking is permitted only on the decks.

Huevo el Plato

An exchange student from Chile named this dish. It is often served with hot cornmeal muffins or toasted whole wheat bagels.

1 16-ounce package frozen potato tots
5 to 6 eggs, separated
1 cup diced green pepper
½ cup diced or finely chopped carrot
½ cup chopped fresh or frozen mushrooms
½ cup white wine (optional)
Salt and pepper to taste
½ teaspoon garlic salt (optional)
½ teaspoon cayenne pepper (optional)
½ cup grated Mozzarella cheese
¼ cup grated sharp Cheddar cheese
Sesame seeds
Black olives
Salsa
Sour cream or yogurt

Grease an 8x10-inch glass pan. Spread the potato tots in the bottom of the pan. In a large bowl beat the egg yolks. Add the green pepper, carrots, mushrooms, white wine, and seasonings. In a separate bowl beat the egg whites until fluffy. Fold the egg whites into the yolk mixture. Pour the mix-ture over the potato tots. Top with Mozzarella and Cheddar cheese, the sesame seeds, and the olives. Bake in a 300° to 325° oven for 30 minutes or until a toothpick inserted in the center comes out clean.

Cut into squares and serve with salsa and sour cream or yogurt.

Serves 6 to 8.

Basic Muffins

This recipe is from the early 1900s.

2 cups all-purpose flour
3 teaspoons baking powder
½ teaspoon salt
1 egg, beaten
1 cup milk
3 tablespoons melted butter (or Wesson oil)

Grease 12 medium or 6 large muffin cups. In a medium bowl sift the flour with the baking powder and salt. In a separate bowl beat the egg and add the milk and butter. Add the dry ingredients to the egg mixture, and stir until just moistened. The batter should be lumpy. Pour into the prepared muffin cups. Bake in a 425° oven for 20 minutes or until a toothpick inserted in the center comes out clean. Serve the muffins piping hot.

Variation: Blueberries, gooseberries, or cranberries may be added to the batter.

Makes 12 medium or 6 large muffins.

The White Swan Guest House

1388 Moore Road
Mount Vernon, Washington 98273
(206) 445-6805

Nestled in the rich farmland of the Skagit Valley, this inn is the perfect spot for long bicycle rides, bird watching, and pleasant walks. The three cozy guest rooms share two bathrooms, and the woodstove in the parlor and fresh-baked cookies on the sideboard are for guests' pleasure. A continental breakfast is served in the dining room. This cozy, informal farmhouse is like "Grandma's house," full of warmth and memories.

The White Swan Guest House

Fresh Blackberry Muffins

This recipe was featured in *Bon Appetit* magazine.

½ cup unsalted butter, room
    temperature
1¼ cups sugar
2 large eggs, room temperature
2 cups all-purpose flour
2 teaspoons baking powder
½ teaspoon salt
½ cup milk
2 cups fresh blackberries (or
    frozen, thawed, and drained)
4 teaspoons sugar

Grease muffin cups. In a large bowl cream the butter and 1¼ cups of sugar with an electric mixer until light. Add the eggs 1 at a time, beating well after each addition. In a small bowl sift together the flour, baking powder, and salt. Add the dry ingredients to the butter mixture alternately with the milk. Fold in the berries. Divide the batter among the prepared muffin cups. Sprinkle the remaining sugar over the batter. Bake in a 375° oven for about 30 minutes. Serve warm or at room temperature.

Makes 12 to 18.

Apple-Oatmeal Crumble

6 tart apples, peeled, cored, and
    chopped
2 tablespoons lemon juice
½ cup golden raisins

    ❧ ❧ ❧

½ cup brown sugar
⅓ cup all-purpose flour
⅓ cup oat bran
½ cup quick-cooking oats
1 teaspoon grated lemon zest
1 tablespoon cinnamon
¼ cup butter, melted

    ❧ ❧ ❧

Vanilla or lemon yogurt

Butter an 8x12-inch pyrex dish. In the prepared dish combine the apples,

lemon juice, and raisins. In a large bowl combine the dry ingredients and the butter. Mix until crumbly. Spread evenly over the apple mixture. Bake in a 375° oven for 30 minutes, or until the apples are tender.

Serve with vanilla or lemon yogurt.

Serves 6 to 8.

Lemon Scones

2 cups all-purpose flour
2 tablespoons sugar
1 tablespoon baking powder
¼ teaspoon salt
1 tablespoon lemon zest
6 tablespoons cold butter, cut into
    pieces
1 egg, beaten
½ cup milk (or half and half)
1 tablespoon vanilla extract

    ❧ ❧ ❧

1 egg, beaten

In a medium bowl or a food processor combine the flour, sugar, baking powder, salt, and lemon zest. Cut in the butter pieces until the mixture is crumbly. In a separate bowl combine the egg, milk, and vanilla. Add the egg mixture to the dry ingredients. Mix until the dough forms a ball. Turn the dough onto a floured board and knead. Roll out to ½-inch thickness. Using a 2-inch cutter (we use a heart shape) cut out scones, or cut into squares. Place on an ungreased baking sheet and brush with beaten egg. Bake in a 400° oven for 10 to 12 minutes, or until light brown.

Makes 14 to 18 scones.

The Tudor Inn

1108 South Oak
Port Angeles, Washington 98362
(206) 452-3138

The Tudor Inn

The Tudor Inn, constructed in 1910, has been restored to capture the charm of that era. The lounge and library, each with its own fireplace, invite guests to relax, whether reading, planning the next day's journey, or enjoying conversation with fellow travelers. The inn's five bedrooms overlook either the Olympic Mountains or the Strait of Juan de Fuca. Queen- and king-size beds are available, as well as two large hallway bathrooms. One bedroom has a private bath.

A full breakfast is served in the formal dining room. Tea is served between 4 and 6 every afternoon.

Wheat and Oat Sourdough Pancakes

    1 cup sourdough starter (made with
        yogurt)
    1 cup warm milk (90°)
    2 eggs, separated
    ¼ cup oil (or butter or margarine)
    Salt to taste
    ½ cup all-purpose flour
    ½ cup whole wheat flour
    ½ cup oats
    ½ teaspoon baking soda
    1 teaspoon baking powder

In a large bowl combine the sourdough starter and warm milk. Stir in the egg yolks, oil, and salt. Mix well. Add the remaining ingredients until just blended. In a separate bowl beat the egg whites. Fold the egg whites into the batter. Bake on a 400° griddle until bubbles rise to the surface, about 3 minutes. Turn and bake the other side, about 1 minute.

Variation: Bake on a 375° waffle iron according to the manufacturer's directions.

Makes about 17 pancakes.

Summer Song

Post Office Box 82
Seabeck, Washington 98380
(206) 830-5089

Summer Song, situated on the shores of Hood Canal, is a cozy cottage completely furnished to accommodate up to four guests. The delicious gourmet breakfast, featuring a wild huckleberry pastry, is served at the cottage or on the beach. The seventy-five-foot beach is perfect for bathing and swimming; a public boat launch is only one mile away. Close-by Green Mountain offers good hiking trails, and beautiful nearby Scenic Beach State Park offers nature trails and a little of Seabeck's history.

The Moody Oyster

    12 oysters in shells
    ⅓ cup butter or margarine
    2 dashes Mexi Pep and white wine
        Worcestershire sauce
    ½ cup Pepperidge Farm seasoned
        bread crumbs
    ⅛ teaspoon paprika
    Dash garlic powder
    ¼ teaspoon Mexican seasoning
    ¼ teaspoon seafood seasoning
    Salt and pepper to taste

Open the oysters, and place on a hot grill in the half shell. In a small saucepan melt the butter and add the Mexi Pep and Worcestershire sauce. In a small bowl combine the seasoned bread crumbs, paprika, garlic powder, Mexican seasoning, seafood seasoning, salt, and pepper. Splash each oyster with the butter mixture. Sprinkle each with the seasoning mixture. Cook to the desired doneness, 5 to 10 minutes.

Serves 12.

Blackberry Mountain Northwest

3 cups Krusteaz oat bran muffin mix
1 cup water
1 to 2 cups fresh or frozen
  blackberries

  &a &a &a

1 cup cooked blackberries
1 tablespoon cornstarch
1 tablespoon corn syrup
¼ cup sugar
¼ cup water

  &a &a &a

Cool Whip
Maraschino cherries
Huckleberry leaves (or other small
  nonpoisonous leaves)

Line 12 muffin cups with paper liners. In a medium bowl mix the muffin mix and water for about 40 strokes. Add the blackberries and stir carefully. Pour the batter into the prepared muffin cups. Bake in a 400° oven for 18 minutes.

In a saucepan combine 1 cup of blackberries, the cornstarch, corn syrup, sugar, and water. Heat to boiling. Strain through a sieve.

Remove the paper liners from the muffins and place the muffins upside down on a cookie sheet. Pour the blackberry sauce over each. Top each with a dollop of Cool Whip, a piece of cherry, and a huckleberry leaf.

Serves 12.

Chambered Nautilus

5005 22nd Avenue, N.E.
Seattle, Washington 98105
(206) 522-2536

Chambered Nautilus, with fine views of the Cascade Mountains, is perched on a peaceful hill in Seattle's University district. Built in 1915, the house is a Georgian colonial house that reflects the English heritage of its first owners. The six guest rooms are large, airy, and comfortably furnished with American and English antiques. Four of the rooms have porches that overlook the grounds. The living room, with its fireplace, piano, and well-stocked bookshelves, is a welcome place for guests to relax. Breakfast is served in the lovely dining room, which has the added warmth of a wood fire on cool mornings. On Sunday mornings a festive buffet is served.

Chambered Nautilus Apple Quiche

1 8-inch deep-dish pie crust,
  partially baked
3 Washington apples, peeled and
  sliced
3 teaspoons cinnamon
3 tablespoons brown sugar
⅔ cup grated Monterey Jack cheese
1 cup heavy cream
3 eggs
Handful dark sweet California
  raisins (optional)

Pile the apples into the pie shell. Sprinkle with cinnamon and sugar. Mound the cheese over the apples, covering the entire surface. In a medium bowl beat together the cream

Chambered Nautilus

and eggs. Poke a small hole in the cheese covering and pour the mixture over the cheese and apples. Smooth the cheese back into place. Bake in a 400° oven for 1 hour. Cool for 10 minutes before serving.

Serves 5 to 6.

Blueberry Serenescene

9 slices sourdough French bread
4 eggs
½ cup half and half
¼ teaspoon baking powder
1 teaspoon vanilla extract

    🍃 🍃 🍃

½ cup sugar
1 teaspoon cinnamon
¼ teaspoon allspice
1½ teaspoons cornstarch
2 12-ounce packages frozen
    blueberries
¼ cup melted butter

Cut the bread into 1-inch fingers. Place the bread fingers on a rimmed baking sheet. In a medium bowl whisk together the eggs, half and half, baking powder, and vanilla. Pour over the bread, coating completely. Cover with plastic wrap and refrigerate overnight.

Grease a 9x12-inch baking dish. In a large bowl combine the sugar, cinnamon, allspice, and cornstarch. Add the frozen berries and coat well. Spread the berry mixture in the prepared baking dish. Cover with the soaked bread fingers. Drizzle with melted butter. Bake in a 450° oven for 30 minutes. Let the dish sit for 10 minutes before serving.

To serve, cut into squares and spoon the juice from the bottom over each serving.

Serves 9.

Albright-Knox Duck Casserole

1 pint sour cream
1 package dry onion soup mix
1 10¾-ounce can cream of
    mushroom soup
3 ducks (baked and cut into bite-
    sized pieces)
2 boxes Uncle Ben's wild and white
    rice mix, prepared
2 cups dry red wine
2 16-ounce cans mandarin oranges

Butter a 2-quart casserole dish. In a medium bowl combine the sour cream and onion soup, and let the mixture stand for 1 hour. Add the mushroom soup to the sour cream mixture. In the prepared casserole, mix the duck, cooked rice, and onion soup mixture. Pour in the red wine to moisten and carefully fold in the oranges. Bake in a 300° oven for 45 minutes or until heated through. Add more wine if needed to moisten.

Serves 8.

Chelsea Station

4915 Linden Avenue North
Seattle, Washington 98103
(206) 547-6077

This elegant 1920 Federal colonial home is located in a peaceful, wooded setting near the south entrance to the Woodland Park Zoo. Chelsea Station is known for its comfort and privacy, with an emphasis on personal service, a perfect place to get away from it all and refresh the spirit. On nearby Shilshole Bay guests can stroll the docks at the marina or enjoy a visit to the Chittenden Locks in Ballard. Several fine restaurants are available nearby. A soothing hot tub in the carriage house is for private

use, and a cookie jar, coffee, tea, and hot chocolate enhance the feeling of being at home.

Ginger Pancakes
with Lemon Sauce

1 cup sugar
1 tablespoon cornstarch
1 cup water
2 tablespoons butter
1 tablespoon grated lemon peel
2 tablespoons lemon juice

    🍃 🍃 🍃

1 cup Krusteaz whole wheat and
    honey pancake mix
1 teaspoon ginger
½ teaspoon cinnamon
¼ teaspoon nutmeg
⅛ teaspoon cloves
1 teaspoon molasses
1 cup water

In a medium saucepan combine the sugar and cornstarch. Mix well. Gradually stir in the water. Bring to a boil. Cook over medium heat, stirring constantly, for 5 minutes or until thickened. Remove from the heat. Add the butter, lemon peel, and lemon juice, and mix well. Keep warm.

In a large bowl combine the pancake mix, spices, molasses, and water. Blend with a wire whisk until smooth and thick. Pour the batter onto a hot griddle to form medium to large pancakes. Turn when the edges are brown and bubbles rise to the surface. Bake until golden. Serve with a slice of fruit on the plate and pour warm lemon sauce over the pancakes.

Serves 2.

Salisbury House

750 16th Avenue East
Seattle, Washington 98112
(206) 328-8682

Salisbury House

Salisbury House is an elegant turn-of-the-century home situated on a tree-lined street minutes from downtown Seattle. Shops, restaurants, Volunteer Park, and the Seattle Art Museum are within walking distance. The inn's four guest rooms are all uniquely decorated, three with queen-size beds and the fourth with two twin beds; and they share two large baths. Some have cushioned window seats for a view of the side yard.

Ginger Pear Muffins

2 cups all-purpose flour
½ cup brown sugar
1 teaspoon baking soda
½ teaspoon salt
2 teaspoons ginger
⅛ teaspoon cloves
⅛ teaspoon nutmeg

ʂ ʂ ʂ

1 cup plain yogurt
½ cup oil
3 tablespoons molasses
1 egg, beaten
1½ cups diced pears, unpeeled
½ cup raisins
½ cup chopped nuts

Grease 12 large muffin cups. In a large bowl mix the first 7 ingredients. In a medium bowl combine the yogurt, oil, molasses, and egg. Blend well. Fold the wet ingredients into the dry ingredients and mix until just blended. Add the pears, raisins, and nuts. Spoon the batter into the prepared muffin cups. Bake in a 400° oven for 20 minutes.

Makes 12 large muffins.

The Williams House

1505 Fourth Avenue North
Seattle, Washington 98109
(206) 285-0810

Williams House is a family bed and breakfast in an Edwardian home that maintains much of its original woodwork and the original gas light fixtures. The five guest rooms have private or semiprivate baths, and most of them offer commanding views of Puget Sound, surrounding lakes, the downtown skyline, and the mountain ranges beyond. A sunny, enclosed porch is shared by all.

Christmas Cookies

**2 16-ounce packages dates (each
date cut into quarters)**
**½ pound candied cherries (each cut
in half)**
**4 candied pineapple slices, cut into
small sections**
1 cup finely chopped pecans
1 cup finely chopped walnuts
Brandy (or rum or whiskey)
2 cups all-purpose flour
1 cup butter
1 cup sugar
1 cup brown sugar
2 eggs
1 teaspoon salt
1 teaspoon baking soda

In a large bowl combine the dates, cherries, pineapple, pecans, and walnuts. Add brandy to cover and soak overnight, or at least 2 hours.

Grease a cookie sheet. Sprinkle ½ cup of flour over the mixture, and stir to blend. In a separate bowl cream the butter and sugars. In a small bowl beat the eggs. Add the eggs and remaining dry ingredients to the creamed mixture. Add the fruit and nut mixture, and blend well. Drop by teaspoonfuls onto the prepared pans. Bake in a 300° oven for 15 to 20 minutes.

Makes about 4 dozen cookies.

West Virginia

Highlawn Inn

304 Market Street
Berkeley Springs, West Virginia 25411
(304) 258-5700

A delightful turn-of-the-century home, today Highlawn Inn welcomes its guests with warm hospitality and superb accommodations for bed and breakfast. The rooms are decorated with furniture and accessories from an earlier era. Day begins with a full country breakfast, featuring hot breads and specialties of the house, served in the Victorian dining room. Gourmet meals are served to guests on major holidays and on murder mystery weekends. A wealth of activities is available within a few miles, from the famed mineral baths just a few blocks away to the picturesque mountains nearby. Guests may choose to laze away their day reading, rocking, or dreaming on the spacious verandah or in front of a comforting fire.

Lemon Tea Bread
with Lemon Glaze

¾ cup milk
2 tablespoons finely chopped lemon balm (fresh or dried)
1 tablespoon finely chopped lemon thyme (fresh or dried)

⁂

2 cups all-purpose flour
1½ teaspoons baking powder
¼ teaspoon salt
6 tablespoons butter, at room temperature
1 cup sugar
2 eggs
1 tablespoon grated lemon zest

⁂

Juice of 2 lemons
Confectioners' sugar

Butter a 9x5-inch loaf pan. In a saucepan heat the milk with the chopped herbs. Let steep until cool.

In a medium bowl combine the flour, baking powder, and salt. In a separate bowl cream the butter and gradually add the sugar, beating until light and fluffy. Beat in the eggs, one at a time, then the lemon zest. Add the flour mixture alternately with the herbed milk, mixing until the batter is just blended. Pour into the prepared pan. Bake in a 325° oven for 50 minutes, or until a toothpick inserted in the center comes out clean. Remove the cake from the pan and set on a wire rack placed over a sheet of waxed paper.

In a saucepan combine the lemon juice and confectioners' sugar, stirring until a thick but pourable glaze forms. Pour over the warm bread.

Decorate with a few sprigs of lemon thyme.
Note: This bread freezes well and is a real favorite with herb gardeners. Makes 1 loaf.

⁂ ⁂ ⁂ ⁂ ⁂

Confetti Squash

This is a real hit because it is colorful and combines different flavors and textures.

2 cups yellow squash, cooked, mashed, and drained
2 eggs, well beaten
½ cup evaporated milk
¼ cup butter or margarine, melted
1 tablespoon sugar
1 tablespoon all-purpose flour
¾ cup grated Swiss cheese
Salt and pepper
1 cup chopped red and green peppers
½ cup chopped onions

⁂ ⁂ ⁂

Bread crumbs

Grease a 1½-quart casserole dish. In a large bowl combine all the ingredients, except the bread crumbs, mixing together well. Pour into the prepared dish and top with the bread crumbs. Bake in a 350° oven for 1 hour, or until the center is set.

Note: This recipe can be assembled the day before refrigerated, and baked the next day.
Serves 6.

Three Oaks and a Quilt

Post Office Box 94
Bramwell, West Virginia 24715
(304) 248-8316

The oak at Three Oaks and a Quilt keeps guests cool in the summer and the quilts keep them warm in the winter in this completely restored Victorian four-square home. The entire town of Bramwell is on the National Register of Historic Places, and walking tours are encouraged. Bramwell was built by coal barons when the Pocahontas Mine Fields were opened.

Amaretto Bread Pudding

This is equally good served cold or without any sauce.

    1 loaf French bread
    1 quart half and half
    ❧   ❧   ❧
    2 tablespoons butter, at room
        temperature
    3 eggs
    1½ cups sugar
    2 tablespoons almond extract
    ¾ cup golden raisins (optional)
    ¾ cup sliced almonds (optional)
    ❧   ❧   ❧
    Amaretto Sauce

Break the bread into small pieces and place in a medium bowl. Cover with the half and half. Cover the bowl and let stand for 1 hour.

Grease a 9x13-inch baking dish with the butter. In a small bowl beat together the eggs, sugar, and almond extract. Stir the mixture into the bread and milk. Gently fold in the raisins and almonds, if desired. Spread the mixture evenly in the prepared dish. Bake in a 325° oven for 50 minutes, until golden. Remove and cool.

Cut the pudding into squares and place on a decorative ovenproof serving dish. Spoon the Amaretto Sauce over the pudding and place under the broiler until the sauce bubbles.

Note: When not using the Amaretto sauce, add 4 tablespoons of Amaretto liqueur to the bread mixture.

Serves 6 to 12.

Amaretto Sauce

    ½ cup unsalted butter, at room
        temperature
    1 cup confectioners' sugar
    1 egg, well beaten
    ¼ cup Amaretto liqueur

In the top of a double boiler over simmering water, stir together the butter and sugar. Stir constantly until the sugar and butter are dissolved and the mixture is very hot. Remove from the heat and whisk in the egg. Continue whisking until the sauce has come to room temperature. Add the liqueur.

Makes about 1 cup.

Spoon Bread

    2 cups boiling water
    1 teaspoon salt
    1 cup white cornmeal
    2 eggs, beaten
    ½ cup Pet or Carnation cream

Grease a soufflé baking dish. In a mixing bowl combine the boiling water and salt. Stir in the cornmeal and set aside to cool. In a separate bowl combine the eggs and cream. Stir into the cornmeal mixture and beat with an electric mixer for 2 minutes. Pour into the prepared baking dish. Bake in a 400° oven for 30 to 40 minutes until nicely browned.

Serves 4 to 6.

Vidalia Onion Pie

    1½ cups crushed crackers
    ½ cup margarine, melted
    ❧   ❧   ❧
    3½ cups sliced Vidalia onions
    1 cup milk, scalded
    3 eggs, slightly beaten
    1 teaspoon salt
    1 pound sharp Cheddar cheese,
        grated

In a medium bowl combine the crackers with ¼ cup of the melted margarine. Press around the bottom and sides of a 10-inch pie plate or baking dish.

In a skillet sauté the onions in the remaining margarine until tender but not brown. Add the milk, eggs, salt, and cheese. Pour the mixture into the prepared pie crust. Bake in a 300° oven for 50 to 60 minutes, or until the pie is golden brown.

Note: I bake in a 325° oven and adjust the time.

Serves 8 to 10.

Kilmarnock Farm

Route 1, Box 91
Orlando, West Virginia 26412
(304) 452-8319

Kilmarnock Farm is nestled in a secluded valley with sparkling brooks and grassy meadows surrounded by deep forests. Nearby is a 970-acre lake that provides some of the East's best musky fishing. Guests of Kilmarnock Farm share the delicious country fare, served family style in the comfortable nineteenth-century farmhouse. Breakfast and dinner are served, and lunch is packed. Special diets are catered upon request. No pets, please.

Sweet Taters 'n Apples Casserole

1 cup sugar
3 tablespoons cornstarch
1¼ cups water
1 teaspoon salt
½ cup butter
5 apples, peeled, cored, and each
  cut into 6 wedges
4 to 5 sweet potatoes, parboiled,
  peeled, and sliced
Cinnamon

In a saucepan combine the sugar, cornstarch, water, salt, and butter. Cook until thickened. Layer the apples and potatoes in a 9x13-inch baking dish, sprinkling cinnamon between the layers. Pour the sauce over the casserole. Bake in a 350° oven for 1 hour.
Serves 10 to 12.

Thomas Shepherd Inn

Thomas Shepherd Inn

Post Office Box 1162
Shepherdstown, West Virginia 25443
(304) 876-3715

Bed and breakfast at the Thomas Shepherd Inn is far more than a comfortable pillow and breakfast. It's a step into the graciousness of the past. Originally a parsonage, the inn was built on land originally owned by Thomas Shepherd, who secured Shepherdstown's charter in 1762. Its six spacious rooms, four with a private bath, are comfortably furnished. The living room, formal dining room, and library are for guests' enjoyment.

Apple Soup

This is nice served for breakfast in place of fruit or juice.

3 pounds tart apples, peeled, cored,
  and sliced
3 cups apple juice
3 cups water
2 teaspoons grated lemon rind
5 teaspoons lemon juice
1 cup sugar
1 teaspoon cinnamon
½ teaspoon nutmeg

½ cup sour cream blended with ¼
  cup milk (optional)
Lemon for garnish

In a large pot combine all the ingredients, except the sour cream and lemon. Simmer about 20 minutes until the apples are soft. Purée the mixture in a blender or food processor. Serve hot or cold and drizzle with the sour cream mixture, if desired. Garnish with a thin slice of lemon.
Serves 12.

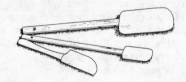

Spiced Shrimp

2 slices bacon
1 to 1½ cups butter
2 tablespoons mustard
1½ teaspoons chili powder
¼ teaspoon basil
¼ teaspoon thyme
2 teaspoons freshly ground black
  pepper
½ teaspoon oregano
2 cloves garlic, crushed
2 tablespoons chopped onion
1 tablespoon crab boil (coriander,
  basil, etc.)
½ teaspoon Tabasco sauce

1½ pounds shrimp

In a skillet sauté the bacon until crisp, then crumble. Remove the bacon drippings and wipe the skillet with paper toweling. Heat the butter until melted and add the mustard, chili powder, basil, thyme, and black pepper. Blend together until heated. Add the oregano, garlic, onions, crab boil, and Tabasco.

Place the shrimp in the hot sauce and cook until done.

Note: The shrimp can be cooked with the sauce in a 375° oven for 20 minutes.
Serves 6.

Rosemary Bread

1 tablespoon rosemary
2 to 3 teaspoons chopped parsley
½ cup butter, softened
1 loaf French bread
Grated cheese

In a small bowl cream together the rosemary, parsley, and butter. Cut the bread lengthwise, spread with the butter mixture, and sprinkle with the cheese. Place under the broiler until lightly browned.

Serves 6 to 8.

Minestrone with Pesto Sauce

1 cup dried white Navy beans
ia ia ia
2 10¾-ounce cans condensed chicken stock
2 quarts water
2 teaspoons salt
ia ia ia
1 small head cabbage, cored, and thinly sliced (1½ pounds)
4 carrots, pared, and ¼-inch diagonally sliced (½ pound)
2 medium potatoes, pared and ½-inch cubed (¾ pound)
1 16-ounce can Italian-style tomatoes
ia ia ia
2 medium onions, thinly sliced (½ pound)
¼ cup olive or vegetable oil
1 stalk celery, ⅛-inch diagonally sliced
2 zucchinis, ¼-inch sliced (½ pound)
1 clove garlic, pressed
½ teaspoon salt
Pepper
¼ cup chopped parsley
1 cup broken thin spaghetti
ia ia ia
Pesto Sauce

The day before cover the beans with cold water. Cover and refrigerate overnight. Drain.

In a 1-quart measure pour the chicken stock, adding water to make 1 quart. Pour into an 8-quart kettle with the 2 quarts of water, 2 teaspoons of salt, and the drained beans.

Bring to a boil, then simmer covered for 1 hour.

Add the cabbage, carrots, potatoes, and tomatoes. Cover and simmer for 30 more minutes.

In a skillet sauté the onions in the oil for 5 minutes. Remove from the heat. Add the celery, zucchini, and garlic with ½ teaspoon of salt and the pepper. Cook slowly uncovered for 20 minutes, stirring occasionally. Add to the bean mixture with the parsley and spaghetti. Cook slowly, covered, for 30 more minutes, stirring occasionally.

Serve the soup hot topped with a spoonful of Pesto Sauce.

Note: The spaghetti can be cooked separately and served individually.

Serves 6 to 8.

Pesto Sauce

¼ cup butter, softened
¼ cup grated Parmesan cheese
½ cup finely chopped parsley
1 clove garlic, crushed
1 teaspoon basil leaves (more, if fresh)
½ teaspoon dried marjoram leaves
¼ cup olive or vegetable oil
¼ cup chopped pine nuts or walnuts

In a medium bowl cream the butter with the Parmesan, parsley, garlic, basil, and marjoram. Gradually add the oil, beating constantly. Add the pine nuts, mixing well. Serve atop the hot Minestrone Soup.

Makes about 1½ cups.

Countryside

Box 57
Summit Point, West Virginia 25446
(304) 725-2614

Countryside was the first bed and breakfast inn in the state of West Virginia. Situated in the quaint, rural village of Summit Point, it is close to many scenic and historic attractions, yet far enough away to be private and relaxing. Countryside is decorated with a cheery mixture of antiques, collectibles, quilts, baskets, and original artwork. Guests enjoy the rural quiet. A complimentary breakfast is served every morning and includes coffee, juice, and rolls. Also served is an afternoon tea. Books, magazines, menus, and area information guides are available to guests.

Good Morning Drink

1 cup orange juice
½ cup strawberries
4 ice cubes

In a blender, combine the orange juice and strawberries. Drop in the ice cubes until crushed.

Serves 1.

Apple Bran Muffins

½ cup whole-bran cereal
1½ cups all-purpose flour
½ cup sugar
½ teaspoon cinnamon
¼ teaspoon nutmeg
4 teaspoons baking powder
½ teaspoon salt
1 cup milk
1 egg
¼ cup butter or margarine, melted
¾ cup finely chopped apple

Grease 12 muffin cups or line with paper liners. In a large bowl combine the cereal, flour, sugar, cinnamon, nutmeg, baking powder, and salt. Stir in the milk, egg, and butter until moistened. Mix in the apple. Spoon the batter evenly into the muffin cups. Bake in a 425° oven for 20 minutes until brown.

Makes 12 muffins.

Wisconsin

The Gallery House

215 North Main Street
Alma, Wisconsin 54610
(608) 685-4975

The Gallery House Mercantile Building, built in 1861, was recently added to the National Register of Historic Places. Perched in the bluffs of the Mississippi River at Lock and Dam No. 4 on the Great River Road, it provides a beautiful view of the Mississippi River. In Alma guests can see homes and buildings carved into the bluffs with stone retaining walls and terraced gardens and stairways instead of streets. A deck on the side of the building provides peaceful surroundings for a morning cup of coffee, an afternoon chat, or an evening of reminiscing. Breakfast is served in the dining room at 8:00 A.M. with a variety of homemade delicacies. Each of the three guest rooms has a double bed, brass appointments, and is decorated in restful shades of yellow and gold. Across the hall is the bath with its claw foot tub and old brass plumbing fixtures.

🐦 🐦 🐦 🐦 🐦

Sandwich Puff

⅔ cup chopped ham
⅔ cup grated yellow cheese
1 teaspoon Dijon mustard
2⅔ teaspoons Miracle Whip salad dressing
4 slices white bread

🐦 🐦 🐦

2 eggs
1⅓ cups milk

Grease 4 ovenproof dishes. In a medium bowl combine the ham, cheese, mustard, and salad dressing. Make two sandwiches with the ham mixture. Cut each sandwich diagonally into 4 pieces. Place two pieces of sandwich in each of the prepared dishes, arranging them so the points are on top.

In a small bowl combine the eggs and milk. Pour over the sandwich pieces. Refrigerate overnight. Bake in a 325° oven for 35 minutes.

Serves 4.

The Old Rittenhouse Inn

Box 584
Bayfield, Wisconsin 54814

Old Rittenhouse Inn, a beautiful Victorian mansion built in 1890 by Civil War General Alen C. Fuller, has twenty-six rooms and twelve working fireplaces. Antique furnishings are used in the dining rooms and overnight guest rooms. Elegant Victorian dining is available nightly. The menu changes daily with such choices as fresh Lake Superior trout aux champagne, chicken cordon bleu with wild rice dressing, prime roast leg of lamb, crêpes de la mer, and scallops provençale. A choice of soups, salads, homemade breads, and a tempting array of desserts accompany each meal. It is open all year by reservation.

Stuffed Mushrooms

This is an original recipe from Mary Phillips.

Giant mushrooms

🐦 🐦 🐦

1 cup grated sharp Cheddar cheese
½ cup cooked wild rice

The Gallery House

2 cups chopped mushroom stems
   (from the mushroom caps)
½ cup fresh broccoli, chopped (or
   frozen and thawed)
2 teaspoons garlic powder (or 6
   medium garlic cloves, puréed)
1 teaspoon dried basil
¾ to 1 cup sour cream

🦐 🦐 🦐

Fresh parsley sprigs for garnish

Wash the mushrooms, removing the stems. Chop the stems and reserve 2 cups.

In a medium bowl combine the remaining ingredients, except the parsley. Cover and refrigerate at least 3 hours. Spoon the mixture into the mushroom caps. Place in a shallow pan with ¼-inch of water and/or chicken stock. Bake in a 300° oven for 10 minutes. Garnish with sprigs of fresh parsley.

Note: Freshly chopped asparagus or green cabbage may be substituted for the broccoli. My goal is to have a green and yellow stuffing with a crunchy texture.

Serves 10 to 12.

🦐 🦐 🦐 🦐 🦐

Lake Superior Trout Meunière

8 small fresh trout or 4 pounds
   fresh fillets
2 cups milk

🦐 🦐 🦐

½ to ¾ cup all-purpose flour
1 teaspoon salt
½ teaspoon coarsely ground black
   pepper
½ teaspoon fresh dill
Oil

🦐 🦐 🦐

¼ cup butter
Lemon slices and fresh parsley for
   garnish

Clean the fish and rinse well under cold running water. Place in a shallow pan, cover with the milk, and let stand for 30 to 45 minutes. Remove from the milk, drain, but do not dry.

In a small bowl combine the flour, salt, pepper, and dill (using additional flour as needed). Coat the fish fillets with the seasoned flour. In a deep heavy skillet heat ½-inch of oil over a medium flame. Add the trout and cook until golden brown on each side. Transfer the fish to a serving platter.

Pour the oil from the skillet and wipe dry with paper toweling. In the skillet heat the butter to sizzling. Pour over the trout and garnish with thin slices of lemon and sprigs of fresh parsley.

Serves 8.

Lemon Chess Pie

2 cups sugar
1 tablespoon all-purpose flour
1 tablespoon cornmeal
4 eggs
¼ cup butter, melted
¼ cup milk
4 tablespoons grated lemon peel
¼ cup lemon juice
1 unbaked 9-inch pie shell

In a small bowl combine the sugar, flour, and cornmeal. Add the eggs, butter, milk, lemon peel, and lemon juice, beating until blended and smooth. Pour into the pie shell. Bake in a 350° oven until the top is golden brown. Cool to room temperature before cutting.

Note: The pie may be frozen.

Serves 6 to 8.

🦐 🦐 🦐 🦐 🦐

The Stagecoach Inn: Bed and Breakfast

W61 N520 Washington Avenue
Cedarburg, Wisconsin 53012
(414) 375-0208
(414) 375-3035

The Stagecoach Inn, housed in a restored 1853 stone building, is on the National Register of Historic Places and is decorated totally with antiques, although the comfortable rooms have modern conveniences. Each room is decorated with wall stenciling and Laura Ashley comforters and has a private bath and central air. A continental breakfast of hot croissants, juice, cereal, coffee, and herbal tea is included. The Stagecoach Pub is on the first floor of the inn, and many special house drinks are available. The pub serves as a pleasant gathering room for guests, and to enhance the warm coffee house feeling of the pub, many games are played in the evenings. Also located on the first floor are two specialty shops. Beerntsen Candy Shop offers an excellent selection of handmade chocolates, nuts, and hard candies. Inn Books carries a complete line of adult and children's books. Because of the historic restoration of the building, smoking is not allowed.

Orange Cake

Serve as a dessert or as a breakfast cake.

½ cup butter
1 cup brown sugar
2 eggs
1 cup buttermilk
1 teaspoon baking soda
2 cups all-purpose flour
1 orange, sliced

Cream together the butter and brown sugar. Add the eggs one at a time. Stir in the buttermilk, baking soda, and flour, blending well. In a blender chop the orange, then add to the batter. Pour into a 9x13-inch pan or bundt pan. Bake in a 350° oven for 40 minutes.

Serves 10 to 12.

The Washington House Inn

The Washington House Inn

Corner of Washington and Center
W62 N573 Washington Avenue
Cedarburg, Wisconsin 53012
(414) 375-3550
(800) 369-4088

The atmosphere of Victorian days comes alive in the Washington House Inn. A collection of antique furniture, a marble-trimmed fireplace, and fresh cut flowers offer guests a warm reception; and the rooms are comfortable, yet elegant, featuring cozy down quilts and flowers. In the late afternoon guests relax in front of a cheery fire and socialize with others

prior to dining at one of the excellent Cedarburg's restaurants. Each morning a continental breakfast is served in the warmth of the gathering room. Muffins, cakes, and breads are baked in the kitchen using recipes from an authentic turn-of-the-century Cedarburg cookbook; fresh fruit, cereal, freshly squeezed juices, and a fine selection of tea and coffee are served as well. The Washington House is on the listing of National Register of Historic Places.

Pistachio Bread

1 3⅝-ounce package instant pistachio pudding
1 18¼-ounce white cake mix, without pudding
1 cup sour cream
¼ cup water
¼ cup oil
4 large eggs

ᴥ ᴥ ᴥ

Cinnamon and sugar
Chopped nuts

Grease and flour 3 loaf pans. In a large bowl combine the pudding and cake mix. Add the sour cream, water, and oil, beating well with an electric mixer. Add the eggs, beating well. Pour a layer of the mixture into each prepared pan and sprinkle with cinnamon and sugar. Add the remaining batter, topping with additional cinnamon and sugar. Sprinkle with chopped nuts. Bake in a 325° oven for 1 hour.

Makes 3 loaves.

Crusty Caraway Rye Rolls

3 cups rye flour
2 ¼-ounce packages active dry yeast
Dash ginger
2 tablespoons caraway seeds

ᴥ ᴥ ᴥ

2¼ cups milk
¼ to ½ cup sugar

3 tablespoons shortening
1 tablespoon salt
2 eggs
4 cups all-purpose flour

ᴥ ᴥ ᴥ

Coarse salt

In a large bowl combine the rye flour, yeast, ginger, and caraway seeds.

In a saucepan combine the milk, sugar, shortening, and salt. Heat to a temperature of 120°. Add to the dry ingredients. Add the eggs, beating for 3 minutes with a wooden spoon. Stir in the flour by hand to make a soft sticky dough. Place in a greased bowl, turn to grease the top and sides, cover, and refrigerate. Two hours before serving shape the dough into balls. Let rise for 1 hour. Brush with water and sprinkle with coarse salt and caraway seeds. Bake in a 350° oven for 20 to 25 minutes.

Makes about 3 dozen rolls.

Rhubarb Raspberry Kuchen

1½ cups sifted all-purpose flour
2 teaspoons sugar
1 teaspoon baking powder
½ teaspoon salt
¼ cup butter
¼ cup lard
1 egg yolk, slightly beaten
2 tablespoons milk
1 3-ounce package raspberry gelatin
6 cups ½-inch sliced rhubarb

ᴥ ᴥ ᴥ

1 cup all-purpose flour
1 cup sugar
6 tablespoons butter

Grease a 9x13-inch pan. In a medium bowl sift together the 1½ cups of flour, 2 teaspoons of sugar, baking powder, and salt. Cut in the ¼ cup of butter and lard with a pastry blender until the mixture resembles coarse meal. In a separate bowl blend together the egg yolk and milk, then add to the flour mixture. Pat the dough into the pan and sprinkle with the dry gelatin. Arrange the rhubarb on top.

In a small bowl combine the 1 cup of flour, 1 cup of sugar, and 6 tablespoons of butter for a streusel topping. Sprinkle over the dough. Bake in a 350° oven for 45 minutes.

Serves 12.

Country Gardens Bed and Breakfast

6421 Highway 42
Egg Harbor, Wisconsin 54209
(414) 743-7434
(414) 743-8604

Country Gardens is situated on a 160-acre farm in Wisconsin's beautiful Door County. While hiking or skiing over farm trails, guests may encounter squirrels, foxes, owls, or other birds and animals. The four guest rooms, which share two baths, range from the spacious master bedroom with massive beams and native stone wall to the Fern Room furnished in wood and wicker. The popular recreational activities of Door County are all available nearby.

Poppy Seed Bread

4 eggs, beaten
½ cup oil
1 package instant lemon or coconut pudding
¼ cup poppy seeds
1 cup boiling water
1 box yellow or white cake mix

Grease and flour 2 medium or 3 small bread pans. In a medium bowl combine the eggs, oil, pudding, and poppy seeds, beating until well blended. Slowly add the boiling water alternately with the cake mix. Beat the mixture until smooth. Pour into the prepared pans. Bake in a 350° oven for 45 to 50 minutes.

Makes 2 medium or 3 small loaves.

Lemon Ginger Carrots

    1 pound carrots
    ❧ ❧ ❧
    ½ cup butter
    ¼ cup sugar
    2 teaspoons grated lemon rind
    1 tablespoon lemon juice
    ½ teaspoon ginger

Peel and shred carrots, measuring 5 cups.

In a medium skillet combine all the ingredients. Heat slowly, stirring frequently until the butter and sugar are melted. Cover and cook for 10 minutes or until the carrots are tender-crisp.

Serves 4.

Cherry Sauce

Good served on waffles, pancakes, bread pudding, custard, or plain cake; over ice cream; or just eaten as a bowl of cherries!

    5 tablespoons cornstarch
    2 cups water
    4 cups pitted red tart cherries with
        juice
    1½ cups sugar
    ½ teaspoon almond extract
    ½ teaspoon cinnamon

In a saucepan blend together the cornstarch and water. Stir in the cherries, juice, and sugar. Cook over medium-high heat until the mixture comes to a boil and thickens, stirring gently so the cherries are not crushed. Remove from the heat and add the extract and cinnamon.

Note: 1 tablespoon of frozen orange juice concentrate may be substituted for the cinnamon.

Makes about 6 cups.

"That" Cherry Dessert

    4 cups sour (tart) red pitted
        cherries with juice
    1 18-ounce box white, yellow, or
        chocolate cake mix
    1 cup butter, melted
    1 cup chopped pecans

Grease a 9x13-inch cake pan. Layer each ingredient in order in the prepared pan, but do not mix together. Bake in a 350° oven for 50 minutes.

Serves 10 to 12.

Steamed Cherry Pudding

    ¼ cup butter
    1 cup sugar
    2 eggs
    ½ cup mild molasses
    2 teaspoons baking soda
    ⅔ cup cherry juice
    3 cups all-purpose flour
    1 teaspoon baking powder
    2 teaspoons red food coloring
    2 cups frozen cherries, thawed and
        drained (or fresh pitted
        cherries)
    ❧ ❧ ❧
    ½ cup butter
    ½ cup whipping cream
    1¼ cups sugar
    1 teaspoon vanilla extract

Grease a 2-quart mold. In a large bowl cream together ¼ cup of butter, 1 cup of sugar, eggs, and molasses. In a separate bowl combine the baking soda and cherry juice. Add the juice mixture, flour, baking powder, food coloring, and 1½ cups of cherries to the creamed mixture. Pour into the prepared mold. Cover with waxed paper and secure with a rubber band. Place in a steamer. Steam at medium heat for 1½ hours. Remove the mold from the steamer. Bake in a 250° oven for 15 minutes. Remove from the oven and let rest for 10 minutes. Unmold, slice, and serve hot, garnished with the remaining ½ cup of cherries.

In the top of a double boiler combine ½ cup of butter, whipping cream, 1¼ cups of sugar, and vanilla. Cook over simmering water, stirring frequently until smooth and hot. Serve over the cherry pudding.

Makes 10 servings.

Rhubarb-Cherry Pie

    1 pound rhubarb, cut in ½-inch
        pieces
    1 16-ounce can tart red cherries,
        drained (or 2 cups pitted fresh
        cherries)
    1½ cups sugar
    ¼ cup quick-cooking tapioca
    5 drops red food coloring
    Pastry for 1 9-inch, 2-crust pie
    2 tablespoons butter, softened

In a large bowl combine the rhubarb, cherries, sugar, tapioca, and food coloring. Let stand for 15 minutes. Roll out half the pastry on a floured surface and prepare the pie shell. Spread 1 tablespoon of the butter over the bottom of the pastry. Add the filling mixture and dot with the remaining butter. Roll out the remaining pastry, cut into strips, and prepare a lattice crust. Seal and flute the edges. Cover the edge of the crust with a strip of aluminum foil. Bake in a 400° oven for 40 to 50 minutes.

Serves 6 to 8.

The Manor House

6536 3rd Avenue
Kenosha, Wisconsin 53143
(414) 658-0014

Listed in the National Register of Historic Places, the Manor House is a stately, sixty-year-old Georgian mansion overlooking Lake Michigan.

The Manor House

Completely redecorated and refurnished with eighteenth-century antiques and accessories, it boasts large, airy rooms, beautiful wood paneling, leaded glass windows, and a grand piano. Formal gardens, including a sunken lily pool with a fountain, and a gazebo, beckon summer guests for sunning or a leisurely stroll. Tennis and bicycles are included. Across the street, Kemper Center, a park and cultural activities facility, boasts tennis courts, a handicapped accessible fishing pier, and an art gallery where local artists work and exhibit. Swimming, charter fishing, boating, golfing, and skiing are nearby. Gourmet lunches and dinners, or a box lunch for picnicking at Kemper Center are available at extra charge.

Jewish Coffee Cake

½ cup butter or margarine, creamed
1 cup sugar
3 eggs
2 cups all-purpose flour
1 teaspoon baking powder
1 teaspoon baking soda
⅛ teaspoon salt
1 8-ounce carton sour cream
1 teaspoon vanilla extract

❧   ❧   ❧

¾ cup chopped nuts
1 cup brown sugar
3 tablespoons all-purpose flour
3 tablespoons butter
1 teaspoon cinnamon

Grease and flour a 10-inch springform pan or angel food pan. In a large bowl cream together ½ cup of butter and the sugar until light and fluffy. Add the eggs, beating well. Mix in the 2 cups of flour, baking powder, baking soda, salt, sour cream, and vanilla, blending well.

In a separate bowl combine the nuts, brown sugar, 3 tablespoons of flour, 3 tablespoons of butter, and cinnamon. Mix together to form a crumb topping.

Spread half of the batter into the prepared pan and sprinkle with half of the topping. Cover with the remaining batter and topping. Bake in a 350° oven for 40 to 45 minutes.

Serves 12 to 16.

Trillium

Route 2, Box 121
La Farge, Wisconsin 54639
(608) 625-4492

Trillium is a cozy, private cottage on an 85-acre farm in a thriving Amish community in southwestern Wisconsin. Named after trilliums, among the first American plants cultivated in English gardens, the inn provides an unusual opportunity for relaxation in the peaceful beauty of rural life. The cottage contains two twin beds and two double beds. Children are welcome.

Crunchy Corn Cakes

3 tablespoons butter
3 tablespoons honey
1 cup milk
1 large egg, beaten
½ cup whole kernel corn, cooked

❧   ❧   ❧

1 cup all-purpose flour
1 cup yellow cornmeal
1 tablespoon baking powder
½ teaspoon salt

Grease a cast-iron corn stick bread tin and heat in a 400° oven until hot. In a small saucepan slowly melt together the butter and honey. Add the milk, heating just until warm. Mix in the egg and corn, then remove from the heat.

In a separate bowl sift together the flour, cornmeal, baking powder, and salt. Form a well in the center of the dry ingredients and pour in the liquid mixture, stirring just until there are no dry lumps. Fill the prepared bread tins half full. Bake in a 400° oven for 20 to 25 minutes.

Makes 15 corn cakes.

The Duke Guest House: Bed and Breakfast

618 Maiden Street
Mineral Point, Wisconsin 53565
(608) 987-2821

In colonial America the pineapple symbolized a hearty welcome and gracious hospitality, and the Duke House has appropriately adopted this symbol. Cool drinks are served between 6:00 and 7:00 P.M. A full breakfast is served featuring coffeecake, muffins, tea biscuits, and scones.

The Duke Guest House

Devonshire Cream

This is a rich and elegant dessert.

    1 teaspoon unflavored gelatin
    ¾ cup cold water

    🍃 🍃 🍃

    1 cup whipping cream
    ½ cup sugar
    1½ teaspoons vanilla extract
    1 8-ounce carton sour cream

In a small saucepan soften the gelatin in the cold water. Heat until the gelatin dissolves, then cool.

In a large mixing bowl beat together the whipping cream, sugar, and vanilla until soft peaks form. Stir the sour cream into the gelatin mixture, then fold into the whipped cream. Serve in stemmed dessert glasses.

Serves 6.

🐦 🐦 🐦 🐦 🐦

Pasta Dijon Salad

    ¼ cup Dijon mustard
    ½ cup olive oil
    ¼ cup red wine vinegar
    2 scallions, thinly sliced
    1 large clove garlic
    1 large tomato, seeded and chopped
    ½ cup peas, cooked
    ½ cup broccoli, cooked
    ½ cup pea pods, cooked
    1 pound pasta, cooked

In a medium bowl combine the mustard, oil, vinegar, scallions, garlic, and tomato. Let stand at room temperature for 1 hour. Add the peas, broccoli, pea pods, and pasta and toss.

Serves 4 to 6.

Halfway House

Route 2, Box 80
Oxford, Wisconsin 53952
(608) 586-5489

Named Halfway House in the 1800s when it was a stage station on the old logging road from Portage to Stevens Point, the inn was remodeled in 1961. Surrounded by a large lawn, flower beds, and flowering trees, Halfway House is on a working farm with Herefords grazing the meadows, and wild game, deer, fox, badger, and many birds abounding.

The house is full of Wisconsin wildlife art and artifacts from Africa, as the innkeepers have traveled through Canada, Mexico, Africa, Holland, Wales, and England. The Halfway House is close to lakes, golf courses, snowmobile trails, and downhill and cross-country skiing. Its four bedrooms share two baths. Children and pets cannot be accommodated. Smoking is not permitted.

Turkey Casserole

7 ounces elbow macaroni, uncooked
13 ounces evaporated milk
1 8-ounce carton sour cream
¼ cup chopped green pepper
¼ cup chopped onion
1½ cups chopped celery
1 small can pimento
¼ pound grated Cheddar cheese
1 10½-ounce can cream of mushroom or cream of chicken soup
1 4-ounce can mushrooms with juice
3 cups chopped cooked turkey (or chicken)
Salt and pepper to taste

❧ ❧ ❧

Buttered bread crumbs
¼ cup blanched almonds

In a large bowl combine all the ingredients, reserving the bread crumbs and almonds for a topping. Spread the mixture in a 9x13-inch baking dish. Sprinkle with the bread crumbs and top with the almonds. Bake in a 375° oven for 25 minutes.

Serves 8 to 10.

Thrasher's Eggs

8 ounces fresh mushrooms, sliced
¼ cup butter
1½ cups shredded Swiss cheese
½ cup whipping cream
¼ teaspoon salt
Dash pepper
¾ teaspoon dry mustard
6 eggs, slightly beaten
1 tablespoon finely chopped parsley for garnish

Grease an 8-inch square baking dish. In a skillet sauté the mushrooms in 2 tablespoons of butter. Set aside. Sprinkle the cheese in the prepared pan and dot with the remaining 2 tablespoons of butter. In a small bowl combine the whipping cream, salt, pepper, and dry mustard. Pour half of the mixture over the cheese. Top with

the mushrooms and eggs. Cover with the remaining cream mixture. Bake in a 325° oven for 35 minutes until the eggs are set. Sprinkle with parsley for garnish.

Serves 4 to 6.

White Lace Inn

16 North 5th Avenue
Sturgeon Bay, Wisconsin 54235
(414) 743-1105

Featured in *Country Home* magazine, White Lace Inn is a recently restored Victorian house that has the feeling of a warm family home from an earlier era. Fifteen guest rooms in three historic houses are individually decorated with fine antiques, coordinated wallpapers, and hardwood floors. The inviting parlor, sitting room, and dining room in the main house serve as the common rooms for the inn. Abundant oak woodwork is accentuated by romantic Laura Ashley prints on the walls and on the furniture. Breakfast is served in the sitting room or in the oak-paneled dining room.

Cherie's Door County Cherry Muffins

4 cups all-purpose flour
1 cup sugar
2 tablespoons baking powder
1 teaspoon cinnamon
3 cups frozen and rinsed Door County cherries

❧ ❧ ❧

1 cup butter, melted
1 cup milk
4 eggs
1 teaspoon vanilla extract

❧ ❧ ❧

1 cup all-purpose flour
½ cup sugar
⅓ cup butter, softened
½ teaspoon cinnamon

Grease muffin cups. In a large bowl blend together the 4 cups of flour, 1 cup of sugar, baking powder, and 1 teaspoon of cinnamon. In a separate bowl toss 1 tablespoon of the dry ingredients with the cherries.

In a small bowl mix together 1 cup of melted butter, milk, eggs, and vanilla. Add to the dry ingredients, stirring until well moistened. Stir in the cherries. Fill muffin cups ¾ full.

In a small bowl combine 1 cup of flour, ½ cup of sugar, ⅓ cup of softened butter, and ½ teaspoon of cinnamon for a topping. Sprinkle over the muffin batter. Bake in a 425° oven for 15 to 20 minutes.

Makes 2 dozen muffins.

Scandinavian Fruit Soup à la White Lace Inn

4 cups water
1 lemon, thinly sliced
1 6-ounce package dried apricots
8 ounces light or dark raisins
1 teaspoon cinnamon

❧ ❧ ❧

2 16-ounce cans sliced pears with juice
2 16-ounce cans sliced peaches with juice
1 16-ounce can red tart Door County cherries, drained

In a large kettle combine the water, lemon, apricots, raisins, and cinnamon. Simmer covered for 30 minutes or until the rinds are soft. Add the pears, peaches, and cherries.

Note: This recipe makes a large amount, but can be kept in the refrigerator for 4 to 5 days and served for breakfast every morning. To reduce this recipe use 3 cups of water and 1 lemon and half of the remaining ingredients. The apricots can be

White Lace Inn

chocolates, and nuts. In a separate bowl combine the eggs, vanilla, oil, and zucchini. Add to the dry ingredients. Fill muffin cups ¾ full. Bake in a 425° oven for 18 to 20 minutes. Do not overbake.

Makes 26 to 28 muffins.

Historic Bennett House

825 Oak Street
Wisconsin Dells, Wisconsin 53965
(608) 254-2500

Built in 1863, this Greek Revival home in the Wisconsin Dells is named after noted photographer Henry H. Bennett. The current owners have restored and decorated the home with a warm, casual elegance. Throughout the home are lace, rich woods, crystal, old china, and collectibles. Guests may choose from among four guest rooms and may use the parlor/dining room with fireplace, along with front or back porches. Outdoor amenities include a gazebo, English garden, and shaded patio. Breakfast is served beside the fireplaces in the country kitchen or in the elegant dining room.

Bennett House Sandwich Supreme

Many guests and innkeepers have requested this recipe because it is so tasty and versatile. This is a personal favorite.

> 2 tablespoons butter, softened
> ¼ teaspoon dry mustard
> 2 slices bran/white bread
> 1 slice Swiss cheese

omitted for a less sweet fruit soup. Serve warm or cold. A spoonful of yogurt can be added on top of the soup before serving.

Serves 6.

Mary's Pineapple Cream Muffins

> 2 cups all-purpose flour
> 2 teaspoons baking powder
> ½ teaspoon baking soda
> 1 3½-ounce package instant vanilla pudding
> ½ cup brown sugar
> 1 egg, well beaten
> 1 cup sour cream
> 1 8¾-ounce can crushed pineapple, with juice
> ½ cup oil

Grease muffin cups. In a large bowl sift together the flour, baking powder, baking soda, and pudding mix. Stir in the brown sugar. In a separate bowl combine the egg and sour cream. Fold in the pineapple and oil. Add the mixture to the dry ingredients, stir-

ring just until moistened. Bake in a 425° oven for 15 minutes.

Note: The batter can be poured into a loaf pan and baked in a 350° oven for 60 to 65 minutes.

Makes 12 muffins.

Bonnie's Chocolate Zucchini Muffins

> 1 cup brown sugar
> 1 cup sugar
> 3 cups all-purpose flour
> 1 teaspoon baking soda
> 1 teaspoon baking powder
> 1 teaspoon salt
> 1 teaspoon cinnamon
> 3 ounces grated Hershey bar
> 1 cup chocolate mini-chips
> ½ cup chopped nuts (optional)
>
> 🍂 🍂 🍂
>
> 3 eggs, beaten
> 1 tablespoon vanilla extract
> 1 cup oil
> 2½ cups grated zucchini

Grease muffin cups. In a large bowl combine the sugars, flour, baking soda, baking powder, salt, cinnamon,

1 slice lean ham
1 slice Mozzarella cheese
1 egg, beaten
2 tablespoons chunky pineapple
   sauce (or applesauce)
1 strawberry, halved

In a small bowl mix together the butter and dry mustard. Spread on both slices of the bread. Layer the Swiss cheese, ham, and Mozzarella cheese between the bread. Dip the sandwich into the egg, coating both sides well. Brown in a lightly buttered skillet, then place on a cookie sheet. Bake in a 400° oven for 10 to 12 minutes or until the cheese melts and the sandwich is heated through, turning frequently to prevent burning. Cut in half diagonally and top with the pineapple sauce and garnish with the strawberry halves.

Serves 1.

Fruit and Fiber Muffins

1 12.5-ounce box of Fruit and Fibre
   cereal
3 cups sugar
5 cups all-purpose flour
5 teaspoons baking soda
1 teaspoon salt
4 large eggs, beaten
1 cup Puritan oil
1 quart buttermilk

Grease muffin tins. In a very large bowl combine all the ingredients, mixing together well. Fill the prepared muffin tins ⅔ full. Bake in a 400° oven for 15 to 18 minutes.

Note: The batter may be stored in a covered container in the refrigerator for up to 6 weeks.

Makes 5 to 6 dozen muffins.

Cinnamon Fruit Breads

Cream cheese, softened
6 slices cinnamon bread
Fresh strawberries, sliced
Ripe bananas, sliced
⅛ teaspoon cinnamon
1 tablespoon sugar

Spread the cream cheese on a slice of the bread. Cut the bread on the diagonal and top with the strawberries or bananas. Combine the cinnamon and sugar and lightly sprinkle over each fruit topped slice of bread.

Serves 6.

Real Custard Rhubarb Pie

1 unbaked 9-inch pie shell
2 cups chopped fresh rhubarb
   (½-inch pieces)

  🐦 🐦 🐦

4 large eggs, slightly beaten
½ cup sugar
¼ teaspoon salt
½ teaspoon vanilla extract
⅛ teaspoon almond extract
2½ cups scalded milk
Dash nutmeg

Cover the bottom of the pie shell with the rhubarb, then chill.

In a medium bowl blend together the eggs, sugar, salt, vanilla, and almond extract. Gradually stir in the milk. Pour into the prepared pie shell. Bake in a 400° oven for 40 to 50 minutes until a knife inserted into the center of the custard comes out clean. Cool and refrigerate.

Note: The rhubarb comes to the top of the custard and adds a festive look of red and green.

Serves 6.

🐦 🐦 🐦 🐦 🐦

Midmorning Delight

1 English muffin
Mayonnaise
2 slices deli ham
Coarse ground mustard with
   horseradish
2 slices mild Cheddar cheese
2 slices tomato
Sour cream
Fresh parsley tips

Separate the English muffin with a fork and toast. Spread each half with the mayonnaise and top with a ham slice. Spread with the mustard and top with the cheese. Place on a cookie sheet. Bake in a 400° oven until the cheese melts. Add the tomato slices, then a dollop of cold sour cream and garnish with the parsley tips.

Serves 2.

Wyoming

Spahn's Big Horn Mountain Lodge

Post Office Box 579
Big Horn, Wyoming 82833
(307) 674-8150

High on the side of the Bighorn Mountains and nestled in a whispering pine forest is a rustic log lodge and guest house built and operated by Ron and Bobbie Spahn, a former Yellowstone Park ranger. The lodge is situated at the edge of the million-acre Bighorn National Forest, and deer, moose, eagles, and turkeys are commonplace. Bear and mountain lions are never far away. Hearty mountain breakfasts are served on the deck with a one-hundred-mile view; binoculars are provided. Western-style supper cookouts followed by evening wildlife safaris are a tradition.

Creamy Eggs

8 eggs
¼ cup milk
¼ teaspoon salt
Dash pepper
2 tablespoons butter
1 8-ounce package cream cheese
    with chives, cubed
Parsley

In a large bowl beat the eggs, milk, salt, and pepper until well blended. In a large skillet melt the butter over low heat, and pour in the egg mixture. Cook until the eggs begin to set, and drop the cream cheese cubes on top. Cook until the eggs are no longer runny and the cheese is melted. Garnish with parsley.
    Serves 6 to 8.

Barbecued Buffalo Sandwiches

2 pounds ground buffalo
1 medium onion, chopped
1 14-ounce bottle catsup
½ cup water
¼ cup chopped celery
2 tablespoons lemon juice
1 tablespoon brown sugar
½ tablespoon Worcestershire sauce
½ tablespoon salt
1 teaspoon vinegar
¼ teaspoon dry mustard

    🍃 🍃 🍃

Toasted wheat buns

In a heavy skillet cook the buffalo and onion, stirring often until the buffalo is brown and tender. Stir in the catsup, water, celery, lemon juice, brown sugar, Worcestershire sauce, salt, vinegar, and dry mustard, and heat to boiling. Reduce the heat, and simmer covered for 30 minutes. Serve on toasted wheat buns.
    Serves 8.

Fresh Spinach Salad

1 10-ounce bag fresh spinach
1 8-ounce can bean sprouts, drained
    and rinsed
8 slices bacon, cooked and
    crumbled
3 hard boiled eggs, diced

    🍃 🍃 🍃

1 cup oil
⅓ cup sugar
⅓ cup catsup
¼ cup vinegar
1 teaspoon Worcestershire sauce
Salt to taste

In a large bowl tear the spinach into bite-sized pieces and toss with the bean sprouts, bacon, and eggs. In a blender container or a medium bowl combine the remaining ingredients, blending or stirring until well mixed. Pour the dressing over the spinach mixture, tossing to mix well.
    Serves 6 to 8.

South Fork Inn

Post Office Box 854
Buffalo, Wyoming 82834

Situated in the Bighorn National Forest, South Fork Inn is a rustic mountain lodge with ten guest cabins and a main lodge containing the dining room and game room. Activities include horseback riding, fishing, hiking, mountain biking, cross-country skiing, and llama trekking.

Peach Muffins

1 cup whole wheat flour
1 cup all-purpose flour
1½ teaspoons baking powder
½ teaspoon cinnamon

❧ ❧ ❧

1 egg
⅔ cup brown sugar
¾ cup buttermilk
¼ cup oil
1 cup diced peaches
½ cup chopped pecans or almonds
    (optional)

Grease 12 muffin cups. In a medium bowl combine the dry ingredients, mixing well. In a large bowl beat the egg and add the brown sugar, buttermilk, and oil. Blend well. Add the dry ingredients, blending until just moistened. Fold in the peaches and pecans. Bake in a 375° oven for 20 minutes.
Makes 12 muffins.

Louise's Perfect Pie Crust

2 cups all-purpose flour
1 teaspoon salt
⅔ cup lard
1 teaspoon vinegar
6 tablespoons cold water

In a food processor fitted with a metal blade combine all of the ingredients. Blend until the dough forms a ball and pulls away from the sides, less than 1 minute. Divide into 2 balls and roll out.
Makes pastry for 2 pies or 1 double crust pie.

Sour Cream Plum Pie

1 unbaked 9-inch pie shell
1 30-ounce can purple plums
2 cups sour cream
2 egg yolks
½ cup sugar
1 teaspoon vanilla extract

Prick the pie crust with a fork. Bake the pie crust in a 400° oven for 12 minutes.
Cut the plums in half and remove the pits. Lay the plum halves skin-side down in the baked pie shell. In a medium bowl combine the sour cream, egg yolks, sugar, and vanilla extract, blending until smooth. Spread the mixture over the plums in the pie shell. Bake in a 350° oven for about 45 minutes or until set. Cool before serving.
Serves 6.

Hunter Peak Ranch

Painter Route
Post Office Box 1731
Cody, Wyoming 82414
(307) 587-3711 (summer)
(307) 754-5878 (winter)

On the banks of the Clarksfork River, nestled among the pines, this guest ranch has operated since 1949. Activities include horseback riding, hiking, photography, lawn games, and fishing in the area's streams, lakes, and river for mouth-watering trout. Rustic cabins and lodge rooms, accommodating two to eleven people, are available for the summer and fall seasons. Facilities include a recreation room, library, television room, and laundry. Delicious home-cooked meals are served family-style in the old lodge, which was built in 1917 and is decorated with Indian rugs, horse tack, and antique tools.

Rhubarb and Strawberry Pie

4 cups diced fresh rhubarb
2 cups fresh strawberries
2 cups sugar
1 tablespoon vanilla extract
½ cup all-purpose flour
Pastry for 9-inch 2-crust pie

In a large bowl combine the rhubarb, strawberries, sugar, vanilla, and flour. Mix well. Fold the mixture into the pie shell and top with a lattice crust. Bake in a 375° oven for 1 hour and 30 minutes.
Variation: Use 2 cups of drained pie cherries for the strawberries, and reduce the vanilla extract to 1½ teaspoons and add 1 teaspoon of almond extract.
Serves 6 to 8.

Corn Pudding

1 17-ounce can whole kernel corn
1 17-ounce can cream-style corn
¼ cup nonfat dry milk
1½ cups bread cubes or cracker
    crumbs (or both)
1 teaspoon parsley flakes
2 large eggs
1 2-ounce jar chopped pimiento,
    drained
2 tablespoons butter or margarine
½ cup bread crumbs or potato chips
1 tablespoon melted butter
1 teaspoon seasoned salt
½ teaspoon pepper

In a large bowl combine the corn, dry milk, bread cubes, parsley flakes, eggs, and pimiento. Pour the mixture into a casserole dish. Cut 2 tablespoons of butter into pieces and dot the pudding with the pieces.

In a small bowl toss the bread crumbs with the melted butter, seasoned salt, and pepper. Sprinkle the mixture over the corn pudding. Bake in a 350° oven for 1 hour.

Serves 8.

Trout Creek Inn

Yellowstone Highway 14, 16, 20 West
Cody, Wyoming 82414
(307) 587-6288

Like other deluxe motels, the Trout Creek Inn offers plush modern rooms with queen-size beds and satellite television. Part of a 7,000-acre mountain ranch, the inn offers hiking, overnight camping in the mountains "far from civilization," and several miles of private stream fishing, plus two private trout ponds that require no Wyoming license. Trout Creek Inn specializes as a vacation "home" where people can spend a week or more taking daily trips to visit Yellowstone or Grand Teton parks and other vacation spots in the area. The inn is in the middle of Theodore Roosevelt's "most beautiful fifty miles in the world."

Norma's Homemade Hash Browns

2 medium-sized potatoes
Oil or butter for frying

Grate the potatoes with the skins. In a skillet heat the oil or butter. Pick up a portion of the potatoes by hand and drop them together into a pile in the hot oil. Do not make patties. Fry, keeping the portion together, until golden brown.

Serves 4 to 6.

Wyoming Scramble

1 cup diced cooked ham
1 2-ounce can mushroom stems and pieces
¼ cup chopped onion
2 tablespoons chopped green pepper
2 tablespoons butter or margarine
8 eggs
⅓ cup milk
¼ teaspoon salt
Dash pepper

In a 10-inch skillet cook the ham, mushrooms, onion, and green pepper in the butter or margarine until the vegetables are tender but not brown.

In a large bowl beat together the eggs, milk, salt, and pepper. Pour the mixture into the skillet with the ham and vegetable mixture and cook without stirring until the mixture begins to set at the bottom and around the edges. Using a spatula, lift the eggs so that the uncooked portion runs under the eggs. Cook for about 4 minutes or until the eggs are cooked.

Serves 4.

4W Ranch Recreation

1162 Lynch Road
Newcastle, Wyoming 82701
(307) 746-2815

Ranch Recreation offers its guests good food, a place to sleep, beautiful weather, clean air, and a chance to participate in the daily life of a working cattle ranch. In the 20,000 acres of meadowland, prairie, woods, and badlands nearby, there are many types of wildlife, including deer, antelope, turkeys, and prairie dogs.

Chocolate Honey Cake

1 18½-ounce box chocolate cake mix
1 cup chocolate chips
1 cup honey
½ cup water

Grease a 9x12-inch pan. Prepare the cake mix batter according to the package directions and pour into the prepared pan. Sprinkle the chocolate chips over the batter. In a small saucepan heat the honey and water to boiling. Pour over the chocolate chips and batter. Bake according to the cake mix package directions.

Serves 12.

Oatmeal Date Cookies

1 cup shortening
2 cups brown sugar
⅓ cup water
1 teaspoon baking soda
2½ cups all-purpose flour
2½ cups oatmeal
1 pound pitted dates
¾ cup water
1 cup sugar

Grease a cookie sheet. In a large bowl cream the shortening and sugar together. In a small bowl combine the water and baking soda, and add to the creamed mixture. Stir in the flour and oatmeal. On heavy waxed paper, roll the dough to about ½-inch thickness.

In a saucepan combine the dates, water, and sugar, and cook until a thick paste forms, stirring constantly. Spread the filling on half of the dough and fold the other half over to make a sandwich. Chill. Cut into 1-inch squares. Place the squares 2 inches apart on the prepared cookie sheet. Bake in a 350° oven for 10 to 12 minutes.

Makes about 2 dozen.

Sour Cream Raisin Pie

1¼ cups sour cream
¼ teaspoon salt
1 cup sugar
1 tablespoon all-purpose flour
1 teaspoon cinnamon
2 egg yolks
½ cup raisins
1 baked 8-inch pie crust

In a saucepan heat the sour cream and salt. In a small bowl combine the sugar, flour, and cinnamon. Beat the egg yolks into the sugar mixture. Stir the sugar mixture into the heated sour cream, and add the raisins. Cook over medium heat, stirring constantly until thickened, about 8 minutes. Pour into the baked pie crust.

Serves 6.

Hotel Wolf

101 East Bridge
Post Office Box 1298
Saratoga, Wyoming 82331
(307) 326-5525

The Hotel Wolf, a three-story structure built for $6,000 in 1893, served as a stagecoach stop on the Walcott Junction stage line. During its early years, the hotel was the hub of the community and was noted for its fine food and convivial atmosphere. Early hotel registers contain names of the famous and the infamous. After extensive renovation, it is now possible to enjoy lunch, dinner, and one's fa-

Hotel Wolf

vorite cocktail in the hotel's comfortable "turn of the century" Victorian atmosphere. Today the hotel rents rooms as they were in 1893, catering to sportsmen, travelers, and the general public. Of its eleven rooms, seven have private baths. The rooms are simple and quaint with cast iron beds and basic wooden dressers. The restaurant enjoys a reputation for excellence, as was true in its earliest days. The luncheon menu features a wide selection of sandwiches, as well as the "Wolf Burger," and a soup and salad bar. The dinner menu offers several steak cuts, prime rib, chicken, shrimp, and crab enhanced by the soup and salad bar.

Split Pea Soup

1 17-ounce can chicken broth
Water
2 cups selected green split peas
¾ cup finely diced celery
¾ cup diced carrot
1 small onion, diced
¼ teaspoon thyme
Pinch cayenne
1 bay leaf
Salt and white pepper to taste
½ cup half and half

In a large kettle combine the chicken broth and enough water to make 2 quarts of liquid. Add the peas, celery, carrot, onion, and seasonings. Boil the mixture for 20 minutes, then reduce the heat to simmer and cook until the peas are tender. Add the half and half and simmer for 15 minutes or until heated through.

Variation: ½ to ¾ cup diced cooked ham may be added.

Serves 8.

Judd's Sailor Soup

1 pound dried small white beans
2 quarts cold water
2 to 3 pounds smoked ham hocks
2 cloves garlic, crushed
Salt and pepper to taste
1 bay leaf
2 tablespoons bacon drippings
1 small onion, chopped

Wash the beans and cover with cold water in a large stock pot or kettle. Bring to a boil, reduce the heat, and boil gently for 2 minutes. Remove from the heat, cover, and let stand for 1 hour. Do not drain. Add the ham hocks, garlic, salt, pepper, and bay leaf. Return to the heat and simmer for approximately 2 hours and 30 minutes.

Remove the ham hocks, cut the meat from the bone, and return the meat to the soup. In a skillet melt the bacon drippings and add the onion, cooking until lightly browned. Add the onion to the soup. Simmer for 30 minutes, or until the meat and beans are tender.

Note: If ham base is available, use a heaping tablespoon to increase the flavor.

Serves 8.

Black Bean Soup

2 cups dried black beans
½ pound cooked ham, cubed
** (optional)**
1 beef bouillon cube
1 chicken bouillon cube
1 green pepper, finely chopped
1 small onion, chopped
¾ cup chopped celery
¾ cup diced carrot
1 bay leaf
2 cloves garlic, crushed
2 tablespoons olive oil
Salt and pepper to taste
¼ cup dry sherry

Pick over and wash the beans. In a large kettle or stock pot cover with water and soak overnight. Drain the beans and add 8 cups of cold water. Cover and simmer for 1 hour and 30 minutes. Add the remaining ingredients except the sherry, and simmer until the beans and vegetables are tender. Add the sherry and cook for 10 minutes to allow the flavors to blend.

Serves 8 to 10.

Teton View Bed and Breakfast

2136 Coyote Loop
Post Office Box 652
Wilson, Wyoming 83014
(307) 733-7954

The three guest rooms of this inn near Jackson Hole have mountain views, large beds, private decks overlooking the Tetons, and cozy country decor. In winter months guests sleep between flannel sheets and warm up with hot cordial drinks. In the summer fresh ice cold water is brought to each room after a day's outing. Guests may relax in the lounge area, enjoy the spacious back yard, or play horseshoes and relax in the hammock.

Lemon-Poppy Seed Coffee Cake

2 cups baking mix
1 cup milk
¼ cup poppy seeds
¼ cup oil
2 eggs
1 3½-ounce package lemon instant
** pudding and pie filling mix**

☙ ☙ ☙

⅔ cup confectioners' sugar
3 to 4 teaspoons lemon juice

Grease a 9-inch square pan. In a large bowl combine the baking mix, milk, poppy seeds, oil, eggs, and lemon pudding mix. Beat with an electric mixer for 30 seconds. Pour the mixture into the prepared pan. Bake in a 350° oven for 35 to 40 minutes, until light golden brown and a toothpick inserted in the center comes out clean. Cool for 10 minutes.

In a small bowl combine the confectioners' sugar and lemon juice. Drizzle over the cooled cake.

High altitude directions: Stir ¼ cup of flour into the baking mix. Increase the eggs to 3. Bake in a 375° oven for 30 to 35 minutes.

Serves 9.

Easy Drop Danish

2 cups baking mix
¼ cup margarine or butter, softened
2 tablespoons sugar
⅔ cup milk
¼ cup raspberry preserves (or any
** flavor)**

☙ ☙ ☙

⅔ cup confectioners' sugar
1 tablespoon warm water
¼ teaspoon vanilla extract

Grease a cookie sheet. In a large bowl combine the baking mix, margarine, and sugar until crumbly. Stir in the milk until a soft dough forms. Beat for 15 strokes. Drop by rounded tablespoons about 2 inches apart onto the cookie sheet. Make a shallow well in the center of each with the back of a spoon and fill with 1 teaspoon of preserves. Bake in a 450° oven for 10 to 15 minutes, until golden.

In a small bowl beat together the confectioners' sugar and water until smooth. Add the vanilla, blending well. Drizzle the glaze over the warm Danishes.

High altitude directions: Stir 2 tablespoons of flour into the baking mix, and decrease the sugar to 1 tablespoon. Bake in a 475° oven 10 to 12 minutes. Cool for 2 minutes before removing from the baking sheet.

Makes 12 Danishes.

Canada

Cougar Creek Inn

Post Office Box 1162
Canmore, Alberta T0L 0M0
(403) 678-4751

Cougar Creek Inn is nestled in the Canadian Rockies backing onto Cougar Creek and a land reserve. With easy access to the townsites of Canmore, Banff, and Lake Louise, it is within a five-minute drive to Canmore Nordic Center. The inn has a private entrance for guests, and the guest rooms have shared full baths, outstanding views, fireplace, sitting and dining areas.

Kahlua Spiced Peaches

1 29-ounce can sliced cling peaches
½ cup Kahlua
½ cup brown sugar
¼ cup tarragon vinegar
2 sticks cinnamon
3 slices lemon peel
3 slices orange peel

In a saucepan combine the drained peach syrup, Kahlua, brown sugar, vinegar, cinnamon, and lemon and orange peel. Simmer over low heat for 5 minutes. In a large bowl combine the peaches and heated syrup mixture. Cool. Pour into four 10-ounce sterilized jars and seal. Refrigerate until needed.

Makes four 10-ounce jars.

Curried Squash Soup

1 30-ounce butternut squash
2 tablespoons butter
4 scallions, finely minced
1 teaspoon parsley
Juice of 1 lemon
4 cups chicken stock
2 cups apple juice
2 to 4 teaspoons curry powder
Pepper to taste

Place the squash in a baking dish. Bake in a 350° oven for 40 minutes. In a food processor or blender purée the squash.

In a small skillet melt the butter and sauté the scallions and parsley. Add the lemon juice. In a saucepan combine the chicken stock, puréed squash, apple juice, curry powder, pepper to taste, and the sautéed mixture. Cook over low heat for 50 minutes, stirring often.

Serves 4.

"The Lookout"

3381 Dolphin Drive
Rural Route 2
Nanoose Bay, British Columbia V0R 2R0
(604) 468-9796

Situated on beautiful Vancouver Island, this lovely contemporary cedar home is in a natural rocky woodland setting that affords a spectacular view of Georgia Strait and many of its islands. From the wraparound deck guests enjoy breathtaking views. Fishing is excellent in this area, and golf is also available. Walks through the woods or by the ocean are a delightful activity many guests enjoy. Breakfast is served on the deck or in the dining room, according to guests' preferences. Reservations are recommended.

Cranberry Breakfast Muffins

½ cup chopped fresh cranberries
5 tablespoons sugar
1⅓ cups all-purpose flour
1 tablespoon baking powder
½ teaspoon salt
1 egg
1 cup milk
3 tablespoons melted butter or margarine
¾ cup Grape Nuts cereal

Grease 12 muffin cups. In a small bowl combine the cranberries and 2 tablespoons of sugar. Set aside. In a large bowl combine the flour, remaining sugar, baking powder, and salt. In a separate bowl beat together the egg, milk, and melted butter. Add the egg mixture to the dry ingredients, mixing until just moistened. Stir in the Grape Nuts and cranberries. Spoon into the prepared muffin cups. Bake in a 400° oven for 15 minutes or until brown.

Makes 12 muffins.

Dutch Cradles
with Orange-Ginger Sauce

¼ cup butter or margarine
4 eggs
1 cup milk
1 cup all-purpose flour

❧ ❧ ❧

2 tablespoons ginger
1 teaspoon grated orange peel
½ cup orange juice
½ cup water
2 tablespoons light corn syrup
1 cup sugar
Corn flour (optional)

In a large casserole dish melt the butter. In a blender combine the eggs and milk, and blend on low speed until well mixed. Add the flour and blend well. Pour the mixture into the bubbling butter. Bake in a 425° oven for 25 minutes.

In a small saucepan combine the remaining ingredients. Bring the mixture to a boil over medium-high heat. Boil for 5 minutes. Serve the sauce over the cradles.

Serves 8.

Ocean View Bed and Breakfast

4024 Dorval Avenue
Powell River, British Columbia V8A 3G2
(604) 485-6880

This inn in central Westview is convenient to ferries and the airport. The four comfortable guest rooms share two bathrooms, and a large sun deck provides guests with an unobstructed view of Malspina Strait and the mountains on Vancouver Island. A full breakfast is served in the dining room, with evening meals by arrangement.

Cooke's Coconut Cookies

When guests arrive, I serve them tea and/or coffee along with freshly baked cookies. This is one of the favorites.

1 cup margarine
¾ cup sugar
¾ cup brown sugar
1 egg
1 cup coconut
1 cup all-purpose flour
2 cups rolled oats
½ teaspoon baking soda
½ teaspoon baking powder
½ teaspoon vanilla extract
Salt to taste

In a large bowl beat together the margarine, sugar, brown sugar, and egg. Add the remaining ingredients. Form into balls and place on an ungreased cookie sheet. Press down with a floured fork. Bake in a 350° oven for 10 to 12 minutes.

Makes about 5 dozen.

Super 'n Easy Sauce

We serve evening meals, and this always goes over well with our guests.

1 cup honey
2 teaspoons dry mustard
2 teaspoons curry powder

In a bowl combine all of the ingredients.

Use the sauce to marinate chicken, pork chops, spare ribs, or white fish. Cover with foil. Bake in a 350° oven for 1 hour for chicken, chops, or ribs, or 30 minutes for fish.

Note: This sauce is delicious served over rice or noodles.

Makes about 1 cup.

Handy Chicken Casserole

1½ cups raw rice (brown or white)
1 package onion soup mix
1 frying chicken, cut into pieces
1 10½-ounce can cream of mushroom soup
1 4-ounce can mushroom pieces (optional)
Paprika
2 cups water

Grease a 9x13-inch baking dish. Sprinkle the rice in the bottom, and sprinkle the onion soup mix over the rice. Place the chicken pieces on top. Spread the cream of mushroom soup over the chicken and top with mushrooms. Sprinkle with paprika. Add the water carefully to the sides of the dish. Cover with a lid or foil and refrigerate for 6 to 8 hours.

Bake in a 350° oven for 1 hour and 15 minutes. Remove the cover and bake for about 15 minutes, until brown. More liquid may be added if necessary.

Serves 6 to 8.

The Ram's Head Inn

Red Mountain Ski Area
Box 636
Rossland, British Columbia V0G 1Y0
(604) 362-9577

At this warm country inn life is informal and comfortable. Limiting itself to eighteen guests, the inn looks after every detail with care. The cooking is unusually good, with hearty breakfasts, memorable dinners, and irresistible desserts. The large cedar hot tub and Swedish sauna under the bright stars are popular with guests. Smoking is not permitted indoors.

🐑 🐑 🐑 🐑 🐑

Almond Jam Cake

Raspberry jam
2 unbaked 9-inch pie shells

🐑 🐑 🐑

¾ cup margarine
1 cup sugar
4 eggs
2 teaspoons almond extract
2 cups sifted all-purpose flour
1 teaspoon baking powder
2 tablespoons milk (or more)
Thin lemon juice frosting

Spread the raspberry jam in the bottoms of the unbaked pie shells. In a large bowl cream the margarine and sugar. Add the eggs, almond extract, flour, baking powder, and milk. Spread over the jam, covering completely. Bake in a 350° oven for 30 to 40 minutes. Ice with lemon juice frosting.
Serves 16.

Barbecue Sauce for Fish

⅔ cup Miracle Whip salad dressing
½ cup melted butter
1 heaping tablespoon honey
1 tablespoon white vinegar
Generous squeeze fresh lemon juice
1 teaspoon fresh dill

In a bowl combine all of the ingredients, mixing until smooth. Brush the sauce on salmon, halibut, or any fish desired. Broil according to the type and size of the fish. The sauce will brown slightly.
Makes about 1¼ cups.

Cool Chicken Curry

¼ cup butter
½ cup honey
⅓ cup Dijon mustard
1 tablespoon curry powder
Juice and grated peel of 1 lime
Pinch salt
1 clove garlic
6 to 8 chicken breasts, skinned
Lime slices for garnish

In a bowl combine the butter, honey, mustard, curry powder, lemon juice, lemon peel, salt, and garlic. Place the chicken in a baking dish. Pour the curry mixture over the chicken breasts. Bake in a 350° oven for about 1 hour, until the chicken is done but not overcooked. Garnish with lime slices.
Serves 6 to 8.

Sooke Harbour House

1528 Whiffen Spit Road
Rural Route 4
Sooke, British Columbia V0S 1N0
(604) 642-3421
(604) 642-4944

The Sooke Harbour House on Whiffen Spit Beach is a sixty-year-old inn known for gracious dining and relaxing accommodations by the sea. The facility provides a magnificent view of Sooke Harbor and the Olympic Mountains, and the homelike atmosphere radiates from the candlelit decor and rustic fireplace. The restaurant, specializing in fresh seafood, is rated one of Canada's best. On the mile-long spit in front of the restaurant, guests can watch seals and otter play.

Abalone and Geoduck
with a Sea Urchin-Gewurztraminer Butter Sauce and Sea Lettuce

1 cup Northwest Gewurztraminer
2 shallots, finely chopped
1 tablespoon apple cider vinegar
2 tablespoons heavy cream
1 cup unsalted butter, cut into pieces
4 ounces sea urchin roe
Pepper to taste

🐑 🐑 🐑

½ pound sea lettuce, thoroughly washed
3 tablespoons soy sauce
1 tablespoon black sesame seeds

🐑 🐑 🐑

1 tablespoon peanut oil

4 pinto (4-inch) abalone, sliced
   diagonally as thinly as possible
1 pound geoduck siphon, peeled
   and sliced diagonally as thinly
   as possible

In a saucepan combine the wine, shallots, and apple cider vinegar and reduce over high heat to a glaze consistency. Add the cream and reduce the heat. Add the butter, a little at a time, stirring constantly until the butter is emulsified. Stir in the sea urchin roe at the very last. Do not cook for more than 15 seconds. Season to taste. Set aside.

Blanch the sea lettuce in boiling water for 5 seconds. In a bowl toss the sea lettuce with the soy sauce and sesame seeds. Set aside.

In a sauté pan heat the oil over high heat until smoking. Sauté the abalone and geoduck for 15 seconds. Remove from the pan. Divide the sea lettuce among 4 serving plates, arranging in the middle. Place the abalone and geoduck decoratively around the sea lettuce. Pour the sauce over the abalone and geoduck. Serve at once.

Serves 4.

Recipe courtesy Co-Chef Kevin Mackenzie.

Broad Bean and Nasturtium Soup

6 tablespoons butter
1 medium onion, diced
4 cloves garlic, finely minced
¼ cup cider vinegar
½ cup dry white wine
2 pounds hulled broad beans
1 quart chicken stock
Pinch nutmeg
1 quart whipping cream
Nasturtium leaves and flowers

In a heavy bottomed pot over medium heat melt the butter. Sweat the onions until translucent, and add the garlic. Stir and sweat the garlic for 30 seconds. Add the cider vinegar and white wine, and reduce until almost dry. Add the broad beans and chicken

Sooke Harbour House

stock. Bring to a boil and season with nutmeg. Reduce the heat and simmer until the broad beans are soft, approximately 3 to 5 minutes. Add the cream and heat through. Purée the soup, and strain. Pour into serving bowls and garnish with coarsely chopped nasturtium greens and flowers.

Serves 6 to 8.

Recipe courtesy Co-Chef Ron Cherry.

Sautéed Geoduck, Kelp, and Sea Lettuce

with Pineapple Sage Butter Sauce

2 ounces kelp fronds (either bull
   kelp, *Nereocystis lvetkeana* or
   giant kelp, *Macrocystis
   intergrafolia* or *M. pyrifera*)
2 ounces sea lettuce (*ulva lactuca*)
4 ounces geoduck siphon
1 tablespoon olive oil
1 teaspoon peeled and minced
   ginger

1 teaspoon sesame oil
2 tablespoons white wine
½ tablespoon rice vinegar
¼ cup plus 2 tablespoons fish stock
3 medium leaves and 10 blossoms
   fresh pineapple sage
6 tablespoons butter

Rinse the kelp fronds and sea lettuce under cold water to remove dirt and small, undesirable sea creatures. Tear the lettuce into bite-sized pieces. Cut the kelp into 2x1-inch strips. Slice the geoduck into thin slices, using pre-cleaned siphon meat.

In a medium sauté pan over high heat add enough olive oil to cover the bottom of the pan. Add the geoduck and toss until heated. Add the sea lettuce and kelp. Toss until completely hot. Divide the mixture between 2 serving plates, arranging in the center.

Return the pan to the heat, and briefly sweat the ginger in sesame oil. Deglaze the pan with white wine. Reduce the mixture to a glaze consistency. Add the rice vinegar and fish stock, and reduce until 1 ounce (or 2 tablespoons) of liquid remains in the pan. Remove from the heat. Add the coarsely chopped sage and whisk in the butter until melted. Pour the sauce around the geoduck mixture. Garnish with pineapple sage blossoms.

Serves 2.

Recipe courtesy Co-Chef Ron Cherry.

Fresh Geoduck, Laminaria, and Pickled Blackberries

1 ounce dried or fresh seaweed (laminaria)
4 ounces peeled and cleaned geoduck siphon
1 tablespoon sesame oil
2 tablespoons dry white wine
½ cup fish stock
¼ cup unsalted butter

   ҙ ҙ ҙ

Pickled blackberries (recipe follows)

Soak the seaweed in lukewarm water for 5 to 10 minutes. Remove and drain thoroughly.

Slice the geoduck neck to ¹⁄₁₆ inch. In a sauté pan heat the sesame oil until smoking. Toss in the geoduck and sauté until heated through, 15 to 30 seconds. Add the seaweed immediately and toss until heated through. Divide the seaweed and geoduck between 2 serving plates, arranging decoratively in the center of the plates. Keep warm.

Return the pan to the heat and deglaze with white wine. Reduce the mixture until almost dry. Add the fish stock and reduce until about 1 ounce (or 2 tablespoons) of liquid remains. Remove from the heat and add the butter, stirring or whisking until melted. Pour the sauce around the geoduck and seaweed.

Garnish the sauce with Pickled Blackberries and decorate with about

1 teaspoon of pickle juice per plate.

Serves 2.

Recipe courtesy Co-Chef Ron Cherry.

Pickled Blackberries

2½ pounds fresh blackberries
1 quart cider vinegar (5% acidity)
3 tablespoons sugar (or ⅓ cup maple syrup or honey)

In a large saucepan or stock pot combine the blackberries, cider vinegar, and sugar. Bring to a boil. Pour the mixture into jars and seal. Refrigerate for at least 24 hours to allow the flavors to blend.

Makes 4½ pints.

Prawn and Anise Hyssop Soup

3 cups fish stock
2 shallots, peeled and chopped
¾ cup white wine
1 tablespoon lemon juice
1 cup whipping cream
½ cup whipped cream
2 teaspoons Pernod
¼ cup chopped fennel
¼ cup chopped anise hyssop leaves
4 prawns, shelled
Freshly ground pepper to taste
4 shelled uncooked prawns, with heads on

   ҙ ҙ ҙ

Fennel and anise hyssop leaves for garnish

In a saucepan combine the fish stock, shallots, white wine, lemon juice, and whipping cream, and bring to a boil. Add the whipped cream, Pernod, chopped fennel, anise hyssop leaves, and 4 shelled prawns. Heat through, and process in a blender until smooth. Divide the soup between 4 warm soup plates, grind fresh pepper over the soup, and place 1 whole

prawn in each bowl. Garnish with sprigs of fennel and anise hyssop leaves.

Serves 4.

Recipe courtesy Michael Stadtlander.

Canadian Abalone
with Wild Sorrel and Nettle Sauce

(Ormeaux aux orties et à l'oseille sauvage)

2 pounds fresh abalone (northern or pinto)
6 tablespoons clarified unsalted butter

   ҙ ҙ ҙ

3 tablespoons finely minced shallots
1 large clove garlic, finely minced
3 tablespoons clarified unsalted butter
24 wild sorrel leaves
24 young nettle leaves (use gloves when handling)
2 cups fish stock
¾ cup dry white wine
1 cup heavy cream
3 tablespoons cold unsalted butter

   ҙ ҙ ҙ

Edible flowers for garnish

Using a spoon, remove the muscle from the shell of the abalone and discard the rest. On a cutting board place the muscle flat-side down and slice vertically into very thin pieces, about ⅛ to ¹⁄₁₆-inch. Set aside.

In a frying pan over medium-high heat melt 6 tablespoons of butter. Sauté the abalone lightly on both sides, about 30 to 45 seconds depending on the thickness.

In a saucepot sauté the shallots and garlic in 3 tablespoons of butter until soft. Add the sorrel and nettles, and sauté gently. Add the fish stock and wine, and bring to a boil. Reduce the liquid by half. Purée the mixture in a blender and pass through a fine sieve.

Pour the strained mixture back into the pot and add the cream. Simmer for 5 minutes or until thickened, remove from the heat, and whisk in the cold butter in small pieces. Spoon the sauce onto plates and arrange the abalone attractively. Garnish with fresh edible flowers such as freesias, calendula, mustard flowers, or chickweed flowers.

Serves 4.

Asparagus Pâté
with Watercress Sauce

1 pound steamed asparagus tips
1 medium dill pickle, diced
Freshly ground black pepper to taste
4 sheets phyllo pastry, halved lengthwise
1 teaspoon finely chopped shallots
½ cup dry white wine
1½ cups whipping cream
1 small bunch watercress, washed and chopped (reserve 4 sprigs)
¼ cup unsalted butter

In a food processor purée the asparagus tips and pickle. Season with pepper. Divide the mixture into 4 portions. Layer 2 phyllo sheet halves and fold lengthwise into a long, narrow strip. Place 1 portion of the filling at one end of the strip, leaving ½ inch clear at either edge. Roll gently toward the center. At the center, fold the edges in and continue to roll to the end, until a neatly rolled asparagus pâté is formed. Place in a dry cloth and refrigerate. Repeat with the remaining phyllo sheets and asparagus mixture.

In a saucepan combine the shallots and wine, and reduce until syrupy. Add the cream and reduce until thick and creamy. Add the watercress, stir well, and cook gently for a few minutes. In a blender or food processor purée the mixture. Season with pepper if desired. Keep warm.

In an ovenproof skillet melt the butter over high heat. Place the pâtés

seam-side up in the butter and brown. Turn the pâtés over and place in a 425° oven for about 4 minutes. Remove from the oven and pour the sauce over the serving plates. Place 1 pâté in the middle of each and garnish with the reserved watercress.

Serves 4.

Grilled Oysters
and Nasturtium Butter Sauce

4 large oysters
½ cup plus 2 tablespoons fish stock
2 tablespoons dry white wine
1 teaspoon nasturtium vinegar (see note)
2 large nasturtium leaves, coarsely chopped
4 nasturtium flowers, coarsely chopped
Nasturtium leaf and flower for garnish

Grill the shelled oysters on both sides until brown, and keep warm. In a sauté pan over high heat reduce the fish stock, white wine, and vinegar until 1 ounce (or 2 tablespoons) of liquid remains. Add the chopped nasturtium leaves and flowers. Remove from the heat and whisk in the butter. Pour the sauce on the plates and arrange the oysters on the sauce. Garnish with a small leaf and flower.

Note: For Nasturtium Vinegar, fill a stainless steel container with nasturtium flowers, leaves, and seed pods. Add apple cider vinegar to cover. Cover the container with plastic wrap, leaving a small opening for breathing. Store in a cool, dry place for a few weeks before using.

Serves 2.

Recipe courtesy Co-Chef Ron Cherry.

Scented Geranium and Loganberry Sorbet

10 to 15 small scented geranium leaves (see note)
3 cups fresh loganberries
1½ cups Gray Monk Cellars Johannisberg Riesling
½ cup maple syrup

Bruise and chop the geranium leaves. In a heavy-bottomed saucepan over medium heat bring the loganberries and ½ cup of wine slowly to a boil, stirring occasionally. Remove from the heat, add the geranium leaves, and cover with a lid. Let the mixture sit for 30 minutes.

In a food processor or blender purée the mixture. Strain out the loganberry seeds and geranium leaves. Add the remaining wine and the maple syrup. Pour into an ice cream machine and prepare according to the manufacturer's directions.

Note: Suggested types of geranium leaves are Rober's Lemon-Rose, M. Ninon (apricot scented), Prince Rupert (lemon scented), Shotesham Pet (filbert scented), Staghorn Oak (sandalwood scented), or Frensham Lemon.

Makes about 1 quart.

Recipe courtesy Co-Chef Ron Cherry.

Scented Geranium and Apple Sorbet

1 apple, peeled, cored and sliced
1 cup dry hard apple cider
1 tablespoon lemon juice
2 tablespoons finely chopped scented geranium leaves

In a medium saucepan combine the apples and cider, and cook until the apples are tender. Add the lemon juice. Remove from the heat and cool. Add the geranium leaves. Pour the mixture into an ice cream maker and process according to the manufacturer's directions.

Serves 2.

Fresh Fir Granite
with Wild Chokecherry Syrup

Fresh Grand Fir needles (from new growth)
Water
1 cup honey

      26 26 26

1 pound chokecherries
1 cup sugar (preferably maple)
2 cups water

Fill a 2-quart container with well-washed Grand Fir needles and weigh with several plates. In a separate pan bring 1 quart of water to a boil and pour over the needles. Steep for 12 hours. Strain through a very fine sieve or cheese cloth. Add the honey. Prepare in an ice cream freezer, sorbetiere, or a shallow pan in the freezer, stirring often.

In a saucepan combine the chokecherries, sugar, and water, and cook over low heat for 30 minutes until the flavors have blended. Strain through a fine chinois.

Serves 4.

Recipe courtesy Gordon Cowen.

The Schroth Farm

Site 6, Comp 25, Rural Route 8
Vernon, British Columbia V1T 8L6
(604) 545-0010

On this farm situated only one mile from Vernon, a cozy, clean vintage home offers guests a self-contained guest room with an adjoining family room. Twin and double beds are available, with private entrance and private bath. All rooms have their own cable television, VCR, and large refrigerator. For relaxing, guests may visit on the large patio and watch cattle graze in the pastures against a mountain backdrop. Nearby are winter skiing, mineral hot springs, sandy beaches, excellent golf courses, trail riding, and more. German is spoken here.

Quick and Easy Cucumber Relish

2 English cucumbers (long), sliced
1 medium onion, sliced
1 tablespoon salt
¾ cup vinegar
¾ cup sugar

In a bowl or glass jar with a cover, combine the cucumbers, onion, and salt. Cover and refrigerate for 2 hours. Drain. Combine the vinegar and sugar, stirring until dissolved. Pour the vinegar mixture over the cucumber mixture, and serve.

Makes about 4 cups.

Abigail's Hotel

Victoria, British Columbia
(604) 388-5363

Following the tradition of European-style inns, Abigail's has been transformed into a small, luxurious hotel. Decorated with soft colors, comfortable furnishings, and crystal chandeliers, the hotel has romantic ambiance. All guest rooms have private bathrooms and goosedown comforters. Guests can relax in a Jacuzzi or soaking tub before a crackling fire in their room. Each afternoon they meet for cheese, fresh fruit, and a glass of port before departing for some of the best restaurants in Victoria. Situated four blocks from the city center, Abigail's is within strolling distance of specialty shops, floral parks, and oceanside delights.

French Breakfast Puffs

⅓ cup shortening
½ cup sugar
1 egg
1½ cups all-purpose flour
1 teaspoon baking powder
½ teaspoon salt
¼ teaspoon nutmeg
½ cup milk
½ cup sugar
1 teaspoon cinnamon
½ cup margarine or butter

Grease 15 muffin cups. In a large bowl combine the shortening, ½ cup of sugar, and the egg. Stir in the flour, baking powder, salt, and nutmeg alternately with the milk. Fill the muffin cups about ⅔ full. Bake in a 350° oven for 20 to 25 minutes, until golden brown. In a small bowl combine ½ cup of sugar and the cinnamon. Immediately after baking, roll the puffs in the melted margarine and then in the cinnamon-sugar mixture.

Makes 15 puffs.

Sunshine Muffins

2 cups whole wheat flour
1 cup sugar
2 teaspoons baking soda
1 tablespoon cinnamon
2 cups grated carrots
⅓ cup chopped dried apricots
⅓ cup sunflower seeds
⅓ cup chocolate chips
⅓ cup coconut
1 banana, mashed
3 eggs
1 cup oil
2 teaspoons vanilla extract

Grease muffin cups. In a large bowl combine the flour, sugar, baking soda, and cinnamon. Mix well. Stir in the carrots, apricots, sunflower seeds, chocolate chips, coconut, and banana. Beat together the eggs, oil, and vanilla. Stir the egg mixture into the dry ingredients until just moistened. Spoon into the prepared muffin cups. Bake in a 375° oven for 15 to 20 minutes.

Makes about 2 dozen muffins.

The Beaconsfield Inn

998 Humboldt Street
Victoria, British Columbia V8V 2Z8
(604) 384-4044

In 1905, at the height of the British Empire, famous architect Samuel McClure was commissioned by R. P. Rithet to build the Beaconsfield for his daughter Gertrude as a wedding gift. A gleaming sun room/conservatory, rich mahogany paneling, period antiques, oil paintings, a book-lined library, and cozy kitchen adorn the main floor. All guest rooms have private bathrooms, goosedown comforters, and luxurious decorations. Some have wood-burning fireplaces, clawfoot tubs, or Jacuzzi baths. Each afternoon guests meet in the library for a sherry hour where an assortment of cheese, crackers, and fresh fruit is served. The inn is only a few minutes' walk from specialty shops, Beacon Hill Park, and the Inner Harbor.

🐚 🐚 🐚 🐚 🐚

Scrambled Eggs
with Shrimp and Green Onion en Brioche

2 brioche shells, unbaked
4 eggs
1 6-ounce can shrimp, mashed
Finely chopped green onion to taste

🐚 🐚 🐚

Sour cream
Paprika
Chopped fresh parsley
Lettuce and fresh fruit accompaniment

Slice the tops off the brioche and scoop out the inside. Place the brioche shells and tops on a baking sheet. Bake in a 375° oven for 10 minutes, until crispy.

In a skillet scramble the eggs. When almost set add the shrimp and green onions. Do not overcook or the eggs will be too dry. Place the scrambled eggs inside the baked brioche. Garnish with a small dollop of sour cream, a sprinkle of paprika, and parsley. Place the tops on the brioche and serve on a bed of lettuce with fresh fruit on the side.

Serves 2.

Fluffy Maple Syrup

2 cups confectioners' sugar
½ cup melted butter
½ cup maple syrup
1 egg, separated

🐚 🐚 🐚

Chopped walnuts

In a mixing bowl reserve the confectioners' sugar. In a blender combine the melted butter and maple syrup. Pour the syrup mixture into the sugar. With an electric mixer blend the mixture well. Add the egg yolk and beat until well combined. Add the egg white and beat well. If the mixture is too thin, add more confectioners' sugar. Serve with chopped walnuts for a garnish.

Serves 6 to 8.

The Captain's Palace

309 Belleville Street
Victoria, British Columbia V8V 1X2
(604) 388-9191

This three-story Victorian mansion was built in 1897 as the home of a prominent businessman and his family. Every detail, from the peppershaker tower to hand-painted frescoed ceilings by Mueller and Stern, has been faithfully restored and preserved. From the moment a guest enters, the opulence of the Victorian era is obvious, from twinkling crystal chandeliers, velvets, tapestries to the stained-glass windows and door and the hand-painted ceramic-tiled fireplace. Each of the eight dining rooms has its own character. There are fourteen unique Victorian suites and bedrooms. Situated on Victoria's Inner Harbor, the Captain's Palace is a five-minute walk to downtown shopping, sightseeing, galleries, and entertainment.

Chef Andres' White Chocolate Pecan Pie

4 unbaked 9-inch pastry shells
2 16-ounce bottles corn syrup
2 cups sugar
3 tablespoons butter

🐚 🐚 🐚

12 eggs
¾ liter whipping cream (about 3 cups)

The Captain's Palace

Baked Shad

The shad is native to the Saint John River in New Brunswick. It is caught in late May and early June and is quite unique in that it has both light and dark meat.

> 4 to 6 slices bread, cubed
> ½ cup butter
> Salt and pepper
> Sage (optional)
> 1 3 to 5-pound shad, cleaned, and
>   head, tail, and fins removed

Cover a cookie sheet with foil and grease the foil. In a bowl combine the bread, butter, and seasonings. Lightly stuff the fish with the stuffing mixture. Place the fish on the prepared cookie sheet. Bake in a 350° oven for 1 hour to 1 hour and 30 minutes, until the fish flakes easily when tested with a fork.

Serves 6 to 8.

> 4 cups pecans
>
> ❧ ❧ ❧
>
> 24 ounces white chocolate
> 1 cup light cream

Bake the pastry shells in a 350° oven until half cooked. Let the shells cool. In a saucepan combine the corn syrup, sugar, and butter. Bring the mixture to a boil, and cook until the sugar is dissolved.

In a large steel mixing bowl beat the eggs with the whippng cream. Add the pecans. Slowly add part of the hot syrup mixture to the eggs. Gradually add the remaining hot syrup mixture, taking care not to cook the eggs with the hot mixture. Place equal amounts of the mixture in each shell. Bake in a 350° oven for 45 minutes. Cool the pies thoroughly.

In a saucepan with a heavy bottom or in the top of a double boiler over simmering water heat the white chocolate until soft. Add the light cream, mixing well. Pour the mixture on top of the cold pies.

Serves 24.

Steamers Stop Inn

Post Office Box 155
Village of Gagetown, New Brunswick E0G
    1V0
(506) 488-2903

Steamers Stop Inn is a colonial-style home on the St. John River in a village established in the mid-1700s. Completely refurbished to its original Victorian charm, it offers a licensed dining room with formal table settings, tastefully decorated guest rooms, sitting rooms, and crackling fireplaces. Guests may relax on the spacious verandah overlooking the river as they watch boaters and wildlife.

❧ ❧ ❧ ❧ ❧

Banana Pancakes

> 1½ cups water
> ½ cup yellow cornmeal
> 1 cup nonfat dry milk
> 2½ cups all-purpose flour
> 2 teaspoons baking powder
> Dash salt
> ⅔ cup brown sugar
> 3 eggs
> ¼ cup oil
> 3½ to 4½ cups cold water
> 3 bananas, mashed
> ½ teaspoon almond flavoring

In a small saucepan bring the water to a boil. Add the cornmeal, stirring constantly, and cook for 5 minutes. Remove from the heat and add ¾ cup of dry milk. Stir and set aside.

In a large bowl mix together the flour, baking powder, salt, and brown sugar. Add the eggs, oil, and about 3 cups of cold water. Stir well. Stir in the cornmeal mixture, the mashed bananas, and the almond flavoring. If the batter is not as thin as desired, add more water. Using a ¼ cup measure, drop the batter on a hot griddle and bake until the edges are

Steamers Stop Inn

browned and bubbles rise to the surface. Turn and bake until golden.

Makes about 36 pancakes.

Dark Chocolate Cake

2 cups sugar
1½ cups all-purpose flour
¾ cup cocoa
2 teaspoons baking soda
1 teaspoon baking powder
½ teaspoon salt
1 cup buttermilk or sour milk
1 cup strong coffee
½ cup oil
2 eggs
1 teaspoon vanilla extract

❧ ❧ ❧

Rich chocolate butter icing

Grease 2 8-inch round cake pans. In a large bowl combine the sugar, flour, cocoa, baking soda, baking powder, and salt in a large bowl. Add the buttermilk, coffee, oil, eggs, and vanilla. Beat with an electric mixer at low speed for 2 minutes. It will be a thin batter when finished. Pour into the prepared cake pans. Bake in a 350° oven for 30 to 35 minutes.

Cool the cakes. Put the cakes together and frost with chocolate icing.

Serves 16.

Oakley House

Lower Jemseg, New Brunswick E0E 1S0
(506) 488-3113

The Lower Saint John River Valley, known as the "Rhine of North America," boasts some of the most scenic waterway country in Canada. The Oakley House is on the Jemseg River and near a popular area for sailing, canoeing, swimming, or birdwatching. A rebuilt 150-year-old farmhouse, the home is comfortably decorated and fully available to guests who may wish to browse through the extensive library, play the piano, listen to records, or bask in the warmth of the fireplace. In addition to the full country breakfasts, additional meals are available on request.

Hearty Fiddlehead Soup

Using frozen fiddleheads is about the only way to enjoy the flavor of this New Brunswick treat during 11 months of the year. This recipe allows us to enjoy a hearty "cream" soup without using dairy products. If a lighter colored soup is preferred, use all-purpose flour. We enjoy the added nuttiness of the whole wheat.

1 small potato
4½ cups chicken broth
6 tablespoons olive oil
2 tablespoons finely chopped onion
6 tablespoons whole wheat flour
1 cup finely chopped steamed
   fiddleheads (about 2 cups
   frozen)
1 teaspoon crushed dried tarragon
Salt and pepper to taste

In a soup pot cook the potato in chicken broth until tender. Cool. In a

blender purée the potato and chicken broth until smooth.

In a soup pot heat the olive oil and sauté the onion until tender. Add the flour and cook for several minutes, stirring frequently until smooth. Whisk in the puréed potato mixture. Add the fiddleheads, tarragon, and salt and pepper to taste. Simmer for about 10 minutes, stirring frequently to allow the tarragon flavor to develop.

Serves 4 to 6.

The Crosstree Guest House

Seal Cove, Grand Manan Island
New Brunswick, Canada E0G 3B0
(506) 662-8263

The Crosstree is nestled in a valley in the prettiest village on Grand Manan Island. Nearby is a nine-hole golf course, Red Point (where magnetic sand can be found on the beach), and a busy harbor. The four guest rooms are lovely and bright, and home cooked meals are served to guests.

Oatmeal Brown Bread

½ cup molasses
1 cup rolled oats
2 cups boiling water
1 tablespoon salt
⅔ cup brown sugar
¼ cup margarine

❧ ❧ ❧

2 teaspoons sugar
½ cup warm water (110° to 115°)
2 tablespoons active dry yeast
2 cups cold water
9 to 10 cups all-purpose flour

Grease 3 loaf pans. In a large bowl combine the first 6 ingredients and let the mixture stand for 10 minutes. In a small bowl combine the sugar, warm water, and the yeast. Let the yeast mixture stand for 10 minutes. To the oat mixture add 2 cups of cold water, and then add the yeast mixture. Add 4 cups of flour, beating well. Add the remaining flour and mix well. Knead for 6 to 8 minutes. Place the dough in a greased bowl, and let rise until doubled in bulk. Punch down and shape into loaves or rolls. Place in the pans. Let the loaves or rolls rise. Bake in a 350° oven for 45 minutes.

Makes 3 loaves.

The Rossmount Inn

St. Andrews-by-the-Sea
New Brunswick E0G 2X0
(506) 529-3351

A three-story manor house with sixteen rooms, Rossmount Inn is part of a private eighty-seven-acre estate at the foot of Chamcook Mountain, the highest point in the Passamaquoddy Bay area. The estate provides scenic hiking, nature trails, a large pool, and spectacular panoramic views. In the atmosphere of this inn all of the services of an elegant small hotel are available. The dining room provides superb home cooked food and good wines in a smoke-free atmosphere. The Victorian decor is complemented by the high ceiling and fine old fireplace, but the focal point is an alcove of three stained-glass windows taken from an eighteenth-century English chapel. The guest rooms are spacious and furnished with unique antiques from all over the world. Each room has its own private bath.

Rossmount Cookie Crumb Pie

1 21-ounce package chocolate chip cookies
½ cup Tia Maria (or Crème de Cacao or Kahlua)
3 cups whipping cream, whipped and slightly sweetened
Chocolate curls for garnish
Strawberries or Maraschino cherries

In a 10 or 12-inch springform pan arrange a layer of cookies. Sprinkle liberally with some of the liqueur. Top with a layer of whipped cream, smoothing with a spatula. Continue layering until the pan is nearly full, ending with a cream layer. Using a pastry bag fitted with a star tip, decorate the top by piping on the remaining whipped cream. Garnish with chocolate curls and strawberries or well-drained Maraschino cherries. Cover with plastic wrap and refrigerate overnight before serving.

Serves 10 to 12.

Rossmount House Dressing

3 6-ounce bags radishes
4 cloves garlic
¼ cup white vinegar
¼ cup wine vinegar
1 cup sour cream
Mayonnaise

In a food processor combine the radishes, garlic, and vinegars. Process until fine. Add the sour cream, mixing well. Pour the mixture into a 4-liter (4¼ quart) container and add enough mayonnaise to almost fill the container. Stir until well blended.

Makes 4¼ quarts.

🐦 🐦 🐦 🐦 🐦

Turkey Divan

2 10-ounce packages frozen broccoli
2 to 3 cups diced or sliced cooked turkey

🐦 🐦 🐦

2 10½-ounce cans cream of chicken soup
1 cup mayonnaise
1 teaspoon lemon juice
½ teaspoon curry powder
½ cup shredded sharp cheese
½ cup toasted bread crumbs
1 tablespoon margarine

In a flat pyrex dish arrange the broccoli and top with the turkey. In a large bowl combine the soup, mayonnaise, lemon juice, curry powder, and cheese. Pour the sauce over the broccoli and turkey. Top with the bread crumbs and margarine. Bake in a 350° oven for 25 to 30 minutes.

Note: This can be prepared ahead and refrigerated until ready to bake.

Serves 6 to 8.

Chez Prime

Rural Route 3
Site 32, Boite 6
Tracadie, New Brunswick E0C 2B0
(506) 395-6884

A wooden house dating from 1917, Chez Prime is decorated with the charm of yesteryear. This is especially evident in the historic library and old-time kitchen with its wood-burning stove. Situated on 115 acres in the beautiful Acadian countryside, it is in the middle of wild flowers, blueberries, and evergreen trees. The four well-kept rooms retain their original decor. The full breakfast has already become well known. Chez Prime has a tea room that is unique in the area. It offers homemade ice cream, King Cole tea, and other irresistible refreshments.

Maritimes Quiche

1 tablespoon butter
½ cup diced onion
½ cup diced celery
½ cup diced red pepper
3 eggs
½ cup homemade mayonnaise
¼ cup white wine
1 tablespoon all-purpose flour
10 ounces crab meat
Salt and pepper to taste
1 unbaked 10-inch pastry shell
5 ounces Gruyère cheese, shredded
Slivered almonds
Paprika

In a small skillet melt the butter and sauté the onions, celery, and red pepper. In a medium bowl whisk together the eggs, mayonnaise, white wine, flour, crab meat, salt, and pepper. In the bottom of the pie shell arrange half of the cheese. Pour the egg mixture over the cheese and top with the remaining cheese. Decorate with slivered almonds and sprinkle with paprika. Bake in a 350° oven for 40 minutes.

Serves 6.

Lina's Baked Eel

4 eels
2 tablespoons minced salted green onions
2 tablespoons butter, cut into pieces
Salt and pepper to taste
1 10½-ounce can tomato soup
½ cup catsup
1 cup water
3 onions, sliced

Butter an oven dish. Cut the eels into 2-inch pieces and arrange in the dish. Scatter the pieces of butter, minced green onion, and sliced onions over the eels. In a bowl combine the soup, catsup, and water, and pour over the eels. Bake in a 375° oven for 1 hour and 30 minutes.

Serves 6.

Rhubarb Marmalade

2 lemons
1 orange
8 cups diced rhubarb
6 cups sugar
¾ cup chopped walnuts

In a food processor chop the lemons and orange. In a saucepan combine the chopped lemons and oranges, rhubarb, and sugar. Simmer over low heat for 45 minutes. Add the walnuts and cook for 15 more minutes. Place the mixture in sterilized jars and seal.

Makes about ten ½ pint jars.

Milford House

South Milford
Rural Route 4
Annapolis Royal, Nova Scotia B0S 1A0
(902) 532-2617

A rustic resort in existence for more than one hundred years, the Milford House has two dozen cottages situated well apart along the wooded shores of two lakes within walking distance of the main lodge. Each cottage has its own lakeside dock, two to five bedrooms, a living room with a fireplace, electricity, and bathroom with tub or shower. Meals in the main lodge dining room feature wholesome country-style cooking: fresh vegetables, home-baked bread, native blueberries and raspberries, homemade soup, fresh fish, and hearty roasts. Tennis, croquet, volleyball, swimming, and a children's play area are on the premises.

Stuffed Trout Papillote

¼ cup butter, melted
1½ cups chopped onion
3 stalks celery, diced
½ cup diced parsley
1 18-ounce package toasted rice cereal
1 pound shrimp, minced
1 pound crab meat, minced
6¼ cups (50 ounces) Newburg sauce

48 8-ounce whole Rainbow trout, cleaned
1 cup butter

In a skillet melt ¼ cup of butter and sauté the onion, celery, and parsley until the onion is transparent. In a large bowl toss together the rice cereal, shrimp, crab meat, and sautéed vegetables. Add the Newburg sauce and blend well.

Season the cleaned fish with salt and pepper. Place on 10 to 12-inch squares of aluminum foil. Fill the fish cavities with 2½ to 3 ounces of stuffing. Close with skewers or wooden picks. Brush the stuffed fish with butter and seal the aluminum foil. Bake in a 400° oven for 20 to 25 minutes. Serve the fish in the opened foil packets.

Serves 48.

Beild House Inn

64 Third Street
Collingwood, Ontario L9Y 1K5
(705) 444-1522

This turn-of-the-century home has been converted into a fourteen-room inn. Each guest room has its own decor, a gentle blending of antique furnishings with modern amenities. At Beild House breakfast is an occasion. In the elegant dining room, homemade preserves, seasonal fruit, and hot dishes are served in generous portions. The inn is a leisurely stroll to downtown shopping and a convenient base close to all the year-round attractions in the Collingwood area.

Mocha Sponge Cake

1 cup strong coffee
9 eggs, separated
1½ cups sugar
Pinch salt
1½ tablespoons baking powder
1 cup plus 2 tablespoons all-
   purpose flour

&ea; &ea; &ea;

3 cups 35% cream
1½ tablespoons sugar
2 cups confectioners' sugar
Strong coffee

In a small saucepan boil 1 cup of coffee until reduced to 4 tablespoons of coffee syrup. Remove from the heat.

In a large bowl beat the egg yolks with 1½ cups of sugar until pale. Add 2 tablespoons of coffee syrup and the salt. In a small bowl combine the baking powder and flour, and add to the egg yolk mixture. In a separate bowl beat the egg whites until stiff but not dry. Fold the beaten egg whites into the yolk mixture. Turn the batter into 3 ungreased springform pans. Bake in a 350° oven for 20 minutes or until a cake tester inserted in the center comes out clean.

Let the layers rest for 5 minutes. Run a knife around the edges and let cool. Whip the cream with 1½ tablespoons of sugar and the remaining 2 tablespoons of coffee syrup. The syrup will color the cream pale beige. Use half of the cream to fill between the layers. Sift the confectioners' sugar and moisten with strong coffee until spreadable. Spread with a wetted knife, allowing the icing to drip down the sides of the cake.

Serves 12 to 16.

Cold Salmon Terrine

3 leeks
4 pounds salmon fillets, skinned
Salt and pepper
⅓ cup dry sherry
Mayonnaise flavored with lemon
   juice

Butter a terrine and set aside. Wash the leeks well and cut off the bottom and any damaged leaves. Cut in half lengthwise. Blanch in boiling water for 30 seconds, and plunge in cold water to refresh. Line the terrine with leeks, leaving enough leaves hanging outside the pan to overlap when filled. Place one layer of salmon on the bottom of the terrine, and add salt and pepper. Pour ⅓ of the sherry over the layer. Repeat until the terrine is filled. Overlap the leeks onto the top. Cover and place in a baking pan of boiling water. Bake in a 350° oven for 45 minutes. Cool.

When cool, place a wooden board slightly smaller than the terrine over the salmon. Place a brick on top, and press firmly. Refrigerate overnight.

Invert the salmon onto a serving platter. Serve with mayonnaise flavored with lemon juice.

Serves 10 to 12.

Asparagus Rolled with Beef Filet

2 4-ounce beef filets
Salt and pepper
½ cup mayonnaise
1 egg yolk
Lemon juice
12 stalks asparagus, cooked firm
   and chilled
Capers
4 slices lemon, cut in half

Slice the beef across the grain as thinly as possible. This is easiest to do when the beef is half frozen. Salt and pepper each slice.

In a small bowl combine the mayonnaise, egg yolk, and lemon juice. Lightly brush the beef slices with the mixture. Wrap the beef, sauce-side in, around each asparagus stalk, leaving the floret end uncovered. Place three wrapped stalks side by side on each serving plate, drizzle with mayonnaise sauce, and sprinkle with capers. Garnish with lemon slices.

Serves 4.

The Union Hotel Bed and Breakfast

Normandale, Ontario

Box 38, Rural Route 1
Vittoria, Ontario N0E 1W0
(519) 426-5568

Situated on the north shore of Lake Erie, the Union Hotel provides a view of the lake from the upper balcony. Inside, it offers an original pioneer setting furnished with period antiques. The three guest rooms have private baths with showers. Breakfast is served daily; Wednesday through Sunday.

Decadent Chocolate Orange Mousse Cake

¾ cup chocolate graham cracker crumbs
¼ cup sugar
½ cup butter

🐦 🐦 🐦

1 12-ounce package orange chocolate chips
¼ cup Triple Sec
3 eggs
3 tablespoons confectioners' sugar
2 cups whipped cream

🐦 🐦 🐦

1 1-ounce square semi-sweet chocolate
2 tablespoons confectioners' sugar

In a large bowl combine the graham cracker crumbs, ¼ cup of sugar, and ½ cup of butter. Set aside.

In the top of a double boiler over simmering water melt the chocolate chips. Add the Triple Sec. Remove from the heat. Add 1 whole egg and 2 egg yolks. Mix well. In a separate bowl beat 2 egg whites until foamy. Add 3 tablespoons of confectioners' sugar and beat until shiny stiff peaks form. Fold the whipped cream into the egg white mixture. Fold the chocolate mixture into the egg white mixture.

Carefully line the inside of a mixing bowl with plastic wrap. Pour the mixture into the lined bowl. Pour the graham cracker crumb mixture over the whipped mixture and pat down. Refrigerate until set, at least 4 hours.

Unmold onto a serving platter and remove the plastic wrap. Decorate with grated chocolate and confectioners' sugar.

Variations: Use mint chocolate chips with mint liqueur, white chocolate with almond liqueur, milk chocolate chips with any liqueur, German chocolate chips with coconut liqueur, semisweet chocolate chips with raspberry liqueur.

Serves 10.

Baked Brie
with Raspberry Sauce

1 17¼-ounce package puff pastry
10½ ounces Brie
1 egg, beaten

🐦 🐦 🐦

2 cups fresh raspberries (or frozen)
1½ ounces Triple Sec

Grease a cookie sheet. Roll out the puff pastry and wrap around the Brie. Do not remove the skin from the Brie. Cut away excess pastry and seal the edges with the egg. Cut 3 leaves and 3 berries from the excess pastry and arrange on the top. Brush with the remaining egg. Pierce several small holes through the top of the pastry. Place on the prepared cookie sheet. Bake in a 325° oven for 20 to 25 minutes.

Purée the raspberries and add the Triple Sec. Heat over low heat, but do not boil. Serve the baked Brie with the raspberry sauce.

Serves 4.

Vegetarian Lasagna

3 8-ounce cans tomato sauce (or 24 ounces spaghetti sauce)
1 tablespoon Italian seasoning
1½ tablespoons garlic powder
1 teaspoon onion powder

🐦 🐦 🐦

3 large carrots
½ green pepper
½ head cauliflower
½ bunch broccoli
1 8-ounce package lasagne noodles, cooked
2 6-ounce jars olives
1 20-ounce can pineapple chunks
4 cups cottage cheese
1½ pounds thinly sliced Mozzarella cheese

In a large saucepan combine the tomato sauce and seasonings. Simmer for 1 hour.

Grease a large deep casserole dish. Cut the raw vegetables into small pieces. In the prepared casserole dish place a small amount of the tomato sauce. Layer some of the noodles, more tomato sauce, some of the vegetables, olives, pineapple, cottage cheese, and Mozzarella cheese. Repeat the layers, ending with a layer of noodles topped with Mozzarella cheese. Bake covered in a 350° oven for 1 hour. Remove the cover and bake for 30 minutes.

Serves 8.

Korean Salad

1 cup oil
¼ cup vinegar
⅓ cup catsup
⅔ cup sugar

🐦 🐦 🐦

1 pound spinach
1 pound bean sprouts
1 5-ounce can sliced water chestnuts
6 slices bacon, cooked and crumbled
¼ pound mushrooms, sliced
1 green pepper, chopped

In a container with a cover combine the oil, vinegar, catsup, and sugar. Blend well and refrigerate for 3 hours. Shake well before serving.

Tear the spinach into small chunks. Toss with the remaining ingredients. Top with dressing and serve.

Serves 6.

Banana Lassi

1½ tablespoons honey
1 banana
1½ cups plain yogurt
2 to 4 tablespoons milk

In a blender combine the honey and banana. Add the yogurt and enough milk to obtain the desired consistency. Serve immediately.

Variations: Instead of bananas, use blueberries, strawberries, raspberries, blackberries, or peaches.

Serves 2.

🐦 🐦 🐦 🐦 🐦

Jakobstettel Guest House

16 Isabella Street
St. Jacobs, Ontario N0B 2N0
(519) 664-2208

This estate home was built in 1898 by William Snider, owner of the village mill. Today it has been beautifully restored, with its grounds bordering the longest mill race in Ontario. The mill is now a shopper's delight. The inn retains all the original stained and leaded windows. To make use of every possible space, when the house was restored, rooms were redesigned and the attic was transformed into six new bedrooms. A total of twelve beautifully decorated guest rooms are available.

Chocolate Eclairs

1 box graham wafers
2 6-ounce packages instant vanilla pudding
3 cups milk
1 pint whipping cream, whipped
᠅ ᠅ ᠅
3 tablespoons cocoa
1½ cups confectioners' sugar
3 tablespoons milk
1 teaspoon corn syrup
1 tablespoon butter

In a 9x13-inch pan place a layer of graham wafers. In a medium bowl beat the pudding with 3 cups of milk. Blend in the whipped cream. Place half of the mixture over the layer of graham wafers. Add a layer of wafers and pour the remaining pudding mixture over the wafers. Top with a layer of graham wafers.

In a small bowl beat together the remaining ingredients. Ice the eclairs with the icing mixture. Refrigerate for 24 hours.
Serves 18.

Rhubarb Jam

5 cups rhubarb, diced
5 cups sugar
1 20-ounce can crushed pineapple
1 6-ounce package strawberry gelatin

In a large saucepan combine the rhubarb, sugar, and pineapple. Bring the mixture to a boil and cook for 20 minutes. Add the gelatin and stir until dissolved. Pour into jars and seal. Store in the refrigerator.
Makes 3 pints.

Oppenheim's

153 Huron Street
Toronto, Ontario M5T 2B6
(416) 598-4562

Situated in the Kensington Market area of Toronto, Oppenheim's is a true find for travelers who are looking for a special place to stay. When guests arrive, they are met by a brindle bulldog named Blossom. All food is freshly prepared. The six bedrooms are furnished with Canadiana and whimsical taste in a farmhouse setting.

Crunchy Apple Crisp

¾ cup brown sugar
½ cup all-purpose flour
½ cup butter, cut into pieces
⅓ cup granola (or graham cracker crumbs)
1 teaspoon cinnamon
᠅ ᠅ ᠅
Apples, peeled, cored and sliced
½ cup raisins
᠅ ᠅ ᠅
Ice cream

Grease a 9-inch square pan or 10-inch round pie plate. In a food processor with a steel blade combine all of the ingredients except the apples, raisins, and ice cream. Process until crumbly, about 8 seconds.

Place the apples and raisins in the prepared pan, tossing to combine. Sprinkle with the crumb mixture. Bake in a 375° oven for 35 to 40 minutes. Serve warm with ice cream.

Variation: This is good with pears, peaches, blackberries, blueberries, raspberries, plums, apricots, or any combination.
Serves 6 to 8.

Chocolate Brownie Muffins

1½ cups all-purpose flour
1 cup brown sugar
⅔ cup cocoa powder
3 teaspoons baking powder
1 teaspoon salt
1 cup granola
2 eggs
1 cup milk
⅓ cup oil
1 teaspoon vanilla extract

Grease 12 muffin cups. In a large bowl combine the first 6 ingredients. In a separate bowl beat the eggs, milk, oil, and vanilla. Pour the liquid ingredients all at once into the dry ingredients. Stir until just blended. Pour the batter into the prepared muffin cups. Bake in a 375° oven for 18 to 20 minutes, or until firm to the touch.
Makes 12 muffins.

Oppenheim's

In a large bowl combine the dry ingredients. Add the butter, milk, and egg, stirring just until the dry ingredients are moistened. Shape the dough into a ball, and turn onto a lightly floured board to form an 8-inch circle. Cut into wedges. Place on a cookie sheet. Bake in a 425° oven for 12 to 15 minutes.

Makes 6 to 8 scones.

Potato Bannock

2¼ cups sifted all-purpose flour
1 teaspoon salt
2 tablespoons baking powder
¼ cup sugar
2 tablespoons shortening
¾ cup mashed potatoes
½ cup cold water
½ cup milk

In a large bowl sift the dry ingredients together. Cut in the shortening with a pastry blender or 2 knives until the mixture resembles coarse meal. Stir in the potatoes. Stir in the water and milk with a fork. Turn onto a lightly floured board and knead gently 8 to 10 times. Place on an ungreased baking sheet and pat down to form an oval shape, about 1-inch thick. Bake in a 450° oven for 7 to 10 minutes.

Serves 6 to 8.

Blue Heron Country Bed and Breakfast

Rural Route 3, North Bedeque
Summerside, Prince Edward Island
    C1N 4J9
(902) 436-4843

The Blue Heron Country Bed and Breakfast is an ideal place for that special visit. Conveniently situated on Route 1A, it overlooks the Wilmot River and the beautiful town of Summerside. The four quiet guest rooms are spacious, bright, and individually decorated. The picturesque verandah is an ideal place on which to relax and enjoy complimentary coffee and a chat in the evening.

Scottish Oat Scones

1½ cups all-purpose flour
1¼ cups quick-cooking rolled oats
¼ cup sugar
1 tablespoon baking powder
1 teaspoon cream of tartar
½ teaspoon salt

   🍃 🍃 🍃

⅔ cup butter, melted
⅓ cup milk
1 egg, slightly beaten
½ cup raisins

West Island Inn

Box 24
Tyne Valley, Prince Edward Island
    C0B 2C0
(902) 831-2495

Situated off the beaten track in unspoiled West Prince County, West Island Inn is a historic late Victorian house furnished with antiques. Its five guest rooms all have private baths. Home cooked meals, served to

guests in the dining room and sun porch, feature fresh oysters, garden vegetables, and local berries in season. Guests enjoy the garden gazebo, hot tub, piano, and laundromat. Breakfast is included in the daily rate.

Quick Cake
with Coconut Topping

For years this recipe has been much requested. It's cheap and easy, and uses accessible ingredients.

    2 eggs, well beaten
    ½ teaspoon vanilla extract
    ¼ cup sugar
    ¾ cup all-purpose flour
    ½ teaspoon salt
    1½ teaspoons baking powder
    1 tablespoon butter
    ½ cup hot milk

        🍂 🍂 🍂

    5 tablespoons brown sugar
    2 tablespoons butter

    2 tablespoons cream (or evaporated
        milk)
    ½ cup coconut, shredded or
        dessicated

Grease an 8-inch square pan. In a large bowl beat the eggs, and add the vanilla and sugar. In a separate bowl mix together the flour, salt, and baking powder. Add the dry ingredients to the egg mixture, blending well. Add the butter to the milk, and add the mixture to the batter. Beat until smooth. Bake in a 350° oven for 20 to 25 minutes, or until a toothpick inserted in the center comes out clean.

In a small saucepan combine the remaining ingredients. Boil for 1 minute. Spread over the cake immediately as it comes out of the oven. Return the cake to the oven and brown lightly.

Good hot or cold.

Serves 9.

MacLeod's Farm Bed and Breakfast

Vernon Bridge Post Office
Uigg, Prince Edward Island C0A 2E0
(902) 651-2303

Guests of this modern farm get to watch a farming operation of one hundred acres on which corn, grain, and vegetables are grown and beef cattle raised. Children will enjoy the kittens, bunnies, and friendly Newfoundland dog named B.J. In the early evening, hayrides are part of the fun. Trout fishing is nearby.

Pumpkin Scones

    1¾ cups all-purpose flour
    4 teaspoons baking powder
    ¾ teaspoon salt
    ¼ cup sugar
    2 teaspoons cinnamon
    ½ teaspoon ginger
    ½ cup chilled shortening
    ½ cup seedless raisins
    1 cup pumpkin

        🍂 🍂 🍂

    Melted butter
    Sugar

In a large bowl combine the dry ingredients. Cut the shortening into the mixture with a pastry blender or 2 knives until the mixture resembles coarse meal. Add the raisins and pumpkin, and blend well. Turn out onto a lightly floured board and pat into a circle. Brush the melted butter over the top and sprinkle with sugar. Cut into wedges. Place on an ungreased cookie sheet. Bake in a 450° oven for 20 to 25 minutes.

Makes 6 to 8 scones.

Index